SOUTH AMERICA

24 SOUTH AMERICA political 1:35M
25 SOUTH AMERICA, SOUTH 1:15M
26-27 SOUTH AMERICA, NORTH 1:15M
28 CENTRAL CHILE-ARGENTINA & URUGUAY 1:7.5M
29 SOUTH-EAST BRAZIL 1:7.5M

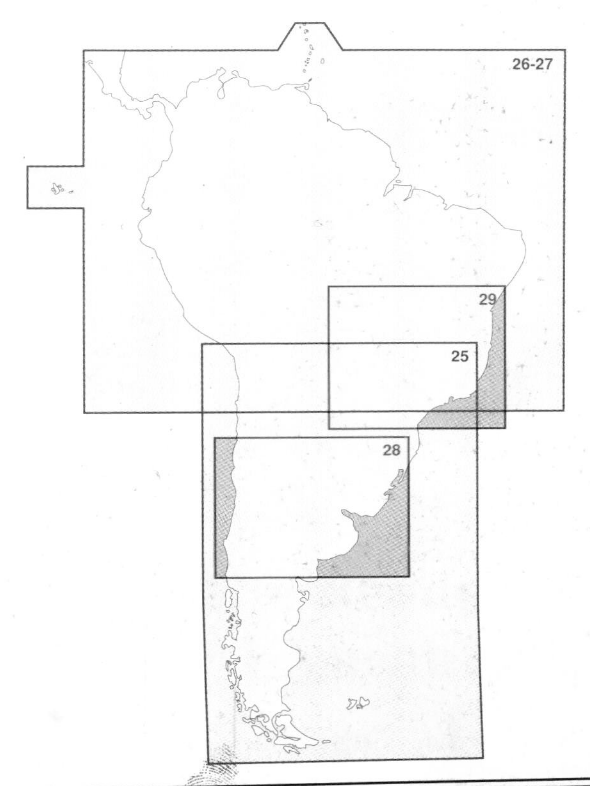

EUROPE

30-31 EUROPE political 1:15M
32 SCANDINAVIA 1:7.5M
33 GREAT BRITAIN & IRELAND 1:5M
34-35 UNITED KINGDOM 1:2.5M
36 LONDON-PARIS-BONN 1:2.5M
37 ALPS 1:2.5M
38 FRANCE 1:5M
39 SPAIN 1:5M
40-41 ITALY & THE BALKANS 1:5M
42-43 NORTH CENTRAL EUROPE 1:5M
44-45 RUSSIAN FEDERATION, WEST & UKRAINE 1:10M

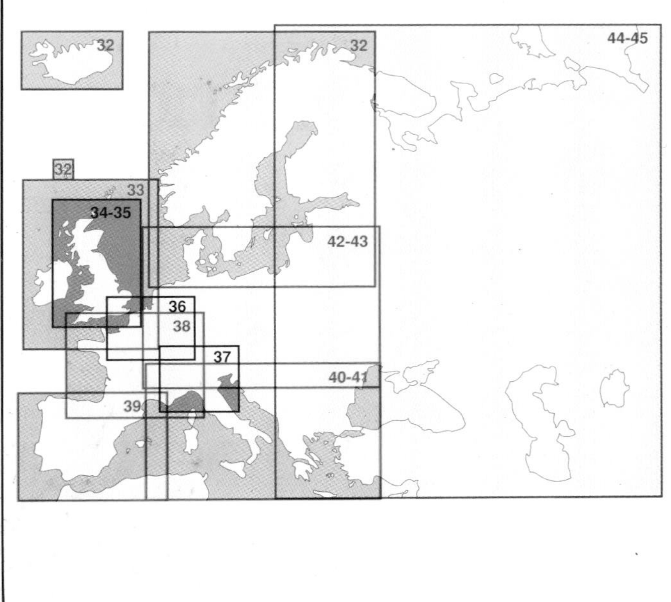

Bartholomew
A Division of HarperCollins Publishers
Duncan Street, Edinburgh EH9 1TA

First published by Bartholomew 1987
Revised edition 1992

ISBN 0-89577-422-4

Printed in Great Britain by HarperCollins Manufacturing, Glasgow

Details included in this atlas are subject to change without notice. Whilst every effort is made to keep information up to date Bartholomew will not be responsible for any loss, damage or inconvenience caused by inaccuracies in this atlas. The publishers are always pleased to acknowledge any corrections brought to their notice, and record their appreciation of the valuable services rendered in the past by map users in assisting to maintain the accuracy of their publications.

E/B4742

Acknowledgements

The Publishers acknowledge the assistance of the following in the preparation of material used in this publication: Dr Walter Stephen, Senior Adviser, Curriculum, Dean Education Centre, Edinburgh; Alister Hendrie, Assistant Headteacher, Portobello High School, Edinburgh; Andrew Grant, Principal Teacher, Geography, Wester Hailes Education Centre, Edinburgh; Stephen Hamilton, Principal Teacher, Geography, Broughton High School, Edinburgh.

The Publishers are grateful to the following for providing the photographs used in this atlas:
(picture number(s) shown in italics)
Travel Photo International: pages xxii-xxiii, savanna, rain forest, prairie, northern forest; page xxii, *7;* page xviii, *2;* page xv , *11;* page xvi , *4, 5, 13, 14;* page xx , *7;* page xxi , *2;* page vi , *3, 4;* page viii,*3,4*. *Photographers' Library:* page xxii-xxiii, scrub *Chris Knaggs photograph*, desert *Oliver Martel photograph;* page x , *8 Clive Sawyer photograph;* page xiv, *8 Ian Wright photograph;* page xvii, *9 Tom Hustler photograph;* page xx , *4 Robyn Beeche photograph. Biofotos:* page x , *5 Heather Angel photograph;* page xx , *6 Andrew Henley photograph;* page xxi , *3 Soames Summerhays photograph. The Photo Source:* page xii , *10;* page xviii, *4;* page xiv, *7. Wade Cooper Associates,* Edinburgh: page xvi , *12;* page xvii, *10;* page vi , *1. Pictor International:* page xiv, *6;* page vi , *2. B. and C. Alexander:* page xxii , tundra. *Bruce Coleman Ltd:* page viii, *6 WWF/Eugen Schuhmacher. Mepha:* page xviii, *1 C. Osborne photograph. Michael Scott:* page xxii , woodland and grass. *Yorkshire and Humberside Tourist Board:* page xi, *2. Spectrum Colour Library:* page xiii, *12, 14.*

CONTENTS

iv-v THE WORLD 1:70M

CONTINENTAL PROFILE

vi-vii NORTH AMERICA
viii-ix SOUTH AMERICA
x-xiii EUROPE
xiv-xvii ASIA
xviii-xix AFRICA
xx-xxi AUSTRALASIA

WORLD PROFILE

xxii-xxiii WORLD ENVIRONMENT
xxiv-xxvi WORLD CLIMATE
xxvii WORLD TRANSPORT
xxviii-xxx WORLD OCEANS
xxxi-xxxii THE WORLD IN FIGURES

1 KEY TO SYMBOLS

NORTH AMERICA

2 NORTH AMERICA political 1:35M
3 WESTERN CANADA 1:7.5M
4-5 EASTERN CANADA 1:7.5M
6-7 CANADA 1:15M
8-9 UNITED STATES OF AMERICA 1:12.5M
10 USA, ALASKA 1:10M
11 USA, NORTH CENTRAL 1:5M
12-13 USA, NORTH-EAST & GREAT LAKES 1:5M
14 USA, ATLANTIC STATES 1:2.5M
15 USA, SOUTH-EAST 1:5M
16-17 USA, CENTRAL & SOUTH 1:5M
18-19 USA, WEST 1:5M
20 USA, CALIFORNIA & HAWAII 1:5M & 1:2.5M
21 CENTRAL AMERICA 1:15M
22 CENTRAL MEXICO 1:5M
23 CARIBBEAN 1:10M

SOUTH AMERICA

24 SOUTH AMERICA political 1:35M
25 SOUTH AMERICA, SOUTH 1:15M
26-27 SOUTH AMERICA, NORTH 1:15M
28 CENTRAL CHILE - ARGENTINA & URUGUAY 1:7.5M
29 SOUTH-EAST BRAZIL 1:7.5M

EUROPE

30-31 EUROPE political 1:15M
32 SCANDINAVIA 1:7.5M
33 GREAT BRITAIN & IRELAND 1:5M
34-35 UNITED KINGDOM 1:2.5M
36 LONDON - PARIS - BONN 1:2.5M
37 ALPS 1:2.5M
38 FRANCE 1:5M
39 SPAIN 1:5M
40-41 ITALY & THE BALKANS 1:5M
42-43 NORTH CENTRAL EUROPE 1:5M
44-45 RUSSIAN FEDERATION, WEST & UKRAINE 1:10M

ASIA

46-47 ASIA & AUSTRALASIA political 1:40M
48-49 ASIA, NORTH 1:20M
50-51 FAR EAST 1:20M
52 CENTRAL CHINA 1:10M
53 JAPAN & KOREA 1:10M
54 CENTRAL JAPAN - KOREA 1:5M
55 SOUTH-EAST ASIA, PENINSULAR 1:10M
56 MALAYSIA & INDONESIA, WEST 1:10M
57 INDONESIA, EAST & PHILIPPINES 1:10M
58-59 SOUTH ASIA & MIDDLE EAST 1:20M
60 INDIA, NORTH-WEST & PAKISTAN 1:7.5M
61 INDIA, NORTH-EAST & BANGLADESH 1:7.5M
62 INDIA, SOUTH & SRI LANKA 1:7.5M
63 IRAN & AFGHANISTAN 1:7.5M
64 TURKEY, SYRIA & IRAQ 1:7.5M
65 ISRAEL, LEBANON & CYPRUS 1:2.5M
66-67 ARABIAN PENINSULA & NILE VALLEY 1:7.5M

AFRICA

68 AFRICA political 1:40M
69 AFRICA, NORTH-EAST 1:15M
70 AFRICA, WEST 1:15M
71 NORTH & WEST AFRICAN COASTS 1:7.5M
72-73 AFRICA, CENTRAL & SOUTHERN 1:15M
74 SOUTH AFRICA 1:7.5M

AUSTRALASIA

75 AUSTRALIA, SOUTH-EAST 1:7.5M
76-77 AUSTRALIA & SOUTH-WEST PACIFIC 1:20M
78 NEW ZEALAND 1:5M

OCEANS & POLAR REGIONS

xxviii-xxix PACIFIC & INDIAN OCEANS 1:60M
xxx ATLANTIC OCEAN 1:60M
79 POLAR REGIONS 1:40M
80 ABBREVIATIONS USED IN REFERENCE MAP SECTION

WORLD INDEX

1-64 ABBREVIATIONS & INDEX

Major Cities by Continent

Africa	Pop. '000
Cairo *Egypt*	9000
Lagos *Nigeria*	7700
Alexandria *Egypt*	3700
Kinshasa *Zaire*	3500
Casablanca *Morocco*	3200
Alger *Algeria*	3000
Cape Town *South Africa*	2300
Abidjan *Ivory Coast*	2200
Tarābulus *Libya*	2100
Ādis Ābeba *Ethiopia*	1900
Khartoum *Sudan*	1900
Dar es Salaam *Tanzania*	1700
Johannesburg *South Africa*	1700
Luanda *Angola*	1700
Maputo *Mozambique*	1600
Tunis *Tunisia*	1600
Dakar *Senegal*	1500
Nairobi *Kenya*	1500

North and Central America	'000
México *Mexico*	20 200
New York *USA*	16 200
Los Angeles *USA*	11 900
Chicago *USA*	7000
Philadelphia *USA*	4300
Detroit *USA*	3700
San Francisco *USA*	3700
Toronto *Canada*	3500
Dallas *USA*	3400
Guadalajara *Mexico*	3200
Houston *USA*	3000
Monterrey *Mexico*	3000
Montréal *Canada*	3000
Washington *USA*	2900
Boston *USA*	2800
Atlanta *USA*	2200
San Diego *USA*	2200
Santo Domingo *Dominican Rep.*	2200
La Habana *Cuba*	2100
Minneapolis *USA*	2000
Phoenix *USA*	2000
Baltimore *USA*	1900
Miami *USA*	1900
St. Louis *USA*	1900
Cleveland *USA*	1700
Pittsburgh *USA*	1700
Denver *USA*	1600
Seattle *USA*	1600
Vancouver *Canada*	1500

South America	'000
São Paulo *Brazil*	17 400
Buenos Aires *Argentina*	11 500
Rio de Janeiro *Brazil*	10 700
Lima *Peru*	6200
Santiago *Chile*	5000
Bogotá *Colombia*	4900
Caracas *Venezuela*	4100
Belo Horizonte *Brazil*	3600
Pôrto Alegre *Brazil*	3100
Recife *Brazil*	2500
Brasília *Brazil*	2400
Salvador *Brazil*	2400
Fortaleza *Brazil*	2100
Curitiba *Brazil*	2000
Guayaquil *Ecuador*	1700
Cali *Colombia*	1600
Medellín *Colombia*	1600
Montevideo *Uruguay*	1200

Asia	'000
Tōkyō *Japan*	18 100
Shanghai *China*	13 400
Calcutta *India*	11 800
Bombay *India*	11 200
Sŏul *South Korea*	11 000
Beijing *China*	10 800
Tianjin *China*	9400
Jakarta *Indonesia*	9300
Delhi *India*	8800
Manila *Philippines*	8500
Ōsaka *Japan*	8500
Karachi *Pakistan*	7700
Bangkok *Thailand*	7200
Tehrān *Iran*	6800

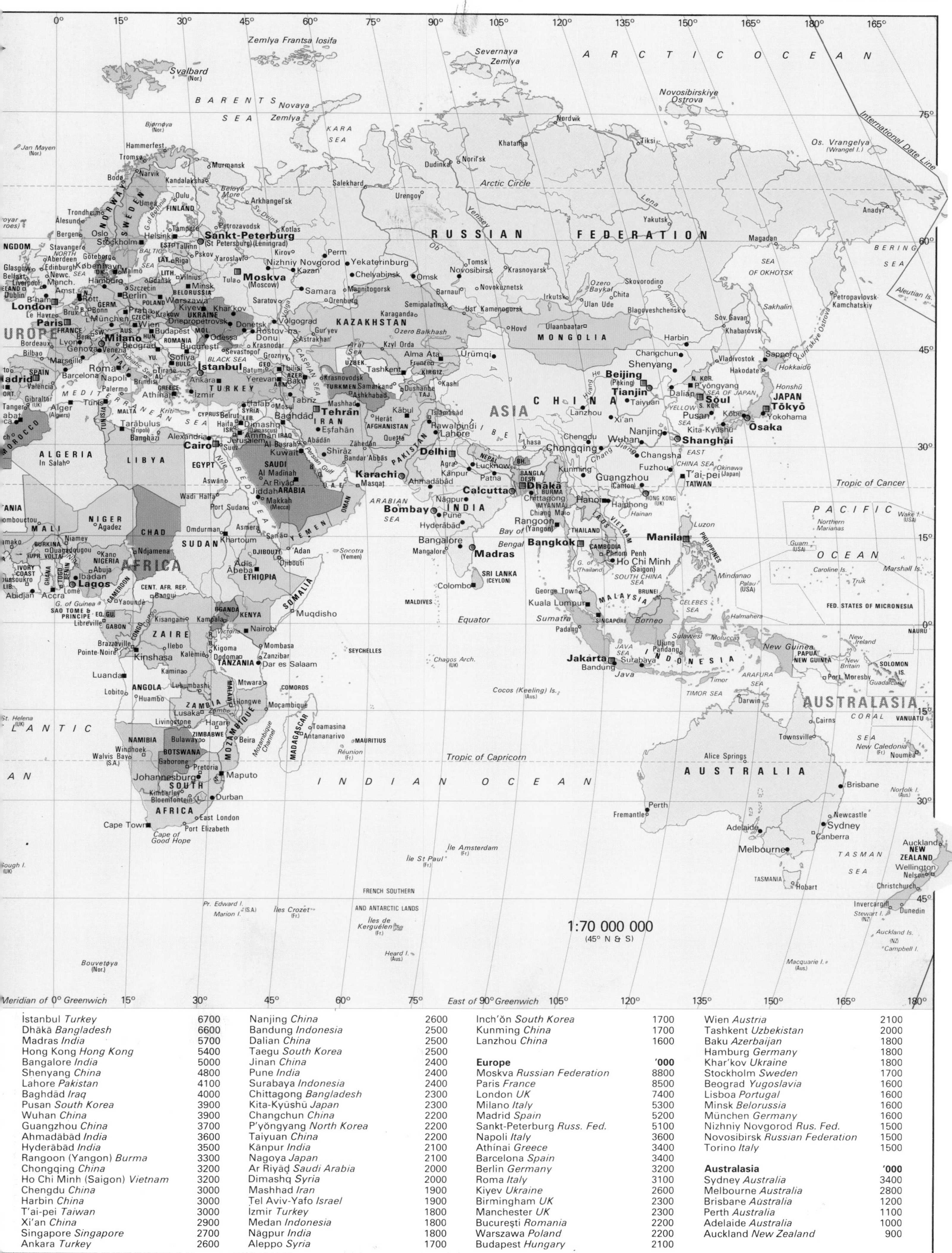

	'000
İstanbul *Turkey*	6700
Dhākā *Bangladesh*	6600
Madras *India*	5700
Hong Kong *Hong Kong*	5400
Bangalore *India*	5000
Shenyang *China*	4800
Lahore *Pakistan*	4100
Baghdād *Iraq*	4000
Pusan *South Korea*	3900
Wuhan *China*	3900
Guangzhou *China*	3700
Ahmadābād *India*	3600
Hyderābād *India*	3500
Rangoon (Yangon) *Burma*	3300
Chongqing *China*	3200
Ho Chi Minh (Saigon) *Vietnam*	3200
Chengdu *China*	3000
Harbin *China*	3000
T'ai-pei *Taiwan*	3000
Xi'an *China*	2900
Singapore *Singapore*	2700
Ankara *Turkey*	2600

	'000
Nanjing *China*	2600
Bandung *Indonesia*	2500
Dalian *China*	2500
Taegu *South Korea*	2500
Jinan *China*	2400
Pune *India*	2400
Surabaya *Indonesia*	2400
Chittagong *Bangladesh*	2300
Kita-Kyūshū *Japan*	2300
Changchun *China*	2200
P'yŏngyang *North Korea*	2200
Taiyuan *China*	2200
Kānpur *India*	2100
Nagoya *Japan*	2100
Ar Riyāḑ *Saudi Arabia*	2000
Dimashq *Syria*	2000
Mashhad *Iran*	1900
Ṭel Aviv-Yafo *Israel*	1900
İzmir *Turkey*	1800
Medan *Indonesia*	1800
Nāgpur *India*	1800
Aleppo *Syria*	1700

Inch'ŏn *South Korea*	1700
Kunming *China*	1700
Lanzhou *China*	1600
Europe	**'000**
Moskva *Russian Federation*	8800
Paris *France*	8500
London *UK*	7400
Milano *Italy*	5300
Madrid *Spain*	5200
Sankt-Peterburg *Russ. Fed.*	5100
Napoli *Italy*	3600
Athínai *Greece*	3400
Barcelona *Spain*	3400
Berlin *Germany*	3200
Roma *Italy*	3100
Kiyev *Ukraine*	2600
Birmingham *UK*	2300
Manchester *UK*	2300
Bucureşti *Romania*	2200
Warszawa *Poland*	2200
Budapest *Hungary*	2100

Wien *Austria*	2100
Tashkent *Uzbekistan*	2000
Baku *Azerbaijan*	1800
Hamburg *Germany*	1800
Khar'kov *Ukraine*	1800
Stockholm *Sweden*	1700
Beograd *Yugoslavia*	1600
Lisboa *Portugal*	1600
Minsk *Belorussia*	1600
München *Germany*	1600
Nizhniy Novgorod *Rus. Fed.*	1500
Novosibirsk *Russian Federation*	1500
Torino *Italy*	1500
Australasia	**'000**
Sydney *Australia*	3400
Melbourne *Australia*	2800
Brisbane *Australia*	1200
Perth *Australia*	1100
Adelaide *Australia*	1000
Auckland *New Zealand*	900

1:35M

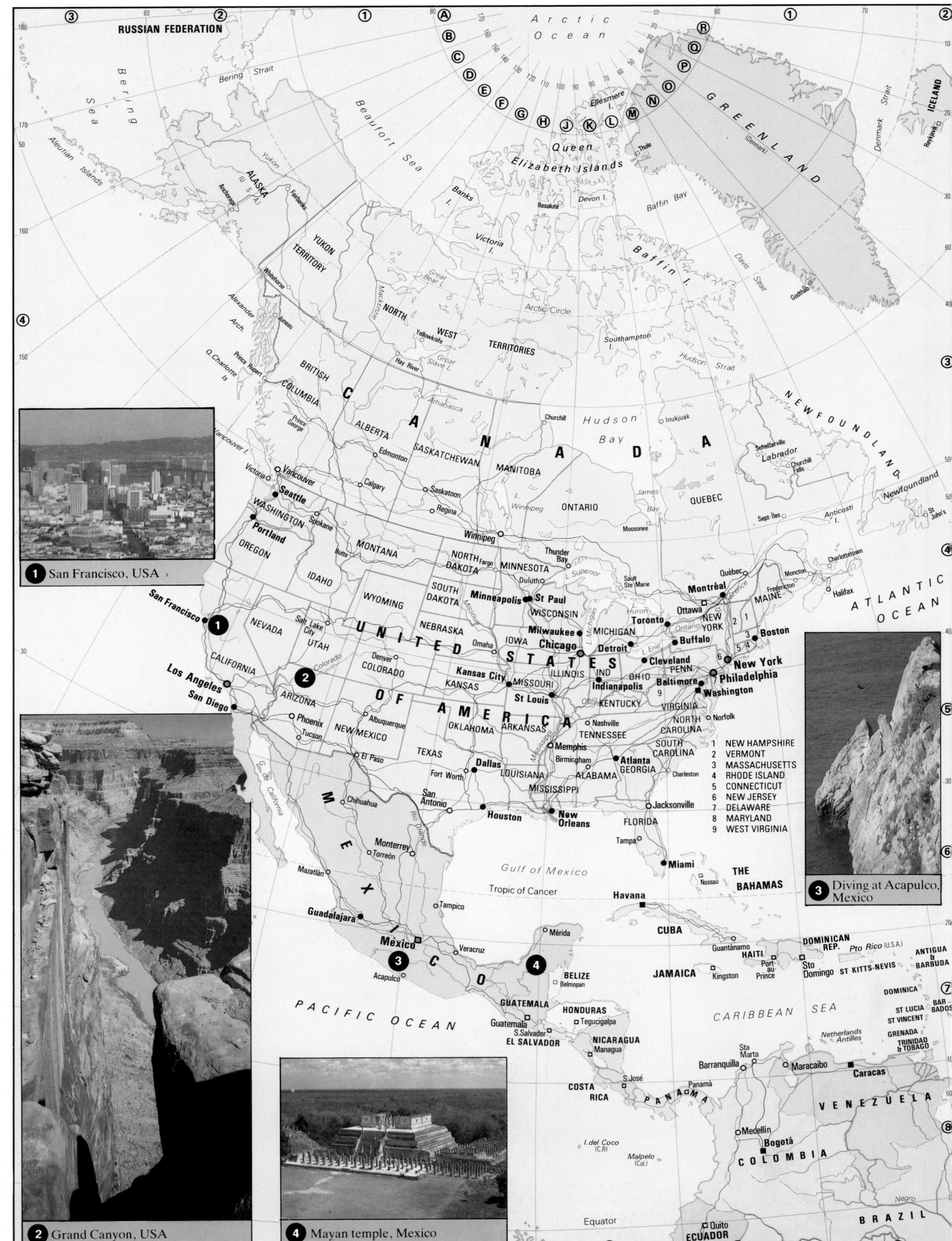

1 San Francisco, USA

2 Grand Canyon, USA

3 Diving at Acapulco, Mexico

4 Mayan temple, Mexico

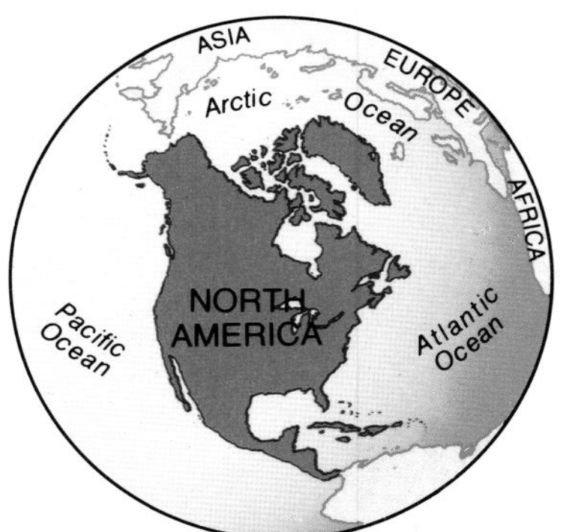

FACTS ABOUT NORTH AMERICA

1 The city of San Francisco was almost destroyed by an earthquake in 1906, and there could be another one soon. Right under the city runs the San Andreas fault, where two of the 'plates' which make up the earth's crust slide against one another. When they get jammed together at any point, pressure builds up, until finally they break apart. This causes an earthquake because of the sudden release of so much energy. The longer the plates stay jammed together, the greater the strength of the final earthquake: in 1906, the plates under San Francisco slid 6 m (20 feet) in a few minutes. Some parts of the fault have not moved for years – and scientists think there will be another big earthquake soon.

2 The huge Grand Canyon in Arizona, USA, was gouged out of the rock by the Colorado River. It is 1.6 km (1 mile) deep, a maximum of 29 km (18 miles) wide and no less than 446 km (227 miles) long! The Grand Canyon is still being carved deeper (though very slowly) by the river.

3 At La Questrada, Acapulco, Mexico, divers often swoop 36 m (118 feet) down into the sea. This is the highest dive which people do regularly.

4 The Maya were a tribe who lived in southern Mexico and Guatemala 1400 years ago. They built great cities with stone temples, public buildings and palaces. The picture shows one of their buildings which can be seen today. It was built without help from any modern machinery.

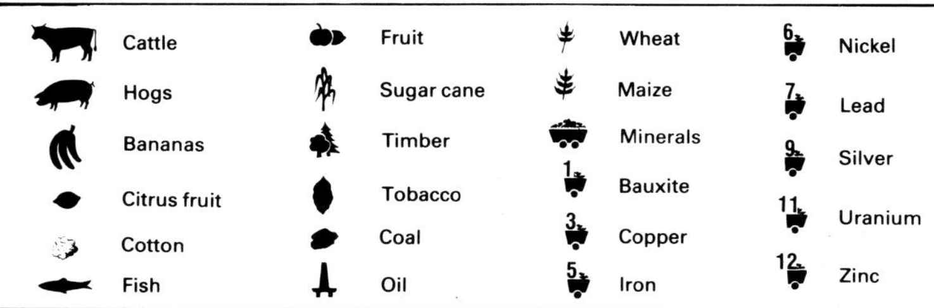

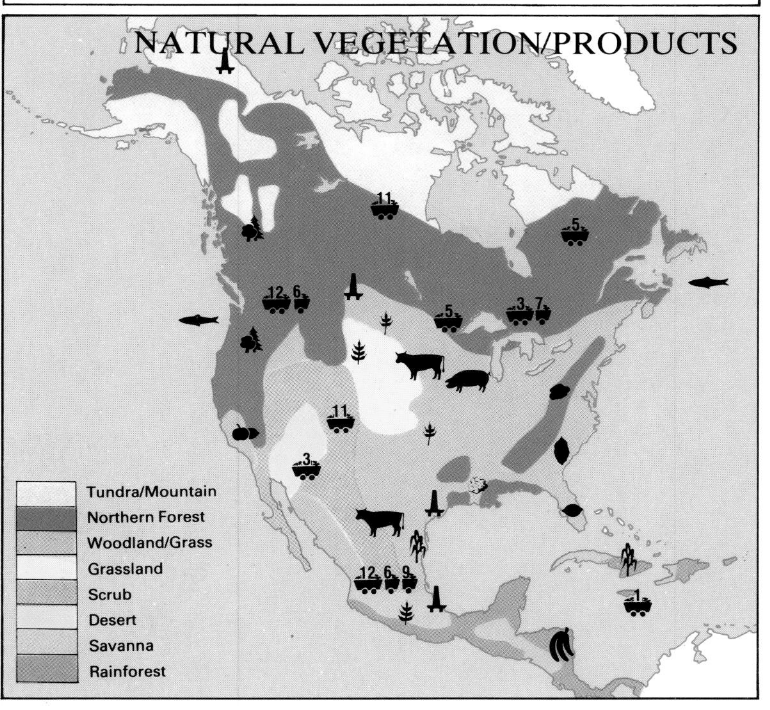

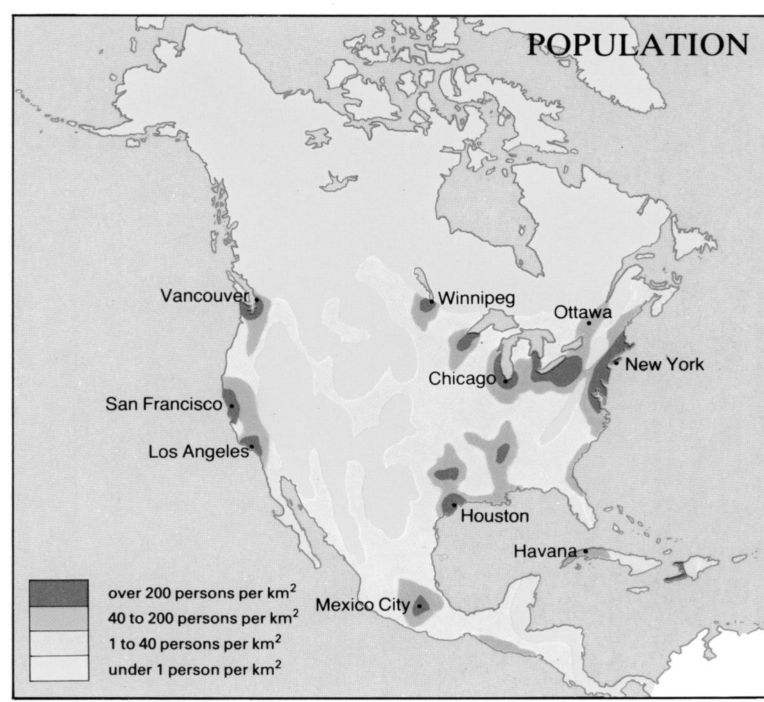

CANADA

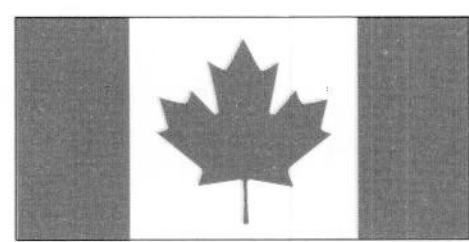

Area: 9 976 147 sq km (3 851 790 sq miles)
Population: 26 500 000
Capital: Ottawa
Languages: English, French
Currency: Canadian Dollar

CUBA

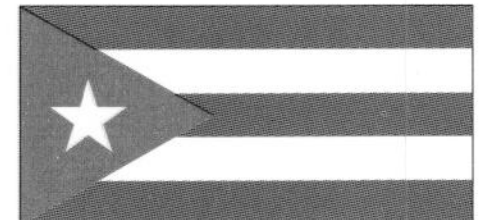

Area: 114 524 sq km (44 218 sq miles)
Population: 10 600 000
Capital: Havana
Language: Spanish
Currency: Cuban Peso

EL SALVADOR

Area: 20 865 sq km (8056 sq miles)
Population: 5 300 000
Capital: San Salvador
Language: Spanish
Currency: Colon

GUATEMALA

Area: 108 888 sq km (42 042 sq miles)
Population: 9 200 000
Capital: Guatemala
Language: Spanish
Currency: Quetzal

JAMAICA

Area: 11 424 sq km (4411 sq miles)
Population: 2 500 000
Capital: Kingston
Language: English
Currency: Jamaican Dollar

MEXICO

Area: 1 967 180 sq km (759 528 sq miles)
Population: 88 600 000
Capital: Mexico City
Language: Spanish
Currency: Mexican Peso

NICARAGUA

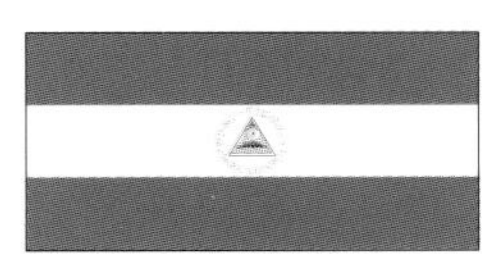

Area: 139 000 sq km (53 668 sq miles)
Population: 3 900 000
Capital: Managua
Language: Spanish
Currency: Cordoba

UNITED STATES OF AMERICA

Area: 9 363 130 sq km (3 615 104 sq miles)
Population: 249 200 000
Capital: Washington
Language: English
Currency: U.S. Dollar

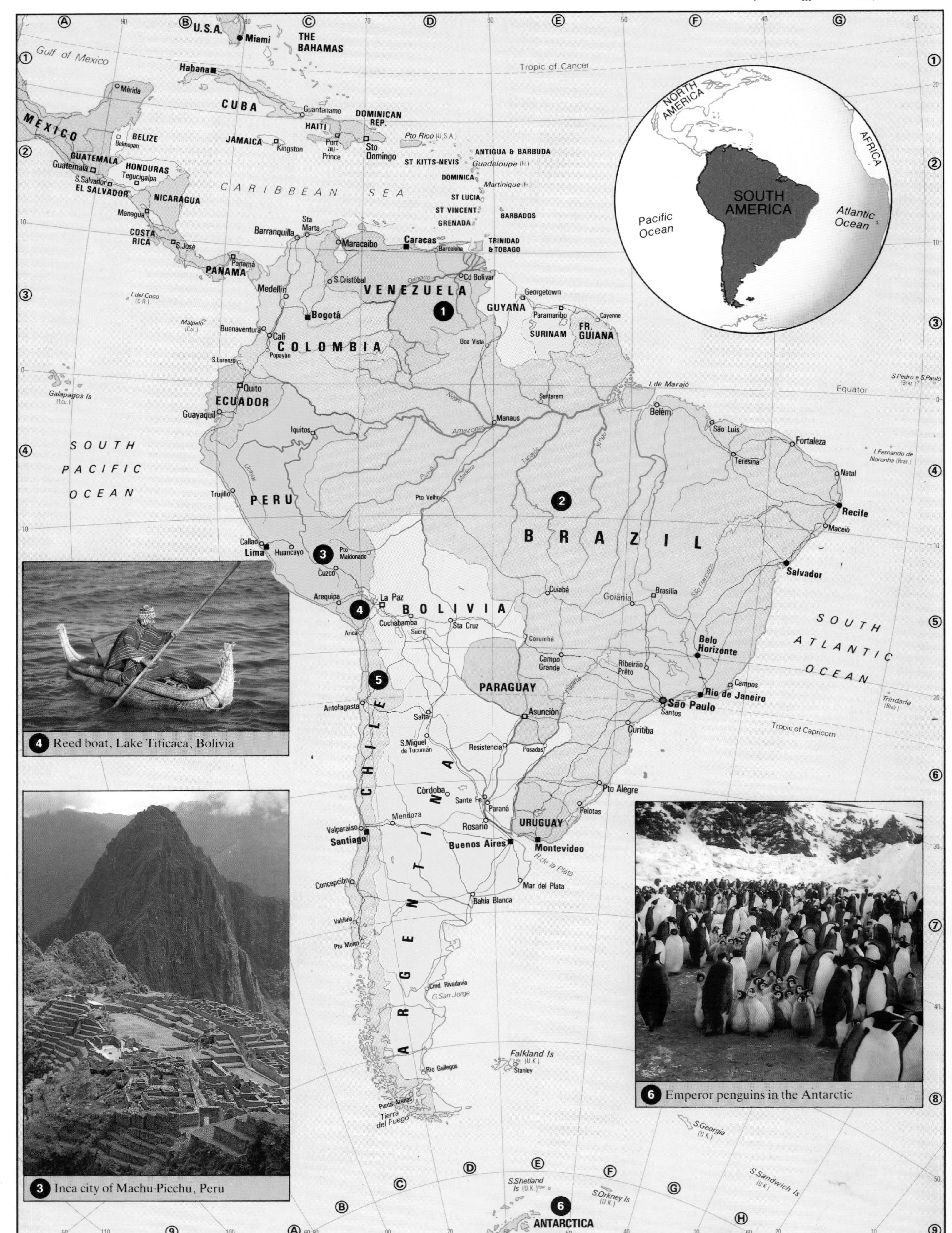

4 Reed boat, Lake Titicaca, Bolivia

3 Inca city of Machu-Picchu, Peru

6 Emperor penguins in the Antarctic

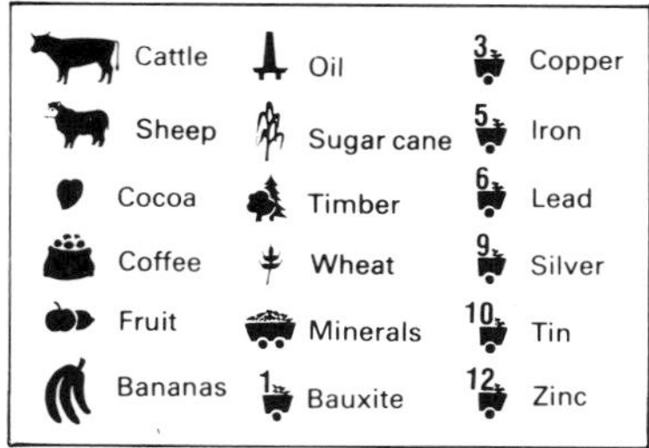

FACTS ABOUT SOUTH AMERICA

1 The Angel Falls, Venezuela, are the highest waterfalls in the world, at 979 m (3212 feet).

2 Deforestation is a major problem in South America. About 1 per cent of the total area of forest is lost each year. Often trees are cut down to clear land for agriculture. On hillsides, the soil soon becomes too poor to grow crops and the land is abandoned. Trees cannot grow again, and so soil is eroded away by rain and wind. Trees are also lost when lakes are made for hydro-electric dams; when new towns are built; and as a result of the way people live – they take too much wood for fuel and timber, allow animals to graze on foliage, and light fires which get out of control.

3 In the Andes Mountains, in the north-west of South America, there are ruins of cities built by the Incas. They ruled the Indians in the area 500 years ago. The Incas had well-developed political and religious systems. They built their cities on terraces engineered from the mountain side. The Spanish, the first Europeans to discover these cities, killed the Incas to seize the gold and silver which they had mined, and their cities were abandoned.

4 The highest navigable lake in the world is Lake Titicaca, on the Peru/Bolivia border. It is no less than 3811 m (12 503 feet) above sea level. The local Indian people make boats from bundles of reeds tied together, to use for fishing. The reeds grow around the edge of the lake.

5 Although in the rain forests of the Amazon Basin it rains every day, in the Atacama Desert, Chile, hundreds of years can pass between one rain storm and the next. A storm in 1971 was the first for 400 years. The desert is the driest place in the world.

6 The Emperor Penguin, found in the Antarctic, does not make a nest. Instead, a single egg is carried on top of the male penguin's feet. It is kept warm by a fold of skin which hangs down and covers it. The penguin does not eat during the two months it takes for the egg to hatch out.

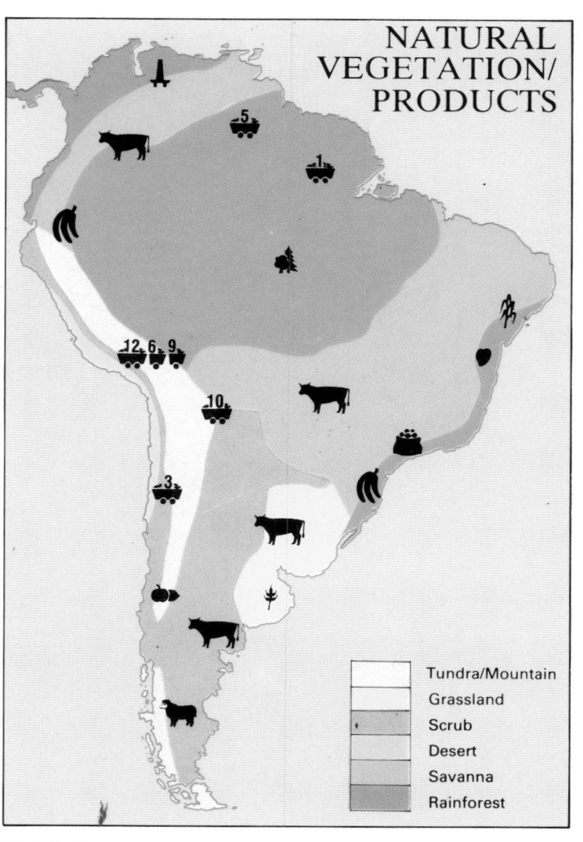

ARGENTINA

Area: 2 777 815 sq km (1 072 514 sq miles)
Population: 32 300 000
Capital: Buenos Aires
Language: Spanish
Currency: Argentine Peso

BOLIVIA

Area: 1,098 575 sq km (424 160 sq miles)
Population: 7 300 000
Capital: La Paz
Languages: Spanish, Aymara, Quechua
Currency: Bolivian Peso

BRAZIL

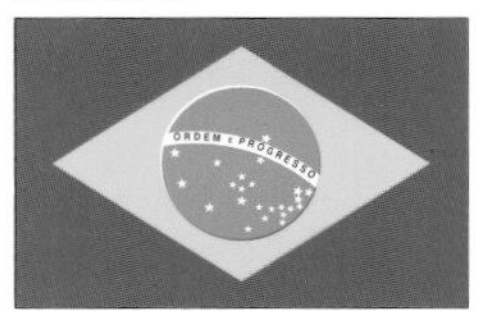

Area: 8 511 968 sq km (3 286 471 sq miles)
Population: 150 400 000
Capital: Brasilia
Language: Portuguese
Currency: Cruzeiro

CHILE

Area: 756 943 sq km (292 256 sq miles)
Population: 13 200 000
Capital: Santiago
Language: Spanish
Currency: Chilean Peso

COLOMBIA

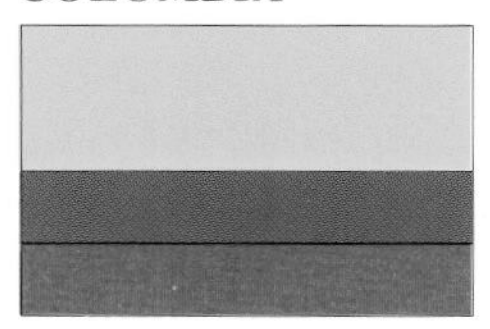

Area: 1 138 907 sq km (439 732 sq miles)
Population: 33 000 000
Capital: Bogota
Language: Spanish
Currency: Colombian Peso

ECUADOR

Area: 455 502 sq km (175 869 sq miles)
Population: 10 600 000
Capital: Quito
Language: Spanish
Currency: Sucre

GUYANA

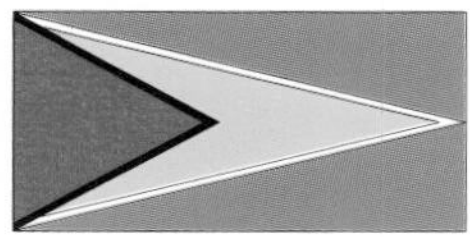

Area: 214 969 sq km (83 000 sq miles)
Population: 800 000
Capital: Georgetown
Language: English
Currency: Guyanese Dollar

PERU

Area: 1 285 215 sq km (496 222 sq miles)
Population: 21 600 000
Capital: Lima
Languages: Spanish, Aymara, Quechua
Currency: Sol

VENEZUELA

Area: 912 047 sq km (352 141 sq miles)
Population: 19 700 000
Capital: Caracas
Language: Spanish
Currency: Bolivar

1:15M

8 Venice, Italy

5 Cork stack and cork oak tree, Portugal

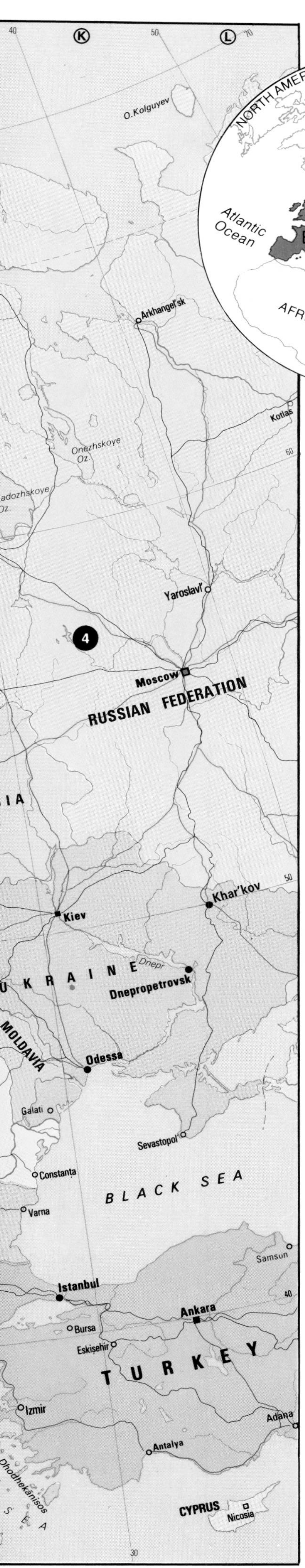

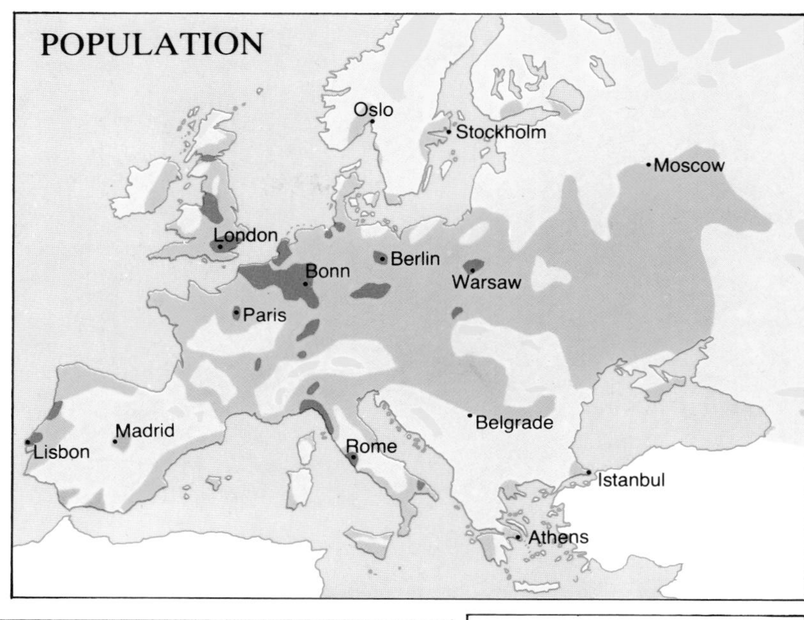

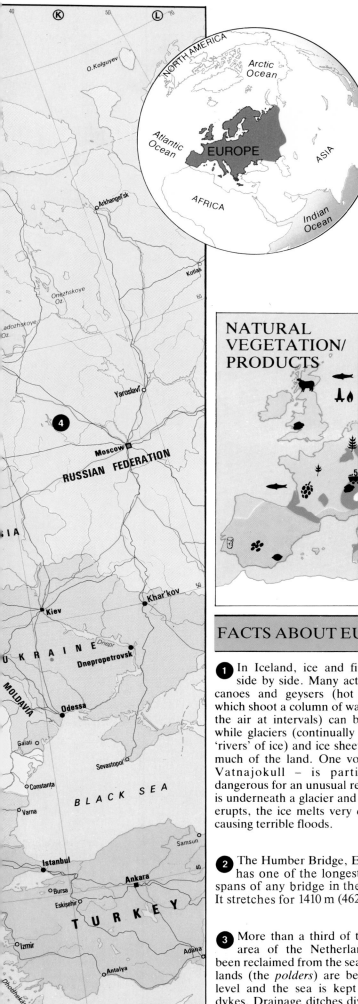

over 500 persons per km^2
100-500 persons per km^2
5-100 persons per km^2
under 5 persons per km^2

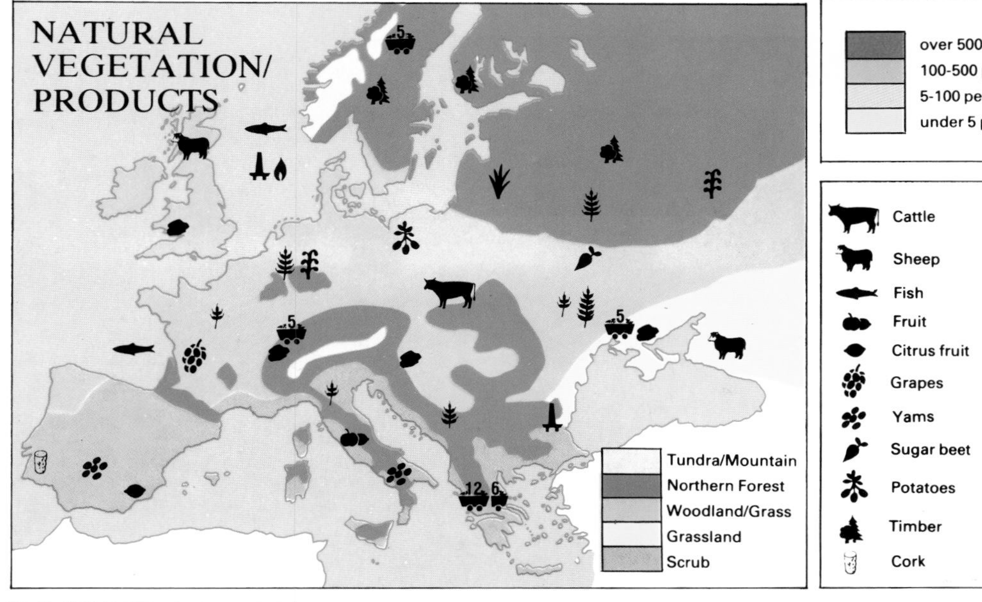

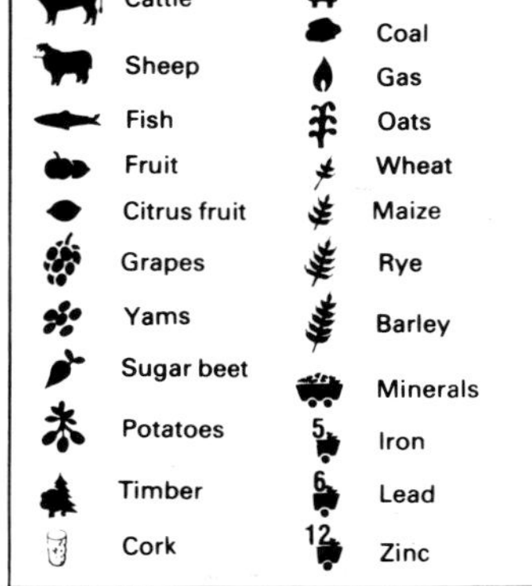

FACTS ABOUT EUROPE

1 In Iceland, ice and fire exist side by side. Many active volcanoes and geysers (hot springs which shoot a column of water into the air at intervals) can be seen, while glaciers (continually moving 'rivers' of ice) and ice sheets cover much of the land. One volcano – Vatnajokull – is particularly dangerous for an unusual reason: it is underneath a glacier and when it erupts, the ice melts very quickly, causing terrible floods.

2 The Humber Bridge, England, has one of the longest single spans of any bridge in the world. It stretches for 1410 m (4626 feet).

3 More than a third of the land area of the Netherlands has been reclaimed from the sea. These lands (the *polders*) are below sea level and the sea is kept out by dykes. Drainage ditches divide the fertile fields. The water from them is pumped into canals and rivers, then out to sea.

4 The longest river in Europe is the Volga, which runs for 3690 km (2292 miles) from the forests north west of Moscow all the way to the Caspian Sea.

5 Portugal is an important source of cork, which is actually the bark of a tree. The cork oak produces cork bark up to 15 cm (6 inches) thick and this is stripped off the trees every 10 to 15 years. Cork oaks grow throughout the western and central Mediterranean region.

6 The Pierre Saint Martin Cavern in the Pyrenees mountains, France, is the deepest cave system yet discovered in the world. It goes 1330 m (4364 feet) into the heart of the mountains.

7 The principality of Monaco is one of the most crowded countries in the world: 28 000 people live on 1.9 sq km (467 acres) of land! By contrast, most of Scandinavia has fewer than 40 people per square kilometre.

8 Venice, Italy, is built on no less than 118 islands. Instead of roads, there are canals, and boats are used for transport. Venice is sinking at a rate of 12 inches each century. Some of the reasons for this include water being extracted from wells, and the compression of the mud on the floor of the lagoon.

9 Mount Etna, Sicily, is the highest volcano in Europe (about 3323 m, 10 902 ft) and is still very active. Despite this, many people live on its lower slopes. This is because the soil there is very fertile and grows good produce.

2 The Humber Bridge, England

ALBANIA

Area: 2 732 sq km
(1 055 sq miles)
Population: 3 200 000
Capital: Tirana
Languages: Albanian
(Tosk and Gheg)
Currency: Lek

ANDORRA

Area: 453 sq km
(175 sq miles)
Population: 47 000
Capital: Andorra-la-Vella
Language: Catalan
Currency: French Franc
and Spanish Peseta

AUSTRIA

Area: 83 848 sq km
(32 374 sq miles)
Population: 7 600 000
Capital: Vienna
Language: German
Currency: Schilling

BELGIUM

Area: 30 512 sq km
(11 781 sq miles)
Population: 9 900 000
Capital: Brussels
Languages: Flemish, French
Currency: Belgian Franc

BULGARIA

Area: 110 911 sq km
(42 822 sq miles)
Population: 9 000 000
Capital: Sofia
Language: Bulgarian
Currency: Lev

CZECHOSLOVAKIA

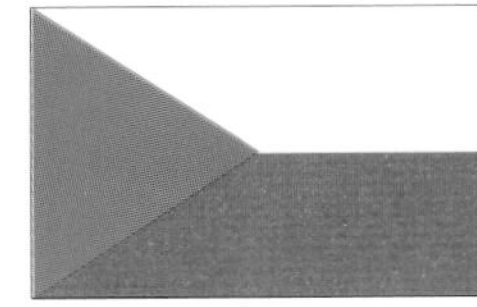

Area: 127 870 sq km
(49 370 sq miles)
Population: 15 700 000
Capital: Prague
Languages: Czech, Slovak
Currency: Koruna

DENMARK

Area: 43 030 sq km
(16 614 sq miles)
Population: 5 100 000
Capital: Copenhagen
Language: Danish
Currency: Krone

ESTONIA

Area: 45 100 sq km
(17 413 sq miles)
Population: 1 600 000
Capital: Tallinn
Language: Estonian
Currency: Ruble, Kroon proposed

FINLAND

Area: 337 032 sq km
(130 128 sq miles)
Population: 5 000 000
Capital: Helsinki
Languages: Finnish, Swedish
Currency: Mark

FRANCE

Area: 551 000 sq km
(212 741 sq miles)
Population: 56 100 000
Capital: Paris
Language: French
Currency: Franc

GERMANY

Area: 357 868 sq km
(138 173 sq miles)
Population: 79 000 000
Capital: Berlin, Bonn
Language: German
Currency: Deutschmark

GREECE

Area: 131 955 sq km
(50 948 sq miles)
Population: 10 000 000
Capital: Athens
Language: Greek
Currency: Drachma

HUNGARY

Area: 93 030 sq km
(35 919 sq miles)
Population: 10 600 000
Capital: Budapest
Language: Magyar
Currency: Forint

ICELAND

Area: 102 828 sq km
(41 131 sq miles)
Population: 250 000
Capital: Reykjavík
Language: Icelandic
Currency: Króna

IRELAND

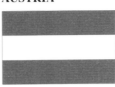

Area: 70·282 sq km
(27 136 sq miles)
Population: 3 700 000
Capital: Dublin
Languages: Irish (Gaelic), English
Currency: Irish Pound
(Punt)

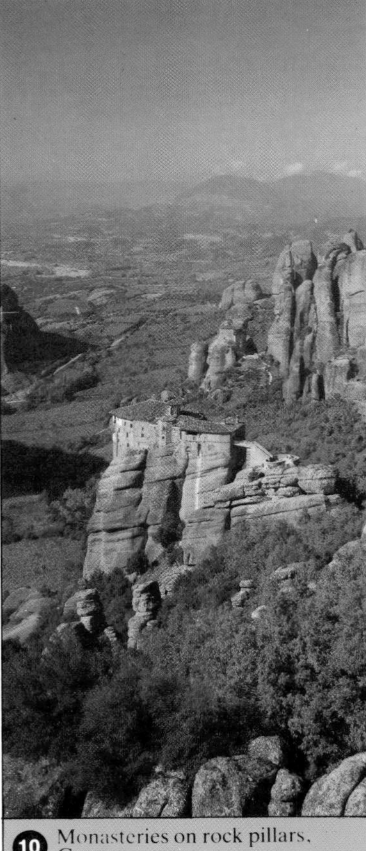

10 Monasteries on rock pillars, Greece

10 Near Kalabaka, Greece, are a group of monasteries built for monks with no fear of heights! They are perched on top of pillars of rock, called meteora, 300 m (1 000 ft) high. The only way up was by ladders or baskets slung on the end of ropes. Now stairways have been constructed so that tourists can visit the buildings.

11 The island of Santorini (Thira) in Greece is the site of the world's largest natural disaster. About 1500 BC this volcanic island erupted leaving a *caldera* (hollow basin shape where the top of the volcano had been) about 13 km (8 miles) across. Many people believe that the destruction of this island is the origin of the story of Atlantis. The people of Atlantis are mentioned by the Greek writer Plato. Crime and corruption spread throughout their island as they became wealthier, until finally the Athenians conquered them. Later the island disappeared into the sea in a single day and night.

7 Monte Carlo, Monaco

12 Loch Ness, in the Highlands of Scotland, is one of the most famous freshwater expanses in the world. Its length and depth are so great that it could accommodate the population of the earth three times over. Its greatest mystery is the world-famous Loch Ness Monster which was first recorded in the 6th century by the Abbot of Iona. 'Nessie', as the monster is affectionately known, has been sighted by many people but evidence of the monster's existence is inconclusive. If it does exist, the most popular theory is that the monster is one of a small colony of unknown creatures which have descended from marine animals trapped in the loch at the end of the last Ice Age 12,000 years ago.

12 Loch Ness, Scotland

13 The stalactite caves of Aggtelek in Hungary form one of the largest cave systems in Europe. They are 23 km (14 miles) long and extend over the border into Czechoslovakia. The stalactites and stalagmites in the caves make a spectacular impact. Stalagmites on the floor of the Aggtelek caves bear a clear resemblance to the human form. Others resemble animals, temples, waterfalls, a 'Great Organ' and even a 'Butcher's Shop'.

14 The spectacularly beautiful Alhambra in Spain is situated on a hill overlooking Granada. From the outside, the fortress walls look plain but they belie the complex and colourful interior. Visitors find the intricate stonework, the sumptuous halls and the attractive gardens with their many fountains quite breathtaking. The Palace of the Alhambra was built as a home for the Moorish rulers in the 14th century and is a well-preserved example of the very best of Moorish art.

14 The Alhambra, Spain

ITALY

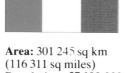

Area: 301 245 sq km (116 311 sq miles)
Population: 57 100 000
Capital: Rome
Language: Italian
Currency: Lira

LATVIA

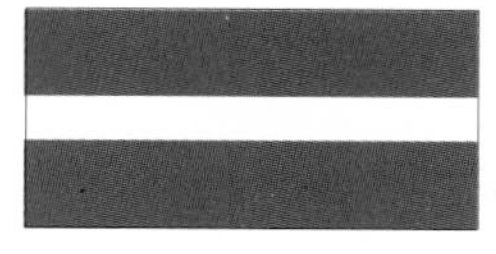

Area: 63 700 sq km (24 595 sq miles)
Population: 2 700 000
Capital: Riga
Language: Latvian
Currency: Ruble, Lat proposed

LIECHTENSTEIN

Area: 161 sq km (62 sq miles)
Population: 28 000
Capital: Vaduz
Language: German
Currency: Swiss Franc

LITHUANIA

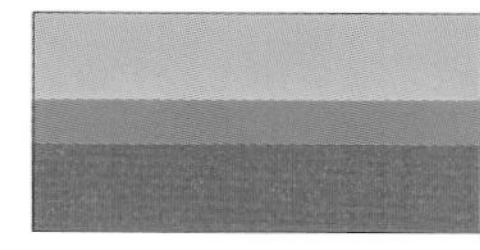

Area: 65 200 sq km (25 170 sq miles)
Population: 3 700 000
Capital: Vilnius
Language: Lithuanian
Currency: Ruble, Litas proposed

LUXEMBOURG

Area: 2 587 sq km (999 sq miles)
Population: 400 000
Capital: Luxembourg
Languages: Letzeburgish, French, German
Currency: Franc

NETHERLANDS

Area: 33 940 sq km (13 104 sq miles)
Population: 15 000 000
Capital: Amsterdam & The Hague
Language: Dutch
Currency: Guilder

NORWAY

Area: 324 218 sq km (125 180 sq miles)
Population: 4 200 000
Capital: Oslo
Language: Norwegian
Currency: Krone

POLAND

Area: 312 683 sq km (120 727 sq miles)
Population: 38 400 000
Capital: Warsaw
Language: Polish
Currency: Zloty

PORTUGAL

Area: 91 671 sq km (35 394 sq miles)
Population: 10 300 000
Capital: Lisbon
Language: Portuguese
Currency: Escudo

ROMANIA

Area: 237 500 sq km (91 699 sq miles)
Population: 23 300 000
Capital: Bucharest
Language: Romanian
Currency: Leu

SPAIN

Area: 504 745 sq km (194 882 sq miles)
Population: 39 200 000
Capital: Madrid
Language: Spanish
Currency: Peseta

SWEDEN

Area: 449 791 sq km (173 664 sq miles)
Population: 8 400 000
Capital: Stockholm
Language: Swedish
Currency: Krona

SWITZERLAND

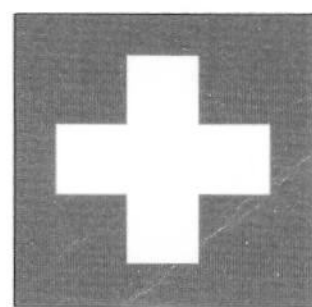

Area: 41 287 sq km (15 941 sq miles)
Population: 6 600 000
Capital: Bern
Languages: German, French, Italian, Romansch
Currency: Franc

UNITED KINGDOM

Area: 244 104 sq km (94 249 sq miles)
Population: 57 200 000
Capital: London
Language: English
Currency: Pound Sterling

YUGOSLAVIA

Area: 255 803 sq km (98 766 sq miles)
Population: 23 800 000
Capital: Belgrade
Languages: Serbo-Croatian, Macedonian, Slovenian
Currency: Dinar

1:40M

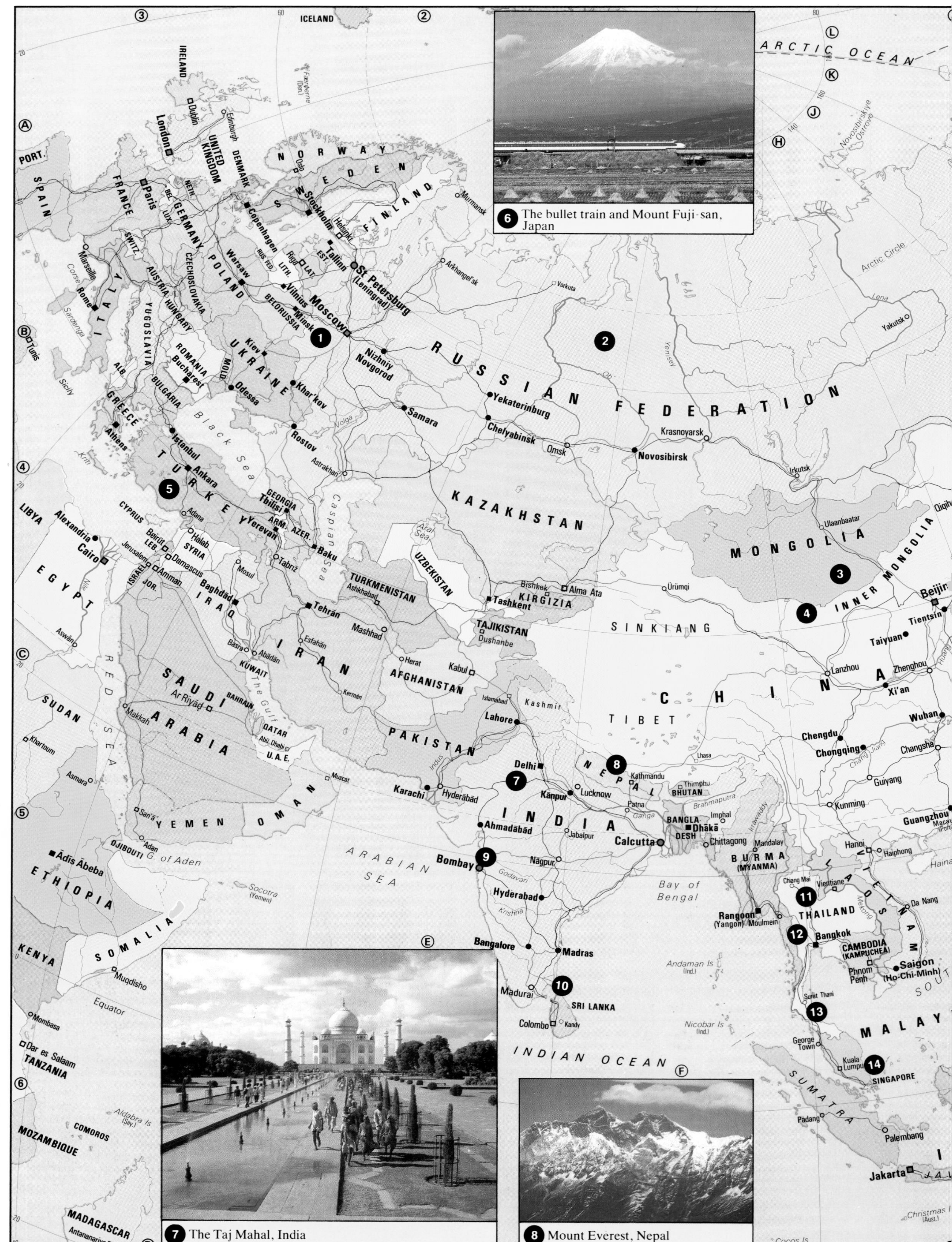

6 The bullet train and Mount Fuji-san, Japan

7 The Taj Mahal, India

8 Mount Everest, Nepal

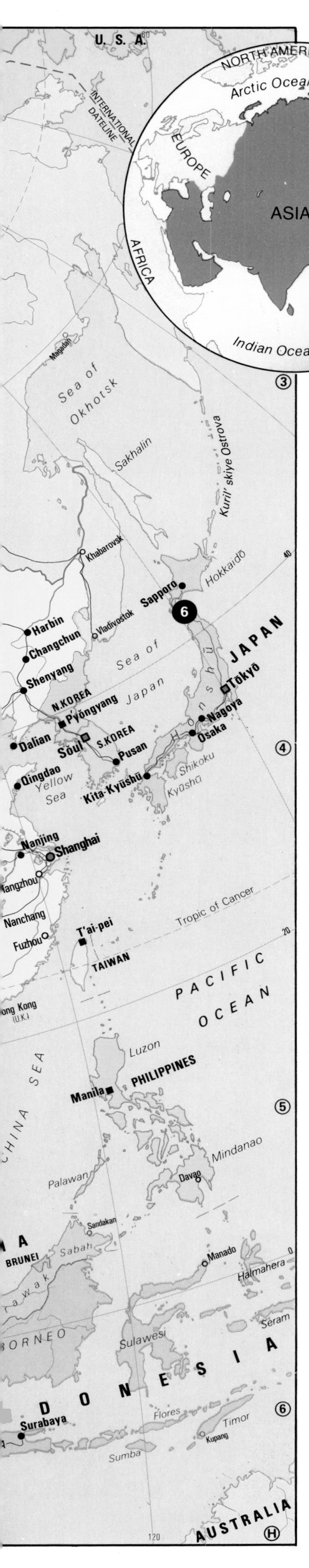

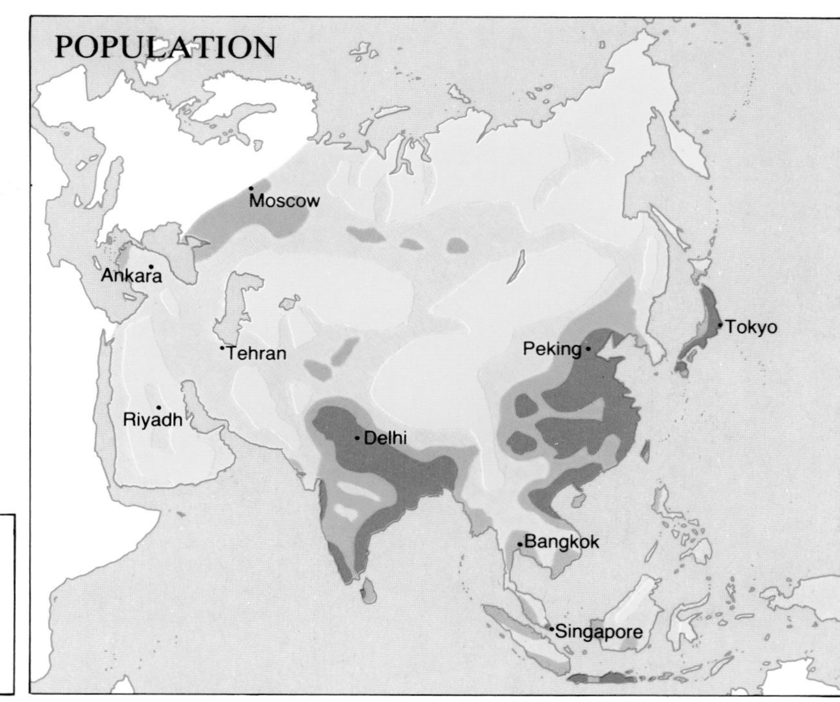

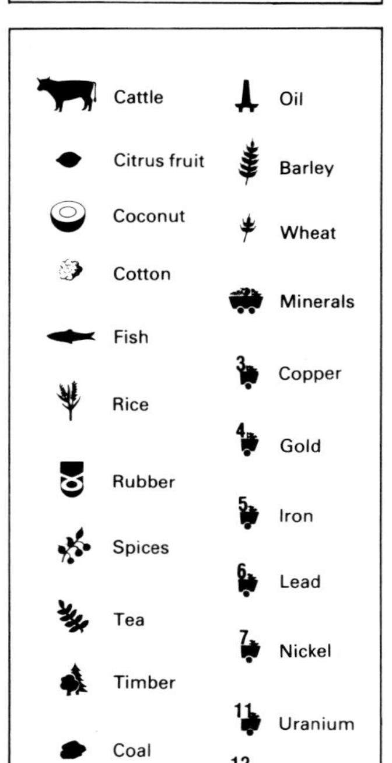

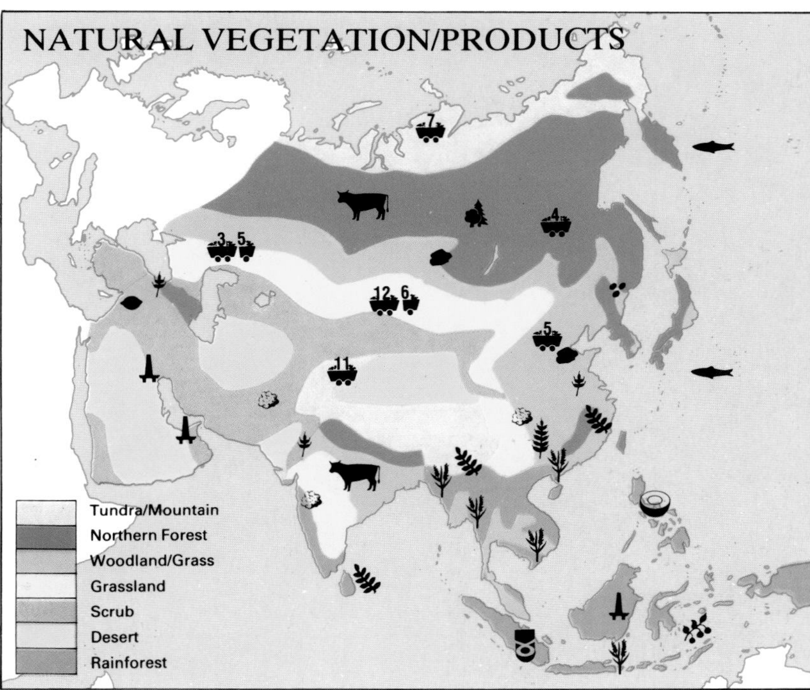

FACTS ABOUT ASIA

1 The world's heaviest bell is the *Czar Bell* in Moscow's Kremlin. It weighs a massive 196 tonnes (193 tons) and is 5.87 m (19 ft 3 in) high. The bell was cast in 1735. It is now cracked, and hasn't been rung since 1836.

2 In Siberia, there is a huge forest called the *taiga*, which makes up a quarter of the total area of forest in the world. The trees are mostly coniferous - pine and larch. Few people used to live in the taiga, as it is a very cold area, but because it is rich in minerals more people are moving into the forest. They live in industrial towns being built deep in its heart, to exploit the minerals.

3 The huge Gobi Desert covers much of Mongolia. The Gobi is a cold, barren region of rocky plains and hills. Water is very scarce and only a few nomads live here. They exist mainly by cattle raising and live in an unusual tent called a *yurt*, which is shaped like an upside-down bowl.

4 The Great Wall of China stretches for 3460 km (2150 miles), making it the longest in the world. It was built for defence in the 3rd century BC and kept in good repair until 400 years ago. Although part of the wall was blown up to make a dam in 1979, the many remaining sections of the wall are still impressive.

11 Floating vegetable market, Thailand

14 Singapore

12 Bangkok, Thailand

5 Cliff dwellings in Cappadocia, Turkey

13 Water buffalo ploughing Chinese paddy fields

FACTS ABOUT ASIA

5 In central Turkey, near Urgup in the region called Cappadocia, an extraordinary landscape can be seen. There was once a plateau here, made up of layers of rock, some hard and some much softer. Over thousands of years the softer rocks have been eroded by the weather, by streams and even by men digging out caves to live in. The rocks are now shaped into strange cones, towers and 'mushrooms', with 'hats' of harder rock balancing on top. There are also complete 'villages' of caves connected to each other by passageways cut through the rock. Each cave has 'cupboards' and 'shelves' cut into its walls. Here many centuries ago people hid from religious persecution. Over 300 churches which they dug out of the rock have been found. Some people still live in caves in this region, today.

6 The Seikan Tunnel in Japan is the longest tunnel in the world. It is an underwater tunnel, stretching for 54 km (34 miles). It was built for Japan's famous *bullet train*, the first passenger train to travel at 200 kph.

7 There should have been two Taj Mahals in India – a black one and a white one. In 1648, Emperor Shah Jahan completed the present Taj Mahal. It was a tomb for his wife, and made of white marble. He then began building a tomb of black marble for himself. Before work had got very far, he was overthrown.

8 At 8848 m (29 028 ft) the peak of Mt Everest in the Himalayas is the Earth's highest point. In May 1953, New Zealander Sir Edmund Hillary was the first man to climb Everest. Twenty two years later, in 1975, the first woman to reach the summit was Junko Tabei of Japan.

9 In India cows are sacred animals and are allowed to wander freely, even in the centre of big cities! Drivers are used to going round cows lying peacefully in the middle of the road.

10 Banyan trees can be seen in India and Sri Lanka. They are very unusual to look at, because what seems to be several trees growing close together, is actually just one tree! Aerial roots grow down from the banyan's branches and root in the ground. They become extra 'trunks' and support a huge canopy of leaves, which gives a lot of shade, very useful in such a hot climate.

11 Throughout Asia there are areas where many people live on boats – because there is not enough room for them to live in houses on land (or they cannot afford to) or because they just prefer to live on water. In these places, even the shops are on boats.

4 The Great Wall, China

10 Banyan tree, India

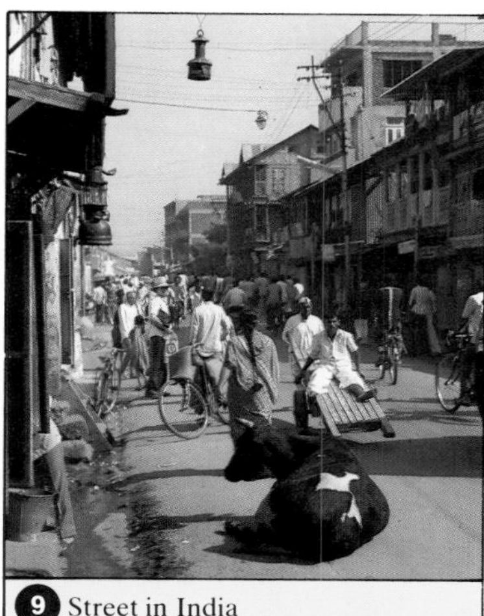

9 Street in India

12 Bangkok, Thailand, once had many canals, called *klongs*, instead of roads. (The city was called the 'Venice of the East' because the klongs reminded visitors of the canals in Venice, Italy.) They were used for transport and also helped to drain the land during the rainy season. After cars and lorries began to be used for transport, many of the klongs were filled in to make roads. Now Bangkok has problems with flooding when the monsoons come.

13 Paddy fields, the irrigated fields in which rice is grown, get their name from *padi*, the Malayan word for rice. Rice is grown throughout Asia in the fertile lowlands near the equator. Millions of people live in these areas, and rice is very important to them as it yields more food per acre than any other crop.

14 Over half the population of the world lives in Asia – that is 3 113 000 000 people. Some parts of Asia have many people living in a small area. One of the most densely populated countries is Singapore, which has an average of 4 420 people for each square kilometre of ground.

AFGHANISTAN

Area: 674 500 sq km
(260 424 sq miles)
Population: 16 600 000
Capital: Kabul
Languages: Pashtu, Dari, Uzbek
Currency: Afghani

CHINA

Area: 9 561 000 sq km
(3 691 502 sq miles)
Population: 1 118 800 000
Capital: Beijing
Language: Chinese (Mandarin)
Currency: Yuan

INDIA

Area: 3 287 593 sq km
(1 269 340 sq miles)
Population: 853 100 000
Capital: Delhi
Languages: Hindi, English
Currency: Indian Rupee

INDONESIA

Area: 1 919 263 sq km
(741 027 miles)
Population: 185 000 000
Capital: Jakarta
Language: Bahasa (Indonesian)
Currency: Rupiah

IRAN

Area: 1 648 184 sq km
(636 364 sq miles)
Population: 54 600 000
Capital: Tehran
Language: Persian (Farsi)
Currency: Rial

IRAQ

Area: 434 924 sq km
(167 924 sq miles)
Population: 18 900 000
Capital: Baghdad
Language: Arabic
Currency: Iraqi Dinar

ISRAEL

Area: 20 770 sq km
(8019 sq miles)
Population: 4 600 000
Capital: Jerusalem
Languages: Hebrew, Arabic
Currency: Shekel

JAPAN

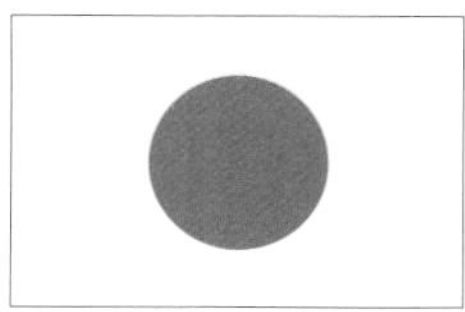

Area: 371 000 sq km
(143 243 sq miles)
Population: 123 500 000
Capital: Tokyo
Language: Japanese
Currency: Yen

MALAYSIA

Area: 330 669 sq km
(127 671 sq miles)
Population: 17 900 000
Capital: Kuala Lumpur
Language: Malay
Currency: Ringgit (Malaysian Dollar)

PAKISTAN

Area: 803 941 sq km
(310 402 sq miles)
Population: 122 600 000
Capital: Islamabad
Language: Urdu
Currency: Pakistan Rupee

PHILIPPINES

Area: 299 765 sq km
(115 739 sq miles)
Population: 62 400 000
Capital: Manila
Language: Philipino
Currency: Philippine Peso

SAUDI ARABIA

Area: 2 400 930 sq km
(927 000 sq miles)
Population: 14 100 000
Capital: Riyadh
Language: Arabic
Currency: Riyal

SINGAPORE

Area: 616 sq km
(238 sq miles)
Population: 2 700 000
Capital: Singapore
Languages: Chinese, Malay, Tamil, English
Currency: Singapore Dollar

THAILAND

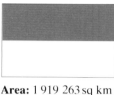

Area: 513 517 sq km
(198 269 sq miles)
Population: 55 700 000
Capital: Bangkok
Languages: Thai, Chinese
Currency: Baht

TURKEY

Area: 780 576 sq km
(301 380 sq miles)
Population: 55 900 000
Capital: Ankara
Language: Turkish
Currency: Turkish Lira

1:40M

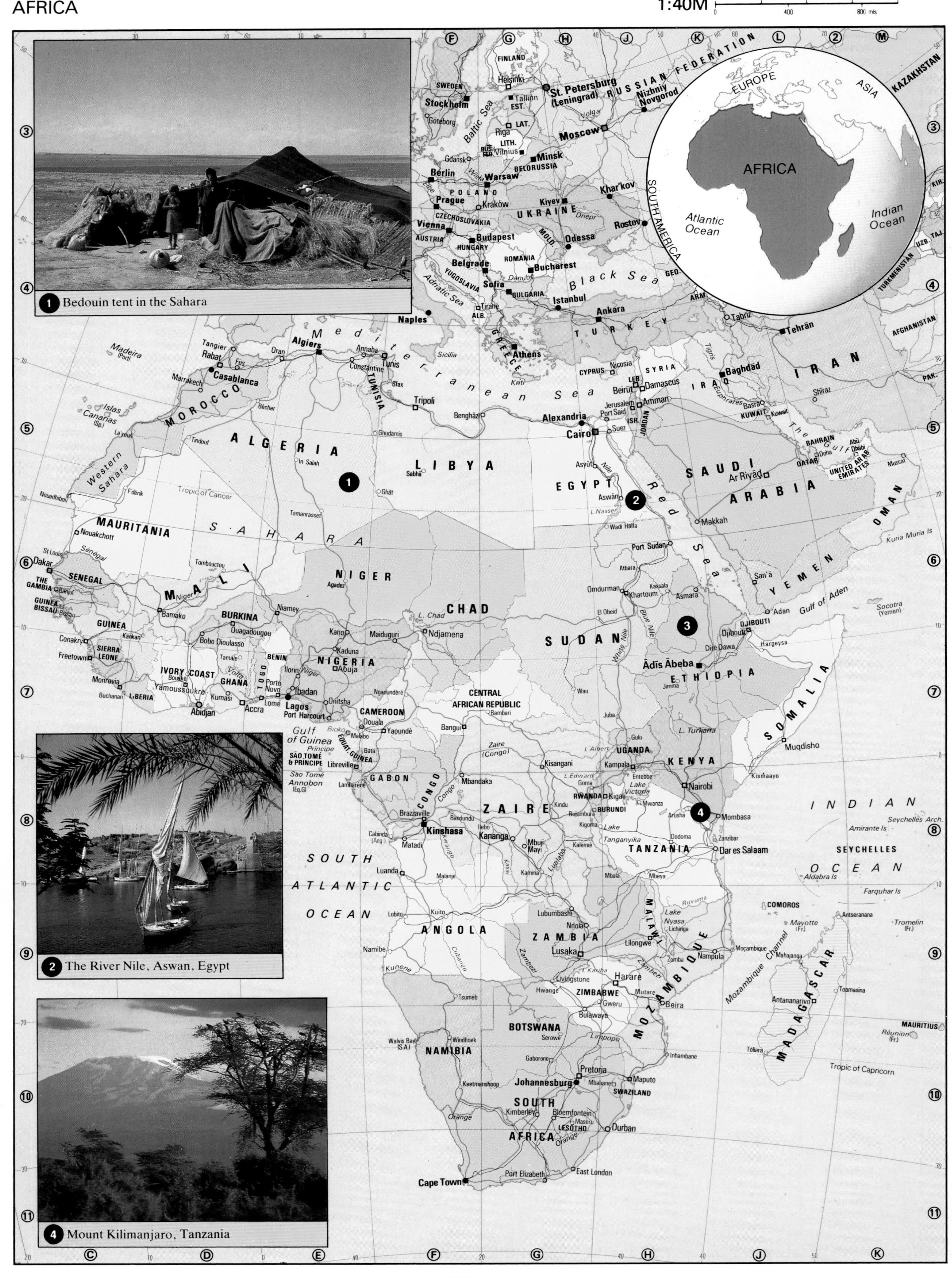

1 Bedouin tent in the Sahara

2 The River Nile, Aswan, Egypt

4 Mount Kilimanjaro, Tanzania

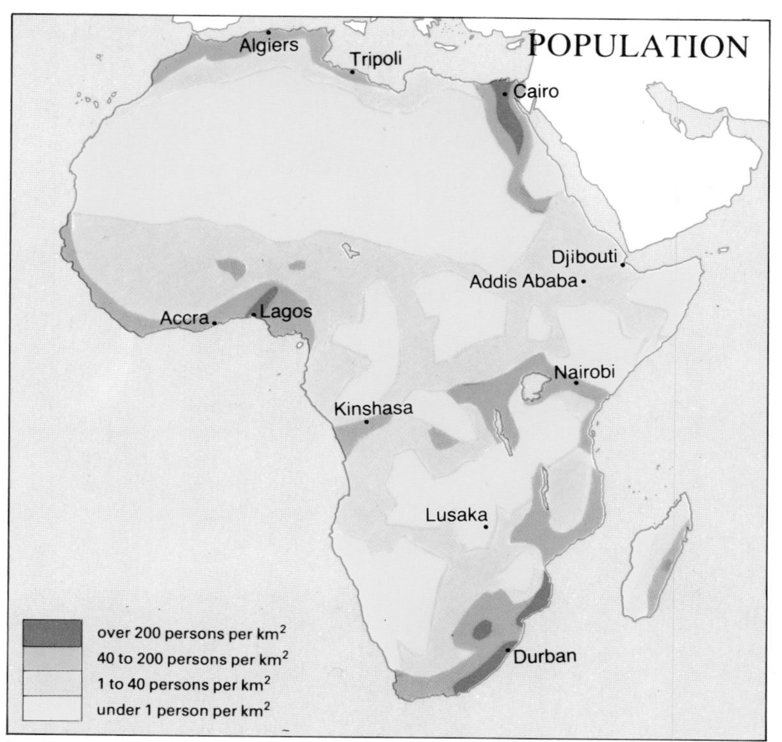

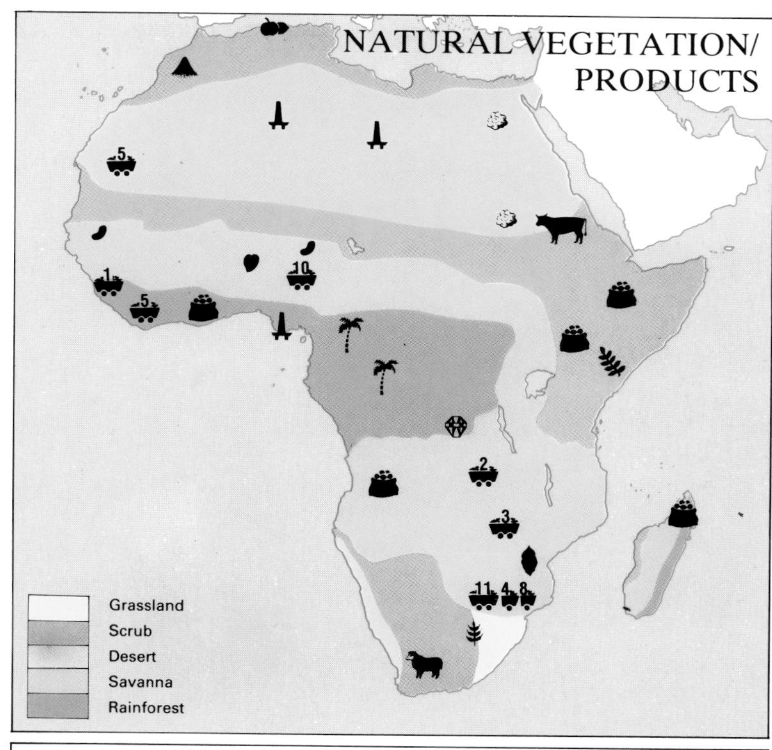

Cattle, Sheep, Cocoa, Coffee, Cotton, Fruit, Peanuts, Palm oil, Tea, Tobacco, Diamonds, Oil, Phosphates, Maize, Minerals, 1 Bauxite, 2 Cobalt, 3 Copper, 4 Gold, 5 Iron, 8 Platinum, 10 Tin, 11 Uranium

FACTS ABOUT AFRICA

1 The largest desert in the world is the Sahara, but only about 30% of it is sand. The rest is rocky waste. People live mainly near oases, where the land is watered by springs rising to the surface and crops can be grown. The desert is very hot and dry, but there are a few plants and animals (like camels) specially adapted to these conditions.

2 The Nile is the longest river in the world and flows for 6650 km (4160 miles) through North Africa to the Mediterranean Sea. The Nile used to flood its banks each year, but now the High Dam at Aswan controls the floods. When the dam was built, the temples of Abu Simbel (3000 years old) were moved to a higher site to stop them being flooded.

3 Some parts of Africa have had no rain, or very little, for several years. Food crops have failed and many people have died from malnutrition and starvation. A further problem has been wars, which have driven many people from their homes and fields. Even if part of a country can grow food, it is difficult to move that food into areas where none can be grown. There are few lorries and, where people are at war, transporting food may be dangerous. Although western countries have sent food supplies, there is still not enough to feed the hundreds of thousands of people who are starving. Governments are trying to find ways of growing more food and distributing it more quickly.

4 Kilimanjaro (now renamed Uhuru, meaning 'freedom') is the highest mountain in Africa (5895 m; 19 340 feet) and its peaks are always covered in snow.

EGYPT

Area: 1 000 250 sq km (386 197 sq miles)
Population: 52 400 000
Capital: Cairo
Language: Arabic
Currency: Egyptian Pound

ETHIOPIA

Area: 1 221 918 sq km (471 783 sq miles)
Population: 49 200 000
Capital: Addis Ababa
Language: Amharic
Currency: Birr

KENYA

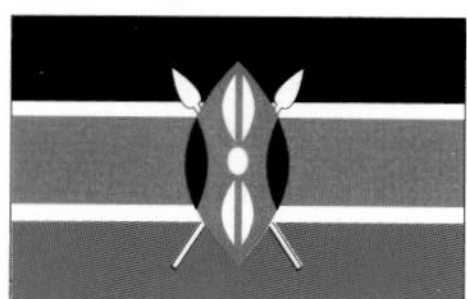

Area: 582 644 sq km (224 959 sq miles)
Population: 24 000 000
Capital: Nairobi
Languages: English, Swahili
Currency: Kenya Shilling

LIBYA

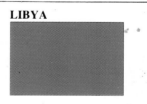

Area: 1 759 530 sq km (679 355 sq miles)
Population: 4 500 000
Capital: Tripoli
Language: Arabic
Currency: Libyan Dinar

NIGERIA

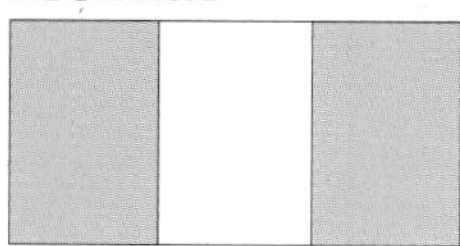

Area: 923 769 sq km (356 667 sq miles)
Population: 108 500 000
Capital: Lagos
Language: English
Currency: Naira

SOUTH AFRICA

Area: 1 221 038 sq km (471 443 sq miles)
Population: 35 300 000
Capital: Pretoria
Languages: Afrikaans, English
Currency: Rand

SUDAN

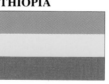

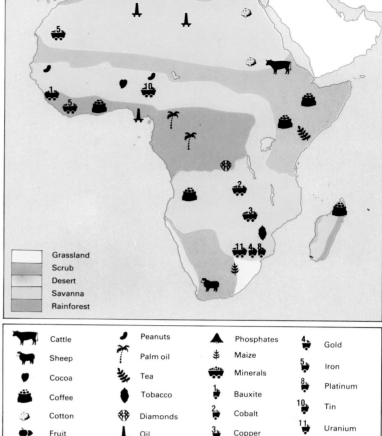

Area: 2 505 792 sq km (967 486 sq miles)
Population: 25 200 000
Capital: Khartoum
Language: Arabic
Currency: Sudanese Pound

ZAIRE

Area: 2 344 885 sq km (905 360 sq miles)
Population: 35 600 000
Capital: Kinshasa
Language: French
Currency: Zaire

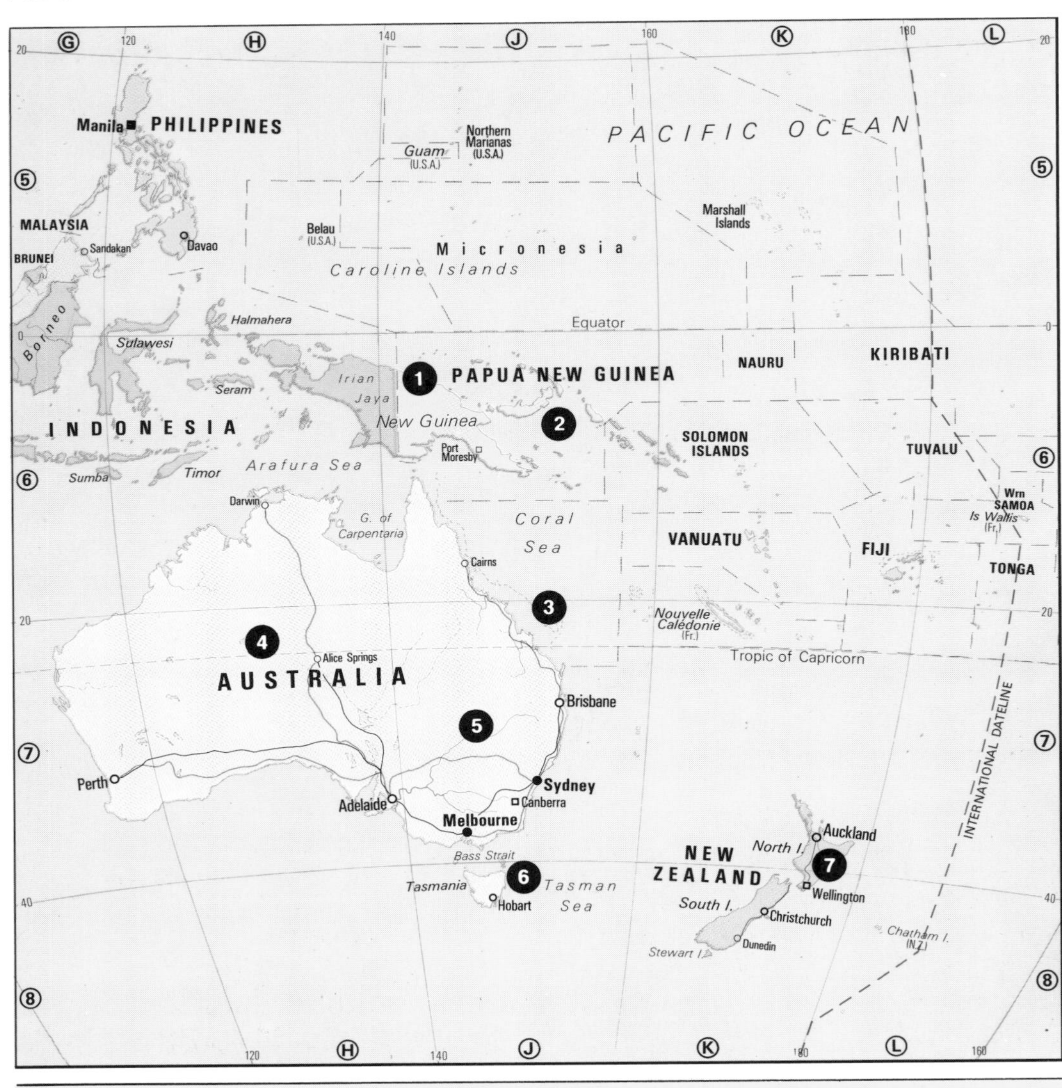

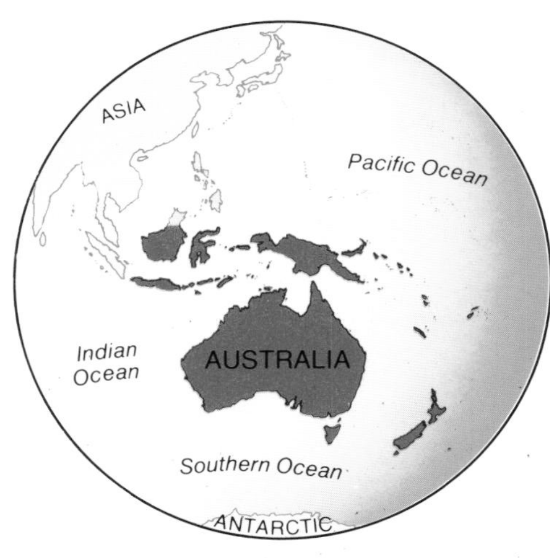

7 Geysers at Whakarewarewa, New Zealand

FACTS ABOUT AUSTRALASIA

1 Over 700 languages are spoken in Papua New Guinea. That is more than a quarter of all the languages spoken in the world. Papua New Guinea's mountains, thick forests and islands meant that different tribes did not mix, so they did not share a common language, but instead each developed its own. Today, Pidgin English and Police Motu have become the languages which the different tribes use to talk to each other.

2 No less than 38 different species of the beautiful Bird of Paradise are to be seen in Papua New Guinea. Another 5 species are found on neighbouring islands and in northern Australia. Their tail feathers are a traditional part of Papua New Guinea tribal costume, although the birds are now protected from hunting to a great extent.

3 Australia's Great Barrier Reef is formed from the shells of millions of tiny sea creatures. It is 2000 km (1250 miles) long and is the world's biggest coral reef. There are many thousands of coral islands or *atolls* in the Pacific region.

4 Ayers Rock is a huge sandstone rock formation which rears up abruptly from the desert in central Australia. The rock is special because it changes colour with the light. Australia's native *aborigine* people believe there is something magical about the rock.

5 Australia is the driest of all the continents in the world. Rainfall is also very unevenly distributed: even though the tropical north has about 2000 mm (79 inches) a year, the central deserts have less than 150 mm (6 inches). Irrigation is important for agriculture, and rivers and artesian wells are used as a source of water. The Snowy Mountains reservoir and irrigation scheme has brought water from the mountains to irrigate farmland in the east of Australia.

6 A Tasmanian Devil is a little bear-like creature found only in Tasmania. It is just 60 cm (2 ft) long, with a big bushy tail. It has very sharp teeth and eats other

4 Ayers Rock, Australia

6 Tasmanian Devil

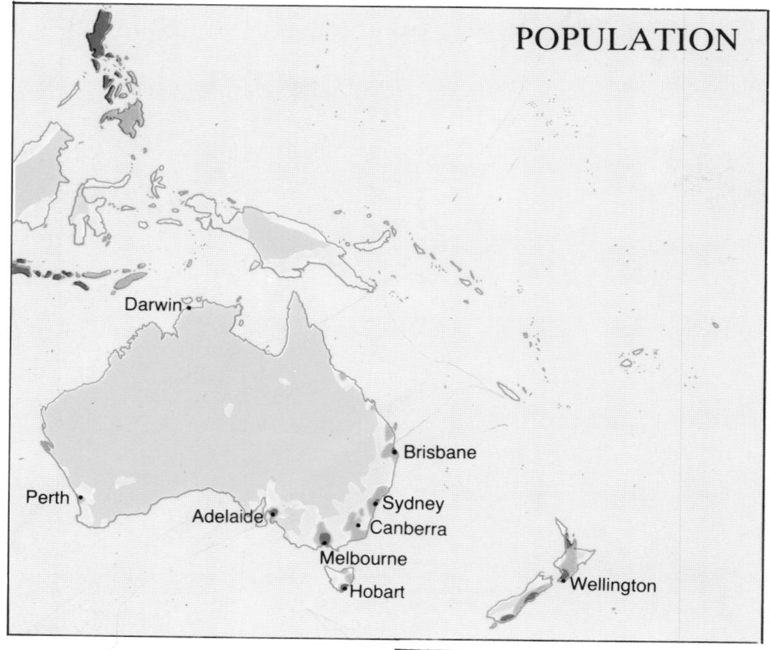

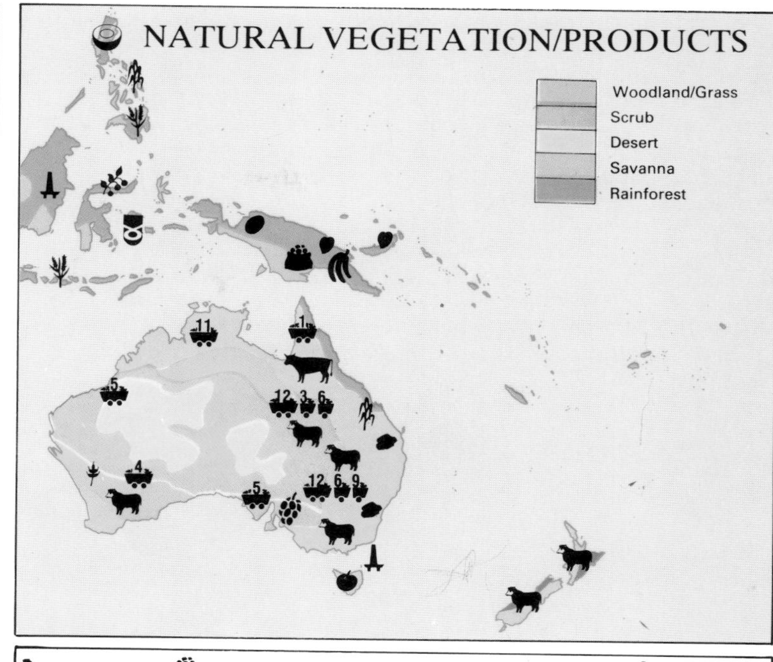

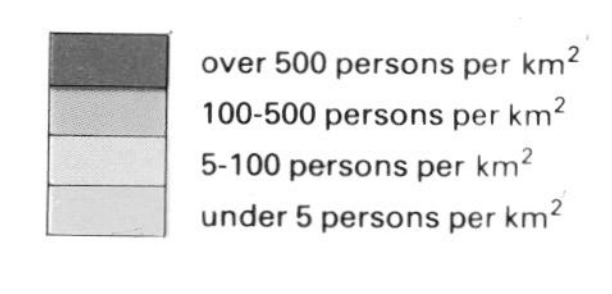

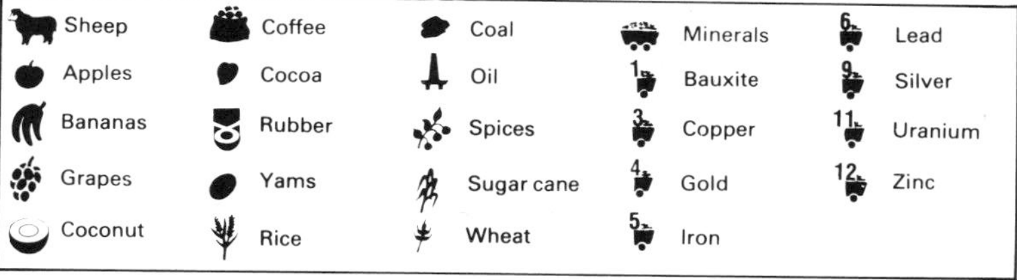

2 Traditional dress, Papua New Guinea

animals and small birds when it comes out at night. The Tasmanian Devil is a *marsupial.* This means it carries its young in a pouch.

7 The tallest geyser ever to have erupted was the Waimangu Geyser in New Zealand. In 1904 it rose to a height of 457 m (1500 ft). It last erupted in 1917, killing four people. Today, steam from New Zealand's hot springs and geysers is harnessed to generate electricity.

3 The Great Barrier Reef, Australia

AUSTRALIA

Area: 7 682 300 sq km
(2 966 136 sq miles)
Population: 16 900 000
Capital: Canberra
Language: English
Currency: Australian Dollar

FIJI

Area: 18 272 sq km
(7055 sq miles)
Population: 800 000
Capital: Suva
Languages: English, Fijian
Currency: Fiji Dollar

KIRIBATI

Area: 800 sq km
(309 sq miles)
Population: 66 000
Capital: Tarawa
Languages: English, I Kiribati
Currency: Australian Dollar

NEW ZEALAND

Area: 268 675 sq km
(103 735 sq miles)
Population: 3 400 000
Capital: Wellington
Language: English
Currency: New Zealand Dollar

PAPUA NEW GUINEA

Area: 461 692 sq km
(178 259 sq miles)
Population: 3 900 000
Capital: Port Moresby
Languages: English, Melanesian Pidgin
Currency: Kina

SOLOMON ISLANDS

Area: 29 785 sq km
(11 500 sq miles)
Population: 320 000
Capital: Honiara
Languages: English, Pidgin
Currency: Solomon Islands Dollar

TONGA

Area: 699 sq km
(270 sq miles)
Population: 100 000
Capital: Nuku'alofa
Languages: English, Tongan
Currency: Pa'anga

VANUATU

Area: 14 763 sq km
(5700 sq miles)
Population: 160 000
Capital: Vila
Languages: Bislama, English, French
Currency: Australian Dollar, Vatu

WESTERN SAMOA

Area: 2831 sq km
(1093 sq miles)
Population: 170 000
Capital: Apia
Languages: Samoan, English
Currency: Tala

The world can be divided into 8 broad 'climatic zones' (these are areas with a particular sort of weather). The natural types of plants and animals found in each zone are different and depend on the weather the zone has. This map shows which parts of the world are in each zone. The colour of the strip at the top of each zone description (for example, Desert, Rainforest) is the same as the colour used for the zone on the big map. The little map beside each zone description pinpoints where that type of habitat is found in the world. (For example, the Desert strip is orange/yellow. The little sketch map shows you where on the big map to look for this colour. You will find this colour in the north of Africa, the west of North America and in parts of Asia and Australia. All these places have deserts. The description tells you what the natural countryside looks like and what plants and animals live there.)

SCRUB OR MEDITERRANEAN

Areas of long, hot, dry summers and short, warm winters. The land used to be covered with trees, but man cleared it for crops and grazed his animals on it. Now there is evergreen scrub – vines and olive trees.

TUNDRA OR MOUNTAIN

Polar areas which are usually frozen over. During the short summers the top layer of soil thaws, creating vast marshes. Compact, wind-resistant plants and lichens and mosses are found here. Animals include lemmings and reindeer.

NORTHERN FOREST (TAIGA)

Forests of conifers growing over a large area. Winters are very cold and long. Summers are short. Trees include spruce and fir. Animals found here include beavers, squirrels and red deer.

WOODLAND AND GRASS

Temperate areas (where the weather is seldom very cold or very hot). Deciduous trees (which lose their leaves in winter) grow in the woodlands. They include oak, beech and maple. Man uses these areas most of all, for farming, building towns and villages, and industry.

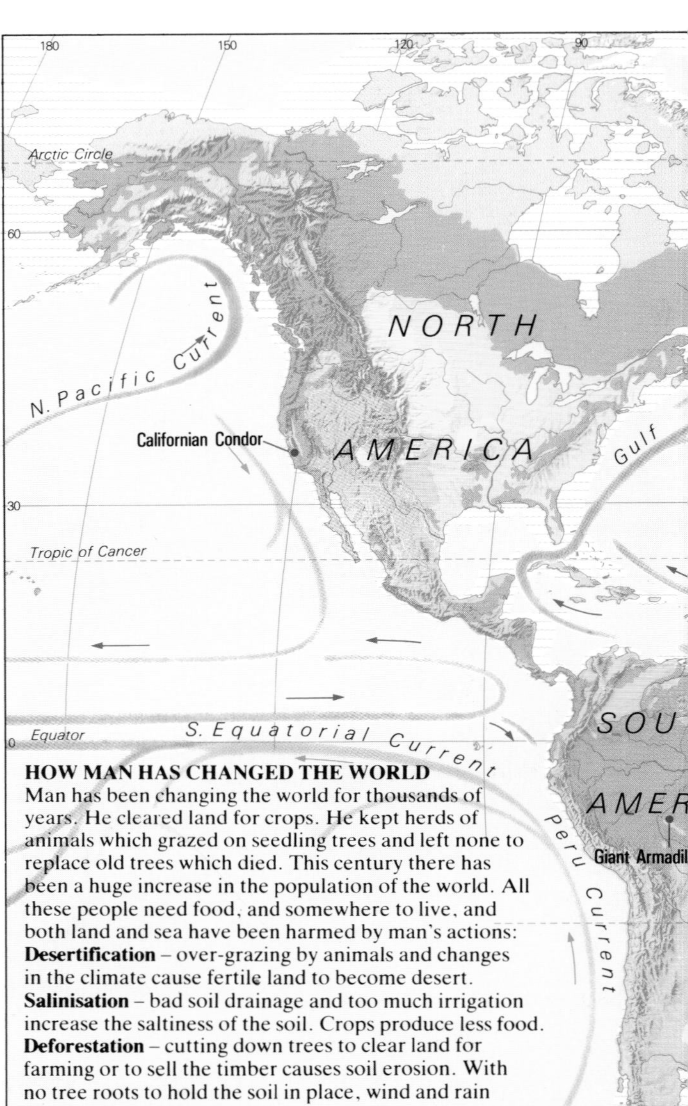

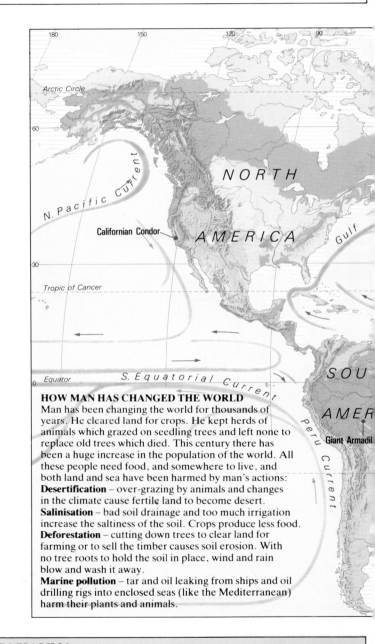

HOW MAN HAS CHANGED THE WORLD

Man has been changing the world for thousands of years. He cleared land for crops. He kept herds of animals which grazed on seedling trees and left none to replace old trees which died. This century there has been a huge increase in the population of the world. All these people need food, and somewhere to live, and both land and sea have been harmed by man's actions:

Desertification – over-grazing by animals and changes in the climate cause fertile land to become desert.

Salinisation – bad soil drainage and too much irrigation increase the saltiness of the soil. Crops produce less food.

Deforestation – cutting down trees to clear land for farming or to sell the timber causes soil erosion. With no tree roots to hold the soil in place, wind and rain blow and wash it away.

Marine pollution – tar and oil leaking from ships and oil drilling rigs into enclosed seas (like the Mediterranean) harm their plants and animals.

GRASSLAND

Hot summers, cold winters and moderate rainfall. Huge area of grassland and 'black' (very fertile) soils. Grain crops grow well, and so does rich pasture for beef cattle. Names for this kind of grassland include steppe, veld, pampas and prairie.

SAVANNA

Tall grasses with thick stems, and flat-topped thorny trees grow here. Animals grazing here include giraffes and zebras. There is a short rainy season. Often it does not rain for a long time (a drought). Fires burn the dried out plants but they have adapted to survive this and grow again.

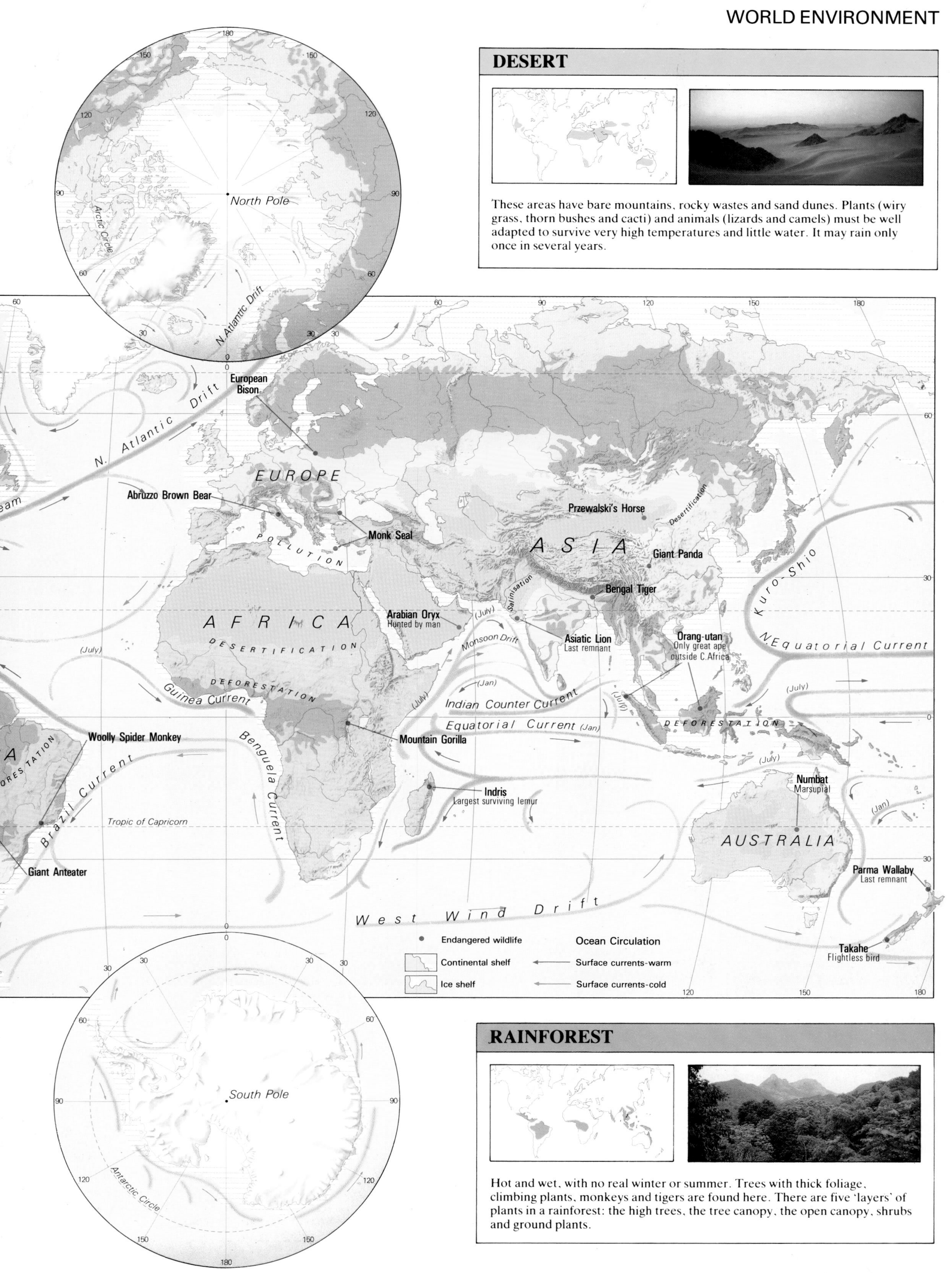

DESERT

These areas have bare mountains, rocky wastes and sand dunes. Plants (wiry grass, thorn bushes and cacti) and animals (lizards and camels) must be well adapted to survive very high temperatures and little water. It may rain only once in several years.

RAINFOREST

Hot and wet, with no real winter or summer. Trees with thick foliage, climbing plants, monkeys and tigers are found here. There are five 'layers' of plants in a rainforest: the high trees, the tree canopy, the open canopy, shrubs and ground plants.

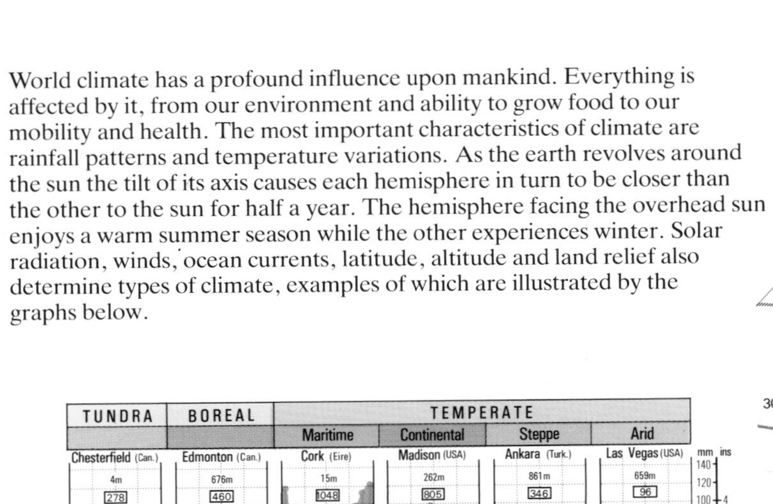

World climate has a profound influence upon mankind. Everything is affected by it, from our environment and ability to grow food to our mobility and health. The most important characteristics of climate are rainfall patterns and temperature variations. As the earth revolves around the sun the tilt of its axis causes each hemisphere in turn to be closer than the other to the sun for half a year. The hemisphere facing the overhead sun enjoys a warm summer season while the other experiences winter. Solar radiation, winds, ocean currents, latitude, altitude and land relief also determine types of climate, examples of which are illustrated by the graphs below.

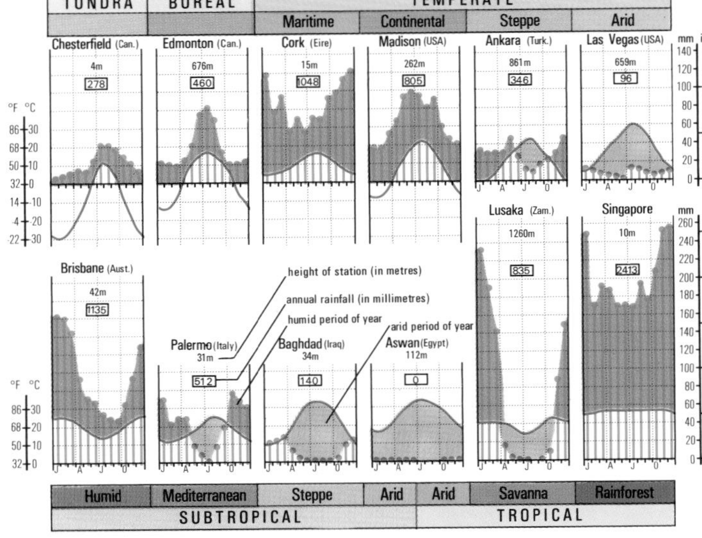

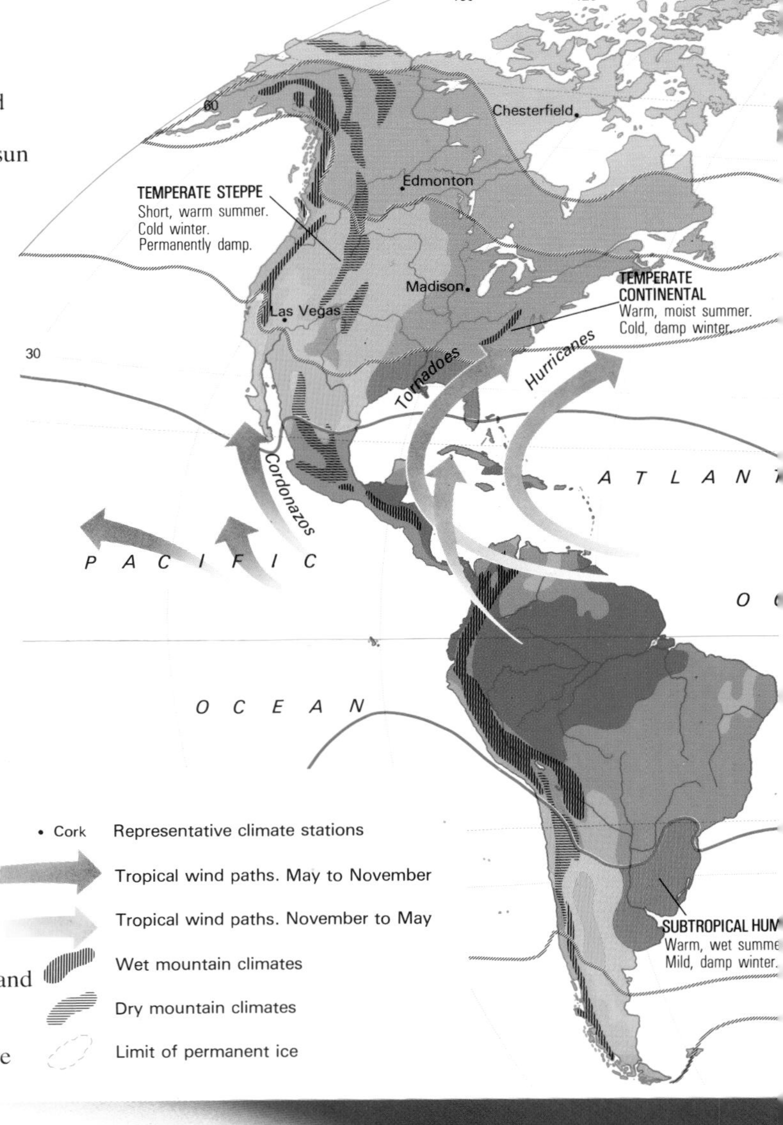

THE RESTLESS ATMOSPHERE

As people who travel by aeroplane at altitude soon discover, all weather is confined to the lower part of the atmosphere, where the air is in a continuous state of unrest. This movement can have tremendous force, eroding land and depositing rain and snow. The map shows the intertropical convergence zone which is where trade winds meet, forcing air to rise upwards and causing torrential rainfall. Circulation of air forms three separate 'cells' in each hemisphere where warm air rises and cold air sinks. These are called the Polar, Ferrel and Hadley cells.

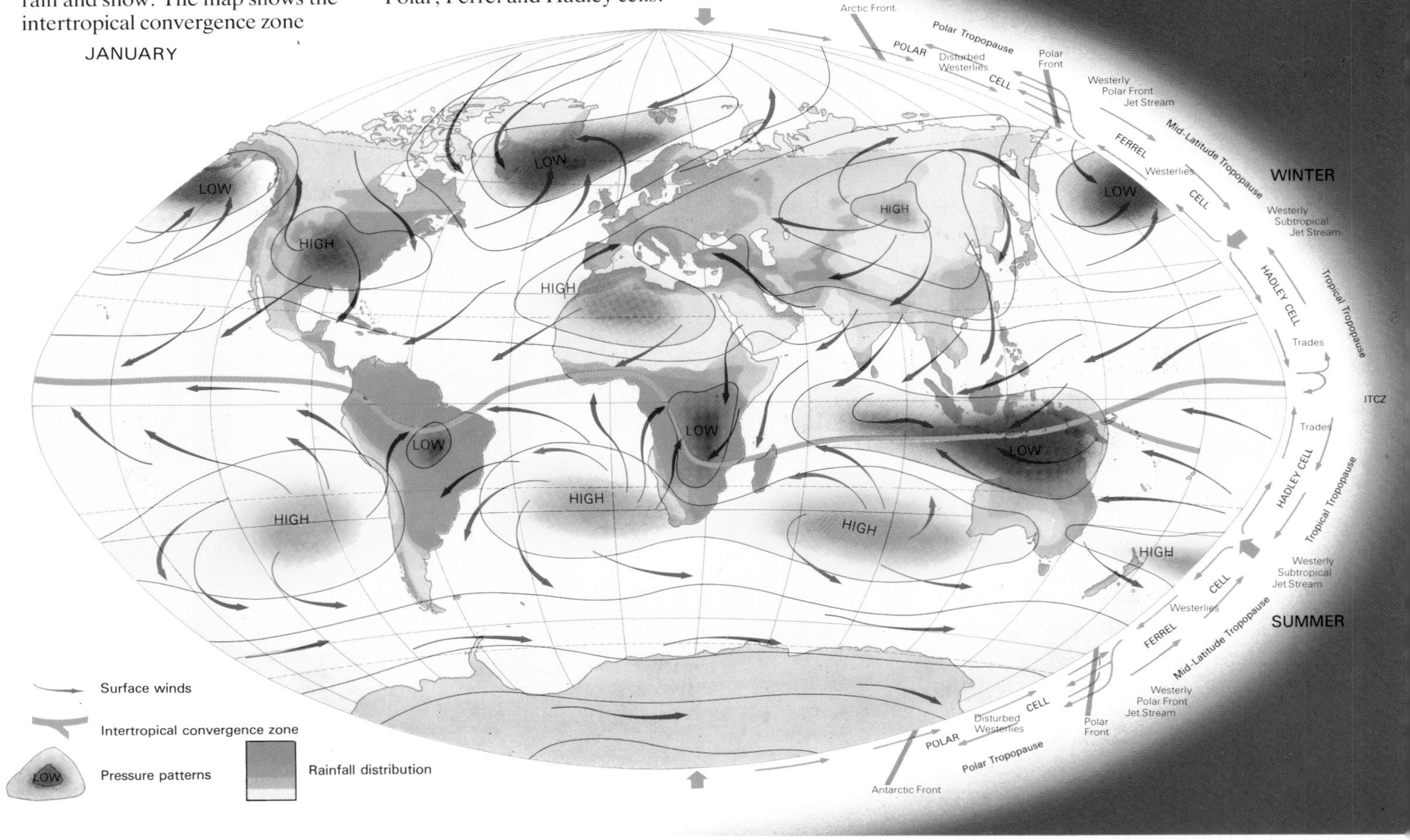

JANUARY

Surface winds

Intertropical convergence zone

Pressure patterns

Rainfall distribution

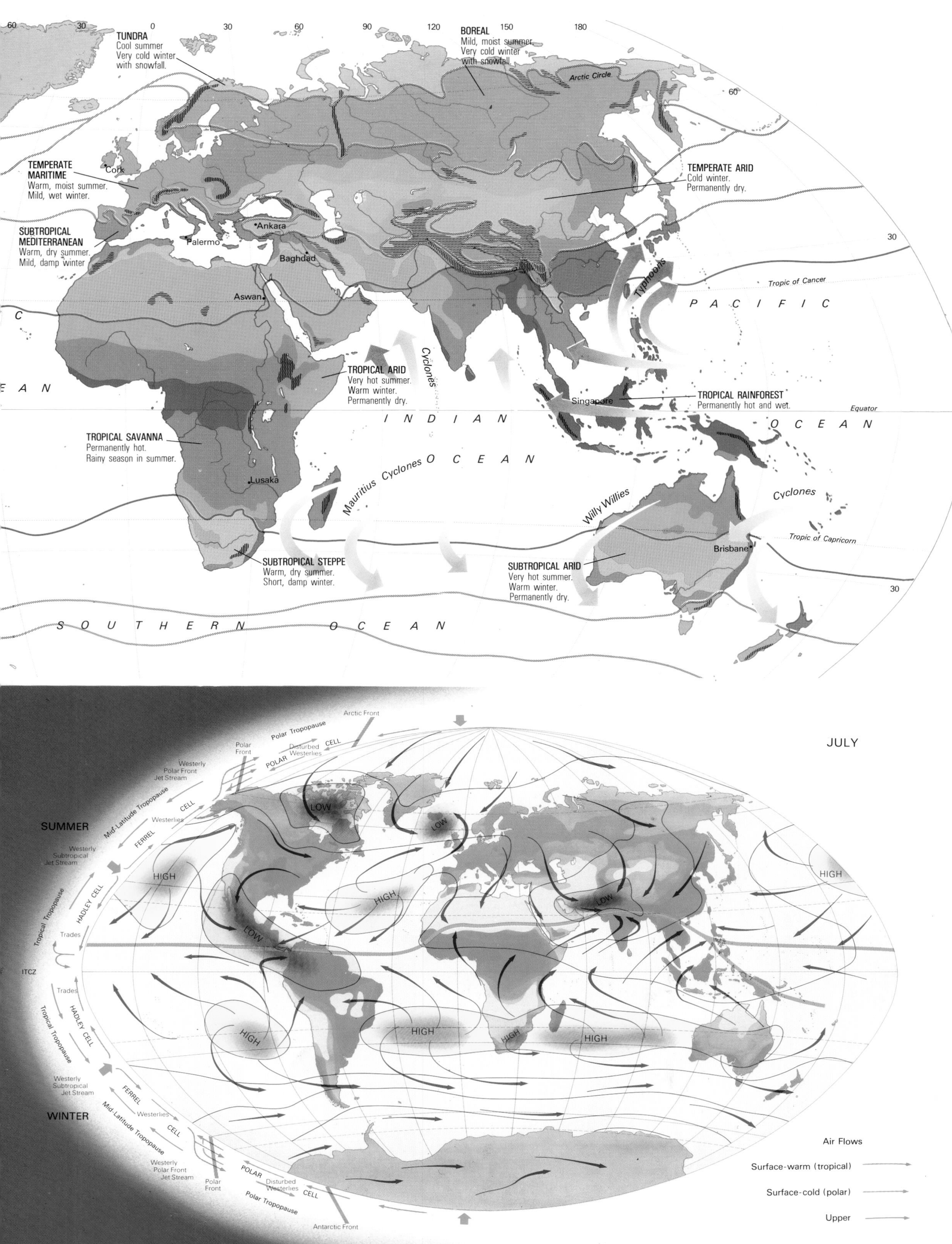
TUNDRA
Cool summer
Very cold winter
with snowfall.
BOREAL
Mild, moist summer.
Very cold winter
with snowfall.
Arctic Circle
TEMPERATE MARITIME
Warm, moist summer.
Mild, wet winter.
Cork
TEMPERATE ARID
Cold winter.
Permanently dry.
SUBTROPICAL MEDITERRANEAN
Warm, dry summer.
Mild, damp winter
Ankara
Palermo
Baghdad
Aswan
Typhoons
Tropic of Cancer
P A C I F I C
Cyclones
TROPICAL ARID
Very hot summer.
Warm winter.
Permanently dry.
TROPICAL RAINFOREST
Permanently hot and wet.
Singapore
Equator
I N D I A N
O C E A N
TROPICAL SAVANNA
Permanently hot.
Rainy season in summer.
Mauritius Cyclones
O C E A N
Lusaka
Willy Willies
Cyclones
Tropic of Capricorn
Brisbane
SUBTROPICAL STEPPE
Warm, dry summer.
Short, damp winter.
SUBTROPICAL ARID
Very hot summer.
Warm winter.
Permanently dry.
S O U T H E R N
O C E A N
JULY
Arctic Front
Polar Tropopause
Polar Front
Disturbed Westerlies
POLAR CELL
Westerly Polar Front Jet Stream
Mid-Latitude Tropopause
FERREL CELL
Westerlies
SUMMER
Westerly Subtropical Jet Stream
HADLEY CELL
Tropical Tropopause
Trades
ITCZ
WINTER
Antarctic Front
LOW
HIGH
Air Flows
Surface-warm (tropical)
Surface-cold (polar)
Upper

CLIMATE INDICATORS

Listed from north to south, is a selection of places from different climate zones of the world (see pp xxiv/xxv), indicating their mean monthly temperatures (in °C and °F) and rainfall (in mm and inches). Also shown are their average temperatures and total rainfall for the year.

REYKJAVIK Iceland 64·1°N 21·9°W *TUNDRA*

	J	F	M	A	M	J	J	A	S	O	N	D	Year
°C	-0·2	0·2	1·5	3·5	6·7	9·7	11·3	10·8	8·5	5·2	3·0	0·4	5·0
°F	32	32	35	38	44	49	52	51	47	41	37	33	41
mm	89	64	62	56	42	42	50	56	67	94	78	79	779
ins	3·5	2·5	2·4	2·2	1·6	1·6	2·0	2·2	2·6	3·7	3·1	3·1	30·7

ANCHORAGE U.S.A. 61·2°N 150·0°W *BOREAL*

	J	F	M	A	M	J	J	A	S	O	N	D	Year
°C	-10·4	-7·6	-4·8	2·0	7·7	12·2	14·1	13·1	8·7	1·8	-5·6	-10·2	1·7
°F	13	18	23	36	46	54	57	56	48	35	22	14	29
mm	20	18	13	11	13	25	47	65	63	47	26	24	372
ins	0·8	0·7	0·5	0·4	0·5	1·0	1·8	2·6	2·5	1·8	1·0	0·9	14·6

STOCKHOLM Sweden 59·3°N 18·1°E *TEMPERATE Continental*

	J	F	M	A	M	J	J	A	S	O	N	D	Year
°C	-3·0	-3·1	-0·5	4·6	10·2	15·0	18·5	16·6	12·3	7·1	2·7	0·0	6·6
°F	27	26	31	40	50	59	65	62	54	45	37	32	44
mm	43	30	25	31	34	45	61	76	60	48	53	48	554
ins	1·7	1·2	1·0	1·2	1·3	1·8	2·4	3·0	2·4	1·9	2·1	1·9	21·8

EDINBURGH U.K. 55·9°N 3·2°W *TEMPERATE Maritime*

	J	F	M	A	M	J	J	A	S	O	N	D	Year
°C	3·3	3·5	5·1	7·4	9·9	12·9	14·8	14·4	12·5	9·4	6·4	4·6	8·6
°F	38	38	41	45	50	55	59	58	54	49	43	40	47
mm	57	39	39	39	54	47	83	77	57	65	62	57	676
ins	2·2	1·5	1·5	1·5	2·1	1·8	3·3	3·0	2·2	2·6	2·4	2·2	26·6

MOSKVA Russian Federation 55·7°N 37·6°E *TEMPERATE Continental*

	J	F	M	A	M	J	J	A	S	O	N	D	Year
°C	-12·7	-9·6	-3·8	5·7	13·3	15·8	17·8	16·9	11·8	5·9	-0·9	-7·0	4·4
°F	9	15	25	42	56	60	64	62	53	43	30	19	40
mm	39	38	36	37	53	58	88	71	58	45	47	54	624
ins	1·5	1·5	1·4	1·5	2·1	2·3	3·5	2·8	2·3	1·8	1·8	2·1	24·6

VANCOUVER Canada 49·2°N 123·2°W *TEMPERATE Maritime*

	J	F	M	A	M	J	J	A	S	O	N	D	Year
°C	2·8	4·1	6·4	9·4	12·6	15·5	17·8	17·2	14·4	10·3	6·3	4·2	10·0
°F	37	39	43	49	55	60	64	63	58	50	43	40	50
mm	214	161	151	90	69	65	39	44	83	172	198	243	1529
ins	8·4	6·3	5·9	3·5	2·7	2·6	1·5	1·7	3·3	6·8	7·8	9·6	60·2

PARIS France 48·8°N 2·3°E *TEMPERATE Maritime*

	J	F	M	A	M	J	J	A	S	O	N	D	Year
°C	3·4	4·3	7·9	11·0	14·6	17·8	19·5	19·1	16·5	11·7	7·2	4·3	11·5
°F	38	40	46	52	58	64	67	66	62	53	45	40	53
mm	56	46	35	42	57	54	59	64	55	50	51	50	619
ins	2·2	1·8	1·4	1·6	2·2	2·1	2·3	2·5	2·2	2·0	2·0	2·0	24·3

BUCUREŞTI Romania 44·5°N 26·0°E *TEMPERATE Steppe*

	J	F	M	A	M	J	J	A	S	O	N	D	Year
°C	-4·2	-1·5	6·2	12·4	17·3	21·2	23·5	22·9·	18·2	13·0	6·4	0·6	8·2
°F	24	29	43	54	63	70	74	73	65	55	43	33	47
mm	46	26	28	59	77	121	53	45	45	29	36	27	592
ins	1·8	1·0	1·1	2·3	3·0	4·8	2·1	1·8	1·8	1·1	1·4	1·1	23·4

NEW YORK U.S.A. 40·7°N 74·0°W *TEMPERATE Continental*

	J	F	M	A	M	J	J	A	S	O	N	D	Year
°C	0·7	0·8	4·7	10·5	16·3	21·2	24·1	23·3	19·8	14·3	8·1	2·2	12·2
°F	33	33	40	51	61	70	75	74	68	58	47	36	54
mm	89	74	104	89	91	86	102	119	89	84	89	84	1100
ins	3·5	2·9	4·1	3·5	3·6	3·4	4·0	4·7	3·5	3·3	3·5	3·3	43·3

TŌKYŌ Japan 35·7°N 139·8°E *TEMPERATE Continental*

	J	F	M	A	M	J	J	A	S	O	N	D	Year
°C	3·3	4·2	7·2	12·5	16·9	20·8	24·7	26·1	22·5	16·7	10·8	5·8	14·4
°F	38	40	45	54	62	69	76	79	72	62	51	42	58
mm	48	74	107	135	147	165	142	152	234	208	96	56	1565
ins	1·9	2·9	4·2	5·3	5·8	6·5	5·6	6·0	9·2	8·2	3·8	2·2	61·6

TANGER Morocco 35·8°N 5·8°W *SUBTROPICAL Mediterranean*

	J	F	M	A	M	J	J	A	S	O	N	D	Year
°C	11·9	12·5	13·6	14·4	17·2	20·0	22·2	23·0	21·4	18·6	14·7	12·4	16·7
°F	53	54	56	58	63	68	72	73	70	65	58	54	62
mm	114	107	122	89	43	15	2	2	23	99	147	137	897
ins	4·5	4·2	4·8	3·5	1·7	0·6	0·1	0·1	0·9	3·9	5·8	5·4	35·3

JERUSALEM Israel 31·8°N 35·2°E *SUBTROPICAL Steppe*

	J	F	M	A	M	J	J	A	S	O	N	D	Year
°C	8·9	9·4	13·0	16·4	20·5	22·5	23·9	24·1	23·0	21·1	16·4	11·1	17·2
°F	48	49	55	61	69	72	75	75	73	70	61	52	63
mm	132	132	63	28	2	1	0	0	1	13	71	87	528
ins	5·2	5·2	2·5	1·1	0·1	0·1	0·0	0·0	0·1	0·5	2·8	3·4	20·8

NEW ORLEANS U.S.A. 30·0°N 90·2°W *SUBTROPICAL Humid*

	J	F	M	A	M	J	J	A	S	O	N	D	Year
°C	12·5	13·9	16·3	19·9	23·5	26·7	27·6	27·7	25·7	21·3	15·5	13·0	20·3
°F	54	57	61	68	74	80	82	82	78	70	60	55	68
mm	97	102	135	114	112	112	170	135	127	71	84	104	1363
ins	3·8	4·0	5·3	4·5	4·4	4·4	6·7	5·3	5·0	2·8	3·3	4·1	53·7

BAHRAIN 26·2°N 50·5°E *SUBTROPICAL Arid*

	J	F	M	A	M	J	J	A	S	O	N	D	Year
°C	16·9	18·0	20·5	25·0	29·4	31·7	33·3	33·6	31·4	28·0	24·2	18·6	25·8
°F	62	64	69	77	85	89	92	92	88	82	75	65	78
mm	8	18	13	8	1	0	0	0	0	0	18	18	79
ins	0·3	0·7	0·5	0·3	0·1	0·0	0·0	0·0	0·0	0·0	0·7	0·7	3·2

HONG KONG 22·3°N 114·2°E *SUBTROPICAL Humid*

	J	F	M	A	M	J	J	A	S	O	N	D	Year
°C	15·5	15·0	17·5	21·7	25·5	27·5	28·0	28·0	27·2	25·0	20·8	17·5	22·5
°F	60	59	63	71	78	81	82	82	81	77	69	63	72
mm	33	46	74	137	292	394	381	361	256	114	43	30	2161
ins	1·3	1·8	2·9	5·4	11·5	15·5	15·0	14·2	10·1	4·5	1·7	1·2	85·1

MIAMI U.S.A. 25·8°N 80·3°W *TROPICAL Savanna*

	J	F	M	A	M	J	J	A	S	O	N	D	Year
°C	19·3	19·9	21·4	23·4	25·3	27·1	27·6	27·9	27·4	25·4	22·4	20·1	23·9
°F	67	68	70	74	77	81	82	82	81	78	72	68	75
mm	51	48	58	99	163	188	170	178	241	208	71	43	1518
ins	2·0	1·9	2·3	3·9	6·4	7·4	6·7	7·0	9·5	8·2	2·8	1·7	59·8

BANGKOK Thailand 13·7°N 100·5°E *TROPICAL Savanna*

	J	F	M	A	M	J	J	A	S	O	N	D	Year
°C	25·8	27·5	28·9	30·0	29·4	28·6	28·3	28·3	28·0	27·5	26·4	25·3	27·7
°F	78	81	84	86	85	83	83	83	82	81	79	77	82
mm	8	20	36	58	198	160	160	175	305	206	66	5	1397
ins	0·3	0·8	1·4	2·3	7·8	6·3	6·3	6·9	12·0	8·1	2·6	0·2	55·0

COLOMBO Sri Lanka 6·9°N 79·9°E *TROPICAL Rainforest*

	J	F	M	A	M	J	J	A	S	O	N	D	Year
°C	26·1	26·4	27·2	27·7	28·0	27·2	27·2	27·2	27·2	26·6	26·1	25·8	26·9
°F	79	80	81	82	82	81	81	81	81	80	79	78	80
mm	89	69	147	231	371	223	135	109	160	348	315	147	2344
ins	3·5	2·7	5·8	9·1	14·6	8·8	5·3	4·3	6·3	13·7	12·4	5·8	92·3

NAIROBI Kenya 1·3°S 36·8°E *TROPICAL Savanna*

	J	F	M	A	M	J	J	A	S	O	N	D	Year
°C	18·6	19·4	19·4	19·2	17·7	16·4	15·5	16·1	17·5	18·6	18·3	18·0	18·0
°F	65	67	67	67	64	61	60	61	63	65	65	64	64
mm	38	63	124	211	157	46	15	23	30	53	109	86	958
ins	1·5	2·5	4·9	8·3	6·2	1·8	0·6	0·9	1·2	2·1	4·3	3·4	37·7

LIMA Peru 12·1°S 77·0°W *TROPICAL Arid*

	J	F	M	A	M	J	J	A	S	O	N	D	Year
°C	23·3	23·8	23·6	21·9	19·4	17·2	16·7	16·1	16·9	18·0	19·4	21·1	20·0
°F	74	75	74	71	67	63	62	61	62	64	67	70	68
mm	1	1	1	1	5	5	8	8	8	2	2	1	41
ins	0·1	0·1	0·1	0·1	0·2	0·2	0·3	0·3	0·3	0·1	0·1	0·1	1·6

RIO DE JANEIRO Brazil 22·9°S 43·2°W *TROPICAL Savanna*

	J	F	M	A	M	J	J	A	S	O	N	D	Year
°C	25·8	26·1	25·3	23·6	21·9	21·1	20·5	21·1	21·1	21·9	23·0	24·7	23·0
°F	78	79	77	74	71	70	69	70	70	71	73	76	73
mm	124	122	130	107	79	53	41	43	66	79	104	137	1085
ins	4·9	4·8	5·1	4·2	3·1	2·1	1·6	1·7	2·6	3·1	4·1	5·4	42·6

JOHANNESBURG S. Africa 26·2°S 28·1°E *SUBTROPICAL Steppe*

	J	F	M	A	M	J	J	A	S	O	N	D	Year
°C	20·0	19·7	18·3	16·1	12·5	10·3	10·5	13·0	15·8	18·3	18·9	19·7	16·1
°F	68	67	65	61	54	50	51	55	60	65	66	67	61
mm	114	109	89	38	25	8	8	8	23	56	107	124	709
ins	4·5	4·3	3·5	1·5	1·0	0·3	0·3	0·3	0·9	2·2	4·2	4·9	27·9

PERTH Australia 31·9°S 115·8°E *SUBTROPICAL Mediterranean*

	J	F	M	A	M	J	J	A	S	O	N	D	Year
°C	23·3	23·3	21·7	19·2	16·1	13·9	13·0	13·3	14·7	16·4	19·2	21·7	17·8
°F	74	74	71	66	61	57	55	56	58	61	66	71	64
mm	8	10	20	43	130	180	170	145	86	56	20	13	881
ins	0·3	0·4	0·8	1·7	5·1	7·1	6·7	5·7	3·4	2·2	0·8	0·5	34·7

WELLINGTON New Zealand 41·3°S 174·8°E *TEMPERATE Maritime*

	J	F	M	A	M	J	J	A	S	O	N	D	Year
°C	16·9	16·9	15·8	13·9	11·4	9·7	8·6	9·2	10·8	12·2	13·6	15·8	12·8
°F	62	62	60	57	52	49	47	48	51	54	56	60	55
mm	81	81	81	97	117	117	137	117	97	102	89	89	1205
ins	3·2	3·2	3·2	3·8	4·6	4·6	5·4	4·6	3·8	4·0	3·5	3·5	47·4

Civilisation depends on trade for growth and travel makes this possible. Shipping is the most important method of world transport but economic progress and moblity are constantly being improved by the development of new routes and new modes of transport.

ROAD AND RAIL

Integrated road and rail networks are the basis of industrial society. Extended highway systems and improved containerisation techniques have made the whole road and rail system much more flexible.

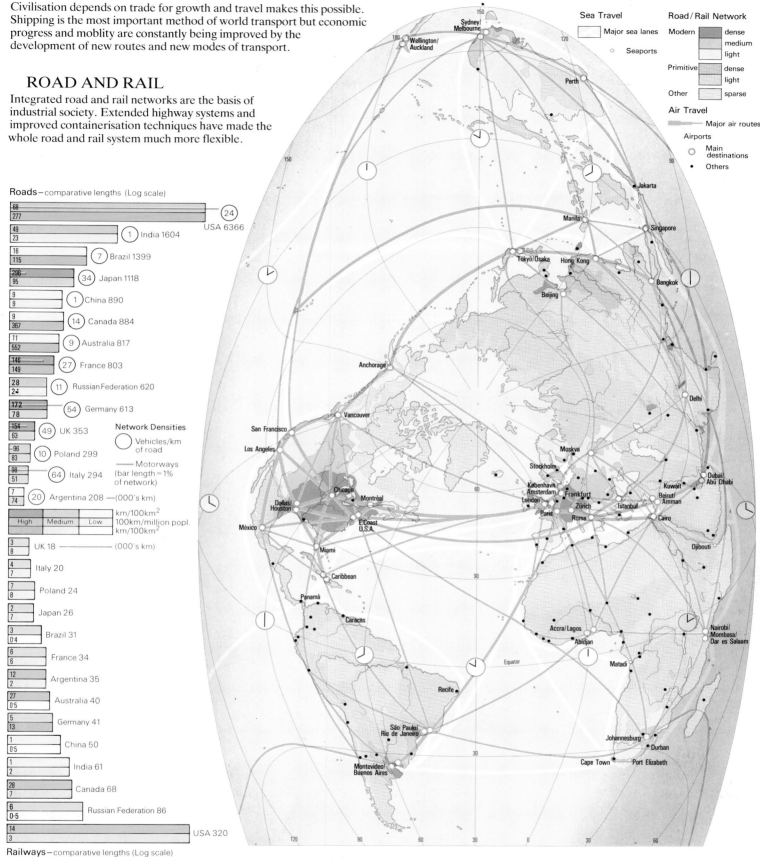

Roads – comparative lengths (Log scale)

Country	Top bar	Bottom bar	Vehicles/km of road	Length (000's km)
USA	68	277	24	6366
India	49	23	1	1604
Brazil	16	115	7	1399
Japan	286	95	34	1118
China	9	9	1	890
Canada	9	367	14	884
Australia	11	552	9	817
France	146	149	27	803
Russian Federation	28	2[illegible]	11	620
Germany	172	78	54	613
UK	154	63	49	353
Poland	96	83	10	299
Italy	98	51	64	294
Argentina	7	74	20	208 —(000's km)

Network Densities

Vehicles/km of road

— Motorways (bar length = 1% of network)

High | Medium | Low

km/100km²
100km/million popl.
km/100km²

Country	Top bar	Bottom bar	Length (000's km)
UK	3	8	18 —(000's km)
Italy	4	7	20
Poland	7	8	24
Japan	2	7	26
Brazil	3	0·4	31
France	6	6	34
Argentina	12	2	35
Australia	27	0·5	40
Germany	5	13	41
China	1	0·5	50
India	1	2	61
Canada	28	7	68
Russian Federation	6	0·5	86
USA	14	3	320

Railways – comparative lengths (Log scale)

Sea Travel
Major sea lanes
Seaports

Road/Rail Network
Modern: dense, medium, light
Primitive: dense, light
Other: sparse

Air Travel
Major air routes
Airports
Main destinations
Others

Sydney/Melbourne
Wellington/Auckland
Perth
Jakarta
Manila
Singapore
Tokyo/Osaka
Hong Kong
Bangkok
Beijing
Anchorage
Delhi
Vancouver
San Francisco
Los Angeles
Moskva
Stockholm
København
Amsterdam
London
Frankfurt
Paris
Zürich
Roma
Istanbul
Kuwait
Dubai/Abū Dhabi
Beirut/Amman
Cairo
Djibouti
Chicago
Montréal
Dallas/Houston
E.Coast U.S.A.
México
Miami
Caribbean
Panamá
Caracas
Accra/Lagos
Abidjan
Nairobi/Mombasa/Dar es Salaam
Matadi
Equator
Recife
São Paulo/Rio de Janeiro
Johannesburg
Durban
Cape Town
Port Elizabeth
Montevideo/Buenos Aires

AIR AND SEA ROUTES

A complex network of primary air routes centred on the Northern Hemisphere provides rapid transit across the world for mass travel, mail and urgent freight. Ships also follow these principal routes, plying the oceans between major ports and transporting the commodities of world trade in bulk.

JOURNEY TIME

The Suez canal cuts 3600 miles off the London-Singapore route, while Concorde halves the London-New York journey time.

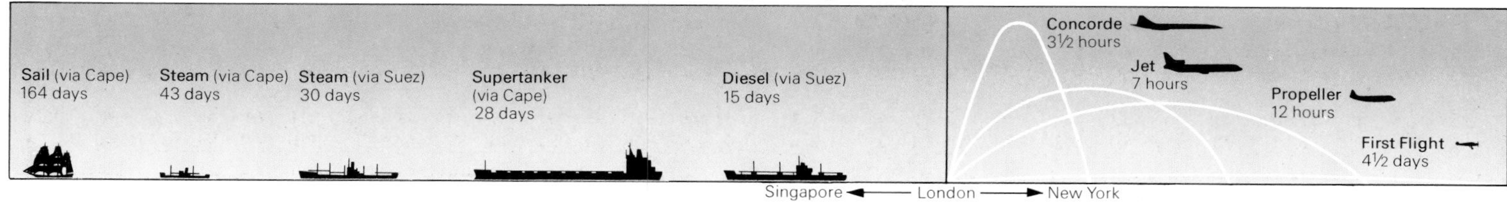

PACIFIC & INDIAN OCEANS

1:60M
0 600 1200 1800 2400 km 
0 600 1200 mls

Barents Sea
Norwegian Basin
Arctic Circle
ICELAND
North Sea
Sea of Okhotsk
Sakhalin
EUROPE
Black Sea
Caspian Sea
Aral Sea
ASIA
Kuril Trench
Vityaz Depth 10542
Mediterranean Sea
Sea of Japan
JAPAN
Huang He
Japan Trench
Chang Jiang
The Gulf
Red Sea
Ganga
TAIWAN
Kyushu-Palau Ridge
S. Honshu Ridge
Arabian Sea
Bay of Bengal
Hainan
South China Sea
Mekong
Mariana Is
Mariana Trench
Guam
Arabian Basin
Raas Caseyr
Andaman Is
PHILIPPINES
Philippine Trench
C. Johnson Depth 10497
11022 Challenger Depth
MICRONESIA
AFRICA
Carlsberg Ridge
Maldives Ridge
SRI LANKA (CEYLON)
Nicobar Is
Belau
Caroline Is
MALDIVES
Celebes Sea
Somali Basin
Sumatra
Borneo
6920
MELANESIA
Celebes
New Guinea
SEYCHELLES
Mascarene Ridge
Chagos Arch.
Ninety-East Ridge
INDONESIA
Java
Planet Deep 9140
Mid Indian Basin
Java Trench
7450
Christmas I.
Timor
Arafura Sea
COMOROS
Mid-Indian Ridge
Cocos Is
West Australian Basin
Coral Sea Basin
Mozambique Channel
INDIAN OCEAN
1737
Great Barrier Reef
MADAGASCAR
Réunion
MAURITIUS
1924
Tropic of Capricorn
AUSTRALIA
Madagascar Basin
S. Madagascar Ridge
Natal Basin
2067
W. Australian Ridge
7102
South West Indian Ridge
1198
C. Agulhas
I. Amsterdam
I. St Paul
South Australia Basin
Tasman Sea
Agulhas Plateau
Crozet Basin
Tasmania
Agulhas Basin
Indian-Antarctic Ridge
Îs Crozet
Pr. Edward Is
Îs Kerguelen
Kerguelen Ridge
1922
Heard I.
Atlantic-Indian Ridge
Macquarie Is
Atlantic-Indian Antarctic Basin
Banzare Seamount 186
Indian-Antarctic Basin
ANTARCTICA

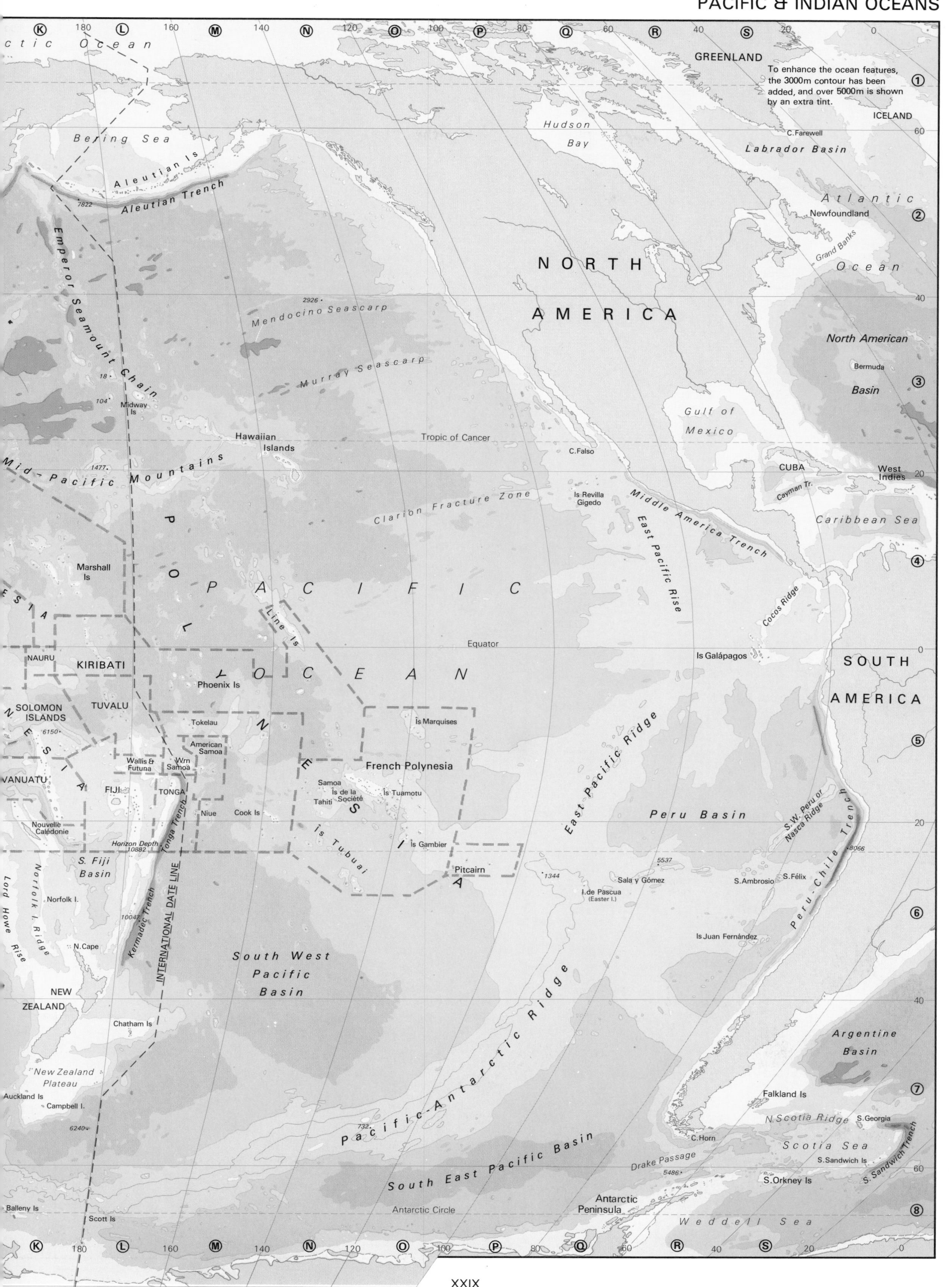
To enhance the ocean features, the 3000m contour has been added, and over 5000m is shown by an extra tint.
GREENLAND
ICELAND
C.Farewell
Labrador Basin
Hudson Bay
Bering Sea
Aleutian Is
Aleutian Trench
7822
Atlantic Ocean
Newfoundland
Grand Banks
NORTH AMERICA
Emperor Seamount Chain
2926
Mendocino Seascarp
Murray Seascarp
North American Basin
Bermuda
Midway Is
Gulf of Mexico
Hawaiian Islands
Tropic of Cancer
C.Falso
Mid-Pacific Mountains
1477
CUBA
West Indies
Cayman Tr.
Is Revilla Gigedo
Middle America Trench
Clarion Fracture Zone
Caribbean Sea
East Pacific Rise
Marshall Is
PACIFIC OCEAN
POLYNESIA
Line Is
Cocos Ridge
Equator
NAURU
KIRIBATI
Is Galápagos
SOUTH AMERICA
Phoenix Is
SOLOMON ISLANDS
TUVALU
Tokelau
Îs Marquises
6150
American Samoa
East Pacific Ridge
Wallis & Futuna
Wrn Samoa
French Polynesia
VANUATU
FIJI
TONGA
Samoa
Îs de la Société
Tahiti
Îs Tuamotu
Peru Basin
S.W. Peru or Nasca Ridge
Nouvelle Calédonie
Niue
Cook Is
Îs Tubuai
Tonga Trench
Horizon Depth 10882
Îs Gambier
Pitcairn
8066
S. Fiji Basin
1344
5537
Sala y Gómez
S.Ambrosio
S.Félix
Norfolk I. Ridge
Lord Howe Rise
Norfolk I.
I.de Pascua (Easter I.)
Peru-Chile Trench
10047
Kermadec Trench
INTERNATIONAL DATE LINE
Is Juan Fernández
N.Cape
South West Pacific Basin
NEW ZEALAND
Pacific-Antarctic Ridge
Chatham Is
Argentine Basin
New Zealand Plateau
Auckland Is
Campbell I.
Falkland Is
N.Scotia Ridge
S.Georgia
6240
732
C.Horn
Scotia Sea
S.Sandwich Is
S.Sandwich Trench
South East Pacific Basin
Drake Passage
5486
S.Orkney Is
Antarctic Peninsula
Balleny Is
Scott Is
Antarctic Circle
Weddell Sea
K L M N O P Q R S
180 160 140 120 100 80 60 40 20 0
1 2 3 4 5 6 7 8

1:60M

0 600 1200 1800 2400 km
0 600 1200 mls

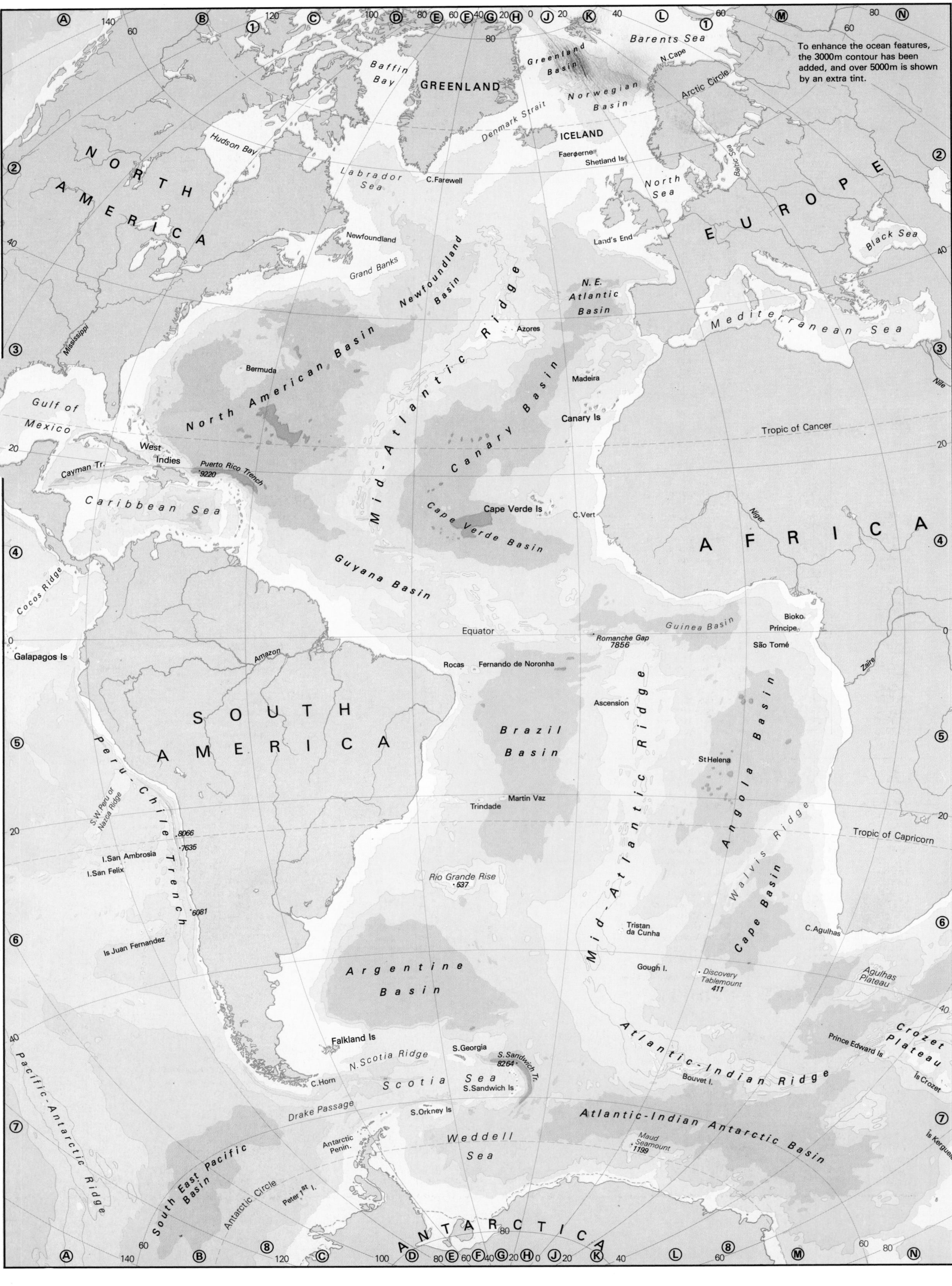

To enhance the ocean features, the 3000m contour has been added, and over 5000m is shown by an extra tint.

Baffin Bay
GREENLAND
Greenland Basin
N.Cape
Barents Sea
Arctic Circle
Norwegian Basin
Denmark Strait
ICELAND
Faerøerne
Shetland Is
Hudson Bay
NORTH AMERICA
Labrador Sea
C.Farewell
North Sea
Baltic Sea
EUROPE
Newfoundland
Land's End
Black Sea
Grand Banks
Newfoundland Basin
N.E. Atlantic Basin
Mediterranean Sea
Azores
Mississippi
North American Basin
Bermuda
Madeira
Nile
Gulf of Mexico
Mid-Atlantic Ridge
Canary Basin
Canary Is
Tropic of Cancer
West Indies
Puerto Rico Trench
9220
Cayman Tr.
Caribbean Sea
Cape Verde Is
C.Vert
Cape Verde Basin
Niger
AFRICA
Guyana Basin
Cocos Ridge
Bioko
Príncipe
Equator
Guinea Basin
Romanche Gap
7856
São Tomé
Galapagos Is
Amazon
Rocas
Fernando de Noronha
Zaire
Ascension
SOUTH AMERICA
Brazil Basin
Angola Basin
St Helena
Peru-Chile Trench
S.W.Peru or Nazca Ridge
Martin Vaz
Trindade
Walvis Ridge
Tropic of Capricorn
8066
7635
I.San Ambrosia
I.San Felix
Rio Grande Rise
637
Cape Basin
6081
Tristan da Cunha
C.Agulhas
Is Juan Fernandez
Argentine Basin
Gough I.
Discovery Tablemount
411
Agulhas Plateau
Falkland Is
Atlantic-Indian Ridge
Crozet Plateau
Prince Edward Is
S.Georgia
S.Sandwich Tr.
8264
N.Scotia Ridge
Is Crozet
C.Horn
Scotia Sea
S.Sandwich Is
Bouvet I.
Pacific-Antarctic Ridge
Drake Passage
S.Orkney Is
Atlantic-Indian Antarctic Basin
Is Kerguelen
Antarctic Penin.
Weddell Sea
Maud Seamount
1199
South East Pacific Basin
Antarctic Circle
Peter 1st I.
ANTARCTICA

MOUNTAIN HEIGHTS

Metres	Feet		Metres	Feet	
8848	29 028	Everest (Qomolangma Feng) *Nepal-Tibet*	6870	22 541	Bonete *Bolivia*
8611	28 250	K2 (Godwin Austen) *Kashmir-Sinkiang*	6800	22 310	Tupungato *Argentina-Chile*
8586	28 168	Kangchenjunga *Nepal-India*	6770	22 211	Mercedario *Argentina*
8475	27 805	Makalu *Tibet-Nepal*	6768	22 205	Huascarán *Peru*
8172	26 810	Dhaulagiri *Nepal*	6723	22 057	Llullaillaco *Argentina-Chile*
8126	26 660	Nanga Parbat *Kashmir*	6714	22 028	Kangrinboqê Feng (Kailas) *Tibet*
8078	26 504	Annapurna *Nepal*	6634	21 765	Yerupaja *Peru*
8068	26 470	Gasherbrum *Kashmir*	6542	21 463	Sajama *Bolivia*
8013	26 291	Xixabangma Feng (Gosainthan) *Tibet*	6485	21 276	Illampu *Bolivia*
7890	25 885	Distaghil Sar *Kashmir*	6425	21 079	Coropuna *Peru*
7820	25 656	Masherbrum *Kashmir*	6402	21 004	Illimani *Bolivia*
7817	25 645	Nanda Devi *India*	6388	20 958	Ancohuma *Bolivia*
7780	25 550	Rakaposhi *Kashmir*	6310	20 702	Chimborazo *Ecuador*
7756	25 447	Kamet *India-Tibet*	6194	20 320	McKinley *USA*
7756	25 447	Namcha Barwa *Tibet*	6050	19 850	Logan *Canada*
7728	25 355	Gurla Mandhata *Tibet*	5895	19 340	Kilimanjaro *Tanzania*
7723	25 338	Muztag (Ulugh Muztagh) *Sinkiang*	5700	18 700	Citlaltepetl *Mexico*
7719	25 325	Kongur Shan (Kungur) *Sinkiang*	5642	18 510	El'bruz *Russian Federation*
7690	25 230	Tirich Mir *Pakistan*	5452	17 887	Popocatepetl *Mexico*
7590	24 903	Gongga Shan (Minya Konka) *China*	5200	17 058	Kirinyaga (Kenya) *Kenya*
7546	24 757	Muztagata (Muztagh Ata) *Sinkiang*	5165	16 946	Ararat *Turkey*
7495	24 590	Pik Kommunizma *Tajikistan*	5140	16 864	Vinson Massif *Antarctica*
7439	24 407	Pik Pobedy (Tomur Feng) *Kirgizia-Sinkiang*	5110	16 763	Stanley *Zaire-Uganda*
7313	23 993	Chomo Lhari *Bhutan-Tibet*	5030	16 500	Jaya (Carstensz) *Indonesia*
7134	23 406	Pik Lenina *Kirgizia-Tajikistan*	4810	15 781	Mont Blanc *France*
6960	22 834	Aconcagua *Argentina*	4508	14 790	Wilhelm *Papua New Guinea*
6908	22 664	Ojos del Salado *Chile-Argentina*	4201	13 784	Mauna Kea *USA*

RIVER LENGTHS

Km	Miles		Km	Miles	
6695	4160	Nile *Africa*	2850	1770	Danube *Europe*
6570	4080	Amazon *South America*	2820	1750	Salween *Asia*
6380	3964	Yangtze *Asia*	2780	1730	São Francisco *South America*
6020	3740	Mississippi-Missouri *North America*	2655	1650	Zambezi *Africa*
5410	3360	Ob-Irtysh *Asia*	2570	1600	Nelson-Saskatchewan *North America*
4840	3010	Huang He (Yellow River) *Asia*	2510	1560	Ganges *Asia*
4630	2880	Zaïre (Congo) *Africa*	2430	1510	Euphrates *Asia*
4500	2796	Paraná *South America*	2330	1450	Arkansas *North America*
4440	2760	Irtysh *Asia*	2330	1450	Colorado *North America*
4416	2745	Amur *Asia*	2285	1420	Dnepr *Europe*
4400	2730	Lena *Asia*	2090	1300	Irrawaddy *Asia*
4240	2630	Mackenzie *North America*	2060	1280	Orinoco *South America*
4180	2600	Mekong *Asia*	2000	1240	Negro *South America*
4100	2550	Niger *Africa*	1870	1160	Don *Europe*
4090	2540	Yenisey *Asia*	1859	1155	Orange *Africa*
3969	2466	Missouri *North America*	1799	1118	Pechora *Europe*
3779	2348	Mississippi *North America*	1609	1000	Marañón *South America*
3750	2330	Murray-Darling *Australia*	1410	876	Dnestr *Europe*
3688	2292	Volga *Europe*	1320	820	Rhine *Europe*
3240	2013	Madeira *South America*	1183	735	Donets *Europe*
3058	1900	St. Lawrence *North America*	1159	720	Elbe *Europe*
3030	1880	Rio Grande *North America*	1094	680	Gambia *Africa*
3020	1870	Yukon *North America*	1080	671	Yellowstone *North America*
2960	1840	Brahmaputra *Asia*	1014	630	Vistula *Europe*
2896	1800	Indus *Asia*	1006	625	Tagus *Europe*

LAKE AND INLAND SEA AREAS

Areas are average and some are subject to seasonal variations.

Sq. Km	Sq. Miles		Sq. Km	Sq. Miles	
371 000	142 240	Caspian *Central Asia (salt)*	22 490	8680	Nyasa (Malawi) *Malawi-Mozambique*
82 900	32 010	Superior *USA-Canada*	19 400	7490	Ontario *USA-Canada*
68 800	26 560	Victoria *Kenya-Uganda-Tanzania*	18 390	7100	Ladoga *Russian Federation*
59 580	23 000	Huron *USA-Canada*	17 400	6700	Balkhash *Kazakhstan*
58 020	22 480	Michigan *USA*	10-26 000	4-10 000	Chad *Nigeria-Niger-Chad-Cameroon*
36 500	14 100	Aral *Central Asia (salt)*	9600	3710	Onega *Russian Federation*
32 900	12 700	Tanganyika *Tanzania-Zambia-Zaire-Burundi*	0-8900	0-3430	Eyre *Australia*
31 330	12 100	Great Bear *Canada*	8340	3220	Titicaca *Peru-Bolivia*
30 500	11 800	Baykal *Russian Federation*	8270	3190	Nicaragua *Nicaragua*
28 570	11 030	Great Slave *Canada*	6410	2470	Turkana (Rudolf) *Kenya-Ethiopia*
25 680	9910	Erie *USA-Canada*	5780	2230	Torrens *Australia (salt)*
24 390	9420	Winnipeg *Canada*	5580	2160	Vänern *Sweden*

GREATEST OCEAN DEPTHS

Metres	Feet	Location	Metres	Feet	Location
		PACIFIC OCEAN			ATLANTIC OCEAN
11 022	36 160	Marianas Trench	9220	30 249	Puerto Rico Trench
10 882	35 702	Tonga Trench	8264	27 113	South Sandwich Trench
10 542	34 586	Kuril Trench	7856	25 774	Romanche Gap
10 497	34 439	Philippine Trench	7500	24 600	Cayman Trench
10 047	32 962	Kermadec Trench			
9810	32 185	Izu-Bonin Trench			INDIAN OCEAN
9165	30 069	New Hebrides Trench	7450	24 442	Java Trench
9140	29 987	South Solomon Trench	7440	24 409	Weber Basin
8412	27 598	Japan Trench	7102	23 300	Diamantina Trench
8066	26 463	Peru-Chile Trench			
7822	25 662	Aleutian Trench			ARCTIC OCEAN
6662	21 857	Middle America	5570	18 274	Nansen Fracture Zone

STATES AND DEPENDENCIES

COUNTRY	Area (sq. km)	Population ('000)	Capital
North and Central America			
Anguilla (UK)	91	7	The Valley
Antigua and Barbuda	442	76	St. John's
The Bahamas	13 864	253	Nassau
Barbados	430	255	Bridgetown
Belize	22 965	187	Belmopan
Bermuda (UK)	53	58	Hamilton
Canada	9 976 147	26 521	Ottawa
Cayman Is. (UK)	259	25	George Town
Costa Rica	50 899	3 015	San José
Cuba	114 524	10 608	La Habana (Havana)
Dominica	751	82	Roseau
Dominican Republic	48 441	7 170	Santo Domingo
El Salvador	20 865	5 252	San Salvador
Grenada	344	85	St. George's
Guadeloupe (Fr.)	1 779	343	Basse Terre
Guatemala	108 888	9 197	Guatemala
Haiti	27 749	6 513	Port-au-Prince
Honduras	112 087	5 138	Tegucigalpa
Jamaica	11 425	2 456	Kingston
Martinique (Fr.)	1 101	341	Fort-de-France
Mexico	1 967 180	107 233	México
Montserrat (UK)	102	12	Plymouth
Netherlands Antilles (Neth.)	993	188	Willemstad
Nicaragua	139 000	3 871	Managua
Panama	75 648	2 418	Panamá
Puerto Rico (USA)	8 897	3 480	San Juan
St. Kitts-Nevis	260	44	Basseterre
St. Lucia	616	150	Castries
St. Vincent	389	116	Kingstown
Trinidad and Tobago	5 128	1 281	Port of Spain
United States of America	9 363 130	249 224	Washington
South America			
Argentina	2 777 815	32 322	Buenos Aires
Bolivia	1 098 575	7 314	La Paz
Brazil	8 511 968	150 368	Brasília
Chile	756 943	13 173	Santiago
Colombia	1 138 907	32 978	Bogotá
Ecuador	455 502	10 587	Quito
French Guiana (Fr.)	91 000	98	Cayenne
Guyana	214 969	796	George Town
Paraguay	406 750	4 277	Asunción
Peru	1 285 215	21 550	Lima
Surinam	163 820	422	Paramaribo
Uruguay	186 925	3 094	Montevideo
Venezuela	912 047	19 735	Caracas
Europe			
Albania	28 752	3 245	Tiranë (Tirana)
Andorra	453	47	Andorra-la-Vella
Armenia	29 800	3 283	Yerevan
Austria	83 848	7 583	Wien (Vienna)
Azerbaijan	86 600	7 029	Baku
Belgium	30 512	9 845	Bruxelles (Brussels)
Belorussia	207 600	10 200	Minsk
Bulgaria	110 911	9 010	Sofiya (Sofia)
Cyprus	9 251	701	Nicosia
Czechoslovakia	127 870	15 667	Praha (Prague)
Denmark	43 030	5 143	København (Copenhagen)
Estonia	45 100	1 573	Tallinn
Faroes (Den.)	1 399	47	Tórshavn
Finland	337 032	4 975	Helsinki
France	551 000	56 138	Paris
Georgia	69 700	5 449	Tbilisi
Germany	357 868	79 070	Berlin, Bonn
Gibraltar (UK)	6	30	Gibraltar
Great Britain and N. Ireland, see United Kingdom			
Greece	131 955	10 047	Athínai (Athens)
Greenland (Den.)	2 175 600	56	Godthåb
Hungary	93 030	10 552	Budapest
Iceland	102 828	253	Reykjavík
Ireland	70 282	3 720	Dublin
Italy	301 245	57 061	Roma (Rome)
Latvia	63 700	2 681	Riga
Liechtenstein	161	28	Vaduz
Lithuania	65 200	3 690	Vilnius
Luxembourg	2 587	373	Luxembourg
Malta	316	353	Valletta
Moldavia	33 700	4 341	Kishinev
Monaco	1.8	28	Monaco
Netherlands	33 940	14 951	Amsterdam/ 's-Gravenhage
Norway	324 218	4 212	Oslo
Poland	312 683	38 423	Warszawa (Warsaw)
Portugal	91 671	10 285	Lisboa (Lisbon)
Romania	237 500	23 272	Bucureşti (Bucharest)
Russian Federation	17 075 000	147 386	Moskva (Moscow)
San Marino	61	23	San Marino
Spain	504 745	39 187	Madrid
Sweden	449 791	8 444	Stockholm
Switzerland	41 287	6 609	Bern
Ukraine	603 700	51 704	Kiyev
United Kingdom	244 104	57 237	London
Vatican City	.4	1	Vatican City
Yugoslavia	255 803	23 807	Beograd (Belgrade)
Asia			
Afghanistan	674 500	16 557	Kābul
Bahrain	660	516	Al Manāmah
Bangladesh	144 020	115 593	Dhaka (Dacca)
Bhutan	46 620	1 516	Thimphu
Brunei	5 765	266	Bandar Seri Begawan
Burma (Myanma)	678 031	41 675	Rangoon (Yangon)
Cambodia	181 035	8 246	Phnom Penh
China	9 561 000	1 118 760	Beijing (Peking)
Hong Kong (UK)	1 062	5 851	
India	3 287 593	853 094	New Delhi
Indonesia	1 919 263	185 020	Jakarta
Iran	1 648 184	54 607	Tehrān
Iraq	434 924	18 920	Baghdād
Israel	20 770	4 600	Jerusalem
Japan	371 000	123 460	Tōkyō
Jordan	97 740	4 009	Amman
Kazakhstan	2 717 300	16 538	Alma Ata
Kirgizia	198 500	4 291	Bishkek (Frunze)
Korea, North	121 248	21 773	P'yŏngyang
Korea, South	98 447	42 793	Sŏul (Seoul)
Kuwait	24 300	2 039	Kuwait
Laos	236 798	4 139	Vientiane
Lebanon	10 399	2 701	Beirut
Macau (Port.)	16	479	Macao
Malaysia	330 669	17 891	Kuala Lumpur
Maldives	298	215	Malé
Mongolia	1 565 000	2 190	Ulaanbaatar (Ulan Bator)
Nepal	141 414	19 143	Kathmandu
Oman	212 379	1 502	Masqaţ (Muscat)
Pakistan	803 941	122 626	Islamabad
Philippines	299 765	62 413	Manila
Qatar	11 437	368	Ad Dawḩah
Saudi Arabia	2 400 930	14 134	Ar Riyāḑ
Singapore	616	2 723	Singapore
Sri Lanka	65 610	17 217	Colombo
Syria	185 179	12 530	Dimashq (Damascus)
Taiwan	35 980	20 300	T'ai-pei
Tajikistan	143 100	5 112	Dushanbe
Thailand	513 517	55 702	Bangkok
Turkey	780 576	55 868	Ankara
Turkmenistan	488 100	3 534	Ashkhabad
United Arab Emirates	83 600	1 589	Abū Ẓabī
Uzbekistan	447 400	19 906	Tashkent
Vietnam	329 566	66 693	Hanoi
Yemen	528 038	11 687	Şan'ā'
Africa			
Algeria	2 381 731	24 960	Alger (El Djezair)
Angola	1 246 694	10 020	Luanda
Benin	112 622	4 630	Porto Novo
Botswana	582 000	1 304	Gaborone
Burkina	274 122	8 996	Ouagadougou
Burundi	27 834	5 472	Bujumbura
Cameroon	475 499	11 833	Yaoundé
Cape Verde	4 033	370	Praia
Central African Republic	622 996	3 039	Bangui
Chad	1 284 000	5 678	N'Djamena
Comoros	1 862	550	Moroni
Congo	342 000	2 271	Brazzaville
Djibouti	21 699	409	Djibouti
Egypt	1 000 250	52 426	Cairo
Equatorial Guinea	28 051	352	Malabo
Ethiopia	1 221 918	49 240	Ādīs Ābeba
Gabon	267 667	1 172	Libreville
The Gambia	10 688	861	Banjul
Ghana	238 538	15 028	Accra
Guinea	245 855	5 755	Conakry
Guinea-Bissau	36 125	964	Bissau
Ivory Coast	322 463	11 997	Yamoussoukro
Kenya	582 644	24 031	Nairobi
Lesotho	30 344	1 774	Maseru
Liberia	111 370	2 575	Monrovia
Libya	1 759 530	4 545	Tripoli
Madagascar	587 042	12 004	Antananarivo
Malawi	94 100	8 754	Lilongwe
Mali	1 240 142	9 214	Bamako
Mauritania	1 030 700	2 024	Nouakchott
Mauritius	1 865	1 082	Port Louis
Morocco	459 000	25 061	Rabat
Mozambique	784 961	15 656	Maputo
Namibia	824 293	1 781	Windhoek
Niger	1 267 000	7 731	Niamey
Nigeria	923 769	108 542	Abuja
Réunion (Fr.)	2 510	598	Saint-Denis
Rwanda	26 338	7 237	Kigali
São Tomé and Principe	964	121	São Tomé
Senegal	196 722	7 327	Dakar
Seychelles	443	69	Victoria
Sierra Leone	71 740	4 151	Freetown
Somalia	637 539	7 497	Muqdisho (Mogadishu)
South Africa	1 221 038	35 282	Pretoria/ Cape Town
Sudan	2 505 792	25 203	Khartoum
Swaziland	17 366	788	Mbabane
Tanzania	942 000	27 318	Dodoma
Togo	56 785	3 531	Lomé
Tunisia	164 148	8 180	Tunis
Uganda	236 036	18 794	Kampala
Western Sahara	266 000	178	-
Zaire	2 344 885	35 568	Kinshasa
Zambia	752 617	8 452	Lusaka
Zimbabwe	390 308	9 709	Harare
Oceania			
American Samoa (USA)	197	38	Fagatogo
Australia	7 682 300	16 873	Canberra
Fiji	18 272	764	Suva
French Polynesia (Fr.)	4 198	206	Papeete
Guam (USA)	549	118	Agaña
Kiribati	800	66	Tarawa
Nauru	21	9	Yaren
New Caledonia (Fr.)	19 104	167	Nouméa
New Zealand	268 675	3 392	Wellington
Niue (NZ)	259	3	Alofi
Federated States of Micronesia	1 300	99	Kolonia
Papua New Guinea	461 692	3 874	Port Moresby
Solomon Islands	29 785	320	Honiara
Tonga	699	95	Nuku'alofa
Tuvalu	25	9	Funafuti
Vanuatu	14 763	158	Vila
Western Samoa	2 831	168	Apia

This page explains the main symbols, lettering style and height/depth colours used on the reference maps on pages 2 to 79. The scale of each map is indicated at the top of each page. Abbreviations used on the maps appear at the beginning of the index.

BOUNDARIES

International

International under Dispute

Cease Fire Line

Autonomous or State

Administrative

Maritime (National)

International Date Line

COMMUNICATIONS

Motorway/Express Highway

Under Construction

Major Highway

Other Roads

Under Construction

Track

Road Tunnel

Car Ferry

Main Railway

Other Railway

Under Construction

Rail Tunnel

Rail Ferry

Canal

International Airport

Other Airport

LAKE FEATURES

Freshwater

Saltwater

Seasonal

Salt Pan

LANDSCAPE FEATURES

Glacier, Ice Cap

Marsh, Swamp

Sand Desert, Dunes

OTHER FEATURES

River

Seasonal River

Pass, Gorge

Dam, Barrage

Waterfall, Rapid

Aqueduct

Reef

4231 Summit, Peak

217 Spot Height, Depth

Well

Oil Field

Gas Field

Gas / Oil Oil/Natural Gas Pipeline

Gemsbok Nat. Pk National Park

UR Historic Site

LETTERING STYLES

CANADA	Independent Nation
FLORIDA	State, Province or Autonomous Region
Gibraltar (U.K.)	Sovereignty of Dependent Territory
Lothian	Administrative Area
LANGUEDOC	Historic Region
Loire *Vosges*	Physical Feature or Physical Region

TOWNS AND CITIES

Square symbols denote capital cities. Each settlement is given a symbol according to its relative importance, with type size to match.

New York	Major City
Montréal	City
Ottawa	Small City
Québec	Large Town
St John's	Town
Yorkton	Small Town
Jasper	Village
	Built-up-area

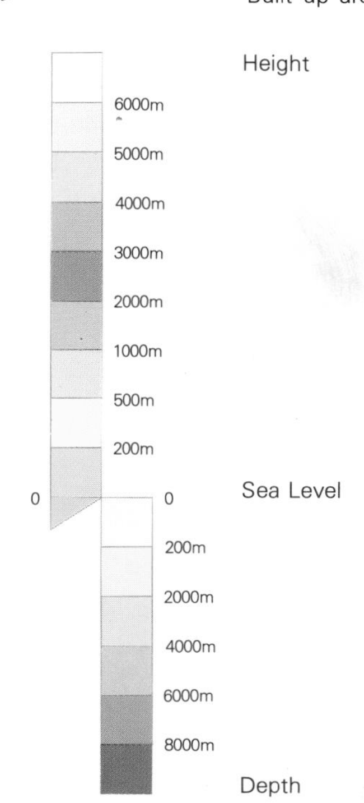

1:35M

0 250 500 750 1000 1250 km

0 250 500 750 mls

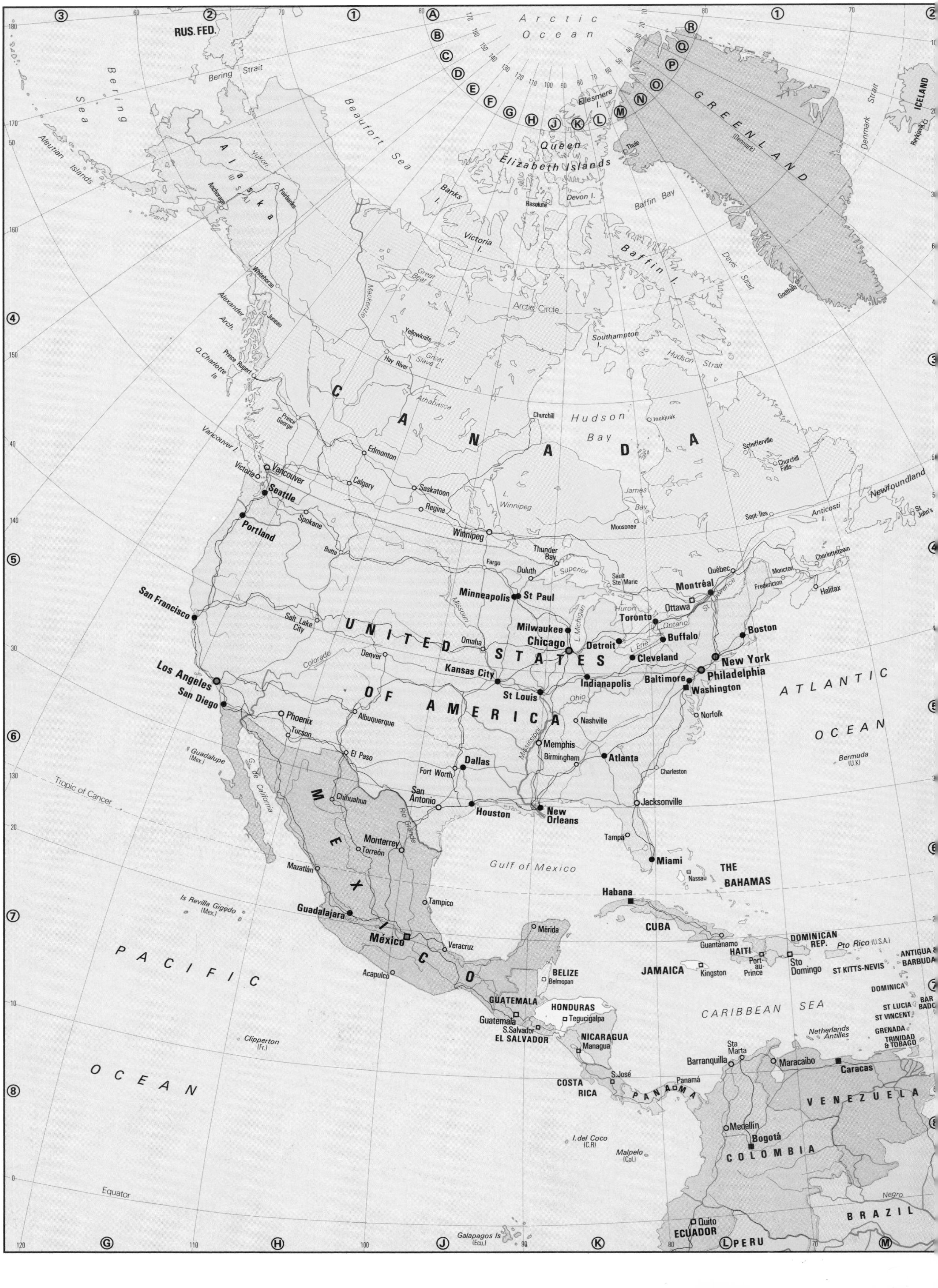

Arctic Ocean
RUS. FED.
Bering Strait
Bering Sea
Aleutian Islands
Alaska (U.S.A.)
Anchorage
Fairbanks
Yukon
Beaufort Sea
Banks I.
Victoria I.
Queen Elizabeth Islands
Ellesmere I.
Devon I.
Resolute
Thule
Baffin Bay
Baffin I.
GREENLAND (Denmark)
Denmark Strait
ICELAND
Reykjavik
Davis Strait
Godthåb
Great Bear L.
Mackenzie
Arctic Circle
Whitehorse
Juneau
Alexander Arch.
Q. Charlotte Is
Prince Rupert
Yellowknife
Hay River
Great Slave L.
Southampton I.
Hudson Strait
Athabasca
Prince George
C A N A D A
Churchill
Hudson Bay
Inukjuak
Schefferville
Churchill Falls
Vancouver I.
Edmonton
Victoria
Vancouver
Calgary
Saskatoon
Regina
L. Winnipeg
James Bay
Newfoundland
Seattle
Portland
Spokane
Winnipeg
Moosonee
Sept-Îles
Anticosti I.
St John's
Butte
Thunder Bay
Charlottetown
Fargo
Duluth
L. Superior
Sault Ste Marie
Québec
Moncton
Fredericton
Halifax
San Francisco
Minneapolis
St Paul
Montréal
Ottawa
St Lawrence
Missouri
L. Huron
Salt Lake City
L. Michigan
Toronto
L. Ontario
Boston
UNITED STATES OF AMERICA
Milwaukee
Chicago
Detroit
L. Erie
Buffalo
Omaha
Colorado
Denver
Cleveland
New York
Kansas City
Indianapolis
Baltimore
Philadelphia
Los Angeles
Washington
San Diego
St Louis
Ohio
ATLANTIC OCEAN
Phoenix
Albuquerque
Nashville
Norfolk
Tucson
Mississippi
Memphis
Guadalupe (Mex.)
El Paso
Birmingham
G. de California
Dallas
Atlanta
Bermuda (U.K.)
Fort Worth
Charleston
Tropic of Cancer
Chihuahua
San Antonio
Houston
New Orleans
Jacksonville
Rio Grande
M E X I C O
Monterrey
Torreón
Tampa
Miami
Mazatlán
Gulf of Mexico
Nassau
THE BAHAMAS
Is Revilla Gigedo (Mex.)
Tampico
Habana
Guadalajara
CUBA
Mérida
México
DOMINICAN REP.
Guantánamo
Pto Rico (U.S.A.)
Veracruz
HAITI
Port-au-Prince
Sto Domingo
ANTIGUA & BARBUDA
PACIFIC OCEAN
JAMAICA
Kingston
ST KITTS-NEVIS
BELIZE
Belmopan
Acapulco
DOMINICA
GUATEMALA
HONDURAS
Tegucigalpa
ST LUCIA
BARBADOS
CARIBBEAN SEA
ST VINCENT
Guatemala
S. Salvador
EL SALVADOR
Netherlands Antilles
GRENADA
TRINIDAD & TOBAGO
NICARAGUA
Managua
Clipperton (Fr.)
Sta Marta
Barranquilla
Maracaibo
Caracas
S. José
COSTA RICA
Panamá
PANAMA
VENEZUELA
Medellín
Bogotá
COLOMBIA
I. del Coco (C.R.)
Malpelo (Col.)
Equator
Negro
BRAZIL
Quito
ECUADOR
Galapagos Is (Ecu.)
PERU

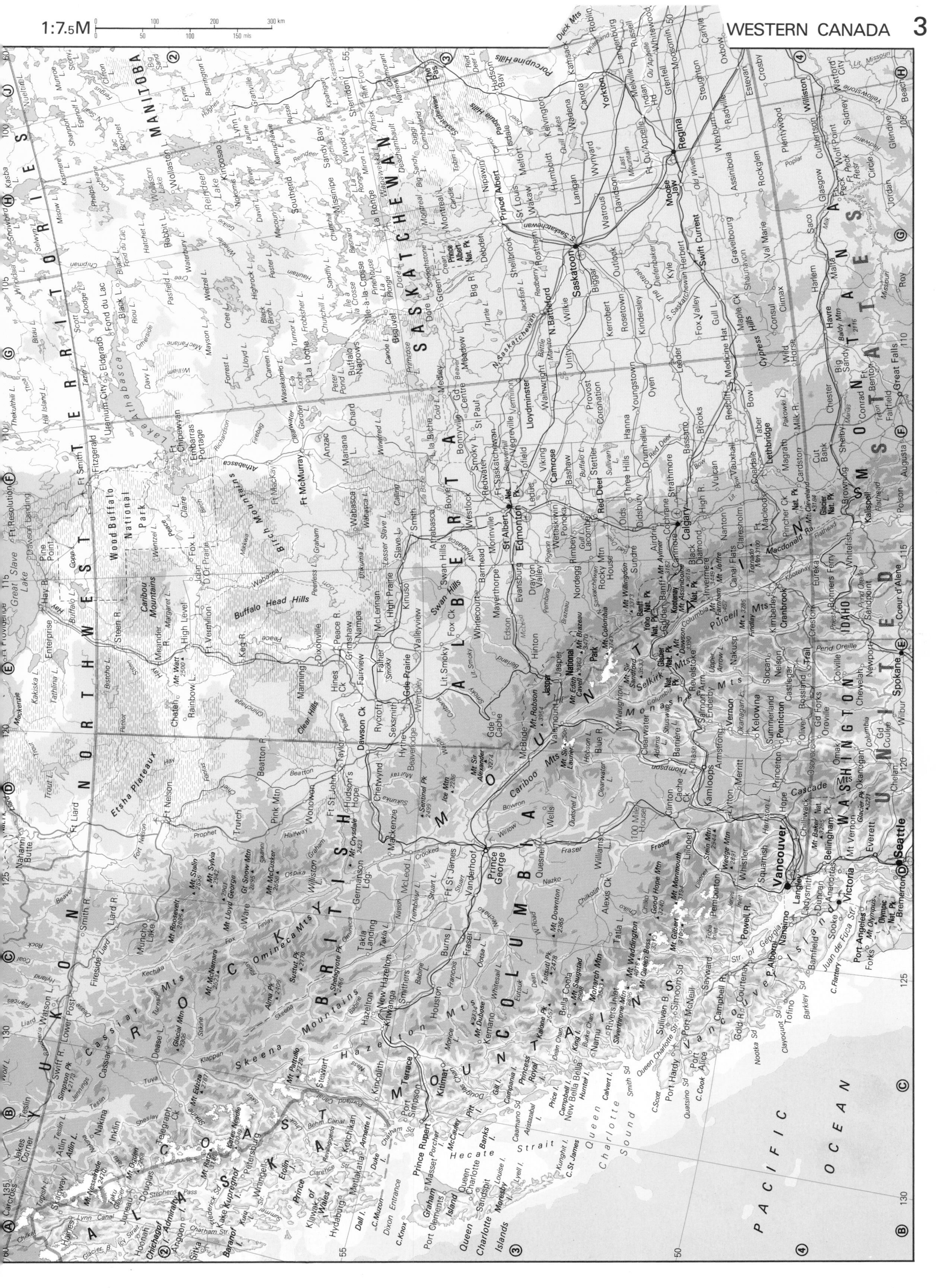
NORTHWEST TERRITORIES
YUKON
MANITOBA
SASKATCHEWAN
ALBERTA
BRITISH COLUMBIA
ALASKA
UNITED STATES
MONTANA
IDAHO
WASHINGTON
PACIFIC OCEAN
ROCKY MOUNTAINS
COAST MOUNTAINS
Cassiar Mts
Skeena Mountains
Omineca Mts
Cariboo Mts
Monashee Mts
Selkirk Mts
Purcell Mts
Caribou Mountains
Buffalo Head Hills
Birch Mountains
Swan Hills
Clear Hills
Etsha Plateau
Wood Buffalo National Park
Great Slave Lake
Lake Athabasca
Queen Charlotte Islands
Queen Charlotte Sound
Hecate Strait
Dixon Entrance
Juan de Fuca Str.
Edmonton
Calgary
Regina
Saskatoon
Vancouver
Victoria
Seattle
Spokane
Prince George
Prince Rupert
Prince Albert
Moose Jaw
Lethbridge
Medicine Hat
Kamloops
Red Deer
Ft McMurray
Jasper
Banff

1:7.5M 0 100 200 300 km 0 50 100 150 mls

A B C D E F
100 95 90 85 80 60
2 3 4 5

HUDSON BAY
James Bay
MANITOBA
ONTARIO
MINNESOTA
WISCONSIN
IOWA
ILLINOIS
MICHIGAN
NEW Y
Q
UNITED STATES
LAKE SUPERIOR
LAKE MICHIGAN
LAKE HURON
LAKE ERIE
LAKE ONTARIO
Georgian Bay
Lake Winnipeg
Lake Winnipegosis
Lake Manitoba
Cedar Lake
Lake Nipigon
Lake of the Woods

Smith I. Akulivik R. Povungnituk Povungnituk Ottawa Is. B. Kogaluc R. Innuksuac L. Qilalugalik Inukjuak Chavigny Sleeper Islands King George Islands Nastapoka Islands L. Minto Nastapoca Belcher Islands L. Guillaume Delisle Petite R. de la Baleine Kuujjuarapik Grande Rivière de la Baleine C. Henrietta Maria Long Island Pointe Louis XIV Kanaaupscow Roggan Roggan L. Chisasibi Radisson La Grande Résr. 2 Duncan L. N. Twin I. S. Twin I. Akimiski Island Sakami L. Sakami Wemindji C. Duncan Opinaca Fort Albany Eastmain Charlton Island Eastmain Pontax Hannah Bay Moosonee Waskaganish Rupert Nottaway Kitchigama Broadback L. Evans Harricana Kesagami L. Turgeon L. Grasset Matagami L. Matagami L. au Goéland Waswanipi L. Olga Miquelon L. Doda

Seal Caribou Tadoule L. Brochet Reindeer Lake Goldsand Wells L. S. Seal Big Sand L. Southern Indian L. N. Knife S. Knife Churchill C. Churchill Churchill Cromarty M'Clintock Owl Silcox Port Nelson Northern Indian L. Lynn Lake Gauer L. Baldock L. Russell L. Sisipuk L. Churchill Highrock Pukatawagan Split L. Ilford Bird Nelson C. Tatnam York Factory Thompson Kississing L. Sherridon Flin Flon Thicket Portage Arnot High Hill Hayes Machichi Kaskattama Kettle Sipiwesk L. Stupart Gods Black Duck Niskibi Wekusko Tyrrell Hayes Beaver Fort Severn Cormorant Kiskitto L. Cross L. The Pas Westray Bolton L. Molson L. Gods L. Severn Polar Bear Provincial Park Winisk Grand Rapids Norway House Stevenson L. Bigstone L. Gunisao Island L. Red Sucker L. Fawn Winisk Sutton Polar Bear Provincial Park Lake River Easterville Gunisao L. Sachigo L. Bearskin Lake Big Trout Lake Opinnagau Swan Chitek L. Poplar Cobham Sandy Lake Opasquia Big Trout L. Shibogama L. Ekwan Berens River Berens Severn Sandy L. Big Beaver House Gypsumville Rorketon L. St. Martin Dauphin Dauphin L. Little Grand Rapids Family L. Wunnummin L. N. Caribou L. Winisk Winisk L. Attawapiskat Attawapiskat Ashern Hodgson Pikangikum Berens Pipestone Alonsa Amaranth Arborg Eriksdale Gimli Riverton Bissett Lansdowne House Attawapiskat L. Cat Lake Cat L. Kapiskau Trout L. Birch L. Pickle Lake Fawcett L. Victoria Beach Pine Falls Red Lake L. St. Joseph Miminiska L. Eabamet L. Fort Hope Albany Ogoki Albany Selkirk Goldpines Portage la Prairie Assiniboine Beausejour Whiteshell Prov. Park Winnipeg St. Boniface Keewatin Minaki Vermilion Lac Seul Sioux Lookout Savant Lake Savant L. Ogoki Resr. Ogoki Stooping Chipie Missinaibi Mattagami Abitibi Steinbach Emerson Roseau Kenora Dryden Minnitaki L. Sturgeon L. Little Current Seseganaga L. Auden Nakina Kenogami Pagwa River Kabinakagami Otter Rapids Langdon Cavalier Warroad Karlstad Paguchi L. Ignace Lynx Longlac Geraldton Macdiarmid White Otter L. Marmion L. English River Ameson Hearst Mattice Opasatika Grafton Warren Fort Frances Thief River Falls Rainy L. International Falls Littlefork Des Mille Lacs Long L. Hillsport Kapuskasing Groundhog Driftwood Cochrane Stimson East Grand Forks Grand Forks Upper Red L. Lower Red L. Quetico Provincial Park Nipigon Nipigon B. Schreiber Heron Bay Coldwell Hornepayne Oba Mahnomen Bemidji Blackduck Ouimet Thunder Bay Pukaskwa Nat. Park White River Franz Elsas Timmins Iroquois Falls Beattyville La Sarre Twin Valley Cass Lake Chisholm Ely Grand Marais Isle Royale Foleyet Abitibi Amos Parent Mégiscane Moorhead Walker Leech L. Virginia Hibbing Grand Rapids Two Harbors Michipicoten I. Dalton Tionaga Ramore Kirkland Lake Swastika Noranda Barraute Rouyn Senneterre Langlade Detroit Lakes Wadena Pine River Mississippi Copper Harbor Wawa Lake Superior Provincial Park Sand Lake Chapleau Matachewan Malartic Val d'Or Monet Fergus Falls Brainerd Alexandria Cloquet Duluth Superior Apostle Is. Keweenaw Pen. Hancock Bayfield Washburn Ashland Keweenaw B. Whitefish B. Sultan Gogama New Liskeard Cobalt L. Simard Résr. Decelles Résr. Dozois La Verendrye Prov. Park Résr. Cabonga Mille Lacs L. Moose Lake Little Falls Solon Springs Rockland Bergland Ironwood Ishpeming Marquette Mekatina Rocky Island L. Laforest Temagami Morris Sauk Centre Pine City St. Cloud Hayward Shingleton Sault Ste. Marie Sault Ste. Marie Elliot Lake Thessalon Copper Cliff Sudbury Sturgeon Falls North Bay L. Kipawa Témiscaming Résr. Baskatong Benson Willmar Litchfield Cambridge Spooner Cumberland Prentice Park Falls Channing Iron Mountain Naubinway Blind River Espanola L. Bryson Mont-Laurier Maniwaki Granite Falls Brooklyn Center Rice Lake Ladysmith Rhinelander Escanaba Manistique St. Ignace North Channel Key Harbour Nipissing Mattawa Ottawa Deep River Gatineau Marshall Tracy Bloomington St. Paul Minneapolis Menomonie Winthrop Red Wing Chippewa Falls Eau Claire Merrill Antigo Elcho Laona Wolf Beaver I. Mackinaw City Cheboygan Manitoulin I. Little Current Brent Petawawa Trout Creek Britt Algonquin Prov. Park Pembroke Fort Coulonge Mankato Windom Faribault Owatonna Whitehall Coleman Oconto Marinette Menominee Green Bay Petoskey Main Channel Emsdale Parry Sound Renfrew Arnprior Hull Ottawa Fairmont Albert Lea Rochester Austin Winona Wisconsin Rapids Shawano Stevens Point Sturgeon Bay Traverse City Mancelona Vanderbilt Alpena Tobermory Bruce Pen. Huntsville Bracebridge Haliburton Highlands Carleton Place Smiths Falls Estherville Spencer Clear Lake Algona Preston Sparta La Crosse Tomah Appleton Oshkosh Green Bay Otsego Lake Black River Stokes Bay L. Muskoka Gravenhurst Penetanguishene Bancroft Haliburton Gilmour Perth Rideau Lakes Brockville Fort Dodge Decorah Osage Mason City Wisconsin Dells Mauston Winnebago Fond du Lac Chilton Manitowoc Cadillac Manistee Ludington Grayling South Branch Tawas City Owen Sound Southampton Nottawasaga B. Orillia Midland Apsley Lindsay Peterborough Madoc Hammond Gananoque Kingston Belmond Iowa Falls Waverly Cedar Falls Waterloo Webster City Ames Oelwein Prairie du Chien Platteville Madison Waukesha Sheboygan Beaver Dam Muskegon Baldwin Reed City Shelby Clare Saginaw Bay Port Austin Kincardine Collingwood Barrie L. Simcoe Belleville Trenton Sac City Carroll Boone Ogden Dubuque Monroe Janesville Beloit Wauwatosa Milwaukee Racine Kenosha Mt. Pleasant Alma Midland Bay City Saginaw Palms Goderich Wingham Guelph Waterloo Kitchener Brampton Oshawa Whitby Cobourg Watertown Marshalltown Vinton Cedar Rapids Freeport Rockford Burlington Waukegan Arlington Heights Grand Rapids Owosso Marlette Stratford Hamilton Toronto Oakville Burlington Lockport Rochester Fulton Oswego Rome Oneida Utica Indianola Des Moines Newton Oskaloosa Iowa City Clinton Davenport Rochelle Dixon Sterling Elgin Evanston Aurora South Haven Holland Kalamazoo Lansing Otsego Battle Creek Pontiac Flint Port Huron Sarnia London Woodstock St. Catharines Niagara Falls Tonawanda Buffalo Syracuse Geneva Auburn Creston Osceola Ottumwa Monmouth Washington Burlington Fort Madison Galesburg Peoria Moline Rock Island Peru Streator Joliet Ottawa Hammond Chicago Gary Michigan City Benton Harbor Niles Elkhart South Bend Albion Coldwater Jackson Ann Arbor Dearborn Warren Detroit Windsor Wyandotte Monroe Toledo Chatham St. Thomas Lackawanna Geneseo Cortland Ithaca Fredonia Jamestown Olean Hornell Corning Binghamton Elmira Endicott Gowanda Bath Warren Erie Conneaut Ashtabula Painesville Corry Meadville Euclid Cleveland Lakewood Lorain Sandusky Maumee Defiance Angola Auburn Plymouth Kankakee Park Forest Pontiac Francesville Bloomfield Princeton Kirksville Trenton Keokuk Hallstead

Ungava Bay
Akpatok I.
C. Chidley
Killinek I.
Killiniq
N. Aulatsivik I.
Torngat Mts.
Mt. Caubvick 1729
Kangirsuk
Aupalak
Tasiujaq
Kuujjuaq
Kangiqsualujjuaq
Saglek Bay
C. Uivak
Hebron
Cod I.
Nutak
C. Kiglapait
S. Aulatsivik I.
Pyramid Hills
Nain
Kamatsuk
Tunungayualok I.
C. Harrigan
Davis Inlet
Mistastin L.
Hopedale
Makkovik
C. Harrison
Indian Harbour
Groswater Bay
Rigolet
Double Mer
N. Head
I. of Ponds
Cartwright
Sandwich Bay
Domino
Stony I.
C. Bluff
George's Cove
Seal Bight
St. Lewis Sound
Port Hope Simpson
Mary's Harbour
Battle Harbour
Belle Isle
Labrador Sea
Labrador
NEWFOUNDLAND
QUEBEC
Smallwood Resr.
Goose Bay
Happy Valley
North West River
L. Melville
Mealy Mountains
Churchill
Schefferville
Attikamagen Lake
Petitsikapau
L. Menihek Lakes
Sawbill
Ossokmanuan L.
Labrador City
Wabush
Ashuanipi L.
Atikonak L.
L. Brûlé
R. du Petit Mécatina
Natashquan
Résr. Caniapiscau
La Grande Résr. 4
L. Bienville
L. Mistassini
Monts Otish 1128
Résr. Manicouagan
Gagnon
Moisie
Romaine
Red Bay
L'Anse au Loup
Blanc Sablon
Strait of Belle Isle
C. Bauld
St. Anthony
Hare Bay
Grandois
Grey Islands
Roddickton
St. John Bay
Englee
Harbour Deep
Long Range Mountains
Fleur-de-Lys
Baie Verte
C. St. John
Notre Dame Bay
Fogo
Fogo I.
Twillingate
C. Freels
Wesleyville
Bonavista Bay
C. Bonavista
Bonavista
Gros Morne Nat. Park
Trout River
Deer Lake
Springdale
Lewisporte
Gander
Gambo
Bay of Islands
Corner Brook
Grand Lake
Windsor
Buchans
Grand Falls
Clarenville
Trinity Bay
Grates Pt.
Carbonear
Harbour Grace
St. John's
Newfoundland
Trans-Canada Highway
Port au Port
Stephenville
St. George's Bay
St. Fintan's
Blue Hills of Couteau
St. Albans
Terrenceville
Argentia
Placentia
Avalon Pen.
Trepassey
C. Race
C. Pine
St. Mary's B.
C. St. Mary's
Placentia Bay
Marystown
Burin Pen.
Fortune Bay
Grand Bank
Belleoram
Burgeo
Rose Blanche
Channel Port-aux-Basques
C. Ray
Saint Pierre & Miquelon (Fr.)
Cabot Strait
Mutton Bay
C. Mécatina
Port Saunders
Daniel's Harbour
St. Augustin-Saguenay
Shekalika Bay
Harrington Harbour
Étamamiou
Gethsémani
Natashquan
Aguanish
Havre St. Pierre
Mingan
Sheldrake
Sept Îles
Détroit de Jacques Cartier
Port Menier
Î. d'Anticosti
Anticosti Prov. Park
Pointe de l'Est
Port Cartier
Rivière Pentecôte
Pointe aux Anglais
Détroit d'Honguedo
Godbout
Baie Comeau
Hauterive
Betsiamites
Ste.-Anne-des-Monts
Cap Chat
Mont Louis
Grande Vallée
Mt. Jacques Cartier 1268
Gaspésie Prov. Park
Gaspé
C. de Gaspé
B. de Malbaie
Péninsule de Gaspé
Grande Rivière
Chandler
Grande Cascapédia
Paspébiac
Matane
Mont Joli
Amqui
Rimouski
Bic
Gulf of St. Lawrence
St. Lawrence
Notre Dame
Miscou I.
B. des Chaleurs
Dalhousie
Campbellton
Shippegan
Tracadie
Îles de la Madeleine (Québec)
C. North
C. Breton Highlands
Chéticamp
Bathurst
Big Bald Mtn. 672
Miramichi Bay
Chatham
Newcastle
Kedgwick
Richibucto
Buctouche
Shediac
North Pt.
Tignish
Alberton
PRINCE EDWARD I.
Summerside
Souris
Charlottetown
Georgetown
Montague
Northumberland Strait
NEW BRUNSWICK
New Waterford
Glace Bay
Sydney
Sydney Mines
C. Breton Island
Bras d'Or L.
Port Hawkesbury
Canso
George B.
NOVA SCOTIA
Moncton
Sackville
Amherst
New Glasgow
Springhill
Stellarton
Truro
Shubenacadie
Minas Basin
Minas Ch.
Chignecto B.
Caledonia Hills
Kentville
Windsor
Sheet Harbour
Middleton
Bridgetown
Dartmouth
Halifax
Bay of Fundy
Grand Manan I.
Digby
Mahone B.
Bridgewater
Liverpool
Shelburne
Lockeport
Port Maitland
Yarmouth
Wedgeport
C. Sable
Sable I. (Nova Scotia)
Freeport
ATLANTIC OCEAN
Saint John
Rothesay
St. George
St. Stephen
Fredericton
Oromocto
Hartland
Bath
Grand Falls
Edmundston
Madawaska
Trans-Canada Hwy.
Houlton
Caribou
Presque Isle
Peaked Mtn. 689
Eagle Lake
Eagle L.
Chesuncook L.
Millinocket
Mattawamkeag
Moosehead L.
MAINE
Bingham
Old Town
Bangor
Machias
Pittsburg
Waterville
Rumford
Belfast
Augusta
Rockland
Lewiston
Auburn
Bath
Brunswick
Portland
Biddeford
Westbrook
Berlin
Mt. Washington 1917
Conway
NEW HAMPSHIRE
VERMONT
St. Johnsbury
Montpelier
Lincoln
Burlington
Lake Champlain
Middlebury
Orford
Rutland
Springfield
Concord
Dover
Portsmouth
Manchester
Nashua
Lawrence
Lowell
Keene
Pittsfield
MASSACHUSETTS
Cambridge
Boston
C. Cod
Cape Cod Bay
Worcester
Springfield
Westfield
Brockton
Providence
Fall River
Hartford
Stamford
Albany
Troy
Schenectady
Amsterdam
Saratoga Springs
Glens Falls
Lake Placid
Mt. Marcy 1629
Adirondack Mountains
Plattsburgh
Malone
St. Albans
Cornwall
Valleyfield
Cowansville
Magog
Granby
St. Jean
Sherbrooke
Windsor
Montréal
Laval
Verdun
St. Laurent
Blainville
Thérèse
St. Jérôme
St. Hyacinthe
Sorel
Drummondville
Victoriaville
Thetford Mines
Joliette
Ste. Agathe-des-Monts
Trois-Rivières
Cap-de-la-Madeleine
Shawinigan
Grand Mère
Québec
Lévis
St. Agapit
Charlesbourg
Ste. Anne de Beaupré
Montmagny
Monts Notre Dame
La Tuque
Festubert
Laurentides Provincial Park
Baie St. Paul
Malbaie
St. Siméon
Tadoussac
Trois Pistoles
Rivière-du-Loup
St. Pacôme
St. Pascal
Chicoutimi
Jonquière
Saguenay
Les Escoumins
Alma
Dolbeau
Mistassini
Roberval
L. St. Jean
Résr. Gouin
Ashuapmushuan Prov. Park
Chibougamau
Chibougamau L.
Mistassini Provincial Park
St. Paul du Nord
Résr. Pipmouacane
Manicouagan
R. aux Outardes
Toulnustouc
Ste. Marguerite
Manouane
Péribonca
Mistassini
Nestaocano
L. Plétipi
Mouchalagane
Gagnon
L. Naococane
Opiscotéo
Nitchequon
L. Sureau
L. Taffanel
Lapointe
L. Rambau
L. Nouveau
L. Holmer
Dalmas
La Grande
L. Néret
L. Delorme
L. Clairambault
L. Mannessier
Sérigny
Wakuach L.
L. aux Goélands
L. Ramusio
Kanairiktok
Naskaupi
Woods L.
Mistinibi L.
Kogaluk
L. Champdoré
L. Guérard
George
Fraser
Kingurutik
Tunulik
R. à la Baleine
Caniapiscau
Nachikapau L.
Wheeler
R. aux Mélèzes
Du Gué
L. Châteauguay
L. à l'Eau-Claire
Koksoak
R. aux Feuilles
L. Bacqueville
L. La Potherie
L. Faribault
L. aux Feuilles
L. Tassialouc
L. Payne
L. Bécard
R. Arnaud
R. Lepellé
R. Vachon
L. Klotz
B. de Keglo
Alexis
Paradise
Eagle
Goose
St. Augustin
St. Paul
Aguanus
Magpie
St. Jean
Wacouno
White Bay
Sop's Arm
Long Range Mtns.
Restigouche
St. John
Penobscot
Mégantic
70
65
60
55
50
45
40
G
H
J
K
L
2
3
4
5

1:15M

0 200 400 600 km

0 100 200 300 mls

Names underlined indicate Province/State capitals

GREENLAND
(Denmark)
DENMARK STRAIT
ICELAND
Reykjavík
BAFFIN BAY
Baffin Island
DAVIS STRAIT
Labrador Sea
HUDSON STRAIT
Ungava Bay
HUDSON BAY
James Bay
NEWFOUNDLAND
Labrador
Newfoundland
St John's
QUEBEC
ONTARIO
Gulf of Saint Lawrence
NOVA SCOTIA
Halifax
NEW BRUNSWICK
PRINCE EDWARD I.
Charlottetown
Cape Breton I.
ATLANTIC OCEAN
LAKE SUPERIOR
MICHIGAN
L. Ontario
Montréal
Québec
Ottawa
Toronto
Hamilton
Buffalo
Detroit
Windsor
Milwaukee
Boston
Providence
Hartford
MAINE
VERMONT
NEW HAMPSHIRE
Thunder Bay
Sudbury
Sault Ste Marie
Duluth
Madison
Churchill
Devon Island
Lancaster Sound
Jones Sound
Ellesmere Island
Axel Heiberg Island
Thule
Melville Peninsula
Foxe Basin
Foxe Channel
Southampton Island
Frobisher Bay
Cumberland Sound
Godthåb
Kap Farvel
Sept-Iles
Gaspé
Chicoutimi
Labrador City
Schefferville
Goose Bay
Corner Brook
Gander
Sydney
Moncton
Fredericton
Saint John
Sherbrooke
Kingston

1:12.5M

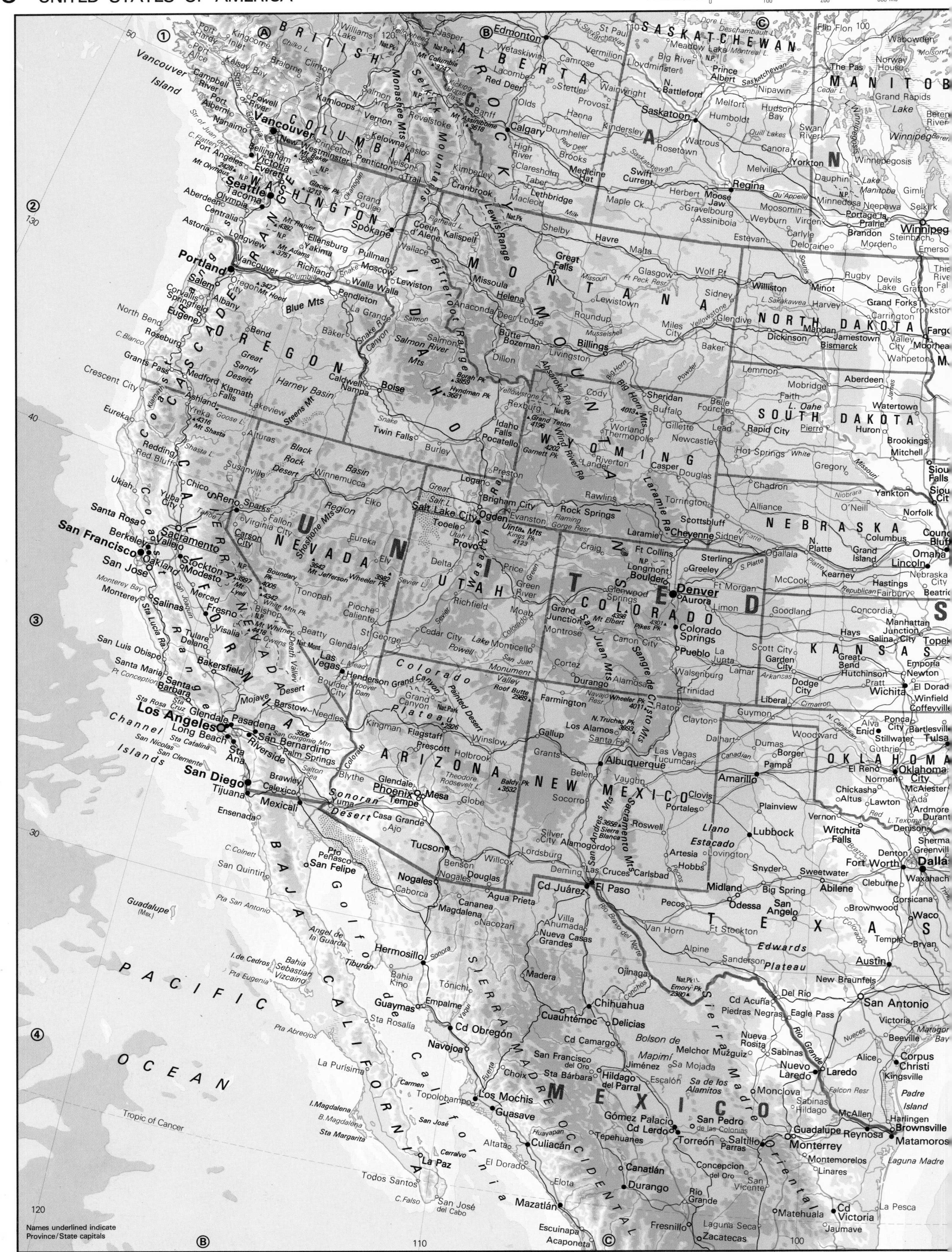

0 100 200 300 400 500 km
0 100 200 300 mls
BRITISH COLUMBIA
ALBERTA
SASKATCHEWAN
MANITOBA
CANADA
ROCKY MOUNTAINS
UNITED STATES
WASHINGTON
OREGON
IDAHO
MONTANA
WYOMING
NORTH DAKOTA
SOUTH DAKOTA
NEBRASKA
KANSAS
OKLAHOMA
TEXAS
NEW MEXICO
ARIZONA
UTAH
COLORADO
NEVADA
CALIFORNIA
MEXICO
BAJA CALIFORNIA
Golfo de California
SIERRA MADRE OCCIDENTAL
Sierra Madre Oriental
CASCADE RANGE
SIERRA NEVADA
Coast Ranges
PACIFIC OCEAN
Vancouver Island
Channel Islands
Great Basin
Black Rock Desert
Great Sandy Desert
Harney Basin
Mojave Desert
Sonoran Desert
Colorado Plateau
Painted Desert
Llano Estacado
Edwards Plateau
Bolson de Mapimí
Great Salt Lake
Tropic of Cancer
Edmonton
Calgary
Saskatoon
Regina
Winnipeg
Vancouver
Victoria
Seattle
Tacoma
Olympia
Portland
Salem
Spokane
Boise
Helena
Billings
Cheyenne
Denver
Salt Lake City
Ogden
Provo
Reno
Carson City
Sacramento
San Francisco
Oakland
San Jose
Fresno
Bakersfield
Los Angeles
San Diego
Las Vegas
Phoenix
Tucson
Albuquerque
Santa Fe
El Paso
Lubbock
Amarillo
Oklahoma City
Wichita
Dallas
Fort Worth
Austin
San Antonio
Laredo
Brownsville
Bismarck
Pierre
Lincoln
Omaha
Topeka
Tijuana
Mexicali
Hermosillo
Chihuahua
Cd Juárez
Monterrey
Saltillo
Torreón
Durango
Mazatlán
Culiacán
La Paz
Cd Obregón
Guaymas
Zacatecas
Cd Victoria
Matamoros
Names underlined indicate Province/State capitals

ONTARIO
QUEBEC
James Bay
LAKE SUPERIOR
LAKE HURON
L. MICHIGAN
L. ONTARIO
LAKE ERIE
MICHIGAN
WISCONSIN
MINNESOTA
IOWA
ILLINOIS
INDIANA
OHIO
PENNSYLVANIA
NEW YORK
VERMONT
NEW HAMPSHIRE
MAINE
MASS.
CONN.
R.I.
N.J.
DEL.
MD
D.C.
WEST VIRGINIA
VIRGINIA
KENTUCKY
TENNESSEE
NORTH CAROLINA
SOUTH CAROLINA
GEORGIA
ALABAMA
MISSISSIPPI
LOUISIANA
ARKANSAS
MISSOURI
FLORIDA
NEW BRUNSWICK
NOVA SCOTIA
PRINCE EDWARD I.
UNITED STATES
APPALACHIAN MOUNTAINS
Ozark Plateau
ATLANTIC OCEAN
GULF OF MEXICO
THE BAHAMAS
CUBA
Straits of Florida
Gulf of Saint Lawrence
St Lawrence
Peninsule de Gaspé
Bay of Fundy
Chesapeake B.
Delaware Bay
Long Island
Cape Cod
C. Hatteras
C. Lookout
C. Fear
C. Canaveral
C. Sable
Lake Okeechobee
Florida Keys
Key West
Tampa B.
Apalachee Bay
Mobile Bay
Galveston Bay
Atchafalaya B.
Great Abaco
Little Abaco
Grand Bahama
Eleuthera
Andros
Nassau
New Providence
Exuma Sound
Great Exuma
Cat
San Salvador
Rum Cay
Long
Crooked
Acklins
Mayaguana
Great Inagua
Little Inagua
Caicos Is
Caicos Passage
Great Bahama Bank
Berry Is
Habana (Havana)
Matanzas
Cardenas
Sta Clara
Cienfuegos
Sancti Spiritus
Ciego de Avila
Camagüey
Holguín
Pinar del Rio
Banes
Colón
Arch. de Camagüey
Cayo Romano
New York
Philadelphia
Boston
Washington
Baltimore
Pittsburgh
Cleveland
Detroit
Chicago
Milwaukee
Toronto
Montréal
Ottawa
Québec
Buffalo
Hartford
Providence
Albany
Newark
Cincinnati
Columbus
Indianapolis
St Louis
Kansas City
Louisville
Nashville
Memphis
Atlanta
Birmingham
Montgomery
Jackson
New Orleans
Baton Rouge
Houston
Galveston
Shreveport
Little Rock
Jacksonville
Savannah
Charleston
Columbia
Charlotte
Raleigh
Durham
Greensboro
Richmond
Norfolk
Newport News
Tampa
Orlando
Miami
Miami Beach
Ft Lauderdale
Hollywood
West Palm Beach
Tallahassee
Pensacola
Mobile
St Paul
Minneapolis
Duluth
Thunder Bay
Sault Ste Marie
Sudbury
Halifax
Saint John
Fredericton
Charlottetown
Sherbrooke
Hamilton
Windsor
Lansing
Flint
Saginaw
Grand Rapids
Toledo
Akron
Dayton
Fort Wayne
South Bend
Gary
Peoria
Springfield
Madison
Green Bay
Des Moines
Cedar Rapids
Davenport
Rockford
Lexington
Knoxville
Chattanooga
Huntsville
Augusta
Macon
Evansville
Portland
Concord
Manchester
Worcester
Syracuse
Rochester
Scranton
Harrisburg
Allentown
Trenton
Atlantic City
Wilmington
Dover
Annapolis
Charleston
Lynchburg
Roanoke
Winston Salem
Asheville
Greenville
Spartanburg
Gainesville
St Augustine
Daytona Beach
Clearwater
St Petersburg
Ft Myers
Lake Charles
Beaumont
Port Arthur
Lafayette
Mt Mitchell 2037
Mt Washington 1916
White Mts
Adirondack Mts
Boston Mts
Ouachita Mts
Everglades
Nat.Pk

1:10M

0 100 200 300 400 km
0 100 200 mls

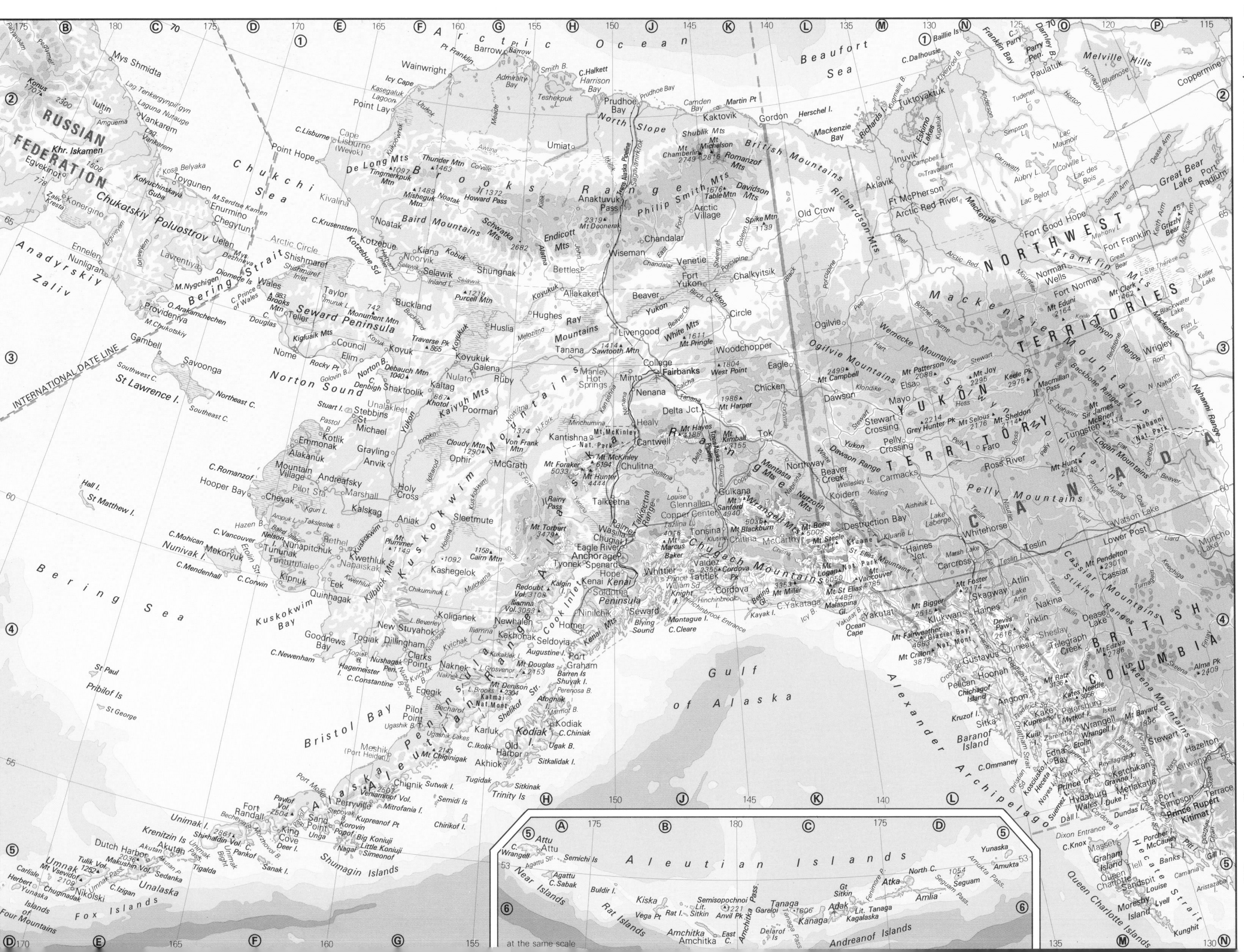

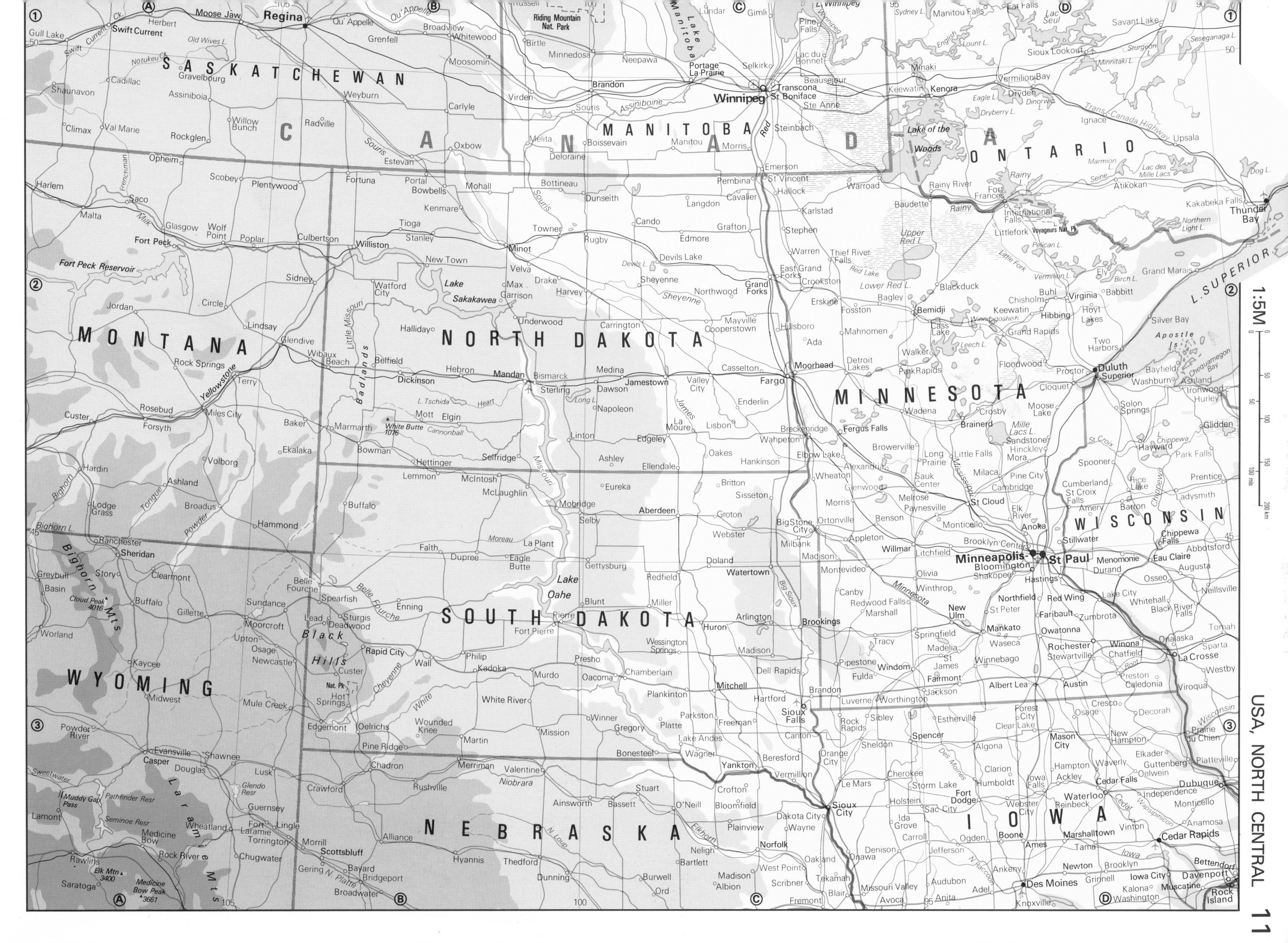
SASKATCHEWAN
MANITOBA
ONTARIO
CANADA
MONTANA
NORTH DAKOTA
SOUTH DAKOTA
MINNESOTA
WISCONSIN
IOWA
NEBRASKA
WYOMING
L. SUPERIOR
Regina
Moose Jaw
Swift Current
Brandon
Winnipeg
Thunder Bay
Duluth
Superior
Minneapolis-
St Paul
Fargo
Moorhead
Bismarck
Mandan
Minot
Grand Forks
Sioux Falls
Sioux City
Rapid City
Pierre
Des Moines
Cedar Rapids
Dubuque
La Crosse
Eau Claire
Rochester
Sheridan
Casper
Black Hills
Badlands
Lake Sakakawea
Lake Oahe
Fort Peck Reservoir
Lake of the Woods
Lake Manitoba
Bighorn Mts
Laramie Mts
Riding Mountain Nat. Park
Voyageurs Nat. Pk
Missouri
Mississippi
Yellowstone
Red
Minnesota
Cloud Peak 4016
White Butte 1076
Medicine Bow Peak 3661
Elk Mtn 3400

1:5M

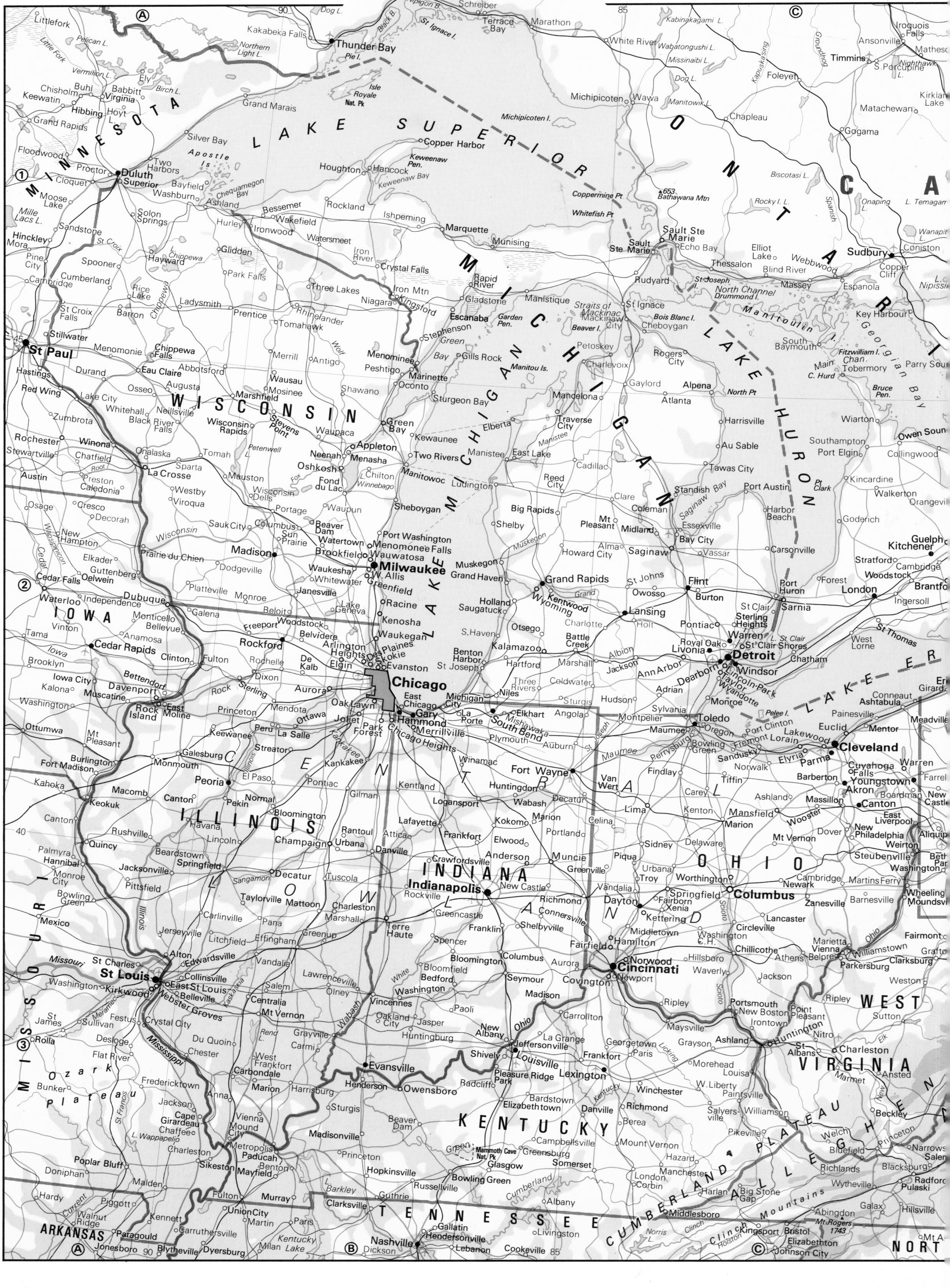
0 50 100 150 200 km
0 50 100 mls
LAKE SUPERIOR
LAKE MICHIGAN
LAKE HURON
LAKE ERIE
MINNESOTA
WISCONSIN
IOWA
ILLINOIS
INDIANA
OHIO
MICHIGAN
KENTUCKY
TENNESSEE
MISSOURI
ARKANSAS
WEST VIRGINIA
ONTARIO
CENTRAL LOWLAND
CUMBERLAND PLATEAU
ALLEGHENY
Ozark Plateau
Thunder Bay
Nipigon
Schreiber
Terrace Bay
Marathon
White River
Wawa
Michipicoten
Chapleau
Timmins
Sault Ste Marie
Sudbury
Isle Royale Nat. Pk
Duluth
Superior
St Paul
Minneapolis
Hibbing
Virginia
Ashland
Marquette
Houghton
Hancock
Copper Harbor
Escanaba
Green Bay
Appleton
Oshkosh
Sheboygan
Manitowoc
Milwaukee
Madison
La Crosse
Eau Claire
Rockford
Chicago
Gary
Hammond
Joliet
Peoria
Springfield
Decatur
Champaign
Bloomington
Quincy
Dubuque
Cedar Rapids
Davenport
Iowa City
Burlington
St Louis
East St Louis
Grand Rapids
Lansing
Flint
Saginaw
Bay City
Detroit
Windsor
Toledo
Cleveland
Akron
Canton
Youngstown
Columbus
Dayton
Cincinnati
Fort Wayne
South Bend
Indianapolis
Terre Haute
Evansville
Louisville
Lexington
Frankfort
Owensboro
Paducah
Nashville
Huntington
Charleston
Parkersburg
Wheeling
Sarnia
London
Kitchener
Georgian Bay
Manitoulin I.
North Channel
Straits of Mackinac
Mammoth Cave Nat. Pk
Mt Rogers 1743
Mississippi
Missouri
Ohio
Wabash
Illinois
Cumberland
Clinch Mountains

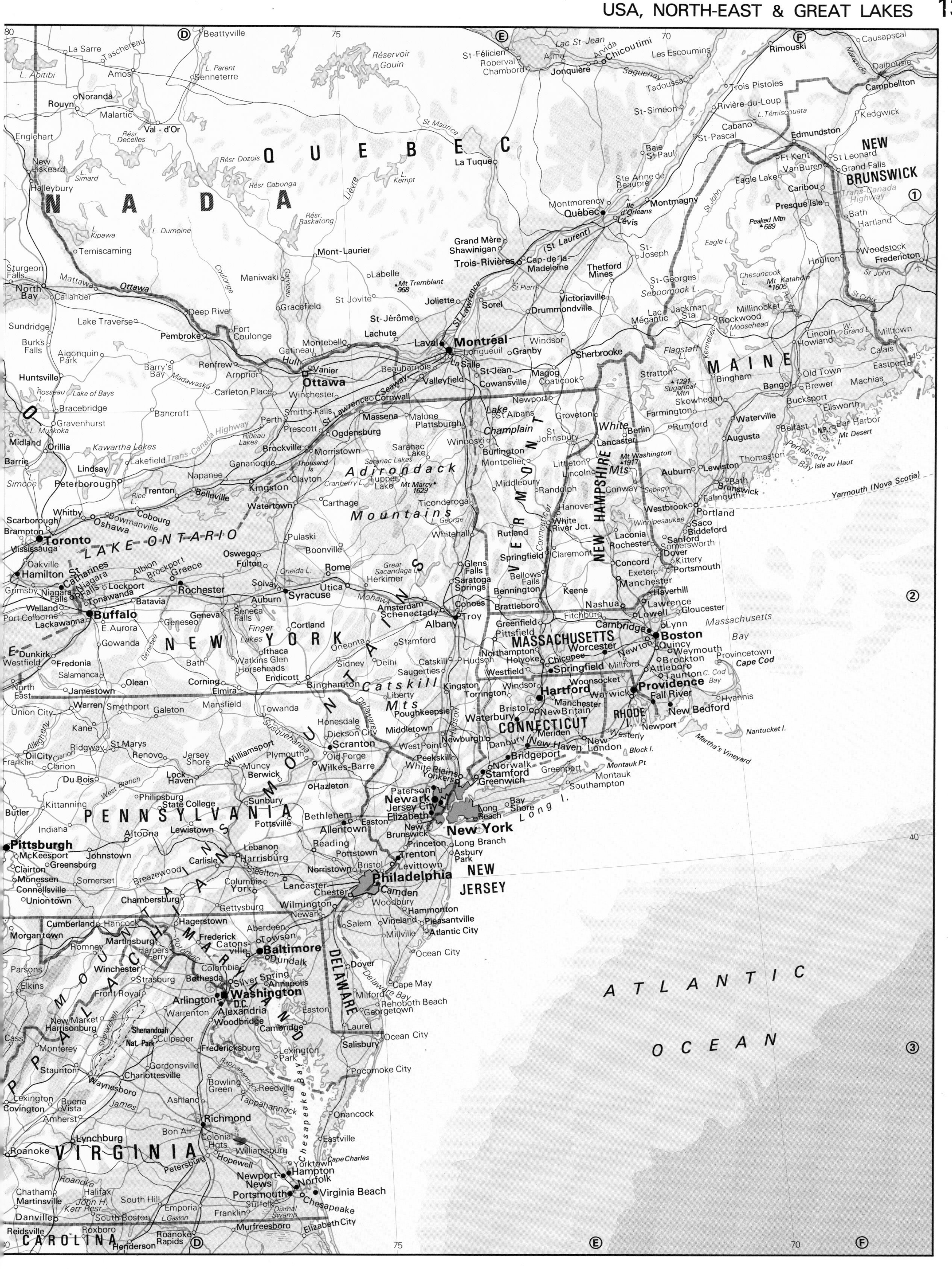
QUEBEC
CANADA
MAINE
NEW BRUNSWICK
VERMONT
NEW HAMPSHIRE
MASSACHUSETTS
RHODE I.
CONNECTICUT
NEW YORK
PENNSYLVANIA
NEW JERSEY
DELAWARE
MARYLAND
VIRGINIA
CAROLINA
ATLANTIC OCEAN
LAKE ONTARIO
Adirondack Mountains
Catskill Mts
APPALACHIAN MOUNTAINS
Massachusetts Bay
Cape Cod
Chesapeake Bay
Delaware Bay
Long I.
Martha's Vineyard
Nantucket I.
Block I.
Montauk Pt
Lake Champlain
St Lawrence
Ottawa
Réservoir Gouin
Trans-Canada Highway
Montréal
Québec
Ottawa
Toronto
Sherbrooke
Trois-Rivières
Fredericton
Edmundston
Campbellton
Rimouski
Chicoutimi
Hamilton
Kingston
Buffalo
Rochester
Syracuse
Utica
Albany
Schenectady
Binghamton
Boston
Worcester
Springfield
Providence
Hartford
New Haven
Bridgeport
Portland
Bangor
Augusta
Manchester
Concord
Burlington
Montpelier
New York
Newark
Jersey City
Philadelphia
Camden
Trenton
Pittsburgh
Harrisburg
Scranton
Allentown
Baltimore
Washington D.C.
Richmond
Norfolk
Virginia Beach
Newport News
Atlantic City
Mt Washington 1917
Mt Katahdin 1605
Mt Marcy 1629
Mt Tremblant 968
Yarmouth (Nova Scotia)
80
75
70
45
40
D
E
F
1
2
3

1:2.5M 0 25 50 75 100 km 0 25 50 mls

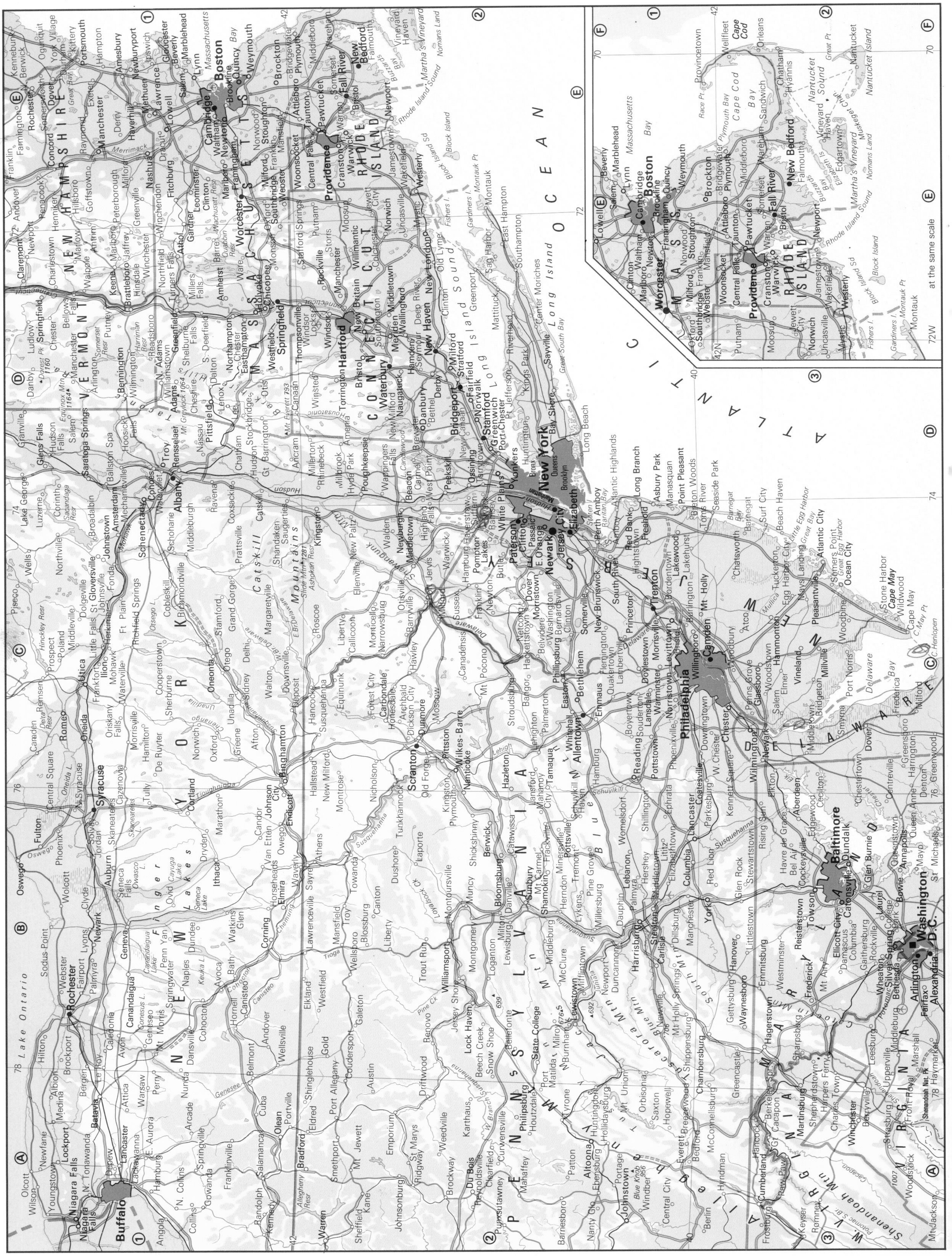

1:5M

0 50 100 150 200 km

0 50 100 mls

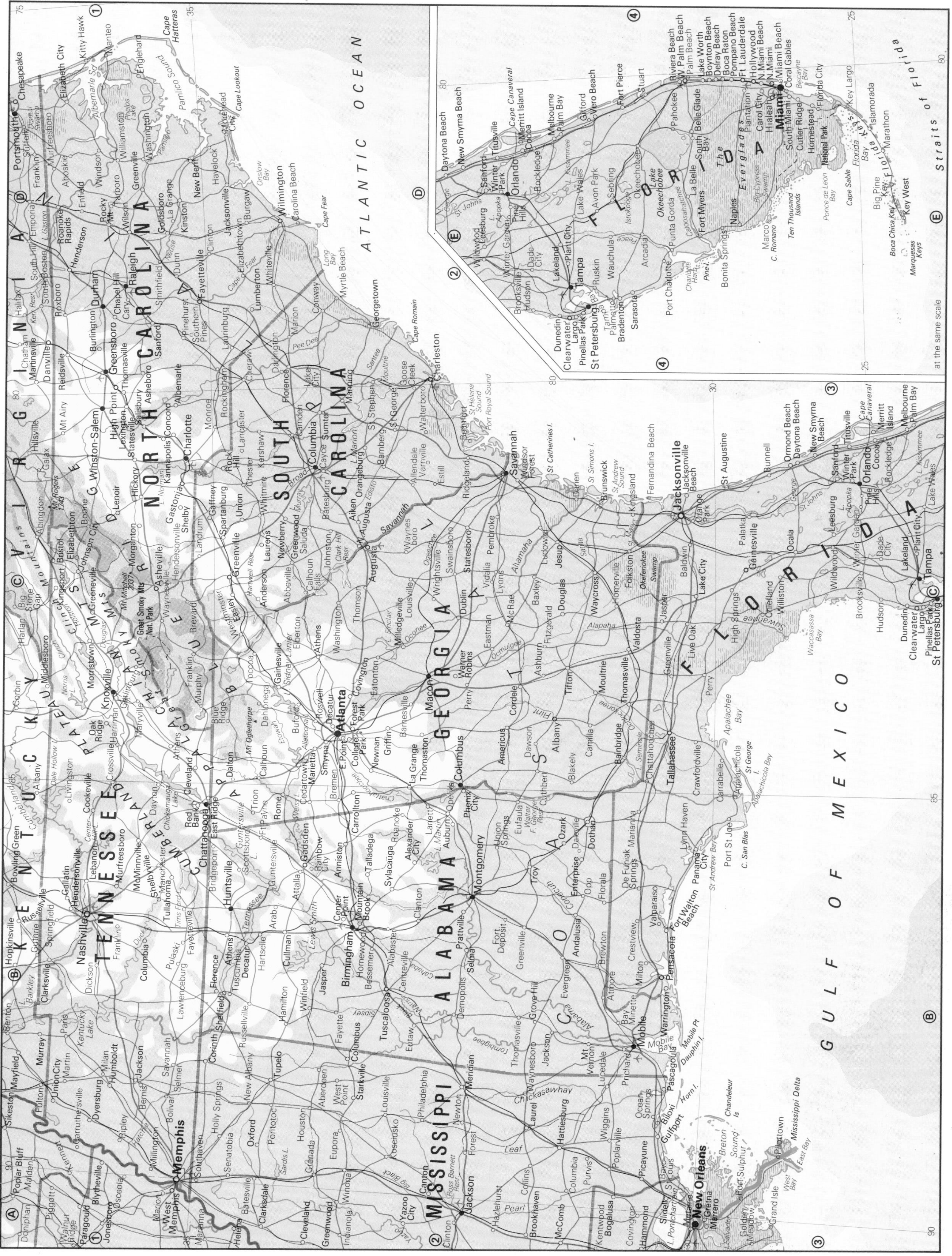

1:5M 0 50 100 150 200 km 0 50 100 mls

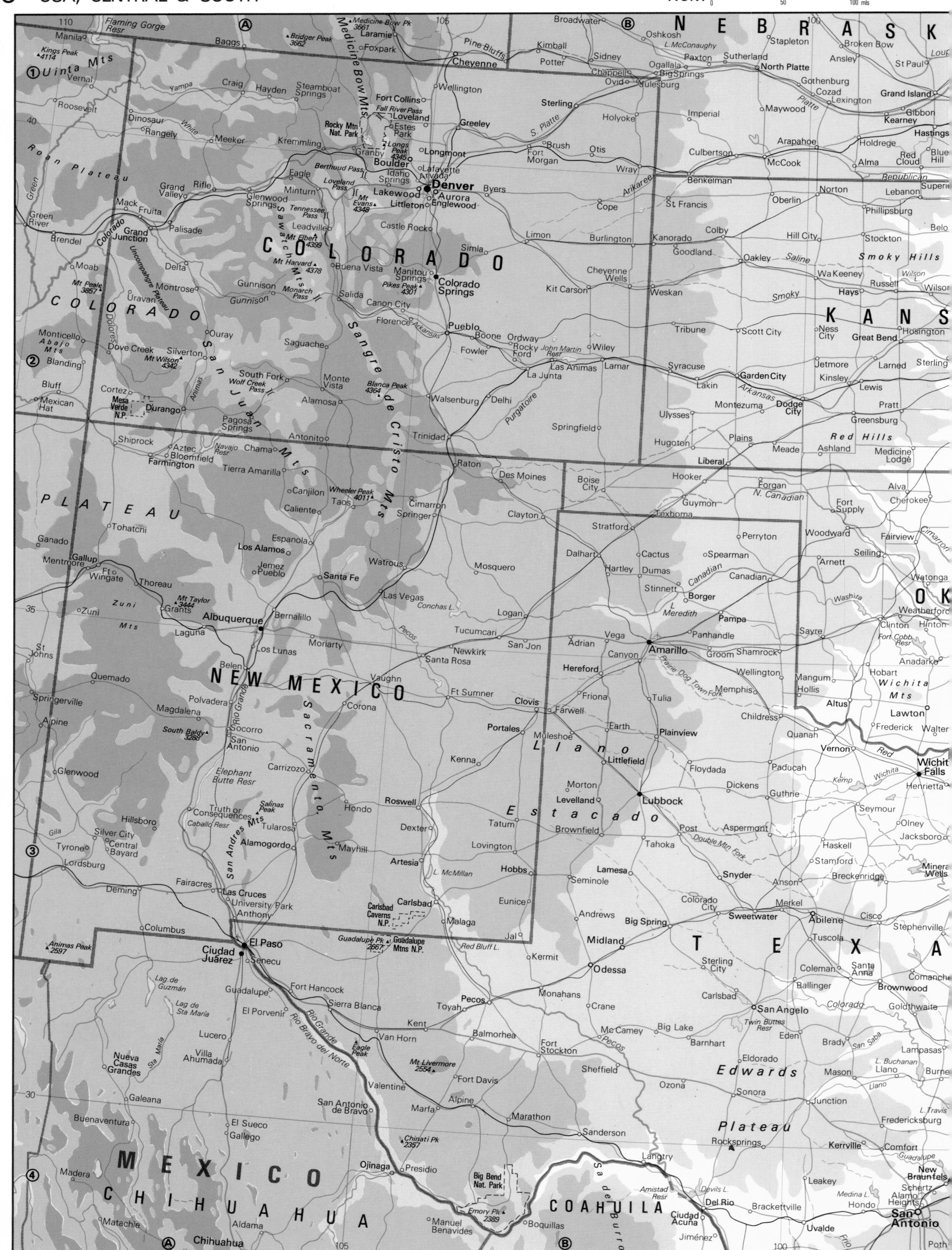

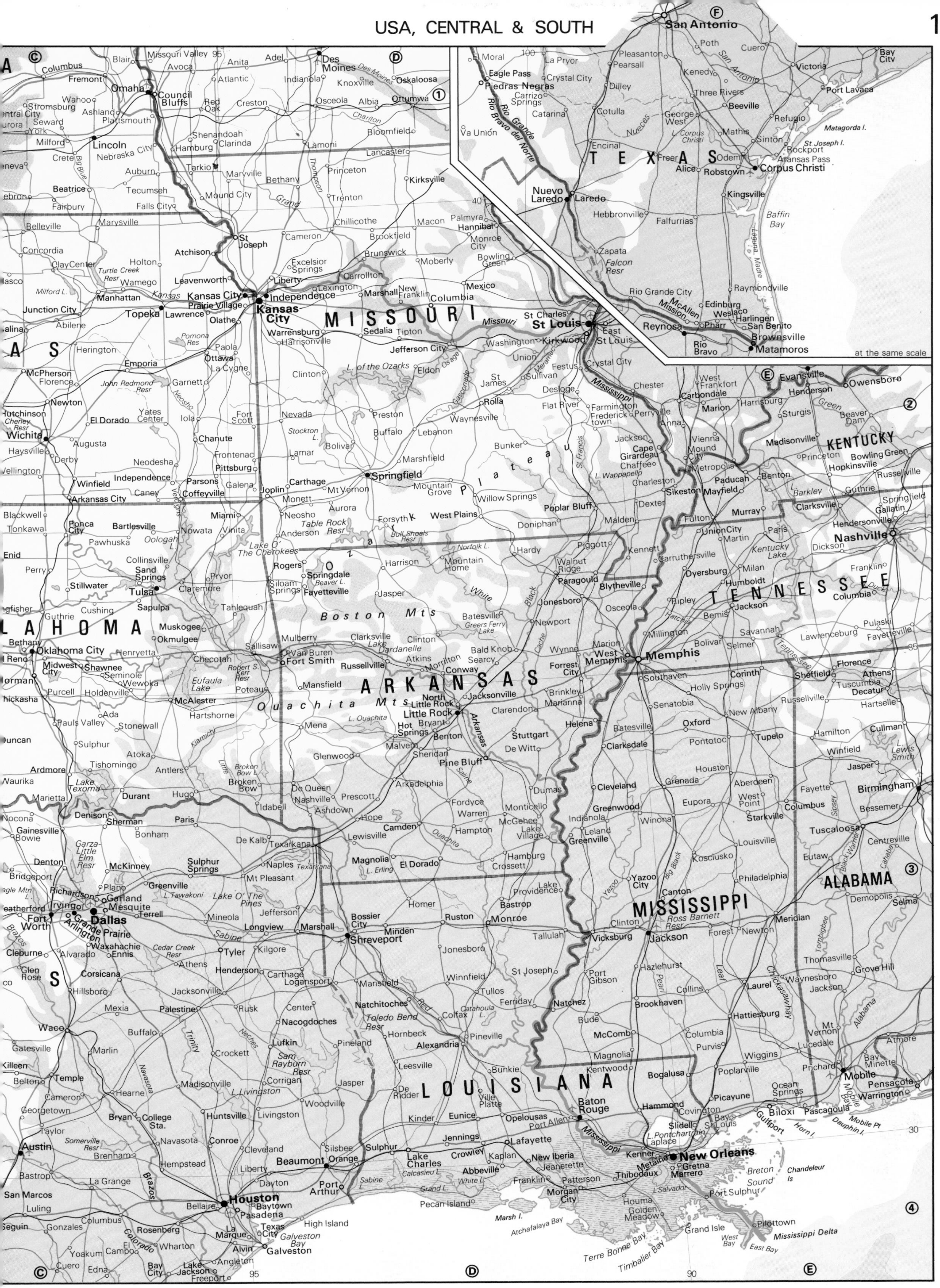
C
D
F
E
1
2
3
4
TEXAS
MISSOURI
KENTUCKY
TENNESSEE
ARKANSAS
MISSISSIPPI
ALABAMA
LOUISIANA
LAHOMA
AS
S
Ozark Plateau
Boston Mts
Ouachita Mts
at the same scale
San Antonio
Pleasanton
Pearsall
Poth
Cuero
Victoria
Bay City
El Moral
La Pryor
Eagle Pass
Crystal City
Piedras Negras
Carrizo Springs
Dilley
Kenedy
San Antonio
Three Rivers
Port Lavaca
Beeville
Catarina
Cotulla
George West
Nueces
L. Corpus Christi
Mathis
Refugio
Matagorda I.
Rio Grande
Rio Bravo del Norte
Va Unión
Encinal
Sinton
St Joseph I.
Rockport
Aransas Pass
Freer
Odem
Alice
Robstown
Corpus Christi
Nuevo Laredo
Laredo
Kingsville
Hebbronville
Falfurrias
Baffin Bay
Laguna Madre
Zapata
Falcon Resr
Raymondville
Rio Grande City
Edinburg
McAllen
Mission
Weslaco
Harlingen
Reynosa
Pharr
San Benito
Brownsville
Rio Bravo
Matamoros
100
40
Columbus
Blair
Missouri Valley
95
Anita
Adel
Des Moines
Fremont
Avoca
Atlantic
Indianola
Knoxville
Des Moines
Oskaloosa
Omaha
Council Bluffs
Red Oak
Creston
Osceola
Albia
Ottumwa
Wahoo
Stromsburg
Ashland
Plattsmouth
Chariton
Central City
Aurora
Seward
York
Shenandoah
Clarinda
Bloomfield
Milford
Lincoln
Hamburg
Lamoni
Crete
Nebraska City
Geneva
Big Blue
Tarkio
Lancaster
Maryville
Princeton
Auburn
Bethany
Kirksville
Thompson
Beatrice
Tecumseh
Mound City
Trenton
Fairbury
Falls City
Grand
Hebron
Marysville
Chillicothe
Macon
Palmyra
Hannibal
Belleville
St Joseph
Cameron
Brookfield
Monroe City
Concordia
Atchison
Brunswick
Bowling Green
Moberly
Clay Center
Holton
Excelsior Springs
Turtle Creek Resr
Wamego
Leavenworth
Liberty
Carrollton
Mexico
Milford L.
Lexington
Marshall
New Franklin
Manhattan
Kansas
Kansas City
Independence
Columbia
Junction City
Prairie Village
Kansas City
Topeka
Lawrence
Olathe
St Charles
St Louis
Abilene
Missouri
Salina
Warrensburg
Sedalia
Tipton
East St Louis
Pomona Res
Harrisonville
Washington
Kirkwood
Paola
Herington
Jefferson City
Union
Ottawa
Emporia
Meramec
Crystal City
La Cygne
L. of the Ozarks
Eldon
Osage
Festus
McPherson
Garnett
Clinton
St James
Sullivan
Chester
West Frankfort
Evansville
Owensboro
Florence
John Redmond Resr
Gasconade
Desloge
Mississippi
Carbondale
Henderson
Neosho
Rolla
Flat River
Farmington
Frederick town
Perryville
Marion
Harrisburg
Green
Beaver Dam
Hutchinson
Newton
Yates Center
Fort Scott
Nevada
Preston
Anna
Sturgis
Cheney Resr
El Dorado
Iola
Waynesville
Wichita
Stockton L.
Buffalo
Lebanon
Jackson
Vienna
Madisonville
Chanute
Bunker
Cape Girardeau
Mound City
Princeton
Bowling Green
Haysville
Augusta
Bolivar
St Francis
Derby
Frontenac
Lamar
Marshfield
Chaffee
Metropolis
Hopkinsville
Wellington
Neodesha
Pittsburg
L. Wappapello
Paducah
Benton
Russellville
Winfield
Independence
Parsons
Galena
Joplin
Carthage
Springfield
Charleston
Caney
Coffeyville
Mt Vernon
Mountain Grove
Willow Springs
Sikeston
Mayfield
Barkley
Guthrie
Springfield
Arkansas City
Verdigris
Monett
Aurora
Dexter
Clarksville
Gallatin
Blackwell
Miami
Neosho
Forsyth
West Plains
Poplar Bluff
Murray
Tonkawa
Ponca City
Bartlesville
Vinita
Table Rock Resr
Malden
Fulton
Paris
Nowata
Anderson
Bull Shoals Resr
Doniphan
Union City
Martin
Hendersonville
Nashville
Pawhuska
Oologah L.
Enid
Lake O' The Cherokees
Norfolk L.
Hardy
Piggott
Kennett
Kentucky Lake
Dickson
Collinsville
Carruthersville
Perry
Sand Springs
Pryor
Rogers
Harrison
Mountain Home
Walnut Ridge
Dyersburg
Milan
Franklin
Stillwater
Tulsa
Claremore
Springdale
Beaver L.
Paragould
Blytheville
Humboldt
Siloam Springs
Fayetteville
White
Black
Duck
Kingfisher
Cushing
Sapulpa
Tahlequah
Jasper
Jonesboro
Osceola
Ripley
Columbia
Guthrie
Batesville
Jackson
Greers Ferry Lake
Bemis
Newport
Hatchie
Pulaski
Bethany
Muskogee
Okmulgee
Mulberry
Clarksville
Clinton
Millington
Savannah
Fayetteville
Lawrenceburg
Oklahoma City
Henryetta
Sallisaw
Lake Dardanelle
Bald Knob
Marion
Bolivar
Selmer
35
Reno
Checotah
Van Buren
Atkins
Searcy
Cache
Wynne
West Memphis
Memphis
Tennessee
Florence
Midwest City
Shawnee
Robert S. Kerr Resr
Fort Smith
Russellville
Morrilton
Conway
Forrest City
Athens
Norman
Seminole
Wewoka
Eufaula Lake
Poteau
Southaven
Corinth
Sheffield
Tuscumbia
Decatur
Purcell
Holdenville
Mansfield
Brinkley
Holly Springs
Chickasha
McAlester
North Little Rock
Jacksonville
Marianna
Senatobia
Russellville
Hartselle
Hartshorne
Little Rock
Clarendon
Ada
L. Ouachita
Bryant
New Albany
Pauls Valley
Stonewall
Mena
Helena
Batesville
Oxford
Cullman
Duncan
Kiamichi
Hot Springs
Benton
Stuttgart
Tupelo
Sulphur
Malvern
Sheridan
De Witt
Clarksdale
Pontotoc
Hamilton
Atoka
Glenwood
Pine Bluff
Winfield
Lewis Smith L.
Tishomingo
Little
Broken Bow L.
Saline
Houston
Jasper
Ardmore
Antlers
Arkadelphia
Grenada
Aberdeen
Waurika
Lake Texoma
Broken Bow
De Queen
Prescott
Dumas
Cleveland
Fayette
Birmingham
Marietta
Durant
Hugo
Nashville
Fordyce
Monticello
Eupora
West Point
Columbus
Sipsey
Idabell
Ashdown
Warren
Greenwood
Winona
Bessemer
Nocona
Denison
Sherman
Paris
Hope
Camden
McGehee
Indianola
Starkville
Tuscaloosa
Gainesville
Bowie
Bonham
Lewisville
Ouachita
Hampton
Lake Village
Leland
Greenville
Louisville
Centreville
Garza-Little Elm Resr
De Kalb
Texarkana
Black Warrior
Cahaba
Denton
Sulphur Springs
Naples
Texarkana
Magnolia
El Dorado
Hamburg
Crossett
Kosciusko
Eutaw
McKinney
Mt Pleasant
L. Erling
Big Black
Bridgeport
Plano
Greenville
Lake
Yazoo
Yazoo City
Philadelphia
Eagle Mtn L.
Richardson
Garland
L. Tawakoni
Lake O' The Pines
Providence
Canton
Demopolis
Weatherford
Irving
Mesquite
Jefferson
Homer
Bastrop
Ross Barnett Resr
Selma
Fort Worth
Grand Prairie
Dallas
Terrell
Mineola
Bossier City
Ruston
Monroe
Clinton
Meridian
Arlington
Longview
Marshall
Minden
Tallulah
Vicksburg
Jackson
Brazos
Waxahachie
Sabine
Shreveport
Forest
Newton
Cleburne
Alvarado
Ennis
Cedar Creek Resr
Tyler
Kilgore
Jonesboro
Tombigbee
Thomasville
Glen Rose
Athens
Henderson
Carthage
St Joseph
Port Gibson
Hazlehurst
Grove Hill
Corsicana
Logansport
Winnfield
Leaf
Chickasawhay
Waynesboro
Hillsboro
Jacksonville
Mansfield
Tullos
Pearl
Collins
Laurel
Jackson
Mexia
Palestine
Rusk
Center
Natchitoches
Red
Catahoula L.
Ferriday
Natchez
Brookhaven
Hattiesburg
Alabama
Waco
Nacogdoches
Toledo Bend Resr
Colfax
Bude
Buffalo
Neches
Lufkin
Hornbeck
Pineville
McComb
Columbia
Mt Vernon
Trinity
Pineland
Alexandria
Purvis
Lucedale
Atmore
Gatesville
Marlin
Crockett
Sam Rayburn Resr
Magnolia
Wiggins
Killeen
Navasota
Leesville
Bunkie
Kentwood
Bogalusa
Poplarville
Prichard
Mobile
Bay Minette
Temple
Belton
Madisonville
Corrigan
Jasper
De Ridder
Ville Platte
Picayune
Ocean Springs
Pensacola
Hearne
L. Livingston
Mobile Bay
Warrington
Cameron
Woodville
Hammond
Covington
Biloxi
Pascagoula
Georgetown
Bryan
College Sta.
Huntsville
Livingston
Kinder
Eunice
Opelousas
Baton Rouge
Slidell
Bay St Louis
Gulfport
Mobile Pt
Dauphin I.
Taylor
Port Allen
L. Pontchartrain
Horn I.
30
Somerville Resr
Navasota
Conroe
Jennings
Lafayette
Laplace
Mississippi
Austin
Brenham
Cleveland
Silsbee
Sulphur
Lake Charles
Crowley
Kaplan
New Iberia
Kenner
New Orleans
Hempstead
Liberty
Beaumont
Orange
Calcasieu L.
Abbeville
Jeanerette
Metairie
Gretna
Marrero
Bastrop
Dayton
Port Arthur
Sabine L.
Grand L.
White L.
Franklin
Patterson
Thibodaux
Breton Sound
Chandeleur Is
La Grange
Morgan City
L. Salvador
Port Sulphur
San Marcos
Bellaire
Houston
Baytown
Pecan Island
Houma
Luling
Pasadena
High Island
Marsh I.
Golden Meadow
Columbus
Texas City
Atchafalaya Bay
Pilottown
Seguin
Gonzales
Rosenberg
La Marque
Galveston Bay
Grand Isle
Mississippi Delta
Colorado
Wharton
Galveston
West Bay
East Bay
Yoakum
Campo
Alvin
Terre Bonne Bay
Timbalier Bay
Cuero
Edna
Bay City
Lake Jackson
Angleton
Freeport
95
90

1:5M

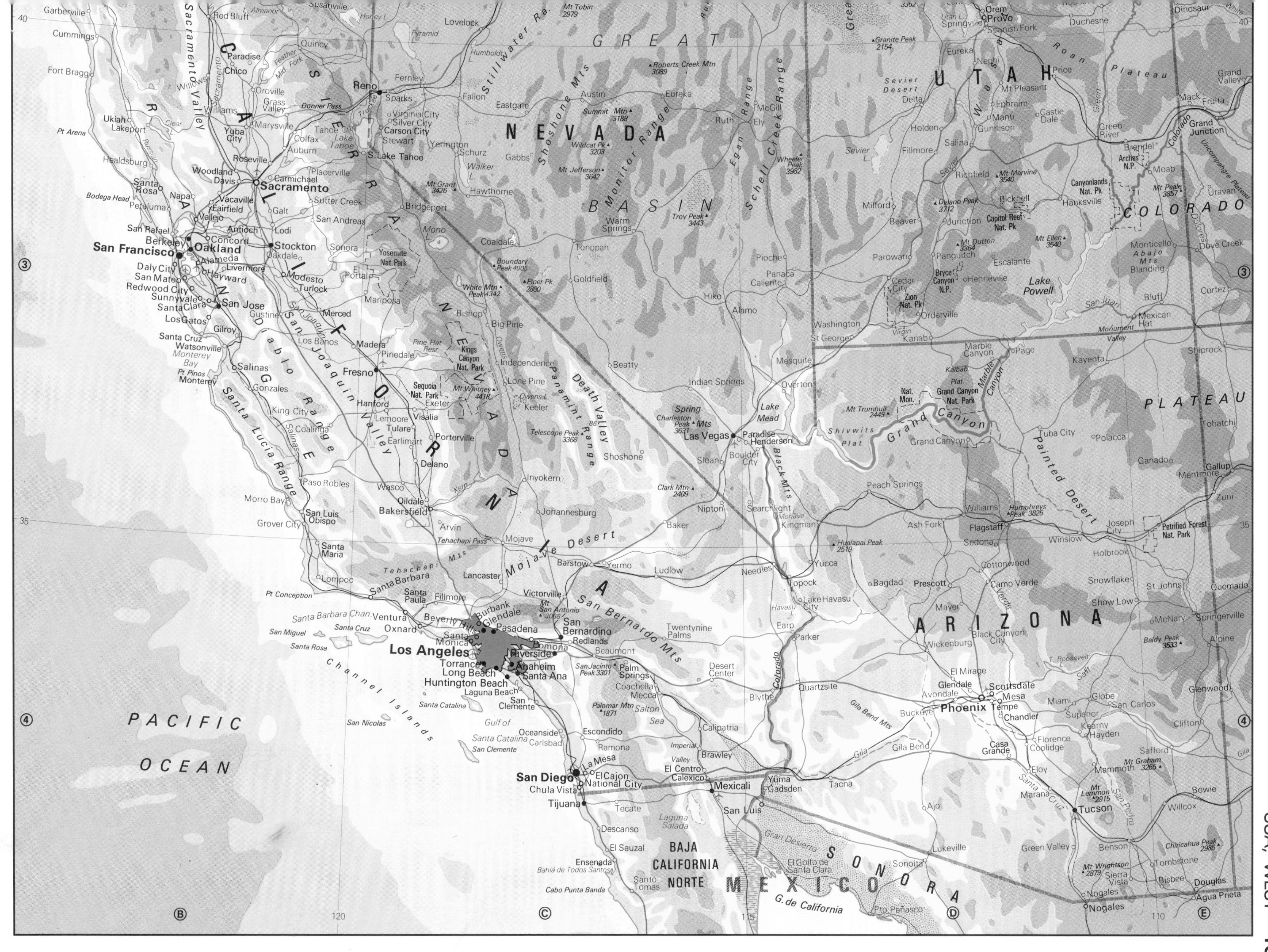
PACIFIC OCEAN
NEVADA
CALIFORNIA
UTAH
ARIZONA
COLORADO
GREAT BASIN
PLATEAU
SIERRA NEVADA
SONORA
MEXICO
BAJA CALIFORNIA NORTE
Sacramento Valley
San Joaquin Valley
Death Valley
Mojave Desert
Painted Desert
Grand Canyon
Lake Mead
Lake Powell
Channel Islands
Santa Lucia Range
Diablo Range
San Bernardino Mts
Panamint Range
Shoshone Mts
Monitor Range
Schell Creek Range
Egan Range
Black Mts
G. de California
San Francisco
Oakland
San Jose
Sacramento
Stockton
Fresno
Bakersfield
Los Angeles
Long Beach
Santa Ana
Anaheim
Riverside
San Bernardino
San Diego
Tijuana
Mexicali
Reno
Carson City
Las Vegas
Henderson
Phoenix
Mesa
Scottsdale
Tempe
Chandler
Tucson
Flagstaff
Prescott
Yuma
Nogales
Provo
Orem
Grand Junction
Moab
Kingman
Barstow
Palm Springs
Santa Barbara
Monterey
Salinas
Modesto
Merced
Visalia
Tonopah
Ely
Eureka
Austin
Fallon
Hawthorne
Needles
Lake Havasu City
Gallup
Winslow
Holbrook
Page
Yosemite Nat. Park
Sequoia Nat. Park
Kings Canyon Nat. Park
Grand Canyon Nat. Park
Zion Nat. Pk
Bryce Canyon N.P.
Canyonlands Nat. Pk
Arches N.P.
Capitol Reef Nat. Pk
Petrified Forest Nat. Park
Mt Whitney 4418
Pt Conception
Pt Arena
Salton Sea
Mono L.
Owens L.

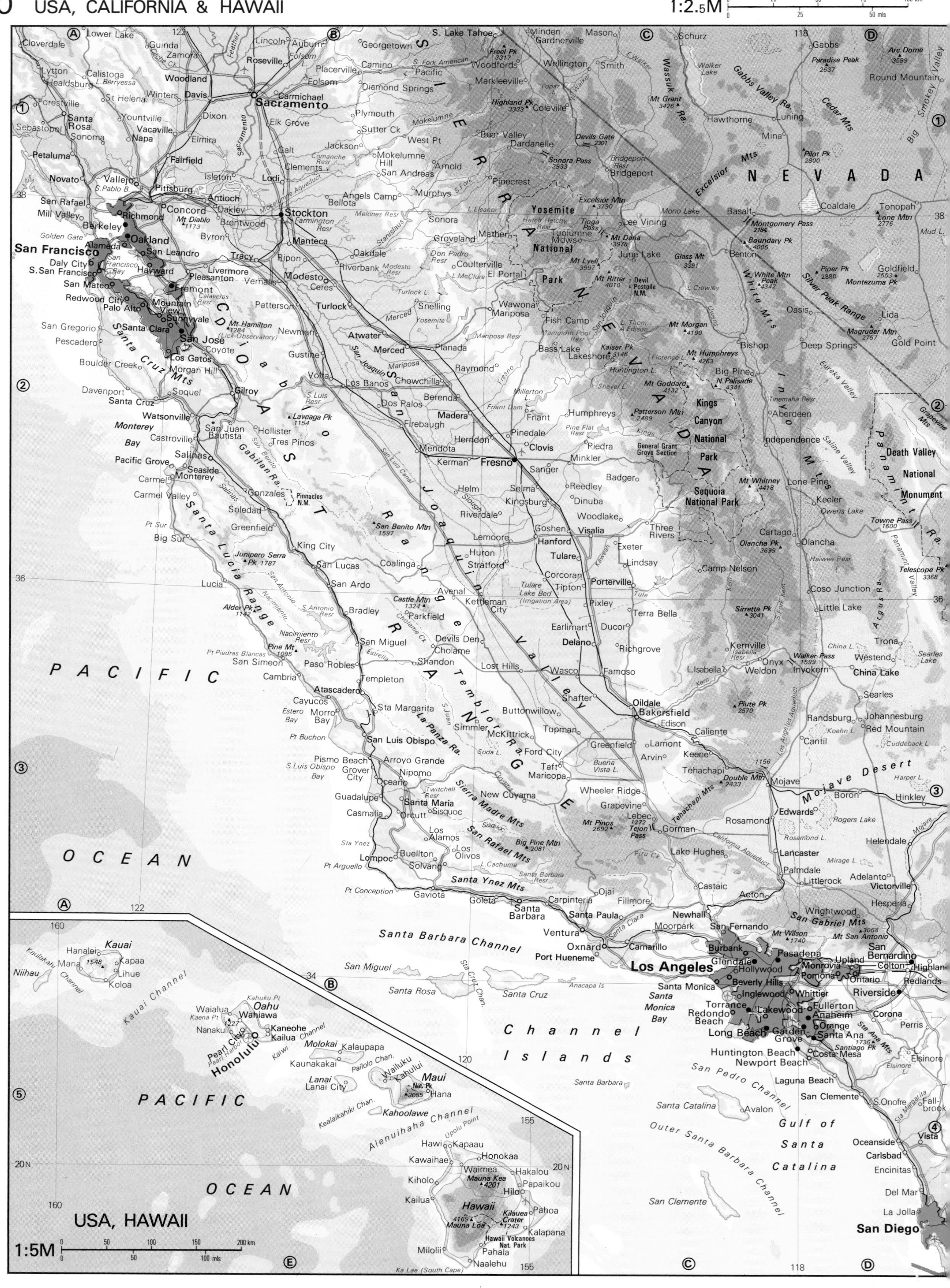
1:2.5M
0 25 50 75 100 km
0 25 50 mls
A B C D
1 2 3 4 5
122 118 38 36 34
Lower Lake
Cloverdale
Guinda
Zamora
Lincoln
Auburn
Georgetown
S. Lake Tahoe
Minden
Gardnerville
Mason
Schurz
Gabbs
Arc Dome 3589
Lytton
Calistoga
Healdsburg
L. Berryessa
Woodland
Roseville
Folsom
Placerville
Camino
Pacific
Woodfords
Freel Pk 3317
Wellington
Smith
Walker Lake
Paradise Peak 2637
Round Mountain
Forestville
St Helena
Winters
Davis
Carmichael
Sacramento
Diamond Springs
Markleeville
Topaz L.
Mt Grant 3426
Gabbs Valley Ra.
Cedar Mts
Big Smokey Valley
Sebastopol
Santa Rosa
Sonoma
Yountville
Vacaville
Napa
Dixon
Elk Grove
Plymouth
Sutter Ck
West Pt
Highland Pk 3333
Coleville
Hawthorne
Luning
Mina
Petaluma
Elmira
Fairfield
Galt
Jackson
Comanche Resr
Mokelumne Hill
Clements
San Andreas
Arnold
Bear Valley
Dardanelle
Devils Gate 2301
Sonora Pass 2933
Bridgeport Resr
Bridgeport
Excelsior Mts
Pilot Pk 2800
NEVADA
Novato
Vallejo
S. Pablo B.
Isleton
Lodi
Pinecrest
Pittsburg
Antioch
San Rafael
Concord
Oakley
Bellota
Angels Camp
Murphys
Excelsior Mtn 3790
Coaldale
Tonopah
Mill Valley
Richmond
Mt Diablo 1173
Brentwood
Stockton
Farmington Resr
Melones Resr
Sonora
L. Eleanor
Yosemite
Hetch Hetchy Resr
Tioga Pass
Mono Lake
Basalt
Montgomery Pass 2184
Lone Mtn 2776
Mud L.
Berkeley
Golden Gate
Oakland
Byron
Manteca
Groveland
Mather
Tuolumne Mdws
Mt Dana 3978
Lee Vining
Boundary Pk 4005
San Francisco
Alameda
San Leandro
Tracy
Ripon
Oakdale
Don Pedro Resr
National
June Lake
Glass Mt 3391
Benton
Daly City
S.San Francisco
Hayward
Livermore
Pleasanton
Riverbank
Modesto Resr
Coulterville
Mt Lyell 3997
Mt Ritter 4010
Devil Postpile N.M.
White Mtn Peak 4342
Piper Pk 2880
Goldfield
2553
Montezuma Pk
San Mateo
Fremont
Vernalis
Modesto
Ceres
L. McClure
El Portal
Park
L.Crowley
Redwood City
Palo Alto
Mountain View
Calaveras Resr
Patterson
Turlock
Turlock L.
Snelling
Wawona
Mariposa
Merced
Yosemite L.
Fish Camp
Oasis
Silver Peak Range
Lida
San Gregorio
Sunnyvale
Santa Clara
Mt Hamilton 1284 (Lick Observatory)
San Jose
Newman
Atwater
Mammoth Pool Resr
L. Thom. A.Edison
Mt Morgan 4190
White Mts
Magruder Mtn 2757
Pescadero
Coyote
Los Gatos
Gustine
Merced
Planada
Mariposa Resr
Bass Lake
Lakeshore
Kaiser Pk 3146
Florence L.
Mt Humphreys 4263
Bishop
Deep Springs
Gold Point
Boulder Creek
Santa Cruz Mts
Morgan Hill
Mariposa
Chowchilla
Raymond
Huntington L.
Big Pine
N.Palisade 4341
Eureka Valley
Davenport
Soquel
Santa Cruz
Gilroy
Volta
Los Banos
Dos Palos
Berenda
S.Luis Resr
Millerton L.
Shaver L.
Mt Goddard 4132
Kings Canyon National Park
Tinemaha Resr
Aberdeen
Grapevine Mts
Watsonville
Laveaga Pk 1154
Madera
Friant Dam
Friant
Humphreys
Patterson Mtn 2489
Monterey Bay
San Juan Bautista
Hollister
Tres Pinos
Firebaugh
Herndon
Pinedale
Pine Flat Resr
Kings
Independence
Death Valley National Monument
Castroville
Salinas
Gabilan Ra.
Mendota
Clovis
Fresno
Kerman
Sanger
Piedra
Minkler
General Grant Grove Section
Saline Valley
Panamint Ra.
Pacific Grove
Seaside
Monterey
Carmel
Gonzales
Pinnacles N.M.
San Luis Canal
Helm
Selma
Kingsburg
Reedley
Dinuba
Badger
Mt Whitney 4418
Lone Pine
Sequoia National Park
Keeler
Owens Lake
Carmel Valley
Soledad
Greenfield
Slough
Riverdale
Woodlake
Three Rivers
Towne Pass 1600
Pt Sur
Big Sur
Santa Lucia Range
San Benito Mtn 1597
King City
Lemoore
Goshen
Visalia
Hanford
Exeter
Tulare
Lindsay
Cartago
Olancha
Olancha Pk 3699
Haiwee Resr
Panamint Valley
Telescope Pk 3368
Junipero Serra Pk 1787
San Lucas
San Ardo
Coalinga
Huron
Stratford
Corcoran
Tipton
Porterville
Camp Nelson
Lucia
San Antonio
Nacimiento
S. Antonio Resr
Avenal
Kettleman City
Tulare Lake Bed (Irrigation Area)
Coso Junction
Argus Ra.
Alder Pk 1142
Bradley
Castle Mtn 1324
Parkfield
Cholame Ck
Pixley
Terra Bella
Little Lake
Sirretta Pk 3041
Earlimart
Ducor
Delano
Nacimiento Resr
San Miguel
Devils Den
Cholame
Richgrove
Kernville
Isabella Resr
Trona
Searles Lake
China L.
Pine Mtn 1095
Pt Piedras Blancas
San Simeon
Estrella
Shandon
Lost Hills
Wasco
Famoso
L.Isabella
Onyx
Walker Pass 1599
Weldon
Inyokern
Westend
China Lake
PACIFIC
Cambria
Paso Robles
Templeton
Temblor Range
Shafter
Kern
Piute Pk 2570
Searles
Atascadero
Cayucos
Estero Bay
Morro Bay
Sta Margarita
S. Juan
Buttonwillow
Oildale
Bakersfield
Edison
Los Angeles Aqueduct
Randsburg
Johannesburg
Koehn L.
Red Mountain
Pt Buchon
San Luis Obispo
La Panza Ra.
Simmler
McKittrick
Tupman
Caliente
Cantil
Cuddeback L.
Soda L.
Ford City
Greenfield
Lamont
Arvin
Keene
Pismo Beach
S.Luis Obispo Bay
Grover City
Arroyo Grande
Nipomo
Taft
Maricopa
Buena Vista L.
Tehachapi
1156
Mojave
Mojave Desert
Harper L.
Oceano
Guadalupe
Twitchell Resr
Santa Maria
Cuyama
New Cuyama
Wheeler Ridge
Grapevine
Double Mtn 2433
Tehachapi Mts
Boron
Hinkley
Casmalia
Orcutt
Sisquoc
Sierra Madre Mts
Edwards
Rogers Lake
Rosamond
Rosamond L.
Sta Ynez
Los Alamos
Sisquoc
San Rafael Mts
Big Pine Mtn 2081
Mt Pinos 2692
Lebec 1272
Tejon Pass
Gorman
California Aqueduct
Helendale
OCEAN
Lompoc
Buellton
Los Olivos
Solvang
L. Cachuma
Piru Ck
Lake Hughes
Lancaster
Mirage L.
Pt Arguello
Santa Ynez Mts
Santa Barbara Resr
Palmdale
Littlerock
Adelanto
Victorville
Pt Conception
Gaviota
Goleta
Santa Barbara
Carpinteria
Ojai
Fillmore
Castaic
Acton
Hesperia
Newhall
Wrightwood
San Gabriel Mts
Santa Paula
Ventura
Santa Clara
Moorpark
San Fernando
Mt Wilson 1740
3068 Mt San Antonio
Oxnard
Camarillo
Port Hueneme
Santa Barbara Channel
Burbank
Pasadena
Glendale
Hollywood
Los Angeles
Monrovia
Pomona
Upland
Ontario
San Bernardino
Colton
Highland
Redlands
San Miguel
Santa Rosa
Sta Cruz Chan.
Santa Cruz
Anacapa Is
Santa Monica
Santa Monica Bay
Beverly Hills
Inglewood
Whittier
Riverside
Torrance
Redondo Beach
Lakewood
Fullerton
Anaheim
Corona
Long Beach
Garden Grove
Orange
Santa Ana
Sta Ana Mts
Perris
Channel Islands
Huntington Beach
Newport Beach
Costa Mesa
Santiago Pk 1736
Elsinore
Santa Barbara
San Pedro Channel
Laguna Beach
San Clemente
Santa Catalina
Avalon
S.Onofre
Fallbrook
Gulf of Santa Catalina
Outer Santa Barbara Channel
Vista
Oceanside
Carlsbad
Encinitas
Del Mar
San Clemente
La Jolla
San Diego
E
160
155
20N
Kauai
Hanalei
Kaulakahi Channel
Mana
1548
Kapaa
Lihue
Niihau
Koloa
Kauai Channel
Kahuku Pt
Oahu
Waialua
Kaena Pt
Wahiawa
1227
Nanakuli
Kaneohe
Kailua
Pearl City
Pearl Harbor
Honolulu
Kaiwi Channel
Molokai
Kalaupapa
Pailolo Chan.
Kaunakakai
Lanai
Lanai City
Wailuku
Kahului
Maui
Nat. Pk 3055
Hana
PACIFIC
Kealaikahiki Chan.
Kahoolawe
Alenuihaha Channel
Upolu Point
Hawi
Kapaau
Honokaa
Kawaihae
Waimea
Hakalou
Mauna Kea 4201
Kiholo
Hilo
Papaikou
OCEAN
Kailua
Hawaii
Pahoa
Kilauea Crater 1243
4169 Mauna Loa
Kalapana
Hawaii Volcanoes Nat. Park
Milolii
Pahala
Naalehu
Ka Lae (South Cape)
USA, HAWAII
1:5M
0 50 100 150 200 km
0 50 100 mls

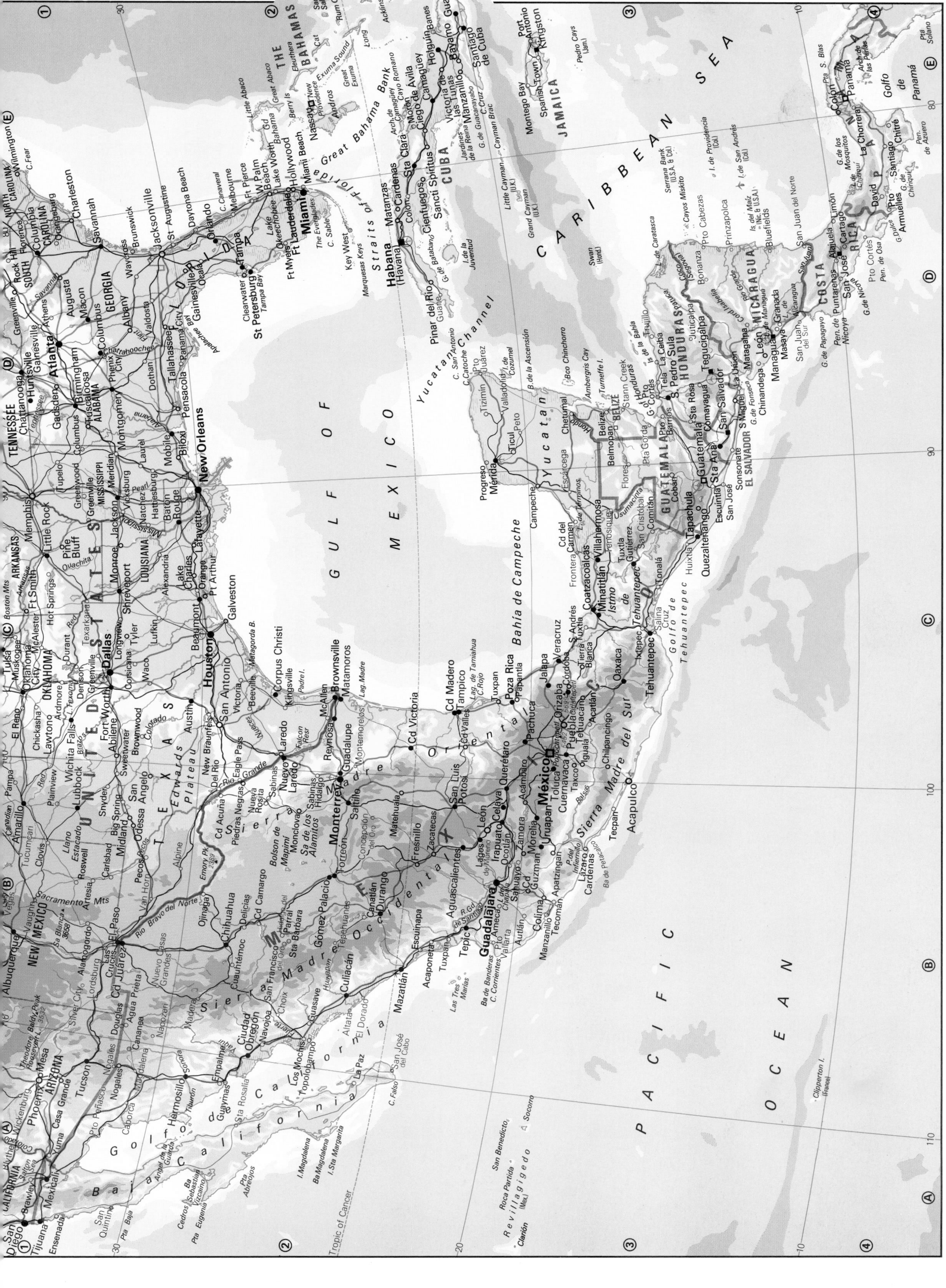

0 200 400 600 km
0 100 200 300 mls

1:5M

0 50 100 150 200 km
0 50 100 mls

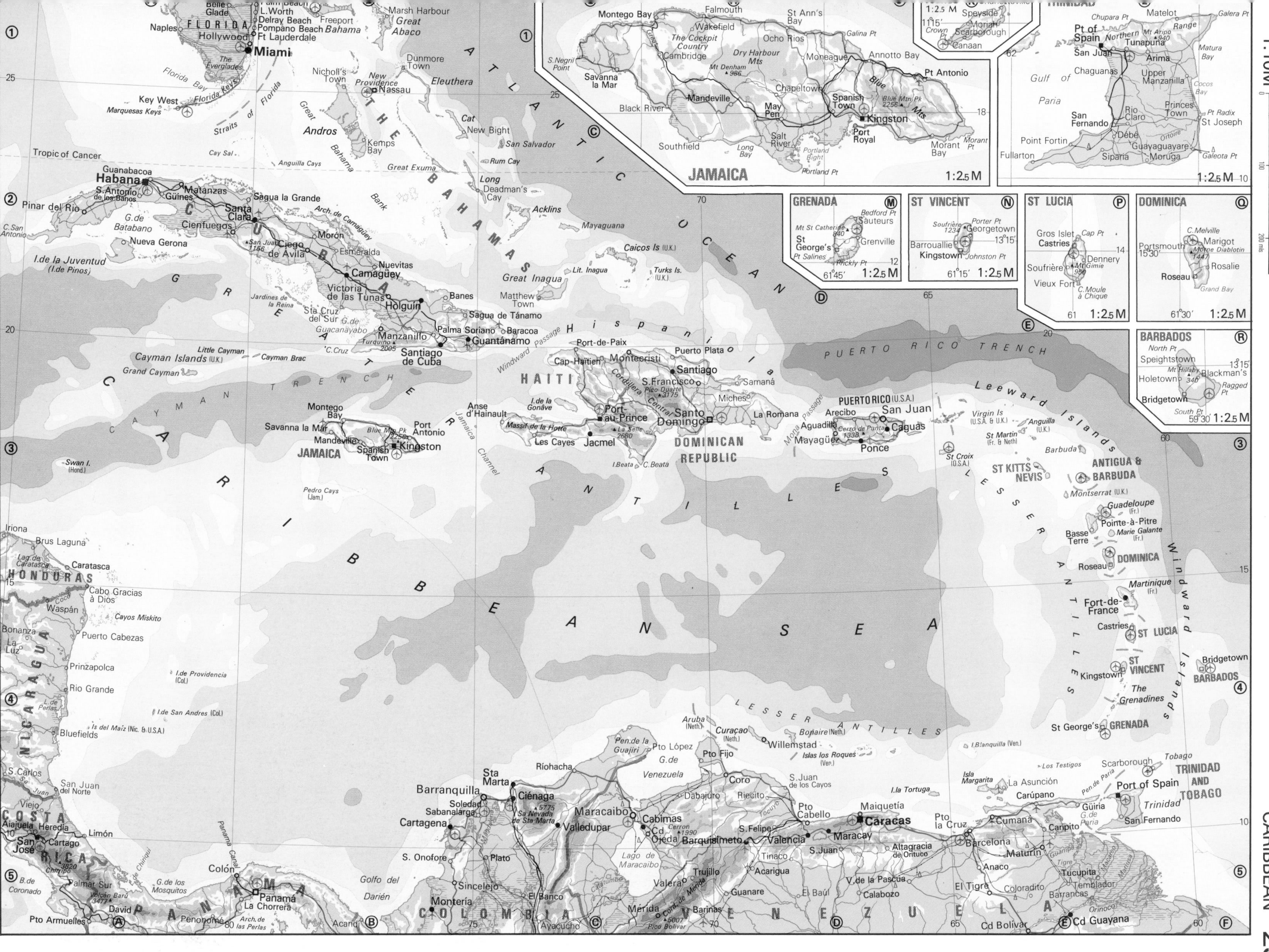
ATLANTIC OCEAN
CARIBBEAN SEA
THE BAHAMAS
CUBA
Hispaniola
HAITI
DOMINICAN REPUBLIC
JAMAICA
PUERTO RICO (U.S.A.)
PUERTO RICO TRENCH
CAYMAN TRENCH
GREATER ANTILLES
LESSER ANTILLES
Leeward Islands
Windward Islands
ANTIGUA & BARBUDA
ST KITTS NEVIS
DOMINICA
ST LUCIA
ST VINCENT
GRENADA
BARBADOS
TRINIDAD AND TOBAGO
VENEZUELA
COLOMBIA
PANAMA
COSTA RICA
NICARAGUA
HONDURAS
FLORIDA
Miami
Habana
Kingston
Santo Domingo
Port-au-Prince
San Juan
Caracas
Maracaibo
Barranquilla
Cartagena
Panamá
Colón
Nassau
Bridgetown
Port of Spain
Roseau
Castries
Kingstown
St George's
Fort-de-France
Basse Terre
Santiago de Cuba
Camagüey
Holguín
Guantánamo
Cayman Islands (U.K.)
Turks Is. (U.K.)
Caicos Is (U.K.)
Great Inagua
Mona Passage
Windward Passage
Jamaica Channel
Panama Canal
Golfo del Darién
Lago de Maracaibo
Tropic of Cancer
GRENADA 1:2.5M
ST VINCENT 1:2.5M
ST LUCIA 1:2.5M
DOMINICA 1:2.5M
BARBADOS 1:2.5M
JAMAICA 1:2.5M
TRINIDAD 1:2.5M

1:35M

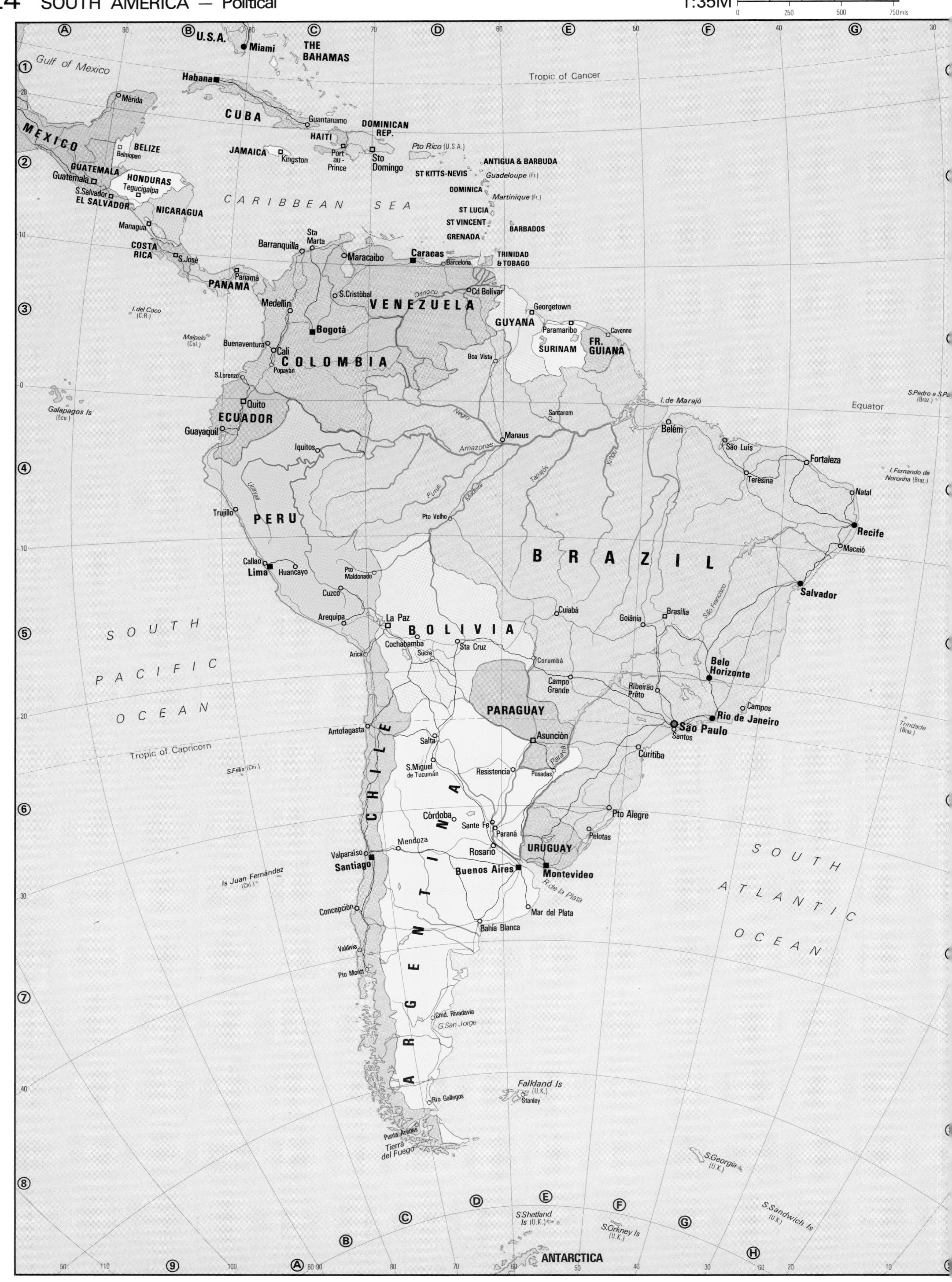

Gulf of Mexico
U.S.A.
Miami
THE BAHAMAS
Habana
Tropic of Cancer
CUBA
Mérida
MEXICO
BELIZE
Belmopan
Guantanamo
DOMINICAN REP.
HAITI
JAMAICA
Kingston
Port-au-Prince
Sto Domingo
Pto Rico (U.S.A.)
ANTIGUA & BARBUDA
ST KITTS-NEVIS
Guadeloupe (Fr.)
DOMINICA
Martinique (Fr.)
ST LUCIA
ST VINCENT
GRENADA
BARBADOS
TRINIDAD & TOBAGO
GUATEMALA
Guatemala
HONDURAS
Tegucigalpa
S.Salvador
EL SALVADOR
NICARAGUA
Managua
CARIBBEAN SEA
COSTA RICA
S.José
Panamá
PANAMA
Barranquilla
Sta Marta
Maracaibo
Caracas
Barcelona
S.Cristóbal
Orinoco
Cd Bolívar
VENEZUELA
Medellín
Bogotá
Georgetown
GUYANA
Paramaribo
Cayenne
SURINAM
FR. GUIANA
I. del Coco (C.R.)
Malpelo (Col.)
Buenaventura
Cali
COLOMBIA
Popayán
Boa Vista
S.Lorenzo
Quito
ECUADOR
Galapagos Is (Ecu.)
Guayaquil
Negro
Santarem
I. de Marajó
Belém
Equator
S.Pedro e S.Paulo (Braz.)
Manaus
Amazonas
Iquitos
Xingu
Tapajós
São Luís
Fortaleza
Teresina
I. Fernando de Noronha (Braz.)
Purus
Madeira
Ucayali
Natal
Trujillo
PERU
Pto Velho
Recife
Maceió
BRAZIL
Callao
Lima
Huancayo
Pto Maldonado
Salvador
Cuzco
Cuiabá
Goiânia
Brasília
São Francisco
Arequipa
La Paz
BOLIVIA
SOUTH PACIFIC OCEAN
Arica
Cochabamba
Sucre
Sta Cruz
Corumbá
Belo Horizonte
Campo Grande
Ribeirão Prêto
PARAGUAY
Campos
Rio de Janeiro
São Paulo
Santos
Antofagasta
Asunción
Trindade (Braz.)
Salta
Tropic of Capricorn
S.Félix (Chi.)
S.Miguel de Tucumán
Resistencia
Posadas
Paraná
Curitiba
CHILE
Córdoba
Sante Fe
Paraná
Pto Alegre
Pelotas
Mendoza
Valparaíso
Santiago
Rosario
URUGUAY
Buenos Aires
Montevideo
R. de la Plata
Is Juan Fernández (Chi.)
SOUTH ATLANTIC OCEAN
Concepción
Mar del Plata
Bahía Blanca
Valdivia
Pto Montt
ARGENTINA
Cmd. Rivadavia
G.San Jorge
Falkland Is (U.K.)
Stanley
Río Gallegos
Punta Arenas
Tierra del Fuego
S.Georgia (U.K.)
S.Shetland Is (U.K.)
S.Orkney Is (U.K.)
S.Sandwich Is (U.K.)
ANTARCTICA

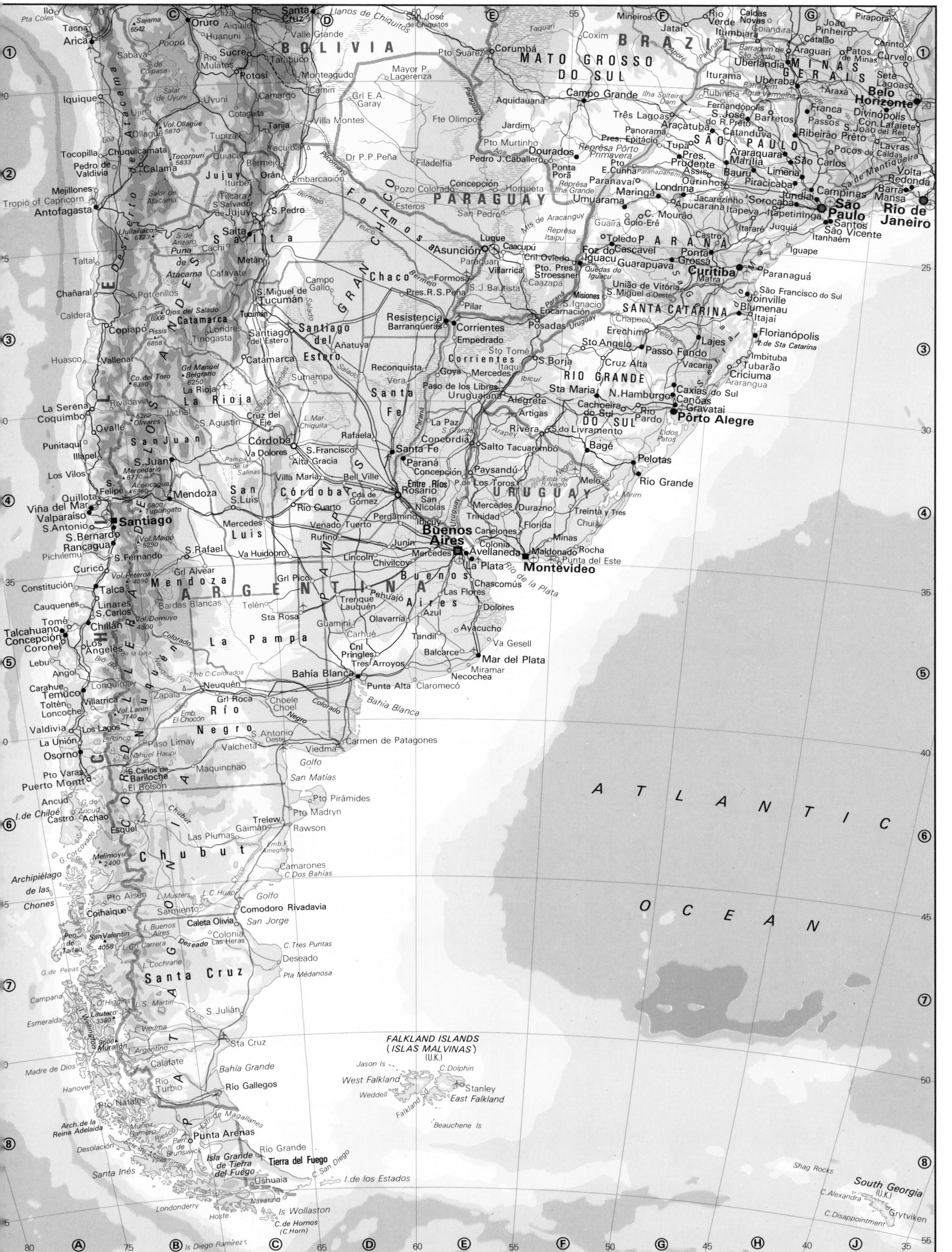
BOLIVIA
BRAZIL
PARAGUAY
URUGUAY
ARGENTINA
CHILE
ATLANTIC OCEAN
FALKLAND ISLANDS (ISLAS MALVINAS) (U.K.)
South Georgia (U.K.)
Buenos Aires
Santiago
Montevideo
Asunción
São Paulo
Rio de Janeiro
Pôrto Alegre
Curitiba
Córdoba
Rosario
Mendoza
Stanley
Punta Arenas
Tierra del Fuego

1:15M

0 200 400 600 km
0 100 200 300 mls

PACIFIC OCEAN

NICARAGUA
COSTA RICA
PANAMA
COLOMBIA
VENEZUELA
ECUADOR
PERU
BOLIVIA
CHILE
ARGENTINA
ACRE
RONDÔNIA
RORAIMA
AMAZONAS
LLANOS
SELVAS
CORDILLERA DE LOS ANDES
Cord. Occidental
Cord. Oriental
Cord. de Mérida
Desierto de Atacama
Neth. Antilles

Tegucigalpa
Comayagua
Siguatepeque
San Miguel
La Unión
Choluteca
Chinandega
Somoto
Estelí
Matagalpa
León
Managua
Masaya
Granada
L. de Nicaragua
Bluefields
Rivas
S. Carlos
San Juan
G. de Papagayo
Puntarenas
Alajuela
Heredia
Limón
San José
Cartago
3815 Chirripó Grande
Pen. de Nicoya
G. de Nicoya
B. de Coronado
3475 Barú
David
G. Dulce
Pto Armuelles
G. de Chiriquí
I. Coiba
Pto Cabezas
I. de Providencia (Col.)
I. de San Andrés (Col.)
Is. de Perlas
Colón
Panamá
La Chorrera
Santiago
Chitré
Pen. de Azuero
Pta Mariato
G. de Panamá
Arch. de las Perlas
La Palma
G. de Urabá
G. de los Mosquitos
L. de Chiriquí
Coco (Segovia)

Pta Gallinas
Pen. de Guajira
Riohacha
Maicao
Sta Marta
Ciénaga
Sa Nevada de Sta Marta 5800
Barranquilla
Cartagena
Valledupar
Machiques
Maracaibo
Cabimas
L. de Maracaibo
G. de Venezuela
Pto Fijo
Aruba
Curaçao (Neth.)
Bonaire
Willemstad
Is. Los Roques (Ven.)
Coro
Riecito
Pto Cabello
Maiquetía
Caracas
Valencia
Maracay
Barquisimeto
Cd Ojeda
Trujillo
Valera
Acarigua
Guanare
Barinas
Mérida
Bolívar 5775
S. Juan
Zarara
V. de la Pascua
Barcelona
Pto la Cruz
Cumaná
Anaco
El Tigre
Maturín
Tucupita
Barrancas
La Tortuga
I. de Margarita
La Asunción
Carúpano
Pen. de Paria
Güiria
G. de Paria
Caripito
Cd Bolívar
Cd Guayana
Upata
Cd Piar
Emb. de Guri
La Paragua
El Dorado
Salto del Ángel
La Gran Sabana
Roraima 2810
Sta Elena
Sa Pacaraima
Sa Parima
S. Fernando
Pto Carreño
Pto Ayacucho
Orinoco
Apure
Arauca
Meta
Vichada
Guaviare
Inírida
Casiquiare
Ventuari
S. Jacinto
Sincelejo
El Banco
Magangué
Montería
Turbo
Caucasia
Ocaña
Cúcuta
Pamplona
San Cristóbal
Bucaramanga
Barrancabermeja
Yarumal
Bello
Pto Berrío
Málaga
Medellín
Itagüí
Barbosa
Sogamoso
Tunja
Quibdó
C. Corrientes
Manizales
5215 Tolima
Pereira
Cartago
Armenia
Chocontá
Bogotá
Tuluá
Ibagué
Buga
Girardot
Villavicencio
Granada
Buenaventura
Palmira
Cali
G. de Tortugas
Santander
Huila 5750
Neiva
Popayán
Vol. Puracé 4700
Pto Rico
Pitalito
Florencia
Calamar
Salto Angostura
Mitú
Vaupés
Apaporis
Caquetá
Salto Grande
Orocué
Guainía
Cucuí
Içana
Tapurucuará
Negro
Tumaco
El Diviso
S. Lorenzo
Pasto
Ipiales
Mocoa
Belén
Tulcán
Pto Asís
Esmeraldas
Ibarra
Otavalo
Cojimíes
Quito
5896 Cotopaxi
Lago Agrio
Coca
Napo
Putumayo
Leguízamo
Jama
Chone
Tena
Manta
Ambato
C. San Lorenzo
Jipijapa
Guaranda
Chimborazo 6310
Guayaquil
Babahoyo
Riobamba
La Libertad
Playas
Milagro
Macas
I. Puná
Cuenca
Azogues
Gualaceo
G. de Guayaquil
Tumbes
Machala
Zaruma
Loja
Zamora
Talara
Negritos
Sullana
Paita
Piura
Chulucanas
Huancabamba
Catacaos
Pta Aguja
Jaén
Moyobamba
Lambayeque
Chiclayo
Ferreñafe
Chachapoyas
Chepén
Cajamarca
Cajabamba
Pacasmayo
Huamachuco
Otusco
Trujillo
Pomabamba
Huallanca
Huascarán 6768
Chimbote
Huaraz
Casma
Huarmey
Pativilca
Barranca
Huacho
Ancón
Callao
Lima
La Oroya
Jauja
Tarma
Huancayo
Acobamba
Cerro de Pasco
Oxapampa
La Merced
Huánuco
La Unión
Tingo María
Pucallpa
Yurimaguas
Tarapoto
Iquitos
Marañón
Huallaga
Ucayali
Pastaza
Tigre
Santiago
Huancavelica
Ayacucho
Andahuaylas
Abancay
Machu Picchu
Quillabamba
Cuzco
Chincha Alta
Pisco
Ica
Pen. de Paracas
Nazca
Coropuna 6425
Sicuani
Ayaviri
Juliaca
Puno
L. Titicaca
Arequipa
Misti 5822
Chala
Camaná
Matarani
Mollendo
Moquegua
Ilo
Pta Coles
Tacna
Arica
Parque Nac. de Manu
Pto Maldonado
Madre de Dios
Leticia
Tabatinga
Solimões (Amazonas)
Yavari (Javari)
Caxias
Elvira
Juruá
Jutaí
Tapauá
Coari
Purus
Tefé
Manacapuru
Japurá
Içá
Cruzeiro do Sul
Feijó
Sena Madureira
Rio Branco
Brasiléia
Cobija
Bôca do Acre
Lábrea
Humaitá
Pôrto Velho
Madeira
Abunã
Guajará-Mirim
Riberalta
Porvenir
Pto Heath
Rurrenabaque
Trinidad
Mamoré
Guaporé
Iténez
L. Rogaguado
Beni
Huanay
Sta Ana
Ancohuma 6388
Sorata
Chulumani
La Paz
Guaqui
Pto Villarroel
Quillacollo
Cochabamba
Santa Cruz
Montero
Llanos de Chiquitos
Oruro
Aiquile
Huanuni
Valle Grande
Sajama 6542
Sabaya
L. Poopó
Sucre
Río Mulatos
Potosí
Tarabuco
Monteagudo
Camiri
Camargo
Salar de Uyuni
Uyuni
Cotagaita
Villa Montes
Iquique
Vol. Ollagüe 5870
Ollagüe
Tupiza
Tarija
Yacuiba
Tocopilla
Chuquicamata
Calama
Tocorpuri 5833
La Quiaca
Bermejo
Orán
Pedro de Valdivia
Jujuy
Embarcación
Mejillones
Salar de Atacama
Tilcara
S. Salvador de Jujuy
Tropic of Capricorn
Antofagasta
Llullaillaco 6723
S. de Anzaro
Salta
S. Pedro
Pilcomayo
Formosa
Roseau
Fort-de-France
Martinique (Fr.)
ST LUCIA
Castries
ST VINCENT
Kingstown
The Grenadines
GRENADA
St George's
Port of Spain
San Fernando

at the same scale
ISLAS GALÁPAGOS (ARCHIPIÉLAGO DO COLÓN) (Equ.)
Culpepper
Wenman
Pinta
Marchena
Genovesa
Fernandina
San Salvador
Santa Cruz
Isabela
Baquerizo Moreno
San Cristóbal
Santa María
Española

at the same scale
Islas Juan Fernández (Chile)
Alejandro Selkirk
Robinson Crusoe
Sta Clara

I. del Coco (C.R.)
Malpelo (Col.)

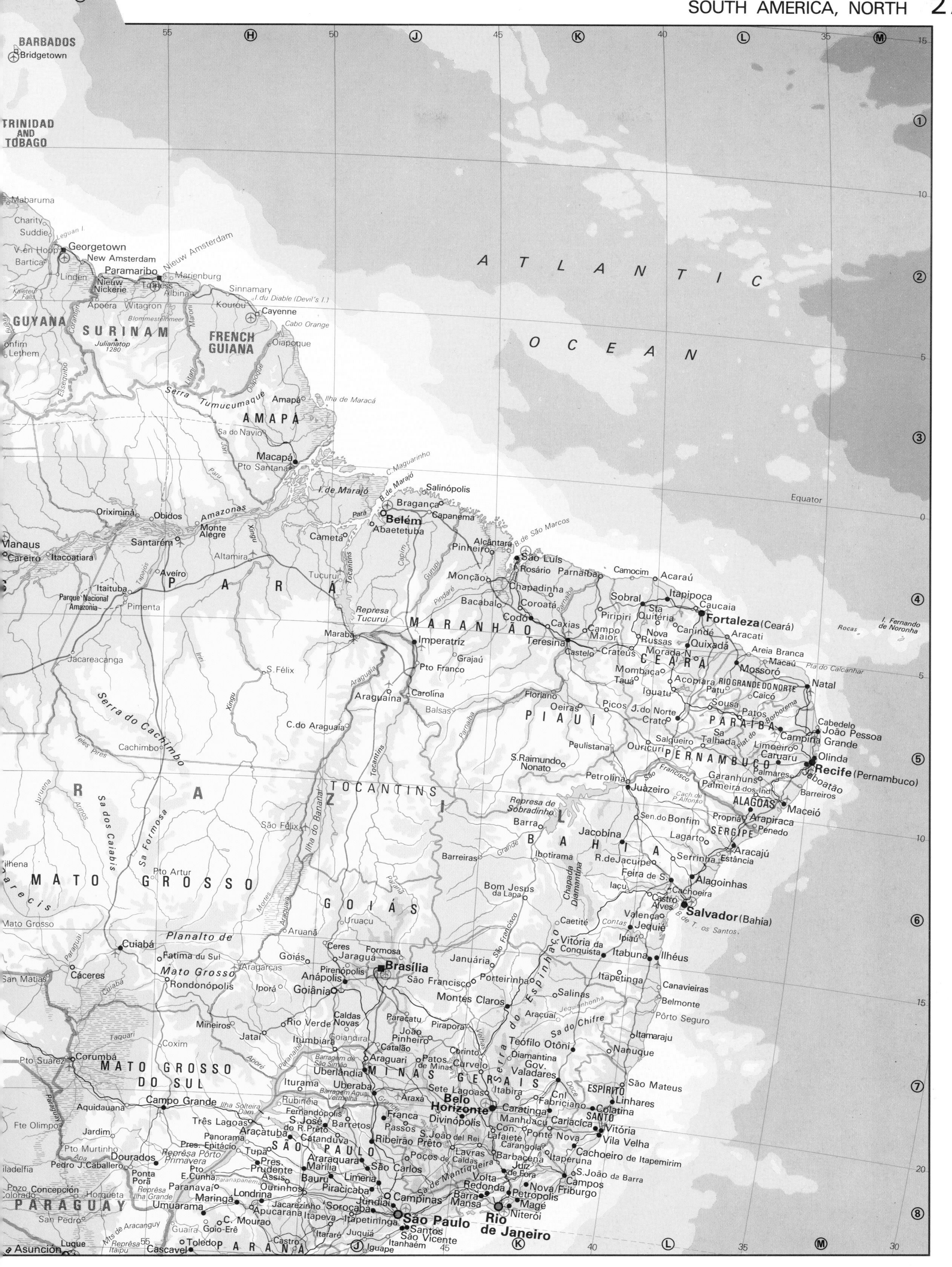
BARBADOS
Bridgetown
TRINIDAD AND TOBAGO
ATLANTIC
OCEAN
Equator
GUYANA
SURINAM
FRENCH GUIANA
Georgetown
New Amsterdam
Paramaribo
Nieuw Amsterdam
Marienburg
Nieuw Nickerie
Albina
Sinnamary
I. du Diable (Devil's I.)
Kourou
Cayenne
Cabo Orange
Oiapoque
Apoera
Witagron
Blommestenmeer
Julianatop 1280
Lethem
Mabaruma
Charity
Suddie
Leguan I.
Bartica
Linden
Kaieteur Falls
Serra Tumucumaque
AMAPÁ
Amapá
Ilha de Maracá
Sa do Navio
Macapá
Pto Santana
C. Maguarinho
I. de Marajó
B. de Marajó
Salinópolis
Bragança
Capanema
Belém
Abaetetuba
Pará
Cametá
Oriximiná
Obidos
Amazonas
Monte Alegre
Santarém
Altamira
Manaus
Careiro
Itacoatiara
Aveiro
Itaituba
Parque Nacional Amazonia
Pimenta
PARÁ
Tucuruí
Represa Tucuruí
Marabá
Alcântara
B. de São Marcos
Pinheiro
São Luís
Rosário
Parnaíba
Camocim
Acaraú
Monção
Chapadinha
Coroatá
Bacabal
Codó
Caxias
MARANHÃO
Imperatriz
Grajaú
Pto Franco
Teresina
Castelo
Campo Maior
Sobral
Itapipoca
Caucaia
Fortaleza (Ceará)
Piripiri
Sta Quitéria
Canindé
Aracati
Nova Russas
Quixadá
Crateús
Morada Nova
CEARÁ
Areia Branca
Macau
Pta do Calcanhar
Mossoró
Mombaça
Tauá
Acopiara
RIO GRANDE DO NORTE
Natal
Iguatu
Patu
Caicó
Sousa
Patos
I. Fernando de Noronha
Rocas
Jacareacanga
S. Félix
Araguaína
Carolina
Balsas
Floriano
Oeiras
PIAUÍ
Picos
J. do Norte
Crato
PARAÍBA
Cabedelo
João Pessoa
Campina Grande
Sa Talhada
Salgueiro
Limoeiro
Caruaru
Olinda
Recife (Pernambuco)
Paulistana
Ouricuri
PERNAMBUCO
Palmares
Garanhuns
Palmeira dos Índ.
Cabo
Barreiros
Maceió
ALAGOAS
Serra do Cachimbo
Cachimbo
Teles Pires
C. do Araguaia
S. Raimundo Nonato
Petrolina
Juazeiro
Cach. de P. Afonso
Represa de Sobradinho
TOCANTINS
Sen. do Bonfim
Propriá
Arapiraca
Penedo
SERGIPE
Barra
Jacobina
Lagarto
BAHIA
Aracajú
Estância
Serrinha
R. de Jacuípe
Feira de S.
Alagoinhas
Cachoeira
Salvador (Bahia)
B. de T. os Santos
Iaçu
Castro Alves
Ibotirama
Chapada Diamantina
Barreiras
Bom Jesus da Lapa
São Félix
Ilha do Bananal
Sa Formosa
Sa dos Caiabis
Pto Artur
MATO GROSSO
Mato Grosso
GOIÁS
Aruanã
Uruaçu
Caetité
Valença
Jequié
Ipiaú
Vitória da Conquista
Itabuna
Ilhéus
Cuiabá
Planalto de Mato Grosso
Fatima du Sul
Cáceres
San Matías
Ceres
Formosa
Jaraguá
Goiás
Pirenópolis
Brasília
Anápolis
Goiânia
Aragarças
Rondonópolis
Iporá
São Francisco
Januária
Porteirinha
Itapetinga
Canavieiras
Belmonte
Salinas
Montes Claros
Pôrto Seguro
Araçuaí
Caldas Novas
Paracatu
Rio Verde
Mineiros
Jataí
João Pinheiro
Pirapora
Sa do Chifre
Itamaraju
Teófilo Otôni
Nanuque
Coxim
Itumbiara
Goiandira
Catalão
Corinto
Curvelo
Diamantina
Serra do Espinhaço
Pto Suarez
Corumbá
MATO GROSSO DO SUL
Araguari
Patos de Minas
Uberlândia
MINAS GERAIS
Gov. Valadares
São Mateus
Iturama
Uberaba
Araxá
Sete Lagoas
Itabira
ESPÍRITO SANTO
Linhares
Campo Grande
Aquidauana
Rubinéia
Fernandópolis
Belo Horizonte
Caratinga
Cnl Fabriciano
Colatina
Fte Olimpo
Três Lagoas
S. José do R. Prêto
Barretos
Franca
Passos
Divinópolis
Manhuaçu
Cariacica
Vitória
Vila Velha
Jardim
Panorama
Araçatuba
Catanduva
Ribeirão Prêto
S. João del Rei
Con. Lafaiete
Ponte Nova
Carangola
Cachoeiro de Itapemirim
Pto Murtinho
Pres. Epitácio
Represa Pôrto Primavera
Tupã
SÃO PAULO
Araraquara
Poços de Caldas
Lavras
Barbacena
Itaperuna
Dourados
Pedro J. Caballero
Ponta Porã
Pres. Prudente
Assis
Marília
São Carlos
Bauru
Limeira
Juiz de Fora
Campos
S. João da Barra
Pto E. Cunha
Paranavaí
Ourinhos
Piracicaba
Sa de Mantiqueira
Volta Redonda
Barra Mansa
Petrópolis
Nova Friburgo
Pozo Colorado
Concepción
Horqueta
Represa Ilha Grande
Londrina
Campinas
Magé
Niterói
PARAGUAY
Umuarama
Maringá
Jacarezinho
Sorocaba
Jundiaí
São Paulo
Rio de Janeiro
San Pedro
Apucarana
Itapeva
Itapetininga
Santos
São Vicente
Mts de Aracanguy
Guaíra
Goio-Erê
C. Mourão
Itararé
Juquiá
Itanhaém
Iguape
Luque
Asunción
Represa Itaipu
Toledo
Cascavel
PARANÁ
Castro

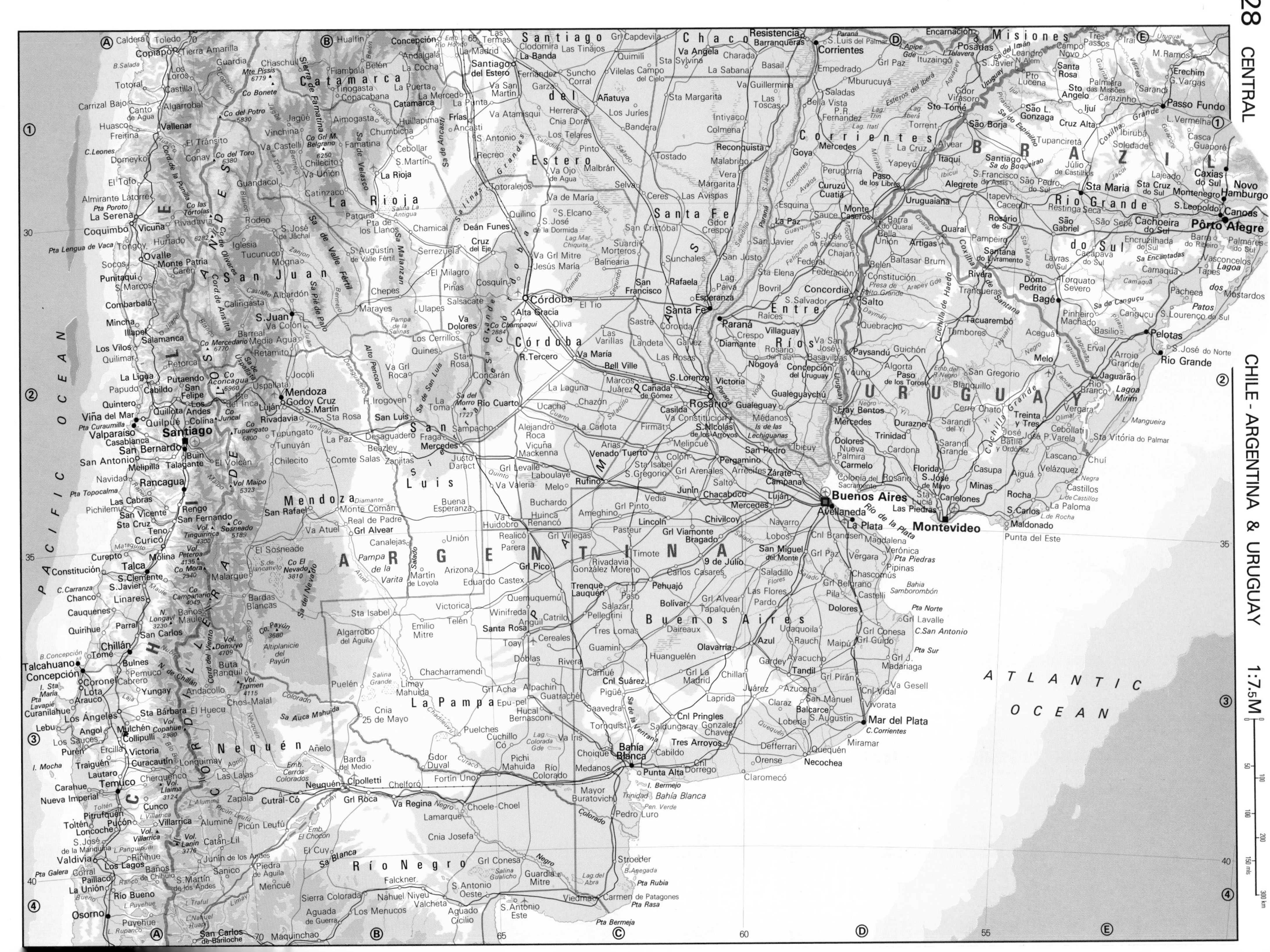

0 100 200 300 km
0 50 100 150 mls
ATLANTIC OCEAN
PACIFIC OCEAN
BRAZIL
URUGUAY
ARGENTINA
CHILE
Buenos Aires
Montevideo
Santiago
Córdoba
Rosario
Mendoza
Pôrto Alegre
Mar del Plata
Bahía Blanca
Valparaíso
Concepción
Río de la Plata

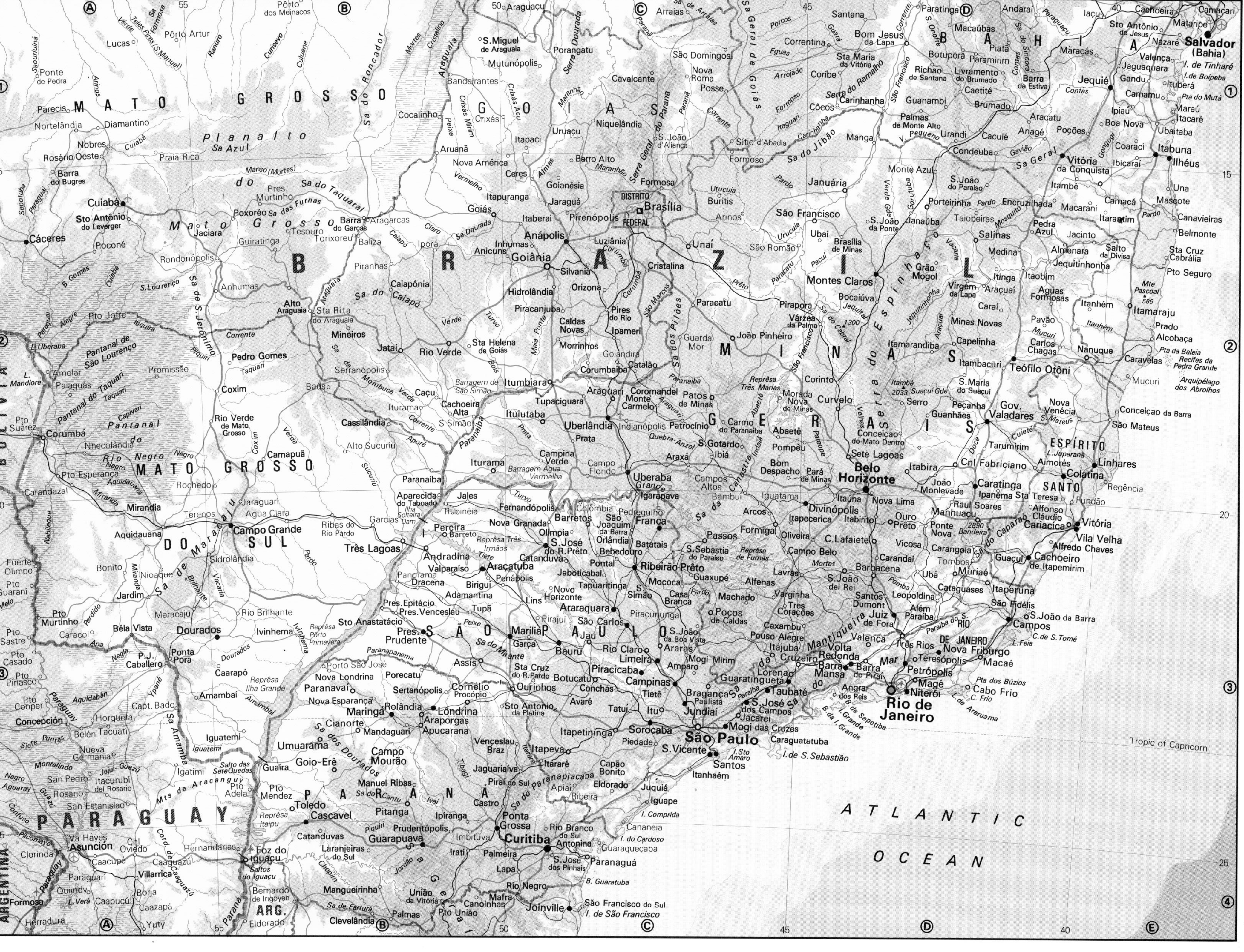
BAHIA
MINAS GERAIS
ESPÍRITO SANTO
RIO DE JANEIRO
SÃO PAULO
PARANÁ
GOIÁS
DISTRITO FEDERAL
MATO GROSSO
MATO GROSSO DO SUL
BRAZIL
PARAGUAY
BOLIVIA
ARGENTINA
ARG.
ATLANTIC OCEAN
Tropic of Capricorn
Salvador (Bahia)
Belo Horizonte
Rio de Janeiro
São Paulo
Brasília
Goiânia
Curitiba
Vitória
Campo Grande
Cuiabá
Asunción
Santos
Niterói
Uberlândia
Londrina
Corumbá
Cáceres
Ilhéus
Teófilo Otôni
Montes Claros
Ribeirão Prêto
Anápolis
Campinas
Juiz de Fora
Planalto do Mato Grosso
Pantanal
Serra do Espinhaço
Serra do Mar
Sa Geral de Goiás

1:15M

0 200 400 600 km
0 100 200 300 mls
ICELAND
Reykjavik
Greenland (Den.)
Kap Farvel
Jan Mayen (Nor.)
ARCTIC
Arctic Circle
NORWEGIAN SEA
Færøerne (Den.)
Shetland
Orkney
ATLANTIC OCEAN
UNITED KINGDOM OF GREAT BRITAIN AND NORTHERN IRELAND
Glasgow
Edinburgh
Aberdeen
Belfast
IRELAND
Dublin
Cork
Newcastle
Liverpool
Manchester
Birmingham
Cardiff
Bristol
London
NORTH SEA
English Channel
NORWAY
SWEDEN
Vesterålen
Lofoten
Narvik
Trondheim
Sundsvall
Bergen
Oslo
Stavanger
Vänern
Stockholm
Gotland
Göteborg
Jonköping
Ålborg
DENMARK
København
Malmö
Öland
Bornholm
Baltic
Rostock
Gdańsk
Hamburg
Amsterdam
's-Gravenhage
Rotterdam
NETHERLANDS
Hannover
Berlin
Poznań
GERMANY
Essen
Bruxelles
BELGIUM
Lille
Köln
Bonn
Leipzig
Dresden
Wrocław
POL
Le Havre
Rouen
Seine
Frankfurt
LUXEMBOURG
Praha
Paris
Nürnberg
CZECHOSLOV
Strasbourg
Stuttgart
Brno
Nantes
Tours
Loire
FRANCE
Rhein
München
Wien
Bratislava
Salzburg
Bern
Zurich
LIECHTENSTEIN
SWITZERLAND
AUSTRIA
Graz
HUNG
La Coruña
Bay of Biscay
Bordeaux
Clermont-Ferrand
Genève
Lyon
Milano
Torino
Trieste
Zagreb
Venezia
Bilbao
Toulouse
Rhône
Porto
Valladolid
Genova
YUGOS
Ebro
ANDORRA
Marseille
MONACO
Firenze
SAN MARINO
Split
ADRIATIC SEA
PORTUGAL
SPAIN
Madrid
Zaragoza
Bastia
Corse
Lisboa
Tajo
Toledo
Barcelona
Ajaccio
ITALY
Roma
Valencia
Is Baleares
Menorca
Mallorca
Ibiza
Sardegna
Olbia
TYRRHENIAN SEA
Napoli
Taranto
Faro
Sevilla
Murcia
Málaga
Cagliari
Madeira (Port.)
Tanger
Gibraltar (U.K.)
Ceuta (Sp.)
MEDITERRANEAN SEA
Palermo
Messina
Reggio di Calabria
Sicilia
Melilla (Sp.)
Oran
Alger
Casablanca
Rabat
Tunis
MOROCCO
ALGERIA
TUNISIA
MALTA
Marrakech
Islas Canarias (Sp.)

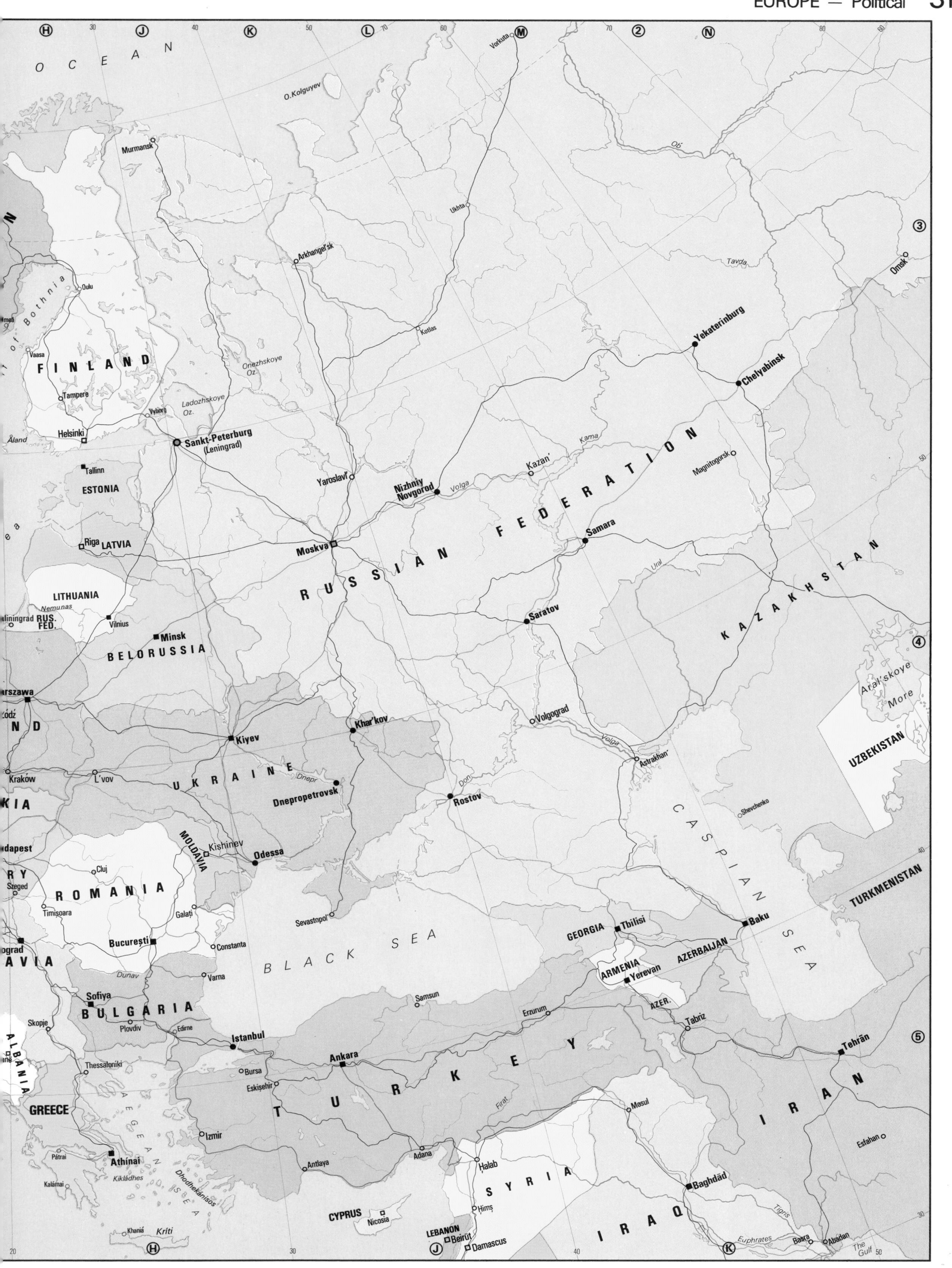
OCEAN
O.Kolguyev
Vorkuta
Murmansk
Ukhta
Ob'
Tavda
Omsk
Arkhangel'sk
Oulu
Gulf of Bothnia
Vaasa
FINLAND
Kotlas
Yekaterinburg
Chelyabinsk
Onezhskoye Oz.
Ladozhskoye Oz.
Tampere
Vyborg
Helsinki
Åland
Sankt-Peterburg (Leningrad)
Kama
Magnitogorsk
Tallinn
ESTONIA
Yaroslavl'
Nizhniy Novgorod
Volga
Kazan'
RUSSIAN FEDERATION
Samara
Riga
LATVIA
Moskva
Ural
KAZAKHSTAN
LITHUANIA
Nemunas
RUS. FED.
Vilnius
Saratov
Minsk
BELORUSSIA
Aral'skoye More
Volgograd
Khar'kov
Kiyev
UZBEKISTAN
Astrakhan'
Kraków
L'vov
UKRAINE
Dnepr
Dnepropetrovsk
Don
Rostov
CASPIAN SEA
Shevchenko
MOLDAVIA
Kishinev
Odessa
Cluj
Szeged
ROMANIA
TURKMENISTAN
Timișoara
Galați
Sevastopol'
Bucuresti
Constanța
BLACK SEA
GEORGIA
Tbilisi
Baku
ARMENIA
Yerevan
AZERBAIJAN
Dunav
Varna
Sofiya
BULGARIA
Samsun
AZER.
Skopje
Plovdiv
Edirne
Erzurum
Tabriz
ALBANIA
Istanbul
Tehrān
Thessaloniki
Ankara
TURKEY
Bursa
Eskişehir
GREECE
AEGEAN SEA
Mosul
Firat
IRAN
Izmir
Esfahan
Pátrai
Athínai
Adana
Antlaya
Halab
SYRIA
Kalámai
Kikládhes
Dhodhekánisos
Baghdād
Ḩimş
CYPRUS
Nicosia
Tigris
IRAQ
Khaniá
Kríti
LEBANON
Beirūt
Damascus
Euphrates
Basra
Abadan
The Gulf

1:7.5M

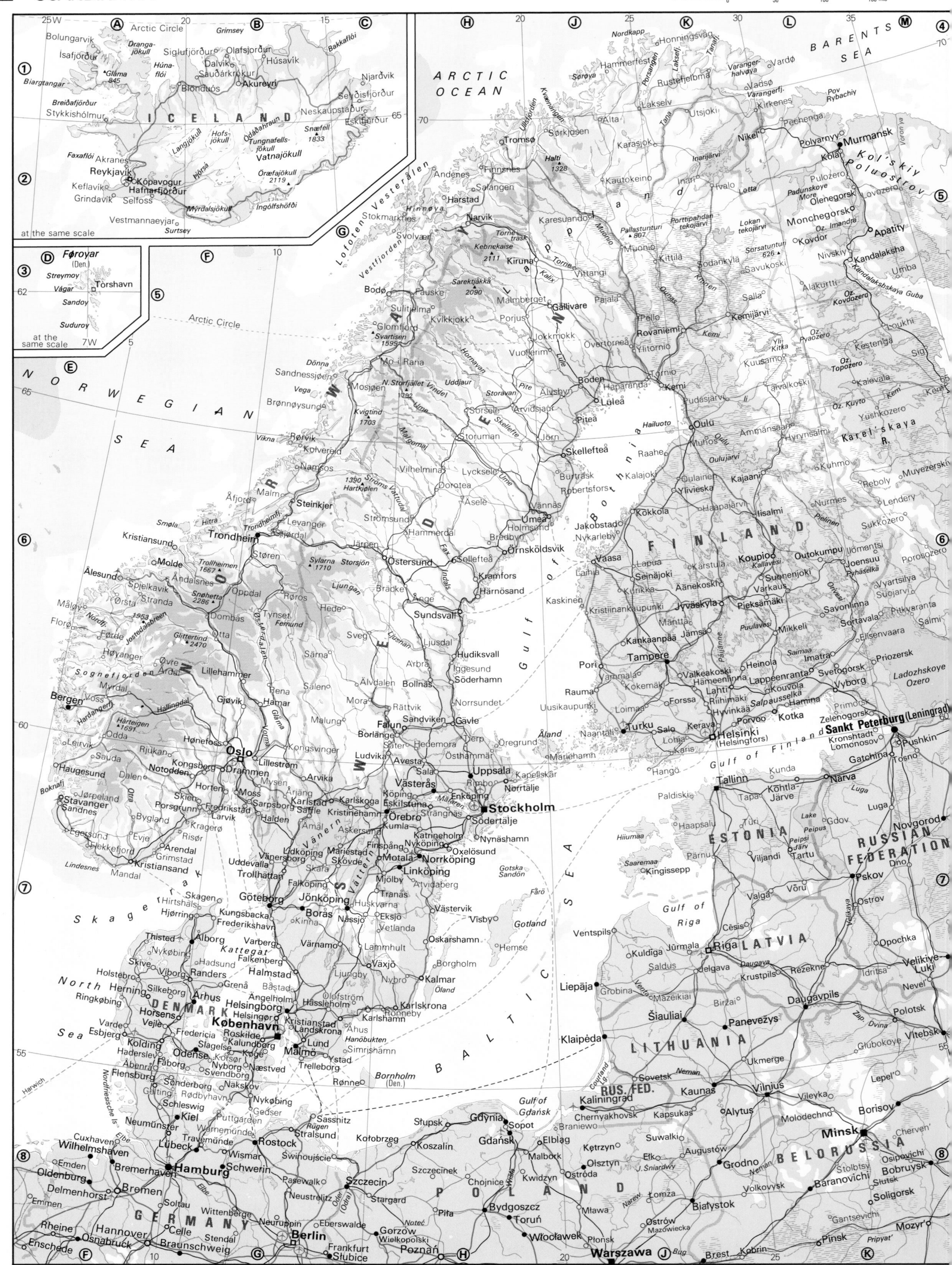

ICELAND
at the same scale
Arctic Circle
Grimsey
Bolungarvik
Ísafjörður
Dranga-jökull
Siglufjörður
Olafsfjörður
Dalvik
Húsavik
Sauðárkrókur
Akureyri
Blönduós
Bakkaflói
Húna-flói
Gláma 845
Biargtangar
Njarðvik
Seyðisfjörður
Neskaupstaður
Eskifjörður
Breiðafjörður
Stykkishólmur
Hofs-jökull
Langjökull
Snæfell 1833
Tungnafells-jökull
Vatnajökull
Faxaflói
Akranes
Reykjavik
Kópavogur
Hafnarfjörður
Keflavik
Grindavik
Selfoss
Þjórsá
Öræfajökull 2119
Mýrdalsjökull
Ingólfshöfði
Vestmannaeyjar
Surtsey
Føroyar (Den.)
Streymoy
Vágar
Tórshavn
Sandoy
Suduroy
at the same scale
Arctic Circle
ARCTIC OCEAN
BARENTS SEA
NORWEGIAN SEA
Nordkapp
Honningsvåg
Hammerfest
Sørøya
Porsangen
Laksefj.
Tanafj.
Varanger-halvøya
Vardø
Vadsø
Varangerfj.
Kirkenes
Pov Rybachiy
Rustefjelbma
Lakselv
Alta
Tana
Utsjoki
Pechenga
Polyarnyy
Murmansk
Kola
Kol'skiy Poluostrov
Nikel'
Tromsø
Sørkjosen
Lyngen
Kvænangen
Ullsfjorden
Karasjok
Halti 1328
Inarijärvi
Inari
Ivalo
Lotta
Kautokeino
Finnsnes
Andenes
Salangen
Harstad
Hinnøya
Vesterålen
Lofoten
Stokmarknes
Narvik
Svolvær
Vestfjorden
Karesuando
Muonio
Pallastunturi 807
Porttipahdan tekojärvi
Lokan tekojärvi
Pulozero
Padunskoye More
Olenegorsk
Lovozero
Monchegorsk
Oz. Imandra
Apatity
Kovdor
Nivskiy
Kandalaksha
Kandalakshskaya Guba
Umba
Torneträsk
Kebnekaise 2111
Kiruna
Torne
Vittangi
Kittilä
Sodankylä
Savukoski
Sorsatunturi 626
Alakurtti
Oz. Kovdozero
Bodø
Fauske
Sulitjelma
Sarektjåkkå 2090
Malmberget
Gällivare
Pajala
Salla
Kemijärvi
Kemi
Glomfjord
Kvikkjokk
Porjus
Svartisen 1599
Jokkmokk
Pello
Rovaniemi
Ylitornio
Övertorneå
Vuollerim
Lule
Oz. Pyaozero
Ylikitka
Loukhi
Kestenga
Dønna
Sandnessjøen
Mo i Rana
Vega
Mosjøen
N. Storfjället 1792
Vindel
Uddjaur
Storavan
Pite
Älvsbyn
Boden
Haparanda
Tornio
Kuusamo
Oz. Topozero
Kalevala
Brønnøysund
Kvigtind 1703
Ume
Sorsele
Arvidsjaur
Luleå
Pudasjärvi
Ii
Taivalkoski
Oz. Kuyto
Kem'
Yushkozero
Piteå
Hailuoto
Oulu
Muhos
Ämmänsaari
Hyrynsalmi
Karel'skaya R.
Vikna
Rørvik
Kolvereid
Malgomaj
Storuman
Jörn
Skellefte
Skellefteå
Raahe
Oulujärvi
Kuhmo
Muyezerskiy
Namsos
Vilhelmina
Lycksele
Burträsk
Kalajoki
Oulainen
Ylivieska
Kajaani
Reboly
Lendery
Malm
Hartkjølen 1390
Ströms Vattudal
Dorotea
Robertsfors
Åsele
Nurmes
Åfjord
Steinkjer
Vännäs
Umeå
Haapajärvi
Iisalmi
Pielinen
Sukkozero
Smøla
Hitra
Trondheimsfj.
Levanger
Strömsund
Holmsund
Kokkola
Jakobstad
Nykarleby
Kristiansund
Trondheim
Stjørdal
Hammerdal
Bredbyn
Örnsköldsvik
FINLAND
Vaasa
Laihia
Lapua
Seinäjoki
Kuopio
Kallavesi
Outokumpu
Joensuu
Pyhäselkä
Ilomantsi
Porosozero
Molde
Trollheimen 1667
Støren
Järpen
Sylarna 1710
Storsjön
Östersund
Sollefteå
Kramfors
Härnösand
Kärstula
Ålesund
Åndalsnes
Oppdal
Ljungan
Bräcke
Indals
Äänekoski
Suonenjoki
Varkaus
Orivesi
Vyartsilya
Suojarvi
Spjelkavik
Stranda
Snøhetta 2286
Røros
Hede
Ånge
Kaskinen
Kristiinankaupunki
Jyväskylä
Pieksämäki
Savonlinna
Pitkyaranta
Måløy
Ørsta
Nordfj.
Dombås
Tynset
Femund
Sundsvall
Mänttä
Puulavesi
Mikkeli
Sortavala
Salmi
Florø
Førde
1953
Jostedalsbreen
Otta
Østerdalen
Sveg
Ljusnan
Ljusdal
Kankaanpää
Jämsä
Päijänne
Elisenvaara
Høyanger
Glittertind 2470
Sårna
Hudiksvall
Tampere
Saimaa
Imatra
Priozersk
Sognefjorden
Øvre Årdal
Lillehammer
Arbrå
Iggesund
Söderhamn
Pori
Valkeakoski
Heinola
Lappeenranta
Svetogorsk
Ladozhskoye Ozero
Myrdal
Voss
Hardangerfj.
Hallingdal
Gjøvik
Rena
Sälen
Älvdalen
Bollnäs
Yammala
Kokemäki
Hämeenlinna
Lahti
Kouvola
Vyborg
Bergen
Hamar
Glåma
Mora
Rättvik
Norrsundet
Rauma
Uusikaupunki
Loimaa
Forssa
Riihimäki
Salpausselkä
Hyvinkää
Hamina
Primorsk
Hårteigen 1691
Odda
Malung
Falun
Sandviken
Gävle
Porvoo
Kotka
Zelenogorsk
Sankt Peterburg (Leningrad)
Leirvik
Hønefoss
Oslo
Vorma
Borlänge
Säter
Hedemora
Tierp
Öregrund
Åland
Naantali
Turku
Salo
Kerava
Helsinki (Helsingfors)
Lohja
Karis
Kronshtadt
Lomonosov
Pushkin
Sauda
Rjukan
Kongsberg
Kongsvinger
Ludvika
Avesta
Östhammar
Mariehamn
Gulf of Finland
Gatchina
Tosno
Haugesund
Notodden
Drammen
Lillestrøm
Sala
Uppsala
Kapellskär
Hangö
Tallinn
Kunda
Narva
Dalen
Horten
Mysen
Arvika
Västerås
Rimbo
Norrtälje
Paldiski
Tapa
Kohtla-Järve
Luga
Bokn fj.
Jørpeland
Stavanger
Sandnes
Skien
Moss
Sarpsborg
Karlstad
Säffle
Karlskoga
Köping
Eskilstuna
Enköping
Mälaren
Stockholm
Porsgrunn
Fredrikstad
Larvik
Halden
Kristinehamn
Örebro
Strängnäs
Södertälje
Bygland
Kragerø
Åmål
Vänern
Askersund
Kumla
Katrineholm
Nynäshamn
Haapsalu
ESTONIA
Türi
Lake Peipus
Gdov
Novgorod
Egersund
Evje
Risør
Arendal
Grimstad
Lidköping
Mariestad
Finspång
Nyköping
Oxelösund
Hiiumaa
Peipsi Järv
Tartu
RUSSIAN FEDERATION
Flekkefjord
Kristiansand
Uddevalla
Vänersborg
Skövde
Motala
Norrköping
Saaremaa
Pärnu
Viljandi
Lindesnes
Mandal
Trollhättan
Skara
Vättern
Linköping
Gotska Sandön
Kingissepp
Dno
Skagerrak
Skagen
Hirtshals
Hjørring
Göteborg
Falköping
Jönköping
Mjölby
Åtvidaberg
Pskov
Valga
Võru
Kungsbacka
Frederikshavn
Borås
Huskvarna
Tranås
Eksjö
Västervik
Fårö
Ostrov
Kinna
Nässjö
Vetlanda
Visby
Gotland
Gulf of Riga
Thisted
Ålborg
Varberg
Kattegat
Värnamo
Lammhult
Oskarshamn
Ventspils
Cēsis
Opochka
Nykøbing
Hadsund
Falkenberg
Hemse
Jūrmala
Riga
LATVIA
Skive
Viborg
Randers
Halmstad
Växjö
Borgholm
Kuldīga
Saldus
Jelgava
Daugava
Krustpils
Rēzekne
Velikiye Luki
Holstebro
Grenå
Båstad
Ljungby
Nybro
Kalmar
Öland
Liepāja
Grobina
Idritsa
Nevel'
North Sea
Herning
Silkeborg
Århus
Ängelholm
Olofström
Venta
Mažeikiai
Biržai
Daugavpils
Ringkøbing
DENMARK
Helsingborg
Hässleholm
Karlskrona
Polotsk
Horsens
Helsingør
Kristianstad
Ronneby
Šiauliai
Panevežys
Zap. Dvina
Varde
Vejle
København
Landskrona
Karlshamn
Esbjerg
Fredericia
Roskilde
Åhus
Kolding
Slagelse
Kalundborg
Lund
Hanöbukten
LITHUANIA
Vitebsk
Haderslev
Odense
Korsør
Køge
Malmö
Simrishamn
Klaipėda
Glubokoye
Åbenrå
Fåborg
Nyborg
Svendborg
Næstved
Ystad
Trelleborg
Ukmerge
Flensburg
Sønderborg
Nakskov
Bornholm (Den.)
Rønne
Curonian Lg.
Neman
Lepel'
Harwich
Nordfriesische Is.
Gelting
Rødbyhavn
Nykøbing
Sovetsk
RUS. FED.
Kaunas
Vilnius
Vileyka
Schleswig
Gedser
Gulf of Gdańsk
Kaliningrad
Alytus
Molodechno
Borisov
Kiel
Neumünster
Puttgarden
Sassnitz
Rügen
Słupsk
Gdynia
Sopot
Chernyakhovsk
Kapsukas
Minsk
Cherven'
Cuxhaven
Elbe
Wilhelmshaven
Lübeck
Travemünde
Rostock
Stralsund
Kołobrzeg
Koszalin
Gdańsk
Braniewo
Elbląg
Kętrzyn
Suwałki
Augustów
BELORUSSIA
Osipovichi
Bobruysk
Emden
Bremerhaven
Hamburg
Wismar
Świnoujście
Malbork
Olsztyn
Ełk
Grodno
Oldenburg
Schwerin
Szczecinek
Chojnice
Wisła
Kwidzyn
Ostróda
J. Śniardwy
Stolbtsy
Slutsk
Baranovichi
Delmenhorst
Bremen
Pasewalk
Szczecin
Oder (Odra)
Stargard
Volkovysk
Soligorsk
Emmen
Soltau
Neustrelitz
POLAND
Narew
Łomża
Mława
Białystok
GERMANY
Wittenberge
Piła
Bydgoszcz
Toruń
Ostrów Mazowiecka
Gantsevichi
Rheine
Hannover
Celle
Neuruppin
Eberswalde
Noteć
Gorzów Wielkopolski
Włocławek
Płock
Mozyr'
Osnabrück
Stendal
Berlin
Frankfurt
Słubice
Poznań
Warszawa
Bug
Brest
Kobrin
Pinsk
Pripyat'
Enschede
Braunschweig

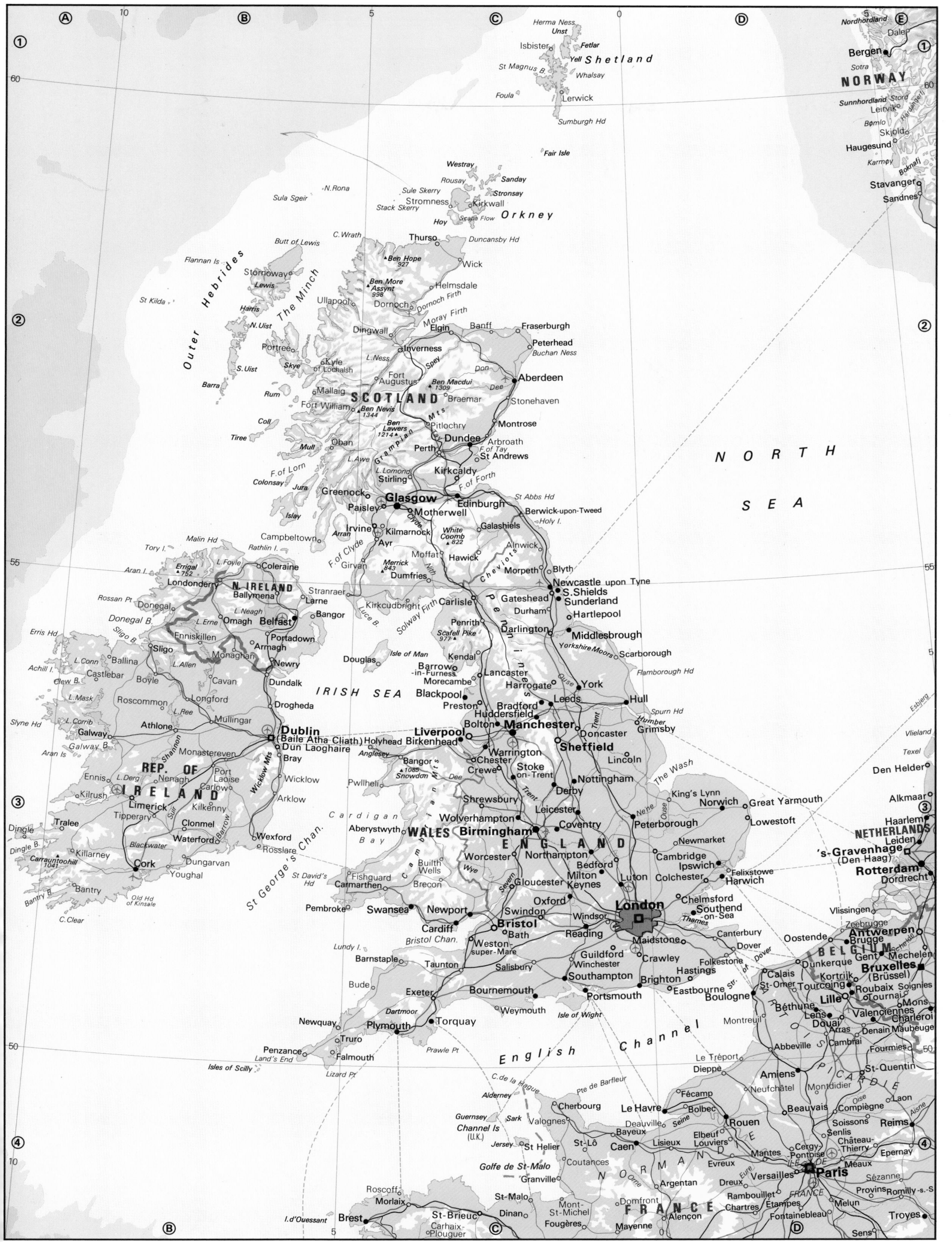
Herma Ness
Unst
Isbister
Fetlar
Yell
Shetland
St Magnus B.
Whalsay
Foula
Lerwick
Sumburgh Hd
Fair Isle
Westray
Rousay
Sanday
Stronsay
N.Rona
Sula Sgeir
Sule Skerry
Stromness
Kirkwall
Stack Skerry
Orkney
Hoy
Scapa Flow
Duncansby Hd
Butt of Lewis
C.Wrath
Thurso
Wick
Flannan Is
Stornoway
Lewis
Outer Hebrides
The Minch
Ben Hope 927
Ben More Assynt 998
Helmsdale
St Kilda
Harris
Ullapool
Dornoch
Dornoch Firth
Moray Firth
N.Uist
Dingwall
Elgin
Banff
Fraserburgh
Peterhead
Buchan Ness
Portree
Inverness
L.Ness
Skye
Kyle of Lochalsh
S.Uist
Spey
Fort Augustus
Don
Aberdeen
Barra
Rum
Mallaig
Ben Macdui 1309
Dee
SCOTLAND
Braemar
Stonehaven
Fort William
Ben Nevis 1344
Coll
Ben Lawers 1214
Grampian Mts
Pitlochry
Montrose
Tiree
Mull
Oban
Dundee
Arbroath
Perth
F. of Tay
St Andrews
L.Awe
F.of Lorn
Colonsay
Jura
L.Lomond
Stirling
Kirkcaldy
F.of Forth
NORTH SEA
Greenock
Glasgow
Edinburgh
St Abbs Hd
Paisley
Motherwell
Berwick-upon-Tweed
Islay
Irvine
Clyde
White Coomb 822
Galashiels
Holy I.
Arran
Kilmarnock
Ayr
Campbeltown
Malin Hd
Tory I.
Rathlin I.
F. of Clyde
Merrick 843
Moffat
Hawick
Alnwick
Cheviots
Errigal 752
L. Foyle
Coleraine
Girvan
Dumfries
Nith
Morpeth
Blyth
Aran I.
Londonderry
N.IRELAND
Ballymena
Stranraer
Larne
Newcastle upon Tyne
S.Shields
Sunderland
Rossan Pt
Donegal
L.Neagh
Kirkcudbright
Carlisle
Gateshead
Durham
Hartlepool
Donegal B.
L.Erne
Omagh
Belfast
Bangor
Luce B.
Solway Firth
Pennines
Penrith
Darlington
Middlesbrough
Sligo B.
Enniskillen
Portadown
Scafell Pike 977
Yorkshire Moors
Scarborough
Erris Hd
Sligo
Armagh
Monaghan
Isle of Man
Douglas
Kendal
L.Conn
Ballina
Newry
Barrow-in-Furness
Lancaster
Flamborough Hd
Achill I.
Castlebar
L.Allen
Cavan
Dundalk
Morecambe
Harrogate
Ouse
York
Clew B.
Boyle
IRISH SEA
Blackpool
L.Mask
Roscommon
Longford
Drogheda
Preston
Bradford
Leeds
Hull
L.Ree
Huddersfield
Spurn Hd
Slyne Hd
L.Corrib
Mullingar
Bolton
Manchester
Trent
Humber
Grimsby
Galway
Athlone
Dublin
(Baile Atha Cliath)
Holyhead
Birkenhead
Liverpool
Doncaster
Galway B.
Shannon
Monasterevin
Dun Laoghaire
Anglesey
Warrington
Sheffield
Aran Is
Bray
Bangor
Chester
Lincoln
REP. OF IRELAND
Port Laoise
Snowdon 1085
Crewe
Stoke-on-Trent
The Wash
Ennis
L.Derg
Nenagh
Wicklow Mts
Wicklow
Dee
Nottingham
Kilrush
Carlow
Pwllheli
Derby
King's Lynn
Limerick
Kilkenny
Arklow
Shrewsbury
Norwich
Great Yarmouth
Tipperary
Suir
Cardigan Bay
Leicester
Nene
Ouse
Dingle
Tralee
Clonmel
Barrow
Aberystwyth
Wolverhampton
Peterborough
Lowestoft
Dingle B.
Waterford
Wexford
WALES
Birmingham
Coventry
ENGLAND
Newmarket
Carrauntoohill 1041
Killarney
Blackwater
Rosslare
St George's Chan.
Cambrian Mts
Worcester
Northampton
Cambridge
Cork
Dungarvan
Builth Wells
Bedford
Ipswich
Felixstowe
Youghal
St David's Hd
Fishguard
Brecon
Wye
Milton Keynes
Colchester
Harwich
Bantry B.
Bantry
Carmarthen
Severn
Gloucester
Luton
Old Hd of Kinsale
Oxford
Chelmsford
C.Clear
Pembroke
Swansea
Newport
Swindon
London
Southend-on-Sea
Cardiff
Bristol
Windsor
Thames
Bristol Chan.
Bath
Reading
Maidstone
Canterbury
Lundy I.
Weston-super-Mare
Dover
Barnstaple
Taunton
Guildford
Crawley
Folkestone
Winchester
Salisbury
Hastings
Str. of Dover
Bude
Southampton
Brighton
Eastbourne
Exeter
Bournemouth
Portsmouth
Boulogne
Dartmoor
Weymouth
Isle of Wight
Newquay
Plymouth
Torquay
Montreuil
Truro
English Channel
Penzance
Falmouth
Prawle Pt
Land's End
Isles of Scilly
Lizard Pt
Le Tréport
Dieppe
C.de la Hague
Pte de Barfleur
Alderney
Cherbourg
Fécamp
Le Havre
Bolbec
Guernsey
Sark
Valognes
Seine
Channel Is (U.K.)
Deauville
Rouen
Bayeux
Jersey
St Helier
St-Lô
Caen
Lisieux
Elbeuf
Louviers
Coutances
Golfe de St-Malo
NORMANDIE
Granville
Orne
Evreux
Argentan
Roscoff
Morlaix
St-Malo
Dinan
Mont-St-Michel
Domfront
Fougères
FRANCE
Alençon
Mayenne
I.d'Ouessant
Brest
St-Brieuc
Carhaix-Plouguer
Nordhordland
Dale
Bergen
Sotra
NORWAY
Sunnhordland
Stord
Leirvik
Hardangerfj.
Bømlo
Skjold
Haugesund
Karmøy
Boknafj.
Stavanger
Sandnes
Esbjerg
Vlieland
Texel
Den Helder
Alkmaar
Haarlem
NETHERLANDS
Leiden
's-Gravenhage (Den Haag)
Rotterdam
Dordrecht
Vlissingen
Zeebrugge
Oostende
Brugge
Antwerpen
BELGIUM
Gent
Mechelen
Dunkerque
Bruxelles (Brüssel)
Calais
Kortrijk
St-Omer
Tourcoing
Roubaix
Soignies
Lille
Tournai
Béthune
Lens
Mons
Douai
Valenciennes
Charleroi
Arras
Denain
Maubeuge
Cambrai
Abbeville
Fourmies
PICARDIE
St-Quentin
Amiens
Neufchâtel
Montdidier
Oise
Laon
Beauvais
Compiègne
Aisne
Soissons
Reims
Senlis
Château-Thierry
Cergy-Pontoise
Epernay
Mantes
Meaux
Versailles
Paris
ILE-DE-FRANCE
Dreux
Sézanne
Rambouillet
Provins
Romilly-s.-S
Chartres
Etampes
Melun
Fontainebleau
Troyes
Sens

1:2.5M

0 25 50 75 100 km

0 25 50 mls

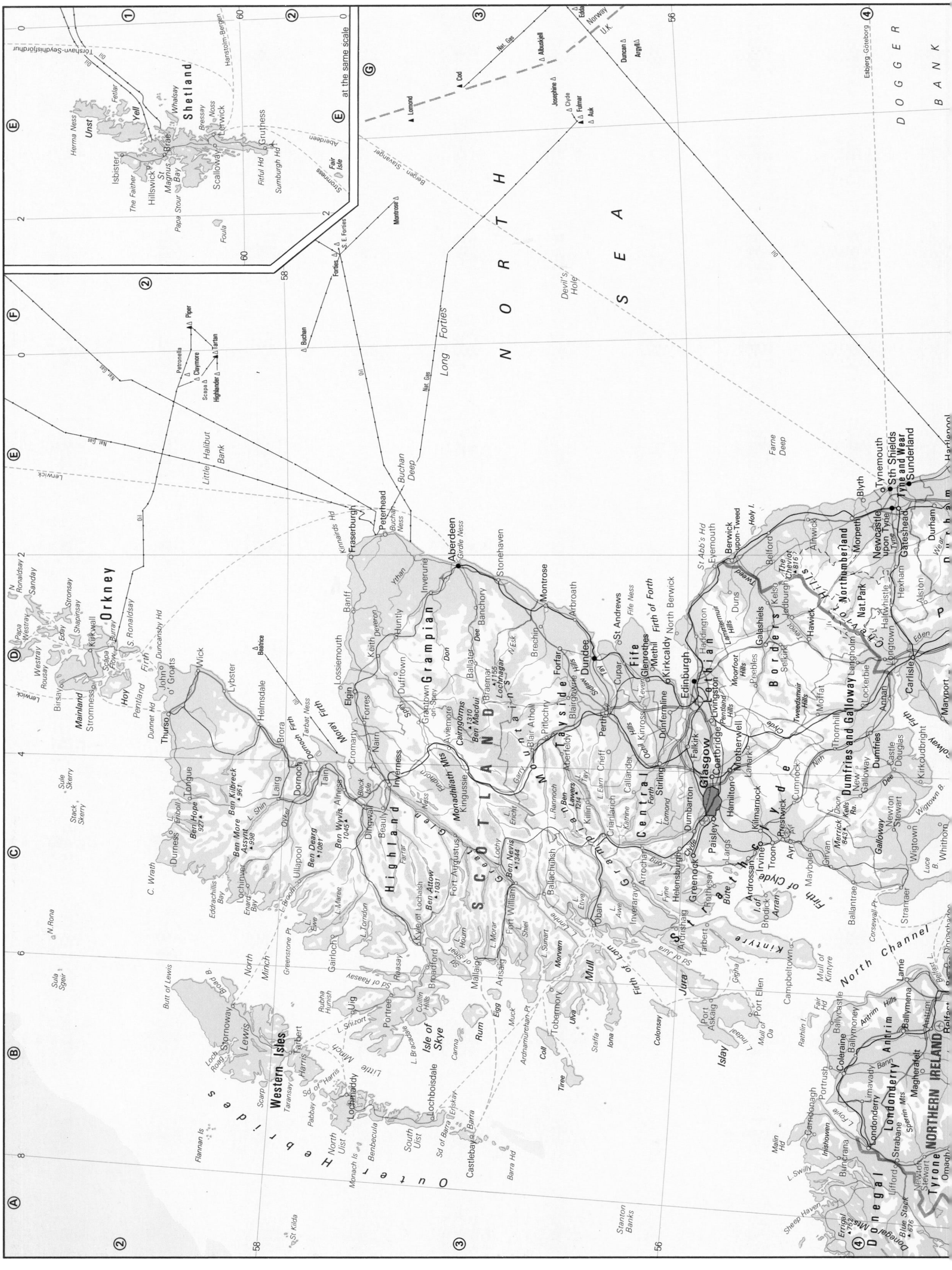

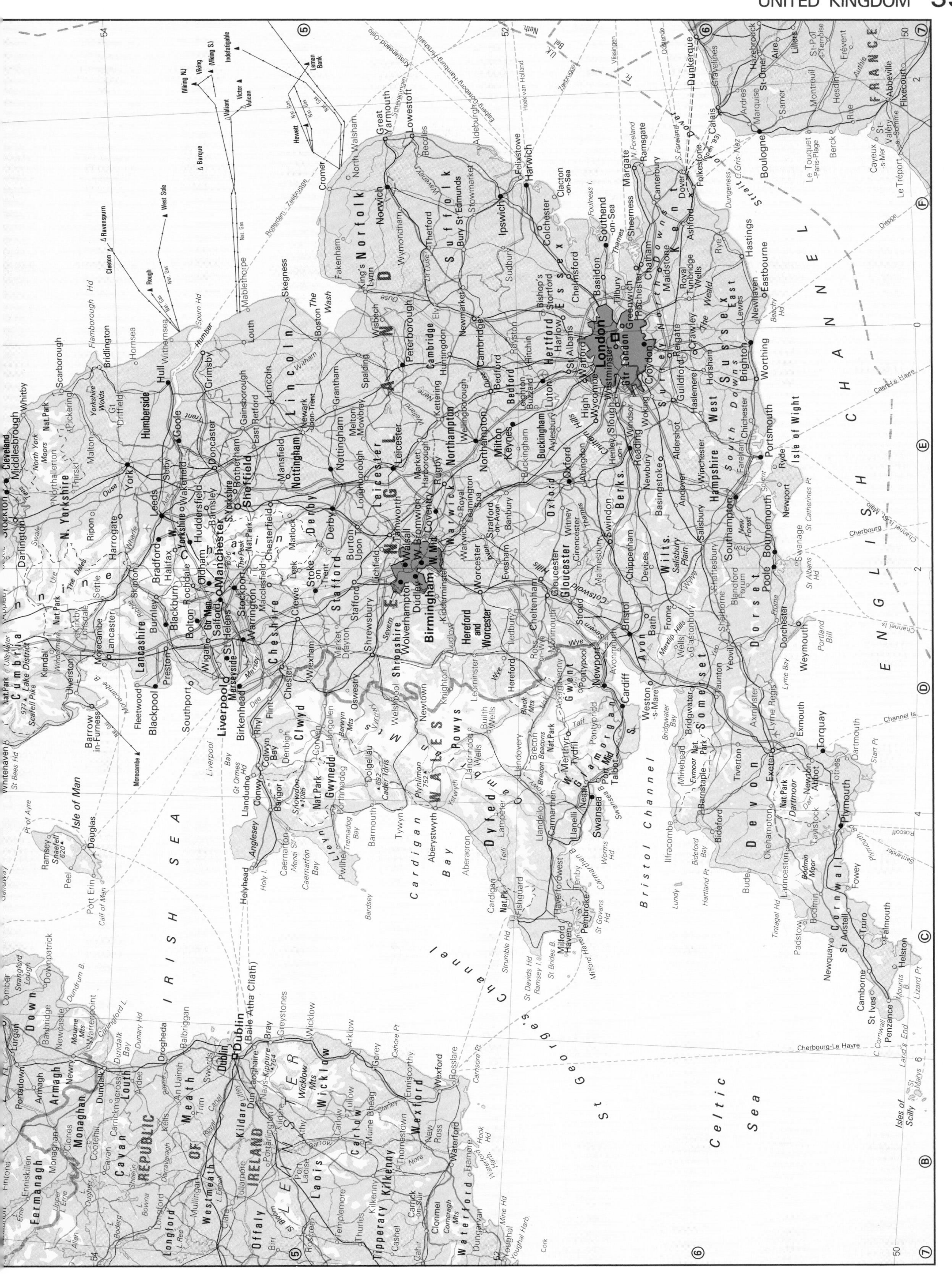

1:2.5M
0 25 50 75 100 km
0 25 50 mls

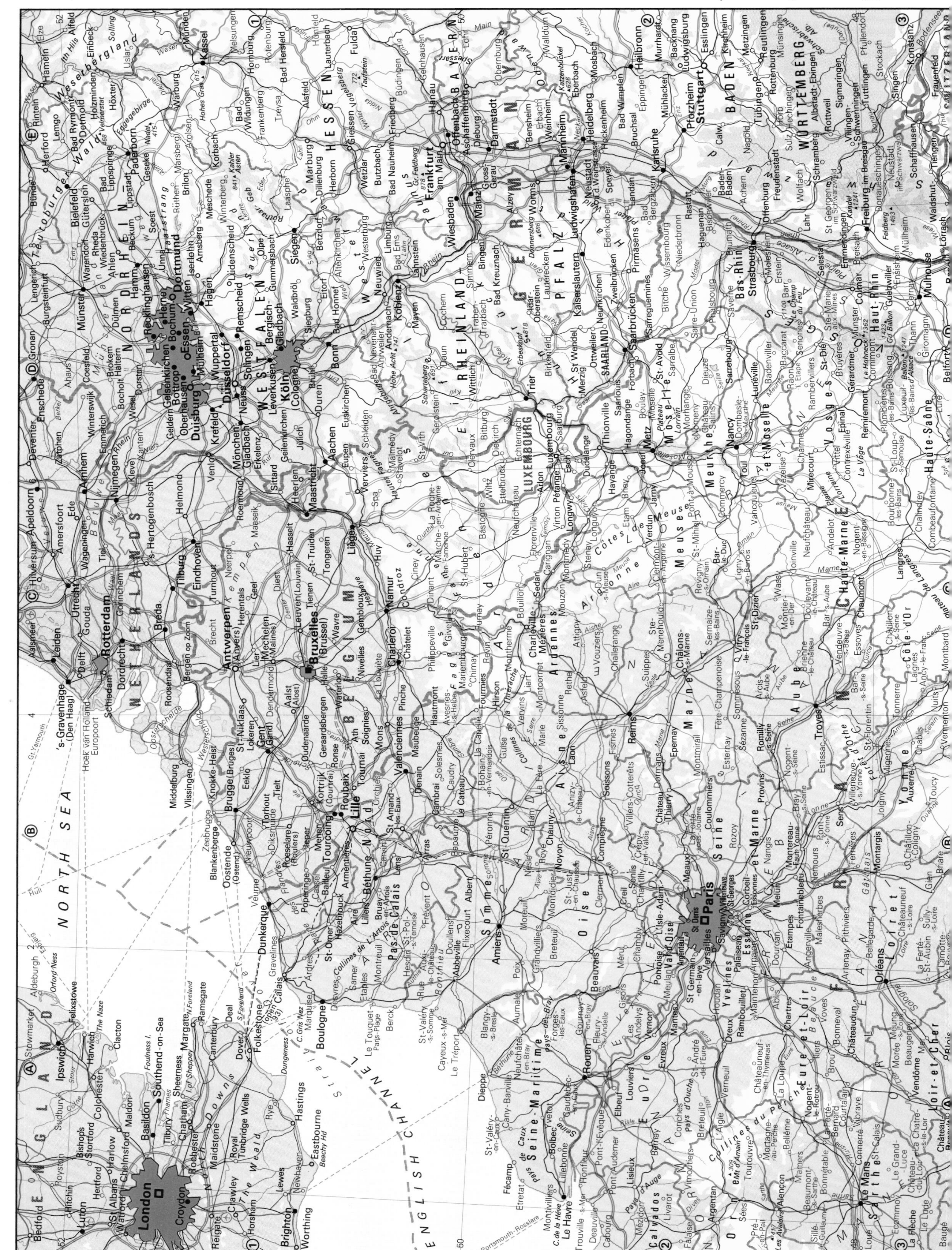

ADRIATIC SEA
LIGURIAN SEA
Golfo di Venezia
Golfo di Genova
AUSTRIA
SWITZERLAND
YUGOSLAVIA
SLOVENIA
CROATIA
MONACO
SAN MARINO
LIECHTENSTEIN
VENETO
PIEMONTE
LOMBARDIA
EMILIA ROMAGNA
TOSCANA
MARCHE
UMBRIA
TRENTINO
FRIULI
VENEZIA GIULIA
VALLE D'AOSTA
PROVENCE
Milano (Milan)
Torino (Turin)
Genova (Genoa)
Venezia (Venice)
Bologna
Firenze (Florence)
Verona
Padova (Padua)
Trieste (Trient)
Marseille
Nice
Grenoble
Genève (Geneva)
Bern (Berne)
Zürich
Basel (Basle)
Innsbruck
Bolzano (Bozen)
Lausanne
Dijon
Besançon
Ancona
Rimini
Livorno
Pisa
La Spezia
Parma
Modena
Brescia
Bergamo
Udine
Perugia
Corse (Fr.)

1:5M 0 50 100 150 200 km 0 50 100 mls

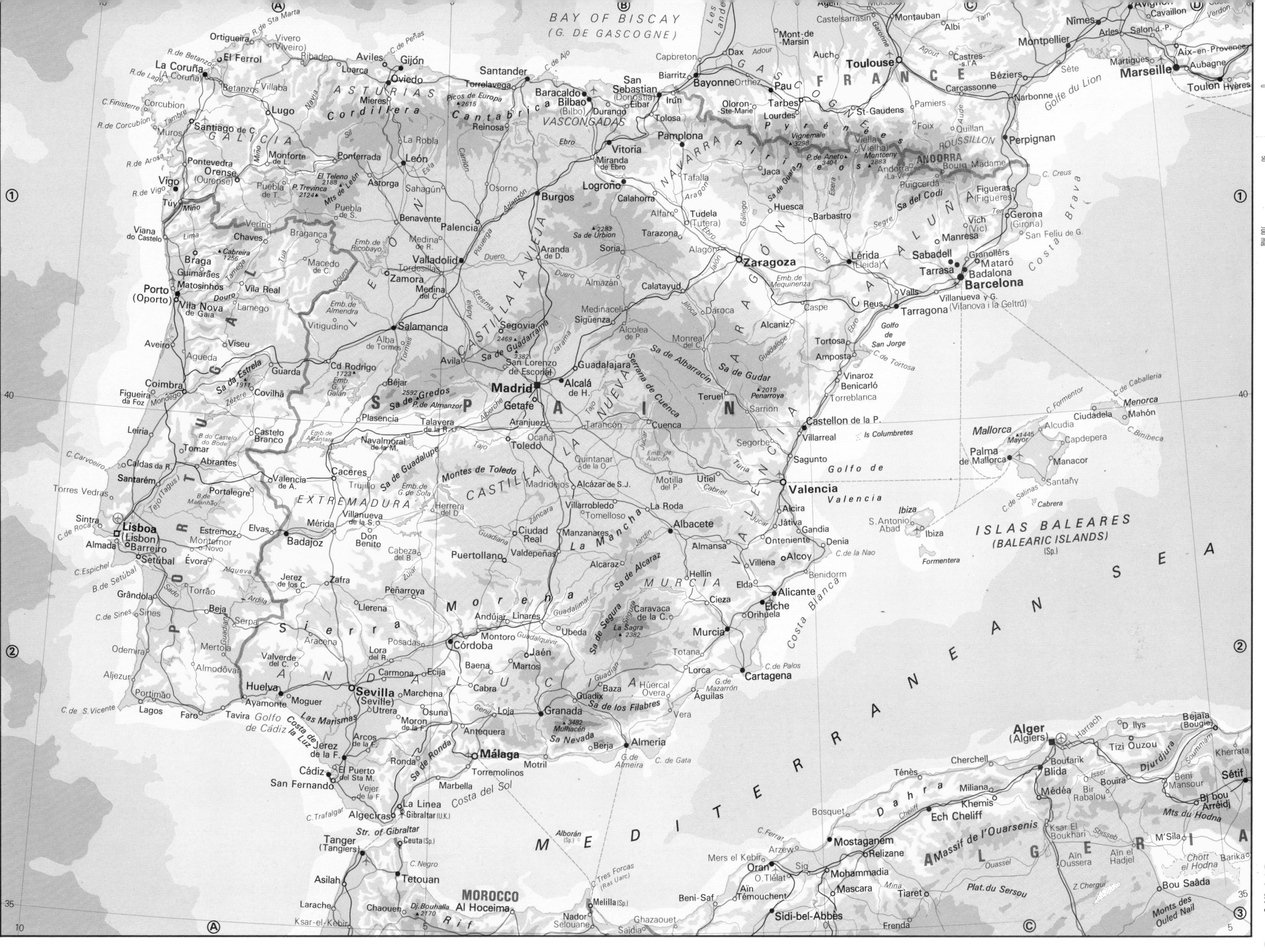
BAY OF BISCAY
(G. DE GASCOGNE)
F R A N C E
ANDORRA
P O R T U G A L
S P A I N
ISLAS BALEARES
(BALEARIC ISLANDS)
M E D I T E R R A N E A N S E A
A L G E R I A
MOROCCO
Golfe du Lion
Golfo de Valencia
Str. of Gibraltar
Madrid
Barcelona
Valencia
Sevilla
(Seville)
Zaragoza
Lisboa
(Lisbon)
Porto
(Oporto)
Málaga
Bilbao
Valladolid
Córdoba
Granada
Murcia
Alicante
Palma de Mallorca
Mallorca
Menorca
Ibiza
Formentera
Alger
(Algiers)
Oran
Toulouse
Marseille
Montpellier
Perpignan
Gibraltar (U.K.)
Ceuta (Sp.)
Melilla (Sp.)
Tanger
(Tangiers)
Tetouan
Pyrénées
Sierra Morena
Sa Nevada
Cordillera Cantabrica
Sa de Guadarrama
CASTILLA LA VIEJA
CASTILLA LA NUEVA
EXTREMADURA
ANDALUCIA
GALICIA
ASTURIAS
ARAGÓN
CATALUÑA
NAVARRA
La Mancha

1:5M
0 50 100 150 200 km
0 50 100 mls
SWITZERLAND
AUSTRIA
GERMANY
FRANCE
SLOVENIA
CROATIA
ITALIA
CORSE (CORSICA)
SARDEGNA (SARDINIA)
SICILIA (SICILY)
ALGERIA
TUNISIA
MALTA
TYRRHENIAN SEA
Ligurian Sea
MEDITERRANEAN SEA
ADRIATIC
Sicilian Channel
Malta Channel
Strait of Bonifacio
Wien
München
Zürich
Bern
Genève
Lyon
Marseille
Torino (Turin)
Milano (Milan)
Genova (Genoa)
Venezia (Venice)
Firenze (Florence)
Roma (Rome)
Napoli (Naples)
Palermo
Messina
Catania
Cagliari
Tunis
Zagreb
Ljubljana
Trieste
Bologna
Ancona
Pescara
Bari
Split (Spalato)

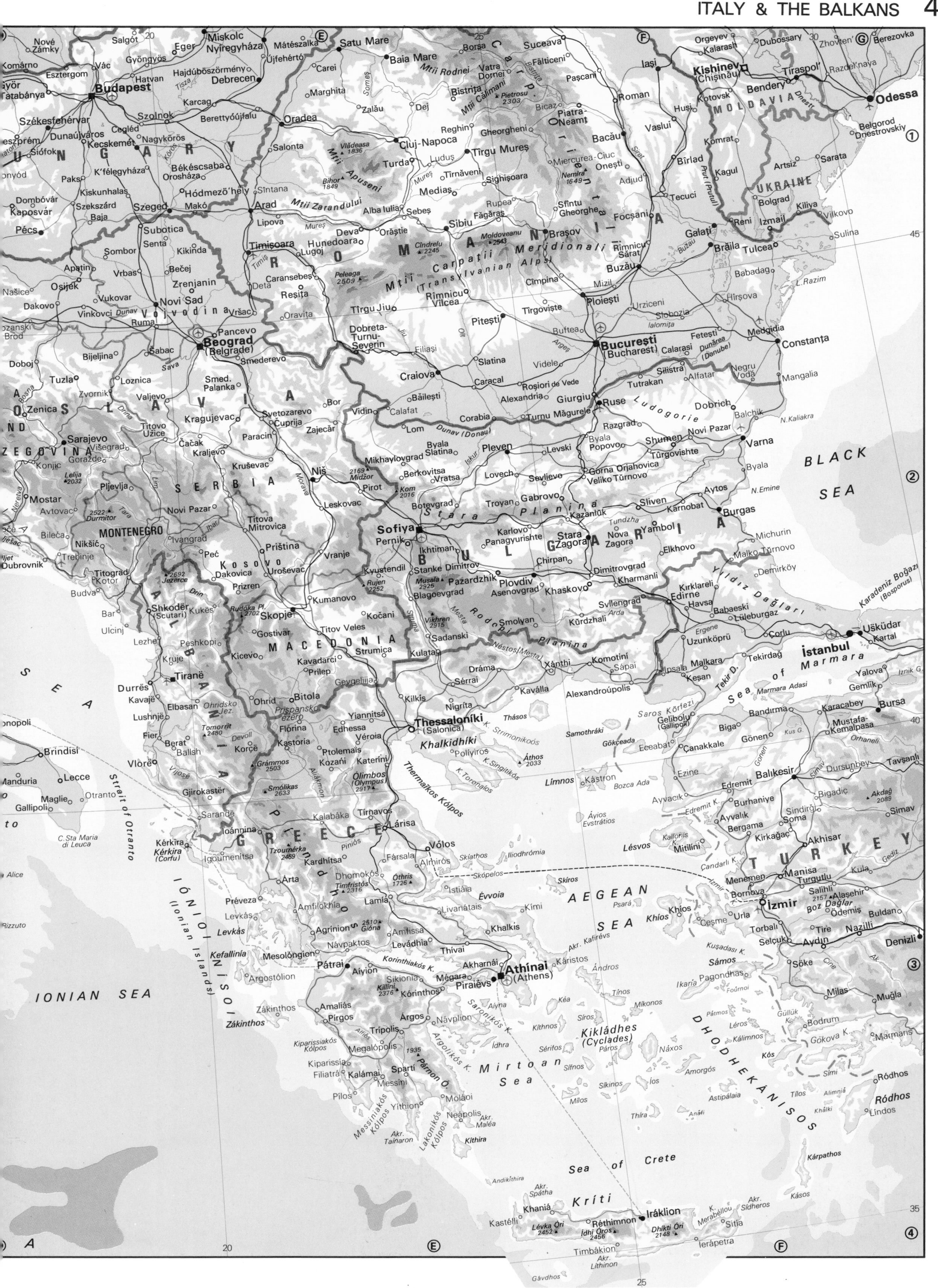

Nové Zámky
Komárno
Esztergom
Győr
Tatabánya
Salgót
Gyöngyös
Vác
Hatvan
Budapest
Eger
Miskolc
Nyíregyháza
Mátészalka
Satu Mare
Újfehértó
Hajdúböszörmény
Debrecen
Carei
Baia Mare
Mtii Rodnei
Borşa
Vatra Dornei
Suceava
Fălticeni
Paşcani
Iaşi
Kishinev (Chişinău)
Orgeyev
Kalarash
Dubossary
Zhovten'
Berezovka
Razdel'naya
Tiraspol'
Bendery
Odessa
Kotovsk
MOLDAVIA
Dnestr
Belgorod Dnestrovskiy
Székesfehérvár
Dunaújváros
Veszprém
Siófok
Kecskemét
Cegléd
Szolnok
Karcag
Berettyóújfalu
Nagykőrös
Oradea
Marghita
Zalău
Dej
Bistriţa
Mtii Călimani
Pietrosu 2303
Bicaz
Piatra-Neamţ
Roman
Huşi
Vaslui
Bacău
Reghin
Gheorgheni
Cluj-Napoca
Tîrgu Mureş
Vlădeasa 1836
Mtii Apuseni
Salonta
Békéscsaba
Orosháza
Hódmezővásárhely
Szeged
Makó
Sîntana
Arad
Turda
Luduş
Tîrnăveni
Sighişoara
Mediaş
Miercurea-Ciuc
Oneşti
Adjud
Nemira 1649
Bîrlad
Komrat
Kagul
Artsiz
Sarata
UKRAINE
Bolgrad
Kiliya
Vilkovo
Tecuci
Reni
Izmail
Sulina
Galaţi
Brăila
Tulcea
Kaposvár
Dombóvár
Pécs
Baja
Szekszárd
Kiskunhalas
Kiskunfélegyháza
Paks
Subotica
Senta
Kikinda
Sombor
Apatin
Vrbas
Bečej
Zrenjanin
Osijek
Našice
Vukovar
Vinkovci
Novi Sad
Vojvodina
Vršac
Dakovo
Ruma
Pancevo
Beograd (Belgrade)
Šabac
Bijeljina
Doboj
Tuzla
Zvornik
Loznica
Valjevo
Smederevo
Smed. Palanka
Lipova
Timişoara
Lugoj
Hunedoara
Deva
Orăştie
Alba Iulia
Sebeş
Mtii Zarandului
Bihor 1849
Sibiu
Făgăraş
Rupea
Sfîntu Gheorghe
Braşov
Focşani
Moldoveanu 2543
Cîndrelu 2245
Peleaga 2509
Carpaţii Meridionali
(Transylvanian Alps)
Rîmnicu Sărat
Buzău
Caransebeş
Reşiţa
Oraviţa
Deta
Rîmnicu Vîlcea
Tîrgu Jiu
Cîmpina
Ploieşti
Mizil
Urziceni
Slobozia
Ialomiţa
Babadag
Hîrşova
L. Razim
Piteşti
Tîrgovişte
Buftea
Bucureşti (Bucharest)
Argeş
Olt
Jiu
Dobreta-Turnu-Severin
Filiaşi
Craiova
Slatina
Caracal
Videle
Roşiori de Vede
Alexandria
Giurgiu
Ruse
Turnu Măgurele
Fetesti
Călăraşi
Dunărea (Danube)
Medgidia
Constanţa
Silistra
Tutrakan
Alfatar
Negru Vodă
Mangalia
Băileşti
Calafat
Vidin
Lom
Dunav (Donau)
Corabia
Ludogorie
Razgrad
Dobrich
Balchik
N. Kaliakra
Shumen
Novi Pazar
Târgovishte
Varna
Byala
Popovo
Levski
Pleven
Byala Slatina
Mikhaylovgrad
Berkovitsa
Vratsa
Lovech
Sevlievo
Gorna Orjahovica
Veliko Tŭrnovo
Iskur
Zenica
Sarajevo
Višegrad
Goražde
Konjic
Lelija 2032
Mostar
Avtovac
Pljevlja
Durmitor 2522
Bileća
Nikšić
Trebinje
Dubrovnik
MONTENEGRO
Titograd
Kotor
Budva
Bar
Ulcinj
Titovo Užice
Čačak
Kraljevo
Kruševac
Kragujevac
Svetozarevo
Ćuprija
Paracin
Zaječar
Bor
Niš
Midžor 2169
Pirot
Kom 2016
Leskovac
SERBIA
Novi Pazar
Titova Mitrovica
Ibar
Morava
Ivangrad
Peć
Priština
Kosovo
Vranje
Dakovica
Uroševac
Prizren
Jezerce 2692
Drin
Shkodër (Scutari)
Kukës
Rudoka Pl. 2702
Skopje
Kumanovo
Kočani
Gostivar
Titov Veles
Kicevo
MACEDONIA
Strumica
Kavadarci
Prilep
Gevgelija
Ohrid
Bitola
Ohridsko Jez.
Prespansko ezero
Lezhë
Peshkopi
Krujë
Tiranë
Durrës
Kavajë
Elbasan
Lushnjë
Fier
Berat
Ballsh
Tomorrit 2480
Devoll
Korçë
Vlorë
Vijosë
Gjirokastër
Sarandë
Grámmos 2503
Smólikas 2633
ALBANIA
Sofiya
Pernik
Ikhtiman
Botevgrad
Stara Planina
Troyan
Gabrovo
Kazanlŭk
Karlovo
Panagyurishte
Stara Zagora
Nova Zagora
Tundzha
Sliven
Yambol
Karnobat
Aytos
Burgas
N. Emine
Michurin
Malko Tŭrnovo
Elkhovo
Kyustendil
Stanke Dimitrov
Rujen 2252
Musala 2925
Pazardzhik
Plovdiv
Asenovgrad
Chirpan
Dimitrovgrad
Kharmanli
Khaskovo
Blagoevgrad
Struma
Mesta
Vikhren 2915
Rodopi Planina
Smolyan
Kŭrdzhali
Arda
Svilengrad
Sadanski
Kulata
Néstos (Mesta)
Demirköy
Yildiz Dağlari
Kirklareli
Edirne
Havsa
Babaeski
Lüleburgaz
Ergene
Uzunköprü
Çorlu
İstanbul
Üsküdar
Kartal
Karadeniz Boğazi (Bosporus)
BULGARIA
BLACK SEA
Dráma
Xánthi
Komotiní
Sápai
Sérrai
Kaválla
Alexandroúpolis
Ipsala
Malkara
Keşan
Tekirdağ
Tekir D.
Sea of Marmara
Marmara Adasi
Yalova
Gemlik
İznik G.
Bursa
Karacabey
Mustafa-Kemalpasa
Bandırma
Orhaneli
Saros Körfezi
Gelibolu (Gallipoli)
Eceabat
Çanakkale
Biga
Gönen
Kus G.
Samothráki
Gökçeada
Thásos
Kilkís
Nigríta
Yiannitsá
Thessaloníki (Salonica)
K. Strimonikós
Khalkidhikí
Políyiros
K. Singitikós
Áthos 2033
K. Toronaíos
Édhessa
Véroia
Flórina
Kastoría
Ptolemaís
Kozaní
Kateríni
Ólimbos (Olympus) 2917
Aliákmon
Thermaïkós Kólpos
Límnos
Kástron
Bozca Ada
Ezine
Balıkesir
Simav
Dursunbey
Tavşanlı
Edremit
Edremit K.
Burhaniye
Ayvacık
Ayvalık
Bergama
Sındırgı
Soma
Bigadiç
Akdağ 2089
Kırkağaç
Akhisar
Gediz
Áyios Evstrátios
Lésvos
Kalloniís K.
Mitilíni
Çandarlı K.
TURKEY
Strait of Otranto
Brindisi
Lecce
Manduria
Maglie
Otranto
Gallipoli
C. Sta Maria di Leuca
Kérkira (Corfu)
Igoumenítsa
Ioánnina
Tzouméрka 2469
Kalabáka
Tírnavos
Lárisa
Piniós
Vólos
Fársala
Almirós
Skíathos
Skópelos
Iliodhrómia
Kardhítsa
Dhomokós
Óthris 1726
Pindhos
Árta
Timfristós 2316
Préveza
Amfilokhía
Lamía
Ístiaia
Évvoia
Skíros
Livanátais
Kími
Khalkís
AEGEAN SEA
Psará
Khíos
Menemen
Manisa
Turgutlu
Kula
Bornova
İzmir
Salihli
Alaşehir
Boz Dağlar
Ödemiş
Buldan
Çeşme
Urla
Torbalı
Tire
Nazilli
Selçuk
Aydın
Denizli
Kuşadası K.
Sámos
Söke
Lefkás
Levkás
Agrínion
Gióna 2510
Ámfissa
Návpaktos
Levádhia
Thívai
Mesolóngion
Kefallinía
Argostólion
Pátrai
Aíyion
Korinthiakós K.
Sikionía
Kilíni 2376
Kórinthos
Mégara
Piraiévs
Akharnaí
Athínai (Athens)
Káristos
Akr. Kafirévs
Ándros
Tínos
Ikaría
Pagondhas
Foúrnoi
Mílas
Muğla
IONIAN SEA
IÓNIOI NÍSOI (Ionian Islands)
Zákinthos
Amaliás
Pírgos
Trípolis
Árgos
Návplion
Saronikós K.
Aíyna
Kéa
Míkonos
Síros
Kíthnos
Kikládhes (Cyclades)
Sérifos
Páros
Náxos
Léros
Pátmos
Kálimnos
Güllük K.
Bodrum
Gökova K.
Marmaris
Kós
Kiparissiakós Kólpos
Megalópolis
Argolikós K.
Ídhra
Kiparissía
Filiatrá
Kalámai
Spartí
Messíni
Párnon Ó.
Mirtoan Sea
Sífnos
Amorgós
DHODHEKÁNISOS
Sími
Tílos
Alimniá
Ródhos
Khálki
Líndos
Pílos
Yíthion
Moláoi
Messiniakós Kólpos
Lakonikós Kólpos
Neápolis
Akr. Maléa
Kíthira
Akr. Taínaron
Síkinos
Mílos
Íos
Thíra
Astipálaia
Anáfi
Kárpathos
Kásos
Sea of Crete
Andikíthira
Akr. Spátha
Khaniá
Kríti
Kastélli
Lévka Óri 2452
Réthimnon
Ídhi Óros 2456
Iráklion
Dhíkti Óri 2148
K. Merabéllou
Sitía
Akr. Sídheros
Timbákion
Ierápetra
Akr. Líthinon
Gávdhos
Rizzuto
Alice

1:5M

0 50 100 150 200 km
0 50 100 mls
NORTH SEA
Kattegat
DENMARK
Jylland (Jutland)
SWEDEN
BALT
København (Copenhagen)
Göteborg
Jönköping
Ålborg
Århus
Odense
Malmö
Helsingborg
Bornholm
SCHLESWIG-HOLSTEIN
MECKLENBURG-VORPOMMERN
NIEDERSACHSEN
BRANDENBURG
SACHSEN-ANHALT
NORDRHEIN-WESTFALEN
HESSEN
THÜRINGEN
SACHSEN
RHEINLAND-PFALZ
SAAR-LAND
BADEN-WÜRTTEMBERG
BAYERN
GERMANY
NETHERLANDS
BELGIUM
LUXEMBOURG
FRANCE
CHAMPAGNE
LORRAINE
BOURGOGNE
FRANCHE-COMTÉ
SAVOIE
DAUPHINÉ
SWITZERLAND
AUSTRIA
ITALY
SLOVENIA
CROATIA
ČESKÉ ZEMĚ
CZECH
Hamburg
Bremen
Hannover
Berlin
Rostock
Kiel
Lübeck
Leipzig
Dresden
Magdeburg
Köln
Düsseldorf
Essen
Dortmund
Duisburg
Frankfurt
Stuttgart
München (Munich)
Nürnberg
Amsterdam
Rotterdam
's-Gravenhage (Den Haag)
Antwerpen (Anvers)
Bruxelles (Brüssel)
Lille
Luxembourg
Strasbourg
Zürich
Bern
Genève
Lyon
Torino (Turin)
Milano (Milan)
Venezia (Venice)
Innsbruck
Salzburg
Wien (Vienna)
Graz
Praha (Prague)
Ljubljana
Zagreb
Szczecin
Poznań
Wrocław (Breslau)

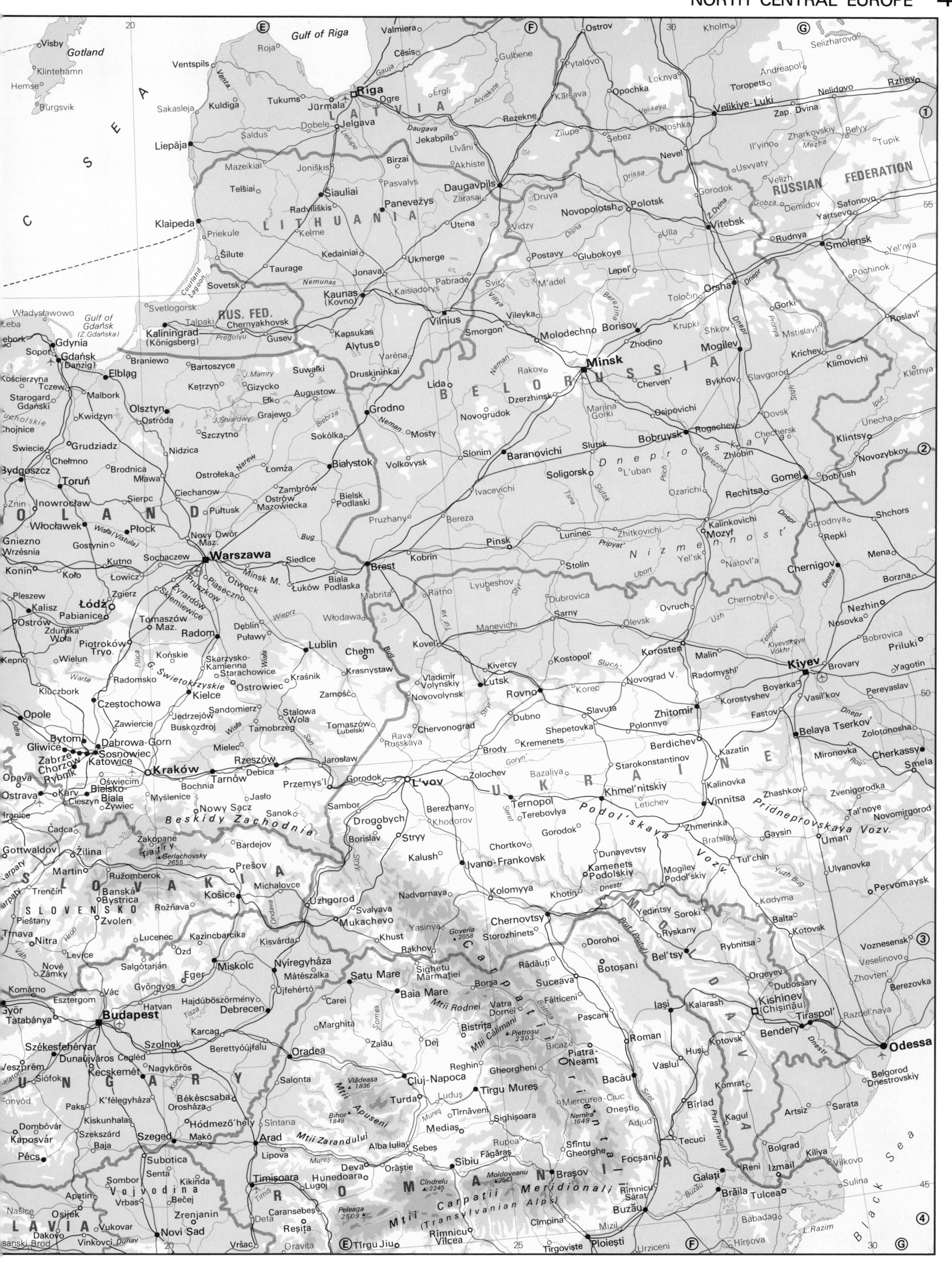
Gulf of Riga
Gotland
Visby
Klintehamn
Hemse
Burgsvik
Ventspils
Roja
Valmiera
Cēsis
Gulbene
Ostrov
Kholm
Selizharovo
Riga
Jūrmala
Tukums
Kuldiga
Sakasleja
Ogre
Ērgli
Jelgava
Dobele
Saldus
Liepāja
L A T V I A
Daugava
Jekabpils
Līvāni
Rezekne
Kārsava
Pytalovo
Opochka
Loknya
Toropets
Andreapol'
Nelidovo
Rzhev
Velikiye-Luki
Zap. Dvina
Pustoshka
Zilupe
Sebez
Nevel
Il'yino
Zharkovskiy
Belyy
Tupik
Mazeikiai
Joniškis
Birzai
Akhiste
Pasvalys
Telšiai
Šiauliai
Panevežys
Daugavpils
Zarasai
Druya
Novopolotsk
Polotsk
Usvyaty
Velizh
Gorodok
RUSSIAN FEDERATION
Demidov
Safonovo
Yartsevo
Radviliškis
Klaipeda
Priekule
L I T H U A N I A
Kelme
Utena
Vidzy
Vitebsk
Ulla
Rudnya
Smolensk
Yel'nya
Šilute
Taurage
Kedainiai
Ukmerge
Postavy
Glubokoye
Lepel'
Pochinok
Nemunas
Jonava
Pabrade
Svir'
M'adel
Kaunas (Kovno)
Kaisiadorys
Sovetsk
Courland Lagoon
Tološin
Orsha
Dnepr
Gorki
Roslavl'
Władysławowo
Gulf of Gdańsk (Z. Gdańska)
Svetlogorsk
RUS. FED.
Talpaki
Chernyakhovsk
Kaliningrad (Königsberg)
Pregolya
Gusev
Kapsukas
Alytus
Vilnius
Vileyka
Smorgon'
Molodechno
Borisov
Krupki
Shkov
Mstislavl'
Zhodino
Mogilev
Krichev
Klimovichi
Klětnya
Gdynia
Sopot
Gdańsk (Danzig)
Braniewo
Elbląg
Bartoszyce
Varėna
Druskininkai
Minsk
Rakov
Lida
B E L O R U S S I A
Cherven'
Bykhov
Slavgorod
Kościerzyna
Tczew
Starogard Gdański
Malbork
Kętrzyn
Gizycko
Ełk
Suwałki
Augustow
Dzerzhinsk
Olsztyn
Ostróda
Kwidzyn
Chojnice
Grajewo
Grodno
Novogrudok
Marjina Gorki
Osipovichi
Dovsk
Unecha
Swiecie
Grudziadz
Szczytno
Sokólka
Mosty
Rogachev
Chechersk
Klintsy
Nidzica
Chełmno
Bydgoszcz
Toruń
Brodnica
Mława
Ostrołęka
Łomża
Białystok
Volkovysk
Slonim
Baranovichi
Slutsk
Bobruysk
Zhlobin
Novozybkov
Soligorsk
L'uban
Dnepro
Gomel
Dobrush
Ciechanow
Zambrów
Ostrów Mazowiecka
Bielsk Podlaski
Ivacevichi
Ozarichi
Rechitsa
Inowrocław
Sierpc
Pułtusk
Pruzhany
Bereza
Shchors
Włocławek
Płock
Nowy Dwór Maz.
Bug
Pinsk
Luninec
Zhitkovichi
Kalinkovichi
Mozyr'
Gorodnya
Repki
Gniezno
Września
Gostynin
Kutno
Sochaczew
Warszawa
Siedlce
Brest
Kobrin
Stolin
Yel'sk
Narovl'a
Chernigov
Mena
Konin
Koło
Łowicz
Minsk M.
Biala Podlaska
Łuków
Otwock
Piaseczno
Pruszków
Żyrardów
Skierniewice
Borzna
Pleszew
Kalisz
Łódź
Zgierz
Pabianice
Mabrita
Ratno
Lyubeshov
Dubrovica
Chernobyl
Ovruch
Nezhin
Ostrów
Zduńska Wola
Tomaszów Maz.
Radom
Dęblin
Puławy
Włodawa
Sarny
Manevichi
Olevsk
Nosovka
Bobrovica
Priluki
Piotrków Tryb.
Wieluń
Kepno
Lublin
Chełm
Kovel'
Korosten'
Malin
Kiyev
Brovary
Yagotin
Końskie
Skarżysko-Kamienna
Starachowice
Kraśnik
Krasnystaw
Kivercy
Kostopol'
Radomysl'
Kluczbork
Radomsko
Kielce
Ostrowiec
Zamość
Vladimir Volynskiy
Novovolynsk
Lutsk
Rovno
Korec
Novograd V.
Boyarka
Vasil'kov
Pereyaslav
Opole
Częstochowa
Jedrzejów
Sandomierz
Stalowa Wola
Zhitomir
Korostyshev
Fastov
Zawiercie
Buskozdroj
Tarnobrzeg
Tomaszów Lubelski
Chervonograd
Dubno
Slavuta
Shepetovka
Polonnye
Belaya Tserkov'
Zolotonosha
Bytom
Gliwice
Zabrze
Chorzów
Rybnik
Dabrowa-Gorn
Sosnowiec
Katowice
Mielec
Rava Russkaya
Brody
Kremenets
Berdichev
Kazatin
Cherkassy
Mironovka
Smela
Kraków
Tarnów
Rzeszów
Debica
Jarosław
Przemysl
Gorodok
L'vov
Zolochev
Bazaliya
Starokonstantinov
Opava
Ostrava
Oświęcim
Bielsko-Biala
Cieszyn
Zywiec
Myślenice
Bochnia
Jasło
Nowy Sącz
Sanok
Sambor
Berezhany
Ternopol
Terebovlya
Khmel'nitskiy
Letichev
Vinnitsa
Kalinovka
Zhashkov
Zvenigorodka
Tal'noye
Novomirgorod
Beskidy Zachodnie
Drogobych
Borislav
Stryy
Khodorov
Gorodok
Podol'skaya Vozv.
Zhmerinka
Pridneprovskaya Vozv.
Uman
Gaysin
Čadca
Žilina
Zakopane
Tatry
Gerlachovsky 2655
Bardejov
Kalush
Chortkov
Dunayevtsy
Bratslav
Tul'chin
Gottwaldov
Martin
Ružomberok
Prešov
Ivano-Frankovsk
Kamenets Podolskiy
Mogilev Podol'skiy
Ulyanovka
Trenčín
Banská Bystrica
Michalovce
Nadvornaya
Kolomyya
Khotin
Dnestr
Pervomaysk
S L O V E N S K O
Rožňava
Košice
Uzhgorod
Svalyava
Mukachevo
Yasinya
Goverla 2058
Chernovtsy
Storozhinets
Yedintsy
Soroki
Kodyma
Piešťany
Zvolen
Balta
Kotovsk
Trnava
Nitra
Lucenec
Kazincbarcika
Kisvárda
Khust
Rakhov
Dorohoi
Ryskany
Rybnitsa
Voznesensk
Levice
Ózd
Salgótarján
Eger
Miskolc
Nyíregyháza
Mátészalka
Sighetu Marmaţiei
Rădăuţi
Botoşani
Bel'tsy
Veselinovo
Nové Zámky
Komárno
Vác
Gyöngyös
Hajdúböszörmény
Újfehértó
Satu Mare
Baia Mare
Borşa
Suceava
Fălticeni
Orgeyev
Dubossary
Zhovten'
Berezovka
Győr
Esztergom
Tatabánya
Budapest
Hatvan
Debrecen
Carei
Mtii Rodnei
Vatra Dornei
Paşcani
Iaşi
Kalarash
Kishinev (Chişinău)
Tiraspol'
Razdel'naya
Karcag
Marghita
Bistriţa
Mtii Căliman
Pietrosu 2303
Roman
Bendery
Odessa
Székesfehérvár
Dunaújváros
Cegléd
Szolnok
Berettyóújfalu
Oradea
Zalău
Dej
Bicaz
Piatra-Neamţ
Vaslui
Huşi
Kotovsk
Veszprém
Siófok
Kecskemét
Nagykőrös
Salonta
Cluj-Napoca
Reghin
Gheorgheni
Bacău
Belgorod Dnestrovskiy
Paks
Kiskunhalas
Kiskunfélegyháza
Békéscsaba
Orosháza
Hódmezővásárhely
Vlădeasa 1836
Mtii Apuseni
Turda
Luduş
Tîrgu Mureş
Tîrnăveni
Miercurea-Ciuc
Oneşti
Komrat
Bîrlad
Artsiz
Sarata
Dombóvár
Kaposvár
Szekszárd
Baja
Szeged
Makó
Sîntana
Arad
Bihor 1849
Mtii Zarandului
Mediaş
Sighişoara
Nemira 1649
Adjud
Kagul
Tecuci
Pécs
Lipova
Alba Iulia
Sebeş
Rupea
Făgăraş
Sfîntu Gheorghe
Focşani
Bolgrad
Kiliya
Vilkovo
Subotica
Senta
Kikinda
Sombor
Timişoara
Hunedoara
Deva
Orăştie
Sibiu
Braşov
Reni
Izmail
Galaţi
Brăila
Tulcea
Sulina
Black Sea
Apatin
Vojvodina
Vrbas
Bečej
Lugoj
Cindrelu 2245
Moldoveanu 2543
Carpaţii Meridionali
Rîmnicu Sărat
Buzău
Našice
Osijek
Vukovar
Zrenjanin
Caransebeş
Peleaga 2509
Mtii Carpaţii (Transylvanian Alps)
Cîmpina
Babadag
Razim
Dakovo
Vinkovci
Novi Sad
Deta
Reşiţa
Rîmnicu Vîlcea
Mizil
Ploieşti
Brod
Vršac
Oravita
Tîrgu Jiu
Tîrgovişte
Urziceni
Hîrşova
U K R A I N E
R O M A N I A
H U N G A R Y
S L O V A K I A
P O L A N D
M O L D A V I A
Nizmennost'
Carpaţii Orientali
20
25
30
45
50
55
E
F
G
1
2
3
4

1:10M 0 100 200 300 400 km 0 100 200 mls

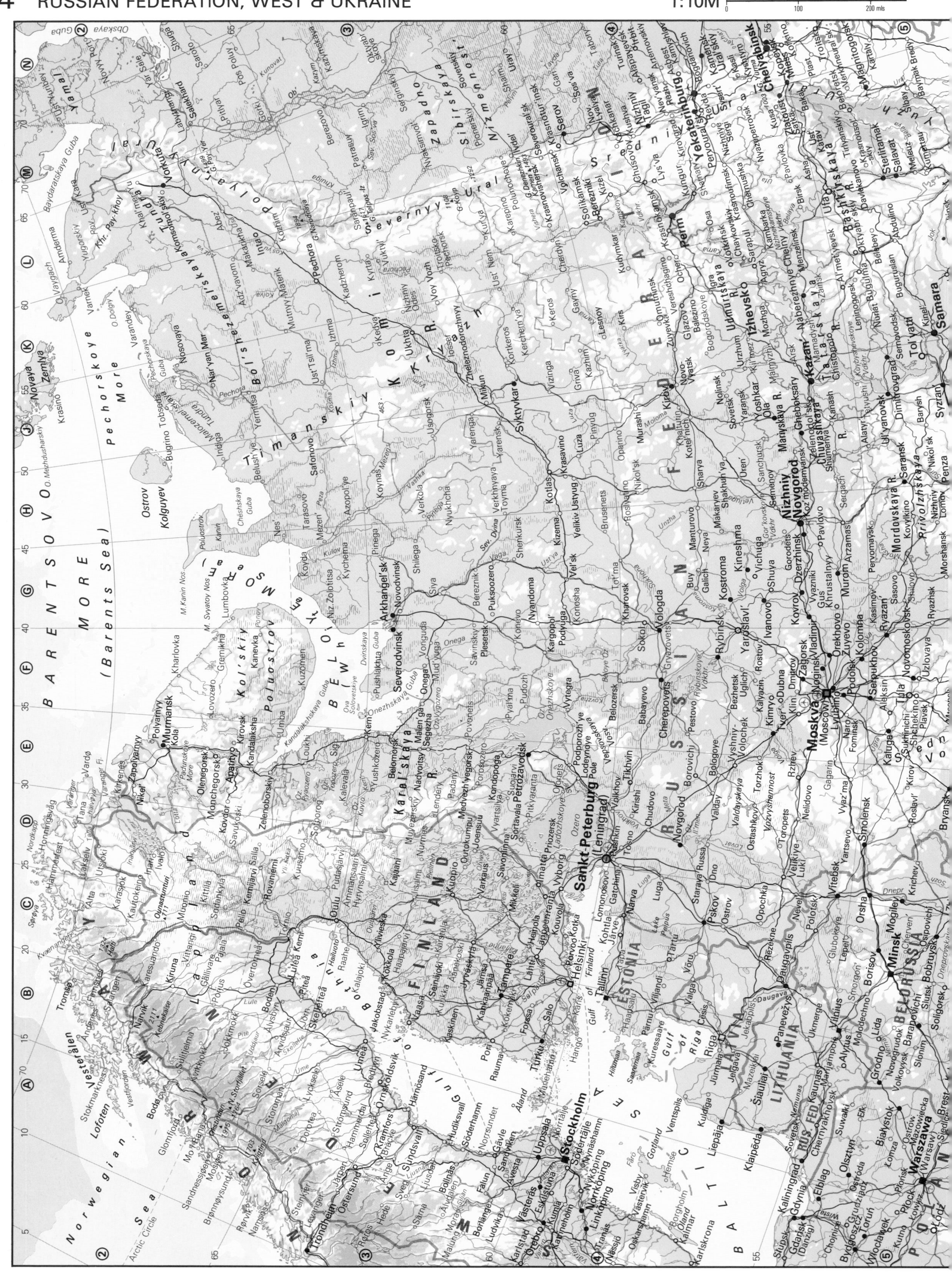

1 Severo-Osetinskaya R.
2 Adzharskaya R.
3 Checheno-Ingushskaya R.
4 Kabardino-Balkarskaya R.
5 Nakhichevanskaya R. (to Azerbaijan)
BLACK SEA
CASPIAN SEA
Azovskoye More
Mediterranean Sea
UKRAINE
KAZAKHSTAN
TURKEY
IRAN
IRAQ
SYRIA
ROMANIA
GEORGIA
ARMENIA
AZERBAIJAN
TURKMENISTAN
UZBEKISTAN
MOLDAVIA
BULGARIA
GREECE
HUNGARY
CYPRUS

1:40M

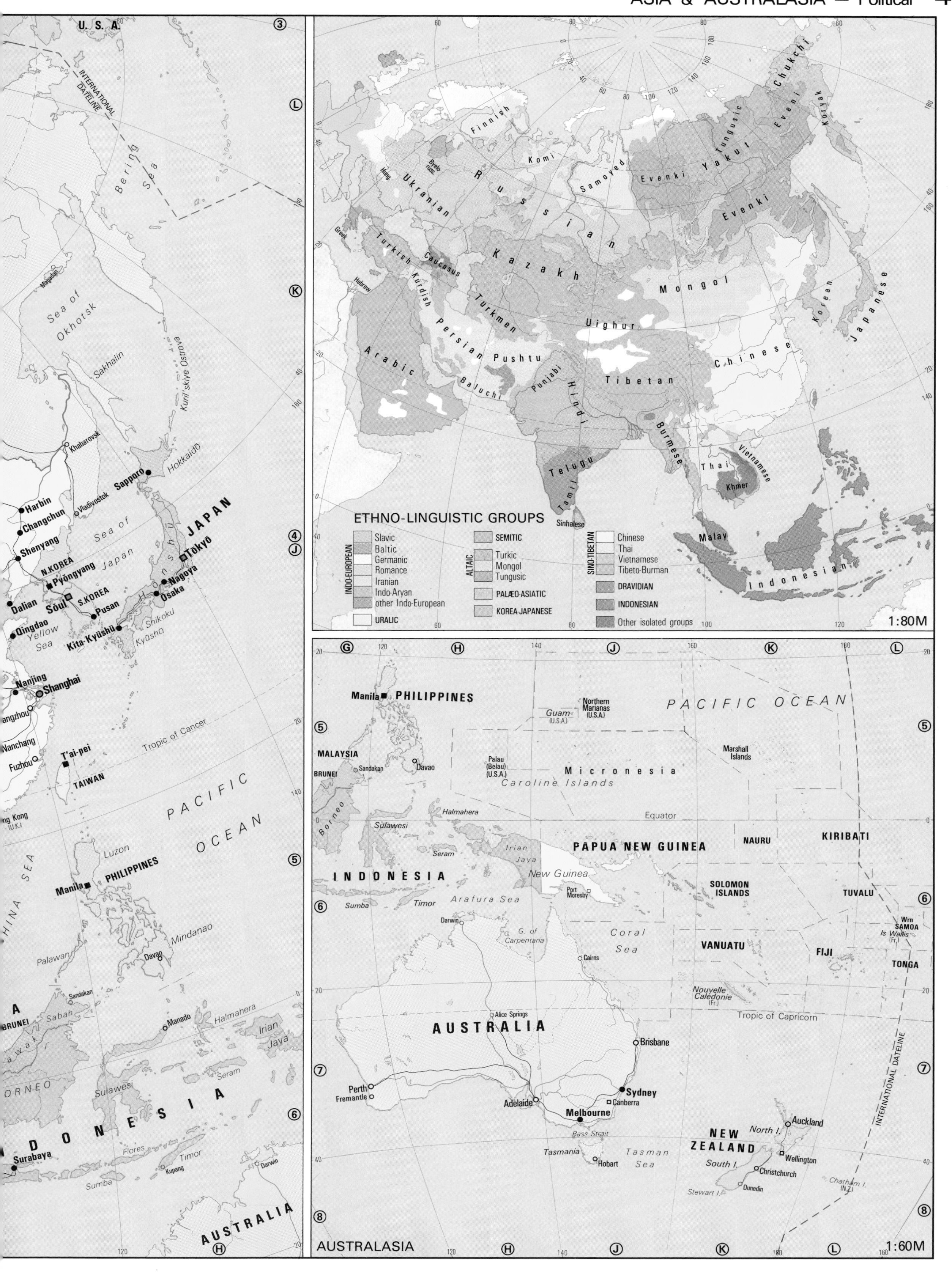

U. S. A.
INTERNATIONAL DATELINE
Bering Sea
Sea of Okhotsk
Sakhalin
Kuril'skiye Ostrova
Magadan
Khabarovsk
Hokkaidō
Sapporo
Harbin
Changchun
Vladivostok
Shenyang
Sea of Japan
JAPAN
Honshū
Tōkyō
Nagoya
Ōsaka
N.KOREA
P'yŏngyang
S.KOREA
Sŏul
Dalian
Pusan
Qingdao
Yellow Sea
Kita-Kyūshū
Shikoku
Kyūshū
Nanjing
Shanghai
Hangzhou
Nanchang
Fuzhou
T'ai-pei
TAIWAN
Tropic of Cancer
Hong Kong (U.K.)
PACIFIC OCEAN
Luzon
Manila
PHILIPPINES
Mindanao
Davao
Palawan
Sandakan
Sabah
BRUNEI
Manado
Halmahera
Irian Jaya
Seram
Sulawesi
BORNEO
INDONESIA
Surabaya
Flores
Timor
Kupang
Sumba
Darwin
AUSTRALIA
Finnish
Komi
Byelorus.
Hung.
Ukranian
Russian
Samoyed
Evenki
Yakut
Tungusic
Eveni
Chukchi
Koryak
Greek
Turkish
Caucasus
Kurdish
Hebrew
Kazakh
Turkmen
Mongol
Uighur
Korean
Japanese
Persian
Arabic
Pushtu
Baluchi
Punjabi
Hindi
Tibetan
Chinese
Burmese
Telugu
Tamil
Sinhalese
Thai
Vietnamese
Khmer
Malay
Indonesian
ETHNO-LINGUISTIC GROUPS
INDO-EUROPEAN
Slavic
Baltic
Germanic
Romance
Iranian
Indo-Aryan
other Indo-European
URALIC
SEMITIC
ALTAIC
Turkic
Mongol
Tungusic
PALÆO-ASIATIC
KOREA-JAPANESE
SINO-TIBETAN
Chinese
Thai
Vietnamese
Tibeto-Burman
DRAVIDIAN
INDONESIAN
Other isolated groups
1:80M
Manila
PHILIPPINES
Guam (U.S.A.)
Northern Marianas (U.S.A.)
PACIFIC OCEAN
MALAYSIA
BRUNEI
Sandakan
Davao
Palau (Belau) (U.S.A.)
Micronesia
Caroline Islands
Marshall Islands
Borneo
Halmahera
Sulawesi
Equator
Seram
Irian Jaya
PAPUA NEW GUINEA
NAURU
KIRIBATI
INDONESIA
New Guinea
Port Moresby
SOLOMON ISLANDS
TUVALU
Sumba
Timor
Arafura Sea
Darwin
G. of Carpentaria
Coral Sea
Cairns
VANUATU
FIJI
Wrn SAMOA
Is Wallis (Fr.)
TONGA
Nouvelle Calédonie (Fr.)
Alice Springs
Tropic of Capricorn
AUSTRALIA
Brisbane
INTERNATIONAL DATELINE
Perth
Fremantle
Sydney
Adelaide
Canberra
Melbourne
Bass Strait
Tasmania
Hobart
Tasman Sea
NEW ZEALAND
North I.
Auckland
Wellington
South I.
Christchurch
Dunedin
Stewart I.
Chatham I. (N.Z.)
AUSTRALASIA
1:60M

1:20M

0 200 400 600 800 km

0 200 400 mls

RUSSIAN FEDERATION
1 Chuvashkaya R.
2 Checheno-Ingushskaya R.
3 Severo-Osetinskaya R.
4 Kabardino- Balkarskaya R.

GEORGIA
5 Abkhazskaya R.
6 Adzharskaya R.

AZERBAIJAN
7 Nakhichevanskaya R.

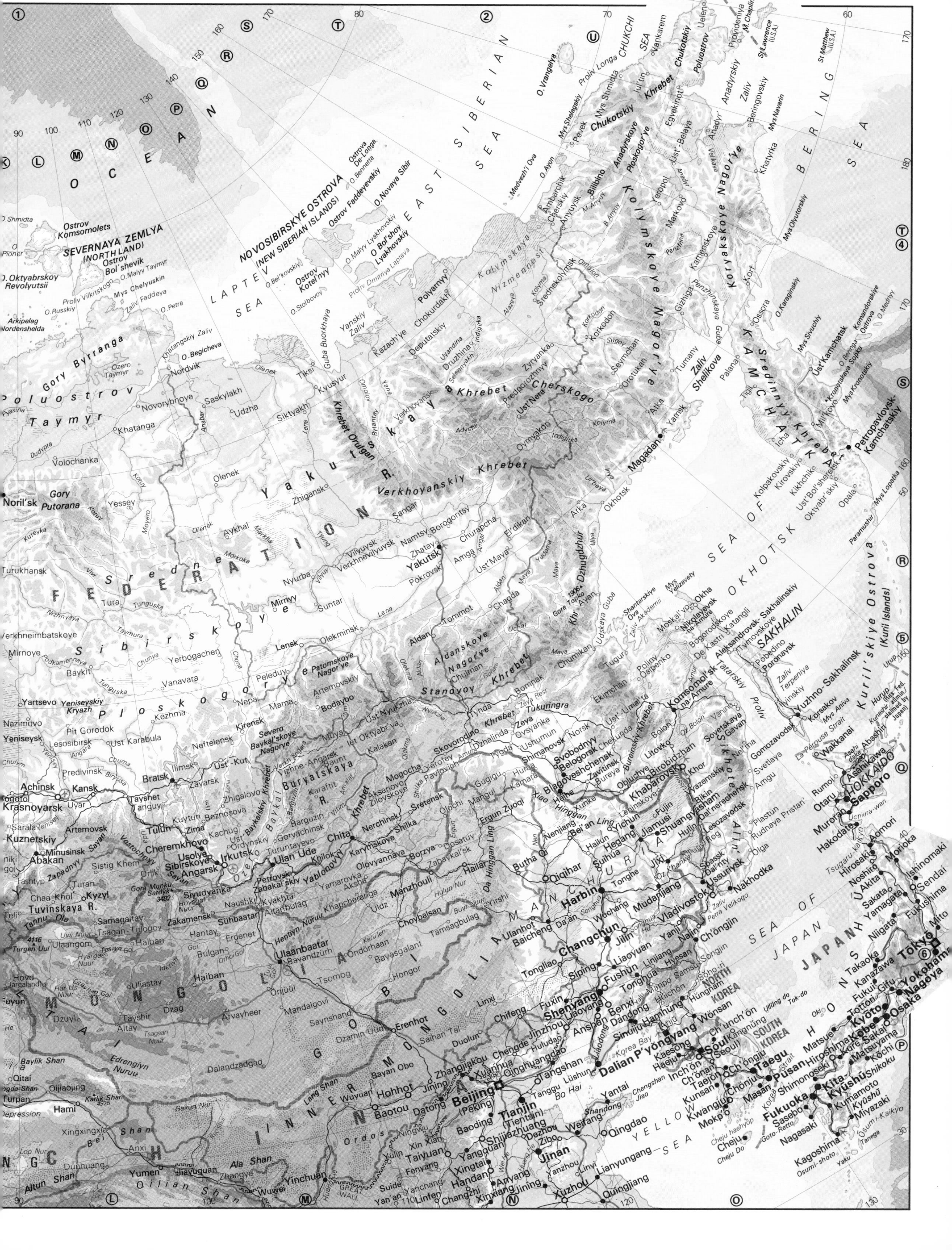

1:20M

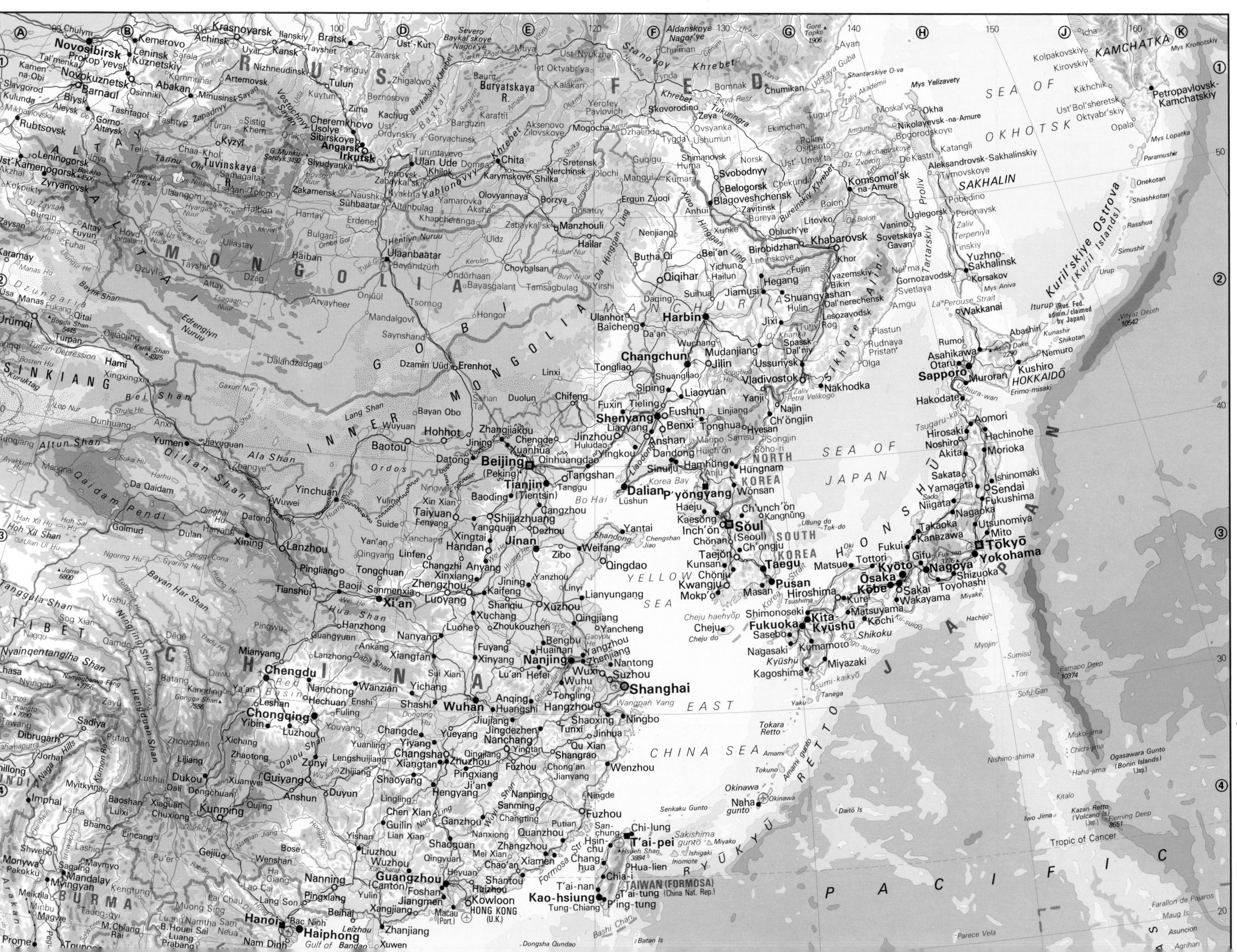
KAMCHATKA
Petropavlovsk-Kamchatskiy
SEA OF OKHOTSK
SAKHALIN
Kuril'skiye Ostrova (Kuril Islands)
HOKKAIDŌ
Sapporo
Tōkyō
Yokohama
Nagoya
Ōsaka
Kyōto
Kōbe
Hiroshima
Kyūshū
Shikoku
SEA OF JAPAN
NORTH KOREA
SOUTH KOREA
P'yŏngyang
Sŏul
Pusan
Taegu
Vladivostok
Khabarovsk
Harbin
Changchun
Shenyang
Dalian
Beijing (Peking)
Tianjin
YELLOW SEA
EAST CHINA SEA
Shanghai
Nanjing
Wuhan
Xi'an
Lanzhou
Chengdu
Chongqing
Kunming
Guangzhou (Canton)
Kowloon
HONG KONG (U.K.)
TAIWAN (FORMOSA)
T'ai-pei
Kao-hsiung
Tropic of Cancer
Hanoi
Haiphong
BURMA
Mandalay
TIBET
Lhasa
SINKIANG
Ürümqi
MONGOLIA
Ulaanbaatar
Irkutsk
Krasnoyarsk
Novosibirsk

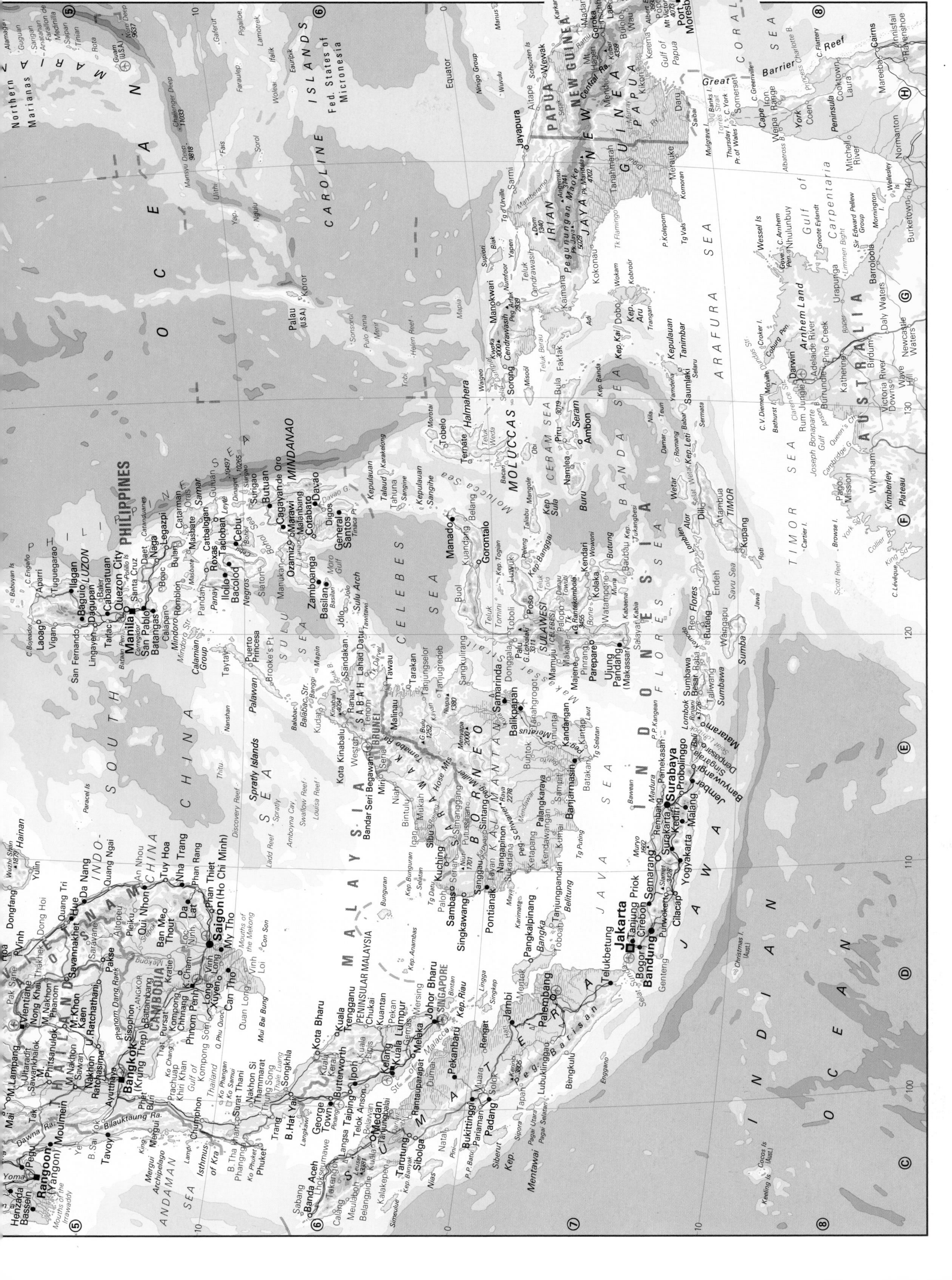

PHILIPPINES
LUZON
MINDANAO
Manila
Quezon City
SOUTH CHINA SEA
SULU SEA
CELEBES SEA
MOLUCCAS
CERAM SEA
BANDA SEA
FLORES SEA
JAVA SEA
ARAFURA SEA
TIMOR SEA
CORAL SEA
INDIAN OCEAN
CAROLINE ISLANDS
Fed. States of Micronesia
NEW GUINEA
PAPUA NEW GUINEA
IRIAN JAYA
BORNEO
SARAWAK
SABAH
BRUNEI
KALIMANTAN
SULAWESI (CELEBES)
INDONESIA
MALAYSIA
PENINSULAR MALAYSIA
SINGAPORE
SUMATERA
JAWA
TIMOR
AUSTRALIA
Arnhem Land
Gulf of Carpentaria
THAILAND
CAMBODIA
VIETNAM
Bangkok (Krung Thep)
Saigon (Ho Chi Minh)
Phnom Penh
Rangoon (Yangon)
Kuala Lumpur
Jakarta
Surabaya
Bandung
Semarang
Medan
Palembang
Port Moresby
Darwin
Hainan
ANDAMAN SEA
Equator

1:10M

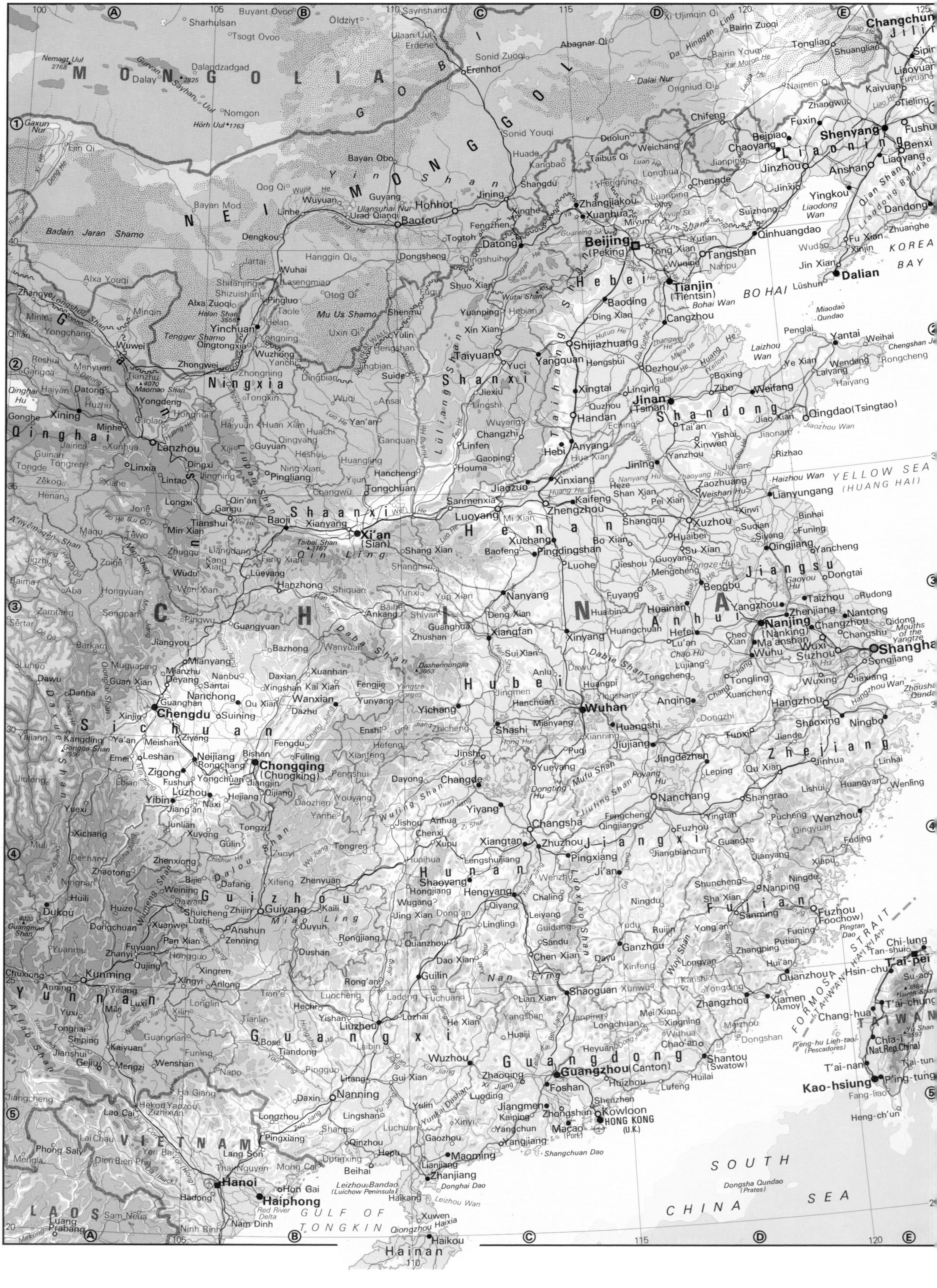
0 100 200 300 400 km
0 100 200 mls
MONGOLIA
GOBI
NEI MONGGOL
CHINA
Qinghai
Ningxia
Shaanxi
Shanxi
Hebei
Shandong
Henan
Jiangsu
Anhui
Hubei
Sichuan
Zhejiang
Jiangxi
Hunan
Guizhou
Fujian
Yunnan
Guangxi
Guangdong
Liaoning
VIETNAM
LAOS
TAIWAN
KOREA BAY
BO HAI
Bohai Wan
YELLOW SEA (HUANG HAI)
SOUTH CHINA SEA
GULF OF TONGKIN
FORMOSA STRAIT (TAIWAN HAIXIA)
Hainan
Changchun
Shenyang
Fushun
Benxi
Anshan
Liaoyang
Jinzhou
Yingkou
Dandong
Dalian
Chifeng
Tongliao
Beijing (Peking)
Tianjin (Tientsin)
Tangshan
Qinhuangdao
Zhangjiakou
Xuanhua
Datong
Hohhot
Baotou
Erenhot
Jining
Shijiazhuang
Taiyuan
Yangquan
Baoding
Cangzhou
Handan
Xingtai
Anyang
Jinan (Tsinan)
Zibo
Weifang
Yantai
Qingdao (Tsingtao)
Xinxiang
Zhengzhou
Kaifeng
Luoyang
Pingdingshan
Xuzhou
Lianyungang
Bengbu
Huainan
Hefei
Nanjing (Nanking)
Zhenjiang
Wuxi
Suzhou
Shanghai
Hangzhou
Ningbo
Wenzhou
Xi'an (Sian)
Baoji
Lanzhou
Xining
Yinchuan
Hanzhong
Xiangfan
Wuhan
Huangshi
Yichang
Shashi
Jiujiang
Jingdezhen
Nanchang
Changsha
Zhuzhou
Xiangtan
Hengyang
Chengdu
Chongqing (Chungking)
Zigong
Neijiang
Yibin
Luzhou
Guiyang
Kunming
Dukou
Liuzhou
Guilin
Nanning
Wuzhou
Guangzhou (Canton)
Foshan
Jiangmen
Shantou (Swatow)
Shaoguan
Fuzhou (Foochow)
Xiamen (Amoy)
Quanzhou
Zhanjiang
Haikou
Macao (Port.)
HONG KONG (U.K.)
Kowloon
Hanoi
Haiphong
T'ai-pei
Kao-hsiung
Chi-lung
Qin Ling
Taihang Shan
Lüliang Shan
Yin Shan
Daba Shan
Dabie Shan
Wuling Shan
Nan Ling
Wuyi Shan
Huang He
Chang Jiang
Dongting Hu
Poyang Hu
Taihu
Hongze Hu
Badain Jaran Shamo
Mu Us Shamo
Tengger Shamo
Great Wall
Taibai Shan 3767
Dashennongjia 3053
Gongga Shan 7556
Hsüeh Shan 3884
Yü Shan 3997

1:10M 0 100 200 300 400 km
0 100 200 mls

1:5M
0 50 100 150 200 km
0 50 100 mls

0
100
200
300
400 km
0
100
200 mls
BURMA
MYANMA
THAILAND
LAOS
VIETNAM
CHINA
CAMBODIA
(KAMPUCHEA)
MALAYSIA
INDONESIA
SUMATERA
MALAYA
PENINSULAR MALAYSIA
SARAWAK
(Malaysia)
BORNEO
Kalimantan
HAINAN
SINGAPORE
ANDAMAN SEA
Bay of Bengal
Gulf of Tongkin
GULF OF THAILAND
SOUTH CHINA SEA
Gulf of Martaban
Mouths of the Irrawaddy
Mouths of the Mekong
Strait of Malacca
Selat Mentawai
Selat Berhala
Paracel Islands
(claimed by China & Vietnam)
NICOBAR ISLANDS
(India)
Little Nicobar
Great Nicobar
Mergui Archipelago
Isthmus of Kra
Bight of Bangkok
Chaîne des Cardamomes
Tonle Sap
Mekong
Salween
Tanen Ra.
Dawna Ra.
Bilauktaung Range
Arakan Yoma
Pegu Yoma
Equator
Lashio
Hsipaw
Kyaukme
Maymyo
Mandalay
Sagaing
Monywa
Shwebo
Myingyan
Meiktila
Pakokku
Chauk
Magwe
Minbu
Taunggyi
Kalaw
Yamethin
Toungoo
Pyinmana
Prome
Thayetmyo
Allanmyo
Henzada
Pegu
Rangoon
(Yangon)
Bassein
Moulmein
Thaton
Kyaikto
Mudon
Ye
Tavoy
Mergui
Tenasserim
Sandoway
Hanoi
Haiphong
Nam Dinh
Ninh Binh
Hoa Binh
Thanh Hoa
Vinh
Ha Tinh
Dong Hoi
Quang Tri
Hue
Da Nang
Quang Ngai
Kontum
Pleiku
Qui Nhon
Tuy Hoa
Nha Trang
Cam Ranh
Da Lat
Phan Rang
Phan Thiet
Ban Me Thuot
Saigon (Ho Chi Minh)
Vung Tau
My Tho
Can Tho
Rach Gia
Long Xuyen
Chau Phu
Vinh Long
Phu Vinh
Khanh Hung
Vinh Loi
Quan Long
Nam Can
Con Son
Lang Son
Cao Bang
Ha Giang
Lao Cai
Lai Chau
Dien Bien Phu
Son La
Vientiane
(Viangchan)
Luang Prabang
Xieng Khouang
Savannakhet
Pakse
Saravane
Attopeu
Thakhek
Nong Khai
Udon Thani
M. Nakhon Phanom
Sam Neua
Phong Saly
Luang Namtha
Sayaboury
Bangkok
Thon Buri
Nakhon Pathom
M. Samut Prakan
Ayutthaya
Lop Buri
Nakhon Ratchasima
Chiang Mai
Chiang Rai
M. Lampang
M. Phitsanulok
M. Nakhon Sawan
Uttaradit
Tak
Khon Kaen
Ubon Ratchathani
Chon Buri
Chanthaburi
Prachuap Khiri Khan
Chumphon
Ranong
Surat Thani
Nakhon Si Thammarat
Phuket
Trang
Songkhla
Hat Yai
Pattani
Yala
Narathiwat
Phnom Penh
Battambang
Siem Reap
ANGKOR
Kompong Thom
Kompong Cham
Kompong Chhnang
Pursat
Kratie
Stung Treng
Sisophon
Kampot
Kompong Som
Sihanoukville
Nanning
Beihai
Zhanjiang
Haikou
Maoming
Yulin
Bose
Qinzhou
Pingxiang
Kota Bharu
Alor Setar
George Town
Pinang
Butterworth
Taiping
Ipoh
Kuala Trengganu
Kuantan
Kuala Lipis
Kuala Lumpur
Kelang
Seremban
Port Dickson
Melaka
Muar
Johor Bharu
Mersing
Kuching
Sibu
Pontianak
Singkawang
Banda Aceh
Sabang
Lhokseumawe
Medan
Binjai
Pematangsiantar
Tanjungbalai
Sibolga
Padangsidempuan
Pekanbaru
Bukittinggi
Padang
Jambi
Dumai
Bengkalis
Tanjungpinang
Kep. Riau
Kep. Lingga
Kep. Anambas
Kep. Bunguran Seletan
Bunguran
Nias
Siberut
Simeulue
Bangka
Karimata

1:10M

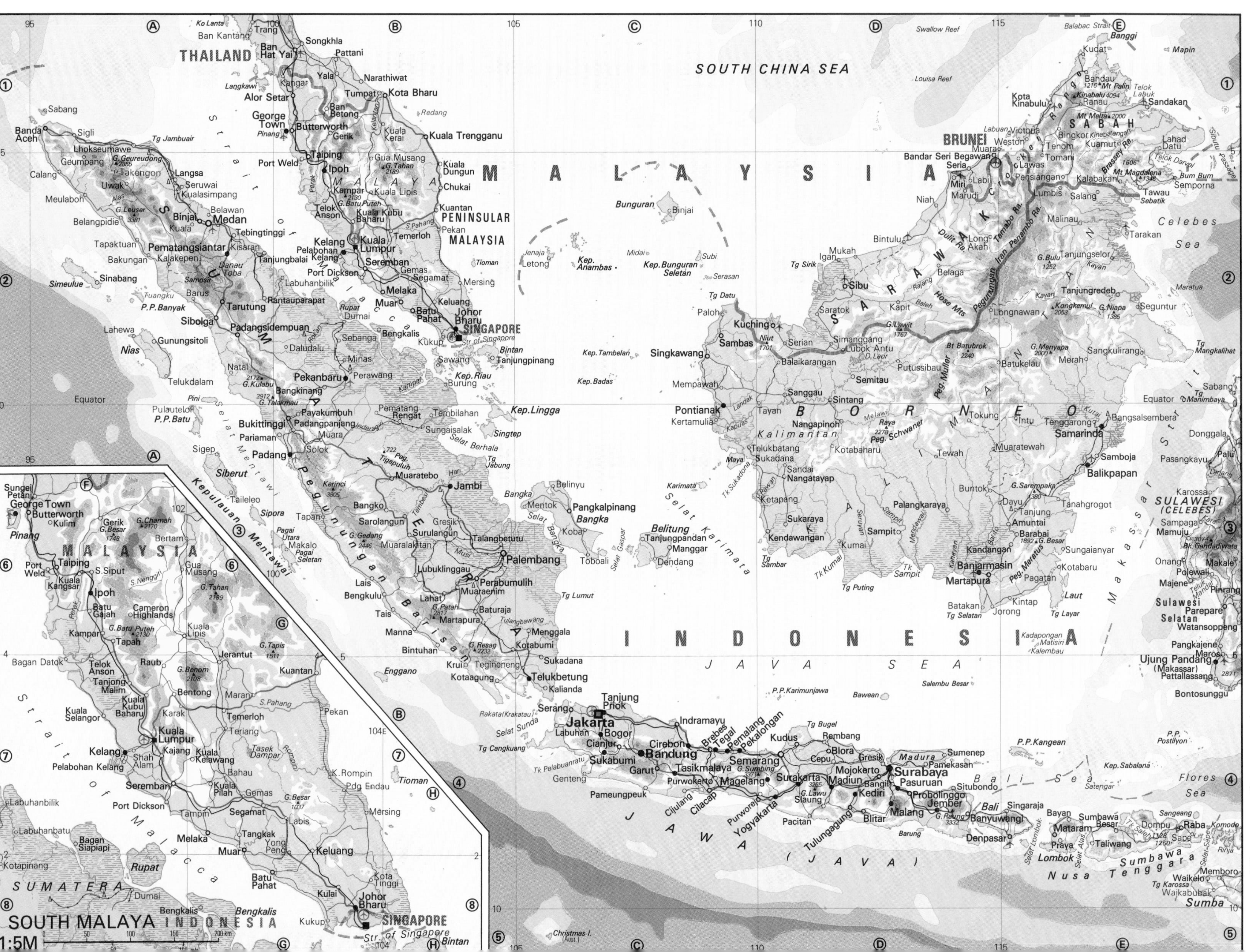
SOUTH CHINA SEA
MALAYSIA
INDONESIA
THAILAND
BRUNEI
SINGAPORE
PENINSULAR MALAYSIA
SABAH
SARAWAK
BORNEO
Kalimantan
SUMATERA
JAVA SEA
JAWA
SULAWESI (CELEBES)
Celebes Sea
Makassar
Flores Sea
Strait of Malacca
Selat Karimata
Selat Sunda
Kepulauan Mentawai
Pegunungan Barisan
Kuala Lumpur
Jakarta
Bandung
Semarang
Surabaya
Palembang
Medan
Padang
Pekanbaru
Jambi
Pontianak
Kuching
Banjarmasin
Balikpapan
Samarinda
Ujung Pandang (Makassar)
Kota Kinabalu
Bandar Seri Begawan
Ipoh
George Town
Banda Aceh
Telukbetung
Yogyakarta
Denpasar
Mataram
Bali
Lombok
Sumbawa
Sumba
Bangka
Belitung
Nias
Siberut
Christmas I. (Aust.)
SOUTH MALAYA
1:5M

1:10M 0 100 200 300 400 km / 0 100 200 mls

1:20M
0 200 400 600 800 km
0 200 400 mls

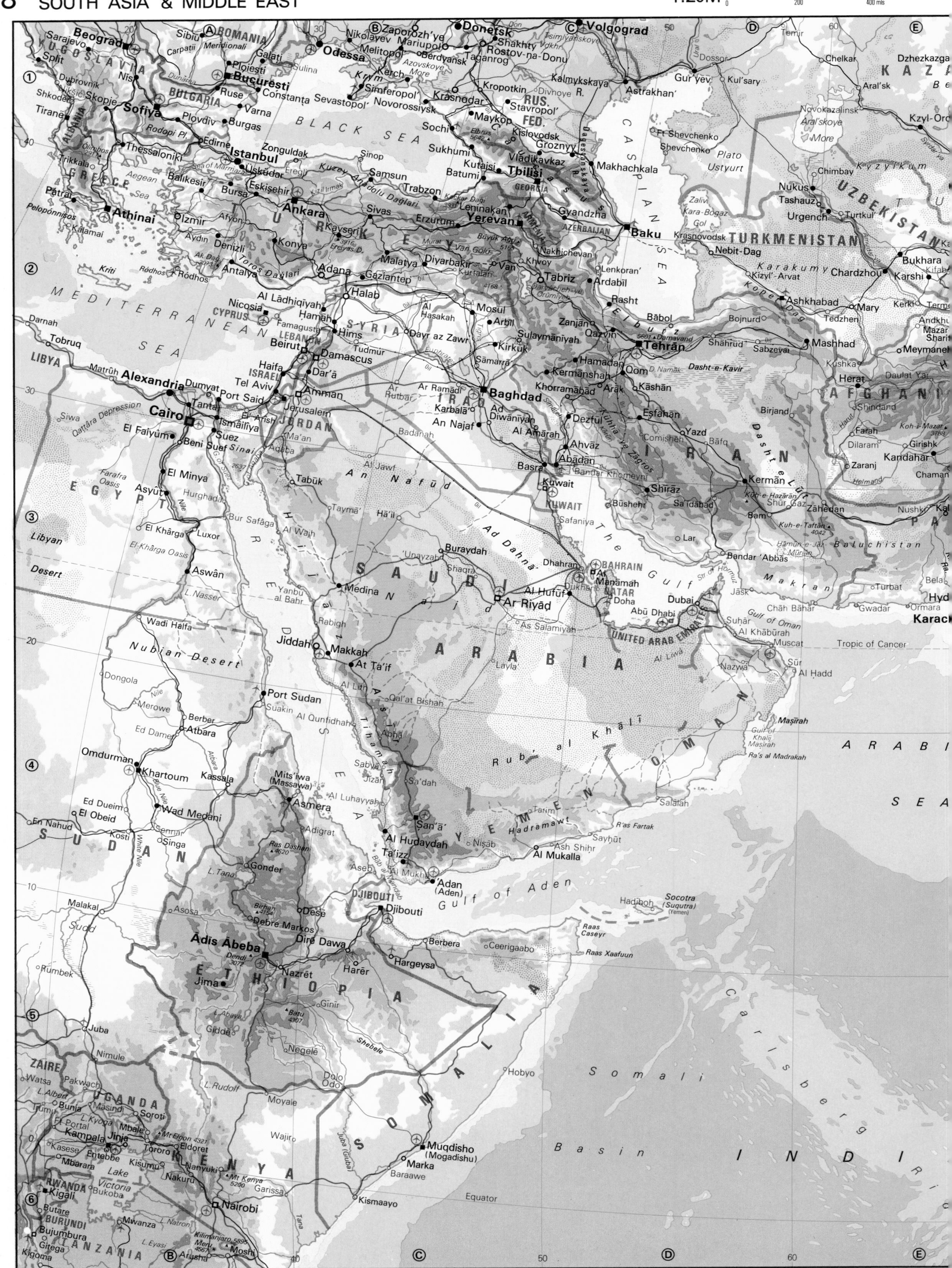

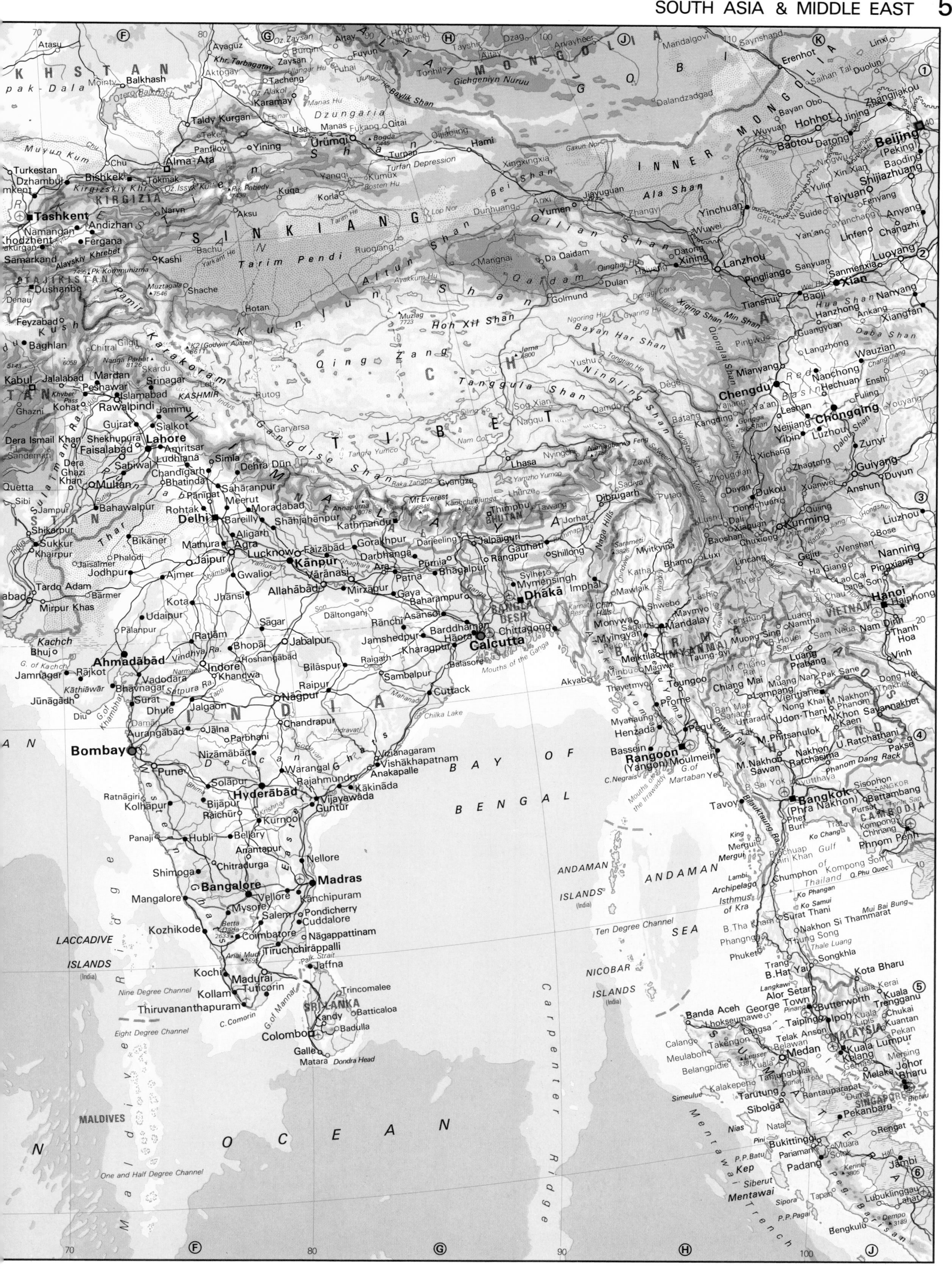
M O N G O L I A
G O B I
INNER MONGOLIA
Dzungaria
Turfan Depression
S I N K I A N G
Tarim Pendi
Kunlun Shan
Altun Shan
Qaidam
Qilian Shan
Qing Zang
T I B E T
C H I N A
Tanggula Shan
Bayan Har Shan
Ningjing Shan
Hoh Xil Shan
Gangdise Shan
Karakoram
H I M A L A Y A
KASHMIR
I N D I A
Thar
Deccan
Eastern Ghats
Western Ghats
BAY OF BENGAL
ANDAMAN SEA
ANDAMAN ISLANDS (India)
NICOBAR ISLANDS (India)
LACCADIVE ISLANDS (India)
MALDIVES
Maldive Ridge
Carpenter Ridge
Mentawai Trench
OCEAN
Ten Degree Channel
Nine Degree Channel
Eight Degree Channel
One and Half Degree Channel
Palk Strait
G. of Mannar
G. of Kachch
G. of Khambhat
G. of Martaban
Gulf of Thailand
Mouths of the Ganga
Mouths of the Irrawaddy
SRI LANKA
BANGLADESH
BHUTAN
NEPAL
BURMA (MYANMA)
THAILAND
LAOS
VIETNAM
CAMBODIA
MALAYSIA
SINGAPORE
SUMATERA
Sichuan Basin
Alma-Ata
Bishkek
Tashkent
Dushanbe
Kabul
Islamabad
Lahore
Delhi
Kathmandu
Thimphu
Dhākā
Calcutta
Bombay
Madras
Hyderābād
Bangalore
Colombo
Rangoon (Yangon)
Bangkok (Phra Nakhon)
Phnom Penh
Hanoi
Vientiane
Kuala Lumpur
Beijing (Peking)
Lhasa
Ürümqi
Kashi
Chengdu
Chongqing
Kunming
Lanzhou
Xian
Mandalay
Chittagong
Karāchi
Ahmadābād
Kānpur
Lucknow
Jaipur
Nāgpur
Medan
Padang
Mt Everest 8848
K2 (Godwin Austen) 8611
Nanga Parbat 8126
Annapurna 8078
Kanchenjunga 8598
Muztagata 7546
Pik Pobedy 7439
Pik Kommunizma 7495
Muzlag 7723
Anai Mudi 2695
70
80
90
100
F
G
H
J
K
1
2
3
4
5
6

1:7.5M

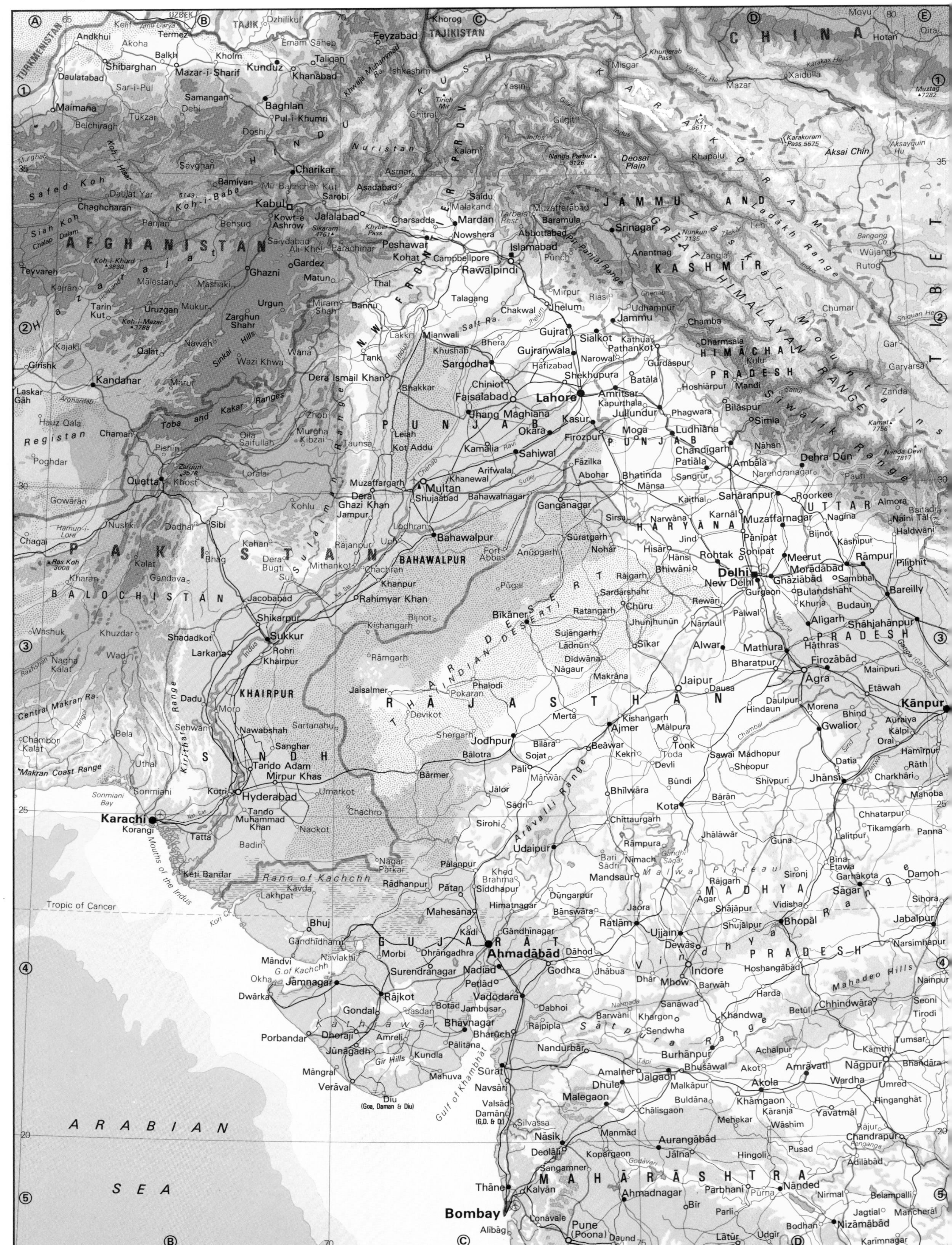

1:7.5M 0 100 200 300 km
0 50 100 150 mls

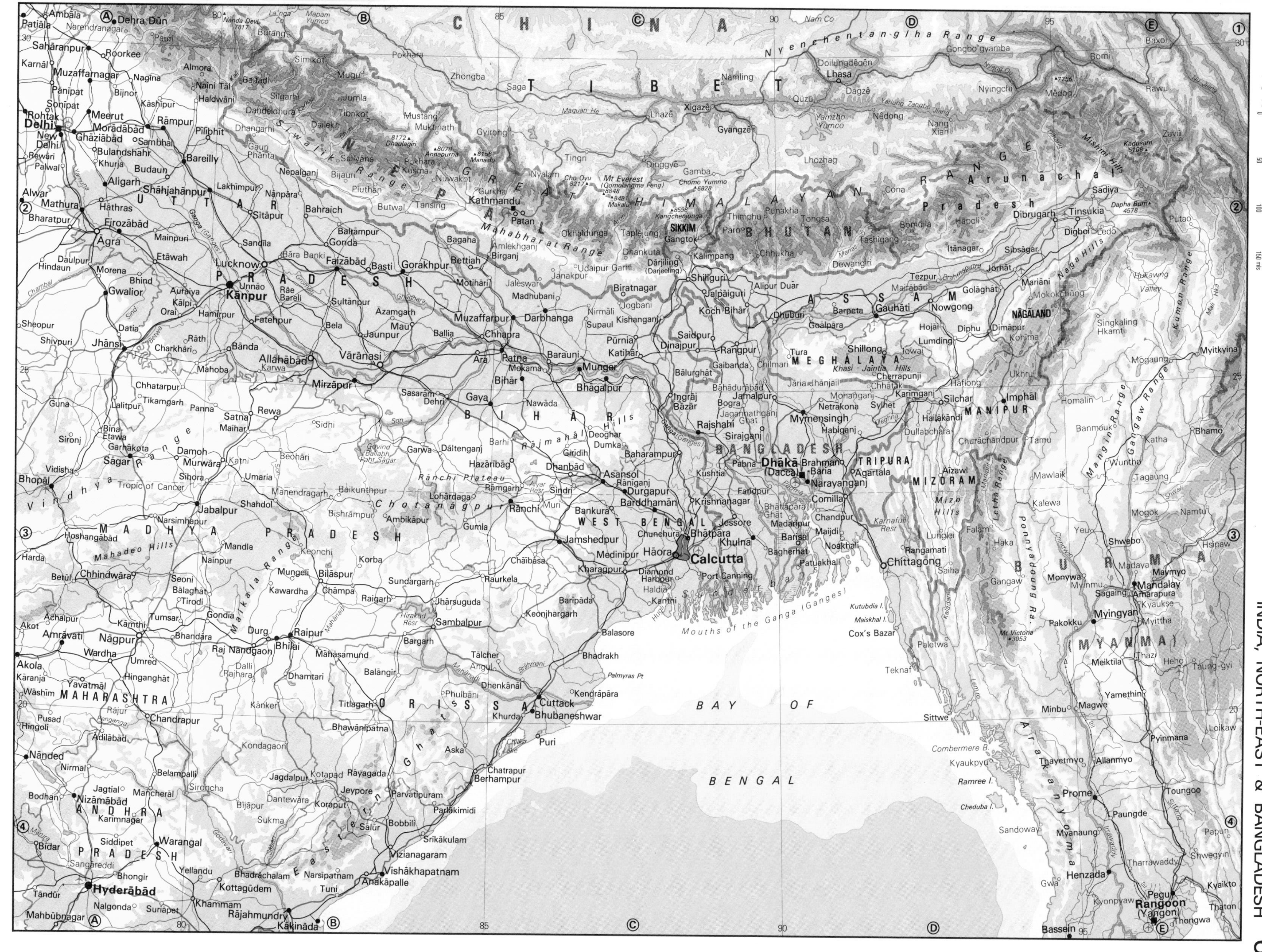

1:7.5M

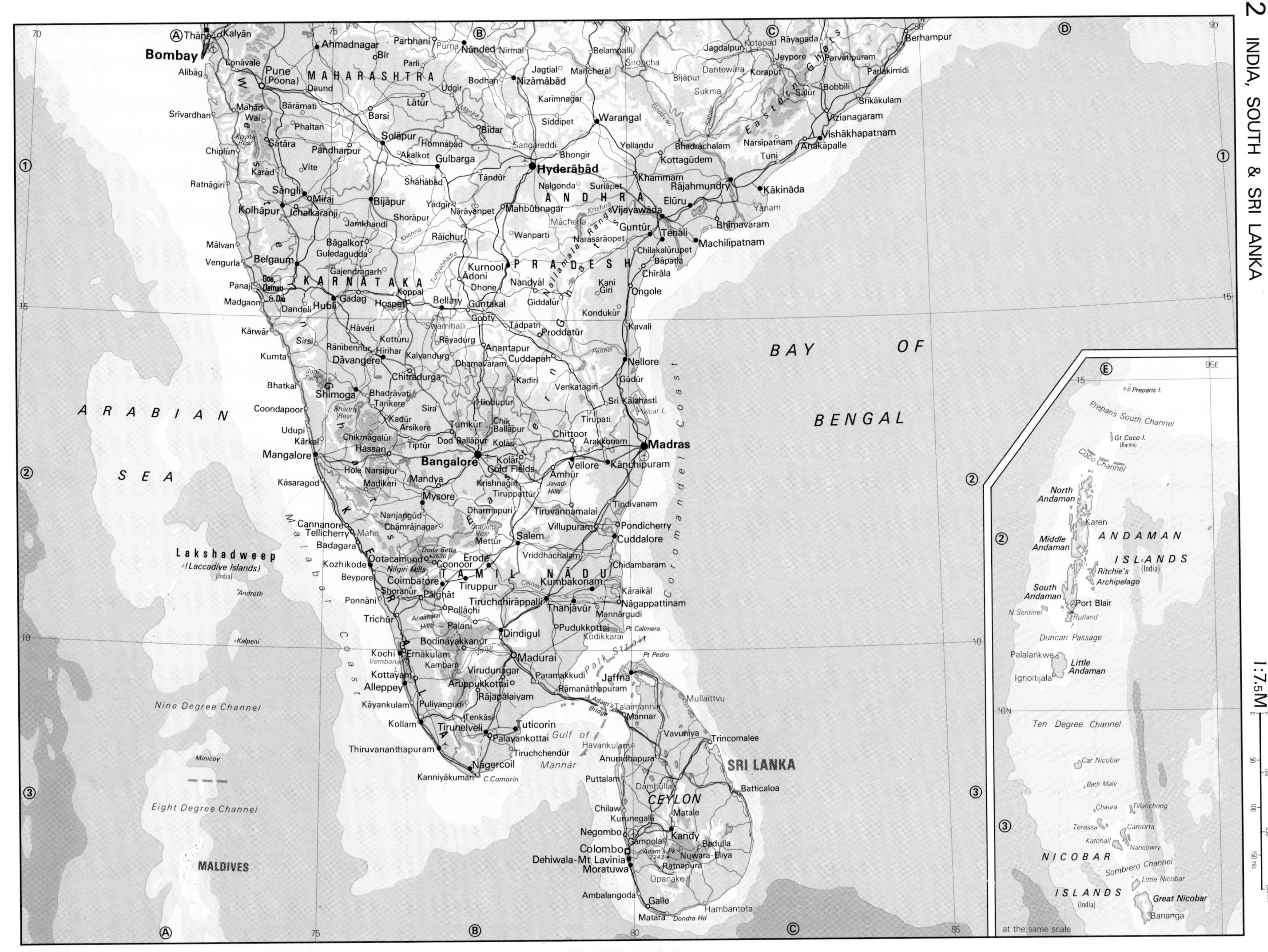

0 100 200 300 km
0 50 100 150 mls
BAY OF BENGAL
ARABIAN SEA
SRI LANKA
CEYLON
MALDIVES
MAHARASHTRA
KARNATAKA
ANDHRA PRADESH
TAMIL NĀDU
KERALA
Lakshadweep (Laccadive Islands) (India)
ANDAMAN ISLANDS
NICOBAR ISLANDS (India)
Bombay
Pune (Poona)
Hyderābād
Bangalore
Madras
Mangalore
Mysore
Coimbatore
Madurai
Colombo
Kandy
Trincomalee
Jaffna
Batticaloa
Galle
Port Blair
Vishākhapatnam
Vijayawada
Guntūr
Nellore
Pondicherry
Tiruchchirāppalli
Thanjāvūr
Salem
Kochi
Alleppey
Kollam
Thiruvananthapuram
Kozhikode
Cannanore
Belgaum
Hubli
Kolhāpur
Solāpur
Gulbarga
Warangal
Kurnool
Bellary
Shimoga
Malabar Coast
Coromandel Coast
Palk Strait
Gulf of Mannār
Adam's Bridge
Nine Degree Channel
Eight Degree Channel
Ten Degree Channel
Duncan Passage
Preparis South Channel
Coco Channel
Sombrero Channel
North Andaman
Middle Andaman
South Andaman
Little Andaman
Car Nicobar
Great Nicobar
Ritchie's Archipelago (India)
Minicoy
C.Comorin
at the same scale

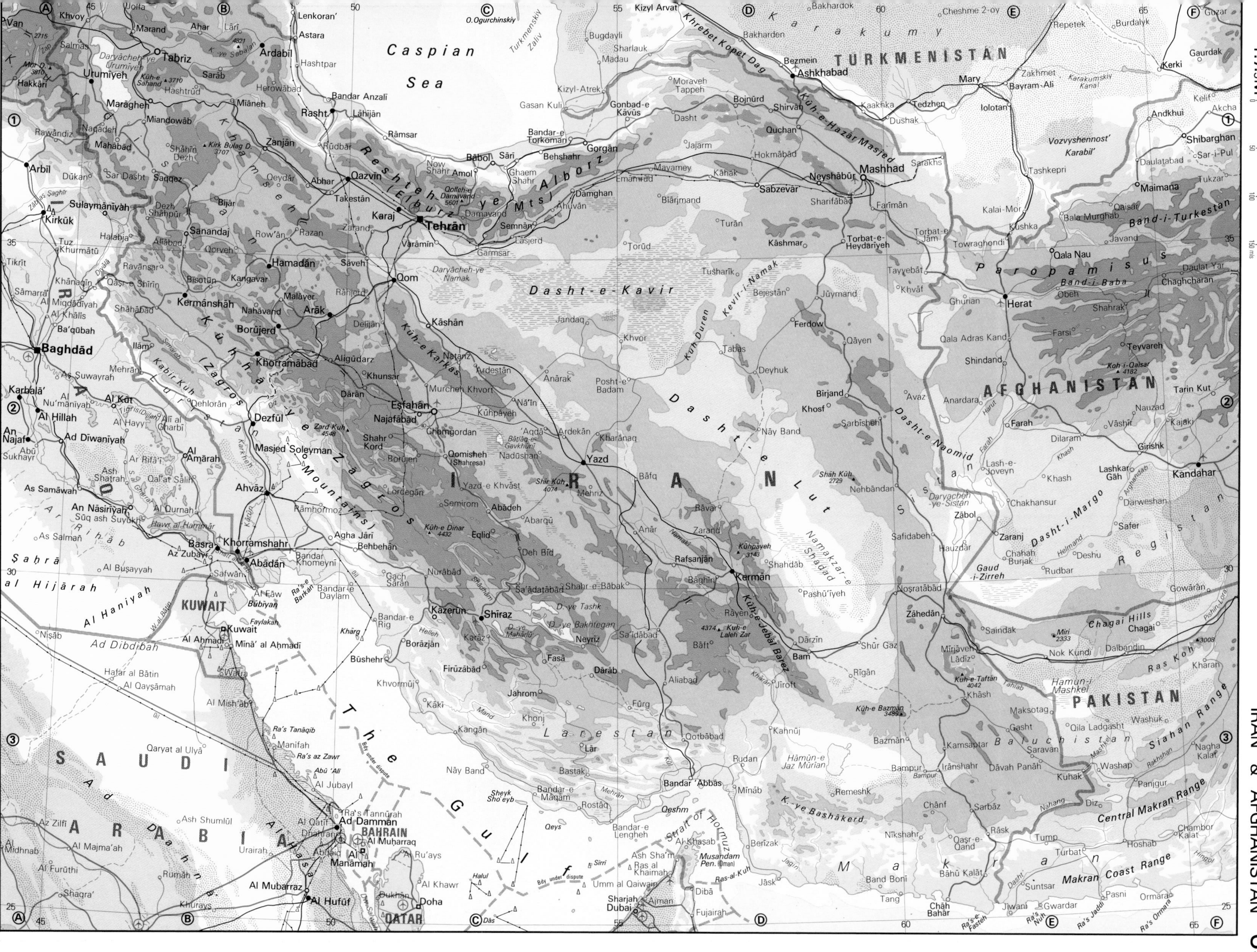
TURKMENISTAN
AFGHANISTAN
PAKISTAN
IRAN
KUWAIT
BAHRAIN
QATAR
SAUDI ARABIA
Caspian Sea
The Gulf
Strait of Hormuz
Dasht-e Kavir
Dasht-e Lut
Zagros Mountains
Elburz Mts
Paropamisus
Central Makran Range
Makran Coast Range
Tehrān
Baghdad
Mashhad
Herat
Kandahar
Eşfahān
Shīrāz
Kermān
Yazd
Tabrīz
Ashkhabad
Kuwait
Doha
Manamah
Dubai
Bandar 'Abbās

1:7.5M

0 100 200 300 km

0 50 100 150 mls

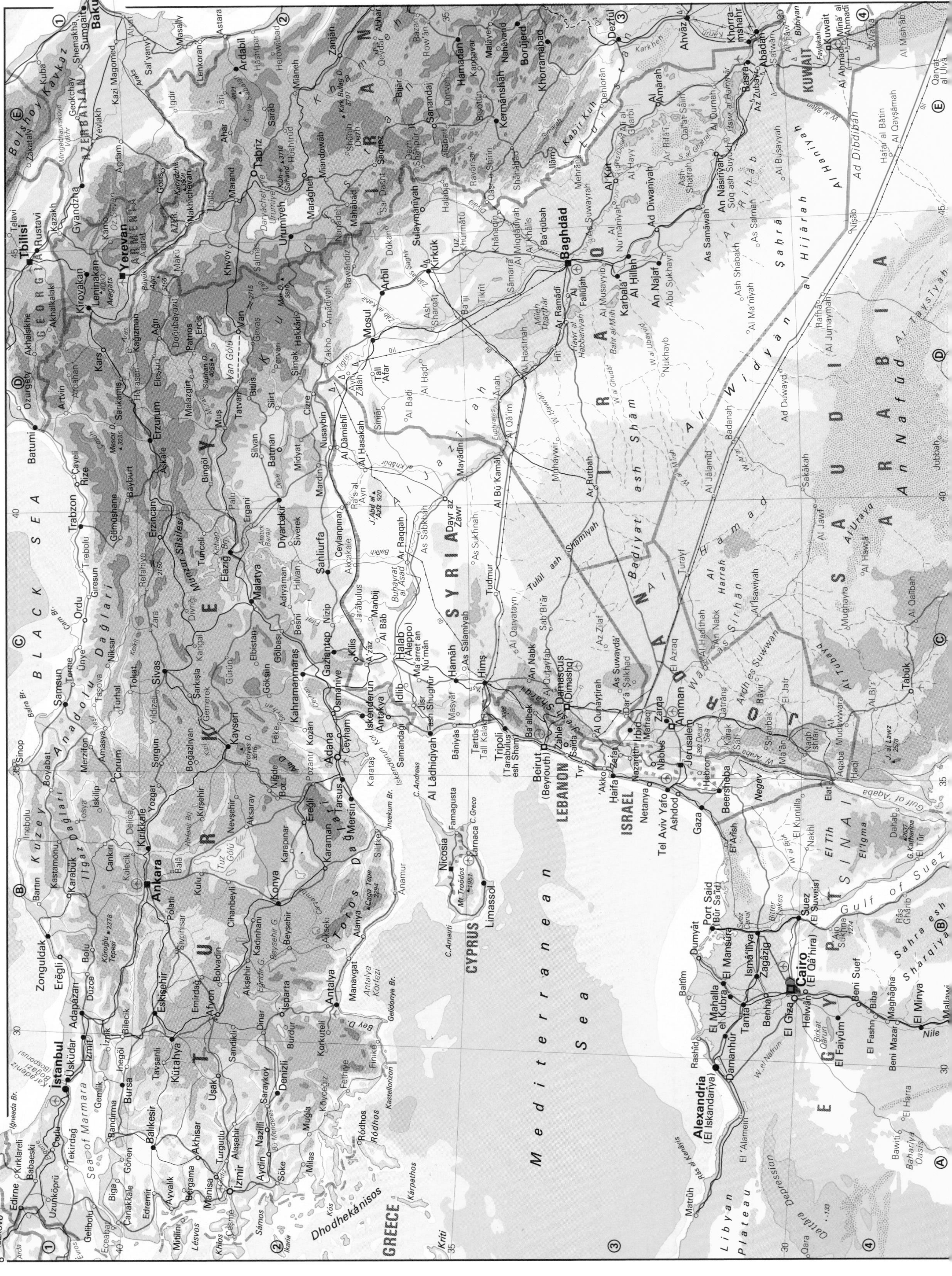

CYPRUS
C.A.Andreas
Rizokaipaso
Yialousa
Leonarisso
C.Kormakiti
Lapithos
Kyrenia
Akanthou
Morphou Bay
Morphou
Kythrea
Trikomo
C.Elea
Lefkoniko
Famagusta Bay
SALAMIS
C.Arnauti
Khrysokhou Bay
Karavostasi
Lefka
Nicosia
ATTILA LINE
Famagusta
Polis
Pedhoulas
Dhali
IDALION
Athna
Mt Olympus
1951
Troodos Range
Paleokhorio
Larnaca
C.Greco
Platres
Larnaca Bay
Lefkara
Paphos
C.Kiti
Zyyi
Episkopi
Limassol
Episkopi B.
Akrotiri Bay
C.Zevgari
C.Gata
MEDITERRANEAN
SEA
Jisr ash Shughūr
Serai
Al Baylūlīyah
Ra's Ibn Hāni'
Al Haffah
Ma'arrat an Nu'mān
Al Lādhiqīyah (Latakia)
SAHYŪN
Silinfah
Shathah
Khān Shaykhūn
at Tahtā'
Al Qardāhah
Jablah
Suqaylibīyah
(Orontes)
Sūrān
'Arab al Mulk
Dayr Shumayyil
Bāniyās
1385
Hamāh
QAL'AT AL MARQAB
Al Qadmūs
Kafr Behum
SYRIA
Masyāf
Bīrīn
Ar Rastan
Tartūs
Duraykīsh
Kafrūn Bashūr
Arwad
Sāfītā
An Nāsirah
Tall Bīsah
Qal'at al Hisn (KRAK DES CHEVALIERS)
Hims (Homs)
Hamīdīyah
Tall Kalakh
Kleiat
Qoubayat
Shinshār
Halba
Al Qusayr
El Mīna
Jūsīyah
Tripoli
Zghorta
El Hermel
Hisyah
(Tarābulus esh Shām)
Qornet es Saouda
3086
Batroun
Amioune
Bcharre
Jabal Halīmah
2464
Laboue
Deir el Ahmar
Jubail
BYBLOS
Kartaba
Dayr 'Atīyah
LEBANON
Rhazīr
2659
An Nabk
Ba'albek
Jounié
Bikfaya
2628
Yabrūd
Baie de St Georges
Beirut (Beyrouth)
Ba'abda
Zahle
Rayak
Jayrūd
Aley
Al J. Ma'lūla
Damour
Az. Zabdānī
Qutayfah
1910
Dumayr
Beit ed Dīne
'Ayn al Fījah
Dūmā
'Adhrā'
Saïda (Sidon)
Machgharab
At Tall
Barada
Damascus (Dimashq)
Jezzine
Rachaya
Qatanā
Hasbaiya
J. ash Shaykh (Mt Hermon)
A'waj
Al Hījānah
Marjayoun
Al Kiswah
Dayr 'Alī
Lītāni
Tyr (Tyre, Sour)
Q.Shemona
Baniyas
Mas'adah
Jouai'ya
CEASE FIRE LINES 1974
Ghabāghib
Burāq
Enn Nâqoûra
Bennt Jbail
Al Qunaytirah
Mismīyah
1208 Har Meron
Yesud Hama'ala
As Sanamayn
Khabab
Nahariya
Ma'alot Tarshīhā
Khushnīyah
Al Lajāh
863
Shaqqā
'Akko (Acre)
Zefat (Safad)
Nawā
B. of Haifa
Izra'
Shahbā
Haifa (Hefa)
Q.Yam
Rama
L. Tiberias (Yam Kinneret) (Sea of Galilee)
Shaykh Miskīn
Shefar'am
Jabal al 'Arab
1735
Tiberias
Tasīl
Q. Ata
Fiq
As Suwaydā'
'Atlit
528 Mt Carmel
Nazareth
Ma'agan
Dar'a
Afula
Zikhron Ya'aqov
MEGIDDO ARMAGEDDON
Deir Abu Sa'id
Irbid
Ramtha
Busrā ash Shām
CAESAREA
Jenin
Beyt Shean
Salkhad
Pardes Hanna
Hadera
Husn
Tisīyah
Qabatiya
Ajlūn
J. Umm ed Daraj
1247
Mafraq
Netanya
Tulkarm
Tubas
Sabhā
Jarash
ISRAEL
Sabastiya
Es Samrā
Herzliyya
Kefar Sava
Nablus
Zarqa
Yarqon
Er Rummān
Bat Yam
Petah Tiqwa
Ramat Gan
Salt
Suweilih
Zarqa
Tel Aviv
Holon
Yafo (Jaffa)
Lod
Ba'al Hazor
1016
Karama
Marka
Rishon le Zion
Ramallah
Amman
Ramla
Wadi es Sir
Rehovot
Jericho (Arīhā)
Sahāb
Latrun
Naur
Ashdod
Jerusalem (El Quds) (Yerushalayim)
Beit Jala
Bethlehem (Bayt Lahm)
Mādabā
Jiza
Ashqelon
Qasr el Kharana
Qiryat Gat
Bet Guvrin
963 Jebel Mudeisisat
Dab'a
Gaza
Sederot
LACHISH
Hebron (El Khalil)
Dead Sea (Bahret Lut)
Dhībān
Khan ez Zabīb
Gaza Strip
Dura
En Gedi
Yatta
Khan Yunis
Edh Dhahiriya
Mazra
Rafah
MEZADA
Rabba
Ofaqim
Beersheba (Be'er Sheva)
Qatrāna
Nevatim
'Arad
El Lisān
Zeelim
Karak
HALUZA
1253 T.el Meise
Sedom
Mazār
Manzil
Dimona
MAMSHIT
Revivim
Safi
El Ghor
1305 J.Ed Dabab
JORDAN
Yeroham
Qeziot
SHIVTA
Sede Boqer
Oron
Tafila
NIZANA
AVEDAT
Hasā
1356 J.Qasred Deir
Hazeva
Rashādīya
Danā
1641 J.el Atā'ita
Jurf ed Darāwīsh
El Quseima
Negev
Mizpe Ramon
Ein Yahav
1305 Har Ramon
Shaubak
1082
Nijil
1615 Jum Suwwāna
Wādi Mūsā
Uneisa
Har Hakippa 467
1006 Har Saggi
PETRA
Beer Menuha
J. Hārūn 1727
Abū el Jurdhān
El Jafr
Taiyiba
J.Mubrak
Ma'ān
Hiyon
Vahel
Naqb Ishtar
Ras en Naqb
El Kuntilla
Yotvata
1242 J.Qatim
Tuwayilel Hāj 1095
El Quwetra
Mikhrot Timna
1420 Ras Um Seisabān
J.el Harad 1274
Beer Ora
J. Bāqir 1592
J.Ram 1754
J.Um Ishrīn 1753
Elat
Ram
Aqaba
G.of Aqaba
1216 J.Um el Hashim
Dumyât (Damietta)
Râs el Barr
Masabb Dumyât
Kafr Sa'd
Fâriskûr
Bahra el Manzala
Port Said (Bûr Saîd)
Bûr Fu'ad
Shirbîn
El Zarqa
El Matarîya
Mit el Nasâra
El Manzala
Râs Burûn
Khalig el Tîna
Sabkhet el Bardawîl
El 'Arîsh
Talkha
El Mansûra
Dîkirnis
El Tîna
PELUSIUM
Români
Samannûd
Aga
El Simbillâwein
DAPHNAE
El Qantara
Bîr el Duweidâr
Bîr Lahfân
Abu 'Aweigîla
Kafr Saqv
El Sâlhîya
Mît Ghamr
Abu Kebir
Hihya
Fâqûs
El Firdân
Ismâ'ilîya
Talata
L. Timsâh
G.Libni 463
Kathib el Henu 207
G.Maghâra 735
892 G.Halâl
Zagâzig
El Abbâsa
Abu Suweir
Minya el Qamn
EGYPT
Khamsa
Great Bitter Lake
Bîr Gifgâfa
Bîr Hasana
Bilbeis
Shibîn el Qanâtir
Fâyid
Saba'a
1094 G.Yi'allaq
El Khânka
Little Bitter Lake
Giddi Pass
704 G.Kharîm
Gineifa
840 G.el Giddi
El Shallûfa
Mitla Pass
520
El Matarîya
Heliopolis
Cairo (El Qâ'hira)
Suez (El Suweis)
El Kûbri
El Shatt
871 G.Ataqa
Bûr Taufiq
El Ma'âdi
Bîr Gindali
Helwân
Nakhl
El Tabbîn
Uyûn Mûsa
El Minya
Gulf of Suez
G.Sinn Bishr 622
SINAI
Sudr
El Thamad
Râs el Sudr
Gebel el Tîh
Bîr el 'Agramîya
'Ain Sukhna
1076
G.Sha'îra 1030
El Saff
Asl
Râs Matarma
1018 G.Abu Rûtha
Gebel el Galâla el Baharîya
1080 Râs el Nafas

1:7.5M

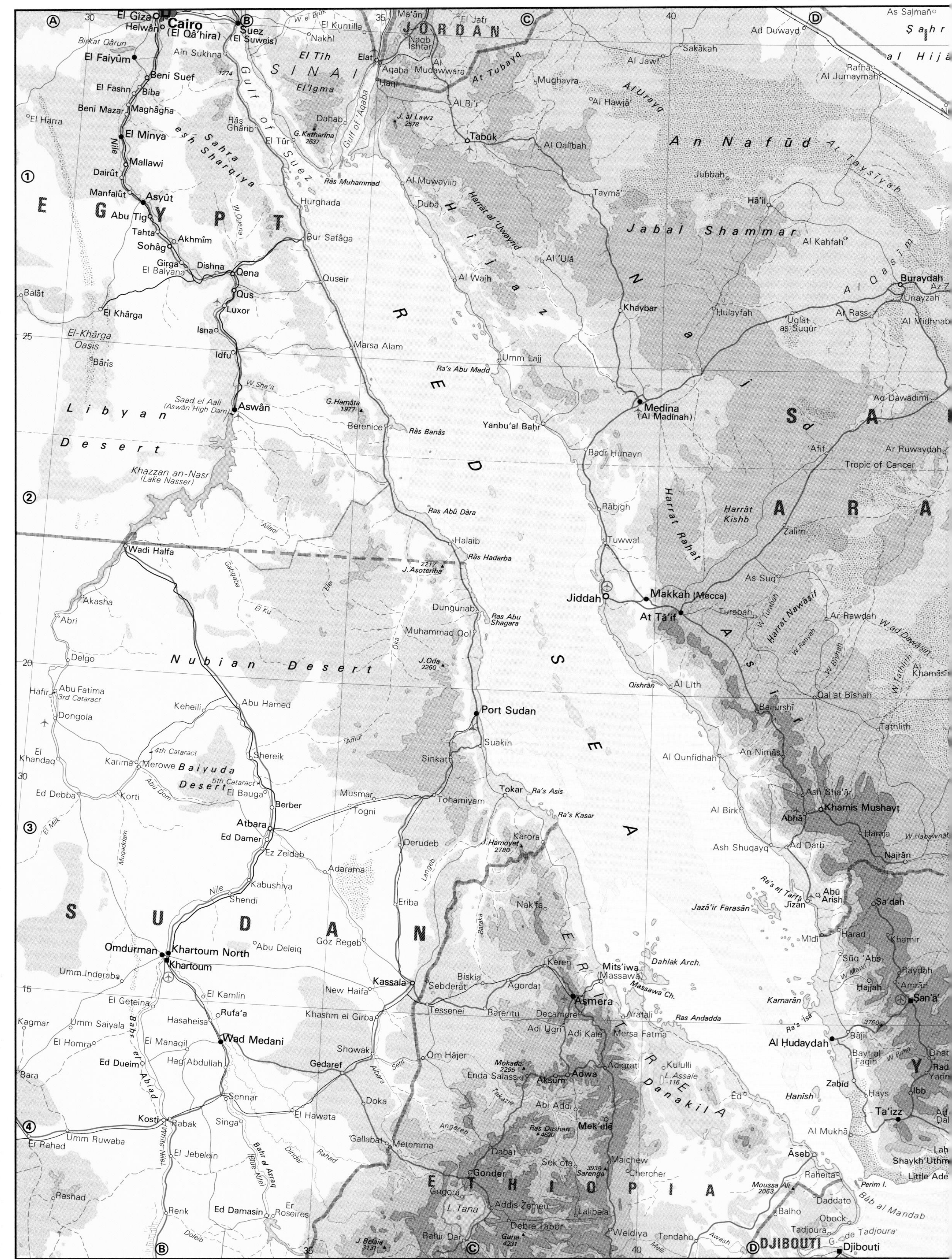
0 100 200 300 km
0 50 100 150 mls
EGYPT
Cairo (El Qâ'hira)
El Gîza
Helwân
Suez (El Suweis)
Birkat Qârun
El Faiyûm
Ain Sukhna
Beni Suef
El Fashn
Biba
Beni Mazar
Maghâgha
El Harra
El Minya
Nile
Mallawi
Dairût
Manfalût
Asyût
Abu Tig
Tahta
Sohâg
Akhmîm
Girga
El Balyana
Dishna
Qena
Qus
Luxor
Balât
El Khârga
El-Khârga Oasis
Bârîs
Isna
Idfu
W. Sha'it
Saad el Aali (Aswân High Dam)
Aswân
Libyan Desert
Khazzan an-Nasr (Lake Nasser)
Sahra esh Sharqiya
W. Qena
Hurghada
Bur Safâga
Quseir
Marsa Alam
Berenice
Râs Banâs
G. Hamâta 1977
Râs Muhammad
Gulf of Suez
SINAI
El Tîh
El 'Igma
Nakhl
El Kuntilla
1274
Râs Ghârib
El Tûr
G. Katharîna 2637
Dahab
Gulf of 'Aqaba
Elat
Aqaba
JORDAN
Ma'ân
Naqb Ishtar
Mudawwara
Haql
El Jafr
At Tubayq
Al Bi'r
J. al Lawz 2578
Tabûk
Mughayra
Al Hawjâ'
Al 'Urayq
Al Qalîbah
Ad Duwayd
Sakâkah
Al Jawf
Rafhâ
Al Jumaymah
Sahr al Hijâ
As Salmân
An Nafûd
At Taysiyah
Jubbah
Hâ'il
Jabal Shammar
Al Kahfah
Al Qasim
Buraydah
'Unayzah
Al Midhnab
Ar Rass
'Uqlat as Suqûr
Hulayfah
Khaybar
Taymâ'
Al Muwaylih
Dubâ
Harrât al 'Uwayrid
Hijaz
Al 'Ulâ
Al Wajh
Umm Lajj
Ra's Abu Madd
Yanbu'al Bahr
Medina (Al Madînah)
Najd
Ad Dawâdimî
'Afîf
Ar Ruwaydah
Tropic of Cancer
SAUDI ARABIA
Harrât Kishb
Zalim
Badr Hunayn
Râbigh
Harrat Rahat
Tuwwal
Jiddah
Makkah (Mecca)
At Tâ'if
Turabah
W. Turabah
Harrat Nawâsif
As Suq
Ar Rawdah
W. ad Dawâsir
W. Ranyah
W. Bîshah
W. Tathlîth
Al Khamâsin
Qal'at Bîshah
Tathlîth
Qishrân
Al Lîth
Baljurshî
Asîr
Al Qunfidhah
An Nimâs
Al Birk
Ash Sha'âr
Khamis Mushayt
Abhâ
Harajah
W. Habawnat
Najrân
Ash Shuqayq
Ad Darb
Ra's at Tarfâ
Jazâ'ir Farasân
Abû Arîsh
Jîzân
Sa'dah
Mîdî
Harad
Khamir
Sûq 'Abs
W. Mawr
Raydah
Hajjah
Amrân
Kamarân
San'â'
Ra's Isa
3760
Al Hudaydah
Bâjil
Bayt al Faqîh
W. Surdud
Zabid
Hays
Ibb
YEMEN
Dhamar
Yarim
Hanîsh
Ta'izz
Al Mukhâ
Lahij
Shaykh 'Uthmân
Little Aden
Perim I.
Bâb al Mandab
RED SEA
Ras Abû Dâra
Halaib
Râs Hadarba
2217 J. Asoteriba
Allaqi
Gabgaba
Wadi Halfa
Akasha
Abri
El Ku
Eleri
Dungunab
Ras Abu Shagara
Muhammad Qol
J. Oda 2260
Oka
Nubian Desert
Delgo
Hafir
Abu Fatima 3rd Cataract
Dongola
Keheili
Abu Hamed
Port Sudan
Suakin
Amur
Shereik
Sinkat
El Khandaq
Karima
Merowe
4th Cataract
Baiyuda Desert
5th Cataract
El Bauga
Abu Dom
Ed Debba
Korti
Berber
Musmar
Togni
Tokar
Ras Asis
Tohamiyam
Ras Kasar
Atbara
Ed Damer
El Milk
Muqaddam
Derudeb
J. Hamoyet 2780
Karora
Ez Zeidab
Adarama
Langeb
Kabushiya
Nile
Shendi
Eriba
Nak'fa
SUDAN
Omdurman
Khartoum North
Khartoum
Abu Deleiq
Goz Regeb
Baraka
Umm Inderaba
Keren
Mits'iwa (Massawa)
Dahlak Arch.
Massawa Ch.
Biskia
Agordat
Kassala
Sebderat
New Haifa
El Kamlin
El Geteina
Kagmar
Umm Saiyala
Rufa'a
Hasaheisa
Khashm el Girba
Tessenei
Barentu
Asmera
Decamere
Aratali
Ras Andadda
ERITREA
Adi Ugri
Adi Kaie
Mersa Fatma
El Homra
El Manaqil
Wad Medani
Showak
Bahr el Abiad
Ed Dueim
Hag Abdullah
Gedaref
Om Hâjer
Setit
Mokada 2295
Enda Salassie
Adwa
Aksum
Adigrat
Kululli
L. Assale -116
Danakil
Bara
Sennar
Atbara
Doka
Tekazie
Abi Addi
Ed
Kosti
Rabak
Singa
El Hawata
Mek'ele
Angareb
Ras Dashan 4620
Umm Ruwaba
Er Rahad
White Nile
El Jebelein
Bahr el Azraq (Blue Nile)
Dinder
Rahad
Gallabat
Metemma
Dabat
Sek'ota
3938 Sarenga
Maichew
Chercher
Âseb
Raheita
Gonder
ETHIOPIA
Gogora
L. Tana
Addis Zemen
Lalibela
Mousaa Ali 2063
Rashad
Renk
Ed Damasin
Er Roseires
Debre Tabor
Balho
Daddato
Obock
Tadjoura
Golfe de Tadjoura
Doleib
J. Belaia 3131
Bahir Dar
Guna 4231
Weldiya
Tendaho
Awash
Mille
DJIBOUTI
Djibouti
Ⓐ Ⓑ Ⓒ Ⓓ
① ② ③ ④
30 35 40
25 20 15

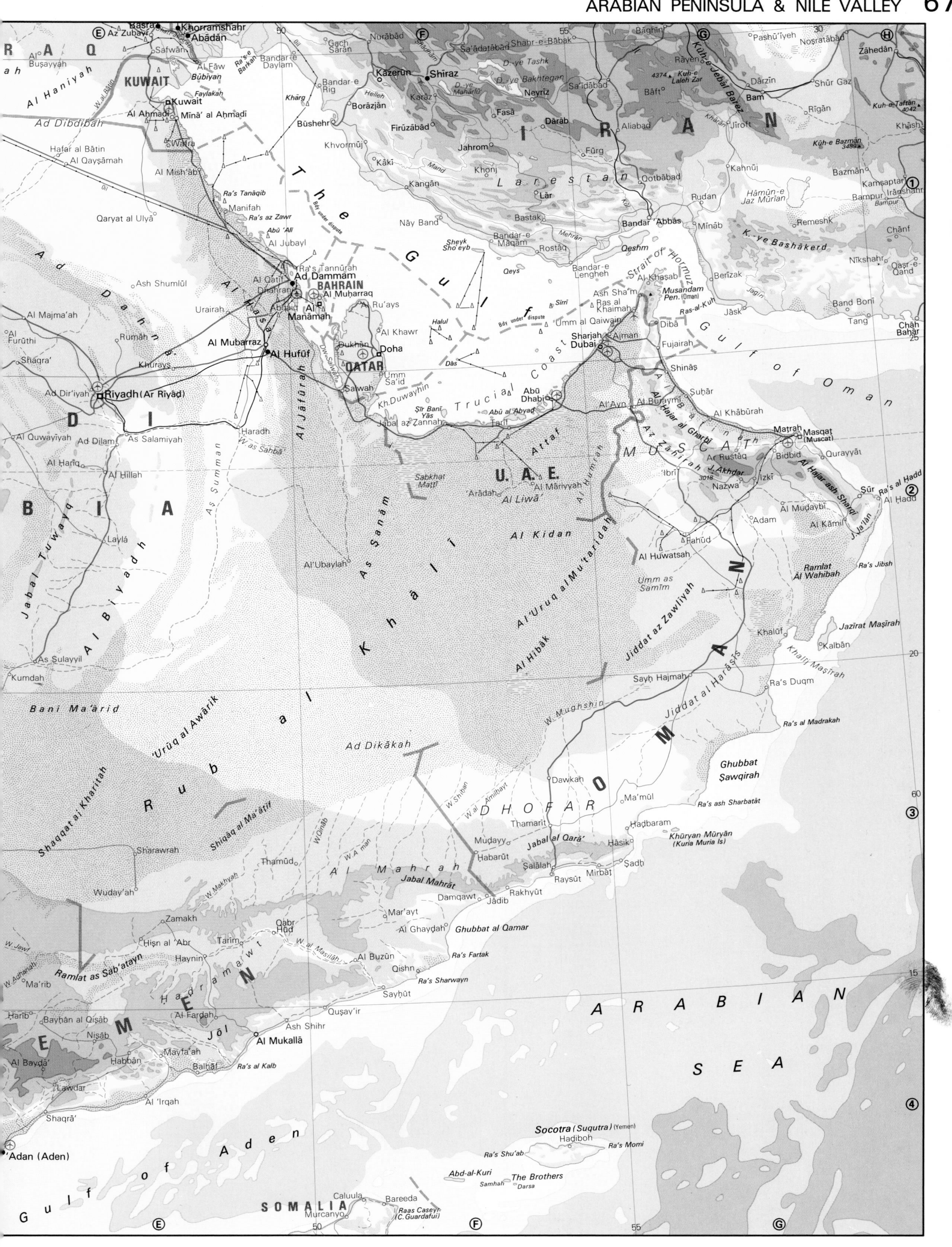

IRAN
KUWAIT
BAHRAIN
QATAR
U.A.E.
MUSCAT
OMAN
YEMEN
SOMALIA
The Gulf
Gulf of Oman
ARABIAN SEA
Gulf of Aden
Strait of Hormuz
Rub al Khali
Trucial Coast
DHOFAR
Riyadh (Ar Riyāḍ)
Kuwait
Ad Dammam
Al Manāmah
Doha
Abū Dhabi
Dubai
Sharjah
Masqat (Muscat)
Shiraz
Bandar 'Abbās
Al Mukallā
'Adan (Aden)
Socotra (Suqutra) (Yemen)
Al Hufūf
Ṣalālah

1:40M

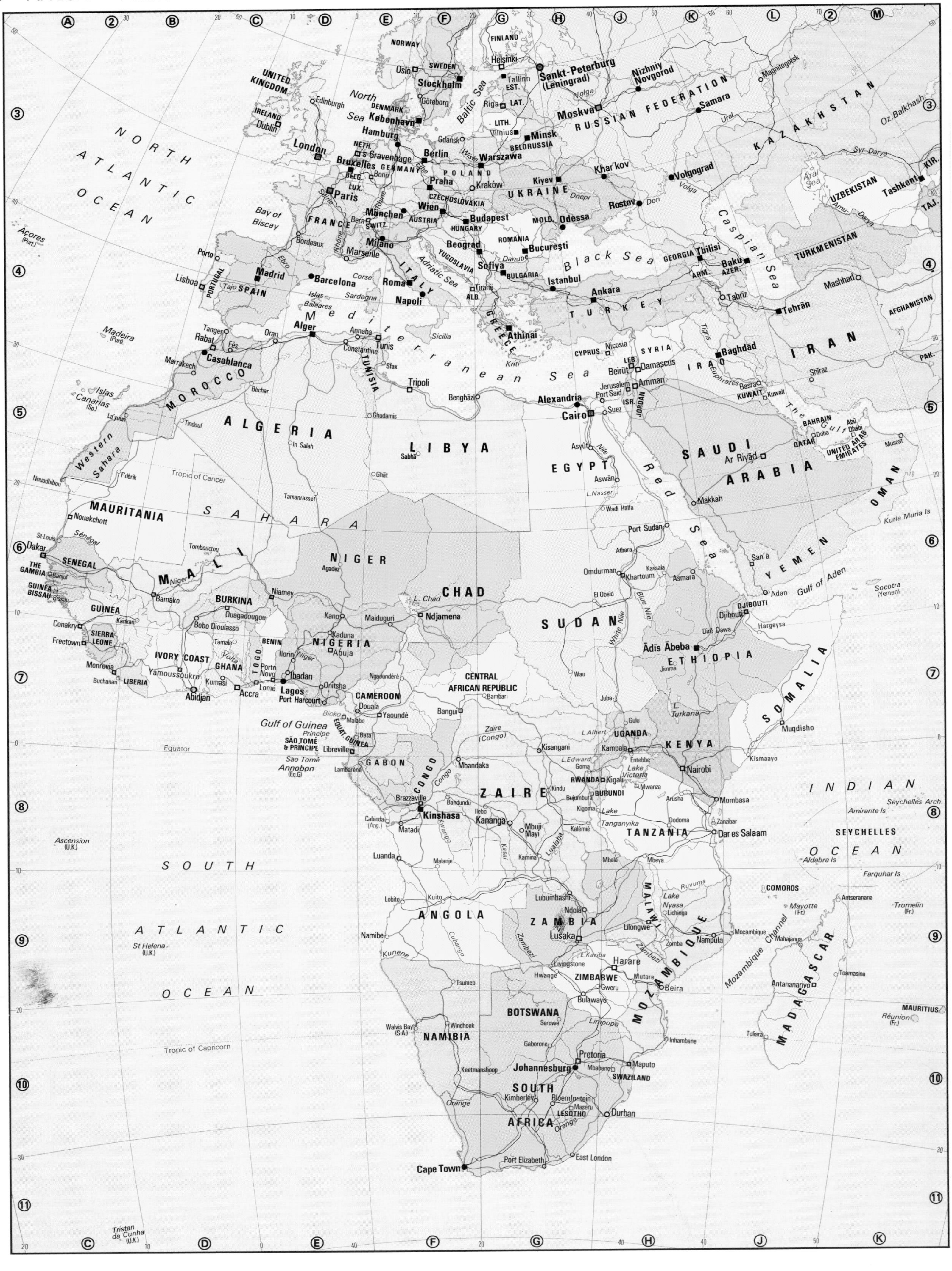

0 400 800 1200 1600 km
0 400 800 mls

NORTH ATLANTIC OCEAN
SOUTH ATLANTIC OCEAN
INDIAN OCEAN
Mediterranean Sea
Black Sea
Caspian Sea
Red Sea
North Sea
Baltic Sea
Adriatic Sea
Bay of Biscay
Gulf of Guinea
Gulf of Aden
The Gulf
Mozambique Channel
SAHARA
Tropic of Cancer
Equator
Tropic of Capricorn

NORWAY
SWEDEN
FINLAND
EST.
LAT.
LITH.
UNITED KINGDOM
IRELAND
DENMARK
NETH.
BELG.
LUX.
GERMANY
POLAND
BELORUSSIA
RUSSIAN FEDERATION
KAZAKHSTAN
UKRAINE
CZECHOSLOVAKIA
AUSTRIA
SWITZ.
FRANCE
HUNGARY
MOLD.
ROMANIA
YUGOSLAVIA
BULGARIA
ALB.
GREECE
ITALY
SPAIN
PORTUGAL
TURKEY
GEORGIA
ARM.
AZER.
TURKMENISTAN
UZBEKISTAN
KIR.
TAJ.
AFGHANISTAN
IRAN
PAK.
CYPRUS
SYRIA
LEB.
IRAQ
ISR.
JORDAN
KUWAIT
BAHRAIN
QATAR
UNITED ARAB EMIRATES
SAUDI ARABIA
OMAN
YEMEN
MOROCCO
Western Sahara
ALGERIA
TUNISIA
LIBYA
EGYPT
MAURITANIA
MALI
NIGER
CHAD
SUDAN
SENEGAL
THE GAMBIA
GUINEA-BISSAU
GUINEA
SIERRA LEONE
LIBERIA
IVORY COAST
BURKINA
GHANA
TOGO
BENIN
NIGERIA
CAMEROON
CENTRAL AFRICAN REPUBLIC
ETHIOPIA
DJIBOUTI
SOMALIA
EQUAT. GUINEA
SÃO TOMÉ & PRINCIPE
GABON
CONGO
ZAIRE
UGANDA
KENYA
RWANDA
BURUNDI
TANZANIA
ANGOLA
ZAMBIA
MALAWI
MOZAMBIQUE
ZIMBABWE
NAMIBIA
BOTSWANA
SOUTH AFRICA
LESOTHO
SWAZILAND
MADAGASCAR
COMOROS
SEYCHELLES
MAURITIUS

Oslo
Stockholm
Helsinki
Sankt-Peterburg (Leningrad)
Tallinn
Riga
Vilnius
Minsk
Moskva
Nizhniy Novgorod
Samara
Magnitogorsk
Edinburgh
Dublin
London
København
Göteborg
Hamburg
Gdańsk
Berlin
's-Gravenhage
Bruxelles
Bonn
Warszawa
Praha
Kraków
Kiyev
Khar'kov
Volgograd
Rostov
Paris
Wien
München
Bern
Budapest
Odessa
Bordeaux
Milano
Marseille
Beograd
Bucureşti
Sofiya
Tbilisi
Baku
Porto
Madrid
Barcelona
Roma
Napoli
Tiranë
Istanbul
Ankara
Tabrīz
Tehrān
Mashhad
Tashkent
Lisboa
Athinai
Nicosia
Beirut
Damascus
Baghdād
Shīrāz
Jerusalem
Amman
Basra
Kuwait
Doha
Abū Dhabi
Muscat
Ar Riyāḍ
Makkah
Şan'ā
Aden
Tanger
Rabat
Fès
Casablanca
Marrakech
Oran
Alger
Annaba
Constantine
Tunis
Sfax
Tripoli
Benghāzī
Alexandria
Port Said
Suez
Cairo
Asyūt
Aswân
Wadi Halfa
Béchar
Tindouf
La'youn
In Salah
Ghudamis
Sabhā
Ghāt
Tamanrasset
F'dérik
Nouadhibou
Nouakchott
St-Louis
Dakar
Banjul
Bissau
Tombouctou
Bamako
Conakry
Kankan
Freetown
Monrovia
Buchanan
Yamoussoukro
Abidjan
Bobo Dioulasso
Ouagadougou
Tamale
Kumasi
Accra
Lomé
Porto Novo
Niamey
Agadez
Kano
Kaduna
Ilorin
Abuja
Ibadan
Lagos
Onitsha
Port Harcourt
Maiduguri
Ndjamena
Ngaoundéré
Douala
Yaoundé
Malabo
Bata
Libreville
Lambaréné
Bangui
Bambari
Port Sudan
Atbara
Omdurman
Khartoum
Kassala
Asmara
El Obeid
Wau
Juba
Djibouti
Dire Dawa
Hargeysa
Ādīs Ābeba
Jimma
Gulu
Kampala
Entebbe
Kisangani
Goma
Kigali
Bujumbura
Nairobi
Mombasa
Kismaayo
Muqdisho
Mbandaka
Brazzaville
Kinshasa
Bandundu
Ilebo
Kananga
Mbuji Mayi
Kindu
Kigoma
Mwanza
Arusha
Dodoma
Zanzibar
Dar es Salaam
Kalémie
Kamina
Mbala
Mbeya
Cabinda (Ang.)
Matadi
Luanda
Malanje
Lobito
Kuito
Lubumbashi
Ndola
Lusaka
Lilongwe
Lichinga
Zomba
Nampula
Moçambique
Namibe
Livingstone
Hwange
Harare
Mutare
Gweru
Bulawayo
Beira
Tsumeb
Windhoek
Walvis Bay (S.A.)
Serowe
Gaborone
Pretoria
Johannesburg
Maputo
Mbabane
Inhambane
Keetmanshoop
Kimberley
Bloemfontein
Maseru
Durban
Cape Town
Port Elizabeth
East London
Antseranana
Mahajanga
Toamasina
Antananarivo
Toliara

Açores (Port.)
Madeira (Port.)
Islas Canarias (Sp.)
Islas Baleares
Corse
Sardegna
Sicilia
Kriti
Bioko
Príncipe
Sao Tomé
Annobon (Eq.G)
Ascension (U.K.)
St Helena (U.K.)
Tristan da Cunha (U.K.)
Socotra (Yemen)
Kuria Muria Is
Seychelles Arch.
Amirante Is
Aldabra Is
Farquhar Is
Mayotte (Fr.)
Tromelin (Fr.)
Réunion (Fr.)

Nile
White Nile
Blue Nile
Niger
Sénégal
Volta
Zaïre (Congo)
Congo
Kwango
Kasai
Lualaba
Zambezi
Kunene
Cubango
Limpopo
Orange
Ruvuma
Tigris
Euphrates
Don
Dnepr
Volga
Ural
Danube
Rhine
Rhône
Seine
Elbe
Wisła
Ebro
Tajo
Syr-Darya
Amu-Darya
Aral Sea
Oz. Balkhash
L. Nasser
L. Chad
L. Albert
L. Edward
Lake Victoria
L. Turkana
Lake Tanganyika
Lake Nyasa
L. Kariba

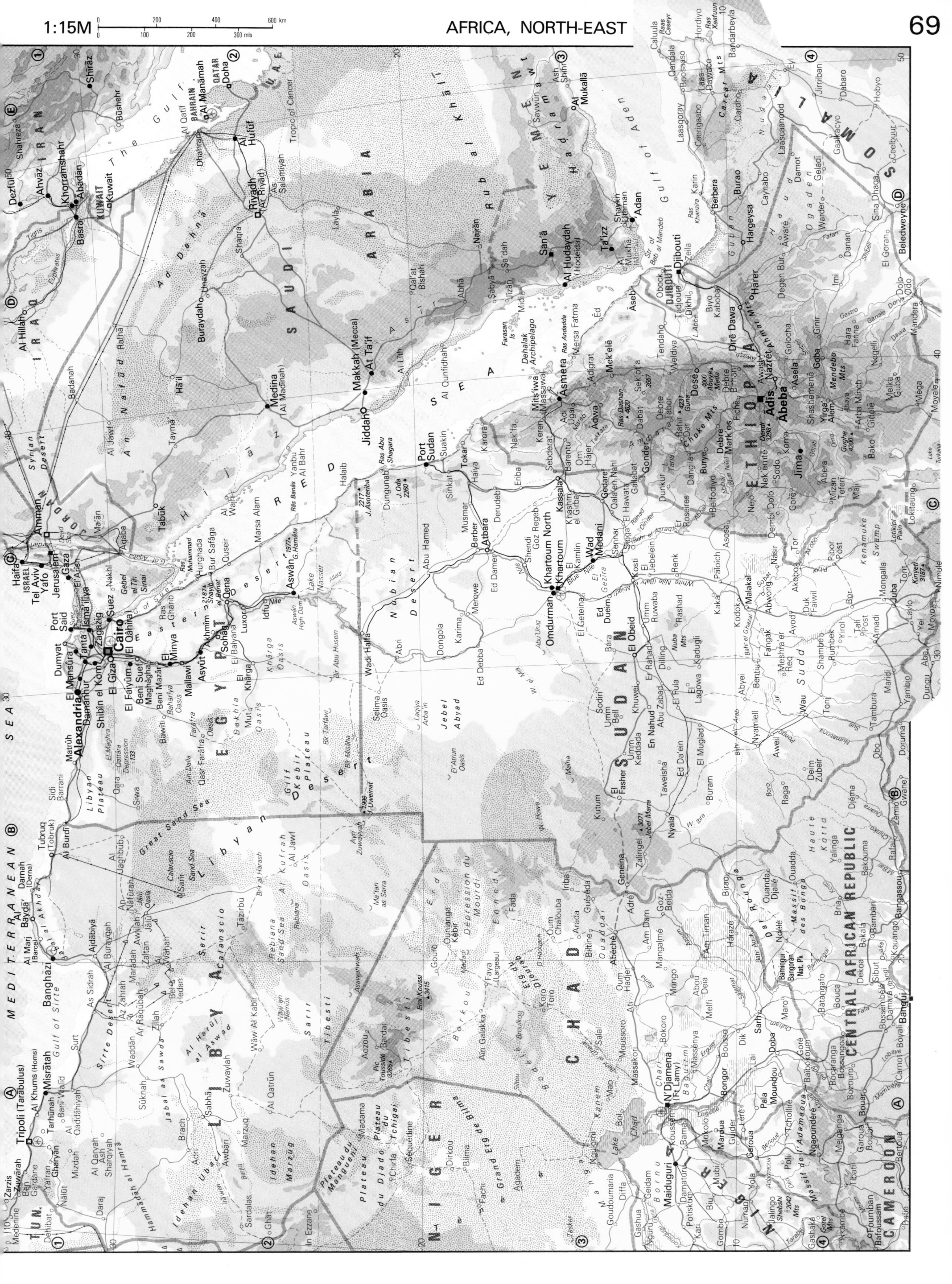
MEDITERRANEAN SEA
LIBYA
EGYPT
SUDAN
CHAD
NIGER
NIGERIA
CAMEROON
CENTRAL AFRICAN REPUBLIC
ETHIOPIA
DJIBOUTI
SOMALIA
SAUDI ARABIA
YEMEN
IRAQ
IRAN
KUWAIT
JORDAN
ISRAEL
BAHRAIN
QATAR
RED SEA
Gulf of Aden
The Gulf
Tropic of Cancer
Libyan Desert
Nubian Desert
Great Sand Sea
Tibesti
Lake Chad
Lake Nasser
Cairo
Alexandria
Khartoum
Omdurman
Tripoli (Tarābulus)
Banghāzī
Adis Abeba
Asmera
Djibouti
Adan
Şan'ā
Makkah (Mecca)
Medina (Al Madīnah)
Jiddah
Riyadh (Ar Riyāḑ)
N'Djamena (Ft Lamy)
Port Sudan
Aswân
Ammān
Jerusalem
Suez
Port Said

1:15M

MEDITERRANEAN SEA
PORTUGAL
SPAIN
MOROCCO
ALGERIA
TUNISIA
Western Sahara
MAURITANIA
MALI
NIGER
SENEGAL
THE GAMBIA
GUINEA-BISSAU
GUINEA
SIERRA LEONE
LIBERIA
IVORY COAST
BURKINA
GHANA
TOGO
BENIN
NIGERIA
CAMEROON
EQUATORIAL GUINEA
S.TOME & PRINCIPE
GULF OF GUINEA
Bight of Benin
Bight of Biafra
Islas Canarias (Canary Islands) (Spain)
Madeira (Portugal)
Açores (Azores) (Portugal)
CAPE VERDE
SAHARA
Tropic of Cancer
Equator
at the same scale

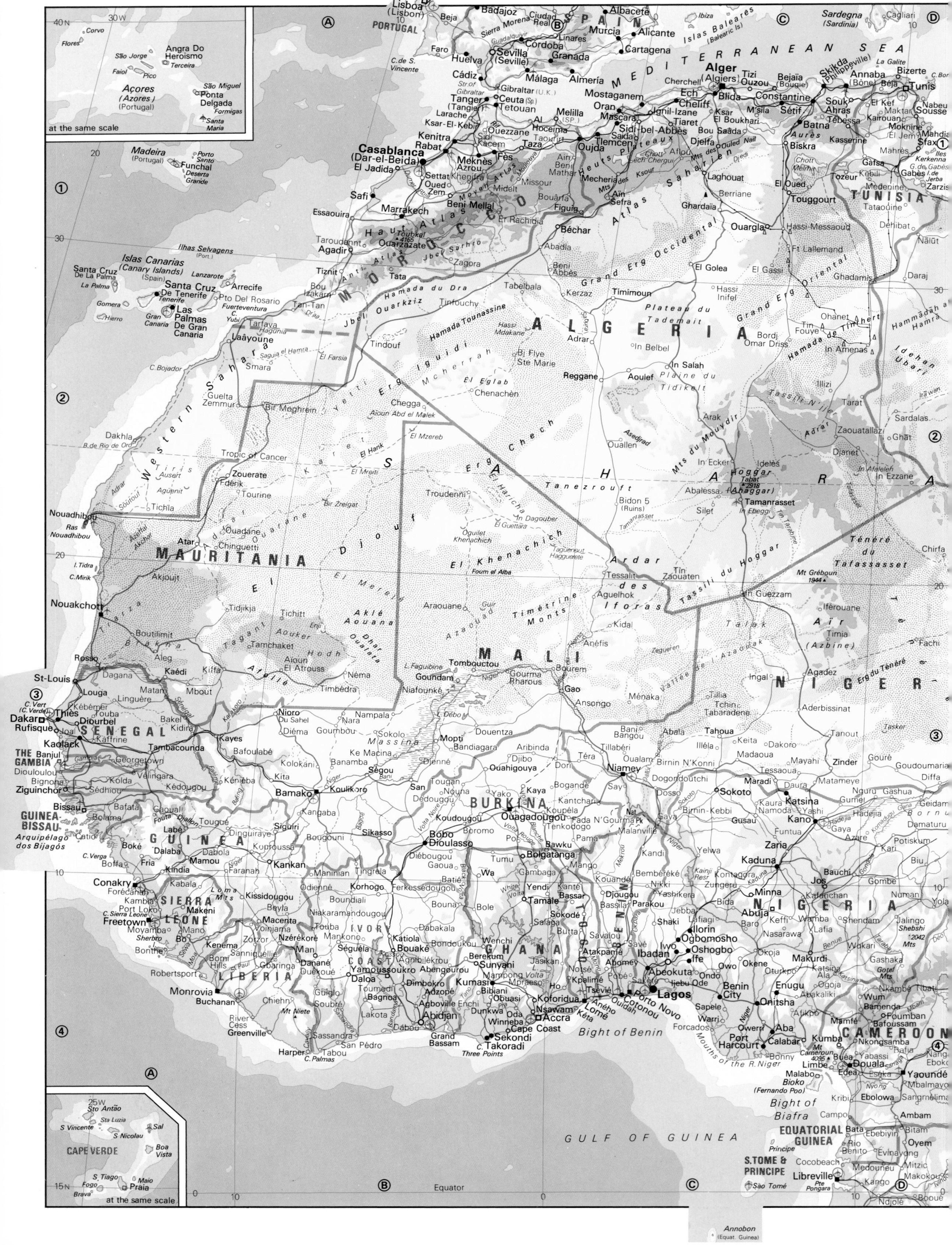

1:7.5M 0 100 200 300 km
0 50 100 150 mls

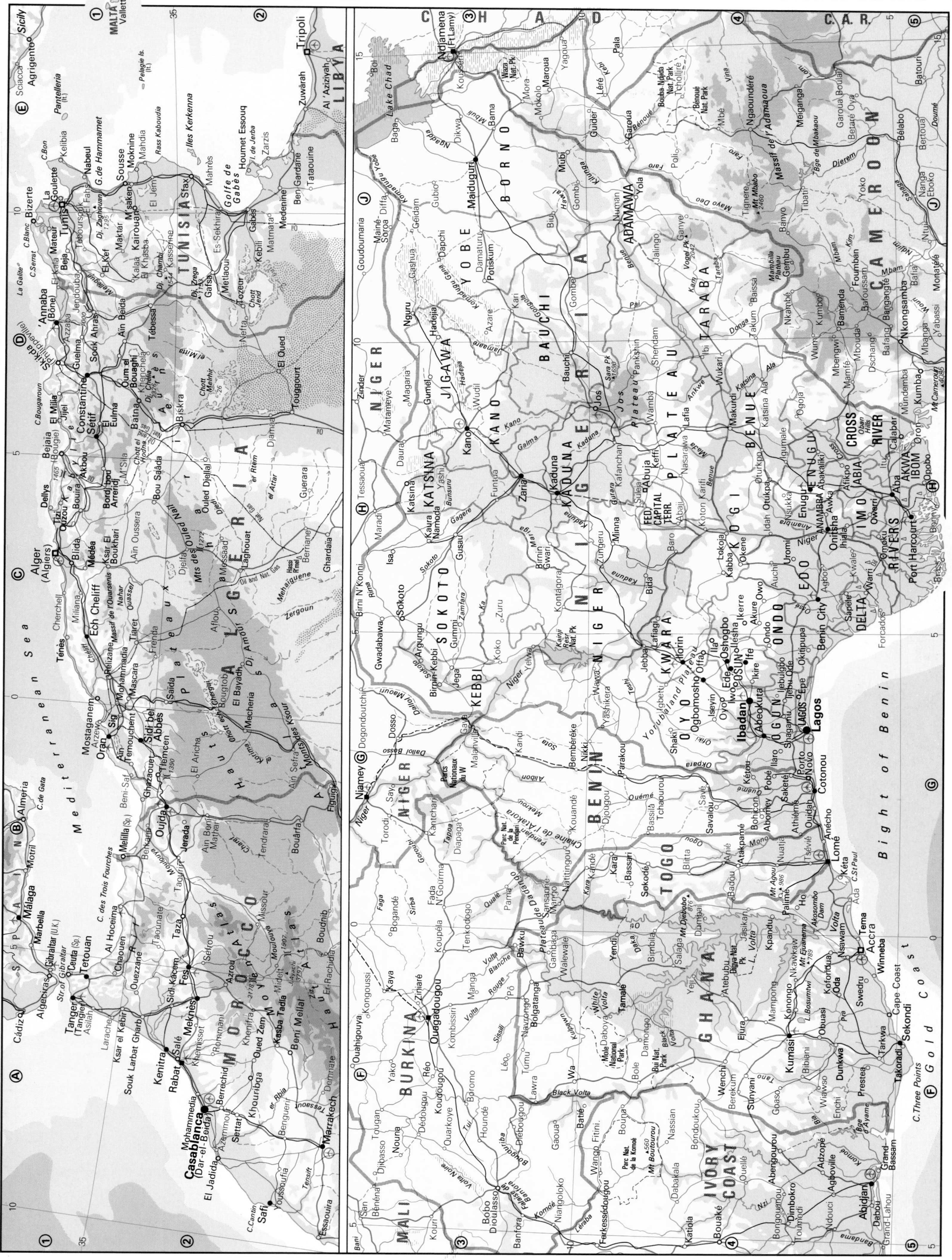

1:15M 0 200 400 600 km
0 100 200 300 mls

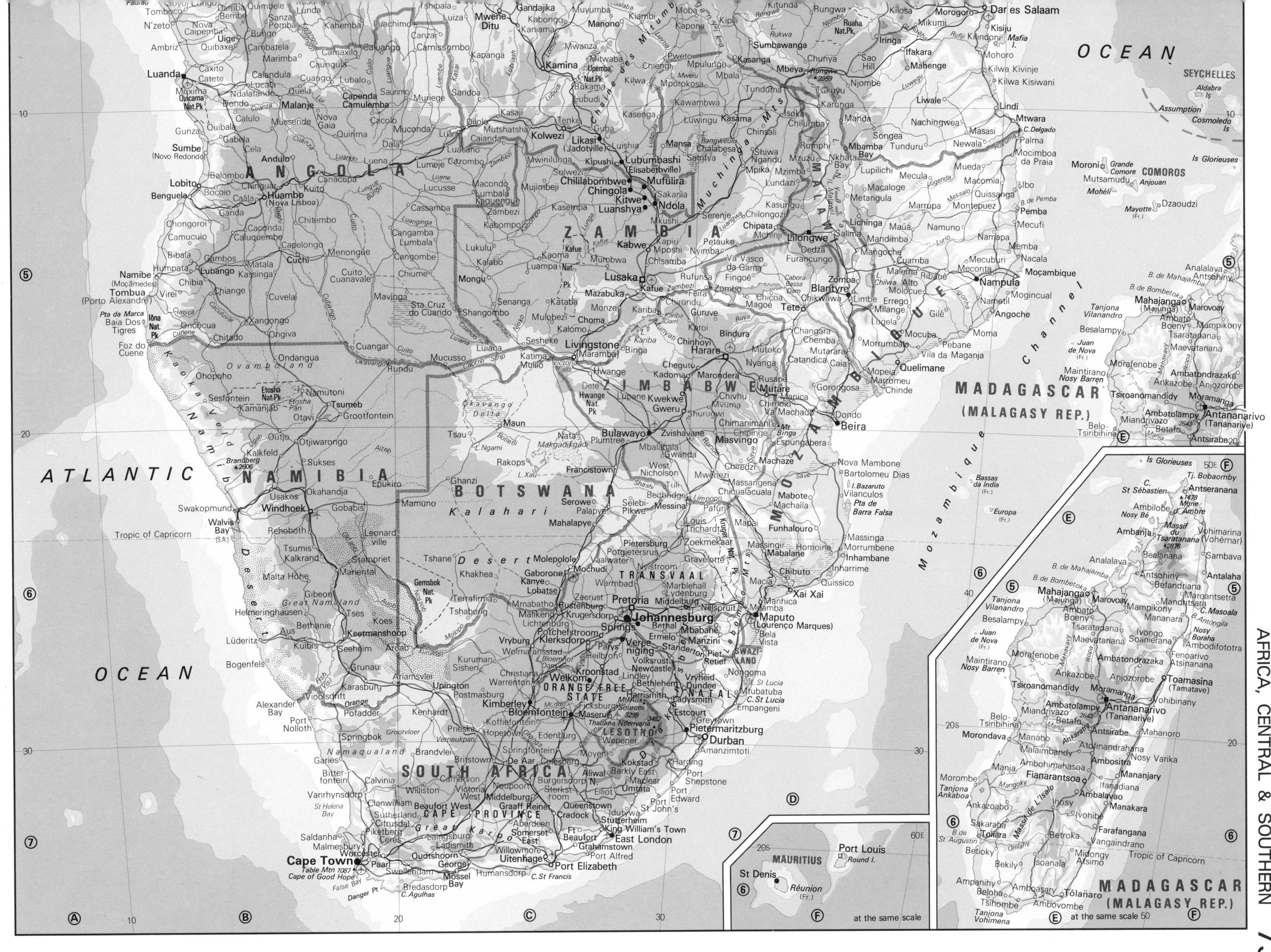
ATLANTIC
OCEAN
OCEAN
Mozambique Channel
ANGOLA
ZAMBIA
MALAWI
MOZAMBIQUE
ZIMBABWE
BOTSWANA
NAMIBIA
SOUTH AFRICA
LESOTHO
SWAZILAND
TRANSVAAL
ORANGE FREE STATE
NATAL
CAPE PROVINCE
MADAGASCAR (MALAGASY REP.)
SEYCHELLES
COMOROS
MAURITIUS
Kalahari
Desert
Tropic of Capricorn
Luanda
Lobito
Benguela
Huambo (Nova Lisboa)
Windhoek
Walvis Bay
Lusaka
Harare
Bulawayo
Gaborone
Pretoria
Johannesburg
Maputo (Lourenço Marques)
Durban
Bloemfontein
Kimberley
Cape Town
Port Elizabeth
East London
Beira
Blantyre
Lilongwe
Dar es Salaam
Antananarivo (Tananarive)
Port Louis
St Denis
Réunion (Fr.)
at the same scale

1:7.5M

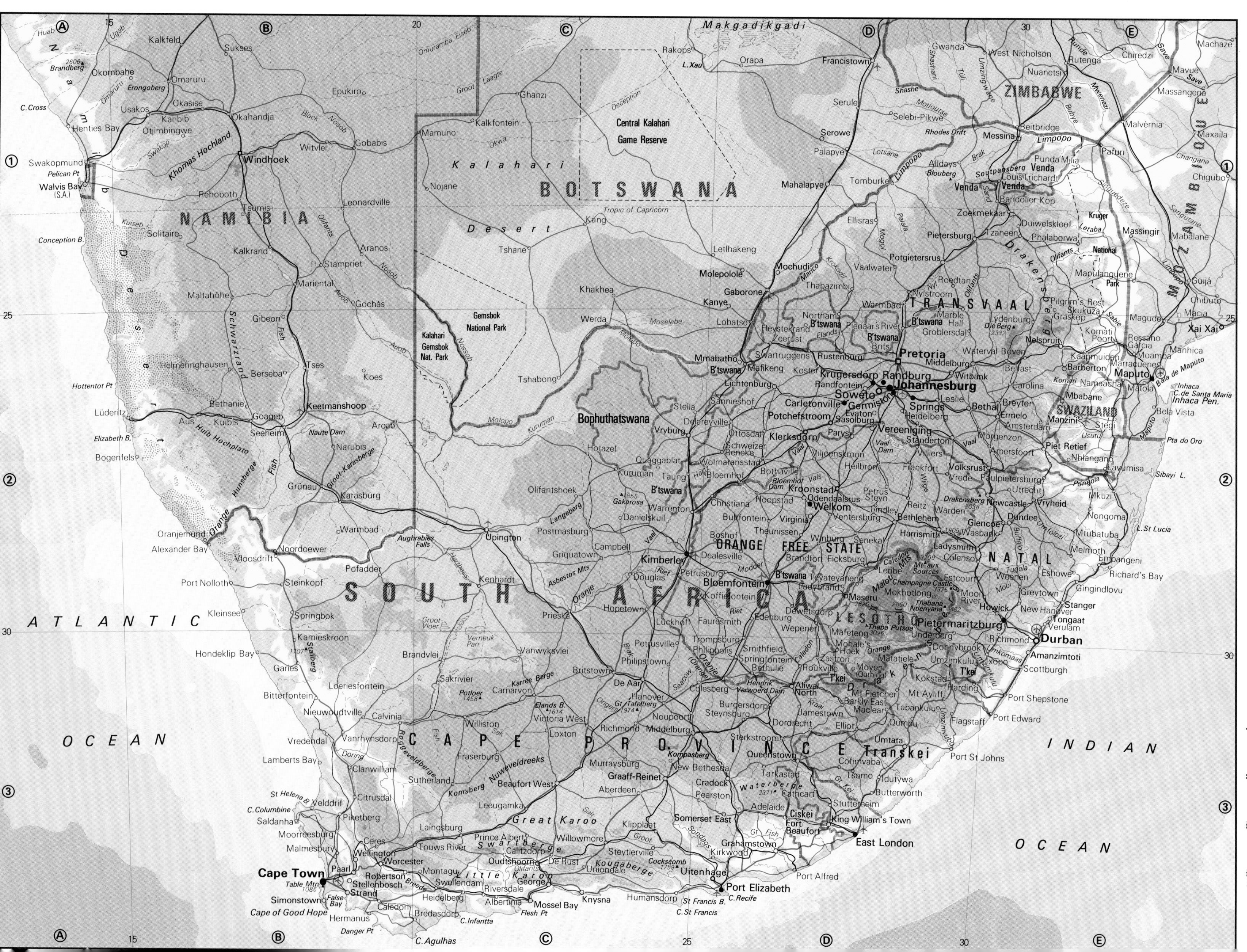
0 100 200 300 km
0 50 100 150 mls
SOUTH AFRICA
BOTSWANA
NAMIBIA
ZIMBABWE
MOZAMBIQUE
LESOTHO
SWAZILAND
TRANSVAAL
ORANGE FREE STATE
NATAL
CAPE PROVINCE
Transkei
Ciskei
Bophuthatswana
Venda
ATLANTIC OCEAN
INDIAN OCEAN
Kalahari Desert
Makgadikgadi
Central Kalahari Game Reserve
Gemsbok National Park
Kalahari Gemsbok Nat. Park
Kruger National Park
Great Karoo
Little Karoo
Tropic of Capricorn
Pretoria
Johannesburg
Soweto
Durban
Pietermaritzburg
Bloemfontein
Kimberley
Welkom
Maseru
Mbabane
Maputo
Windhoek
Walvis Bay (S.A.)
Gaborone
Cape Town
Port Elizabeth
East London
Cape of Good Hope
C. Agulhas
Table Mtn 1086

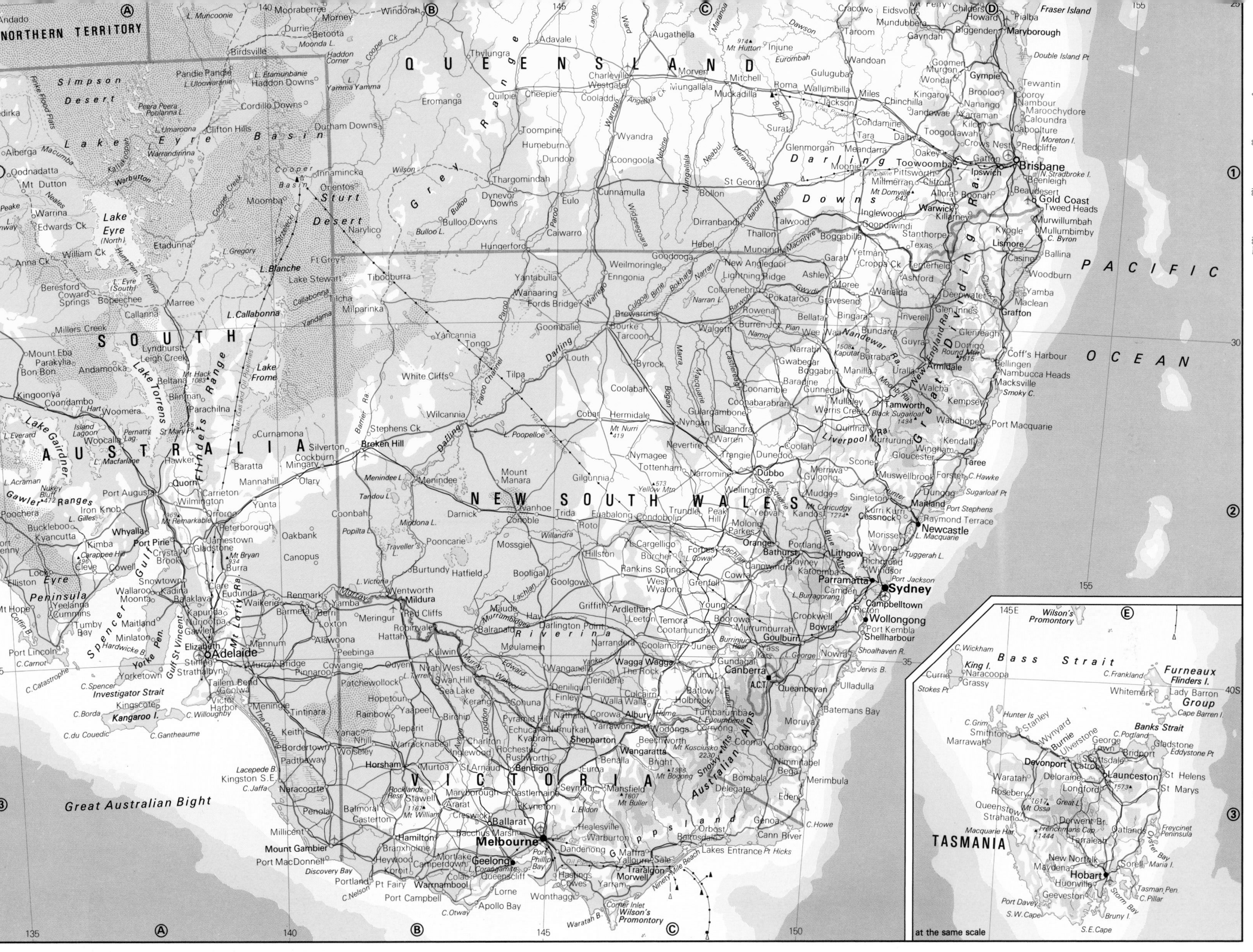
0 100 200 300 km
0 50 100 150 mls
QUEENSLAND
NEW SOUTH WALES
VICTORIA
SOUTH AUSTRALIA
NORTHERN TERRITORY
TASMANIA
PACIFIC OCEAN
Great Australian Bight
Bass Strait
Simpson Desert
Sturt Desert
Great Dividing Ra.
Darling Downs
Australian Alps
Snowy Mts.
Flinders Range
Gawler Ranges
Eyre Peninsula
Yorke Pen.
Spencer Gulf
Gulf St Vincent
Kangaroo I.
Investigator Strait
Lake Eyre (North)
L. Eyre (South)
Lake Torrens
Lake Gairdner
Lake Frome
L. Blanche
L. Callabonna
Lake Eyre Basin
Riverina
Gippsland
Brisbane
Sydney
Melbourne
Adelaide
Canberra
Hobart
Newcastle
Wollongong
Geelong
Launceston
Devonport
Toowoomba
Ipswich
Gold Coast
Broken Hill
Mildura
Dubbo
Orange
Bathurst
Wagga Wagga
Albury
Bendigo
Ballarat
Shepparton
Wangaratta
Horsham
Hamilton
Warrnambool
Mount Gambier
Port Augusta
Port Pirie
Whyalla
Port Lincoln
Tamworth
Armidale
Lismore
Grafton
Goulburn
Queanbeyan
Parramatta
Maryborough
Gympie
Warwick
Fraser Island
Wilson's Promontory
Flinders I.
Furneaux Group
King I.
at the same scale

1:20M

0 200 400 600 800 km

0 200 400 mls

BORNEO
Samarinda
Balikpapan
Banjarmasin
Makassar Strait
SULAWESI (CELEBES)
Manado
Gorontalo
Palu
Poso
Palopo
Kendari
Parepare
Watampone
Ujung Pandang (Makassar)
Ternate
Halmahera
Morotai
Tubelo
MOLUCCAS
Molucca Sea
Ceram Sea
Banda Sea
Ambon
Buru
Seram
Namlea
Sorong
Manokwari
Biak
Fakfak
IRIAN JAYA
Jayapura
Sarmi
Merauke
Kep. Aru
Kep. Kai
Kep. Tanimbar
Flores Sea
Flores
Timor
Dili
Kupang
Sumbawa
Bali
Lombok
Denpasar
Mataram
Waingapu
Ende
Ruteng
INDONESIA

Bismarck Archipelago
Bismarck Sea
Admiralty Is
Kavieng
Wewak
Madang
Lae
Morobe
Mt Hagen
Mendi
Goroka
Mt Wilhelm 4508
Port Moresby
Gulf of Papua
Daru
Kikori
PAPUA NEW GUINEA
NEW GUINEA
Torres Strait

Arafura Sea
Timor Sea
Java Trench
INDIAN OCEAN
Gulf of Carpentaria
Coral Sea
Great Barrier Reef
Great Australian Bight
Bass Strait

AUSTRALIA
WESTERN AUSTRALIA
NORTHERN TERRITORY
SOUTH AUSTRALIA
QUEENSLAND
NEW SOUTH WALES
VICTORIA
TASMANIA
A.C.T.

Darwin
Rum Jungle
Arnhem Land
Nhulunbuy
Katherine
Pine Creek
Adelaide River
Wyndham
Kununurra
Daly Waters
Borroloola
Newcastle Waters
Tennant Creek
Barrow Creek
Alice Springs
Macdonnell Ranges
Simpson Desert
Ayers Rock
Mt Woodroffe 1440
Musgrave Ra.
Great Sandy Desert
Gibson Desert
Great Victoria Desert
Nullarbor Plain
Lake Eyre
Lake Eyre Basin
L. Torrens
L. Gairdner
L. Frome
Broome
Derby
Fitzroy Crossing
Hall's Creek
Port Hedland
Dampier
Roebourne
Onslow
Carnarvon
Newman
Paraburdoo
Hamersley Ra.
Mt Augustus 1106
Meekatharra
Wiluna
Mt Magnet
Leonora
Geraldton
Northampton
Kalgoorlie
Coolgardie
Norseman
Esperance
Perth
Fremantle
Bunbury
Busselton
Albany
Cape Leeuwin
Cape Naturaliste
Eucla
Ooldea
Tarcoola
Coober Pedy
Oodnadatta
Woomera
Port Augusta
Whyalla
Port Pirie
Port Lincoln
Ceduna
Adelaide
Kangaroo I.
Spencer Gulf
Mount Gambier
Murray Bridge
Mt Isa
Cloncurry
Camooweal
Burketown
Normanton
Croydon
Weipa
Cape York
Cooktown
Cairns
Townsville
Charters Towers
Mackay
Rockhampton
Gladstone
Emerald
Longreach
Barcaldine
Winton
Birdsville
Windorah
Charleville
Roma
Toowoomba
Brisbane
Cunnamulla
St George
Bourke
Broken Hill
Wilcannia
Menindee
Dubbo
Orange
Bathurst
Sydney
Wollongong
Newcastle
Canberra
Wagga Wagga
Griffith
Albury
Mildura
Melbourne
Geelong
Ballarat
Bendigo
Shepparton
Horsham
Hamilton
Portland
Warrnambool
Launceston
Burnie
Devonport
Hobart
Queenstown
Mt Kosciusko 2230
Great Dividing Range
Darling
Murray
Murrumbidgee

110 120 130 140 150

A B C D

1 2 3 4 5

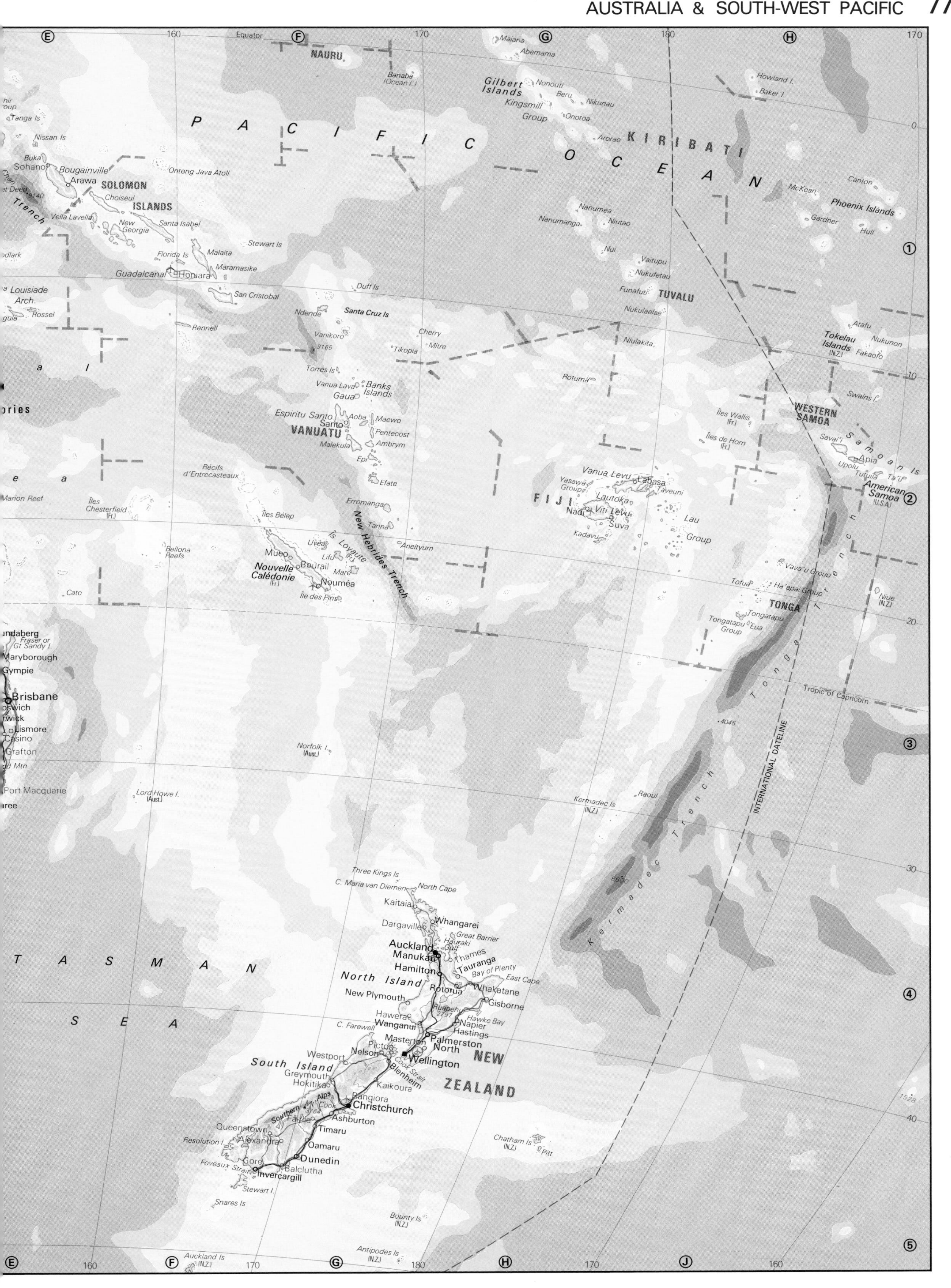

PACIFIC OCEAN
Equator
NAURU
Banaba (Ocean I.)
Maiana
Abemama
Gilbert Islands
Nonouti
Beru
Nikunau
Kingsmill Group
Onotoa
Arorae
KIRIBATI
Howland I.
Baker I.
Canton
McKean
Phoenix Islands
Gardner
Hull
Tanga Is
Nissan Is
Buka
Sohano
Bougainville
Arawa
Ontong Java Atoll
SOLOMON ISLANDS
Choiseul
Vella Lavella
New Georgia
Santa Isabel
Stewart Is
Florida Is
Malaita
Maramasike
Guadalcanal
Honiara
San Cristobal
Louisiade Arch.
Rossel
Rennell
Duff Is
Ndende
Santa Cruz Is
Vanikoro
9165
Cherry
Tikopia
Mitre
Torres Is
Vanua Lava
Banks Islands
Gaua
Espiritu Santo
Santo
Aoba
Maewo
VANUATU
Pentecost
Malekula
Ambrym
Epi
Efate
Erromanga
Tanna
Aneityum
Récifs d'Entrecasteaux
Îles Chesterfield (Fr.)
Marion Reef
Îles Bélep
Bellona Reefs
Uvéa
Is Loyauté (Fr.)
Lifu
Maré
Mueo
Bourail
Nouvelle Calédonie (Fr.)
Nouméa
Île des Pins
Cato
New Hebrides Trench
Nanumea
Nanumanga
Niutao
Nui
Vaitupu
Nukufetau
Funafuti
TUVALU
Nukulaelae
Niulakita
Rotuma
Atafu
Nukunon
Tokelau Islands (N.Z.)
Fakaofo
Swains I.
WESTERN SAMOA
Savai'i
Apia
Upolu
Samoa Is
Tutuila
Ta'ū
American Samoa (U.S.A.)
Îles Wallis (Fr.)
Îles de Horn (Fr.)
Vanua Levu
Labasa
Taveuni
Yasawa Group
Lautoka
FIJI
Viti Levu
Nadi
Suva
Kadavu
Lau Group
Vava'u Group
Tofua
Ha'apai Group
TONGA
Niue (N.Z.)
Tongatapu Group
Tongatapu
'Eua
Tonga Trench
Tropic of Capricorn
4045
INTERNATIONAL DATELINE
Kermadec Is (N.Z.)
Raoul
Kermadec Trench
Bundaberg
Fraser or Gt Sandy I.
Maryborough
Gympie
Brisbane
Ipswich
Lismore
Casino
Grafton
Port Macquarie
Norfolk I. (Aust.)
Lord Howe I. (Aust.)
TASMAN SEA
Three Kings Is
C. Maria van Diemen
North Cape
Kaitaia
Whangarei
Dargaville
Great Barrier
Hauraki Gulf
Auckland
Manukau
Thames
Hamilton
Tauranga
Bay of Plenty
East Cape
North Island
Rotorua
Whakatane
New Plymouth
Gisborne
Ruapehu
Hawke Bay
Hawera
Napier
Wanganui
Hastings
C. Farewell
Masterton
Palmerston North
Picton
Nelson
Westport
Wellington
Cook Strait
Blenheim
NEW ZEALAND
South Island
Greymouth
Hokitika
Kaikoura
Rangiora
Christchurch
Southern Alps
Cook
Fairlie
Ashburton
Queenstown
Timaru
Resolution I.
Alexandra
Oamaru
Dunedin
Gore
Foveaux Strait
Balclutha
Invercargill
Stewart I.
Snares Is
Chatham Is (N.Z.)
Pitt
Bounty Is (N.Z.)
Antipodes Is (N.Z.)
Auckland Is (N.Z.)
1528
E
F
G
H
J
160
170
180
170
160
0
10
20
30
40
1
2
3
4
5

1:5M
0 50 100 150 200 km 
0 50 100 mls

Three Kings Is
C. Maria van Diemen
North Cape
Ninety Mile Beach
Rangaunu B.
Doubtless B.
Ahipara B.
Tauroa Pt
Kaitaia
Bay of Islands
C.Brett
Russell
Kaikohe
Kawakawa
Hikurangi
Hokianga Har.
Whangarei
Hen & Chickens Is
Bream B.
Dargaville
Little Barrier I.
Great Barrier I.
Kaipara Har.
Wellsford
Hauraki Gulf
C.Colville
Mercury Is
Mercury Bay
Coromandel Ra.
Coromandel Peninsula
Takapuna
Auckland
Papatoetoe
Manukau
Papakura
Pukekohe
Waiuku
Thames
Mayor I.
NORTH ISLAND
Paeroa
Waihi
Huntly
Te Aroha
Matakana I.
Tauranga Har.
White I.
C. Runaway
Hicks Bay
East C.
Glen Afton
Ngaruawahia
Morrinsville
Tauranga
Hamilton
Cambridge
Te Puke
Bay of Plenty
Whakatane
Te Awamutu
Putaruru
Opotiki
Kawhia
Otorohanga
Rotorua
Kawerau
Te Teko
Raukumara Ra.
Waitomo
Te Kuiti
Tokomaru Bay
Tolaga Bay
Mangakino
Murupara
Huiarau Ra.
Taupo
L. Taupo
Gisborne
N. Taranaki Bight
Ohura
Waitara
Taumarunui
Waikaremoana
Poverty Bay
New Plymouth
Inglewood
Mt Ngauruhoe 2291
Kaimanawa Mts
Mt Makorako 1727
C. Egmont
Mt Egmont 2518
Stratford
Mt Ruapehu 2797
Tarawera
Wairoa
Mahia Peninsula
Hawke Bay
Opunake
Eltham
Raetihi
Ohakune
Portland I.
Hawera
Waiouru
Eskdale
Taradale
Napier
S.Taranaki Bight
Patea
Taihape
Hastings
C. Kidnappers
Havelock North
Wanganui
Marton
Rangitikei
Ruahine Ra.
Waipukurau
Palmerston N.
Feilding
Dannevirke
Foxton
Woodville
Pahiatua
C. Farewell
Farewell Spit
Golden Bay
Separation Pt
COOK STRAIT
C.Turnagain
Herbertville
Collingwood
Levin
Eketahuna
Rocks Pt
C.Stephens
D'Urville I.
Otaki
Takaka
Tasman Mts
Tasman Bay
Paraparaumu
C.Jackson
Masterton
Carterton
Motueka
The Twins 1826
Picton
Porirua
Tawa
Upper Hutt
Karamea
Karamea Bight
Nelson
Richmond
Wellington
Lower Hutt
Wairarapa
Martinborough
Seddonville
Richmond Ra.
Wairau
Blenheim
Palliser Bay
Mt Ross 983
C. Palliser
Westport
C. Foulwind
Murchison
Buller
C. Campbell
Awatere
L. Rotoroa
L. Rotoiti
Reefton
Victoria Ra.
Spenser Mts
Mt Travers 2338
Kaikoura Ra.
Tapuaenuku 2885
Clarence
Runanga
Greymouth
Grey
Lewis Pass
Hanmer Springs
Kaikoura
Kaikoura Pen.
Hokitika
L. Brunner
Waiau
L. Sumner
Culverden
Hurunui
Cheviot
Ross
Arthurs Pass
Puketeraki Ra.
Waipara
SOUTH ISLAND
Abut Hd
Pegasus Bay
Rangiora
Kaiapoi
Franz Josef Gl.
L. Coleridge
Rakaia
Waimakariri
Hornby
Christchurch
Lyttelton
SOUTHERN ALPS
Mt Cook 3764
Mt Sefton 3157
Methven
Lincoln
Banks Peninsula
Akaroa
Hermitage
Canterbury Plains
L. Ellesmere
L. Tekapo
Geraldine
Ashburton
Jackson Hd
Cascade Pt
Pollux 2542
Young Ra.
L. Pukaki
Ohau
Lake Pukaki
Fairlie
Canterbury Bight
Temuka
Awarua Pt
L. Benmore
Timaru
Mt Aspiring 3027
L. Wanaka
L. Hawea
Omarama
Hawkdun Ra.
L. Aviemore
Milford Sd
Milford Sd
Homer Tunnel
Wanaka
Kurow
Waimate
PACIFIC OCEAN
TASMAN SEA
Mt Pyramid 2326
George Sd
Arrowtown
Dunstan Mts
Waitaki
Caswell Sd
Queenstown
Cromwell
Clyde
Ranfurly
Oamaru
Secretary I.
Fiordland
L. Te Anau
L. Wakatipu
Alexandra
Hampden
Doubtful Sd
Te Anau
Kingston
Nat. Park
L. Manapouri 718
Manapouri
Roxburgh
Palmerston
Breaksea Sd
Mt Ward
Waikouaiti
Resolution I.
Dusky Sd
Waiau
Lumsden
Riversdale
Heriot
Taieri
Port Chalmers
Otago Peninsula
Mosgiel
Dunedin
Cameron Mts
Ohai
L. Hauroko
Oreti
Tapanui
Clutha
Lawrence
Milton
Tuatapere
Gore
Winton
Puysegur Pt
Te Waewae Bay
Mataura
Balclutha
Edendale
Kaitangata
Riverton
Owaka
Invercargill
Foveaux Strait
Solander I.
Bluff
Codfish I.
Oban
Paterson Inlet
Stewart Island
Mt Allen 730
Shelter Pt
Port Pegasus

35 40 45 170 175
A B C 1 2 3

1:40M 0 400 800 1200 1600 km / 0 400 800 mls

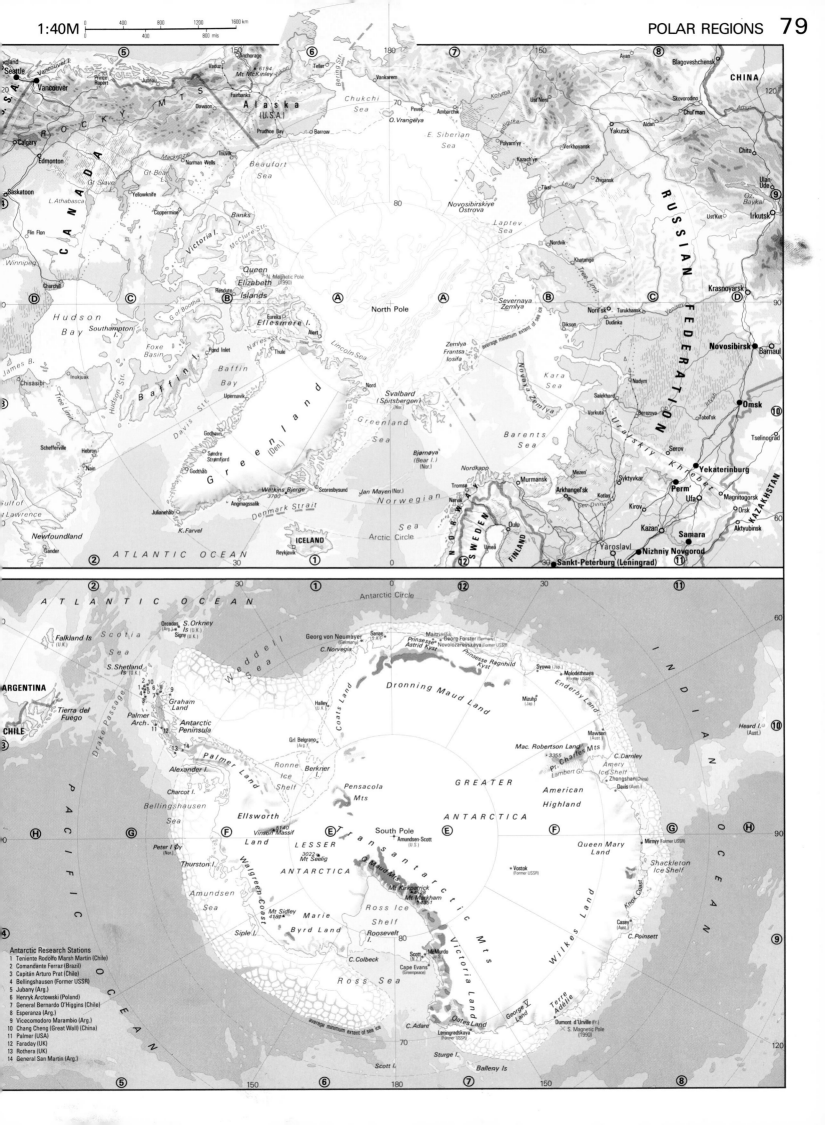

Antarctic Research Stations

1 Teniente Rodolfo Marsh Martin (Chile)
2 Comandante Ferraz (Brazil)
3 Capitán Arturo Prat (Chile)
4 Bellingshausen (Former USSR)
5 Jubany (Arg.)
6 Henryk Arctowski (Poland)
7 General Bernardo O'Higgins (Chile)
8 Esperanza (Arg.)
9 Vicecomodoro Marambio (Arg.)
10 Chang Cheng (Great Wall) (China)
11 Palmer (USA)
12 Faraday (UK)
13 Rothera (UK)
14 General San Martin (Arg.)

Abbreviations

Abbreviations used in Reference Map Section

A

	Full Form	English Form	Language
a.d.	an der	**on the**	German
Akr.	Akra, Akrotírion	**cape**	Greek
Appno	Appennino	**mountain range**	Italian
Arch.	Archipelago	**archipelago**	English

B

	Full Form	English Form	Language
B.	1. Baai, Bahía, Baía, Baie, Bay, Bucht, Bukhta, Bugt	**bay**	Dutch, Spanish, Portuguese, French, English, German, Russian, Danish
	2. Ban	**village**	Indo-Chinese
	3. Barrage	**dam**	French
Bol.	Bol'sh/aya, -oy, -oye	**big**	Russian
Br.	1. Branch	**branch**	English
	2. Bridge, Brücke	**bridge**	English, German
	3. Burun	**cape**	Turkish
Brj	Baraj,-i	**dam**	Turkish

C

	Full Form	English Form	Language
C.	Cabo, Cap, Cape	**cape**	Spanish, French, English
Can.	Canal	**canal**	English
Cd	Ciudad	**town**	Spanish
Chan.	Channel	**channel**	English
Ck	Creek	**creek**	English
Cord.	Cordillera	**mountain range**	Spanish

D

	Full Form	English Form	Language
D.	1. Dağ,Dägh, Daği, Dağlari	**mountain, range**	Persian, Turkish
	2. Daryācheh	**lake**	Persian
Dj.	Djebel	**mountain**	Arabic

E

	Full Form	English Form	Language
E.	East	**east**	English
Emb.	Embalse	**reservoir**	Spanish
Escarp.	Escarpment	**escarpment**	English
Estr.	Estrecho	**strait**	Spanish

F

	Full Form	English Form	Language
F.	Firth	**estuary**	Gaelic
Fj.	1. Fjell	**mountain**	Norwegian
	2. Fjord, Fjorður	**fjord**	Norwegian, Icelandic
Ft	Fort	**fort**	English

G

	Full Form	English Form	Language
G.	1. Gebel	**mountain**	Arabic
	2. Göl, Gölü	**lake**	Turkish
	3. Golfe, Golfo, Gulf	**gulf**	French, Italian, Portuguese, Spanish, English
	4. Gora, -gory	**mountain, range**	Russian
	5. Gunung	**mountain**	Malay, Indonesian
Gd, Gde	Grand, Grande	**grand**	English, French
Geb.	Gebirge	**mountain range**	German
Gl.	Glacier	**glacier**	French, English
Grl	General	**general**	Spanish
Gt, Gtr	Great, Groot, -e, Greater	**greater**	English, Dutch

H

	Full Form	English Form	Language
Har.	Harbour	**harbour**	English
Hd	Head	**head**	English

I

	Full Form	English Form	Language
I.	Ile, Ilha, Insel, Isla, Island Isle, Isola, Isole	**island**	French, Portuguese, German Spanish, English, Italian
In.	1. Indre, Inner	**inner**	Norwegian, English
	2. Inlet	**inlet**	English
Is	Iles, Ilhas, Islands, Isles, Islas	**islands**	French, Portuguese, English, Spanish
Isth.	Isthmus	**isthmus**	English

J

	Full Form	English Form	Language
J.	Jabal, Jebel, Jibal	**mountain**	Arabic

K

	Full Form	English Form	Language
K.	1. Kaap, Kap, Kapp	**cape**	Dutch, German, Norwegian, Swedish
	2. Koh, Kuh, Kuhha	**mountain**	Persian
	3. Kolpos	**gulf**	Greek
Kep.	Kepulauan	**islands**	Indonesian
Khr.	Khrebet	**mountain range**	Russian
Kör.	Körfez, -i	**gulf, bay**	Turkish

L

	Full Form	English Form	Language
L.	1. Lac, Lago, Lagoa, Lake, Liman, Limni, Loch, Lough	**lake**	French, Italian, Spanish, Portuguese, English, Russian, Greek, Gaelic
Lag.	Lagoon, Laguna, -e, Lagôa	**lagoon**	English, Spanish, French, Portuguese
Ld	Land	**land**	English
Lit.	Little	**little**	English

M

	Full Form	English Form	Language
M.	1. Muang	**town**	Thai
	2. Mys	**cape**	Russian
m	metre, -s	**metre(s)**	English, French
Mal.	Mali, -o, -yy	**small**	Russian
Mf	Massif	**mountain group**	French
Mgne	Montagne(s)	**mountain(s)**	French
Mont	Monument	**monument**	English
Mt	Mont, Mount	**mountain**	French, English
Mte	Monte	**mountain**	Italian, Portuguese, Spanish
Mti	Monti	**mountain, range**	Italian
Mtn	Mountain	**mountain**	English
Mts	Monts, Mountains Montañas, Montes	**mountains**	French, English, Spanish, Italian, Portuguese

N

	Full Form	English Form	Language
N.	1. Neu, Ny	**new**	German
	2. Nevado	**snow capped mtns**	Spanish
	3. Noord, Nord, Norte Nørre, North	**north**	Danish, French, Portuguese, Spanish, Danish, English
Nat.	National	**national**	English
Nat. Pk	National Park	**national park**	English
Ndr	Neder, Nieder	**lower**	Dutch, Swedish, German
N.E.	North East	**north east**	English
N.M.	National Monument	**national monument**	English
N.P.	National Park	**national park**	English
N.W.	North West	**north west**	English

O

	Full Form	English Form	Language
O.	1. Oost, Ost	**east**	Dutch, German
	2. Ostrov	**island**	Russian
Ø	Øy	**island**	Norwegian
Oz.	Ozero, Ozera	**lake(s)**	Russian

P

	Full Form	English Form	Language
P.	1. Pass, Passo	**pass**	English, German, Italian
	2. Pic, Pico, Pizzo	**peak**	French, Portuguese, Spanish, Italian
	3. Pulau	**island**	Malay, Indonesian
P.P.	Pulau-pulau	**islands**	Indonesian
Pass.	Passage	**passage**	English
Peg.	Pegunungan	**mountains**	Indonesian
Pen.	Peninsula, Peninsola	**peninsula**	English, Italian
Pk	1. Park	**park**	English
	2. Peak, Pik	**peak**	English, Russian
Plat.	Plateau, Planalto	**plateau**	English, French, Portuguese
Pov	Poluostrov	**peninsula**	Russian
Pr.	Prince	**prince**	English
Pres.	President, Presidente	**president**	English, Spanish, Portuguese
Promy	Promontory	**promontory**	English
Pt	Point	**point**	English
Pta	1. Ponta, Punta	**point**	Portuguese, Italian, Spanish
	2. Puerta	**pass**	Spanish
Pte	Pointe	**point**	French
Pto	Porto, Puerto	**port**	Spanish

R

	Full Form	English Form	Language
R.	1. Rio, River, Rivière,	**river**	Portuguese, Spanish, English, French
	2. Ría	**river mouth**	Spanish
Ra.	Range	**range**	English
Rap.	Rapids	**rapids**	English
Res.	Reserve, Reservation	**reserve, reservation**	English
Resr	Reservoir	**reservoir**	English
Résr	Réservoir	**reservoir**	French

S

	Full Form	English Form	Language
S.	1. Salar, Salina	**salt marsh**	Spanish
	2. San, São	**saint**	Spanish, Portuguese
	3. See	**sea, lake**	German
	4. South, Sud	**south**	English, French
s.	sur	**on**	French
Sa	Serra, Sierra	**mountain range**	Portuguese, Spanish
Sd	Sound, Sund	**sound**	English, German, Swedish
S.E.	South East	**south east**	English
Sev.	Sever, Severnaya	**north**	Russian
Sp.	Spitze	**peak**	German
Spr.	Spring,(s)	**spring(s)**	English
St	Saint	**saint**	English
Sta	Santa	**saint**	Spanish
Sta.	Station	**station**	English
Ste	Sainte	**saint**	French
Sto	Santo	**saint**	Portuguese, Spanish
Str.	Strait	**strait**	English
S.W.	South West	**south west**	English

T

	Full Form	English Form	Language
T.	Tall, Tel	**hill, mountain**	Arabic, Hebrew
Tg	Tanjong, Tandjong	**cape**	Malay, Indonesian
Tk	Têluk, Télok	**bay**	Indonesian
Tr.	Trench, Trough	**trench, trough**	English

U

	Full Form	English Form	Language
U.	Uad	**wadi**	Arabic
Ug	Ujung	**cape**	Malay
Upr	Upper	**upper**	English

V

	Full Form	English Form	Language
V.	1. Val, Valle	**valley**	French, Italian, Spanish
	2. Ville	**town**	French
Va	Villa	**town**	Spanish
Vdkhr.	Vodokhranilishche	**reservoir**	Russian
Vol.	Volcán, Volcano	**volcano**	Spanish, English
Vozv.	Vozvyshennost'	**upland**	Russian

W

	Full Form	English Form	Language
W.	1. Wadi	**wadi**	Arabic
	2. Water	**water**	English
	3. Well	**well**	English
	4. West	**west**	English

Y

	Full Form	English Form	Language
Yuzh.	Yuzhnaya, Yuzhno, Yuzhnyy	**south**	Russian

Z

	Full Form	English Form	Language
Z.	Zaliv	**gulf, bay**	Russian
Zap.	Zapadnyy, -aya, -o, -oye	**western**	Russian
Zem.	Zemlya	**country, land**	Russian

Index

Introduction to the index

In the index, the first number refers to the page, and the following letter and number to the section of the map in which the index entry can be found. For example, 38C2 **Paris** means that Paris can be found on page 38 where column C and row 2 meet.

Abbreviations used in the index

Afghan	Afghanistan
Alb	Albania
Alg	Algeria
Ant	Antarctica
Arg	Argentina
Aust	Australia
Bang	Bangladesh
Belg	Belgium
Bol	Bolivia
Bulg	Bulgaria
Camb	Cambodia
Can	Canada
CAR	Central African Republic
Czech	Czechoslovakia
Den	Denmark
Dom Rep	Dominican Republic
El Sal	El Salvador
Eng	England
Eq Guinea	Equatorial Guinea
Eth	Ethiopia
Fin	Finland
Hung	Hungary
Ind	Indonesia
Irish Rep	Irish Republic
N Ire	Ireland, Northern
Leb	Lebanon
Lib	Liberia
Liech	Liechtenstein
Lux	Luxembourg
Madag	Madagascar
Malay	Malaysia
Maur	Mauritania
Mor	Morocco
Mozam	Mozambique
Neth	Netherlands
NZ	New Zealand
Nic	Nicaragua
Nig	Nigeria
Nor	Norway
Pak	Pakistan
PNG	Papua New Guinea
Par	Paraguay
Phil	Philippines
Pol	Poland
Port	Portugal
Rom	Romania
Russian Fed	Russian Federation
S Arabia	Saudi Arabia
Scot	Scotland
Sen	Senegal
S Africa	South Africa
Switz	Switzerland
Tanz	Tanzania
Thai	Thailand
Turk	Turkey
USA	United States of America
Urug	Uruguay
Ven	Venezuela
Viet	Vietnam
Yugos	Yugoslavia
Zim	Zimbabwe
Arch	Archipelago
B	Bay
C	Cape
Chan	Channel
Gl	Glacier
I(s)	Island(s)
Lg	Lagoon
L	Lake
Mt(s)	Mountain(s)
O	Ocean
P	Pass
Pass	Passage
Pen	Peninsula
Plat	Plateau
Pt	Point
Res	Reservoir
R	River
S	Sea
Sd	Sound
Str	Strait
V	Valley

A

42B2 **Aachen** Germany
36C1 **Aalst** Belg
32K6 **Äänekoski** Fin
37C1 **Aarau** Switz
37B1 **Aare** *R* Switz
52A3 **Aba** China
71H4 **Aba** Nig
72D3 **Aba** Zaïre
63B2 **Abādān** Iran
63C2 **Abādeh** Iran
70B1 **Abadla** Alg
29C2 **Abaeté** Brazil
29C2 **Abaeté** *R* Brazil
27J4 **Abaetetuba** Brazil
52D1 **Abagnar Qi** China
71H4 **Abaji** Nig
19E3 **Abajo Mts** USA
71H4 **Abakaliki** Nig
49L4 **Abakan** Russian Fed
70C3 **Abala** Niger
70C2 **Abalessa** Alg
26D6 **Abancay** Peru
63C2 **Abarqū** Iran
53E3 **Abashiri** Japan
53E3 **Abashiri-wan** *B* Japan
22C1 **Abasolo** Mexico
51H7 **Abau** PNG
72D3 **Abaya** *L* Eth
72D2 **Abbai** *R* Eth
72E2 **Abbe** *L* Eth
38C1 **Abbeville** France
17D4 **Abbeville** Louisiana, USA
15C2 **Abbeville** S Carolina, USA
37C2 **Abbiategrasso** Italy
18B1 **Abbotsford** Can
12A2 **Abbotsford** USA
60C2 **Abbottabad** Pak
67F4 **Abd-al-Kuri** *I* Yemen
44J5 **Abdulino** Russian Fed
72C2 **Abéché** Chad
71F4 **Abengourou** Ivory Coast
32F7 **Åbenrå** Den
42B1 **Åbenra** Den
71G4 **Abeokuta** Nig
72D3 **Abera** Eth
35C5 **Aberaeron** Wales
20C2 **Aberdeen** California, USA
13D3 **Aberdeen** Maryland, USA
15B2 **Aberdeen** Mississippi, USA
74C3 **Aberdeen** S Africa
34D3 **Aberdeen** Scot
8D2 **Aberdeen** S Dakota, USA
8A2 **Aberdeen** Washington, USA
6J3 **Aberdeen L** Can
34D3 **Aberfeldy** Scot
35D6 **Abergavenny** Wales
35C5 **Aberystwyth** Wales
44L2 **Abez'** Russian Fed
66D3 **Abhā** S Arabia
63B1 **Abhar** Iran
71H4 **Abia** *State* Nigeria
66C4 **Abi Addi** Eth
71F4 **Abidjan** Ivory Coast
17C2 **Abilene** Kansas, USA
16C3 **Abilene** Texas, USA
35E6 **Abingdon** Eng
12C3 **Abingdon** USA
7K4 **Abitibi** *R* Can
7L5 **Abitibi,L** Can
45G7 **Abkhazskaya** Respublika, Georgia
36A2 **Ablis** France
60C2 **Abohar** India
71G4 **Abomey** Benin
72B3 **Abong Mbang** Cam
57E9 **Aborlan** Phil
72B2 **Abou Deïa** Chad
67E1 **Abqaiq** S Arabia
39A2 **Abrantes** Port
72D1 **'Abri** Sudan
76A3 **Abrolhos** *Is* Aust
8B2 **Absaroka Range** *Mts* USA
67F2 **Abū al Abyad** *I* UAE
67E1 **Abū 'Ali** *I* S Arabia
66D3 **Abū Arish** S Arabia
66B3 **Abu Deleiq** Sudan
67F2 **Abū Dhabi** UAE
66B3 **'Abu Dom** *Watercourse* Sudan
65C3 **Ābū el Jurdhān** Jordan
66B3 **Abu Fatima** Sudan
72D2 **Abu Hamed** Sudan
68E7 **Abuja** Nigeria
65A3 **Abu Kebir Hihya** Egypt
26E5 **Abunã** Brazil
26E6 **Abuna** *R* Bol
64D3 **Abū Sukhayr** Iraq
65B3 **Abu Suweir** Egypt
78B2 **Abut Head** *C* NZ
66B1 **Abu Tig** Egypt
72D2 **Abu'Urug** *Well* Sudan
72D2 **Abuye Meda** *Mt* Eth
72C2 **Abu Zabad** Sudan
72D3 **Abwong** Sudan
42B1 **Åby** Den
65C3 **Aby 'Aweigīla** *Well* Egypt
72C3 **Abyei** Sudan
13F2 **Acadia Nat Pk** USA
21B2 **Acambaro** Mexico
23B5 **Acandi** Colombia
21B2 **Acaponeta** Mexico
21B3 **Acapulco** Mexico
27L4 **Acaraú** Brazil
26E2 **Acarigua** Ven
22C2 **Acatlán** Mexico
22C2 **Acatzingo** Mexico
22D2 **Acayucan** Mexico
71F4 **Accra** Ghana
28E2 **Aceguá** Urug
60D4 **Achalpur** India
25B6 **Achao** Chile
53B2 **Acheng** China
37D1 **Achensee** *L* Austria
36E2 **Achern** Germany
33A3 **Achill** *I* Irish Rep
49L4 **Achinsk** Russian Fed
40D3 **Acireale** Italy
11D3 **Ackley** USA
23C2 **Acklins** *I* Caribbean
26D6 **Acobamba** Peru
25B4 **Aconcagua** *Mt* Chile
27L5 **Acopiara** Brazil
68B4 **Açores** *Is* Atlantic O
A Coruna = La Coruña
37C2 **Acqui** Italy
75A2 **Acraman,L** Aust
Acre = 'Akko
26D5 **Acre State,** Brazil
20C3 **Acton** USA
22C1 **Actopan** Mexico
71G4 **Ada** Ghana
17C3 **Ada** USA
39B1 **Adaja** *R* Spain
10C6 **Adak** *I* USA
67G2 **Adam** Oman
72D3 **Adama** Eth
29B3 **Adamantina** Brazil
72B3 **Adamaoua** Region, Nig/Cam
71J4 **Adamawa** State, Nigeria
37D1 **Adamello** *Mt* Italy
14D1 **Adams** USA
62B3 **Adam's Bridge** India/Sri Lanka
3E3 **Adams L** Can
8A2 **Adams,Mt** USA
62C3 **Adam's Peak** *Mt* Sri Lanka
67E4 **'Adan** Yemen
45F8 **Adana** Turk
45E7 **Adapazari** Turk
66B3 **Adarama** Sudan
79F7 **Adare,C** Ant
57D4 **Adaut** Indon
75B1 **Adavale** Aust
37C2 **Adda** *R* Italy
67E1 **Ad Dahna'** Region, S Arabia
66D4 **Ad Dālī'** Yemen
67F1 **Ad Damman** S Arabia
66D3 **Ad Darb** S Arabia
66D2 **Ad Dawādimī** S Arabia
67E1 **Ad Dibdibah** Region, S Arabia
67F3 **Ad Dikākah** Region, S Arabia
67E2 **Ad Dilam** S Arabia
67E2 **Ad Dir'iyah** S Arabia
66C4 **Addis Zeman** Eth
64D3 **Ad Dīwanīyah** Iraq
64D3 **Ad Duwayd** S Arabia
11D3 **Adel** USA
76C4 **Adelaide** Aust
6J3 **Adelaide Pen** Can
51G8 **Adelaide River** Aust
20D3 **Adelanto** USA
Aden = 'Adan
58C4 **Aden,G of** Yemen/Somalia
70C3 **Aderbissinat** Niger
65D2 **Adhra** Syria
51G7 **Adi** *I* Indon
40C1 **Adige** *R* Italy
72D2 **Adigrat** Eth
66C4 **Adi Kale** Eth
60D5 **Adilābād** India
18B2 **Adin** USA
13E2 **Adirondack Mts** USA
72D3 **Ādīs Ābeba** Eth
72D2 **Adi Ugai** Eth
64C2 **Adıyaman** Turk
41F1 **Adjud** Rom
10G1 **Admiralty B** USA
6E4 **Admiralty I** USA
7K2 **Admiralty Inlet** *B* Can
76D1 **Admiralty Is** PNG
57B4 **Adonara** *I* Indon
62B1 **Ādoni** India
38B3 **Adour** *R* France
70A2 **Adrar** Region, Maur
70C2 **Adrar** *Mts* Alg
70A2 **Adrar Soutouf** Region, Mor
72C2 **Adré** Chad
69A2 **Adri** Libya
37E2 **Adria** Italy
12C2 **Adrian** Michigan, USA
16B2 **Adrian** Texas, USA
40C2 **Adriatic S** Italy/Yugos
72D2 **Adwa** Eth
49P3 **Adycha** *R* Russian Fed
71F4 **Adzopé** Ivory Coast
44K2 **Adz'va** *R* Russian Fed
44K2 **Adz'vavom** Russian Fed
41E3 **Aegean** *S* Greece
58E2 **Afghanistan** Republic, Asia
72E3 **Afgooye** Somalia
66D2 **'Afif** S Arabia
71H4 **Afikpo** Nig
32G6 **Åfjord** Nor
71C2 **Aflou** Alg
72E3 **Afmado** Somalia
70A3 **Afollé** Region, Maur
14C1 **Afton** New York, USA
18D2 **Afton** Wyoming, USA
65C2 **Afula** Israel
45E8 **Afyon** Turk
65A3 **Aga** Egypt
72B2 **Agadem** Niger
70C3 **Agadez** Niger
70B1 **Agadir** Mor
60D4 **Agar** India
61D3 **Agartala** India
18B1 **Agassiz** Can
10A6 **Agattu** *I* USA
10A5 **Agattu Str** USA
71H4 **Agbor** Nig
71F4 **Agboville** Ivory Coast
64E1 **Agdam** Azerbaijan
54C3 **Agematsu** Japan
38C3 **Agen** France
63B2 **Agha Jārī** Iran
45G8 **Ağn** Turk
37D2 **Agno** *R* Italy
66C3 **Agordat** Eth
37E1 **Agordo** Italy
71G4 **Agou,Mt** Togo
38C3 **Agout** *R* France
60D3 **Āgra** India
64D2 **Ağri** Turk
40D2 **Agri** *R* Italy
40C3 **Agrigento** Italy
41E3 **Agrinion** Greece
28A3 **Agrio** *R* Chile
40C2 **Agropoli** Italy
44J4 **Agryz** Russian Fed
7N3 **Agto** Greenland
29B3 **Agua Clara** Brazil
28B4 **Aguada de Guerra** Arg
23D3 **Aguadilla** Puerto Rico

28B4 **Aguado Cicilio** Arg
22B1 **Aguanava** *R* Mexico
5J3 **Aguanish** Can
5J3 **Aguanus** *R* Can
28D1 **Aguapey** *R* Arg
21B1 **Agua Prieta** Mexico
29A3 **Aguaray Guazu** Par
21B2 **Aguascalientes** Mexico
22B1 **Aguascalientes** State, Mexico
29D2 **Aguas Formosas** Brazil
25G1 **Agua Vermelha, Barragem** *Res* Brazil
39A1 **Agueda** Port
70C3 **Aguelhok** Mali
70A2 **Agüenit** *Well* Mor
39B2 **Aguilas** Spain
22B2 **Aguililla** Mexico
xxviiiC7 **Agulhas Basin** Indian O
73C7 **Agulhas,C** S Africa
xxviiiC6 **Agulhas Plat** Indian O
57G9 **Agusan** *R* Phil
Ahaggar = Hoggar
45H8 **Ahar** Iran
78B1 **Ahipara B** NZ
36D1 **Ahlen** Germany
60C4 **Ahmadābād** India
62A1 **Ahmadnagar** India
72E3 **Ahmar** *Mts* Eth
15D1 **Ahoskie** USA
36D1 **Ahr** *R* Germany
36D1 **Ahrgebirge** Region, Germany
22B1 **Ahuacatlán** Mexico
22B1 **Ahualulco** Mexico
32G7 **Åhus** Sweden
63C1 **Āhuvān** Iran
63B2 **Ahvāz** Iran
23A4 **Aiajuela** Costa Rica
37B1 **Aigle** Switz
28E2 **Aiguá** Urug
37B2 **Aiguille d'Arves** *Mt* France
37B2 **Aiguille de la Grand Sassière** *Mt* France
53B1 **Aihui** China
54C3 **Aikawa** Japan
15C2 **Aiken** USA
52A5 **Ailao Shan** *Upland* China
28B1 **Aimogasta** Arg
29D2 **Aimorés** Brazil
37A1 **Ain** *R* France
71D1 **Aïn Beïda** Alg
71B2 **Ain Beni Mathar** Mor
69B2 **Ain Dalla** *Well* Egypt
39C2 **Aïn el Hadjel** Alg
72B2 **Aïn Galakka** Chad
71C1 **Aïn Oussera** Alg
71B2 **Aïn Sefra** Alg
64B4 **'Ain Sukhna** Egypt
11C3 **Ainsworth** USA
71B1 **Aïn Temouchent** Alg
54B4 **Aioi** Japan
70B2 **Aioun Abd el Malek** *Well* Maur
70B3 **Aïoun El Atrouss** Maur
26E7 **Aiquile** Bol
70C3 **Aïr** *Desert Region* Niger
3F3 **Airdrie** Can
36B1 **Aire** France
35E5 **Aire** *R* Eng
36C2 **Aire** *R* France
7L3 **Airforce I** Can
37C1 **Airolo** Switz
6E3 **Aishihik** Can
10L3 **Aishihik L** Can
36B2 **Aisne** Department, France
38C2 **Aisne** *R* France
76D1 **Aitape** PNG
43F1 **Aiviekste** *R* Latvia
52B2 **Aixa Zuogi** China
38D3 **Aix-en-Provence** France
37A2 **Aix-les-Bains** France
61C3 **Aiyar Res** India
41E3 **Aíyion** Greece
41E3 **Aíyna** *I* Greece
61D3 **Āīzawl** India
73B6 **Aizeb** *R* Namibia
53E4 **Aizu-Wakamatsu** Japan
40B2 **Ajaccio** Corse
22C2 **Ajalpan** Mexico
69B1 **Ajdabiyak** Libya
37E2 **Ajdovščina** Slovenia, Yugos
53E3 **Ajigasawa** Japan
65C2 **Ajlūn** Jordan
67G1 **Ajman** UAE
60C3 **Ajmer** India
19D4 **Ajo** USA
41F2 **Ajtos** Bulg
22B2 **Ajuchitan** Mexico
41F3 **Ak** *R* Turk
54D2 **Akabira** Japan
54C3 **Akaishi-sanchi** *Mts* Japan
62B1 **Akalkot** India
65B1 **Akanthou** Cyprus
78B2 **Akaroa** NZ
66B2 **Akasha** Sudan
54B4 **Akashi** Japan
71C1 **Akbou** Alg
45K5 **Akbulak** Russian Fed
64C2 **Akçakale** Turk
70A2 **Akchar** *Watercourse* Maur
41F3 **Ak Dağ** *Mt* Turk
57C2 **Akelamo** Indon
72C3 **Aketi** Zaïre
64D1 **Akhalkalaki** Georgia
64D1 **Akhalsikhe** Georgia
41E3 **Akharnái** Greece
10H4 **Akhiok** USA
64A2 **Akhisar** Turk
43F1 **Akhiste** Latvia
69C2 **Akhmim** Egypt
45H6 **Akhtubinsk** Russian Fed
45E5 **Akhtyrka** Ukraine
54B4 **Aki** Japan
7K4 **Akimiski I** Can
53E4 **Akita** Japan
70A3 **Akjoujt** Maur
65C2 **'Akko** Israel
10L2 **Aklavik** Can
70B3 **Aklé Aouana** *Desert Region* Maur
72D3 **Akobo** Sudan
72D3 **Akobo** *R* Sudan
60B1 **Akoha** Afghan
60D4 **Akola** India
71G4 **Akosombo Dam** Ghana
60D4 **Akot** India
7M3 **Akpatok I** Can
41E3 **Ákra Kafirévs** *C* Greece
41E4 **Ákra Líthinon** *C* Greece
41E3 **Ákra Maléa** *C* Greece
32A2 **Akranes** Iceland
41F3 **Ákra Sídheros** *C* Greece
41E3 **Ákra Spátha** *C* Greece
41E3 **Ákra Taínaron** *C* Greece
9E2 **Akron** USA
65B1 **Akrotiri B** Cyprus
60D1 **Aksai Chin** *Mts* China
45E8 **Aksaray** Turk
45J5 **Aksay** Kazakhstan
60D1 **Aksayquin Hu** *L* China
64B2 **Akşehir** Turk
64B2 **Akseki** Turk
49N4 **Aksenovo Zilovskoye** Russian Fed
50E1 **Aksha** Russian Fed
59G1 **Aksu** China
66C4 **Aksum** Eth
48J5 **Aktogay** Kazakhstan
45K6 **Aktumsyk** Kazakhstan
45K5 **Aktyubinsk** Kazakhstan
4F1 **Akulivik** Can
71H4 **Akure** Nig
32B1 **Akureyri** Iceland
10E5 **Akutan** USA
10E5 **Akutan** *I* USA
10E5 **Akutan Pass** USA
71H5 **Akwa Ibom** *State* Nigeria
48K5 **Akzhal** Kazakhstan
9E3 **Alabama** State, USA
15B2 **Alabama** *R* USA
15B2 **Alabaster** USA
64C2 **Ala Dağlari** *Mts* Turk
45G7 **Alagir** Russian Fed
37B2 **Alagna** Italy
27L5 **Alagoas** State, Brazil
27L6 **Alagoinhas** Brazil
39B1 **Alagón** Spain
64E4 **Al Ahmadi** Kuwait
21D3 **Alajuela** Costa Rica
10F3 **Alakanuk** USA
48K5 **Alakol, Ozero** *L* Russian Fed/Kazakhstan
32L5 **Alakurtti** Russian Fed
64E3 **Al Amārah** Iraq
19B3 **Alameda** USA
22C1 **Alamo** Mexico
19C3 **Alamo** USA
16A3 **Alamogordo** USA
16C4 **Alamo Heights** USA
16A2 **Alamosa** USA
32H6 **Åland** *I* Fin
45E8 **Alanya** Turk
15C2 **Alapaha** *R* USA
44L4 **Alapayevsk** Russian Fed
56A2 **Alas** *R* Indon
64A2 **Alaşehir** Turk
50D3 **Ala Shan** *Mts* China
6C3 **Alaska** State, USA
6D4 **Alaska,G of** USA
10G4 **Alaska Pen** USA
6C3 **Alaska Range** *Mts* USA
40B2 **Alassio** Italy
37C3 **Alássio** Region, Italy
10H2 **Alatna** *R* USA
44H5 **Alatyr'** Russian Fed
75B2 **Alawoona** Aust
67G2 **Al'Ayn** UAE
59F2 **Alayskiy Khrebet** *Mts* Tajikistan
49R3 **Alazeya** *R* Russian Fed
71E2 **Al'Azīzīyah** Libya
38D3 **Alba** Italy
64C2 **Al Bāb** Syria
39B2 **Albacete** Spain
39A1 **Alba de Tormes** Spain
64D2 **Al Badi** Iraq
41E1 **Alba Iulia** Rom
41D2 **Albania** Republic, Europe
76A4 **Albany** Aust
15C2 **Albany** Georgia, USA
12B3 **Albany** Kentucky, USA
13E2 **Albany** New York, USA
8A2 **Albany** Oregon, USA
4E3 **Albany** *R* Can
66C4 **Albara** *R* Sudan
28B2 **Albardón** Arg
67G2 **Al Batinah** Region, Oman
51H8 **Albatross B** Aust
69B1 **Al Bayḍā** Libya
67E4 **Al Bayḍā'** Yemen
65C1 **Al Baylūlīyah** Syria
15C1 **Albemarle** USA
15D1 **Albemarle Sd** USA
37C2 **Albenga** Region, Italy
39B1 **Alberche** *R* Spain
75A1 **Alberga** Aust
36B1 **Albert** France
6G4 **Alberta** Province, Can
51H7 **Albert Edward** *Mt* PNG
74C3 **Albertinia** S Africa
72D3 **Albert,L** Uganda/Zaïre
9D2 **Albert Lea** USA
72D3 **Albert Nile** *R* Uganda
18D1 **Alberton** USA
5J4 **Alberton** Can
38D2 **Albertville** France
38C3 **Albi** France
17D1 **Albia** USA
27H2 **Albina** Surinam
12C2 **Albion** Michigan, USA
11C3 **Albion** Nebraska, USA
13D2 **Albion** New York, USA
64C4 **Al Bi'r** S Arabia
66D3 **Al Birk** S Arabia
67E2 **Al Biyadh** Region, S Arabia
39B2 **Alborán** *I* Spain
32G7 **Ålborg** Den
36E2 **Albstadt-Ebingen** Germany
64D3 **Al Bū Kamāl** Syria
37C1 **Albula** *R* Switz
8C3 **Albuquerque** USA
67G2 **Al Buraymi** Oman
69A1 **Al Burayqah**
69B1 **Al Burdī** Libya
76D4 **Albury** Aust
64E3 **Al Buşayyah** Iraq
34G3 **Albuskjell** *Oilfield* N Sea
67F3 **Al Buzūn** Yemen
39B1 **Alcalá de Henares** Spain
40C3 **Alcamo** Italy
39B1 **Alcaniz** Spain
27K4 **Alcântara** Brazil
39B2 **Alcaraz** Spain
39B2 **Alcázar de San Juan** Spain
39B2 **Alcira** Spain
29E2 **Alcobaça** Brazil
39B1 **Alcolea de Pinar** Spain
39B2 **Alcoy** Spain
39C2 **Alcudia** Spain
68J8 **Aldabra** *Is* Indian O
16A4 **Aldama** Mexico
22C1 **Aldama** Mexico
49O4 **Aldan** Russian Fed
49P4 **Aldan** *R* Russian Fed
49O4 **Aldanskoye Nagor'ye** *Upland* Russian Fed
35F5 **Aldeburgh** Eng
38B2 **Alderney** *I* UK
35E6 **Aldershot** Eng
70A3 **Aleg** Maur
29A2 **Alegre** *R* Brazil
25E3 **Alegrete** Brazil
28C2 **Alejandro Roca** Arg
49Q4 **Aleksandrovsk Sakhalinskiy** Russian Fed
48J4 **Alekseyevka** Kazakhstan
44F5 **Aleksin** Russian Fed
42D1 **Ålem** Sweden
29D3 **Além Paraíba** Brazil
38C2 **Alençon** France
20E5 **Alenuihaha Chan** Hawaiian Is
Aleppo = Ḩalab
7M1 **Alert** Can
38C3 **Alès** France
40B2 **Alessandria** Italy
48B3 **Ålesund** Nor
10B5 **Aleutian Is** USA
10G4 **Aleutian Range** *Mts* USA
xxixL2 **Aleutian Trench** Pacific O
6E4 **Alexander Arch** USA
74B2 **Alexander Bay** S Africa
15B2 **Alexander City** USA
79G3 **Alexander I** Ant
78A3 **Alexandra** NZ
25J8 **Alexandra,C** South Georgia
7L2 **Alexandra Fjord** Can
69B1 **Alexandria** Egypt
9D3 **Alexandria** Louisiana, USA
9D2 **Alexandria** Minnesota, USA
9F3 **Alexandria** Virginia, USA
41F2 **Alexandroúpolis** Greece
5K3 **Alexis** *R* Can
3D3 **Alexis Creek** Can
65C2 **Aley** Leb
48K4 **Aleysk** Russian Fed
64D3 **Al Fallūjah** Iraq
67E4 **Al Fardah** Yemen
39B1 **Alfaro** Spain
41F2 **Alfatar** Bulg
64E3 **Al Fāw** Iraq
36E1 **Alfeld** Germany
29C3 **Alfensas** Brazil
41E3 **Alfiós** *R* Greece
37D2 **Alfonsine** Italy
29D3 **Alfonzo Cláudio** Brazil
29D3 **Alfredo Chaves** Brazil
67E1 **Al Furūthi** S Arabia
45K6 **Alga** Kazakhstan
28A1 **Algarrobal** Chile
28B3 **Algarrobo del Águila** Arg
39A2 **Algeciras** Spain
71C1 **Alger** Alg
70B2 **Algeria** Republic, Africa
67F3 **Al Ghaydah** Yemen
40B2 **Alghero** Sardegna
Algiers = Alger
11D3 **Algona** USA
13D1 **Algonquin Park** Can
4F4 **Algonquin Prov Park** Can
28D2 **Algorta** Urug
67G2 **Al Hadd** Oman
64D3 **Al Hadithah** Iraq
64C3 **Al Hadithah** S Arabia
64D2 **Al Hadr** Iraq
65D1 **Al Haffah** Syria
67G2 **Al Hajar al Gharbī** *Mts* Oman
67G2 **Al Hajar ash Sharqī** *Mts* Oman
64C3 **Al Hamad** *Desert Region* Jordan/S Arabia
64E4 **Al Haniyah** *Desert Region* Iraq
67E2 **Al Harīq** S Arabia
64C3 **Al Harrah** *Desert Region* S Arabia
69A2 **Al Harūj al Aswad** *Upland* Libya
67E1 **Al Hasa** Region, S Arabia
64D2 **Al Hasakah** Syria
64C4 **Al Hawjā'** S Arabia
64E3 **Al Hayy** Iraq
67F2 **Al Hibāk** Region, S Arabia
65D2 **Al Hījānah** Syria
64D3 **Al Hillah** Iraq
67E2 **Al Hillah** S Arabia
71B1 **Al Hoceima** Mor
66D4 **Al Hudaydah** Yemen
67E1 **Al Hufūf** S Arabia
67F2 **Al Humrah** Region, UAE
67G2 **Al Huwatsah** Oman
63B1 **Alīābad** Iran
63D3 **Aliabad** Iran
41E2 **Aliákmon** *R* Greece
64E3 **Alī al Gharbī** Iraq
62A1 **Alībāg** India
71B3 **Alibori** *R* Benin
39B2 **Alicante** Spain
8D4 **Alice** USA
76C3 **Alice Springs** Aust
40C3 **Alicudi** *I* Italy
60D3 **Aligarh** India
63B2 **Aligūdarz** Iran
60B2 **Ali-Khel** Afghan
41F3 **Alimniá** *I* Greece
61C2 **Alīpur Duār** India
12C2 **Aliquippa** USA
67E4 **Al'Irqah** Yemen
64C3 **Al'Īsawiyah** S Arabia
74D3 **Aliwal North** S Africa
69B2 **Al Jaghbūb** Libya
64D3 **Al Jālamīd** S Arabia
69B2 **Al Jawf** Libya
64C4 **Al Jawf** S Arabia
45G8 **Al Jazīrah** Syria
64D2 **Al Jazīrah** *Desert* Region Syria/Iraq
39A2 **Aljezur** Port
67E1 **Al Jubayl** S Arabia
65D4 **Al Kabid** *Desert* Jordan
66D1 **Al Kahfah** S Arabia
67G2 **Al Kāmil** Oman
64D2 **Al Khābūr** *R* Syria
67G2 **Al Khābūrah** Oman
64D3 **Al Khālis** Iraq
66D2 **Al Khamāsīn** S Arabia
67G1 **Al Khasab** Oman
67F1 **Al Khawr** Qatar
69A1 **Al Khums** Libya
67F2 **Al Kidan** Region, S Arabia
65D2 **Al Kiswah** Syria
42A2 **Alkmaar** Neth
69B2 **Al Kufrah Oasis** Libya
64E3 **Al Kūt** Iraq
64C2 **Al Lādhiqīyah** Syria
61B2 **Allahābād** India
65D2 **Al Lajāh** *Mt* Syria
10H2 **Allakaket** USA
55B2 **Allanmyo** Burma
66B2 **'Allaqi** *Watercourse* Egypt
15C2 **Allatoona L** USA
74D1 **Alldays** S Africa
13D2 **Allegheny** *R* USA
9F3 **Allegheny Mts** USA
14A2 **Allegheny Res** USA
15C2 **Allendale** USA
78A3 **Allen,Mt** NZ
13D2 **Allentown** USA
62B3 **Alleppey** India
38C2 **Aller** *R* France
37D1 **Allgäu** *Mts* Germany
11B3 **Alliance** USA
66D2 **Al Līth** S Arabia
67F2 **Al Liwā** Region, UAE
75D1 **Allora** Aust
37B2 **Allos** France
12C2 **Alma** Michigan, USA
16C1 **Alma** Nebraska, USA
59F1 **Alma Ata** Kazakhstan
39A2 **Almada** Port
Al Madīnah = Medina S Arabia
51H5 **Almagan** I Pacific O
67F3 **Al Mahrah** Region, Yemen
67E1 **Al Majma'ah** S Arabia
67F1 **Al Manāmah** Bahrain
64D3 **Al Ma'nīyah** Iraq
19B2 **Almanor,L** USA
39B2 **Almansa** Spain
3C2 **Alma Peak** *Mt* Can
67F2 **Al Māriyyah** UAE
5G4 **Alma** Can
69B1 **Al Marj** Libya
39B1 **Almazán** Spain
36E1 **Alme** *R* Germany
29D2 **Almenara** Brazil
39B2 **Almeria** Spain
29C2 **Almes** *R* Brazil
44J5 **Al'met'yevsk** Russian Fed
42C1 **Älmhult** Sweden
66D1 **Al Midhnab** S Arabia
64E3 **Al Miqdādīyah** Iraq
79G3 **Almirante Brown** *Base* Ant
28A1 **Almirante Latorre** Chile
41E3 **Almirós** Greece
67E1 **Al Mish'ab** A Arabia
39A2 **Almodôvar** Port
60D3 **Almora** India
67E1 **Al Mubarraz** S Arabia
64C4 **Al Mudawwara** Jordan
67G2 **Al Mudaybi** Oman
67F1 **Al Muharraq** Bahrain
67E4 **Al Mukallā** Yemen
66D4 **Al Mukhā** Yemen
64D3 **Al Musayyib** Iraq
66C1 **Al Muwaylih** S Arabia
34C3 **Alness** Scot
64E3 **Al Nu'mānīyah** Iraq
34E4 **Alnwick** Eng
4B3 **Alonsa** Can
57B4 **Alor** *I* Indon
55C4 **Alor Setar** Malay
Alost = Aalst
76E2 **Alotau** PNG
76B3 **Aloysius,Mt** Aust
28C3 **Alpachiri** Arg
37D2 **Alpe di Succiso** *Mt* Italy
12C1 **Alpena** USA
37B1 **Alpes du Valais** *Mts* Switz
37B2 **Alpes Maritimes** *Mts* France
37E1 **Alpi Carniche** *Mts* Italy
40C1 **Alpi Dolomitiche** *Mts* Italy
37B2 **Alpi Graie** *Mts* Italy
19E4 **Alpine** Arizona, USA
16B3 **Alpine** Texas, USA
18D2 **Alpine** Wyoming, USA
37C1 **Alpi Orobie** *Mts* Italy
37B2 **Alpi Penine** *Mts* Italy
37C1 **Alpi Retiche** *Mts* Switz
37D1 **Alpi Venoste** *Mts* Italy
40B1 **Alps** *Mts* Europe
69A1 **Al Qaddāhiyah** Libya
65D1 **Al Qadmūs** Syria
64D3 **Al Qā'im** Iraq
64C4 **Al Qalībah** S Arabia
64D2 **Al Qāmishlī** Syria
65D1 **Al Qardāhah** Syria

69A1 **Al Qaryah Ash Sharqiyah** Libya
64C3 **Al Qaryatayn** Syria
66D1 **Al Qasīm** Region, S Arabia
67E1 **Al Qāṭif** S Arabia
69A2 **Al Qatrūn** Libya
67E1 **Al Qayṣāmah** S Arabia
65D2 **Al Quatayfah** Syria
39A2 **Alquera** *Res* Port/Spain
64C3 **Al Qunayṭirah** Syria
66D3 **Al Qunfidhah** S Arabia
64E3 **Al Qurnah** Iraq
65D1 **Al Quṣayr** Syria
64C3 **Al Qutayfah** Syria
67E2 **Al Quwayīyah** S Arabia
42B1 **Als** *I* Den
38D2 **Alsace** Region, France
42B2 **Alsfeld** Germany
34D4 **Alston** Eng
32J5 **Alta** Nor
25D4 **Alta Gracia** Arg
23D5 **Altagracia de Orituco** Ven
50B2 **Altai** *Mts* Mongolia
15C2 **Altamaha** *R* USA
27H4 **Altamira** Brazil
22C1 **Altamira** Mexico
40D2 **Altamura** Italy
50D1 **Altanbulag** Mongolia
49M5 **Altanbulag** Russian Fed
51H7 **Altape** PNG
21B2 **Altata** Mexico
48K5 **Altay** China
49L5 **Altay** Mongolia
48K4 **Altay** *Mts* Russian Fed
37C1 **Altdorf** Switz
36D1 **Altenkirchen** Germany
28B3 **Altiplanicie del Payún** *Plat* Arg
37B1 **Altkirch** France
29B2 **Alto Araguaia** Brazil
73D5 **Alto Molócue** Mozam
12A3 **Alton** USA
13D2 **Altoona** USA
28B2 **Alto Pencoso** *Mts* Arg
29B2 **Alto Sucuriú** Brazil
22C2 **Altotonga** Mexico
22B2 **Altoyac de Alvarez** Mexico
59G2 **Altun Shan** *Mts* China
18B2 **Alturas** USA
16C3 **Altus** USA
67F2 **Al'Ubaylah** S Arabia
66C1 **Al'Ulā** S Arabia
28A3 **Aluminé** Arg
64C4 **Al Urayq** *Desert Region* S Arabia
67F2 **Al'Uruq al Mu'taridah** Region, S Arabia
16C2 **Alva** USA
22C2 **Alvarado** Mexico
17C3 **Alvarado** USA
32G6 **Ålvdalen** Sweden
28D1 **Alvear** Arg
17C4 **Alvin** USA
32J5 **Alvsbyn** Sweden
69A2 **Al Wāha** Libya
66C1 **Al Wajh** S Arabia
60D3 **Alwar** India
64D3 **Al Widyān** *Desert Region* Iraq/S Arabia
52A2 **Alxa Yougi** China
64E2 **Alyat** Azerbaijan
32J8 **Alytus** Lithuania
36E2 **Alzey** Germany
22C2 **Amacuzac** *R* Mexico
72D3 **Amadi** Sudan
64D2 **Amādīyah** Iraq
7L3 **Amadjuak L** Can
57C3 **Amahai** Indon
53B5 **Amakusa-shotō** *I* Japan
32G7 **Åmål** Sweden
49N4 **Amalat** *R* Russian Fed
41E3 **Amaliás** Greece
60C4 **Amalner** India
29A3 **Amambai** Brazil
29B3 **Amambai** *R* Brazil
50F4 **Amami** *I* Japan
50F4 **Amami gunto** *Arch* Japan
27H3 **Amapá** Brazil
27H3 **Amapá** State, Brazil
4B3 **Amaranth** Can
61E3 **Amarapura** Burma
16B2 **Amarillo** USA
45F7 **Amasya** Turk
22B1 **Amatitan** Mexico
22C1 **Amaulipas** Mexico
Amazonas = Solimões
27H4 **Amazonas** Brazil
26E4 **Amazonas** State, Brazil
24D4 **Amazonas** *R* Brazil
60D2 **Ambāla** India
62C3 **Ambalangoda** Sri Lanka
73E6 **Ambalavao** Madag
72B3 **Ambam** Cam
73E5 **Ambanja** Madag
49S3 **Ambarchik** Russian Fed
26C4 **Ambato** Ecuador
73E5 **Ambato-Boeny** Madag
73E5 **Ambatolampy** Madag
73E5 **Ambatondrazaka** Madag
42C3 **Amberg** Germany
21D3 **Ambergris Cay** *I* Belize
37A2 **Ambérieu** France
61B3 **Ambikāpur** India
73E5 **Ambilobe** Madag
73E6 **Amboasary** Madag
73E5 **Ambodifototra** Madag
73E6 **Ambohimahasoa** Madag
57C3 **Ambon** Indon
57C3 **Ambon** *I* Indon
73E6 **Ambositra** Madag
73E6 **Ambovombe** Madag
73B4 **Ambriz** Angola
77F2 **Ambrym** *I* Vanuatu
10B6 **Amchitka** USA
10B6 **Amchitka** *I* USA
10C6 **Amchitka Pass** USA
72C2 **Am Dam** Chad
44L2 **Amderma** Russian Fed
21B2 **Ameca** Mexico
22A1 **Ameca** *R* Mexico
22C2 **Amecacameca** Mexico
28C2 **Ameghino** Arg
42B2 **Ameland** *I* Neth
14D2 **Amenia** USA
18D2 **American Falls** USA
18D2 **American Falls Res** USA
19D2 **American Fork** USA
79F10 **American Highland** *Upland* Ant
xxixL5 **American Samoa** *Is* Pacific O
15C2 **Americus** USA
42B2 **Amersfoort** Neth
74D2 **Amersfoort** S Africa
11D2 **Amery** USA
79G10 **Amery Ice Shelf** Ant
11D3 **Ames** USA
14E1 **Amesbury** USA
4E4 **Ameson** Can
41E3 **Amfilokhía** Greece
41E3 **Amfissa** Greece
49P3 **Amga** Russian Fed
49P3 **Amgal** *R* Russian Fed
53D2 **Amgu** Russian Fed
10C2 **Amguema** *R* Russian Fed
53D1 **Amgun'** *R* Russian Fed
72D2 **Amhara** *Region* Eth
7M5 **Amherst** Can
14D1 **Amherst** Massachusetts, USA
13D3 **Amherst** Virginia, USA
62B2 **Amhūr** India
38C2 **Amiens** France
54C3 **Amino** Japan
65C1 **Amioune** Leb
68K8 **Amirante Is** Indian O
3H3 **Amisk L** Can
16B4 **Amistad Res** Mexico
61C2 **Amlekhgan** Nepal
10D6 **Amlia** *I* USA
64C3 **Amman** Jordan
32K6 **Ämmänsaario** Fin
54A3 **Amnyong-dan** *C* N Korea
63C1 **Amol** Iran
7L5 **Amos** Can
Amoy = Xiamen
57B3 **Ampana** Indon
73E6 **Ampanihy** Madag
29C3 **Amparo** Brazil
39C1 **Amposta** Spain
5H4 **Amqui** Can
66D3 **Amrān** Yemen
60D4 **Amrāvati** India
60C4 **Amreli** India
60C2 **Amritsar** India
42A2 **Amsterdam** Neth
74E2 **Amsterdam** S Africa
13E2 **Amsterdam** USA
72C2 **Am Timan** Chad
48H5 **Amu Darya** *R* Uzbekistan
10D6 **Amukta** *I* USA
10D6 **Amukta Pass** USA
7J2 **Amund Ringnes I** Can
6F2 **Amundsen G** Can
79F4 **Amundsen S** Ant
79E **Amundsen-Scott** *Base* Ant
56E3 **Amuntai** Indon
49O4 **Amur** *R* Russian Fed
66C3 **Amur** *Watercourse* Sudan
57B2 **Amurang** Indon
53D1 **Amursk** Russian Fed
53E1 **Amurskiy Liman** *Str* Russian Fed
53C2 **Amurzet** Russian Fed
49N2 **Anabar** *R* Russian Fed
26F2 **Anaco** Ven
8B2 **Anaconda** USA
18B1 **Anacortes** USA
16C2 **Anadarko** USA
49T3 **Anadyr'** Russian Fed
49T3 **Anadyr'** *R* Russian Fed
49U3 **Anadyrskiy Zaliv** *S* Russian Fed
49T3 **Anadyrskoye Ploskogor'ye** *Plat* Russian Fed
41F3 **Anáfi** *I* Greece
29D1 **Anagé** Brazil
64D3 **'Ānah** Iraq
19C4 **Anaheim** USA
62B2 **Anaimalai Hills** India
62C1 **Anakāpalle** India
10J2 **Anaktuvuk P** USA
73E5 **Analalaya** Madag
71H4 **Anambra** *State* Nig
71H4 **Anambra** *R* Nig
12A2 **Anamosa** USA
45E8 **Anamur** Turk
54B4 **Anan** Japan
62B2 **Anantapur** India
60D2 **Anantnag** India
27J7 **Anápolis** Brazil
63D2 **Anār** Iran
63C2 **Anārak** Iran
63E2 **Anardara** Afghan
51H5 **Anatahan** *I* Pacific O
25D3 **Añatuya** Arg
53B4 **Anbyŏn** N Korea
20C4 **Ancapa Is** USA
28B1 **Ancasti** Arg
6D3 **Anchorage** USA
26E7 **Ancohuma** *Mt* Bol
26C6 **Ancón** Peru
40C2 **Ancona** Italy
14D1 **Ancram** USA
25B6 **Ancud** Chile
36C3 **Ancy-le-Franc** France
26D6 **Andabuaylas** Peru
28A3 **Andacollo** Arg
75A1 **Andado** Aust
28B1 **Andagalá** Arg
32F6 **Andalsnes** Nor
39A2 **Andalucia** Region, Spain
15B2 **Andalusia** USA
59H4 **Andaman Is** Burma
59H4 **Andaman S** Burma
75A2 **Andamooka** Aust
29D1 **Andaraí** Brazil
35B5 **Andee** Irish Rep
36C2 **Andelot** France
32H5 **Andenes** Nor
37C1 **Andermatt** Switz
42B2 **Andernach** Germany
12B2 **Anderson** Indiana, USA
17D2 **Anderson** Missouri, USA
15C2 **Anderson** S Carolina, USA
6F3 **Anderson** *R* Can
62B1 **Andhra Pradesh** State, India
41E3 **Andikíthira** *I* Greece
48J5 **Andizhan** Uzbekistan
48H6 **Andkhui** Afghan
53B4 **Andong** S Korea
39C1 **Andorra** Principality, SW Europe
39C1 **Andorra-La-Vella** Andorra
35E6 **Andover** Eng
14E1 **Andover** New Hampshire, USA
14B1 **Andover** New York, USA
29B3 **Andradina** Brazil
10F3 **Andreafsky** USA
10C6 **Andreanof Is** USA
43G1 **Andreapol'** Russian Fed
64B2 **Andreas,C** Cyprus
16B3 **Andrews** USA
40D2 **Andria** Italy
9F4 **Andros** *I* Bahamas
41E3 **Ándros** *I* Greece
62A2 **Androth** *I* India
39B2 **Andújar** Spain
73B5 **Andulo** Angola
71G4 **Anécho** Togo
70C3 **Anéfis** Mali
77F3 **Aneityum** *I* Vanuatu
28B3 **Añelo** Arg
66C4 **Angareb** *Watercourse* Eth
49M4 **Angarsk** Russian Fed
44A3 **Ånge** Sweden
21A2 **Angel de la Guarda** *I* Mexico
57F7 **Angeles** Phil
32G7 **Angelholm** Sweden
75C1 **Angellala Creek** *R* Aust
20B1 **Angels Camp** USA
51G7 **Angemuk** *Mt* Indon
38B2 **Angers** France
36B2 **Angerville** France
55C3 **Angkor** *Hist Site* Camb
33C3 **Anglesey** *I* Wales
17C4 **Angleton** USA
7P3 **Angmagssalik** Greenland
73E5 **Angoche** Mozam
25B5 **Angol** Chile
12C2 **Angola** Indiana, USA
14A1 **Angola** New York, USA
73B5 **Angola** Republic, Africa
xxxJ5 **Angola Basin** Atlantic O
10M4 **Angoon** USA
38C2 **Angoulême** France
70A1 **Angra do Heroismo** Açores
29D3 **Angra dos Reis** Brazil
28C3 **Anguil** Arg
23E3 **Anguilla** *I* Caribbean
23B2 **Anguilla Cays** *Is* Caribbean
61C3 **Angul** India
72C4 **Angumu** Zaïre
42C1 **Anholt** *I* Den
52C4 **Anhua** China
52D3 **Anhui** Province, China
29B2 **Anhumas** Brazil
54A3 **Anhŭng** S Korea
10G3 **Aniak** USA
29C2 **Anicuns** Brazil
71G4 **Anié** Togo
16A2 **Animas** *R* USA
16A3 **Animas Peak** *Mt* USA
11D3 **Anita** USA
36B2 **Anizy-le-Château** France
38B2 **Anjou** Republic, France
73E5 **Anjouan** *I* Comoros
73E5 **Anjozorobe** Madag
53B4 **Anju** N Korea
52B3 **Ankang** China
45E8 **Ankara** Turk
73E5 **Ankaratra** *Mt* Madag
73E6 **Ankazoabo** Madag
73E5 **Ankazobe** Madag
11D3 **Ankeny** USA
42C2 **Anklam** Germany
71H4 **Ankwe** *R* Nig
55D3 **An Loc** Viet
52B4 **Anlong** China
52C3 **Anlu** China
12B3 **Anna** USA
71D1 **'Annaba** Alg
64C3 **An Nabk** S Arabia
64C3 **An Nabk** Syria
75A1 **Anna Creek** Aust
69B2 **An Nāfūrah** Libya
64D3 **An Najaf** Iraq
34D4 **Annan** Scot
13D3 **Annapolis** USA
61B2 **Annapurna** *Mt* Nepal
12C2 **Ann Arbor** USA
65D1 **An Nāsirah** Syria
64E3 **An Nāsirīyah** Iraq
37B2 **Annecy** France
37B1 **Annemasse** France
3B2 **Annette I** USA
55D3 **An Nhon** Viet
66D3 **An Nimās** S Arabia
52A5 **Anning** China
15B2 **Anniston** USA
70C4 **Annobon, I** Eq Guinea
38C2 **Annonay** France
37B3 **Annot** France
23J1 **Annotto Bay** Jamaica
52D3 **Anqing** China
52B2 **Ansai** China
42C3 **Ansbach** Germany
23C3 **Anse d'Hainault** Haiti
52E1 **Anshan** China
52B4 **Anshun** China
16C1 **Ansley** USA
16C3 **Anson** USA
51F8 **Anson B** Aust
70C3 **Ansongo** Mali
12C1 **Ansonville** Can
12C3 **Ansted** USA
45F8 **Antakya** Turk
73F5 **Antalaha** Madag
45E8 **Antalya** Turk
45E8 **Antalya Körfezi** *B* Turk
73E5 **Antananarivo** Madag
79G1 **Antarctic Circle** Ant
79G3 **Antarctic Pen** Ant
39B2 **Antequera** Spain
16A3 **Anthony** USA
70B1 **Anti-Atlas** *Mts* Mor
37B3 **Antibes** France
7M5 **Anticosti, Î d'** Can
5J4 **Anticosti Prov Park** Can
12B1 **Antigo** USA
23E3 **Antigua** *I* Caribbean
Anti Lebanon = Jebel esh Sharqi
19B3 **Antioch** USA
77G5 **Antipodes Is** NZ
17C3 **Antlers** USA
25B2 **Antofagasta** Chile
29C4 **Antonina** Brazil
16A2 **Antonito** USA
34B4 **Antrim** County, N Ire
34B4 **Antrim** N Ire
14E1 **Antrim** USA
34B4 **Antrim Hills** N Ire
73E5 **Antseranana** Madag
73E5 **Antsirabe** Madag
73E5 **Antsohiny** Madag
55D3 **An Tuc** Viet
28C1 **Añtuya** Arg
36C1 **Antwerpen** Belg
35B5 **An Uaimh** Irish Rep
54A3 **Anui** S Korea
60C3 **Anupgarh** India
62C3 **Anuradhapura** Sri Lanka
Anvers = Antwerpen
6B3 **Anvik** USA
10B6 **Anvil Pk** *Mt* USA
49L5 **Anxi** China
52C2 **Anyang** China
52A3 **A'nyêmaqên Shan** *Upland* China
49S3 **Anyuysk** Russian Fed
37C2 **Anza** *R* Italy
3F2 **Anzac** Can
48K4 **Anzhero-Sudzhensk** Russian Fed
40C2 **Anzio** Italy
77F2 **Aoba** *I* Vanuatu
53E3 **Aomori** Japan
40B1 **Aosta** Italy
70B3 **Aoukar** *Desert Region* Maur
70C2 **Aoulef** Alg
72B1 **Aozou** Chad
25E2 **Apa** *R* Brazil/Par
9E4 **Apalachee B** USA
15C3 **Apalachicola** USA
15B3 **Apalachicola B** USA
22C2 **Apan** Mexico
26D3 **Apaporis** *R* Colombia
29B3 **Aparecida do Taboado** Brazil
57F7 **Aparri** Phil
41D1 **Apatin** Croatia, Yugos
44E2 **Apatity** Russian Fed
21B3 **Apatzingan** Mexico
42B2 **Apeldoorn** Neth
77H2 **Apia** Western Samoa
29C3 **Apiai** Brazil
22B1 **Apizolaya** Mexico
27G2 **Apoera** Surinam
75B3 **Apollo Bay** Aust
57G9 **Apo,Mt** Phil
15C3 **Apopka,L** USA
27H7 **Aporé** *R* Brazil
12A1 **Apostle Is** USA
22B1 **Apozol** Mexico
9E3 **Appalachian Mts** USA
37D2 **Appenino Tosco-Emiliano** *Mts* Italy
40C2 **Appennino Abruzzese** *Mts* Italy
40B2 **Appennino Ligure** *Mts* Italy
40D2 **Appennino Lucano** *Mts* Italy
40D2 **Appennino Napoletano** *Mts* Italy
40C2 **Appennino Tosco-Emilliano** *Mts* Italy
40C2 **Appennino Umbro-Marchigiano** *Mts* Italy
37C1 **Appenzell** Switz
35D4 **Appleby** Eng
11C2 **Appleton** Minnesota, USA
12B2 **Appleton** Wisconsin, USA
45J7 **Apsheronskiy Poluostrov** *Pen* Azerbaijan
4F5 **Apsley** Can
37A3 **Apt** France
25F2 **Apucarana** Brazil
22C1 **Apulco** Mexico
26E2 **Apure** *R* Ven
26D6 **Apurimac** *R* Peru
64C4 **'Aqaba** Jordan
64B4 **'Aqaba,G of** Egypt/S Arabia
63C2 **'Aqdā** Iran
27G8 **Aqidauana** Brazil
22A1 **Aqua Nueva** Mexico
29A3 **Aquidabán** *R* Par
25E2 **Aquidauana** Brazil
29A2 **Aquidauana** *R* Brazil
22B2 **Aquila** Mexico
61B2 **Ara** India
15B2 **Arab** USA
65C1 **'Arab al Mulk** Syria
58E4 **Arabian** *S* Asia/Arabian Pen
xxviiiE4 **Arabian Basin** Indian O
27L6 **Aracajú** Brazil
25E2 **Aracanguy, Mts de** *Mts* Brazil
29A3 **Aracanguy, Mts de** Par
27L4 **Aracati** Brazil
29D1 **Aracatu** Brazil
27H8 **Araçatuba** Brazil
39A2 **Aracena** Spain
27K7 **Araçuai** Brazil
65C3 **Arad** Israel
45C6 **Arad** Rom

72C2 Arada Chad
67F2 'Arādah UAE
76C1 Arafura S Indon/Aust
27H7 Aragarças Brazil
45G7 Aragats *Mt* Armenia
39B1 Aragón Region, Spain
39B1 Aragon *R* Spain
29C1 Araguaçu Brazil
27H6 Araguaia *R* Brazil
27J5 Araguaína Brazil
27J7 Araguari Brazil
29C2 Araguari *R* Brazil
54C3 Arai Japan
70C2 Arak Alg
63B2 Arāk Iran
10D3 Arakamchechen, Ostrov *Is* Russian Fed
55A2 Arakan Yoma *Mts* Burma
62B2 Arakkonam India
64E2 Araks *R* Azerbaijan
48H5 Aral'sk Kazakhstan
48G5 Aral'skoye More *S* Kazakhstan/Uzbekistan
22C1 Aramberri Mexico
33B2 Aran *I* Irish Rep
39B1 Aranda de Duero Spain
22B1 Arandas Mexico
39B1 Aranjuez Spain
74B1 Aranos Namibia
17F4 Aransas Pass USA
54B4 Arao Japan
70B3 Araouane Mali
16C1 Arapahoe USA
25E4 Arapey *R* Urug
28D2 Arapey Grande *R* Urug
27L6 Arapiraca Brazil
29B3 Araporgas Brazil
25G3 Ararangua Brazil
27J8 Araraquara Brazil
29C3 Araras Brazil
76D4 Ararat Aust
64D2 Ararat Armenia
64D1 Aras *R* Turk
45H8 Aras *R* Azerbaijan/Iran
66C3 Aratali Eth
54D3 Arato Japan
26E2 Arauca *R* Ven
28A3 Arauco Chile
26D2 Arauea Colombia
60C3 Arāvalli Range *Mts* India
77E1 Arawa PNG
27J7 Araxá Brazil
45G8 Araxes *R* Iran
72D3 Arba Minch Eth
40B3 Arbatax Sardegna
45G8 Arbīl Iraq
37A1 Arbois France
4B3 Arborg Can
32H6 Arbrå Sweden
34D3 Arbroath Scot
37A3 Arc *R* France
37B2 Arc *R* France
38B3 Arcachon France
14A1 Arcade USA
15E4 Arcadia USA
18B2 Arcata USA
20D1 Arc Dome, Mt USA
22B2 Arcelia Mexico
14C2 Archbald USA
20E3 Arches Nat Pk USA
23B2 Archipiélago de Camaguey *Arch* Cuba
25B8 Archipiélago de la Reina Adelaida *Arch* Chile
25B6 Archipiélago de las Chones *Arch* Chile
26C2 Archipiélago de las Perlas *Arch* Panama
36C2 Arcis-sur-Aube France
18D2 Arco USA
29C3 Arcos Brazil
39A2 Arcos de la Frontera Spain
37A1 Arc Senans France
79C1 Arctic Circle
6E3 Arctic Red Can
6E3 Arctic Red River Can
6D3 Arctic Village USA
79G2 Arctowski *Base* Ant
41F2 Arda *R* Bulg
45H8 Ardabīl Iran
45G7 Ardahan Turk
70C2 Ardar des Iforas *Upland* Alg/Mali
63C2 Ardekān Iran
32F6 Ardel Nor
36C2 Ardennes Department, France
42B2 Ardennes Region, Belg
63C2 Ardestan Iran
64C3 Ardh es Suwwan *Desert Region* Jordan
39A2 Ardila *R* Port
75C2 Ardlethan Aust
8D3 Ardmore USA
34B3 Ardnamurchan *Pt* Scot
35F6 Ardres France
36A1 Ardres France
34C3 Ardrishaig Scot
34C4 Ardrossan Scot
23D3 Arecibo Puerto Rico
27L4 Areia Branca Brazil
19B3 Arena,Pt USA
32F7 Arendal Nor
26D7 Arequipa Peru
40C2 Arezzo Italy
37B3 Argens *R* France
40C2 Argenta Italy
38C2 Argentan France
36B2 Argenteuil France
5L4 Argentia Can
24D7 Argentina Republic, S America
xxxF7 Argentine Basin Atlantic O
38C2 Argenton-sur-Creuse France
41F2 Argeşul *R* Rom
60B2 Arghardab *R* Afghan
41E3 Argolikós Kólpos *G* Greece
36C2 Argonne Region, France
41E3 Árgos Greece
41E3 Argostólion Greece
20B3 Arguello,Pt USA
71G3 Argungu Nig
20D3 Argus Range *Mts* USA
76B2 Argyle,L Aust
34G3 Argyll *Oilfield* N Sea
42C1 Århus Den
73C6 Ariamsvlei Namibia
39B1 Arian zón *R* Spain
28C2 Arias Venado Arg
70B3 Aribinda Burkina
25B1 Arica Chile
60C2 Arifwala Pak
Arihā = Jericho
16B2 Arikaree, R USA
23L1 Arima Trinidad
29C2 Arinos Brazil
27G6 Arinos *R* Brazil
22B2 Ario de Rosales Mexico
23L1 Aripo,Mt Trinidad
26F5 Aripuana Brazil
26F5 Aripuanã *R* Brazil
34C3 Arisaig Scot
62B2 Ariskere India
22B1 Arista Mexico
22D2 Arista Mexico
3C3 Aristazabal I Can
28B3 Arizona Arg
8B3 Arizona State, USA
32G7 Årjäng Sweden
49Q4 Arka Russian Fed
45G5 Arkadak Russian Fed
17D3 Arkadelphia USA
48H4 Arkalyk Kazakhstan
9D3 Arkansas State, USA
9D3 Arkansas *R* USA
17C2 Arkansas City USA
44G3 Arkhangel'sk Russian Fed
53C2 Arkhara Russian Fed
49K2 Arkipelag Nordenshelda *Arch* Russian Fed
33B3 Arklow Irish Rep
5G5 Arkville USA
37D1 Arlberg P Austria
38C3 Arles France
11C3 Arlington S Dakota, USA
17C3 Arlington Texas, USA
13D3 Arlington Virginia, USA
18B1 Arlington Washington, USA
12B2 Arlington Heights USA
42B3 Arlon Belg
Armageddon = Megido
35B4 Armagh County, N Ire
35B4 Armagh N Ire
41F3 Armagós *I* Greece
36B3 Armançon *R* France
45G7 Armavir Russian Fed
22B2 Armena Mexico
45G7 Armenia *Republic* Europe
26C3 Armenia Colombia
76E4 Armidale Aust
3E3 Armstrong Can
53D2 Armu *R* Russian Fed
7L3 Arnaud *R* Can
64B2 Arnauti *C* Cyprus
16C2 Arnett USA
42B2 Arnhem Neth
76C2 Arnhem,C Aust
76C2 Arnhem Land Aust
37D3 Arno *R* Italy
20B1 Arnold USA
37E1 Arnoldstein Austria
4B2 Arnot Can
4F4 Arnprior Can
36E1 Arnsberg Germany
74B2 Aroab Namibia
36E1 Arolsen Germany
37C2 Arona Italy
10F3 Aropuk L USA
77G1 Arorae *I* Kiribati
40B1 Arosa Switz
36B2 Arpajon France
29E2 Arquipélago dos Abrolhos *Arch* Brazil
70A3 Arquipélago dos Bijagós *Arch* Guinea-Bissau
29C1 Arraias Brazil
64D3 Ar Ramādī Iraq
34C4 Arran *I* Scot
64C2 Ar Raqqah Syria
69A2 Ar Rāqūbah Libya
38C1 Arras France
66D1 Ar Rass S Arabia
65D1 Ar Rastan Syria
66D2 Ar Rawdah S Arabia
70A2 Arrecife Canary Is
28C2 Arrecifes Arg
22B1 Arriaga Mexico
22D2 Arriaga Mexico
64E3 Ar Rifā't Iraq
64E3 Ar Rihāb *Desert Region* Iraq
Ar Riyād = Riyadh
34C3 Arrochar Scot
28E2 Arroio Grande Brazil
29C1 Arrojado *R* Brazil
18C2 Arrowrock Res USA
78A2 Arrowtown NZ
20B3 Arroyo Grande USA
22C1 Arroyo Seco Mexico
67F1 Ar Ru'ays Qatar
67G2 Ar Rustaq Oman
64D3 Ar Rutbah Iraq
66D2 Ar Ruwaydah S Arabia
53C3 Arsen'yev Russian Fed
37D2 Arsiero Italy
38D2 Arsizio Italy
44H4 Arsk Russian Fed
41E3 Árta Greece
22B2 Arteaga Mexico
53C3 Artem Russian Fed
49L4 Artemovsk Russian Fed
49N4 Artemovskiy Russian Fed
36A2 Artenay France
8C3 Artesia USA
78B2 Arthurs P NZ
32G7 Årthus Den
7K2 Artic Bay Can
25E4 Artigas Urug
28D2 Artigas Urug
6H3 Artillery L Can
38C1 Artois Region, France
43F3 Artsiz Ukraine
79G2 Arturo Prat *Base* Ant
45G7 Artvin Turk
72D3 Aru Zaïre
27H6 Aruanã Brazil
23C4 Aruba *I* Caribbean
61C2 Arun *R* Nepal
61D2 Arunāchal Pradesh Union Territory, India
53A2 Arun He *R* China
53A2 Arun Qi China
62B3 Aruppukkottai India
72D4 Arusha Tanz
72C3 Aruwimi *R* Zaïre
16A2 Arvada USA
50D2 Arvayheer Mongolia
37B2 Arve *R* France
7L5 Arvida Can
32H5 Arvidsjaur Sweden
44B2 Arvidsjaur Sweden
32G7 Arvika Sweden
19C3 Arvin USA
65C1 Arwad *I* Syria
57C4 Arwala Indon
44G4 Arzamas Russian Fed
71B1 Arzew Alg
60C2 Asadabad Afghan
54B4 Asahi *R* Japan
53E3 Asahi dake *Mt* Japan
53E3 Asahikawa Japan
54A3 Asan-man *B* S Korea
61C3 Asansol India
69A2 Asawanwah *Well* Libya
44L4 Asbest Russian Fed
74C2 Asbestos Mts S Africa
13E2 Asbury Park USA
xxxH5 Ascension *I* Atlantic O
42B3 Aschaffenburg Germany
42C2 Aschersleben Germany
40C2 Ascoli Piceno Italy
37C1 Ascona Switz
72E2 Āseb Eth
70C2 Asedjirad *Upland* Alg
72D3 Asela Eth
32H6 Åsele Sweden
41E2 Asenovgrad Bulg
36C2 Asfeld France
44K4 Asha Russian Fed
15C2 Ashburn USA
77G5 Ashburton NZ
76A3 Ashburton *R* Aust
64B3 Ashdod Israel
17D3 Ashdown USA
15D1 Asheboro USA
4B3 Ashern Can
9E3 Asheville USA
75D1 Ashford Aust
35F6 Ashford Eng
19D3 Ash Fork USA
54D2 Ashibetsu Japan
53D4 Ashikaga Japan
54B4 Ashizuri-misaki *Pt* Japan
48G6 Ashkhabad Turkmenistan
16C2 Ashland Kansas, USA
9E3 Ashland Kentucky, USA
11A2 Ashland Montana, USA
17C1 Ashland Nebraska, USA
12C2 Ashland Ohio, USA
8A2 Ashland Oregon, USA
13D3 Ashland Virginia, USA
11D2 Ashland Wisconsin, USA
75C1 Ashley Aust
11C2 Ashley USA
14C2 Ashokan Res USA
65C3 Ashqelon Israel
64D3 Ash Shabakh Iraq
67G1 Ash Sha'm UAE
66D3 Ash Sh'ār S Arabia
64D2 Ash Sharqāt Iraq
64E3 Ash Shatrah Iraq
67E4 Ash Shihr Yemen
67E1 Ash Shumlul S Arabia
66D3 Ash Shuqayq S Arabia
12C2 Ashtabula USA
7M4 Ashuanipi L Can
5G4 Ashuapmushuan Prov Park Can
45F8 'Āsī *R* Syria
37D2 Asiago Italy
71A1 Asilah Mor
40B2 Asinara *I* Medit S
48K4 Asino Russian Fed
66D2 Asir Region, S Arabia
61B4 Aska India
64D2 Aşkale Turk
32G7 Askersund Sweden
65B4 Asl Egypt
60C1 Asmar Afghan
72D2 Asmera Eth
54B4 Āso Japan
72D2 Asosa Eth
16B3 Aspermont USA
78A2 Aspiring,Mt NZ
37A2 Aspres-sur-Buëch France
64C2 As Sabkhah Syria
67E2 As Salamiyah S Arabia
64C2 As Salamīyah Syria
66D4 Assale,L Eth
64D3 As Salmān Iraq
61D2 Assam State, India
64E3 As Samāwah Iraq
67F2 AsŞanām Region, S Arabia
65D2 As Sanamayn Syria
37B3 Asse *R* France
42B2 Assen Neth
42C1 Assens Den
69A1 As Sidrah Libya
6H5 Assiniboia Can
6G4 Assiniboine,Mt Can
4B4 Assiniboine *R* Can
5G3 Assinica Prov Park Can
37E3 Assissi Italy
64C3 As Sukhnah Syria
67E2 As Sulayyil S Arabia
67E2 As Summan Region, S Arabia
73E4 Assumption *I* Seychelles
66D2 As Suq S Arabia
64C3 As Suwaydā' Syria
64D3 As Suwayrah Iraq
64E2 Astara Azerbaijan
40B2 Asti Italy
41F3 Astipálaia *I* Greece
39A1 Astorga Spain
8A2 Astoria USA
45H6 Astrakhan' Russian Fed
39A1 Asturias Region, Spain
25E3 Asunción Par
72D3 Aswa *R* Uganda
66B2 Aswân Egypt
69C2 Aswân High Dam Egypt
69C2 Asyût Egypt
64C3 As Zilaf Syria
77H1 Atafu *I* Tokelau Is
71G4 Atakpamé Togo
57B5 Atambua Indon
7N3 Atangmik Greenland
57B4 Atapupu Indon
70A2 Atar Maur
20B3 Atascadero USA
48J5 Atasu Kazakhstan
57C4 Atauro *I* Indon
72D2 Atbara Sudan
48H4 Atbasar Kazakhstan
9D4 Atchafalaya B USA
9D3 Atchison USA
14C3 Atco USA
71F4 Atebubu Ghana
22B1 Atenguillo Mexico
40C2 Atessa Italy
36B1 Ath Belg
3F3 Athabasca Can
6G4 Athabasca *R* Can
6H4 Athabasca, L Can
Athens = Athínai
15B2 Athens Alabama, USA
9E3 Athens Georgia, USA
12C3 Athens Ohio, USA
14B2 Athens Pennsylvania, USA
15C1 Athens Tennessee, USA
17C3 Athens Texas, USA
71G4 Athiémé Benin
41E3 Athínai Greece
33B3 Athlone Irish Rep
65B1 Athna Cyprus
14D1 Athol USA
41E2 Áthos *Mt* Greece
35B5 Athy Irish Rep
72B2 Ati Chad
7J5 Atikoken Can
5J3 Atikonak L Can
49R3 Atka Russian Fed
10D6 Atka *I* USA
45G5 Atkarsk Russian Fed
17D2 Atkins USA
22C2 Atlacomulco Mexico
9E3 Atlanta Georgia, USA
12C2 Atlanta Michigan, USA
17C1 Atlantic USA
9F3 Atlantic City USA
14C2 Atlantic Highlands USA
xxxH8 Atlantic Indian Basin Atlantic O
xxxH7 Atlantic Indian Ridge Atlantic O
70C1 Atlas Saharien *Mts* Alg
6E4 Atlin Can
6E4 Atlin L Can
65C2 'Atlit Israel
22C2 Atlixco Mexico
9E3 Atmore USA
73E6 Atofinandrahana Madag
10H4 Atognak I USA
17C3 Atoka USA
22B1 Atotonilco Mexico
22C2 Atoyac *R* Mexico
26C2 Atrato *R* Colombia
67F2 Attaf Region, UAE
66D2 At Tā'if S Arabia
65D2 At Tall Syria
15B2 Attalla USA
7K4 Attawapiskat Can
4D3 Attawapiskat L Can
7K4 Attawapiskat *R* Can
64D3 At Taysiyah *Desert Region* S Arabia
12B2 Attica Indiana, USA
14A1 Attica New York, USA
36C2 Attigny France
5H2 Attikamagen L Can
65B1 Attila Line Cyprus
13E2 Attleboro Massachusetts, USA
55D3 Attopeu Laos
10A5 Attu USA
10A5 Attu *I* USA
64C4 At Tubayq *Upland* S Arabia
28B3 Atuel *R* Arg
32H7 Atvidaberg Sweden
20B2 Atwater USA
38D3 Aubagne France
36C2 Aube Department, France
36C2 Aube *R* France
38C3 Aubenas France
10N2 Aubry L Can
15B2 Auburn Alabama, USA
19B3 Auburn California, USA
12B2 Auburn Indiana, USA
13E2 Auburn Maine, USA
17C1 Auburn Nebraska, USA
13D2 Auburn New York, USA
18B1 Auburn Washington, USA
38C3 Auch France
71H4 Auchi Nig
77G4 Auckland NZ
xxixK7 Auckland Is NZ
38C3 Aude *R* France
7K4 Auden Can
37B1 Audincourt France
11D3 Audubon USA
75C1 Augathella Aust
74B2 Aughrabies Falls S Africa
42C3 Augsburg Germany
76A4 Augusta Aust
9E3 Augusta Georgia, USA
17C2 Augusta Kansas, USA
9G2 Augusta Maine, USA
18D1 Augusta Montana, USA
12A2 Augusta Wisconsin, USA
10H4 Augustine I USA

43E2 **Augustow** Pol
76A3 **Augustus,Mt** Aust
34G3 **Auk** *Oilfield* N Sea
37C2 **Aulla** Italy
36A2 **Aumale** France
74B1 **Auob** *R* Namibia
5H2 **Aupalak** Can
57C3 **Auponhia** Indon
37B3 **Aups** France
60D3 **Auraiya** India
60D5 **Aurangābād** India
71D1 **Aurès** *Mts* Alg
38C3 **Aurillac** France
8C3 **Aurora** Colorado, USA
12B2 **Aurora** Illinois, USA
12C3 **Aurora** Indiana, USA
17D2 **Aurora** Mississippi, USA
17C1 **Aurora** Nebraska, USA
74B2 **Aus** Namibia
12C2 **Au Sable** USA
70A2 **Ausert** *Well* Mor
9D2 **Austin** Minnesota, USA
19C3 **Austin** Nevada, USA
14A2 **Austin** Pennsylvania, USA
8D3 **Austin** Texas, USA
76D4 **Australian Alps** *Mts* Aust
30G4 **Austria,** *Fed Republic* Europe
36A1 **Authie** *R* France
21B3 **Autlán** Mexico
38C2 **Autun** France
38C2 **Auvergne** Region, France
38C2 **Auxerre** France
36A1 **Auxi-le-Château** France
37A1 **Auxonne** France
38C2 **Avallon** France
20C4 **Avalon** USA
7N5 **Avalon Pen** Can
28D1 **Avalos** *R* Arg
29C3 **Avaré** Brazil
63E2 **Avaz** Iran
65C3 **Avedat** *Hist Site* Israel
27G4 **Aveiro** Brazil
39A1 **Aveiro** Port
25E4 **Avellaneda** Arg
40C2 **Avellino** Italy
20B3 **Avenal** USA
36B1 **Avesnes-sur-Helpe** France
32H6 **Avesta** Sweden
40C2 **Avezzano** Italy
34D3 **Aviemore** Scot
78B2 **Aviemore,L** NZ
37B2 **Avigliana** Italy
38C3 **Avignon** France
39B1 **Avila** Spain
39A1 **Aviles** Spain
37D1 **Avisio** *R* Italy
11C3 **Avoca** Iowa, USA
14B1 **Avoca** New York, USA
75B3 **Avoca** *R* Aust
35D6 **Avon** County, Eng
14B1 **Avon** USA
35E6 **Avon** *R* Dorset, Eng
35E5 **Avon** *R* Warwick, Eng
19D4 **Avondale** USA
35D6 **Avonmouth** Wales
15E4 **Avon Park** USA
36B2 **Avre** *R* France
41D2 **Avtovac** Bosnia & Herzegovina, Yugos
65D2 **A'waj** *R* Syria
53D5 **Awaji-shima** *B* Japan
72E3 **Awarē** Eth
78A2 **Awarua Pt** NZ
72E3 **Awash** Eth
72E3 **Awash** *R* Eth
54C3 **Awa-shima** *I* Japan
78B2 **Awatere** *R* NZ
69A2 **Awbārī** Libya
72C3 **Aweil** Sudan
69B2 **Awjilah** Libya
71H4 **Awka** Nig
10G2 **Awuna** *R* USA
7J1 **Axel Heiberg I** Can
35D6 **Axminster** Eng
54C3 **Ayabe** Japan
25E5 **Ayacucho** Arg
23C5 **Ayacucho** Colombia
26D6 **Ayacucho** Peru
48K5 **Ayaguz** Kazakhstan
59G2 **Ayakkum Hu** *L* China
39A2 **Ayamonte** Spain
49P4 **Ayan** Russian Fed
26D6 **Ayauiri** Peru
45D8 **Aydin** Turk
41F3 **Áyios Evstrátios** *I* Greece
49N3 **Aykhal** Russian Fed
35E5 **Aylesbury** Eng
3E3 **Aylmer,Mt** Can
65D2 **'Ayn al Fijah** Syria
64D2 **Ayn Zālah** Iraq
69B2 **Ayn Zuwayyah** *Well* Libya
72D3 **Ayod** Sudan
49S3 **Ayon, Ostrov** *I* Russian Fed
76D2 **Ayr** Aust
34C4 **Ayr** Scot
34C4 **Ayr** *R* Scot
35C4 **Ayre,Pt of** Eng
55C3 **Aytthaya** Thai
22B1 **Ayutla** Mexico
41F3 **Ayvacik** Turk
41F3 **Ayvalik** Turk
61B2 **Āzamgarh** India
70B3 **Azaouad** *Desert Region* Mali
71J3 **Azare** Nig
64C2 **A'Zāz** Syria
Azbine = Aïr
70A2 **Azeffal,** *Watercourse* Maur
71A2 **Azemmour** Mor
45H7 **Azerbaijan** *Republic* Europe
26C4 **Azogues** Ecuador
44H2 **Azopol'ye** Russian Fed
Azores = Açores
72C2 **Azoum, R** Chad
45F6 **Azovskoye More** *S* Russian Fed/Ukraine
71A2 **Azrou** Mor
16A2 **Aztec** USA
28D3 **Azucena** Arg
26B2 **Azuero,Pen de** Panama
25E5 **Azúl** Arg
71D1 **Azzaba** Alg
65D2 **Az-Zabdānī** Syria
67G2 **Az Zāhirah** *Mts* Oman
69A2 **Az Zahrah** Libya
66D1 **Az Zilfi** S Arabia
64E3 **Az Zubayr** Iraq

B

57B5 **Baa** Indon
65C2 **Ba'abda** Leb
64C3 **Ba'albek** Leb
65C3 **Ba'al Hazor** *Mt* Israel
72E3 **Baardheere** Somalia
41F2 **Babadag** Rom
64A1 **Babaeski** Turk
66D4 **Bāb al Mandab** *Str* Djibouti/Yemen
26C4 **Babanoyo** Ecuador
57C4 **Babar** *I* Indon
72D4 **Babati** Tanz
44F4 **Babayevo** Russian Fed
11D2 **Babbitt** USA
12C2 **Baberton** USA
3C2 **Babine** *R* Can
3C3 **Babine L** Can
76C1 **Babo** Indon
63C1 **Bābol** Iran
57F7 **Babuyan Chan** Phil
57F7 **Babuyan Is** Phil
27J4 **Bacabal** Brazil
57C3 **Bacan** *I* Indon
45D6 **Bacău** Rom
55D1 **Bac Can** Viet
36D2 **Baccarat** France
75B3 **Bacchus Marsh** Aust
59F2 **Bachu** China
6J3 **Back** *R* Can
10N3 **Backbone Ranges** *Mts* Can
36E2 **Backnang** Germany
55D1 **Bac Ninh** Viet
57F8 **Bacolod** Phil
57F8 **Baco,Mt** Phil
62B2 **Badagara** India
52A1 **Badain Jaran Shamo** *Desert* China
39A2 **Badajoz** Spain
39C1 **Badalona** Spain
64D3 **Badanah** S Arabia
37E1 **Bad Aussee** Austria
36E2 **Bad Bergzabern** Germany
36D1 **Bad Ems** Germany
38D2 **Baden** Region, Germany
37C1 **Baden** Switz
42B3 **Baden-Baden** Germany
36D2 **Badenviller** France
42B3 **Baden-Württemberg** State, Germany
42C3 **Badgastein** Austria
20C2 **Badger** USA
42B2 **Bad-Godesberg** Germany
42B2 **Bad Hersfeld** Germany
36D1 **Bad Honnef** Germany
60B4 **Badin** Pak
40C1 **Bad Ischl** Austria
64C3 **Badiyat ash Sham** *Desert Region* Jordan/Iraq
42B3 **Bad-Kreuznach** Germany
11B2 **Badlands** USA
36E1 **Bad Lippspringe** Germany
36E1 **Bad Nauheim** Germany
36D1 **Bad Nevenahr-Ahrweiler** Germany
71G4 **Badou** Togo
37C1 **Bad Ragaz** Switz
66C2 **Badr Hunayn** S Arabia
36E1 **Bad Ryrmont** Germany
42C3 **Bad Tolz** Germany
62C3 **Badulla** Sri Lanka
36E1 **Bad Wildungen** Germany
36E2 **Bad Wimpfen** Germany
53C1 **Badzhal'skiy Khrebet** *Mts* Russian Fed
39B2 **Baena** Spain
71J4 **Bafang** Cam
70A3 **Bafatá** Guinea-Bissau
7L2 **Baffin B** Greenland/Can
17F4 **Baffin B** USA
7L2 **Baffin I** Can
72B3 **Bafia** Cam
70A3 **Bafing** *R* Mali
70A3 **Bafoulabé** Mali
72B3 **Bafoussam** Cam
63D2 **Bāfq** Iran
45F7 **Bafra Burun** *Pt* Turk
63D3 **Bāft** Iran
72C3 **Bafwasende** Zaïre
71J3 **Baga** Nig
61B2 **Bagaha** India
62B1 **Bāgalkot** India
73D4 **Bagamoyo** Tanz
56F7 **Bagan Datok** Malay
56F7 **Bagan Siapiapi** Indon
19D4 **Bagdad** USA
25F4 **Bagé** Brazil
16A1 **Baggs** USA
64D3 **Baghdād** Iraq
61C3 **Bagherhat** Bang
63D2 **Bāghīn** Iran
60B1 **Baghlan** Afghan
11C2 **Bagley** USA
70B4 **Bagnoa** Ivory Coast
38C3 **Bagnols-sur-Cèza** France
70B3 **Bagoé** *R* Mali
57F7 **Baguio** Phil
61C2 **Bāhādurābād** India
9F4 **Bahamas,The** *Is* Caribbean
61C3 **Baharampur** India
64A4 **Baharîya Oasis** Egypt
56G7 **Bahau** Malay
60C3 **Bahawahpur** Province, Pak
60C3 **Bahawalpur** Pak
60C3 **Bahawathagar** Pak
Bahia = Salvador
27K6 **Bahia State,** Brazil
28C4 **Bahia Anegada** Arg
25D5 **Bahía Blanca** Arg
25D5 **Bahía Blanca** *B* Arg
28A3 **Bahía Concepción** *B* Chile
29D3 **Bahia da Ilha Grande** *B* Brazil
21B2 **Bahía de Banderas** *B* Mexico
21C2 **Bahía de Campeche** *B* Mexico
26B2 **Bahía de Corando** *B* Costa Rica
21D3 **Bahía de la Ascension** *B* Mexico
21B3 **Bahía de Petacalco** *B* Mexico
70A2 **Bahía de Rio de Oro** *B* Mor
29D3 **Bahia de Sepetiba** *B* Brazil
19C4 **Bahiá de Todos Santos** *B* Mexico
25C8 **Bahía Grande** *B* Arg
8B4 **Bahía Kino** Mexico
21A2 **Bahía Magdalena** *B* Mexico
28A1 **Bahía Salada** *B* Chile
28D3 **Bahía Samborombon** *B* Arg
21A2 **Bahía Sebastia Vizcaino** *B* Mexico
66C4 **Bahir Dar** Eth
65A3 **Bahrael Manzala** *L* Egypt
61B2 **Bahraich** India
58D3 **Bahrain** Sheikdom, Arabian Pen
64D3 **Bahr al Milh** *L* Iraq
72C3 **Bahr Aouk** *R* Chad/CAR
Bahrat Lut = Dead S
Bahr el Abiad = White Nile
66B4 **Bahr el Abiad** *R* Sudan
72C3 **Bahr el Arab** *Watercourse* Sudan
Bahr el Azraq = Blue Nile
66B4 **Bahr el Azraq** *R* Sudan
72D3 **Bahr el Ghazal** *R* Sudan
72B2 **Bahr el Ghazal** *Watercourse* Chad
65A3 **Bahr Fâqûs** *R* Egypt
63E3 **Bāhū-Kalāt** Iran
57B3 **Bahumbelu** Indon
5H2 **Baie de Keglo** *B* Can
5J4 **Baie de Malbaie** *B* Can
74E2 **Baia de Maputo** *B* Mozam
27J4 **Baia de Marajó** *B* Brazil
73E5 **Baiá de Pemba** *B* Mozam
27K4 **Baia de São Marcos** *B* Brazil
5H4 **Baie des Chaleurs** *B* Can
39A2 **Baia de Setúbal** *B* Port
27L6 **Baia de Todos os Santos** *B* Brazil
73B5 **Baia dos Tigres** Angola
29C4 **Baiá Guaratuba** Brazil
45C6 **Baia Mare** Rom
72B3 **Baïbokoum** Chad
53A2 **Baicheng** China
73F5 **Baie Antongila** *B* Madag
7M5 **Baie-Comeau** Can
73E5 **Baie de Bombetoka** *B* Madag
73E5 **Baie de Mahajamba** *B* Madag
73E6 **Baie de St Augustin** *B* Madag
65C2 **Baie de St Georges** *B* Leb
7L4 **Baie-du-Poste** Can
5F2 **Baie Kogaluc** *B* Can
5G4 **Baie Saint Paul** Can
7N5 **Baie Verte** Can
52B3 **Baihe** China
52C3 **Bai He** *R* China
64D3 **Ba'ījī** Iraq
61B3 **Baikunthpur** India
Baile Atha Cliath = Dublin
41E2 **Băileşti** Rom
36B1 **Bailleul** France
10N1 **Baillie Is** Can
52A3 **Baima** China
15C2 **Bainbridge** USA
57B5 **Baing** Indon
53B2 **Baiquan** China
10F3 **Baird Inlet** USA
6B3 **Baird Mts** USA
52D1 **Bairin Youqi** China
52D1 **Bairin Zuoqi** China
76D4 **Bairnsdale** Aust
57F9 **Bais** Phil
71J4 **Baissa** Nig
61B2 **Baitadi** Nepal
66B3 **Baiyuda** *Desert* Sudan
41D1 **Baja** Hung
21A1 **Baja California** *Pen* Mexico
19C4 **Baja California Norte** Mexico
57B4 **Bajawi** Indon
66D4 **Bājil** Yemen
57B2 **Bajo** Indon
44K5 **Bakal** Russian Fed
72C3 **Bakala** CAR
70A3 **Bakel** Sen
19C3 **Baker** California, USA
8C2 **Baker** Montana, USA
8B2 **Baker** Oregon, USA
7J3 **Baker Foreland** *Pt* Can
6J3 **Baker L** Can
6J3 **Baker Lake** Can
8A2 **Baker,Mt** USA
8B3 **Bakersfield** USA
63D1 **Bakharden** Turkmenistan
63D1 **Bakhardok** Turkmenistan
45E5 **Bakhmach** Ukraine
32C1 **Bakkaflói** *B* Iceland
72D3 **Bako** Eth
72C3 **Bakouma** CAR
45H7 **Baku** Azerbaijan
57B3 **Bakudek** *I* Indon
56A2 **Bakungan** Indon
64B2 **Balâ** Turk
57E9 **Balabac** *I* Phil
56E1 **Balabac** *Str* Malay
61B3 **Bālaghāt** India
56D2 **Balaikarangan** Indon
75A2 **Balaklava** Aust
45H5 **Balakovo** Russian Fed
63E1 **Bala Murghab** Afghan
61B3 **Balāngīr** India
45G5 **Balashov** Russian Fed
61C3 **Balasore** India
66A1 **Balât** Egypt
41D1 **Balaton** *L* Hung
35B5 **Balbniggan** Irish Rep
25E5 **Balcarce** Arg
41F2 **Balchik** Bulg
77F5 **Balclutha** NZ
17D2 **Bald Knob** USA
4B2 **Baldock L** Can
15C2 **Baldwin** USA
4D5 **Baldwin** Michigan, USA
18E1 **Baldy Mt** USA
8C3 **Baldy Peak** *Mt* USA
Balearic Is = Islas Baleares
56D2 **Baleh, R** Malay
57F7 **Baler** Phil
44J4 **Balezino** Russian Fed
67E4 **Balhāf** Yemen
66D4 **Balho** Djibouti
76A1 **Bali** *I* Indon
64A2 **Balıkesir** Turk
64C2 **Balīkh** *R* Syria
56E3 **Balikpapan** Indon
57F7 **Balintang Chan** Phil
56D4 **Bali S** Indon
29B2 **Baliza** Brazil
66D3 **Baljurshī** S Arabia
60B1 **Balkh** Afghan
48J5 **Balkhash** Kazakhstan
48J5 **Balkhash, Ozero** *L* Kazakhstan
34C3 **Ballachulish** Scot
34C4 **Ballantrae** Scot
6G2 **Ballantyne Str** Can
62B2 **Ballapur** India
76D4 **Ballarat** Aust
34D3 **Ballater** Scot
79F7 **Balleny Is** Ant
61B2 **Ballia** India
75D1 **Ballina** Aust
33B3 **Ballina** Irish Rep
16C3 **Ballinger** USA
36D3 **Ballon d'Alsace** *Mt* France
41D2 **Ballsh** Alb
14D1 **Ballston Spa** USA
34B4 **Ballycastle** N Ire
34B4 **Ballymena** N Ire
34B4 **Ballymoney** N Ire
35A4 **Ballyshannon** Irish Rep
75B3 **Balmoral** Aust
16B3 **Balmorhea** USA
28C2 **Balnearia** Arg
60B3 **Balochistān** Region, Pak
73B5 **Balombo** Angola
75C1 **Balonn** *R* Aust
60C3 **Balotra** India
61B2 **Balrāmpur** India
76D4 **Balranald** Aust
27J5 **Balsas** Brazil
22C2 **Balsas** Mexico
21B3 **Balsas** *R* Mexico
45D6 **Balta** Ukraine
28D2 **Baltasar Brum** Urug
32H7 **Baltic S** N Europe
64B3 **Baltîm** Egypt
9F3 **Baltimore** USA
61C2 **Bālurghāt** India
45J6 **Balykshi** Kazakhstan
63D3 **Bam** Iran
72B2 **Bama** Nig
70B3 **Bamako** Mali
72C3 **Bambari** CAR
15C2 **Bamberg** USA
42C3 **Bamberg** Germany
72C3 **Bambili** Zaïre
29C3 **Bambui** Brazil
72B3 **Bamenda** Cam
3C4 **Bamfield** Can
72B3 **Bamingui** *R* CAR
72B3 **Bamingui Bangoran** National Park, CAR
60B2 **Bamiyan** Afghan
63E3 **Bampur** Iran
63E3 **Bampur** *R* Iran
77F1 **Banaba** *I* Kiribati
72C3 **Banalia** Zaïre
70B3 **Banamba** Mali
62E3 **Bananga** Nicobar Is
55C3 **Ban Aranyaprathet** Thai
55C2 **Ban Ban** Laos
55C4 **Ban Betong** Thai
35B4 **Banbridge** N Ire
35E5 **Banbury** Eng
34D3 **Banchory** Scot
21D3 **Banco Chinchorro** *Is* Mexico
4F4 **Bancroft** Can
61B2 **Bānda** India
56A1 **Banda Aceh** Indon
70B4 **Bandama** *R* Ivory Coast
63D3 **Bandar Abbās** Iran
45H8 **Bandar Anzalī** Iran
63C3 **Bandar-e Daylam** Iran
63C3 **Bandar-e Lengheh** Iran
63C3 **Bandar-e Māqām** Iran
63C3 **Bandar-e Rig** Iran
45J8 **Bandar-e Torkoman** Iran
63B2 **Bandar Khomeynī** Iran
56D2 **Bandar Seri Begawan** Brunei
51F7 **Banda S** Indon
56E1 **Bandau** Malay
63D3 **Band Bonī** Iran
29D3 **Bandeira** *Mt* Brazil
28C1 **Bandera** Arg
29B1 **Banderantes** Brazil
70B3 **Bandiagara** Mali
63E2 **Band-i-Baba** *Upland* Afghan
45D7 **Bandirma** Turk
63E1 **Band-i-Turkestan** *Mts* Afghan
37A3 **Bandol** France
74D1 **Bandolier Kop** S Africa

72B4 **Bandundu** Zaïre
56C4 **Bandung** Indon
45H8 **Baneh** Iran
57C2 **Banermo** Indon
21E2 **Banes** Cuba
3E3 **Banff** Can
34D3 **Banff** Scot
6G4 **Banff** *R* Can
3E3 **Banff Nat Pk** Can
71F3 **Banfora** Burkina
62B2 **Bangalore** India
71J4 **Bangangté** Cam
72C3 **Bangassou** CAR
56E1 **Banggi** *I* Malay
55D2 **Bang Hieng** *R* Laos
56C3 **Bangka** *I* Indon
56B2 **Bangkinang** Indon
56B3 **Bangko** Indon
55C3 **Bangkok** Thai
59H3 **Bangladesh** Republic, Asia
60D2 **Bangong Co** *L* China
9G2 **Bangor** Maine, USA
34B4 **Bangor** N Ire
14C2 **Bangor** Pennsylvania, USA
35C5 **Bangor** Wales
56E3 **Bangsalsembera** Indon
55B3 **Bang Saphan Yai** Thai
57F7 **Bangued** Phil
72B3 **Bangui** CAR
73D5 **Bangweulu** *L* Zambia
55C4 **Ban Hat Yai** Thai
55C2 **Ban Hin Heup** Laos
55C1 **Ban Houei Sai** Laos
55B3 **Ban Hua Hin** Thai
70B3 **Bani** *R* Mali
70C3 **Bani Bangou** Niger
67E3 **Banī Ma'arid** Region, S Arabia
69A1 **Banī Walīd** Libya
64C2 **Bāniyās** Syria
65C2 **Baniyas** Syria
40D2 **Banja Luka** Bosnia & Herzegovina, Yugos
56D3 **Banjarmasin** Indon
70A3 **Banjul** The Gambia
55B4 **Ban Kantang** Thai
55D2 **Ban Khemmarat** Laos
55B4 **Ban Khok Kloi** Thai
77F2 **Banks** *Is* Vanuatu
51H8 **Banks I** Aust
6E4 **Banks I** British Columbia, Can
6F2 **Banks I** Northwest Territories, Can
18C1 **Banks L** USA
78B2 **Banks Pen** NZ
75E3 **Banks Str** Aust
61C3 **Bankura** India
55B2 **Ban Mae Sariang** Thai
55B2 **Ban Mae Sot** Thai
61E3 **Banmauk** Burma
55D3 **Ban Me Thuot** Viet
34B4 **Bann** *R* N Ire
55B4 **Ban Na San** Thai
60C2 **Bannu** Pak
28A4 **Baños de Chihuio** Chile
28A3 **Baños Maule** Chile
55C2 **Ban Pak Neun** Laos
55C4 **Ban Pak Phanang** Thai
55D3 **Ban Ru Kroy** Camb
55B3 **Ban Sai Yok** Thai
55C3 **Ban Sattahip** Thai
43D3 **Banská Bystrica** Czech
60C4 **Bānswāra** India
57B4 **Bantaeng** Indon
55B4 **Ban Tha Kham** Thai
55D2 **Ban Thateng** Laos
55C2 **Ban Tha Tum** Thai
33B3 **Bantry** Irish Rep
33A3 **Bantry** *B* Irish Rep
55D3 **Ban Ya Soup** Viet
71J4 **Banyo** Cam
56D4 **Banyuwangi** Indon
xxviiiE7 **Banzare Seamount** Indian O
52C3 **Baofeng** China
55C1 **Bao Ha** Viet
52B3 **Baoji** China
55D3 **Bao Loc** Viet
53C2 **Baoqing** China
50C4 **Baoshan** China
52C1 **Baotou** China
62C1 **Bāpatla** India
36B1 **Bapaume** France
64D3 **Ba'Qūbah** Iraq
41D2 **Bar** Montenegro, Yugos
57C3 **Bara** Indon
72D2 **Bara** Sudan
72E3 **Baraawe** Somalia
56E3 **Barabai** Indon
61B2 **Bāra Banki** India
48J4 **Barabinsk** Russian Fed
48J4 **Barabinskaya Step** *Steppe* Kazakhstan/Russian Fed
39B1 **Baracaldo** Spain
23C2 **Baracoa** Cuba
65D2 **Baradá** *R* Syria
75C2 **Baradine** Aust
66C3 **Baraka** *Watercourse* Eth
62A1 **Bārāmati** India
60C2 **Baramula** Pak
60D3 **Bārān** India
57F8 **Barangas** Phil
6E4 **Baranof I** USA
44D5 **Baranovichi** Belorussia
75A2 **Baratta** Aust
61C2 **Barauni** India
27K8 **Barbacena** Brazil
23F4 **Barbados** *I* Caribbean
39C1 **Barbastro** Spain
74E2 **Barberton** S Africa
38B2 **Barbezieux** France
26D2 **Barbòsa** Colombia
23E3 **Barbuda** *I* Caribbean
76D3 **Barcaldine** Aust
Barce = Al Marj
40D3 **Barcellona** Italy
39C1 **Barcelona** Spain
26F1 **Barcelona** Ven
37B2 **Barcelonnette** France
76D3 **Barcoo** *R* Aust
28B3 **Barda del Medio** Arg
72B1 **Bardai** Chad
25C5 **Bardas Blancas** Arg
61C3 **Barddhamān** India
43E3 **Bardejov** Czech
37C2 **Bardi** Italy
37B2 **Bardonecchia** Italy
35C5 **Bardsey** *I* Wales
12B3 **Bardstown** USA
67F4 **Bareeda** Somalia
60D3 **Bareilly** India
44F1 **Barentsovo More** *S* Russian Fed
48D2 **Barentsøya** *I* Barents S
Barents S = Barentsovo More
72D2 **Barentu** Eth
61B3 **Bargarh** India
37B2 **Barge** Italy
49M4 **Barguzin** Russian Fed
49N4 **Barguzin** *R* Russian Fed
13F2 **Bar Harbor** USA
61C3 **Barhi** India
40D2 **Bari** Italy
39D2 **Barika** Alg
26D2 **Barinas** Ven
61C3 **Baripāda** India
66B2 **Bâris** Egypt
60C4 **Bari Sādri** India
61D3 **Barisal** Bang
56D3 **Barito** *R* Indon
37B3 **Barjols** France
69A2 **Barjuj** *Watercourse* Libya
52A3 **Barkam** China
17E2 **Barkley,L** USA
3C4 **Barkley Sd** Can
74D3 **Barkly East** S Africa
76C2 **Barkly Tableland** *Mts* Aust
36C2 **Bar-le-Duc** France
76A3 **Barlee,L** Aust
76A3 **Barlee Range** *Mts* Aust
40D2 **Barletta** Italy
60C3 **Barmer** India
75B2 **Barmera** Aust
35C5 **Barmouth** Wales
35E4 **Barnard Castle** Eng
48K4 **Barnaul** Russian Fed
14C3 **Barnegat** USA
14C3 **Barnegat B** USA
14A2 **Barnesboro** USA
7L2 **Barnes Icecap** Can
15C2 **Barnesville** Georgia, USA
12C3 **Barnesville** Ohio, USA
16B3 **Barnhart** USA
35E5 **Barnsley** Eng
35C6 **Barnstaple** Eng
71H4 **Baro** Nig
61D2 **Barpeta** India
26E1 **Barquisimeto** Ven
35F5 **Barqe** *Oilfield* N Sea
36D2 **Barr** France
27K6 **Barra** Brazil
34B3 **Barra** *I* Scot
75D2 **Barraba** Aust
29D1 **Barra da Estiva** Brazil
22B2 **Barra de Navidad** Mexico
29D3 **Barra de Piraí** Brazil
22D2 **Barra de Tonalá** Mexico
29A2 **Barra do Bugres** Brazil
29B2 **Barra do Garças** Brazil
28D2 **Barra do Quarai** Brazil
28E2 **Barra do Ribeiro** Brazil
71F4 **Barrage d'Ayama** Ivory Coast
71J4 **Barrage de Mbakaou** *Dam* Cam
27K6 **Barragem de Sobradinho** Brazil
39A2 **Barragem do Castelo do Bode** *Res* Port
39A2 **Barragem do Maranhão** Port
34B3 **Barra Head** *Pt* Scot
27K8 **Barra Mansa** Brazil
26C6 **Barranca** Peru
26D2 **Barrancabermeja** Colombia
26F2 **Barrancas** Ven
105E3 **Barranqueras** Arg
26D1 **Barranquilla** Colombia
34B3 **Barra,Sound of** *Chan* Scot
4F4 **Barraute** Can
14D1 **Barre** USA
28B2 **Barreal** Arg
27K6 **Barreiras** Brazil
39A2 **Barreiro** Port
27L5 **Barreiros** Brazil
76D5 **Barren,C** Aust
10H4 **Barren Is** USA
27J8 **Barretos** Brazil
3F3 **Barrhead** Can
4F5 **Barrie** Can
3D3 **Barrière** Can
75B2 **Barrier Range** *Mts* Aust
3H2 **Barrington L** Can
76E4 **Barrington,Mt** Aust
29C2 **Barro Alto** Brazil
51G8 **Barroloola** Aust
12A1 **Barron** USA
23N2 **Barrouaillie** St Vincent
6C2 **Barrow** USA
35B5 **Barrow** *R* Irish Rep
76C3 **Barrow Creek** Aust
76A3 **Barrow I** Aust
35D4 **Barrow-in-Furness** Eng
6C2 **Barrow,Pt** USA
7J2 **Barrow Str** Can
13D1 **Barry's Bay** Can
14C2 **Barryville** USA
62B1 **Barsi** India
8B3 **Barstow** USA
38C2 **Bar-sur-Aube** France
36C2 **Bar-sur-Seine** France
27G2 **Bartica** Guyana
64B1 **Bartın** Turk
76D2 **Bartle Frere,Mt** Aust
8D3 **Bartlesville** USA
11C3 **Bartlett** USA
73D6 **Bartolomeu Dias** Mozam
43E2 **Bartoszyce** Pol
26B2 **Barú** Panama
56D4 **Barung** *I* Indon
56A2 **Barus** Indon
60D4 **Barwāh** India
60C4 **Barwāni** India
75C1 **Barwon** *R* Aust
44H5 **Barysh** Russian Fed
28D1 **Basail** Arg
20C1 **Basalt** USA
72B3 **Basankusu** Zaïre
28D2 **Basavilbas** Arg
57F6 **Basco** Phil
36D3 **Basel** France
40B1 **Basel** Switz
40D2 **Basento** *R* Italy
3F3 **Bashaw** Can
57F6 **Bashi Chan** Phil
44J5 **Bashkirskaya** Respublika, Russian Fed
57B3 **Basiano** Indon
57F9 **Basilan** *I* Phil
35F6 **Basildon** Eng
28E2 **Basilio** Brazil
18E2 **Basin** USA
35E6 **Basingstoke** Eng
8B2 **Basin Region** USA
64E3 **Basra** Iraq
36D2 **Bas-Rhin** Department, France
55D3 **Bassac** *R* Camb
3F3 **Bassano** Can
40C1 **Bassano** Italy
37D2 **Bassano del Grappa** Italy
71G4 **Bassari** Togo
73D6 **Bassas da India** *I* Mozam Chan
55A2 **Bassein** Burma
23E3 **Basse Terre** Guadeloupe
11C3 **Bassett** USA
71G4 **Bassila** Benin
20C2 **Bass Lake** USA
76D5 **Bass Str** Aust
32G7 **Båstad** Sweden
63C3 **Bastak** Iran
61B2 **Basti** India
40B2 **Bastia** Corse
42B3 **Bastogne** Belg
17D3 **Bastrop** Louisiana, USA
17C3 **Bastrop** Texas, USA
72A3 **Bata** Eq Guinea
56D3 **Batakan** Indon
60D2 **Batala** India
50C3 **Batang** China
72B3 **Batangafo** CAR
57F6 **Batan Is** Phil
57D3 **Batanta** *I* Indon
29C3 **Batatais** Brazil
13D2 **Batavia** USA
75D3 **Batemans Bay** Aust
15C2 **Batesburg** USA
17D2 **Batesville** Arkansas, USA
17E3 **Batesville** Mississippi, USA
5H4 **Bath** Can
35D6 **Bath** Eng
13F2 **Bath** Maine, USA
13D2 **Bath** New York, USA
72B2 **Batha** *R* Chad
12C1 **Bathawana Mt** Can
76D4 **Bathurst** Aust
7M5 **Bathurst** Can
6F2 **Bathurst,C** Can
76C2 **Bathurst I** Aust
6H2 **Bathurst I** Can
6H3 **Bathurst Inlet** *B* Can
71F4 **Batié** Burkina
63C2 **Bātlāq-e-Gavkhūnī** *Salt Flat* Iran
75C3 **Batlow** Aust
64D2 **Batman** Turk
71D1 **Batna** Alg
9D3 **Baton Rouge** USA
65C1 **Batroun** Leb
55C3 **Battambang** Camb
62C3 **Batticaloa** Sri Lanka
62E3 **Batti Malv** *I* Indian O
3G3 **Battle** *R* Can
9E2 **Battle Creek** USA
7N4 **Battle Harbour** Can
18C2 **Battle Mountain** USA
56F6 **Batu Gajah** Malay
56E2 **Batukelau** Indon
45G7 **Batumi** Georgia
55C5 **Batu Pahat** Malay
56B3 **Baturaja** Indon
65C2 **Bat Yam** Israel
76B1 **Baubau** Indon
71H3 **Bauchi** Nig
71H3 **Bauchi** State, Nig
11D2 **Baudette** USA
37B2 **Bauges** *Mts* France
7N4 **Bauld,C** Can
37B1 **Baumes-les-Dames** France
49N4 **Baunt** Russian Fed
27J8 **Bauru** Brazil
29B2 **Baus** Brazil
42C2 **Bautzen** Germany
56D4 **Baween** *I* Indon
69B2 **Bawîti** Egypt
71F3 **Bawku** Ghana
55B2 **Bawlake** Burma
75A2 **Bawlen** Aust
15C2 **Baxley** USA
61E1 **Baxoi** China
21E2 **Bayamo** Cuba
53B2 **Bayan** China
56E4 **Bayan** Indon
50D2 **Bayandzürh** Mongolia
50C3 **Bayan Har Shan** *Mts* China
52A1 **Bayan Mod** China
52B1 **Bayan Obo** China
11B3 **Bayard** Nebraska, USA
16A3 **Bayard** New Mexico, USA
37B2 **Bayard** *P* France
10N4 **Bayard,Mt** Can
49N5 **Bayasgalant** Mongolia
57F8 **Baybay** Phil
64D1 **Bayburt** Turk
9E2 **Bay City** Michigan, USA
17C4 **Bay City** Texas, USA
64B2 **Bay Dağlari** Turk
44M2 **Baydaratskaya Guba** *B* Russian Fed
72E3 **Baydhabo** Somalia
38B2 **Bayeaux** France
37D1 **Bayerische Alpen** *Mts* Germany
42C3 **Bayern** State, Germany
12A1 **Bayfield** USA
67E4 **Bayhan al Qisāb** Yemen
64C3 **Bāyir** Jordan
49M6 **Baykal, Ozero** *L* Kazakhstan
50D1 **Baykalskiy Khrebet** *Mts* Russian Fed
49L3 **Baykit** Russian Fed
49L5 **Baylik Shan** *Mts* China/ Mongolia
44K5 **Baymak** Russian Fed
15B2 **Bay Minette** USA
57F7 **Bayombang** Phil
38B3 **Bayonne** France
63E1 **Bayram Ali** Turkmenistan
42C3 **Bayreuth** Germany
17E3 **Bay St Louis** USA
13E2 **Bay Shore** USA
13D1 **Bays,L of** Can
66D4 **Bayt al Faqih** Yemen
50B2 **Baytik Shan** *Mts* China
Bayt Lahm = Bethlehem
17D4 **Baytown** USA
39B2 **Baza** Spain
43F3 **Bazaliya** Ukraine
45H7 **Bazar-Dyuzi** *Mt* Azerbaijan
38B3 **Bazas** France
52B3 **Bazhong** China
63E3 **Bazmān** Iran
65D1 **Bcharre** Leb
11B2 **Beach** USA
14C3 **Beach Haven** USA
35F6 **Beachy Head** Eng
14D2 **Beacon** USA
73E5 **Bealanana** Madag
18D2 **Bear** *R* USA
12A2 **Beardstown** USA
Bear I = Bjørnøya
18D2 **Bear L** USA
4C3 **Bearskin Lake** Can
20B1 **Bear Valley** USA
8D2 **Beatrice** USA
34D2 **Beatrice** *Oilfield* N Sea
3D2 **Beatton** *R* Can
6F4 **Beatton River** Can
8B3 **Beatty** USA
4F4 **Beattyville** Can
36A2 **Beauce** Region, France
25E8 **Beauchene Is** Falkland Is
75D1 **Beaudesert** Aust
79B5 **Beaufort S** Can
74C3 **Beaufort West** S Africa
36A3 **Beaugeney** France
13E1 **Beauharnois** Can
34C3 **Beauly** Scot
19C4 **Beaumont** California, USA
9D3 **Beaumont** Texas, USA
36A2 **Beaumont-sur-Sarthe** France
38C2 **Beaune** France
4B3 **Beauséjour** Can
38C2 **Beauvais** France
3G2 **Beauval** Can
10J2 **Beaver** Alaska, USA
19D3 **Beaver** Utah, USA
4D2 **Beaver** *R* Can
3G3 **Beaver** *R* Saskatchewan, Can
3C1 **Beaver** *R* Yukon, Can
6D3 **Beaver Creek** Can
10J2 **Beaver Creek** USA
12B3 **Beaver Dam** Kentucky, USA
12B2 **Beaver Dam** Wisconsin, USA
18D1 **Beaverhead Mts** USA
3F3 **Beaverhill L** Can
12B1 **Beaver I** USA
17D2 **Beaver L** USA
3E2 **Beaverlodge** Can
60C3 **Beawar** India
28B2 **Beazley** Arg
29C3 **Bebedouro** Brazil
35F5 **Beccles** Eng
41E1 **Bečej** Serbia, Yugos
70B1 **Béchar** Alg
10G4 **Becharof L** USA
10F4 **Bechevin B** USA
9E3 **Beckley** USA
36E1 **Beckum** Germany
35E5 **Bedford** County, Eng
35E5 **Bedford** Eng
12B3 **Bedford** Indiana, USA
14A3 **Bedford** Pennsylvania, USA
23M2 **Bedford Pt** Grenada
14B2 **Beech Creek** USA
6D2 **Beechey Pt** USA
75C3 **Beechworth** Aust
75D1 **Beenleigh** Aust
65C3 **Beer Menuha** Israel
65C4 **Beer Ora** Israel
64B3 **Beersheba** Israel
Beèr Sheva = Beersheba
65C3 **Beér Sheva,** *R* Israel
8D4 **Beeville** USA
72C3 **Befale** Zaïre
73E5 **Befandriana** Madag
75C3 **Bega** Aust
49N2 **Begicheva, Ostrov** *I* Russian Fed
63C2 **Behbehān** Iran
10M4 **Behm Canal** *Sd* USA
63C1 **Behshahr** Iran
60B2 **Behsud** Afghan
53B2 **Bei'an** China
52B5 **Beihai** China
55D1 **Beihai** China
52D2 **Beijing** China
55E1 **Beiliu** China
52B4 **Beipan Jiang** *R* China
52E1 **Beipiao** China
73D5 **Beira** Mozam
64C3 **Beirut** Leb
50C2 **Bei Shan** *Mts* China

74E1 **Beitbridge** Zim
65C2 **Beit ed Dīne** Leb
65C3 **Beit Jala** Israel
39A2 **Beja** Port
71D1 **Beja** Tunisia
71D1 **Bejaïa** Alg
39A1 **Béjar** Spain
63D2 **Bejestān** Iran
43E3 **Békéscsaba** Hung
73E6 **Bekily** Madag
61B2 **Bela** India
60B3 **Bela** Pak
56D2 **Belaga** Malay
14B3 **Bel Air** USA
62B1 **Belamoalli** India
57B2 **Belang** Indon
56A2 **Belangpidie** Indon
xxviiiH4 **Belau** *I* Pacific O
Belau = Palau
74E2 **Bela Vista** Mozam
29A3 **Béla Vista** Par/Brazil
56A2 **Belawan** Indon
44K4 **Belaya** *R* Ukraine
43G3 **Belaya Tserkov'** Russian Fed
7J2 **Belcher Chan** Can
7L4 **Belcher Is** Can
60B1 **Belchiragh** Afghan
44J5 **Belebey** Russian Fed
72E3 **Beled Weyne** Somalia
27J4 **Belém** Brazil
28B1 **Belén** Arg
26C3 **Belén** Colombia
29A3 **Belén** Par
28D2 **Belén** Urug
8C3 **Belen** USA
28B1 **Belén** *R* Arg
34B4 **Belfast** N Ire
74E2 **Belfast** S Africa
5H5 **Belfast** USA
34B4 **Belfast Lough** *Estuary* N Ire
11B2 **Belfield** USA
72D2 **Bēlfodiyo** Eth
34E4 **Belford** Eng
38D2 **Belfort** France
62A1 **Belgaum** India
42A2 **Belgium** Kingdom, N W Europe
45F5 **Belgorod** Russian Fed
45E6 **Belgorod Dnestrovskiy** Ukraine
Belgrade = Beograd
18D1 **Belgrade** USA
69A2 **Bel Hedan** Libya
56C3 **Belinyu** Indon
56C3 **Belitung** *I* Indon
21D3 **Belize** Belize
21D3 **Belize** Republic, C America
49P2 **Bel'kovskiv, Ostrov** *I* Russian Fed
38C2 **Bellac** France
6F4 **Bella Coola** Can
37C2 **Bellagio** Italy
17C4 **Bellaire** USA
37C1 **Bellano** Italy
62B1 **Bellary** India
75C1 **Bellata** Aust
28D2 **Bella Union** Urug
28D1 **Bella Vista** Arg
37B2 **Belledonne** *Mts* France
14B2 **Bellefonte** USA
8C2 **Belle Fourche** USA
11B3 **Belle Fourche** *R* USA
38D2 **Bellegarde** France
15E4 **Belle Glade** USA
7N4 **Belle I** Can
38B2 **Belle-Ile** *I* France
7N4 **Belle Isle,Str of** Can
36A2 **Bellême** France
5K4 **Belleoram** Can
7L5 **Belleville** Can
12B3 **Belleville** Illinois, USA
17C2 **Belleville** Kansas, USA
18D2 **Bellevue** Idaho, USA
12A2 **Bellevue** Iowa, USA
18B1 **Bellevue** Washington, USA
37A2 **Belley** France
75D2 **Bellingen** Aust
8A2 **Bellingham** USA
79G2 **Bellingshausen** *Base* Ant
79G3 **Bellingshausen S** Ant
40B1 **Bellinzona** Switz
26C2 **Bello** Colombia
77E3 **Bellona Reefs** Nouvelle Calédonie
20B1 **Bellota** USA
13E2 **Bellows Falls** USA
7K3 **Bell Pen** Can
40C1 **Belluno** Italy
25D4 **Bell Ville** Arg
4C5 **Belmond** USA
14B1 **Belmont** USA
27L7 **Belmonte** Brazil
21D3 **Belmopan** Belize
53B1 **Belogorsk** Russian Fed
73E6 **Beloha** Madag
27K7 **Belo Horizonte** Brazil
16C2 **Beloit** Kansas, USA
9E2 **Beloit** Wisconsin, USA
44E3 **Belomorsk** Russian Fed
44K5 **Beloretsk** Russian Fed
44D5 **Belorussia** *Republic* Europe
73E5 **Belo-Tsiribihina** Madag
44F2 **Beloye More** *S*
44F3 **Beloye Ozero** *L* Russian Fed
44F3 **Belozersk** Russian Fed
12C3 **Belpre** USA
75A2 **Beltana** Aust
17C3 **Belton** USA
43F3 **Bel'tsy** Moldavia
48K5 **Belukha** *Mt* Russian Fed
44H2 **Belush'ye** Russian Fed
12B2 **Belvidere** Illinois, USA
14C2 **Belvidere** New Jersey, USA
48J2 **Belyy, Ostrov** *I* Russian Fed
73B4 **Bembe** Angola
71G3 **Bembéréke** Benin
9D2 **Bemidji** USA
15B1 **Bemis** USA
32G6 **Bena** Nor
72C4 **Bena Dibele** Zaïre
75C3 **Benalla** Aust
34C2 **Ben Attow** *Mt* Scot
39A1 **Benavente** Spain
34B3 **Benbecula** *I* Scot
76A4 **Bencubbin** Aust
8A2 **Bend** USA
69E3 **Bendarbeyla** Somalia
34C3 **Ben Dearg** *Mt* Scot
43F3 **Bendery** Moldavia
76D4 **Bendigo** Aust
71F3 **Bénéna** Mali
42C3 **Benešov** Czech
40C2 **Benevento** Italy
59G4 **Bengal,B of** Asia
69A1 **Ben Gardane** Libya
71E2 **Ben Gardane** Tunisia
52D3 **Bengbu** China
57B3 **Benggai** *I* Indon
69B1 **Benghāzī** Libya
56B2 **Bengkalis** Indon
56B3 **Bengkulu** Indon
73B5 **Benguela** Angola
71A2 **Benguerir** Mor
64B3 **Benha** Egypt
34C2 **Ben Hope** *Mt* Scot
72C3 **Beni** Zaïre
26E6 **Béni** *R* Bol
70B1 **Beni Abbes** Alg
39C1 **Benicarló** Spain
39B2 **Benidorm** Spain
39C2 **Beni Mansour** Alg
69C2 **Beni Mazar** Egypt
71A2 **Beni Mellal** Mor
70C4 **Benin** Republic, Africa
71H4 **Benin City** Nig
71B1 **Beni-Saf** Alg
69C2 **Beni Suef** Egypt
16B2 **Benkelman** USA
34C2 **Ben Kilbreck** *Mt* Scot
33C2 **Ben Lawers** *Mt* Scot
34D3 **Ben Macdui** *Mt* Scot
34C2 **Ben More Assynt** *Mt* Scot
78B2 **Benmore,L** NZ
49R2 **Bennetta, Ostrov** *I* Russian Fed
34C3 **Ben Nevis** *Mt* Scot
13E2 **Bennington** USA
65C2 **Bennt Jbail** Leb
72B3 **Bénoué** *R* Cam
71J4 **Bénoué Nat Pk** Cam
36E2 **Bensheim** Germany
8B3 **Benson** Arizona, USA
11C2 **Benson** Minnesota, USA
72C3 **Bentiu** Sudan
29A2 **Bento Gomes** *R* Brazil
17D3 **Benton** Arkansas, USA
20C2 **Benton** California, USA
12B3 **Benton** Kentucky, USA
12B2 **Benton Harbor** USA
71H4 **Benue** State, Nig
71H4 **Benue** *R* Nig
34C3 **Ben Wyvis** *Mt* Scot
52E1 **Benxi** China
57C2 **Beo** Indon
41E2 **Beograd** Serbia, Yugos
61B3 **Beohāri** India
53C5 **Beppu** Japan
41D2 **Berat** Alb
72D2 **Berber** Sudan
72E2 **Berbera** Somalia
72B3 **Berbérati** CAR
36A1 **Berck** France
43F3 **Berdichev** Ukraine
45F6 **Berdyansk** Ukraine
12C3 **Berea** USA
57C2 **Berebere** Indon
71F4 **Berekum** Ghana
20B2 **Berenda** USA
66C2 **Berenice** Egypt
4C3 **Berens** *R* Can
6J4 **Berens River** Can
75A1 **Beresford** Aust
11C3 **Beresford** USA
43E3 **Berettyoújfalu** Hung
43E2 **Bereza** Belorussia
43E3 **Berezhany** Ukraine
43F2 **Berezina** *R* Belorussia
44G3 **Bereznik** Russian Fed
44K4 **Berezniki** Russian Fed
45E6 **Berezovka** Ukraine
44L3 **Berezovo** Russian Fed
53D1 **Berezovyy** Russian Fed
64A2 **Bergama** Turk
40B1 **Bergamo** Italy
32F6 **Bergen** Nor
14B1 **Bergen** USA
36C1 **Bergen op Zoom** Neth
38C3 **Bergerac** France
36D1 **Bergisch-Gladbach** Germany
4D4 **Bergland** USA
62C1 **Berhampur** India
49S4 **Beringa, Ostrov** *I* Russian Fed
10K3 **Bering Gl** USA
49T3 **Beringovskiy** Russian Fed
xxixK2 **Bering S** Russian Fed/USA
79C6 **Bering Str** Russian Fed/ USA
63D3 **Berīzak** Iran
39B2 **Berja** Spain
71B2 **Berkane** Mor
8A3 **Berkeley** USA
14A3 **Berkeley Spring** USA
79F2 **Berkner I** Ant
41E2 **Berkovitsa** Bulg
35E6 **Berkshire** County, Eng
14D1 **Berkshire Hills** USA
3E3 **Berland** *R* Can
42C2 **Berlin** Germany
13E2 **Berlin** New Hampshire, USA
14A3 **Berlin** Pennsylvania, USA
42C2 **Berlin** State, Germany
26F8 **Bermejo** Bol
25E3 **Bermejo** *R* Arg
2M5 **Bermuda** *I* Atlantic O
40B1 **Bern** Switz
16A2 **Bernalillo** USA
29B4 **Bernardo de Irigoyen** Arg
14C2 **Bernardsville** USA
28C3 **Bernasconi** Arg
36A2 **Bernay** France
42C2 **Bernburg** Germany
37B1 **Berner Orberland** *Mts* Switz
7K2 **Bernier B** Can
42C3 **Berounka** *R* Czech
71A2 **Berrechid** Mor
75B2 **Berri** Aust
71C2 **Berriane** Alg
38C2 **Berry** Region, France
20A1 **Berryessa,L** USA
9F4 **Berry Is** Bahamas
14B3 **Berryville** USA
74B2 **Berseba** Namibia
56F6 **Bertam** Malay
16A2 **Berthoud P** USA
72B3 **Bertoua** Cam
77G1 **Beru** *I* Kiribati
13D2 **Berwick** USA
34D4 **Berwick-upon-Tweed** Eng
35D5 **Berwyn** *Mts* Wales
73E5 **Besalampy** Madag
38D2 **Besançon** France
43E3 **Beskidy Zachodnie** *Mts* Pol
3G2 **Besnard L** Can
64C2 **Besni** Turk
65C3 **Besor** *R* Israel
15B2 **Bessemer** Alabama, USA
12B1 **Bessemer** Michigan, USA
73E5 **Betafo** Madag
39A1 **Betanzos** Spain
71J4 **Betaré Oya** Cam
65C3 **Bet Guvrin** Israel
74D2 **Bethal** S Africa
74B2 **Bethanie** Namibia
17D1 **Bethany** Missouri, USA
17C2 **Bethany** Oklahoma, USA
6B3 **Bethel** Alaska, USA
14D2 **Bethel** Connecticut, USA
12C2 **Bethel Park** USA
13D3 **Bethesda** USA
65C3 **Bethlehem** Israel
74D2 **Bethlehem** S Africa
13D2 **Bethlehem** USA
74D3 **Bethulie** S Africa
38C1 **Bethune** France
36A2 **Béthune** *R* France
73E6 **Betioky** Madag
75B1 **Betoota** Aust
72B3 **Betou** Congo
59E1 **Betpak Dala** *Steppe* Kazakhstan
73E6 **Betroka** Madag
7M5 **Betsiamites** Can
12A2 **Bettendorf** USA
61B2 **Bettiah** India
10H2 **Bettles** USA
37C2 **Béttola** Italy
60D4 **Bētul** India
36C1 **Betuwe** Region, Neth
60D3 **Betwa** *R* India
36D1 **Betzdorf** Germany
10G4 **Beverley,L** USA
14E1 **Beverly** USA
20C3 **Beverly Hills** USA
70B4 **Beyla** Guinea
62B2 **Beypore** India
Beyrouth = Beirut
64B2 **Beyşehir** Turk
45E8 **Beysehir Gölü** *L* Turk
65C2 **Beyt Shean** Israel
37C1 **Bezan** Austria
44F4 **Bezhetsk** Russian Fed
38C3 **Béziers** France
63D1 **Bezmein** Turkmenistan
50D1 **Beznosova** Russian Fed
61C2 **Bhadgaon** Nepal
62C1 **Bhadrāchalam** India
61C3 **Bhadrakh** India
62B2 **Bhadra Res** India
62B2 **Bhadrāvati** India
60B3 **Bhag** Pak
61C2 **Bhāgalpur** India
60C2 **Bhakkar** Pak
61E3 **Bhamo** Burma
60D4 **Bhandāra** India
60D3 **Bharatpur** India
60C4 **Bharūch** India
61C3 **Bhātiāpāra Ghat** Bang
60C2 **Bhatinda** India
62A2 **Bhatkal** India
61C3 **Bhātpāra** India
60C4 **Bhāvnagar** India
61B4 **Bhawānipatna** India
60C2 **Bhera** Pak
61B2 **Bheri** *R* Nepal
61B3 **Bhilai** India
60C3 **Bhīlwāra** India
62C1 **Bhīmavaram** India
60D3 **Bhind** India
60D3 **Bhiwāni** India
62B1 **Bhongir** India
60D4 **Bhopāl** India
61C3 **Bhubaneshwar** India
60B4 **Bhuj** India
60D4 **Bhusāwal** India
59H3 **Bhutan** Kingdom, Asia
71F4 **Bia** *R* Ghana
51G7 **Biak** *I* Indon
43E2 **Biala Podlaska** Pol
42D2 **Bialograd** Pol
43E2 **Bialystok** Pol
32A1 **Biargtangar** *C* Iceland
63D1 **Bīarjmand** Iran
57C2 **Biaro** *I* Indon
38B3 **Biarritz** France
37C1 **Biasca** Switz
64B4 **Biba** Egypt
53E3 **Bibai** Japan
73B5 **Bibala** Angola
37D3 **Bibbiena** Italy
42B3 **Biberach** Germany
71F4 **Bibiani** Ghana
5H4 **Bic** Can
41F1 **Bicaz** Rom
53D1 **Bichi** *R* Russian Fed
19D3 **Bicknell** USA
71H4 **Bida** Nig
62B1 **Bīdar** India
67G2 **Bidbid** Oman
13E2 **Biddeford** USA
35C6 **Bideford** Eng
35C6 **Bideford B** Eng
70C2 **Bidon 5** Alg
43E2 **Biebrza** Pol
40B1 **Biel** Switz
42D2 **Bielawa** Pol
42B2 **Bielefeld** Germany
37B1 **Bieler See** *L* Switz
40B1 **Biella** Italy
43E2 **Bielsk Podlaski** Pol
55D3 **Bien Hoa** Viet
40C2 **Biferno** *R* Italy
64A1 **Biga** Turk
41F3 **Bigadiç** Turk
5H4 **Big Bald Mt** Can
4D3 **Big Beaver House** Can
16B4 **Big Bend Nat Pk** USA
18D1 **Big Belt Mts** USA
17E3 **Big Black** *R* USA
17C1 **Big Blue** *R* USA
15E4 **Big Cypress Swamp** USA
6D3 **Big Delta** USA
38D2 **Bigent** Germany
3G3 **Biggar** Can
75D1 **Biggenden** Aust
10L4 **Bigger,Mt** Can
18D1 **Big Hole** *R* USA
11A2 **Bighorn** *R* USA
11A2 **Bighorn L** USA
11A3 **Bighorn Mts** USA
55C3 **Bight of Bangkok** *B* Thai
70C4 **Bight of Benin** *B* W Africa
70C4 **Bight of Biafra** *B* Cam
7L3 **Big I** Can
10G4 **Big Koniuji** *I* USA
16B3 **Big Lake** USA
37C1 **Bignasco** Switz
70A3 **Bignona** Sen
19C3 **Big Pine** USA
15E4 **Big Pine Key** USA
20C3 **Big Pine Mt** USA
12B2 **Big Rapids** USA
6H4 **Big River** Can
4B2 **Big Sand L** Can
18D1 **Big Sandy** USA
3H3 **Big Sandy L** Can
11C3 **Big Sioux** *R* USA
20D1 **Big Smokey V** USA
8C3 **Big Spring** USA
16B1 **Big Springs** USA
11C2 **Big Stone City** USA
12C3 **Big Stone Gap** USA
4B3 **Bigstone L** Can
20B2 **Big Sur** USA
18E1 **Big Timber** USA
7J4 **Big Trout L** Can
4D3 **Big Trout Lake** Can
40D2 **Bihać** Bosnia & Herzegovina, Yugos
61C2 **Bihār** India
61C3 **Bihar** State, India
72D4 **Biharamulo** Tanz
45C6 **Bihor** *Mt* Rom
62B1 **Bijāpur** India
62C1 **Bijāpur** India
63B1 **Bījār** Iran
61B2 **Bijauri** Nepal
41D2 **Bijeljina** Bosnia & Herzegovina, Yugos
52B4 **Bijie** China
60D3 **Bijnor** India
60C3 **Bijnot** Pak
60C3 **Bikāner** India
65C2 **Bikfaya** Leb
53C2 **Bikin** Russian Fed
53D2 **Bikin** *R* Russian Fed
72B4 **Bikoro** Zaïre
53A2 **Bila He** *R* China
60C3 **Bilara** India
60D2 **Bilaspur** India
61B3 **Bilāspur** India
55B3 **Bilauktaung Range** *Mts* Thai
39B1 **Bilbao** Spain
65A3 **Bilbeis** Egypt
Bilbo = Bilbao
42D3 **Bílé** *R* Czech
41D2 **Bileća** Bosnia & Herzegovina, Yugos
64B1 **Bilecik** Turk
72C3 **Bili** *R* Zaïre
49S3 **Bilibino** Russian Fed
57F8 **Biliran** *I* Phil
8C2 **Billings** USA
72B2 **Bilma** Niger
9E3 **Biloxi** USA
72C2 **Biltine** Chad
71F4 **Bimbita** Ghana
60D4 **Bina-Etawa** India
57F8 **Binalbagan** Phil
73D5 **Bindura** Zim
73C5 **Binga** Zim
73D5 **Binga** *Mt* Zim
75D1 **Bingara** Aust
42B3 **Bingen** Germany
13F1 **Bingham** USA
9F2 **Binghamton** USA
56E1 **Bingkor** Malay
64D2 **Bingöl** Turk
52D3 **Binhai** China
56A2 **Binjai** Indon
56C2 **Binjai** Indon
57B4 **Binongko** *I* Indon
56B2 **Bintan** *I* Indon
56B3 **Bintuhan** Indon
56D2 **Bintulu** Malay
25B5 **Bió Bió** *R* Chile
xxxJ4 **Bioko** *I* Atlantic O
62B1 **Bīr** India
53C2 **Bira** Russian Fed
69B2 **Bîr Abu Husein** *Well* Egypt
69B2 **Bi'r al Harash** *Well* Libya
72C2 **Birao** CAR
61C2 **Biratnagar** Nepal

3F2 **Birch** *R* Can
10J2 **Birch Creek** USA
75B3 **Birchip** Aust
11D2 **Birch L** USA
4C3 **Birch L** Can
6G4 **Birch Mts** Can
7J4 **Bird** Can
76C3 **Birdsville** Aust
76C2 **Birdum** Aust
65A4 **Bîr el 'Agramîya** *Well* Egypt
65B3 **Bir el Duweidâr** *Well* Egypt
61B2 **Birganj** Nepal
65B3 **Bîr Gifgâfa** *Well* Egypt
65A4 **Bîr Gindali** *Well* Egypt
65B3 **Bîr Hasana** *Well* Egypt
29B3 **Birigui** Brazil
65D1 **Bīrīn** Syria
63D2 **Birjand** Iran
64B4 **Birkat Qarun** *L* Egypt
36D2 **Birkenfeld** Germany
35D5 **Birkenhead** Eng
45D6 **Bîrlad** Rom
65B3 **Bir Lahfân** *Well* Egypt
35D5 **Birmingham** Eng
9E3 **Birmingham** USA
69B2 **Bir Misâha** *Well* Egypt
70A2 **Bir Moghrein** Maur
71H3 **Birnin Gwari** Nig
71G3 **Birnin Kebbi** Nig
71H3 **Birni N'Konni** Nig
53C2 **Birobidzhan** Russian Fed
35B5 **Birr** Irish Rep
39C2 **Bir Rabalou** Alg
75C1 **Birrie** *R* Aust
34D2 **Birsay** Scot
44K4 **Birsk** Russian Fed
69B2 **Bîr Tarfâwi** *Well* Egypt
11B1 **Birtle** Can
65B4 **Bîr Udelb** *Well* Egypt
49L4 **Biryusa** *R* Russian Fed
32J7 **Biržai** Lithuania
70B2 **Bir Zreigat** *Well* Maur
57C3 **Bisa** *I* Indon
19E4 **Bisbee** USA
38A2 **Biscay,B of** Spain/France
15E4 **Biscayne B** USA
37E1 **Bischofshofen** Austria
36D2 **Bischwiller** France
12C1 **Biscotasi L** Can
52B4 **Bishan** China
59F1 **Bishkek** Kirgizia
8B3 **Bishop** USA
35E4 **Bishop Auckland** Eng
35F6 **Bishop's Stortford** Eng
61B3 **Bishrāmpur** India
53A1 **Bishui** China
66C3 **Biskia** Eth
71D2 **Biskra** Alg
57G9 **Bislig** Phil
8C2 **Bismarck** USA
76D1 **Bismarck Arch** PNG
76D1 **Bismarck Range** *Mts* PNG
76D1 **Bismarck S** PNG
63B2 **Bīsotūn** Iran
70A3 **Bissau** Guinea-Bissau
4B3 **Bissett** Can
6G4 **Bistcho L** Can
41F1 **Bistrita** *R* Rom
72B3 **Bitam** Gabon
3G1 **Bitau L** Can
42B3 **Bitburg** Germany
36D2 **Bitche** France
64D2 **Bitlis** Turk
41E2 **Bitola** Macedonia, Yugos
42C2 **Bitterfeld** Germany
74B3 **Bitterfontein** S Africa
64B3 **Bitter Lakes** Egypt
8B2 **Bitteroot Range** *Mts* USA
57C2 **Bitung** Indon
71J3 **Biu** Nig
53D4 **Biwa-ko** *L* Japan
72E2 **Biyo Kaboba** Eth
48K4 **Biysk** Russian Fed
71D1 **Bizerte** Tunisia
39C2 **Bj bou Arréridj** Alg
40D1 **Bjelovar** Croatia, Yugos
70B2 **Bj Flye Ste Marie** Alg
48C2 **Bjørnøya** *I* Barents S
10K2 **Black** *R* USA
17D2 **Black** *R* USA
76D3 **Blackall** Aust
12B1 **Black B** Can
3G2 **Black Birch L** Can
35D5 **Blackburn** Eng
6D3 **Blackburn,Mt** USA
19D4 **Black Canyon City** USA
3F3 **Black Diamond** Can
11D2 **Blackduck** USA
4D2 **Black Duck** *R* Can
18D1 **Black Eagle** USA
18D2 **Blackfoot** USA
18D1 **Blackfoot** *R* USA
6H5 **Black Hills** USA
34C3 **Black Isle** *Pen* Scot
3G2 **Black L** Can
3G2 **Black Lake** Can
23Q2 **Blackman's** Barbados
19D3 **Black Mts** USA
35D6 **Black Mts** Wales
74B1 **Black Nossob** *R* Namibia
35D5 **Blackpool** Eng
23H1 **Black River** Jamaica
4E5 **Black River** USA
12A2 **Black River Falls** USA
8B2 **Black Rock Desert** USA
45D7 **Black S** Europe/Asia
12C3 **Blacksburg** USA
75D2 **Black Sugarloaf** *Mt* Aust
71F4 **Black Volta** *R* Ghana
15B2 **Black Warrior** *R* USA
33B3 **Blackwater** *R* Irish Rep
10O3 **Blackwater L** Can
17C2 **Blackwell** USA
41E2 **Blagoevgrad** Bulg
49O4 **Blagoveshchensk** Russian Fed
18D1 **Blaikiston,Mt** Can
18B1 **Blaine** USA
11C3 **Blair** USA
34D3 **Blair Atholl** Scot
34D3 **Blairgowrie** Scot
15C2 **Blakely** USA
16A2 **Blanca Peak** *Mt* USA
75A1 **Blanche,L** Aust
28A2 **Blanco** *R* Arg
28B1 **Blanco** *R* Arg
22C1 **Blanco** *R* Mexico
8A2 **Blanco,C** USA
7N4 **Blanc Sablon** Can
35D6 **Blandford Forum** Eng
19E3 **Blanding** USA
36A2 **Blangy-sur-Bresle** France
36B1 **Blankenberge** Belg
28D2 **Blanquillo** Urug
73D5 **Blantyre** Malawi
38B2 **Blaye** France
75C2 **Blayney** Aust
77G5 **Blenheim** NZ
37B2 **Bléone** *R* France
71C1 **Blida** Alg
4E4 **Blind River** Can
75A2 **Blinman** Aust
56D4 **Blitar** Indon
71G4 **Blitta** Togo
13E2 **Block I** USA
14E2 **Block Island Sd** USA
74D2 **Bloemfontin** S Africa
74D2 **Bloemhof** S Africa
74D2 **Bloemhof Dam** *Res* S Africa
36A3 **Blois** France
27G3 **Blommesteinmeer** *L* Surinam
32A1 **Blönduós** Iceland
12B3 **Bloomfield** Indiana, USA
17D1 **Bloomfield** Iowa, USA
11C3 **Bloomfield** Nebraska, USA
16A2 **Bloomfield** New Mexico, USA
12B2 **Bloomington** Illinois, USA
12B3 **Bloomington** Indiana, USA
11D3 **Bloomington** Minnesota, USA
14B2 **Bloomsburg** USA
56D4 **Blora** Indon
14B2 **Blossburg** USA
7Q3 **Blosseville Kyst** *Mts* Greenland
74D1 **Blouberg** *Mt* S Africa
42B3 **Bludenz** Austria
9E3 **Bluefield** USA
26B1 **Bluefields** Nic
16C1 **Blue Hill** USA
14A2 **Blue Knob** *Mt* USA
23B3 **Blue Mountain Peak** *Mt* Jamaica
14B2 **Blue Mt** USA
75D2 **Blue Mts** Aust
23J1 **Blue Mts** Jamaica
8A2 **Blue Mts** USA
72D2 **Blue Nile, R** Sudan
6G3 **Bluenose L** Can
15C2 **Blue Ridge** USA
9E3 **Blue Ridge Mts** USA
3E3 **Blue River** Can
34A4 **Blue Stack** *Mt* Irish Rep
78A3 **Bluff** NZ
19E3 **Bluff** USA
5K3 **Bluff,C** Can
76A4 **Bluff Knoll** *Mt* Aust
25G3 **Blumenau** Brazil
38D2 **Blundez** Austria
11C3 **Blunt** USA
18B2 **Bly** USA
10J4 **Blying Sd** USA
34E4 **Blyth** Eng
8B3 **Blythe** USA
9E3 **Blytheville** USA
70A4 **Bo** Sierra Leone
57F8 **Boac** Phil
52D2 **Boading** China
57C3 **Boano** *I* Indon
29D1 **Boa Nova** Brazil
12C2 **Boardman** USA
49M5 **Boatou** China
26F3 **Boa Vista** Brazil
70A4 **Boa Vista** *I* Cape Verde
55E1 **Bobai** China
62C1 **Bobbili** India
37C2 **Bóbbio** Italy
71F3 **Bobo Dioulasso** Burkina
43G2 **Bobrovica** Ukraine
44D5 **Bobruysk** Belorussia
15E4 **Boca Chica Key** *I* USA
26E4 **Bõca do Acre** Brazil
29D2 **Bocaiúva** Brazil
22C1 **Boca Jesús Maria** Mexico
72B3 **Bocaranga** CAR
15E4 **Boca Raton** USA
43E3 **Bochnia** Pol
42B2 **Bocholt** Germany
36D1 **Bochum** Germany
73B5 **Bocoio** Angola
72B3 **Boda** CAR
49N4 **Bodaybo** Russian Fed
19B3 **Bodega Head** *Pt* USA
72B2 **Bodélé** *Desert Region* Chad
32J5 **Boden** Sweden
37C1 **Bodensee** *L* Switz/ Germany
62B1 **Bodhan** India
62B2 **Bodināyakkanūr** India
35C6 **Bodmin** Eng
35C6 **Bodmin Moor** *Upland* Eng
32G5 **Bodø** Nor
41F3 **Bodrum** Turk
72C4 **Boende** Zaïre
70A3 **Boffa** Guinea
55B2 **Bogale** Burma
17E3 **Bogalusa** USA
75C2 **Bogan** *R* Aust
71F3 **Bogandé** Burkina
64C2 **Boğazlıyan** Turk
44L4 **Bogdanovich** Russian Fed
50B2 **Bogda Shan** *Mt* China
74B2 **Bogenfels** Namibia
75D1 **Boggabilla** Aust
75C2 **Boggabri** Aust
57F8 **Bogo** Phil
75C3 **Bogong,Mt** Aust
56C4 **Bogor** Indon
44J4 **Bogorodskoye** Russian Fed
26D3 **Bogotá** Colombia
49K4 **Bogotol** Russian Fed
61C3 **Bogra** Bang
52D2 **Bo Hai** *B* China
36B2 **Bohain-en-Vermandois** France
52D2 **Bohai Wan** *B* China
37E1 **Boh Bistrica** Slovenia, Yugos
71G4 **Bohicon** Benin
42C3 **Bohmer-wald** *Upland* Germany
57F9 **Bohol** *I* Phil
57F9 **Bohol S** Phil
29B2 **Bois** *R* Brazil
12C1 **Bois Blanc I** USA
8B2 **Boise** USA
16B2 **Boise City** USA
11B2 **Boissevain** Can
70A2 **Bojador,C** Mor
57F7 **Bojeador,C** Phil
63D1 **Bojnūrd** Iran
70A3 **Boké** Guinea
75C1 **Bokhara** *R* Aust
32F7 **Boknafjord** *Inlet* Nor
72B4 **Boko** Congo
55C3 **Bokor** Camb
72B2 **Bokoro** Chad
72C4 **Bokungu** Zaïre
72B2 **Bol** Chad
22B1 **Bolaãnos** Mexico
70A3 **Bolama** Guinea-Bissau
22B1 **Bolanos** *R* Mexico
38C2 **Bolbec** France
71F4 **Bole** Ghana
53D1 **Bolen** Russian Fed
42D2 **Boleslawiec** Pol
71F3 **Bolgatanga** Ghana
45D6 **Bolgrad** Ukraine
53C2 **Boli** China
28C3 **Bolívar** Arg
17D2 **Bolivar** Missouri, USA
17E2 **Bolivar** Tennessee, USA
26E7 **Bolivia** Republic, S America
32H6 **Bollnas** Sweden
75C1 **Bollon** Aust
26D2 **Bollvar** *Mt* Ven
72B4 **Bolobo** Zaire
40C2 **Bologna** Italy
44E4 **Bologoye** Russian Fed
53D2 **Bolon'** Russian Fed
53D2 **Bolon', Ozero** *L* Russian Fed
49M2 **Bol'shevik, Ostrov** *I* Russian Fed
44J2 **Bol'shezemel'skaya Tundra** *Plain* Russian Fed
49S3 **Bol'shoy Anyuy** *R* Russian Fed
53E1 **Bol'shoye Kizi, Ozero** *L* Russian Fed
45H5 **Bol'shoy Irgiz** *R* Russian Fed
53C3 **Bol'shoy Kamen** Russian Fed
45F5 **Bol'shoy Kavkaz** *Mts* Georgia
49Q2 **Bol'shoy Lyakhovskiy, Ostrov** *I* Russian Fed
45H6 **Bol'shoy Uzen** *R* Kazakhstan
8C4 **Bolson de Mapimi** *Desert* Mexico
35D5 **Bolton** Eng
4B3 **Bolton L** Can
64B1 **Bolu** Turk
32A1 **Bolugarvik** Iceland
64B2 **Bolvadin** Turk
40C1 **Bolzano** Italy
72B4 **Boma** Zaïre
76D4 **Bombala** Aust
62A1 **Bombay** India
72D3 **Bombo** Uganda
61D2 **Bomdila** India
61E2 **Bomi** China
70A4 **Bomi Hills** Lib
27K6 **Bom Jesus da Lapa** Brazil
49O4 **Bomnak** Russian Fed
72C3 **Bomokandi** *R* Zaïre
72C3 **Bomu** *R* CAR/Zaïre
13D3 **Bon Air** USA
23D4 **Bonaire** *I* Caribbean
10K3 **Bona,Mt** USA
21D3 **Bonanza** Nic
7N5 **Bonavista** Can
5L4 **Bonavista B** Can
5L4 **Bonavista,C** Can
75A2 **Bon Bon** Aust
29C2 **Bon Despacho** Brazil
72C3 **Bondo** Zaïre
71F4 **Bondoukou** Ivory Coast
Bône = 'Annaba
57B4 **Bone** Indon
57B3 **Bonelipu** Indon
11C3 **Bonesteel** USA
27G3 **Bonfim** Guyana
72C3 **Bongandanga** Zaïre
57B3 **Bongka** *R* Indon
72B2 **Bongor** Chad
71F4 **Bongouanou** Ivory Coast
17C3 **Bonham** USA
40B2 **Bonifacio** Corse
40B2 **Bonifacio,Str of** *Chan* Medit S
Bonin Is = Ogasawara Gunto
15E4 **Bonita Springs** USA
29A3 **Bonito** Brazil
42B2 **Bonn** Germany
18C1 **Bonners Ferry** USA
36A2 **Bonnétable** France
10M2 **Bonnet Plume** *R* Can
36A2 **Bonneval** France
3F3 **Bonnyville** Can
76A1 **Bonthain** Indon
70A4 **Bonthe** Sierra Leone
57A4 **Bontosunggu** Indon
69D3 **Booaaso** Somalia
75B2 **Booligal** Aust
75D1 **Boonah** Aust
16B2 **Boone** Colorado, USA
11D3 **Boone** Iowa, USA
15C1 **Boone** North Carolina, USA
13D2 **Boonville** USA
75C2 **Boorowa** Aust
7J2 **Boothia,G of** Can
7J2 **Boothia Pen** Can
72B4 **Booué** Gabon
75A1 **Bopeechee** Aust
74C2 **Bophuthatswana** Self governing homeland, S Africa
16B4 **Boquillas** Mexico
72D3 **Bor** Sudan
64B2 **Bor** Turk
41E2 **Bor** Serbia, Yugos
8B2 **Borah Peak** *Mt* USA
32G7 **Borås** Sweden
63C3 **Borāzjān** Iran
75A3 **Borda,C** Aust
38B3 **Bordeaux** France
6G2 **Borden I** Can
7K2 **Borden Pen** Can
14C2 **Bordentown** USA
34D4 **Borders** Region, Scot
75B3 **Bordertown** Aust
37B3 **Bordighera** Italy
70C2 **Bordi Omar Dris** Alg
71C1 **Bordj bou Arreridj** Alg
32K6 **Borgå** Fin
32A2 **Borgarnes** Iceland
8C3 **Borger** USA
32H7 **Borgholm** Sweden
37D3 **Borgo San Lorenzo** Italy
37C2 **Borgosia** Italy
37C2 **Borgo Val di Taro** Italy
37D1 **Borgo Valsugana** Italy
43E3 **Borislav** Ukraine
45G5 **Borisoglebsk** Russian Fed
44D5 **Borisov** Belorussia
45F5 **Borisovka** Russian Fed
29A4 **Borja** Par
72B2 **Borkou** *Desert Region* Chad
32H6 **Borlänge** Sweden
37C2 **Bormida** Italy
37D1 **Bormio** Italy
32H7 **Bornholm** *I* Den
71J3 **Borno** State, Nig
41F3 **Bornova** Turk
72C3 **Boro** *R* Sudan
49P3 **Borogontsy** Russian Fed
71F3 **Boromo** Burkina
20D3 **Boron** USA
44E4 **Borovichi** Russian Fed
76C2 **Borroloola** Aust
41E1 **Borsa** Rom
63B2 **Borūjed** Iran
63C2 **Borūjen** Iran
42D2 **Bory Tucholskie** Region, Pol
43G2 **Borzna** Ukraine
49N4 **Borzya** Russian Fed
52B5 **Bose** China
53E2 **Boshnyakovo** Russian Fed
74D2 **Boshof** S Africa
41D2 **Bosna** *R* Bosnia & Herzegovina, Yugos
40D2 **Bosnia and Herzegovina** *Republic* Yugos
54D3 **Bōsō-hantō** *B* Japan
Bosporus = Karadeniz Boğazi
39C2 **Bosquet** Alg
72B3 **Bossangoa** CAR
72B3 **Bossèmbélé** CAR
17D3 **Bossier City** USA
48K5 **Bosten Hu** *L* China
35E5 **Boston** Eng
9F2 **Boston** USA
9D3 **Boston Mts** USA
71F4 **Bosumtwi,L** Ghana
60C4 **Botād** India
41E2 **Botevgrad** Bulg
74D2 **Bothaville** S Africa
44B3 **Bothnia,G of** Sweden/Fin
73C6 **Botletli** *R* Botswana
45D6 **Botosani** Rom
73C6 **Botswana** Republic, Africa
40D3 **Botte Donato** *Mt* Italy
11B2 **Bottineau** USA
36D1 **Bottrop** Germany
29C3 **Botucatu** Brazil
29D1 **Botupora** Brazil
7N5 **Botwood** Can
70B4 **Bouaflé** Ivory Coast
68D7 **Bouaké** Ivory Coast
72B3 **Bouar** CAR
71B2 **Bouârfa** Mor
71J4 **Bouba Ndija Nat Pk** Cam
72B3 **Bouca** CAR
71B2 **Boudnib** Mor
39C2 **Boufarik** Alg
77E1 **Bougainville** *I* PNG
Bougie = Bejaïa
70B3 **Bougouni** Mali
71F3 **Bougouriba** *R* Burkina
71C2 **Bougtob** Alg
36C2 **Bouillon** France
71C1 **Bouira** Alg
70B2 **Bou Izakarn** Mor
36D2 **Boulay-Moselle** France
8C2 **Boulder** Colorado, USA
18D1 **Boulder** Montana, USA
8B3 **Boulder City** USA
20A2 **Boulder Creek** USA
38C1 **Boulogne** France
72B3 **Boumba** *R* CAR
71F4 **Bouna** Ivory Coast
8B3 **Boundary Peak** *Mt* USA
70B4 **Boundiali** Ivory Coast
18D2 **Bountiful** USA
77G5 **Bounty Is** NZ
77F3 **Bourail** Nouvelle Calédonie
36C3 **Bourbonne-les-Bains** France
70B3 **Bourem** Mali
38D2 **Bourg** France

38D2 **Bourg de Péage** France
37A1 **Bourg-en-Bresse** France
38C2 **Bourges** France
38C3 **Bourg-Madame** France
38C2 **Bourgogne** Region, France
37A2 **Bourgoin-Jallieu** France
37B2 **Bourg-St-Maurice** France
75C2 **Bourke** Aust
35E6 **Bournemouth** Eng
71C1 **Bou Saâda** Alg
72B2 **Bousso** Chad
70A3 **Boutilmit** Maur
71F4 **Boutourou,Mt** Ivory Coast
xxxJ7 **Bouvet I** Atlantic O
28D2 **Bovril** Arg
3F3 **Bow** *R* Can
11B2 **Bowbells** USA
76D2 **Bowen** Aust
19E4 **Bowie** Arizona, USA
17C3 **Bowie** Texas, USA
3F4 **Bow Island** Can
9E3 **Bowling Green** Kentucky, USA
17D2 **Bowling Green** Missouri, USA
12C2 **Bowling Green** Ohio, USA
13D3 **Bowling Green** Virginia, USA
11B2 **Bowman** USA
13D2 **Bowmanville** Can
75D2 **Bowral** Aust
3D3 **Bowron** *R* Can
52D3 **Bo Xian** China
52D2 **Boxing** China
64B1 **Boyabat** Turk
72B3 **Boyali** CAR
43G2 **Boyarka** Ukraine
6J4 **Boyd** Can
14C2 **Boyertown** USA
3F3 **Boyle** Can
33B3 **Boyle** Irish Rep
35B5 **Boyne** *R* Irish Rep
15E4 **Boynoton Beach** USA
72C3 **Boyoma Falls** Zaïre
18E2 **Boysen Res** USA
41F3 **Bozcaada** *I* Turk
41F3 **Boz Dağlari** *Mts* Turk
8B2 **Bozeman** USA
Bozen = Bolzano
72B3 **Bozene** Zaïre
72B3 **Bozoum** CAR
37B2 **Bra** Italy
40D2 **Brač** *I* Croatia, Yugos
4F4 **Bracebridge** Can
69A2 **Brach** Libya
32H6 **Bräcke** Sweden
16B4 **Brackettville** USA
15E4 **Bradenton** USA
35E5 **Bradford** Eng
14A2 **Bradford** USA
20B3 **Bradley** USA
16C3 **Brady** USA
34E1 **Brae** Scot
34D3 **Braemar** Scot
39A1 **Braga** Port
28C3 **Bragado** Arg
39A1 **Bragana** Port
27J4 **Bragança** Brazil
29C3 **Bragança Paulista** Brazil
61D3 **Brahman-Baria** Bang
61C3 **Brāhmani** *R* India
61D2 **Brahmaputra** *R* India
45D6 **Brăila** Rom
9D2 **Brainerd** USA
74C3 **Brak** *R* S Africa
74D1 **Brak** *R* S Africa
70A3 **Brakna** Region, Maur
6F4 **Bralorne** Can
4F5 **Brampton** Can
26F3 **Branco** *R* Brazil
73B6 **Brandberg** *Mt* Namibia
42C2 **Brandenburg** Germany
42C2 **Brandenburg** State, Germany
74D2 **Brandfort** S Africa
8D2 **Brandon** Can
11C3 **Brandon** USA
74C3 **Brandvlei** S Africa
42C2 **Brandys nad Lebem** Czech
43D2 **Braniewo** Pol
9E2 **Brantford** Can
75B3 **Branxholme** Aust
7M5 **Bras d'Or L** Can
29D2 **Brasíla de Minas** Brazil
26E6 **Brasiléia** Brazil
27J7 **Brasilia** Brazil
41F1 **Brasov** Rom
56E2 **Brassay Range** *Mts* Malay
42D3 **Bratislava** Czech
49M4 **Bratsk** Russian Fed
43F3 **Bratslav** Ukraine
13E2 **Brattleboro** USA
42C2 **Braunschweig** Germany
70A4 **Brava** *I* Cape Verde
8B3 **Brawley** USA
35B5 **Bray** Irish Rep
7L3 **Bray I** Can
36B2 **Bray-sur-Seine** France
3E3 **Brazeau** *R* Can
3E3 **Brazeau,Mt** Can
24E5 **Brazil** Republic, S America
xxxG5 **Brazil Basin** Atlantic O
8D3 **Brazos** *R* USA
72B4 **Brazzaville** Congo
42C3 **Brdy** *Upland* Czech
78A3 **Breaksea Sd** NZ
78B1 **Bream B** NZ
56C4 **Brebes** Indon
34D3 **Brechin** Scot
36C1 **Brecht** Belg
11C2 **Breckenridge** Minnesota, USA
16C3 **Breckenridge** Texas, USA
42D3 **Břeclav** Czech
35D6 **Brecon** Wales
35D6 **Brecon Beacons** *Mts* Wales
35C5 **Brecon Beacons Nat Pk** Wales
42A2 **Breda** Neth
74C3 **Bredasdorp** S Africa
32H6 **Bredby** Sweden
44B3 **Bredbyn** Sweden
44K5 **Bredy** Russian Fed
74B3 **Breede** *R* S Africa
13D2 **Breezewood** USA
37C1 **Bregenz** Austria
37C1 **Bregenzer Ache** *R* Austria
32A1 **Breiðafjörður** *B* Iceland
36D2 **Breisach** Germany
37C2 **Brembo** Italy
37C2 **Brembo** *R* Italy
15B2 **Bremen** USA
42B2 **Bremen** Germany
42B2 **Bremerhaven** Germany
18B1 **Bremerton** USA
19E3 **Brendel** USA
17C3 **Brenham** USA
38E2 **Brenner** *Mt* Austria
42C3 **Brenner** *P* Austria/Italy
37D2 **Breno** Italy
4F4 **Brent** Can
37D2 **Brenta** *R* Italy
20B2 **Brentwood** USA
40C1 **Brescia** Italy
Breslau = Wrocław
37D1 **Bressanone** Italy
34E1 **Bressay** *I* Scot
38B2 **Bressuire** France
38B2 **Brest** France
43E2 **Brest** Belorussia
38B2 **Bretagne** Region, France
36B2 **Breteuil** France
36A2 **Bretevil** France
15B3 **Breton Sd** USA
14C2 **Breton Woods** USA
78B1 **Brett,C** NZ
15C1 **Brevard** USA
75C1 **Brewarrina** Aust
13F2 **Brewer** USA
14D2 **Brewster** New York, USA
18C1 **Brewster** Washington, USA
15B2 **Brewton** USA
74D2 **Breyten** S Africa
40D1 **Brežice** Slovenia, Yugos
72C3 **Bria** CAR
38D3 **Briancon** France
38C2 **Briare** France
15B2 **Bridgeport** Alabama, USA
19C3 **Bridgeport** California, USA
13E2 **Bridgeport** Connecticut, USA
11B3 **Bridgeport** Nebraska, USA
17C3 **Bridgeport** Texas, USA
20C1 **Bridgeport Res** USA
18E1 **Bridger** USA
16A1 **Bridger Peak** USA
14C3 **Bridgeton** USA
23F4 **Bridgetown** Barbados
5H5 **Bridgetown** Can
7M5 **Bridgewater** Can
14E2 **Bridgewater** USA
35D6 **Bridgwater** Eng
35D6 **Bridgwater B** Eng
35E4 **Bridlington** Eng
75E3 **Bridport** Aust
36C2 **Brienne-le-Château** France
37B1 **Brienzer See** *L* Switz
36C2 **Briey** France
40B1 **Brig** Switz
8B2 **Brigham City** USA
75C3 **Bright** Aust
35E6 **Brighton** Eng
37B3 **Brignoles** France
29A3 **Brilhante** *R* Brazil
36E1 **Brilon** Germany
41D2 **Brindisi** Italy
17D3 **Brinkley** USA
77E3 **Brisbane** Aust
13E2 **Bristol** Connecticut, USA
35D6 **Bristol** Eng
13E2 **Bristol** Pennsylvania, USA
14E2 **Bristol** Rhode Island, USA
9E3 **Bristol** Tennessee, USA
10F4 **Bristol B** USA
35C6 **Bristol Chan** Eng/Wales
6F4 **British Columbia** Province, Can
7K1 **British Empire Range** *Mts* Can
10K2 **British Mts** USA/Can
74D2 **Brits** S Africa
74C3 **Britstown** S Africa
4E4 **Britt** Can
11C2 **Britton** USA
38C2 **Brive** France
42D3 **Brno** Czech
15C2 **Broad** *R* USA
14C1 **Broadalbin** USA
7L4 **Broadback** *R* Can
34B2 **Broad Bay** *Inlet* Scot
34C3 **Broadford** Scot
11A2 **Broadus** USA
11B1 **Broadview** Can
11B3 **Broadwater** USA
6H4 **Brochet** Can
6G2 **Brock I** Can
13D2 **Brockport** USA
14E1 **Brockton** USA
4F5 **Brockville** Can
14A2 **Brockway** USA
7K2 **Brodeur Pen** Can
34C4 **Brodick** Scot
43D2 **Brodnica** Pol
45D5 **Brody** Ukraine
36D1 **Brokem Haltern** Germany
16C1 **Broken Bow** Nebraska, USA
17D3 **Broken Bow** Oklahoma, USA
17D3 **Broken Bow L** USA
76D4 **Broken Hill** Aust
37C2 **Broni** Italy
32G5 **Brønnøysund** Nor
14D2 **Bronx** *Borough* New York, USA
57E9 **Brooke's Point** Phil
17D2 **Brookfield** Missouri, USA
12B2 **Brookfield** Wisconsin, USA
9D3 **Brookhaven** USA
18B2 **Brookings** Oregon, USA
8D2 **Brookings** South Dakota, USA
14E1 **Brookline** USA
11D3 **Brooklyn** USA
14D2 **Brooklyn** *Borough* New York, USA
11D2 **Brooklyn Center** USA
6G4 **Brooks** Can
10G4 **Brooks,L** USA
10E2 **Brooks Mt** USA
6C3 **Brooks Range** *Mts* USA
15C3 **Brooksville** USA
13E2 **Brookton** USA
75D1 **Brooloo** Aust
76B2 **Broome** Aust
34D2 **Brora** Scot
18B2 **Brothers** USA
67F4 **Brothers,The** *Is* Yemen
36A2 **Brou** France
72B2 **Broulkou** *Well* Chad
43G2 **Brovary** Ukraine
11D2 **Browerville** USA
16B3 **Brownfield** USA
3F4 **Browning** USA
8D4 **Brownsville** USA
8D3 **Brownwood** USA
51F8 **Browse** *I* Aust
36B1 **Bruay-en-Artois** France
76A3 **Bruce,Mt** Aust
4E5 **Bruce Pen** Can
36E2 **Bruchsal** Germany
37E1 **Bruck** Austria
42D3 **Bruck an der Mur** Austria
Bruges = Brugge
36B1 **Brugge** Belg
36D1 **Brühl** Germany
29D1 **Brumado** Brazil
36D2 **Brumath** France
18C2 **Bruneau** USA
18C2 **Bruneau** *R* USA
56D2 **Brunei** Sultanate, S E Asia
40C1 **Brunico** Italy
78B2 **Brunner,L** NZ
9E3 **Brunswick** Georgia, USA
13F2 **Brunswick** Maine, USA
17D2 **Brunswick** Mississippi, USA
25B8 **Brunswick,Pen de** Chile
75E3 **Bruny I** Aust
44G3 **Brusenets** Russian Fed
16B1 **Brush** USA
23A3 **Brus Laguna** Honduras
Brussel = Bruxelles
42A2 **Bruxelles** Belg
36D2 **Bruyères** France
8D3 **Bryan** USA
75A2 **Bryan,Mt** Aust
44E5 **Bryansk** Russian Fed
17D3 **Bryant** USA
20D3 **Bryce Canyon Nat Pk** USA
42D2 **Brzeg** Pol
64E4 **Būbīyan** *I* Kuwait/Iraq
72D4 **Bubu** *R* Tanz
74E1 **Bubye** *R* Zim
26D2 **Bucaramanga** Colombia
34E3 **Buchan** *Oilfield* N Sea
70A4 **Buchanan** Lib
16C3 **Buchanan,L** USA
34E3 **Buchan Deep** N Sea
7L2 **Buchan G** Can
33C2 **Buchan Ness** *Pen* Scot
7N5 **Buchans** Can
28C2 **Buchardo** Arg
Bucharest = Bucureşti
20B3 **Buchon, Pt** USA
37C1 **Buchs** Switz
19D4 **Buckeye** USA
35E5 **Buckingham** Eng
10F2 **Buckland** USA
10F2 **Buckland** *R* USA
75A2 **Buckleboo** Aust
13F2 **Bucksport** USA
72B4 **Buco Zau** Congo
5J4 **Buctouche** Can
41F2 **Bucureşti** Rom
43D3 **Budapest** Hung
60D3 **Budaun** India
35C6 **Bude** Eng
17D3 **Bude** USA
45G7 **Budennovsk** Russian Fed
36E1 **Büdingen** Germany
41D2 **Budva** Montenegro, Yugos
72A3 **Buéa** Cam
37A2 **Buech** *R* France
20B3 **Buellton** USA
28B2 **Buena Esperanza** Arg
26C3 **Buenaventura** Colombia
16A4 **Buenaventura** Mexico
16A2 **Buena Vista** Colorado, USA
22B2 **Buenavista** Mexico
13D3 **Buena Vista** Virginia, USA
20C3 **Buena Vista L** USA
28A4 **Bueno** *R* Chile
25E4 **Buenos Aires** Arg
25E5 **Buenos Aires** State, Arg
17D2 **Buffalo** Mississipi, USA
9F2 **Buffalo** New York, USA
11B2 **Buffalo** South Dakota, USA
17C3 **Buffalo** Texas, USA
8C2 **Buffalo** Wyoming, USA
74E2 **Buffalo** *R* S Africa
3E2 **Buffalo Head Hills** *Mts* Can
18C1 **Buffalo Hump** USA
3F3 **Buffalo L** Alberta, Can
3E1 **Buffalo L** Northwest Territories, Can
6H4 **Buffalo Narrows** Can
15C2 **Buford** USA
41F2 **Buftea** Rom
43E2 **Bug** *R* Pol/Ukraine
26C3 **Buga** Colombia
63C1 **Bugdayli** Turkmenistan
44H2 **Bugrino** Russian Fed
53A2 **Bugt** China
44J5 **Bugulma** Russian Fed
44J5 **Buguruslan** Russian Fed
64C2 **Buhayrat al Asad** *Res* Syria
18D2 **Buhl** Idaho, USA
11D2 **Buhl** Minnesota, USA
71F4 **Bui Dam** Ghana
35D5 **Builth Wells** Wales
28A2 **Buin** Chile
37A2 **Buis-les-Baronnies** France
37E2 **Buje** Croatia, Yugos
72C4 **Bujumbura** Burundi
77E1 **Buka** *I* PNG
73C4 **Bukama** Zaïre
72C4 **Bukavu** Zaïre
58E2 **Bukhara** Uzbekistan
56D2 **Bukit Batubrok** *Mt* Indon
56B3 **Bukittinggi** Indon
72D4 **Bukoba** Tanz
57B3 **Buku Gandadiwata** *Mt* Indon
57C2 **Buku Saolat** *Mt* Indon
51G7 **Bula** Indon
57F8 **Bulan** Phil
60D3 **Bulandshahr** India
73C6 **Bulawayo** Zim
41F3 **Buldan** Turk
60D4 **Buldāna** India
10B6 **Buldir I** USA
50D2 **Bulgan** Mongolia
41E2 **Bulgaria** Republic, Europe
57C2 **Buli** Indon
37B1 **Bulle** Switz
78B2 **Buller** *R* NZ
75C3 **Buller,Mt** Aust
76A4 **Bullfinch** Aust
75B1 **Bulloo** *R* Aust
75B1 **Bulloo Downs** Aust
75B1 **Bulloo L** Aust
17D2 **Bull Shoals Res** USA
28A3 **Bulnes** Chile
76D1 **Bulolo** PNG
74D2 **Bultfontein** S Africa
57B4 **Bulukumba** Indon
72C3 **Bumba** Zaïre
56E2 **Bum Bum** *I* Malay
45D8 **Bu Menderes** *R* Turk
55B2 **Bumphal Dam** Thai
72D3 **Buna** Kenya
76A4 **Bunbury** Aust
34B4 **Buncrana** Irish Rep
77E3 **Bundaberg** Aust
75D2 **Bundarra** Aust
60D3 **Būndi** India
75C1 **Bungil** *R* Aust
73B4 **Bungo** Angola
54B4 **Bungo-suidō** *Str* Japan
56C2 **Bunguran** *I* Indon
72D3 **Bunia** Zaïre
17D2 **Bunker** USA
17D3 **Bunkie** USA
15C3 **Bunnell** USA
71H3 **Bunsuru** *R* Nig
56D3 **Buntok** Indon
57B2 **Buol** Indon
65D2 **Burāg** Syria
72C2 **Buram** Sudan
61B1 **Burang** China
72E3 **Burao** Somalia
57G8 **Burauen** Phil
66D1 **Buraydah** S Arabia
19C4 **Burbank** USA
75C2 **Burcher** Aust
63E1 **Burdalyk** Turkmenistan
45E8 **Burdur** Turk
53C1 **Bureinskiy Khrebet** *Mts* Russian Fed
50F2 **Bureya** Russian Fed
53C1 **Bureya** *R* Russian Fed
65B3 **Bûr Fu'ad** Egypt
42C2 **Burg** Germany
41F2 **Burgas** Bulg
15D2 **Burgaw** USA
37B1 **Burgdorf** Switz
5K4 **Burgeo** Can
74D3 **Burgersdorp** S Africa
48K5 **Burgin** China
22C1 **Burgos** Mexico
39B1 **Burgos** Spain
43D1 **Burgsvik** Sweden
41F3 **Burhaniye** Turk
60D4 **Burhānpur** India
57F8 **Burias** *I* Phil
5K4 **Burin Pen** Can
55C2 **Buriram** Thai
29C2 **Buritis** Brazil
3C3 **Burke Chan** Can
76C2 **Burketown** Aust
70B3 **Burkina** Republic, Africa
13D1 **Burk's Falls** Can
8B2 **Burley** USA
4F5 **Burlington** Can
16B2 **Burlington** Colorado, USA
9D2 **Burlington** Iowa, USA
14C2 **Burlington** New Jersey, USA
15D1 **Burlington** North Carolina, USA
9F2 **Burlington** Vermont, USA
18B1 **Burlington** Washington, USA
4D5 **Burlington** Wisconsin, USA
59H3 **Burma** Republic, Asia
16C3 **Burnet** USA
18B2 **Burney** USA
14B2 **Burnham** USA
76D5 **Burnie** Aust
35D5 **Burnley** Eng
18C2 **Burns** USA
6F4 **Burns Lake** Can
59G1 **Burqin** China
75A2 **Burra** Aust
75D2 **Burragorang,L** Aust
34D2 **Burray** *I* Scot
75C2 **Burren Junction** Aust
75C2 **Burrinjuck Res** Aust
51G8 **Burrundie** Aust
45D7 **Bursa** Turk
66B1 **Bur Safâga** Egypt
Bûr Sa'îd = Port Said
65B4 **Bûr Taufiq** Egypt
12C2 **Burton** USA
35E5 **Burton upon Trent** Eng
32J6 **Burtrask** Sweden
75B2 **Burtundy** Aust
57C3 **Buru** Indon
72C4 **Burundi** Republic, Africa

56B2 **Burung** Indon
11C3 **Burwell** USA
49N4 **Buryatskaya** Respublika, Russian Fed
72D2 **Burye** Eth
45J6 **Burynshik** Kazakhstan
35F5 **Bury St Edmunds** Eng
63C3 **Būshehr** Iran
72B4 **Busira** *R* Zaïre
43E2 **Buskozdroj** Pol
65D2 **Busrā ash Shām** Syria
36D3 **Bussang** France
76A4 **Busselton** Aust
38D2 **Busto** Italy
40B1 **Busto Arsizio** Italy
57E8 **Busuanga** *I* Phil
72C3 **Buta** Zaïre
28B3 **Buta Ranquil** Arg
72C4 **Butare** Rwanda
34C4 **Bute** *I* Scot
53A2 **Butha Qi** China
13D2 **Butler** USA
8B2 **Butte** USA
55C4 **Butterworth** Malay
74D3 **Butterworth** S Africa
33B2 **Butt of Lewis** *C* Scot
7M3 **Button Is** Can
20C3 **Buttonwillow** USA
57G9 **Butuan** Phil
57B4 **Butung** *I* Indon
45G5 **Buturlinovka** Russian Fed
61B2 **Butwal** Nepal
36E1 **Butzbach** Germany
72E3 **Buulobarde** Somalia
72E3 **Buurhaakaba** Somalia
44G4 **Buy** Russian Fed
52B1 **Buyant Ovvo** Mongolia
45H7 **Buynaksk** Russian Fed
49N5 **Buyr Nuur** *L* Mongolia
45G8 **Büyük Ağri Daği** *Mt* Turk
53E2 **Buyukly** Russian Fed
64A2 **Büyük Menderes** *R* Turk
41F1 **Buzău** Rom
41F1 **Buzău** *R* Rom
44J5 **Buzuluk** Russian Fed
14E2 **Buzzards B** USA
41F2 **Byala** Bulg
41E2 **Byala Slatina** Bulg
6H2 **Byam Martin Chan** Can
6H2 **Byam Martin I** Can
65C1 **Byblos** *Hist. Site* Leb
43D2 **Bydgoszcz** Pol
16B2 **Byers** USA
32F7 **Bygland** Nor
43G2 **Bykhov** Belorussia
53E2 **Bykov** Russian Fed
7K2 **Bylot I** Can
75C2 **Byrock** Aust
20B2 **Byron** USA
75D1 **Byron,C** Aust
49P3 **Bytantay** *R* Russian Fed
43D2 **Bytom** Pol

C

25E3 **Caacupé** Par
29A4 **Caaguazú** Par
73B5 **Caála** Angola
3C3 **Caamano Sd** Can
29A4 **Caapucú** Par
29B3 **Caarapó** Brazil
25E3 **Caazapá** Par
16A3 **Caballo Res** USA
57F7 **Cabanatuan** Phil
13F1 **Cabano** Can
27M5 **Cabedelo** Brazil
39A2 **Cabeza del Buey** Spain
28C3 **Cabildo** Arg
28A2 **Cabildo** Chile
26D1 **Cabimas** Ven
72B4 **Cabinda** Angola
72B4 **Cabinda** Province, Angola
18C1 **Cabinet Mts** USA
23C3 **Cabo Beata** Dom Rep
39C2 **Cabo Binibeca** *C* Spain
71A2 **Cabo Cantin** *C* Mor
40B3 **Cabo Carbonara** *C* Sardegna
28A3 **Cabo Carranza** *C* Chile
39A2 **Cabo Carvoeiro** *C* Port
8B3 **Cabo Colnett** *C* Mexico
28D3 **Cabo Corrientes** *C* Arg
26C2 **Cabo Corrientes** *C* Colombia
21B2 **Cabo Corrientes** *C* Mexico
23B3 **Cabo Cruz** *C* Cuba
39B1 **Cabo de Ajo** *C* Spain
39C1 **Cabo de Caballeria** *C* Spain
39C1 **Cabo de Creus** *C* Spain
25C9 **Cabo de Hornos** *C* Chile
39C2 **Cabo de la Nao** *C* Spain
39A1 **Cabo de Peñas** *C* Spain
39A2 **Cabo de Roca** *C* Port
39C2 **Cabo de Salinas** *C* Spain
74E2 **Cabo de Santa Maria** *C* Mozam
29D3 **Cabo de São Tomé** *C* Brazil
39A2 **Cabo de São Vicente** *C* Port
39B2 **Cabo de Sata** *C* Spain
39A2 **Cabo de Sines** *C* Port
39C1 **Cabo de Tortosa** *C* Spain
25C6 **Cabo Dos Bahias** *C* Arg
39A2 **Cabo Espichel** *C* Port
8B4 **Cabo Falso** *C* Mexico
39B2 **Cabo Ferrat** *C* Alg
39A1 **Cabo Finisterre** *C* Spain
39C1 **Cabo Formentor** *C* Spain
29D3 **Cabo Frio** Brazil
29D3 **Cabo Frio** *C* Brazil
23A4 **Cabo Gracias à Dios** Honduras
28A1 **Cabo Leones** *C* Chile
27J4 **Cabo Maguarinho** *C* Brazil
39A2 **Cabo Negro** *C* Mor
75D1 **Caboolture** Aust
27H3 **Cabo Orange** *C* Brazil
19C4 **Cabo Punta Banda** *C* Mexico
73D5 **Cabora Bassa Dam** Mozam
21A1 **Caborca** Mexico
21C2 **Cabo Rojo** *C* Mexico
22C1 **Cabos** Mexico
28D3 **Cabo San Antonio** *C* Arg
23A2 **Cabo San Antonio** *C* Cuba
25C8 **Cabo San Diego** *C* Arg
26B4 **Cabo San Lorenzo** *C* Ecuador
40B3 **Cabo Teulada** *C* Sardegna
39A2 **Cabo Trafalgar** *C* Spain
39B2 **Cabo Tres Forcas** *C* Mor
25C7 **Cabo Tres Puntas** *C* Arg
7M5 **Cabot Str** Can
39B2 **Cabra** Spain
39A1 **Cabreira** *Mt* Port
39C2 **Cabrera** *I* Spain
28A3 **Cabrero** Chile
39B2 **Cabriel** *R* Spain
22C2 **Cacahuamilpa** Mexico
41E2 **Čačak** Serbia, Yugos
28E2 **Cacapava do Sul** Brazil
14A3 **Cacapon** *R* USA
22C2 **C A Carillo** Mexico
28E1 **Caceoul** Brazil
27G7 **Cáceres** Brazil
39A2 **Caceres** Spain
17D2 **Cache** *R* USA
3D3 **Cache Creek** Can
20A1 **Cache Creek, R** USA
18D2 **Cache Peak** *Mt* USA
25C3 **Cachi** Arg
27G5 **Cachimbo** Brazil
27L6 **Cachoeira** Brazil
29B2 **Cachoeira Alta** Brazil
27L5 **Cachoeira de Paulo Afonso** *Waterfall* Brazil
25F4 **Cachoeira do Sul** Brazil
27K8 **Cachoeiro de Itapemirim** Brazil
20C3 **Cachuma, L** USA
73B5 **Cacolo** Angola
73B5 **Caconda** Angola
16B2 **Cactus** USA
29B2 **Caçu** Brazil
29D1 **Caculé** Brazil
73B5 **Caculuvar** *R* Angola
43D3 **Čadca** Czech
35D5 **Cader Idris** *Mts* Wales
11A2 **Cadillac** Can
9E2 **Cadillac** USA
57F8 **Cadiz** Phil
39A2 **Cadiz** Spain
27K6 **Caeité** Brazil
38B2 **Caen** France
35C5 **Caernarfon** Wales
35C5 **Caernarfon B** Wales
65C2 **Caesarea** *Hist Site* Israel
29D1 **Caetité** Brazil
25C3 **Cafayate** Arg
64B2 **Caga Tepe** Turk
57F7 **Cagayan** *R* Phil
57F9 **Cagayan de Oro** Phil
57F9 **Cagayan Is** Phil
37E3 **Cagli** Italy
40B3 **Cagliari** Sardegna
23D3 **Caguas** Puerto Rico
15B2 **Cahaba** *R* USA
35B5 **Cahir** Irish Rep
35B5 **Cahone Pt** Irish Rep
38C3 **Cahors** France
73D5 **Caia** Mozam
73C5 **Caianda** Angola
29B2 **Caiapó** *R* Brazil
29B2 **Caiapônia** Brazil
27L5 **Caicó** Brazil
23C2 **Caicos Is** Caribbean
9F4 **Caicos Pass** Bahamas
10G3 **Cairn Mt** USA
76D2 **Cairns** Aust
64B3 **Cairo** Egypt
9E3 **Cairo** USA
75B1 **Caiwarro** Aust
26C5 **Cajabamba** Peru
26C5 **Cajamarca** Peru
23D5 **Calabozo** Ven
41E2 **Calafat** Rom
25B8 **Calafate** Arg
57F8 **Calagua Is** Phil
39B1 **Calahorra** Spain
38C1 **Calais** France
13F1 **Calais** USA
25C2 **Calama** Chile
26D3 **Calamar** Colombia
57E8 **Calamian Group** *Is* Phil
73B4 **Calandula** Angola
56A2 **Calang** Indon
69B2 **Calanscio Sand Sea** Libya
57F8 **Calapan** Phil
41F2 **Calarasi** Rom
39B1 **Calatayud** Spain
20B2 **Calaveras Res** USA
57F8 **Calbayog** Phil
17D4 **Calcasieu L** USA
61C3 **Calcutta** India
39A2 **Caldas da Rainha** Port
27J7 **Caldas Novas** Brazil
25B3 **Caldera** Chile
8B2 **Caldwell** USA
74B3 **Caledon** S Africa
74D3 **Caledon** *R* S Africa
12A2 **Caledonia** Minnesota, USA
14B1 **Caledonia** New York, USA
5H4 **Caledonia Hills** Can
22B1 **Calera** Mexico
25C7 **Caleta Olivia** Arg
8B3 **Calexico** USA
6G4 **Calgary** Can
15C2 **Calhoun** USA
15C2 **Calhoun Falls** USA
26C3 **Cali** Colombia
20C3 **Caliente** California, USA
8B3 **Caliente** Nevada, USA
16A2 **Caliente** New Mexico, USA
20C3 **California Aqueduct** USA
8A3 **California** State, USA
62B2 **Calimera,Pt** India
28B2 **Calingasta** Arg
19C4 **Calipatria** USA
74C3 **Calitzdorp** S Africa
75B1 **Callabonna** *R* Aust
75A1 **Callabonna,L** Aust
13D1 **Callander** Can
34C3 **Callander** Scot
75A1 **Callanna** Aust
26C6 **Callao** Peru
22C1 **Calles** Mexico
14C2 **Callicoon** USA
3F2 **Calling L** Can
22C1 **Calnali** Mexico
15E4 **Caloosahatchee** *R* USA
75D1 **Caloundra** Aust
22C2 **Calpulalpan** Mexico
40C3 **Caltanissetta** Italy
73B4 **Caluango** Angola
73B5 **Calulo** Angola
73B5 **Caluquembe** Angola
67F4 **Caluula** Somalia
3C3 **Calvert I** Can
40B2 **Calvi** Corse
22B1 **Calvillo** Mexico
74B3 **Calvinia** S Africa
36E2 **Calw** Germany
29E1 **Camacari** Brazil
22B1 **Camacho** Mexico
28E2 **Camaguã** Brazil
28E2 **Camaguã** *R* Brazil
21E2 **Camagüey** Cuba
21E2 **Camagüey,Arch de** *Is* Cuba
29E1 **Camamu** Brazil
26D7 **Camaná** Peru
10N5 **Camania** *I* Can
29B2 **Camapuã** Brazil
26E8 **Camargo** Bol
20C3 **Camarillo** USA
25C6 **Camarones** Arg
18B1 **Camas** USA
73B4 **Camaxilo** Angola
73B4 **Cambatela** Angola
55C3 **Cambodia** Republic, S E Asia
35C6 **Camborne** Eng
38C1 **Cambrai** France
20B3 **Cambria** USA
35D5 **Cambrian Mts** Wales
12C2 **Cambridge** Can
35E5 **Cambridge** County, Eng
35F5 **Cambridge** Eng
23H1 **Cambridge** Jamaica
13D3 **Cambridge** Maryland, USA
13E2 **Cambridge** Massachussets, USA
11D2 **Cambridge** Minnesota, USA
78C1 **Cambridge** NZ
12C2 **Cambridge** Ohio, USA
6H3 **Cambridge Bay** Can
51F8 **Cambridge G** Aust
45F7 **Cam Burun** *Pt* Turk
9D3 **Camden** Arkansas, USA
75D2 **Camden** Aust
13E3 **Camden** New Jersey, USA
14C1 **Camden** New York, USA
15C2 **Camden** South Carolina, USA
10J1 **Camden B** USA
37E3 **Camerino** Italy
17D2 **Cameron** Missouri, USA
17C3 **Cameron** Texas, USA
56F6 **Cameron Highlands** Malay
6H2 **Cameron I** Can
78A3 **Cameron Mts** NZ
72B3 **Cameroon** Federal Republic, Africa
72A3 **Cameroun** *Mt* Cam
27J4 **Cametá** Brazil
57F9 **Camiguin** *I* Phil
57F7 **Camiling** Phil
15C2 **Camilla** USA
20B1 **Camino** USA
26F8 **Camiri** Bol
73C4 **Camissombo** Angola
27K4 **Camocim** Brazil
76C2 **Camooweal** Aust
62E3 **Camorta** *I* Indian O
28D2 **Campana** Arg
25A7 **Campana** *I* Chile
3C3 **Campania I** Can
74C2 **Campbell** S Africa
78B2 **Campbell,C** NZ
3C3 **Campbell I** Can
xxixN7 **Campbell I** NZ
10M2 **Campbell L** Can
6E3 **Campbell,Mt** Can
60C2 **Campbellpore** Pak
6F5 **Campbell River** Can
12B3 **Campbellsville** USA
7M5 **Campbellton** Can
75D2 **Campbelltown** Aust
34C4 **Campbeltown** Scot
21C3 **Campeche** Mexico
75B3 **Camperdown** Aust
27L5 **Campina Grande** Brazil
27J8 **Campinas** Brazil
29C2 **Campina Verde** Brazil
57B5 **Camplong** Indon
20C2 **Camp Nelson** USA
72A3 **Campo** Cam
40C2 **Campobasso** Italy
29C3 **Campo Belo** Brazil
28C1 **Campo del Cielo** Arg
29C2 **Campo Florido** Brazil
25D3 **Campo Gallo** Arg
25F2 **Campo Grande** Brazil
27K4 **Campo Maior** Brazil
25F2 **Campo Mourão** Brazil
28E1 **Campo Novo** Brazil
29D3 **Campos** Brazil
29C2 **Campos Altos** Brazil
37D1 **Campo Tures** Italy
19D4 **Camp Verde** USA
55D3 **Cam Ranh** Viet
6G4 **Camrose** Can
73B5 **Camucuio** Angola
23K1 **Canaan** Tobago
14D1 **Canaan** USA
73B5 **Canacupa** Angola
2F3 **Canada** Dominion, N America
25D4 **Cañada de Gomez** Arg
14C2 **Canadensis** USA
16B2 **Canadian** USA
8C3 **Canadian** *R* USA
45D7 **Canakkale** Turk
28B3 **Canalejas** Arg
3E3 **Canal Flats** Can
14B1 **Canandaigua** USA
14B1 **Canandaigua L** USA
21A1 **Cananea** Mexico
29C4 **Cananeia** Brazil
xxxG3 **Canary Basin** Atlantic O
Canary Is = Islas Canarias
22B2 **Canas** Mexico
21B2 **Canatlán** Mexico
9E4 **Canaveral,C** USA
27L7 **Canavieiras** Brazil
76D4 **Canberra** Aust
18B2 **Canby** California, USA
11C3 **Canby** Minnesota, USA
41F3 **Çandarli Körfezi** *B* Turk
3G3 **Candle L** Can
14D2 **Candlewood,L** USA
11C2 **Cando** USA
14B1 **Candor** USA
25E4 **Canelones** Urug
17C2 **Caney** USA
73C5 **Cangamba** Angola
73C5 **Cangombe** Angola
28E2 **Canguçu** Brazil
52D2 **Cangzhou** China
7M4 **Caniapiscau** *R* Can
7M4 **Caniapiscau, Réservoir** *Res* Can
40C3 **Canicatti** Italy
27L4 **Canindé** Brazil
14B1 **Canisteo** USA
14B1 **Canisteo** *R* USA
22B1 **Canitas de Felipe Pescador** Mexico
16A2 **Canjilon** USA
64B1 **Çankırı** Turk
3E3 **Canmore** Can
34B3 **Canna** *I* Scot
62B2 **Cannanore** India
38D3 **Cannes** France
11B2 **Cannonball** *R* USA
75C3 **Cann River** Aust
25F3 **Canõas** Brazil
3G2 **Canoe L** Can
29B4 **Canoinhas** Brazil
16A2 **Canon City** USA
75B2 **Canopus** Aust
6H4 **Canora** Can
75C2 **Canowindra** Aust
5J4 **Canso** Can
35B5 **Cansore Pt** Irish Rep
35F6 **Canterbury** Eng
78B2 **Canterbury Bight** *B* NZ
78B2 **Canterbury Plains** NZ
55D4 **Can Tho** Viet
20D3 **Cantil** USA
28A1 **Canto de Augua** Chile
Canton = Guangzhou
17E3 **Canton** Mississippi, USA
12A2 **Canton** Missouri, USA
9E2 **Canton** Ohio, USA
14B2 **Canton** Pensylvania, USA
11C3 **Canton** S Dakota, USA
77H1 **Canton** *I* Phoeniz Is
10J3 **Cantwell** USA
36A2 **Cany-Barville** France
16B3 **Canyon** USA
18C2 **Canyon City** USA
18D1 **Canyon Ferry L** USA
19D3 **Canyonlands Nat Pk** USA
10N3 **Canyon Range** *Mts* Can
18B2 **Canyonville** USA
73C4 **Canzar** Angola
55D1 **Cao Bang** Viet
27J4 **Capanema** Brazil
29C3 **Capão Bonito** Brazil
37B3 **Cap Bénat** *C* France
71D1 **Cap Blanc** *C* Tunisia
71E1 **Cap Bon** *C* Tunisia
71D1 **Cap Bougaron** *C* Alg
38B3 **Capbreton** France
37B3 **Cap Camarat** *C* France
5H4 **Cap Chat** Can
22A1 **Cap Corrientes** *C* Mexico
40B2 **Cap Corse** *C* Corse
73E5 **Cap d'Ambre** *C* Madag
37B3 **Cap d'Antibes** *C* France
5J4 **Cap de Gaspé** *C* Can
38B2 **Cap de la Hague** *C* France
5G4 **Cap-de-la-Madeleine** Can
7L3 **Cap de Nouvelle-France** *C* Can
39C2 **Capdepera** Spain
22B2 **Cap de Tancitiario** *C* Mexico
71B1 **Cap des Trois Fourches** *C* Mor
75E3 **Cape Barren I** Aust
xxxJ6 **Cape Basin** Atlantic O
7N5 **Cape Breton I** Can
71F4 **Cape Coast** Ghana
13E2 **Cape Cod B** USA
7M3 **Cape Dyer** Can
79F7 **Cape Evans** *Base* Ant.
15D2 **Cape Fear** *R* USA
17E2 **Cape Girardeau** USA
Cape Horn = Cabo de Hornos
xxviiiH4 **Cape Johnston Depth** Pacific O
29D2 **Capelinha** Brazil
10E2 **Cape Lisburne** USA
73B5 **Capelongo** Angola
13E3 **Cape May** USA
73B4 **Capenda Camulemba** Angola
6F2 **Cape Parry** Can
74C3 **Cape Province** S Africa
74B3 **Cape Town** S Africa
xxxG4 **Cape Verde** *Is* Atlantic O
xxxG4 **Cape Verde Basin** Atlantic O
10K4 **Cape Yakataga** USA
76D2 **Cape York Pen** Aust
37B3 **Cap Ferrat** *C* France
36A1 **Cap Gris Nez** *C* France
23C3 **Cap-Haitien** Haiti

27J4 **Capim** *R* Brazil
29A3 **Capitán Bado** Par
20D3 **Capitol Reef Nat Pk** USA
29A2 **Capivari** *R* Brazil
5K3 **Cap Mécatina** *C* Can
23P2 **Cap Moule à Chique** *C* St Lucia
37C2 **Capo di Noli** *C* Italy
40D3 **Capo Isola de Correnti** *C* Italy
40D3 **Capo Rizzuto** *C* Italy
41D3 **Capo Santa Maria di Leuca** *C* Italy
40C3 **Capo San Vito** Italy
40D3 **Capo Spartivento** *C* Italy
23P2 **Cap Pt** St Lucia
40C2 **Capri** *I* Italy
73C5 **Caprivi Strip** Region, Namibia
40B2 **Cap Rosso** *C* Corse
71D1 **Cap Serrat** *C* Tunisia
37A3 **Cap Sicié** *C* France
70A3 **Cap Vert** *C* Sen
26D4 **Caquetá** *R* Colombia
41E2 **Caracal** Rom
26F3 **Caracaraí** Brazil
26E1 **Caracas** Ven
29A3 **Caracol** Brazil
29C3 **Caraguatatuba** Brazil
25B5 **Carahue** Chile
29D2 **Caraí** Brazil
29D3 **Carandaí** Brazil
29A2 **Carandazal** Brazil
27K8 **Carangola** Brazil
41E1 **Caransebeş** Rom
75A2 **Carappee Hill** *Mt* Aust
23A3 **Caratasca** Honduras
29D2 **Caratinga** Brazil
39B2 **Caravaca** Spain
29E2 **Caravelas** Brazil
28E1 **Carazinho** Brazil
12B3 **Carbondale** Illinois, USA
14C2 **Carbondale** Pennsylvania, USA
7N5 **Carbonear** Can
40B3 **Carbonia** Sardegna
6G4 **Carcajou** Can
69D3 **Carcar Mts** Somalia
38C3 **Carcassonne** France
6E3 **Carcross** Can
22C2 **Cardel** Mexico
21D2 **Cardenas** Cuba
22C1 **Cárdenas** Mexico
22D2 **Cárdenas** Mexico
35D6 **Cardiff** Wales
35C5 **Cardigan** Wales
35C5 **Cardigan B** Wales
28D2 **Cardóna** Urug
3F4 **Cardston** Can
3G2 **Careen L** Can
41E1 **Carei** Rom
27G4 **Careiro** Brazil
28A2 **Carén** Chile
12C2 **Carey** USA
38B2 **Carhaix-Plouguer** France
25D5 **Carhué** Arg
27K8 **Cariacica** Brazil
24C2 **Caribbean S** C America
4B2 **Caribou** Can
13F1 **Caribou** USA
10N3 **Caribou** *R* Can
6G4 **Caribou Mts** Alberta, Can
6F4 **Caribou Mts** British Columbia, Can
57F8 **Carigara** Phil
36C2 **Carignan** France
36B1 **Carin** France
29D1 **Carinhanha** Brazil
29D1 **Carinhanha** *R* Brazil
26F1 **Caripito** Ven
4F4 **Carleton Place** Can
74D2 **Carletonville** S Africa
18C2 **Carlin** USA
12B3 **Carlinville** USA
34D4 **Carlisle** Eng
13D2 **Carlisle** USA
10D5 **Carlisle** *I* USA
28C3 **Carlos** Arg
29D2 **Carlos Chagas** Brazil
35B5 **Carlow** County, Irish Rep
35B5 **Carlow** Irish Rep
19C4 **Carlsbad** California, USA
8C3 **Carlsbad** New Mexico, USA
16B3 **Carlsbad Caverns Nat Pk** USA
xxviiiE4 **Carlsberg Ridge** Indian O
6H5 **Carlyle** Can
10L3 **Carmacks** Can
37B2 **Carmagnola** Italy
35C6 **Carmarthen** Wales
35C6 **Carmarthen B** Wales
20B2 **Carmel** California, USA
14D2 **Carmel** New York, USA
65C2 **Carmel,Mt** Israel
28D2 **Carmelo** Urug
20B2 **Carmel Valley** USA
8B4 **Carmen** *I* Mexico
25D6 **Carmen de Patagones** Arg
12B3 **Carmi** USA
19B3 **Carmichael** USA
29C2 **Carmo do Paranaiba** Brazil
39A2 **Carmona** Spain
76A3 **Carnarvon** Aust
74C3 **Carnarvon** S Africa
29E2 **Carncacá** Brazil
34B4 **Carndonagh** Irish Rep
76B3 **Carnegi,L** Aust
34D3 **Carngorms** *Mts* Scot
62E3 **Car Nicobar** *I* Indian O
72B3 **Carnot** CAR
75A2 **Carnot,C** Aust
10N2 **Carnwath** *R* Can
15E4 **Carol City** USA
27J5 **Carolina** Brazil
74E2 **Carolina** S Africa
15D2 **Carolina Beach** USA
xxviiiJ4 **Caroline Is** Pacific O
45C6 **Carpathians** *Mts* E Europe
43F3 **Carpatii Orientali** *Mts* Rom
76C2 **Carpentaria,G of** Aust
59H5 **Carpenter Ridge** Indian O
38D3 **Carpentras** France
40C2 **Carpi** Italy
20C3 **Carpinteria** USA
15C3 **Carrabelle** USA
40C2 **Carrara** Italy
33B3 **Carrauntoohill** *Mt* Irish Rep
35B5 **Carrickmacross** Irish Rep
35B5 **Carrick-on-Suir** Irish Rep
75A2 **Carrieton** Aust
8D2 **Carrington** USA
39B1 **Carrión** *R* Spain
28A1 **Carrizal Bajo** Chile
17F4 **Carrizo Spring** USA
16A3 **Carrizozo** USA
9D2 **Carroll** USA
15B2 **Carrollton** Georgia, USA
12B3 **Carrollton** Kentucky, USA
17D2 **Carrollton** Missouri, USA
3H3 **Carrot** *R* Can
17E2 **Carruthersville** USA
45F7 **Carsamba** Turk
45E8 **Carsamba** *R* Turk
8B3 **Carson City** USA
12C2 **Carsonville** USA
23B4 **Cartagena** Colombia
39B2 **Cartagena** Spain
26C3 **Cartago** Colombia
21D4 **Cartago** Costa Rica
20C2 **Cartago** USA
26D1 **Cartegena** Colombia
78C2 **Carterton** NZ
17D2 **Carthage** Missouri, USA
13D2 **Carthage** New York, USA
17D3 **Carthage** Texas, USA
76B2 **Cartier I** Timor S
7N4 **Cartwright** Can
27L5 **Caruaru** Brazil
26F1 **Carúpano** Ven
15D1 **Cary** USA
28A2 **Casablanca** Chile
71A2 **Casablanca** Mor
29C3 **Casa Branca** Brazil
8B3 **Casa Grande** USA
40B1 **Casale Monferrato** Italy
37D2 **Casalmaggiore** Italy
28C3 **Casares** Arg
22C1 **Casas** Mexico
28E1 **Casca** Brazil
18D1 **Cascade** USA
3D4 **Cascade Mts** Can/USA
78A2 **Cascade Pt** NZ
8A2 **Cascade Range** *Mts* USA
18C2 **Cascade Res** USA
25F2 **Cascavel** Brazil
37D3 **Casciana** Italy
37D3 **Cascina** Italy
40C2 **Caserta** Italy
79G9 **Casey** *Base* Ant
35B5 **Cashel** Irish Rep
28C2 **Casilda** Arg
77E3 **Casino** Aust
26C5 **Casma** Peru
20B3 **Casmalia** USA
39C1 **Caspe** Spain
8C2 **Casper** USA
45H7 **Caspian S** Asia/Europe
13D3 **Cass** USA
73C5 **Cassamba** Angola
36B1 **Cassel** France
11C2 **Casselton** USA
3C2 **Cassiar** Can
6E3 **Cassiar Mts** Can
29B2 **Cassilândia** Brazil
40C2 **Cassino** Italy
11D2 **Cass Lake** USA
20C3 **Castaic** USA
28B2 **Castaño** *R* Arg
37D2 **Castelfranco** Italy
38D3 **Castellane** France
28D3 **Castelli** Arg
39C1 **Castellon de la Plana** Spain
37D2 **Castelnovo ne'Monti** Italy
37D2 **Castelnuovo di Garfagnana** Italy
27K5 **Castelo** Brazil
39A2 **Castelo Branco** Port
38C3 **Castelsarrasin** France
40C3 **Castelvetrano** Italy
75B3 **Casterton** Aust
37D3 **Castiglion Fiorentino** Italy
28A1 **Castilla** Chile
39B2 **Castilla La Nueva** Region, Spain
39B1 **Castilla La Vieja** Region, Spain
28E2 **Castillos** Urug
33B3 **Castlebar** Irish Rep
34B3 **Castlebay** Scot
19D3 **Castle Dale** USA
34D4 **Castle Douglas** Scot
18C1 **Castlegar** Can
75B3 **Castlemain** Aust
20B3 **Castle,Mt** USA
18D2 **Castle Peak** USA
75C2 **Castlereagh** Aust
16B2 **Castle Rock** USA
38C3 **Castres-sur-l'Agout** France
23E4 **Castries** St Lucia
25B6 **Castro** Arg
25F2 **Castro** Brazil
27L6 **Castro Alves** Brazil
40D3 **Castrovillari** Italy
20B2 **Castroville** USA
28D2 **Casupa** Urug
78A2 **Caswell Sd** NZ
21E2 **Cat** *I* Bahamas
57F8 **Catabalogan** Phil
26B5 **Catacaos** Peru
29D3 **Cataguases** Brazil
17D3 **Catahoula L** USA
29C2 **Catalão** Brazil
39C1 **Cataluña** Region, Spain
25C3 **Catamarca** Arg
25C3 **Catamarca** State, Arg
73D5 **Catandica** Mozam
57F8 **Catanduanes** *I* Phil
25G2 **Catanduva** Brazil
29B4 **Catanduvas** Brazil
40D3 **Catania** Italy
28A3 **Catan-Lil** Arg
40D3 **Catanzaro** Italy
17F4 **Catarina** USA
57F8 **Catarman** Phil
75A2 **Catastrophe,C** Aust
23C5 **Catatumbo** *R* Ven
14B2 **Catawissa** USA
22C2 **Catemaco** Mexico
38D3 **Cater** Corse
40B2 **Cateraggio** Corse
73B4 **Catete** Angola
74D3 **Cathcart** S Africa
28B1 **Catinzaco** Arg
70A3 **Catio** Guinea-Bissau
4C3 **Cat L** Can
4C3 **Cat Lake** Can
77E3 **Cato** *I* Aust
21D2 **Catoche,C** Mexico
14B3 **Catoctin Mt** USA
13D3 **Catonsville** USA
28C3 **Catrilo** Arg
13E2 **Catskill** USA
13E2 **Catskill Mts** USA
5J2 **Caubvick,Mt** Can
26D2 **Cauca** *R* Colombia
21L4 **Caucaia** Brazil
26C2 **Caucasia** Colombia
45G7 **Caucasus** *Mts* Georgia
36A2 **Caudebec-en-Caux** France
36B1 **Caudry** France
73B4 **Caungula** Angola
25B5 **Cauquenes** Chile
13F1 **Causapscal** Can
62B2 **Cauvery** *R* India
38D3 **Cavaillon** France
29C1 **Cavalcanta** Brazil
37D1 **Cavalese** italy
11C2 **Cavalier** USA
70B4 **Cavally** *R* Lib
35B5 **Cavan** County, Irish Rep
35B5 **Cavan** Irish Rep
57F8 **Cavite** Phil
26D4 **Caxias** Brazil
27K4 **Caxias** Brazil
25F3 **Caxias do Sul** Brazil
73B4 **Caxito** Angola
15C2 **Cayce** USA
64D1 **Çayeli** Turk
27H3 **Cayenne** French Guiana
36A1 **Cayeux-sur-Mer** France
21E3 **Cayman Brac** *I* Caribbean
23A3 **Cayman Is** Caribbean
23A3 **Cayman Trench** Caribbean
72E3 **Caynabo** Somalia
20B3 **Cayncos** USA
21E2 **Cayo Romana** *I* Cuba
21D3 **Cayos Mistikos** *Is* Nic
23A2 **Cay Sal** *I* Caribbean
14B1 **Cayuga L** USA
14C1 **Cazenovia** USA
73C5 **Cazombo** Angola
5J4 **C Breton Highlands** Can
Ceará = Fortaleza
27K5 **Ceara** State, Brazil
28B1 **Cebollar** Arg
28E2 **Cebollati** Urug
57F8 **Cebu** Phil
57F8 **Cebu** *I* Phil
14C3 **Cecilton** USA
40C2 **Cecina** Italy
37D3 **Cecina** *R* Italy
11D3 **Cedar** *R* USA
8B3 **Cedar City** USA
17C3 **Cedar Creek Res** USA
11D3 **Cedar Falls** USA
6H4 **Cedar L** Can
20D1 **Cedar Mts** USA
9D2 **Cedar Rapids** USA
15B2 **Cedartown** USA
22B1 **Cedral** Mexico
21A2 **Cedros** *I* Mexico
76C4 **Ceduna** Aust
72E3 **Ceelbuur** Somalia
69D3 **Ceerigaabo** Somalia
40C3 **Cefalù** Italy
43D3 **Cegléd** Hung
73B5 **Cela** Angola
21B2 **Celaya** Mexico
Celebes = Sulawesi
51F6 **Celebes S** S E Asia
12C2 **Celina** USA
40D1 **Celje** Slovenia, Yugos
42C2 **Celle** Germany
35B6 **Celtic S** UK
51G7 **Cendrawasih** *Pen* Indon
37C2 **Ceno** *R* Italy
17D3 **Center** USA
15B1 **Center Hill L** USA
14D2 **Center Moriches** USA
37D2 **Cento** Italy
34C3 **Central** Region, Scot
16A3 **Central** USA
72B3 **Central African Republic** Africa
17C1 **Central City** Nebraska, USA
14A2 **Central City** Pennsylvania, USA
12B3 **Centralia** Illinois, USA
8A2 **Centralia** Washington, USA
74C1 **Central Kalahari Game Res** Botswana
63E3 **Central Makran Range** *Mts* Pak
18B2 **Central Point** USA
51H7 **Central Range** *Mts* PNG
14B1 **Central Square** USA
15B2 **Centre Point** USA
15B2 **Centreville** Alabama, USA
14B3 **Centreville** Maryland, USA
56D4 **Cepu** Indon
Ceram = Seram
51F7 **Ceram Sea** Indonesia
28C3 **Cereales** Arg
28C1 **Ceres** Arg
27J7 **Ceres** Brazil
74B3 **Ceres** S Africa
20B2 **Ceres** USA
38C2 **Cergy-Pontoise** France
40D2 **Cerignola** Italy
45D7 **Cernavodă** Rom
36D3 **Cernay** France
8C4 **Cerralvo** *I* Mexico
22B1 **Cerritos** Mexico
28B2 **Cerro Aconcagua** *Mt* Arg
22C1 **Cerro Azul** Mexico
28B1 **Cerro Boneta** *Mt* Arg
28A3 **Cerro Campanario** *Mt* Chile
28C2 **Cerro Champaqui** *Mt* Arg
28D2 **Cerro Chatto** Urug
22B2 **Cerro Cuachaia** *Mt* Mexico
22C1 **Cerro de Astillero** Mexico
28B1 **Cerro del Potro** *Mt* Chile/Arg
22C1 **Cerro del Tigre** *Mt* Mexico
28B1 **Cerro del Toro** *Mt* Chile/Arg
28B2 **Cerro de Olivares** *Mt* Arg
26C6 **Cerro de Pasco** Peru
23D3 **Cerro de Punta** *Mt* Puerto Rico
22B2 **Cerro El Cantado** *Mt* Mexico
28B3 **Cerro El Nevado** Arg
28B1 **Cerro General M Belgrano** *Mt* Arg
22B2 **Cerro Grande** *Mts* Mexico
22A1 **Cerro Huehueto** *Mt* Mexico
28A2 **Cerro Juncal** *Mt* Arg/Chile
22B1 **Cerro la Ardilla** *Mts* Mexico
28A1 **Cerro las Tortolas** *Mt* Chile
22B2 **Cerro Laurel** *Mt* Mexico
28A2 **Cerro Mercedario** *Mt* Arg
28A3 **Cerro Mora** *Mt* Chile
23C4 **Cerron** *Mt* Ven
28B3 **Cerro Payún** *Mt* Arg
22C1 **Cerro Peña Nevada** *Mt* Mexico
22C2 **Cerro Penón del Rosario** *Mt* Mexico
28B2 **Cerro Sosneado** *Mt* Arg
22B2 **Cerro Teotepec** *Mt* Mexico
28B2 **Cerro Tupungato** *Mt* Arg
22C2 **Cerro Yucuyacau** *Mt* Mexico
37E2 **Cervia** Italy
37C2 **Cervo** *R* Italy
40C2 **Cesena** Italy
44D4 **Cēsis** Latvia
42C3 **České Budějovice** Czech
42C3 **České Zemé** Region, Czech
42D3 **Českomoravská Vysočina** *Mts* Czech
41F3 **Çeşme** Turk
76E4 **Cessnock** Aust
40D2 **Cetina** *R* Croatia, Yugos
71A1 **Ceuta** N W Africa
64C2 **Ceyham** Turk
64C2 **Ceyhan** *R* Turk
64C2 **Ceylanpınar** Turk
Ceylon = Sri Lanka
49L4 **Chaa-Khol** Russian Fed
38C2 **Chaâteaudun** France
37B1 **Chablais** Region, France
36B3 **Chablis** France
28C2 **Chacabuco** Arg
26C5 **Chachapoyas** Peru
28B3 **Chacharramendi** Arg
60C3 **Chachran** Pak
25D3 **Chaco** State, Arg
72B2 **Chad** Republic, Africa
72B2 **Chad** *L* C Africa
28B3 **Chadileuvu** *R* Arg
8C2 **Chadron** USA
17E2 **Chaffee** USA
60A3 **Chagai** Pak
63E3 **Chagai Hills** Pak
49P4 **Chagda** Russian Fed
60B2 **Chaghcharan** Afghan
xxviiiE5 **Chagos Arch** Indian O
23L1 **Chaguanas** Trinidad
63E2 **Chahah Burjak** Afghan
63E3 **Chāh Bahār** Iran
54A2 **Ch'aho** N Korea
55C2 **Chai Badan** Thai
61C3 **Chāībāsa** India
71G3 **Chaîne de l'Atakor** *Mts* Benin
55C3 **Chaîne des Cardamomes** *Mts* Camb
73C4 **Chaîne des Mitumba** *Mts* Zaïre
55C2 **Chaiyaphum** Thai
28D2 **Chajari** Arg
63E2 **Chakhansur** Afghan
60C2 **Chakwal** Pak
26D7 **Chala** Peru
73D5 **Chalabesa** Zambia
60A2 **Chalap Dalam** *Mts* Afghan
36C3 **Chalindrey** France
52C4 **Chaling** China
60D4 **Chālisgaon** India
10K2 **Chalkyitsik** USA
36C2 **Challerange** France
18D2 **Challis** USA
36C2 **Châlons sur Marne** France
38C2 **Chalon sur Saône** France
42C3 **Cham** Germany
16A2 **Chama** USA
60B2 **Chaman** Pak
60D2 **Chamba** India
60D3 **Chambal** *R* India
11C3 **Chamberlain** USA
10J2 **Chamberlin,Mt** USA
13D3 **Chambersburg** USA
38D2 **Chambéry** France
36B2 **Chambly** France
13E1 **Chambord** Can
60A3 **Chambor Kalat** Pak
22A2 **Chamela** Mexico
63C2 **Chamgordan** Iran
28B2 **Chamical** Arg
37B2 **Chamonix** France
61B3 **Champa** India

38C2 **Champagne** Region, France
74D2 **Champagne Castle** *Mt* Lesotho
37A1 **Champagnole** France
9E2 **Champaign** USA
55D3 **Champassak** Laos
9F2 **Champlain,L** USA
37A1 **Champlitte** France
62B2 **Chāmrājnagar** India
25B3 **Chañaral** Chile
28A3 **Chanco** Chile
6D3 **Chandalar** USA
6D3 **Chandalar** *R* USA
15B3 **Chandeleur Is** USA
60D2 **Chandīgarh** India
5J4 **Chandler** Can
19D4 **Chandler** USA
61D3 **Chandpur** Bang
60D5 **Chandrapur** India
63E3 **Chānf** Iran
74E1 **Changane** *R* Mozam
73D5 **Changara** Mozam
53B3 **Changbai** China
53B3 **Changchun** China
52C4 **Changde** China
54A3 **Changdo** N Korea
54A3 **Changhang** S Korea
54A3 **Changhowan** S Korea
50E4 **Chang-hua** Taiwan
54A4 **Changhung** S Korea
55D2 **Changjiang** China
52D3 **Chang Jiang** *R* China
53B3 **Changjin** N Korea
54A2 **Changjin** *R* N Korea
54A2 **Changjin Res** N Korea
53A3 **Changling** China
52C4 **Changsha** China
52E3 **Changshu** China
53A3 **Changtu** China
52B2 **Changwu** China
53B4 **Changyŏn** N Korea
52C2 **Changzhi** China
52E3 **Changzhou** China
38B2 **Channel Is** UK
8B3 **Channel Is** USA
7N5 **Channel Port-aux-Basques** Can
4D4 **Channing** USA
55C3 **Chanthaburi** Thai
36B2 **Chantilly** France
7J3 **Chantrey Inlet** *B* Can
17C2 **Chanute** USA
48J4 **Chany, Ozero** *L* Russian Fed
52D5 **Chaoàn** China
52D5 **Chao'an** China
52D3 **Chao Hu** *L* China
55C3 **Chao Phraya** *R* Thai
53A2 **Chaor He** *R* China
71A1 **Chaouen** Mor
52E1 **Chaoyang** China
53A1 **Chaozhong** China
27K6 **Chapada Diamantina** *Mts* Brazil
27K4 **Chapadinha** Brazil
22B1 **Chapala** Mexico
22B1 **Chapala,Lac de** *L* Mexico
45J5 **Chapayevo** Kazakhstan
25F3 **Chapecó** Brazil
15D1 **Chapel Hill** USA
23H1 **Chapeltown** Jamaica
7K5 **Chapleau** Can
44G5 **Chaplygin** Russian Fed
16B1 **Chappell** USA
28D1 **Charada** Arg
79G3 **Charcot I** Ant
58E2 **Chardzhou** Turkmenistan
71B2 **Charef** Mor
38C2 **Charente** *R* France
72B2 **Chari** *R* Chad
72B2 **Chari Baguirmi** Region, Chad
60B1 **Charikar** Afghan
17D1 **Chariton** *R* USA
27G2 **Charity** Guyana
60D3 **Charkhāri** India
36C1 **Charleroi** Belg
5G4 **Charlesbourg** Can
9F3 **Charles,C** USA
12B3 **Charleston** Illinois, USA
17E2 **Charleston** Missouri, USA
9F3 **Charleston** S Carolina, USA
9E3 **Charleston** W Virginia, USA
19C3 **Charleston Peak** *Mt* USA
14B3 **Charles Town** USA
14D1 **Charlestown** USA
72C4 **Charlesville** Zaïre
76D3 **Charleville** Aust
38C2 **Charleville-Mézières** France
12B1 **Charlevoix** USA
12C2 **Charlotte** Michigan, USA
9E3 **Charlotte** N Carolina, USA
15E4 **Charlotte Harbor** *B* USA
9F3 **Charlottesville** USA
7M5 **Charlottetown** Can
23K1 **Charlotteville** Tobago
75B3 **Charlton** Aust
4F3 **Charlton I** Can
36D2 **Charmes** France
60C2 **Charsadda** Pak
76D3 **Charters Towers** Aust
38C2 **Chartres** France
28B1 **Chaschuil** Arg
25E5 **Chascomús** Arg
3E3 **Chase** Can
54A2 **Chasong** N Korea
37A2 **Château-Arnoux** France
38B2 **Châteaubriant** France
36A3 **Château-du-Loir** France
36A2 **Châteaudun** France
38B2 **Châteaulin** France
36A2 **Châteauneuf-en Thymerais** France
36B3 **Châteauneuf-sur-Loire** France
36A3 **Château Renault** France
38C2 **Châteauroux** France
36D2 **Château-Salins** France
38C2 **Château-Thierry** France
3E2 **Chateh** Can
36C1 **Châtelet** Belg
38C2 **Châtellerault** France
11D3 **Chatfield** USA
35F6 **Chatham** Eng
14E2 **Chatham** Massachusets, USA
7M5 **Chatham** New Brunswick, Can
14D1 **Chatham** New York, USA
4E5 **Chatham** Ontario, Can
13D3 **Chatham** Virginia, USA
77H5 **Chatham Is** NZ
3B3 **Chatham Sd** Can/USA
10M4 **Chatham Str** USA
5J4 **Chéticamp** Can
38C2 **Châtillon** France
36B3 **Châtillon-Coligny** France
36C3 **Châtillon-sur-Siene** France
61B4 **Chatrapur** India
14C3 **Chatsworth** USA
15C2 **Chattahoochee** USA
15B2 **Chattahoochee** *R* USA
9E3 **Chattanooga** USA
37B2 **Châttilon** Italy
55A1 **Chauk** Burma
38D2 **Chaumont** France
36B2 **Chauny** France
55D3 **Chau Phu** Viet
62E3 **Chaura** *I* Indian O
37A1 **Chaussin** France
39A1 **Chaves** Port
44J4 **Chaykovskiy** Russian Fed
39B2 **Chazaouet** Alg
28C2 **Chazón** Arg
26D2 **Chcontá** Colombia
42C2 **Cheb** Czech
44H4 **Cheboksary** Russian Fed
43G2 **Chechersk** Belorussia
53B4 **Chech'on** S Korea
60C3 **Chechro** Pak
17C2 **Checotah** USA
55A2 **Cheduba** *I* Burma
75B1 **Cheepie** Aust
53C1 **Chegdomyn** Russian Fed
70B2 **Chegga** Maur
73D5 **Chegutu** Zim
10D2 **Chegytun'** Russian Fed
18B1 **Chehalis** USA
53B5 **Cheju** S Korea
53B5 **Cheju do** *I* S Korea
53B5 **Cheju-haehyŏp** *Str* S Korea
53E2 **Chekhov** Russian Fed
49P4 **Chekunda** Russian Fed
3D4 **Chelan** USA
18B1 **Chelan,L** USA
45J8 **Cheleken** Turkmenistan
28B3 **Chelforo** Arg
71C1 **Chéliff** *R* Alg
58D1 **Chelkar** Kazakhstan
43E2 **Chelm** Pol
43D2 **Chelmno** Pol
35F6 **Chelmsford** Eng
35D6 **Cheltenham** Eng
44L4 **Chelyabinsk** Russian Fed
73D5 **Chemba** Mozam
42C2 **Chemnitz** USA
14B1 **Chemung** *R* USA
60D2 **Chenab** *R* India/Pak
70B2 **Chenachen** Alg
14C1 **Chenango** *R* USA
18C1 **Cheney** USA
17C2 **Cheney Res** USA
52D1 **Chengda** China
52A3 **Chengdu** China
52E2 **Chengshan Jiao** *Pt* China
52C4 **Chenxi** China
52C4 **Chen Xian** China
52D3 **Cheo Xian** China
26C5 **Chepén** Peru
28B2 **Chepes** Arg
12A1 **Chequamegon B** USA
38C2 **Cher** *R* France
22B2 **Cheran** Mexico
15D2 **Cheraw** USA
38B2 **Cherbourg** France
22B1 **Chercas** Mexico
71C1 **Cherchell** Alg
66C4 **Chercher** Eth
44K3 **Cherdyn** Russian Fed
49M4 **Cheremkhovo** Russian Fed
44F4 **Cherepovets** Russian Fed
45E6 **Cherkassy** Ukraine
45G7 **Cherkessk** Russian Fed
45E5 **Chernigov** Ukraine
43G2 **Chernobyl** Ukraine
45D6 **Chernovtsy** Ukraine
44K4 **Chernushka** Russian Fed
44C5 **Chernyakhovsk** Russian Fed
45H6 **Chernyye Zemli** *Region* Russian Fed
11C3 **Cherokee** Iowa, USA
16C2 **Cherokee** Oklahoma, USA
17C2 **Cherokees,L o'the** USA
28A3 **Cherquenco** Chile
61D2 **Cherrapunji** India
77F2 **Cherry** *I* Solomon Is
49S3 **Cherskiy** Russian Fed
44D5 **Cherven'** Belorussia
43E2 **Chervonograd** Ukraine
13D3 **Chesapeake** USA
13D3 **Chesapeake B** USA
35D5 **Cheshire** County, Eng
14D1 **Cheshire** USA
44H2 **Chëshskaya Guba** *B* Russian Fed
19B2 **Chester** California, USA
35D5 **Chester** Eng
12B3 **Chester** Illinois, USA
14D1 **Chester** Massachusets, USA
18D1 **Chester** Montana, USA
13D3 **Chester** Pennsylvania, USA
15C2 **Chester** S Carolina, USA
3F4 **Chester** USA
14D1 **Chester** Vermont, USA
14B3 **Chester** *R* USA
35E5 **Chesterfield** Eng
7J3 **Chesterfield Inlet** Can
14B3 **Chestertown** USA
13F1 **Chesuncook L** USA
21D3 **Chetumal** Mexico
3D2 **Chetwynd** Can
10E3 **Chevak** USA
78B2 **Cheviot** NZ
33C2 **Cheviots** *Hills* Eng/Scot
3E4 **Chewelah** USA
16B1 **Cheyenne** USA
11B3 **Cheyenne** *R* USA
16B2 **Cheyenne Wells** USA
61B2 **Chhapra** India
61D2 **Chhātak** Bang
60D4 **Chhatarpur** India
60D4 **Chhindwāra** India
61C2 **Chhuka** Bhutan
52E5 **Chia'i** Taiwan
73B5 **Chiange** Angola
55C2 **Chiang Kham** Thai
55B2 **Chiang Mai** Thai
22D2 **Chiapa** *R* Mexico
37C2 **Chiavari** Italy
37C1 **Chiavenna** Italy
53E4 **Chiba** Japan
73B5 **Chibia** Angola
7L4 **Chibougamau** Can
5G4 **Chibougamau L** Can
53B3 **Chiburi-jima** *I* Japan
74E1 **Chibuto** Mozam
9E2 **Chicago** USA
12B2 **Chicago Heights** USA
10L4 **Chichagof I** USA
35E6 **Chichester** Eng
54C3 **Chichibu** Japan
50H4 **Chichi-jima** *I* Japan
9E3 **Chickamauga L** USA
17E3 **Chickasawhay** *R* USA
8D3 **Chickasha** USA
10K3 **Chicken** USA
26B5 **Chiclayo** Peru
8A3 **Chico** USA
25C6 **Chico** *R* Arg
73D5 **Chicoa** Mozam
13E2 **Chicopee** USA
7L5 **Chicoutimi** Can
73D6 **Chicualacuala** Mozam
62B2 **Chidambaram** India
7M3 **Chidley,C** Can
3D2 **Chief** *R* Can
15C3 **Chiefland** USA
70B4 **Chiehn** Lib
73C4 **Chiengi** Zambia
37E3 **Chienti** *R* Italy
37B2 **Chieri** Italy
36C2 **Chiers** *R* France
37C1 **Chiesa** Italy
37D2 **Chiese** *R* Italy
40C2 **Chieti** Italy
52D1 **Chifeng** China
10G4 **Chiginigak,Mt** USA
6C3 **Chigmit Mts** USA
22C2 **Chignahuapán** Mexico
5J4 **Chignecto B** Can
10G4 **Chignik** USA
74E1 **Chigubo** Mozam
21B2 **Chihuahua** Mexico
16A4 **Chihuahua** State, Mexico
62B2 **Chik Ballāpur** India
62B2 **Chikmagalūr** India
10G3 **Chikuminuk L** USA
73D5 **Chikwawa** Malawi
55A1 **Chi-kyaw** Burma
62C1 **Chilakalūrupet** India
22C2 **Chilapa** Mexico
62B3 **Chilaw** Sri Lanka
75D1 **Childers** Aust
16B3 **Childress** USA
24C6 **Chile** Republic
28B1 **Chilecito** La Rioja, Arg
28B2 **Chilecito** Mendoza, Arg
73C5 **Chililabombwe** Zambia
61C3 **Chilka** *L* India
3D3 **Chilko** *R* Can
6F4 **Chilko L** Can
3D3 **Chilkotin** *R* Can
28A3 **Chillán** Chile
28C3 **Chillar** Arg
17D2 **Chillicothe** Missouri, USA
12C3 **Chillicothe** Ohio, USA
3D4 **Chilliwack** Can
61C2 **Chilmari** India
26C4 **Chilmborazo** *Mt* Ecuador
73D5 **Chilongozi** Zambia
18B2 **Chiloquin** USA
21C3 **Chilpancingo** Mexico
35E6 **Chiltern Hills** *Upland* Eng
12B2 **Chilton** USA
73D5 **Chilumba** Malawi
50F4 **Chi-lung** Taiwan
73D5 **Chilwa** *L* Malawi
73D5 **Chimanimani** Zim
36C1 **Chimay** Belg
48G5 **Chimbay** Uzbekistan
26C5 **Chimbote** Peru
48H5 **Chimkent** Kazakhstan
73D5 **Chimoio** Mozam
46F4 **China** Republic, Asia
22A1 **Chinacates** Mexico
20D3 **China L** USA
20D3 **China Lake** USA
China National Republic = Taiwan
21D3 **Chinandega** Nic
16B4 **Chinati Peak** *Mt* USA
26C6 **Chincha Alta** Peru
3E2 **Chinchaga** *R* Can
75D1 **Chinchilla** Aust
73D5 **Chinde** Mozam
54A4 **Chindo** S Korea
61D3 **Chindwin** *R* Burma
73C5 **Chingola** Zambia
73B5 **Chinguar** Angola
70A2 **Chinguetti** Maur
53B4 **Chinhae** S Korea
73D5 **Chinhoyi** Zim
10H4 **Chiniak,C** USA
60C2 **Chiniot** Pak
53B4 **Chinju** S Korea
72C3 **Chinko** *R* CAR
54C3 **Chino** Japan
73D5 **Chinsali** Zambia
40C1 **Chioggia** Italy
73D5 **Chipata** Zambia
4E3 **Chipie** *R* Can
73D6 **Chipinge** Zim
62A1 **Chiplūn** India
3H2 **Chipman** *R* Can
35D6 **Chippenham** Eng
12A1 **Chippewa** *R* USA
9D2 **Chippewa Falls** USA
12A1 **Chippewa,L** USA
26B4 **Chira** *R* Peru
62C1 **Chirāla** India
73D6 **Chiredzi** Zim
72B1 **Chirfa** Niger
19E4 **Chiricahua Peak** *Mt* USA
10G4 **Chirikof I** USA
41F2 **Chirpan** Bulg
26B2 **Chirrípo Grande** *Mt* Costa Rica
77G5 **Chirstchurch** NZ
73C5 **Chirundu** Zim
73C5 **Chisamba** Zambia
7L4 **Chisasibi** Can
11D2 **Chisholm** USA
52B4 **Chishui He** *R* China
68J8 **Chisimaio** Somalia
Chişinău = Kishinev
37B2 **Chisone** Italy
44J4 **Chistopol** Russian Fed
50E1 **Chita** Russian Fed
73B5 **Chitado** Angola
4B3 **Chitek L** Can
73B5 **Chitembo** Angola
10K3 **Chitina** USA
10K3 **Chitina** *R* USA
54D2 **Chitose** Japan
62B2 **Chitradurga** India
60C1 **Chitral** Pak
26B2 **Chitré** Panama
61D3 **Chittagong** Bang
60C4 **Chittaurgarh** India
62B2 **Chittoor** India
73C5 **Chiume** Angola
37D1 **Chiusa** Italy
37D3 **Chiusi** Italy
37B2 **Chivasso** Italy
25D4 **Chivilcoy** Arg
73D5 **Chivu** Zim
53E1 **Chiya, Ozero** *L* Russian Fed
54B3 **Chizu** Japan
54A3 **Choch'iwŏn** S Korea
54A4 **Ch'o-do** *I* S Korea
25C5 **Choele Choel** Arg
28C3 **Choique** Arg
77E1 **Choiseul** *I* Solomon Is
21B2 **Choix** Mexico
43D2 **Chojnice** Pol
54D3 **Chokai-san** *Mt* Japan
72D2 **Choke** *Mts* Eth
49Q2 **Chokurdakh** Russian Fed
20B3 **Cholame** USA
20B3 **Cholame Creek** *R* USA
38B2 **Cholet** France
22C2 **Cholula** Mexico
26A1 **Choluteca** Honduras
73C5 **Choma** Zambia
54A3 **Chŏmch'ŏn** S Korea
61C2 **Chomo Yummo** *Mt* China/India
42C2 **Chomutov** Czech
49M3 **Chona** *R* Russian Fed
53B4 **Ch'ŏnan** S Korea
55C3 **Chon Buri** Thai
54A2 **Chonchon** N Korea
26C4 **Chone** Ecuador
54A3 **Chongdo** S Korea
53B3 **Ch'ŏngjin** N Korea
53B4 **Chongju** N Korea
53B4 **Ch'ŏngju** S Korea
73B5 **Chongoroi** Angola
54A3 **Chongpyong** N Korea
52B4 **Chongqing** China
54A3 **Chŏngsŏn** S Korea
53B4 **Chŏngŭp** S Korea
53B4 **Chŏnju** S Korea
61C2 **Chooyu** *Mt* China/Nepal
29B4 **Chopim** *R* Brazil
43F3 **Chortkov** Ukraine
53B4 **Ch'ŏrwŏn** N Korea
43D2 **Chorzow** Pol
54A2 **Chosan** N Korea
53E4 **Choshi** Japan
28A3 **Chos-Malal** Arg
42D2 **Choszczno** Pol
61B3 **Chotanāgpur** Region, India
18D1 **Choteau** USA
71B2 **Chott ech Chergui** Alg
71D1 **Chott el Hodna** Alg
71D2 **Chott Jerid** Tunisia
71D2 **Chott Melrhir** Alg
20B2 **Chowchilla** USA
49N5 **Choybalsan** Mongolia
78B2 **Christchurch** NZ
74D2 **Christiana** S Africa
7M2 **Christian,C** Can
10M4 **Christian Sd** USA
7N3 **Christianshåb** Greenland
xxviiiG5 **Christmas I** Indian O
48J5 **Chu** Kazakhstan
48J5 **Chu** *R* Kazakhstan
18D2 **Chubbuck** USA
25C6 **Chubut** State, Arg
25C6 **Chubut** *R* Arg
44E4 **Chudovo** Russian Fed
44D1 **Chudskoye, Ozero** *L* Estonia/Russian Fed
6D3 **Chugach Mts** USA
10J3 **Chugiak** USA
10E5 **Chuginadak** *I* USA
54B3 **Chūgoku-sanchi** *Mts* Japan
11B3 **Chugwater** USA
28E2 **Chuí** Brazil
25B5 **Chuillán** Chile
55C5 **Chukai** Malay
Chukchagirskoye, Ozero *L* Russian Fed
10E2 **Chukchi S** Russian Fed/USA

49T3 Chukotskiy Khrebet Mts Russian Fed
49U3 Chukotskiy Poluostrov Pen Russian Fed
55D2 Chu Lai Viet
19C4 Chula Vista USA
10J3 Chulitna USA
50F1 Chulman Russian Fed
26B5 Chulucanas Peru
26E7 Chulumani Bol
48K4 Chulym Russian Fed
49K4 Chulym R Russian Fed
49L4 Chuma R Russian Fed
60D2 Chumar India
28B1 Chumbicha Arg
49P4 Chumikan Russian Fed
55B3 Chumphon Thai
53B4 Ch'unch'ŏn S Korea
61C3 Chunchura India
53B4 Ch'ungju S Korea
Chungking = Chongqing
54A4 Ch'ungmu S Korea
54A3 Chungwa N Korea
73D4 Chunya Tanz
49M3 Chunya R Russian Fed
54A3 Ch'unyang S Korea
23L1 Chupara Pt Trinidad
25C2 Chuquicamata Chile
40B1 Chur Switz
61D3 Churāchāndpur India
49P3 Churapcha Russian Fed
7J4 Churchill Can
7M4 Churchill R Labrador, Can
7J4 Churchill R Manitoba, Can
7J4 Churchill,C Can
7M4 Churchill Falls Can
6H4 Churchill L Can
60C3 Chūru India
22B2 Churumuco Mexico
44K4 Chusovoy Russian Fed
44H4 Chuvashkaya Respublika, Russian Fed
50C4 Chuxiong China
55D3 Chu Yang Sin Mt Viet
56C4 Cianjur Indon
37D2 Ciano d'Enza Italy
29B3 Cianorte Brazil
43E2 Ciechanow Pol
22B2 Ciedad Altamirano Mexico
26D1 Ciedad Ojeda Ven
21E2 Ciego de Avila Cuba
26D1 Ciénaga Colombia
21D2 Cienfuegos Cuba
43D3 Cieszyn Pol
39B2 Cieza Spain
64B2 Cihanbeyli Turk
22B2 Cihuatlán Mexico
56C4 Cijulang Indon
56C4 Cilacap Indon
16B2 Cimarron USA
16C2 Cimarron R USA
37B3 Cime du Cheiron Mt France
41F1 Cîmpina Rom
39C1 Cinca R Spain
40D2 Činčer Mt Bosnia & Herzegovina, Yugos
9E3 Cincinnati USA
41E1 Cindrelu Mt Rom
41F3 Cine R Turk
36C1 Ciney Belg
22D2 Cintalapa Mexico
28B3 Cipolletti Arg
6D3 Circle Alaska, USA
11A2 Circle Montana, USA
12C3 Circleville USA
56C4 Cirebon Indon
35E6 Cirencester Eng
16C3 Cisco USA
37D2 Citadella Italy
21C3 Citlaltepetl Mt Mexico
74B3 Citrusdal S Africa
40C2 Citta del Vaticano Italy
40C2 Città di Castello Italy
21B2 Ciudad Acuña Mexico
26F2 Ciudad Bolivar Ven
21B2 Ciudad Camargo Mexico
21C3 Ciudad del Carmen Mexico
39C2 Ciudadela Spain
26F2 Ciudad Guayana Ven
21B3 Ciudad Guzman Mexico
22B2 Ciudad Hidalgo Mexico
21B1 Ciudad Juárez Mexico
8C4 Ciudad Lerdo Mexico
21C2 Ciudad Madero Mexico
22C2 Ciudad Mendoza Mexico
21B2 Ciudad Obregon Mexico
23C4 Ciudad Ojeda Ven
26F2 Ciudad Piar Ven
39B2 Ciudad Real Spain
39A1 Ciudad Rodrigo Spain
21C2 Ciudad Valles Mexico
21C2 Ciudad Victoria Mexico
37E1 Cividale del Friuli Italy
37E3 Civitanova Marche Italy
40C2 Civitavecchia Italy
64D2 Cizre Turk
35F6 Clacton-on-Sea Eng
6G4 Claire,L Can
13D2 Clairton USA
37A1 Clairvaux France
15B2 Clanton USA
74B3 Clanwilliam S Africa
35B5 Clara Irish Rep
28D3 Claraz Arg
12C2 Clare USA
13E2 Claremont USA
17C2 Claremore USA
75D1 Clarence R Aust
78B2 Clarence R NZ
76C2 Clarence Str Aust
10M4 Clarence Str USA
17D3 Clarendon USA
5L4 Clarenville Can
7N5 Clarenville Can
6G4 Claresholm Can
17C1 Clarinda USA
11D3 Clarion Iowa, USA
13D2 Clarion Pennsylvania, USA
21A3 Clarión I Mexico
13D2 Clarion R USA
xxixM4 Clarion Fracture Zone Pacific O
9E3 Clark Hill Res USA
10O3 Clark,Mt Can
19C3 Clark Mt USA
12C2 Clark,Pt Can
12C3 Clarksburg USA
9D3 Clarksdale USA
10G4 Clarks Point USA
18C1 Clarkston USA
17D2 Clarksville Arkansas, USA
15B1 Clarksville Tennessee, USA
29B2 Claro R Brazil
25E5 Claromecó Arg
17C2 Clay Center USA
34E2 Claymore Oilfield N Sea
3C4 Clayoquot Sd Can
8C3 Clayton New Mexico, USA
13D2 Clayton New York, USA
33B3 Clear C Irish Rep
10J4 Cleare,C USA
14A2 Clearfield Pennsylvania, USA
18D2 Clearfield Utah, USA
3E2 Clear Hills Mts Can
19B3 Clear L USA
11D3 Clear Lake USA
18B2 Clear Lake Res USA
11A3 Clearmont USA
3D3 Clearwater Can
9E4 Clearwater USA
3F2 Clearwater R Can
3D3 Clearwater L Can
18C1 Clearwater Mts USA
8D3 Cleburne USA
35F4 Cleeton Oilfield N Sea
20B1 Clements USA
57E8 Cleopatra Needle Mt Phil
76D3 Clermont Aust
36B2 Clermont France
36C2 Clermont-en-Argonne France
38C2 Clermont-Ferrand France
36D1 Clervaux Germany
37D1 Cles Italy
75A2 Cleve Aust
35E4 Cleveland County, Eng
17D3 Cleveland Mississippi, USA
9E2 Cleveland Ohio, USA
15C1 Cleveland Tennessee, USA
17C3 Cleveland Texas, USA
29B4 Clevelândia Brazil
18D1 Cleveland,Mt USA
33B3 Clew B Irish Rep
19E4 Clifton Arizona, USA
75D1 Clifton Aust
14C2 Clifton New Jersey, USA
75A1 Clifton Hills Aust
3J2 Clifton L Can
3G4 Climax Can
15C1 Clinch R USA
15C1 Clinch Mts USA
17D2 Clinton Arkansas, USA
6F4 Clinton Can
14D2 Clinton Connecticut, USA
12A2 Clinton Iowa, USA
14E1 Clinton Massachusetts, USA
17D3 Clinton Mississippi, USA
17D2 Clinton Missouri, USA
15D2 Clinton N Carolina, USA
14C2 Clinton New Jersey, USA
16C2 Clinton Oklahoma, USA
6H3 Clinton-Colden L Can
21B3 Clipperton I Pacific O
26E7 Cliza Bol
28C1 Clodomira Arg
76D3 Cloncurry Aust
35B4 Clones Irish Rep
35B5 Clonmel Irish Rep
9D2 Cloquet USA
29A4 Clorinda Arg
11A3 Cloud Peak Mt USA
10G3 Cloudy Mt USA
20A1 Cloverdale USA
20C2 Clovis California, USA
8C3 Clovis New Mexico, USA
45C6 Cluj Rom
41E1 Cluj-Napoca Rom
37B1 Cluses France
37C2 Clusone Italy
78A3 Clutha R NZ
35D5 Clwyd County, Wales
7M2 Clyde Can
78A3 Clyde NZ
14B1 Clyde USA
34C4 Clyde R Scot
19C4 Coachella USA
22B2 Coahuayana Mexico
16B4 Coahuila State, Mexico
10N3 Coal R Can
22B2 Coalcomán Mexico
3F4 Coaldale Can
19C3 Coaldale USA
19B3 Coalinga USA
18D2 Coalville USA
29E1 Coaraci Brazil
26F5 Coari R Brazil
15B2 Coastal Plain USA
6E4 Coast Mts Can
8A2 Coast Ranges Mts USA
34C4 Coatbridge Scot
22C2 Coatepec Mexico
14C3 Coatesville USA
13E1 Coaticook Can
7K3 Coats I Can
79F1 Coats Land Region, Ant
21C3 Coatzacoalcas Mexico
22D2 Coatzacoalcos R Mexico
7L5 Cobalt Can
21C3 Cobán Guatemala
76D4 Cobar Aust
75C3 Cobargo Aust
4C3 Cobham R Can
26E6 Cobija Bol
14C1 Cobleskill USA
39B2 Cobo de Palos C Spain
7L5 Cobourg Can
76C2 Cobourg Pen Aust
42C2 Coburg Germany
26C4 Coca Ecuador
15C3 Coca USA
29B1 Cocalinho Brazil
26E7 Cochabamba Bol
36D1 Cochem Germany
3F3 Cochrane Alberta, Can
7K5 Cochrane Ontario, Can
3H2 Cochrane R Can
75B2 Cockburn Aust
14B3 Cockeysville USA
23H1 Cockpit Country,The Jamaica
74C3 Cockscomb Mt S Africa
21D3 Coco R Honduras/Nic
72A3 Cocobeach Gabon
62E2 Coco Channel Andaman Is
29D1 Côcos Brazil
23L1 Cocos B Trinidad
xxviiiF5 Cocos Is Indian O
xxixP4 Cocos Ridge Pacific O
22B1 Cocula Mexico
34G3 Cod Oilfield N Sea
9F2 Cod,C USA
78A3 Codfish I NZ
7M4 Cod I Can
37E2 Codigoro Italy
27K4 Codó Brazil
37C2 Codogno Italy
8C2 Cody USA
51H8 Coen Aust
42B2 Coesfeld Germany
3E4 Coeur d'Alene USA
8D3 Coffeyville USA
75A2 Coffin B Aust
75D2 Coff's Harbour Aust
74D3 Cofimvaba S Africa
22C2 Cofre de Perote Mt Mexico
38B2 Cognac France
14B1 Cohocton USA
14B1 Cohocton R USA
13E2 Cohoes USA
75B3 Cohuna Aust
25B7 Coihaique Chile
62B2 Coimbatore India
39A1 Coimbra Port
26B3 Cojimies Ecuador
18D2 Cokeville USA
76D4 Colac Aust
27K7 Colatina Brazil
79F6 Colbeck,C Ant
16B2 Colby USA
35F6 Colchester Eng
14D2 Colchester USA
37B1 Col de la Faucille France
3F3 Cold L Can
40B1 Col du Grand St Bernard P Switz/Italy
37B2 Col du Lautaret P France
40B1 Col du Mont Cenis P Italy/France
38D2 Col du Mt Cenis P Italy
12C2 Coldwater USA
4D4 Coldwell Can
10K2 Coleen R USA
18D1 Coleman Can
12C2 Coleman Michigan, USA
16C3 Coleman Texas, USA
74D2 Colenso S Africa
34B4 Coleraine N Ire
78B2 Coleridge,L NZ
74D3 Colesberg S Africa
20C1 Coleville USA
19B3 Colfax California, USA
17D3 Colfax Louisiana, USA
18C1 Colfax Washington, USA
21B3 Colima Mexico
22B2 Colima State, Mexico
28A2 Colina Chile
34B3 Coll I Scot
75C1 Collarenebri Aust
40B2 Colle de Tende P Italy/France
37D3 Colle di Val d'Elsa Italy
10J3 College USA
15C2 College Park Georgia, USA
14B3 College Park Washington, USA
17C3 College Station USA
76A4 Collie Aust
76B2 Collier B Aust
37D3 Colline Metallifere Mts Italy
36A1 Collines de L'Artois Mts France
36B2 Collines De Thiérache France
36A2 Collines du Perche Mts France
4E5 Collingwood Can
78B2 Collingwood NZ
17E3 Collins Mississippi, USA
14A1 Collins New York, USA
6H2 Collinson Pen Can
76D3 Collinsville Aust
12B3 Collinsville Illinois, USA
17C2 Collinsville Oklahoma, USA
28A3 Collipulli Chile
38D2 Colmar France
28C1 Colmena Arg
36A1 Colne R Eng
Cologne = Köln
29C3 Colômbia Brazil
26D3 Colombia Republic, S America
13D3 Colombia USA
62B3 Colombo Sri Lanka
25E4 Colón Arg
21D2 Colon Cuba
26C2 Colón Panama
25E4 Colonia Urug
28D2 Colonia del Sacramento Urug
28B3 Colonia 25 de Mayo Arg
28C1 Colonia Dora Arg
28B3 Colonia Josefa Arg
25C7 Colonia Las Heras Arg
13D3 Colonial Heights USA
34B3 Colonsay I Scot
23E5 Coloradito Ven
8C3 Colorado State, USA
8B3 Colorado R Arizona, USA
25D5 Colorado R Buenos Aires, Arg
28B1 Colorado R La Rioja, Arg
8D3 Colorado R Texas, USA
16B3 Colorado City USA
8B3 Colorado Plat USA
8C3 Colorado Springs USA
22B1 Colptlán Mexico
14B3 Columbia Maryland, USA
17E3 Columbia Mississippi, USA
9D3 Columbia Missouri, USA
13D2 Columbia Pennsylvania, USA
9E3 Columbia S Carolina, USA
9E3 Columbia Tennessee, USA
3E3 Columbia R Can
8A2 Columbia R USA
18D1 Columbia Falls USA
6G4 Columbia,Mt Can
18C1 Columbia Plat USA
74B3 Columbine,C S Africa
9E3 Columbus Georgia, USA
12B3 Columbus Indiana, USA
9E3 Columbus Mississippi, USA
18E1 Columbus Montana, USA
8D2 Columbus Nebraska, USA
16A3 Columbus New Mexico, USA
9E2 Columbus Ohio, USA
17C4 Columbus Texas, USA
12B2 Columbus Wisconsin, USA
18C1 Colville USA
6C3 Colville R USA
78C1 Colville,C NZ
6F3 Colville L Can
35D5 Colwyn Bay Wales
37E2 Comacchio Italy
22D2 Comalcalco Mexico
16C3 Comanche USA
20B1 Comanche Res USA
21D3 Comayagua Honduras
28A2 Combarbalá Chile
35C4 Comber N Ire
61D4 Combermere B Burma
36C3 Combeufontaine France
37E1 Comeglians Italy
35B5 Comeragh Mts Irish Rep
16C3 Comfort USA
61D3 Comilla Bang
21C3 Comitán Mexico
36C2 Commercy France
7K3 Committee B Can
40B1 Como Italy
25C7 Comodoro Rivadavia Arg
22B1 Comonfort Mexico
62B3 Comorin,C India
73E5 Comoros Is Indian O
38C2 Compiègne France
22B1 Compostela Mexico
28B2 Comte Salas Arg
61D2 Cona China
70A4 Conakry Guinea
28A1 Conay Chile
28B2 Concarán Arg
38B2 Concarneau France
29E2 Conceiçao da Barra Brazil
27J5 Conceição do Araguaia Brazil
29D2 Conceiçao do Mato Dentro Brazil
28B1 Concepción Arg
29A3 Concepción Brazil/Par
25B5 Concepción Chile
25E2 Concepción Par
25E4 Concepción R Arg
21B2 Concepcion del Oro Mexico
28D2 Concepcion del Uruguay Arg
74A1 Conception B Namibia
8A3 Conception,Pt USA
29C3 Conchas Brazil
16B2 Conchas L USA
36A2 Conches France
8C4 Conchos R Mexico
19B3 Concord California, USA
9F2 Concord New Hampshire, USA
15C1 Concord North Carolina, USA
25E4 Concordia Arg
22A1 Concordia Mexico
8D3 Concordia USA
18B1 Concrete USA
75D1 Condamine Aust
29D1 Condeuba Brazil
76D4 Condobolin Aust
18B1 Condon USA
36C1 Condroz, Mts Belg
27H8 Condrina Brazil
15B2 Conecuh R USA
37E2 Conegliano Italy
14B1 Conesus L USA
29A3 Confuso R Par
68F8 Congo Republic, Africa
68F8 Congo R Congo
Congo,R = Zaïre,R
12C1 Coniston Can
12C2 Conneaut USA
9F2 Connecticut State, USA
13E2 Connecticut R USA
13D2 Connellsville USA
36A2 Connerré France
12B3 Connersville USA
75B2 Conoble Aust
18D1 Conrad USA
17C3 Conroe USA
29D3 Conselheiro Lafaiete Brazil
55D4 Con Son Is Viet
Constance,L = Bodensee
45D7 Constanta Rom
71D1 Constantine Alg
10G4 Constantine,C USA
25B5 Constitución Chile
28D2 Constitución Urug
3G4 Consul Can
18D2 Contact USA
37E2 Contarina Italy
27K6 Contas R Brazil
22C2 Contreras Mexico

36C2 **Contrexéville** France
6H3 **Contwoyto L** Can
9D3 **Conway** Arkansas, USA
13E2 **Conway** New Hampshire, USA
15D2 **Conway** South Carolina, USA
75A1 **Conway,L** Aust
35D5 **Conwy** Wales
76C3 **Coober Pedy** Aust
3C3 **Cook,C** Can
15B1 **Cookeville** USA
6C3 **Cook Inlet** *B* USA
xxixL5 **Cook Is** Pacific O
78B2 **Cook,Mt** NZ
77G5 **Cook Str** NZ
76D2 **Cooktown** Aust
75C2 **Coolabah** Aust
75C1 **Cooladdi** Aust
75C2 **Coolah** Aust
75C2 **Coolamon** Aust
76B4 **Coolgardie** Aust
19D4 **Coolidge** USA
75C3 **Cooma** Aust
75C2 **Coonabarabran** Aust
75C2 **Coonambie** Aust
75B2 **Coonbah** Aust
75A2 **Coondambo** Aust
62A2 **Coondapoor** India
75C1 **Coongoola** Aust
62B2 **Coonoor** India
75B1 **Cooper Basin** Aust
76C3 **Cooper Creek** Aust
75B1 **Cooper Creek** *R* Aust
14C1 **Cooperstown** New York, USA
11C2 **Cooperstown** North Dakota, USA
75A3 **Coorong,The** Aust
75D1 **Cooroy** Aust
18B2 **Coos B** USA
18B2 **Coos Bay** USA
76D4 **Cootamundra** Aust
35B4 **Cootehill** Irish Rep
28B1 **Copacabana** Arg
22C2 **Copala** Mexico
22C2 **Copalillo** Mexico
16B2 **Cope** USA
Copenhagen = København
25B3 **Copiapó** Chile
28B1 **Copiapó** *R* Chile
37D2 **Copparo** Italy
10K3 **Copper** *R* USA
6D3 **Copper Center** USA
4E4 **Copper Cliff** Can
12B1 **Copper Harbor** USA
6G3 **Coppermine** Can
6G3 **Coppermine** *R* Can
12C1 **Coppermine Pt** Can
22A1 **Co Prieto** *Mt* Mexico
Coquilhatville = Mbandaka
25B3 **Coquimbo** Chile
41E2 **Corabia** Rom
15E4 **Coral Gables** USA
7K3 **Coral Harbour** Can
76E2 **Coral S** Aust/PNG
xxviiiJ5 **Coral Sea Basin** Pacific O
76E2 **Coral Sea Island Territories** Aust
75B3 **Corangamite,L** Aust
27G3 **Corantijn** *R* Surinam/Guyana
36B2 **Corbeil-Essonnes** France
12C3 **Corbin** USA
20C2 **Corcoran** USA
39A1 **Corcubion** Spain
38A3 **Cord Cantabrica** *Mts* Spain
9E3 **Cordele** USA
39A1 **Cordillera Cantabrica** *Mts* Spain
23C3 **Cordillera Central** *Mts* Dom Rep
57F7 **Cordillera Central** *Mts* Phil
28B2 **Cordillera de Ansita** *Mts* Arg
29A4 **Cordillera de Caaguazú** Par
28A1 **Cordillera de la Punilla** *Mts* Chile
26C5 **Cordillera de los Andes** *Mts* Peru
25C3 **Cordillera del Toro** *Mt* Arg
26D2 **Cordillera de Mérida** Ven
28A3 **Cordillera de Viento** *Mts* Arg
21D3 **Cordillera Isabelia** *Mts* Nicaragua
26C2 **Cordillera Occidental** *Mts* Colombia
26C3 **Cordillera Oriental** *Mts* Colombia
75B1 **Cordillo Downs** Aust
25D4 **Córdoba** Arg
21C3 **Córdoba** Mexico
39B2 **Córdoba** Spain
25D4 **Córdoba** State, Arg
6D3 **Cordova** USA
10M5 **Cordova B** USA
Corfu = Kérkira
29D1 **Coribe** Brazil
75D2 **Coricudgy,Mt** Aust
40D3 **Corigliano Calabro** Italy
9E3 **Corinth** Mississippi, USA
14D1 **Corinth** New York, USA
27K7 **Corinto** Brazil
33B3 **Cork** Irish Rep
64A1 **Çorlu** Turk
4A3 **Cormorant** Can
3H3 **Cormorant L** Can
27K7 **Cornel Fabriciano** Brazil
29B3 **Cornelio Procópio** Brazil
7N5 **Corner Brook** Can
75C3 **Corner Inlet** *B* Aust
36D3 **Cornimont** France
13D2 **Corning** USA
7L5 **Cornwall** Can
35C6 **Cornwall** County, Eng
35C6 **Cornwall,C** Eng
6H2 **Cornwall I** Can
7J2 **Cornwallis I** Can
26D1 **Coro** Ven
27K4 **Coroatá** Brazil
26E7 **Coroico** Bol
29C2 **Coromandel** Brazil
62C2 **Coromandel Coast** India
78C1 **Coromandel Pen** NZ
78C1 **Coromandel Range** *Mts* NZ
20D4 **Corona** California, USA
16A3 **Corona** New Mexico, USA
3F3 **Coronation** Can
6G3 **Coronation G** Can
28C2 **Coronda** Arg
25B5 **Coronel** Chile
28D3 **Coronel Brandsen** Arg
28C3 **Coronel Dorrego** Arg
29D2 **Coronel Fabriciano** Brazil
25E3 **Coronel Oviedo** Par
25D5 **Coronel Pringles** Arg
28C3 **Coronel Suárez** Arg
28D3 **Coronel Vidal** Arg
26D7 **Coropuna** *Mt* Peru
75C3 **Corowa** Aust
38D3 **Corps** France
8D4 **Corpus Christi** USA
17F4 **Corpus Christi,L** USA
28A3 **Corral** Chile
57F8 **Corregidor** *I* Phil
29D1 **Corrente** *R* Bahia, Brazil
29C1 **Corrente** *R* Goias, Brazil
29B2 **Corrente** *R* Mato Grosso, Brazil
29D1 **Correntina** Brazil
25E3 **Corrientes** Arg
25E3 **Corrientes** State, Arg
28D1 **Corrientes** *R* Arg
17D3 **Corrigan** USA
76A4 **Corrigin** Aust
76E2 **Corringe Is** Aust
4F5 **Corry** USA
75C3 **Corryong** Aust
40B2 **Corse** *I* Medit S
34C4 **Corsewall** *Pt* Scot
Corsica = Corse
8D3 **Corsicana** USA
40B2 **Corte** Corse
8C3 **Cortez** USA
40C1 **Cortina d'Ampezzo** Italy
13D2 **Cortland** USA
37D3 **Cortona** Italy
22B2 **Coruca de Catalan** Mexico
45G7 **Çoruh** *R* Turk
45F7 **Çorum** Turk
27G7 **Corumbá** Brazil
29C2 **Corumba** *R* Brazil
29C2 **Corumbaiba** Brazil
18B2 **Corvallis** USA
70A1 **Corvo** *I* Açores
35D5 **Corwen** Wales
10E4 **Corwin,C** USA
22A1 **Cosala** Mexico
22C2 **Coscomatopec** Mexico
40D3 **Cosenza** Italy
73E5 **Cosmoledo** *Is* Seychelles
20D2 **Coso Junction** USA
28C2 **Cosquín** Arg
39B2 **Costa Blanca** Region, Spain
39C1 **Costa Brava** Region, Spain
39B2 **Costa de la Luz** Region, Spain
39B2 **Costa del Sol** Region, Spain
20D4 **Costa Mesa** USA
21D3 **Costa Rica** Republic, C America
57F9 **Cotabato** Phil
26E8 **Cotagaita** Bol
3G3 **Coteau, The** Region, Can
38D3 **Côte d'Azur** Region, France
36C3 **Côte-d'Or** Department, France
36C2 **Côtes de Meuse** *Mts* France
71G4 **Cotonou** Benin
26C4 **Cotopaxi** *Mt* Ecuador
35D6 **Cotswold Hills** *Upland* Eng
18B2 **Cottage Grove** USA
42C2 **Cottbus** Germany
19D4 **Cottonwood** USA
17F4 **Cotulla** USA
14A2 **Coudersport** USA
75A3 **Couedic,C du** Aust
18C1 **Couer d'Alene L** USA
36B2 **Coulommiers** France
37A3 **Coulon** *R* France
4F4 **Coulonge** *R* Can
20B2 **Coulterville** USA
6B3 **Council** USA
8D2 **Council Bluffs** USA
43E1 **Courland Lagoon** *Lg* Lithuania/Russian Fed
37B2 **Courmayeur** Italy
36A2 **Courtalain** France
3C4 **Courtenay** Can
Courtrai = Kortrijk
38B2 **Coutances** France
5K4 **Couteau,Blue Hills of** Can
35E5 **Coventry** Eng
39A1 **Covilhã** Spain
15C2 **Covington** Georgia, USA
12C3 **Covington** Kentucky, USA
17D3 **Covington** Louisiana, USA
13D3 **Covington** Virginia, USA
75C2 **Cowal,L** Aust
75B3 **Cowangie** Aust
5G4 **Cowansville** Can
75A1 **Coward Springs** Aust
75A2 **Cowell** Aust
75C3 **Cowes** Aust
18B1 **Cowichan L** Can
18B1 **Cowiltz** *R* USA
75C2 **Cowra** Aust
28D2 **Coxilha de Santana** *Mts* Brazil/Urug
28E1 **Coxilha Grande** *Mts* Brazil
27H7 **Coxim** Brazil
29B2 **Coxim** *R* Brazil
14D1 **Coxsackie** USA
61D3 **Cox's Bazar** Bang
22A1 **Coyobitan** Mexico
22B2 **Coyuca de Benitez** Mexico
16C1 **Cozad** USA
75D1 **Cracow** Aust
43D2 **Cracow** Pol
74D3 **Cradock** S Africa
8C2 **Craig** USA
42C3 **Crailsheim** Germany
41E2 **Craiova** Rom
13E2 **Cranberry L** USA
6G5 **Cranbrook** Can
18C2 **Crane** Oregon, USA
16B3 **Crane** Texas, USA
14E2 **Cranston** USA
18B2 **Crater L** USA
18B2 **Crater Lake Nat Pk** USA
27K5 **Crateus** Brazil
27L5 **Crato** Brazil
11B3 **Crawford** USA
12B2 **Crawfordsville** USA
15C2 **Crawfordville** USA
35E6 **Crawley** Eng
18D1 **Crazy Mts** USA
3G3 **Crean L** Can
3G2 **Cree** *R* Can
6H4 **Cree L** Can
36B2 **Creil** France
37C2 **Crema** Italy
37A2 **Crémieu** France
40C1 **Cremona** Italy
14E2 **Crentral Falls** USA
36B2 **Crépy-en-Valois** France
40C2 **Cres** *I* Croatia, Yugos
18B2 **Crescent** USA
8A2 **Crescent City** USA
11D3 **Cresco** USA
28C2 **Crespo** Arg
3E4 **Creston** Can
17D1 **Creston** USA
15B2 **Crestview** USA
75B3 **Creswick** Aust
37A1 **Crêt de la Neige** *Mt* France
Crete = Kríti
17C1 **Crete** USA
41E3 **Crete,S of** Greece
38C2 **Creuse** *R* France
35D5 **Crewe** Eng
34C3 **Crianlarich** Scot
25G3 **Criciuma** Brazil
34D3 **Crieff** Scot
10L4 **Crillon,Mt** USA
29C2 **Cristalina** Brazil
29B1 **Cristalina** *R* Brazil
29C1 **Crixás** Brazil
29C1 **Crixás Acu** *R* Brazil
29B1 **Crixás Mirim** *R* Brazil
40D1 **Croatia** Republic, Yugos
56E1 **Crocker Range** *Mts* Malay
17C3 **Crockett** USA
11C3 **Crofton** USA
76C2 **Croker I** Aust
4C2 **Cromarty** Can
34D3 **Cromarty** Scot
35F5 **Cromer** Eng
78A3 **Cromwell** NZ
9F4 **Crooked** *I* Bahamas
3D3 **Crooked** *R* Can
8D2 **Crookston** USA
75C2 **Crookwell** Aust
75D1 **Croppa Creek** Aust
11D2 **Crosby** USA
4B3 **Cross L** Can
71H4 **Cross** *R* Nig
74A1 **Cross,C** *C* Namibia
9D3 **Crossett** USA
71H4 **Cross River** State, Nig
10L4 **Cross Sd** USA
15B1 **Crossville** USA
40D3 **Crotone** Italy
17D3 **Crowley** USA
20C2 **Crowley,L** USA
23K1 **Crown Pt** Tobago
75D1 **Crows Nest** Aust
76D2 **Croydon** Aust
35E6 **Croydon** Eng
xxviiiE6 **Crozet Basin** Indian O
6F2 **Crozier Chan** Can
22C1 **Cruillas** Mexico
25F3 **Cruz Alta** Brazil
21E3 **Cruz,C** Cuba
25D4 **Cruz del Eje** Arg
29D3 **Cruzeiro** Brazil
26D5 **Cruzeiro do Sul** Brazil
3D2 **Crysdale,Mt** Can
75A2 **Crystal Brook** Aust
17D2 **Crystal City** Missouri, USA
17F4 **Crystal City** Texas, USA
12B1 **Crystal Falls** USA
73D5 **Cuamba** Mozam
73C5 **Cuando** *R* Angola
73B5 **Cuangar** Angola
Cuango,R = Kwango,R
28C2 **Cuarto, R** Arg
21B2 **Cuauhtémoc** Mexico
22C2 **Cuautla** Mexico
21D2 **Cuba** Republic, Caribbean
14A1 **Cuba** USA
73B5 **Cubango** *R* Angola
73B5 **Cuchi** Angola
73B5 **Cuchi** *R* Angola
28D2 **Cuchilla de Haedo** *Mts* Urug
28D2 **Cuchilla Grande** *Mts* Urug
28C3 **Cuchillo Có** Arg
26E3 **Cucui** Brazil
26D2 **Cúcuta** Colombia
62B2 **Cuddalore** India
62B2 **Cuddapah** India
20D3 **Cuddeback L** USA
76A3 **Cue** Aust
26C4 **Cuenca** Ecuador
39B1 **Cuenca** Spain
22B1 **Cuencame** Mexico
21C3 **Cuernavaca** Mexico
17C4 **Cuero** USA
27G7 **Cuiabá** Brazil
29A1 **Cuiabá** *R* Brazil
22C2 **Cuicatlan** Mexico
29D2 **Cuieté** *R* Brazil
34B3 **Cuillin Hills** *Mts* Scot
73B4 **Cuilo** *R* Angola
37A1 **Cuiseaux** France
73B5 **Cuito** *R* Angola
73B5 **Cuito Cunavale** Angola
22B2 **Cuitzeo** Mexico
55D3 **Cu Lao Hon** *I* Viet
11B2 **Culbertson** Montana, USA
16B1 **Culbertson** Nebraska, USA
75C3 **Culcairn** Aust
75C1 **Culgoa** *R* Aust
21B2 **Culiacán** Mexico
57E8 **Culion** *I* Phil
15B2 **Cullman** USA
37A2 **Culoz** France
13D3 **Culpeper** USA
15E4 **Culter Ridge** USA
29B1 **Culuene** *R* Brazil
78B2 **Culverden** NZ
26F1 **Cumaná** Ven
9F3 **Cumberland** Maryland, USA
12A1 **Cumberland** Wisconsin, USA
9E3 **Cumberland** *R* USA
3H3 **Cumberland L** Can
7M3 **Cumberland Pen** Can
12C3 **Cumberland Plat** USA
7M3 **Cumberland Sd** Can
35D4 **Cumbria** Eng
19B3 **Cummings** USA
75A2 **Cummins** Aust
34C4 **Cumnock** Scot
28A3 **Cunco** Chile
73B5 **Cunene** *R* Angola/Namibia
40B2 **Cuneo** Italy
76D3 **Cunnamulla** Aust
34D3 **Cupar** Scot
41E2 **Čuprija** Serbia, Yugos
23D4 **Curaçao** *I* Caribbean
28A3 **Curacautin** Chile
28B3 **Curaco** *R* Arg
28A3 **Curanilahue** Chile
28A3 **Curepto** Chile
25B4 **Curicó** Chile
29B1 **Curisevo** *R* Brazil
25G3 **Curitiba** Brazil
75A2 **Curnamona** Aust
73B5 **Curoca** *R* Angola
28D1 **Curuzú Cuatiá** Arg
27K7 **Curvelo** Brazil
14A2 **Curwensville** USA
17C2 **Cushing** USA
18E1 **Custer** Montana, USA
11B3 **Custer** S Dakota, USA
18D1 **Cut Bank** USA
3E3 **Cutbank** *R* Can
15C2 **Cuthbert** USA
28B3 **Cutral-Có** Arg
61C3 **Cuttack** India
73B5 **Cuvelai** Angola
42B2 **Cuxhaven** Germany
12C2 **Cuyahoga Falls** USA
20C3 **Cuyama,R** USA
57F8 **Cuyo Is** Phil
26D6 **Cuzco** Peru
72C4 **Cyangugu** Zaïre
Cyclades = Kikládhes
3F4 **Cypress Hills, Mts** Can
64B3 **Cyprus** Republic, Medit S
7M3 **Cyrus Field B** Can
43D3 **Czechoslovakia** Republic, Europe
43D2 **Częstochowa** Pol

D

55C1 **Da** *R* Viet
53A2 **Da'an** China
65D3 **Dab'a** Jordan
23C4 **Dabajuro** Ven
69D4 **Dabaro** Somalia
52B3 **Daba Shan** *Mts* China
72D2 **Dabat** Eth
60C4 **Dabhoi** India
52C3 **Dabie Shan** *U* China
70A3 **Dabola** Guinea
70B4 **Dabou** Ivory Coast
71F4 **Daboya** Ghana
43D2 **Dabrowa Gorn** Pol
42C3 **Dachau** Germany
40C1 **Dachstein** *Mt* Austria
52A3 **Dada He** *R* China
66D4 **Daddato** Djibouti
15C3 **Dade City** USA
60B3 **Dadhar** Pak
60B3 **Dadu** Pak
50D3 **Dadu He** *R* China
57F8 **Daet** Phil
52B4 **Dafang** China
55B2 **Daga** *R* Burma
70A3 **Dagana** Sen
72E3 **Dageh Bur** Eth
45H7 **Dagestanskaya** Respublika, Russian Fed
57F7 **Dagupan** Phil
61D2 **Dagzê** China
64B4 **Dahab** Egypt
49O5 **Da Hinggan Line** *Mts* China
15C2 **Dahlonega** USA
60C4 **Dāhod** India
39C2 **Dahra** Region, Alg
61B2 **Dailekh** Nepal
28C3 **Daireaux** Arg
66B1 **Dairût** Egypt
50G4 **Daitō** *Is* Pacific Oc
76C3 **Dajarra** Aust
71F4 **Daka** *R* Ghana
70A3 **Dakar** Sen
70A2 **Dakhla** Mor
69B2 **Dakhla Oasis** Egypt
70C3 **Dakoro** Niger
11C3 **Dakota City** USA
41E2 **Dakovica** Serbia, Yugos
41D1 **Dakovo** Croatia, Yugos
73C5 **Dala** Angola
70A3 **Dalaba** Guinea
52D1 **Dalai Nur** *L* China
44B3 **Dalälven** *R* Sweden
50D2 **Dalandzadgad** Mongolia
57F8 **Dalanganem Is** Phil
55D3 **Da Lat** Viet

52A1 **Dalay** Mongolia
63E3 **Dalbandin** Pak
76E3 **Dalby** Aust
15B1 **Dale Hollow L** USA
32F7 **Dalen** Nor
35D4 **Dales,The** *Upland* Eng
15B2 **Daleville** USA
8C3 **Dalhart** USA
5H4 **Dalhousie** Can
6E2 **Dalhousie,C** Can
52E2 **Dalian** China
65B1 **Dalion** *Hist Site* Cyprus
8D3 **Dallas** USA
18B1 **Dalles,The** USA
10M5 **Dall I** USA
61B3 **Dalli Rajhara** India
70C3 **Dallol** *R* Niger
71G3 **Dallol Bosso** *R* Niger
71G3 **Dallol Maouri** *R* Niger
40D2 **Dalmatia** *Region* Bosnia & Herzegovina, Yugos
53D3 **Dal'negorsk** Russian Fed
53C2 **Dal'nerechensk** Russian Fed
70B4 **Daloa** Ivory Coast
52B4 **Dalou Shan** *Mts* China
61B3 **Dāltenganj** India
4E4 **Dalton** Can
15C2 **Dalton** Georgia, USA
14D1 **Dalton** Massachusetts, USA
56B2 **Daludalu** Indon
76C2 **Daly** *R* Aust
19B3 **Daly City** USA
76C2 **Daly Waters** Aust
57F9 **Damaguete** Phil
60C4 **Damān** India
64B3 **Damanhûr** Egypt
76B1 **Damar** *I* Indon
72B3 **Damara** CAR
64C3 **Damascus** Syria
14B3 **Damascus** USA
71J3 **Damaturu** Nig
63C1 **Damavand** Iran
73B4 **Damba** Angola
62C3 **Dambulla** Sri Lanka
63C1 **Damghan** Iran
Damietta = Dumyât
60D4 **Damoh** India
71F4 **Damongo** Ghana
72E3 **Damot** Eth
65C2 **Damour** Leb
76A3 **Dampier** Aust
67F3 **Damqawt** Yemen
65C3 **Danā** Jordan
66D4 **Danakil** Region, Eth
20C2 **Dana,Mt** USA
70B4 **Danané** Lib
55D2 **Da Nang** Viet
57F8 **Danao** Phil
57B3 **Danau Poso** *Mt* Indon
56A2 **Danau Tobu** *L* Indon
57B3 **Danau Tuwuti** *L* Indon
52A3 **Danbu** China
13E2 **Danbury** USA
14D1 **Danby** USA
61B2 **Dandeldhura** Nepal
62A1 **Dandeli** India
75C3 **Dandenong** Aust
53A3 **Dandong** China
74B3 **Danger Pt** S Africa
72D2 **Dangila** Eth
18D2 **Daniel** USA
7N4 **Daniel's Harbour** Can
74C2 **Danielskuil** S Africa
7P3 **Dannebrogs Øy** *I* Greenland
78C2 **Dannevirke** NZ
14B1 **Dansville** USA
62C1 **Dantewāra** India
Danube = Dunărea
Danube = Donau
45G8 **Danuk** Iraq
9E2 **Danville** Illinois, USA
9E3 **Danville** Kentucky, USA
14B2 **Danville** Pennsylvania, USA
9F3 **Danville** Virginia, USA
Danzig = Gdańsk
52C4 **Dao Xian** China
52B4 **Daozhen** China
71J3 **Dapchi** Nig
61E2 **Dapha Bum** *Mt* India
65B3 **Daphnae** *Hist Site* Egypt
57F9 **Dapiak,Mt** Phil
57F9 **Dapitan** Phil
50C3 **Da Qaidam** China
53B2 **Daqing** China
65D2 **Dar'a** Syria
63C3 **Dārāb** Iran
69A1 **Daraj** Libya
63C2 **Dārān** Iran
64C3 **Dar'ā Salkhad** Syria
61C2 **Darbhanga** India
20C1 **Dardanelle** USA
17D2 **Dardanelle,L** USA
Dar-el-Beida = Casablanca Mor
73D4 **Dar Es Salaam** Tanz
78B1 **Dargaville** NZ
15C2 **Darien** USA
Darjeeling = Dārjiling
61C2 **Dārjiling** India
76D4 **Darling** *R* Aust
75C1 **Darling Downs** Aust
7L1 **Darling Pen** Can
75B2 **Darlington** Aust
35E4 **Darlington** Eng
15D2 **Darlington** USA
42B3 **Darmstadt** Germany
69B1 **Darnah** Libya
75B2 **Darnick** Aust
6F3 **Darnley B** Can
79G10 **Darnley,C** Ant
39B1 **Daroca** Spain
72C3 **Dar Rounga** Region, CAR
67F4 **Darsa** *I* Yemen
35D6 **Dart** *R* Eng
33C3 **Dartmoor** *Moorland* Eng
35D6 **Dartmoor Nat Pk** Eng
7M5 **Dartmouth** Can
35D6 **Dartmouth** Eng
76D1 **Daru** PNG
40D1 **Daruvar** Croatia, Yugos
63E3 **Darweshan** Afghan
76C2 **Darwin** Aust
63C3 **Daryacheh-ye Bakhtegan** *L* Iran
63C3 **Daryacheh-ye Mahārlū** *L* Iran
63C2 **Daryācheh-ye Namak** *Salt Flat* Iran
63E2 **Daryacheh-ye-Sistan** *Salt Lake* Iran/Afghan
63C3 **Daryacheh-ye Tashk** *L* Iran
45H8 **Daryācheh-ye Urumīyeh** *L* Iran
63D3 **Dārzīn** Iran
67F1 **Das** *I* UAE
52C3 **Dashennonglia** *Mt* China
63D1 **Dasht** Iran
63E3 **Dasht** *R* Pak
63C2 **Dasht-e-Kavir** *Salt Desert* Iran
63D2 **Dasht-e Lut** *Salt Desert* Iran
63E2 **Dasht-e Naomid** *Desert Region* Iran
63E2 **Dasht-i-Margo** *Desert* Afghan
54D2 **Date** Japan
60D3 **Datia** India
52A2 **Datong** China
52C1 **Datong** China
52A2 **Datong He** *R* China
57F9 **Datu Piang** Phil
44D4 **Daugava** *R* Latvia
44D4 **Daugavpils** Latvia
38D2 **Dauphiné** Region, France
7M1 **Dauguard Jensen Land** Greenland
60A1 **Daulatabad** Afghan
60D3 **Daulpur** India
36D1 **Daun** Germany
62A1 **Daund** India
6H4 **Dauphin** Can
14B2 **Dauphin** USA
15B2 **Dauphin I** USA
4B3 **Dauphin L** Can
70C3 **Daura** Nig
60D3 **Dausa** India
63E3 **Dāvah Panāh** Iran
62B2 **Dāvangere** India
57G9 **Davao** Phil
57G9 **Davao G** Phil
20A2 **Davenport** California, USA
9D2 **Davenport** Iowa, USA
26B2 **David** Panama
3G3 **Davidson** Can
6D3 **Davidson Mts** USA
3H2 **Davin L** Can
19B3 **Davis** USA
79G10 **Davis** *Base* Ant
7M4 **Davis Inlet** Can
7N3 **Davis Str** Greenland/Can
44K5 **Davlekanovo** Russian Fed
37C1 **Davos** Switz
3G2 **Davy L** Can
72E3 **Dawa** *R* Eth
52A4 **Dawan** China
60B2 **Dawat Yar** Afghan
67F1 **Dawḥat Salwah** *B* Qatar/S Arabia
67F3 **Dawkah** Oman
55B2 **Dawna Range** *Mts* Burma
6E3 **Dawson** Can
15C2 **Dawson** Georgia, USA
11C2 **Dawson** N Dakota, USA
76D3 **Dawson** *R* Aust
6F4 **Dawson Creek** Can
3F1 **Dawson Landing** Can
3E3 **Dawson,Mt** Can
10L3 **Dawson Range** *Mts* Can
52A3 **Dawu** China
52C3 **Dawu** China
38B3 **Dax** France
52B3 **Daxian** China
52B5 **Daxin** China
52A3 **Daxue Shan** *Mts* China
28D2 **Dayman** *R* Urug
52C4 **Dayong** China
65D2 **Dayr'Ali** Syria
65D1 **Dayr'Atīyah** Syria
64D2 **Dayr az Zawr** Syria
65D1 **Dayr Shumayyil** Syria
9E3 **Dayton** Ohio, USA
15B1 **Dayton** Tennessee, USA
17D4 **Dayton** Texas, USA
18C1 **Dayton** Washington, USA
9E4 **Daytona Beach** USA
52C4 **Dayu** China
56E3 **Dayu** Indon
52D2 **Da Yunhe** China
52D2 **Da Yunhe** *R* China
18C2 **Dayville** USA
52B3 **Dazhu** China
74C3 **De Aar** S Africa
23C2 **Deadman's Cay** Bahamas
64C3 **Dead S** Israel/Jordan
11B3 **Deadwood** USA
36A1 **Deal** Eng
74D2 **Dealesville** S Africa
3C3 **Dean** *R* Can
3C3 **Dean Chan** Can
28C2 **Deán Funes** Arg
12C2 **Dearborn** USA
3B2 **Dease Lake** Can
3C2 **Dease** *R* Can
6F3 **Dease Arm** *B* Can
8B3 **Death V** USA
20D2 **Death Valley Nat Mon** USA
38C2 **Deauville** France
71F4 **Debakala** Ivory Coast
10F3 **Debauch Mt** USA
3G3 **Debden** Can
23L1 **Débé** Trinidad
43E2 **Debica** Pol
43E2 **Deblin** Pol
70B3 **Débo,L** Mali
72D3 **Debre Birhan** Eth
43E3 **Debrecen** Hung
72D2 **Debre Mark'os** Eth
72D2 **Debre Tabor** Eth
66C3 **Decamere** Eth
9E3 **Decatur** Alabama, USA
15C2 **Decatur** Georgia, USA
9E3 **Decatur** Illinois, USA
12C2 **Decatur** Indiana, USA
38C3 **Decazeville** France
74C1 **Deception** *R* Botswana
52A4 **Dechang** China
11D3 **Decorah** USA
71F3 **Dedougou** Burkina
53B2 **Dedu** China
73D5 **Dedza** Malawi
34C4 **Dee** *R* Dumfries and Galloway, Scot
35D5 **Dee** *R* Eng/Wales
34D3 **Dee** *R* Grampian, Scot
4F4 **Deep River** Can
14D2 **Deep River** USA
20D2 **Deep Springs** USA
75D1 **Deepwater** Aust
10F5 **Deer I** USA
7N5 **Deer Lake** Can
8B2 **Deer Lodge** USA
26E7 **Deésaguadero** *R* Bol
18C2 **Deeth** USA
28D3 **Defferrari** Arg
4E5 **Defiance** USA
15B2 **De Funiak Springs** USA
50C3 **Dêgê** China
76A3 **De Grey** *R* Aust
66D3 **Dehalak** *Arch* Eth
63C2 **Deh Bīd** Iran
60B1 **Dehi** Afghan
70D1 **Dehibat** Tunisia
62B3 **Dehiwala-Mt Lavinia** Sri Lanka
63B2 **Dehlorān** Iran
60D2 **Dehra Dūn** India
61B3 **Dehri** India
53B3 **Dehui** China
72C3 **Deim Zubeir** Sudan
65C2 **Deir Abu Sa'id** Jordan
65D1 **Deir el Ahmar** Leb
45C6 **Dej** Rom
12B2 **De Kalb** Illinois, USA
17D3 **De Kalb** Texas, USA
49Q4 **De Kastri** Russian Fed
72C4 **Dekese** Zaïre
72B3 **Dekoa** CAR
8B3 **Delano** USA
19D3 **Delano Peal** *Mt* USA
74D2 **Delareyville** S Africa
10C6 **Delarof Is** USA
9F3 **Delaware** State, USA
12C2 **Delaware** USA
13D2 **Delaware** *R* USA
9F3 **Delaware B** USA
75C3 **Delegate** Aust
37B1 **Delemont** Switz
73E5 **Delgado** *C* Mozam
66B2 **Delgo** Sudan
16B2 **Delhi** Colorado, USA
60D3 **Delhi** India
13E2 **Delhi** New York, USA
64B1 **Delice** Turk
21B2 **Delicias** Mexico
63C2 **Delījān** Iran
37B1 **Delle** France
11C3 **Dell Rapids** USA
71C1 **Dellys** Alg
20D4 **Del Mar** USA
32F8 **Delmenhorst** Germany
10F2 **De Long Mts** USA
49R2 **De-Longa, Ostrov** *I* Russian Fed
75E3 **Deloraine** Aust
6H5 **Deloraine** Can
15E4 **Delray Beach** USA
8C4 **Del Rio** USA
8B3 **Delta** USA
10J3 **Delta** *R* USA
71H4 **Delta** *State* Nigeria
10J3 **Delta Junction** USA
14C1 **Delta Res** USA
72D3 **Dembī Dolo** Eth
36C1 **Demer** *R* Belg
43G1 **Demidov** Russian Fed
16A3 **Deming** USA
41F2 **Demirköy** Turk
71A2 **Demnate** Mor
37B2 **Demonte** Italy
15B2 **Demopolis** USA
48H4 **Demyanskoya** Russian Fed
38C1 **Denain** France
59E2 **Denau** Uzbekistan
35D5 **Denbigh** Wales
10F3 **Denbigh,C** USA
56C3 **Dendang** Indon
36C1 **Dendermond** Belg
72D3 **Dendi** *Mt* Eth
36B1 **Dèndre** *R* Belg
52B1 **Dengkou** China
52C3 **Deng Xian** China
Den Haag = 's-Gravenhage
23H1 **Denham,Mt** Jamaica
42A2 **Den Helder** Neth
39C2 **Denia** Spain
76D4 **Deniliquin** Aust
18C2 **Denio** USA
11C3 **Denison** Iowa, USA
8D3 **Denison** Texas, USA
10H4 **Denison,Mt** USA
45D8 **Denizli** Turk
32F7 **Denmark** Kingdom, Europe
79C1 **Denmark Str** Greenland/ Iceland
23P2 **Dennery** St Lucia
56E4 **Denpasar** Indon
14C3 **Denton** Maryland, USA
8D3 **Denton** Texas, USA
76E1 **D'Entrecasteaux Is** PNG
37B1 **Dents du Midi** *Mt* Switz
8C3 **Denver** USA
4F2 **Denys** *R* Can
72B3 **Déo** *R* Cam
61C3 **Deoghar** India
60C5 **Deolāli** India
60D1 **Deosai Plain** India
14A1 **Depew** USA
14C1 **Deposit** USA
72C2 **Dépression du Mourdi** *Desert Region* Chad
49P3 **Deputatskiy** Russian Fed
17D3 **De Queen** USA
60C3 **Dera** Pak
60B3 **Dera Bugti** Pak
60B2 **Dera Ismail Khan** Pak
45H7 **Derbent** Russian Fed
76B2 **Derby** Aust
14D2 **Derby** Connecticut, USA
35E5 **Derby** County, Eng
35E5 **Derby** Eng
17C2 **Derby** Kansas, USA
45F5 **Dergachi** Ukraine
17D3 **De Ridder** USA
69B1 **Derna** Libya
72E3 **Derri** Somalia
14E1 **Derry** USA
72D2 **Derudeb** Sudan
74C3 **De Rust** S Africa
14C1 **De Ruyter** USA
75E3 **Derwent Bridge** Aust
28B2 **Desaguadero** Arg
28B2 **Desaguadero** *R* Arg
19C4 **Descanso** Mexico
3H3 **Deschambault L** Can
18B2 **Deschutes** *R* USA
72D2 **Desē** Eth
25C7 **Deseado** Arg
25C7 **Deseado** *R* Arg
37D2 **Desenzano** Italy
70A1 **Deserta Grande** *I* Medeira
19C4 **Desert Centre** USA
19D2 **Desert Peak** *Mt* USA
63E2 **Deshu** Afghan
25C2 **Desierto de Atacama** *Desert* Chile
17D2 **Desloge** USA
9D2 **Des Moines** Iowa, USA
16B2 **Des Moines** New Mexico, USA
11D3 **Des Moines** *R* USA
45E5 **Desna** *R* Russian Fed
25B8 **Desolación** *I* Chile
12B2 **Des Plaines** USA
42C2 **Dessau** Germany
10L3 **Destruction Bay** Can
36A1 **Desvres** France
41E1 **Deta** Rom
73C5 **Dete** Zim
36E1 **Detmold** Germany
9E2 **Detroit** USA
5J4 **Détroit d'Honguedo** *Str* Can
5J3 **Détroit de Jacques Cartier** *Str* Can
11C2 **Detroit Lakes** USA
55D3 **Det Udom** Thai
41E1 **Deva** Rom
42B2 **Deventer** Neth
34D3 **Deveron** *R* Scot
60C3 **Devikot** India
20C2 **Devil Postpile Nat Mon** USA
20C3 **Devils Den** USA
20C1 **Devils Gate** *P* USA
34F3 **Devil's Hole** *Region* N Sea
Devil's Island = Isla du Diable
11C2 **Devils L** N Dakota, USA
16B4 **Devils L** Texas, USA
8D2 **Devils Lake** USA
10M4 **Devils Paw** *Mt* Can
35E6 **Devizes** Eng
60D3 **Devli** India
41E2 **Devoll** *R* Alb
37A2 **Dévoluy** *Mts* France
35C6 **Devon** County, Eng
7J2 **Devon I** Can
76D5 **Devonport** Aust
61D2 **Dewangiri** Bhutan
60D4 **Dewās** India
74D2 **Dewetsdorp** S Africa
9E3 **Dewey Res** USA
17D3 **De Witt** USA
17E2 **Dexter** Missouri, USA
16B3 **Dexter** New Mexico, USA
52A3 **Deyang** China
63D2 **Deyhuk** Iran
63B2 **Dezfūl** Iran
52D2 **Dezhou** China
63B1 **Dezh Shāhpūr** Iran
67F1 **Dhahran** S Arabia
61D3 **Dhākā** Bang
65B1 **Dhali** Cyprus
66D4 **Dhamār** Yemen
62B2 **Dhamavaram** India
61B3 **Dhamtari** India
61C3 **Dhanbād** India
61B2 **Dhangarhi** Nepal
61C2 **Dhankuta** Nepal
60D4 **Dhār** India
62B2 **Dharmapuri** India
60D2 **Dharmsāla** India
70B3 **Dhar Oualata** *Desert Region* Maur
61B2 **Dhaulagiri** *Mt* Nepal
61C3 **Dhenkānāi** India
65C3 **Dhibah** Jordan
41F3 **Dhíkti Óri** *Mt* Greece
67F3 **Dhofar** Region, Oman
41E3 **Dhomokós** Greece
62B1 **Dhone** India
60C4 **Dhoraji** India
60C4 **Dhrāngadhra** India
61C2 **Dhuburi** India
60C4 **Dhule** India
20B2 **Diablo,Mt** USA
19B3 **Diablo Range** *Mts* USA
28C2 **Diamante** Arg
28B2 **Diamante** *R* Arg
27K7 **Diamantina** Brazil
76D3 **Diamantina** *R* Aust
29A1 **Diamantino** Brazil
61C3 **Diamond Harbours** India
20B1 **Diamond Springs** USA
18D2 **Diamondville** USA
71G3 **Diapaga** Burkina
67G1 **Dibā** UAE
73C4 **Dibaya** Zaïre
61D2 **Dibrugarh** India

16B3 **Dickens** USA
8C2 **Dickinson** USA
15B1 **Dickson** USA
13D2 **Dickson City** USA
45G8 **Dicle** *R* Turk
3F3 **Didsbury** Can
60C3 **Dīdwāna** India
37A2 **Die** France
74E2 **Die Berg** *Mt* S Africa
71F3 **Diebougou** Burkina
36E2 **Dieburg** Germany
3G3 **Diefenbaker,L** Can
36D2 **Diekirch** Lux
70B3 **Diéma** Mali
55C1 **Dien Bien Phu** Viet
42B2 **Diepholz** Germany
38C2 **Dieppe** France
53B3 **Dier Songhua Jiang** *R* China
36C1 **Diest** Belg
36D2 **Dieuze** France
71J3 **Diffa** Niger
61E2 **Digboi** India
7M5 **Digby** Can
38D3 **Digne** France
38C2 **Digoin** France
57G9 **Digos** Phil
76C1 **Digul** *R* Indon
71F4 **Digya Nat Pk** Ghana
61D2 **Dihang** *R* India
Dijlah = Tigris
37A1 **Dijon** France
72B3 **Dik** Chad
72E2 **Dikhil** Djibouti
65A3 **Dikirnis** Egypt
36B1 **Diksmuide** Belg
48K2 **Dikson** Russian Fed
71J3 **Dikwa** Nig
63E2 **Dilaram** Afghan
57C4 **Dili** Indon
55D3 **Di Linh** Viet
36E1 **Dillenburg** Germany
17F4 **Dilley** USA
72C2 **Dilling** Sudan
10G4 **Dillingham** USA
8B2 **Dillon** USA
14B2 **Dillsburg** USA
73C5 **Dilolo** Zaïre
22A1 **Dimas** Mexico
Dimashq = Damascus
72C4 **Dimbelenge** Zaïre
71F4 **Dimbokro** Ivory Coast
41F2 **Dimitrovgrad** Bulg
44H5 **Dimitrovgrad** Russian Fed
65C3 **Dimona** Israel
61D2 **Dimpāpur** India
57G8 **Dinagat** *I* Phil
61C2 **Dinajpur** India
38B2 **Dinan** France
36C1 **Dinant** Belg
64B2 **Dinar** Turk
72D2 **Dinder** *R* Sudan
62B2 **Dindigul** India
52B2 **Dingbian** China
61C2 **Dinggyê** China
33A3 **Dingle** Irish Rep
33A3 **Dingle** *B* Irish Rep
70A3 **Dinguiraye** Guinea
34C3 **Dingwall** Scot
52A2 **Dingxi** China
52D2 **Ding Xian** China
55D1 **Dinh Lap** Viet
11D2 **Dinorwic L** Can
16A1 **Dinosaur** USA
20C2 **Dinuba** USA
10E2 **Diomede Is** Russian Fed/USA
70A3 **Diouloulou** Sen
61D2 **Diphu** India
72E3 **Diredawa** Eth
76A3 **Dirk Hartog** *I* Aust
72B2 **Dirkou** Niger
75C1 **Dirranbandi** Aust
25J8 **Disappointment,C** South Georgia
18B1 **Disappointment,C** USA
76B3 **Disappointment,L** Aust
75B3 **Discovery B** Aust
xxxJ6 **Discovery Tablemount** Atlantic O
37C1 **Disentis Muster** Switz
66B1 **Dishna** Egypt
7N3 **Disko** *I* Greenland
7N3 **Disko Bugt** *B* Greenland
7N3 **Diskofjord** Greenland
13D3 **Dismal Swamp** USA
43F1 **Disna** *R* Belorussia
29C2 **Distrito Federal** Federal District, Brazil
60C4 **Diu** India
57G9 **Diuat Mts** Phil
36A2 **Dives** *R* France
27K8 **Divinópolis** Brazil
45G6 **Divnoye** Russian Fed
64C2 **Divriği** Turk
20B1 **Dixon** California, USA
12B2 **Dixon** Illinois, USA
18D1 **Dixon** Montana, USA
6E4 **Dixon Entrance** *Sd* Can/USA
3E2 **Dixonville** Can
64E3 **Diyālā** *R* Iraq
45G8 **Diyarbakir** Turk
63E3 **Diz** Pak
63B2 **Diz** *R* Iran
72B3 **Dja** *R* Cam
71C2 **Djadi** *R* Alg
72B1 **Djado,Plat du** Niger
71D2 **Djamaa** Alg
72B4 **Djambala** Congo
70C2 **Djanet** Alg
71C2 **Djebel Amour** *Mts* Alg
39A2 **Djebel Bouhalla** *Mt* Mor
71D1 **Djebel Chambi** *Mt* Tunisia
71D1 **Djebel Chélia** *Mts* Alg
71E1 **Djebel Zaghouan** *Mt* Tunisia
71D2 **Djebel Zrega** *Mt* Tunisia
71G4 **Djebobo** *Mt* Ghana
71C2 **Djelfa** Alg
72C3 **Djéma** CAR
70B3 **Djenné** Mali
71J4 **Djerem** *R* Cam
71F3 **Djibasso** Burkina
70B3 **Djibo** Burkina
72E2 **Djibouti** Djibouti
72E2 **Djibouti** Republic, E Africa
72C3 **Djolu** Zaïre
71G4 **Djougou** Benin
72D3 **Djugu** Zaïre
32C2 **Djúpivogur** Iceland
39C2 **Djurdjura** *Mts* Alg
44F4 **Dmitrov** Russian Fed
45E6 **Dnepr** *R* Ukraine
45E6 **Dneprodzerzhinsk** Ukraine
45F6 **Dnepropetrovsk** Ukraine
44D5 **Dneprovskaya Nizmennost'** Region, Belorussia
45C6 **Dnestr** *R* Ukraine
44E4 **Dno** Russian Fed
72B3 **Doba** Chad
43E1 **Dobele** Latvia
28C3 **Doblas** Arg
76C1 **Dobo** Indon
41D2 **Doboj** Bosnia & Herzegovina, Yugos
41F2 **Dobrich** Bulg
45E5 **Dobrush** Belorussia
27K7 **Doce** *R* Brazil
25D2 **Doctor R P Peña** Arg
62B2 **Dod** India
62B2 **Doda Betta** *Mt* India
Dodecanese = Sporádhes
8C3 **Dodge City** USA
3G2 **Dodge L** Can
12A2 **Dodgeville** USA
72D4 **Dodoma** Tanz
34G4 **Dogger Bank** *Sand-bank* N Sea
12B1 **Dog L** Can
12C1 **Dog L** Can
54B3 **Dōgo** *I* Japan
70C3 **Dogondoutchi** Niger
64D2 **Doğubayazit** Turk
67F1 **Doha** Qatar
61D2 **Doilungdêqên** China
66C4 **Doka** Sudan
76C1 **Dolak** *I* Indon
11C3 **Doland** USA
7L5 **Dolbeau** Can
38D2 **Dôle** France
66B4 **Doleib** *Watercourse* Sudan
35D5 **Dolgellau** Wales
14C1 **Dolgeville** USA
44K2 **Dolgiy, Ostrov** *I* Russian Fed
53E2 **Dolinsk** Russian Fed
37D1 **Dolomitche** *Mts* Italy
72E3 **Dolo Odo** Eth
25E5 **Dolores** Arg
28D2 **Dolores** Urug
16A2 **Dolores** *R* USA
22B1 **Dolores Hidalgo** Mexico
6G3 **Dolphin and Union Str** Can
25E8 **Dolphin,C** Falkland Is
51G7 **Dom** *Mt* Indon
45K5 **Dombarovskiy** Russian Fed
32F6 **Dombas** Nor
36D2 **Dombasle-sur-Meurthe** France
41D1 **Dombóvár** Hung
28A1 **Domeyko** Chile
38B2 **Domfront** France
23E3 **Dominica** *I* Caribbean
23C3 **Dominican Republic** Caribbean
7L3 **Dominion,C** Can
7N4 **Domino** Can
50E1 **Domna** Russian Fed
40B1 **Domodossola** Italy
28E2 **Dom Pedrito** Brazil
56E4 **Dompu** Indon
25B5 **Domuyo** *Mt* Arg
75D1 **Domville,Mt** Aust
34D3 **Don** *R* Scot
45G6 **Don** *R* Russian Fed
34B4 **Donaghadee** N Ire
22B1 **Donato Guerta** Mexico
Donau = Dunav Bulg
42C3 **Donau, R** Austria
42C3 **Donau** *R* Germany
36E3 **Donaueschingen** Germany
42C3 **Donauwörth** Germany
39A2 **Don Benito** Spain
35E5 **Doncaster** Eng
73B4 **Dondo** Angola
73D5 **Dondo** Mozam
62C3 **Dondra Head** *C* Sri Lanka
34B4 **Donegal** County, Irish Rep
33B3 **Donegal** Irish Rep
33B3 **Donegal** *B* Irish Rep
34A4 **Donegal** *Mts* Irish Rep
45F6 **Donetsk** Ukraine
71J4 **Donga** *R* Nig
52C4 **Dong'an** China
76A3 **Dongara** Aust
52A4 **Dongchuan** China
55D2 **Dongfang** China
53B3 **Dongfeng** China
76A1 **Donggala** Indon
50C3 **Donggi Cona** *L* China
53A4 **Donggou** China
52C5 **Donghai Dao** *I* China
52A1 **Dong He** *R* China
55D2 **Dong Hoi** Viet
52C5 **Dong Jiang** *R* China
53C2 **Donglanghong** China
53C3 **Dongning** China
72D2 **Dongola** Sudan
52D5 **Dongshan** China
50E4 **Dongsha Qundao** *I* China
52C2 **Dongsheng** China
52E3 **Dongtai** China
52C4 **Dongting Hu** *L* China
52B5 **Dongxing** China
52D3 **Dongzhi** China
17D2 **Doniphan** USA
40D2 **Donji Vakuf** Bosnia & Herzegovina, Yugos
32G5 **Dönna** *I* Nor
19B3 **Donner** *P* USA
36D2 **Donnersberg** *Mt* Germany
74D2 **Donnybrook** S Africa
38B3 **Donostia** Spain
20B2 **Don Pedro Res** USA
10H2 **Doonerak,Mt** USA
57F9 **Dopolong** Phil
52A3 **Do Qu** *R* China
37B2 **Dora Baltea** *R* Italy
38D2 **Dorbirn** Austria
53A2 **Dorbod** China
35D6 **Dorchester** Eng
7L3 **Dorchester,C** Can
38C2 **Dordogne** *R* France
42A2 **Dordrecht** Neth
74D3 **Dordrecht** S Africa
3G3 **Doré L** Can
3G3 **Doré Lake** Can
14D1 **Dorest Peak** *Mt* USA
70B3 **Dori** Burkina
74B3 **Doring** *R* S Africa
36B2 **Dormans** France
42B3 **Dornbirn** Austria
34C3 **Dornoch** Scot
34C3 **Dornoch Firth** *Estuary* Scot
32H6 **Dorotea** Sweden
75D2 **Dorrigo** Aust
18B2 **Dorris** USA
35D6 **Dorset** County, Eng
36D1 **Dorsten** Germany
42B2 **Dortmund** Germany
72C3 **Doruma** Zaïre
49N4 **Dosatuy** Russian Fed
60B1 **Doshi** Afghan
20B2 **Dos Palos** USA
71G3 **Dosso** Niger
48G5 **Dossor** Kazakhstan
9E3 **Dothan** USA
38C1 **Douai** France
72A3 **Douala** Cam
75D1 **Double Island Pt** Aust
5K3 **Double Mer** *B* Can
16B3 **Double Mountain Fork** *R* USA
20C3 **Double Mt** USA
38D2 **Doubs** *R* France
78A3 **Doubtful Sd** NZ
70B3 **Douentza** Mali
3B2 **Douglas** Alaska, USA
8C3 **Douglas** Arizona, USA
35C4 **Douglas** Eng
15C2 **Douglas** Georgia, USA
74C2 **Douglas** S Africa
8C2 **Douglas** Wyoming, USA
10E2 **Douglas,C** USA
3C3 **Douglas Chan** Can
15C1 **Douglas L** USA
10H4 **Douglas,Mt** USA
36C2 **Doulevant-le-Château** France
36B1 **Doullens** France
35B4 **Doun** County, N Ire
27H8 **Dourados** Brazil
29B3 **Dourados** *R* Brazil
36B2 **Dourdan** France
39A1 **Douro** *R* Port
16A2 **Dove Creek** USA
13D3 **Dover** Delaware, USA
35F6 **Dover** Eng
13E2 **Dover** New Hampshire, USA
14C2 **Dover** New Jersey, USA
12C2 **Dover** Ohio, USA
35E5 **Dover** *R* Eng
35F6 **Dover,Str of** Eng/France
43G2 **Dovsk** Belorussia
14C3 **Downington** USA
35C4 **Downpatrick** N Ire
14C1 **Downsville** USA
3D3 **Downton,Mt** Can
14C2 **Doylestown** USA
54B3 **Dōzen** *I* Japan
70A2 **Dr'aa** *R* Mor
37A2 **Drac** *R* France
29B3 **Dracena** Brazil
14E1 **Dracut** USA
38D3 **Draguignan** France
11B2 **Drake** USA
73D6 **Drakensberg** *Mts* S Africa
xxxE7 **Drake Pass** Pacific/Atlantic O
41E2 **Dráma** Greece
32G6 **Drammen** Nor
32A1 **Drangajökull** Iceland
22B1 **Dr Arroyo** Mexico
37E1 **Drau** *R* Austria
40D1 **Drava** *R* Slovenia, Yugos
3F3 **Drayton Valley** Can
38C2 **Dreaux** France
42C2 **Dresden** Germany
36A2 **Dreux** France
18C2 **Drewsey** USA
4E4 **Driftwood** Can
14A2 **Driftwood** USA
41E2 **Drin** *R* Alb
41D2 **Drina** *R* Bosnia & Herzegovina/Serbia
43F1 **Drissa** *R* Belorussia
35B5 **Drogheda** Irish Rep
43E3 **Drogobych** Ukraine
37A2 **Drôme** *R* France
37B2 **Dronera** Italy
79F12 **Dronning Maud Land** Region, Ant
26F8 **Dr P.P. Pená** Par
6G4 **Drumheller** Can
18D1 **Drummond** USA
12C1 **Drummond I** USA
5G4 **Drummondville** Can
43E2 **Druskininksi** Lithuania
49Q3 **Druzhina** Russian Fed
10L4 **Dry B** USA
11D2 **Dryberry L** Can
7J5 **Dryden** Can
14B1 **Dryden** USA
23H1 **Dry Harbour Mts** Jamaica
71J4 **Dschang** Cam
55B3 **Duang** *I* Burma
66C1 **Dubā** S Arabia
67G1 **Dubai** UAE
6H3 **Dubawnt** *R* Can
6H3 **Dubawnt L** Can
76D4 **Dubbo** Aust
35B5 **Dublin** County, Irish Rep
35B5 **Dublin** Irish Rep
15C2 **Dublin** USA
44F4 **Dubna** Russian Fed
45D5 **Dubno** Ukraine
18D2 **Dubois** Idaho, USA
13D2 **Du Bois** USA
18E2 **Dubois** Wyoming, USA
3C3 **Dubose,Mt** Can
43F3 **Dubossary** Moldavia
43F2 **Dubrovica** Ukraine
41D2 **Dubrovnik** Croatia, Yugos
9D2 **Dubuque** USA
19D2 **Duchesne** USA
15B1 **Duck** *R* USA
3H3 **Duck Mts** Can
20C3 **Ducor** USA
36D2 **Dudelange** Lux
48K3 **Dudinka** Russian Fed
35D5 **Dudley** Eng
49L2 **Dudypta** *R* Russian Fed
70B4 **Duekoué** Ivory Coast
39B1 **Duero** *R* Spain
77F1 **Duff Is** Solomon Is
34D3 **Dufftown** Scot
40C2 **Dugi Otok** *I* Croatia, Yugos
5G2 **Du Gué** *R* Can
42B2 **Duisburg** Germany
74E1 **Duiwelskloof** S Africa
64E3 **Dūkan** Iraq
10M5 **Duke I** USA
72D3 **Duk Faiwil** Sudan
67F1 **Dukhān** Qatar
52A4 **Dukou** China
50C3 **Dulan** China
28C2 **Dulce** *R* Arg
56D2 **Dulit Range** *Mts* Malay
61D3 **Dullabchara** India
36D1 **Dülmen** Germany
9D2 **Duluth** USA
65D2 **Dūmā** Syria
56B2 **Dumai** Indon
57E8 **Dumaran** *I* Phil
8C3 **Dumas** USA
65D2 **Dumayr** Syria
71G4 **Dumbai** Ghana
34C4 **Dumbarton** Scot
34D4 **Dumfries** Scot
34C4 **Dumfries and Galloway** Region, Scot
61C3 **Dumka** India
57B2 **Dumoga Kecil** Indon
13D1 **Dumoine,L** Can
79G8 **Dumont d'Urville** *Base* Ant
69C1 **Dumyât** Egypt
41F2 **Dunărea** *R* Rom
35B5 **Dunary Head** *Pt* Irish Rep
41E2 **Dunav** *R* Bulg
41D1 **Dunav** *R* Croatia/Serbia
43F3 **Dunayevtsy** Ukraine
3D4 **Duncan** Can
17C3 **Duncan** USA
4E3 **Duncan,C** Can
4F3 **Duncan L** Can
14B2 **Duncannon** USA
62E2 **Duncan Pass** Andaman Is
34D2 **Duncansby Head** *Pt* Scot
35B4 **Dundalk** Irish Rep
14B3 **Dundalk** USA
35B5 **Dundalk B** Irish Rep
7M2 **Dundas** Greenland
10M5 **Dundas I** Can
6G2 **Dundas Pen** Can
51G8 **Dundas Str** Aust
74E2 **Dundee** S Africa
34D3 **Dundee** Scot
14B1 **Dundee** USA
75B1 **Dundoo** Aust
35C4 **Dundrum** *B* N Ire
77G5 **Dunedin** NZ
15C3 **Dunedin** USA
75C2 **Dunedoo** Aust
34D3 **Dunfermline** Scot
60C4 **Dungarpur** India
35B5 **Dungarvan** Irish Rep
35F6 **Dungeness** Eng
75D2 **Dungog** Aust
72C3 **Dungu** Zaïre
72D1 **Dungunab** Sudan
53B3 **Dunhua** China
50C2 **Dunhuang** China
36B1 **Dunkerque** France
9F2 **Dunkirk** USA
72D2 **Dunkur** Eth
71F4 **Dunkwa** Ghana
33B3 **Dun Laoghaire** Irish Rep
14C2 **Dunmore** USA
23B1 **Dunmore Town** Bahamas
15D1 **Dunn** USA
34D2 **Dunnet Head** *Pt* Scot
11B3 **Dunning** USA
34D4 **Duns** Scot
11B2 **Dunseith** USA
18B2 **Dunsmuir** USA
78A2 **Dunstan Mts** NZ
36C2 **Dun-sur-Meuse** France
52D1 **Duolun** China
11B2 **Dupree** USA
73B4 **Duque de Braganca** Angola
12B3 **Du Quoin** USA
65C3 **Dura** Israel
38D3 **Durance** *R* France
12A2 **Durand** USA
21B2 **Durango** Mexico
39B1 **Durango** Spain
22A1 **Durango** State, Mexico
8C3 **Durango** USA
8D3 **Durant** USA
65D1 **Duraykīsh** Syria
25E4 **Durazho** Urug
74E2 **Durban** S Africa
36D1 **Duren** Germany
61B3 **Durg** India
61C3 **Durgapur** India
34E4 **Durham** County, Eng
34E4 **Durham** Eng

9F3 Durham N Carolina, USA
14E1 Durham New Hampshire, USA
75B1 Durham Downs Aust
41D2 Durmitor *Mt* Montenegro, Yugos
34C2 Durness Scot
41D2 Durrës Alb
75B1 Durrie Aust
41F3 Dursunbey Turk
78B2 D'Urville I NZ
63E1 Dushak Turkmenistan
52B4 Dushan China
59E2 Dushanbe Tajikistan
14B2 Dushore USA
78A3 Dusky Sd NZ
42B2 Düsseldorf Germany
10E5 Dutch Harbor USA
19D3 Dutton,Mt USA
52B4 Duyun China
64B1 Düzce Turk
44F2 Dvinskaya Guba *B* Russian Fed
60B4 Dwārka India
18C1 Dworshak Res USA
9E3 Dyersburg USA
35C5 Dyfed County, Wales
45G7 Dykh Tau *Mt* Russian Fed
75B1 Dynevor Downs Aust
50C2 Dzag Mongolia
50D2 Dzamïn Uüd Mongolia
73E5 Dzaoudzi Mayotte
50C2 Dzavhan Gol *R* Mongolia
44G4 Dzerzhinsk Russian Fed
49O4 Dzhalinda Russian Fed
48J5 Dzhambul Kazakhstan
45E6 Dzhankoy Ukraine
48H5 Dzhezkazgan Kazakhstan
60B1 Dzhilikul' Tajikistan
48J5 Dzhungarskiy Alatau *Mts* Kazakhstan
42D2 Dzierzoniow Pol
59G1 Dzungaria Basin, China
49L5 Dzüyl Mongolia

E

7K4 Eabamet L Can
10K3 Eagle Alaska, USA
16A2 Eagle Colorado, USA
5K3 Eagle *R* Can
11B2 Eagle Butte USA
18B2 Eagle L California, USA
11D2 Eagle L Can
13F1 Eagle L Maine, USA
13F1 Eagle Lake USA
17C3 Eagle Mountain L USA
8C4 Eagle Pass USA
16A3 Eagle Peak *Mt* USA
6E3 Eagle Plain Can
10J3 Eagle River USA
11D1 Ear Falls Can
19C3 Earlimart USA
19D4 Earp USA
16B3 Earth USA
15C2 Easley USA
13D2 East Aurora USA
15B3 East B USA
35F6 Eastbourne Eng
14C1 East Branch Delaware *R* USA
77G4 East,C NZ
10B6 East C USA
12B2 East Chicago USA
50F3 East China Sea China/ Japan
61B4 Eastern Ghats *Mts* India
4B3 Easterville Can
25E8 East Falkland *I* Falkland Is
10J2 East Fork *R* USA
19C3 Eastgate USA
11C2 East Grand Forks USA
14D1 Easthampton USA
14D2 East Hampton USA
12B2 East Lake USA
12C2 East Liverpool USA
74D3 East London S Africa
7L4 Eastmain Can
7L4 Eastmain *R* Can
15C2 Eastman USA
12A2 East Moline USA
13D3 Easton Maryland, USA
13D2 Easton Pennsylvania, USA
14C2 East Orange USA
xxixO5 East Pacific Ridge Pacific O
xxixO4 East Pacific Rise Pacific O
15C2 East Point USA
13F2 Eastport USA
35E5 East Retford Eng
15B1 East Ridge USA
9D3 East St Louis USA
49R2 East Siberian S Russian Fed
35F6 East Sussex County, Eng
13D3 Eastville USA
20C1 East Walker USA
15C2 Eatonton USA
11D3 Eau Claire USA
51H6 Eauripik *I* Pacific O
22C1 Ebano Mexico
72B3 Ebebiyin Eq Guinea
14A2 Ebensburg USA
36E2 Eberbach Germany
42C2 Eberswalde Germany
54D2 Ebetsu Japan
52A4 Ebian China
48K5 Ebinur *L* China
40D2 Eboli Italy
72B3 Ebolowa Cam
39B1 Ebro *R* Spain
64A1 Eceabat Turk
71C1 Ech Cheliff Alg
52D2 Eching China
18C1 Echo USA
Echo Bay = Port Radium
6G3 Echo Bay Can
36D2 Echternach Lux
75B3 Echuca Aust
39A2 Ecija Spain
7K2 Eclipse Sd Can
36A3 Ecommoy France
26C4 Ecuador Republic, S America
34D2 Eday *I* Scot
72E2 Ed Eth
34G3 Edda *Oilfield* N Sea
72C2 Ed Da'ein Sudan
66B4 Ed Damasin Sudan
72D2 Ed Damer Sudan
72D2 Ed Debba Sudan
34C2 Eddrachillis *B* Scot
72D2 Ed Dueim Sudan
75E3 Eddystone Pt Aust
71G4 Ede Nig
72A3 Edea Cam
75C3 Eden Aust
16C3 Eden Texas, USA
18E2 Eden Wyoming, USA
34D4 Eden *R* Eng
74D2 Edenburg S Africa
78A3 Edendale NZ
36D2 Edenkoben Germany
36E1 Eder *R* Germany
11C2 Edgeley USA
7M3 Edgell I Can
11B3 Edgemont USA
48D2 Edgeøya *I* Barents S
14B3 Edgewood USA
65C3 Edh Dhahiriya Israel
41E2 Edhessa Greece
17F4 Edinburg USA
34D3 Edinburgh Scot
45D7 Edirne Turk
20C3 Edison USA
15C2 Edisto *R* USA
18B1 Edmonds USA
6G4 Edmonton Can
11C2 Edmore USA
7M5 Edmundston Can
17C4 Edna USA
10M4 Edna Bay USA
71H4 Edo *State* Nigeria
40C1 Edolo Italy
65C3 Edom Region, Jordan
45D8 Edremit Turk
41F3 Edremit Körfezi *B* Turk
50C2 Edrengiyn Nuruu *Mts* Mongolia
6G4 Edson Can
28C3 Eduardo Castex Arg
10N3 Eduni,Mt Can
75B3 Edward *R* Aust
72C4 Edward,L Zaïre/Uganda
20D3 Edwards USA
75A1 Edwards Creek Aust
8C3 Edwards Plat USA
12B3 Edwardsville USA
3B2 Edziza,Mt Can
10F3 Eek USA
36B1 Eeklo Belg
77F2 Efate *I* Vanuatu
9E3 Effingham USA
19D3 Egan Range *Mts* USA
7N3 Egedesminde Greenland
10G4 Egegik USA
3H2 Egenolf L Can
43E3 Eger Hung
32F7 Egersund Nor
36E1 Eggegebirge Region, Germany
14C3 Egg Harbor City USA
6G2 Eglinton I Can
78B1 Egmont,C NZ
78B1 Egmont,Mt NZ
64B2 Eğridir Gölü *L* Turk
29C1 Eguas *R* Brazil
49U3 Egvekinot Russian Fed
69B2 Egypt Republic, Africa
32K6 Ehsenvaara Fin
39B1 Eibar Spain
38C2 Eibeuf France
75D1 Eidsvolo Aust
36D1 Eifel Region, Germany
34B3 Eigg *I* Scot
59F5 Eight Degree Chan Indian O
76B2 Eighty Mile Beach Aust
75C3 Eildon,L Aust
36E1 Einbeck Germany
42B2 Eindhoven Neth
37C1 Einsiedeln Switz
65C3 Ein Yahav Israel
42C2 Eisenach Germany
42C3 Eisenerz Austria
37E1 Eisenhut *Mt* Austria
36D1 Eitorf Germany
52A1 Ejin qi China
71F4 Ejuanema,Mt Ghana
71F4 Ejura Ghana
22C2 Ejutla Mexico
11B2 Ekalaka USA
78C2 Eketahuna NZ
48J4 Ekibastuz Kazakhstan
49P4 Ekimchan Russian Fed
64B3 Ek Mahalla el Kubra Egypt
32H7 Eksjo Sweden
4D3 Ekwan *R* Can
65A3 El Abbâsa Egypt
64A3 El'Alamein Egypt
74D2 Elands *R* S Africa
74C3 Elands Berg S Africa
22B1 El Arenal Mexico
71B2 El Aricha Alg
64B3 El'Arîsh Egypt
64B4 Elat Israel
72C2 El' Atrun Oasis Sudan
71C2 el Attar *R* Alg
45F8 Elazig Turk
64C3 El Azraq Jordan
40C2 Elba *I* Italy
69C2 El Balyana Egypt
53D1 El'ban Russian Fed
26D2 El Banco Colombia
41E2 Elbasan Alb
66B3 El Bauga Sudan
23D5 El Baúl Ven
71C2 El Bayadh Alg
42C2 Elbe *R* Germany
65D1 El Bega'a *R* Leb
12B2 Elberta USA
8C3 Elbert,Mt USA
15C2 Elberton USA
36A2 Elbeuf France
64C2 Elbistan Turk
43D2 Elblag Pol
25B6 El Bolson Arg
11C2 Elbow Lake USA
22B1 El Bozal Mexico
45G7 Elbrus *Mt* Russian Fed
Elburz Mts = Reshteh-ye Alborz
19C4 El Cajon USA
17C4 El Campo USA
19C4 El Centro USA
39B2 Elche Spain
4D4 Elcho USA
28B3 El Cuy Arg
39B2 Elda Spain
49P3 El'dikan Russian Fed
26C3 El Diviso Colombia
70B2 El Djouf *Desert* Region Maur
17D2 Eldon USA
29B4 Eldorado Arg
9D3 El Dorado Arkansas, USA
29C3 Eldorado Brazil
3G2 Eldorado Can
8D3 El Dorado Kansas, USA
21B2 El Dorado Mexico
16B3 Eldorado Texas, USA
26F2 El Dorado Ven
72D3 Eldoret Kenya
14A2 Eldred USA
65C1 Elea,C Cyprus
18D2 Electric Peak *Mt* USA
70B2 El Eglab Region, Alg
66B2 Elel *Watercourse* Egypt
16A3 Elephant Butte Res USA
39B1 El Escorial Spain
64D2 Eleşkirt Turk
71D1 El Eulma Alg
9F4 Eleuthera *I* Bahamas
71D1 El Fahs Tunisia
64B4 El Faiyûm Egypt
70B2 El Farsia *Well* Mor
72C2 El Fasher Sudan
64B4 El Fashn Egypt
39A1 El Ferrol del Caudillo Spain
65B3 El Firdân Egypt
72C2 El Fula Sudan
70C1 El Gassi Alg
72D2 El Geteina Sudan
72D2 El Gezîra Region, Sudan
65C3 El Ghor *V* Israel/Jordan
9E2 Elgin Illinois, USA
11B2 Elgin N Dakota, USA
34D3 Elgin Scot
64B3 El Gîza Egypt
70C1 El Golea Alg
19D4 El Golfo de Santa Clara Mexico
72D3 Elgon,Mt Uganda/Kenya
72E3 El Goran Eth
22B2 El Grullo Mexico
70B2 El Guettara *Well* Mali
70B2 El Haricha *Desert Region* Mali
64A4 El Harra Egypt
39C2 El Harrach Alg
66B4 El Hawata Sudan
22C1 El Hig Mexico
66B4 El Homra Sudan
28A3 El Huecu Arg
64B4 El'Igma *Desert Region* Egypt
10F3 Elim USA
Elisabethville = Lubumbashi
32K6 Elisenvaara Russian Fed
El Iskandarîya = Alexandria Egypt
45G6 Elista Russian Fed
76C4 Elizabeth Aust
13E2 Elizabeth USA
74B2 Elizabeth B Namibia
9F3 Elizabeth City USA
14E2 Elizabeth Is USA
15C1 Elizabethton Tennessee, USA
12B3 Elizabethtown Kentucky, USA
15D2 Elizabethtown N Carolina, USA
14B2 Elizabethtown Pennsylvania, USA
71A2 El Jadida Mor
64C3 El Jafr Jordan
65D3 El Jafr *L* Jordan
72D2 El Jebelein Sudan
71E1 El Jem Tunisia
43E2 Elk Pol
14C3 Elk *R* Maryland, USA
12C3 Elk *R* W Virginia, USA
11D3 Elkader USA
71D1 El Kala Alg
72D2 El Kamlin Sudan
71D1 El Kef Tunisia
20B1 Elk Grove USA
El Khalil = Hebron Israel
66B3 El Khandaq Sudan
65A3 El Khânka Egypt
66B1 El Khârga Egypt
66B1 El-Khârga Oasis Egypt
12B2 Elkhart USA
70B2 El Khenachich *Desert* Region Mali
11C3 Elkhorn *R* USA
41F2 Elkhovo Bulg
13D3 Elkins USA
14B2 Elkland USA
11A3 Elk Mt USA
18C1 Elko Can
8B2 Elko USA
71B2 el Korima *R* Alg
14C3 Elkton USA
66B2 El Ku *Watercourse* Egypt
65B3 El Kûbri Egypt
64B3 El Kuntilla Egypt
72C2 El Lagowa Sudan
6H2 Ellef Ringnes I Can
11C2 Ellendale USA
19D3 Ellen,Mt USA
8A2 Ellensburg USA
14C2 Ellenville USA
7K2 Ellesmere I Can
78B2 Ellesmere,L NZ
14B3 Ellicott City USA
74D3 Elliot S Africa
7K5 Elliot Lake Can
18D2 Ellis USA
65C3 El Lisan *Pen* Jordan
74D1 Ellisras S Africa
13F2 Ellsworth USA
79F3 Ellsworth Land *Region* Ant
65A4 El Ma'âdi Egypt
69B1 El Maghra *L* Egypt
66B4 El Manaqil Sudan
64B3 El Mansûra Egypt
65A3 El Manzala Egypt
65A3 El Matarîya Egypt
65B3 El Matarîya Egypt
14C3 Elmer USA
70B3 El Merelé *Desert Region* Maur
28B2 El Milagro Arg
71D1 El Milia Alg
66B3 El Milk *Watercourse* Sudan
65C1 El Mîna Leb
64B4 El Minya Egypt
20B1 Elmira California, USA
9F2 Elmira New York, USA
19D4 El Mirage USA
71D2 el Mitta *R* Alg
17F4 El Moral Mexico
70B2 El Mreitl *Well* Maur
42B2 Elmsborn Germany
72C2 El Muglad Sudan
70B2 El Mzereb *Well* Mali
57E8 El Nido Phil
72D2 El Obeid Sudan
22B2 El Oro Mexico
22A1 Elota Mexico
71D2 El Oued Alg
19D4 Eloy USA
8C3 El Paso USA
19B3 El Porta USA
20C2 El Portal USA
16A3 El Porvenir Mexico
22B1 El Potosí Mexico
39A2 El Puerto del Sta Maria Spain
El Qâhira = Cairo
65B3 El Qantara Egypt
El Quds = Jerusalem
22A1 El Quelite Mexico
65C3 El Quseima Egypt
65C4 El Quwetra Jordan
8D3 El Reno USA
6E3 Elsa Can
37D3 Elsa *R* Italy
65A4 El Saff Egypt
65B3 El Sâlhîya Egypt
22A1 El Salto Mexico
21D3 El Salvador Republic, C America
4E4 Elsas Can
19C4 El Sauzal Mexico
65B3 El Shallûfa Egypt
65B4 El Shatt Egypt
65A3 El Simbillâwein Egypt
20D4 Elsinore L USA
28B3 El Sosneade Arg
42C2 Elsterwerde Germany
16A4 El Sueco Mexico
El Suweis = Suez
65A4 El Tabbin Egypt
39A1 El Teleno *Mt* Spain
78B1 Eltham NZ
65C4 El Thamad Egypt
26F2 El Tigre Ven
64B4 El Tîh *Desert Region* Egypt
65B3 El Tîna Egypt
28C2 El Tio Arg
18C1 Eltopia USA
28A1 El Toro Chile
28A1 El Transito Chile
22A1 El Tuito Mexico
64B4 El Tûr Egypt
62C1 Elūru India
39A2 Elvas Port
26D5 Elvira Brazil
6H2 Elvira,C Can
28A2 El Volcán Chile
12B2 Elwood USA
35F5 Ely Eng
9D2 Ely Minnesota, USA
8B3 Ely Nevada, USA
12C2 Elyria USA
65A3 El Zarqa Egypt
63D1 Emāmrūd Iran
60B1 Emām Sāheb Afghan
42D1 Eman *R* Sweden
45K6 Emba Kazakhstan
45K6 Emba *R* Kazakhstan
25C5 Embalse Cerros Colorados *L* Arg
39B2 Embalse de Alarcón *Res* Spain
39A2 Embalse de Alcántarà *Res* Spain
39A1 Embalse de Almendra *Res* Spain
39A2 Embalse de Garcia de Sola *Res* Spain
26F2 Embalse de Guri *L* Ven
39B1 Embalse de Mequinenza *Res* Spain
39A1 Embalse de Ricobayo *Res* Spain
25E4 Embalse de Rio Negro *Res* Urug
28B3 Embalse El Choc1on *Res* Arg
25C5 Embalse Ezequil Ramos Mexia *L* Arg
25C6 Embalse Florentine Ameghino *L* Arg
39A1 Embalse Gabriel y Galan *Res* Spain
28B1 Embalse Rio Hondo *Res* Arg
25D2 Embarcación Arg
6G4 Embarras Portage Can

37B2 Embrun France
72D4 Embu Kenya
42B2 Emden Germany
52A4 Emei China
76D3 Emerald Aust
7M4 Emeril Can
6J5 Emerson Can
18C2 Emigrant P USA
72B1 Emi Koussi Mt Chad
28B3 Emilo Mitre Arg
64B2 Emirdağ Turk
14C2 Emmaus USA
42B2 Emmen Neth
36D2 Emmendingen Germany
36D1 Emmerich Germany
18C2 Emmett USA
14B3 Emmitsburg USA
10F3 Emmonak USA
8C4 Emory Peak Mt USA
21A2 Empalme Mexico
74E2 Empangeni S Africa
25E3 Empedrado Arg
xxixK2 Emperor Seamount Chain Pacific O
37D3 Empoli Italy
17C2 Emporia Kansas, USA
13D3 Emporia Virginia, USA
14A2 Emporium USA
42B2 Ems R Germany
4F4 Emsdale Can
34C2 Enard B Scot
22B1 Encarnacion Mexico
25E3 Encarnación Par
71F4 Enchi Ghana
17F4 Encinal USA
20D4 Encinitas USA
29D2 Encruzilhada Brazil
28E2 Encruzilhada do Sul Brazil
66C4 Enda Salassie Eth
76B1 Endeh Indon
3E3 Enderby Can
79G11 Enderby Land Region, Ant
11C2 Enderlin USA
13D2 Endicott USA
10H2 Endicott Mts USA
15D1 Enfield USA
37D1 Engadin Mts Switz
57F7 Engaño,C Phil
54D2 Engaru Japan
65C3 En Gedi Israel
37C1 Engelberg Switz
45H5 Engel's Russian Fed
56B4 Enggano I Indon
33C3 England Country, UK
7N4 Englee Can
15D1 Englehard USA
13D1 Englehart Can
16B2 Englewood USA
11D1 English R Can
33C3 English Channel Eng/France
4C4 English River Can
17C2 Enid USA
54D2 Eniwa Japan
70B3 Enji Well Maur
32H7 Enkoping Sweden
40C3 Enna Italy
72C2 En Nahud Sudan
72C2 Ennedi Desert Region Chad
10C2 Ennelen Russian Fed
75C1 Enngonia Aust
11B3 Enning USA
33B3 Ennis Irish Rep
18D1 Ennis Montana, USA
17C3 Ennis Texas, USA
35B5 Enniscorthy Irish Rep
35B4 Enniskillen N Ire
65C2 Enn Nâqoûra Leb
42C3 Enns R Austria
57A3 Enrekang Indon
32F8 Enschede Neth
21A1 Ensenada Mexico
52B3 Enshi China
36D3 Ensisheim France
72D4 Entebbe Uganda
15B2 Enterprise Alabama, USA
3E1 Enterprise Can
18C1 Enterprise Oregon, USA
71H4 Enugu Nig
71H4 Enugu State Nig
10D2 Enurmino Russian Fed
36E2 Enz R w Germ
54C3 Enzan Japan
71G4 Epe Nig
38C2 Epernay France
19D3 Ephraim USA
14B2 Ephrata Pennsylvania, USA
18C1 Ephrata Washington, USA
77F2 Epi I Vanuatu
38D2 Épinal France
65B1 Episkopi Cyprus
65B1 Episkopi B Cyprus
36E2 Eppingen Germany
36A2 Epte R France
74B1 Epukiro Namibia
28C3 Epu pel Arg
63C2 Eqlid Iran
68D7 Equator
72A3 Equatorial Guinea Republic, Africa
14D1 Equinox Mt USA
14C2 Equinunk USA
37C2 Erba Italy
36E2 Erbach Germany
36D2 Erbeskopf Mt Germany
28A3 Ercilla Chile
64D2 Erciş Turk
45F8 Erciyas Daglari Mt Turk
53B3 Erdaobaihe China
52C1 Erdene Mongolia
50D2 Erdenet Mongolia
72C2 Erdi Desert Region Chad
25F3 Erechim Brazil
64B1 Ereğli Turk
64B2 Ereğli Turk
50E2 Erenhot China
39B1 Eresma R Spain
36D1 Erft R Germany
42C2 Erfurt Germany
64C2 Ergani Turk
70B2 Erg Chech Desert Region Alg
72B2 Erg du Djourab Desert Region Chad
70D3 Erg Du Ténéré Desert Region Niger
64A1 Ergene R Turk
70B2 Erg Iguidi Region Alg
43F1 Ērgli Latvia
72B2 Erguig R Chad
50E1 Ergun R China/Russian Fed
49O4 Ergun Zuoqi China
10C2 Erguveyem R Russian Fed
72D2 Eriba Sudan
9F2 Erie USA
9E2 Erie,L USA/Can
4B3 Eriksdale Can
54D2 Erimo-misaki C Japan
35C4 Erin Port Eng
34B3 Eriskay I Scot
66C3 Eritrea Region, Eth
36D1 Erkelenz Germany
42C3 Erlangen Germany
17D3 Erling,L USA
74D2 Ermelo S Africa
62B3 Ernākulam India
62B2 Erode India
75B1 Eromanga Aust
74B1 Erongoberg Mt Namibia
71B2 Er Rachidia Mor
72D2 Er Rahad Sudan
73D5 Errego Mozam
33B2 Errigal Mt Irish Rep
33A3 Erris Head Pt Irish Rep
77F2 Erromanga I Vanuatu
72D2 Er Roseires Sudan
71C2 er Rtem R Alg
65C2 Er Rummān Jordan
11C2 Erskine USA
36D2 Erstein France
28E2 Erval Brazil
42C2 Erzgebirge Upland Germany
45F8 Erzincan Turk
45G8 Erzurum Turk
54D2 Esan-misaki C Japan
38C3 Esara R Spain
54D2 Esashi Japan
42B1 Esbjerg Den
19D3 Escalante USA
8C4 Escalón Mexico
9E2 Escanaba USA
21C3 Escárcega Mexico
36C2 Esch Luxembourg
19C4 Escondido USA
21B2 Escuinapa Mexico
21C3 Escuintla Guatemala
72B3 Eséka Cam
39C1 Esera R Spain
63C2 Eşfahān Iran
74E2 Eshowe S Africa
65C3 Esh Sharā Upland Jordan
37E3 Esino Italy
78C1 Eskdale NZ
32C1 Eskifjörður Iceland
32H7 Eskilstuna Sweden
6E3 Eskimo L Can
7J3 Eskimo Point Can
45E8 Eskisehir Turk
39A1 Esla R Spain
26C3 Esmeraldas Ecuador
23B2 Esmerelda Cuba
25A7 Esmerelda I Chile
38C3 Espalion France
4E4 Espanola Can
16A2 Espanola USA
76B4 Esperance Aust
28C2 Esperanza Arg
79G2 Esperanza Base Ant
29D2 Espírito Santo State, Brazil
77F2 Espiritu Santo I Vanuatu
73D6 Espungabera Mozam
25B6 Esquel Arg
18B1 Esquimalt Can
28D2 Esquina Arg
65D2 Es Samra Jordan
71A2 Essaourira Mor
71E2 Es-Sekhira Tunisia
42B2 Essen Germany
27G3 Essequibo Guyana
35F6 Essex County, Eng
12C2 Essexville USA
42B3 Esslingen Germany
36B2 Essonne France
36C2 Essoyes France
27L6 Estância Brazil
74D2 Estcourt S Africa
37D2 Este Italy
26A1 Esteli Nic
36B2 Esternay France
20B3 Estero B USA
22C1 Esteros Mexico
25D2 Esteros Par
28D1 Esteros del Iberá Swamp Arg
16A1 Estes Park USA
6H5 Estevan Can
11D3 Estherville USA
15C2 Estill USA
36B2 Estissac France
44C4 Estonia Republic Europe
25B8 Estrecho de Magallanes Str Chile
20B3 Estrella R USA
39A2 Estremoz Port
43D3 Esztergom Hung
75A1 Etadunna Aust
7L2 Etah Can
36C2 Etam France
5K3 Etamamiou Can
38C2 Etampes France
75A1 Etamunbanie,L Aust
36A1 Etaples France
60D3 Etāwah India
72D3 Ethiopia Republic, Africa
22C2 Etla Mexico
40C3 Etna Mt Italy
10M4 Etolin I USA
10E3 Etolin Str USA
73B5 Etosha Nat Pk Namibia
73B5 Etosha Pan Salt L Namibia
15C2 Etowah R USA
36A2 Etretat France
3D2 Etsha Plateau Can
36C2 Ettelbruck Lux
77H3 Eua I Tonga
75C2 Euabalong Aust
12C2 Euclid USA
75C3 Eucumbene,L Aust
75A2 Eudunda Aust
17C2 Eufala L USA
15B2 Eufaula USA
8A2 Eugene USA
75C1 Eulo Aust
17D3 Eunice Louisiana, USA
16B3 Eunice New Mexico, USA
36D1 Eupen Germany
64D3 Euphrates R Iraq
17E3 Eupora USA
36A2 Eure Department, France
38C2 Eure R France
36A2 Eure-et-Loir Department, France
18B2 Eureka California, USA
7K1 Eureka Can
18C1 Eureka Montana, USA
8B3 Eureka Nevada, USA
11C2 Eureka S Dakota, USA
19D3 Eureka Utah, USA
7K2 Eureka Sound Can
20D2 Eureka V USA
75C3 Euroa Aust
75C1 Eurombah R Aust
73E6 Europa I Mozam Chan
36C1 Europoort Neth
42B2 Euskirchen Germany
15B2 Eutaw USA
3C3 Eutsuk L Can
3F3 Evansburg Can
7K1 Evans,C Can
7L4 Evans,L Can
16A2 Evans,Mt Colorado, USA
18D1 Evans,Mt Montana, USA
7K3 Evans Str Can
12B2 Evanston Illinois, USA
8B2 Evanston Wyoming, USA
9E3 Evansville Indiana, USA
11A3 Evansville Wyoming, USA
74D2 Evaton S Africa
76C4 Everard,L Aust
59G3 Everest,Mt Nepal/China
14A2 Everett Pennsylvania, USA
8A2 Everett Washington, USA
14D1 Everett,Mt USA
9E4 Everglades,The Swamp USA
15B2 Evergreen USA
35E5 Evesham Eng
72B3 Evinayong Eq Guinea
32F7 Evje Nor
37B1 Evolène Switz
39A2 Évora Port
38C2 Evreux France
41E3 Évvoia I Greece
72B4 Ewo Congo
20C1 Excelisor Mt USA
20C1 Excelisor Mts USA
17D2 Excelsior Springs USA
19C3 Exeter California, USA
35D6 Exeter Eng
13E2 Exeter New Hampshire, USA
35D6 Exmoor Nat Pk Eng
35D6 Exmouth Eng
39A2 Extremadura Region, Spain
21E2 Exuma Sd Bahamas
72D4 Eyasi L Tanz
34D4 Eyemouth Scot
69D4 Eyl Somalia
76B4 Eyre Aust
76C3 Eyre Creek R Aust
76C3 Eyre,L Aust
76C4 Eyre Pen Aust
3H2 Eyrie L Can
57F8 Eyte I Phil
22B1 Ezatlan Mexico
41F3 Ezine Turk
66B3 Ez Zeidab Sudan

F

4G3 Faber L Can
32F7 Fåborg Den
40C2 Fabriano Italy
37B2 Fabrosa Italy
72B2 Fachi Niger
72C2 Fada Chad
71G3 Fada N'Gourma Burkina
49Q2 Faddeyevskiy, Ostrov I Russian Fed
40C2 Faenza Italy
7N3 Faeringehavn Greenland
30E2 Faeroerne Is, N Atlantic
72B3 Fafa R CAR
72E3 Fafan R Eth
71G3 Faga R Burkina
41E1 Făgăraş Rom
36C1 Fagnes Region, Belg
70B3 Faguibine,L Mali
67G2 Fahud Oman
70A1 Faiol I Açores
16A3 Fairacres USA
6D3 Fairbanks USA
12C3 Fairborn USA
8D2 Fairbury USA
14B3 Fairfax USA
19B3 Fairfield California, USA
14D2 Fairfield Connecticut, USA
18D2 Fairfield Idaho, USA
18D1 Fairfield Montana, USA
12C3 Fairfield Ohio, USA
34B4 Fair Head Pt N Ire
33C2 Fair Isle I Scot
78B2 Fairlie NZ
11D3 Fairmont Minnesota, USA
12C3 Fairmont W Virginia, USA
14B1 Fairport USA
3E2 Fairview Can
16C2 Fairview USA
6E4 Fairweather,Mt USA
51H6 Fais I Pacific O
60C2 Faisalabad Pak
11B2 Faith USA
34E1 Faither,The Pen Scot
61B2 Faizābād India
77H1 Fakaofo I Tokeau Is
35F5 Fakenham Eng
76C1 Fakfak Indon
32G7 Faköping Sweden
71F3 Falaise de Banfora Burkina
61D3 Falam Burma
28B4 Falckner Arg
21C2 Falcon Res USA/Mexico
70A3 Falémé R Mali/Sen
17F4 Falfurrias USA
3E2 Falher Can
32G7 Falkenberg Sweden
34D4 Falkirk Scot
25D8 Falkland Is Dependency, S Atlantic
25E8 Falkland Sd Falkland Is
20D4 Fallbrook USA
8B3 Fallon USA
13E2 Fall River USA
16A1 Fall River P USA
17C1 Falls City USA
35C6 Falmouth Eng
23H1 Falmouth Jamaica
13E2 Falmouth Maine, USA
14E2 Falmouth Massachusetts, USA
74B3 False B S Africa
21A2 Falso,C Mexico
42C2 Falster I Den
41F1 Fălticeni Rom
32H6 Falun Sweden
64B2 Famagusta Cyprus
65B1 Famagusta B Cyprus
28B1 Famatina Arg
36C1 Famenne Region, Belg
4B3 Family L Can
20C3 Famoso USA
55B2 Fang Thai
72D3 Fangak Sudan
52E5 Fang liao Taiwan
53B2 Fangzheng China
40C2 Fano Italy
65A3 Fâqûs Egypt
79G3 Faraday Base Ant
72C3 Faradje Zaïre
73E6 Farafangana Madag
69B2 Farafra Oasis Egypt
63E2 Farah Afghan
63E2 Farah R Afghan
51H5 Farallon de Medinilla I Pacific O
70A3 Faranah Guinea
51H6 Faraulep I Pacific O
35E6 Fareham Eng
Farewell,C = Kap Farvel
77G5 Farewell,C NZ
78B2 Farewell Spit Pt NZ
8D2 Fargo USA
65C2 Fari'a R Israel
9D2 Faribault USA
61C3 Faridpur Bang
63D1 Farimān Iran
65A3 Fâriskûr Egypt
13E2 Farmington Maine, USA
17D2 Farmington Missouri, USA
14E1 Farmington New Hampshire, USA
8C3 Farmington New Mexico, USA
18D2 Farmington Utah, USA
20B2 Farmington Res USA
34E4 Farne Deep N Sea
3E3 Farnham,Mt Can
10M3 Faro Can
39A2 Faro Port
32H7 Fåro I Sweden
71J4 Faro R Cam
68K8 Farquhar Is Indian O
34C3 Farrar R Scot
12C2 Farrell USA
41E3 Fársala Greece
63E2 Farsi Afghan
16B3 Farwell USA
63C3 Fasā Iran
45D5 Fastov Ukraine
61B2 Fatehpur India
27H7 Fatima du Sul Brazil
18C1 Fauquier Can
74D2 Fauresmith S Africa
37B2 Faverges France
4C3 Fawcett L Can
7K4 Fawn R Can
32H6 Fax R Sweden
32A2 Faxaflóri B Iceland
72B2 Faya Chad
15B2 Fayette USA
9D3 Fayetteville Arkansas, USA
9F3 Fayetteville N Carolina, USA
15B1 Fayetteville Tennessee, USA
65B3 Fâyid Egypt
64E4 Faylakah I Kuwait
60C2 Fāzilka India
70A2 Fdérik Maur
9F3 Fear,C USA
19B3 Feather Middle Fork R USA
36A2 Fécamp France
28D2 Federación Arg
28D2 Federal Arg
71H4 Federal Capital Territory Nig
51H6 Federated States of Micronesia Is Pacific O
42C2 Fehmarn I Germany
26D5 Feijó Brazil
52C5 Feilai Xai Bei Jiang R China
78C2 Feilding NZ
73D5 Feira Zambia
27L6 Feira de Santan Brazil
64C2 Feke Turk
36D3 Feldberg Mt Germany
42B3 Feldkirch Austria
28D2 Feliciano R Arg
33D3 Felixstowe Eng
37D1 Feltre Italy
32G6 Femund L Nor

53A3 **Fengcheng** China
52B4 **Fengdu** China
52D1 **Fenging** China
52B3 **Fengjie** China
53A1 **Fengshui Shan** *Mt* China
52B3 **Feng Xian** China
52C1 **Fengzhen** China
52C2 **Fen He** *R* China
10C6 **Fenimore Pass** USA
73E5 **Fenoarivo Atsinanana** Madag
45F7 **Feodosiya** Ukraine
63D2 **Ferdow** Iran
36B2 **Fère** France
36B2 **Fère-Champenoise** France
59F2 **Fergana** Uzbekistan
3J2 **Fergus** *R* Can
11C2 **Fergus Falls** USA
35B4 **Fermanagh** County, N Ire
37E3 **Fermo** Italy
37D1 **Fern** *Mt* Austria
28C1 **Fernandez** Arg
15C2 **Fernandina Beach** USA
xxxG5 **Fernando de Noronha** *I* Atlantic O
29B3 **Fernandópolis** Brazil
70C4 **Fernando Poo** *I* Eq Guinea
18B1 **Ferndale** USA
18C1 **Fernie** Can
19C3 **Fernley** USA
40C2 **Ferrara** Italy
26C5 **Ferreñafe** Peru
17D3 **Ferriday** USA
36B2 **Ferriéres** France
71A2 **Fès** Mor
5G4 **Festubert** Can
17D2 **Festus** USA
41F2 **Feteşti** Rom
64A2 **Fethiye** Turk
45J7 **Fetisovo** Kazakhstan
34E1 **Fetlar** *I* Scot
53C1 **Fevral'skoye** Russian Fed
48J6 **Feyzabad** Afghan
28B1 **Fiambalá** Arg
73E6 **Fianarantsoa** Madag
72D3 **Fichē** Eth
74D2 **Ficksburg** S Africa
37D2 **Fidenza** Italy
41D2 **Fier** Alb
37D1 **Fiera Di Primeiro** Italy
34D3 **Fife** Region, Scot
34D3 **Fife Ness** *Pen* Scot
38C3 **Figeac** France
39A1 **Figueira da Foz** Port
39C1 **Figueras** Spain
Figueres = Figueras
71B2 **Figuig** Mor
77G2 **Fiji** *Is* Pacific O
27G8 **Filadelpia** Par
41E2 **Filiaşi** Rom
41E3 **Filiatrá** Greece
40C3 **Filicudi** *I* Italy
19C4 **Fillmore** California, USA
19D3 **Fillmore** Utah, USA
37C2 **Finale Ligure** Italy
34C3 **Findhorn** *R* Scot
9E2 **Findlay** USA
3E3 **Findlay,Mt** Can
13D2 **Finger Lakes** USA
73D5 **Fingoè** Mozam
45E8 **Finike** Turk
76C3 **Finke** *R* Aust
75A1 **Finke Flood Flats** Aust
44C3 **Finland** Republic, N Europe
32J7 **Finland,G of** N Europe
6F4 **Finlay** *R* Can
6F4 **Finlay Forks** Can
75C3 **Finley** Aust
32H5 **Finnsnes** Nor
51H7 **Finschhafen** PNG
37C1 **Finsteraarhorn** *Mt* Switz
42C2 **Finsterwalde** Germany
35B4 **Fintona** N Ire
78A3 **Fiordland Nat Pk** NZ
65C2 **Fīq** Syria
45F8 **Firat** *R* Turk
3F2 **Firebag** *R* Can
20B2 **Firebaugh** USA
40C2 **Firenze** Italy
37D2 **Firenzuola** Italy
3C2 **Fireside** Can
28C2 **Firmat** Arg
60D3 **Firozābād** India
60C2 **Firozpur** India
32H7 **Firspång** Sweden
34C4 **Firth of Clyde** *Estuary* Scot
34D3 **Firth of Forth** *Estuary* Scot
34B3 **Firth of Lorn** *Estuary* Scot
33C2 **Firth of Tay** *Estuary* Scot
63C3 **Fīrūzābād** Iran
74B2 **Fish** *R* Namibia
74C3 **Fish** *R* S Africa
20C2 **Fish Camp** USA
14D2 **Fishers I** USA
7K3 **Fisher Str** Can
35C6 **Fishguard** Wales
10O3 **Fish L** Can
7N3 **Fiskenaesset** Greenland
36B2 **Fismes** France
13E2 **Fitchburg** USA
34E2 **Fitful Head** *Pt* Scot
15C2 **Fitzgerald** USA
3F2 **Fitzgerald** Can
76B2 **Fitzroy** *R* Aust
76B2 **Fitzroy Crossing** Aust
12C1 **Fitzwilliam I** Can
Fiume = Rijeka
72C4 **Fizi** Zaïre
74D3 **Flagstaff** S Africa
8B3 **Flagstaff** USA
13E1 **Flagstaff L** USA
35E4 **Flamborough Head** *C* Eng
8C2 **Flaming Gorge Res** USA
34B2 **Flannan Isles** *Is* Scot
10N3 **Flat** *R* Can
3F4 **Flathead** *R* USA
8B2 **Flathead L** USA
17D2 **Flat River** USA
51H8 **Flattery,C** Aust
8A2 **Flattery,C** USA
35D5 **Fleetwood** Eng
32F7 **Flekkefjord** *Inlet* Nor
50H4 **Fleming Deep** Pacific Oc
14C2 **Flemington** USA
42B2 **Flensburg** Germany
5K3 **Fleur-de-Lys** Can
37B1 **Fleurier** Switz
36A2 **Fleury-sur-Andelle** France
76C4 **Flinders I** Aust
76D5 **Flinders** *I* Aust
76C4 **Flinders Range** *Mts* Aust
6H4 **Flin Flon** Can
9E2 **Flint** USA
35D5 **Flint** Wales
9E3 **Flint** *R* USA
36B1 **Flixecourt** France
12A1 **Floodwood** USA
15B2 **Florala** USA
Florence = Firenze
9E3 **Florence** Alabama, USA
19D4 **Florence** Arizona, USA
16A2 **Florence** Colorado, USA
17C2 **Florence** Kansas, USA
18B2 **Florence** Oregon, USA
9F3 **Florence** S Carolina, USA
20C2 **Florence,L** USA
26C3 **Florencia** Colombia
36C2 **Florenville** Belg
21D3 **Flores** Guatemala
70A1 **Flores** *I* Açores
76B1 **Flores** *I* Indon
28D3 **Flores** *R* Arg
51E7 **Flores S** Indon
27K5 **Floriano** Brazil
25G3 **Florianópolis** Brazil
21D2 **Florida** State, USA
25E4 **Florida** Urug
15E4 **Florida B** USA
15E4 **Florida City** USA
77E1 **Florida Is** Solomon Is
9E4 **Florida Keys** *Is* USA
9E4 **Florida,Strs of** USA
41E2 **Flórina** Greece
32F6 **Florø** Nor
16B3 **Floydada** USA
37D1 **Fluchthorn** *Mt* Austria
57C3 **Fluk** Indon
76D1 **Fly** *R* PNG
37E2 **Foci del Po** *Delta* Italy
41F1 **Focsani** Rom
40D2 **Foggia** Italy
37E3 **Foglia** *R* Italy
5L4 **Fogo** Can
5L4 **Fogo I** Can
70A4 **Fogo** *I* Cape Verde
38C3 **Foix** France
4E4 **Foleyet** Can
7L3 **Foley I** Can
40C2 **Foligno** Italy
35F6 **Folkestone** Eng
15C2 **Folkston** USA
40C2 **Follonica** Italy
20B1 **Folsom** USA
14C1 **Fonda** USA
6H4 **Fond-du-Lac** Can
9E2 **Fond du Lac** USA
38C2 **Fontainebleau** France
3D2 **Fontas** *R* Can
17D2 **Fontenac** USA
38B2 **Fontenay-le-Comte** France
41D1 **Fonyód** Hung
Foochow = Fuzhou
10H3 **Foraker,Mt** USA
36D2 **Forbach** France
75C2 **Forbes** Aust
71H4 **Forcados** Nig
37A3 **Forcalquier** France
20C3 **Ford City** USA
32F6 **Forde** Nor
75C1 **Fords Bridge** Aust
17D3 **Fordyce** USA
70A4 **Forécariah** Guinea
7P3 **Forel,Mt** Greenland
18D1 **Foremost** Can
12C2 **Forest** Can
15B2 **Forest** USA
11D3 **Forest City** Iowa, USA
14C2 **Forest City** Pennsylvania, USA
15C2 **Forest Park** USA
20A1 **Forestville** USA
36B2 **Forêt d'Othe** France
34D3 **Forfar** Scot
16B2 **Forgan** USA
36A2 **Forges-les-Eaux** France
18B1 **Forks** USA
40C2 **Forlì** Italy
39C2 **Formentera** *I* Spain
40C2 **Formia** Italy
70A1 **Formigas** *I* Açores
Formosa = Taiwan
25E3 **Formosa** Arg
27J7 **Formosa** Brazil
25D2 **Formosa** State, Arg
52D5 **Formosa Str** Taiwan/China
29C1 **Formoso** Brazil
29C1 **Formoso** *R* Brazil
37D2 **Fornovo di Taro** Italy
34D3 **Forres** Scot
76B4 **Forrest** Aust
9D3 **Forrest City** USA
3G2 **Forrest L** Can
76D2 **Forsayth** Aust
32J6 **Forssa** Fin
75D2 **Forster** Aust
17D2 **Forsyth** Missouri, USA
11A2 **Forsyth** Montana, USA
60C3 **Fort Abbas** Pak
7K4 **Fort Albany** Can
27L4 **Fortaleza** Brazil
34C3 **Fort Augustus** Scot
74D3 **Fort Beaufort** S Africa
18D1 **Fort Benton** USA
19B3 **Fort Bragg** USA
3F2 **Fort Chipewyan** Can
16C2 **Fort Cobb Res** USA
8C2 **Fort Collins** USA
4F4 **Fort Coulonge** Can
16B3 **Fort Davis** USA
23E4 **Fort de France** Martinique
15B2 **Fort Deposit** USA
9D2 **Fort Dodge** USA
76A3 **Fortescue** *R* Aust
7J5 **Fort Frances** Can
6F3 **Fort Franklin** Can
6F3 **Fort Good Hope** Can
75B1 **Fort Grey** Aust
34C3 **Forth** *R* Scot
16A3 **Fort Hancock** USA
7K4 **Fort Hope** Can
34F3 **Forties** *Oilfield* N Sea
28B3 **Fortin Uno** Arg
13F1 **Fort Kent** USA
70C1 **Fort Lallemand** Alg
Fort Lamy = Ndjamena
11B3 **Fort Laramie** USA
9E4 **Fort Lauderdale** USA
3D1 **Fort Liard** Can
6G4 **Fort Mackay** Can
6G5 **Fort Macleod** Can
6G4 **Fort McMurray** Can
6E3 **Fort McPherson** Can
12A2 **Fort Madison** USA
8C2 **Fort Morgan** USA
9E4 **Fort Myers** USA
6F4 **Fort Nelson** Can
3D2 **Fort Nelson** *R* Can
6F3 **Fort Norman** Can
15B2 **Fort Payne** USA
11A2 **Fort Peck** USA
8C2 **Fort Peck Res** USA
9E4 **Fort Pierce** USA
11B3 **Fort Pierre** USA
14C1 **Fort Plain** USA
6G3 **Fort Providence** Can
3H3 **Fort Qu'Appelle** Can
10F4 **Fort Randall** USA
6G3 **Fort Resolution** Can
72B4 **Fort Rousset** Congo
6F4 **Fort St James** Can
3D2 **Fort St John** Can
3F3 **Fort Saskatchewan** Can
17D2 **Fort Scott** USA
6E3 **Fort Selkirk** Can
7K4 **Fort Severn** Can
45J7 **Fort Shevchenko** Kazakhstan
6F3 **Fort Simpson** Can
6G3 **Fort Smith** Can
9D3 **Fort Smith** USA
6F3 **Fort Smith** Region, Can
8C3 **Fort Stockton** USA
16B3 **Fort Sumner** USA
16C2 **Fort Supply** USA
18B2 **Fortuna** California, USA
11B2 **Fortuna** N Dakota, USA
5K4 **Fortune B** Can
6G4 **Fort Vermilion** Can
15B2 **Fort Walton Beach** USA
9E2 **Fort Wayne** USA
34C3 **Fort William** Scot
16A2 **Fort Wingate** USA
8D3 **Fort Worth** USA
10K3 **Fortymile** *R* USA
10J2 **Fort Yukon** USA
52C5 **Foshan** China
7K2 **Fosheim** *Pen* Can
37B2 **Fossano** Italy
37E3 **Fossombrone** Italy
11C2 **Fosston** USA
3G2 **Foster L** Can
10L4 **Foster,Mt** USA
72B4 **Fougamou** Gabon
38B2 **Fougères** France
34D1 **Foula** *I* Scot
35F6 **Foulness I** Eng
78B2 **Foulwind,C** NZ
72B3 **Foumban** Cam
38C1 **Fourmies** France
10E5 **Four Mountains,Is of** USA
41F3 **Foúrnoi** *I* Greece
70A3 **Fouta Djallon** *Mts* Guinea
77F5 **Foveaux Str** NZ
35C6 **Fowey** Eng
16B2 **Fowler** USA
12B2 **Fox** *R* USA
3E3 **Fox Creek** Can
7K3 **Foxe Basin** *G* Can
7K3 **Foxe Chan** Can
7L3 **Foxe Pen** Can
10E5 **Fox Is** USA
3F2 **Fox Lake** Can
16A1 **Foxpark** USA
78C2 **Foxton** NZ
3G3 **Fox Valley** Can
73B5 **Foz do Cuene** Angola
25F3 **Foz do Iquaçu** Brazil
22B1 **Fracisco I Madero** Mexico
14B2 **Frackville** USA
28B2 **Fraga** Arg
14E1 **Framingham** USA
27J8 **Franca** Brazil
38C2 **France** Republic, Europe
10N3 **Frances** *R* Can
4D5 **Francesville** USA
38D2 **Franche Comté** Region, France
74D1 **Francistown** Botswana
3C3 **Francois L** Can
18E2 **Francs Peak** *Mt* USA
36E1 **Frankenberg** Germany
12B2 **Frankfort** Indiana, USA
9E3 **Frankfort** Kentucky, USA
14C1 **Frankfort** New York, USA
42B2 **Frankfurt** Germany
74D2 **Frankfurt** S Africa
36E1 **Frankfurt am Main** Germany
42C2 **Frankfurt-an-der-Oder** Germany
42C3 **Fränkischer Alb** *Upland* Germany
18D2 **Franklin** Idaho, USA
12B3 **Franklin** Indiana, USA
17D4 **Franklin** Louisiana, USA
14E1 **Franklin** Massachusetts, USA
15C1 **Franklin** N Carolina, USA
14E1 **Franklin** New Hampshire, USA
14C2 **Franklin** New Jersey, USA
13D2 **Franklin** Pennsylvania, USA
15B1 **Franklin** Tennessee, USA
13D3 **Franklin** Virginia, USA
6F2 **Franklin B** Can
18C1 **Franklin D Roosevelt** *L* USA
6F3 **Franklin Mts** Can
10G1 **Franklin,Pt** USA
6J2 **Franklin Str** Can
14A1 **Franklinville** USA
4E4 **Franz** Can
78B2 **Franz Josef Glacier** NZ
Franz-Joseph-Land = Zemlya Franza Josifa
4F5 **Fraser** *R* Can
74C3 **Fraserburg** S Africa
34D3 **Fraserburgh** Scot
75D1 **Fraser I** Aust
3C3 **Fraser Lake** Can
5J2 **Fraser** *R* Can
37B1 **Frasne** France
37C1 **Frauenfield** Switz
28D2 **Fray Bentos** Urug
33C2 **Frazerburgh** Scot
14C3 **Frederica** USA
42B1 **Fredericia** Den
13D3 **Frederick** Maryland, USA
16C3 **Frederick** Oklahoma, USA
16C3 **Fredericksburg** Texas, USA
13D3 **Fredericksburg** Virginia, USA
10M4 **Frederick Sd** USA
17D2 **Fredericktown** USA
7M5 **Fredericton** Can
7N3 **Frederikshåb** Greenland
32G7 **Frederikshavn** Den
13D2 **Fredonia** USA
32G7 **Fredrikstad** Nor
14C2 **Freehold** USA
20C1 **Freel Peak** *Mt* USA
5L4 **Freels,C** Can
11C3 **Freeman** USA
23B1 **Freeport** Bahamas
5H5 **Freeport** Can
12B2 **Freeport** Illinois, USA
17C4 **Freeport** Texas, USA
17F4 **Freer** USA
70A4 **Freetown** Sierra Leone
42B3 **Freiburg** Germany
36D2 **Freiburg im Breisgau** Germany
28A1 **Freirina** Chile
42C3 **Freistadt** Austria
37B3 **Fréjus** France
76A4 **Fremantle** Aust
20B2 **Fremont** California, USA
17C1 **Fremont** Nebraska, USA
12C2 **Fremont** Ohio, USA
27H3 **French Guiana** Dependency, S America
11A2 **Frenchman** *R* USA
75E3 **Frenchmans Cap** *Mt* Aust
xxixM5 **French Polynesia** *Is* Pacific O
71C1 **Frenda** Alg
21B2 **Fresnillo** Mexico
8B3 **Fresno** USA
20C2 **Fresno** *R* USA
18D1 **Fresno Res** USA
37A1 **Fretigney** France
36E2 **Freudenstadt** Germany
36B1 **Frévent** France
75E3 **Freycinet Pen** Aust
70A3 **Fria** Guinea
20C2 **Friant** USA
20C2 **Friant Dam** USA
28B1 **Frías** Arg
40B1 **Fribourg** Switz
36E1 **Friedberg** Germany
42B3 **Friedrichshafen** Germany
16C4 **Frio** *R* USA
16B3 **Friona** USA
37E1 **Friuli** Region, Italy
7M3 **Frobisher B** Can
7M3 **Frobisher Bay** Can
6H4 **Frobisher L** Can
45G6 **Frolovo** Russian Fed
35D6 **Frome** Eng
75A1 **Frome** *R* Aust
35D6 **Frome** *R* Eng
76C4 **Frome,L** Aust
21C3 **Frontera** Mexico
13D3 **Front Royal** USA
40C2 **Frosinone** Italy
14A3 **Frostburg** USA
16A2 **Fruita** USA
52C5 **Fuchuan** China
52E4 **Fuding** China
21B2 **Fuerte** *R* Mexico
29A3 **Fuerte Olimpo** Brazil
25E2 **Fuerte Olimpo** Par
70A2 **Fuerteventura** *I* Canary Is
52C2 **Fugu** China
50B2 **Fuhai** China
67G1 **Fujairah** UAE
54C3 **Fuji** Japan
52D4 **Fujian** Province, China
53C2 **Fujin** China
54C3 **Fujinomiya** Japan
53D4 **Fuji-san** *Mt* Japan
54C3 **Fujisawa** Japan
54C3 **Fuji-Yoshida** Japan
54D2 **Fukagawa** Japan
48K5 **Fukang** China
53C4 **Fukuchiyima** Japan
54A4 **Fukue** Japan
54A4 **Fukue** *I* Japan
53D4 **Fukui** Japan
53C5 **Fukuoka** Japan
53E4 **Fukushima** Japan
53C5 **Fukuyama** Japan
11C3 **Fulda** USA
42B2 **Fulda** Germany
42B2 **Fulda** *R* Germany
52B4 **Fuling** China
23L1 **Fullarton** Trinidad
20D4 **Fullerton** USA
12A2 **Fulton** Illinois, USA
12B3 **Fulton** Kentucky, USA
13D2 **Fulton** New York, USA
36C1 **Fumay** France
54D3 **Funabashi** Japan
77G1 **Funafuti** *I* Tuvalu

70A1 **Funchal** Medeira
29D2 **Fundão** Brazil
7M5 **Fundy,B of** Can
73D6 **Funhalouro** Mozam
52B5 **Funing** China
52D3 **Funing** China
71H3 **Funtua** Nig
52D4 **Fuqing** China
73D5 **Furancungo** Mozam
54D2 **Furano** Japan
63D3 **Fürg** Iran
37C1 **Furka** *P* Switz
76D5 **Furneaux Group** *Is* Aust
42C2 **Fürstenwalde** Germany
42C3 **Fürth** Germany
54D2 **Furubira** Japan
53D4 **Furukawa** Japan
7K3 **Fury and Hecla Str** Can
53A3 **Fushun** Liaoning, China
52A4 **Fushun** Sichuan, China
53B3 **Fusong** China
42C3 **Füssen** Germany
52E2 **Fu Xian** China
52E1 **Fuxin** China
52D3 **Fuyang** China
53A2 **Fuyu** China
53C2 **Fuyuan** Heilongjiang, China
52E1 **Fuyuan** Liaoning, China
52A4 **Fuyuan** Yunnan, China
50B2 **Fuyun** China
52D4 **Fuzhou** China
42C1 **Fyn** *I* Den

G

72E3 **Gaalkacyo** Somalia
19C3 **Gabbs** USA
20C1 **Gabbs Valley Range** *Mts* USA
73B5 **Gabela** Angola
71E2 **Gabe's** Tunisia
66B2 **Gabgaba** *Watercourse* Egypt
20B2 **Gabilan Range** *Mts* USA
72B4 **Gabon** Republic, Africa
74D1 **Gaborone** Botswana
41F2 **Gabrovo** Bulg
63C2 **Gach Sārān** Iran
15B2 **Gadsden** Alabama, USA
19D4 **Gadsden** Arizona, USA
40C2 **Gaeta** Italy
51H6 **Gaferut** *I* Pacific O
15C1 **Gaffney** USA
71D2 **Gafsa** Tunisia
44E4 **Gagarin** Russian Fed
71H3 **Gagere** *R* Nig
7M4 **Gagnon** Can
45G7 **Gagra** Georgia
61C2 **Gaibanda** India
37E1 **Gailtaler Alpen** *Mts* Austria
25C6 **Gaimán** Arg
15C3 **Gainesville** Florida, USA
15C2 **Gainesville** Georgia, USA
17C3 **Gainesville** Texas, USA
35E5 **Gainsborough** Eng
75A2 **Gairdner,L** Aust
34C3 **Gairloch** Scot
14B3 **Gaithersburg** USA
62B1 **Gajendragarh** India
52D4 **Ga Jiang** *R* China
74C2 **Gakarosa** *Mt* S Africa
72D4 **Galana** *R* Kenya
xxxD4 **Galapagos Is** Pacific O
34D4 **Galashiels** Scot
41F1 **Galaţi** Rom
12C3 **Galax** USA
16A3 **Galeana** Mexico
57C2 **Galela** Indon
6C3 **Galena** Alaska, USA
12A2 **Galena** Illinois, USA
17D2 **Galena** Kansas, USA
23L1 **Galeota Pt** Trinidad
23L1 **Galera Pt** Trinidad
12A2 **Galesburg** USA
14B2 **Galeton** USA
44G4 **Galich** Russian Fed
39A1 **Galicia** Region, Spain
Galilee,S of = Tiberias,L
23J1 **Galina Pt** Jamaica
66C4 **Gallabat** Sudan
37C2 **Gallarate** Italy
15B1 **Gallatin** USA
18D1 **Gallatin** *R* USA
62C3 **Galle** Sri Lanka
16A4 **Gallego** Mexico
39B1 **Gállego** *R* Spain
Gallipoli = Gelibolu
41D2 **Gallipoli** Italy
44C2 **Gällivare** Sweden
34C4 **Galloway** District
35C4 **Galloway,Mull of** *C* Scot
16A2 **Gallup** USA
71H3 **Galma** *R* Nig
21C2 **Galveston** USA
9D4 **Galveston B** USA
28C2 **Galvez** Arg
38D3 **Galvi** Corse
33B3 **Galway** Irish Rep
33B3 **Galway** *B* Irish Rep
57D3 **Gam** *I* Indon
61C2 **Gamba** China
71F3 **Gambaga** Ghana
10D3 **Gambell** USA
70A3 **Gambia** *R* The Gambia/ Sen
70A3 **Gambia,The** Republic, Africa
5L4 **Gambo** Can
72B4 **Gamboma** Congo
73B5 **Gambos** Angola
62C3 **Gampola** Sri Lanka
19E3 **Ganado** USA
72E3 **Ganale Dorya** *R* Eth
4F5 **Gananoque** Can
Gand = Gent
73B5 **Ganda** Angola
73C4 **Gandajika** Zaïre
60B3 **Gandava** Pak
7N5 **Gander** Can
60B4 **Gāndhīdhām** India
60C4 **Gāndhīnagar** India
60D4 **Gāndhi Sāgar** *L* India
39B2 **Gandia** Spain
29E1 **Gandu** Brazil
61C3 **Ganga** *R* India
60C3 **Ganganar** India
61D3 **Gangaw** Burma
61E3 **Gangaw Range** *Mts* Burma
52A2 **Gangca** China
59G2 **Gangdise Shan** *Mts* China
Ganges = Ganga
61C2 **Gangtok** India
52B3 **Gangu** China
53A1 **Gan He** *R* China
57C3 **Gani** Indon
53A2 **Gannan** China
18E2 **Gannett Peak** *Mt* USA
52B2 **Ganquan** China
75A3 **Gantheaume** *C* Aust
32K8 **Gantsevichi** Belorussia
71J4 **Ganye** Nig
52D4 **Ganzhou** China
70C3 **Gao** Mali
52A2 **Gaolan** China
52C2 **Gaoping** China
71F3 **Gaoua** Burkina
70A3 **Gaoual** Guinea
52D3 **Gaoyou Hu** *L* China
52C5 **Gaozhou** China
38D3 **Gap** France
57F7 **Gapan** Phil
60D2 **Gar** China
75C1 **Garah** Aust
27L5 **Garanhuns** Brazil
19B2 **Garberville** USA
29C3 **Garça** Brazil
29B3 **Garcias** Brazil
37D2 **Garda** Italy
37A3 **Gardanne** France
16B2 **Garden City** USA
12B1 **Garden Pen** USA
28D3 **Gardey** Arg
60B2 **Gardez** Afghan
18D1 **Gardiner** USA
14D2 **Gardiners I** USA
14E1 **Gardner** USA
77H1 **Gardner** *I* Phoenix Is
20C1 **Gardnerville** USA
37D2 **Gardone** Italy
10C6 **Gareloi** *I* USA
37D2 **Gargano** Italy
60D4 **Garhākota** India
44L4 **Gari** Russian Fed
74B3 **Garies** S Africa
72D4 **Garissa** Kenya
17C3 **Garland** USA
42C3 **Garmisch-Partenkirchen** Germany
63C1 **Garmsar** Iran
17C2 **Garnett** USA
8B2 **Garnett Peak** *Mt* USA
38C3 **Garonne** *R* France
71J4 **Garoua** Cam
71J4 **Garoua Boulai** Cam
11B2 **Garrison** USA
34C3 **Garry** *R* Scot
6H3 **Garry L** Can
56C4 **Garut** Indon
61B3 **Garwa** India
12B2 **Gary** USA
59G2 **Garyarsa** China
6H3 **Gary L** Can
28C1 **Garza** Arg
17C3 **Garza-Little Elm** *Res* USA
63C1 **Gasan Kuli** Turkmenistan
38B3 **Gascogne** Region, France
17D2 **Gasconade** *R* USA
76A3 **Gascoyne** *R* Aust
72B3 **Gashaka** Nig
63E3 **Gasht** Iran
71J3 **Gashua** Nig
5J4 **Gaspé** Can
5H4 **Gaspésie Prov Park** Can
15C1 **Gastonia** USA
15D1 **Gaston,L** USA
65B1 **Gata,C** Cyprus
44D4 **Gatchina** Russian Fed
34D4 **Gateshead** Eng
17C3 **Gatesville** USA
36B2 **Gâtinais** Region, France
4F4 **Gatineau** Can
4F4 **Gatineau** *R* Can
15C1 **Gatlinburg** USA
75D1 **Gatton** Aust
77F2 **Gaua** *I* Vanuatu
63E2 **Gaud-i-Zirreh** *Salt Desert* Afghan
4B2 **Gauer L** Can
61D2 **Gauháti** India
43E1 **Gauja** *R* Latvia
63F1 **Gaurdak** Turkmenistan
61B2 **Gauri Phanta** India
41E4 **Gavdhos** *I* Greece
29D1 **Gavião** *R* Brazil
20B3 **Gaviota** USA
32H6 **Gävle** Sweden
75A2 **Gawler Ranges** *Mts* Aust
52A1 **Gaxun Nur** *L* China
61B3 **Gaya** India
71G3 **Gaya** Niger
53B3 **Gaya** *R* China
12C1 **Gaylord** USA
75D1 **Gayndah** Aust
44J3 **Gayny** Russian Fed
43F3 **Gaysin** Ukraine
64B3 **Gaza** Israel
64C2 **Gaziantep** Turk
70B4 **Gbaringa** Lib
43D2 **Gdańsk** Pol
43D2 **Gdańsk,G of** Pol
32K7 **Gdov** Russian Fed
43D2 **Gdynia** Pol
57C3 **Gebe** *I* Indon
65C4 **Gebel Abu Rûtha** *Mt* Egypt
65C3 **Gebel Araif el Naqa** *Mt* Egypt
65B4 **Gebel Ataqa** *Mt* Egypt
65B4 **Gebel Budhiya** Egypt
65A4 **Gebel el Galâla Bahariya** *Desert* Egypt
65B3 **Gebel El Giddi** *Mt* Egypt
65B4 **Gebel El Tîh** *Upland* Egypt
65B3 **Gebel Halâl** *Mt* Egypt
66C2 **Gebel Hamata** *Mt* Egypt
64B4 **Gebel Katherina** *Mt* Egypt
65B4 **Gebel Kharim** *Mt* Egypt
65B3 **Gebel Libni** *Mt* Egypt
65B3 **Gebel Maghâra** *Mt* Egypt
65C4 **Gebel Sha'îra** *Mt* Egypt
65B4 **Gebel Sinn Bishr** *Mt* Egypt
65B3 **Gebel Yi'allaq** *Mt* Egypt
71E2 **Gebès** Tunisia
22C1 **Gedad del Maiz** Mexico
66C4 **Gedaref** Sudan
41F3 **Gediz** *R* Turk
42C2 **Gedser** Den
36C1 **Geel** Belg
75B3 **Geelong** Aust
75E3 **Geeveston** Aust
71J3 **Geidam** Nig
3H2 **Geikie** *R* Can
36D1 **Geilenkirchen** Germany
72D4 **Geita** Tanz
52A5 **Gejiu** China
40C3 **Gela** Italy
72E3 **Geladi** Eth
36D1 **Geldern** Germany
41F2 **Gelibolu** Turk
64B2 **Gelidonya Burun** Turk
22B1 **Gelleana** Mexico
36E1 **Gelnhausen** Germany
36D1 **Gelsenkirchen** Germany
32F8 **Gelting** Germany
55C5 **Gemas** Malay
36C1 **Gembloux** Belg
71J4 **Gembut** Nig
72B3 **Gemena** Zaïre
64C2 **Gemerek** Turk
64A1 **Gemlik** Turk
40C1 **Gemona** Italy
37E1 **Gemona del Friuli** Italy
74C2 **Gemsbok Nat Pk** Botswana
72C2 **Geneina** Sudan
28C3 **General Acha** Arg
28C3 **General Alvear** Buenos Aires, Arg
28B2 **General Alvear** Mendoza, Arg
28C2 **General Arenales** Arg
28D3 **General Belgrano** Arg
79F2 **General Belgrano** *Base* Ant
79G2 **General Bernardo O'Higgins** *Base* Ant
28C1 **General Capdevia** Arg
28D3 **General Conesa** Buenos Aires, Arg
28C4 **General Conesa** Rio Negro, Arg
26F8 **General Eugenio A Garay** Par
20C2 **General Grant Grove Section** *Region* USA
28D3 **General Guido** Arg
28C3 **General La Madrid** Arg
28D3 **General Lavalle** Arg
28C2 **General Levalle** Arg
28D3 **General Madariaga** Arg
25C3 **General Manuel Belgrano** *Mt* Arg
28D3 **General Paz** Buenos Aires, Arg
28D1 **General Paz** Corrientes, Arg
28C3 **General Pico** Arg
28C2 **General Pinto** Arg
28D3 **General Pirán** Arg
25C5 **General Roca** Arg
22B1 **General San Bolivar** Mexico
57G9 **General Santos** Phil
28C3 **General Viamonte** Arg
28C3 **General Villegas** Arg
13D2 **Genesee** *R* USA
13D2 **Geneseo** USA
Geneva = Genève
17C10 **Geneva** Nebraska, USA
14B1 **Geneva** New York, USA
Geneva,L of = Lac Léman
40B1 **Genève** Switz
39B2 **Genil** *R* Spain
Genoa = Genova
75C3 **Genoa** Aust
40B2 **Genova** Italy
36B1 **Gent** Belg
56C4 **Genteng** Indon
42C2 **Genthin** Germany
45H7 **Geokchay** Azerbaijan
74C3 **George** S Africa
7M4 **George** *R* Can
5J4 **George B** Can
75C2 **George,L** Aust
15C3 **George,L** Florida, USA
13E2 **George,L** New York, USA
5K3 **George's Cove** Can
78A2 **George Sd** NZ
75E3 **George Town** Aust
5J4 **Georgetown** Can
20B1 **Georgetown** California, USA
13D3 **Georgetown** Delaware, USA
27G2 **Georgetown** Guyana
12C3 **Georgetown** Kentucky, USA
55C4 **George Town** Malay
23N2 **Georgetown** St Vincent
15D2 **Georgetown** S Carolina, USA
17C3 **Georgetown** Texas, USA
70A3 **Georgetown** The Gambia
79G8 **George V Land** Region, Ant
17F4 **George West** USA
79F12 **Georg Forster** *Base* Ant
45G7 **Georgia** *Republic* Europe
15C2 **Georgia** State, USA
4E3 **Georgian B** Can
3D4 **Georgia,Str of** Can
76C3 **Georgina** *R* Aust
45G7 **Georgiyevsk** Russian Fed
42C2 **Gera** Germany
36B1 **Geraardsbergen** Belg
78B2 **Geraldine** NZ
76A3 **Geraldton** Aust
4D4 **Geraldton** Can
65C3 **Gerar** *R* Israel
36D2 **Gérardmer** France
6C3 **Gerdine,Mt** USA
10J3 **Gerdova Peak** *Mt* USA
55C4 **Gerik** Malay
11B3 **Gering** USA
45C6 **Gerlachovsky** *Mt* Pol
3D2 **Germanson Lodge** Can
42B2 **Germany** Republic
74D2 **Germiston** S Africa
36D1 **Gerolstein** Germany
39C1 **Gerona** Spain
36E1 **Geseke** Germany
72E3 **Gestro** *R* Eth
39B1 **Getafe** Spain
5J3 **Gethsémani** Can
14B3 **Gettysburg** Pennsylvania, USA
11C2 **Gettysburg** S Dakota, USA
28E1 **Getúlio Vargas** Brazil
56A2 **Geumpang** Indon
64D2 **Gevaş** Turk
41E2 **Gevgelija** Macedonia, Yugos
37B1 **Gex** France
65D2 **Ghabāghib** Syria
70C1 **Ghadamis** Libya
63C1 **Ghaem Shahr** Iran
61B2 **Ghāghara** *R* India
70B4 **Ghana** Republic, Africa
74C1 **Ghanzi** Botswana
71C2 **Ghardaïa** Alg
69A1 **Gharyan** Libya
69A2 **Ghāt** Libya
71B1 **Ghazaouet** Alg
60D3 **Ghāziābād** India
60C3 **Ghazi Khan** Pak
60B2 **Ghazni** Afghan
41F1 **Gheorgheni** Rom
67F3 **Ghubbat al Qamar** *B* Yemen
67G3 **Ghubbat Sawqirah** *B* Oman
68E4 **Ghudamis** Alg
63E2 **Ghurian** Afghan
40D3 **Giarre** Italy
16C1 **Gibbon** USA
74B2 **Gibeon** Namibia
39A2 **Gibraltar** Colony, SW Europe
39A2 **Gibraltar,Str of** Spain/Africa
76B3 **Gibson Desert** Aust
18B1 **Gibsons** Can
62B1 **Giddalūr** India
65B3 **Giddi P** Egypt
72D3 **Gīdolē** Eth
36B3 **Gien** France
42B2 **Giessen** Germany
15C3 **Gifford** USA
53D4 **Gifu** Japan
34C4 **Gigha** *I* Scot
40C2 **Giglio** *I* Italy
39A1 **Gijon** Spain
19D4 **Gila** *R* USA
19D4 **Gila Bend** USA
19D4 **Gila Bend Mts** USA
76D2 **Gilbert** *R* Aust
77G1 **Gilbert Is** Pacific O
3D3 **Gilbert,Mt** Can
18D1 **Gildford** USA
73D5 **Gilé** Mozam
65C2 **Gilead** Region, Jordan
69B2 **Gilf Kebir Plat** Egypt
75C2 **Gilgandra** Aust
60C1 **Gilgit** Pak
60C1 **Gilgit** *R* Pak
75C2 **Gilgunnia** Aust
7J4 **Gillam** Can
75A2 **Gilles** *L* Aust
11A3 **Gillette** USA
3C3 **Gill I** Can
12B1 **Gills Rock** USA
12B2 **Gilman** USA
4F5 **Gilmour** Can
20B2 **Gilroy** USA
4B3 **Gimli** Can
65B3 **Gineifa** Egypt
74E2 **Gingindlovu** S Africa
57G9 **Gingoog** Phil
72E3 **Gīnīr** Eth
41E3 **Gióna** *Mt* Greece
75C3 **Gippsland** *Mts* Aust
12C2 **Girard** USA
26D3 **Girardot** Colombia
34D3 **Girdle Ness** *Pen* Scot
64C1 **Giresun** Turk
66B1 **Girga** Egypt
60C4 **Gir Hills** India
72B3 **Giri** *R* Zaïre
61C3 **Girīdīh** India
60A2 **Girishk** Afghan
36D3 **Giromagny** France
Girona = Gerona
38B2 **Gironde** *R* France
34C4 **Girvan** Scot
78C2 **Gisborne** NZ
36A2 **Gisors** France
72C4 **Gitega** Burundi
Giuba,R = Juba,R
37E2 **Giulia Region,** Italy
41F2 **Giurgiu** Rom
36C1 **Givet** Belg
49S3 **Gizhiga** Russian Fed
43E2 **Gizycko** Pol
41E2 **Gjirokastër** Alb
6J3 **Gjoatlaven** Can
32G6 **Gjøvik** Nor
7M5 **Glace Bay** Can
3C2 **Glacial Mt** Can
3A2 **Glacier B** USA
10L4 **Glacier Bay Nat Mon** USA
3F4 **Glacier Nat Pk** USA
18B1 **Glacier Peak** *Mt* USA
7K2 **Glacier Str** Can
76E3 **Gladstone** Queensland, Aust
75A2 **Gladstone** S Aust, Aust
75E3 **Gladstone** Tasmania, Aust
12B1 **Gladstone** USA
32A1 **Glama** *Mt* Iceland

32G6 Glåma R Nor
36D2 Glan R Germany
37C1 Glarner Mts Switz
37C1 Glarus Switz
17C2 Glasco USA
12B3 Glasgow Kentucky, USA
11A2 Glasgow Montana, USA
34C4 Glasgow Scot
14C3 Glassboro USA
20C2 Glass Mt USA
35D6 Glastonbury Eng
44J4 Glazov Russian Fed
42D3 Gleisdorf Austria
78C1 Glen Afton NZ
14B3 Glen Burnie USA
74E2 Glencoe S Africa
19D4 Glendale Arizona, USA
20C3 Glendale California, USA
11B2 Glendive USA
11B3 Glendo Res USA
10J3 Glenhallen USA
75D1 Glen Innes Aust
75C1 Glenmorgan Aust
75D2 Glenreagh Aust
14B3 Glen Rock USA
17C3 Glen Rose USA
14D1 Glens Falls USA
17D3 Glenwood Arkansas, USA
11C2 Glenwood Minnesota, USA
16A3 Glenwood New Mexico, USA
16A2 Glenwood Springs USA
12A1 Glidden USA
32F6 Glittertind Mt Nor
43D2 Gliwice Pol
19D4 Globe USA
42D2 Głogów Pol
32G5 Glomfjord Nor
75D2 Gloucester Aust
35D6 Gloucester Eng
14E1 Gloucester USA
14C1 Gloversville USA
43F1 Glubokoye Belorussia
45E5 Glukhov Russian Fed
42D3 Gmünd Austria
42C3 Gmunden Austria
43D2 Gniezno Pol
74B2 Goabeg Namibia
62A1 Goa, Daman and Diu Union Territory, India
61D2 Goālpāra India
71F4 Goaso Ghana
72D3 Goba Eth
74B1 Gobabis Namibia
28C2 Gobernador Crespo Arg
28B3 Gobernador Duval Arg
52B1 Gobi Desert China/Mongolia
54C4 Gobo Japan
43G1 Gobza R Russian Fed
74B1 Gochas Namibia
62B1 Godag India
62C1 Godāvari R India
5H4 Godbout Can
20C2 Goddard,Mt USA
4E5 Goderich Can
7N3 Godhavn Greenland
60C4 Godhra India
28B2 Godoy Cruz Arg
4C2 Gods R Can
7J4 Gods L Can
7N3 Godthåb Greenland
Godwin Austen = K2
14E1 Goffstown USA
4E4 Gogama Can
66C4 Gogora Eth
29C2 Goiandira Brazil
29C2 Goianésia Brazil
29C2 Goiânia Brazil
29B2 Goiás Brazil
27J6 Goiás State, Brazil
29B3 Goio-Erê Brazil
72D3 Gojab R Eth
41F2 Gökçeada I Turk
45F8 Goksu R Turk
64C2 Göksun Turk
49M5 Gol R Mongolia
61D2 Golāghāt India
64C2 Gölbaşi Turk
48K2 Gol'chikha Russian Fed
18C2 Golconda USA
14B2 Gold USA
18B2 Gold Beach USA
75D1 Gold Coast Aust
3E3 Golden Can
78B2 Golden B NZ
18B1 Goldendale USA
20A2 Golden Gate Chan USA
17D4 Golden Meadow USA
19C3 Goldfield USA
4C3 Goldpines Can
20D2 Gold Point USA
4A2 Goldsand L Can
16C3 Goldthwaite USA
42C2 Goleniów Pol
20C3 Goleta USA
40B2 Golfe d'Ajaccio G Corse
71E2 Golfe de Gabes G Tunisia
Golfe de Gascogne = Biscay,Bay of
71E1 Golfe de Hammamet G Tunisia
37B3 Golfe de la Napoule G France
40B2 Golfe de St Florent G Corse
38B2 Golfe de St-Malo B France
38C3 Golfe du Lion G France
25B6 Golfo Corcovado G Chile
39B2 Golfo de Almeira G Spain
25B6 Golfo de Ancud G Chile
21D2 Golfo de Batabano G Cuba
23A2 Golfo de Batano G Cuba
39A2 Golfo de Cadiz G Spain
40B3 Golfo de Cagliari G Sardegna
21A1 Golfo de California G Mexico
21D4 Golfo de Chiriqui G Panama
21D3 Golfo de Fonseca Honduras
23B2 Golfo de Guacanayabo G Cuba
26B4 Golfo de Guayaquil G Ecuador
23B5 Golfo del Darien G Colombia/Panama
26B2 Golfo de los Mosquitos G Panama
26A1 Golfo del Papagaya G Nic
39B2 Golfo de Mazarrón G Spain
26A2 Golfo de Nicoya G Costa Rica
40B3 Golfo de Oristano G Sardegna
21E4 Golfo de Panamá G Panama
21D3 Golfo de Papagayo G Costa Rica
23E4 Golfo de Paria G Ven
26F1 Golfo de Paris G Ven
25B7 Golfo de Penas G Chile
38D3 Golfo de St Florent Corse
39C1 Golfo de San Jorge G Spain
21C3 Golfo de Tehuantepec G Mexico
26C3 Golfo de Torugas G Colombia
26C2 Golfo de Uraba G Colombia
39C2 Golfo de Valencia G Spain
37E2 Golfo de Venezia G Italy
23C4 Golfo de Venezuela G Ven
40B2 Golfo di Genova G Italy
40D3 Golfo di Policastro G Italy
40D3 Golfo di Squillace G Italy
40D2 Golfo di Taranto G Italy
37E2 Golfo di Trieste G Italy
40C1 Golfo di Venezia G Italy
21D4 Golfo Dulce G Costa Rica
25C7 Golfo San Jorge G Arg
25D6 Golfo San Matías G Arg
50C3 Golmud China
72E3 Golocha Eth
10F3 Golovin B USA
53F3 Golovnino Russian Fed
72C4 Goma Zaïre
71J3 Gombe Nig
71J3 Gombi Nig
43G2 Gomel Belorussia
70A2 Gomera I Canary Is
21B2 Gómez Palacio Mexico
49O4 Gonam R Russian Fed
63D1 Gonbad-e Kāvūs Iran
61B2 Gonda India
60C4 Gondal India
72D2 Gonder Eth
61B3 Gondia India
64A1 Gönen Turk
41F3 Gonen R Turk
35B5 Goney Irish Rep
61D1 Gongbo'gyamba China
52A4 Gongga Shan Mt China
52A2 Gonghe China
29D1 Gongogi R Brazil
71J3 Gongola R Nig
20B2 Gonzales California, USA
17C4 Gonzales Texas, USA
22C1 Gonzalez Mexico
28C3 Gonzalez Chaves Arg
74B3 Good Hope,C of S Africa
3D3 Good Hope Mt Can
18D2 Gooding USA
16B2 Goodland USA
10F4 Goodnews Bay USA
75C1 Goodooga R Aust
35E5 Goole Eng
75C2 Goolgowi Aust
75A3 Goolwa Aust
76A4 Goomalling Aust
75C2 Goombalie Aust
75D1 Goomer Aust
75D1 Goomeri Aust
75D1 Goondiwindi Aust
7N4 Goose Bay Can
15D2 Goose Creek USA
5J3 Goose R Can
18B2 Goose L USA
62B1 Gooty India
76D1 Goraka PNG
44K3 Gora Koyp Mt Russian Fed
49M4 Gora Munku Sardyk Mt Mongolia/Russian Fed
44K3 Gora Narodnaya Mt Russian Fed
44L2 Gora Pay-Yer Mt Russian Fed
44K3 Gora Telpos-Iz Mt Russian Fed
41D2 Goražde Bosnia & Herzegovina, Yugos
10K2 Gordon USA
3F2 Gordon L Can
13D3 Gordonsville USA
72B3 Goré Chad
72D3 Gorē Eth
78A3 Gore NZ
49P4 Gore Topko Mt Russian Fed
63C1 Gorgān Iran
37C3 Gorgona I Italy
36C1 Gorinchem Neth
64E2 Goris Armenia
40C1 Gorizia Italy
43G2 Gorki Belorussia
44M2 Gorki Russian Fed
44G4 Gor'kovskoye Vodokhranilishche Res Russian Fed
42C2 Gorlitz Germany
45F6 Gorlovka Ukraine
20C3 Gorman USA
41F2 Gorna Orjahovica Bulg
50B1 Gorno-Altaysk Russian Fed
53E1 Gorno Lopatina Mt Russian Fed
53D2 Gorno Medvezh'ya Mt Russian Fed
53C3 Gorno Oblachnaya Mt Russian Fed
53D2 Gorno Tardoki Yani Mt Russian Fed
53E2 Gornozavodsk Russian Fed
53D1 Gornyy Russian Fed
44K3 Goro Denezhkin Kamen' Mt Russian Fed
44G4 Gorodets Russian Fed
43G2 Gorodnya Ukraine
43F1 Gorodok Belorussia
43E3 Gorodok Ukraine
43F3 Gorodok Ukraine
51H7 Goroka PNG
61B2 Gorokhpur India
57D3 Gorong I Indon
73D5 Gorongosa Mozam
57B2 Gorontalo Indon
71G3 Goroubi R Burkina
44L4 Goro Yurma Mt Russian Fed
29D2 Gorutuba R Brazil
49M4 Goryachinsk Russian Fed
45J7 Gory Akkyr Upland Turkmenistan
49L2 Gory Byrranga Mts Russian Fed
43F3 Goryn' R Ukraine
49L3 Gory Putorana Mts Russian Fed
43E2 Góry Świetokrzyskie Upland Pol
32H8 Gorzow Wielkopolski Pol
20C2 Goshen USA
53E3 Goshogawara Japan
45F8 Gosku R Turk
40D2 Gospić Croatia, Yugos
41E2 Gostivar Macedonia, Yugos
43D2 Gostynin Pol
32G7 Göteborg Sweden
72B3 Gotel Mts Nig
16B1 Gothenburg USA
32H7 Gotland I Sweden
53B5 Gotō-retto I Japan
32H7 Gotska Sandōn I Sweden
53C4 Gōtsu Japan
43D3 Gottwaldov Czech
36C1 Gouda Neth
72B2 Goudoumaria Niger
xxxH7 Gough I Atlantic O
75C2 Goulburn Aust
70B3 Goumbou Mali
70B3 Goundam Mali
72B2 Gouré Niger
70B3 Gourma Rharous Mali
36A2 Gournay-en-Bray France
72B2 Gouro Chad
18E1 Govenlock Can
51G8 Gove Pen Aust
45C6 Goverla Mt Ukraine
29D2 Governador Valadares Brazil
28D1 Governador Virasoro Arg
61B3 Govind Ballabh Paht Sāgar L India
14A1 Gowanda USA
60B3 Gowārān Afghan
28D1 Goya Arg
72C2 Goz-Beïda Chad
40C3 Gozo I Medit S
66C3 Goz Regeb Sudan
74C3 Graaff-Reinet S Africa
13D1 Gracefield Can
37E2 Grado Italy
75D1 Grafton Aust
11C2 Grafton N Dakota, USA
12C3 Grafton W Virginia, USA
3D2 Graham R Can
3B3 Graham I Can
3F2 Graham L Can
19E4 Graham,Mt USA
74D3 Grahamstown S Africa
27J5 Grajaú Brazil
43E2 Grajewo Pol
41E2 Grámmos Mt Greece/Alb
34D3 Grampian Region, Scot
34C3 Grampian Mts Scot
26D3 Granada Colombia
26A1 Granada Nic
39B2 Granada Spain
5G4 Granby Can
16A1 Granby USA
70A2 Gran Canaria I Canary Is
25D3 Gran Chaco Region Arg
12B2 Grand R Michigan, USA
17D1 Grand R Missouri, USA
23Q2 Grand B Dominica
9F4 Grand Bahama I Bahamas
36D3 Grand Ballon Mt France
7N5 Grand Bank Can
xxxF1 Grand Banks Atlantic O
71F4 Grand Bassam Ivory Coast
37B2 Grand Bérard Mt France
19D3 Grand Canyon USA
19D3 Grand Canyon Nat Pk USA
23A3 Grand Cayman I Caribbean
3F3 Grand Centre Can
18C1 Grand Coulee USA
28B3 Grande R Arg
27K6 Grande R Bahia, Brazil
29C2 Grande R Minas Gerais/São Paulo, Brazil
3E3 Grande Cache Can
5H4 Grande Cascapédia Can
37A2 Grande Chartreuse Region, France
73E5 Grande Comore I Comoros
3E2 Grande Prairie Can
17C3 Grande Prairie USA
72B2 Grand Erg de Bilma Desert Region Niger
70B2 Grand erg Occidental Mts Alg
70C2 Grand erg Oriental Mts Alg
5J4 Grande Rivière Can
7L4 Grande Rivière de la Baleine R Can
18C1 Grande Ronde R USA
19D4 Gran Desierto USA
5H4 Grande Vallée Can
7M5 Grand Falls New Brunswick, Can
7N5 Grand Falls Newfoundland, Can
18C1 Grand Forks Can
11C2 Grand Forks USA
14C1 Grand Gorge USA
12B2 Grand Haven USA
16C1 Grand Island USA
17E3 Grand Isle USA
16A2 Grand Junction USA
5K4 Grand L Can
17D4 Grand L USA
5H5 Grand Manan I Can
12A1 Grand Marais USA
5G4 Grand Mère Can
5K3 Grandois Can
39A2 Grândola Port
6J4 Grand Rapids Can
12B2 Grand Rapids Michigan, USA
12A1 Grand Rapids Minnesota, USA
37B2 Grand St Bernard P Italy/Switz
8B2 Grand Teton Mt USA
18D2 Grand Teton Nat Pk USA
16A2 Grand Valley USA
36A2 Grandvilliers France
21D1 Grangeburg USA
18C1 Grangeville USA
4B5 Granite Falls USA
18E1 Granite Peak Mt Montana, USA
19D2 Granite Peak Mt Utah, USA
39C1 Granollérs Spain
40B1 Gran Paradiso Mt Italy
37D1 Gran Pilastro Mt Austria/Italy
35E5 Grantham Eng
20C1 Grant,Mt USA
34D3 Grantown-on-Spey Scot
16A2 Grants USA
18B2 Grants Pass USA
38B2 Granville France
14D1 Granville USA
6H4 Granville L Can
29D2 Grão Mogol Brazil
20C3 Grapevine USA
20D2 Grapevine Mts USA
74E1 Graskop S Africa
38D3 Grasse France
18E1 Grassrange USA
19B3 Grass Valley USA
5L4 Grates Pt Can
25F4 Gravatai Brazil
6H5 Gravelbourg Can
36B1 Gravelines France
73D6 Gravelotte S Africa
4F5 Gravenhurst Can
18D1 Grave Peak Mt USA
75D1 Gravesend Aust
10M4 Gravina I USA
37A1 Gray France
10F3 Grayling USA
4E5 Grayling Michigan, USA
18B1 Grays Harbor B USA
18D2 Grays L USA
12C3 Grayson USA
12B3 Grayville USA
42D3 Graz Austria
23H1 Great R Jamaica
9F4 Great Abaco I Bahamas
76B4 Great Australian Bight G Aust
14E1 Great B New Hampshire, USA
14C3 Great B New Jersey, USA
21E2 Great Bahama Bank Bahamas
78C1 Great Barrier I NZ
76D2 Great Barrier Reef Is Aust
14D1 Great Barrington USA
19C2 Great Basin USA
10O2 Great Bear R Can
6F3 Great Bear L Can
16C2 Great Bend USA
65B3 Great Bitter L Egypt
14A3 Great Cacapon USA
62E2 Great Coco I Burma
76D3 Great Dividing Range Mts Aust
35E4 Great Driffield Eng
14C3 Great Egg Harbor B USA
79F10 Greater Antarctic Region, Ant
23B2 Greater Antilles Is Caribbean
35E6 Greater London County, Eng
35D5 Greater Manchester County, Eng
21E2 Great Exuma I Bahamas
18D1 Great Falls USA
74D3 Great Fish R S Africa
34C3 Great Glen V Scot
61C2 Great Himalayan Range Mts Asia
9F4 Great Inagua I Bahamas
74C3 Great Karroo Mts S Africa
74D3 Great Kei R S Africa
75E3 Great L Aust
73B6 Great Namaland Region, Namibia
62E3 Great Nicobar I Indian O
35D5 Great Ormes Head C Wales
14E2 Great Pt USA
9F4 Great Ragged I Bahamas
73D4 Great Ruaha R Tanz
13E2 Great Sacandaga L USA
18D2 Great Salt L USA
18D2 Great Salt Lake Desert USA
69B2 Great Sand Sea Libya/Egypt
76B3 Great Sandy Desert Aust
8A2 Great Sandy Desert USA
Great Sandy I = Fraser I
10C6 Great Sitkin, I USA
6G3 Great Slave L Can

15C1 **Great Smoky Mts** USA
15C1 **Great Smoky Mts Nat Pk** USA
3D2 **Great Snow Mt** Can
14D2 **Great South B** USA
74C3 **Great Tafelberg** *Mt* S Africa
76B3 **Great Victoria Desert** Aust
52B2 **Great Wall** China
35F5 **Great Yarmouth** Eng
65C1 **Greco,C** Cyprus
41E3 **Greece** Republic, Europe
13D2 **Greece** USA
16B1 **Greeley** USA
7K1 **Greely Fjord** Can
12B3 **Green** *R* Kentucky, USA
19D3 **Green** *R* Utah, USA
12B1 **Green B** USA
12B2 **Green Bay** USA
48H1 **Green Bell, Ostrov** *I* Russian Fed
12B3 **Greencastle** Indiana, USA
14B3 **Greencastle** Pennsylvania, USA
14C1 **Greene** USA
15C1 **Greeneville** USA
20B2 **Greenfield** California, USA
20C3 **Greenfield** California, USA
14D1 **Greenfield** Massachusetts, USA
12B2 **Greenfield** Wisconsin, USA
5G4 **Greening** Can
3G3 **Green Lake** Can
7O2 **Greenland** Dependency, N Atlantic
xxxH1 **Greenland Basin** Greenland S
79B1 **Greenland S** Greenland
34C4 **Greenock** Scot
14D2 **Greenport** USA
19D3 **Green River** Utah, USA
18E2 **Green River** Wyoming, USA
14C3 **Greensboro** Maryland, USA
15D1 **Greensboro** N Carolina, USA
16C2 **Greensburg** Kansas, USA
12B3 **Greensburg** Kentucky, USA
13D2 **Greensburg** Pennsylvania, USA
34C3 **Greenstone** *Pt* Scot
12B3 **Greenup** USA
19D4 **Green Valley** USA
15B2 **Greenville** Alabama, USA
70B4 **Greenville** Lib
17D3 **Greenville** Mississippi, USA
15D1 **Greenville** N Carolina, USA
14E1 **Greenville** N Hampshire, USA
12C2 **Greenville** Ohio, USA
15C2 **Greenville** S Carolina, USA
17C3 **Greenville** Texas, USA
51H8 **Greenville,C** Aust
35F6 **Greenwich** Eng
14D2 **Greenwich** USA
14C3 **Greenwood** Delaware, USA
17D3 **Greenwood** Mississippi, USA
15C2 **Greenwood** S Carolina, USA
17D2 **Greers Ferry L** USA
11C3 **Gregory** USA
75A1 **Gregory,L** Aust
76D2 **Gregory Range** *Mts* Aust
42C2 **Greifswald** Germany
44F2 **Gremikha** Russian Fed
42C1 **Grenå** Den
17E3 **Grenada** USA
23E4 **Grenada** *I* Caribbean
23E4 **Grenadines,The** *Is* Caribbean
75C2 **Grenfell** Aust
3H3 **Grenfell** Can
38D2 **Grenoble** France
23M2 **Grenville** Grenada
76D2 **Grenville,C** Aust
18B1 **Gresham** USA
56D4 **Gresik** Jawa, Indon
56B3 **Gresik** Sumatera, Indon
17D4 **Gretna** USA
78B2 **Grey** *R* NZ
18E2 **Greybull** USA
10L3 **Grey Hunter Pk** *Mt* Can
7N4 **Grey Is** Can
14D1 **Greylock,Mt** USA
78B2 **Greymouth** NZ
76D3 **Grey Range** *Mts* Aust
35B5 **Greystones** Irish Rep
74E2 **Greytown** S Africa
74C2 **Griekwastad** S Africa
15C2 **Griffin** USA
75C2 **Griffith** Aust
76D5 **Grim,C** Aust
13D2 **Grimsby** Can
35E5 **Grimsby** Eng
32B1 **Grimsey** *I* Iceland
3E2 **Grimshaw** Can
32F7 **Grimstad** Nor
37C1 **Grindelwald** Switz
11D3 **Grinnell** USA
7J2 **Grinnell Pen** Can
7K2 **Grise Fjord** Can
44J3 **Griva** Russian Fed
10O2 **Grizzly Bear** *Mt* Can
32J7 **Grobina** Latvia
74D2 **Groblersdal** S Africa
37E1 **Gröbming** Austria
43E2 **Grodno** Belorussia
61B2 **Gromati** *R* India
42B2 **Groningen** Neth
16B2 **Groom** USA
74C3 **Groot** *R* S Africa
76C2 **Groote Eylandt** *I* Aust
73B5 **Grootfontein** Namibia
74B2 **Groot-Karasberge** *Mts* Namibia
74C1 **Groot Laagte** *R* Botswana
74C2 **Groot Vloer** *Salt L* S Africa
23P2 **Gros Islet** St Lucia
5K4 **Gros Morne Nat Park** Can
36E1 **Grosser Feldberg** *Mt* Germany
40C2 **Grosseto** Italy
36E2 **Gross-Gerau** Germany
42C3 **Grossglockner** *Mt* Austria
37E1 **Gross Venediger** *Mt* Austria
10G4 **Grosvenor,L** USA
18D2 **Gros Ventre Range** *Mts* USA
5K3 **Groswater B** Can
11C2 **Groton** USA
4E4 **Groundhog** *R* Can
15B2 **Grove Hill** USA
20B2 **Groveland** USA
20B3 **Grover City** USA
13E2 **Groveton** USA
45H7 **Groznyy** Russian Fed
43D2 **Grudziadz** Pol
74B2 **Grünau** Namibia
34E2 **Grutness** Scot
45G5 **Gryazi** Russian Fed
44G4 **Gryazovets** Russian Fed
25J8 **Grytviken** South Georgia
29D3 **Guaçuí** Brazil
22B1 **Guadalajara** Mexico
39B1 **Guadalajara** Spain
77E1 **Guadalcanal** *I* Solomon Is
39B2 **Guadalimar** *R* Spain
39B1 **Guadalope** *R* Spain
39B2 **Guadalqivir** *R* Spain
21B2 **Guadalupe** Mexico
20B3 **Guadalupe** USA
2G6 **Guadalupe** *I* Mexico
16C4 **Guadalupe** *R* USA
16B3 **Guadalupe Nat Pk** USA
16B3 **Guadalupe Peak** *Mt* USA
22B1 **Guadalupe Victoria** Mexico
22B1 **Guadarupe** Mexico
23E3 **Guadeloupe** *I* Caribbean
39B2 **Guadian** *R* Spain
39A2 **Guadiana** *R* Port
39B2 **Guadian** *R* Spain
39B2 **Guadix** Spain
29B3 **Guaira** Brazil
26E6 **Guajará Mirim** Brazil
26D1 **Guajira,Pen de** Colombia
26C4 **Gualaceo** Ecuador
37E3 **Gualdo Tadino** Italy
28D2 **Gualeguay** Arg
28D2 **Gualeguaychú** Arg
51H5 **Guam** *I* Pacific O
28C3 **Guamini** Arg
55C5 **Gua Musang** Malay
22B1 **Guanajuato** Mexico
22B1 **Guanajuato** State, Mexico
29D1 **Guanambi** Brazil
26E2 **Guanare** Ven
28B1 **Guandacol** Arg
21D2 **Guane** Cuba
52C5 **Guangdong** Province, China
52A3 **Guanghan** China
52C3 **Guanghua** China
52A4 **Guangmao Shan** *Mt* China
52A5 **Guangnan** China
52B3 **Guangyuan** China
52D4 **Guangze** China
52C5 **Guangzhon** China
46G4 **Guangzhou** China
29D2 **Guanhães** Brazil
26E3 **Guania** *R* Colombia
23E5 **Guanipa** *R* Ven
23B2 **Guantánamo** Cuba
52D1 **Guanting Shuiku** *Res* China
52B5 **Guanxi** Province, China
52A3 **Guan Xian** China
26C2 **Guapa** Colombia
28E1 **Guaporé** Brazil
28E1 **Guaporé** *R* Brazil
26F6 **Guaporé** *R* Brazil/Bol
26E7 **Guaquí** Bol
29D1 **Guará** *R* Brazil
29B4 **Guarapuava** Brazil
29C4 **Guaraqueçaba** Brazil
29C3 **Guaratinguetá** Brazil
39A1 **Guarda** Port
29C2 **Guarda Mor** Brazil
28B1 **Guardia** Chile
28C4 **Guardia Mitre** Arg
28E1 **Guarita** *R* Brazil
8C4 **Guasave** Mexico
37D2 **Guastalla** Italy
21C3 **Guatemala** Guatemala
21C3 **Guatemala** Republic, C America
28C3 **Guatraché** Arg
26D3 **Guavrare** *R* Colombia
29C3 **Guaxupé** Brazil
23L1 **Guayaguayare** Trinidad
26B4 **Guayaquil** Ecuador
21A2 **Guaymas** Mexico
28D2 **Guayquiraro** *R* Arg
73C5 **Guba** Zaïre
49P2 **Guba Buorkhaya** *B* Russian Fed
72E3 **Guban** *Region* Somalia
57F8 **Gubat** Phil
37E3 **Gubbio** Italy
42C2 **Gubin** Pol
71J3 **Gubio** Nig
62B2 **Güdür** India
36D3 **Guebwiller** France
71D1 **Guelma** Alg
4E5 **Guelph** Can
70A2 **Guelta Zemmur** Mor
22C1 **Güemez** Mexico
23A2 **Guenabacoa** Cuba
71C2 **Guerara** Alg
72C2 **Guéréda** Chad
38C2 **Guéret** France
11B3 **Guernsey** USA
38B2 **Guernsey** *I* UK
22B2 **Guerrero** State, Mexico
72D3 **Gughe** *Mt* Eth
49O4 **Gugigu** China
51H5 **Guguan** *I* Pacific O
75C2 **Guiargambone** Aust
28D2 **Guichón** Urug
71J4 **Guider** Cam
52C4 **Guidong** China
70B4 **Guiglo** Ivory Coast
74E1 **Guija** Mozam
52C5 **Gui Jiang** *R* China
35E6 **Guildford** Eng
52C4 **Guilin** China
37B2 **Guillestre** France
52A2 **Guinan** China
20A1 **Guinda** USA
70A3 **Guinea** Republic, Africa
xxxH4 **Guinea Basin** Atlantic O
70A3 **Guinea-Bissau** Republic, Africa
70C4 **Guinea,G of** W Africa
23A2 **Güines** Cuba
70B3 **Guir** *Well* Mali
60C2 **Guiranwala** Pak
29B2 **Guiratinga** Brazil
26F1 **Güiria** Ven
36B2 **Guise** France
57G8 **Guiuan** Phil
52B5 **Gui Xian** China
52B4 **Guiyang** China
52B4 **Guizhou** Province, China
60C4 **Gujarāt** State, India
60C2 **Gujrat** Pak
62B1 **Gulbarga** India
43F1 **Gulbene** Latvia
62B1 **Guledagudda** India
15B2 **Gulfport** USA
58D3 **Gulf,The** S W Asia
75C2 **Gulgong** Aust
53A1 **Gulian** China
52B4 **Gulin** China
10J3 **Gulkana** USA
10J3 **Gulkana** *R* USA
3F3 **Gull L** Can
3G3 **Gull Lake** Can
72D3 **Gulu** Uganda
75C1 **Guluguba** Aust
56F6 **Gulung Chamah** *Mt* Malay
71H3 **Gumel** Nig
36D1 **Gummersbach** Germany
71H3 **Gummi** Nig
61B3 **Gumpla** India
64C1 **Gümüşhane** Turk
60D4 **Guna** India
72D2 **Guna** *Mt* Eth
75C3 **Gundagai** Aust
72B4 **Gungu** Zaïre
4B3 **Gunisao** *R* Can
4B3 **Gunisao L** Can
7Q3 **Gunnbjørn Fjeld** *Mt* Greenland
75D2 **Gunnedah** Aust
16A2 **Gunnison** USA
16A2 **Gunnison** *R* USA
62B1 **Guntakal** India
15B2 **Guntersville** USA
15B2 **Guntersville L** USA
62C1 **Guntūr** India
55C5 **Gunung Batu Putch** *Mt* Malay
56G7 **Gunung Benom** *Mt* Malay
56E3 **Gunung Besar** *Mt* Indon
56F6 **Gunung Besar** *Mt* Malay
56G7 **Gunung Besar** *Mt* Malay
56E2 **Gunung Bulu** *Mt* Indon
56B3 **Gunung Gedang** *Mt* Indon
56A2 **Gunung Geureudong** *Mt* Indon
56A2 **Gunung Kulabu** *Mt* Indon
56D2 **Gunung Lawit** *Mt* Malay
56D4 **Gunung Lawu** *Mt* Indon
56A2 **Gunung Leuser** *Mt* Indon
57B3 **Gunung Lokilalaka** *Mt* Indon
57B3 **Gunung Mekongga** *Mt* Indon
56E2 **Gunung Menyapa** *Mt* Indon
56E2 **Gunung Niapa** *Mt* Indon
57B2 **Gunung Ogoamas** *Mt* Indon
56B3 **Gunung Patah** *Mt* Indon
56D4 **Gunung Raung** *Mt* Indon
56B3 **Gunung Resag** *Mt* Indon
56E3 **Gunung Sarempaka** *Mt* Indon
56A2 **Gunungsitoli** Indon
56D4 **Gunung Sumbing** *Mt* Indon
55C5 **Gunung Tahan** *Mt* Malay
56B2 **Gunung Talakmau** *Mt* Indon
56G7 **Gunung Tapis** *Mt* Malay
57B3 **Gunung Tokala** *Mt* Indon
73B5 **Gunza** Angola
52D3 **Guoyang** China
26C4 **Guranda** Ecuador
71H4 **Gurara** Nig
60D2 **Gurdāspur** India
60D3 **Gurgaon** India
61B2 **Gurkha** Nepal
37E1 **Gurktaler Alpen** *Mts* Austria
53D1 **Gurskoye** Russian Fed
64C2 **Gürün** Turk
27J4 **Gurupi** *R* Brazil
73D5 **Guruve** Zim
52A1 **Gurvan Sayhan Uul** *Upland* Mongolia
45J6 **Gur'yev** Kazakhstan
71H3 **Gusau** Nig
43E2 **Gusev** Russian Fed
53A4 **Gushan** China
44G4 **Gus'Khrustalnyy** Russian Fed
10L4 **Gustavus** USA
20B2 **Gustine** USA
42B2 **Gütersloh** Germany
12B3 **Guthrie** Kentucky, USA
17C2 **Guthrie** Oklahoma, USA
16B3 **Guthrie** Texas, USA
22C1 **Gutiérrez Zamora** Mexico
11D3 **Guttenberg** USA
27G3 **Guyana** Republic, S America
xxxF4 **Guyana Basin** Atlantic O
52C1 **Guyang** China
38B3 **Guyenne** Region, France
16B2 **Guymon** USA
75D2 **Guyra** Aust
52B2 **Guyuan** China
63F1 **Guzar** Turkmenistan
61D4 **Gwa** Burma
75C2 **Gwabegar** Aust
71H3 **Gwadabawa** Nig
60D3 **Gwalior** India
74D1 **Gwanda** Zim
72C3 **Gwane** Zaïre
63E3 **Gwardar** Pak
68G9 **Gwelo** Zim
35D6 **Gwent** County, Wales
73C5 **Gweru** Zim
75C1 **Gwydir** *R* Aust
35D4 **Gwynedd** Wales
45H7 **Gyandzha** Azerbaijan
61C2 **Gyangzê** China
50C3 **Gyaring Hu** *L* China
48J2 **Gydanskiy Poluostrov** *Pen* Russian Fed
61C2 **Gyirong** China
7O3 **Gyldenløves** *Fjord* Greenland
75D1 **Gympie** Aust
43D3 **Gyöngyös** Hung
43D3 **Györ** Hung
4B3 **Gypsumville** Can

H

77H2 **Ha'apai Group** *Is* Tonga
32K6 **Haapajärvi** Fin
44C4 **Haapsalu** Estonia
42A2 **Haarlem** Neth
36D1 **Haarstrang** Region, Germany
21D2 **Habana** Cuba
67F3 **Habarūt** Oman
67E4 **Habbān** Yemen
61D3 **Habiganj** Bang
53F3 **Habomai Shoto** *I* Russian Fed
53D5 **Hachijō-jima** *I* Japan
54C3 **Hachiman** Japan
53E3 **Hachinohe** Japan
54C3 **Hachioji** Japan
14C2 **Hackettstown** USA
75A2 **Hack,Mt** Aust
67G3 **Hadbaram** Oman
34D4 **Haddington** Scot
75B1 **Haddon Corner** Aust
75B1 **Haddon Downs** Aust
71J3 **Hadejia** Nig
71H3 **Hadejia** *R* Nig
65C2 **Hadera** Israel
42B1 **Haderslev** Den
67F4 **Hadiboh** Socotra
6H2 **Hadley B** Can
54A3 **Hadong** S Korea
52B5 **Hadong** Vietnam
67E3 **Haḍramawt** Region, Yemen
42C1 **Hadsund** Den
53B4 **Haeju** N Korea
54A3 **Haeju-man** *B* N Korea
54A4 **Haenam** S Korea
67E1 **Hafar al Bātin** S Arabia
7M2 **Haffners Bjerg** *Mt* Greenland
66B3 **Hafir** Sudan
60C2 **Hafizabad** Pak
61D2 **Hāflong** India
32A2 **Hafnafjörður** Iceland
66B4 **Hag'Abdullah** Sudan
10F4 **Hagemeister** *I* USA
42B2 **Hagen** Germany
14B3 **Hagerstown** USA
54B4 **Hagi** Japan
52A5 **Ha Giang** Vietnam
36D2 **Hagondange** France
36D2 **Haguenan** France
70A2 **Hagunia** *Well* Mor
50H4 **Haha-jima** *I* Japan
50C3 **Hah Xil Hu** *L* China
53A3 **Haicheng** China
55D1 **Hai Duong** Viet
65C2 **Haifa** Israel
65C2 **Haifa,B of** Israel
52D2 **Hai He** *R* China
52C5 **Haikang** China
55E1 **Haikou** China
66D1 **Ha'il** S Arabia
61D3 **Hailākāndi** India
49N5 **Hailar** China
53B3 **Hailong** China
53B2 **Hailun** China
32J5 **Hailuoto** *I* Fin
55D2 **Hainan** *I* China
10L4 **Haines** USA
10L3 **Haines Junction** Can
42D3 **Hainfeld** Austria
52B5 **Haiphong** Vietnam
23C3 **Haiti** Republic, Caribbean
20D2 **Haiwee Res** USA
72D2 **Haiya** Sudan
52A2 **Haiyan** China
52B2 **Haiyuan** China
52D3 **Haizhou Wan** *B* China
43E3 **Hajdúböszörmény** Hung
66D3 **Hajfah** Yemen
54C3 **Hajiki-saki** *Pt* Japan
61D3 **Haka** Burma
20E5 **Hakalau** Hawaiian Is
64D2 **Hakkâri** Turk
53E3 **Hakodate** Japan
54C3 **Hakui** Japan
54C3 **Haku-san** *Mt* Japan
45F8 **Ḥalab** Syria
64E3 **Halabja** Iraq
72D1 **Halaib** Sudan
65D1 **Halba** Leb
50C2 **Halban** Mongolia
42C2 **Halberstadt** Germany
57F8 **Halcon,Mt** Phil
32G7 **Halden** Nor
61C3 **Haldia** India
60D3 **Haldwāni** India
3D2 **Halfway** *R* Can
4F4 **Haliburton** Can
4F4 **Haliburton Highlands** Can
7M5 **Halifax** Can
35E5 **Halifax** Eng
13D3 **Halifax** USA
10H1 **Halkett,C** USA

54A4 **Halla-San** *Mt* S Korea
7M1 **Hall Basin** *Sd* Can/ Greenland
7K3 **Hall Beach** Can
36C1 **Halle** Belg
42C2 **Halle** Germany
79F1 **Halley** *Base* Ant
13D1 **Halleybury** Can
10D3 **Hall I** USA
11B2 **Halliday** USA
32F6 **Hallingdal** *R* Nor
11C2 **Hallock** USA
7M3 **Hall Pen** Can
76B2 **Hall's Creek** Aust
14C2 **Hallstead** USA
57C2 **Halmahera** *I* Indon
57C3 **Halmahera S** Indon
32G7 **Halmstad** Sweden
42B2 **Haltern** Germany
32J5 **Haltia** *Mt* Nor
34D4 **Haltwhistle** Eng
67F1 **Halul** *I* Qatar
65C3 **Haluza** *Hist Site* Israel
54B4 **Hamada** Japan
70C2 **Hamada de Tinrhert** *Desert Region* Alg
70B2 **Hamada du Dra** *Upland* Alg
63B2 **Hamadān** Iran
70B2 **Hamada Tounassine** Region, Alg
45F8 **Ḩamāh** Syria
54C4 **Hamamatsu** Japan
32G6 **Hamar** Nor
54D1 **Hama-Tombetsu** Japan
62C3 **Hambantota** Sri Lanka
17D3 **Hamburg** Arkansas, USA
17C1 **Hamburg** Iowa, USA
14A1 **Hamburg** New York, USA
14C2 **Hamburg** Pennsylvania, USA
42B2 **Hamburg** Germany
14D2 **Hamden** USA
32J6 **Hämeeninna** Fin
76A3 **Hamersley Range** *Mts* Aust
53B3 **Hamgyong Sanmaek** *Mts* N Korea
53B3 **Hamhŭng** N Korea
50C2 **Hami** China
65C1 **Hamīdīyah** Syria
15B2 **Hamilton** Alabama, USA
75B3 **Hamilton** Aust
4F5 **Hamilton** Can
18D1 **Hamilton** Montana, USA
14C1 **Hamilton** New York, USA
78C1 **Hamilton** NZ
12C3 **Hamilton** Ohio, USA
34C4 **Hamilton** Scot
20B2 **Hamilton,Mt** USA
32K6 **Hamina** Fin
61B2 **Hamirpur** India
54A3 **Hamju** N Korea
42B2 **Hamm** Germany
69A2 **Hammādāh al Hamra** *Upland* Libya
32H6 **Hammerdal** Sweden
32J4 **Hammerfest** Nor
4F5 **Hammond** Can
12B2 **Hammond** Illinois, USA
17D3 **Hammond** Louisiana, USA
11B2 **Hammond** Montana, USA
14C3 **Hammonton** USA
78B3 **Hampden** NZ
35E6 **Hampshire** County, Eng
17D3 **Hampton** Arkansas, USA
11D3 **Hampton** Iowa, USA
14E1 **Hampton** New Hampshire, USA
13D3 **Hampton** Virginia, USA
63D3 **Hāmūn-e Jaz Mūrīan** *L* Iran
60B3 **Hamun-i-Lora** *Salt L* Pak
63E3 **Hamun-i Mashkel** *Salt Plain* Pak
54A3 **Han** *R* S Korea
20E5 **Hana** Hawaiian Is
20E5 **Hanalei** Hawaiian Is
53E4 **Hanamaki** Japan
36E1 **Hanau** Germany
52C2 **Hancheng** China
52C3 **Hanchuan** China
13D3 **Hancock** Maryland, USA
12B1 **Hancock** Michigan, USA
14C2 **Hancock** New York, USA
54C4 **Handa** Japan
52C2 **Handan** China
72D4 **Handeni** Tanz
20C2 **Hanford** USA
52B2 **Hanggin Qi** China
32J7 **Hangö** Fin
52E3 **Hangzhou** China
52E3 **Hangzhou Wan** *B* China
66D4 **Hanīsh** *I* Yemen
11C2 **Hankinson** USA
19D3 **Hanksville** USA
78B2 **Hanmer Springs** NZ
3F3 **Hanna** Can
4E3 **Hannah B** Can
17D2 **Hannibal** USA
42B2 **Hannover** Germany
32G7 **Hanöbukten** *B* Sweden
55D1 **Hanoi** Viet
74C3 **Hanover** S Africa
14B3 **Hanover** USA
25B8 **Hanover** *I* Chile
52B3 **Han Shui** China
52C3 **Han Shui** *R* China
60D3 **Hānsi** India
50D2 **Hantay** Mongolia
52B3 **Hanzhong** China
61C3 **Hāora** India
32J5 **Haparanda** Sweden
54A3 **Hapch'on** S Korea
28D1 **Hapevi** Brazil
61D2 **Hāpoli** India
5J3 **Happy Valley** Can
64C4 **Haql** S Arabia
66D3 **Harad** Yemen
67E2 **Haradh** S Arabia
72E3 **Hara Fanna** Eth
66D3 **Haraja** S Arabia
54D3 **Haramachi** Japan
72E3 **Harar** Eth
73D5 **Harare** Zim
72C2 **Harazé** Chad
53B2 **Harbin** China
12C2 **Harbor Beach** USA
5K3 **Harbour Deep** Can
5L4 **Harbour Grace** Can
60D4 **Harda** India
32F6 **Hardangerfjord** *Inlet* Nor
11A2 **Hardin** USA
36D2 **Hardt** Region, Germany
75A2 **Hardwicke B** Aust
17D2 **Hardy** USA
5K3 **Hare B** Can
72E3 **Harēr** Eth
72E3 **Hargeysa** Somalia
65C3 **Har Hakippa** *Mt* Israel
50C3 **Harhu** *L* China
56B3 **Hari** *R* Indon
67E4 **Harīb** Yemen
54B4 **Harima-nada** *B* Japan
12C3 **Harlan** USA
18E1 **Harlem** USA
42B2 **Harlingen** Neth
17F4 **Harlingen** USA
35F6 **Harlow** Eng
18E1 **Harlowtown** USA
65C2 **Har Meron** *Mt* Israel
18C2 **Harney Basin** USA
18C2 **Harney L** USA
32H6 **Härnösand** Sweden
49L5 **Har Nuur** *L* Mongolia
70B4 **Harper** Lib
20D3 **Harper L** USA
10K3 **Harper,Mt** USA
13D3 **Harpers Ferry** USA
65C3 **Har Ramon** *Mt* Israel
66C1 **Harrāt al 'Uwayrid** *Upland* Region, S Arabia
66D2 **Harrāt Kishb** Region, S Arabia
66D2 **Harrat Nawāāsīf** Region, S Arabia
66D2 **Harrat Rahat** Region, S Arabia
7L4 **Harricana** *R* Can
5J2 **Harrigan,C** Can
15C1 **Harriman** USA
14D1 **Harriman Res** USA
14C3 **Harrington** USA
7N4 **Harrington Harbour** Can
34B3 **Harris** *District* Scot
12B3 **Harrisburg** Illinois, USA
14B2 **Harrisburg** Pennsylvania, USA
74D2 **Harrismith** S Africa
17D2 **Harrison** USA
10H1 **Harrison B** USA
13D3 **Harrisonburg** USA
7N4 **Harrison,C** Can
3D4 **Harrison L** Can
17D2 **Harrisonville** USA
34B3 **Harris,Sound of** *Chan* Scot
12C2 **Harrisville** USA
35E4 **Harrogate** Eng
65C3 **Har Saggi** *Mt* Israel
32H5 **Harstad** Nor
10L3 **Hart** *R* Can
74C2 **Hartbees** *R* S Africa
32F6 **Hårteigen** *Mt* Nor
14D2 **Hartford** Connecticut, USA
12B2 **Hartford** Michigan, USA
11C3 **Hartford** S Dakota, USA
32G6 **Hartkjølen** *Mt* Nor
75A2 **Hart,L** Aust
5H4 **Hartland** Can
35C6 **Hartland Pt** Eng
34E4 **Hartlepool** Eng
16B2 **Hartley** USA
15B2 **Hartselle** USA
17C3 **Hartshorne** USA
15C2 **Hartwell Res** USA
74C2 **Hartz** *R* S Africa
50C2 **Har Us Nuur** *L* Mongolia
63E2 **Harut** *R* Afghan
16A2 **Harvard,Mt** USA
11B2 **Harvey** USA
35F6 **Harwich** Eng
60D3 **Haryāna** State, India
65C3 **Hāsā** Jordan
66B4 **Hasaheisa** Sudan
65C2 **Hāsbaiya** Leb
35E6 **Haselmere** Eng
54C4 **Hashimoto** Japan
63B1 **Hashtpar** Iran
63B1 **Hashtrūd** Iran
67G3 **Hāsik** Oman
16C3 **Haskell** USA
62B2 **Hassan** India
42B2 **Hasselt** Belg
70C2 **Hassi Inifel** Alg
70B2 **Hassi Mdakane** *Well* Alg
70C1 **Hassi Messaoud** Alg
71C2 **Hassi R'mel** Alg
32G4 **Hassleholm** Sweden
75C3 **Hastings** Aust
35F6 **Hastings** Eng
11D3 **Hastings** Minnesota, USA
8D2 **Hastings** Nebraska, USA
78C1 **Hastings** NZ
3H2 **Hatchet L** Can
15B1 **Hatchie** *R* USA
75B2 **Hatfield** Aust
10F2 **Hatham Inlet** USA
60D3 **Hāthras** India
55D2 **Ha Tinh** Viet
75B2 **Hattah** Aust
9F3 **Hatteras,C** USA
17E3 **Hattiesburg** USA
43D3 **Hatvan** Hung
55D3 **Hau Bon** Viet
72E3 **Haud** Region, Eth
32F7 **Haugesund** Nor
78C1 **Hauhungaroa Range** *Mts* NZ
3G2 **Haultain** *R* Can
78B1 **Hauraki G** NZ
78A3 **Hauroko,L** NZ
37C1 **Hausstock** *Mt* Switz
71A2 **Haut Atlas** *Mts* Mor
72C3 **Haute Kotto** Region, CAR
36C2 **Haute-Marne** Department, France
5H4 **Hauterive** Can
36C3 **Haute-Saône** Department, France
36C1 **Hautes Fagnes** *Mts* Belg
37A2 **Hauteville-Lompnès** France
36C1 **Hautmont** Belg
36D3 **Haut-Rhin** Department, France
71B2 **Hauts Plateaux** *Mts* Alg
63E2 **Hauzdar** Iran
60A2 **Hauz Qala** Afghan
12A2 **Havana** USA
Havana = Habana
62B3 **Havankulam** Sri Lanka
19D4 **Havasu L** USA
15D2 **Havelock** USA
78C1 **Havelock North** NZ
35C6 **Haverfordwest** West
14E1 **Haverhill** USA
62B2 **Hāveri** India
14D2 **Haverstraw** USA
42D3 **Havlíčkův Brod** Czech
18E1 **Havre** USA
14B3 **Havre de Grace** USA
7M4 **Havre-St-Pierre** Can
41F2 **Havsa** Turk
20E5 **Hawaii** Hawaiian Is
20E5 **Hawaii Volcanoes Nat Pk** Hawaiian Is
71J3 **Hawal** *R* Nig
78A2 **Hawea,L** NZ
78B1 **Hawera** NZ
20E5 **Hawi** Hawaiian Is
34D4 **Hawick** Scot
78A2 **Hawkdun Range** *Mts* NZ
78C1 **Hawke B** NZ
75D2 **Hawke,C** Aust
75A2 **Hawker** Aust
14C2 **Hawley** USA
55B1 **Hawng Luk** Burma
64D3 **Hawr al Habbaniyah** *L* Iraq
64E3 **Hawr al Hammár** *L* Iraq
20C1 **Hawthorne** USA
75B2 **Hay** Aust
6G3 **Hay** *R* Can
36C2 **Hayange** France
6B3 **Haycock** USA
19D4 **Hayden** Arizona, USA
16A1 **Hayden** Colorado, USA
4C2 **Hayes** *R* Can
7J4 **Hayes** *R* Can
7M2 **Hayes Halvø** *Region* Greenland
10J3 **Hayes,Mt** USA
14B3 **Haymarket** USA
67E3 **Haynin** Yemen
6G3 **Hay River** Can
16C2 **Hays** USA
66D4 **Hays** Yemen
17C2 **Haysville** USA
12A1 **Hayward** Wisconsin, USA
12C3 **Hazard** USA
61C3 **Hazārībāg** India
36B1 **Hazebrouck** France
17D3 **Hazelhurst** USA
6F4 **Hazelton** Can
3C2 **Hazelton Mts** Can
10E3 **Hazen B** USA
7M1 **Hazen L** Can
6G2 **Hazen Str** Can
65C3 **Hazeva** Israel
14C2 **Hazleton** USA
75C3 **Healesville** Aust
10J3 **Healy** USA
xxviiiE7 **Heard I** Indian O
17C3 **Hearne** USA
4E4 **Hearst** Can
11B2 **Heart** *R* USA
17F4 **Hebbronville** USA
52D2 **Hebei** Province, China
75C1 **Hebel** Aust
18D2 **Heber City** USA
18D2 **Hebger L** USA
52C2 **Hebi** China
52C2 **Hebian** China
7M4 **Hebron** Can
65C3 **Hebron** Israel
11B2 **Hebron** N. Dakota, USA
17C1 **Hebron** Nebraska, USA
3B3 **Hecate Str** Can
10M4 **Heceta I** USA
52B5 **Hechi** China
36E2 **Hechingen** Germany
6G2 **Hecla and Griper B** Can
78C2 **Hector,Mt** NZ
32G6 **Hede** Sweden
32H6 **Hedemora** Sweden
18C1 **He Devil Mt** USA
42B2 **Heerenveen** Neth
36C1 **Heerlen** Neth
Hefa = Haifa
52D3 **Hefei** China
52B4 **Hefeng** China
53C2 **Hegang** China
54C3 **Hegura-jima** *I* Japan
61E3 **Heho** Burma
65C3 **Heidan** *R* Jordan
42B2 **Heide** Germany
74C3 **Heidelberg** Cape Province, S Africa
74D2 **Heidelberg** Transvaal, S Africa
42B3 **Heidelberg** Germany
49O4 **Heihe** China
74D2 **Heilbron** S Africa
42B3 **Heilbronn** Germany
42C2 **Heiligenstadt** Germany
53B2 **Heilongjiang** Province, China
53A1 **Heilong Jiang** *R* China
32K6 **Heinola** Fin
52B4 **Hejiang** China
7R3 **Hekla** *Mt* Iceland
55C1 **Hekou** Viet
52A5 **Hekou Yaozou Zizhixian** China
52B2 **Helan** China
52B2 **Helan Shan** *Mt* China
17D3 **Helena** Arkansas, USA
18D1 **Helena** Montana, USA
20D3 **Helendale** USA
57D2 **Helen Reef** *I* Pacific O
34C3 **Helensburgh** Scot
65A3 **Heliopolis** Egypt
63C3 **Helleh** *R* Iran
39B2 **Hellin** Spain
18C1 **Hells Canyon** *R* USA
36D1 **Hellweg** Region, Germany
20B2 **Helm** USA
63E2 **Helmand** *R* Afghan
74B2 **Helmeringhausen** Namibia
36C1 **Helmond** Neth
34D2 **Helmsdale** Scot
53B3 **Helong** China
32G7 **Helsingborg** Sweden
Helsingfors = Helsinki
42C1 **Helsingør** Den
32J6 **Helsinki** Fin
35C6 **Helston** Eng
64B4 **Helwân** Egypt
17C3 **Hempstead** USA
32H7 **Hemse** Sweden
52A3 **Henan** China
52C3 **Henan** Province, China
78B1 **Hen and Chicken Is** NZ
54C2 **Henashi-zaki** *C* Japan
12B3 **Henderson** Kentucky, USA
15D1 **Henderson** N. Carolina, USA
19D3 **Henderson** Nevada, USA
17D3 **Henderson** Texas, USA
15C1 **Hendersonville** N. Carolina, USA
15B1 **Hendersonville** Tennessee, USA
74D3 **Hendrik Verwoerd Dam** S Africa
52E5 **Heng-ch'un** Taiwan
50C4 **Hengduan Shan** *Mts* China
42B2 **Hengelo** Neth
52B2 **Hengshan** China
52D2 **Hengshui** China
55D1 **Heng Xian** China
52C4 **Hengyang** China
55A4 **Henhoaha** Nicobar Is
35E6 **Henley-on-Thames** Eng
14C3 **Henlopen,C** USA
14E1 **Henniker** USA
16C3 **Henrietta** USA
7K4 **Henrietta Maria,C** Can
19D3 **Henrieville** USA
17C2 **Henryetta** USA
7M3 **Henry Kater Pen** Can
74A1 **Henties Bay** Namibia
50D2 **Hentiyn Nuruu** *Mts* Mongolia
55B2 **Henzada** Burma
52B5 **Hepu** China
63E2 **Herat** Afghan
6H4 **Herbert** Can
10D5 **Herbert** *I* USA
78C2 **Herbertville** NZ
36E1 **Herborn** Germany
23A4 **Heredia** Costa Rica
35D5 **Hereford** Eng
16B3 **Hereford** USA
35D5 **Hereford & Worcester** County, Eng
36C1 **Herentals** Belg
37B1 **Héricourt** France
17C2 **Herington** USA
78A3 **Heriot** NZ
37C1 **Herisau** Switz
14C1 **Herkimer** USA
37E1 **Hermagor** Austria
34E1 **Herma Ness** *Pen* Scot
74B3 **Hermanus** S Africa
75C2 **Hermidale** Aust
78B2 **Hermitage** NZ
76D1 **Hermit Is** PNG
Hermon,Mt = Jebel ash Shaykh
21A2 **Hermosillo** Mexico
29B4 **Hernandarias** Par
14B2 **Herndon** USA
36D1 **Herne** Germany
42B1 **Herning** Den
4D4 **Heron Bay** Can
63B1 **Herowābad** Iran
29A4 **Herradura** Arg
28C1 **Herrera** Arg
39B2 **Herrera del Duque** Spain
10L2 **Herschel I** Can
14B2 **Hershey** USA
35E6 **Hertford** County, Eng
65C2 **Herzliyya** Israel
36C1 **Hesbaye** Region, Belg
36A1 **Hesdin** France
52B2 **Heshui** China
20D3 **Hesperia** USA
10M3 **Hess** *R* Can
42B2 **Hessen** State, Germany
20C2 **Hetch Hetchy Res** USA
11B2 **Hettinger** USA
35F5 **Heweth** *Oilfield* N Sea
34D4 **Hexham** Eng
52C5 **He Xian** China
74D2 **Heystekrand** S Africa
52C5 **Heyuan** China
75B3 **Heywood** Aust
52D2 **Heze** China
15E4 **Hialeah** USA
11D2 **Hibbing** USA
15C1 **Hickory** USA
78C1 **Hicks Bay** NZ
75C3 **Hicks,Pt** Aust
17C3 **Hico** USA
54D2 **Hidaka-sammyaku** *Mts* Japan
22C1 **Hidalgo** Mexico
22C1 **Hidalgo** State, Mexico
21B2 **Hidalgo del Parral** Mexico
29C2 **Hidrolândia** Brazil
70A2 **Hierro** *I* Canary Is
54D3 **Higashine** Japan
53B5 **Higashi-suidō** *Str* Japan
18B2 **High Desert** USA
4B2 **High Hill** *R* Can

17D4 **High Island** USA
34C2 **Highland** Region, Scot
20D3 **Highland** USA
20C1 **Highland Peak** *Mt* USA
14C2 **Highland Falls** USA
3E2 **High Level** Can
15C1 **High Point** USA
3E2 **High Prairie** Can
6G4 **High River** Can
3G2 **Highrock L** Can
4A2 **Highrock L** Can
15C3 **High Springs** USA
14C2 **Hightstown** USA
35E6 **High Wycombe** Eng
32J7 **Hiiumaa** *I* Estonia
66C1 **Hijaz** Region, S Arabia
54C4 **Hikigawa** Japan
19C3 **Hiko** USA
54C3 **Hikone** Japan
78B1 **Hikurangi** NZ
8C4 **Hildago del Parral** Mexico
42B2 **Hildesheim** Germany
23Q2 **Hillaby,Mt** Barbados
16C2 **Hill City** USA
42C1 **Hillerød** Den
3G1 **Hill Island L** Can
11C2 **Hillsboro** N. Dakota, USA
14E1 **Hillsboro** New Hampshire, USA
16A3 **Hillsboro** New Mexico, USA
12C3 **Hillsboro** Ohio, USA
18B1 **Hillsboro** Oregon, USA
17C3 **Hillsboro** Texas, USA
4D4 **Hillsport** Can
75C2 **Hillston** Aust
12C3 **Hillsville** USA
34E1 **Hillswick** Scot
20E5 **Hilo** Hawaiian Is
14B1 **Hilton** USA
64C2 **Hilvan** Turk
42B2 **Hilversum** Neth
60D2 **Himachal Pradesh** State, India
59G3 **Himalaya, Mts** Asia
60C4 **Himatnagar** India
53C5 **Himeji** Japan
53D4 **Himi** Japan
45F9 **Himş** Syria
10J3 **Hinchinbrook Entrance** USA
10J3 **Hinchinbrook I** USA
11D2 **Hinckley** Minnesota, USA
14C1 **Hinckley Res** USA
60D3 **Hindaun** India
60B1 **Hindu Kush** *Mts* Afghan
62B2 **Hindupur** India
3E2 **Hines Creek** Can
60D4 **Hinganghāt** India
53B2 **Hinggan Ling** *Upland* China
60B3 **Hingol** *R* Pak
60D5 **Hingoli** India
20D3 **Hinkley** USA
32H5 **Hinnøya** *I* Nor
14D1 **Hinsdale** USA
3E3 **Hinton** Can
16C2 **Hinton** USA
28B2 **Hipolito Itrogoyen** Arg
54A4 **Hirado** Japan
54A4 **Hirado-shima** *I* Japan
61B3 **Hirakud Res** India
64B2 **Hirfanli Baraji** *Res* Turk
62B2 **Hirihar** India
54D2 **Hiroo** Japan
53E3 **Hirosaki** Japan
53C5 **Hiroshima** Japan
36C2 **Hirson** France
41F2 **Hirşova** Rom
42B1 **Hirtshals** Den
60D3 **Hisār** India
67E3 **Hisn al 'Abr** Yemen
23C3 **Hispaniola** *I* Caribbean
65D1 **Hisyah** Syria
64D3 **Hīt** Iraq
53E4 **Hitachi** Japan
54D3 **Hitachi-Ota** Japan
35E6 **Hitchin** Eng
32F6 **Hitra** *I* Nor
54B4 **Hiuchi-nada** *B* Japan
54B4 **Hiwasa** Japan
65C3 **Hiyon** *R* Israel
42B1 **Hjørring** Den
55B1 **Hka** *R* Burma
71G4 **Ho** Ghana
55D1 **Hoa Binh** Viet
55D3 **Hoa Da** Viet
75E3 **Hobart** Aust
16C3 **Hobart** USA
16B3 **Hobbs** USA
42B1 **Hobro** Den
3D3 **Hobson L** Can
69D4 **Hobyo** Somalia
37E1 **Hochalm Spitze** *Mt* Austria
37E1 **Hochgolling** *Mt* Austria
Ho Chi Minh = Saigon
42C3 **Hochkonig, Mt** Austria
54A2 **Hochon** N Korea
36E2 **Hockenheim** Germany
37E1 **Hockönig** *Mt* Austria
4B3 **Hodgson** Can
41E1 **Hódmezö'hely** Hung
42D3 **Hodonin** Czech
36C1 **Hoek van Holland** Neth
54A3 **Hoengsŏng** S Korea
53B3 **Hoeryong** N Korea
54A3 **Hoeyang** N Korea
42C2 **Hof** Germany
32B2 **Hofsjökull** *Mts* Iceland
7R3 **Höfn** Iceland
53C5 **Hōfu** Japan
70C2 **Hoggar** *Upland* Alg
36D1 **Hohe Acht** *Mt* Germany
36E1 **Hohes Gras** *Mts* Germany
37E1 **Hohe Tauern** *Mts* Austria
52C1 **Hohhot** China
50C3 **Hoh Sai Hu** *L* China
59G2 **Hoh Xil Shan** *Mts* China
72D3 **Hoima** Uganda
61D2 **Hojāi** India
54B4 **Hojo** Japan
78B1 **Hokianga Harbour** *B* NZ
78B2 **Hokitika** NZ
53E3 **Hokkaidō** Japan
63D1 **Hokmābād** Iran
54D3 **Hokota** Japan
75C3 **Holbrook** Aust
19D4 **Holbrook** USA
19D3 **Holden** USA
17C2 **Holdenville** USA
16C1 **Holdrege** USA
62B2 **Hole Narsipur** India
23Q2 **Holetown** Barbados
23B2 **Holguín** Cuba
78B2 **Holitika** NZ
10G3 **Holitna** *R* USA
42D3 **Hollabrunn** Austria
12B2 **Holland** USA
14A2 **Hollidaysburg** USA
16C3 **Hollis** USA
20B2 **Hollister** USA
17E3 **Holly Springs** USA
20C3 **Hollywood** California, USA
15E4 **Hollywood** Florida, USA
6G2 **Holman Island** Can
32J6 **Holmsund** Sweden
65C2 **Holon** Israel
42B1 **Holstebro** Den
11C3 **Holstein** USA
7N3 **Holsteinsborg** Greenland
15C1 **Holston** *R* USA
12C2 **Holt** USA
17C2 **Holton** USA
10G3 **Holy Cross** USA
35C5 **Holyhead** Wales
34E4 **Holy I** Eng
35C5 **Holy I** Wales
16B1 **Holyoke** Colorado, USA
14D1 **Holyoke** Massachusetts, USA
36E1 **Holzminden** Germany
61D3 **Homalin** Burma
36E1 **Homburg** Germany
7M3 **Home B** Can
10H4 **Homer** Alaska, USA
17D3 **Homer** Louisiana, USA
78A2 **Homer Tunnel** NZ
15C2 **Homerville** USA
15E4 **Homestead** USA
15B2 **Homewood** USA
62B1 **Homnābād** India
73D6 **Homoine** Mozam
74B3 **Hondeklip B** S Africa
16A3 **Hondo** New Mexico, USA
16C4 **Hondo** Texas, USA
21C3 **Hondo** *R* Mexico
21D3 **Honduras** Republic, C America
21D3 **Honduras,G of** Honduras
32G6 **Hønefoss** Nor
14C2 **Honesdale** USA
19B2 **Honey L** USA
36A2 **Honfleur** France
55C1 **Hong, R** Viet
55D1 **Hon Gai** Viet
54A3 **Hongchŏn** S Korea
52A4 **Hongguo** China
52C4 **Hong Hu** *L* China
52B2 **Honghui** China
52C4 **Hongjiang** China
52C5 **Hong Kong** Colony, S E Asia
50E2 **Hongor** Mongolia
52B5 **Hongshui He** *R* China
54A3 **Hongsong** S Korea
54A3 **Hongwon** N Korea
52A3 **Hongyuan** China
52D3 **Hongze Hu** *L* China
77E1 **Honiara** Solomon Is
54D3 **Honjō** Japan
55C4 **Hon Khoai** *I* Camb
55D3 **Hon Lan** *I* Viet
32K4 **Honnigsvåg** Nor
44D1 **Honningsvåg** Nor
20E5 **Honokaa** Hawaiian Is
20E5 **Honolulu** Hawaiian Is
55C4 **Hon Panjang** *I* Viet
53D4 **Honshu** *I* Japan
18B1 **Hood,Mt** USA
18B1 **Hood River** USA
16B2 **Hooker** USA
35B5 **Hook Head** *C* Irish Rep
10L4 **Hoonah** USA
10E3 **Hooper Bay** USA
74D2 **Hoopstad** S Africa
42A2 **Hoorn** Neth
14D1 **Hoosick Falls** USA
8B3 **Hoover Dam** USA
10J3 **Hope** Alaska, USA
17D3 **Hope** Arkansas, USA
3D4 **Hope** Can
7M4 **Hopedale** Can
48D2 **Hopen** *I* Barents S
7M3 **Hopes Advance,C** Can
75B3 **Hopetoun** Aust
74C2 **Hopetown** S Africa
14A2 **Hopewell** Pennsylvania, USA
13D3 **Hopewell** Virginia, USA
12B3 **Hopkinsville** USA
18B1 **Hoquiam** USA
64D2 **Horasan** Turk
36E2 **Horb** Germany
69E3 **Hordiyo** Somalia
37C1 **Horgen** Switz
xxixL6 **Horizon Depth** Pacific O
67G1 **Hormuz,Str of** Oman/Iran
42D3 **Horn** Austria
7Q3 **Horn** *C* Iceland
10O2 **Hornaday** *R* Can
32H5 **Hornavan** *L* Sweden
17D3 **Hornbeck** USA
18B2 **Hornbrook** USA
78B2 **Hornby** NZ
20C2 **Horndon** USA
14B1 **Hornell** USA
7K5 **Hornepayne** Can
15B2 **Horn I** USA
6F3 **Horn Mts** Can
35E5 **Hornsea** Eng
52B1 **Horn Uul** *Mt* Mongolia
53A2 **Horqin-Youyi Qianqi** China
53A3 **Horqin Zuoyi** China
25E2 **Horqueta** Par
14B1 **Horseheads** USA
42C1 **Horsens** Den
18B1 **Horseshoe Bay** Can
18C2 **Horseshoe Bend** USA
75B3 **Horsham** Aust
35E6 **Horsham** Eng
32G7 **Horten** Nor
10O2 **Horton** *R* Can
56D2 **Hose Mts** Malay
63E3 **Hoshab** Pak
60D4 **Hoshangābād** India
60D2 **Hoshiārpur** India
16C2 **Hosington** USA
62B1 **Hospet** India
25C9 **Hoste** *I* Chile
59F2 **Hotan** China
74C2 **Hotazel** S Africa
17D3 **Hot Springs** Arkansas, USA
11B3 **Hot Springs** S. Dakota, USA
6G3 **Hottah L** Can
74A2 **Hottentot Pt** Namibia
36A2 **Houdan** France
12B1 **Houghton** USA
13F1 **Houlton** USA
52C2 **Houma** China
17D4 **Houma** USA
71E2 **Houmet Essouq** Tunisia
71F3 **Houndé** Burkina
53A3 **Houqi** China
14D2 **Housatonic** *R* USA
3C3 **Houston** Can
17E3 **Houston** Mississippi, USA
17C4 **Houston** Texas, USA
76A3 **Houtman** *Is* Aust
14A2 **Houtzdale** USA
50C2 **Hovd** Mongolia
50D1 **Hövsgol Nuur** *L* Mongolia
75D1 **Howard** Aust
12B2 **Howard City** USA
10G2 **Howard P** USA
75C3 **Howe,C** Aust
18B1 **Howe Sd** Can
74E2 **Howick** S Africa
13F1 **Howland** USA
36E1 **Höxter** Germany
34D2 **Hoy** *I* Scot
32F6 **Høyanger** Nor
11D2 **Hoyt Lakes** USA
42D2 **Hradeç-Královė** Czech
43D3 **Hranice** Czech
43D3 **Hron** *R* Czech
52E5 **Hsin-chu** Taiwan
61E3 **Hsipaw** Burma
52E5 **Hsüeh Shan** *Mt* Taiwan
54A4 **Hsuyong** S Korea
74A1 **Huab** *R* Namibia
52B2 **Huachi** China
26C6 **Huacho** Peru
52C1 **Huade** China
52D3 **Huaibei** China
52D3 **Huaibin** China
53A3 **Huaide** China
52D3 **Huai He** *R* China
52C4 **Huaihua** China
52C5 **Huaiji** China
52D3 **Huainan** China
19D3 **Hualapai Peak** *Mt* USA
28B1 **Hualfin** Arg
50F4 **Hua-lien** Taiwan
26C5 **Huallaga** *R* Peru
26C5 **Huallanca** Peru
26C5 **Huamachuco** Peru
73B5 **Huambo** Angola
53C2 **Huanan** China
26E7 **Huanay** Bol
26C5 **Huancabamba** Peru
26C6 **Huancavelica** Peru
26C6 **Huancayo** Peru
52D3 **Huangchuan** China
52A3 **Huange He** *R* China
Huang Hai = Yellow Sea
52D2 **Huang He, R** China
52B2 **Huangling** China
55D2 **Huangliu** China
53B3 **Huangnihe** China
52C3 **Huangpi** China
52D3 **Huangshi** China
28C3 **Huanguelén** Arg
52E4 **Huangyan** China
53B3 **Huanren** China
26C5 **Huānuco** Peru
25C1 **Huanuni** Bol
52B2 **Huan Xian** China
26C5 **Huaráz** Peru
26C6 **Huarmey** Peru
26C5 **Huascarán** *Mt* Peru
28A1 **Huasco** Chile
28A1 **Huasco** *R* Chile
22C2 **Huatusco** Mexico
22C1 **Huauchinango** Mexico
22B1 **Huaunamota** *R* Mexico
22C2 **Huautla** Mexico
52C2 **Hua Xian** China
21B2 **Huayapan** *R* Mexico
52C3 **Hubei** Province, China
37E1 **Huben** Austria
62B1 **Hubli** India
28C3 **Hucal** Arg
53B3 **Huch'ang** N Korea
35E5 **Huddersfield** Eng
32H6 **Hudiksvall** Sweden
15C3 **Hudson** Florida, USA
12C2 **Hudson** Michigan, USA
14D1 **Hudson** New York, USA
14D1 **Hudson** *R* USA
7K4 **Hudson B** Can
6H4 **Hudson Bay** Can
14D1 **Hudson Falls** USA
3D2 **Hudson's Hope** Can
7L3 **Hudson Str** Can
55D2 **Hue** Viet
22B1 **Huejuqvilla** Mexico
22C1 **Huejutla** Mexico
39A2 **Huelva** Spain
22B2 **Hueramo** Mexico
39B2 **Húercal Overa** Spain
22B1 **Huertecillas** Mexico
39B1 **Huesca** Spain
22C2 **Huexotla** *Hist Site* Mexico
76D3 **Hughenden** Aust
10H2 **Hughes** USA
3H2 **Hughes** *R* Can
61C3 **Hugli** *R* India
17C3 **Hugo** USA
16B2 **Hugoton** USA
52D4 **Hui'an** China
78C1 **Huiarau Range** *Mts* NZ
74B2 **Huib hochplato** *Plat* Namibia
53B3 **Hüich'ŏn** N Korea
53B3 **Huifa He** *R* China
52D5 **Huilai** China
52A4 **Huili** China
28B1 **Huillapima** Arg
22D2 **Huimanguillo** Mexico
53B3 **Huinan** China
28C2 **Huinca Renancó** Arg
36A2 **Huisne** *R* France
21C3 **Huixtla** Mexico
22B1 **Huizache** Mexico
52A4 **Huize** China
52C5 **Huizhou** China
22C2 **Hujuápan de Léon** Mexico
61E2 **Hukawng Valley** Burma
53B2 **Hulan** China
66D1 **Hulayfah** S Arabia
53C2 **Hulin** China
4F4 **Hull** Can
35E5 **Hull** Eng
77H1 **Hull** *I* Phoenix Is
26C3 **Hulla** *Mt* Colombia
42D1 **Hultsfred** Sweden
49N5 **Hulun Nur** *L* China
53B1 **Huma** China
53A1 **Huma He** *R* China
26F5 **Humaita** Brazil
74C3 **Humansdorp** S Africa
35E5 **Humber** *R* Eng
35E5 **Humberside** County, Eng
6H4 **Humboldt** Can
11D3 **Humboldt** Iowa, USA
15B1 **Humboldt** Tennessee, USA
18C2 **Humboldt** *R* USA
18B2 **Humboldt B** USA
7M2 **Humboldt Gletscher** *Gl* Greenland
19C3 **Humboldt L** USA
75C1 **Humeburn** Aust
75C3 **Hume,L** Aust
73B5 **Humpata** Angola
20C2 **Humphreys** USA
20C2 **Humphreys,Mt** California, USA
19D3 **Humphreys Peak** *Mt* Arizona, USA
32A1 **Húnaflóri** *B* Iceland
52C4 **Hunan** Province, China
53C3 **Hunchun** China
3D3 **Hundred Mile House** Can
41E1 **Hunedoara** Rom
36E1 **Hünfeld** Germany
43D3 **Hungary** Republic, Europe
75B1 **Hungerford** Aust
53B4 **Hüngnam** N Korea
18D1 **Hungry Horse Res** USA
53B3 **Hunjiang** China
74B2 **Hunsberge** *Mts* Namibia
36D2 **Hunsrück** Mts, Germany
75D2 **Hunter** *R* Aust
3C3 **Hunter I** Can
75E3 **Hunter Is** Aust
10H3 **Hunter,Mt** USA
12B3 **Huntingburg** USA
35E5 **Huntingdon** Eng
12B2 **Huntingdon** Indiana, USA
14A2 **Huntingdon** Pennsylvania, USA
12C3 **Huntington** USA
20C4 **Huntington Beach** USA
20C2 **Huntington L** USA
78C1 **Huntly** NZ
34D3 **Huntly** Scot
10N3 **Hunt,Mt** Can
75A1 **Hunt Pen** Aust
15B2 **Huntsville** Alabama, USA
4F4 **Huntsville** Can
17C3 **Huntsville** Texas, USA
53B2 **Huolongmen** China
55D2 **Huong Khe** Viet
51H7 **Huon Peninsula** *Pen* PNG
75E3 **Huonville** Anst
12C1 **Hurd,C** Can
66B1 **Hurghada** Egypt
12A1 **Hurley** USA
20B2 **Huron** California, USA
11C3 **Huron** S. Dakota, USA
12C1 **Huron,L** USA/Can
28A2 **Hurtado** Chile
78B2 **Hurunui** *R* NZ
32B1 **Husavik** Iceland
41F1 **Huşi** Rom
32G7 **Huskvarna** Sweden
10G2 **Huslia** USA
65C2 **Husn** Jordan
42B2 **Husum** Germany
17C2 **Hutchinson** USA
75C1 **Hutton,Mt** Aust
52D2 **Hutuo He** *R* China
36C1 **Huy** Belg
52A2 **Huzhu** China
40D2 **Hvar** *I* Croatia, Yugos
54A2 **Hwadae** N Korea
73C5 **Hwange** Zim
73C5 **Hwange Nat Pk** Zim
54A2 **Hwapyong** N Korea
14E2 **Hyannis** Massachusetts, USA
11B3 **Hyannis** Nebraska, USA
50C2 **Hyaryas Nuur** *L* Mongolia
3B2 **Hydaburg** USA
14D2 **Hyde Park** USA
62B1 **Hyderābād** India
60B3 **Hyderabad** Pak
37B3 **Hyères** France
10N3 **Hyland** *R* Can
14A3 **Hyndman** USA
8B2 **Hyndman Peak** *Mt* USA
44D3 **Hyrynsalmi** Fin
3E2 **Hythe** Can
53C5 **Hyūga** Japan
32J6 **Hyvikää** Fin

I

27K6 **Iaçu** Brazil
41F2 **Ialomiţa** *R* Rom
32G6 **Iärpen** Sweden
41F1 **Iaşi** Rom
71G4 **Ibadan** Nig
26C3 **Ibagué** Colombia
41E2 **Ibar** *R* Montenegro/Serbia
26C3 **Ibarra** Ecuador
66D4 **Ibb** Yemen
71H4 **Ibi** Nig
29C2 **Ibiá** Brazil
29E1 **Ibicaraí** Brazil
28D1 **Ibicui** *R* Brazil
28D2 **Ibicuy** Arg
28E1 **Ibirubá** Brazil
39C2 **Ibiza** Spain
39C2 **Ibiza** *I* Spain
73E5 **Ibo** Mozam
27K6 **Ibotirama** Brazil
67G2 **'Ibrī** Oman
26C6 **Ica** Peru
26E4 **Içá** *R* Brazil
26E3 **Icana** Brazil
32A1 **Iceland** Republic, N Atlantic O
3D3 **Ice Mt** Can
49R4 **Icha** Russian Fed
62A1 **Ichalkaranji** India
53E4 **Ichihara** Japan
54C3 **Ichinomiya** Japan
53E4 **Ichinoseki** Japan
10K4 **Icy B** USA
10F1 **Icy C** USA
3A2 **Icy Str** USA
17D3 **Idabell** USA
11C3 **Ida Grove** USA
71H4 **Idah** Nig
18D2 **Idaho** State, USA
18C2 **Idaho City** USA
18D2 **Idaho Falls** USA
16A2 **Idaho Springs** USA
18B2 **Idanha** USA
36D2 **Idar Oberstein** Germany
69A2 **Idehan Marzūg** *Desert* Libya
69A2 **Idehan Ubari** *Desert* Libya
70C2 **Idelés** Alg
50C2 **Iderlym Gol** *R* Mongolia
66B2 **Idfu** Egypt
41E3 **Ídhi Óros** *Mt* Greece
41E3 **Ídhra** *I* Greece
72B4 **Idiofa** Zaïre
10G3 **Iditarod** *R* USA
64C2 **Idlib** Syria
37E2 **Idrija** Slovenia, Yugos
32K7 **Idritsa** Russian Fed
74D3 **Idutywa** S Africa
36B1 **Ieper** Belg
41F3 **Ierápetra** Greece
37E3 **Iesi** Italy
73D4 **Ifakara** Tanz
51H6 **Ifalik** *I* Pacific
73E6 **Ifanadiana** Madag
71G4 **Ife** Nig
70C3 **Iférouane** Niger
56D2 **Igan** Malay
29C3 **Igaranava** Brazil
48K3 **Igarka** Russian Fed
29A3 **Igatimi** Par
71G4 **Igbetti** Nig
64E2 **Igdir** Iran
32H6 **Iggesund** Sweden
28B2 **Iglesia** Arg
40B3 **Iglesias** Sardegna
7K3 **Igloolik** Can
4C4 **Ignace** Can
64A1 **Iğneada Burun** *Pt* Turk
62E2 **Ignoitijala** Andaman Is
41E3 **Igoumenítsa** Greece
44J4 **Igra** Russian Fed
44L3 **Igrim** Russian Fed
22C2 **Iguala** Mexico
25G2 **Iguape** Brazil
29C3 **Iguatama** Brazil
29B3 **Iguatemi** Brazil
29A3 **Iguatemi** *R* Brazil
27L5 **Iguatu** Brazil
72A4 **Iguéla** Gabon
71H4 **Igumale** Nig
71H4 **Ihiala** Nig
73E6 **Ihosy** Madag
53D4 **Iida** Japan
54C3 **Iide-san** *Mt* Japan
32K6 **Iisalmi** Fin
54B4 **Iizuka** Japan
71G4 **Ijebulgbo** Nig
71G4 **Ijebu Ode** Nig
42B2 **IJsselmeer** *S* Neth
28E1 **Ijuí** Brazil
28D1 **Ijui** *R* Brazil
41F3 **Ikaría** *I* Greece
53E3 **Ikeda** Japan
72C4 **Ikela** Zaïre
71H4 **Ikerre** Nig
41E2 **Ikhtiman** Bulg
54A4 **Iki** *I* Japan
71G4 **Ikire** Nig
10H4 **Ikolik,C** USA
73E5 **Ikopa** *R* Madag
71G4 **Ila** Nig
57F7 **Ilagan** Phil
63B2 **Īlām** Iran
50C1 **Ilanskiy** Russian Fed
37C1 **Ilanz** Switz
71G4 **Ilaro** Nig
3G2 **Île à la Crosse** Can
3G2 **Île à la Crosse,L** Can
68G8 **Ilebo** Zaire
36B2 **Île De France** Region, France
71E2 **Île de Jerba** *I* Tunisia
38B2 **Ile de Noirmoutier** *I* France
38B2 **Ile de Ré** *I* France
77F3 **Île des Pins** *I* Nouvelle Calédonie
13E1 **Ile d'Orleans** Can
38A2 **Ile d'Ouessant** *I* France
38B2 **Ile d'Yeu** *I* France
45K5 **Ilek** *R* Russian Fed
22A1 **Ile María Cleofas** *I* Mexico
22A1 **Ile María Madre** *I* Mexico
22A1 **Ile María Magdalena** Mexico
22A1 **Ile San Juanico** *I* Mexico
77F2 **Îles Bélèp** Nouvelle Calédonie
77E2 **Îles Chesterfield** Nouvelle Calédonie
77H2 **Îles de Horn** *Is* Pacific O
38D3 **Iles d'Hyères** *Is* France
71G4 **Ilesha** Nig
71E2 **Iles Kerkenna** *Is* Tunisia
4B2 **Ilford** Can
35C6 **Ilfracombe** Eng
64B1 **Ilgaz Dağları** *Mts* Turk
73D6 **Ilha Bazaruto** *I* Mozam
29C3 **Ilha Comprida** *I* Brazil
29E1 **Ilha de Boipeba** *I* Brazil
27H3 **Ilha De Maracá** *I* Brazil
27H4 **Ilha de Marajó** *I* Brazil
29C4 **Ilha de São Francisco** *I* Brazil
29C3 **Ilha de São Sebastião** *I* Brazil
29E1 **Ilha de Tinharé** *I* Brazil
27H6 **Ilha do Bananal** *Region* Brazil
29C4 **Ilha do Cardoso** *I* Brazil
25F2 **Ilha Grande, Reprêsa** *Res* Brazil
29D3 **Ilha Grande** *I* Brazil
29B3 **Ilha Grande ou Sete Quedas** *I* Brazil
29C3 **Ilha Santo Amaro** *I* Brazil
29B3 **Ilha Solteira Dam** Brazil
70A2 **Ilhas Selvegens** *I* Atlantic O
27L6 **Ilhéus** Brazil
48J5 **Ili** *R* Kazakhstan
10G4 **Iliamna L** USA
10H3 **Iliamna V** USA
36A2 **Iliers** France
57F9 **Iligan** Phil
49M4 **Ilim** *R* Russian Fed
49M4 **Ilimsk** Russian Fed
53E2 **Il'inskiy** Russian Fed
41E3 **Iliodhrómia** *I* Greece
14C1 **Ilion** USA
57F9 **Illana B** Phil
28A2 **Illapel** Chile
28A2 **Illapel** *R* Chile
70C3 **Illéla** Niger
37D1 **Iller** *R* Germany
22B1 **Illescas** Mexico
77H2 **Îlles Wallis** *Is* Pacific O
12B2 **Illinois** State, USA
12A3 **Illinois** *R* USA
70C2 **Illizi** Alg
44E4 **Il'men, Ozero** *L* Russian Fed
26D7 **Ilo** Peru
57F8 **Iloilo** Phil
32L6 **Ilomantsi** Fin
71G4 **Ilorin** Nig
57C4 **Ilwaki** Indon
43G1 **Il'yino** Russian Fed
54B4 **Imabari** Japan
54C3 **Imalchi** Japan
32L5 **Imandra, Ozero** *L* Russian Fed
54A4 **Imari** Japan
44D3 **Imatra** Fin
25G3 **Imbituba** Brazil
29B4 **Imbitura** Brazil
72E3 **Imi** Eth
54A3 **Imjin** *R* N Korea
18C2 **Imlay** USA
37D1 **Immenstadt** Germany
71H4 **Imo** State, Nig
40C2 **Imola** Italy
27J5 **Imperatriz** Brazil
40B2 **Imperia** Italy
16B1 **Imperial** USA
19C4 **Imperial V** USA
72B3 **Impfondo** Congo
61D3 **Imphāl** India
37D1 **Imst** Austria
10F2 **Imuruk L** USA
54C3 **Ina** Japan
70C2 **In Afahleleh** *Well* Alg
54C4 **Inamba-jima** *I* Japan
70C2 **In Amenas** Alg
32K5 **Inari** Fin
32K5 **Inarijärvi** *L* Fin
54D3 **Inawashiro-ko** *L* Japan
70C2 **In Belbel** Alg
45F7 **Ince Burun** *Pt* Turk
64B2 **Incekum Burun** *Pt* Turk
53B4 **Inch'ŏn** S Korea
70B2 **In Dagouber** *Well* Mali
29C2 **Indaiś** *R* Brazil
32H6 **Indals** *R* Sweden
35G5 **Indefatigable** *Gasfield* N Sea
20C2 **Independence** California, USA
11D3 **Independence** Iowa, USA
17C2 **Independence** Kansas, USA
17D2 **Independence** Missouri, USA
18C2 **Independence Mts** USA
56B3 **Inderagiri** *R* Indon
45J6 **Inderborskiy** Kazakhstan
59F4 **India** Federal Republic, Asia
12B2 **Indiana** State, USA
13D2 **Indiana** USA
xxviiiF7 **Indian-Antarctic Basin** Indian O
xxviiiF7 **Indian-Antarctic Ridge** Indian O
12B3 **Indianapolis** USA
Indian Desert = Thar Desert
7N4 **Indian Harbour** Can
3H3 **Indian Head** Can
xxviiiE5 **Indian O**
17D1 **Indianola** Iowa, USA
17D3 **Indianola** Mississippi, USA
29C2 **Indianópolis** Brazil
19C3 **Indian Springs** USA
44H2 **Indiga** Russian Fed
49Q3 **Indigirka** *R* Russian Fed
55D2 **Indo China** Region, S E Asia
51F7 **Indonesia** Republic, S E Asia
60D4 **Indore** India
56C4 **Indramayu** Indon
38C2 **Indre** *R* France
60B3 **Indus** *R* Pak
45E7 **Inebdu** Turk
70C2 **In Ebeggi** *Well* Alg
64B1 **Inebolu** Turk
70C2 **In Ecker** Alg
64A1 **Inegöl** Turk
70D2 **In Ezzane** Alg
74C3 **Infante,C** S Africa
70C3 **Ingal** Niger
12C2 **Ingersoll** Can
76D2 **Ingham** Aust
7M2 **Inglefield Land** *Region* Greenland
78B1 **Inglewood** NZ
75D1 **Inglewood** Queensland, Aust
20C4 **Inglewood** USA
75B3 **Inglewood** Victoria, Aust
32B2 **Ingólfshöfði** *I* Iceland
42C3 **Ingolstadt** Germany
61C3 **Ingrāj Bāzār** India
70C3 **In-Guezzam** *Well* Alg
74E2 **Inhaca** *I* Mozam
74E2 **Inhaca Pen** Mozam
73D6 **Inhambane** Mozam
73D6 **Inharrime** Mozam
29C2 **Inhumas** Brazil
26E3 **Inirida** *R* Colombia
34B4 **Inishowen** District, Irish Rep
75C1 **Injune** Aust
3B2 **Inklin** Can
10M4 **Inklin** *R* Can
10G2 **Inland L** USA
37D1 **Inn** *R* Austria
75B1 **Innamincka** Aust
50D2 **Inner Mongolia** Autonomous Region, China
76D2 **Innisfail** Aust
53E2 **Innokent'yevskiy** Russian Fed
10G3 **Innoko** *R* USA
42C3 **Innsbruck** Austria
72B4 **Inongo** Zaïre
43D2 **Inowrocław** Pol
70C2 **In Salah** Alg
54A3 **Insil** S Korea
44L2 **Inta** Russian Fed
37B1 **Interlaken** Switz
77H3 **International Date Line**
11D2 **International Falls** USA
28C1 **Intiyaco** Arg
37C2 **Intra** Italy
56E3 **Intu** Indon
54D3 **Inubo-saki** *C* Japan
7L4 **Inukjuak** Can
6E3 **Inuvik** Can
6E3 **Inuvik** Region, Can
34C3 **Inveraray** Scot
78A3 **Invercargill** NZ
75D1 **Inverell** Aust
3E3 **Invermere** Can
34C2 **Inverness** Scot
34D3 **Inverurie** Scot
75A3 **Investigator Str** Aust
50B1 **Inya** Russian Fed
49Q3 **Inya** *R* Russian Fed
73D5 **Inyanga** Zim
20D3 **Inyokern** USA
20C2 **Inyo Mts** USA
72B4 **Inzia** *R* Zaïre
41E3 **Ioánnina** Greece
17C2 **Iola** USA
63E1 **Iolotan** Turkmenistan
34B3 **Iona** *I* Scot
73B5 **Iôna Nat Pk** Angola
18C1 **Ione** USA
Ionian Is = Ioníoi Nísoi
41D3 **Ionian S** Italy/Greece
41E3 **Ioníoi Nísoi** *Is* Greece
10D2 **Ioniveyem** *R* Russian Fed
41F3 **Íos** *I* Greece
44J3 **Iosser** Russian Fed '
11D3 **Iowa** State, USA
11D3 **Iowa** *R* USA
12A2 **Iowa City** USA
11D3 **Iowa Falls** USA
29C2 **Ipameri** Brazil
29D2 **Ipanema** Brazil
45G6 **Ipatovo** Russian Fed
26C3 **Ipiales** Colombia
29E1 **Ipiaú** Brazil
29B4 **Ipiranga** Brazil
55C5 **Ipoh** Malay
27H7 **Iporá** Brazil
41F2 **Ipsala** Turk
75D1 **Ipswich** Aust
35F5 **Ipswich** Eng
14E1 **Ipswich** USA
43G2 **Iput** *R* Russian Fed
29C3 **Iquape** Brazil
25B2 **Iquique** Chile
26D4 **Iquitos** Peru
28E1 **Irai** Brazil
41F3 **Iráklion** Greece
58D2 **Iran** Republic, S W Asia
63E3 **Irānshahr** Iran
22B1 **Irapuato** Mexico
64D3 **Iraq** Republic, S W Asia
29B4 **Irati** Brazil
69A2 **Irā Wan** *Watercourse* Libya
65C2 **Irbid** Jordan
44L4 **Irbit** Russian Fed
27G3 **Ireng** *R* Guyana
53B4 **Iri** S Korea
51G7 **Irian Jaya** Province, Indon
72C2 **Iriba** Chad
57F8 **Iriga** Phil
73D4 **Iringa** Tanz
50F4 **Iriomote** *I* Japan
23A3 **Iriona** Honduras
27H5 **Iriri** *R* Brazil
35C5 **Irish S** Eng/Irish Rep
10H2 **Irkillik** *R* USA
49M4 **Irkutsk** Russian Fed
75A2 **Iron Knob** Aust
12B1 **Iron Mountain** USA
76D2 **Iron Range** Aust
12B1 **Iron River** USA
12C3 **Irontown** USA
12A1 **Ironwood** USA
4E4 **Iroquois Falls** Can
54C4 **Iro-zaki** *C* Japan
61E4 **Irrawaddy** *R* Burma
55A2 **Irrawaddy,Mouths of the** Burma
48H4 **Irtysh** *R* Russian Fed
39B1 **Irun** Spain
34C4 **Irvine** Scot
17C3 **Irving** USA
71H3 **Isa** Nig
57F9 **Isabela** Phil
20C3 **Isabella Res** USA
6H2 **Isachsen** Can
6H2 **Isachsen,C** Can
7Q3 **Ísafjörður** Iceland
53C5 **Isahaya** Japan
72C3 **Isangi** Zaïre
37D1 **Isar** *R* Germany
37D1 **Isarco** *R* Italy
34E1 **Isbister** Scot
37D1 **Ischgl** Austria
40C2 **Ischia** *I* Italy
54C4 **Ise** Japan
37D2 **Iseo** Italy
37A2 **Isère** *R* France
36D1 **Iserlohn** Germany
40C2 **Isernia** Italy
54C4 **Ise-wan** *B* Japan
71G4 **Iseyin** Nig
50F4 **Ishigaki** *I* Japan
53E3 **Ishikari** *R* Japan
53E3 **Ishikari-wan** *B* Japan
48H4 **Ishim** Russian Fed
48H4 **Ishim** *R* Kazakhstan
53E4 **Ishinomaki** Japan
54D3 **Ishioka** Japan
60C1 **Ishkashim** Afghan
12B1 **Ishpeming** USA
48J4 **Isil'kul'** Russian Fed
57B2 **Isimu** Indon
72D3 **Isiolo** Kenya
72C3 **Isiro** Zaïre
64C2 **Iskenderun** Turk
64C2 **Iskenferun Körfezi** *B* Turk
64B1 **Iskilip** Turk
48K4 **Iskitim** Russian Fed
41E2 **Iskur** *R* Bulg
10M4 **Iskut** *R* Can/USA
22C2 **Isla** Mexico
28D1 **Isla Apipe Grande** Arg
23C3 **Isla Beata** Dom Rep
28C3 **Isla Bermejo** *I* Arg
23E4 **Isla Blanquilla** Ven
26B2 **Isla Coiba** *I* Panama
8B4 **Isla de Cedros** *I* Mexico
25B6 **Isla de Chiloé** *I* Chile
21D2 **Isla de Cozumel** *I* Mexico
23C3 **Isla de la Gonâve** Cuba
23A2 **Isla de la Juventud** *I* Cuba
28D2 **Isla de las Lechiguanas** *I* Arg
2K8 **Isla del Coco** *I* Costa Rica
21D3 **Isla del Maiz** *I* Caribbean
22C1 **Isla de Lobos** *I* Mexico
25D8 **Isla de los Estados** *I* Arg
24F4 **Isla de Marajó** *I* Brazil
xxixO6 **Isla de Pascua** *I* Pacific O
23A4 **Isla de Providencia** *I* Caribbean
23A4 **Isla de San Andres** *I* Caribbean
25G3 **Isla de Santa Catarina** *I* Brazil
27H2 **Isla du Diable** *I* French Guiana
27M4 **Isla Fernando de Noronha** *I* Brazil
25C8 **Isla Grande de Tierra del Fuego** *I* Arg/Chile
23D4 **Isla la Tortuga** *I* Ven
60C2 **Islamabad** Pak
21A2 **Isla Magdalena** *I* Mexico
23E4 **Isla Margarita** Ven
28A3 **Isla Mocha** Chile
15E4 **Islamorada** USA
4C3 **Island L** Can
75A2 **Island Lg** Aust
18D2 **Island Park** USA
5K4 **Islands,B of** Can
78B1 **Islands,B of** NZ
26B1 **Isla Providencia** *I* Colombia
26B4 **Isla Puná** *I* Ecuador
xxxD6 **Isla San Ambrosia** *I* Pacific O
xxxD6 **Isla San Felix** *I* Pacific O
21A2 **Isla Santa Margarita** *I* Mexico
28A3 **Isla Santa Maria** *I* Chile
39C2 **Islas Baleares** *Is* Spain
70A2 **Islas Canarias** *Is* Atlantic O
39C2 **Islas Columbretes** *Is* Spain
21D3 **Islas de la Bahia** *Is* Honduras
23A4 **Islas del Maiz** *Is* Caribbean
26F1 **Islas de Margarita** *Is* Ven
25C9 **Islas Diego Ramírez** *Is* Chile
26N0 **Islas Galapagos** *Is* Pacific O
26Q0 **Islas Juan Fernandez** *Is* Pacific O
26E1 **Islas los Roques** *Is* Ven
Islas Malvinas = Falkland Is
xxixO4 **Islas Revilla Gigedo** *Is* Pacific O
25C9 **Islas Wollaston** *Is* Chile
70A3 **Isla Tidra** *I* Maur
25B7 **Isla Wellington** *I* Chile
34B4 **Islay** *I* Scot
38C2 **Isle** *R* France
xxviiiE6 **Isle Amsterdam** *I* Indian O
13F2 **Isle au Haut** *I* USA
35E6 **Isle of Wight** *I* Eng

12B1 **Isle Royale** *I* USA
12B1 **Isle Royale Nat Pk** USA
xxviiiE6 **Isle St Paul** *I* Indian O
xxviiiD7 **Îsles Crozet** *I* Indian O
xxixM5 **Îsles de la Société** Pacific O
xxixN6 **Îsles Gambier** *Is* Pacific O
73E5 **Isles Glorieuses** *Is* Madag
xxviiiE7 **Îsles Kerguelen** *Is* Indian O
77F3 **Îsles Loyauté** *Is* Nouvelle Calédonie
xxixN5 **Îsles Marquises** *Is* Pacific O
xxixM5 **Îsles Tuamotu** *Is* Pacific O
xxixM6 **Îsles Tubai** *Is* Pacific O
20B1 **Isleton** USA
64B3 **Ismâ'ilîya** Egypt
66B1 **Isna** Egypt
73E6 **Isoanala** Madag
73D5 **Isoka** Zambia
37C3 **Isola di Capraia** *I* Italy
40C3 **Isola Egadi** *I* Italy
40C2 **Isola Ponziane** *I* Italy
40C3 **Isole Lipari** *Is* Italy
40D2 **Isoles Tremiti** *Is* Italy
54C3 **Isosaki** Japan
64B2 **Isparta** Turk
65C2 **Israel** Republic, S W Asia
39C2 **Isser** *R* Alg
38C2 **Issoire** France
38C2 **Issoudun** France
37A1 **Is-sur-Tille** France
59F1 **Issyk Kul, Ozero** *I* Kirgizia
64A1 **Istanbul** Turk
41E3 **Istiáia** Greece
22D2 **Istmo de Tehuantepec** *Isthmus* Mexico
15E4 **Istokpoga,L** USA
40C1 **Istra** *Pen* Croatia, Yugos
41F2 **Istranca Dağlari** *Upland* Turk
29C2 **Itaberai** Brazil
29D2 **Itabira** Brazil
29D3 **Itabirito** Brazil
29E1 **Itabuna** Brazil
29E1 **Itacaré** Brazil
27G4 **Itacoatiara** Brazil
29A3 **Itacurubi del Rosario** Par
26C2 **Itagui** Colombia
25F2 **Itaipu, Reprêsa** *Res* Brazil
27G4 **Itaituba** Brazil
25G3 **Itajaí** Brazil
29C3 **Itajuba** Brazil
40C2 **Italy** Repubic, Europe
29E2 **Itamaraju** Brazil
29D2 **Itamarandiba** Brazil
29D2 **Itambacuri** Brazil
29D2 **Itambe** Brazil
29D2 **Itambé** *Mt* Brazil
61D2 **Itānagar** India
29C3 **Itanhaém** Brazil
29D2 **Itanhém** Brazil
29D2 **Itanhém** *R* Brazil
29D2 **Itaobím** Brazil
29C1 **Itapaci** Brazil
29C3 **Itapecerica** Brazil
29D3 **Itaperuna** Brazil
27K7 **Itapetinga** Brazil
29C3 **Itapetininga** Brazil
29C3 **Itapeva** Brazil
27L4 **Itapipoca** Brazil
29C2 **Itapuranga** Brazil
29C1 **Itaquari** *R* Brazil
28D1 **Itaqui** Brazil
29D2 **Itarantim** Brazil
29C3 **Itararé** Brazil
29C3 **Itararé** *R* Brazil
29D3 **Itaúna** Brazil
26F6 **Iténez** *R* Brazil/Bol
13D2 **Ithaca** USA
36E1 **Ith Hills** *Mts* Germany
72C3 **Itimbiri** *R* Zaïre
29D2 **Itinga** Brazil
29A2 **Itiquira** *R* Brazil
7N3 **Itivdleq** Greenland
32G6 **Itjørdal** Nor
54C4 **Ito** Japan
53D4 **Itoigawa** Japan
36A2 **Iton** *R* France
26F6 **Itonomas** *R* Bol
29C3 **Itu** Brazil
71H4 **Itu** Nig
29E1 **Ituberá** Brazil
29C2 **Itumbiara** Brazil
29B2 **Iturama** Brazil
25C2 **Iturbe** Arg
22C1 **Iturbide** Mexico
53F3 **Iturup, Ostrov** *I* Russian Fed
29C2 **Iturutaba** Brazil
28D1 **Ituzzaingó** Arg
42B2 **Itzehoe** Germany
49U3 **Iul'tin** Russian Fed
43F2 **Ivacevichi** Belorussia
29B3 **Ivai** *R* Brazil
32K5 **Ivalo** Fin
41D2 **Ivangrad** Montenegro, Yugos
75B2 **Ivanhoe** Aust
43E3 **Ivano-Frankovsk** Ukraine
44G4 **Ivanovo** Russian Fed
44L3 **Ivdel'** Russian Fed
72B3 **Ivindo** *R* Gabon
29B3 **Ivinhema** Brazil
29B3 **Ivinhema** *R* Brazil
73E6 **Ivohibe** Madag
73E5 **Ivongo Soanierana** Madag
70B4 **Ivory Coast** Republic, Africa
40B1 **Ivrea** Italy
7L3 **Ivujivik** Can
53E4 **Iwaki** Japan
54D2 **Iwaki** *R* Japan
54D2 **Iwaki-san** *Mt* Japan
53C5 **Iwakuni** Japan
54D2 **Iwamizawa** Japan
53E3 **Iwanai** Japan
71G4 **Iwo** Nig
50H4 **Iwo Jima** *I* Japan
22B1 **Ixcuintla** Mexico
22C1 **Ixmiquilpa** Mexico
22B2 **Ixtapa** Mexico
22C2 **Ixtepec** Mexico
22B1 **Ixtlán** Mexico
54B4 **Iyo** Japan
54B4 **Iyo-nada** *B* Japan
44J4 **Izhevsk** Russian Fed
44J2 **Izhma** Russian Fed
44J2 **Izhma** *R* Russian Fed
10E5 **Izigan,C** USA
67G2 **Izkī** Oman
43F3 **Izmail** Ukraine
64A2 **İzmir** Turk
41F3 **Izmir Körfezi** *B* Turk
64A1 **İzmit** Turk
64A1 **İznik** Turk
41F2 **Iznik Golü** *L* Turk
65D2 **Izra'** Syria
22C2 **Izúcar de Matamoros** Mexico
54A4 **Izuhara** Japan
54C4 **Izumi-sano** Japan
54B3 **Izumo** Japan
53D5 **Izu-shotō** *Is* Japan
53C2 **Izvestkovyy** Russian Fed

J

69B1 **Jabal al Akhdar** *Mts* Libya
65D2 **Jabal al 'Arab** Syria
67F3 **Jabal al Qara'** *Mts* Oman
65D1 **Jabal an Nuşayrīyah** *Mts* Syria
69A2 **Jabal as Sawdā** *Mts* Libya
67F2 **Jabal aẓẒannah** UAE
65D1 **Jabal Halīmah** *Mt* Syria/Leb
67F3 **Jabal Mahrāt** *Mts* Yemen
61B3 **Jabalpur** India
66D1 **Jabal Shammar** Region, S Arabia
67E2 **Jabal Tuwayq** *Mts* S Arabia
65C1 **Jablah** Syria
42D2 **Jablonec nad Nisou** Czech
27L5 **Jaboatão** Brazil
39B1 **Jaca** Spain
22C1 **Jacala** Mexico
27G5 **Jacareacanga** Brazil
27H8 **Jacarezinho** Brazil
29C3 **Jacarie** Brazil
25C4 **Jáchal** Arg
29B2 **Jaciara** Brazil
29D2 **Jacinto** Brazil
3G3 **Jackfish L** Can
13E1 **Jackman Station** USA
16C3 **Jacksboro** USA
14B2 **Jacks Mt** USA
15B2 **Jackson** Alabama, USA
75C1 **Jackson** Aust
20B1 **Jackson** California, USA
12C2 **Jackson** Michigan, USA
11D3 **Jackson** Minnesota, USA
17D3 **Jackson** Mississippi, USA
12B3 **Jackson** Missouri, USA
12C3 **Jackson** Ohio, USA
15B1 **Jackson** Tennessee, USA
18D2 **Jackson** Wyoming, USA
78B2 **Jackson,C** NZ
78A2 **Jackson Head** *Pt* NZ
18D2 **Jackson L** USA
17D3 **Jacksonville** Arkansas, USA
15C2 **Jacksonville** Florida, USA
12A3 **Jacksonville** Illinois, USA
15D2 **Jacksonville** N Carolina, USA
17C3 **Jacksonville** Texas, USA
15C2 **Jacksonville Beach** USA
23C3 **Jacmel** Haiti
60B3 **Jacobabad** Pak
27K6 **Jacobina** Brazil
22B2 **Jacona** Mexico
28E1 **Jacui** *R* Brazil
67F3 **Jādib** Yemen
Jadotville = Likasi
26C5 **Jaén** Peru
39B2 **Jaén** Spain
Jaffa = Tel Aviv Yafo
75A3 **Jaffa** *C* Aust
62B3 **Jaffna** Sri Lanka
14D1 **Jaffrey** USA
61C3 **Jagannathganj Ghat** Bang
62C1 **Jagdalpur** India
53A1 **Jagdaqi** China
63D3 **Jagin** *R* Iran
62B1 **Jagtial** India
29E1 **Jaguaquara** Brazil
28E2 **Jaguarão** Brazil
28E2 **Jaguarão** *R* Brazil
29C3 **Jaguarialva** Brazil
28B1 **Jagüé** Arg
28B1 **Jagüé** *R* Arg
45H8 **Jahan Dāgh** *Mt* Iran
63C3 **Jahrom** Iran
57C2 **Jailolo** Indon
60D5 **Jāina** India
52A2 **Jainca** China
60D3 **Jaipur** India
60C3 **Jaisalmer** India
63D1 **Jajarm** Iran
40D2 **Jajce** Bosnia & Herzegovina, Yugos
56C4 **Jakarta** Indon
3B1 **Jakes Corner** Can
7N3 **Jakobshavn** Greenland
32J6 **Jakobstad** Fin
16B3 **Jal** USA
22C2 **Jalaca** Mexico
53A2 **Jalaid Qi** China
60C2 **Jalalabad** Afghan
22C2 **Jalapa** Mexico
29B3 **Jales** Brazil
61C2 **Jaleswar** Nepal
60D4 **Jalgaon** India
71J4 **Jalingo** Nig
22A2 **Jalisco** State, Mexico
39B1 **Jalón** *R* Spain
60C3 **Jālor** India
22B1 **Jalostotitlan** Mexico
61C2 **Jalpāiguri** India
22C1 **Jalpan** Mexico
69B2 **Jālū** Libya
69B2 **Jālū Oasis** Libya
26B4 **Jama** Ecuador
72E3 **Jamaame** Somalia
71H3 **Jamaaré** *R* Nig
23B3 **Jamaica** *I* Caribbean
23B3 **Jamaica Chan** Caribbean
61C3 **Jamalpur** Bang
56B3 **Jambi** Indon
60C4 **Jambussar** India
11C2 **James** *R* N Dakota, USA
13D3 **James** *R* Virginia, USA
7K4 **James B** Can
75A2 **Jamestown** Aust
11C2 **Jamestown** N Dakota, USA
13D2 **Jamestown** New York, USA
14E2 **Jamestown** Rhode Island, USA
74D3 **Jamestown** S Africa
22C2 **Jamiltepec** Mexico
62B1 **Jamkhandi** India
60C2 **Jammu** India
60D2 **Jammu and Kashmir** State, India
60B4 **Jamnagar** India
60C3 **Jampur** Pak
44C3 **Jämsä** Fin
61C3 **Jamshedpur** India
61C2 **Janakpur** Nepal
29D2 **Janaúba** Brazil
63C2 **Jandaq** Iran
75D1 **Jandowae** Aust
12B2 **Janesville** USA
79B1 **Jan Mayen** *I* Norwegian S
29D2 **Januária** Brazil
60D4 **Jaora** India
53 **Japan** Empire, E Asia
53C4 **Japan,S of** S E Asia
xxviiiJ3 **Japan Trench** Pacific O
26E4 **Japurá** *R* Brazil
64C2 **Jarābulus** Syria
29C2 **Jaraguá** Brazil
29B3 **Jaraguari** Brazil
39B1 **Jarama** *R* Spain
65C2 **Jarash** Jordan
29A3 **Jardim** Brazil
39B2 **Jardin** *R* Spain
23B2 **Jardines de la Reina** *Is* Cuba
Jargalant = Hovd
27H3 **Jari** *R* Brazil
61D2 **Jaria Jhānjail** Bang
36C2 **Jarny** France
42D2 **Jarocin** Pol
43E2 **Jaroslaw** Pol
44A3 **Järpen** Sweden
52B2 **Jartai** China
60C4 **Jasdan** India
71G4 **Jasikan** Ghana
63D3 **Jāsk** Iran
43E3 **Jaslo** Pol
25D8 **Jason Is** Falkland Is
15B2 **Jasper** Alabama, USA
17D2 **Jasper** Arkansas, USA
3E3 **Jasper** Can
15C2 **Jasper** Florida, USA
12B3 **Jasper** Indiana, USA
17D3 **Jasper** Texas, USA
3E3 **Jasper Nat Pk** Can
42D2 **Jastrowie** Pol
29B2 **Jatai** Brazil
39B2 **Játiva** Spain
29C3 **Jau** Brazil
26C6 **Jauja** Peru
22C1 **Jaumave** Mexico
61B2 **Jaunpur** India
Java = Jawa
62B2 **Javadi Hills** India
63E1 **Javand** Afghan
Javari = Yavari
51D7 **Java S** Indon
76A2 **Java Trench** Indon
56C4 **Jawa** *I* Indon
51H7 **Jayapura** Indon
65D2 **Jayrūd** Syria
66D3 **Jazā'ir Farasān** *Is* S Arabia
67G2 **Jazīrat Maşirah** *I* Oman
22B1 **Jazminal** Mexico
71B2 **Jbel Ayachi** *Mt* Mor
70B2 **Jbel Ouarkziz** *Mts* Mor
70B1 **Jbel Sarhro** *Mt* Mor
17D4 **Jeanerette** USA
71G4 **Jebba** Nig
64D2 **Jebel 'Abd al 'Azīz** *Mt* Syria
72C2 **Jebel Abyad** *Desert Region* Sudan
67G2 **Jebel Akhdar** *Mt* Oman
64C4 **Jebel al Lawz** *Mt* S Arabia
65C2 **Jebel ash Shaykh** *Mt* Syria
72D1 **Jebel Asoteriba** *Mt* Sudan
65D1 **Jebel az Zāwīyah** *Upland* Syria
65C4 **Jebel Bāqir** *Mt* Jordan
66C4 **Jebel Belaia** *Mt* Eth
65C3 **Jebel Ed Dabab** *Mt* Jordan
65C3 **Jebel el Ata'ita** *Mt* Jordan
65C4 **Jebel el Harad** *Mt* Jordan
64C3 **Jebel esh Sharqi** *Mts* Leb/Syria
66C3 **Jebel Hamoyet** *Mt* Sudan
65C3 **Jebel Hārūn** *Mt* Jordan
65D3 **Jebel Ithrīyat** *Mt* Jordan
67G2 **Jebel Ja'lan** *Mt* Oman
65C2 **Jebel Liban** *Mts* Leb
65D2 **Jebel Ma'lūlā** *Mt* Syria
72C2 **Jebel Marra** *Mt* Sudan
65C3 **Jebel Mubrak** *Mt* Jordan
65D3 **Jebel Mudeisisat** *Mt* Jordan
66C2 **Jebel Oda** *Mt* Sudan
65C3 **Jebel Qasr ed Deir** *Mt* Jordan
65C4 **Jebel Qatim** *Mt* Jordan
65C4 **Jebel Ram** Jordan
65C2 **Jebel Um ed Daraj** *Mt* Jordan
65C4 **Jebel Um el Hashim** *Mt* Jordan
65C4 **Jebel Um Ishrīn** *Mt* Jordan
72C1 **Jebel Uweinat** *Mt* Sudan
34D4 **Jedburgh** Scot
Jedda = Jiddah
43E2 **Jedrzejów** Pol
11D3 **Jefferson** Iowa, USA
17D3 **Jefferson** Texas, USA
18D1 **Jefferson** *R* USA
9D3 **Jefferson City** USA
8B3 **Jefferson,Mt** USA
12B3 **Jeffersonville** USA
71G3 **Jega** Nig
29A3 **Jejui-Guazú** *R* Par
44D4 **Jekabpils** Latvia
42D2 **Jelena Gora** Pol
44C4 **Jelgava** Latvia
56D4 **Jember** Indon
16A2 **Jemez Pueblo** USA
42C2 **Jena** Germany
56C2 **Jenaja** *I* Indon
37D1 **Jenbach** Austria
71D1 **Jendouba** Tunisia
65C2 **Jenin** Israel
17D3 **Jennings** USA
3B2 **Jennings** *R* Can
42D2 **Jenseniky** *Upland* Czech
7O3 **Jensen Nunatakker** *Mt* Greenland
7K3 **Jens Munk I** Can
75B3 **Jeparit** Aust
27L6 **Jequié** Brazil
29D2 **Jequital** *R* Brazil
29D2 **Jequitinhonha** Brazil
27K7 **Jequitinhonha** *R* Brazil
71B2 **Jerada** Mor
56G7 **Jerantut** Malay
22B1 **Jerez** Mexico
39A2 **Jerez de la Frontera** Spain
39A2 **Jerez de los Caballeros** Spain
65C3 **Jericho** Israel
75C3 **Jerilderie** Aust
18D2 **Jerome** USA
38B2 **Jersey** *I* UK
9F2 **Jersey City** USA
13D2 **Jersey Shore** USA
12A3 **Jerseyville** USA
64C3 **Jerusalem** Israel
75D3 **Jervis B** Aust
3D3 **Jervis Inlet** *Sd* Can
40C1 **Jesenice** Slovenia, Yugos
61C3 **Jessore** Bang
9E3 **Jesup** USA
22D2 **Jesus Carranza** Mexico
28C2 **Jesus Maria** Arg
16C2 **Jetmore** USA
14E2 **Jewett City** USA
62C1 **Jeypore** India
41D2 **Jezerce** *Mt* Alb
43E2 **Jezioro Mamry** *L* Pol
43E2 **Jezioro80Sniardwy** *L* Pol
65C2 **Jezzine** Leb
60C4 **Jhābua** India
60D4 **Jhālāwār** India
60C2 **Jhang Maghiana** Pak
60D3 **Jhānsi** India
61B3 **Jhārsuguda** India
60C2 **Jhelum** Pak
60C2 **Jhelum** *R* Pak
9F3 **J H Kerr L** USA
60D3 **Jhunjhunūn** India
53C2 **Jiamusi** China
52C4 **Ji'an** Jiangxi, China
53B3 **Ji'an** Jilin, China
52D4 **Jiande** China
52B4 **Jiang'an** China
52D4 **Jiangbiancun** China
52A5 **Jiangcheng** China
52B3 **Jiang Jiang** *R* China
52B4 **Jiangjin** China
52C5 **Jiangmen** China
52D3 **Jiangsu** Province, China
52C4 **Jiangxi** Province, China
52A3 **Jiangyou** China
52D1 **Jianping** China
52A5 **Jianshui** China
52D4 **Jian Xi** *R* China
52D4 **Jianyang** China
53B3 **Jiaohe** China
52E2 **Jiaonan** China
52E2 **Jiao Xian** China
52E2 **Jiaozhou Wan** *B* China
52C2 **Jiaozuo** China
52E3 **Jiaxiang** China
53C2 **Jiayin** China
50C3 **Jiayuguan** China
66C2 **Jiddah** S Arabia
67G3 **Jiddat Al Harāsīs** Region, Oman
67G2 **Jiddat az Zawlīyah** Region, Oman
52D3 **Jieshou** China
52C2 **Jiexiu** China
71H3 **Jigawa** *State* Nig
52A3 **Jigzhi** China
42D3 **Jihlava** Czech
71D1 **Jijel** Alg
72E3 **Jilib** Somalia
53B3 **Jilin** China
53B3 **Jilin** Province, China
53A1 **Jiliu He** *R* China
39B1 **Jiloca** *R* Spain
72D3 **Jima** Eth
16B4 **Jiménez** Coahuila, Mexico
22C1 **Jiménez** Tamaulipas, Mexico
52D2 **Jinan** China
60D3 **Jind** India
52B2 **Jingbian** China
52D4 **Jingdezhen** China
55C1 **Jinghong** China
52C3 **Jingmen** China
52B2 **Jingning** China
52B4 **Jing Xiang** China
52D4 **Jinhua** China
52C1 **Jining** Nei Monggol, China
52D2 **Jining** Shandong, China
72D3 **Jinja** Uganda
55C1 **Jinping** China
52A4 **Jinsha Jiang** *R* China
52C4 **Jinshi** China
52E1 **Jinxi** China
52E2 **Jin Xian** China
52E1 **Jinzhou** China
26F5 **Jiparaná** *R* Brazil
26B4 **Jipijapa** Ecuador
22B2 **Jiquilpan** Mexico

63D3 **Jīroft** Iran
69D4 **Jirriban** Somalia
52B4 **Jishou** China
64C2 **Jisr ash Shughūr** Syria
41E2 **Jiu** *R* Rom
52D4 **Jiujiang** China
52A4 **Jiulong** China
52D4 **Jiulong Jiang** *R* China
53B3 **Jiutai** China
63E3 **Jiwani** Pak
53C2 **Jixi** China
65C3 **Jiza** Jordan
66D3 **Jīzan** S Arabia
70A3 **Joal** Sen
29D2 **João Monlevade** Brazil
27M5 **João Pessoa** Brazil
29C2 **João Pinheiro** Brazil
29C3 **Joboticabal** Brazil
28B2 **Jocoli** Arg
60C3 **Jodhpur** India
32K6 **Joensuu** Fin
36C2 **Joeuf** France
3E3 **Joffre,Mt** Can
61C2 **Jogbani** India
62A2 **Jog Falls** India
74D2 **Johannesburg** S Africa
19C3 **Johannesburg** USA
7L2 **Johan Pen** Can
10H2 **John** *R* USA
18C2 **John Day** USA
18B1 **John Day** *R* USA
3E2 **John d'Or Prairie** Can
13D3 **John H. Kerr Res** USA
16B2 **John Martin Res** USA
34D2 **John O'Groats** Scot
17C2 **John Redmond Res** USA
14A2 **Johnsonburg** USA
14C1 **Johnson City** New York, USA
15C1 **Johnson City** Tennessee, USA
15C2 **Johnston** USA
23N2 **Johnston Pt** St Vincent
14C1 **Johnstown** New York, USA
13D2 **Johnstown** Pennsylvania, USA
55C5 **Johor Bharu** Malay
38C2 **Joigny** France
25G3 **Joinville** Brazil
36C2 **Joinville** France
44J5 **Jok** *R* Russian Fed
32H5 **Jokkmokk** Sweden
67E4 **Jōl** *Mts* Yemen
45H8 **Jolfa** Iran
9E2 **Joliet** USA
7L5 **Joliette** Can
57F9 **Jolo** Phil
57F9 **Jolo** *I* Phil
59H2 **Joma** *Mt* China
43E1 **Jonava** Lithuania
52A3 **Jonê** China
9D3 **Jonesboro** Arkansas, USA
17D3 **Jonesboro** Louisiana, USA
7K2 **Jones Sd** Can
43E1 **Joniškis** Lithuania
32G7 **Jönköping** Sweden
5G4 **Jonquière** Can
9D3 **Joplin** USA
64C3 **Jordan** Kingdom, S W Asia
11A2 **Jordan** Montana, USA
14B1 **Jordan** New York, USA
65C2 **Jordan** *R* Israel
18C2 **Jordan Valley** USA
29B4 **Jordão** *R* Brazil
61D2 **Jorhāt** India
44C2 **Jörn** Sweden
56D3 **Jorong** Indon
32F7 **Jørpeland** Nor
71H4 **Jos** Nig
28E2 **José Batlle y Ordoñez** Urug
57F8 **Jose Pañganiban** Phil
28E2 **José Pedro Varela** Urug
76B2 **Joseph Bonaparte G** Aust
19D3 **Joseph City** USA
34G3 **Josephine** *Oilfield* N Sea
71H4 **Jos Plat** Nig
48B3 **Jotunheimen** *Mt* Nor
65C2 **Jouai'ya** Leb
65C2 **Jounié** Leb
61D2 **Jowai** India
72E3 **Jowhar** Somalia
10M3 **Joy,Mt** Can
27K5 **Juàjeiro** Brazil
22B1 **Juan Aldama** Mexico
6F5 **Juan de Fuca,Str of** USA/Can
73E5 **Juan de Nova** *I* Mozam Chan
28D3 **Juárez** Arg
27L5 **Juazeiro do Norte** Brazil
72D3 **Juba** Sudan
72E3 **Juba** *R* Somalia
65C1 **Jubail** Leb
64D3 **Jubbah** S Arabia
39B2 **Jucar** *R* Spain
22C2 **Juchatengo** Mexico
22B1 **Juchipila** *R* Mexico
22C2 **Juchitán** Mexico
22B1 **Juchitlan** Mexico
42C3 **Judenburg** Austria
26D7 **Juilaca** Peru
52C4 **Juiling Shan** *Hills* China
27K8 **Juiz de Fora** Brazil
25C2 **Jujuy** State, Arg
16B1 **Julesburg** USA
26E7 **Juli** Peru
27G3 **Julianatop** *Mt* Surinam
7O3 **Julianehåb** Greenland
36D1 **Jülich** Germany
37E1 **Julijske Alpen** *Mts* Slovenia, Yugos
28E1 **Júlio de Castilhos** Brazil
60D2 **Jullundur** India
61B2 **Jumla** Nepal
65C3 **Jum Suwwāna** *Mt* Jordan
60C4 **Jūnāgadh** India
52D2 **Junan** China
16C3 **Junction** Texas, USA
19D3 **Junction** Utah, USA
8D3 **Junction City** USA
25G2 **Jundiaí** Brazil
6E4 **Juneau** USA
76D4 **Junee** Aust
20C2 **June Lake** USA
40B1 **Jungfrau** *Mt* Switz
14B2 **Juniata** *R* USA
25D4 **Junín** Arg
28A3 **Junin de los Andes** Arg
20B2 **Junipero Serra Peak** *Mt* USA
52A4 **Junlian** China
25G2 **Juquiá** Brazil
72C3 **Jur** *R* Sudan
34C4 **Jura** *I* Scot
38D2 **Jura** *Mts* France
34C3 **Jura,Sound of** *Chan* Scot
65C3 **Jurf ed Darāwīsh** Jordan
48K4 **Jurga** Russian Fed
44C4 **Jūrmala** Latvia
26E4 **Juruá** *R* Brazil
27G6 **Juruena** *R* Brazil
53B2 **Jusheng** China
65D1 **Jūsīyah** Syria
28B2 **Justo Daract** Arg
26E4 **Jutai** *R* Brazil
21D3 **Juticalpa** Honduras
Jutland = Jylland
63D2 **Jūymand** Iran
42B1 **Jylland** *Pen* Den
32K6 **Jyväskyla** Fin

K

59F2 **K2** *Mt* China/India
71H3 **Ka** *R* Nig
63D1 **Kaakhka** Turkmenistan
74E2 **Kaapmuiden** S Africa
76B1 **Kabaena** *I* Indon
70A4 **Kabala** Sierra Leone
72D4 **Kabale** Rwanda
72C4 **Kabalo** Zaïre
72C4 **Kabambare** Zaïre
72D3 **Kabarole** Uganda
71H4 **Kabba** Nig
76B1 **Kabia** *I* Indon
12C1 **Kabinakagami L** Can
4E3 **Kabinakagami** *R* Can
72C4 **Kabinda** Zaïre
65C1 **Kabīr** *R* Syria
63B2 **Kabir Kuh** *Mts* Iran
73C5 **Kabompo** Zambia
73C5 **Kabompo** *R* Zambia
73C4 **Kabongo** Zaïre
60B2 **Kabul** Afghan
57C2 **Kaburuang** *I* Indon
66B3 **Kabushiya** Sudan
60B4 **Kachchh,G of** India
44K4 **Kachkanar** Russian Fed
49M4 **Kachug** Russian Fed
55B3 **Kadan** Burma
56E3 **Kadapongan** *I* Indon
77G2 **Kadavu** *I* Fiji
60C4 **Kadi** India
75A2 **Kadina** Aust
64B2 **Kadınhanı** Turk
62B2 **Kadiri** India
45F6 **Kadiyevka** Ukraine
11B3 **Kadoka** USA
73C5 **Kadoma** Zim
72C2 **Kadugli** Sudan
71H3 **Kaduna** Nig
71H3 **Kaduna** State, Nig
71H3 **Kaduna** *R* Nig
62B2 **Kadūr** India
61E2 **Kadusam** *Mt* China
44K3 **Kadzherom** Russian Fed
54A3 **Kaechon** N Korea
70A3 **Kaédi** Maur
20E5 **Kaena Pt** Hawaiian Is
53B4 **Kaesŏng** N Korea
71H4 **Kafanchan** Nig
70A3 **Kaffrine** Sen
65D1 **Kafr Behum** Syria
65A3 **Kafr Sa'd** Egypt
65A3 **Kafr Saqv** Egypt
65D1 **Kafrūn Bashūr** Syria
73C5 **Kafue** Zambia
73C5 **Kafue** *R* Zambia
73C5 **Kafue Nat Pk** Zambia
53D4 **Kaga** Japan
10C6 **Kagalaska** *I* USA
48H6 **Kagan** Uzbekistan
45G7 **Kağizman** Turk
66B4 **Kagmar** Sudan
53C5 **Kagoshima** Japan
43F3 **Kagul** Moldavia
63D1 **Kāhak** Iran
72D4 **Kahama** Tanz
60B3 **Kahan** Pak
56D3 **Kahayan** *R* Indon
73B4 **Kahemba** Zaïre
36E1 **Kahler Asten** *Mt* Germany
63D3 **Kahnūj** Iran
12A2 **Kahoka** USA
20E5 **Kahoolawe** *I* Hawaiian Is
64C2 **Kahramanmaraş** Turk
20E5 **Kahuku Pt** Hawaiian Is
20E5 **Kahului** Hawaiian Is
78B2 **Kaiapoi** NZ
19D3 **Kaibab Plat** USA
27G2 **Kaieteur Fall** Guyana
52C3 **Kaifeng** China
78B1 **Kaikohe** NZ
77G5 **Kaikoura** NZ
78B2 **Kaikoura Pen** NZ
78B2 **Kaikoura Range** *Mts* NZ
52B4 **Kaili** China
20E5 **Kailua** Hawaiian Is
51G7 **Kaimana** Indon
54C4 **Kainan** Japan
71G3 **Kainji Res** Nig
78B1 **Kaipara Harbour** *B* NZ
52C5 **Kaiping** China
71E1 **Kairouan** Tunisia
20C2 **Kaiser Peak** *Mt* USA
42B3 **Kaiserslautern** Germany
53B3 **Kaishantun** China
43E2 **Kaisiadorys** Lithuania
78B1 **Kaitaia** NZ
78A3 **Kaitangata** NZ
60D3 **Kaithal** India
20E5 **Kaiwi Chan** Hawaiian Is
52B3 **Kai Xian** China
52A5 **Kaiyuan** Liaoning, China
53A3 **Kaiyuan** Yunnan, China
10G3 **Kaiyuh Mts** USA
32K6 **Kajaani** Fin
60B2 **Kajaki** Afghan
56F7 **Kajang** Malay
72D4 **Kajiado** Kenya
60B2 **Kajrān** Afghan
72D2 **Kaka** Sudan
12B1 **Kakabeka Falls** Can
72D3 **Kakamega** Kenya
54B4 **Kake** Japan
10M4 **Kake** USA
10H4 **Kakhonak** USA
45E6 **Kakhovskoye Vodokhranilishche** *Res* Ukraine
63C3 **Kākī** Iran
62C1 **Kākināda** India
3E1 **Kakiska L** Can
54B4 **Kakogawa** Japan
10K1 **Kaktovik** USA
54D3 **Kakuda** Japan
71D1 **Kalaa El Khasba** Tunisia
57B4 **Kalabahi** Indon
41E3 **Kalabáka** Greece
56E2 **Kalabakan** Malay
73C5 **Kalabo** Zambia
45G5 **Kalach** Russian Fed
45G6 **Kalach-na-Donu** Russian Fed
61D3 **Kaladan** *R* Burma
20E5 **Ka Lae** *C* Hawaiian Is
73C6 **Kalahari Desert** Botswana
74C2 **Kalahari Gemsbok Nat Pk** S Africa
63E1 **Kalai-Mor** Turkmenistan
44C3 **Kalajoki** Fin
49N4 **Kalakan** Russian Fed
56A2 **Kalakepen** Indon
60C1 **Kalam** Pak
41E3 **Kalámai** Greece
9E2 **Kalamazoo** USA
57B4 **Kalao** *I* Indon
57B4 **Kalaotoa** *I* Indon
20E5 **Kalapana** Hawaiian Is
43F3 **Kalarsh** Moldavia
60B3 **Kalat** Pak
20E5 **Kalaupapa** Hawaiian Is
67G2 **Kalbān** Oman
64B1 **Kalecik** Turk
57B4 **Kaledupa** *I* Indon
56E3 **Kalembau** *I* Indon
72C4 **Kalémié** Zaïre
44E2 **Kalevala** Russian Fed
61D3 **Kalewa** Burma
10H3 **Kalgin I** USA
76B4 **Kalgoorlie** Aust
61B2 **Kali** *R* India
56C4 **Kalianda** Indon
57F8 **Kalibo** Phil
72C4 **Kalima** Zaïre
56D3 **Kalimantan** Province, Indon
41F3 **Kálimnos** *I* Greece
61C2 **Kālimpang** India
32J8 **Kaliningrad** Russian Fed
45D5 **Kalinkovichi** Belorussia
43F3 **Kalinovka** Ukraine
8B2 **Kalispell** USA
43D2 **Kalisz** Pol
72D4 **Kaliua** Tanz
32J5 **Kalix** *R* Sweden
73B6 **Kalkfeld** Namibia
74C1 **Kalkfontein** Botswana
74B1 **Kalkrand** Namibia
75A1 **Kallakoopah** *R* Aust
32K6 **Kallávesi** *L* Fin
41F3 **Kallonis Kólpos** *B* Greece
32H7 **Kalmar** Sweden
45H6 **Kalmytskaya** Respublika, Russian Fed
57B3 **Kalolio** Indon
73C5 **Kalomo** Zambia
12A2 **Kalona** USA
3C3 **Kalone Peak** *Mt* Can
62A2 **Kalpeni** *I* India
60D3 **Kālpi** India
10F3 **Kalskag** USA
10G3 **Kaltag** USA
44F5 **Kaluga** Russian Fed
32G7 **Kalundborg** Den
43E3 **Kalush** Ukraine
62A1 **Kalyān** India
62B2 **Kalyandurg** India
44F4 **Kalyazin** Russian Fed
71J4 **Kam** *R* Nig
44J3 **Kama** *R* Russian Fed
53E4 **Kamaishi** Japan
60C2 **Kamalia** Pak
78C1 **Kamanawa Mts** NZ
73B5 **Kamanjab** Namibia
49O4 **Kamara** China
66D3 **Kamarān** *I* Yemen
5J2 **Kamarsuk** Can
60D2 **Kamat** *Mt* India
62B3 **Kamban** India
44J4 **Kambarka** Russian Fed
70A4 **Kambia** Sierra Leone
49S4 **Kamchatka** *Pen* Russian Fed
43F3 **Kamenets Podolskiy** Ukraine
44G5 **Kamenka** Russian Fed
48K4 **Kamen-na-Obi** Russian Fed
53C3 **Kamen' Rybolov** Russian Fed
49S3 **Kamenskoya** Russian Fed
44L4 **Kamensk-Ural'skiy** Russian Fed
74B3 **Kamieskroon** S Africa
6H3 **Kamilukuak L** Can
73C4 **Kamina** Zaïre
7J3 **Kaminak L** Can
54D3 **Kaminoyama** Japan
6F4 **Kamloops** Can
64E1 **Kamo** Armenia
54D3 **Kamogawa** Japan
72D3 **Kampala** Uganda
55C5 **Kampar** Malay
56B2 **Kampar** *R* Indon
42B2 **Kampen** Neth
55B2 **Kamphaeng Phet** Thai
55C3 **Kampot** Camb
Kampuchea = Cambodia
3H3 **Kamsack** Can
63E3 **Kamsaptar** Iran
44K4 **Kamskoye Vodokhranilishche** *Res* Russian Fed
60D4 **Kāmthi** India
3H2 **Kamuchawie L** Can
45H5 **Kamyshin** Russian Fed
44L4 **Kamyshlov** Russian Fed
7L4 **Kanaaupscow** *R* Can
19D3 **Kanab** USA
10C6 **Kanaga** *I* USA
37E1 **Kanal** Slovenia, Yugos
72C4 **Kananga** Zaïre
44H4 **Kanash** Russian Fed
54C3 **Kanayama** Japan
53D4 **Kanazawa** Japan
62B2 **Kānchipuram** India
60B2 **Kandahar** Afghan
5J3 **Kanairiktok** *R* Can
44E2 **Kandalaksha** Russian Fed
32L5 **Kandalakshskaya Guba** *B* Russian Fed
71G4 **Kandé** Togo
36D2 **Kandel** *Mt* Germany
71G3 **Kandi** Benin
75C2 **Kandos** Aust
62C3 **Kandy** Sri Lanka
13D2 **Kane** USA
7L1 **Kane Basin** *B* Can
72B2 **Kanem** *Desert Region* Chad
20E5 **Kaneohe** Hawaiian Is
44F2 **Kanevka** Russian Fed
37E2 **Kanfanar** Slovenia, Yugos
74C1 **Kang** Botswana
70B3 **Kangaba** Mali
64C2 **Kangal** Turk
7N3 **Kangâmiut** Greenland
63C3 **Kangān** Iran
55C4 **Kangar** Malay
76C4 **Kangaroo I** Aust
7N3 **Kangâtsiaq** Greenland
63B2 **Kangavar** Iran
52C1 **Kangbao** China
59G3 **Kangchenjunga** *Mt* Nepal
52A4 **Kangding** China
7P3 **Kangerdlugssuaq** *B* Greenland
7P3 **Kangerdlugssuatsaiq** *B* Greenland
72D3 **Kangetet** Kenya
53B3 **Kanggye** N Korea
7M4 **Kangiqsualujjuaq** Can
7L3 **Kangiqsujuak** Can
7L3 **Kangirsuk** Can
53B4 **Kangnŭng** S Korea
72B3 **Kango** Gabon
50C4 **Kan94gto** *Mt* China
52B3 **Kang Xian** China
55D4 **Kanh Hung** Viet
73C4 **Kaniama** Zaïre
62B1 **Kani Giri** India
44G2 **Kanin, Poluostrov** *Pen* Russian Fed
32J6 **Kankaanpää** Fin
12B2 **Kankakee** USA
12B2 **Kankakee** *R* USA
70B3 **Kankan** Guinea
61B3 **Kānker** India
15C1 **Kannapolis** USA
62B3 **Kanniyākuman** India
71H3 **Kano** Nig
71H3 **Kano** State, Nig
71H3 **Kano** *R* Nig
16B2 **Kanorado** USA
53C5 **Kanoya** Japan
61B2 **Kānpur** India
8D3 **Kansas** State, USA
17C2 **Kansas** *R* USA
9D3 **Kansas City** USA
52D5 **Kanshi** China
49L4 **Kansk** Russian Fed
54A3 **Kansŏng** S Korea
71G3 **Kantchari** Burkina
61C3 **Kanthi** India
10H3 **Kantishna** USA
10H3 **Kantishna** *R* USA
74D1 **Kanye** Botswana
50E4 **Kao-hsiung** Taiwan
73B5 **Kaoka Veld** *Plain* Namibia
70A3 **Kaolack** Sen
73C5 **Kaoma** Zambia
20E5 **Kapaa** Hawaiian Is
20E5 **Kapaau** Hawaiian Is
73C4 **Kapanga** Zaïre
7O3 **Kap Cort Adelaer** *C* Greenland
7Q3 **Kap Dalton** *C* Greenland
32H7 **Kapellskär** Sweden
7O4 **Kap Farvel** *C* Greenland
7P3 **Kap Gustav Holm** *C* Greenland
73C5 **Kapiri** Zambia
4E3 **Kapiskau** *R* Can
56D2 **Kapit** Malay
17D3 **Kaplan** USA
42C3 **Kaplice** Czech
55B4 **Kapoe** Thai
73C4 **Kapona** Zaïre
41D1 **Kaposvár** Hung
7L2 **Kap Parry** *C* Greenland
7Q3 **Kap Ravn** *C* Greenland
54A2 **Kapsan** N Korea
44C5 **Kapsukas** Lithuania
56C3 **Kapuas** *R* Indon
75A2 **Kapunda** Aust
60D2 **Kapurthala** India
7K5 **Kapuskasing** Can
12C1 **Kapuskasing** *R* Can
75D2 **Kaputar** *Mt* Aust
45H8 **Kapydzhik** *Mt* Armenia
54A3 **Kapyŏng** S Korea
7M2 **Kap York** *C* Greenland
71G4 **Kara** Togo
71G4 **Kara** *R* Togo
64B1 **Karabük** Turk
41F2 **Karacabey** Turk

60B4 **Karachi** Pak
62A1 **Karād** India
45F7 **Kara Daglari** *Mt* Turk
45D7 **Karadeniz Boğazi** *Sd* Turk
50E1 **Karaftit** Russian Fed
48J5 **Karaganda** Kazakhstan
48J5 **Karagayly** Kazakhstan
49S4 **Karaginskiy, Ostrov** *I* Russian Fed
62B2 **Kāraikāl** India
63C1 **Karaj** Iran
64C3 **Karak** Jordan
56F7 **Karak** Malay
48G5 **Kara Kalpakskaya** Respublika, Uzbekistan
60D1 **Karakax He** *R* China
57C2 **Karakelong** *I* Indon
60D1 **Karakoram** *Mts* India
60D1 **Karakoram** *P* India/China
70A3 **Karakoro** *R* Maur/Sen
63E1 **Karakumskiy Kanal** Turkmenistan
48G6 **Karakumy** *Desert* Russian Fed
65C3 **Karama** Jordan
57A3 **Karama** *R* Indon
45E8 **Karaman** Turk
48K5 **Karamay** China
78B2 **Karamea** NZ
78B2 **Karamea Bight** *B* NZ
45E8 **Karanhk** *R* Turk
60D4 **Kāranja** India
64B2 **Karapınar** Turk
48J2 **Kara S** Russian Fed
74B2 **Karasburg** Namibia
32K5 **Karasjok** Nor
48J4 **Karasuk** Russian Fed
64C2 **Karataş** Turk
48H5 **Kara Tau** *Mts* Kazakhstan
55B3 **Karathuri** Burma
53B5 **Karatsu** Japan
48K2 **Karaul** Russian Fed
65B1 **Karavostasi** Cyprus
37E1 **Karawanken** *Mts* Austria
63C3 **Karāz** Iran
64D3 **Karbalā'** Iraq
43E3 **Karcag** Hung
41E3 **Kardhítsa** Greece
44E3 **Karel'skaya** Respublika, Russian Fed
62E2 **Karen** Andaman Is
44K3 **Karepino** Russian Fed
32J5 **Karesvando** Sweden
70B2 **Karet** *Desert Region* Maur
48K4 **Kargasok** Russian Fed
44F3 **Kargopol'** Russian Fed
45G8 **Karh** *R* Turk
71J3 **Kari** Nig
73C5 **Kariba** Zim
73C5 **Kariba** *L* Zim/Zambia
73C5 **Kariba Dam** Zim/Zambia
74B1 **Karibib** Namibia
72D2 **Karima** Sudan
56C3 **Karimata** *I* Indon
61D3 **Karimganj** Bang
62B1 **Karīmnagar** India
72E2 **Karin** Somalia
32J6 **Karis** Fin
72C4 **Karishimbe** *Mt* Zaïre
41E3 **Káristos** Greece
62A2 **Kārkal** India
51H7 **Karkar** *I* PNG
63B2 **Karkheh** *R* Iran
45E6 **Karkinitskiy Zaliv** *B* Ukraine
49L5 **Karlik Shan** *Mt* China
42D2 **Karlino** Pol
40D2 **Karlobag** Croatia, Yugos
40D1 **Karlovac** Croatia, Yugos
41E2 **Karlovo** Bulg
42C2 **Karlovy Vary** Czech
32G7 **Karlshamn** Sweden
32G7 **Karlskoga** Sweden
32H7 **Karlskrona** Sweden
42B3 **Karlsruhe** Germany
32G7 **Karlstad** Sweden
11C2 **Karlstad** USA
10H4 **Karluk** USA
61D3 **Karnafuli Res** Bang
60D3 **Karnal** India
62A1 **Karnataka** State, India
41F2 **Karnobat** Bulg
37E1 **Kärnten** Province, Austria
73C5 **Karoi** Zim
73D4 **Karonga** Malawi
72D2 **Karora** Sudan
57A3 **Karossa** Indon
41F3 **Kárpathos** *I* Greece
7N2 **Karrats Fjord** Greenland
74C3 **Karree Berge** S Africa
45G7 **Kars** Turk
48H5 **Karsakpay** Kazakhstan
43F1 **Kārsava** Latvia
58E2 **Karshi** Uzbekistan
32J6 **Karstula** Fin
65C1 **Kartaba** Leb
41F2 **Kartal** Turk
44L5 **Kartaly** Russian Fed
14A2 **Karthaus** USA
63B2 **Kārūn** *R* Iran
61B2 **Karwa** India
62A2 **Kārwār** India
50E1 **Karymskoye** Russian Fed
72B4 **Kasai** *R* Zaïre
73C5 **Kasaji** Zaïre
73D5 **Kasama** Zambia
73D4 **Kasanga** Tanz
62A2 **Kāsaragod** India
6H3 **Kasba L** Can
71A2 **Kasba Tadla** Mor
10F1 **Kasegaluk Lg** USA
73C5 **Kasempa** Zambia
73C5 **Kasenga** Zaïre
72D3 **Kasese** Uganda
63C2 **Kāshān** Iran
10G3 **Kashegelok** USA
59F2 **Kashi** China
54B4 **Kashima** Japan
60D3 **Kāshipur** India
53D4 **Kashiwazaki** Japan
63D1 **Kashmar** Iran
46E4 **Kashmir** State, India
44G5 **Kasimov** Russian Fed
57C3 **Kasiruta** *I* Indon
12B3 **Kaskaskia** *R* USA
4C2 **Kaskattama** *R* Can
32J6 **Kasko** Fin
44L4 **Kasli** Russian Fed
6G5 **Kaslo** Can
3H2 **Kasmere L** Can
72C4 **Kasonga** Zaïre
73B4 **Kasongo-Lunda** Zaïre
41F3 **Kásos** *I* Greece
45H6 **Kaspiyskiy** Russian Fed
72D2 **Kassala** Sudan
42B2 **Kassel** Germany
71D1 **Kasserine** Tunisia
73B5 **Kassinga** Angola
64B1 **Kastamonou** Turk
41E3 **Kastélli** Greece
64A2 **Kastellorizon** *I* Greece
41E2 **Kastoría** Greece
41F3 **Kástron** Greece
53D4 **Kasugai** Japan
54B3 **Kasumi** Japan
73D5 **Kasungu** Malawi
60C2 **Kasur** Pak
73C5 **Kataba** Zambia
13F1 **Katahdin,Mt** USA
72C4 **Katako-kombe** Zaïre
6D3 **Katalla** USA
49Q4 **Katangli** Russian Fed
76A4 **Katanning** Aust
62E3 **Katchall** *I* Indian O
41E2 **Kateríni** Greece
6E4 **Kates Needle** *Mt* Can/USA
61E3 **Katha** Burma
76C2 **Katherine** Aust
60C4 **Kāthiāwār** *Pen* India
65B3 **Kathib El Henu** Egypt
61C2 **Kathmandu** Nepal
60D2 **Kathua** India
61C2 **Katihār** India
73C5 **Katima Mulilo** Namibia
6C4 **Katmai,Mt** USA
10H4 **Katmai Nat Mon** USA
61B3 **Katni** India
75D2 **Katoomba** Aust
43D2 **Katowice** Pol
32H7 **Katrineholm** Sweden
71H3 **Katsina** Nig
71H3 **Katsina** *Region* Nig
71H3 **Katsina** *State* Nig
71H4 **Katsina Ala** Nig
54D3 **Katsuta** Japan
54D3 **Katsuura** Japan
54C3 **Katsuy** Japan
48H6 **Kattakurgan** Uzbekistan
32G7 **Kattegat** *Str* Denmark/ Sweden
36E2 **Katzenbuckel** *Mt* Germany
57C2 **Kau** Indon
20E5 **Kauai** *I* Hawaiian Is
20E5 **Kauai Chan** Hawaiian Is
20E5 **Kaulakahi Chan** Hawaiian Is
20E5 **Kaunakaki** Hawaiian Is
44C5 **Kaunas** Lithuania
71H3 **Kaura Namoda** Nig
32J5 **Kautokeino** Nor
41E2 **Kavadarci** Macedonia, Yugos
41D2 **Kavajë** Alb
53D3 **Kavalerovo** Russian Fed
62B2 **Kavali** India
41E2 **Kavālla** Greece
60B4 **Kāvda** India
76E1 **Kavieng** PNG
54C3 **Kawagoe** Japan
54C3 **Kawaguchi** Japan
20E5 **Kawaihae** Hawaiian Is
78B1 **Kawakawa** NZ
73C4 **Kawambwa** Zambia
61B3 **Kawardha** India
13D2 **Kawartha Lakes** Can
53D4 **Kawasaki** Japan
20C2 **Kaweah** *R* USA
78C1 **Kawerau** NZ
78B1 **Kawhia** NZ
71F3 **Kaya** Burkina
10K4 **Kayak I** USA
56E2 **Kayan** *R* Indon
62B3 **Kāyankulam** India
11A3 **Kaycee** USA
57C3 **Kayeli** Indon
19D3 **Kayenta** USA
70A3 **Kayes** Mali
45F8 **Kayseri** Turk
49P2 **Kazach'ye** Russian Fed
64E1 **Kazakh** Azerbaijan
48G5 **Kazakhstan** *Republic* Europe
44H4 **Kazan'** Russian Fed
41F2 **Kazanlük** Bulg
50H4 **Kazan Retto** *Is* Japan
43F3 **Kazatin** Ukraine
45G7 **Kazbek** *Mt* Georgia
63C3 **Kāzerūn** Iran
44J3 **Kazhim** Russian Fed
64E1 **Kazi Magomed** Azerbaijan
43E3 **Kazincbarcika** Hung
44M3 **Kazym** *R* Russian Fed
44M3 **Kazymskaya** Russian Fed
41E3 **Kéa** *I* Greece
20E5 **Kealaikahiki Chan** Hawaiian Is
8D2 **Kearney** USA
19D4 **Kearny** USA
64C2 **Keban Baraji** *Res* Turk
71G3 **Kebbi** *State* Nig
70A3 **Kébémer** Sen
71J4 **Kebi** *R* Chad
71D2 **Kebili** Tunisia
65D1 **Kebīr** *R* Syria/Leb
32H5 **Kebrekaise** *Mt* Sweden
3C2 **Kechika** *R* Can
43D3 **Kecskemet** Hung
43E1 **Kedainiai** Lithuania
5H4 **Kedgwick** Can
53B2 **Kedong** China
70A3 **Kédougou** Sen
44J3 **Kedva** Russian Fed
10N4 **Keechiga** *R* Can
10N3 **Keele** *R* Can
10M3 **Keele Pk** *Mt* Can
19C3 **Keeler** USA
20C3 **Keene** California, USA
13E2 **Keene** New Hampshire, USA
74B2 **Keetmanshoop** Namibia
12B2 **Keewanee** USA
4C4 **Keewatin** Can
12A1 **Keewatin** USA
6J3 **Keewatin** *Region* Can
41E3 **Kefallinía** *I* Greece
57B4 **Kefamenanu** Indon
65C2 **Kefar Sava** Israel
71H4 **Keffi** Nig
32A2 **Keflavik** Iceland
6G4 **Keg River** Can
66B3 **Keheili** Sudan
55B1 **Kehsi Mansam** Burma
75B3 **Keith** Aust
34D3 **Keith** Scot
6F3 **Keith Arm** *B* Can
7M3 **Kekertuk** Can
60D3 **Kekri** India
55C5 **Kelang** Malay
57C3 **Kelang** *I* Indon
55C4 **Kelantan** *R* Malay
71E1 **Kelibia** Tunisia
60B1 **Kelif** Turkmenistan
64C1 **Kelkit** *R* Turk
72B4 **Kellé** Congo
10O3 **Keller L** Can
6F2 **Kellet,C** Can
18C1 **Kellogg** USA
48D3 **Kelloselka** Fin
35B5 **Kells** Irish Rep
34C4 **Kells Range** *Hills* Scot
43E1 **Kelme** Lithuania
6G5 **Kelowna** Can
6F4 **Kelsey Bay** Can
34D4 **Kelso** Scot
18B1 **Kelso** USA
3H3 **Kelvington** Can
44E3 **Kem'** Russian Fed
44E3 **Kem'** *R* Russian Fed
70B3 **Ke Macina** Mali
3C3 **Kemano** Can
48K4 **Kemerovo** Russian Fed
32J5 **Kemi** Fin
32K5 **Kemi** *R* Fin
32K5 **Kemijärvi** Fin
18D2 **Kemmerer** USA
36C1 **Kempen** Region, Belg
16C3 **Kemp,L** USA
23B2 **Kemps Bay** Bahamas
75D2 **Kempsey** Aust
42C3 **Kempten** Germany
10H3 **Kenai** USA
10H4 **Kenai Mts** USA
10H3 **Kenai Pen** USA
72D3 **Kenamuke Swamp** Sudan
35D4 **Kendal** Eng
75D2 **Kendall** Aust
76B1 **Kendari** Indon
56D3 **Kendawangan** Indon
61C3 **Kendrāpāra** India
18C1 **Kendrick** USA
17F4 **Kenedy** USA
70A4 **Kenema** Sierra Leone
72B4 **Kenge** Zaïre
55B1 **Kengtung** Burma
74C2 **Kenhardt** S Africa
70A3 **Kéniéba** Mali
71A2 **Kenitra** Mor
11B2 **Kenmare** USA
16B3 **Kenna** USA
13F1 **Kennebec** *R* USA
14E1 **Kennebunk** USA
14A1 **Kennedy** USA
17D4 **Kenner** USA
17E2 **Kennett** USA
14C3 **Kennett Square** USA
18C1 **Kennewick** USA
6F4 **Kenny Dam** Can
4D3 **Kenogami** *R* Can
7J5 **Kenora** Can
9E2 **Kenosha** USA
35F6 **Kent** County, Eng
16B3 **Kent** Texas, USA
18B1 **Kent** Washington, USA
12B2 **Kentland** USA
12C2 **Kenton** USA
6H3 **Kent Pen** Can
9E3 **Kentucky** State, USA
12C3 **Kentucky** *R* USA
9E3 **Kentucky L** USA
5J4 **Kentville** Can
17D3 **Kentwood** Louisiana, USA
12B2 **Kentwood** Michigan, USA
72D3 **Kenya** Republic, Africa
72D4 **Kenya,Mt** Kenya
12A2 **Keokuk** USA
61B3 **Keonchi** India
61C3 **Keonjhargarh** India
51G7 **Kepaluan Tanimbar** *Arch* Indon
43D2 **Kepno** Pol
57C3 **Kepualuan Widi** *Arch* Indon
57B4 **Kepulauan Alor** *Arch* Indon
56C2 **Kepulauan Anambas** *Arch* Indon
51G7 **Kepulauan Aru** *Arch* Indon
76B1 **Kepulauan Babar** *I* Indon
56C2 **Kepulauan Badas** *Is* Indon
51G7 **Kepulauan Banda** *Arch* Indon
76B1 **Kepulauan Banggai** *I* Indon
76B1 **Kepulauan Barat Daya** *Is* Indon
56C2 **Kepulauan Bunguran Seletan** *Arch* Indon
57D3 **Kepulauan Gorong** *Arch* Indon
51G7 **Kepulauan Kai** *Arch* Indon
57C2 **Kepulauan Kawio** *Arch* Indon
76B1 **Kepulauan Leti** *I* Indon
56B3 **Kepulauan Lingga** *Is* Indon
57C2 **Kepulauan Loloda** *Arch* Indon
56A3 **Kepulauan Mentawi** *Arch* Indon
57C2 **Kepulauan Nenusa** *Arch* Indon
57C3 **Kepulauan Obi** *Arch* Indon
56B2 **Kepulauan Riau** *Arch* Indon
56E4 **Kepulauan Sabalana** *Arch* Indon
57C2 **Kepulauan Sangihe** *Arch* Indon
76B1 **Kepulauan Sermata** *I* Indon
76B1 **Kepulauan Sula** *I* Indon
57C2 **Kepulauan Talaud** *Arch* Indon
56C2 **Kepulauan Tambelan** *Is* Indon
76C1 **Kepulauan Tanimbar** *I* Indon
76B1 **Kepulauan Togian** *I* Indon
76B1 **Kepulauan Tukangbesi** *Is* Indon
57D3 **Kepulauan Watubela** *Arch* Indon
57C3 **Kepulauan Yef Fam** *Arch* Indon
57B4 **Kepulaun Solor** *Arch* Indon
62B2 **Kerala** State, India
75B3 **Kerang** Aust
32J6 **Kerava** Fin
53D1 **Kerbi** *R* Russian Fed
45F6 **Kerch'** Ukraine
44J3 **Kerchem'ya** Russian Fed
76D1 **Kerema** PNG
18C1 **Keremeps** Can
72D2 **Keren** Eth
xxviiiE7 **Kerguelen Ridge** Indian O
72D4 **Kericho** Kenya
56B3 **Kerinci** *Mt* Indon
72D3 **Kerio** *R* Kenya
58E2 **Kerki** Turkmenistan
41D3 **Kérkira** Greece
41D3 **Kérkira** *I* Greece
77H3 **Kermadec Is** NZ
77H4 **Kermadec Trench** Pacific O
63D2 **Kerman** Iran
20B2 **Kerman** USA
63B2 **Kermānshāh** Iran
41F3 **Kerme Kōrfezi** *B* Turk
16B3 **Kermit** USA
19C3 **Kern** *R* USA
20C3 **Kernville** USA
44J3 **Keros** Russian Fed
3G3 **Kerrobert** Can
16C3 **Kerrville** USA
15C2 **Kershaw** USA
56C3 **Kertamulia** Indon
49N5 **Kerulen** *R* Mongolia
70B2 **Kerzaz** Alg
4F3 **Kesagami L** Can
41F2 **Keşan** Turk
53E4 **Kesennuma** Japan
53B2 **Keshan** China
45G7 **Kesir Daglari** *Mt* Turk
32L5 **Kesten'ga** Russian Fed
35D4 **Keswick** Eng
71G4 **Kéta** Ghana
56D3 **Ketapang** Indon
6E4 **Ketchikan** USA
70C3 **Ketia** Niger
60B4 **Keti Bandar** Pak
71G4 **Kétou** Benin
43E2 **Ketrzyn** Pol
35E5 **Kettering** Eng
12C3 **Kettering** USA
4D2 **Kettle** *R* Manitoba, Can
18C1 **Kettle** *R* British Columbia, Can
20C2 **Kettleman City** USA
18C1 **Kettle River Range** *Mts* USA
7L3 **Kettlestone B** Can
14B1 **Keuka L** USA
63D2 **Kevir-i Namak** *Salt Flat* Iran
12B2 **Kewaunee** USA
12B1 **Keweenaw B** USA
12B1 **Keweenaw Pen** USA
4E4 **Key Harbour** Can
15E4 **Key Largo** USA
14A3 **Keyser** USA
9E4 **Key West** USA
49M4 **Kezhma** Russian Fed
41D1 **K'félegháza** Hung
10F3 **Kgun L** USA
65D2 **Khabab** Syria
53D2 **Khabarovsk** Russian Fed
45G8 **Khabur** *R* Syria
60B3 **Khairpur** Pak
60B3 **Khairpur** Region, Pak
74C1 **Khakhea** Botswana
65B3 **Khalig El Tîna** *B* Egypt
67G2 **Khalīj Maşirah** *B* Oman
41F3 **Khálki** *I* Greece
41E2 **Khalkidhíki** *Pen* Greece
41E3 **Khalkís** Greece
44L2 **Khal'mer-Yu** Russian Fed
44H4 **Khalturin** Russian Fed
67G2 **Khalūf** Oman
60C4 **Khambhāt,G of** India
60D4 **Khāmgaon** India
66D3 **Khamir** Yemen
66D3 **Khamis Mushayt** S Arabia
55C2 **Kham Keut** Laos
62C1 **Khammam** India
65B3 **Khamsa** Egypt
63B1 **Khamseh** *Mts* Iran
55C2 **Khan** *R* Laos
60B1 **Khanabad** Afghan
64E3 **Khānaqīn** Iraq
60D4 **Khandwa** India
60C2 **Khanewal** Pak
65D3 **Khan ez Zabib** Jordan
55D4 **Khanh Hung** Viet
41E3 **Khaniá** Greece
53C3 **Khanka, Ozero** *L* China

Khankendy = Stepanakert
60C3 **Khanpur** Pak
65D1 **Khān Shaykhūn** Syria
48H3 **Khanty-Mansiysk** Russian Fed
65C3 **Khan Yunis** Egypt
60D1 **Khapalu** India
50E2 **Khapcheranga** Russian Fed
45H6 **Kharabali** Russian Fed
61C3 **Kharagpur** India
63D3 **Khārān** Iran
60B3 **Kharan** Pak
63C2 **Kharānaq** Iran
63C3 **Khārg** *Is* Iran
69C2 **Khârga Oasis** Egypt
60D4 **Khargon** India
45F6 **Khar'kov** Ukraine
44F2 **Kharlovka** Russian Fed
41F2 **Kharmanli** Bulg
44G4 **Kharovsk** Russian Fed
72D2 **Khartoum** Sudan
72D2 **Khartoum North** Sudan
53C3 **Khasan** Russian Fed
63E2 **Khash** Afghan
63E3 **Khāsh** Iran
63E2 **Khash** *R* Afghan
72D2 **Khashm el Girba** Sudan
61D2 **Khasi-Jaintia Hills** India
41F2 **Khaskovo** Bulg
49M2 **Khatanga** Russian Fed
49N2 **Khatangskiy Zaliv** *Estuary* Russian Fed
49T3 **Khatyrka** Russian Fed
55B3 **Khawsa** Burma
66C1 **Khaybar** S Arabia
66B2 **Khazzan an-Nasr** *L* Egypt
55C2 **Khe Bo** Viet
60C4 **Khed Brahma** India
39C2 **Khemis** Alg
71A2 **Khemisset** Mor
71D1 **Khenchela** Alg
71A2 **Khenifra** Mor
39D2 **Kherrata** Alg
45E6 **Kherson** Ukraine
49N4 **Khilok** Russian Fed
41F3 **Khíos** Greece
41F3 **Khíos** *I* Greece
45D6 **Khmel'nitskiy** Ukraine
43E3 **Khodorov** Ukraine
59E1 **Khodzhent** Taji
60B1 **Kholm** Afghan
43G1 **Kholm** Russian Fed
53E2 **Kholmsk** Russian Fed
74B1 **Khomas Hochland, Mts** Namibia
55D3 **Khong** Laos
63C3 **Khonj** Iran
53C2 **Khor** Russian Fed
53D2 **Khor** *R* Russian Fed
63B2 **Khoramshahr** Iran
67F2 **Khōr Duwayhin** *B* UAE
60C1 **Khorog** Tajikistan
63B2 **Khorramābad** Iran
63D2 **Khosf** Iran
60B2 **Khost** Pak
45D6 **Khotin** Ukraine
10G3 **Khotol** *Mt* USA
71A2 **Khouribga** Mor
45D5 **Khoyniki** Belorussia
49Q3 **Khrebet Cherskogo** *Mts* Russian Fed
53B1 **Khrebet Dzhagdy** *Mts* Russian Fed
49P4 **Khrebet Dzhugdzhur** *Mts* Russian Fed
10C2 **Khrebet Iskamen** *Mts* Russian Fed
49O3 **Khrebet Orulgan** *Mts* Russian Fed
44L2 **Khrebet Pay-khoy** *Mts* Russian Fed
53D2 **Khrebet Sikhote Alin'** *Mts* Russian Fed
59G1 **Khrebet Tarbagatay** *Mts* Kazakhstan
49O4 **Khrebet Tukuringra** *Mts* Russian Fed
53C1 **Khrebet Turana** *Upland* Russian Fed
65B1 **Khrysokhou B** Cyprus
44L3 **Khulga** *R* Russian Fed
61C3 **Khulna** Bang
60D1 **Khunjerab** *P* China/India
63C2 **Khunsar** Iran
67E1 **Khurays** S Arabia
61C3 **Khurda** India
60D3 **Khurja** India
67G3 **Khūryan Mūryān** *Is* Oman
60C2 **Khushab** Pak
65C2 **Khushnīyah** Syria
43E3 **Khust** Ukraine
72C2 **Khuwei** Sudan
60B3 **Khuzdar** Pak
63E2 **Khvāf** Iran
45H5 **Khvalynsk** Russian Fed
63D2 **Khvor** Iran
63C3 **Khvormūj** Iran
45G8 **Khvoy** Iran
60C1 **Khwaja Muhammad** *Mts* Afghan
60C2 **Khyber P** Afghan/Pak
73C4 **Kiambi** Zaïre
17C3 **Kiamichi** *R* USA
10F2 **Kiana** USA
72B4 **Kibangou** Congo
72D4 **Kibaya** Tanz
72C4 **Kibombo** Zaïre
72D4 **Kibondo** Tanz
72D4 **Kibungu** Rwanda
41E2 **Kičevo** Macedonia, Yugos
6G4 **Kicking Horse P** Can
70C3 **Kidal** Mali
35D5 **Kidderminster** Eng
70A3 **Kidira** Sen
78C1 **Kidnappers,C** NZ
42C2 **Kiel** Germany
43E2 **Kielce** Pol
42C2 **Kieler Bucht** *B* Germany
Kiev = Kiyev
58E2 **Kifab** Uzbekistan
70A3 **Kiffa** Maur
68H8 **Kigali** Rwanda
5J2 **Kiglapatt,C** Can
10E3 **Kigluaik Mts** USA
72C4 **Kigoma** Tanz
20E5 **Kiholo** Hawaiian Is
54C4 **Kii-sanchi** *Mts* Japan
53C5 **Kii-suido** *B* Japan
49R4 **Kikhchik** Russian Fed
41E1 **Kikinda** Serbia, Yugos
41E3 **Kikládhes** *Is* Greece
76D1 **Kikon** PNG
54D2 **Kikonai** Japan
51H7 **Kikori** PNG
72B4 **Kikwit** Zaïre
20E5 **Kilauea Crater** *Mt* Hawaiian Is
6C3 **Kilbuck Mts** USA
53B3 **Kilchu** N Korea
75D1 **Kilcoy** Aust
35B5 **Kildane** County, Irish Rep
35B5 **Kildare** Irish Rep
17D3 **Kilgore** USA
72E4 **Kilifi** Kenya
72D4 **Kilimanjaro** *Mt* Tanz
73D4 **Kilindoni** Tanz
64C2 **Kilis** Turk
43F3 **Kiliya** Ukraine
35B5 **Kilkenny** County, Irish Rep
35B5 **Kilkenny** Irish Rep
41E2 **Kilkis** Greece
75D1 **Killarney** Aust
33B3 **Killarney** Irish Rep
17C3 **Killeen** USA
10H2 **Killik** *R* USA
34C3 **Killin** Scot
5J1 **Killinek I** Can
41E3 **Killíni** *Mt* Greece
34C4 **Kilmarnock** Scot
44J4 **Kil'mez** Russian Fed
73D4 **Kilosa** Tanz
33B3 **Kilrush** Irish Rep
71J4 **Kilunga** *R* Nig
73C4 **Kilwa** Zaïre
73D4 **Kilwa Kisiwani** Tanz
73D4 **Kilwa Kivinje** Tanz
71J4 **Kim** *R* Cam
75A2 **Kimba** Aust
16B1 **Kimball** USA
10K3 **Kimball,Mt** USA
3E4 **Kimberley** Can
74C2 **Kimberley** S Africa
76B2 **Kimberley Plat** Aust
53B3 **Kimch'aek** N Korea
53B4 **Kimch'ŏn** S Korea
54A3 **Kimhae** S Korea
41E3 **Kími** Greece
54A3 **Kimje** S Korea
44F4 **Kimry** Russian Fed
54A3 **Kimwha** N Korea
56E1 **Kinabalu** *Mt* Malay
56E1 **Kinabatangan** *R* Malay
4E5 **Kincardine** Can
3C2 **Kincolith** Can
17D3 **Kinder** USA
3G3 **Kindersley** Can
70A3 **Kindia** Guinea
72C4 **Kindu** Zaïre
44J5 **Kinel'** Russian Fed
44G4 **Kineshma** Russian Fed
75D1 **Kingaroy** Aust
19B3 **King City** USA
6F4 **Kingcome Inlet** Can
10F4 **King Cove** USA
17C2 **Kingfisher** USA
7L4 **King George Is** Can
76D5 **King I** Aust
3C3 **King I** Can
76B2 **King Leopold Range** *Mts* Aust
8B3 **Kingman** USA
72C4 **Kingombe** Zaïre
75A2 **Kingoonya** Aust
20C2 **Kingsburg** USA
19C3 **Kings Canyon Nat Pk** USA
75A3 **Kingscote** Aust
76B2 **King Sd** Aust
12B1 **Kingsford** USA
15C2 **Kingsland** USA
35F5 **King's Lynn** Eng
77G1 **Kingsmill Group** *Is* Kiribati
14D2 **Kings Park** USA
8B2 **Kings Peak** *Mt* USA
15C1 **Kingsport** USA
76C4 **Kingston** Aust
7L5 **Kingston** Can
21E3 **Kingston** Jamaica
13E2 **Kingston** New York, USA
78A3 **Kingston** NZ
14C2 **Kingston** Pennsylvania, USA
23E4 **Kingstown** St Vincent
8D4 **Kingsville** USA
5J2 **Kingurutik** *R* Can
34C3 **Kingussie** Scot
6J3 **King William I** Can
74D3 **King William's Town** S Africa
72B4 **Kinkala** Congo
32G7 **Kinna** Sweden
34D3 **Kinnairds Head** *Pt* Scot
54C3 **Kinomoto** Japan
34D3 **Kinross** Scot
72B4 **Kinshasa** Zaïre
16C2 **Kinsley** USA
15D1 **Kinston** USA
56E3 **Kintap** Indon
34C4 **Kintyre** *Pen* Scot
3E2 **Kinuso** Can
72D3 **Kinyeti** *Mt* Sudan
36E1 **Kinzig** *R* Germany
3H2 **Kipahigan L** Can
41E3 **Kiparissía** Greece
41E3 **Kiparissiakós Kólpos** *G* Greece
13D1 **Kipawa,L** Can
73D4 **Kipili** Tanz
10F4 **Kipnuk** USA
35B5 **Kippure** *Mt* Irish Rep
73C5 **Kipushi** Zaïre
36E2 **Kirchheim** Germany
49M4 **Kirensk** Russian Fed
48J5 **Kirgizia** *Republic* Europe
59F1 **Kirgizskiy Khrebet** *Mts* Kirgizia
72B4 **Kiri** Zaïre
77G1 **Kiribati** *Is* Pacific O
64B2 **Kırıkkale** Turk
44E4 **Kirishi** Russian Fed
60B3 **Kirithar Range** *Mts* Pak
41F3 **Kirkağaç** Turk
45H8 **Kirk Bulāg Dāgh** *Mt* Iran
35D4 **Kirkby** Eng
34D3 **Kirkcaldy** Scot
34C4 **Kirkcudbright** Scot
32K5 **Kirkenes** Nor
7K5 **Kirkland Lake** Can
64A1 **Kırklareli** Turk
79E **Kirkpatrick,Mt** Ant
9D2 **Kirksville** USA
64D2 **Kirkūk** Iraq
34D2 **Kirkwall** Scot
17D2 **Kirkwood** USA
74D3 **Kirkwood** *R* S Africa
44E5 **Kirov** Russian Fed
44H4 **Kirov** Russian Fed
64D1 **Kirovakan** Armenia
44K4 **Kirovgrad** Russian Fed
45E6 **Kirovograd** Ukraine
44E2 **Kirovsk** Russian Fed
49R4 **Kirovskiy** Kamchatka, Russian Fed
53C2 **Kirovskiy** Primorskiykray, Russian Fed
44J4 **Kirs** Russian Fed
64B2 **Kirşehir** Turk
42C2 **Kiruna** Sweden
54C3 **Kiryū** Japan
72C3 **Kisangani** Zaïre
57C4 **Kisar** *I* Indon
56A2 **Kisaran** Indon
54C3 **Kisarazu** Japan
61C2 **Kishanganj** India
60C3 **Kishangarh** India
43F3 **Kishinev** Moldavia
54C4 **Kishiwada** Japan
72D4 **Kisii** Kenya
73D4 **Kisiju** Tanz
10B6 **Kiska** *I* USA
4B3 **Kiskitto L** Can
43D3 **Kiskunhalas** Hung
45G7 **Kislovodsk** Russian Fed
72E4 **Kismaayo** Somalia
54C3 **Kiso-sammyaku** *Mts* Japan
70B4 **Kissidougou** Guinea
15C3 **Kissimmee,L** USA
3H2 **Kississing L** Can
72D4 **Kisumu** Kenya
43E3 **Kisvárda** Hung
70B3 **Kita** Mali
48H6 **Kitab** Uzbekistan
54D3 **Kitakami** Japan
54D3 **Kitakami** *R* Japan
54D3 **Kitakata** Japan
53C5 **Kita-Kyūshū** Japan
72D3 **Kitale** Kenya
50H4 **Kitalo** *I* Japan
53E3 **Kitami** Japan
54D2 **Kitami-Esashi** Japan
16B2 **Kit Carson** USA
7K5 **Kitchener** Can
4F3 **Kitchigama** *R* Can
72D3 **Kitgum** Uganda
41E3 **Kíthira** *I* Greece
41E3 **Kíthnos** *I* Greece
65B1 **Kiti,C** Cyprus
6G2 **Kitikmeot** Region, Can
6F4 **Kitimat** Can
32K5 **Kitnen** *R* Fin
54B4 **Kitsuki** Japan
13D2 **Kittanning** USA
13E2 **Kittery** USA
32J5 **Kittilä** Fin
15D1 **Kitty Hawk** USA
73D4 **Kitunda** Tanz
10N4 **Kitwanga** Can
73C5 **Kitwe** Zambia
42C3 **Kitzbühel** Austria
37E1 **Kitzbühler Alpen** *Mts* Austria
42C3 **Kitzingen** Germany
72C4 **Kiumbi** Zaïre
10F2 **Kivalina** USA
43F2 **Kivercy** Ukraine
72C4 **Kivu,L** Zaïre/Rwanda
6B3 **Kiwalik** USA
45E5 **Kiyev** Ukraine
43G2 **Kiyevskoye Vodokhranilishche** *Res* Ukraine
44K4 **Kizel** Russian Fed
44G3 **Kizema** Russian Fed
64C2 **Kizil** *R* Turk
58D2 **Kizyl-Arvat** Turkmenistan
45J8 **Kizyl-Atrek** Turkmenistan
42C2 **Kladno** Czech
42C3 **Klagenfurt** Austria
44C4 **Klaipėda** Lithuania
18B2 **Klamath** USA
8A2 **Klamath** *R* USA
8A2 **Klamath Falls** USA
18B2 **Klamath Mts** USA
3C2 **Klappan** *R* Can
42C3 **Klatovy** Czech
10M4 **Klawak** USA
65C1 **Kleiat** Leb
74B2 **Kleinsee** S Africa
74D2 **Klerksdorp** S Africa
43G2 **Kletnya** Russian Fed
36D1 **Kleve** Germany
43G2 **Klimovichi** Belorussia
44F4 **Klin** Russian Fed
43D1 **Klintehamn** Sweden
45E5 **Klintsy** Russian Fed
74C3 **Klipplaat** S Africa
40D2 **Ključ** Bosnia & Herzegovina, Yugos
42D2 **Kłodzko** Pol
10L3 **Klondike** *R* USA/Can
6D3 **Klondike Plat** USA/Can
42D3 **Klosterneuburg** Austria
10L3 **Kluane** *R* Can
10L3 **Kluane L** Can
10L3 **Kluane Nat Pk** Can
43D2 **Kluczbork** Pol
10L4 **Klukwan** USA
10J3 **Klutina L** USA
10J3 **Knight I** USA
35D5 **Knighton** Wales
40D2 **Knin** Croatia, Yugos
76A4 **Knob,C** Aust
36B1 **Knokke-Heist** Belg
10M5 **Knox,C** Can
79G9 **Knox Coast** Ant
11D3 **Knoxville** Iowa, USA
9E3 **Knoxville** Tennessee, USA
7Q3 **Knud Ramsussens Land** *Region* Greenland
74C3 **Knysna** S Africa
56C3 **Koba** Indon
7O3 **Kobberminebugt** *B* Greenland
53D5 **Kobe** Japan
42C1 **København** Den
37E1 **Kobiard** Slovenia, Yugos
42B2 **Koblenz** Germany
53C1 **Koboldo** Russian Fed
44C5 **Kobrin** Russian Fed
51G7 **Kobroör** *I* Indon
10G2 **Kobuk** *R* USA
41E2 **Kočani** Macedonia, Yugos
54A3 **Kŏch'ang** S Korea
55C3 **Ko Chang** *I* Thai
61C2 **Koch Bihār** India
37D1 **Kochel** Germany
36E2 **Kocher** *R* Germany
7L3 **Koch I** Can
62B3 **Kochi** India
53C5 **Kōchi** Japan
10H4 **Kodiak** USA
10H4 **Kodiak I** USA
62B2 **Kodikkarai** India
72D3 **Kodok** Sudan
54D2 **Kodomari-misaki** *C* Japan
43F3 **Kodyma** Ukraine
20D3 **Koehn L** USA
74B2 **Koes** Namibia
74D2 **Koffiefontein** S Africa
71F4 **Koforidua** Ghana
53D4 **Kōfu** Japan
54C3 **Koga** Japan
5J2 **Kogaluk** *R* Can
32G7 **Køge** Den
71H4 **Kogi** *State* Nig
60C2 **Kohat** Pak
60B2 **Koh-i-Baba** *Mts* Afghan
60B1 **Koh-i-Hisar** *Mts* Afghan
60B2 **Koh-i-Khurd** *Mt* Afghan
61D2 **Kohima** India
60B1 **Koh-i-Mazar** *Mt* Afghan
63E2 **Koh-i-Qaisar** *Mt* Afghan
60B3 **Kohlu** Pak
44D4 **Kohtla Järve** Estonia
54A4 **Kohung** S Korea
54A4 **Kohyon** S Korea
54C3 **Koide** Japan
10K3 **Koidern** Can
55A4 **Koihoa** *Is* Nicobar Is
54A2 **Koin** N Korea
53B5 **Kōje-do** *I* S Korea
54C2 **Ko-jima** *I* Japan
48H4 **Kokchetav** Kazakhstan
32J6 **Kokemaki** *L* Fin
32J6 **Kokkola** Fin
71G3 **Koko** Nig
76D1 **Kokoda** PNG
12B2 **Kokomo** USA
51G7 **Kokonau** Indon
50B2 **Kokpekty** Kazakhstan
54A3 **Koksan** N Korea
7M4 **Koksoak** *R* Can
54A3 **Koksŏng** S Korea
74D3 **Kokstad** S Africa
55C3 **Ko Kut** *I* Thai
44E2 **Kola** Russian Fed
57B3 **Kolaka** Indon
55B4 **Ko Lanta** *I* Thai
62B2 **Kolār** India
62B2 **Kolār Gold Fields** India
70A3 **Kolda** Sen
32F7 **Kolding** Den
53E1 **Kolendo** Russian Fed
44H2 **Kolguyev, Ostrov** *I* Russian Fed
62A1 **Kolhāpur** India
10G4 **Koliganek** USA
42D2 **Kolín** Czech
62B3 **Kollam** India
42B2 **Köln** Germany
43D2 **Kolo** Pol
20E5 **Koloa** Hawaiian Is
42D2 **Kolobrzeg** Pol
70B3 **Kolokani** Mali
44F4 **Kolomna** Russian Fed
45D6 **Kolomyya** Ukraine
57B3 **Kolono** Indon
57B3 **Kolonodale** Indon
49R4 **Kolpakovskiy** Russian Fed
48K4 **Kolpashevo** Russian Fed
41F3 **Kólpos Merabéllou** *B* Greece
41E2 **Kólpos Singitikós** *G* Greece
41E2 **Kólpos Strimonikós** *G* Greece
41E2 **Kólpos Toronaíos** *G* Greece
44F2 **Kol'skiy Poluostrov** *Pen* Russian Fed
44K2 **Kolva** *R* Russian Fed
32G6 **Kolvereid** Nor
73C5 **Kolwezi** Zaïre
49R3 **Kolyma** *R* Russian Fed
49R3 **Kolymskaya Nizmennost** *Lowland* Russian Fed
49S3 **Kolymskoye Nagor'ye** *Mts* Russian Fed
10D2 **Kolyuchinskaya Guba** *B* Russian Fed
41E2 **Kom** *Mt* Bulg/Serbia
72D3 **Koma** Eth

54D3 **Koma** Japan
71J3 **Komaduga Gana** *R* Nig
71J3 **Komadugu Yobé** *R* Nig
54D2 **Komaga take** *Mt* Japan
49S4 **Komandorskiye Ostrova** *I* Russian Fed
43D3 **Komárno** Czech
74E2 **Komati,R** S Africa
74E2 **Komati Poort** S Africa
53D4 **Komatsu** Japan
54B4 **Komatsushima** Japan
71F3 **Kombissiri** Burkina
44J3 **Komi** Respublika, Russian Fed
50B1 **Kommunar** Russian Fed
57A4 **Komodo** *I* Indon
71F4 **Komoé** *R* Ivory Coast
51G7 **Komoran** *I* Indon
54C3 **Komoro** Japan
41F2 **Komotiní** Greece
74C3 **Kompasberg** *Mt* S Africa
55D3 **Kompong Cham** Camb
55C3 **Kompong Chhnang** *Mts* Camb
55C3 **Kompong Som** Camb
55D3 **Kompong Thom** Camb
55D3 **Kompong Trabek** Camb
43F3 **Komrat** Moldavia
74C3 **Komsberg** *Mts* S Africa
49Li **Komsomolets, Ostrov** *I* Russian Fed
44L2 **Komsomol'skiy** Russian Fed
49P4 **Komsomol'sk na Amure** Russian Fed
48H4 **Konda** *R* Russian Fed
61B4 **Kondagaon** India
72D4 **Kondoa** Tanz
53D1 **Kondon** Russian Fed
44E3 **Kondopoga** Russian Fed
62B1 **Kondukūr** India
10C2 **Konergino** Russian Fed
44F3 **Konevo** Russian Fed
7P3 **Kong Christian IX Land** *Region* Greenland
7O3 **Kong Frederik VI Kyst** *Region* Greenland
54A3 **Kongju** S Korea
48D2 **Kong Karls Land** *Is* Barents S
56E2 **Kongkemul** *Mt* Indon
72C4 **Kongolo** Zaïre
71F3 **Kongoussi** Burkina
32F7 **Kongsberg** Den
32G6 **Kongsvinger** Nor
Königsberg = Kaliningrad
37E1 **Königsee, L** Germany
43D2 **Konin** Pol
41D2 **Konjic** Bosnia & Herzegovina, Yugos
71F4 **Konongo** Ghana
44G3 **Konosha** Russian Fed
54C3 **Konosu** Japan
45E5 **Konotop** Ukraine
43E2 **Końskie** Pol
36E3 **Konstanz** Germany
71H3 **Kontagora** Nig
55D3 **Kontum** Viet
10B2 **Konus** *Mt* Russian Fed
45E8 **Konya** Turk
18C1 **Kootenay** *L* Can
3E4 **Kootenay** *R* Can
60C5 **Kopargaon** India
7R3 **Kópasker** Iceland
32A2 **Kópavogur** Iceland
40C1 **Koper** Slovenia, Yugos
58D2 **Kopet Dag** *Mts* Iran/ Turkmenistan
44L4 **Kopeysk** Russian Fed
55C4 **Ko Phangan** *I* Thai
55B4 **Ko Phuket** *I* Thai
32H7 **Köping** Sweden
54A3 **Kopo-ri** S Korea
62B1 **Koppal** India
40D1 **Koprivnica** Croatia, Yugos
60B4 **Korangi** Pak
62C1 **Koraput** India
61B3 **Korba** India
42B2 **Korbach** Germany
41E2 **Korçë** Alb
40D2 **Korčula** *I* Croatia, Yugos
52E2 **Korea B** China/Korea
53B5 **Korea Str** S Korea/Japan
43F2 **Korec** Ukraine
49S3 **Korf** Russian Fed
64B1 **Körğlu Tepesi** *Mt* Turk
70B4 **Korhogo** Ivory Coast
60B4 **Kori Creek** India
41E3 **Korinthiakós Kólpos** *G* Greece
41E3 **Kórinthos** Greece
53E4 **Kōriyama** Japan
44L5 **Korkino** Russian Fed
49R3 **Korkodon** Russian Fed
49R3 **Korkodon** *R* Russian Fed
64B2 **Korkuteli** Turk
59G1 **Korla** China
65B1 **Kormakiti,C** Cyprus
40D2 **Kornat** *I* Croatia, Yugos
45E7 **Köroğlu Tepesi** *Mt* Turk
72D4 **Korogwe** Tanz
75B3 **Koroit** Aust
51G6 **Koror** Palau Is, Pacific O
43E3 **Körös** *R* Hung
45D5 **Korosten** Ukraine
43F2 **Korostyshev** Ukraine
72B2 **Koro Toro** Chad
10F4 **Korovin** *I* USA
53E2 **Korsakov** Russian Fed
32G7 **Korsør** Den
66B3 **Korti** Sudan
44J3 **Kortkeroz** Russian Fed
42A2 **Kortrijk** Belg
49S3 **Koryakskoye Nagor'ye** *Mts* Russian Fed
54A3 **Koryong** S Korea
41F3 **Kós** *I* Greece
10D2 **Kosa Belyaka** *B* Russian Fed
55C4 **Ko Samui** *I* Thai
54A3 **Kosan** N Korea
43D2 **Koscierzyna** Pol
15B2 **Kosciusko** USA
76D4 **Kosciusko** *Mt* Aust
10M4 **Kosciusko I** USA
53B5 **Koshikijima-retto** *I* Japan
43E3 **Kosiče** Czech
44J2 **Kosma** *R* Russian Fed
53B4 **Kosong** N Korea
41E2 **Kosovo** *Aut Republic* Serbia, Yugos
70B4 **Kossou** *L* Ivory Coast
74D2 **Koster** S Africa
72D2 **Kosti** Sudan
43F2 **Kostopol'** Ukraine
44G4 **Kostroma** Russian Fed
42C2 **Kostrzyn** Pol
44K2 **Kos'yu** *R* Russian Fed
32H8 **Koszalin** Pol
60D3 **Kota** India
56B4 **Kotaagung** Indon
56D3 **Kotabaharu** Indon
56E3 **Kotabaru** Indon
55C4 **Kota Bharu** Malay
56C3 **Kotabum** Indon
60C2 **Kot Addu** Pak
56E1 **Kota Kinabulu** Malay
57B2 **Kotamobagu** Indon
62C1 **Kotapad** India
56F7 **Kotapinang** *I* Indon
56G8 **Kota Tinggi** Malay
44H4 **Kotel'nich** Russian Fed
45G6 **Kotel'nikovo** Russian Fed
49P2 **Kotel'nyy, Ostrov** *I* Russian Fed
32K6 **Kotka** Fin
44H3 **Kotlas** Russian Fed
10F3 **Kotlik** USA
71H4 **Koton Karifi** Nig
41D2 **Kotor** Montenegro, Yugos
45D6 **Kotovsk** Ukraine
60B3 **Kotri** Pak
37E1 **Kötschach** Austria
62C1 **Kottagūdem** India
62B3 **Kottayam** India
72C3 **Kotto** *R* CAR
62B2 **Kottūru** India
49L3 **Kotuy** *R* Russian Fed
10F2 **Kotzebue** USA
6B3 **Kotzebue Sd** USA
71G3 **Kouande** Benin
72C3 **Kouango** CAR
71F3 **Koudougou** Burkina
74C3 **Kougaberge** *Mts* S Africa
72B4 **Koulamoutou** Gabon
70B3 **Koulikoro** Mali
71F3 **Koupéla** Burkina
71F3 **Kouri** Mali
27H2 **Kourou** French Guiana
70B3 **Kouroussa** Guinea
72B2 **Kousséri** Cam
32K6 **Kouvola** Fin
32L5 **Kovdor** Russian Fed
32L5 **Kovdozero, Ozero** *L* Russian Fed
43E2 **Kovel'** Ukraine
Kovno = Kaunas
44G4 **Kovrov** Russian Fed
44G5 **Kovylkino** Russian Fed
44F3 **Kovzha** *R* Russian Fed
55C4 **Ko Way** *I* Thai
52C5 **Kowloon** Hong Kong
54A3 **Kowōn** N Korea
60B2 **Kowt-e-Ashrow** Afghan
64A2 **Köyceğiz** Turk
44G2 **Koyda** Russian Fed
62A1 **Koyna Res** India
44H3 **Koynas** Russian Fed
57C2 **Koyoa** *I* Indon
10F3 **Koyuk** USA
10F2 **Koyuk** *R* USA
10G3 **Koyukuk** USA
10G2 **Koyukuk** *R* USA
64C2 **Kozan** Turk
41E2 **Kozańi** Greece
62B2 **Kozhikode** India
44K2 **Kozhim** Russian Fed
44H4 **Koz'modemyansk** Russian Fed
54C4 **Kōzu-shima** *I* Japan
71G4 **Kpandu** Ghana
74D3 **Kraai** *R* S Africa
32F7 **Kragerø** Nor
41E2 **Kragujevac** Serbia, Yugos
55B3 **Kra,Isthmus of** Burma/ Malay
Krakatau = Rakata
65D1 **Krak des Chevaliers** *Hist Site* Syria
Kraków = Cracow Pol
41E2 **Kraljevo** Serbia, Yugos
45F6 **Kramatorsk** Ukraine
32H6 **Kramfors** Sweden
40C1 **Kranj** Slovenia, Yugos
44H3 **Krasavino** Russian Fed
44J1 **Krasino** Russian Fed
43E2 **Kraśnik** Pol
45H5 **Krasnoarmeysk** Russian Fed
45F6 **Krasnodar** Russian Fed
53E2 **Krasnogorsk** Russian Fed
44K4 **Krasnokamsk** Russian Fed
44L4 **Krasnotur'insk** Russian Fed
44K4 **Krasnoufimsk** Russian Fed
44K5 **Krasnousol'-skiy** Russian Fed
44K3 **Krasnovishersk** Russian Fed
45J7 **Krasnovodsk** Turkmenistan
49L4 **Krasnoyarsk** Russian Fed
43E2 **Krasnystaw** Pol
45H5 **Krasnyy Kut** Russian Fed
45F6 **Krasnyy Luch** Ukraine
45H6 **Krasnyy Yar** Russian Fed
55D3 **Kratie** Camb
7N2 **Kraulshavn** Greenland
42B2 **Krefeld** Germany
45E6 **Kremenchug** Ukraine
45E6 **Kremenchugskoye Vodokhranilische** *Res* Ukraine
43F2 **Kremenets** Ukraine
16A1 **Kremming** USA
10E5 **Krenitzin Is** USA
72A3 **Kribi** Cam
44E5 **Krichev** Belorussia
37E1 **Krimml** Austria
32J6 **Krinstinestad** Fin
62B1 **Krishna** *R* India
62B2 **Krishnagiri** India
61C3 **Krishnangar** India
32F7 **Kristiansand** Nor
32G7 **Kristianstad** Sweden
48B3 **Kristiansund** Nor
32G7 **Kristineham** Sweden
41E3 **Kriti** *I* Greece
45E6 **Krivoy Rog** Ukraine
40C1 **Krk** *I* Croatia, Yugos
74D1 **Krokodil** *R* S Africa
49S4 **Kronotskaya Sopka** *Mt* Russian Fed
7P3 **Kronpris Frederik Bjerge** *Mts* Greenland
32K7 **Kronshtadt** Russian Fed
74D2 **Kroonstad** S Africa
45G6 **Kropotkin** Russian Fed
74E1 **Kruger Nat Pk** S Africa
74D2 **Krugersdorp** S Africa
56B4 **Krui** Indon
41D2 **Kruje** Alb
43F2 **Krupki** Belorussia
10F2 **Krusenstern,C** USA
41E2 **Kruzevac** Serbia, Yugos
32K7 **Krustpils** Latvia
10L4 **Kruzof I** USA
45E6 **Krym** *Pen* Ukraine
45F7 **Krymsk** Russian Fed
42D2 **Krzyz** Pol
71C1 **Ksar El Boukhari** Alg
71A2 **Ksar el Kebir** Mor
56A2 **Kuala** Indon
55C5 **Kuala Dungun** Malay
56F6 **Kuala Kangsar** Malay
56G7 **Kuala Kelawang** Malay
55C4 **Kuala Kerai** Malay
55C5 **Kuala Kubu Baharu** Malay
55C5 **Kuala Lipis** Malay
55C5 **Kuala Lumpur** Malay
56G7 **Kuala Pilah** Malay
56F7 **Kuala Selangor** Malay
56A2 **Kualasimpang** Indon
55C4 **Kuala Trengganu** Malay
56E1 **Kuamut** Malay
53A3 **Kuandian** China
55C5 **Kuantan** Malay
45H7 **Kuba** Azerbaijan
51H7 **Kubar** PNG
56D2 **Kuching** Malay
56E1 **Kudat** Malay
56D4 **Kudus** Indon
44J4 **Kudymkar** Russian Fed
42C3 **Kufstein** Austria
10M2 **Kugaluk** *R* Can
10M2 **Kugmallit B** Can
63E3 **Kuhak** Iran
63D2 **Kuh Duren** *Upland* Iran
63D3 **Kūh e Bazmān** *Mt* Iran
63C2 **Kūh-e Dinar** *Mt* Iran
63D1 **Kūh-e-Hazār Masjed** *Mts* Iran
63D3 **Kūh-e Jebāl Barez** *Mts* Iran
63C2 **Kūh-e Karkas** *Mts* Iran
63D3 **Kuh-e Laleh Zar** *Mt* Iran
63B1 **Kūh-e Sahand** *Mt* Iran
63E3 **Kuh e Taftān** *Mt* Iran
45H9 **Kūhhaye Alvand** *Mts* Iran
45H8 **Kūhhaye Sabalan** *Mts* Iran
63B2 **Kūhhā-ye Zāgros** *Mts* Iran
32K6 **Kuhmo** Fin
63C2 **Kūhpāyeh** Iran
63D2 **Kūhpāyeh** *Mt* Iran
63D3 **Kūh ye Bashākerd** *Mts* Iran
63B1 **Kūh ye Sabalan** *Mt* Iran
74B2 **Kuibis** Namibia
74B1 **Kuiseb** *R* Namibia
73B5 **Kuito** Angola
10M4 **Kuiu I** USA
54A3 **Kujang** N Korea
53E3 **Kuji** Japan
54B4 **Kuju-san** *Mt* Japan
10G4 **Kukaklek L** USA
41E2 **Kukës** Alb
10F2 **Kukpowruk** *R* USA
55C5 **Kukup** Malay
63D3 **Kūl** *R* Iran
41F3 **Kula** Turk
56G8 **Kulai** Malay
45K6 **Kulakshi** Kazakhstan
72D3 **Kulal,Mt** Kenya
41E2 **Kulata** Bulg
44C4 **Kuldīga** Latvia
56F6 **Kulim** Malay
44G2 **Kulov** *R* Russian Fed
71F3 **Kulpawn** *R* Ghana
45J6 **Kul'sary** Kazakhstan
60D2 **Kulu** India
64B2 **Kulu** Turk
66D4 **Kululli** Eth
48J4 **Kulunda** Russian Fed
75B2 **Kulwin** Aust
45H7 **Kuma** *R* Russian Fed
54C3 **Kumagaya** Japan
56D3 **Kumai** Indon
45L5 **Kumak** Russian Fed
53C5 **Kumamoto** Japan
54C4 **Kumano** Japan
41E2 **Kumanovo** Macedonia, Yugos
53B1 **Kumara** China
71F4 **Kumasi** Ghana
72A3 **Kumba** Cam
62B2 **Kumbakonam** India
71J4 **Kumbo** Cam
54A3 **Kūmch'ŏn** N Korea
67E2 **Kumdah** S Arabia
44K5 **Kumertau** Russian Fed
54A3 **Kumgang** N Korea
53B4 **Kūmhwa** S Korea
32H7 **Kumla** Sweden
54A4 **Kūmnyŏng** S Korea
54A4 **Kūmo-do** *I* S Korea
61E2 **Kumon Range** *Mts* Burma
62A2 **Kumta** India
59G1 **Kümüx** China
60C2 **Kunar** *R* Afghan
53F3 **Kunashir, Ostrov** *I* Russian Fed
32K7 **Kunda** Estonia
60C4 **Kundla** India
60B1 **Kunduz** Afghan
68F9 **Kunene** *R* Angola
10M5 **Kunghit** *I* Can
32G7 **Kungsbacka** Sweden
44K4 **Kungur** Russian Fed
55B1 **Kunhing** Burma
59G2 **Kunlun Shan** *Mts* China
52A4 **Kunming** China
44M3 **Kunovat** *R* Russian Fed
53B4 **Kunsan** S Korea
32K6 **Kuopio** Fin
40D1 **Kupa** *R* Croatia/Bosnia & Herzegovina, Yugos
76B2 **Kupang** Indon
76D2 **Kupiano** PNG
10M4 **Kupreanof I** USA
10G4 **Kupreanof Pt** USA
45F6 **Kupyansk** Ukraine
59G1 **Kuqa** China
53C2 **Kur** *R* Russian Fed
45H8 **Kura** *R* Azerbaijan
54C3 **Kurabe** Japan
53C5 **Kurashiki** Japan
54B3 **Kurayoshi** Japan
63B1 **Kurdistan** Region, Iran
41F2 **Kūrdzhali** Bulg
53C5 **Kure** Japan
44C4 **Kuressaare** Estonia
49L3 **Kureyka** *R* Russian Fed
48H4 **Kurgan** Russian Fed
Kuria Muria Is = Khūryan Mūryān
32J6 **Kurikka** Fin
Kuril Is = Kuril'skiye Ostrova
53F2 **Kuril'sk** Russian Fed
49Q5 **Kuril'skiye Ostrova** *Is* Russian Fed
xxviiiJ2 **Kuril Trench** Pacific O
45H8 **Kurinskaya Kosa** *Sand Spit* Azerbaijan
62B1 **Kurnool** India
54D2 **Kuroishi** Japan
54D3 **Kuroiso** Japan
78B2 **Kurow** NZ
75D2 **Kurri Kurri** Aust
45F5 **Kursk** Russian Fed
50B2 **Kuruktag** *R* China
74C2 **Kuruman** S Africa
74C2 **Kuruman** *R* S Africa
53C5 **Kurume** Japan
62C3 **Kurunegala** Sri Lanka
48K5 **Kurunktag** *R* China
44K3 **Kur'ya** Russian Fed
44K4 **Kusa** Russian Fed
41F3 **Kuşadasi Körfezi** *B* Turk
41F2 **Kus Golü** *L* Turk
53D5 **Kushimoto** Japan
53E3 **Kushiro** Japan
63E1 **Kushka** Afghan
61C3 **Kushtia** Bang
45J5 **Kushum** *R* Kazakhstan
44K4 **Kushva** Russian Fed
10F3 **Kuskokwim** *R* USA
10F4 **Kuskokwim B** USA
10G3 **Kuskokwim Mts** USA
61B2 **Kusma** Nepal
53E3 **Kussharo-ko** *L* Japan
48H4 **Kustanay** Kazakhstan
45D8 **Kütahya** Turk
56E3 **Kutai** *R* Indon
45G7 **Kutaisi** Georgia
54D2 **Kutchan** Japan
42D3 **Kutná Hora** Czech
43D2 **Kutno** Pol
72B4 **Kutu** Zaïre
61D3 **Kutubdia I** Bang
72C2 **Kutum** Sudan
7M4 **Kuujjuaq** Can
7L4 **Kuujjuarapik** Can
32K5 **Kuusamo** Fin
45K5 **Kuvandyk** Russian Fed
64E4 **Kuwait** Kuwait
58C3 **Kuwait** Sheikdom, S W Asia
54C3 **Kuwana** Japan
48J4 **Kuybyshev** Russian Fed
44H5 **Kuybyshevskoye Vodokhranilishche** *Res* Russian Fed
44E2 **Kuyto, Ozero** *L* Russian Fed
49M4 **Kuytun** Russian Fed
45F7 **Kuzey Anadolu Daglari** *Mts* Turk
44H5 **Kuznetsk** Russian Fed
44F2 **Kuzomen** Russian Fed
44C2 **Kvaenangen** *Sd* Nor
10G4 **Kvichak** USA
10G4 **Kvichak** *R* USA
10G4 **Kvichak B** USA
32G5 **Kvigtind** *Mt* Nor
44B2 **Kvikkjokk** Sweden
72D4 **Kwale** Kenya
71H4 **Kwale** Nig
53B4 **Kwangju** S Korea
72B4 **Kwango** *R* Zaïre
54A3 **Kwangyang** S Korea
54A2 **Kwanmo-bong** *Mt* N Korea
71H4 **Kwara** State, Nig
73C5 **Kwekwe** Zim
10F3 **Kwethluk** USA
10F3 **Kwethluk** *R* USA
43D2 **Kwidzyn** Pol
6B4 **Kwigillingok** USA
51G7 **Kwoka** *Mt* Indon
75C3 **Kyabram** Aust
55B2 **Kyaikkami** Burma
55B2 **Kyaikto** Burma
50D1 **Kyakhta** Russian Fed
75A2 **Kyancutta** Aust
55B1 **Kyaukme** Burma
55B1 **Kyauk-padaung** Burma
55A2 **Kyaukpyu** Burma

61E3 **Kyaukse** Burma
44G2 **Kychema** Russian Fed
3G3 **Kyle** Can
33B2 **Kyle of Lochalsh** Scot
36D1 **Kyll** *R* Germany
75B3 **Kyneton** Aust
72D3 **Kyoga** *L* Uganda
75D1 **Kyogle** Aust
53B4 **Kyŏngju** S Korea
54A3 **Kyongsang Sanmaek** *Mts* S Korea
54A2 **Kyŏngsŏng** N Korea
61E4 **Kyonpyaw** Burma
53D4 **Kyoto** Japan
65B1 **Kyrenia** Cyprus
44K3 **Kyrta** Russian Fed
44L4 **Kyshtym** Russian Fed
65B1 **Kythrea** Cyprus
53C5 **Kyūshū** *I* Japan
xxviiiH4 **Kyushu-Palau Ridge** Pacific O
41E2 **Kyustendil** Bulg
49O2 **Kyusyur** Russian Fed
50C1 **Kyzyl** Russian Fed
48H5 **Kyzylkum** *Desert* Uzbekistan
48H5 **Kzyl Orda** Kazakhstan

L

72E3 **Laascaanood** Somalia
22C1 **La Ascensión** Mexico
69D3 **Laas Dawaco** Somalia
36E1 **Laasphe** Germany
69D3 **Laasqoray** Somalia
26F1 **La Asunción** Ven
70A2 **Laâyoune** Mor
28C1 **La Banda** Arg
22B1 **La Barca** Mexico
18D2 **La Barge** USA
77G2 **Labasa** Fiji
70A3 **Labé** Guinea
42D2 **Labe** *R* Czech
13E1 **Labelle** Can
15E4 **La Belle** USA
10L3 **Laberge,L** Can
56D2 **Labi** Brunei
45G7 **Labinsk** Russian Fed
56G7 **Labis** Malay
65D1 **Laboué** Leb
28C2 **Laboulaye** Arg
7M4 **Labrador** *Region* Can
7M4 **Labrador City** Can
7N4 **Labrador S** Greenland/Can
26F5 **Lábrea** Brazil
56E1 **Labuan** *I* Malay
57C3 **Labuha** Indon
56C4 **Labuhan** Indon
57B4 **Labuhanbajo** Indon
56F7 **Labuhanbatu** Indon
56B2 **Labuhanbilik** Indon
55A2 **Labutta** Burma
44M2 **Labytnangi** Russian Fed
7L4 **Lac à l'Eau Claire** Can
4F2 **Lac Anuc** *L* Can
36B1 **La Capelle** France
28C2 **La Carlota** Arg
57F8 **La Carlota** Phil
4F4 **Lac au Goéland** *L* Can
5G2 **Lac aux Feuilles** *L* Can
5J2 **Lac aux Goélands** *L* Can
5G2 **Lac Bacquerville** *L* Can
5G2 **Lac Bécard** *L* Can
10N2 **Lac Belot** *L* Can
7L4 **Lac Bienville** *L* Can
3H2 **Lac Brochet** Can
5J3 **Lac Brûlé** *R* Can
4F4 **Lac Bryson** *L* Can
Laccadive Is = Lakshadweep
59F4 **Laccadive Is** India
5J2 **Lac Champdoré** *L* Can
5G2 **Lac Châteauguay** *L* Can
5F2 **Lac Chavigny** *L* Can
5H3 **Lac Clairambault** *L* Can
4F1 **Lac Couture** *L* Can
5G3 **Lac Dalmas** *L* Can
37B2 **Lac d'Annecy** *L* France
6G3 **Lac de Gras** *L* Can
37B1 **Lac de Joux** *L* Switz
5G3 **Lac Delorme** *L* Can
37B1 **Lac de Neuchâtel** *L* Switz
22B2 **Lac de Patzcuaro** *L* Mexico
22B2 **Lac de Sayula** *L* Mexico
6F3 **Lac des Bois** *L* Can
4C4 **Lac des Mille Lacs** *L* Can
4F4 **Lac Doda** *L* Can
11C1 **Lac du Bonnet** Can
37A2 **Lac du Bourget** *L* France
21D3 **La Ceiba** Honduras
75A3 **Lacepede B** Aust
5G2 **Lac Faribault** *L* Can
4F3 **Lac Grasset** *L* Can
5J2 **Lac Gruéard** *L* Can
4F2 **Lac Guillaume-Delisle** *L* Can
38C2 **La Châtre** France
36A3 **La Châtre-sur-le-Loir** France
37B1 **La-Chaux-de-Fonds** Switz
65C3 **Lachish** *Hist Site* Israel
76D4 **Lachlan** *R* Aust
5G3 **Lac Holmer** *L* Can
26C2 **La Chorrera** Panama
13E1 **Lachute** Can
37A3 **La Ciotat** France
22A1 **La Ciudad** Mexico
7M4 **Lac Joseph** *L* Can
13D2 **Lackawanna** USA
5G4 **Lac Kempt** *L* Can
4F4 **Lac Kipawa** *L* Can
5G1 **Lac Klotz** *L* Can
3F3 **Lac la Biche** Can
6F3 **Lac la Martre** *L* Can
5H3 **Lac Lapointe** *L* Can
5G2 **Lac La Potherie** *L* Can
6H4 **Lac la Ronge** *L* Can
40B1 **Lac Léman** *L* Switz/France
5F2 **Lac Le Roy** *L* Can
5G2 **Lac Mannessier** *L* Can
7L4 **Lac Manouane** Can
4F4 **Lac Matagami** *L* Can
10N2 **Lac Maunoir** *L* Can
7L4 **Lac Mistassini** *L* Can
4F4 **Lac Muskoka** *L* Can
5G3 **Lac Naococane** *L* Can
5G3 **Lac Néret** *L* Can
5H3 **Lac Nouveau** *L* Can
28B1 **La Cocha** Arg
3F3 **Lacombe** Can
13E2 **Laconia** USA
5H3 **Lac Opiscotéo** *L* Can
39A1 **La Coruña** Spain
37A2 **La Côte-St-André** France
4F4 **Lac Parent** *L* Can
5F2 **Lac Qilalugalik** *L* Can
5H3 **Lac Rambau** *L* Can
5J2 **Lac Ramusio** *L* Can
9D2 **La Crosse** USA
28D1 **La Cruz** Arg
22A1 **La Cruz** Mexico
5G4 **Lac Saint Jean** *L* Can
4F3 **Lac Sakami** *L* Can
7J4 **Lac Seul** *L* Can
4F4 **Lac Simard** *L* Can
5G3 **Lac Sureau** *L* Can
5G3 **Lac Taffanel** *L* Can
5G2 **Lac Tassialouc** *L* Can
17D2 **La Cygne** USA
60D2 **Ladākh Range** India
63E3 **Lādīz** Iran
60C3 **Lādnūn** India
52B5 **Ladong** China
44E3 **Ladozhskoye Ozero** *L* Ukraine
7K2 **Lady Ann Str** Can
75E3 **Lady Barron** Aust
74D2 **Ladybrand** S Africa
3D4 **Ladysmith** Can
74D2 **Ladysmith** S Africa
12A1 **Ladysmith** USA
76D1 **Lae** PNG
55C3 **Laem Ngop** Thai
42C1 **Laesø** *I* Den
16A2 **Lafayette** Colorado, USA
9E2 **Lafayette** Indiana, USA
9D3 **Lafayette** Louisiana, USA
36B2 **La Fène** France
36A2 **La-Ferté-Barnard** France
36B2 **La Ferté-St-Aubin** France
36B2 **La-Ferté-sous-Jouarre** France
71H4 **Lafia** Nig
71H4 **Lafiagi** Nig
38B2 **La Flèche** France
4E4 **Laforest** Can
71D1 **La Galite** *I* Tunisia
42C1 **Lagan** *R* Sweden
27L6 **Lagarto** Brazil
71C2 **Laghouat** Alg
29D3 **Lagoa de Araruama** Brazil
28E2 **Lagoa de Castillos** *L* Urug
28E2 **Lagoa de Rocha** Urug
25F4 **Lagoa dos Patos** *Lg* Brazil
29D3 **Lagoa Feia** Brazil
26C4 **Lago Agrio** Ecuador
29D2 **Lagoa Juparanã** *L* Brazil
29A2 **Lagoa Mandiore** *L* Brazil
28E2 **Lagoa Mangueira** *L* Brazil
25D4 **Lagoa mar Chiguita** *L* Arg
25F4 **Lagoa Mirim** *L* Urug/Brazil
28E2 **Lagoa Negra** *L* Urug
25B8 **Lago Argentino** *L* Arg
29A2 **Lagoa Uberaba** *L* Brazil
28E1 **Lagoa Vermelha** Brazil
25B7 **Lago Buenos Aries** *L* Arg
25B7 **Lago Cochrane** *L* Chile/Arg
25C7 **Lago Colhué Huapi** *L* Arg
21B2 **Lago de Chapala** *L* Mexico
26B2 **Lago de Chiriqui** *L* Panama
22B2 **Lago de Cuitzeo** *L* Mexico
25B5 **Lago de la Laja** *L* Chile
40B2 **Lago del Coghinas** *L* Sardegna
26D2 **Lago de Maracaibo** *L* Ven
26A1 **Lago de Nicaragua** *L* Nic
26B1 **Lago de Perlas** *L* Nic
22B1 **Lago de Santiaguillo** *L* Mexico
40C2 **Lago di Bolsena** *L* Italy
40C2 **Lago di Bracciano** *L* Italy
40B1 **Lago di Como** *L* Italy
37D2 **Lago d'Idro** *L* Italy
40C1 **Lago di Garda** *L* Italy
37C2 **Lago di Lecco** *L* Italy
37C2 **Lago di Lugano** *L* Italy
37D2 **Lago d'Iseo** *L* Italy
37C2 **Lago d'Orta** *L* Italy
25B7 **Lago General Carrera** *L* Chile
40B1 **Lago Maggiore** *L* Italy
25C7 **Lago Musters** *L* Arg
38B3 **Lagon** France
25B6 **Lago Nahuel Haupi** *L* Arg
25B7 **Lago O'Higgins** *L* Chile
40B2 **Lago Omodeo** *L* Sardegna
26E7 **Lago Poopó** *L* Bol
25B6 **Lago Ranco** *L* Chile
26E6 **Lago Rogaguado** *L* Bol
71G4 **Lagos** Nig
39A2 **Lagos** Port
71G4 **Lagos** State, Nig
25B7 **Lago San Martin** *L* Chile/Arg
21B2 **Lagos de Moreno** Mexico
26E7 **Lago Titicaca** Bol/Peru
37E3 **Lago Trasimeno** *L* Italy
71E1 **La Goulette** Tunisia
25B7 **Lago Viedma** *L* Arg
8B2 **La Grande** USA
4F3 **La Grande Réservoir 2** *Res* Can
5G3 **La Grande Réservoir 3** *Res* Can
5G3 **La Grande Réservoir 4** *Res* Can
76B2 **Lagrange** Aust
9E3 **La Grange** Georgia, USA
12B3 **La Grange** Kentucky, USA
15D1 **La Grange** N Carolina, USA
17C4 **La Grange** Texas, USA
26F2 **La Gran Sabana** *Mts* Ven
37B2 **La Grave** France
38B3 **Lagronño** Spain
16A3 **Laguna** USA
22A1 **Laguna Agua Brava** Mexico
28A3 **Laguna Aluminé** *L* Arg
19C4 **Laguna Beach** USA
28C3 **Laguna Colorada Grande** *L* Arg
57F8 **Laguna de Bay** *Lg* Phil
21D3 **Laguna de Caratasca** *Lg* Honduras
21D4 **Laguna de Chiriqui** *L* Panama
16A3 **Laguna de Guzmán** *L* Mexico
28C4 **Laguna del Abra** *L* Arg
22A1 **Laguna del Caimanero** *L* Mexico
21D3 **Laguna de Managua** *L* Nicaragua
21D3 **Laguna de Nicaragua** *L* Nicaragua
23A4 **Laguna de Perlas** *Lg* Nic
22C1 **Laguna de Pueblo Viejo** *L* Mexico
16A3 **Laguna de Santa Maria** *L* Mexico
21C2 **Laguna de Tamiahua** *Lg* Mexico
21C3 **Laguna de Términos** *Lg* Mexico
22B1 **Laguna de Yuriria** *L* Mexico
28D1 **Laguna Iberá** Arg
28D1 **Laguna Itati** *L* Arg
22C1 **Laguna le Altamira** Mexico
21C2 **Laguna Madre** *Lg* Mexico
17F4 **Laguna Madre** *Lg* USA
28C2 **Laguna Mar Chiquita** *L* Arg
28A4 **Laguna Nahuel Huapi** *L* Arg
10C2 **Laguna Nutauge** *Lg* Russian Fed
28C2 **Laguna Paiva** Arg
28A3 **Laguna Panguipulli** *L* Chile
28A4 **Laguna Puyehue** *L* Chile
28A4 **Laguna Ranco** Chile
28A4 **Laguna Repanco** *L* Chile
19C4 **Laguna Salada** *L* Mexico
8C4 **Laguna Seca** Mexico
22C2 **Laguna Superior** *L* Mexico
10C2 **Laguna Tenkergynpil'gyn** *Lg* Russian Fed
22C1 **Laguna Tortugas** *L* Mexico
28A4 **Laguna Traful** *L* Arg
28D1 **Laguna Trin** *L* Arg
10C2 **Laguna Vankarem** *Lg* Russian Fed
37E2 **Laguna Veneta** *Lg* Italy
28A3 **Laguna Villarrica** *L* Chile
22B1 **Lagund Seca** Mexico
56E1 **Lahad Datu** Malay
56B3 **Lahat** Indon
56A2 **Lahewa** Indon
32J6 **Lahia** Fin
66D4 **Lahij** Yemen
63C1 **Lāhījān** Iran
36D1 **Lahn** *R* Germany
36D1 **Lahnstein** Germany
60C2 **Lahore** Pak
36D2 **Lahr** France
32K6 **Lahti** Fin
22B2 **La Huerta** Mexico
72B3 **Lai** Chad
52B5 **Laibin** China
55C1 **Lai Chau** Viet
36A2 **L'Aigle** France
74C3 **Laingsburg** S Africa
34C2 **Lairg** Scot
56B3 **Lais** Indon
57G9 **Lais** Phil
57C3 **Laiwui** Indon
52E2 **Laiyang** China
52D2 **Laizhou Wan** *B* China
28A3 **Laja** *R* Chile
28E1 **Lajeado** Brazil
25F3 **Lajes** Brazil
20D4 **La Jolla** USA
8C3 **La Junta** USA
11C3 **Lake Andes** USA
75C2 **Lake Cargelligo** Aust
9D3 **Lake Charles** USA
15C2 **Lake City** Florida, USA
11D3 **Lake City** Minnesota, USA
15D2 **Lake City** S Carolina, USA
35D4 **Lake District** *Region* Eng
20D4 **Lake Elsinore** USA
76C3 **Lake Eyre Basin** Aust
13D2 **Lakefield** Can
12B2 **Lake Geneva** USA
14D1 **Lake George** USA
7M3 **Lake Harbour** Can
19D4 **Lake Havasu City** USA
20C3 **Lake Hughes** USA
14C2 **Lakehurst** USA
20C3 **Lake Isabella** USA
17C4 **Lake Jackson** USA
3F3 **Lake la Biche** Can
15C3 **Lakeland** USA
7J5 **Lake of the Woods** Can
18B1 **Lake Oswego** USA
5G5 **Lake Placid** USA
19B3 **Lakeport** USA
17D3 **Lake Providence** USA
78B2 **Lake Pukaki** NZ
4E3 **Lake River** Can
75C3 **Lakes Entrance** Aust
20C2 **Lakeshore** USA
75B1 **Lake Stewart** Aust
4E4 **Lake Superior Prov Park** Can
13D1 **Lake Traverse** Can
8A2 **Lakeview** USA
18B1 **Lakeview Mt** Can
17D3 **Lake Village** USA
15C3 **Lake Wales** USA
20C4 **Lakewood** California, USA
16A2 **Lakewood** Colorado, USA
14C2 **Lakewood** New Jersey, USA
12C2 **Lakewood** Ohio, USA
15E4 **Lake Worth** USA
61B2 **Lakhīmpur** India
60B4 **Lakhpat** India
16B2 **Lakin** USA
60C2 **Lakki** Pak
41E3 **Lakonikós Kólpos** *G* Greece
57C4 **Lakor** *I* Indon
70B4 **Lakota** Ivory Coast
32K4 **Laksefjord** *Inlet* Nor
32K4 **Lakselv** Nor
62A2 **Lakshadweep** *Is* India
28C2 **La Laguna** Arg
66C4 **Lalibela** Eth
26B4 **La Libertad** Ecuador
28A2 **La Ligua** Chile
57B5 **Lalindi** Indon
57B3 **Lalindu** *R* Indon
39A2 **La Linea** Spain
60D4 **Lalitpur** India
57B3 **Laloa** Indon
6H4 **La Loche** Can
3G2 **La Loche,L** Can
36A2 **La Loupe** France
36C1 **La Louvière** Belg
23A4 **La Luz** Nic
28B1 **La Madrid** Arg
7L5 **La Malbaie** Can
22C2 **La Malinche** *Mt* Mexico
22B1 **La Mancha** Mexico
39B2 **La Mancha** Region, Spain
8C3 **Lamar** Colorado, USA
17D2 **Lamar** Missouri, USA
28B3 **Lamarque** Arg
17C4 **La Marque** USA
72B4 **Lambaréné** Gabon
26B5 **Lambayeque** Peru
79F10 **Lambert Gl** Ant
74B3 **Lamberts Bay** S Africa
14C2 **Lambertville** USA
37C2 **Lambro** *R* Italy
6F2 **Lambton,C** Can
55C2 **Lam Chi** *R* Thai
39A1 **Lamego** Port
37B2 **La Meije** *Mt* France
28B1 **La Merced** Arg
26C6 **La Merced** Peru
16B3 **Lamesa** USA
19C4 **La Mesa** USA
41E3 **Lamía** Greece
34D4 **Lammermuir Hills** Scot
32G7 **Lammhult** Sweden
57F8 **Lamon B** Phil
37D2 **Lamone** *R* Italy
17D1 **Lamoni** USA
20C3 **Lamont** California, USA
11A3 **Lamont** Wyoming, USA
51H6 **Lamotrek** *I* Pacific O
36B3 **Lamotte Beuvron** France
11C2 **La Moure** USA
16C3 **Lampasas** USA
35C5 **Lampeter** Wales
72E4 **Lamu** Kenya
37A2 **La Mure** France
37D1 **Lana** Italy
20E5 **Lanai** *I* Hawaiian Is
20E5 **Lanai City** Hawaiian Is
34D4 **Lanark** Scot
55B3 **Lanbi** *I* Burma
55C1 **Lancang** *R* China
35D5 **Lancashire** County, Eng
19C4 **Lancaster** California, USA
35D4 **Lancaster** Eng
17D1 **Lancaster** Mississippi, USA
13E2 **Lancaster** New Hampshire, USA
14A1 **Lancaster** New York, USA
12C3 **Lancaster** Ohio, USA
9F3 **Lancaster** Pennsylvania, USA
15C2 **Lancaster** S Carolina, USA
7K2 **Lancaster Sd** Can
56C3 **Landak** *R* Indon
36E2 **Landan** Germany
42C3 **Landeck** Austria
8C2 **Lander** USA
28C2 **Landeta** Arg
15C1 **Landrum** USA
42C3 **Landsberg** Germany
6F2 **Lands End** *C* Can
35C6 **Land's End** *Pt* Eng
42C3 **Landshut** Germany
32G7 **Làndskrona** Sweden
15B2 **Lanett** USA
61B1 **La'nga Co** *L* China
11C2 **Langdon** USA
66C3 **Langeb** *Watercourse* Sudan
74C2 **Langeberg** *Mt* S Africa
3H3 **Langenburg** Can
42B2 **Langenhagen** Germany
37B1 **Langenthal** Switz
34D4 **Langholm** Scot
32A2 **Langjökull** *Mts* Iceland
55B4 **Langkawi** *I* Malay
4F4 **Langlade** Can
3D4 **Langley** Can
75C1 **Langlo** *R* Aust
37B1 **Langnau** Switz
38D2 **Langres** France
56A2 **Langsa** Indon
50D2 **Lang Shan** *Mts* China
55D1 **Lang Son** Viet
16B4 **Langtry** USA
38C3 **Languedoc** Region, France
3G3 **Lanigan** Can
25B5 **Lanin** *Mt* Arg
57F9 **Lanoa,L** Phil
14C2 **Lansdale** USA
4D3 **Lansdowne House** Can
5K3 **L'Anse au Loup** Can
14C2 **Lansford** USA
9E2 **Lansing** USA
37B2 **Lanslebourg** France
70A2 **Lanzarote** *I* Canary Is
52A2 **Lanzhou** China
37B2 **Lanzo Torinese** Italy
57F7 **Laoag** Phil
55C1 **Lao Cai** Viet
52D1 **Laoha He** *R* China
35B5 **Laois** County, Irish Rep
35B5 **Laoise Port** Irish Rep

54A2 **Laoling** China
36B2 **Laon** France
4D4 **Laona** USA
26C6 **La Orova** Peru
55C2 **Laos** Republic, S E Asia
29C4 **Lapa** Brazil
38C2 **Lapalisse** France
70A2 **La Palma** *I* Canary Is
26C2 **La Palmas** Panama
28E2 **La Paloma** Urug
28B3 **La Pampa** State, Arg
20B3 **La Panza Range** *Mts* USA
26F2 **La Paragua** Ven
25E4 **La Paz** Arg
28B2 **La Paz** Arg
26E7 **La Paz** Bol
21A2 **La Paz** Mexico
53E2 **La Perouse Str** Russian Fed/Japan
22C1 **La Pesca** Mexico
22B1 **La Piedad** Mexico
18B2 **La Pine** USA
65B1 **Lapithos** Cyprus
17D3 **Laplace** USA
22B2 **La Placita** Mexico
11B2 **La Plant** USA
25E4 **La Plata** Arg
3G2 **La Plonge,L** Can
12B2 **La Porte** USA
14B2 **Laporte** USA
32K6 **Lappeenranta** Fin
32H5 **Lappland** *Region* Sweden/Fin
28C3 **Laprida** Arg
17F4 **La Pryor** USA
49O2 **Laptev S** Russian Fed
32J6 **Lapua** Fin
28B1 **La Puerta** Arg
57F8 **Lapu-Lapu** Phil
28C1 **La Punta** Arg
8B4 **La Purísima** Mexico
72C1 **Laqiya Arbain** *Well* Sudan
25C2 **La Quiaca** Arg
40C2 **L'Aquila** Italy
63C3 **Lār** Iran
71A1 **Larache** Mor
37A2 **Laragne** France
8C2 **Laramie** USA
11A3 **Laramie Mts** USA
8C2 **Laramie Range** *Mts* USA
29B4 **Laranjeiras do Sul** Brazil
57B4 **Larantuka** Indon
57D4 **Larat** *I* Indon
39B2 **Larca** Spain
8D4 **Laredo** USA
63C3 **Larestan** Region, Iran
Largeau = Faya
37B2 **L'Argentière** France
15C3 **Largo** USA
34C4 **Largs** Scot
63B1 **Lārī** Iran
57A3 **Lariang** *R* Indon
25C3 **La Rioja** Arg
25C3 **La Rioja** State, Arg
41E3 **Lárisa** Greece
60B3 **Larkana** Pak
64B3 **Larnaca** Cyprus
65B1 **Larnaca B** Cyprus
34B4 **Larne** N Ire
16C2 **Larned** USA
39A1 **La Robla** Spain
36C1 **La Roche-en-Ardenne** Belg
38B2 **La Rochelle** France
37B1 **La Roche-sur-Foron** France
38B2 **La Roche-sur-Yon** France
39B2 **La Roda** Spain
23D3 **La Romana** Dom Rep
6H4 **La Ronge** Can
32F7 **Larvik** Nor
48J3 **Laryak** Russian Fed
28D1 **La Sabana** Arg
39B2 **La Sagra** *Mt* Spain
13E1 **La Salle** Can
12B2 **La Salle** USA
16B2 **Las Animas** USA
7L5 **La Sarre** Can
28C1 **Las Avispas** Arg
28A2 **Las Cabras** Chile
28E2 **Lascano** Urug
16A3 **Las Cruces** USA
23C3 **La Selle** *Mt* Haiti
52B2 **Lasengmia** China
25B3 **La Serena** Chile
37A3 **La Seyne** France
25E5 **Las Flores** Arg
63E2 **Lash-e-Joveyn** Afghan
55B1 **Lashio** Burma
40D3 **La Sila** *Mts* Italy
63C1 **Lāsjerd** Iran
60A2 **Laskar Grah** Afghan
28A3 **Las Lajas** Chile
39A2 **Las Marismas** *Marshland* Spain
22B1 **La Soledad** Mexico
57B3 **Lasolo** Indon
57B3 **Lasolo** *R* Indon
70A2 **Las Palmas de Gran Canaria** Canary Is
40B2 **La Spezia** Italy
8C3 **Las Cruces** USA
28D2 **Las Piedras** Urug
25C6 **Las Plumas** Arg
28C2 **Las Rosas** Arg
18B2 **Lassen Peak** *Mt* USA
18B2 **Lassen Volcanic Nat Pk** USA
28C1 **Las Termas** Arg
22C2 **Las Tinaja** Mexico
28C1 **Las Tinajos** Arg
3G3 **Last Mountain L** Can
28D1 **Las Toscas** Arg
72B4 **Lastoursville** Gabon
40D2 **Lastovo** *I* Croatia, Yugos
21B2 **Las Tres Marias** *Is* Mexico
22A1 **Las Varas** Mexico
28C2 **Las Varillas** Arg
8C3 **Las Vegas** New Mexico, USA
8B3 **Las Vegas** Nevada, USA
Latakia = Al Lādhiqīyah
40C2 **Latina** Italy
28B2 **La Toma** Arg
26E1 **La Tortuga** *I* Ven
57F7 **La Trinidad** Phil
75E3 **Latrobe** Aust
28B1 **La Troya** *R* Arg
65C3 **Latrun** Israel
7L5 **La Tuque** Can
62B1 **Lātūr** India
44C4 **Latvia** *Republic* Europe
35B4 **Laugh Allen** *L* Irish Rep
35B5 **Laugh Boderg** *L* Irish Rep
35B5 **Laugh Bouna** *L* Irish Rep
35B4 **Laugh Carlingford** *L* N Ire
35B5 **Laugh Derravaragh** *L* Irish Rep
35B4 **Laugh Erne** *L* N Ire
35B4 **Laugh Oughter** *L* Irish Rep
35B5 **Laugh Ree** *L* Irish Rep
35B5 **Laugh Sheelin** *L* Irish Rep
77H2 **Lau Group** *Is* Fiji
76D5 **Launceston** Aust
35C6 **Launceston** Eng
25B6 **La Unión** Chile
21D3 **La Union** El Salvador
22B2 **La Union** Mexico
26C5 **La Unión** Peru
76D2 **Laura** Aust
13D3 **Laurel** Delaware, USA
14B3 **Laurel** Maryland, USA
9E3 **Laurel** Mississippi, USA
18E1 **Laurel** Montana, USA
15C2 **Laurens** USA
5G4 **Laurentides Prov Park** Can
3H2 **Laurie L** Can
15D2 **Laurinburg** USA
40B1 **Lausanne** Switz
56E3 **Laut** *I* Indon
25B7 **Lautaro** Chile
36E1 **Lauterbach** Germany
36D2 **Lauterecken** Germany
77G2 **Lautoka** *I* Fiji
5G4 **Laval** Can
38B2 **Laval** France
20B2 **Laveaga Peak** *Mt* USA
37C2 **Laveno** Italy
22B1 **La Ventura** Mexico
29A4 **La Verá** Par
4F4 **La Verendrye Prov Park** Can
18E1 **Lavina** USA
36C2 **La Vôge** Region, France
27K8 **Lavras** Brazil
28E2 **Lavras do Sul** Brazil
10D2 **Lavrentiya** Russian Fed
74E2 **Lavumisa** Swaziland
56E2 **Lawas** Malay
67E4 **Lawdar** Yemen
57B4 **Lawele** Indon
55B1 **Lawksawk** Burma
71F3 **Lawra** Ghana
17C2 **Lawrence** Kansas, USA
13E2 **Lawrence** Massachusetts, USA
78A3 **Lawrence** NZ
15B1 **Lawrenceburg** USA
12B3 **Lawrenceville** Illinois, USA
14B2 **Lawrenceville** Pennsylvania, USA
8D3 **Lawton** USA
67E2 **Layla** S Arabia
72D3 **Laylo** Sudan
53E1 **Lazarev** Russian Fed
22B2 **Lázaro Cárdenas** Mexico
57F9 **Lazi** Phil
53C3 **Lazo** Russian Fed
8C2 **Lead** USA
3G3 **Leader** Can
16A2 **Leadville** USA
15B2 **Leaf** *R* USA
16C4 **Leakey** USA
28D1 **Leandro N Alem** Arg
17C2 **Leavenworth** USA
43D2 **Leba** Pol
16C2 **Lebanon** Kansas, USA
17D2 **Lebanon** Missouri, USA
18B2 **Lebanon** Oregon, USA
13D2 **Lebanon** Pennsylvania, USA
64C3 **Lebanon** Republic, S W Asia
12B3 **Lebanon** Tennessee, USA
20C3 **Lebec** USA
73D6 **Lebombo** *Mts* Mozam/S Africa/Swaziland
43D2 **Lebork** Pol
37B2 **Le Bourg-d'Oisans** France
37B1 **Le Brassus** Switz
25B5 **Lebu** Chile
37B1 **Le Buet** *Mt* France
36B1 **Le Cateau** France
41D2 **Lecce** Italy
40B1 **Lecco** Italy
37D1 **Lech** *R* Austria
36D2 **Le Champ de Feu** *Mt* France
37D1 **Lechtaler Alpen** *Mts* Austria
38C2 **Le Creusot** France
35D5 **Ledbury** Eng
61E2 **Ledo** India
3F3 **Leduc** Can
14D1 **Lee** USA
11D2 **Leech L** USA
33C3 **Leeds** Eng
35D5 **Leek** Eng
42B2 **Leer** Germany
15C3 **Leesburg** Florida, USA
14B3 **Leesburg** Virginia, USA
17D3 **Leesville** USA
75C2 **Leeton** Aust
74C3 **Leeugamka** S Africa
42B2 **Leeuwarden** Neth
76A4 **Leeuwin,C** Aust
20C2 **Lee Vining** USA
23E3 **Leeward Is** Caribbean
65B1 **Lefka** Cyprus
65B1 **Lefkara** Cyprus
65B1 **Lefkoniko** Cyprus
57F8 **Legazpi** Phil
37D2 **Legnago** Italy
42D2 **Legnica** Pol
36A3 **Le Grand-Luce** France
37A2 **Le Grand Veymont** *Mt* France
26D4 **Legulzamo** Colombia
27G2 **Legvan Inlet** Guyana
60D2 **Leh** India
38C2 **Le Havre** France
19D2 **Lehi** USA
14C2 **Lehigh** *R* USA
14C2 **Lehighton** USA
36D2 **Le Hohneck** *Mt* France
60C2 **Leiah** Pak
42D3 **Leibnitz** Austria
35E5 **Leicester** County, Eng
35E5 **Leicester** Eng
76C2 **Leichhardt** *R* Aust
42A2 **Leiden** Neth
36B1 **Leie** *R* Belg
76C4 **Leigh Creek** Aust
35E6 **Leighton Buzzard** Eng
42B2 **Leine** *R* Germany
35B5 **Leinster** Region, Irish Rep
42C2 **Leipzig** Germany
39A2 **Leiria** Port
32F7 **Leirvik** Nor
52C4 **Leiyang** China
52B5 **Leizhou Bandao** *Pen* China
52C5 **Leizhou Wan** *B* China
42A2 **Lek** *R* Neth
57B3 **Lekitobi** Indon
57C3 **Leksula** Indon
17D3 **Leland** USA
37B3 **Le Lavendou** France
41D2 **Lelija** *Mt* Bosnia & Herzegovina, Yugos
37B1 **Le Locle** France
36A3 **Le Lude** France
22B1 **Lema** *R* Mexico
38C2 **Le Mans** France
11C3 **Le Mars** USA
18D2 **Lemhi Range** *Mts* USA
7M3 **Lemicux Is** Can
8C2 **Lemmon** USA
19D4 **Lemmon,Mt** USA
35G5 **Lemon Bank** *Oilfield* N Sea
19C3 **Lemoore** USA
38C2 **Lempdes** France
61D3 **Lemro** *R* Burma
40D2 **Le Murge** Region, Italy
49O3 **Lena** *R* Russian Fed
37E1 **Lend** Austria
44E3 **Lendery** Russian Fed
52C4 **Lengshujiang** China
45G7 **Leninakan** Armenia
Leningrad = Sankt Peterburg
79F7 **Leningradskaya** *Base* Ant
44J5 **Leninogorsk** Tatar ASSR, Russian Fed
50B1 **Leninogorsk** Kazakhstan
48K4 **Leninsk-Kuznetskiy** Russian Fed
53C2 **Leninskoye** Russian Fed
45H8 **Lenkoran'** Azerbaijan
36E1 **Lenne** *R* Germany
15C1 **Lenoir** USA
14D1 **Lenox** USA
36B1 **Lens** France
49N3 **Lensk** Russian Fed
40C3 **Lentini** Italy
55B3 **Lenya** *R* Burma
71F3 **Léo** Burkina
40C1 **Leoben** Austria
35D5 **Leominster** Eng
14E1 **Leominster** USA
21B2 **Leon** Mexico
26A1 **León** Nic
39A1 **Leon** Region, Spain
39A1 **León** Spain
22C1 **León** State, Mexico
74B1 **Leonardville** Namibia
65C1 **Leonarisso** Cyprus
53E2 **Leonidovo** Russian Fed
76B3 **Leonora** Aust
29D3 **Leopoldina** Brazil
Léopoldville = Kinshasa
44D5 **Lepel** Belorussia
36B1 **Leper** Belg
52D4 **Leping** China
38C2 **Le Puy** France
71F4 **Léraba** *R* Ivory Coast
72B3 **Léré** Chad
74D2 **Leribe** Lesotho
37C2 **Lerici** Italy
39C1 **Lérida** Spain
37D1 **Lermoos** Austria
41F3 **Léros** *I* Greece
14B1 **Le Roy** USA
33C1 **Lerwick** Scot
36A2 **Les Andelys** France
37B3 **Les Arcs** France
23C3 **Les Cayes** Haiti
37A2 **Les Echelles** France
37B2 **Les Ecrins** *Mt* France
5H4 **Les Escoumins** Can
52A4 **Leshan** China
41E2 **Leskovac** Serbia, Yugos
38B3 **Les Landes** Region, France
74D2 **Leslie** S Africa
44J4 **Lesnoy** Russian Fed
53E2 **Lesogorsk** Russian Fed
49L4 **Lesosibirsk** Russian Fed
74D2 **Lesotho** Kingdom, S Africa
53C2 **Lesozavodsk** Russian Fed
38B2 **Les Sables-d'Olonne** France
79E **Lesser Antarctica** Region, Ant
23D4 **Lesser Antilles** *Is* Caribbean
3F2 **Lesser Slave L** Can
37B2 **Les Trois Evêchés** *Mt* France
41F3 **Lésvos** *I* Greece
42D2 **Leszno** Pol
74E1 **Letaba** *R* S Africa
74D1 **Lethakeng** Botswana
61D3 **Letha Range** *Mts* Burma
6G5 **Lethbridge** Can
27G3 **Lethem** Guyana
57C4 **Leti** *I* Indon
43F3 **Letichev** Ukraine
56C2 **Letong** Indon
35F6 **le Touquet-Paris-Plage** France
55B2 **Letpadan** Burma
38C1 **Le Tréport** France
37B1 **Leuk** Switz
42A2 **Leuven** Belg
41E3 **Levádhia** Greece
32G6 **Levanger** Nor
37B2 **Levanna** *Mt* Italy
37C2 **Levanto** Italy
16B3 **Levelland** USA
37B3 **Levens** France
76B2 **Lévêque,C** Aust
36D1 **Leverkusen** Germany
43D3 **Levice** Czech
37D2 **Levico** Italy
78C2 **Levin** NZ
7L5 **Lévis** Can
13E2 **Levittown** USA
41E3 **Lévka Óri** *Mt* Greece
41E3 **Levkás** Greece
41E3 **Levkás** *I* Greece
41F2 **Levski** Bulg
35F6 **Lewes** Eng
16C2 **Lewis** USA
33B2 **Lewis** *I* Scot
14B2 **Lewisburg** USA
78B2 **Lewis P** NZ
5K4 **Lewisporte** Can
8B2 **Lewis Range** *Mts* USA
15B2 **Lewis Smith,L** USA
8B2 **Lewiston** Idaho, USA
9F2 **Lewiston** Maine, USA
8C2 **Lewistown** Montana, USA
13D2 **Lewistown** Pennsylvania, USA
17D3 **Lewisville** USA
9E3 **Lexington** Kentucky, USA
17D2 **Lexington** Missouri, USA
15C1 **Lexington** N Carolina, USA
16C1 **Lexington** Nebraska, USA
13D3 **Lexington** Virginia, USA
13D3 **Lexington Park** USA
57G8 **Leyte G** Phil
41D2 **Lezhe** Alb
59H2 **Lhasa** China
61C2 **Lhazê** China
56A1 **Lhokseumawe** Indon
61D2 **Lhozhag** China
50C4 **Lhunze** China
Liancourt Rocks = Tok-do
57G9 **Lianga** Phil
52B3 **Liangdang** China
52C5 **Lianjiang** China
52C5 **Lianping** China
52C5 **Lian Xian** China
52D3 **Lianyungang** China
52E1 **Liaoding Bandao** *Pen* China
52E1 **Liaodong Wan** *B* China
52E1 **Liao He** *R* China
52E1 **Liaoning** Province, China
52E1 **Liaoyang** China
52E1 **Liaoyuan** China
6F3 **Liard** *R* Can
6F4 **Liard River** Can
36C2 **Liart** France
18C1 **Libby** USA
72B3 **Libenge** Zaïre
8C3 **Liberal** USA
42C2 **Liberec** Czech
70A4 **Liberia** Republic, Africa
17D2 **Liberty** Missouri, USA
13E2 **Liberty** New York, USA
14B2 **Liberty** Pennsylvania, USA
17D3 **Liberty** Texas, USA
38B3 **Libourne** France
22C2 **Libres** Mexico
72A3 **Libreville** Gabon
69A2 **Libya** Republic, Africa
69B2 **Libyan Desert** Libya
69B1 **Libyan Plat** Egypt
40C3 **Licata** Italy
35E5 **Lichfield** Eng
73D5 **Lichinga** Mozam
74D2 **Lichtenburg** S Africa
12C3 **Licking** *R* USA
20B2 **Lick Observatory** USA
44D5 **Lida** Belorussia
20D2 **Lida** USA
32G7 **LidKöping** Sweden
40C2 **Lido di Ostia** Italy
40B1 **Liechtenstein** Principality, Europe
42B2 **Liège** Belg
43E1 **Lielupe** *R* Latvia
72C3 **Lienart** Zaïre
42C3 **Lienz** Austria
32J7 **Liepāja** Latvia
36C1 **Lier** Belg
37B1 **Liestal** Switz
42C3 **Liezen** Austria
35B5 **Liffey** *R* Irish Rep
34B4 **Lifford** Irish Rep
77F3 **Lifu** *I* Nouvelle Calédonie
75C1 **Lightning Ridge** Aust
36C2 **Ligny-en-Barrois** France
73D5 **Ligonha** *R* Mozam
37C2 **Liguria** Region, Italy
40B2 **Ligurian** *S* Italy
77E1 **Lihir Group** *Is* PNG
20E5 **Lihue** Hawaiian Is
73C5 **Likasi** Zaïre
57C2 **Likupang** Indon
38C1 **Lille** France
36A2 **Lillebonne** France
32G6 **Lillehammer** Nor
36B1 **Lillers** France
32G6 **Lillestøm** Nor
3D3 **Lillooet** Can
3D3 **Lillooet** *R* Can
73D5 **Lilongwe** Malawi
57F9 **Liloy** Phil
41D2 **Lim** *R* Montenegro/Serbia, Yugos
26C6 **Lima** Peru
39A1 **Lima** Spain
9E2 **Lima** USA
18D2 **Lima Res** USA

64B3 Limassol Cyprus
34B4 Limavady N Ire
28B3 Limay *R* Arg
28B3 Limay Mahuida Arg
73D5 Limbe Malawi
57B2 Limbotto Indon
42B2 Limburg W Gem
27J8 Limeira Brazil
33B3 Limerick Irish Rep
42B1 Limfjorden *L* Den
76C2 Limmen Bight *B* Aust
41F3 Límnos *I* Greece
27L5 Limoeiro Brazil
38C2 Limoges France
21D4 Limón Costa Rica
8C3 Limon USA
37B2 Limone Italy
38C2 Limousin Region, France
74E1 Limpopo *R* Mozam
22C1 Linanes Mexico
57E8 Linapacan Str Phil
25B5 Linares Chile
8D4 Linares Mexico
39B2 Linares Spain
50C4 Lincang China
25D4 Lincoln Arg
17C1 Lincoln California, USA
35E5 Lincoln County, Eng
35E5 Lincoln Eng
12B2 Lincoln Illinois, USA
13F1 Lincoln Maine, USA
8D2 Lincoln Nebraska, USA
13E2 Lincoln New Hampshire, USA
78B2 Lincoln NZ
79A Lincoln *S* Greenland
18B2 Lincoln City USA
12C2 Lincoln Park USA
40B2 L'Incudina *Mt* Corse
42B3 Lindau Germany
27G2 Linden Guyana
32F7 Lindesnes *C* Nor
73D4 Lindi Tanz
72C3 Lindi *R* Zaïre
74D2 Lindley S Africa
41F3 Lindos Greece
4F5 Lindsay Can
20C2 Lindsay California, USA
11A2 Lindsay Montana, USA
xxixM4 Line Is Pacific O
52C2 Linfen China
55D2 Lingao China
57F7 Lingayen Phil
42B2 Lingen Germany
11B3 Lingle USA
52C4 Lingling China
52B5 Lingshan China
52C2 Lingshi China
70A3 Linguère Sen
53A1 Linhai Heilongjiang, China
52E4 Linhai Rhejiang, China
27L7 Linhares Brazil
52B1 Linhe China
53B3 Linjiang China
32H7 Linköping Sweden
53C2 Linkou China
52D2 Linqing China
29C3 Lins Brazil
52A2 Lintao China
37C1 Linthal Switz
11B2 Linton USA
50E2 Linxi China
52A2 Linxia China
42C3 Linz Austria
57F8 Lipa Phil
40C3 Lipari *I* Italy
45F5 Lipetsk Russian Fed
41E1 Lipova Rom
42B2 Lippe *R* Germany
36E1 Lippstadt Germany
72D3 Lira Uganda
72B4 Liranga Congo
72C3 Lisala Zaïre
39A2 Lisboa Port
Lisbon = Lisboa
11C2 Lisbon USA
35B4 Lisburn N Ire
10E2 Lisburne,C USA
52D4 Lishui China
52C4 Li Shui *R* China
45F6 Lisichansk Ukraine
38C2 Lisieux France
45F5 Liski Russian Fed
36B2 L'Isle-Adam France
37B1 L'Isle-sur-le-Doubs France
77E3 Lismore Aust
52B5 Litang China
65C2 Lītanī *R* Leb
27H3 Litani *R* Surinam
12B3 Litchfield Illinois, USA
11D2 Litchfield Minnesota, USA
76E4 Lithgow Aust
44C4 Lithuania *Republic* Europe
14B2 Lititz USA
53E1 Litke Russian Fed
53D2 Litovko Russian Fed
17C3 Little *R* USA
9F4 Little Abaco *I* Bahamas
66D4 Little Aden Yemen
62E2 Little Andaman *I* Andaman Is
78C1 Little Barrier I NZ
18D1 Little Belt Mts USA
65B3 Little Bitter L Egypt
3F3 Little Bow *R* Can
21D3 Little Cayman *I* Caribbean
4D3 Little Current Can
4E4 Little Current Can
14C3 Little Egg Harbor *B* USA
11D2 Little Falls Minnesota, USA
14C1 Little Falls New York, USA
16B3 Littlefield USA
11D2 Littlefork USA
11D2 Little Fork *R* USA
4B3 Little Grand Rapids Can
34E2 Little Halibut Bank *Sandbank* Scot
23C2 Little Inagua *I* Caribbean
74C3 Little Karroo *R* S Africa
10G4 Little Koniuji *I* USA
20D3 Little Lake USA
11B2 Little Missouri *R* USA
55A4 Little Nicobar *I* Nicobar Is
9D3 Little Rock USA
20D3 Littlerock USA
10B6 Little Sitkin *I* USA
3E3 Little Smoky Can
3E3 Little Smoky *R* Can
14B3 Littlestown USA
10C6 Little Tanaga *I* USA
16A2 Littleton Colorado, USA
13E2 Littleton New Hampshire, USA
53B3 Liuhe China
52B5 Liuzhou China
41E3 Livanátais Greece
43F1 Līvāni Latvia
36A2 Livarot France
10J2 Livengood USA
37E2 Livenza *R* Italy
15C2 Live Oak USA
19B3 Livermore USA
16B3 Livermore,Mt USA
7M5 Liverpool Can
35D5 Liverpool Eng
6E2 Liverpool B Can
35D5 Liverpool B Eng
7L2 Liverpool,C Can
75D2 Liverpool Range *Mts* Aust
8B2 Livingston Montana, USA
15B1 Livingston Tennessee, USA
17D3 Livingston Texas, USA
73C5 Livingstone Zambia
17C3 Livingston,L USA
40D2 Livno Bosnia & Herzegovina, Yugos
45F5 Livny Russian Fed
12C2 Livonia USA
40C2 Livorno Italy
29D1 Livramento do Brumado Brazil
73D4 Liwale Tanz
35C7 Lizard Pt Eng
40C1 Ljubljana Slovenia, Yugos
32G6 Ljungan *R* Sweden
32G7 Ljungby Sweden
32H6 Ljusdal Sweden
44B3 Ljusnan *R* Sweden
35D6 Llandeilo Wales
35D6 Llandovery Wales
35D5 Llandrindod Wells Wales
35D5 Llandudno Wales
35C6 Llanelli Wales
35D5 Llangollen Wales
16C3 Llano USA
16C3 Llano *R* USA
8C3 Llano Estacado *Plat* USA
Z4D2 Llanos Region, Colombia/ Ven
26F7 Llanos de Chiquitos Region, Bol
Lleida = Lérida
22C1 Llera Mexico
39A2 Llerena Spain
35C5 Lleyn *Pen* Wales
68E7 Llorin Nigeria
3C2 Lloyd George,Mt Can
3G2 Lloyd L Can
6H4 Lloydminster Can
25C2 Llullaillaco *Mt* Chile/Arg
25C2 Loa *R* Chile
38C2 Loan France
72B4 Loange *R* Zaïre
74D2 Lobatse Botswana
72B3 Lobaye *R* CAR
28D3 Loberia Arg
73B5 Lobito Angola
28D3 Lobos Arg
37B2 Locano Italy
37C1 Locarno Switz
34C3 Loch Awe *L* Scot
34B3 Lochboisdale Scot
34B3 Loch Bracadale *Inlet* Scot
34C3 Loch Broom *Estuary* Scot
34C4 Loch Doon *L* Scot
34C3 Loch Earn *L* Scot
34C2 Loch Eriboll *Inlet* Scot
34C3 Loch Ericht *L* Scot
38C2 Loches France
34C3 Loch Etive *Inlet* Scot
34C3 Loch Ewe *Inlet* Scot
34C3 Loch Fyne *Inlet* Scot
34C3 Loch Hourn *Inlet* Scot
34B4 Loch Indaal *Inlet* Scot
34C2 Lochinver Scot
34C3 Loch Katrine *L* Scot
34D3 Loch Leven *L* Scot
34C3 Loch Linnhe *Inlet* Scot
34C3 Loch Lochy *L* Scot
34C3 Loch Lomond *L* Scot
34C3 Loch Long *Inlet* Scot
34B3 Lochmaddy Scot
34C3 Loch Maree *L* Scot
34C3 Loch Morar *L* Scot
34D3 Lochnagar *Mt* Scot
34C3 Loch Ness *L* Scot
34C3 Loch Rannoch *L* Scot
34B2 Loch Roag *Inlet* Scot
18C1 Lochsa *R* USA
34C3 Loch Sheil *L* Scot
34C2 Loch Shin *L* Scot
34B3 Loch Snizort *Inlet* Scot
34C3 Loch Sunart *Inlet* Scot
34C3 Loch Tay *L* Scot
34C3 Loch Torridon *Inlet* Scot
75A2 Lock Aust
5H5 Lockeport Can
34D4 Lockerbie Scot
13D2 Lock Haven USA
13D2 Lockport USA
55D3 Loc Ninh Viet
40D3 Locri Italy
65C3 Lod Israel
75B3 Loddon *R* Aust
44E3 Lodeynoye Pole Russian Fed
18E1 Lodge Grass USA
60C3 Lodhran Pak
40B1 Lodi Italy
19B3 Lodi USA
72C4 Lodja Zaïre
37B1 Lods France
72D3 Lodwar Kenya
43D2 Łódź Pol
74B3 Loeriesfontein S Africa
37E1 Lofer Austria
32G5 Lofoten *Is* Nor
16B2 Logan New Mexico, USA
8B2 Logan Utah, USA
6D3 Logan,Mt Can
10N3 Logan Mts Can
12B2 Logansport Indiana, USA
17D3 Logansport Louisiana, USA
14B2 Loganton USA
39B1 Logroño Spain
61B3 Lohārdaga India
32J6 Lohja Fin
36E2 Lohr Germany
55B2 Loikaw Burma
32J6 Loimaa Fin
36B2 Loing *R* France
38C2 Loir *R* France
36A3 Loir et Cher Department, France
38C2 Loire *R* France
36B3 Loiret Department, France
26C4 Loja Ecuador
39B2 Loja Spain
57C3 Loji Indon
32K5 Lokan Tekojärvi *Res* Fin
36B1 Lokeren Belg
72D3 Lokitaung Kenya
43F1 Loknya Russian Fed
71H4 Lokoja Nig
72C4 Lokolo *R* Zaïre
72C4 Lokoro *R* Zaïre
7M3 Loks Land *I* Can
42C2 Lolland *I* Den
57C2 Loloda Indon
18D1 Lolo P USA
41E2 Lom Bulg
71J4 Lom *R* Cam
73C4 Lomami *R* Zaïre
70A4 Loma Mts Sierra Leone/ Guinea
57B2 Lombagin Indon
37C2 Lombardia Region, Italy
57B4 Lomblen *I* Indon
56E4 Lombok *I* Indon
71G4 Lomé Togo
72C4 Lomela Zaïre
72C4 Lomela *R* Zaïre
34G3 Lomond *Oilfield* N Sea
44D4 Lomonosov Russian Fed
37B1 Lomont Region, France
19B4 Lompoc USA
43E2 Łomza Pol
62A1 Lonāvale India
25B5 Loncoche Chile
7K5 London Can
35E6 London Eng
12C3 London USA
34B4 Londonderry County, N Ire
34B4 Londonderry N Ire
25B9 Londonderry *I* Chile
76B2 Londonderry,C Aust
25C3 Londres Arg
25F2 Londrina Brazil
20D1 Lone Mt USA
20C2 Lone Pine USA
9F4 Long *I* Bahamas
51H7 Long *I* PNG
56D2 Long Akah Malay
37E1 Longarone Italy
28A3 Longavi *Mt* Chile
23H2 Long B Jamaica
15D2 Long B USA
8B3 Long Beach California, USA
13E2 Long Beach New York, USA
13E2 Long Branch USA
52D5 Longchuan China
18C2 Long Creek USA
75E3 Longford Aust
35B5 Longford County, Irish Rep
35B5 Longford Irish Rep
34E3 Long Forties *Region* N Sea
52D1 Longhua China
7L4 Long I Can
76D1 Long I PNG
9F2 Long I USA
14D2 Long Island Sd USA
53A2 Longjiang China
4D4 Long L Can
11B2 Long L USA
7K5 Longlac Can
52B5 Longlin China
8C2 Longmont USA
56E2 Longnawan Indon
36C2 Longny France
11D2 Long Prairie USA
25B5 Longquimay Chile
5K4 Long Range Mts Can
76D3 Longreach Aust
52A2 Longshou Shan *Upland* China
16A1 Longs Peak *Mt* USA
34D4 Longtown Eng
13E1 Longueuil Can
28A3 Longuimay Chile
36C2 Longuyon France
9D3 Longview Texas, USA
8A2 Longview Washington, USA
38D2 Longwy France
52A3 Longxi China
55D3 Long Xuyen Viet
52D4 Longyan China
52B5 Longzhou China
37D2 Lonigo Italy
38D2 Lons-le-Saunier France
9F3 Lookout,C USA
72D4 Loolmalasin *Mt* Tanz
3E2 Loon *R* Can
55C3 Lop Buri Thai
72A4 Lopez *C* Gabon
50C2 Lop Nur *L* China
39A2 Lora del Rio Spain
9E2 Lorain USA
60B2 Loralai Pak
63C2 Lordegān Iran
77E4 Lord Howe *I* Aust
xxixK5 Lord Howe Rise Pacific O
7J3 Lord Mayor B Can
8C3 Lordsburg USA
29C3 Lorena Brazil
37E2 Loreo Italy
22B1 Loreto Mexico
38B2 Lorient France
75B3 Lorne Aust
42B3 Lörrach Germany
38D2 Lorraine *Region* France
8C3 Los Alamos USA
28A2 Los Andes Chile
25B5 Los Angeles Chile
8B3 Los Angeles USA
20C3 Los Angeles Aqueduct USA
19B3 Los Banos USA
28B2 Los Cerrillos Arg
22A1 Los Corchos Mexico
19B3 Los Gatos USA
40C2 Lozinj *I* Croatia, Yugos
28C1 Los Juries Arg
28A3 Los Lagos Chile
22C1 Los Laiaderoz Mexico
28A1 Los Loros Chile
16A3 Los Luncas USA
28B4 Los Menucos Arg
21B2 Los Mochis Mexico
20B3 Los Olivos USA
28A3 Los Sauces Chile
34D3 Lossiemouth Scot
28C1 Los Telares Arg
23E4 Los Testigos *Is* Ven
20C3 Lost Hills USA
18D1 Lost Trail P USA
25B4 Los Vilos Chile
38C3 Lot *R* France
28A3 Lota Chile
34D4 Lothian Region, Scot
72D3 Lotikipi Plain Sudan/Kenya
72C4 Loto Zaïre
74D1 Lotsane *R* Botswana
37B1 Lötschberg Tunnel Switz
32K5 Lotta *R* Fin/Russian Fed
38B2 Loudéac France
70A3 Louga Sen
33B3 Lough Allen *L* Irish Rep
35E5 Loughborough Eng
33B3 Lough Conn *L* Irish Rep
33B3 Lough Corrib *L* Irish Rep
33B3 Lough Derg *L* Irish Rep
6H2 Lougheed I Can
35B5 Lough Ennell *L* Irish Rep
33B3 Lough Erne *L* N Ire
33B2 Lough Foyle *Estuary* N Ire/ Irish Rep
33B3 Lough Neagh *L* N Ire
33B3 Lough Ree *L* Irish Rep
35C4 Lough Strangford *L* Irish Rep
34B4 Lough Swilly *Estuary* Irish Rep
37A1 Louhans France
12C3 Louisa USA
56D1 Louisa Reef *I* S E Asia
10M5 Louise *I* Can
10J3 Louise,L USA
77E2 Louisiade Arch Solomon Is
9D3 Louisiana State, USA
74D1 Louis Trichardt S Africa
15C2 Louisville Georgia, USA
9E3 Louisville Kentucky, USA
15B2 Louisville Mississippi, USA
44E2 Loukhi Russian Fed
11D1 Lount L Can
37B3 Loup *R* France
16C1 Loup *R* USA
38B3 Lourdes France
75C2 Louth Aust
35B5 Louth County, Irish Rep
35E5 Louth Eng
Louvain = Leuven
38C2 Louviers France
44E4 Lovat *R* Russian Fed
41E2 Lovech Bulg
16A1 Loveland USA
16A2 Loveland P USA
18E2 Lovell USA
19C2 Lovelock USA
40C1 Lóvere Italy
16B3 Lovington USA
44F2 Lovozero Russian Fed
7K3 Low,C Can
9F2 Lowell Massachusetts, USA
18B2 Lowell Oregon, USA
14E1 Lowell USA
18C1 Lower Arrow L Can
78B2 Lower Hutt NZ
20A1 Lower Lake USA
10N4 Lower Post Can
11C2 Lower Red L USA
35F5 Lowestoft Eng
43D2 Lowicz Pol
75B2 Loxton Aust
74C3 Loxton S Africa
14B2 Loyalsock Creek *R* USA
41D2 Loznica Serbia, Yugos
22B2 loz Reyes Mexico
48H3 Lozva *R* Russian Fed
73C5 Luacano Angola
73C4 Luachimo Angola
72C4 Lualaba *R* Zaïre
73C5 Luampa Zambia
73C5 Luân Angola
52D3 Lu'an China
73B4 Luanda Angola
73B5 Luando *R* Angola
73C5 Luanginga *R* Angola
55C1 Luang Namtha Laos
55C2 Luang Prabang Laos
73B4 Luangue *R* Angola
73D5 Luangwa *R* Zambia
52D1 Luan He *R* China
52D1 Luanping China
73C5 Luanshya Zambia
73C5 Luapula *R* Zaïre
39A1 Luarca Spain
73B4 Lubalo Angola
43F2 L'uban Belorussia
57F8 Lubang Is Phil
73B5 Lubango Angola
8C3 Lubbock USA
42C2 Lübeck Germany
72C4 Lubefu Zaïre

72C4 **Lubefu** *R* Zaïre
72C3 **Lubero** Zaïre
37A3 **Lubéron** *R* France
73C4 **Lubilash** *R* Zaïre
43E2 **Lublin** Pol
45E5 **Lubny** Ukraine
56D2 **Lubok Antu** Malay
73C4 **Lubudi** Zaïre
73C4 **Lubudi** *R* Zaïre
56B3 **Lubuklinggau** Indon
73C5 **Lubumbashi** Zaïre
72C4 **Lubutu** Zaïre
29A1 **Lucas** Brazil
57F8 **Lucban** Phil
40C2 **Lucca** Italy
34C4 **Luce** *B* Scot
17E3 **Lucedale** USA
57F8 **Lucena** Phil
43D3 **Lucenec** Czech
Lucerne = Luzern
16A3 **Lucero** Mexico
53C2 **Luchegorsk** Russian Fed
52C5 **Luchuan** China
20B2 **Lucia** USA
42C2 **Luckenwalde** Germany
74C2 **Luckhoff** S Africa
61B2 **Lucknow** India
73C5 **Lucusse** Angola
50E2 **Lüda** China
36D1 **Lüdenscheid** Germany
74B2 **Lüderitz** Namibia
60D2 **Ludhiana** India
12B2 **Ludington** USA
19C4 **Ludlow** California, USA
35D5 **Ludlow** Eng
14D1 **Ludlow** Vermont, USA
41F2 **Ludogorie** *Upland* Bulg
15C2 **Ludowici** USA
41E1 **Luduş** Rom
32H6 **Ludvika** Sweden
42B3 **Ludwigsburg** Germany
42B3 **Ludwigshafen** Germany
42C2 **Ludwigslust** Germany
72C4 **Luebo** Zaïre
72C4 **Luema** *R* Zaïre
73C4 **Luembe** *R* Angola
73B5 **Luena** Angola
73C5 **Luene** *R* Angola
52B3 **Lüeyang** China
52D5 **Lufeng** China
9D3 **Lufkin** USA
44D4 **Luga** Russian Fed
44D4 **Luga** *R* Russian Fed
40B1 **Lugano** Switz
45F6 **Lugansk** Ukraine
73D5 **Lugela** Mozam
73D5 **Lugenda** *R* Mozam
37D2 **Lugo** Italy
39A1 **Lugo** Spain
41E1 **Lugoj** Rom
52A3 **Luhuo** China
73B4 **Lui** *R* Angola
73C5 **Luiana** Angola
73C5 **Luiana** *R* Angola
Luichow Peninsula = Leizhou Bandao
37C2 **Luino** Italy
72B3 **Luionga** *R* Zaïre
52B2 **Luipan Shan** *Upland* China
44D2 **Luiro** *R* Fin
73C5 **Luishia** Zaïre
50C4 **Luixi** China
73C4 **Luiza** Zaïre
28B2 **Luján** Arg
28D2 **Luján** Arg
52D3 **Lujiang** China
72B4 **Lukenie** *R* Zaïre
19D4 **Lukeville** USA
72B4 **Lukolela** Zaïre
43E2 **Łuków** Pol
72C4 **Lukuga** *R* Zaïre
73C5 **Lukulu** Zambia
44C2 **Lule** *R* Sweden
32J5 **Luleå** Sweden
41F2 **Lüleburgaz** Turk
52C2 **Lüliang Shan** *Mts* China
17C4 **Luling** USA
26E8 **Lullaillaco** *Mt* Chile
72C3 **Lulonga** *R* Zaïre
Luluabourg = Kananga
73C5 **Lumbala Kaquengue** Angola
9F3 **Lumberton** USA
56E2 **Lumbis** Indon
44G2 **Lumbovka** Russian Fed
61D2 **Lumding** India
73C5 **Lumeje** Angola
78A3 **Lumsden** NZ
32G7 **Lund** Sweden
11C1 **Lundar** Can
73D5 **Lundazi** Zambia
73D6 **Lundi** *R* Zim
35C6 **Lundy** *I* Eng
42C2 **Lüneburg** Germany
36D2 **Lunéville** France
73C5 **Lunga** *R* Zambia
61D3 **Lunglei** India
73B5 **Lungue Bungo** *R* Angola
43F2 **Luninec** Belorussia
20C1 **Luning** USA
53C2 **Luobei** China
72B4 **Luobomo** Congo
52B5 **Luocheng** China
52C5 **Luoding** China
52C3 **Luohe** China
52C3 **Luo He** *R* Henan, China
52B2 **Luo He** *R* Shaanxi, China
52C4 **Luoxiao Shan** *Hills* China
52C3 **Luoyang** China
72B4 **Luozi** Zaïre
73C5 **Lupane** Zim
73D5 **Lupilichi** Mozam
Lu Qu = Tao He
25E3 **Luque** Par
36D3 **Lure** France
35B4 **Lurgan** N Ire
73D5 **Lurio** *R* Mozam
63B2 **Luristan** Region, Iran
73C5 **Lusaka** Zambia
72C4 **Lusambo** Zaïre
41D2 **Lushnjë** Alb
72D4 **Lushoto** Tanz
50C4 **Lushui** China
52E2 **Lüshun** China
11B3 **Lusk** USA
35E6 **Luton** Eng
45D5 **Lutsk** Ukraine
72E3 **Luuq** Somalia
11C3 **Luverne** USA
73C4 **Luvua** *R* Zaïre
73D4 **Luwegu** *R* Tanz
73D5 **Luwingu** Zambia
57B3 **Luwuk** Indon
36D2 **Luxembourg** Grand Duchy, N W Europe
38D2 **Luxembourg** Lux
36D3 **Luxeuil-les-Bains** France
52A5 **Luxi** China
69C2 **Luxor** Egypt
44H3 **Luza** Russian Fed
44H3 **Luza** *R* Russian Fed
40B1 **Luzern** Switz
14D1 **Luzerne** USA
52B5 **Luzhai** China
52B4 **Luzhi** China
52B4 **Luzhou** China
29C2 **Luziânia** Brazil
57F7 **Luzon** *I* Phil
57F6 **Luzon Str** Phil
43E3 **L'vov** Ukraine
34D2 **Lybster** Scot
32H6 **Lycksele** Sweden
73C6 **Lydenburg** S Africa
3B3 **Lyell I** Can
8B3 **Lyell,Mt** USA
14B2 **Lykens** USA
18D2 **Lyman** USA
35D6 **Lyme B** Eng
35D6 **Lyme Regis** Eng
9F3 **Lynchburg** USA
75A2 **Lyndhurst** Aust
13E2 **Lynn** USA
3A2 **Lynn Canal** *Sd* USA
15B2 **Lynn Haven** USA
3H2 **Lynn Lake** Can
4D3 **Lynx** Can
6H3 **Lynx L** Can
38C2 **Lyon** France
10L4 **Lyon Canal** *Sd* USA
15C2 **Lyons** Georgia, USA
14B1 **Lyons** New York, USA
76A3 **Lyons** *R* Aust
37B2 **Lys** *R* Italy
44K4 **Lys'va** Russian Fed
78B2 **Lyttelton** NZ
3D3 **Lytton** Can
20A1 **Lytton** USA
43F2 **Lyubeshov** Ukraine
44F4 **Lyublino** Russian Fed

M

55C1 **Ma** *R* Viet
65C2 **Ma'agan** Jordan
65C2 **Ma'alot Tarshīha** Israel
64C3 **Ma'an** Jordan
52D3 **Ma'anshan** China
65D1 **Ma'arrat an Nu'mān** Syria
36C1 **Maas** *R* Neth
36C1 **Maaseik** Belg
57F8 **Maasin** Phil
42B2 **Maastricht** Belg
74E1 **Mabalane** Mozam
27G2 **Mabaruma** Guyana
35F5 **Mablethorpe** Eng
73D6 **Mabote** Mozam
43E2 **Mabrita** Belorussia
43F2 **M'adel** Belorussia
29D3 **Macaé** Brazil
8D3 **McAlester** USA
8D4 **McAllen** USA
73D5 **Macaloge** Mozam
52C5 **Macao** Dependency, China
27H3 **Macapá** Brazil
29D2 **Macarani** Brazil
26C4 **Macas** Ecuador
27L5 **Macaú** Brazil
29D1 **Macaúbas** Brazil
72C3 **M'Bari** *R* CAR
3D3 **McBride** Can
18C2 **McCall** USA
16B3 **McCamey** USA
18D2 **McCammon** USA
10K3 **McCarthy** USA
3B3 **McCauley I** Can
35D5 **Macclesfield** Eng
7K1 **McClintock B** Can
6H2 **McClintock Chan** Can
14B2 **McClure** USA
20B2 **McClure,L** USA
6G2 **McClure Str** Can
17D3 **McComb** USA
16B1 **McConaughy,L** USA
14B3 **McConnellsburg** USA
8C2 **McCook** USA
7L2 **Macculloch,C** Can
3D2 **McCusker,Mt** Can
6F4 **McDame** Can
18C2 **McDermitt** USA
4D4 **Macdiarmid** Can
18D1 **Mcdonald Peak** *Mt* USA
76C3 **Macdonnell Ranges** *Mts* Aust
39A1 **Macedo de Cavaleiros** Port
41E2 **Macedonia** *Republic* Serbia, Yugos
27L5 **Maceió** Brazil
70B4 **Macenta** Guinea
40C2 **Macerata** Italy
3G2 **Macfarlane** *R* Can
75A2 **Macfarlane,L** Aust
17D3 **McGehee** USA
19D3 **McGill** USA
6C3 **McGrath** USA
18D1 **McGuire,Mt** USA
29C3 **Machado** Brazil
73D6 **Machaíla** Mozam
72D4 **Machakos** Kenya
26C4 **Machala** Ecuador
73D6 **Machaze** Mozam
62B1 **Mācherla** India
65C2 **Machgharab** Leb
13F2 **Machias** USA
4C2 **Machichi** *R* Can
62C1 **Machilīpatnam** India
26D1 **Machiques** Ven
26D6 **Machu-Picchu** *Hist Site* Peru
73D6 **Macia** Mozam
Macias Nguema = Fernando Poo
11B2 **McIntosh** USA
75C1 **MacIntyre** *R* Aust
16A2 **Mack** USA
76D3 **Mackay** Aust
18D2 **Mackay** USA
76B3 **Mackay,L** Aust
77H1 **McKean** *I* Phoenix Is
13D2 **McKeesport** USA
3D2 **Mackenzie** Can
6F3 **Mackenzie** *R* Can
6E3 **Mackenzie B** Can
6G2 **Mackenzie King I** Can
6E3 **Mackenzie Mts** Can
12C1 **Mackinac,Str of** USA
12C1 **Mackinaw City** USA
10H3 **McKinley,Mt** USA
17C3 **McKinney** USA
7L2 **Mackinson Inlet** *B* Can
20C3 **McKittrick** USA
75D2 **Macksville** Aust
18B2 **Mclaoughlin,Mt** USA
11B2 **McLaughlin** USA
75D1 **Maclean** Aust
74D3 **Maclear** S Africa
6G4 **McLennan** Can
3E3 **McLeod** *R* Can
6G3 **McLeod B** Can
76A3 **McLeod,L** Aust
3D2 **McLeod Lake** Can
6E3 **Macmillan** *R* Can
16B3 **McMillan,L** USA
10M3 **Macmillan P** Can
18B1 **McMinnville** Oregon, USA
15B1 **McMinnville** Tennessee, USA
79F7 **McMurdo** *Base* Ant
3C2 **McNamara,Mt** Can
19E4 **McNary** USA
3E3 **McNaughton L** Can
12A2 **Macomb** USA
40B2 **Macomer** Sardegna
73D5 **Macomia** Mozam
38C2 **Mâcon** France
9E3 **Macon** Georgia, USA
17D2 **Macon** Missouri, USA
73C5 **Macondo** Angola
3H2 **Macoun L** Can
17C2 **McPherson** USA
xxviiiJ7 **Macquarie** *Is* Aust
75C2 **Macquarie** *R* Aust
75E3 **Macquarie Harbour** *B* Aust
75D2 **Macquarie,L** Aust
15C2 **McRae** USA
79F11 **Mac Robertson Land** Region, Ant
71E1 **M'saken** Tunisia
71C1 **M'Sila** Alg
6G3 **McTavish Arm** *B* Can
75A1 **Macumba** *R* Aust
37C2 **Macunaga** Italy
6F3 **McVicar Arm** *B* Can
42D3 **M'yaróvár** Hung
71H4 **Mada** *R* Nig
65C3 **Mādabā** Jordan
72C2 **Madadi** *Well* Chad
68J9 **Madagascar** *I* Indian O
xxviiiD6 **Madagascar Basin** Indian O
72B1 **Madama** Niger
76D1 **Madang** PNG
70C3 **Madaoua** Niger
61D3 **Madaripur** Bang
63C1 **Madau** Turkmenistan
5H4 **Madawaska** USA
13D1 **Madawaska** *R* Can
61E3 **Madaya** Burma
70A1 **Madeira** *I* Atlantic O
26F5 **Madeira** *R* Brazil
7M5 **Madeleine, Îles de la** Can
11D3 **Madelia** USA
21B2 **Madera** Mexico
19B3 **Madera** USA
62A1 **Madgaon** India
61C2 **Madhubani** India
61B3 **Madhya Pradesh** State, India
62B2 **Madikeri** India
72B4 **Madimba** Zaïre
72B4 **Madingo Kayes** Congo
72B4 **Madingou** Congo
9E3 **Madison** Indiana, USA
11C2 **Madison** Minnesota, USA
11C3 **Madison** Nebraska, USA
11C3 **Madison** S Dakota, USA
9E2 **Madison** Wisconsin, USA
18D1 **Madison** *R* USA
12B3 **Madisonville** Kentucky, USA
17C3 **Madisonville** Texas, USA
56D4 **Madiun** Indon
4F5 **Madoc** Can
72D3 **Mado Gashi** Kenya
37D1 **Madonna Di Campiglio** Italy
62C2 **Madras** India
18B2 **Madras** USA
25A8 **Madre de Dios** *I* Chile
26E6 **Madre de Dios** *R* Bol
39B1 **Madrid** Spain
39B2 **Madridejos** Spain
56D4 **Madura** *I* Indon
62B3 **Madurai** India
54C3 **Maebashi** Japan
55B3 **Mae Khlong** *R* Thai
55B4 **Mae Nam Lunang** *R* Thai
55C2 **Mae Nam Mun** *R* Thai
55B2 **Mae Nam Ping** *R* Thai
54A3 **Maengsan** N Korea
73E5 **Maevatanana** Madag
77F2 **Maewo** *I* Vanuatu
74D2 **Mafeking** S Africa
74D2 **Mafeteng** Lesotho
75C3 **Maffra** Aust
73D4 **Mafia** *I* Tanz
25G3 **Mafra** Brazil
64C3 **Mafraq** Jordan
49R4 **Magadan** Russian Fed
26D2 **Magargué** Colombia
71H3 **Magaria** Niger
53B1 **Magdagachi** Russian Fed
28D3 **Magdalena** Arg
8B3 **Magdalena** Mexico
16A3 **Magdalena** USA
23C4 **Magdalena** *R* Colombia
56E2 **Magdalena,Mt** Malay
42C2 **Magdeburg** Germany
26D2 **Magdelena** *R* Colombia
27K8 **Magé** Brazil
56D4 **Magelang** Indon
37C1 **Maggia** *R* Switz
64B4 **Maghâgha** Egypt
34B4 **Magherafelt** N Ire
41D2 **Maglie** Italy
44K5 **Magnitogorsk** Russian Fed
17D3 **Magnolia** USA
53E1 **Mago** Russian Fed
13E1 **Magog** Can
22C1 **Magosal** Mexico
5J3 **Magpie** *R* Can
37C2 **Magra** *R* Italy
3F3 **Magrath** Can
20D2 **Magruder Mt** USA
74E2 **Magude** Mozam
7J3 **Maguse River** Can
55B1 **Magwe** Burma
45H8 **Mahābād** Iran
61C2 **Mahabharat Range** *Mts* Nepal
62A1 **Mahād** India
60D4 **Mahadeo Hills** India
14A2 **Mahaffey** USA
73E5 **Mahajanga** Madag
74D1 **Mahalapye** Botswana
61B3 **Mahānadi** *R* India
73E5 **Mahanoro** Madag
14B2 **Mahanoy City** USA
62A1 **Maharashtra** State, India
61B3 **Māhāsamund** India
55C2 **Maha Sarakham** Thai
73E5 **Mahavavy** *R* Madag
62B1 **Mahbūbnagar** India
71E1 **Mahdia** Tunisia
62B2 **Mahe** India
60D4 **Mahekar** India
61B3 **Mahendragarh** India
73D4 **Mahenge** Tanz
60C4 **Mahesāna** India
78C1 **Mahia Pen** NZ
11C2 **Mahnomen** USA
60D3 **Mahoba** India
39C2 **Mahón** Spain
5J5 **Mahone B** Can
10N2 **Mahony L** Can
71E2 **Mahrés** Tunisia
60C4 **Mahuva** India
26D1 **Maicao** Colombia
37B1 **Maîche** France
66C4 **Maichew** Eth
35F6 **Maidstone** Eng
72B2 **Maiduguri** Nig
44B3 **Maigomaj** *R* Sweden
61B3 **Maihar** India
61D3 **Maijdi** Bang
55B3 **Mail Kyun** *I* Burma
60A1 **Maimana** Afghan
36E2 **Main** *R* Germany
4E4 **Main Chan** Can
72B4 **Mai-Ndombe** *L* Zaïre
9G2 **Maine** State, USA
36A3 **Maine** *Region* France
71J3 **Mainé-Soroa** Niger
34D2 **Mainland** *I* Scot
60D3 **Mainpuri** India
36A2 **Maintenon** France
73E5 **Maintirano** Madag
42B2 **Mainz** Germany
70A4 **Maio** *I* Cape Verde
25C4 **Maipó** *Mt* Arg/Chile
28D3 **Maipú** Arg
26E1 **Maiquetía** Ven
37B2 **Maira** *R* Italy
61D2 **Mairābāri** India
61D3 **Maiskhal I** Bang
76E4 **Maitland** New South Wales, Aust
75A2 **Maitland** S Australia, Aust
79F12 **Maitri** *Base* Ant
38D1 **Maiz** Germany
53D4 **Maizuru** Japan
76A1 **Majene** Indon
26D7 **Majes** *R* Peru
72D3 **Maji** Eth
52D2 **Majia He** *R* China
Majunga = Mahajanga
72D2 **Makale** Eth
57A3 **Makale** Indon
56B3 **Makalo** Indon
61C2 **Makalu** *Mt* China/Nepal
44K2 **Makarikha** Russian Fed
53E2 **Makarov** Russian Fed
40D2 **Makarska** Croatia, Yugos
44G4 **Makaryev** Russian Fed
Makassar Ujung Pandang
56E3 **Makassar Str** Indon
45J6 **Makat** Kazakhstan
70A4 **Makeni** Sierra Leone
45F6 **Makeyevka** Ukraine
73C6 **Makgadikgadi** *Salt Pan* Botswana
45H7 **Makhachkala** Russian Fed
64D1 **Makharadze** Georgia
57C2 **Makian** *I* Indon
72D4 **Makindu** Kenya
Makkah = Mecca S Arabia
7N4 **Makkovik** Can
43E3 **Makó** Hung
72B3 **Makokou** Gabon
78C1 **Makorako,Mt** NZ
72B3 **Makoua** Congo
60C3 **Makrāna** India
60A3 **Makran Coast Range** *Mts* Pak
53D2 **Maksimovka** Russian Fed
63E3 **Maksotag** Iran
71D1 **Maktar** Tunisia
45G8 **Mākū** Iran
72C4 **Makumbi** Zaïre

53C5 Makurazaki Japan
71H4 Makurdi Nig
10E5 Makushin V USA
57F9 Malabang Phil
62B2 Malabar Coast India
68E7 Malabo Bioko
28D1 Malabrigo Arg
55C5 Malacca,Str of S E Asia
18D2 Malad City USA
26D2 Málaga Colombia
39B2 Malaga Spain
16B3 Malaga USA
73E6 Malaimbandy Madag
77F1 Malaita I Solomon Is
72D3 Malakal Sudan
60C2 Malakand Pak
57B3 Malamala Indon
56D4 Malang Indon
73B4 Malange Angola
71G3 Malanville Benin
49S3 Mal Anyuy R Russian Fed
32H7 Mälaren L Sweden
28B3 Malargüe Arg
4F4 Malartic Can
10K4 Malaspina Gl USA
45F8 Malatya Turk
73D5 Malawi Republic, Africa
Malawi,L = Nyasa,L
53D2 Malaya Sidima Russian Fed
57G9 Malaybalay Phil
63B2 Malāyer Iran
51D6 Malaysia Federation, S E Asia
64D2 Malazgirt Turk
43D2 Malbork Pol
28C1 Malbrán Arg
42C2 Malchin Germany
17E2 Malden USA
59F5 Maldives Is Indian O
xxviiiE4 Maldives Ridge Indian O
36A1 Maldon Eng
25F4 Maldonado Urug
37D1 Male Italy
60C4 Malegaon India
42D3 Malé Karpaty Upland Czech
77F2 Malekula I Vanuatu
73D5 Malema Mozam
44F3 Malen'ga Russian Fed
36B2 Malesherbes France
60B2 Mālestān Afghan
32H5 Malgomaj L Sweden
72C2 Malha Well Sudan
18C2 Malheur L USA
70B3 Mali Republic, Africa
61E2 Mali Hka R Burma
57B3 Malili Indon
43F2 Malin Ukraine
56E2 Malinau Indon
72E4 Malindi Kenya
Malines = Mechelen
33B2 Malin Head Pt Irish Rep
61B3 Malkala Range Mts India
60D4 Malkāpur India
41F2 Malkara Turk
41F2 Malko Tŭrnovo Bulg
34C3 Mallaig Scot
69C2 Mallawi Egypt
37D1 Málles Venosta Italy
39C2 Mallorca I Spain
32G6 Malm Nor
32J5 Malmberget Sweden
36D1 Malmédy Germany
35D6 Malmesbury Eng
74B3 Malmesbury S Africa
32G7 Malmö Sweden
44J4 Malmyzh Russian Fed
57F8 Malolos Phil
13E2 Malone USA
74D2 Maloti Mts Lesotho
32F6 Måloy Nor
44J2 Malozemel'skaya Tundra Plain Russian Fed
22B1 Mal Paso Mexico
22D2 Malpaso Mexico
24B3 Malpelo I Colombia
28A2 Malpo R Chile
60D3 Mālpura India
18D2 Malta Idaho, USA
8C2 Malta Montana, USA
40C3 Malta Chan Malta/Italy
40C3 Malta I Medit S
74B1 Maltahöhe Namibia
35E4 Malton Eng
32G6 Malung Sweden
62A1 Mālvan India
17D3 Malvern USA
74E1 Malvérnia Mozam
60D4 Malwa Plat India
45G7 Malyy Kavkaz Mts Georgia/Azerbaijan
49Q2 Malyy Lyakchovskiy, Ostrov I Russian Fed
49M2 Malyy Taymyr, Ostrov I Russian Fed
45H6 Malyy Uzen' R Kazakhstan
49N4 Mama Russian Fed
44J4 Mamadysh Russian Fed
72C3 Mambasa Zaïre
76C1 Mamberamo R Aust
51G7 Mamberamo R Indon
72B3 Mambéré R CAR
57A3 Mamciju Indon
36A2 Mamers France
72A3 Mamfé Cam
19D4 Mammoth USA
12B3 Mammoth Cave Nat Pk USA
20C2 Mammoth Pool Res USA
26E6 Mamoré R Bol
70A3 Mamou Guinea
73E5 Mampikony Madag
71F4 Mampong Ghana
65C3 Mamshit Hist Site Israel
67G3 Ma'mūl Oman
74C1 Mamuno Botswana
70B4 Man Ivory Coast
20E5 Mana Hawaiian Is
73E6 Manabo Madag
26F4 Manacapuru Brazil
39C2 Manacor Spain
57B2 Manado Indon
26A1 Managua Nic
73E6 Manakara Madag
76D1 Manam I PNG
73E5 Mananara Madag
73E6 Mananjary Madag
78A3 Manapouri NZ
78A3 Manapouri,L NZ
61D2 Manas Bhutan
59G1 Manas China
48K5 Manas Hu L China
61B2 Manaslu Mt Nepal
14C2 Manasquan USA
27G4 Manaus Brazil
45E8 Manavgat Turk
64C2 Manbij Syria
71J4 Manbilla Plat Nig
35C4 Man,Calf of I Eng
12B2 Mancelona USA
62B1 Mancheral India
13E2 Manchester Connecticut, USA
35D5 Manchester Eng
12C3 Manchester Kentucky, USA
9F2 Manchester New Hampshire, USA
14B2 Manchester Pennsylvania, USA
15B1 Manchester Tennessee, USA
14D1 Manchester Vermont, USA
53B2 Manchuria Hist Region, China
63C3 Mand R Iran
73D5 Manda Tanz
29B3 Mandaguari Brazil
32F7 Mandal Nor
55B1 Mandalay Burma
50D2 Mandalgovĭ Mongolia
41F3 Mandalya Körfezi B Turk
8C2 Mandan USA
72E3 Mandera Eth
23B3 Mandeville Jamaica
73D5 Mandimba Mozam
57C3 Mandioli I Indon
61B3 Mandla India
73E5 Mandritsara Madag
60D4 Mandsaur India
41D2 Manduria Italy
60B4 Māndvi India
62B2 Mandya India
43F2 Manevichi Ukraine
66B1 Manfalût Egypt
35E5 Manfield Eng
40D2 Manfredonia Italy
29D1 Manga Brazil
71F3 Manga Burkina
72B2 Manga Desert Region Niger
78C1 Mangakino NZ
41F2 Mangalia Rom
72C2 Mangalmé Chad
62A2 Mangalore India
56C3 Manggar Indon
61E3 Mangin Range Mts Burma
50C3 Mangnia China
73D5 Mangoche Malawi
73E6 Mangoky R Madag
57C3 Mangole I Indon
60B4 Māngral India
29B4 Manguerinha Brazil
49O4 Mangui China
16C3 Mangum USA
45J7 Mangyshiak, Poluostrov Pen Kazakhstan
8D3 Manhattan USA
74E2 Manhica Mozam
27K8 Manhuacu Brazil
73E5 Mania R Madag
37E1 Maniago Italy
73D5 Manica Mozam
7M5 Manicouagan R Can
7M4 Manicouagan, Réservoir Res Can
67E1 Manifah S Arabia
57F8 Manila Phil
18E2 Manila USA
75D2 Manilla Aust
70B3 Maninian Ivory Coast
57C3 Manipa I Indon
61D3 Manipur State, India
61D3 Manipur R Burma
45D8 Manisa Turk
33C3 Man,Isle of Irish Sea
12B2 Manistee USA
12B2 Manistee R USA
12B1 Manistique USA
6J4 Manitoba Province, Can
6J4 Manitoba,L Can
3G3 Manito L Can
11C2 Manitou Can
11D1 Manitou Falls Can
12B1 Manitou Is USA
7K5 Manitoulin I Can
16B2 Manitou Springs USA
12C1 Manitowik L Can
12B2 Manitowoc USA
4F4 Maniwaki Can
26C2 Manizales Colombia
73E6 Manja Madag
76A4 Manjimup Aust
62B1 Mānjra R India
9D2 Mankato USA
70B4 Mankono Ivory Coast
10H3 Manley Hot Springs USA
78B1 Manly NZ
60C4 Manmād India
56B3 Manna Indon
75A2 Mannahill Aust
62B3 Mannar Sri Lanka
62B3 Mannār,G of India
62B2 Mannārgudi India
42B3 Mannheim Germany
3E2 Manning Can
15C2 Manning USA
75A2 Mannum Aust
70A4 Mano Sierra Leone
76C1 Manokwari Indon
73C4 Manono Zaïre
55B3 Manoron Burma
37A3 Manosque France
5G3 Manouane R Can
54C3 Mano-wan B Japan
53B3 Manp'o N Korea
60D2 Mānsa India
73C5 Mansa Zambia
7K3 Mansel I Can
17D2 Mansfield Arkansas, USA
75C3 Mansfield Aust
17D3 Mansfield Louisiana, USA
14E1 Mansfield Massachusetts, USA
9E2 Mansfield Ohio, USA
13D2 Mansfield Pennsylvania, USA
29B2 Manso R Brazil
51G5 Mansyu Deep Pacific O
57E9 Mantalingajan,Mt Phil
54A2 Mantap-san Mt N Korea
26C6 Mantaro R Peru
20B2 Manteca USA
15D1 Manteo USA
38C2 Mantes France
19D3 Manti USA
40C1 Mantova Italy
32J6 Mantta Fin
44G4 Manturovo Russian Fed
22C1 Manuel Mexico
16B4 Manuel Benavides Mexico
29B3 Manuel Ribas Brazil
57B3 Manui I Indon
57F9 Manukan Phil
77G4 Manukau NZ
51H7 Manus I Pacific O
39B2 Manzanares Spain
21E2 Manzanillo Cuba
21B3 Manzanillo Mexico
49N5 Manzhouli China
65D3 Manzil Jordan
73D6 Manzini Swaziland
72B2 Mao Chad
52A2 Maomao Shan Mt China
52C5 Maoming China
73D6 Mapai Mozam
61B1 Mapam Yumco L China
51G6 Mapia Is Pacific O
57E9 Mapin I Phil
6H5 Maple Creek Can
74E1 Mapulanguene Mozam
74E2 Maputo Mozam
74E2 Maputo R Mozam
Ma Qu = Huange He
52A3 Maqu China
61C2 Maquan He R China
72B4 Maquela do Zombo Angola
25C6 Maquinchao Arg
27J5 Marabá Brazil
26D1 Maracaibo Ven
29A3 Maracaju Brazil
29D1 Máracás Brazil
26E1 Maracay Ven
69A2 Marādah Libya
70C3 Maradi Niger
45H8 Marāgheh Iran
30E5 Marakech Mor
72D3 Maralal Kenya
77F1 Maramasike I Solomon Is
Maramba = Livingstone
56G7 Maran Malay
19D4 Marana USA
45H8 Marand Iran
29C1 Maranhão R Brazil
27J4 Maranhōa State, Brazil
75C1 Maranoa R Aust
26C4 Marañón R Peru
45F8 Maras Turk
7K5 Marathon Can
15E4 Marathon Florida, USA
14B1 Marathon New York, USA
16B3 Marathon Texas, USA
56E2 Maratua I Indon
29E1 Maraú Brazil
22B2 Maravatio Mexico
57F9 Marawi Phil
28B2 Marayes Arg
67F3 Mar'ayt Yemen
39B2 Marbella Spain
76A3 Marble Bar Aust
19D3 Marble Canyon USA
74D2 Marble Hall S Africa
14E1 Marblehead USA
42B2 Marburg Germany
28E1 Marcelino Ramos Brazil
42B2 Marche Belg
37E3 Marche Region, Italy
39A2 Marchean Spain
36C1 Marche-en-Famenne Belg
15E4 Marco USA
28C2 Marcos Juárez Arg
10J3 Marcus Baker,Mt USA
13E2 Marcy,Mt USA
45G8 Mar Dağlari Mt Turk
60C2 Mardan Pak
25E5 Mar del Plata Arg
45G8 Mardin Turk
77F3 Maré I Nouvelle Calédonie
72D2 Mareb R Eth
51H8 Mareeba Aust
72E3 Mareeq Somalia
16B3 Marfa USA
14C1 Margaretville USA
28C1 Margarita Arg
35F6 Margate Eng
41E1 Marghita Rom
75E3 Maria I Aust
xxviiiJ3 Mariana Is Pacific O
3F2 Mariana Lake Can
xxviiiJ4 Marianas Trench Pacific O
61D2 Mariāni India
17D3 Marianna Arkansas, USA
15B2 Marianna Florida, USA
77G4 Maria Van Diemen,C NZ
42D3 Mariazell Austria
67E3 Ma'rib Yemen
40D1 Maribor Slovenia, Yugos
74D1 Marico R Botswana/S Africa
20C3 Maricopa USA
72C3 Maridi Sudan
79F5 Marie Byrd Land Region, Ant
23E3 Marie Galante I Caribbean
32H6 Mariehamn Fin
36C1 Mariembourg Belg
27H2 Marienburg Surinam
74B1 Mariental Namibia
32G7 Mariestad Sweden
15C2 Marietta Georgia, USA
12C3 Marietta Ohio, USA
17C3 Marietta Oklahoma, USA
71H3 Mariga R Nig
23Q2 Marigot Dominica
25G2 Marilia Brazil
73B4 Marimba Angola
57F8 Marinduque I Phil
9E2 Marinette USA
25F2 Maringá Brazil
72C3 Maringa R Zaïre
17D2 Marion Arkansas, USA
12B3 Marion Illinois, USA
9E2 Marion Indiana, USA
9E2 Marion Ohio, USA
15D2 Marion S Carolina, USA
9E3 Marion,L USA
77E2 Marion Reef Aust
19C3 Mariposa USA
20B2 Mariposa R USA
20B2 Mariposa Res USA
57B2 Marisa Indon
45F6 Mariupol Ukraine
45D7 Marista R Bulg
44H4 Mariyskaya Respublika, Russian Fed
65C2 Marjayoun Leb
43F2 Marjina Gorki Belorussia
65C3 Marka Jordan
72E3 Marka Somalia
42C1 Markaryd Sweden
35D5 Market Drayton Eng
35E5 Market Harborough Eng
79E Markham,Mt Ant
20C1 Markleeville USA
49T3 Markovo Russian Fed
14E1 Marlboro Massachusetts, USA
14D1 Marlboro New Hampshire, USA
76D3 Marlborough Aust
36B2 Marle France
4E5 Marlette USA
17C3 Marlin USA
14D1 Marlow USA
38C3 Marmande France
41F2 Marmara Adi I Turk
64A1 Marmara,S of Turk
41F3 Marmaris Turk
11B2 Marmarth USA
12C3 Marmet USA
4C4 Marmion L Can
40C1 Marmolada Mt Italy
10H4 Marmot B USA
22D2 Mar Muerto Lg Mexico
37A1 Marnay France
36C2 Marne Department, France
36B2 Marne R France
72B3 Maro Chad
73E5 Maroantsetra Madag
73D5 Marondera Zim
27H3 Maroni R French Guiana
75D1 Maroochydore Aust
57A3 Maros Indon
72B2 Maroua Cam
73E5 Marovoay Madag
9E4 Marquesas Keys Is USA
9E2 Marquette USA
36A1 Marquise France
75C2 Marra R Aust
74E2 Marracuene Mozam
70B1 Marrakech Mor
76C3 Marree Aust
17D4 Marrero USA
73D5 Marromeu Mozam
73D5 Marrupa Mozam
66B1 Marsa Alam Egypt
72D3 Marsabit Kenya
40C3 Marsala Italy
36E1 Marsberg Germany
38D3 Marseille France
10F3 Marshall Alaska, USA
12B3 Marshall Illinois, USA
12C2 Marshall Michigan, USA
11C3 Marshall Minnesota, USA
17D2 Marshall Missouri, USA
9D3 Marshall Texas, USA
14B3 Marshall Virginia, USA
xxixK4 Marshall Is Pacific O
11D3 Marshalltown USA
17D2 Marshfield Missouri, USA
12A2 Marshfield Wisconsin, USA
23B1 Marsh Harbour Bahamas
17D4 Marsh I USA
10M3 Marsh L Can
26B4 Marta Ecuador
55B2 Martaban,G of Burma
56B3 Martapura Indon
56D3 Martapura Indon
13E2 Martha's Vineyard I USA
38D2 Martigny Switz
43D3 Martin Czech
11B3 Martin S Dakota, USA
15B1 Martin Tennessee, USA
78C2 Martinborough NZ
28B3 Martín de Loyola Arg
22C1 Martínez de la Torre Mexico
23E4 Martinique I Caribbean
15B2 Martin,L USA
10K1 Martin Pt USA
13D3 Martinsburg USA
12C2 Martins Ferry USA
13D3 Martinsville USA
xxxG5 Martin Vaz I Atlantic O
38D3 Martiques France
78C2 Marton NZ
39B2 Martos Spain
45G7 Martvili Georgia
56D2 Marudi Malay
60B2 Maruf Afghan
54B4 Marugame Japan
19D3 Marvine,Mt USA
60C3 Mārwār India
48H6 Mary Turkmenistan
77E3 Maryborough Queensland, Aust

75B3 **Maryborough** Victoria, Aust
6F4 **Mary Henry,Mt** Can
9F3 **Maryland** State, USA
34D4 **Maryport** Eng
5K3 **Mary's Harbour** Can
5K4 **Marystown** Can
19B3 **Marysville** California, USA
17C2 **Marysville** Kansas, USA
18B1 **Marysville** Washington, USA
17D1 **Maryville** Missouri, USA
15C1 **Maryville** Tennessee, USA
69A2 **Marzuq** Libya
65A3 **Masabb Dumyât** *C* Egypt
Masada = Mezada
65C2 **Mas'adah** Syria
72D4 **Masai Steppe** *Upland* Tanz
72D4 **Masaka** Uganda
64E2 **Masally** Azerbaijan
57B3 **Masamba** Indon
53B4 **Masan** S Korea
73D5 **Masasi** Tanz
21D3 **Masaya** Nic
57F8 **Masbate** Phil
57F8 **Masbate** *I* Phil
71C1 **Mascara** Alg
xxviiiD5 **Mascarene Ridge** Indian O
22B1 **Mascota** Mexico
29E2 **Mascote** Brazil
57C4 **Masela** *I* Indon
74D2 **Maseru** Lesotho
60B2 **Mashaki** Afghan
63D1 **Mashhad** Iran
63E3 **Mashkel** *R* Pak
72B4 **Masi-Manimba** Zaïre
72D3 **Masindi** Uganda
72C4 **Masisi** Zaïre
63B2 **Masjed Soleyman** Iran
73F5 **Masoala** *C* Madag
20C1 **Mason** Nevada, USA
16C3 **Mason** Texas, USA
9D2 **Mason City** USA
67G2 **Masqat** Oman
42B2 **Mass** *R* Neth
40C2 **Massa** Italy
9F2 **Massachusetts** State, USA
13E2 **Massachusetts B** USA
72B2 **Massakori** Chad
37D3 **Massa Marittima** Italy
73D6 **Massangena** Mozam
Massawa = Mits'iwa
66C3 **Massawa Chan** Eth
13E2 **Massena** USA
72B2 **Massénya** Chad
3B3 **Masset** Can
12C1 **Massey** Can
38C2 **Massif Central** *Mts* France
71C1 **Massif de l'Ouarsenis** *Mts* Alg
72B3 **Massif de l'Adamaoua** *Mts* Cam
23C3 **Massif de la Hotte** *Mts* Haiti
73E6 **Massif de l'Isalo** *Upland* Madag
72C3 **Massif des Bongo** *Upland* CAR
38D2 **Massif du Pelvoux** *Mts* France
73E5 **Massif du Tsaratanana** *Mt* Madag
12C2 **Massillon** USA
70B3 **Massina** Region, Mali
73D6 **Massinga** Mozam
74E1 **Massingir** Mozam
45J6 **Masteksay** Kazakhstan
77G5 **Masterton** NZ
53C5 **Masuda** Japan
72B4 **Masuku** Gabon
64C2 **Maşyāf** Syria
4E4 **Matachewan** Can
16A4 **Matachie** Mexico
72B4 **Matadi** Zaïre
26A1 **Matagalpa** Nic
7L5 **Matagami** Can
8D4 **Matagorda B** USA
17F4 **Matagorda I** USA
78C1 **Matakana I** NZ
73B5 **Matala** Angola
62C3 **Matale** Sri Lanka
70A3 **Matam** Sen
70C3 **Matameye** Niger
21C2 **Matamoros** Mexico
69B2 **Ma'tan as Sarra** *Well* Libya
7M5 **Matane** Can
21D2 **Matanzas** Cuba
13F1 **Matapédia** *R* Can
28A2 **Mataquito** *R* Chile
62C3 **Matara** Sri Lanka
76A1 **Mataram** Indon
26D7 **Matarani** Peru
29E1 **Mataripe** Brazil
39C1 **Mataró** Spain
74D3 **Matatiele** S Africa
78A3 **Mataura** NZ
21B2 **Matehuala** Mexico
37E3 **Matelica** Italy
23L1 **Matelot** Trinidad
40D2 **Matera** Italy
43E3 **Mátészalka** Hung
71D1 **Mateur** Tunisia
20C2 **Mather** USA
12C1 **Matheson** Can
17F4 **Mathis** USA
60D3 **Mathura** India
57G9 **Mati** Phil
22C2 **Matías Romero** Mexico
56E3 **Matisiri** *I* Indon
35E5 **Matlock** Eng
71D2 **Matmatma** Tunisia
27G6 **Mato Grosso** Brazil
27G6 **Mato Grosso** State, Brazil
27G7 **Mato Grosso do Sul** State, Brazil
74E2 **Matola** Mozam
67G2 **Matrah** Oman
37E1 **Matrel im Osttirol** Austria
64A3 **Matrûh** Egypt
53C4 **Matsue** Japan
53E3 **Matsumae** Japan
53D4 **Matsumoto** Japan
53D5 **Matsusaka** Japan
53C5 **Matsuyama** Japan
7K5 **Mattagami** *R* Can
4F4 **Mattawa** Can
5H4 **Mattawamkeag** USA
40B1 **Matterhorn** *Mt* Switz/Italy
18C2 **Matterhorn** *Mt* USA
23C2 **Matthew Town** Bahamas
4E4 **Mattice** Can
14D2 **Mattituck** USA
12B3 **Mattoon** USA
60B2 **Matun** Afghan
23L1 **Matura B** Trinidad
26F2 **Maturin** Ven
61B2 **Mau** India
73D5 **Maúa** Mozam
38C1 **Maubeuge** France
75B2 **Maude** Aust
xxxJ8 **Maud Seamount** Atlantic O
20E5 **Maui** *I* Hawaiian Is
28A3 **Maule** *R* Chile
12C2 **Maumee** USA
12C2 **Maumee** *R* USA
57B4 **Maumere** Indon
73C5 **Maun** Botswana
20E5 **Mauna Kea** *Mt* Hawaiian Is
20E5 **Mauna Loa** *Mt* Hawaiian Is
6F3 **Maunoir,L** Can
37B3 **Maures** *Mts* France
38C2 **Mauriac** France
70A2 **Mauritania** Republic, Africa
68K10 **Mauritius** *I* Indian O
12A2 **Mauston** USA
37E1 **Mauterndorf** Austria
73C5 **Mavinga** Angola
74E1 **Mavue** Mozam
61D3 **Mawlaik** Burma
79G10 **Mawson** *Base* Ant
11B2 **Max** USA
74E1 **Maxaila** Mozam
22C1 **Maxcaltzin** Mexico
56C3 **Maya** *I* Indon
49P4 **Maya** *R* Russian Fed
64D2 **Mayādīn** Syria
9F4 **Mayaguana** *I* Bahamas
23D3 **Mayagüez** Puerto Rico
70C3 **Mayahi** Niger
72B4 **Mayama** Congo
63D1 **Mayamey** Iran
57D4 **Mayanobab** Indon
34C4 **Maybole** Scot
9F3 **May,C** USA
75E3 **Maydena** Aust
36D1 **Mayen** Germany
38B2 **Mayenne** France
19D4 **Mayer** USA
3E3 **Mayerthorpe** Can
67E4 **Mayfa'ah** Yemen
12B3 **Mayfield** USA
16A3 **Mayhill** USA
45G7 **Maykop** Russian Fed
48H6 **Maymaneh** Afghan
55B1 **Maymyo** Burma
6E3 **Mayo** Can
14B3 **Mayo** USA
71J4 **Mayo Deo** *R* Cam
57F8 **Mayon** *Mt* Phil
39C2 **Mayor** *Mt* Spain
28C3 **Mayor Buratovich** Arg
78C1 **Mayor I** NZ
25D1 **Mayor P Lagerenza** Par
73E5 **Mayotte** *I* Indian O
23H2 **May Pen** Jamaica
14C3 **May Point,C** USA
37D1 **Mayrhofen** Austria
53B1 **Mayskiy** Russian Fed
14C3 **Mays Landing** USA
3G2 **Mayson L** Can
12C3 **Maysville** USA
72B4 **Mayumba** Gabon
11C2 **Mayville** USA
16B1 **Maywood** USA
73C5 **Mazabuka** Zambia
22B1 **Mazapil** Mexico
60D1 **Mazar** China
65C3 **Mazār** Jordan
40C3 **Mazara del Vallo** Italy
60B1 **Mazar-i-Sharif** Afghan
21B2 **Mazatlán** Mexico
44C4 **Mazeikiai** Lithuania
65C3 **Mazra** Jordan
73D6 **Mbabane** Swaziland
71J4 **Mbabo,Mt** Cam
72B3 **Mbaïki** CAR
73D4 **Mbala** Zambia
73C6 **Mbalabala** Zim
72D3 **Mbale** Uganda
72B3 **Mbalmayo** Cam
72B3 **Mbam** *R* Cam
73D5 **Mbamba Bay** Tanz
72B3 **Mbandaka** Zaïre
72B4 **Mbanza Congo** Angola
72B4 **Mbanza-Ngungu** Zaïre
72D4 **Mbarara** Uganda
71J4 **Mbé** Cam
71J4 **Mbengwi** Cam
72B3 **Mbènza** Congo
72B3 **Mbére** *R* Cam
73D4 **Mbeya** Tanz
72B4 **Mbinda** Congo
71J4 **Mbouda** Cam
70A3 **Mbout** Maur
72C4 **Mbuji-Mayi** Zaïre
71J3 **Mbuli** *R* Nig
72D4 **Mbulu** Tanz
28D1 **Mburucuyá** Arg
70B2 **Mcherrah** Region, Alg
73D5 **Mchinji** Malawi
4C2 **M'Clintock** Can
55D3 **Mdrak** Viet
16B2 **Meade** USA
10G1 **Meade** *R* USA
8B3 **Mead,L** USA
6H4 **Meadow Lake** Can
12C2 **Meadville** USA
54D2 **Me-akan dake** *Mt* Japan
7N4 **Mealy Mts** Can
75C1 **Meandarra** Aust
6G4 **Meander River** Can
35B5 **Meath** Irish Rep
38C2 **Meaux** France
66C2 **Mecca** S Arabia
19C4 **Mecca** USA
14D1 **Mechanicville** USA
48G2 **Mechdusharskiy, Ostrov** *I* Russian Fed
42A2 **Mechelen** Belg
71B2 **Mecheria** Alg
42C2 **Mecklenburger Bucht** *B* Germany
42C2 **Mecklenburg-Vorpommern** State, Germany
73D5 **Meconta** Mozam
73D5 **Mecuburi** Mozam
73E5 **Mecufi** Mozam
73D5 **Mecula** Mozam
56A2 **Medan** Indon
28C3 **Médanos** Arg
28D2 **Médanos** Arg
71C1 **Médéa** Alg
26C2 **Medellín** Colombia
71E2 **Medenine** Tunisia
8A2 **Medford** USA
41F2 **Medgidia** Rom
28B2 **Media Agua** Arg
41E1 **Mediaş** Rom
18C1 **Medical Lake** USA
11A3 **Medicine Bow** USA
16A1 **Medicine Bow Mts** USA
11A3 **Medicine Bow Peak** *Mt* USA
6G5 **Medicine Hat** Can
16C2 **Medicine Lodge** USA
29D2 **Medina** Brazil
11C2 **Medina** N Dakota, USA
14A1 **Medina** New York, USA
66C2 **Medina** S Arabia
39B1 **Medinaceli** Spain
39A1 **Medina del Campo** Spain
39A1 **Medina de Rio Seco** Spain
16C4 **Medina L** USA
61C3 **Medinīpur** India
68E4 **Mediterranean S** Europe
3F3 **Medley** Can
45K5 **Mednogorsk** Russian Fed
49S4 **Mednyy, Ostrov** *I* Russian Fed
61E2 **Mêdog** China
72B3 **Medouneu** Gabon
45G5 **Medvedista** *R* Russian Fed
49S2 **Medvezh'i Ova** *I* Russian Fed
44E3 **Medvezh'yegorsk** Russian Fed
76A3 **Meekatharra** Aust
16A1 **Meeker** USA
60D3 **Meerut** India
18E2 **Meeteetse** USA
72D3 **Mēga** Eth
41E3 **Megalópolis** Greece
41E3 **Mégara** Greece
61D2 **Meghālaya** State, India
61D3 **Meghna** *R* Bang
65C2 **Megido** *Hist Site* Israel
4F4 **Mégiscane** *R* Can
71C2 **Mehaïguene** *R* Alg
10E3 **Mehoryuk** USA
63C3 **Mehran** *R* Iran
63C2 **Mehriz** Iran
29C2 **Meia Ponte** *R* Brazil
72B3 **Meiganga** Cam
55B1 **Meiktila** Burma
37C1 **Meiringen** Switz
52A4 **Meishan** China
42C2 **Meissen** Germany
52D5 **Mei Xian** China
52D5 **Meizhou** China
26D8 **Mejillones** Chile
72B3 **Mekambo** Gabon
4E4 **Mekatina** Can
71C4 **Mek'elē** Eth
71A2 **Meknès** Mor
Mekong = Lancang
55D3 **Mekong, R** Camb
71G3 **Mekrou** *R* Benin
55C5 **Melaka** Malay
xxviiiJ5 **Melanesia** *Region* Pacific O
56D3 **Melawi** *R* Indon
76D4 **Melbourne** Aust
9E4 **Melbourne** USA
8C4 **Melchor Muźguiz** Mexico
44K5 **Meleuz** Russian Fed
72B2 **Melfi** Chad
6H4 **Melfort** Can
71B1 **Melilla** N W Africa
25B6 **Melimoyu** *Mt* Chile
28C2 **Melincué** Arg
28A2 **Melipilla** Chile
11B2 **Melita** Can
45F6 **Melitopol'** Ukraine
7M2 **Meliville Bugt** *B* Greenland
72D3 **Melka Guba** Eth
71D1 **Mellègue** *R* Tunisia
66D4 **Melli** *R* Eth
74E2 **Melmoth** S Africa
28C2 **Melo** Arg
25F4 **Melo** Urug
29A3 **Melo** *R* Brazil
20B2 **Melones Res** USA
10H2 **Melozitna** *R* USA
11D2 **Melrose** USA
37C1 **Mels** Switz
36E1 **Melsungen** Germany
56E1 **Melta,Mt** Malay
35E5 **Melton Mowbray** Eng
38C2 **Melun** France
6H4 **Melville** Can
23Q2 **Melville,C** Dominica
6F3 **Melville Hills** *Mts* Can
76C2 **Melville I** Aust
6G2 **Melville I** Can
7N4 **Melville,L** Can
7K3 **Melville Pen** Can
73E5 **Memba** Mozam
76A1 **Memboro** Indon
42C3 **Memmingen** Germany
56C2 **Mempawan** Indon
9E3 **Memphis** Tennessee, USA
16B3 **Memphis** Texas, USA
17D3 **Mena** USA
43G2 **Mena** Ukraine
35C5 **Menai Str** Wales
70C3 **Ménaka** Mali
12B2 **Menasha** USA
28B4 **Mencué** Arg
56D3 **Mendawai** *R* Indon
38C3 **Mende** France
72D3 **Mendebo** *Mts* Eth
10E4 **Mendenhall,C** USA
76D1 **Mendi** PNG
35D6 **Mendip Hills** *Upland* Eng
18B2 **Mendocino,C** USA
xxixM3 **Mendocino Seascarp** Pacific O
20B2 **Mendota** California, USA
12B2 **Mendota** Illinois, USA
25C4 **Mendoza** Arg
25C5 **Mendoza** State, Arg
41F3 **Menemen** Turk
36B1 **Menen** Belg
52D3 **Mengcheng** China
56C3 **Menggala** Indon
55B1 **Menghai** China
52A5 **Mengla** China
55B1 **Menglian** China
52A5 **Mengzi** China
5H3 **Menihek Lakes** Can
76D4 **Menindee** Aust
75B2 **Menindee L** Aust
75A3 **Meningie** Aust
12B1 **Menominee** USA
12B2 **Menomonee Falls** USA
12A2 **Menomonie** USA
73B5 **Menongue** Angola
39C1 **Menorca** *I* Spain
10K3 **Mentasta Mts** USA
16A2 **Mentmore** USA
56C3 **Mentok** Indon
37B3 **Menton** France
12C2 **Mentor** USA
36B2 **Ménu** France
52A2 **Menyuan** China
44J4 **Menzelinsk** Russian Fed
42B2 **Meppen** Germany
36A3 **Mer** France
56E2 **Merah** Indon
17D2 **Meramec** *R* USA
40C1 **Merano** Italy
76D1 **Merauke** Indon
8A3 **Merced** USA
20B2 **Merced** *R* USA
25B4 **Mercedario** *Mt* Chile
25C4 **Mercedes** Arg
25E4 **Mercedes** Buenos Aires, Arg
25E3 **Mercedes** Corrientes, Arg
25E4 **Mercedes** Urug
78C1 **Mercury B** NZ
78C1 **Mercury Is** NZ
6F2 **Mercy B** Can
7M3 **Mercy,C** Can
16B2 **Meredith,L** *L* USA
55B3 **Mergui** Burma
55B3 **Mergui Arch** Burma
21D2 **Mérida** Mexico
39A2 **Mérida** Spain
26D2 **Mérida** Ven
9E3 **Meridian** USA
75C3 **Merimbula** Aust
75B2 **Meringur** Aust
16B3 **Merkel** USA
72D2 **Merowe** Sudan
76A4 **Merredin** Aust
34C4 **Merrick** *Mt* Scot
12B1 **Merrill** USA
12B2 **Merrillville** USA
14E1 **Merrimack** *R* USA
11B3 **Merriman** USA
3D3 **Merritt** Can
15C3 **Merritt Island** USA
75D2 **Merriwa** Aust
66D4 **Mersa Fatma** Eth
39B2 **Mers el Kebir** Alg
35D5 **Mersey** *R* Eng
35D5 **Merseyside** County, Eng
45E8 **Mersin** Turk
55C5 **Mersing** Malay
60C3 **Merta** India
35D6 **Merthyr Tydfil** Wales
39A2 **Mertola** Port
72D4 **Meru** *Mt* Tanz
45F7 **Merzifon** Turk
36D2 **Merzig** Germany
8B3 **Mesa** USA
16A2 **Mesa Verde Nat Pk** USA
36E1 **Meschede** Germany
64D1 **Mescit Dağ** *Mt* Turk
10G4 **Meshik** USA
72C3 **Meshra'er Req** Sudan
37C1 **Mesocco** Switz
41E3 **Mesolóngion** Greece
19D3 **Mesquite** Nevada, USA
17C3 **Mesquite** Texas, USA
71C2 **Messaad** Alg
73D5 **Messalo** *R* Mozam
40D3 **Messina** Italy
74D1 **Messina** S Africa
41E3 **Messíni** Greece
41E3 **Messiniakós Kólpos** *G* Greece
Mesta = Néstos
41E2 **Mesta, R** Bulg
40C1 **Mestre** Italy
26D3 **Meta** *R* Colombia
44E4 **Meta** *R* Russian Fed
26E2 **Meta** *R* Ven
7L3 **Meta Incognita Pen** Can
17D4 **Metairie** USA
18C1 **Metaline Falls** USA
25D3 **Metán** Arg
73D5 **Metangula** Mozam
40D2 **Metaponto** Italy
37E3 **Metauro** *R* Italy
66C4 **Metemma** Eth
34D3 **Methil** Scot
14E1 **Methuen** USA
78B2 **Methven** NZ
10M4 **Metlakatla** USA

71D2 **Metlaoui** Tunisia
12B3 **Metropolis** USA
62B2 **Mettūr** India
38D2 **Metz** France
36E2 **Metzingen** Germany
56A2 **Meulaboh** Indon
36A2 **Meulan** France
36A3 **Meung-sur-Loire** France
36D2 **Meurthe** *R* France
36D2 **Meurthe-et-Moselle** Department, France
36C2 **Meuse** Department, France
36C1 **Meuse** *R* Belg
38D2 **Meuse** *R* France
17C3 **Mexia** USA
21A1 **Mexicali** Mexico
19E3 **Mexican Hat** USA
21B2 **Mexico** Federal Republic, Central America
21C3 **México** Mexico
22B2 **México** State, Mexico
17D2 **Mexico** USA
21C2 **Mexico,G of** C America
37A2 **Meximieux** France
65C3 **Mezada** *Hist Site* Israel
22C2 **Mezcala** Mexico
22D2 **Mezcalapa** *R* Mexico
44G2 **Mezen'** Russian Fed
44H3 **Mezen'** *R* Russian Fed
43G1 **Mezha** *R* Russian Fed
44J1 **Mezhdusharskiy, Ostrov** *I* Russian Fed
22B1 **Mezquital** Mexico
22B1 **Mezquital** *R* Mexico
53E1 **Mgachi** Russian Fed
60D4 **Mhow** India
22C2 **Miahuatlán** Mexico
19D4 **Miami** Arizona, USA
9E4 **Miami** Florida, USA
17D2 **Miami** Oklahoma, USA
9E4 **Miami Beach** USA
45H8 **Miandowāb** Iran
73E5 **Miandrivazo** Madag
45H8 **Mīāneh** Iran
60C2 **Mianwali** Pak
52A3 **Mianyang** Sichuan, China
52C3 **Mianyang** Hubei, China
52A3 **Mianzhu** China
52E2 **Miaodao Qundao** *Arch* China
52B4 **Miao Ling** *Upland* China
44L5 **Miass** Russian Fed
43E3 **Michalovce** Czech
18D1 **Michel** Can
23D3 **Miches** Dom Rep
9E2 **Michigan** State, USA
12B2 **Michigan City** USA
9E2 **Michigan,L** USA
12C1 **Michipicoten** Can
7K5 **Michipicoten I** Can
22B2 **Michoacan** State, Mexico
41F2 **Michurin** Bulg
45G5 **Michurinsk** Russian Fed
xxviiiJ4 **Micronesia** *Region* Pacific O
56C2 **Midai** *I* Indon
xxxF4 **Mid Atlantic Ridge** Atlantic O
36B1 **Middelburg** Neth
18B2 **Middle Alkali L** USA
xxixO4 **Middle America Trench** Pacific O
62E2 **Middle Andaman** *I* Indian O
14E2 **Middleboro** USA
74C3 **Middleburg** Cape Province, S Africa
14B2 **Middleburg** Pennsylvania, USA
74D2 **Middleburg** Transvaal, S Africa
14B3 **Middleburg** Virginia, USA
14C1 **Middleburgh** USA
13E2 **Middlebury** USA
9E3 **Middlesboro** USA
35E4 **Middlesbrough** Eng
5H5 **Middleton** Can
14D2 **Middletown** Connecticut, USA
14C3 **Middletown** Delaware, USA
13E2 **Middletown** New York, USA
12C3 **Middletown** Ohio, USA
14B2 **Middletown** Pennsylvania, USA
14C1 **Middleville** USA
71B2 **Midelt** Mor
35D6 **Mid Glamorgan** County, Wales
66D3 **Midī** Yemen
xxviiiE5 **Mid Indian Basin** Indian O
xxviiiE5 **Mid Indian Ridge** Indian O
7L5 **Midland** Can
12C2 **Midland** Michigan, USA
8C3 **Midland** Texas, USA
73E6 **Midongy Atsimo** Madag
xxixK4 **Mid Pacific Mts** Pacific O
18C2 **Midvale** USA
xxixL3 **Midway Is** Pacific O
11A3 **Midwest** USA
17C2 **Midwest City** USA
64D2 **Midyat** Turk
41E2 **Midžor** *Mt* Serbia, Yugos
43E2 **Mielec** Pol
41F1 **Miercurea-Ciuc** Rom
39A1 **Mieres** Spain
14B2 **Mifflintown** USA
22B1 **Miguel Auza** Mexico
22C1 **Miguihuana** Mexico
54B4 **Mihara** Japan
52D1 **Mijun Shuiku** *Res* China
41E2 **Mikhaylovgrad** Bulg
45G5 **Mikhaylovka** Russian Fed
48J4 **Mikhaylovskiy** Russian Fed
65C4 **Mikhrot Timna** Israel
32K6 **Mikkeli** Fin
3F2 **Mikkwa** *R* Can
41F3 **Míkonos** *I* Greece
42D3 **Mikulov** Czech
73D4 **Mikumi** Tanz
44J3 **Mikun** Russian Fed
53D4 **Mikuni-sammyaku** *Mts* Japan
54C4 **Mikura-jima** *I* Japan
11D2 **Milaca** USA
26C4 **Milagro** Ecuador
Milan = Milano
15B1 **Milan** USA
39C2 **Milana** Alg
73D5 **Milange** Mozam
57B2 **Milango** *R* Indon
40B1 **Milano** Italy
45D8 **Milas** Turk
11C2 **Milbank** USA
76D4 **Mildura** Aust
52A5 **Mile** China
64D3 **Mileh Tharthār** *L* Iraq
76E3 **Miles** Aust
8C2 **Miles City** USA
14D2 **Milford** Connecticut, USA
13D3 **Milford** Delaware, USA
13E2 **Milford** Massachusetts, USA
17C1 **Milford** Nebraska, USA
14E1 **Milford** New Hampshire, USA
14C2 **Milford** Pennsylvania, USA
19D3 **Milford** Utah, USA
35C6 **Milford Haven** Wales
35C6 **Milford Haven** *Sd* Wales
17C2 **Milford L** USA
78A2 **Milford Sd** NZ
71C1 **Miliana** Alg
11A2 **Milk** *R* USA
49R4 **Mil'kovo** Russian Fed
3F4 **Milk River** Can
38C3 **Millau** France
14D2 **Millbrook** USA
15C2 **Milledgeville** USA
11D2 **Mille Lacs L** USA
11C3 **Miller** USA
10K3 **Miller,Mt** USA
45G6 **Millerovo** Russian Fed
14B2 **Millersburg** USA
75A1 **Millers Creek** Aust
14D1 **Millers Falls** USA
14D2 **Millerton** USA
20C2 **Millerton L** USA
75B3 **Millicent** Aust
15B1 **Millington** USA
13F1 **Millinocket** USA
75D1 **Millmerran** Aust
37E1 **Millstätter See** *L* Austria
13F1 **Milltown** Can
18D1 **Milltown** USA
20A2 **Mill Valley** USA
13E3 **Millville** USA
7Q2 **Milne Land** *I* Greenland
20E5 **Milolii** Hawaiian Is
41E3 **Mílos** *I* Greece
76D3 **Milparinka** Aust
14B2 **Milroy** USA
15B2 **Milton** Florida, USA
78A3 **Milton** NZ
14B2 **Milton** Pennsylvania, USA
9E2 **Milwaukee** USA
4D3 **Miminiska L** Can
54D2 **Mimmaya** Japan
20C1 **Mina** USA
39C2 **Mina** *R* Alg
64E4 **Mīnā' al Ahmadī** Kuwait
63D3 **Mīnāb** Iran
57B2 **Minahassa Pen** Indon
4C4 **Minaki** Can
53C5 **Minamata** Japan
56B2 **Minas** Indon
25E4 **Minas** Urug
5J4 **Minas Basin** Can
5J4 **Minas Chan** Can
27J7 **Minas Gerais** State, Brazil
29D2 **Minas Novas** Brazil
21C3 **Minatitlan** Mexico
55A1 **Minbu** Burma
55A1 **Minbya** Burma
28A2 **Mincha** Chile
34B3 **Minch,Little** *Sd* Scot
34B2 **Minch,North** *Sd* Scot
33B2 **Minch,The** *Sd* Scot
10H3 **Minchumina,L** USA
37D2 **Mincio** *R* Italy
57F9 **Mindanao** *I* Phil
17D3 **Minden** Louisiana, USA
20C1 **Minden** Nevada, USA
42B2 **Minden** Germany
75B2 **Mindona L** Aust
57F8 **Mindoro** *I* Phil
57F8 **Mindoro Str** Phil
35D6 **Minehead** Eng
27H7 **Mineiros** Brazil
17C3 **Mineola** USA
22C1 **Mineral de Monte** Mexico
16C3 **Mineral Wells** USA
14B2 **Minersville** USA
5J3 **Mingan** Can
75B2 **Mingary** Aust
45H7 **Mingechaurskoye Vodokhranilische** *Res* Azerbaijan
53B2 **Mingshui** China
52A2 **Minhe** China
37D3 **Minialo** Italy
62A3 **Minicoy** *I* India
52D4 **Min Jiang** *R* Fujian, China
52A4 **Min Jiang** *R* Sichuan, China
20C2 **Minkler** USA
75A2 **Minlaton** Aust
52A2 **Minle** China
71H4 **Minna** Nig
9D2 **Minneapolis** USA
6J4 **Minnedosa** Can
9D2 **Minnesota** State, USA
11C3 **Minnesota** *R* USA
4C4 **Minnitaki L** Can
39A1 **Miño** *R* Spain
8C2 **Minot** USA
52A2 **Minqin** China
52A3 **Min Shan** *Upland* China
44D5 **Minsk** Belorussia
43E2 **Minsk Mazowiecki** Pol
10J3 **Minto** USA
6G2 **Minto Inlet** *B* Can
7L4 **Minto,L** Can
16A2 **Minturn** USA
50C1 **Minusinsk** Russian Fed
52A3 **Min Xian** China
65A3 **Minyael Qamn** Egypt
4F4 **Miquelon** Can
7N5 **Miquelon** *I* France
20D3 **Mirage L** USA
62A1 **Miraj** India
25E5 **Miramar** Arg
5J4 **Miramichi B** Can
60B2 **Miram Shah** Pak
29A2 **Miranda** *R* Brazil
39B1 **Miranda de Ebro** Spain
29A3 **Mirandia** Brazil
37D2 **Mirandola** Italy
60B2 **Mir Bachchen Kūt** Afghan
67F3 **Mirbāt** Oman
37A1 **Mirebeau** France
36C2 **Mirecourt** France
56D2 **Miri** Malay
63E3 **Miri** *Mt* Pak
70A3 **Mirik,C** Maur
28D1 **Mirinay** *R* Arg
63E3 **Mīrjāveh** Iran
37E2 **Mirna** *R* Croatia, Yugos
49K3 **Mirnoye** Russian Fed
49N3 **Mirnyy** Russian Fed
79G9 **Mirnyy** *Base* Ant
3H2 **Miron L** Can
43G3 **Mironovka** Ukraine
60C2 **Mirpur** Pak
60B3 **Mirpur Khas** Pak
41E3 **Mirtoan S** Greece
53B4 **Miryang** S Korea
61B2 **Mirzāpur** India
22C2 **Misantla** Mexico
5J4 **Miscou I** Can
60C1 **Misgar** Pak
53C2 **Mishan** China
12B2 **Mishawaka** USA
10F2 **Misheguk Mt** USA
54B4 **Mi-shima** *I* Japan
61E2 **Mishmi Hills** India
77E2 **Misima** *I* Solomon Is
25F3 **Misiones** State, Arg
43E3 **Miskolc** Hung
65D2 **Mismīyah** Syria
51G7 **Misoöl** *I* Indon
3H2 **Misow L** Can
69A1 **Misrātah** Libya
7K5 **Missinaibi** *R* Can
12C1 **Missinaibi L** Can
3H2 **Missinipe** Can
11B3 **Mission** S Dakota, USA
17F4 **Mission** Texas, USA
18B1 **Mission City** Can
13D2 **Mississauga** Can
9D3 **Mississippi** State, USA
9D3 **Mississippi** *R* USA
17E3 **Mississippi Delta** USA
8B2 **Missoula** USA
71B2 **Missour** Mor
9D3 **Missouri** State, USA
9D3 **Missouri** *R* USA
11C3 **Missouri Valley** USA
5G4 **Mistassini** Can
5G4 **Mistassini** *R* Can
5G3 **Mistassini Provincial Park** Can
5J2 **Mistastin L** Can
26D7 **Misti** *Mt* Peru
5J2 **Mistinibi L** Can
75C1 **Mitchell** Aust
8D2 **Mitchell** USA
76D2 **Mitchell** *R* Aust
9E3 **Mitchell,Mt** USA
51H8 **Mitchell River** Aust
65A3 **Mit el Nasâra** Egypt
65A3 **Mit Ghamr** Egypt
60B3 **Mithankot** Pak
41F3 **Mitilíni** Greece
22C2 **Mitla** Mexico
65B3 **Mitla P** Egypt
77G2 **Mitre** *I* Solomon Is
10G4 **Mitrofania I** USA
72D2 **Mits'iwa** Eth
37E1 **Mittersill** Austria
26D3 **Mitu** Colombia
72C4 **Mitumbar** *Mts* Zaïre
73C4 **Mitwaba** Zaïre
72B3 **Mitzic** Gabon
54C3 **Miura** Japan
52C3 **Mi Xian** China
50G3 **Miyake** *I* Japan
54C4 **Miyake-jima** *I* Japan
50F4 **Miyako** *I* Japan
53C5 **Miyakonojō** Japan
53C5 **Miyazaki** Japan
54C3 **Miyazu** Japan
53C5 **Miyoshi** Japan
52D1 **Miyun** China
54D2 **Mi-zaki** *Pt* Japan
72D3 **Mīzan Teferī** Eth
69A1 **Mizdah** Libya
41F1 **Mizil** Rom
61D3 **Mizo Hills** India
61D3 **Mizoram** Union Territory, India
65C3 **Mizpe Ramon** Israel
79F11 **Mizuho** *Base* Ant
53E4 **Mizusawa** Japan
32H7 **Mjolby** Sweden
73C5 **Mkushi** Zambia
74E2 **Mkuzi** S Africa
42C2 **Mladá Boleslav** Czech
43E2 **Mława** Pol
41D2 **Mljet** *I* Croatia, Yugos
74D2 **Mmabatho** S Africa
60D2 **Mnadi** India
57C4 **Moa** *I* Indon
70A4 **Moa** *R* Sierra Leone
65C3 **Moab** Region, Jordan
8C3 **Moab** USA
74E2 **Moamba** Mozam
72B4 **Moanda** Congo
72B4 **Moanda** Gabon
73C4 **Moba** Zaïre
54D3 **Mobara** Japan
72C3 **Mobaye** CAR
72C3 **Mobayi** Zaire
9D3 **Moberly** USA
9E3 **Mobile** USA
9E3 **Mobile B** USA
15B2 **Mobile Pt** USA
8C2 **Mobridge** USA
73E5 **Moçambique** Mozam
Moçâmedes = Namibe
55C1 **Moc Chau** Viet
74D1 **Mochudi** Botswana
73E5 **Mocimboa da Praia** Mozam
26C3 **Mocoa** Colombia
29C3 **Mococa** Brazil
28D2 **Mocoreta** *R* Arg
22C1 **Moctezulma** *R* Mexico
22B1 **Moctezuma** Mexico
73D5 **Mocuba** Mozam
37B2 **Modane** France
74D2 **Modder** *R* S Africa
40C2 **Modena** Italy
36D2 **Moder** *R* France
8A3 **Modesto** USA
20B2 **Modesto Res** USA
40C3 **Modica** Italy
42D3 **Mödling** Austria
76D4 **Moe** Aust
37C1 **Moesa** *R* Switz
34D4 **Moffat** Scot
60D2 **Moga** India
68J7 **Mogadiscio** Somalia
61E2 **Mogaung** Burma
29C3 **Mogi das Cruzes** Brazil
43G2 **Mogilev** Belorussia
45D6 **Mogilev Podol'skiy** Ukraine
29C3 **Mogi-Mirim** Brazil
73E5 **Mogincual** Mozam
37E2 **Mogliano** Italy
28B2 **Mogna** Arg
50E1 **Mogocha** Russian Fed
48K4 **Mogochin** Russian Fed
61E3 **Mogok** Burma
74D1 **Mogol** *R* S Africa
39A2 **Moguer** Spain
78C1 **Mohaka** *R* NZ
74D3 **Mohale's Hoek** Lesotho
11B2 **Mohall** USA
71C1 **Mohammadia** Alg
71A2 **Mohammedia** Mor
61D3 **Mohanganj** Bang
19D3 **Mohave,L** USA
14C1 **Mohawk** USA
13E2 **Mohawk** *R* USA
73E5 **Mohéli,I** Comoros
10E3 **Mohican,C** USA
73D4 **Mohoro** Tanz
48J5 **Mointy** Kazakhstan
32G5 **Mo i Rana** Nor
5H3 **Moisie** *R* Can
38C3 **Moissac** France
19C3 **Mojave** USA
20D3 **Mojave** *R* USA
8B3 **Mojave Desert** USA
56D4 **Mojokerto** Indon
66C4 **Mokada** *Mt* Eth
61C2 **Mokama** India
78B1 **Mokau** *R* NZ
20B1 **Mokelumne Aqueduct** USA
20B1 **Mokelumne Hill** USA
20B1 **Mokelumne North Fork** *R* USA
74D2 **Mokhotlong** Lesotho
71E1 **Moknine** Tunisia
61D2 **Mokokchūng** India
72B2 **Mokolo** Cam
53B5 **Mokp'o** S Korea
44G5 **Moksha** *R* Russian Fed
22C1 **Molango** Mexico
41E3 **Moláoi** Greece
45D6 **Moldavia** *Republic* Europe
32F6 **Molde** Nor
41E1 **Moldoveanu** *Mt* Rom
71F4 **Mole Nat Pk** Ghana
74D1 **Molepolole** Botswana
36D2 **Molesheim** France
40D2 **Molfetta** Italy
28A3 **Molina** Chile
37E1 **Möll** *R* Austria
26D7 **Mollendo** Peru
44D5 **Molodechno** Belorussia
79G11 **Molodezhnaya** *Base* Ant
20E5 **Molokai** *I* Hawaiian Is
44H4 **Moloma** *R* Russian Fed
75C2 **Molong** Aust
74C2 **Molopo** *R* S Africa/ Botswana
72B3 **Molounddu** Cam
4B3 **Molson L** Can
76B1 **Molucca S** Indon
51F7 **Moluccas** *Is* Indon
73D5 **Moma** Mozam
27K5 **Mombaca** Brazil
72D4 **Mombasa** Kenya
54D2 **Mombetsu** Japan
72C3 **Mompono** Zaïre
42C2 **Mon** *I* Den
34B3 **Monach** *Is* Scot
38D3 **Monaco** Principality, Europe
34C3 **Monadhliath** *Mts* Scot
35B4 **Monaghan** County, Irish Rep
35B4 **Monaghan** Irish Rep
16B3 **Monahans** USA
23D3 **Mona Pass** Caribbean
3C3 **Monarch Mt** Can
16A2 **Monarch P** USA
6G4 **Monashee Mts** Can
33B3 **Monastereven** Irish Rep
54D2 **Monbetsu** Japan
37B2 **Moncalieri** Italy
27J4 **Monção** Brazil
32L5 **Monchegorsk** Russian Fed
42B2 **Mönchen-gladbach** Germany
21B2 **Monclova** Mexico
7M5 **Moncton** Can
39A1 **Mondego** *R* Port
40B2 **Mondovi** Italy
23H1 **Moneague** Jamaica
13D2 **Monessen** USA
4F4 **Monet** Can
17D2 **Monett** USA

40C1 **Monfalcone** Italy
39A1 **Monforte de Lemos** Spain
72C3 **Monga** Zaïre
72C3 **Mongala** *R* Zaïre
72D3 **Mongalla** Sudan
55D1 **Mong Cai** Viet
72B2 **Mongo** Chad
50C2 **Mongolia** Republic, Asia
73C5 **Mongu** Zambia
19C3 **Monitor Range** *Mts* USA
72C4 **Monkoto** Zaïre
35D6 **Monmouth** Eng
12A2 **Monmouth** USA
3D3 **Monmouth,Mt** Can
71G4 **Mono** *R* Togo
19C3 **Mono L** USA
41D2 **Monopoli** Italy
39B1 **Monreal del Campo** Spain
17D3 **Monroe** Louisiana, USA
12C2 **Monroe** Michigan, USA
15C2 **Monroe** N Carolina, USA
18B1 **Monroe** Washington, USA
12B2 **Monroe** Wisconsin, USA
17D2 **Monroe City** USA
70A4 **Monrovia** Lib
20D3 **Monrovia** USA
42A2 **Mons** Belg
37D2 **Monselice** Italy
14D1 **Monson** USA
42D1 **Mönsterås** Sweden
73E5 **Montagne d'Ambre** *Mt* Madag
71C2 **Montagnes des Ouled Naïl** *Mts* Alg
74C3 **Montagu** S Africa
5J4 **Montague** Can
10J4 **Montague I** USA
38B2 **Montaigu** France
40D3 **Montallo** *Mt* Italy
8B2 **Montana** State, USA
39A1 **Montañas de León** *Mts* Spain
38C2 **Montargis** France
38C3 **Montauban** France
13E2 **Montauk** USA
13E2 **Montauk Pt** USA
36C3 **Montbard** France
38D2 **Montbéliard** France
40B1 **Mont Blanc** *Mt* France/Italy
Montblanc = Montblanch
39C1 **Montblanch** Spain
38C2 **Montceau les Mines** France
39C1 **Montceny** *Mt* Spain
38D3 **Mont Cinto** *Mt* Corse
36C2 **Montcornet** France
36A2 **Mont d'Amain** *Mt* France
38B3 **Mont-de-Marsin** France
38C2 **Montdidier** France
26F7 **Monteagudo** Bol
27H4 **Monte Alegre** Brazil
40C2 **Monte Amiata** *Mt* Italy
29D2 **Monte Azul** Brazil
37D2 **Monte Baldo** *Mt* Italy
13D1 **Montebello** Can
76A3 **Monte Bello Is** Aust
37E2 **Montebelluna** Italy
37B3 **Monte Carlo** France
29C2 **Monte Carmelo** Brazil
28D2 **Monte Caseros** Arg
37D3 **Montecatini** Italy
37E3 **Monte Catria** *Mt* Italy
40C2 **Monte Cimone** *Mt* Italy
40B2 **Monte Cinto** *Mt* Corse
28B2 **Monte Coman** Arg
40C2 **Monte Corno** *Mt* Italy
23C3 **Montecristi** Dom Rep
40C2 **Montecristo** *I* Italy
22B1 **Monte Escobedo** Mexico
37D3 **Monte Falterona** *Mt* Italy
40D2 **Monte Gargano** *Mt* Italy
23B3 **Montego Bay** Jamaica
37D2 **Monte Grappa** *Mt* Italy
37C2 **Monte Lesima** *Mt* Italy
38C3 **Montélimar** France
29A3 **Montelindo** *R* Par
40C2 **Monte Miletto** *Mt* Italy
39A2 **Montemo-o-Novo** Port
21C2 **Montemorelos** Mexico
23B5 **Montená** Colombia
41D2 **Montenegro** Republic, Yugos
28E1 **Montengero** Brazil
37C3 **Monte Orsaro** *Mt* Italy
29E2 **Monte Pascoal** *Mt* Brazil
28A2 **Monte Patria** Chile
37E3 **Monte Pennino** *Mt* Italy
28B1 **Monte Pississ** *Mt* Arg
40D3 **Monte Pollino** *Mt* Italy
37E2 **Monte Pramaggiore** *Mt* Italy
73D5 **Montepuez** Mozam
37D3 **Montepulciano** Italy
36B2 **Montereau-Faut-Yonne** France
8A3 **Monterey** California, USA
13D3 **Monterey** Virginia, USA
8A3 **Monterey B** USA
26C2 **Montería** Colombia
26F7 **Montero** Bol
37B2 **Monte Rosa** *Mt* Italy/Switz
21B2 **Monterrey** Mexico
27K7 **Montes Claros** Brazil
39B2 **Montes de Toledo** *Mts* Spain
37D3 **Montevarchi** Italy
25E4 **Montevideo** Urug
11C3 **Montevideo** USA
35F6 **Montevil** France
40B2 **Monte Viso** *Mt* Italy
16A2 **Monte Vista** USA
16B2 **Montezuma** USA
20D2 **Montezuma Peak** *Mt* USA
23P2 **Mont Gimie** *Mt* St Lucia
9E3 **Montgomery** Alabama, USA
14B2 **Montgomery** Pennsylvania, USA
20C2 **Montgomery P** USA
70C2 **Mont Gréboun** Niger
36C2 **Montherme** France
37B1 **Monthey** Switz
17D3 **Monticello** Arkansas, USA
12A2 **Monticello** Iowa, USA
11D2 **Monticello** Minnesota, USA
14C2 **Monticello** New York, USA
8C3 **Monticello** Utah, USA
40B2 **Monti del Gennargentu** *Mt* Sardegna
36C2 **Montier-en-Der** France
37D2 **Monti Lessini** *Mts* Italy
40C3 **Monti Nebrodi** *Mts* Italy
36A2 **Montivilliers** France
5H4 **Mont Joli** Can
4F4 **Mont-Laurier** Can
5H4 **Mont Louis** Can
38C2 **Montluçon** France
7L5 **Montmagny** Can
36C2 **Montmédy** France
36B2 **Montmirail** France
13E1 **Montmorency** Can
37B2 **Mont Mounier** *Mt* France
39B2 **Montoro** Spain
14B2 **Montoursville** USA
38D3 **Mont Pelat** *Mt* France
18D2 **Montpelier** Idaho, USA
12C2 **Montpelier** Ohio, USA
9F2 **Montpelier** Vermont, USA
38C3 **Montpellier** France
7L5 **Montréal** Can
3G3 **Montreal L** Can
3G3 **Montreal Lake** Can
38C1 **Montreuil** France
40B1 **Montreux** Switz
37A1 **Montrevel** France
37B1 **Mont Risoux** *Mt* France
8C3 **Montrose** Colorado, USA
14C2 **Montrose** Pennsylvania, USA
33C2 **Montrose** Scot
34F3 **Montrose** *Oilfield* N Sea
38B2 **Mont-St-Michel** France
71B2 **Monts des Ksour** *Mts* Alg
39C3 **Monts des Ouled Neil** *Mts* Alg
39C2 **Monts du Hodna** *Mts* Alg
23E3 **Montserrat** *I* Caribbean
5H4 **Monts Notre Dame** *Mts* Can
5G3 **Monts Otish** *Mts* Can
5G4 **Mont Tremblant Prov Park** Can
37A2 **Mont Ventoux** *Mt* France
10F2 **Monument Mt** USA
8B3 **Monument V** USA
72C3 **Monveda** Zaïre
55B1 **Monywa** Burma
40B1 **Monza** Italy
73C5 **Monze** Zambia
74E2 **Mooi** *R* S Africa
74D2 **Mool River** S Africa
75B1 **Moomba** Aust
75D2 **Moonbi Range** *Mts* Aust
75B1 **Moonda L** Aust
75D1 **Moonie** Aust
75C1 **Moonie** *R* Aust
75A2 **Moonta** Aust
76A4 **Moora** Aust
75B1 **Mooraberree** Aust
11B3 **Moorcroft** USA
76A3 **Moore,L** Aust
34D4 **Moorfoot Hills** Scot
8D2 **Moorhead** USA
20C3 **Moorpark** USA
74B3 **Moorreesburg** S Africa
7K4 **Moose** *R* Can
13F1 **Moosehead L** USA
6H4 **Moose Jaw** Can
11D2 **Moose Lake** USA
6H4 **Moosomin** Can
7K4 **Moosonee** Can
14E2 **Moosup** USA
73D5 **Mopeia** Mozam
70B3 **Mopti** Mali
26D7 **Moquegua** Peru
71J3 **Mora** Cam
32G6 **Mora** Sweden
11D2 **Mora** USA
27L5 **Morada** Brazil
60D3 **Morādābād** India
29C2 **Morada Nova de Minas** *L* Brazil
73E5 **Morafenobe** Madag
73E5 **Moramanga** Madag
18D2 **Moran** USA
23J2 **Morant Bay** Jamaica
23J2 **Morant Pt** Jamaica
62B3 **Moratuwa** Sri Lanka
42D3 **Morava** *R* Austria/Czech
41E2 **Morava** *R* Serbia, Yugos
63D1 **Moraveh Tappeh** Iran
33C2 **Moray Firth** *Estuary* Scot
37C1 **Morbegno** Italy
60C4 **Morbi** India
22B1 **Morcillo** Mexico
64D2 **Mor Dağ** *Mt* Turk
6J5 **Morden** Can
44G5 **Mordovskaya** Respublika, Russian Fed
11B2 **Moreau** *R* USA
35D4 **Morecambe** Eng
35D4 **Morecambe B** Eng
76D3 **Moree** Aust
36A3 **Morée** France
12C3 **Morehead** USA
15D2 **Morehead City** USA
37C1 **Mörel** Switz
21B3 **Morelia** Mexico
22B1 **Morelos** Mexico
22C1 **Morelos** Mexico
22C2 **Morelos** State, Mexico
60D3 **Morena** India
6E4 **Moresby I** Can
75D1 **Moreton I** Aust
36B2 **Moreuil** France
37B1 **Morez** France
17D4 **Morgan City** USA
20B2 **Morgan Hill** USA
20C2 **Morgan,Mt** USA
15C1 **Morganton** USA
13D3 **Morgantown** USA
74D2 **Morgenzon** S Africa
37B1 **Morges** Switz
36D2 **Morhange** France
53E3 **Mori** Japan
16A3 **Moriarty** USA
23K1 **Moriatio** Tobago
3C3 **Morice L** Can
53A2 **Morin Dawa** China
3F3 **Morinville** Can
53E4 **Morioka** Japan
75D2 **Morisset** Aust
49N3 **Morkoka** *R* Russian Fed
38B2 **Morlaix** France
23Q2 **Morne Diablotin** *Mt* Dominica
75B1 **Morney** Aust
76C2 **Mornington** *I* Aust
60B3 **Moro** Pak
76D1 **Morobe** PNG
70B1 **Morocco** Kingdom, Africa
57F9 **Moro G** Phil
73D4 **Morogoro** Tanz
22B1 **Moroleon** Mexico
73E6 **Morombe** Madag
23B2 **Morón** Cuba
73E6 **Morondava** Madag
39A2 **Moron de la Frontera** Spain
73E5 **Moroni** Comoros
57C2 **Morotai** *I* Indon
72D3 **Moroto** Uganda
45G6 **Morozovsk** Russian Fed
34E4 **Morpeth** Eng
65B1 **Morphou** Cyprus
65B1 **Morphou B** Cyprus
11B3 **Morrill** USA
17D2 **Morrilton** USA
29C2 **Morrinhos** Brazil
78C1 **Morrinsville** NZ
11C2 **Morris** Can
11C2 **Morris** USA
14C2 **Morristown** New Jersey, USA
13D2 **Morristown** New York, USA
15C1 **Morristown** Tennessee, USA
14C1 **Morrisville** New York, USA
14C2 **Morrisville** Pennsylvania, USA
20B3 **Morro Bay** USA
22B2 **Morro de Papanoa** Mexico
22B2 **Morro de Petatlán** Mexico
73D5 **Morrumbala** Mozam
73D6 **Morrumbene** Mozam
44G5 **Morshansk** Russian Fed
36A2 **Mortagne-au-Perche** France
37C2 **Mortara** Italy
28C2 **Morteros** Arg
Mortes = Manso
27H6 **Mortes** *R* Malo Grosso, Brazil
29D3 **Mortes** *R* Minas Gerais, Brazil
75B3 **Mortlake** Aust
16B3 **Morton** USA
23L1 **Moruga** Trinidad
75D3 **Moruya** Aust
75C1 **Morven** Aust
34C3 **Morvern** *Pen* Scot
75C3 **Morwell** Aust
10F4 **Morzhovoi B** USA
36E2 **Mosbach** Germany
55B3 **Moscos Is** Burma
Moscow = Moskva
18C1 **Moscow** Idaho, USA
14C2 **Moscow** Pennsylvania, USA
42B2 **Mosel** *R* Germany
74C2 **Moselebe** *R* Botswana
36D2 **Moselle** Department, France
36D2 **Moselle** *R* France
18C1 **Moses Lake** USA
78B3 **Mosgiel** NZ
72D4 **Moshi** Tanz
12B2 **Mosinee** USA
32G5 **Mosjøen** Nor
49Q4 **Moskal'vo** Russian Fed
44F4 **Moskva** Russian Fed
16B2 **Mosquero** USA
29D2 **Mosquito** *R* Brazil
32G7 **Moss** Nor
72B4 **Mossaka** Congo
Mossâmedes = Moçâmedes
74C3 **Mossel Bay** S Africa
72B4 **Mossendjo** Congo
75B2 **Mossgiel** Aust
27L5 **Mossoró** Brazil
42C2 **Most** Czech
71C1 **Mostaganem** Alg
41D2 **Mostar** Bosnia & Herzegovina, Yugos
28E2 **Mostardos** Brazil
43E2 **Mosty** Belorussia
64D2 **Mosul** Iraq
32G7 **Motala** Sweden
34D4 **Motherwell** Scot
61B2 **Motihāri** India
39B2 **Motilla del Palancar** Spain
74D1 **Motloutse** *R* Botswana
37E2 **Motovun** Croatia, Yugos
39B2 **Motril** Spain
11B2 **Mott** USA
78B2 **Motueka** NZ
78B2 **Motueka** *R* NZ
5H3 **Mouchalagane** *R* Can
37B1 **Moudon** Switz
72B4 **Mouila** Gabon
75B2 **Moulamein** Aust
6G2 **Mould Bay** Can
38C2 **Moulins** France
55B2 **Moulmein** Burma
71B2 **Moulouya** *R* Mor
15C2 **Moultrie** USA
15D2 **Moultrie,L** USA
12B3 **Mound City** Illinois, USA
17C1 **Mound City** Missouri, USA
72B3 **Moundou** Chad
12C3 **Moundsville** USA
38C3 **Mount Aigoual** *Mt* France
10N2 **Mountain** *R* Can
15B2 **Mountain Brook** USA
17D2 **Mountain Grove** USA
17D2 **Mountain Home** Arkansas, USA
18C2 **Mountain Home** Idaho, USA
20A2 **Mountain View** USA
10F3 **Mountain Village** USA
14B3 **Mount Airy** Maryland, USA
15C1 **Mount Airy** N Carolina, USA
74D3 **Mount Ayliff** S Africa
14B2 **Mount Carmel** USA
13F2 **Mount Desert I** USA
75A1 **Mount Dutton** Aust
75A2 **Mount Eba** Aust
74D3 **Mount Fletcher** S Africa
75B3 **Mount Gambier** Aust
76D1 **Mount Hagen** PNG
14C3 **Mount Holly** USA
14B2 **Mount Holly Springs** USA
75A2 **Mount Hope** Aust
76C3 **Mount Isa** Aust
14A3 **Mount Jackson** USA
5H4 **Mt Jacques Cartier** Can
14A2 **Mount Jewett** USA
75A2 **Mount Lofty Range** *Mts* Aust
10H3 **Mount McKinley Nat Pk** USA
76A3 **Mount Magnet** Aust
75B2 **Mount Manara** Aust
38C3 **Mount Mézenc** *Mt* France
76E3 **Mount Morgan** Aust
14B1 **Mount Morris** USA
75D1 **Mount Perry** Aust
4E5 **Mt Pleasant** Michigan, USA
17D3 **Mount Pleasant** Texas, USA
19D3 **Mount Pleasant** Utah, USA
14C2 **Mount Pocono** USA
18B1 **Mount Rainier Nat Pk** USA
35C6 **Mounts B** Eng
18B2 **Mount Shasta** USA
14B2 **Mount Union** USA
15B2 **Mount Vernon** Alabama, USA
12B3 **Mount Vernon** Illinois, USA
17C3 **Mount Vernon** Kentucky, USA
18B1 **Mount Vernon** Washington, USA
35B4 **Mourne Mts** N Ire
66D4 **Moussa Ali** *Mt* Djibouti
72B2 **Moussoro** Chad
37B3 **Moustiers Ste Marie** France
60B4 **Mouth of the Indus** Pak
61C3 **Mouths of the Ganga** India/Bang
55D4 **Mouths of the Mekong** Viet
70C4 **Mouths of the Niger** Nigeria
37B1 **Moutier** Switz
37B2 **Moûtiers** France
57B2 **Moutong** Indon
70C2 **Mouydir** *Mts* Alg
72B4 **Mouyondzi** Congo
36C2 **Mouzon** France
22B1 **Moyahua** Mexico
72D3 **Moyale** Kenya
70A4 **Moyamba** Sierra Leone
71A2 **Moyen Atlas** *Mts* Mor
74D3 **Moyeni** Lesotho
49M3 **Moyero** *R* Russian Fed
72D3 **Moyo** Uganda
26C5 **Moyobamba** Peru
60D1 **Moyu** China
73D6 **Mozambique** Republic, Africa
73D6 **Mozambique Chan** Mozam/Madag
44J4 **Mozhga** Russian Fed
32K8 **Mozyr'** Belorussia
72D4 **Mpanda** Tanz
73D5 **Mpika** Zambia
73D4 **Mporokosa** Zambia
73C5 **Mposhi** Zambia
73D4 **Mpulungu** Zambia
72D4 **Mpwapwa** Tanz
43G2 **Mstislavl'** Belorussia
44F5 **Mtsensk** Russian Fed
74E2 **Mtubatuba** S Africa
73E5 **Mtwara** Tanz
55C2 **Muang Chainat** Thai
55C2 **Muang Chiang Rai** Thai
55C2 **Muang Kalasin** Thai
55C2 **Muang Khon Kaen** Thai
55B2 **Muang Lampang** Thai
55B2 **Muang Lamphun** Thai
55C2 **Muang Loei** Thai
55C2 **Muang Lom Sak** Thai
55C2 **Muang Nakhon Phanom** Thai
55B2 **Muang Nakhon Sawan** Thai
55C2 **Muang Nan** Thai
55C2 **Muang Phayao** Thai
55C2 **Muang Phetchabun** Thai
55C2 **Muang Phichit** Thai
55C2 **Muang Phitsanulok** Thai
55C2 **Muang Phrae** Thai
55C2 **Muang Roi Et** Thai
55C2 **Muang Sakon Nakhon** Thai
55C3 **Muang Samut Prakan** Thai
55C2 **Muang Uthai Thani** Thai
55C2 **Muang Yasothon** Thai
55C5 **Muar** Malay
56D2 **Muara** Brunei
56B3 **Muara** Indon
56B3 **Muaralakitan** Indon
56B3 **Muaratebo** Indon
56E3 **Muaratewah** Indon
56B3 **Muarenim** Indon
55A2 **Muaungmaya** Burma
72D3 **Mubende** Uganda
71J3 **Mubi** Nig
73D5 **Muchinga** *Mts* Zambia
34B3 **Muck** *I* Scot
75C1 **Muckadilla** Aust
73C5 **Muconda** Angola
29E2 **Mucuri** Brazil
29D2 **Mucuri** *R* Brazil
73C5 **Mucusso** Angola

53B3 **Mudanjiang** China
67F3 **Mudayy** Oman
11A3 **Muddy Gap P** USA
75C2 **Mudgee** Aust
20D2 **Mud L** USA
55B2 **Mudon** Burma
44F3 **Mud'yuga** Russian Fed
77F3 **Mue** Nouvelle Calédonie
73D5 **Mueda** Mozam
73C5 **Mufulira** Zambia
52C4 **Mufu Shan** *Hills* China
Mugadishu = Muqdisho
45K6 **Mugodzhary** *Mts* Kazakhstan
64C4 **Mughayra** S Arabia
64A2 **Muğla** Turk
45K6 **Mugodzhary** *Mts* Kazakhstan
61B2 **Mugu** Nepal
52A3 **Muguaping** China
66C2 **Muhammad Qol** Sudan
64D3 **Muhaywir** Iraq
36E2 **Mühlacker** Germany
42C3 **Mühldorf** Germany
42C2 **Muhlhausen** Germany
32K6 **Muhos** Fin
55C4 **Mui Bai Bung** *C* Camb
35B5 **Muine Bheag** Irish Rep
73C5 **Mujimbeji** Zambia
43E3 **Mukachevo** Ukraine
56D2 **Mukah** Malay
54D2 **Mukawa** Japan
50H4 **Muko-jima** *I* Japan
61B2 **Muktinath** Nepal
60B2 **Mukur** Afghan
53B2 **Mulan** China
17D2 **Mulberry** USA
10G3 **Mulchatna** *R* USA
28A3 **Mulchén** Chile
42C2 **Mulde** *R* Germany
11B3 **Mule Creek** USA
16B3 **Muleshoe** USA
51H8 **Mulgrave I** Aust
39B2 **Mulhacén** *Mt* Spain
36D1 **Mülheim** Germany
36D3 **Mulhouse** France
52A4 **Muli** China
53C3 **Muling** China
53C2 **Muling He** *R* China
34C3 **Mull** *I* Scot
62C3 **Mullaitvu** Sri Lanka
75C2 **Mullaley** Aust
76A3 **Mullewa** Aust
36D3 **Müllheim** Germany
14C3 **Mullica** *R* USA
35B5 **Mullingar** Irish Rep
34C4 **Mull of Kintyre** *Pt* Scot
34B4 **Mull of Oa** *C* Scot
75D1 **Mullumbimby** Aust
73C5 **Mulobezi** Zambia
60C2 **Multan** Pak
57C3 **Muluku** *Is* Indon
73C5 **Mumbwa** Zambia
45H6 **Mumra** Russian Fed
57B4 **Muna** *I* Indon
42C3 **München** Germany
3C2 **Muncho Lake** Can
54A3 **Munchŏn** N Korea
12B2 **Muncie** USA
75A1 **Munconnie,L** Aust
14B2 **Muncy** USA
42B2 **Münden** Germany
75D1 **Mundubbera** Aust
75C1 **Mungallala** Aust
75C1 **Mungallala** *R* Aust
72C3 **Mungbere** Zaïre
61B3 **Mungeli** India
61C2 **Munger** India
75C1 **Mungindi** Aust
Munich = München
12B1 **Munising** USA
25B8 **Muñoz Gomero,Pen** Chile
3J2 **Munroe L** Can
54A3 **Munsan** S Korea
36E2 **Münsingen** Germany
36D2 **Munster** France
37C1 **Münster** Switz
42B2 **Münster** Germany
36D1 **Münsterland** Region, Germany
41E1 **Muntii Apuseni** *Mts* Rom
41E1 **Muntii Călimanilor** *Mts* Rom
41E1 **Muntii Carpaţii Meridionali** *Mts* Rom
41E1 **Muntii Rodnei** *Mts* Rom
41E1 **Muntii Zarandului** *Mts* Rom
64C2 **Munzur Silsilesi** *Mts* Turk
48D3 **Muomio** Fin
55C1 **Muong Khoua** Laos
55D3 **Muong Man** Viet
55D2 **Muong Nong** Laos
55C1 **Muong Ou Neua** Laos
55C1 **Muong Sai** Laos
55C2 **Muong Sen** Viet
55C1 **Muong Sing** Laos
55C1 **Muong Son** Laos
32J5 **Muonio** Fin
32J5 **Muonio** *R* Sweden/Fin
66B3 **Muqaddam** *Watercourse* Sudan
72E3 **Muqdisho** Somalia
40C1 **Mur** *R* Austria
53D4 **Murakami** Japan
25B7 **Murallón** *Mt* Chile/Arg
44H4 **Murashi** Russian Fed
64D2 **Murat** *R* Turk
40B3 **Muravera** Sardegna
54D3 **Murayama** Japan
67F4 **Murcanyo** Somalia
63C2 **Murcheh Khvort** Iran
78B2 **Murchison** NZ
76A3 **Murchison** *R* Aust
39B2 **Murcia** Region, Spain
39B2 **Murcia** Spain
11B3 **Murdo** USA
41E1 **Mureş** *R* Rom
41E1 **Muresui** *R* Rom
15B1 **Murfreesboro** USA
15D1 **Murfreesboro** USA
36E2 **Murg** *R* Germany
48H6 **Murgab** *R* Turkmenistan
60B2 **Murgha Kibzai** Pak
75D1 **Murgon** Aust
61C3 **Muri** India
29D3 **Muriaé** Brazil
73C4 **Muriege** Angola
44E2 **Murmansk** Russian Fed
44G4 **Murom** Russian Fed
53E3 **Muroran** Japan
39A1 **Muros** Spain
53C5 **Muroto** Japan
54B4 **Muroto-zaki** *C* Japan
18C2 **Murphy** Idaho, USA
15C1 **Murphy** N Carolina, USA
20B1 **Murphys** USA
12B3 **Murray** Kentucky, USA
18D2 **Murray** Utah, USA
75B2 **Murray** *R* Aust
3D2 **Murray** *R* Can
75A3 **Murray Bridge** Aust
51H7 **Murray,L** PNG
15C2 **Murray,L** USA
74C3 **Murraysburg** S Africa
xxixM3 **Murray Seacarp** Pacific O
36E2 **Murrhardt** Germany
75B2 **Murrumbidgee** *R* Aust
75C2 **Murrumburrah** Aust
75D2 **Murrurundi** Aust
37B1 **Murten** Switz
75B3 **Murtoa** Aust
78C1 **Murupara** NZ
61B3 **Murwāra** India
75D1 **Murwillimbah** Aust
64D2 **Muş** Turk
41E2 **Musala** *Mt* Bulg
53B3 **Musan** N Korea
67G1 **Musandam** *Pen* Oman
Muscat = Masqat
67G2 **Muscat** *Region* Oman
11D3 **Muscatine** USA
76C3 **Musgrave Range** *Mts* Aust
72B4 **Mushie** Zaïre
14E2 **Muskeget Chan** USA
12B2 **Muskegon** USA
12B2 **Muskegon** *R* USA
17C2 **Muskogee** USA
66C3 **Musmar** Sudan
72D4 **Musoma** Tanz
76D1 **Mussau** *I* PNG
18E1 **Musselshell** *R* USA
73B5 **Mussende** Angola
38C2 **Mussidan** France
41F2 **Mustafa-Kemalpasa** Turk
61B2 **Mustang** Nepal
54A2 **Musu-dan** *C* N Korea
75D2 **Muswelibrook** Aust
69B2 **Mut** Egypt
73D5 **Mutarara** Mozam
73D5 **Mutare** Zim
57B4 **Mutis** *Mt* Indon
44K2 **Mutnyy Materik** Russian Fed
73D5 **Mutoko** Zim
73E5 **Mutsamudu** Comoros
73C5 **Mutshatsha** Zaïre
53E3 **Mutsu** Japan
53E3 **Mutsu-wan** *B* Japan
5K3 **Mutton Bay** Can
29C1 **Mutunópolis** Brazil
52B2 **Mu Us Shamo** *Desert* China
73B4 **Muxima** Angola
49N4 **Muya** Russian Fed
44E3 **Muyezerskiy** Russian Fed
72D4 **Muyinga** Burundi
73C4 **Muyumba** Zaïre
59E1 **Muyun Kum** *Desert* Kazakhstan
60C2 **Muzaffarābad** Pak
60C2 **Muzaffargarh** Pak
60D3 **Muzaffarnagar** India
61C2 **Muzaffarpur** India
48H3 **Muzhi** Russian Fed
59G2 **Muzlag** *Mt* China
3B3 **Muzon,C** USA
59F2 **Muztagala** *Mt* China
73D5 **Mvuma** Zim
72D4 **Mwanza** Tanz
73C4 **Mwanza** Zaïre
72C4 **Mweka** Zaïre
73C4 **Mwene Ditu** Zaïre
73D6 **Mwenezi** Zim
72C4 **Mwenga** Zaïre
73C4 **Mweru** *L* Zambia
73C5 **Mwinilunga** Zambia
61E4 **Myanaung** Burma
Myanma = Burma
61E3 **Myingyan** Burma
55B1 **Myingyao** Burma
55B3 **Myinmoletkat** *Mt* Burma
61E3 **Myinmu** Burma
61E2 **Myitkyina** Burma
55B3 **Myitta** Burma
61E3 **Myittha** Burma
61D3 **Mymensingh** Bang
50G3 **Myojin** *I* Japan
54A2 **Myongchon** N Korea
54A2 **Myonggan** N Korea
32F6 **Myrdal** Nor
32B2 **Myrdalsjökur** *Mts* Iceland
15D2 **Myrtle Beach** USA
18B2 **Myrtle Creek** USA
49U3 **Mys Chaplino** *C* Russian Fed
49M2 **Mys Chelyuskin** *C* Russian Fed
10D3 **Mys Chukotskiy** *Pt* Russian Fed
10E2 **Mys Dezhneva** *Pt* Russian Fed
32G7 **Mysen** Nor
42C2 **Mysiloborz** Pol
44G2 **Mys Kanin Nos** *C* Russian Fed
49S4 **Mys Kronotskiy** *C* Russian Fed
43D3 **Myślenice** Pol
49R4 **Mys Lopatka** *C* Russian Fed
49T3 **Mys Navarin** *C* Russian Fed
10D2 **Mys Nygchigen** *Pt* Russian Fed
49T4 **Mys Olyutorskiy** *C* Russian Fed
62B2 **Mysore** India
45E7 **Mys Sarych** *C* Ukraine
10D2 **Mys Serdtse Kamen** *Pt* Russian Fed
49T2 **Mys Shelagskiy** *C* Russian Fed
49U3 **Mys Shmidta** Russian Fed
49S4 **Mys Sivuchiy** *C* Kirgizia
44F2 **Mys Svyatoy Nos** *C* Russian Fed
14E2 **Mystic** USA
45J7 **Mys Tyub-Karagan** *Pt* Kazakhstan
49Q4 **Mys Yelizavety** *C* Russian Fed
48H2 **Mys Zhelaniya** *C* Russian Fed
55D3 **My Tho** Viet
18B2 **Mytle Point** USA
73D5 **Mzimba** Malawi
73D5 **Mzuzú** Malawi

N

20E5 **Naalehu** Hawaiian Is
32J6 **Naantali** Fin
35B5 **Naas** Irish Rep
54C4 **Nabari** Japan
44J4 **Naberezhnyye Chelny** Russian Fed
10K3 **Nabesna** *R* USA
71E1 **Nabeul** Tunisia
29A3 **Nabileque** *R* Brazil
65C2 **Nablus** Israel
73E5 **Nacala** Mozam
18B1 **Naches** USA
5H2 **Nachikapau L** Can
73D5 **Nachingwea** Tanz
20B3 **Nacimiento** *R* USA
20B3 **Nacimiento Res** USA
17D3 **Nacogdoches** USA
55A3 **Nacondam** *I* Indian O
21B1 **Nacozari** Mexico
36E1 **Nadel** *Mt* Germany
77G2 **Nadi** Fiji
60C4 **Nadiād** India
39B2 **Nador** Mor
63C2 **Nadūshan** Iran
44E3 **Nadvoitsy** Russian Fed
43E3 **Nadvornaya** Ukraine
42C1 **Naestved** Den
54B4 **Nagahama** Japan
61E2 **Naga Hills** Burma
54C3 **Nagai** Japan
10G5 **Nagal** *I* USA
61D2 **Nāgāland** State, India
53D4 **Nagano** Japan
53D4 **Nagaoka** Japan
62B2 **Nāgappattinam** India
60C4 **Nagar Parkar** Pak
53B5 **Nagasaki** Japan
54C4 **Nagashima** Japan
54B4 **Nagato** Japan
60C3 **Nāgaur** India
62B3 **Nāgercoil** India
60B3 **Nagha Kalat** Pak
60D3 **Nagīna** India
36E2 **Nagold** Germany
53D4 **Nagoya** Japan
60D4 **Nāgpur** India
59H2 **Nagqu** China
42D3 **Nagykanizsa** Hung
43D3 **Nagykörös** Hung
50F4 **Naha** Japan
60D2 **Nāhan** India
63E3 **Nahang** *R* Iran
6F3 **Nahanni Butte** Can
10N3 **Nahanni Nat Pk** Can
10O3 **Nahanni Range** *Mts* Can
65C2 **Nahariya** Israel
71C1 **Nahar Ouassel** *R* Alg
63B2 **Nahāvand** Iran
36D2 **Nahe** *R* Germany
52D2 **Nahpu** China
28B4 **Nahuel Niyeu** Arg
57B4 **Naikliu** Indon
52E1 **Naimen Qi** China
7M4 **Nain** Can
63C2 **Nā'īn** Iran
60D3 **Naini Tai** India
61B3 **Nainpur** India
34D3 **Nairn** Scot
72D4 **Nairobi** Kenya
63C2 **Najafābād** Iran
66D1 **Najd** Region, S Arabia
53C3 **Najin** N Korea
66D3 **Najrān** S Arabia
54A3 **Naju** S Korea
54A4 **Nakadori-jima** Japan
54B4 **Nakama** Japan
53E4 **Nakaminato** Japan
54B4 **Nakamura** Japan
54C3 **Nakano** Japan
54B3 **Nakano-shima** *I* Japan
53C5 **Nakatsu** Japan
54C3 **Nakatsu-gawa** Japan
66C3 **Nak'fa** Eth
45H8 **Nakhichevan** Azerbaijan
65B4 **Nakhl** Egypt
53C3 **Nakhodka** Russian Fed
55C3 **Nakhon Pathom** Thai
55C3 **Nakhon Ratchasima** Thai
55C4 **Nakhon Si Thammarat** Thai
3B2 **Nakina** British Columbia, Can
7K4 **Nakina** Ontario, Can
3B2 **Nakina** *R* Can
10G4 **Naknek** USA
10G4 **Naknek L** USA
32G7 **Nakskov** Den
54A3 **Naktong** *R* S Korea
72D4 **Nakuru** Kenya
3E3 **Nakusp** Can
45G7 **Nal'chik** Russian Fed
62B1 **Nalgonda** India
62B1 **Nallamala Range** *Mts* India
44C2 **Naltia** *Mt* Nor/Fin
69A1 **Nālūt** Libya
74E2 **Namaacha** Mozam
48G6 **Namak** *L* Iran
63D2 **Namakzar-e Shadad** *Salt Flat* Iran
48J5 **Namangan** Uzbekistan
73D5 **Namapa** Mozam
73B7 **Namaqualand** Region, S Africa
75D1 **Nambour** Aust
75D2 **Nambucca Heads** Aust
55D4 **Nam Can** Viet
59H2 **Nam Co** *L* China
55D1 **Nam Dinh** Viet
73D5 **Nametil** Mozam
3H3 **Namew L** Can
53B5 **Namhae-do** *I* S Korea
74A1 **Namib Desert** Namibia
73B5 **Namibe** Angola
73B6 **Namibia** Republic, Africa
57C3 **Namlea** Indon
61C2 **Namling** China
57B3 **Namo** Indon
75C2 **Namoi** *R* Aust
3E2 **Nampa** Can
18C2 **Nampa** USA
70B3 **Nampala** Mali
55C2 **Nam Phong** Thai
53B4 **Namp'o** N Korea
73D5 **Nampula** Mozam
32G6 **Namsos** Nor
55B1 **Namton** Burma
49O3 **Namtsy** Russian Fed
61E3 **Namtu** Burma
3C3 **Namu** Can
73D5 **Namuno** Mozam
36C1 **Namur** Belg
73B5 **Namutoni** Namibia
53B4 **Namwŏn** S Korea
3D4 **Nanaimo** Can
53B3 **Nanam** N Korea
75D1 **Nanango** Aust
53D4 **Nanao** Japan
54C3 **Nanatsu-jima** *I* Japan
52B3 **Nanbu** China
53B2 **Nancha** China
52D4 **Nanchang** China
52B3 **Nanchong** China
62E3 **Nancowry** *I* Indian O
38D2 **Nancy** France
61B1 **Nanda Devi** *Mt* India
62B1 **Nānded** India
75D2 **Nandewar Range** *Mts* Aust
60C4 **Nandurbar** India
62B1 **Nandyāl** India
72B3 **Nanga Eboko** Cam
57B4 **Nangahale** Indon
60C1 **Nanga Parbat** *Mt* Pak
56D3 **Nangapinoh** Indon
56D3 **Nangatayap** Indon
36B2 **Nangis** France
54A2 **Nangnim** N Korea
53B3 **Nangnim Sanmaek** *Mts* N Korea
61D2 **Nang Xian** China
62B2 **Nanjangūd** India
52D3 **Nanjing** China
Nanking = Nanjing
54B4 **Nankoku** Japan
52C4 **Nan Ling** Region, China
55D1 **Nanliu** *R* China
52B5 **Nanning** China
7O3 **Nanortalik** Greenland
52A5 **Nanpan Jiang** *R* China
61B2 **Nānpāra** India
52D4 **Nanping** China
7J1 **Nansen Sd** Can
72D4 **Nansio** Tanz
38B2 **Nantes** France
14C2 **Nanticoke** USA
3F3 **Nanton** Can
52E3 **Nantong** China
37A1 **Nantua** France
14E2 **Nantucket** USA
14E2 **Nantucket I** USA
14E2 **Nantucket Sd** USA
14A2 **Nanty Glo** USA
77G1 **Nanumanga** *I* Tuvalu
77G1 **Nanumea** *I* Tuvalu
29D2 **Nanuque** Brazil
52C3 **Nanyang** China
52D2 **Nanyang Hu** *L* China
72D3 **Nanyuki** Kenya
53D4 **Naoetsu** Japan
60B4 **Naokot** Pak
20A1 **Napa** USA
10F3 **Napaiskak** USA
13D2 **Napanee** Can
48K4 **Napas** Russian Fed
7N3 **Napassoq** Greenland
55D2 **Nape** Laos
78C1 **Napier** NZ
Naples = Napoli
15E4 **Naples** Florida, USA
14B1 **Naples** New York, USA
17D3 **Naples** Texas, USA
52B5 **Napo** China
26D4 **Napo** *R* Peru/Ecuador
11C2 **Napoleon** USA
40C2 **Napoli** Italy
63B1 **Naqadeh** Iran
65C3 **Naqb Ishtar** Jordan
54C4 **Nara** Japan
70B3 **Nara** Mali
76D4 **Naracoorte** Aust
22C1 **Naranjos** Mexico
62B1 **Narasarāopet** India
55C4 **Narathiwat** Thai
61D3 **Narayanganj** Bang
62B1 **Nārāyenpet** India
38C3 **Narbonne** France
60D2 **Narendranagar** India
7L2 **Nares Str** Can
43E2 **Narew** *R* Pol
54D3 **Narita** Japan
60C4 **Narmada** *R* India
60D3 **Nārnaul** India
44F4 **Naro Fominsk** Russian Fed
72D4 **Narok** Kenya
43F2 **Narovl'a** Belorussia

60C2 **Narowal** Pak
76D4 **Narrabri** Aust
75C1 **Narran** *L* Aust
75C1 **Narran** *R* Aust
75C2 **Narrandera** Aust
76A4 **Narrogin** Aust
75C2 **Narromine** Aust
12C3 **Narrows** USA
14C2 **Narrowsburg** USA
60D4 **Narsimhapur** India
62C1 **Narsipatnam** India
7O3 **Narssalik** Greenland
7O3 **Narssaq** Greenland
7O3 **Narssarssuaq** Greenland
74B2 **Narubis** Namibia
54D3 **Narugo** Japan
54B4 **Naruto** Japan
44D4 **Narva** Russian Fed
32H5 **Narvik** Nor
60D3 **Narwāna** India
44J2 **Nar'yan Mar** Russian Fed
75B1 **Narylico** Aust
48J5 **Naryn** Kazakhstan
71H4 **Nasarawa** Nig
xxxD5 **Nasca Ridge** Pacific O
14E1 **Nashua** USA
17D3 **Nashville** Arkansas, USA
15B1 **Nashville** Tennessee, USA
41D1 **Našice** Croatia, Yugos
60C4 **Nāsik** India
72D3 **Nasir** Sudan
5J3 **Naskaupi** *R* Can
3C2 **Nass** *R* Can
23B1 **Nassau** Bahamas
14D1 **Nassau** USA
69C2 **Nasser,L** Egypt
71F4 **Nassian** Ivory Coast
32G7 **Nässjö** Sweden
7L4 **Nastapoka Is** Can
4F2 **Nastapoca** *R* Can
73C6 **Nata** Botswana
27L5 **Natal** Brazil
56A2 **Natal** Indon
74E2 **Natal** Province, S Africa
xxviiiC6 **Natal Basin** Indian O
63C2 **Natanz** Iran
7M4 **Natashquan** Can
7M4 **Natashquan** *R* Can
17D3 **Natchez** USA
17D3 **Natchitoches** USA
75C3 **Nathalia** Aust
7Q2 **Nathorsts Land** *Region* Greenland
3D2 **Nation** *R* Can
19C4 **National City** USA
National Republic of China = Taiwan
71G3 **Natitingou** Benin
54D3 **Natori** Japan
72D4 **Natron** *L* Tanz
76A4 **Naturaliste,C** Aust
4D4 **Naubinway** USA
37D1 **Nauders** Austria
42C2 **Nauen** Germany
14D2 **Naugatuck** USA
42C2 **Naumburg** Germany
65C3 **Naur** Jordan
77F1 **Nauru** *I* Pacific O
49M4 **Naushki** Russian Fed
74B2 **Naute Dam** *Res* Namibia
22C1 **Nautla** Mexico
63E2 **Nauzad** Afghan
8C3 **Navajo Res** USA
39A2 **Navalmoral de la Mata** Spain
25C9 **Navarino** *I* Chile
39B1 **Navarra** Province, Spain
28D3 **Navarro** Arg
17C3 **Navasota** USA
17C3 **Navasota** *R* USA
39A1 **Navia** *R* Spain
28A2 **Navidad** Chile
60C4 **Navlakhi** India
45E5 **Navlya** Russian Fed
21B2 **Navojoa** Mexico
41E3 **Návpaktos** Greece
41E3 **Návplion** Greece
71F3 **Navrongo** Ghana
60C4 **Navsāri** India
65D2 **Nawá** Syria
61C3 **Nawāda** India
60B2 **Nawah** Afghan
60B3 **Nawrabshah** Pak
52B4 **Naxi** China
41F3 **Náxos** *I* Greece
22B1 **Nayar** Mexico
22A1 **Nayarit** State, Mexico
63C3 **Nāy Band** Iran
63D2 **Nāy Band** Iran
53E3 **Nayoro** Japan
29E1 **Nazaré** Brazil
65C2 **Nazareth** Israel
38B2 **Nazay** France
26D6 **Nazca** Peru
64A2 **Nazilli** Turk
49L4 **Nazimovo** Russian Fed
3D3 **Nazko** *R* Can
58B5 **Nazrēt** Eth
67G2 **Nazwa** Oman
48J4 **Nazyvayevsk** Russian Fed
73B4 **Ndalatando** Angola
72C3 **Ndélé** CAR
72B4 **Ndendé** Gabon
77F2 **Ndende** *I* Solomon Is
72B2 **Ndjamena** Chad
72B4 **Ndjolé** Gabon
73C5 **Ndola** Zambia
71F4 **Ndouci** Ivory Coast
75C1 **Neabul** Aust
75A1 **Neales** *R* Aust
41E3 **Neápolis** Greece
10A6 **Near Is** USA
35D6 **Neath** Wales
75C1 **Nebine** *R* Aust
48G6 **Nebit Dag** Turkmenistan
8C2 **Nebraska** State, USA
17C1 **Nebraska City** USA
3D3 **Nechako** *R* Can
17C3 **Neches** *R* USA
36E2 **Neckar** *R* Germany
28D3 **Necochea** Arg
61D2 **Nêdong** China
19D4 **Needles** USA
12B2 **Neenah** USA
6J4 **Neepawa** Can
36C1 **Neerpelt** Belg
71D2 **Nefta** Tunisia
53E1 **Neftegorsk** Russian Fed
49M4 **Neftelensk** Russian Fed
72D3 **Negelli** Eth
65C3 **Negev** *Desert* Israel
29A3 **Negla** *R* Par
45C6 **Negolu** *Mt* Rom
62B3 **Negombo** Sri Lanka
55A2 **Negrais,C** Burma
26B4 **Negritos** Peru
26F4 **Negro** *R* Amazonas, Brazil
28C4 **Negro** *R* Arg
29A2 **Negro** *R* Mato Grosso de Sul, Brazil
29A3 **Negro** *R* Par
28D2 **Negro** *R* Urug
57F8 **Negros** *I* Phil
41F2 **Negru Voda** Rom
63E2 **Nehbāndan** Iran
53A2 **Nehe** China
52B4 **Neijiang** China
12A2 **Neillsville** USA
52B1 **Nei Monggol** Autonomous Region, China
26C3 **Neira** Colombia
72D3 **Nejo** Eth
72D3 **Nek'emte** Eth
44E4 **Nelidovo** Russian Fed
11C3 **Neligh** USA
62B2 **Nellore** India
53D2 **Nel'ma** Russian Fed
3E4 **Nelson** Can
78B2 **Nelson** NZ
6J4 **Nelson** *R* Can
75B3 **Nelson,C** Aust
10F3 **Nelson I** USA
74E2 **Nelspruit** S Africa
70B3 **Néma** Maur
52A1 **Nemagt Uul** *Mt* Mongolia
53D1 **Nemilen** *R* Russian Fed
41F1 **Nemira** *Mt* Rom
53B2 **Nemor He** *R* China
36B2 **Nemours** France
43E1 **Nemunas** *R* Lithuania
53F3 **Nemuro** Japan
49O5 **Nen** *R* China
33B3 **Nenagh** Irish Rep
10J3 **Nenana** USA
10J3 **Nenana** *R* USA
35E5 **Nene** *R* Eng
56F6 **Nenggiri** *R* Malay
53B2 **Nenjiang** China
17C2 **Neodesha** USA
17D2 **Neosho** USA
49M4 **Nepa** Russian Fed
59G3 **Nepal** Kingdom, Asia
61B2 **Nepalganj** Nepal
19D3 **Nephi** USA
65C3 **Neqarot** *R* Israel
28A3 **Nequén** State, Arg
50E1 **Nerchinsk** Russian Fed
41D2 **Neretva** *R* Bosnia & Herzegovina/Croatia, Yugos
51H5 **Nero Deep** Pacific O
44G2 **Nes'** Russian Fed
32C1 **Neskaupstaður** Iceland
36B2 **Nesle** France
16C2 **Ness City** USA
3B2 **Nesselrode,Mt** Can/USA
5G3 **Nestaocano** *R* Can
41E2 **Néstos** *R* Greece
65C2 **Netanya** Israel
14C2 **Netcong** USA
42B2 **Netherlands** Kingdom, Europe
2M7 **Netherlands Antilles** *Is* Caribbean
49N4 **Net Oktyobr'ya** Russian Fed
61D3 **Netrakona** Bang
7L3 **Nettilling L** Can
42C2 **Neubrandenburg** Germany
37B1 **Neuchâtel** Switz
36C2 **Neufchâteau** Belg
36C2 **Neufchâteau** France
38C2 **Neufchâtel** France
36A2 **Neufchâtel-en-Bray** France
42B2 **Neumünster** Germany
40D1 **Neunkirchen** Austria
36D2 **Neunkirchen** Germany
28B3 **Neuquén** Arg
25B6 **Neuquén** State, Arg
28B3 **Neuquén** *R* Arg
42C2 **Neuruppin** Germany
15D1 **Neuse** *R* USA
36D1 **Neuss** Germany
42C2 **Neustadt** Germany
36E2 **Neustadt an der Weinstrasse** Germany
36E3 **Neustadt im Schwarzwald** Germany
42C2 **Neustrelitz** Germany
36D1 **Neuwied** Germany
8B3 **Nevada** State, USA
17D2 **Nevada** USA
28A3 **Nevada de Chillán** *Mts* Chile/Arg
22B2 **Nevada de Collima** Mexico
22C2 **Nevada de Toluca** *Mt* Mexico
65C3 **Nevatim** Israel
44D4 **Nevel'** Russian Fed
53E2 **Nevel'sk** Russian Fed
53A1 **Never** Russian Fed
38C2 **Nevers** France
75C2 **Nevertire** Aust
64B2 **Nevşehir** Turk
44L4 **Nev'yansk** Russian Fed
12C3 **New** *R* USA
73D5 **Newala** Tanz
12B3 **New Albany** Indiana, USA
17E3 **New Albany** Mississippi, USA
27G2 **New Amsterdam** Guyana
75C1 **New Angledool** Aust
13D3 **Newark** Delaware, USA
9F2 **Newark** New Jersey, USA
14B1 **Newark** New York, USA
12C2 **Newark** Ohio, USA
35E5 **Newark-upon-Trent** Eng
13E2 **New Bedford** USA
3C3 **New Bella Bella** Can
18B1 **Newberg** USA
15D1 **New Bern** USA
15C2 **Newberry** USA
74C3 **New Bethesda** S Africa
23B2 **New Bight** Bahamas
12C3 **New Boston** USA
16C4 **New Braunfels** USA
14D2 **New Britain** USA
76E1 **New Britain** *I* PNG
76E1 **New Britain Trench** PNG
7M5 **New Brunswick** Province, Can
14C2 **New Brunswick** USA
14C2 **Newburgh** USA
35E6 **Newbury** Eng
14E1 **Newburyport** USA
14D2 **New Canaan** USA
75D2 **Newcastle** Aust
5H4 **Newcastle** Can
12B3 **New Castle** Indiana, USA
35C4 **Newcastle** N Ire
12C2 **New Castle** Pennsylvania, USA
74D2 **Newcastle** S Africa
11B3 **Newcastle** Wyoming, USA
34E4 **Newcastle upon Tyne** Eng
76C2 **Newcastle Waters** Aust
20C3 **New Cuyama** USA
60D3 **New Delhi** India
75D2 **New England Range** *Mts* Aust
10F4 **Newenham,C** USA
14A1 **Newfane** USA
35E6 **New Forest,The** Eng
7M4 **Newfoundland** Province, Can
7N5 **Newfoundland** *I* Can
xxxF2 **Newfoundland Basin** Atlantic O
17D2 **New Franklin** USA
34C4 **New Galloway** Scot
77E1 **New Georgia** *I* Solomon Is
7M5 **New Glasgow** Can
76D1 **New Guinea** *I* S E Asia
66C3 **New Haifa** Sudan
10H4 **Newhalen** USA
20C3 **Newhall** USA
9F2 **New Hampshire** State, USA
11D3 **New Hampton** USA
74E2 **New Hanover** S Africa
76E1 **New Hanover** *I* PNG
35F6 **Newhaven** Eng
13E2 **New Haven** USA
3C2 **New Hazelton** Can
77F3 **New Hebrides Trench** Pacific O
17D3 **New Iberia** USA
76E1 **New Ireland** *I* PNG
9F2 **New Jersey** State, USA
16B3 **Newkirk** USA
7L5 **New Liskeard** Can
14D2 **New London** USA
76A3 **Newman** Aust
20B2 **Newman** USA
35F5 **Newmarket** Eng
13D3 **New Market** USA
18C2 **New Meadows** USA
8C3 **New Mexico** State, USA
14D2 **New Milford** Connecticut, USA
14C2 **New Milford** Pennsylvania, USA
15C2 **Newnan** USA
75E3 **New Norfolk** Aust
9D3 **New Orleans** USA
14C2 **New Paltz** USA
12C2 **New Philadelphia** USA
78B1 **New Plymouth** NZ
17D2 **Newport** Arkansas, USA
35E6 **Newport** Eng
12C3 **Newport** Kentucky, USA
14D1 **Newport** New Hampshire, USA
18B2 **Newport** Oregon, USA
14B2 **Newport** Pennsylvania, USA
13E2 **Newport** Rhode Island, USA
13E2 **Newport** Vermont, USA
35D6 **Newport** Wales
18C1 **Newport** Washington, USA
20D4 **Newport Beach** USA
9F3 **Newport News** USA
23B1 **New Providence** *I* Caribbean
35C6 **Newquay** Eng
7L3 **New Quebec Crater** Can
35B5 **New Ross** Irish Rep
35B4 **Newry** N Ire
New Siberian Is = Novosibirskye Ostrova
15C3 **New Smyrna Beach** USA
76D4 **New South Wales** State, Aust
10G4 **New Stuyahok** USA
11D3 **Newton** Iowa, USA
17C2 **Newton** Kansas, USA
14E1 **Newton** Massachusetts, USA
17E3 **Newton** Mississippi, USA
14C2 **Newton** New Jersey, USA
35D6 **Newton Abbot** Eng
34B4 **Newton Stewart** N Ire
34C4 **Newton Stewart** Scot
11B2 **New Town** USA
35D5 **Newtown** Wales
35C4 **Newtownards** N Ire
11D3 **New Ulm** USA
14B2 **Newville** USA
5J4 **New Waterford** Can
6F5 **New Westminster** Can
9F2 **New York** State, USA
9F2 **New York** USA
77G5 **New Zealand** Dominion, SW Pacific O
xxixK7 **New Zealand Plat** Pacific O
44G4 **Neya** Russian Fed
63C3 **Neyrīz** Iran
63D1 **Neyshābūr** Iran
45E5 **Nezhin** Ukraine
72B4 **Ngabé** Congo
71J3 **Ngadda** Nig
73C6 **Ngami** *L* Botswana
71J4 **N'Gaoundéré** Cam
78C1 **Ngaruawahia** NZ
78C1 **Ngaruroro** *R* NZ
78C1 **Ngauruhoe,Mt** NZ
72B4 **Ngo** Congo
55D2 **Ngoc Linh** *Mt* Viet
72B3 **Ngoko** *R* Cam
50C3 **Ngoring Hu** *L* China
72D4 **Ngorongoro Crater** Tanz
72B4 **N'Gounié** *R* Gabon
72B2 **Nguigmi** Niger
51G6 **Ngulu** *I* Pacific O
71J3 **Nguru** Nig
55D3 **Nha Trang** Viet
29A2 **Nhecolandia** Brazil
75B3 **Nhill** Aust
74E2 **Nhlangano** Swaziland
55D2 **Nhommarath** Laos
76C2 **Nhulunbuy** Aust
70B3 **Niafounké** Mali
12B1 **Niagara** USA
13D2 **Niagara Falls** Can
13D2 **Niagara Falls** USA
56D2 **Niah** Malay
70B4 **Niakaramandougou** Ivory Coast
70C3 **Niamey** Niger
72C3 **Niangara** Zaïre
71F3 **Niangoloko** Burkina
72C3 **Nia Nia** Zaïre
53A2 **Nianzishan** China
56A2 **Nias** *I* Indon
21D3 **Nicaragua** Republic, C America
40D3 **Nicastro** Italy
38D3 **Nice** France
23B1 **Nicholl's Town** Bahamas
14C2 **Nicholson** USA
59H5 **Nicobar Is** Indian O
65B1 **Nicosia** Cyprus
21D3 **Nicoya,Pen de** Costa Rica
36E1 **Nidda** *R* Germany
43E2 **Nidzica** Pol
36D2 **Niederbronn** France
37E1 **Niedere Tauern** *Mts* Austria
42B2 **Niedersachsen** State, Germany
72C4 **Niemba** Zaïre
42B2 **Nienburg** Germany
36D1 **Niers** *R* Germany
70B4 **Niete,Mt** Lib
27G2 **Nieuw Amsterdam** Surinam
27G2 **Nieuw Nickeire** Surinam
74B3 **Nieuwoudtville** S Africa
36B1 **Nieuwpoort** Belg
22B1 **Nieves** Mexico
64B2 **Niğde** Turk
70C3 **Niger** Republic, Africa
71H4 **Niger** State, Nig
71H4 **Niger** *R* Nig
70C4 **Nigeria** Federal Republic, Africa
12C1 **Nighthawk L** Can
41E2 **Nigríta** Greece
54D3 **Nihommatsu** Japan
53D4 **Niigata** Japan
53C5 **Niihama** Japan
54C4 **Nii-jima** *I* Japan
54B4 **Niimi** Japan
53D4 **Niitsu** Japan
65C3 **Nijil** Jordan
42B2 **Nijmegen** Neth
44E2 **Nikel'** Russian Fed
71G3 **Nikki** Benin
53D4 **Nikko** Japan
45E6 **Nikolayev** Ukraine
45H6 **Nikolayevsk** Russian Fed
49Q4 **Nikolayevsk-na-Amure** Russian Fed
44H5 **Nikol'sk** Penza, Russian Fed
•4H4 **Nikol'sk** Russian Fed
10E5 **Nikolski** USA
45E6 **Nikopol** Ukraine
64C1 **Niksar** Turk
63E3 **Nīkshahr** Iran
41D2 **Nikšić** Montenegro, Yugos
77G1 **Nikunau** *I* Kiribati
57C4 **Nila** *I* Indon
58B3 **Nile** *R* N E Africa
12B2 **Niles** USA
62B2 **Nilgiri Hills** India
22D2 **Niltepec** Mexico
60C4 **Nimach** India
38C3 **Nîmes** France
75C3 **Nimmitabel** Aust
72D3 **Nimule** Sudan
59F5 **Nine Degree Chan** Indian O
xxviiiF5 **Ninety-East Ridge** Indian O
75C3 **Ninety Mile Beach** Aust
53B3 **Ning'an** China
52D4 **Ningde** China
52D4 **Ningdu** China
50C3 **Ningjing Shan** *Mts* China
55D1 **Ningming** China
52A4 **Ningnan** China
52B2 **Ningxia** Province, China
52B2 **Ning Xian** China
52B5 **Ninh Binh** Vietnam
76D1 **Ninigo Is** PNG
10H3 **Ninilchik** USA
29A3 **Nioaque** Brazil
11B3 **Niobrara** *R* USA
72B4 **Nioki** Zaïre
70B3 **Nioro du Sahel** Mali
38B2 **Niort** France
6H4 **Nipawin** Can
7K5 **Nipigon** Can
4D4 **Nipigon B.** Can
7K5 **Nipigon,L** Can
7K5 **Nipissing,L** *R* Can
20B3 **Nipomo** USA

19C3 **Nipton** USA
29C1 **Niquelândia** Brazil
62B1 **Nirmal** India
61C2 **Nirmāli** India
41E2 **Niš** Serbia, Yugos
67E4 **Nisāb** Yemen
53C5 **Nishinoomote** Japan
50G4 **Nishino-shima** *I* Japan
54B3 **Nishino-shima** *I* Japan
54A4 **Nishi-suidō** *Str* S Korea
54B4 **Nishiwaki** Japan
4D2 **Niskibi** *R* Can
10L3 **Nisling** *R* Can
77E1 **Nissan Is** PNG
10M3 **Nisutlin** *R* Can
7L4 **Nitchequon** Can
27K8 **Niterói** Brazil
34D4 **Nith** *R* Scot
57B4 **Nitibe** Indon
43D3 **Nitra** Czech
12C3 **Nitro** USA
77J2 **Niue** *I* Pacific O
77G2 **Niulakita** *I* Tuvalu
56D2 **Niut** *Mt* Malay
77G1 **Niutao** *I* Tuvalu
36C1 **Nivelles** Belg
38C2 **Nivernais** Region, France
32L5 **Nivskiy** Russian Fed
62B1 **Nizāmābād** India
65C3 **Nizana** *Hist Site* Israel
44J4 **Nizhnekamskoye Vodokhranilische** *Res* Russian Fed
50C1 **Nizhneudinsk** Russian Fed
44K4 **Nizhniye Sergi** Russian Fed
44G5 **Nizhniy Lomov** Russian Fed
44G4 **Nizhniy Novgorod** Russian Fed
44J3 **Nizhniy Odes** Russian Fed
44K4 **Nizhniy Tagil** Russian Fed
49L3 **Nizhnyaya Tunguska** *R* Russian Fed
44G2 **Nizhnyaya Zolotitsa** Russian Fed
64C2 **Nizip** Turk
73C5 **Njoko** *R* Zambia
73D4 **Njombe** Tanz
72B3 **Nkambé** Cam
71F4 **Nkawkaw** Ghana
73D5 **Nkhata Bay** Malawi
72B3 **Nkongsamba** Cam
70C3 **N'Konni** Niger
61D3 **Noakhali** Bang
10F2 **Noatak** USA
10G2 **Noatak** *R* USA
53C5 **Nobeoka** Japan
54D2 **Noboribetsu** Japan
29A1 **Nobres** Brazil
37D1 **Noce** *R* Italy
22B1 **Nochistlán** Mexico
22C2 **Nochixtlán** Mexico
17C3 **Nocona** USA
21A1 **Nogales** Sonora, Mexico
19D4 **Nogales** USA
22C2 **Nogales** Veracruz, Mexico
37D2 **Nogara** Italy
54B4 **Nogata** Japan
36C2 **Nogent-en-Bassigny** France
36A2 **Nogent-le-Rotrou** France
36B2 **Nogent-sur-Seine** France
44F4 **Noginsk** Russian Fed
53E1 **Nogliki** Russian Fed
28D2 **Nogoyá** Arg
28D2 **Nogoyá** *R* Arg
60C3 **Nohar** India
54D2 **Noheji** Japan
74C1 **Nojane** Botswana
54C4 **Nojima-zaki** *C* Japan
63E3 **Nok Kundi** Pak
3H2 **Nokomis L** Can
72B3 **Nola** CAR
44H4 **Nolinsk** Russian Fed
14E2 **Nomans Land** *I* USA
22B1 **Nombre de Dioz** Mexico
10E3 **Nome** USA
36D2 **Nomeny** France
52B1 **Nomgon** Mongolia
54A4 **Nomo-saki** *Pt* Japan
6H3 **Nonachol L** Can
53B3 **Nong'an** China
55C2 **Nong Khai** Thai
74E2 **Nongoma** S Africa
77G1 **Nonouti** *I* Kiribati
54A3 **Nonsan** S Korea
74B2 **Noordoewer** Namibia
10F2 **Noorvik** USA
3C4 **Nootka Sd** Can
22C2 **Nopala** Mexico
72B4 **Noqui** Angola
7L5 **Noranda** Can
36B1 **Nord** Department, France
48D2 **Nordaustlandet** *I* Barents S
3E3 **Nordegg** Can
32F6 **Nordfjord** *Inlet* Nor
32F8 **Nordfriesische** *Is* Germany
42C2 **Nordhausen** Germany
32J4 **Nordkapp** *C* Nor
7N3 **Nordre Strømfjord** Greenland
42B2 **Nordrhein Westfalen** State, Germany
32G5 **Nord Stronfjället** *Mt* Sweden
49N2 **Nordvik** Russian Fed
35B5 **Nore** *R* Irish Rep
35F5 **Norfolk** County, Eng
11C3 **Norfolk** Nebraska, USA
13D3 **Norfolk** Virginia, USA
77F3 **Norfolk I** Aust
17D2 **Norfolk L** USA
xxixK5 **Norfolk Ridge** Pacific O
49K3 **Noril'sk** Russian Fed
12B2 **Normal** USA
17C2 **Norman** USA
38B2 **Normandie** Region, France
15C1 **Norman,L** USA
76D2 **Normanton** Aust
10N2 **Norman Wells** Can
44B2 **Norra Storfjället** *Mt* Sweden
15C1 **Norris L** USA
13D2 **Norristown** USA
32H7 **Norrköping** Sweden
32H6 **Norrsundet** Sweden
32H7 **Norrtälje** Sweden
76B4 **Norseman** Aust
53C1 **Norsk** Russian Fed
29A1 **Nortelândia** Brazil
xxxJ2 **North** *S* N W Europe
35E4 **Northallerton** Eng
76A4 **Northam** Aust
74D2 **Northam** S Africa
xxxE3 **North American Basin** Atlantic O
76A3 **Northampton** Aust
35E5 **Northampton** County, Eng
35E5 **Northampton** Eng
13E2 **Northampton** USA
62E2 **North Andaman** *I* Indian O
6G3 **North Arm** *B* Can
15C2 **North Augusta** USA
7M4 **North Aulatsivik I** Can
3G3 **North Battleford** Can
7L5 **North Bay** Can
18B2 **North Bend** USA
34D3 **North Berwick** Scot
14E1 **North Berwick** USA
7M5 **North,C** Can
77G4 **North C** NZ
10D5 **North C** USA
16B2 **North Canadian** *R* USA
4C3 **North Caribou L** Can
9E3 **North Carolina** State, USA
18B1 **North Cascade Nat Pk** USA
4E4 **North Chan** Can
34C4 **North Chan** Ire/Scot
14A1 **North Collins** USA
8C2 **North Dakota** State, USA
35F6 **North Downs** Eng
36A1 **North Downs** *Upland* Eng
13D2 **North East** USA
xxxH1 **North East Atlantic Basin** Atlantic O
10E3 **Northeast C** USA
4B2 **Northern Indian L** Can
33B3 **Northern Ireland** UK
11D2 **Northern Light L** Can
23L1 **Northern Range** *Mts* Trinidad
76C2 **Northern Territory** Aust
34D3 **North Esk** *R* Scot
14D1 **Northfield** Massachusetts, USA
11D3 **Northfield** Minnesota, USA
35F6 **North Foreland** Eng
36A1 **North Foreland** *Pt* Eng
10H3 **North Fork** *R* USA
4E3 **North French** *R* Can
5K3 **North Head** *C* Can
78B1 **North I** NZ
4B2 **North Knife** *R* Can
53B4 **North Korea** Republic, S E Asia
North Land = Severnaya Zemlya
17D3 **North Little Rock** USA
11B3 **North Loup** *R* USA
79B4 **North Magnetic Pole** Can
15E4 **North Miami** USA
15E4 **North Miami Beach** USA
10O3 **North Nahanni** *R* Can
20C2 **North Palisade** *Mt* USA
16B1 **North Platte** USA
8C2 **North Platte** *R* USA
5J4 **North Pt** *C* Can
79A **North Pole** Arctic
23Q2 **North Pt** Barbados
12C1 **North Pt** USA
11D3 **North Raccoon** *R* USA
33B2 **North Rona** *I* Scot
34D2 **North Ronaldsay** *I* Scot
3G3 **North Saskatchewan** *R* Can
33D2 **North Sea** N W Europe
3H2 **North Seal** *R* Can
62E2 **North Sentinel** Andaman Is
10J2 **North Slope** USA
6D3 **North Slope** *Region* USA
75D1 **North Stradbroke** *I* Aust
14B1 **North Syracuse** USA
78B1 **North Taranaki Bight** *B* NZ
14A1 **North Tonawanda** USA
8C3 **North Truchas Peak** *Mt* USA
4F3 **North Twin I** Can
34B3 **North Uist** *I* Scot
34D4 **Northumberland** County, Eng
76E3 **Northumberland Is** Aust
7M5 **Northumberland Str** Can
18B1 **North Vancouver** Can
14C1 **Northville** USA
35F5 **North Walsham** Eng
10K3 **Northway** USA
76A3 **North West C** Aust
60C2 **North West Frontier** Province, Pak
7M4 **North West River** Can
6G3 **North West Territories** Can
11C2 **Northwood** USA
35E4 **North York Moors Nat Pk** Eng
16C2 **Norton** *R* USA
10F3 **Norton B** USA
10F3 **Norton Sd** USA
79F1 **Norvegia,C** Ant
14D2 **Norwalk** Connecticut, USA
12C2 **Norwalk** Ohio, USA
32F6 **Norway** Kingdom, Europe
6J4 **Norway House** Can
7J2 **Norwegian B** Can
xxxH1 **Norwegian Basin** Norewegian S
48B3 **Norwegian S** N W Europe
14D2 **Norwich** Connecticut, USA
35F5 **Norwich** Eng
14C1 **Norwich** New York, USA
14E1 **Norwood** Massachusetts, USA
12C3 **Norwood** Ohio, USA
41F2 **Nos Emine** *C* Bulg
53D3 **Noshiro** Japan
41F2 **Nos Kaliakra** *C* Bulg
44J2 **Nosovaya** Russian Fed
43G2 **Nosovka** Ukraine
34E1 **Noss** *I* Scot
74B1 **Nossob** *R* Namibia
63E3 **Nostrābād** Iran
73E5 **Nosy Barren** *I* Madag
73E5 **Nosy Bé** *I* Madag
73F5 **Nosy Boraha** *I* Madag
73E6 **Nosy Varika** Madag
42D2 **Notéc** *R* Pol
6G4 **Notikewin** Can
40D3 **Noto** Italy
32F7 **Notodden** Nor
54C3 **Noto-hantō** *Pen* Japan
7N5 **Notre Dame B** Can
4E5 **Nottawasaga B** Can
4F3 **Nottaway** *R* Can
35E5 **Nottingham** County, Eng
35E5 **Nottingham** Eng
7L3 **Nottingham I** Can
11A2 **Notukeu Creek** *R* Can
70A2 **Nouadhibou** Maur
70A3 **Nouakchott** Maur
77F3 **Nouméa** Nouvelle Calédonie
71F3 **Nouna** Burkina
74C3 **Noupoort** S Africa
77F3 **Nouvelle Calédonie** *I* S W Pacific O
29C2 **Nova América** Brazil
73B4 **Nova Caipemba** Angola
29B3 **Nova Esperança** Brazil
29D3 **Nova Friburgo** Brazil
73B5 **Nova Gaia** Angola
29C3 **Nova Granada** Brazil
29C3 **Nova Herizonte** Brazil
29D3 **Nova Lima** Brazil
Nova Lisboa = Huambo
29B3 **Nova Londrina** Brazil
73D6 **Nova Mambone** Mozam
37C2 **Novara** Italy
29C1 **Nova Roma** Brazil
57C4 **Nova Sagres** Indon
7M5 **Nova Scotia** Province, Can
20A1 **Novato** USA
29D2 **Nova Venécia** Brazil
45E6 **Novaya Kakhovka** Ukraine
49R2 **Novaya Sibir, Ostrov** *I* Russian Fed
48G2 **Novaya Zemlya** *I* Russian Fed
41F2 **Nova Zagora** Bulg
27K4 **Nove Russas** Brazil
41D1 **Nové Zámky** Czech
44E4 **Novgorod** Russian Fed
37E2 **Novigrad** Croatia, Yugos
53E2 **Novikovo** Russian Fed
37C2 **Novi Ligure** Italy
22A1 **Novillero** Mexico
41F2 **Novi Pazar** Bulg
41E2 **Novi Pazar** Serbia, Yugos
41D1 **Novi Sad** Serbia, Yugos
45K5 **Novoalekseyevka** Kazakhstan
45G5 **Novoanninskiy** Russian Fed
53C2 **Novobureyskiy** Russian Fed
45G6 **Novocherkassk** Russian Fed
44G3 **Novodvinsk** Russian Fed
45D5 **Novograd Volynskiy** Ukraine
43F2 **Novogrudok** Belorussia
28E1 **Novo Hamburgo** Brazil
48H5 **Novokazalinsk** Kazakhstan
48K4 **Novokuznetsk** Russian Fed
79F12 **Novolazarevskaya** *Base* Ant
40D1 **Novo Mesto** Slovenia, Yugos
43G3 **Novomirgorod** Ukraine
44F5 **Novomoskovsk** Russian Fed
Novo Redondo = Sumbe
45F7 **Novorossiysk** Russian Fed
49M2 **Novorybnoye** Russian Fed
48K4 **Novosibirsk** Russian Fed
49P2 **Novosibirskye Ostrova** *Is* Russian Fed
45K5 **Novotroitsk** Russian Fed
45H5 **Novo Uzensk** Russian Fed
43E2 **Novovolynsk** Ukraine
44H4 **Novo Vyatsk** Russian Fed
45E5 **Novozybkov** Russian Fed
48J3 **Novvy Port** Russian Fed
43E2 **Novy Dwór Mazowiecki** Pol
44L4 **Novyy Lyalya** Russian Fed
44N2 **Novyy Port** Russian Fed
45J7 **Novyy Uzen** Kazakhstan
42D2 **Nowa Sól** Pol
17C2 **Nowata** USA
61D2 **Nowgong** India
10H3 **Nowitna** *R* USA
75D2 **Nowra** Aust
63C1 **Now Shahr** Iran
60C2 **Nowshera** Pak
43E3 **Nowy SSącz** Pol
10M4 **Noyes I** USA
36B2 **Noyon** France
71F4 **Nsawam** Ghana
71H4 **Nsukka** Nig
74E1 **Nuanetsi** Zim
74E1 **Nuanetsi** *R* Zim
71G4 **Nuatja** Togo
72D2 **Nuba** *Mts* Sudan
66B2 **Nubian Desert** Sudan
28A3 **Nuble** *R* Chile
8D4 **Nueces** *R* USA
6J3 **Nueltin L** Can
21B1 **Nueva Casas Grandes** Mexico
29A3 **Nueva Germania** Par
23A2 **Nueva Gerona** Cuba
28A3 **Nueva Imperial** Chile
28D2 **Nueva Palmira** Urug
21B2 **Nueva Rosita** Mexico
23B2 **Nuevitas** Cuba
22B1 **Nuevo** State, Mexico
21B1 **Nuevo Casas Grandes** Mexico
22A1 **Nuevo Ideal** Mexico
21C2 **Nuevo Laredo** Mexico
69D4 **Nugaal** Region, Somalia
7N2 **Nûgâtsiaq** Greenland
7N2 **Nûgussuaq** *Pen* Greenland
7N2 **Nûgussuaq** *I* Greenland
77G1 **Nui** *I* Tuvalu
52A5 **Nui Con Voi** *R* Vietnam
36C3 **Nuits** France
61E2 **Nu Jiang** *R* China
75A2 **Nukey Bluff** *Mt* Aust
64D3 **Nukhayb** Iraq
77G1 **Nukufetau** *I* Tuvalu
77G1 **Nukulaelae** *I* Tuvalu
77H1 **Nukunon** *I* Tokelau Is
48G5 **Nukus** Uzbekistan
10G3 **Nulato** USA
76B4 **Nullarbor Plain** Aust
71J4 **Numan** Nig
54C3 **Numata** Japan
72C3 **Numatinna** *R* Sudan
53D4 **Numazu** Japan
51G7 **Numfoor** *I* Indon
75C3 **Numurkah** Aust
10F3 **Nunapitchuk** USA
14A1 **Nunda** USA
10E3 **Nunivak I** USA
60D2 **Nunkun** *Mt* India
10C3 **Nunligran** Russian Fed
53A1 **Nuomin He** *R* China
40B2 **Nuoro** Sardegna
63C2 **Nurābād** Iran
37C2 **Nure** *R* Italy
75A2 **Nuriootpa** Aust
60C1 **Nuristan** *Upland* Afghan
44J5 **Nurlat** Russian Fed
32K6 **Nurmes** Fin
42C3 **Nürnberg** Germany
75C2 **Nurri,Mt** Aust
56E4 **Nusa Tenggara** *Is* Indon
57B4 **Nusa Tenggara Timor** Province, Indon
64D2 **Nusaybin** Turk
10G4 **Nushagak** *R* USA
10G4 **Nushagak B** USA
10G4 **Nushagak Pen** USA
60B3 **Nushki** Pak
7M4 **Nutak** Can
10K3 **Nutzotin Mts** USA
7L3 **Nuvukjuak** Can
61B2 **Nuwakot** Nepal
62C3 **Nuwara-Eliya** Sri Lanka
74C3 **Nuweveldreeks** *Mts* S Africa
45C3 **Nyac** USA
14D2 **Nyack** USA
72D3 **Nyahururu Falls** Kenya
75B3 **Nyah West** Aust
50C3 **Nyaingentanglha Shan** *Mts* China
72D4 **Nyakabindi** Tanz
44L3 **Nyaksimvol'** Russian Fed
72C2 **Nyala** Sudan
61C2 **Nyalam** China
72C3 **Nyamlell** Sudan
73D6 **Nyanda** Zim
44G3 **Nyandoma** Russian Fed
72B4 **Nyanga** *R* Gabon
61D2 **Nyang Qu** China
73D5 **Nyasa L** Malawi/Mozam
55B2 **Nyaunglebin** Burma
44K4 **Nyazepetrovsk** Russian Fed
32G7 **Nyborg** Den
32H7 **Nybro** Sweden
48J3 **Nyda** Russian Fed
7M1 **Nyeboes Land** *Region* Can
61D1 **Nyenchentanglha Range** *Mts* China
72D4 **Nyeri** Kenya
73D5 **Nyimba** Zambia
59H2 **Nyingchi** China
43E3 **Nyíregyháza** Hung
72D3 **Nyiru,Mt** Kenya
32J6 **Nykarleby** Fin
32F7 **Nykøbing** Den
32G8 **Nykøbing** Den
32H7 **Nyköping** Sweden
74D1 **Nyl** *R* S Africa
74D1 **Nylstroom** S Africa
75C2 **Nymagee** Aust
32H7 **Nynäshamn** Sweden
75C2 **Nyngan** Aust
37B1 **Nyon** Switz
72B3 **Nyong** *R* Cam
54A3 **Nyongwol** S Korea
54A3 **Nyongwon** N Korea
38D3 **Nyons** France
42D2 **Nysa** Pol
53E1 **Nysh** Russian Fed
18C2 **Nyssa** USA
44H3 **Nyukhcha** Russian Fed
50F1 **Nyukzha** *R* Russian Fed
49N3 **Nyurba** Russian Fed
72D4 **Nzega** Tanz
70B4 **Nzérékore** Guinea
73B4 **N'zeto** Angola
71F4 **Nzi** *R* Ivory Coast

O

11C3 **Oacoma** USA
11B3 **Oahe,L** *Res* USA
20E5 **Oahu,I** Hawaiian Is
75B2 **Oakbank** Aust
20B2 **Oakdale** USA
11C2 **Oakes** USA
75D1 **Oakey** Aust
19B3 **Oakland** California, USA
11C3 **Oakland** Nebraska, USA
18B2 **Oakland** Oregon, USA
12B3 **Oakland City** USA
12B2 **Oak Lawn** USA
20B2 **Oakley** California, USA
16B2 **Oakley** Kansas, USA
15C1 **Oak Ridge** USA
18B2 **Oakridge** USA
4F5 **Oakville** Can
78B3 **Oamaru** NZ
20D2 **Oasis** California, USA
18D2 **Oasis** Nevada, USA

79F7 Oates Land Region, Ant
75E3 Oatlands Aust
22C2 Oaxaca Mexico
22C2 Oaxaca State, Mexico
48H3 Ob' R Russian Fed
4E4 Oba Can
54C3 Obama Japan
78A3 Oban NZ
34C3 Oban Scot
54D3 Obanazawa Japan
71H4 Oban Hills Nig
63E2 Obeh Afghan
37D1 Oberammergau Germany
37E1 Oberdrauburg Austria
36D1 Oberhausen Germany
16B2 Oberlin USA
36E2 Obernburg Germany
37D1 Oberstdorf Germany
37E1 Obervellach Austria
57C3 Obi I Indon
27G4 Obidos Brazil
53E3 Obihiro Japan
53C2 Obluch'ye Russian Fed
72C3 Obo CAR
72E2 Obock Djibouti
42D2 Oborniki Pol
45F5 Oboyan' Russian Fed
18B2 O'Brien USA
45J5 Obshchiy Syrt Mts Russian Fed
48J3 Obskaya Guba B Russian Fed
71F4 Obuasi Ghana
15C3 Ocala USA
22C1 Ocampo Mexico
26D2 Ocana Colombia
39B2 Ocaño Spain
10L4 Ocean C USA
13D3 Ocean City Maryland, USA
14C3 Ocean City New Jersey, USA
6F4 Ocean Falls Can
Ocean I = Banaba
20B3 Oceano USA
20D4 Oceanside USA
17E3 Ocean Springs USA
44J4 Ocher Russian Fed
34D3 Ochil Hills Scot
15C2 Ochlockonee R USA
23H1 Ocho Rios Jamaica
15C2 Ocmulgee R USA
15C2 Oconee R USA
12B2 Oconto USA
22B1 Ocotlán Jalisco, Mexico
22C2 Ocotlán Oaxaca, Mexico
22D2 Ocozocoautla Mexico
71F4 Oda Ghana
54B3 Oda Japan
54A2 Ŏdaejin N Korea
32B2 Ódáðahraun Region, Iceland
53E3 Odate Japan
53D4 Odawara Japan
32F6 Odda Nor
17F4 Odem USA
39A2 Odemira Port
41F3 Ödemiş Turk
74D2 Odendaalsrus S Africa
32G7 Odense Den
36E2 Odenwald Region, Germany
42C2 Oder R Pol/Germany
37E2 Oderzo Italy
16B3 Odessa Texas, USA
45E6 Odessa Ukraine
18C1 Odessa Washington, USA
70B4 Odienné Ivory Coast
Odra = Oder
43D2 Odra, R Pol
27K5 Oeiras Brazil
11B3 Oelrichs USA
11D3 Oelwein USA
40D2 Ofanto R Italy
65C3 Ofaqim Israel
71G4 Offa Nig
35B5 Offaly County, Irish Rep
36E1 Offenbach Germany
36D2 Offenburg Germany
54D3 Ofunato Japan
53D4 Oga Japan
72E3 Ogaden Region, Eth
53D4 Ogaki Japan
16B1 Ogallala USA
50H4 Ogasawara Gunto Is Japan
71G4 Ogbomosho Nig
11D3 Ogden Iowa, USA
18D2 Ogden Utah, USA
3B2 Ogden,Mt. Can/USA
13D2 Ogdensburg USA
15C2 Ogeechee R USA
10L2 Ogilvie Can
6E3 Ogilvie Mts Can
15C2 Oglethorpe,Mt USA
37D2 Oglio R Italy
37B1 Ognon R France
71H4 Ogoja Nig
4D3 Ogoki Can
4D3 Ogoki R Can
4D3 Ogoki Res Can
72A4 Ogooué R Gabon
71G4 Ogou R Togo
43E1 Ogre Latvia
70B2 Oguilet Khenachich Well Mali
40D1 Ogulin Croatia, Yugos
71G4 Ogun State, Nig
14E1 Ogunquit USA
45J8 Ogurchinskiy, Ostov I Turkmenistan
78A3 Ohai NZ
78C1 Ohakune NZ
70C2 Ohanet Alg
54D2 Ōhata Japan
78A2 Ohau,L NZ
9E2 Ohio State, USA
12B3 Ohio R USA
36E1 Ohm R Germany
73B5 Ohopoho Namibia
42C2 Ohre R Czech
41E2 Ohrid Macedonia, Yugos
41E2 Ohridsko Jezero L Macedonia, Yugos/Alb
78B1 Ohura NZ
27H3 Oiapoque French Guiana
50C2 Oijiaojing China
13D2 Oil City USA
20C3 Oildale USA
49L6 Oilian Shan Mts China
36B2 Oise Department, France
38C2 Oise R France
53C5 Ōita Japan
20C3 Ojai USA
21B2 Ojinaga Mexico
22C2 Ojitlán Mexico
54C3 Ojiya Japan
22B1 Ojocaliente Mexico
25C3 Ojos del Salado Mt Arg
22B1 Ojueloz Mexico
44F5 Oka R Russian Fed
74B1 Okahandja Namibia
18C1 Okanagan Falls Can
3E3 Okanagan L Can
18C1 Okanogan USA
18C1 Okanogan R USA
18B1 Okanogan Range Mts Can/USA
60C2 Okara Pak
74B1 Okasise Namibia
73B5 Okavango R Namibia/Angola
73C5 Okavango Delta Marsh Botswana
53D4 Okaya Japan
53C5 Okayama Japan
54C4 Okazaki Japan
15E4 Okeechobee USA
15E4 Okeechobee,L USA
15C2 Okefenokee Swamp USA
71H4 Okene Nig
60B4 Okha India
53E1 Okha Russian Fed
61C2 Okhaldunga Nepal
49Q4 Okhotsk Russian Fed
49Q4 Okhotsk,S of Russian Fed
50F4 Okinawa, I Japan
50F4 Okinagunto Arch Japan
53C4 Oki-shoto, Is Japan
71G4 Okitipupa Nig
8D3 Oklahoma State, USA
17C2 Oklahoma City USA
17C2 Okmulgee USA
74B1 Okombahe Namibia
72B4 Okondja Gabon
54D2 Okoppe Japan
72B4 Okoyo Congo
71G4 Okpara R Nig
44A2 Okstindan Mt Nor
45K6 Oktyabr'sk Kazakhstan
53B1 Oktyabr'skiy Amurskaya, Russian Fed
44J5 Oktyabr'skiy Bashkirskaya, Russian Fed
50J1 Oktyabr'skiy Kamchatka, Russian Fed
49L2 Oktyabrskoy Revolyutsii, Ostrov I Russian Fed
44M3 Oktyabr'skoye Russian Fed
53D3 Okushiri-tō I Japan
74C1 Okwa R Botswana
32A2 Olafsvik Iceland
20D2 Olancha USA
20C2 Olanch Peak Mt USA
32H7 Öland I Sweden
75B2 Olary Aust
17D2 Olathe USA
25D5 Olavarría Arg
40B2 Olbia Sardegna
14A1 Olcott USA
10L2 Old Crow Can
42B2 Oldenburg Niedersachsen, Germany
42C2 Oldenburg Schleswig-Holstein, Germany
14C2 Old Forge USA
35D5 Oldham Eng
10H4 Old Harbor USA
33B3 Old Head of Kinsale C Scot
14D2 Old Lyme USA
3F3 Olds Can
13F2 Old Town USA
3G3 Old Wives L Can
52B1 Öldziyt
14A1 Olean USA
49O4 Olekma R Russian Fed
49O3 Olekminsk Russian Fed
44E2 Olenegorsk Russian Fed
49N3 Olenek Russian Fed
49O2 Olenek R Russian Fed
43F2 Olevsk Ukraine
53D3 Ol'ga Russian Fed
4F4 Olga L Can
74C3 Olifants R Cape Province, S Africa
74B1 Olifants R Namibia
74E1 Olifants R Transvaal, S Africa
74C2 Olifantshoek S Africa
28E2 Olimar R Urug
41E2 Ólimbos Mt Greece
29C3 Olímpia Brazil
22C2 Olinala Mexico
27M5 Olinda Brazil
28C2 Oliva Arg
25C4 Olivares Mt Arg
29D3 Oliveira Brazil
3E4 Oliver Can
3H2 Oliver L Can
11D3 Olivia USA
25C2 Ollagüe Chile
25C2 Ollagüe Mt Bol
12B3 Olney Illinois, USA
16C3 Olney Texas, USA
50E1 Olochi Russian Fed
32G7 Olofstrom Sweden
72B4 Olombo Congo
42D3 Olomouc Czech
44E3 Olonets Russian Fed
57F8 Olongapa Phil
38B3 Oloron ste Marie France
50E1 Olovyannaya Russian Fed
36D1 Olpe Germany
43E2 Olsztyn Pol
37B1 Olten Switz
41E2 Olt R Rom
18B1 Olympia USA
18B1 Olympic Nat Pk USA
Olympus = Ólimbos
65B1 Olympus,Mt Cyprus
18B1 Olympus,Mt USA
54C3 Omachi Japan
54C4 Omae-zaki C Japan
34B4 Omagh N Ire
17C1 Omaha USA
18C1 Omak USA
67G2 Oman Sultanate, Arabian Pen
67G2 Oman,G of UAE
74B1 Omaruru Namibia
74A1 Omaruru R Namibia
54D2 Ōma-saki C Japan
72A4 Omboué Gabon
72D2 Omdurman Sudan
22C2 Ometepec Mexico
72D2 Om Häjer Eth
54D2 Ōminato Japan
3C2 Omineca R Can
3C2 Omineca Mts Can
54C3 Omiya Japan
10M4 Ommaney,C USA
6H2 Ommanney B Can
72D3 Omo R Eth
71H4 Omoku Nig
49R3 Omolon R Russian Fed
49P3 Omoloy R Russian Fed
54D3 Omono R Japan
48J4 Omsk Russian Fed
54D2 Ōmu Japan
53B5 Omura Japan
74C1 Omuramba Eiseb R Botswana
53C5 Ōmuta Japan
44J4 Omutninsk Russian Fed
12A2 Onalaska USA
13D3 Onancock USA
57A3 Onang Indon
12C1 Onaping L Can
11C3 Onawa USA
73B5 Oncócua Angola
73B5 Ondangua Namibia
43E3 Ondava R Czech
71G4 Ondo Nig
71G4 Ondo State, Nig
50E2 Öndörhaan Mongolia
59F5 One and Half Degree Chan Indian O
44F3 Onega Russian Fed
44F3 Onega R Russian Fed
14C1 Oneida USA
14B1 Oneida L USA
11C3 O'Neill USA
50J2 Onekotan I Russian Fed
72C4 Onema Zaïre
14C1 Oneonta USA
41F1 Oneşti Rom
44F3 Onezhskaya Guba B Russian Fed
44F3 Onezhskoye, Ozero L Russian Fed
74C3 Ongers R S Africa
73B5 Ongiva Angola
53B4 Ongjin N Korea
52D1 Ongniud Qi China
62C1 Ongole India
13D2 Onieda L USA
73E6 Onilahy R Madag
71H4 Onitsha Nig
50D2 Onjüül Mongolia
54C3 Ono Japan
54C4 Ōnohara-jima I Japan
53C5 Onomichi Japan
77G1 Onotoa I Kiribati
76A3 Onslow Aust
15D2 Onslow B USA
54C3 Ontake-san Mt Japan
20D3 Ontario California, USA
18C2 Ontario Oregon, USA
7J4 Ontario Province, Can
13D2 Ontario,L USA/Can
39B2 Onteniente Spain
77E1 Ontong Java Atoll Solomom Is
54A3 Onyang S Korea
20C3 Onyx USA
76C3 Oodnadatta Aust
76C4 Ooldea Aust
17C2 Oologah L USA
36B1 Oostende Belg
36B1 Oosterschelde Estuary Neth
62B2 Ootacamund India
3C3 Ootsa L Can
22B1 Opal Mexico
49R4 Opala Russian Fed
72C4 Opala Zaïre
62C3 Opanake Sri Lanka
44H4 Oparino Russian Fed
4E4 Opasatika Can
4E4 Opasatika R Can
4C3 Opasquia Can
43D3 Opava Czech
15B2 Opelika USA
17D3 Opelousas USA
11A2 Opheim USA
10G3 Ophir USA
4F3 Opinaca R Can
4E3 Opinnagau R Can
43F1 Opochka Russian Fed
43D2 Opole Pol
Oporto = Porto
78C1 Opotiki NZ
15B2 Opp USA
32F6 Oppdal Nor
78B1 Opunake NZ
41E1 Oradea Rom
32B2 Oraefajökull Mts Iceland
60D3 Orai India
71B1 Oran Alg
25D2 Orán Arg
54A2 Orang N Korea
75C2 Orange Aust
20D4 Orange California, USA
38C3 Orange France
17D3 Orange Texas, USA
74B2 Orange R S Africa
15C2 Orangeburg USA
11C3 Orange City USA
74D2 Orange Free State Province, S Africa
15C2 Orange Park USA
12C2 Orangeville Can
42C2 Oranienburg Germany
74C2 Oranje R S Africa
74B2 Oranjemund Namibia
74D1 Orapa Botswana
57G8 Oras Phil
41E1 Orăstie Rom
41E1 Oraviţa Rom
40C2 Orbetello Italy
14B2 Orbisonia USA
75C3 Orbost Aust
36B1 Orchies France
37B2 Orco R Italy
20B3 Orcutt USA
11C3 Ord USA
76B2 Ord R Aust
19D3 Orderville USA
76B2 Ord,Mt Aust
49M6 Ordos Desert China
64C1 Ordu Turk
16B2 Ordway USA
32H7 Örebro Sweden
8A2 Oregon State, USA
12C2 Oregon USA
18B1 Oregon City USA
32H6 Oregrund Sweden
44F4 Orekhovo Zuyevo Russian Fed
45F5 Orel Russian Fed
53D1 Orel, Ozero' L Russian Fed
19D2 Orem USA
45J5 Orenburg Russian Fed
28D3 Orense Arg
39A1 Orense Spain
42C1 Oresund Str Den/Sweden
78A3 Oreti R NZ
5G5 Orford USA
43F3 Orgeyev Moldavia
41F3 Orhaneli R Turk
50D2 Orhon Gol R Mongolia
22C2 Oriental Mexico
75B1 Orientos Aust
39B2 Orihuela Spain
4F5 Orillia Can
26F2 Orinoco R Ven
14C1 Oriskany Falls USA
61B3 Orissa State, India
40B3 Oristano Sardegna
32K6 Orivesi L Fin
27G4 Oriximina Brazil
22C2 Orizaba Mexico
29C2 Orizona Brazil
34D2 Orkney I Scot
29C3 Orlândia Brazil
15C3 Orlando USA
38C2 Orléanais Region France
38C2 Orléans France
14E2 Orleans USA
49L4 Orlik Russian Fed
63E3 Ormara Pak
37B2 Ormea Italy
57F8 Ormoc Phil
15C3 Ormond Beach USA
36C2 Ornain R France
37B1 Ornans France
38B2 Orne R France
32H6 Örnsköldsvik Sweden
54A2 Oro N Korea
26D3 Orocué Colombia
18C1 Orofino USA
5H4 Oromocto Can
65C3 Oron Israel
Orontes = 'Āsī,R
53A1 Oroqen Zizhiqi China
57F9 Oroquieta Phil
43E3 Orosháza Hung
49R3 Orotukan Russian Fed
19B3 Oroville California, USA
18C1 Oroville Washington, USA
32F6 Ørsba Nor
43G2 Orsha Belorussia
37B1 Orsières Switz
45K5 Orsk Russian Fed
38B3 Orthez France
39A1 Ortigueira Spain
37D1 Ortles Mts Italy
38E2 Ortles Mt Italy
23L1 Ortoire R Trinidad
11C2 Ortonville USA
26E7 Oruro Bol
44K4 Osa Russian Fed
11D3 Osage Iowa, USA
11B3 Osage Wyoming, USA
17D2 Osage R USA
54C3 Osaka Japan
21D4 Osa,Pen de Costa Rica
49P2 Osbrov Stolbovoy I Russian Fed
17E2 Osceola Arkansas, USA
17D1 Osceola Iowa, USA
18C2 Osgood Mts USA
54D2 Oshamambe Japan
4F5 Oshawa Can
54C2 Ō-shima I Japan
54C4 Ō-shima I Japan
16B1 Oshkosh Nebraska, USA
12B2 Oshkosh Wisconsin, USA
45H8 Oshnoviyeh Iran
71G4 Oshogbo Nig
72B4 Oshwe Zaïre
41D1 Osijek Croatia, Yugos
37E3 Osimo Italy
48K4 Osinniki Russian Fed
43F2 Osipovichi Belorussia
17D1 Oskaloosa USA
44B4 Oskarshamn Sweden
32G6 Oslo Nor
64C2 Osmaniye Turk
42B2 Osnabrück Germany
25B6 Osorno Chile
39B1 Osorno Spain
18C1 Osoyoos Can
3D2 Ospika R Can
76D5 Ossa,Mt Aust

71H4 Ossé R Nig
12A2 Osseo USA
37E1 Ossiacher See L Austria
14D2 Ossining USA
5J3 Ossokmanuan L Can
49S4 Ossora Russian Fed
44E4 Ostashkov Russian Fed
Ostend = Oostende
32G6 Østerdalen, V Nor
32G6 Östersund Sweden
32H6 Östhammär Sweden
40C2 Ostia Italy
37D2 Ostiglia Italy
43D3 Ostrava Czech
43D2 Ostróda Pol
43E2 Ostroleka Pol
44D4 Ostrov Russian Fed
43D2 Ostrów Pol
43E2 Ostrowiec Pol
43E2 Ostrów Mazowiecka Pol
53C5 Ōsumi-kaikyō Str Japan
53C5 Ōsumi-shotō Is Japan
71G4 Osun State Nigeria
39A2 Osuna Spain
14B1 Oswego USA
14B1 Oswego R USA
35D5 Oswestry Eng
43D3 OświȘecim Pol
54C3 Ota Japan
78B3 Otago Pen NZ
78C2 Otaki NZ
53E3 Otaru Japan
26C3 Otavalo Ecuador
73B5 Otavi Namibia
54D3 Otawara Japan
14C1 Otego USA
18C1 Othello USA
3G2 Otherside R Can
41E3 Óthris Mt Greece
71G4 Oti R Ghana
71G4 Otiki R Nig
16B1 Otis Colorado, USA
14D1 Otis Massachusetts, USA
14C2 Otisville USA
74B1 Otjimbingwe Namibia
73B6 Otjiwarongo Namibia
52B2 Otog Qi China
54D2 Otoineppu Japan
78C1 Otorohanga NZ
41D2 Otranto Italy
41D2 Otranto,Str of Chan Italy/Alb
12B2 Otsego USA
14C1 Otsego L USA
4E5 Otsego Lake USA
54C3 Otsu Japan
32F6 Otta Nor
32F7 Otta R Nor
4F4 Ottawa Can
4F4 Ottawa R Can
12B2 Ottawa Illinois, USA
17C2 Ottawa Kansas, USA
7K4 Ottawa Is Can
7K4 Otter Rapids Can
7K1 Otto Fjord Can
74D2 Ottosdal S Africa
12A2 Ottumwa USA
36D2 Ottweiler Germany
71H4 Otukpa Nig
71H4 Oturkpo Nig
26C5 Otusco Peru
75B3 Otway,C Aust
43E2 Otwock Pol
37D1 Ötz Austria
37D1 Ötzal Mts Austria
55C1 Ou R Laos
17D3 Ouachita R USA
17D3 Ouachita,L USA
17D3 Ouachita Mts USA
70A2 Ouadane Maur
72C3 Ouadda CAR
72C2 Ouaddai Desert Region Chad
71F3 Ouagadougou Burkina
71F3 Ouahigouya Burkina
72C3 Ouaka CAR
70C3 Oualam Niger
71G3 Oualé R Burkina
70C2 Ouallen Alg
72C3 Ouanda Djallé CAR
36B3 Ouanne R France
70A2 Ouarane Region, Maur
70C1 Ouargla Alg
72C3 Ouarra R CAR
70B1 Ouarzazate Mor
39C2 Ouassel R Alg
72B3 Oubangui R Congo
36B1 Oudenaarde Belg
74C3 Oudtshoorn S Africa
39B2 Oued Tlělat Alg
71A2 Oued Zem Mor
71F4 Ouellé Ivory Coast
72B3 Ouesso Congo
71A2 Ouezzane Mor
72B3 Ouham R Chad
71G4 Ouidah Benin
4D4 Ouimet Can
71B2 Oujda Mor
32J6 Oulainen Fin
32K5 Oulu Fin
32K6 Oulu R Fin
32K6 Oulujärvi L Fin
72C2 Oum Chalouba Chad
71D1 Oum el Bouaghi Alg
71A2 Oumer Rbia R Mor
72B2 Oum Hadjer Chad
72C2 Oum Haouach Watercourse Chad
32K5 Ounas R Fin
44C2 Ounasjoki R Fin
44C2 Ounastunturi Mt Fin
72C2 Ounianga Kebir Chad
36D1 Our R Germany
16A2 Ouray USA
36C2 Ource R France
Ourense = Orense Spain
36B2 Ourcq R France
27K5 Ouricurí Brazil
29C3 Ourinhos Brazil
29D3 Ouro Prêto Brazil
36C1 Ourthe R Belg
35E4 Ouse R Eng
35F5 Ouse R Eng
33B2 Outer Hebrides Is Scot
20C4 Outer Santa Barbara Chan USA
73B6 Outjo Namibia
3G3 Outlook Can
32K6 Outokumpu Fin
37A2 Ouvèze R France
75B3 Ouyen Aust
37C2 Ovada Italy
28A2 Ovalle Chile
73B5 Ovamboland Region, Namibia
19D3 Overton USA
32J5 Övertorneå Sweden
16B1 Ovid Colorado, USA
14B1 Ovid New York, USA
39A1 Oviedo Spain
45D5 Ovruch Ukraine
49O4 Ovsyanka Russian Fed
78A3 Owaka NZ
14B1 Owasco L USA
54C4 Owase Japan
11D3 Owatonna USA
14B1 Owego USA
20C2 Owens R USA
12B3 Owensboro USA
20D2 Owens L USA
4E5 Owen Sound Can
76D1 Owen Stanley Range Mts PNG
71H4 Owerri Nig
4C2 Owl R Can
18E2 Owl Creek Mts USA
71H4 Owo Nig
12C2 Owosso USA
18C2 Owyhee USA
18C2 Owyhee R USA
18C2 Owyhee Mts USA
26C6 Oxampampa Peru
3H4 Oxbow Can
32H7 Oxelösund Sweden
35E6 Oxford County, Eng
35E5 Oxford Eng
14E1 Oxford Massachusetts, USA
17E3 Oxford Mississippi, USA
14C1 Oxford New York, USA
20C3 Oxnard USA
53D4 Oyama Japan
3F3 Oyen Can
72B3 Oyen Gabon
34C3 Oykel R Scot
49Q3 Oymyakon Russian Fed
71G4 Oyo Nig
37A1 Oyonnax France
32F6 Øyre Nor
75E3 Oyster B Aust
57F9 Ozamiz Phil
43F2 Ozarichi Belorussia
15B2 Ozark USA
17D2 Ozark Plat USA
17D2 Ozarks,L of the USA
43E3 Ózd Hung
53E2 Ozerskiy Russian Fed
16B3 Ozona USA
22C1 Ozuluama Mexico

P

74B3 Paarl S Africa
34B3 Pabbay I Scot
43D2 Pabianice Pol
61C3 Pabna Bang
43F1 Pabrade Lithuania
26C5 Pacasmayo Peru
28E2 Pacheca Brazil
22B1 Pacheco Mexico
22C1 Pachuca Mexico
20B1 Pacific USA
xxixN7 Pacific-Antarctic Ridge Pacific O
20B2 Pacific Grove USA
xxixG8 Pacific O
56D4 Pacitan Indon
29D2 Pacuí R Brazil
56B3 Padang Indon
57B4 Padang Indon
56B3 Padangpanjang Indon
56A2 Padangsidempuan Indon
44E3 Padany Russian Fed
42B2 Paderborn Germany
6J3 Padlei Can
61D3 Padma R Bang
37D2 Padova Italy
8D4 Padre I USA
35C6 Padstow Eng
75B3 Padthaway Aust
Padua = Padova
12B3 Paducah Kentucky, USA
16B3 Paducah Texas, USA
32L5 Padunskoye More L Russian Fed
54A2 Paegam N Korea
53A4 Paengnyŏng-do I S Korea
78C1 Paeroa NZ
74E1 Pafuri Mozam
40C2 Pag I Croatia, Yugos
57F9 Pagadian Phil
56B3 Pagai Seletan I Indon
56B3 Pagai Utara I Indon
51H5 Pagan I Pacific O
56E3 Pagatan Indon
19D3 Page USA
51F8 Pago Mission Aust
41F3 Pagondhas Greece
16A2 Pagosa Springs USA
4C4 Paguchi L Can
4D3 Pagwa River Can
20E5 Pahala Hawaiian Is
78C2 Pahiatua NZ
20E5 Pahoa Hawaiian Is
15E4 Pahokee USA
71J4 Pai R Nig
32K6 Päijänna L Fin
28A4 Paillaco Chile
20E5 Pailola Chan Hawaiian Is
12C2 Painesville USA
19D3 Painted Desert USA
12C3 Paintsville USA
34C4 Paisley Scot
26B5 Paita Peru
32J5 Pajala Sweden
57B4 Pajeti Indon
58E3 Pakistan Republic, Asia
55C2 Pak Lay Laos
61E3 Pakokku Burma
3F4 Pakowki L Can
40D1 Pakrac Croatia, Yugos
41D1 Paks Hung
55C2 Pak Sane Laos
55D2 Pakse Laos
72D3 Pakwach Uganda
72B3 Pala Chad
40D2 Palagruža I Croatia, Yugos
36B2 Palaiseau France
74D1 Palala R S Africa
62E2 Palalankwe Andaman Is
49S4 Palana Russian Fed
56D3 Palangkaraya Indon
62B2 Palani India
60C4 Palanpur India
74D1 Palapye Botswana
15C3 Palatka USA
51G6 Palau Is Pacific O
55B3 Palaw Burma
57E9 Palawan I Phil
57E9 Palawan Pass Phil
62B3 Palayankottai India
32J7 Paldiski Estonia
57B2 Paleleh Indon
56B3 Palembang Indon
39B1 Palencia Spain
65B1 Paleokhorio Cyprus
40C3 Palermo Italy
65C3 Palestine Region, Israel
17C3 Palestine USA
61D3 Paletwa Burma
62B2 Pālghāt India
60C3 Pāli India
71G4 Palimé Togo
56E1 Palin,Mt Malay
16A2 Palisade USA
60C4 Pālitāna India
62B3 Palk Str India/Sri Lanka
45H5 Pallasovka Russian Fed
32J5 Pallastunturi Mt Fin
78B2 Palliser B NZ
78C2 Palliser,C NZ
73E5 Palma Mozam
39C2 Palma de Mallorca Spain
27L5 Palmares Brazil
28E2 Palmares do Sul Brazil
23A5 Palmar Sur Costa Rica
29B4 Palmas Brazil
70B4 Palmas,C Lib
29D1 Palmas de Monte Alto Brazil
23B2 Palma Soriano Cuba
15C3 Palm Bay USA
15E4 Palm Beach USA
20C3 Palmdale USA
29C4 Palmeira Brazil
27L5 Palmeira dos Indos Brazil
10J3 Palmer USA
79G3 Palmer Base Ant
79G3 Palmer Arch Ant
79F3 Palmer Land Region Ant
78B3 Palmerston NZ
78C2 Palmerston North NZ
14C2 Palmerton USA
15E4 Palmetto USA
40D3 Palmi Italy
28E1 Palmiera das Missões Brazil
22C1 Palmillas Mexico
26C3 Palmira Colombia
76D2 Palm Is Aust
4E5 Palms USA
19C4 Palm Springs USA
12A3 Palmyra Missouri, USA
14B1 Palmyra New York, USA
14B2 Palmyra Pennsylvania, USA
61C3 Palmyras Pt India
20A2 Palo Alto USA
56C2 Paloh Indon
72D2 Paloích Sudan
22C2 Palomares Mexico
19C4 Palomar Mt USA
57B3 Palopo Indon
57A3 Palu Indon
64C2 Palu Turk
60D3 Palwal India
10B2 Palyavaam R Russian Fed
71G3 Pama Burkina
56D4 Pamekasan Indon
56C4 Pameungpeuk Indon
38C3 Pamiers France
59F2 Pamir Mts China
48J6 Pamir R Russian Fed
15D1 Pamlico R USA
15D1 Pamlico Sd USA
16B2 Pampa USA
28B2 Pampa de la Salinas Salt pan Arg
28B3 Pampa de la Varita Plain Arg
57B3 Pampanua Indon
28D2 Pampeiro Brazil
26D2 Pamplona Colombia
39B1 Pamplona Spain
12B3 Pana USA
19D3 Panaca USA
41E2 Panagyurishte Bulg
62A1 Panaji India
26C2 Panamá Panama
26B2 Panama Republic, C America
23B5 Panama Canal Panama
15B2 Panama City USA
19C3 Panamint Range Mts USA
20D2 Panamint V USA
37D2 Panaro R Italy
57F8 Panay I Phil
41E2 Pancevo Serbia, Yugos
57F8 Pandan Phil
62B1 Pandharpur India
75A1 Pandie Pandie Aust
43E1 Panevežys Lithuania
48K5 Panfilov Kazakhstan
55B1 Pang R Burma
72D4 Pangani Tanz
72D4 Pangani R Tanz
72C4 Pangi Zaïre
57A3 Pangkajene Indon
56C3 Pangkalpinang Indon
7M3 Pangnirtung Can
55B1 Pangtara Burma
19D3 Panguitch USA
57F9 Pangutaran Group Is Phil
16B2 Panhandle USA
60D3 Panipat India
60B2 Panjao Afghan
63E3 Panjgur Pak
10F5 Pankof,C USA
71H4 Pankshin Nig
53B4 P'anmunjŏm N Korea
61B3 Panna India
29B3 Panorama Brazil
29A2 Pantanal de São Lourenço Swamp Brazil
29A2 Pantanal do Rio Negro Swamp Brazil
29A2 Pantanal do Taquari Swamp Brazil
57B4 Pantar I Indon
40C3 Pantelleria I Medit S
22C1 Pantepec Mexico
22C1 Panuco Mexico
22C1 Pánuco R Mexico
52A4 Pan Xian China
40D3 Paola Italy
17D2 Paola USA
12B3 Paoli USA
42D3 Papa Hung
20E5 Papaikou Hawaiian Is
78B1 Papakura NZ
22C2 Papaloapan R Mexico
22C1 Papantla Mexico
34E1 Papa Stour I Scot
78B1 Papatoetoe NZ
34D2 Papa Westray I Scot
65B1 Paphos Cyprus
76D1 Papua,G of PNG
76D1 Papua New Guinea Republic, S E Asia
28A2 Papudo Chile
55B2 Papun Burma
27H4 Para State, Brazil
27J4 Pará R Brazil
76A3 Paraburdoo Aust
26C6 Paracas,Pen de Peru
29C2 Paracatu Brazil
29C2 Paracatu R Brazil
55E2 Paracel Is S E Asia
75A2 Parachilna Aust
60C2 Parachinar Pak
41E2 Paracin Serbia, Yugos
29D2 Pará de Minas Brazil
19B3 Paradise California, USA
19D3 Paradise Nevada, USA
5K3 Paradise R Can
20D1 Paradise Peak Mt USA
17D2 Paragould USA
26F6 Paraguá R Bol
26F2 Paragua R Ven
29D1 Paraguaçu R Brazil
27G7 Paraguai R Brazil
29A4 Paraguarí Par
25E2 Paraguay Republic, S America
25E2 Paraguay R Par
27L5 Paraiba State, Brazil
29D3 Paraíba do Sul R Brazil
22D2 Paraiso Mexico
71G4 Parakou Benin
75A2 Parakylia Aust
62B3 Paramakkudi India
27G2 Paramaribo Surinam
29D1 Paramirim Brazil
49R4 Paramushir, Ostrov I Russian Fed
29B4 Paraná Brazil
25F2 Paraná State, Brazil
28C2 Paraná Urug
25E4 Paraná R Arg
27J6 Paranã R Brazil
29C4 Paranaguá Brazil
29B2 Paranaiba Brazil
29B2 Paranaiba R Brazil
29B3 Paranapanema R Brazil
29B3 Paranavai Brazil
57F9 Parang Phil
29D2 Paraope R Brazil
78B2 Paraparaumu NZ
29D1 Paratinga Brazil
62B1 Parbhani India
71G3 Parc National d'Arly Burkina
71F4 Parc National de la Komoé Ivory Coast
71G3 Parc National de la Pendjari Benin
71G3 Parcs Nationaux du W Benin
65C2 Pardes Hanna Israel
28D3 Pardo Arg
29E2 Pardo R Bahia, Brazil
29B3 Pardo R Mato Grosso do Sul, Brazil
29C2 Pardo R Minas Gerais, Brazil
29C3 Pardo R Sao Paulo, Brazil
42D2 Pardubice Czech
50G4 Parece Vela Reef Pacific O
29A1 Parecis Brazil
4G4 Parent Can
57A3 Parepare Indon
28C3 Parera Arg
56B3 Pariaman Indon
26F1 Paria,Pen de Ven
57B3 Parigi Indon
38C2 Paris France
12C3 Paris Kentucky, USA
15B1 Paris Tennessee, USA
17C3 Paris Texas, USA
19D4 Parker USA
12C3 Parkersburg USA
75C2 Parkes Aust
14C3 Parkesburg USA
12A1 Park Falls USA
20B3 Parkfield USA
12B2 Park Forest USA
11C2 Park Rapids USA
11C3 Parkston USA

18B1 **Parksville** Can
18D2 **Park Valley** USA
62C1 **Parlākimidi** India
62B1 **Parli** India
37D2 **Parma** Italy
12C2 **Parma** USA
27K4 **Parnaiba** Brazil
27K4 **Parnaiba** *R* Brazil
41E3 **Párnon Óros** *Mts* Greece
44C4 **Pärnu** Estonia
61C2 **Paro** Bhutan
75B1 **Paroo** *R* Aust
75B2 **Paroo Channel** *R* Aust
63E2 **Paropamisus** *Mts* Afghan
41F3 **Páros** *I* Greece
19D3 **Parowan** USA
37B2 **Parpaillon** *Mts* France
28A3 **Parral** Chile
75D2 **Parramatta** Aust
8C4 **Parras** Mexico
7K3 **Parry B** Can
10O1 **Parry,C** Can
6G2 **Parry Is** Can
10O2 **Parry Pen** Can
12C1 **Parry Sound** Can
42C3 **Parsberg** Germany
6F4 **Parsnip** *R* Can
17C2 **Parsons** Kansas, USA
13D3 **Parsons** West Virginia, USA
38B2 **Parthenay** France
40C3 **Partinico** Italy
53C3 **Partizansk** Russian Fed
27H4 **Paru** *R* Brazil
22A1 **Páruco** Mexico
62C1 **Parvatipuram** India
74D2 **Parys** S Africa
17C4 **Pasadena** Texas, USA
20C3 **Pasadena** USA
57A3 **Pasangkayu** Indon
57B4 **Pasarwajo** Indon
55B2 **Pasawing** Burma
17E3 **Pascagoula** USA
41F1 **Paşcani** Rom
18C1 **Pasco** USA
36B1 **Pas-de-Calais** Department, France
32G8 **Pasewalk** Germany
3G2 **Pasfield L** Can
63D3 **Pashū'īyeh** Iran
76B4 **Pasley,C** Aust
63E3 **Pasni** Pak
28D1 **Paso de los Libres** Arg
25E4 **Paso de los Toros** Urug
25B6 **Paso Limay** Arg
20B3 **Paso Robles** USA
5H4 **Paspébiac** Can
3H3 **Pasquia Hills** Can
14C2 **Passaic** USA
42C3 **Passau** Germany
25E3 **Passo de los Libres** Arg
22B1 **Passo del Toro** *Mt* Mexico
37D1 **Passo di Stelvio** *Mt* Italy
37D1 **Passo di Tonale** Italy
28E1 **Passo Fundo** Brazil
29C3 **Passos** Brazil
37B2 **Passy** France
26C4 **Pastaza** *R* Peru
28C3 **Pasteur** Arg
6H4 **Pas,The** Can
26C3 **Pasto** Colombia
10F3 **Pastol B** USA
37D2 **Pasubio** *Mt* Italy
56D4 **Pasuruan** Indon
43E1 **Pasvalys** Lithuania
60C4 **Pātan** India
61C2 **Patan** Nepal
75B3 **Patchewollock** Aust
78B1 **Patea** NZ
78B2 **Patea** *R* NZ
40C3 **Paterno** Italy
14C2 **Paterson** USA
78A3 **Paterson Inlet** *B* NZ
60D2 **Pathankot** India
11A3 **Pathfinder Res** USA
60D2 **Patiāla** India
26C6 **Pativilca** Peru
41F3 **Pátmos** *I* Greece
61C2 **Patna** India
64D2 **Patnos** Turk
49N4 **Patomskoye Nagor'ye** *Upland* Russian Fed
27L5 **Patos** Brazil
29C2 **Patos de Minas** Brazil
28B2 **Patquia** Arg
41E3 **Pátrai** Greece
44L3 **Patrasuy** Russian Fed
29C2 **Patrocinio** Brazil
72E4 **Patta** *I* Kenya
57A4 **Pattallasang** Indon
55C4 **Pattani** Thai
20B2 **Patterson** California, USA
17D4 **Patterson** Louisiana, USA
10M3 **Patterson,Mt** Can
20C2 **Patterson Mt** USA
14A2 **Patton** USA
3C2 **Pattullo,Mt** Can
27L5 **Patu** Brazil
61D3 **Patuakhali** Bang
21D3 **Patuca** *R* Honduras
22B2 **Patzcuaro** Mexico
38B3 **Pau** France
10O2 **Paulatuk** Can
27K5 **Paulistana** Brazil
74E2 **Paulpietersburg** S Africa
17C3 **Pauls Valley** USA
55B2 **Paungde** Burma
60D2 **Pauri** India
32H5 **Pauskie** Nor
29D2 **Pavão** Brazil
37C2 **Pavia** Italy
48J4 **Pavlodar** Kazakhstan
10F4 **Pavlof V** USA
10F4 **Pavlov B** USA
44K4 **Pavlovka** Russian Fed
44G4 **Pavlovo** Russian Fed
45G5 **Pavlovsk** Russian Fed
37D2 **Pavullo nel Frigano** Italy
56D3 **Pawan** *R* Indon
17C2 **Pawhuska** USA
14A3 **Paw Paw** USA
14E2 **Pawtucket** USA
16B1 **Paxton** USA
56B3 **Payakumbuh** Indon
37B1 **Payerne** Switz
18C2 **Payette** USA
7L4 **Payne,L** Can
11D2 **Paynesville** USA
28D2 **Paysandu** Urug
36A2 **Pays d'Auge** Region, France
36A2 **Pays-de-Bray** Region, France
36A2 **Pays de Caux** Region, France
36A2 **Pays d'Ouche** Region, France
41E2 **Pazardzhik** Bulg
37E2 **Pazin** Croatia, Yugos
3E2 **Peace** *R* Can
15E4 **Peace** *R* USA
3E2 **Peace River** Can
19D3 **Peach Springs** USA
35E5 **Peak District Nat Pk** Eng
75A1 **Peake** *R* Aust
13F1 **Peaked Mt** USA
75C2 **Peak Hill** Aust
51G7 **Peak Mandala** *Mt* Indon
35E5 **Peak,The** *Mt* Eng
19E3 **Peale,Mt** USA
17D3 **Pearl** *R* USA
20E5 **Pearl City** Hawaiian Is
20E5 **Pearl Harbor** Hawaiian Is
17F4 **Pearsall** USA
74D3 **Pearston** S Africa
6H2 **Peary Chan** Can
73D5 **Pebane** Mozam
41E2 **Peć** Serbia, Yugos
29D2 **Peçanha** Brazil
17D4 **Pecan Island** USA
32L5 **Pechenga** Russian Fed
44K2 **Pechora** Russian Fed
44J2 **Pechora** *R* Russian Fed
44J2 **Pechorskaya Guba** *G* Russian Fed
44J2 **Pechorskoye More** *S* Russian Fed
40D3 **Pecoraro** *Mt* Italy
16B3 **Pecos** USA
16B3 **Pecos** *R* USA
43D3 **Pécs** Hung
56G7 **Pedang Endau** Malay
65B1 **Pedhoulas** Cyprus
75A1 **Pedirka** Aust
29D2 **Pedra Azul** Brazil
29C3 **Pedregulho** Brazil
23B3 **Pedro Cays** *Is* Caribbean
25C2 **Pedro de Valdivia** Chile
29B2 **Pedro Gomes** Brazil
29A3 **Pedro Juan Caballero** Par
28C3 **Pedro Luro** Arg
22C1 **Pedro Mentova** Mexico
62C3 **Pedro,Pt** Sri Lanka
28D1 **Pedro R Fernandez** Arg
75B2 **Peebinga** Aust
34D4 **Peebles** Scot
15D2 **Pee Dee** *R* USA
14D2 **Peekskill** USA
35C4 **Peel** Eng
10M2 **Peel** *R* Can
6J2 **Peel Sd** Can
75A1 **Peera Peera Poolanna** *L* Aust
3F2 **Peerless L** Can
51G7 **Peg Arfak** *Mt* Indon
78B2 **Pegasus B** NZ
10B2 **Pegtymel'** *R* Russian Fed
61E4 **Pegu** Burma
56B3 **Pegunungan Barisan** *Mts* Indon
56D2 **Pegunungan Iran** *Mts* Malay Indon
76C1 **Pegunungan Maoke** *Mts* Indon
56E3 **Pegunungan Meratus** *Mts* Indon
56D2 **Pegunungan Muller** *Mts* Indon
56D3 **Pegunungan Schwanet** *Mts* Indon
56B3 **Pegunungan Tigapuluh** *Mts* Indon
55B2 **Pegu Yoma** *Mts* Burma
28C3 **Pehuajó** Arg
32K7 **Peipsi Järv** *L* Estonia
32K7 **Peipus, Lake** *L* Russian Fed
29B1 **Peixe** *R* Mato Grosso, Brazil
29B3 **Peixe** *R* Sao Paulo, Brazil
52D3 **Pei Xian** China
56C4 **Pekalongan** Indon
55C5 **Pekan** Malay
56B2 **Pekanbaru** Indon
12B2 **Pekin** USA
Peking = Beijing
55C5 **Pelabohan Kelang** Malay
71E1 **Pelagie Is** Mediterranean S
57C3 **Pelau Pelau Boö** *Is* Indon
56E4 **Pelau Pelau Kangean** *Is* Indon
56D4 **Pelau Pelau Karimunjawa** *Arch* Indon
57C4 **Pelau Pelau Maisel** *Is* Indon
57C4 **Pelau Pelau Penyu** *Is* Indon
56E4 **Pelau Pelau Postilyon** *Is* Indon
57B3 **Pelau Pelau Salabangka** *Is* Indon
41E1 **Peleaga** *Mt* Rom
49N4 **Peleduy** Russian Fed
12C2 **Pelee I** Can
76B1 **Peleng** *I* Indon
10L4 **Pelican** USA
11D2 **Pelican L** USA
74A1 **Pelican Pt** S Africa
41D2 **Peljeẓac** *Pen* Croatia, Yugos
28C3 **Pellegrini** Arg
32J5 **Pello** Fin
10M3 **Pelly** *R* Can
7J3 **Pelly Bay** Can
10L3 **Pelly Crossing** Can
10M3 **Pelly Mts** Can
28E2 **Pelotas** Brazil
25F3 **Pelotas** *R* Brazil
65B3 **Pelusium** *Hist Site* Egypt
37B2 **Pelvoux** Region, France
44L3 **Pelym** *R* Russian Fed
56C4 **Pemalang** Indon
56B3 **Pematang** Indon
56A2 **Pematangsiantar** Indon
73E5 **Pemba** Mozam
72D4 **Pemba** *I* Tanz
3D3 **Pemberton** Can
11C2 **Pembina** USA
3E3 **Pembina** *R* Can
4F4 **Pembroke** Can
15C2 **Pembroke** USA
35C6 **Pembroke** Wales
28A3 **Pemuco** Chile
14E1 **Penacook** USA
56E2 **Penambo Range** *Mts* Malay
29B3 **Penápolis** Brazil
39A2 **Peñarroya** Spain
39B1 **Penarroya** *Mt* Spain
39A1 **Peña Trevina** *Mt* Spain
72B3 **Pende** *R* Chad
10N4 **Pendelton,Mt** Can
71G3 **Pendjari** *R* Benin
18C1 **Pendleton** USA
18C1 **Pend Oreille** *R* USA
27L6 **Penedo** Brazil
4F5 **Penetanguishene** Can
60D5 **Penganga** *R* India
52D5 **P'eng hu Lieh tao** *Is* Taiwan
52E2 **Penglai** China
52B4 **Pengshui** China
51G7 **Pengunungan Maoke** *Mts* Indon
5H4 **Peninsule de Gaspé** *Pen* Can
23C4 **Península de la Guajiri** *Pen* Colombia
23E4 **Península de Paria** *Pen* Ven
55C5 **Peninsular Malaysia** Malay
22B1 **Penjamo** Mexico
37E3 **Pennabilli** Italy
62B2 **Penner** *R* India
34D4 **Pennine Chain** *Mts* Eng
14C3 **Penns Grove** USA
9F2 **Pennsylvania** State, USA
14B1 **Penn Yan** USA
7M3 **Penny Highlands** *Mts* Can
13F1 **Penobscot** *R* USA
13F2 **Penobscot B** USA
75B3 **Penola** Aust
76C4 **Penong** Aust
23A5 **Penonomé** Panama
35D4 **Penrith** Eng
15B2 **Pensacola** USA
79E **Pensacola Mts** Ant
56E2 **Pensiangan** Malay
77F2 **Pentecost** *I* Vanuatu
3E4 **Penticton** Can
34D2 **Pentland Firth** *Chan* Scot
34D4 **Pentland Hills** Scot
44H5 **Penza** Russian Fed
35C6 **Penzance** Eng
49S3 **Penzhina** *R* Russian Fed
49S3 **Penzhinskaya Guba** *B* Russian Fed
12B2 **Peoria** USA
56B3 **Perabumulih** Indon
55C5 **Perak** *R* Malay
56B2 **Perawang** Indon
29A3 **Perdido** *R* Brazil
26C3 **Pereira** Colombia
29B3 **Pereira Barreto** Brazil
45G6 **Perelazovskiy** Russian Fed
10H4 **Perenosa B** USA
43G2 **Pereyaslav** Ukraine
53D2 **Pereyaslavka** Russian Fed
28C2 **Pergamino** Arg
37E3 **Pergola** Italy
7L4 **Péribonca** *R* Can
66D4 **Perim** *I* Yemen
38C2 **Périqueux** France
21E4 **Perlas Arch de** *Is* Panama
44K4 **Perm'** Russian Fed
Pernambuco = Recife
27L5 **Pernambuco State,** Brazil
75A2 **Pernatty Lg** Aust
41E2 **Pernik** Bulg
36B2 **Péronne** France
22C2 **Perote** Mexico
38C3 **Perpignan** France
20D4 **Perris** USA
15C2 **Perry** Florida, USA
15C2 **Perry** Georgia, USA
14A1 **Perry** New York, USA
17C2 **Perry** Oklahoma, USA
6H3 **Perry River** Can
12C2 **Perrysburg** USA
16B2 **Perryton** USA
10G4 **Perryville** Alaska, USA
17E2 **Perryville** Missouri, USA
4F5 **Perth** Can
13D2 **Perth** Can
34D3 **Perth** Scot
14C2 **Perth Amboy** USA
37A3 **Pertuis** France
26D6 **Peru** Republic, S America
12B2 **Peru** USA
xxixP5 **Peru Basin** Pacific O
xxxE6 **Peru-Chile Trench** Pacific O
40C2 **Perugia** Italy
28D1 **Perugorria** Arg
40D2 **Peruẓic** Croatia, Yugos
64D2 **Pervari** Turk
44G5 **Pervomaysk** Russian Fed
45E6 **Pervomaysk** Ukraine
44K4 **Pervoural'sk** Russian Fed
37E3 **Pesaro** Italy
20A2 **Pescadero** USA
Pescadores = P'eng-hu Lieh-tao
40C2 **Pescara** Italy
37D2 **Peschiera** Italy
37D3 **Pescia** Italy
60C2 **Peshawar** Pak
41E2 **Peshkopi** Alb
12B1 **Peshtigo** USA
44F4 **Pestovo** Russian Fed
65C2 **Petah Tiqwa** Israel
19B3 **Petaluma** USA
36C2 **Pétange** Lux
22B2 **Petatlán** Mexico
73D5 **Petauke** Zambia
4F4 **Petawawa** Can
12B2 **Petenwell L** USA
75A2 **Peterborough** Aust
4F5 **Peterborough** Can
35E5 **Peterborough** Eng
14E1 **Peterborough** USA
34E3 **Peterhead** Scot
7M1 **Petermann Gletscher** *Gl* Greenland
76B3 **Petermann Range** *Mts* Aust
25B5 **Peteroa** *Mt* Chile/Arg
3G2 **Peter Pond L** Can
10M4 **Petersburg** Alaska, USA
13D3 **Petersburg** Virginia, USA
4F2 **Petite Rivière de la Baleine** *R* Can
3E2 **Petitot** *R* Can
5H3 **Petitsikapau L** Can
60C4 **Petlād** India
22C2 **Petlalcingo** Mexico
21D2 **Peto** Mexico
28A2 **Petorca** Chile
12C1 **Petoskey** USA
65C3 **Petra** *Hist Site* Jordan
79G2 **Petral** *Base* Ant
49N2 **Petra, Ostrov** *I* Russian Fed
19E3 **Petrified Forest Nat Pk** USA
27K5 **Petrolina** Brazil
48H4 **Petropavlovsk** Kazakhstan
50J1 **Petropavlovsk-Kamchatskiy** Russian Fed
29D3 **Petrópolis** Brazil
45H5 **Petrovsk** Russian Fed
49M4 **Petrovsk Zabakal'skiy** Russian Fed
50D1 **Petrovsk Zabaykal'skiy** Russian Fed
44E3 **Petrozavodsk** Russian Fed
74D2 **Petrus** S Africa
74D2 **Petrusburg** S Africa
74C3 **Petrusville** S Africa
49T3 **Pevek** Russian Fed
44H2 **Peza** *R* Russian Fed
36D2 **Pfälzer Wald** Region, Germany
42B3 **Pforzheim** Germany
60D2 **Phagwara** India
74E1 **Phalaborwa** S Africa
60C3 **Phalodi** India
36D2 **Phalsbourg** France
62A1 **Phaltan** India
55B4 **Phangnga** Thai
55C3 **Phanom Dang** *Mts* Camb
55D3 **Phan Rang** Viet
55D3 **Phan Thiet** Viet
17F4 **Pharr** USA
3H2 **Phelps L** Can
15D1 **Phelps L** USA
15B2 **Phenix City** USA
55B3 **Phet Buri** Thai
55D3 **Phiafay** Laos
17E3 **Philadelphia** Mississippi, USA
14C2 **Philadelphia** Pennsylvania, USA
11B3 **Philip** USA
Philippeville = Skikda
36C1 **Philippeville** Belg
51F5 **Philippine S** Pacific O
51F5 **Philippines** Republic, S E Asia
xxviiiH4 **Philippine Trench** Pacific O
74D3 **Philippolis** S Africa
18D1 **Philipsburg** Montana, USA
13D2 **Philipsburg** Pennsylvania, USA
10J2 **Philip Smith Mts** USA
74C3 **Philipstown** S Africa
57F7 **Phillipine S** Phil
7K1 **Phillips B** Can
16C2 **Phillipsburg** Kansas, USA
14C2 **Phillipsburg** New Jersey, USA
7L2 **Philpots Pen** Can
55C3 **Phnom Penh** Camb
19D4 **Phoenix** Arizona, USA
14B1 **Phoenix** New York, USA
77H1 **Phoenix** *Is* Pacific O
14C2 **Phoenixville** USA
55C1 **Phong Saly** Laos
Phra Nakhon = Bangkok
55C2 **Phu Bia** *Mt* Laos
55D3 **Phu Cuong** Viet
55B4 **Phuket** Thai
61B3 **Phulbāni** India
55C2 **Phu Miang** *Mt* Thai
55D2 **Phu Set** *Mt* Laos
55D1 **Phu Tho** Viet
55D4 **Phu Vinh** Viet
32K6 **Phyäselkä** *L* Fin
37C2 **Piacenza** Italy
75D1 **Pialba** Aust
75C2 **Pian** *R* Aust
37D2 **Pianoro** Italy
40C2 **Pianosa** *I* Italy
40D2 **Pianosa** *I* Italy
43E2 **Piaseczno** Pol
29D1 **Piata** Brazil
41F1 **Piatra-Neamţ** Rom
27K5 **Piaui** State, Brazil
37E2 **Piave** Italy
37E1 **Piave** *R* Italy
72D3 **Pibor** *R* Sudan
72D3 **Pibor Post** Sudan
36B2 **Picardie** Region, France
17E3 **Picayune** USA
37B2 **Pic de Rochebrune** *Mt* France
28A2 **Pichilemu** Chile

28C3 **Pichi Mahuida** Arg
22D2 **Pichucalco** Mexico
35E4 **Pickering** Eng
7J4 **Pickle Lake** Can
70A1 **Pico** *I* Açores
37C1 **Pico Bernina** *Mt* Switz
23C5 **Pico Bolivar** *Mt* Ven
39C1 **Pico de Anito** *Mt* Spain
21B3 **Pico del Infiernillo** *Mt* Mexico
23C3 **Pico Duarte** *Mt* Dom Rep
27K5 **Picos** Brazil
39B1 **Picos de Europa** *Mt* Spain
75D2 **Picton** Aust
78B2 **Picton** NZ
72B1 **Pic Toussidé** *Mt* Chad
28A3 **Picún Leufú** *R* Arg
29C3 **Piedade** Brazil
20C2 **Piedra** USA
28B4 **Piedra de Aguila** Arg
20B3 **Piedras Blancas,Pt** USA
21B2 **Piedras Negras** Mexico
12B1 **Pie I** Can
32K6 **Pieksämäki** Fin
32K6 **Pielinen** *L* Fin
37B2 **Piemonte** Region, Italy
74D2 **Pienaarsrivier** S Africa
11B3 **Pierre** USA
43D3 **Pieztany** Czech
74E2 **Pietermaritzburg** S Africa
74D1 **Pietersburg** S Africa
37D3 **Pietrasanta** Italy
74E2 **Piet Retief** S Africa
45C6 **Pietrosu** *Mt* Rom
41F1 **Pietrosul** *Mt* Rom
37E1 **Pieve di Cadore** Italy
51H6 **Pigailoe** *I* Pacific O
3F3 **Pigeon L** Can
17D2 **Piggott** USA
28C3 **Pigüé** Arg
22D2 **Pijijapan** Mexico
4C3 **Pikangikum** Can
7J4 **Pikangikum L** Can
16A2 **Pikes Peak** USA
74B3 **Piketberg** S Africa
12C3 **Pikeville** USA
7O3 **Pikiutaleq** Greenland
59F2 **Pik Kommunizma** *Mt* Tajikistan
72B3 **Pikounda** Congo
59G1 **Pik Pobedy** *Mt* China/Kirgizia
28D3 **Pila** Arg
42D2 **Pila** Pol
25E3 **Pilar** Par
25D2 **Pilcomayo** *R* Arg/Par
74E1 **Pilgrim's Rest** S Africa
60D3 **Pīlībhīt** India
43D2 **Pilica** *R* Pol
75E3 **Pillar,C** Aust
41E3 **Pílos** Greece
18C1 **Pilot Knob Mt** USA
20D1 **Pilot Peak** *Mt* USA
10G4 **Pilot Point** USA
10F3 **Pilot Station** USA
17E3 **Pilottown** USA
27G4 **Pimenta** Brazil
55C4 **Pinang** *I* Malay
23A2 **Pinar del Rio** Cuba
28B2 **Pinas** Arg
36C1 **Pinche** Belg
3F4 **Pincher Creek** Can
27J4 **Pindaré** *R* Brazil
41E3 **Pindhos** *Mts* Greece
17D3 **Pine Bluff** USA
16B1 **Pine Bluffs** USA
5L4 **Pine,C** Can
11D2 **Pine City** USA
76C2 **Pine Creek** Aust
14B2 **Pine Creek** *R* USA
20C1 **Pinecrest** USA
20C2 **Pinedale** California, USA
18E2 **Pinedale** Wyoming, USA
4B3 **Pine Falls** Can
20C2 **Pine Flat Res** USA
44G3 **Pinega** Russian Fed
44H3 **Pinega** *R* Russian Fed
14B2 **Pine Grove** USA
15C3 **Pine Hills** USA
3G2 **Pinehouse L** Can
15D1 **Pinehurst** USA
15E4 **Pine I** USA
17D3 **Pineland** USA
15C3 **Pinellas Park** USA
20B3 **Pine Mt** USA
3F1 **Pine Point** Can
11B3 **Pine Ridge** USA
4C4 **Pine River** USA
37B2 **Pinerolo** Italy
17D3 **Pines,Lo'the** USA
17D3 **Pineville** USA
52C3 **Pingdingshan** China
52B5 **Pingguo** China
52B2 **Pingliang** China
52B2 **Pingluo** China
52D4 **Pingtan Dao** *I* China
52E5 **P'ing tung** Taiwan
52A3 **Pingwu** China
52B5 **Pingxiang** Guangxi, China
52C4 **Pingxiang** Jiangxi, China
27J4 **Pinheiro** Brazil
28E2 **Pinheiro Machado** Brazil
56A2 **Pini** *I* Indon
41E3 **Piniós** *R* Greece
57B2 **Pinjang** Indon
76A4 **Pinjarra** Aust
3D2 **Pink Mountain** Can
75B3 **Pinnaroo** Aust
Pinos,I de = Isla de la Juventud
20C3 **Pinos,Mt** USA
19B3 **Pinos,Pt** USA
22C2 **Pinotepa Nacional** Mexico
57A3 **Pinrang** Indon
45D5 **Pinsk** Belorussia
28C1 **Pinto** Arg
44H3 **Pinyug** Russian Fed
19D3 **Pioche** USA
40C2 **Piombino** Italy
49K2 **Pioner, Ostrov** *I* Russian Fed
18D1 **Pioneer Mts** USA
44L3 **Pionerskiy** Russian Fed
43D2 **Piotroków Trybunalski** Pol
34F2 **Piper** *Oilfield* N Sea
20D2 **Piper Peak** *Mt* USA
11C3 **Pipestone** USA
4C3 **Pipestone** *R* Can
28D3 **Pipinas** Arg
5M4 **Pipmudcan, Réservoir** *Res* Can
12C2 **Piqua** USA
29B4 **Piquiri** *R* Brazil
29C2 **Piracanjuba** Brazil
29C3 **Piracicaba** Brazil
29C3 **Piraçununga** Brazil
29C3 **Pirai do Sul** Brazil
41E3 **Piraiévs** Greece
29C3 **Pirajui** Brazil
37E2 **Piran** Slovenia, Yugos
29B2 **Piranhas** Brazil
29D2 **Pirapora** Brazil
28D1 **Piratina** *R* Brazil
28E2 **Piratini** *R* Brazil
41E2 **Pirdop** Bulg
29C2 **Pirenópolis** Brazil
29C2 **Pires do Rio** Brazil
41E3 **Pírgos** Greece
Pirineos = Pyrénées
38B3 **Pirineos** *Mts* Spain
27K4 **Piripiri** Brazil
36D2 **Pirmasens** Germany
41E2 **Pirot** Serbia, Yugos
60C2 **Pīr Panjāl Range** *Mts* Pak
57C3 **Piru** Indon
20C3 **Piru Creek** *R* USA
37D3 **Pisa** Italy
26C6 **Pisco** Peru
14C1 **Piseco** USA
42C3 **Písek** Czech
60B2 **Pishin** Pak
20B3 **Pismo Beach** USA
25C3 **Pissis** *Mt* Arg
37D3 **Pistoia** Italy
39B1 **Pisuerga** *R* Spain
18B2 **Pit** *R* USA
26C3 **Pitalito** Colombia
xxixN6 **Pitcairn** *I* Pacific O
32H5 **Pite** *R* Sweden
32J5 **Piteå** Sweden
41E2 **Piteşti** Rom
49L4 **Pit Gorodok** Russian Fed
36B2 **Pithiviers** France
44E3 **Pitkyaranta** Russian Fed
34D3 **Pitlochry** Scot
44M2 **Pitlyar** Russian Fed
28A3 **Pitrutquén** Chile
77H5 **Pitt** *I* NZ
3C3 **Pitt I** Can
20B1 **Pittsburg** California, USA
17D2 **Pittsburg** Kansas, USA
5G4 **Pittsburg** New Hampshire, USA
13D2 **Pittsburgh** USA
12A3 **Pittsfield** Illinois, USA
14D1 **Pittsfield** Massachusetts, USA
14C2 **Pittston** USA
75D1 **Pittsworth** Aust
20C3 **Piute Peak** *Mt* USA
61B2 **Piuthan** Nepal
53D1 **Pivan'** Russian Fed
20C3 **Pixley** USA
37D1 **Pizzo Redorta** *Mt* Italy
32B2 **Pjórsá** Iceland
26B5 **Pjura** Peru
5L4 **Placentia** Can
7N5 **Placentia B** Can
20B1 **Placerville** USA
36D2 **Plaine d'Alsace** *Plain* France
36B1 **Plaine des Flandres** *Plain* France/Belg
70C2 **Plaine du Tidikelt** *Desert* Region
36C2 **Plaine Lorraine** Region, France
16B2 **Plains** USA
11C3 **Plainview** Nebraska, USA
16B3 **Plainview** Texas, USA
20B2 **Planada** USA
27H7 **Planalto de Mato Grosso** *Plat* Brazil
27L5 **Planalto do Borborema** *Plat* Brazil
26B1 **Planalto do Mato Grosso** *Mts* Brazil
77E1 **Planet Deep** PNG
11C3 **Plankinton** USA
17C3 **Plano** USA
15E4 **Plantation** USA
15C3 **Plant City** USA
39A1 **Plasencia** Spain
44L5 **Plast** Russian Fed
53D3 **Plastun** Russian Fed
71H4 **Plateau** State, Nig
71G3 **Plateau de Dadango** Togo
36C3 **Plateau de Langres** *Plat* France
37A2 **Plateau De St Christol** Region, France
70C2 **Plateau du Tademait** Alg
36D2 **Plateau Lorrain** *Plat* France
38C2 **Plateaux de Limousin** *Plat* France
39C2 **Plateaux du Sersou** *Plat* Alg
23C5 **Plato** Colombia
45J7 **Plato Ustyurt** *Plat* Kazakhstan
65B1 **Platres** Cyprus
11C3 **Platte** USA
16B1 **Platte** *R* USA
12A2 **Platteville** USA
13E2 **Plattsburgh** USA
17C1 **Plattsmouth** USA
42C2 **Plauen** Germany
44F5 **Plavsk** Russian Fed
22B2 **Playa Azul** Mexico
26B4 **Playas** Ecuador
22C2 **Playa Vincente** Mexico
39A1 **Plaza de Moro Almanzor** *Mt* Spain
20B2 **Pleasanton** California, USA
17F4 **Pleasanton** Texas, USA
14C3 **Pleasantville** USA
12B3 **Pleasure Ridge Park** USA
55D3 **Pleiku** Viet
78C1 **Plenty,B of** NZ
11B2 **Plentywood** USA
44G3 **Plesetsk** Russian Fed
43D2 **Pleszew** Pol
7L4 **Pletipi,L** Can
41E2 **Pleven** Bulg
41D2 **Pljevlja** Montenegro, Yugos
41D2 **Ploče** Bosnia & Herzegovina, Yugos
43D2 **Płock** Pol
38B2 **Ploërmel** France
41F2 **Ploieşti** Rom
36D3 **Plombières-les-Bains** France
44C5 **Płońsk** Pol
41E2 **Plovdiv** Bulg
18C1 **Plummer** USA
10G3 **Plummer,Mt** USA
73C6 **Plumtree** Zim
20B1 **Plymouth** California, USA
35C6 **Plymouth** Eng
12B2 **Plymouth** Indiana, USA
14E2 **Plymouth** Massachusetts, USA
14C2 **Plymouth** Pennsylvania, USA
14E2 **Plymouth B** USA
35C6 **Plymouth Sd** Eng
35D5 **Plynlimon** *Mt* Wales
42C3 **Plzeň** Czech
42D2 **Pniewy** Pol
71F3 **Pô** Burkina
37E2 **Po** *R* Italy
71G4 **Pobé** Benin
53E2 **Pobedino** Russian Fed
18D2 **Pocatello** USA
43G2 **Pochinok** Russian Fed
22C2 **Pochutla** Mexico
29D1 **Poções** Brazil
13D3 **Pocomoke City** USA
29A2 **Poconé** Brazil
29C3 **Pocos de Caldas** Brazil
37D2 **Po di Volano** *R* Italy
49L3 **Podkamennaya Tunguska** *R* Russian Fed
44F4 **Podol'sk** Russian Fed
43F3 **Podol'skaya Vozvyshennost'** *Upland* Ukraine
44E3 **Podporozh'ye** Russian Fed
44G3 **Podyuga** Russian Fed
74B2 **Pofadder** S Africa
37D3 **Poggibonsi** Italy
60A2 **Poghdar** Afghan
53C3 **Pogranichnyy** Russian Fed
57B3 **Poh** Indon
53B4 **P'ohang** S Korea
79G9 **Poinsett,C** Ant
75C2 **Point** Aust
23E3 **Pointe-à-Pitre** Guadeloupe
5H4 **Pointe aux Anglais** Can
38B2 **Pointe de Barfleur** *Pt* France
5J4 **Pointe de l'Est** *C* Can
4F3 **Pointe Louis XIV** *C* Can
72B4 **Pointe Noire** Congo
72A3 **Pointe Pongara** *Pt* Gabon
75B3 **Point Fairy** Aust
23L1 **Point Fortin** Trinidad
10E2 **Point Hope** USA
6G3 **Point L** Can
10F2 **Point Lay** USA
14C2 **Point Pleasant** New Jersey, USA
12C3 **Point Pleasant** W Virginia, USA
37B2 **Point St Bernard** *Mt* France
38C2 **Poitiers** France
38B2 **Poitou** Region, France
36A2 **Poix** France
60C3 **Pokaran** India
75C1 **Pokataroo** Aust
61B2 **Pokhara** Nepal
49O3 **Pokrovsk** Russian Fed
19D3 **Polacca** USA
43D2 **Poland** Republic, Europe
14C1 **Poland** USA
4E3 **Polar Bear Prov Park** Can
45E8 **Polath** Turk
64B2 **Polatli** Turk
57B3 **Poleang** Indon
57A3 **Polewali** Indon
71J4 **Poli** Cam
37A1 **Poligny** France
49P4 **Poliny Osipenko** Russian Fed
65B1 **Polis** Cyprus
41E2 **Políyiros** Greece
62B2 **Pollāchi** India
57F8 **Polollo Is** Phil
43F2 **Polonnye** Ukraine
43F1 **Polotsk** Belorussia
18D1 **Polson** USA
45E6 **Poltava** Ukraine
40D1 **Pölten** Austria
44K3 **Polunochoye** Russian Fed
16A3 **Polvadera** USA
44E2 **Polyarnyy** Murmansk, Russian Fed
49Q2 **Polyarnyy** Yakutskaya, Russian Fed
44L2 **Polyarnyy Ural** *Mts* Russian Fed
xxixL4 **Polynesia** *Region* Pacific O
26C5 **Pomabamba** Peru
29D3 **Pomba** *R* Brazil
20D3 **Pomona** USA
17C2 **Pomona Res** USA
15E4 **Pompano Beach** USA
14C2 **Pompton Lakes** USA
17C2 **Ponca City** USA
23D3 **Ponce** Puerto Rico
15E4 **Ponce de Leon B** USA
62B2 **Pondicherry** India
7L2 **Pond Inlet** Can
5K3 **Ponds,I of** Can
39A1 **Ponferrade** Spain
72C3 **Pongo** *R* Sudan
74E2 **Pongola** *R* S Africa
62B2 **Ponnāni** India
61D3 **Ponnyadoung Range** *Mts* Burma
3F3 **Ponoka** Can
48F3 **Ponoy** Russian Fed
44G2 **Ponoy** *R* Russian Fed
38B2 **Pons** France
29E2 **Ponta da Baleia** *Pt* Brazil
70A1 **Ponta Delgada** Açores
29E1 **Ponta do Mutá** *Pt* Brazil
72B4 **Ponta do Padrão** *Pt* Angola
29D3 **Ponta dos Búzios** *Pt* Brazil
29B4 **Ponta Grossa** Brazil
37A1 **Pontailler-sur-Saône** France
29C3 **Pontal** Brazil
36C2 **Pont-à-Mousson** France
29A3 **Ponta Pora** Brazil
38D2 **Pontarlier** France
37D3 **Pontassieve** Italy
4F3 **Pontax** *R* Can
17D3 **Pontchartrain,L** USA
37A1 **Pont d'Ain** France
29A1 **Ponte de Pedra** Brazil
40C2 **Pontedera** Italy
40B2 **Ponte Lecca** Corse
39A1 **Pontevedra** Spain
12B2 **Pontiac** Illinois, USA
12C2 **Pontiac** Michigan, USA
56C3 **Pontianak** Indon
38B2 **Pontivy** France
36B2 **Pontoise** France
17E3 **Pontotoc** USA
37C2 **Pontremoli** Italy
36B2 **Pont-sur-Yonne** France
35D6 **Pontypool** Wales
35D6 **Pontypridd** Wales
35E6 **Poole** Eng
Poona = Pune
75B2 **Pooncarie** Aust
75B2 **Poopelloe,L** Aust
10G3 **Poorman** USA
26C3 **Popayán** Colombia
36B1 **Poperinge** Belg
75B2 **Popilta L** Aust
11A2 **Poplar** USA
4B3 **Poplar** *R* Can
3G4 **Poplar** *R* USA
17D2 **Poplar Bluff** USA
17E3 **Poplarville** USA
76D1 **Popndetta** PNG
22C2 **Popocatepetl** *Mt* Mexico
10F4 **Popof** *I* USA
72B4 **Popokabaka** Zaïre
51H7 **Popondetta** PNG
41F2 **Popovo** Bulg
29C3 **Poraiba** *R* Brazil
29C1 **Porangatu** Brazil
60B4 **Porbandar** India
3B3 **Porcher I** Can
29C1 **Porcos** *R* Brazil
10K2 **Porcupine** *R* USA/Can
3H3 **Porcupine Hills** Can
37E2 **Pordenone** Italy
40C1 **Poreč** Croatia, Yugos
29B3 **Porecatu** Brazil
32J6 **Pori** Fin
78B2 **Porirua** NZ
32H5 **Porjus** Sweden
53E1 **Poronay** *R* Russian Fed
53E2 **Poronaysk** Russian Fed
44E3 **Porosozero** Russian Fed
37B1 **Porrentruy** Switz
37D3 **Porretta** Italy
32K4 **Porsangen** *Inlet* Nor
32F7 **Porsgrunn** Nor
35B4 **Portadown** N Ire
12B2 **Portage** USA
4B4 **Portage la Prairie** Can
11B2 **Portal** USA
3D4 **Port Alberni** Can
39A2 **Portalegre** Port
16B3 **Portales** USA
74D3 **Port Alfred** S Africa
3C3 **Port Alice** Can
14A2 **Port Allegany** USA
17D3 **Port Allen** USA
18B1 **Port Angeles** USA
23B3 **Port Antonio** Jamaica
35B5 **Portarlington** Irish Rep
17D4 **Port Arthur** USA
34B4 **Port Askaig** Scot
36A2 **Port-Audemer** France
75A2 **Port Augusta** Aust
23C3 **Port-au-Prince** Haiti
12C2 **Port Austin** USA
62E2 **Port Blair** Andaman Is
75B3 **Port Campbell** Aust
61C3 **Port Canning** India
7M5 **Port Cartier** Can
78B3 **Port Chalmers** NZ
15E4 **Port Charlotte** USA
14D2 **Port Chester** USA
3B3 **Port Clements** Can
12C2 **Port Clinton** USA
13D2 **Port Colborne** Can
75E3 **Port Davey** Aust
23C3 **Port-de-Paix** Haiti
55C5 **Port Dickson** Malay
74E3 **Port Edward** S Africa
29D2 **Porteirinha** Brazil
12C2 **Port Elgin** Can
74D3 **Port Elizabeth** S Africa
34B4 **Port Ellen** Scot
23N2 **Porter Pt** St Vincent
20C2 **Porterville** USA
76D4 **Port Fairy** Aust
72A4 **Port Gentil** Gabon
17D3 **Port Gibson** USA
10H4 **Port Graham** USA
18B1 **Port Hammond** Can
68E7 **Port Harcourt** Nigeria
3C3 **Port Hardy** Can
7M5 **Port Hawkesbury** Can
76A3 **Port Hedland** Aust

Port Heiden = Meshik
35C5 Porthmadog Wales
7N4 Port Hope Simpson Can
20C3 Port Hueneme USA
12C2 Port Huron USA
39A2 Portimão Port
75D2 Port Jackson *B* Aust
14D2 Port Jefferson USA
14C2 Port Jervis USA
75D2 Port Kembla Aust
12C2 Portland Indiana, USA
13E2 Portland Maine, USA
75C2 Portland New South Wales, Aust
18B1 Portland Oregon, USA
75B3 Portland Victoria, Aust
23H2 Portland Bight *B* Jamaica
35D6 Portland Bill *Pt* Eng
75E3 Portland,C Aust
3B2 Portland Canal *Sd* USA/Can
78C1 Portland I NZ
23H2 Portland Pt Jamaica
33B3 Port Laoise Irish Rep
17F4 Port Lavaca USA
36A2 Port-l'Evêque France
75A2 Port Lincoln Aust
70A4 Port Loko Sierra Leone
73F6 Port Louis Mauritius
75B3 Port MacDonnell Aust
3C3 Port McNeill Can
75D2 Port Macquarie Aust
5H5 Port Maitland Can
14A2 Port Matilda USA
5J4 Port Menier Can
10F4 Port Moller USA
76D1 Port Moresby PNG
4C2 Port Nelson Can
74B2 Port Nolloth S Africa
14C3 Port Norris USA
39A1 Porto Port
25F4 Pôrto Alegre Brazil
Porto Alexandre = Tombula
23A5 Porto Armuelles Panama
29A1 Pôrto Artur Brazil
29B3 Pôrto de Novembro Brazil
29B1 Pôrto dos Meinacos Brazil
25F2 Pôrto E Cunha Brazil
29A2 Pôrto Esperança Brazil
40C2 Portoferraio Italy
23E4 Port of Spain Trinidad
37E2 Portogruaro Italy
29A2 Porto Jofre Brazil
28D1 Porto Lucena Brazil
37D2 Portomaggiore Italy
29B3 Porto Mendez Brazil
29A3 Porto Murtinho Brazil
71G4 Porto Novo Benin
25F2 Pôrto Primavera, Reprêsa *Res* Brazil
18B1 Port Orchard USA
37E3 Porto Recanati Italy
18B2 Port Orford USA
70A1 Porto Santo *I* Medeira
29B3 Porto São José Brazil
27L7 Pôrto Seguro Brazil
40B2 Porto Torres Sardegna
29B4 Porto União Brazil
40B2 Porto Vecchio Corse
26F5 Pôrto Velho Brazil
78A3 Port Pegasus *B* NZ
75B3 Port Phillip B Aust
75A2 Port Pirie Aust
10P2 Port Radium Can
34B3 Portree Scot
18B1 Port Renfrew Can
23J2 Port Royal Jamaica
15C2 Port Royal Sd USA
34B4 Portrush N Ire
65B3 Port Said Egypt
15B3 Port St Joe USA
74D3 Port St Johns S Africa
7N4 Port Saunders Can
74E3 Port Shepstone S Africa
3B3 Port Simpson Can
23Q2 Portsmouth Dominica
35E6 Portsmouth Eng
14E1 Portsmouth New Hampshire, USA
12C3 Portsmouth Ohio, USA
13D3 Portsmouth Virginia, USA
75D2 Port Stephens *B* Aust
72D2 Port Sudan Sudan
17E3 Port Sulphur USA
32K5 Porttipahdan Tekojärvi *Res* Fin
39A2 Portugal Republic, Europe
14A1 Portville USA
12B2 Port Washington USA
55C5 Port Weld Malay
26E6 Porvenir Bol
25E3 Posadas Arg
39A2 Posadas Spain
37D1 Poschiavo Switz
63D2 Posht-e Badam Iran
57B3 Poso Indon
54A4 Posŏng S Korea
44M2 Pos Polvy Russian Fed
29C1 Posse Brazil
16B3 Post USA
43F1 Postavy Belorussia
74C2 Postmasburg S Africa
40C1 Postojna Slovenia, Yugos
53C3 Pos'yet Russian Fed
57B4 Pota Indon
74D2 Potchetstroom S Africa
17D2 Poteau USA
40D2 Potenza Italy
74D1 Potgietersrus S Africa
16C4 Poth USA
45G7 Poti Georgia
71J3 Potiskum Nig
18C1 Potlatch USA
74C3 Potloer *Mt* S Africa
18C1 Pot Mt USA
13D3 Potomac *R* USA
14A3 Potomac South Branch *R* USA
26E7 Potosi Bol
25C3 Potrerillos Chile
42C2 Potsdam Germany
5G5 Potsdam USA
16B1 Potter USA
14C2 Pottstown USA
14B2 Pottsville USA
14D2 Poughkeepsie USA
29C3 Pouso Alegre Brazil
78C1 Poverty B NZ
44E3 Povonets Russian Fed
45G5 Povorino Russian Fed
7L4 Povungnituk Can
11A2 Powder *R* USA
11A3 Powder River USA
18E2 Powell USA
76C2 Powell Creek Aust
19D3 Powell,L USA
3D4 Powell River Can
35D5 Powys County, Wales
29B2 Poxoréo Brazil
52D4 Poyang Hu *L* China
53B2 Poyarkovo Russian Fed
64C2 Pozantı Turk
22C1 Poza Rica Mexico
42D2 Poznań Pol
25E2 Pozo Colorado Par
40C2 Pozzuoli Italy
71F4 Pra *R* Ghana
55C3 Prachin Buri Thai
55B3 Prachuap Khiri Khan Thai
42D2 Praděd *Mt* Czech
38C3 Pradelles France
29E2 Prado Brazil
Prague = Praha
42C2 Praha Czech
70A4 Praia Cape Verde
29A1 Praia Rica Brazil
26F5 Prainha Brazil
16B3 Prairie Dog Town Fork *R* USA
12A2 Prairie du Chien USA
17D2 Prairie Village USA
55C3 Prakhon Chai Thai
29C2 Prata Brazil
29C2 Prata *R* Brazil
Prates = Dongsha Qundao
37D3 Prato Italy
37D3 Pratomagno *Mt* Italy
14C1 Prattsville USA
15B2 Prattville USA
38B1 Prawle Pt Eng
56E4 Praya Indon
37D1 Predazzo Italy
49L4 Predivinsk Russian Fed
49Q3 Predporozhnyy Russian Fed
43E2 Pregolyu *R* Russian Fed
55D3 Prek Kak Camb
12A1 Prentice USA
42C2 Prenzlau Germany
62E2 Preparis I Burma
55A2 Preparis North Chan Burma
55A3 Preparis South Chan Burma
42D3 Přerov Czech
22C1 Presa de les Adjuntas Mexico
22B2 Presa del Infiernillo Mexico
28D2 Presa de Salto Grande Urug
22D2 Presa Netzahualcóyotl Mexico
19D4 Prescott Arizona, USA
17D3 Prescott Arkansas, USA
13D2 Prescott Can
11B3 Presho USA
25D3 Presidencia Roque Sáenz Peña Arg
29B3 Presidente Epitácio Brazil
79G2 Presidente Frei *Base* Ant
22C2 Presidente Migúel Aleman *L* Mexico
29B2 Presidente Murtinho Brazil
29B3 Presidente Prudente Brazil
29B3 Presidente Venceslau Brazil
16B4 Presidio USA
22A1 Presidio *R* Mexico
43E3 Prezov Czech
41E2 Prespansko Jezero *L* Macedonia, Yugos
13F1 Presque Isle USA
71F4 Prestea Ghana
35D5 Preston Eng
8B2 Preston Idaho, USA
11D3 Preston Minnesota, USA
17D2 Preston Missouri, USA
34C4 Prestwick Scot
27J8 Prêto Brazil
29C2 Prêto *R* Brazil
74D2 Pretoria S Africa
41E3 Préveza Greece
55D3 Prey Veng Camb
10E4 Pribilof Is USA
19D3 Price USA
3C3 Price I Can
15B2 Prichard USA
45E6 Prichernomorskaya Nizmennost' *Lowland* Ukraine
23M2 Prickly Pt Grenada
43F3 Pridneprovskaya Vozvyshennost' *Upland* Ukraine
43E1 Priekule Lithuania
74C2 Prieska S Africa
18C1 Priest L USA
18C1 Priest River USA
45H6 Prikaspiyskaya Nizmennost' *Region* Kazakhstan
41E2 Prilep Macedonia, Yugos
45E5 Priluki Ukraine
28C2 Primero *R* Arg
32K6 Primorsk Russian Fed
45F6 Primorsko-Akhtarsk Russian Fed
3G3 Primrose L Can
3G3 Prince Albert Can
74C3 Prince Albert S Africa
6F2 Prince Albert,C Can
3G3 Prince Albert Nat Pk Can
6G2 Prince Albert Pen Can
6G2 Prince Albert Sd Can
7L3 Prince Charles I Can
79G10 Prince Charles Mts Ant
xxviiiC7 Prince Edward *I* Indian O
7M5 Prince Edward I Province, Can
3D3 Prince George Can
6H2 Prince Gustaf Adolp Sea Can
10E2 Prince of Wales,C USA
51H8 Prince of Wales I Aust
6H2 Prince of Wales I Can
3B2 Prince of Wales I USA
6G2 Prince of Wales Str Can
6G2 Prince Patrick I Can
7J2 Prince Regent Inlet *Str* Can
3B3 Prince Rupert Can
76D2 Princess Charlotte B Aust
3C3 Princess Royal I Can
23L1 Princes Town Trinidad
3D4 Princeton Can
12B2 Princeton Illinois, USA
12B3 Princeton Kentucky, USA
17D1 Princeton Missouri, USA
14C2 Princeton New Jersey, USA
12C3 Princeton W Virginia, USA
10J3 Prince William Sd USA
70C4 Principe *I* W Africa
18B2 Prineville USA
10J2 Pringle,Mt USA
7O3 Prins Christian Sund *Sd* Greenland
79F12 Prinsesse Astrid Kyst Region, Ant
79F12 Prinsesse Ragnhild Kyst Region, Ant
48C2 Prins Karls Forland *I* Barents S
21D3 Prinzapolca Nic
44E3 Priozersk Russian Fed
43F2 Pripyat' *R* Belorussia
41E2 Priztina Serbia, Yugos
42C2 Pritzwalk Germany
44G5 Privolzhskaya Vozvyshennost' *Upland* Russian Fed
41E2 Prizren Serbia, Yugos
56D4 Probolinggo Indon
11D2 Proctor USA
62B2 Proddatūr India
21D2 Progreso Mexico
53B2 Progress Russian Fed
18B2 Project City USA
45G7 Prokhladnyy Russian Fed
48K4 Prokop'yevsk Russian Fed
45G6 Proletarskaya Russian Fed
49P2 Proliv Dmitriya Lapteva *Str* Russian Fed
48G2 Proliv Karskiye Vorota *Str* Russian Fed
49T2 Proliv Longa *Str* Russian Fed
49L2 Proliv Vilkitskogo *Str* Russian Fed
61E4 Prome Burma
29A2 Promissão Brazil
43G2 Pronya *R* Belorussia
3D2 Prophet *R* Can
27L6 Propriá Brazil
14C1 Prospect New York, USA
18B2 Prospect Oregon, USA
76D3 Prosperine Aust
42D3 Prostějov Czech
7N2 Prøven Greenland
38D3 Provence Region, France
14E2 Providence USA
49U3 Provideniya Russian Fed
14E1 Provincetown USA
36B2 Provins France
19D2 Provo USA
3F3 Provost Can
29B4 Prudentópolis Brazil
10J1 Prudhoe B USA
10J1 Prudhoe Bay USA
7M2 Prudhoe Land *Region* Greenland
43E2 Pruszkow Pol
43F3 Prut *R* Rom/Moldavia
45D6 Prutul *R* Rom
43E2 Pruzhany Belorussia
17C2 Pryor USA
43E3 Przemys'l Pol
41F3 Psará *I* Greece
44D4 Pskov Russian Fed
43F2 Ptich *R* Belorussia
41E2 Ptolemaïs Greece
54A3 Puan S Korea
26D5 Pucallpa Peru
52D4 Pucheng China
28A3 Pucón Chile
32K5 Pudasjärvi Fin
44F3 Pudozh Russian Fed
62B2 Pudukkottai India
39A1 Puebai de Trives Spain
22C2 Puebla Mexico
22C2 Puebla State, Mexico
39A1 Puebla de Sanabria Spain
16B2 Pueblo USA
28B3 Puelches Arg
28B3 Puelén Arg
22B2 Puenta Ixbapa Mexico
28B2 Puente del Inca Arg
26B5 Puerta Aguja Peru
26D7 Puerta Coles Peru
28B2 Puerta de los Llanos Arg
22A1 Puerta de Mita Mexico
27L5 Puerta do Calcanhar *Pt* Brazil
74E2 Puerta do Oro *Pt* S Africa
22C2 Puerta Galera Mexico
26D1 Puerta Gallinas Colombia
22C2 Puerta Maldonado *Pt* Mexico
26B2 Puerta Mariato Panama
25C7 Puerta Médanosa *Pt* Arg
22B2 Puerta Mongrove Mexico
22C2 Puerta Roca Partida Mexico
21E4 Puerta San Blas *Pt* Panama
22B2 Puerta San Telmo Mexico
29B3 Puerto Adela Brazil
25B7 Puerto Aisén Chile
22C2 Puerto Angel Mexico
21D4 Puerto Armuelles Panama
27G6 Puerto Artur Brazil
26C3 Puerto Asis Colombia
26E2 Puerto Ayacucho Ven
21D3 Puerto Barrios Guatemala
26D2 Puerto Berrio Colombia
26E1 Puerto Cabello Ven
21D3 Puerto Cabezas Nic
26E2 Puerto Carreño Ven
29A3 Puerto Casado Brazil
26B1 Puerto Cavezas Nic
29A3 Puerto Cooper Brazil
21D4 Puerto Cortes Costa Rica
21D3 Puerto Cortés Honduras
70A2 Puerto del Rosario Canary Is
27H8 Puerto E Cunha Brazil
22C2 Puerto Escondido Mexico
26D1 Puerto Fijo Ven
27J5 Puerto Franco Brazil
29A3 Puerto Guarani Brazil
26E6 Puerto Heath Bol
21D2 Puerto Juarez Mexico
26F1 Puerto la Cruz Ven
39B2 Puertollano Spain
23C4 Puerto Lopez Colombia
25D6 Puerto Madryn Arg
26E6 Puerto Maldonado Peru
22C2 Puerto Marquéz Mexico
25B6 Puerto Montt Chile
24C7 Puerto Moritt Chile
27G8 Puerto Murtinho Brazil
25B8 Puerto Natales Chile
21A1 Puerto Peñasco Mexico
29A3 Puerto Pinasco Brazil
25D6 Puerto Pirámides Arg
23C3 Puerto Plata Dom Rep
57E9 Puerto Princesa Phil
26C3 Puerto Rico Colombia
23D3 Puerto Rico *I* Caribbean
23D3 Puerto Rico Trench Caribbean
22B2 Puerto San Juan de Lima Mexico
27H4 Puerto Santanga Brazil
29A3 Puerto Sastre Brazil
25E1 Puerto Suárez Bol
22A1 Puerto Vallarta Mexico
25B6 Puerto Varas Chile
26F7 Puerto Villarroel Bol
45H5 Pugachev Russian Fed
60C3 Pugal India
39C1 Puigcerdá Spain
54A2 Pujŏn N Korea
54A2 Pujŏn Res N Korea
78B2 Pukaki,L NZ
4D4 Pukaskwa Nat Park Can
4A2 Pukatawagan Can
54A2 Pukchin N Korea
53B3 Pukch'ŏng N Korea
78B1 Pukekobe NZ
78B2 Puketeraki Range *Mts* NZ
44G3 Puksoozero Russian Fed
40C2 Pula Croatia, Yugos
13D2 Pulaski New York, USA
15B1 Pulaski Tennessee, USA
12C3 Pulaski Virginia, USA
51G7 Pulau Kolepom *I* Indon
57D2 Pulau Pulau Asia *Is* Indon
57D2 Pulau Pulau Ayu *Is* Indon
56A2 Pulau Pulau Banyak *Arch* Indon
56A3 Pulau Pulau Batu *Is* Indon
76A1 Pulau Pulau Kangean *Is* Indon
76B1 Pulau Pulau Macan *Is* Indon
57D3 Pulau Pulau Pisang *Is* Indon
56A3 Pulautelo Indon
43E2 Pulawy Pol
62C2 Pulicat,L India
60B1 Pul-i-Khumri Afghan
62B3 Puliyangudi India
36E3 Pullendorf Germany
18C1 Pullman USA
51G6 Pulo Anna Merir *I* Pacific I
57F7 Pulog,Mt Phil
32L5 Pulozero Russian Fed
43E2 Pultusk Pol
25C3 Puna de Atacama Arg
61C2 Punakha Bhutan
60C2 Punch Pak
74E1 Punda Milia S Africa
62A1 Pune India
22B2 Punéper Mexico
54A2 Pungsan N Korea
54A2 Pungso N Korea
72C4 Punia Zaïre
28A2 Punitaqui Chile
60C2 Punjab Province, Pak
60D2 Punjab State, India
26D7 Puno Peru
21A2 Punta Abreojos *Pt* Mexico
40D3 Punta Alice *Pt* Italy
28C3 Punta Alta Arg
25B8 Punta Arenas Chile
21A2 Punta Baja *Pt* Mexico
28C4 Punta Bermeja *Pt* Arg
28A2 Punta Curaumilla *Pt* Chile
73B5 Punta da Marca *Pt* Angola
73D6 Punta de Barra Falsa *Pt* Mozam
28E2 Punta del Este Urug
37C2 Punta di Portofino *Pt* Italy
21A2 Punta Eugenia *Pt* Mexico
28A3 Punta Galera Chile
21D3 Punta Gorda Belize
15E4 Punta Gorda USA
28A3 Punta Lavapié *Pt* Chile
28A2 Punta Lengua de Vaca *Pt* Chile
40C2 Punta Licosa *Pt* Italy
28D3 Punta Norte *Pt* Arg
28D3 Punta Piedras *Pt* Arg
28A1 Punta Poroto *Pt* Chile
28C4 Punta Rasa *Pt* Arg
26B1 Puntarenas Costa Rica
28C4 Punta Rubia *Pt* Arg

8B4 **Punta San Antonio** *Pt* Mexico
28D3 **Punta Sur** Arg
28A2 **Punta Topocalma** Chile
57B4 **Puntjak Ranakah** *Mt* Indon
14A2 **Punxsutawney** USA
57D3 **Puper** Indon
52C4 **Puqi** China
46J3 **Pur** *R* Russian Fed
17C2 **Purcell** USA
10G2 **Purcell Mt** USA
3E3 **Purcell Mts** Can
28A3 **Purén** Chile
16B2 **Purgatoire** *R* USA
61C3 **Puri** India
62B1 **Pūrna** India
61C2 **Pūrnia** India
55C3 **Pursat** Camb
22B1 **Puruandro** Mexico
26F4 **Purus** *R* Brazil
17E3 **Purvis** USA
56C4 **Purwokerto** Indon
48J3 **Pur** *R* Russian Fed
56D4 **Purworejo** Indon
60D5 **Pusad** India
53B4 **Pusan** S Korea
44E4 **Pushkin** Russian Fed
44F3 **Pushlakhta** Russian Fed
43F1 **Pustoshka** Russian Fed
28A2 **Putaendo** Chile
61E2 **Putao** Burma
78C1 **Putaruru** NZ
52D4 **Putian** China
14E2 **Putnam** USA
14D1 **Putney** USA
62B3 **Puttalam** Sri Lanka
42C2 **Puttgarden** Germany
26C4 **Putumayo** *R* Ecuador
56D2 **Putussibau** Indon
32K6 **Puulavesl** *L* Fin
18B1 **Puyallup** USA
38C2 **Puy de Sancy** *Mt* France
28A4 **Puyehue** Chile
78A3 **Puysegur Pt** NZ
73C4 **Pweto** Zaïre
35C5 **Pwllheli** Wales
44F3 **Pyal'ma** Russian Fed
44E2 **Pyaozero, Ozero** *L* Russian Fed
55B2 **Pyapon** Burma
49K2 **Pyasina** *R* Russian Fed
45G7 **Pyatigorsk** Russian Fed
61E4 **Pyinmana** Burma
54A2 **Pyŏktong** N Korea
54A3 **Pyonggang** N Korea
54A3 **Pyŏnggok-dong** S Korea
54A3 **P'Yŏngsann** N Korea
54A3 **P'yongt'aek** S Korea
53B4 **P'yŏngyang** N Korea
75B3 **Pyramid Hill** Aust
5J2 **Pyramid Hills** Can
19C2 **Pyramid L** USA
78A2 **Pyramid,Mt** NZ
38B3 **Pyrénées** *Mts* France
43F1 **Pytalovo** Russian Fed
55B2 **Pyu** Burma

Q

65C2 **Qabatiya** Israel
67E3 **Qabr Hūd** Yemen
65D3 **Qā'el Hafīra** *Mud Flats* Jordan
65D3 **Qa'el Jinz** *Mud Flats* Jordan
7O3 **Qagssimiut** Greenland
50C3 **Qaidam Pendi** *Salt Flat* China
63E1 **Qaisar** Afghan
65D2 **Qa Khanna** *Salt Marsh* Jordan
63E2 **Qala Adras Kand** Afghan
72D2 **Qala'en Nahl** Sudan
63E2 **Qala Nau** Afghan
60B2 **Qalat** Afghan
65D1 **Qal'at al Hisn** Syria
65C1 **Qal'at al Marqab** *Hist Site* Syria
66D2 **Qal'at Bīshah** S Arabia
64E3 **Qal'at Sālih** Iraq
50C3 **Qamdo** China
69E3 **Qandala** Somalia
69B2 **Qara** Egypt
45H8 **Qareh Dāgh** *Mts* Iran
63B2 **Qaṛe Shīrīn** Iran
67E1 **Qaryat al Ulyā** S Arabia
65D3 **Qasr el Kharana** Jordan
63E3 **Qasr-e-Qand** Iran
69B2 **Qasr Farafra** Egypt
65D2 **Qaṭana** Syria
67F1 **Qatar** Emirate, Arabian Pen
65D3 **Qatrāna** Jordan
69B2 **Qattāra Depression** Egypt
63D2 **Qāyen** Iran
63C1 **Qazvīn** Iran
66B1 **Qena** Egypt
63B1 **Qeydār** Iran
63C3 **Qeys** *I* Iran
45H8 **Qezel Owzan** *R* Iran
65C3 **Qeziot** Israel
53A3 **Qian'an** China
53A2 **Qian Gorlos** China
52B5 **Qian Jiang** *R* China
52E1 **Qian Shan** *Upland* China
52E3 **Qidong** China
52B4 **Qijiang** China
63E3 **Qila Ladgasht** Pak
60B2 **Qila Saifullah** Pak
52A2 **Qilian** China
50C3 **Qilian Shan** China
52B3 **Qin'an** China
52E2 **Qingdao** China
53B2 **Qinggang** China
52A2 **Qinghai** Province, China
50C3 **Qinghai Hu** *L* China
52D3 **Qingjiang** Jiangsu, China
52D4 **Qingjiang** Jiangxi, China
52B3 **Qing Jiang** *R* China
52C2 **Qingshuihe** China
52B2 **Qingshui He** *R* China
52B2 **Qingtonxia** China
52B2 **Qingyang** China
53B3 **Qingyuan** Liaoning, China
52D4 **Qingyuan** Zhejiang, China
59G2 **Qing Zang** *Upland* China
52B5 **Qingzhou** China
52D2 **Qinhuangdao** China
52B3 **Qin Ling** *Mts* China
55E2 **Qionghai** China
52A3 **Qionglai Shan** *Upland* China
55D1 **Qiongzhou Haixia** *Str* China
53A2 **Qiqihar** China
65C2 **Qiryat Ata** Israel
65C3 **Qiryat Gat** Israel
65C2 **Qiryat Shemona** Israel
65C2 **Qiryat Yam** Israel
67F3 **Qishn** Yemen
65C2 **Qishon** *R* Israel
66C2 **Qishran** *I* S Arabia
49K5 **Qitai** China
53C2 **Qitaihe** China
53C2 **Qixing He** *R* China
52C4 **Qiyang** China
52B1 **Qog Qi** China
45J8 **Qolleh-ye-Damavand** *Mt* Iran
63C1 **Qolleh-ye Damavand** *Mt* Iran
63C2 **Qom** Iran
63C2 **Qomisheh** Iran
Qomolangma Feng = Everest,Mt
65D1 **Qornet es Saouda** *Mt* Leb
7N3 **Qôrnoq** Greenland
63B1 **Qorveh** Iran
63D3 **Qotābad** Iran
45H8 **Qotúr** *R* Iran
14D1 **Quabbin Res** USA
74C2 **Quaggablat** S Africa
14C2 **Quakertown** USA
55C3 **Quam Phu Quoc** *I* Viet
16C3 **Quanah** USA
55D2 **Quang Ngai** Viet
55D2 **Quang Tri** Viet
55D4 **Quan Long** Viet
52D5 **Quanzhou** Fujian, China
52C4 **Quanzhou** Guangxi, China
11B1 **Qu'Appelle** Can
6H4 **Qu' Appelle** *R* Can
28D2 **Quarai** *R* Urug
28D2 **Quaral** Brazil
67G2 **Quarayyāt** Oman
69D4 **Quardho** Somalia
71F3 **Quarkoye** Burkina
19D4 **Quartzsite** USA
3C3 **Quatsino Sd** Can
63D1 **Quchan** Iran
75C3 **Queanbeyan** Aust
5G4 **Québec** Can
7L4 **Quebec** Province, Can
29C2 **Quebra-Anzol** *R* Brazil
28D2 **Quebracho** Urug
25F3 **Quedas do Iguaçu** Brazil/Arg
14C3 **Queen Anne** USA
3C3 **Queen Bess,Mt** Can
3B3 **Queen Charlotte** Can
3B3 **Queen Charlotte Is** Can
3B3 **Queen Charlotte Sd** Can
3C3 **Queen Charlotte Str** Can
6H1 **Queen Elizabeth Is** Can
79G9 **Queen Mary Land** Region, Ant
6H3 **Queen Maud G** Can
79E **Queen Maud Mts** Ant
14D2 **Queens** *Borough* New York, USA
51F8 **Queens Ch** Aust
75B3 **Queenscliff** Aust
76D3 **Queensland** State, Aust
75E3 **Queenstown** Aust
78A3 **Queenstown** NZ
74D3 **Queenstown** S Africa
14B3 **Queenstown** USA
73B4 **Quela** Angola
73D5 **Quelimane** Mozam
16A3 **Quemado** USA
71G4 **Quémé** *R* Benin
28C3 **Quemuquemú** Arg
4C4 **Quentico Prov Park** Can
28D3 **Quequén** Arg
28D3 **Quequén** *R* Arg
22B1 **Querétaro** Mexico
22B1 **Queretaro** *State* Mexico
3D3 **Quesnel** Can
3D3 **Quesnel** *L* Can
60B2 **Quetta** Pak
21C3 **Quezaltenango** Guatemala
57F8 **Quezon City** Phil
73B5 **Quibala** Angola
73B4 **Quibaxe** Angola
26C2 **Quibdó** Colombia
38B2 **Quiberon** France
73B4 **Quicama Nat Pk** Angola
29A4 **Quiindy** Par
52A4 **Quijing** China
28A2 **Quilima** Chile
28C2 **Quilino** Arg
26D6 **Quillabamba** Peru
26E7 **Quillacollo** Bol
38C3 **Quillan** France
3H3 **Quill Lakes** Can
28A2 **Quillota** Chile
75B1 **Quilpie** Aust
28A2 **Quilpué** Chile
73B4 **Quimbele** Angola
28C1 **Quimili** Arg
38B2 **Quimper** France
38B2 **Quimperlé** France
19B3 **Quincy** California, USA
12A3 **Quincy** Illinois, USA
14E1 **Quincy** Massachusetts, USA
28B2 **Quines** Arg
10F4 **Quinhagak** USA
55D3 **Qui Nhon** Viet
39B2 **Quintanar de la Orden** Spain
28A2 **Quintero** Chile
28C2 **Quinto** *R* Arg
28A3 **Quirihue** Chile
73B5 **Quirima** Angola
75D2 **Quirindi** Aust
73E5 **Quissanga** Mozam
73D6 **Quissico** Mozam
26C4 **Quito** Ecuador
27L4 **Quixadá** Brazil
74D3 **Qumbu** S Africa
75A2 **Quorn** Aust
66B1 **Qus** Egypt
67F4 **Quṣayir** Oman
66B1 **Quseir** Egypt
7N3 **Qutdligssat** Greenland
Quthing = Moyeni
52B3 **Qu Xian** Sichuan, China
52D4 **Qu Xian** Zhejiang, China
55D2 **Quynh Luu** Viet
52C2 **Quzhou** China
61D2 **Qūzū** China

R

32J6 **Raahe** Fin
34B3 **Raasay** *I* Scot
34B3 **Raasay,Sound of** *Chan* Scot
67F4 **Raas Caseyr** *C* Somalia
40C2 **Rab** *I* Croatia, Yugos
56E4 **Raba** Indon
42D3 **Rába** *R* Hung
66B4 **Rabak** Sudan
71A2 **Rabat** Mor
76E1 **Rabaul** PNG
65C3 **Rabba** Jordan
3H2 **Rabbit Lake** Can
66C2 **Rabigh** S Arabia
37B2 **Racconigi** Italy
7N5 **Race,C** Can
14E1 **Race Pt** USA
65C2 **Rachaya** Leb
42C3 **Rachel** *Mt* Germany
55D3 **Rach Gia** Viet
12B2 **Racine** USA
66D4 **Radā'** Yemen
43F3 **Rădăuţi** Rom
12B3 **Radcliff** USA
12C3 **Radford** USA
60C4 **Radhanpur** India
23L1 **Radix,Pt** Trinidad
43E2 **Radom** Pol
43D2 **Radomsko** Pol
43F2 **Radomyshl'** Ukraine
37E1 **Radstadt** Austria
43E1 **Radviližkis** Lithuania
3H4 **Radville** Can
6G3 **Rae** Can
61B2 **Rāe Bareli** India
7K3 **Rae Isthmus** Can
6G3 **Rae L** Can
78C1 **Raetihi** NZ
28C2 **Rafaela** Arg
65C3 **Rafah** Egypt
72C3 **Rafai** CAR
64D3 **Rafhā Al Jumaymah** S Arabia
63D2 **Rafsanjān** Iran
72C3 **Raga** Sudan
23Q2 **Ragged Pt** Barbados
40C3 **Ragusa** Italy
57B3 **Raha** Indon
66C4 **Rahad** *R* Sudan
66D4 **Raheita** Eth
60C3 **Rahimyar Khan** Pak
63C2 **Rāhjerd** Iran
28D2 **Raíces** Arg
62B1 **Rāichur** India
61B3 **Raigarh** India
75B3 **Rainbow** Aust
15B2 **Rainbow City** USA
3E2 **Rainbow Lake** Can
18B1 **Rainier** USA
18B1 **Rainier,Mt** USA
11D2 **Rainy** *R* USA
4C4 **Rainy L** Can
10H3 **Rainy P** USA
11D2 **Rainy River** Can
61B3 **Raipur** India
62C1 **Rājahmundry** India
56D2 **Rajang** *R* Malay
60C3 **Rajanpur** Pak
62B3 **Rājapālaiyam** India
60C3 **Rājasthan** State, India
60D3 **Rājgarh** India
60D4 **Rājgarh** State, India
60C4 **Rājkot** India
61C3 **Rājmahāl Hills** India
61B3 **Raj Nāndgaon** India
60C4 **Rājpīpla** India
61C3 **Rajshahi** Bang
60D4 **Rajur** India
78B2 **Rakaia** *R* NZ
56C4 **Rakata** *I* Indon
59G3 **Raka Zangbo** *R* China
43E3 **Rakhov** Ukraine
63E3 **Rakhshan** *R* Pak
67F3 **Rakhyūt** Oman
74C1 **Rakops** Botswana
43F2 **Rakov** Belorussia
15D1 **Raleigh** USA
65C4 **Ram** Jordan
65C2 **Rama** Israel
65C3 **Ramallah** Israel
62B3 **Rāmanāthapuram** India
50H3 **Ramapo Deep** Pacific O
4E4 **Ramore** Can
65C2 **Ramat Gan** Israel
36D2 **Rambervillers** France
36A2 **Rambouillet** France
61C3 **Rāmgarh** Bihar, India
60C3 **Rāmgarh** Rajosthan, India
63B2 **Rāmhormoz** Iran
65C3 **Ramla** Israel
67G2 **Ramlat Al Wahibah** Region, Oman
67E3 **Ramlat as Sab'atayn** Region, Yemen
19C4 **Ramona** USA
60D3 **Rāmpur** India
60D4 **Rāmpura** India
61D4 **Ramree** *I* Burma
45J8 **Rāmsar** Iran
35C4 **Ramsey** Eng
14C2 **Ramsey** USA
35C6 **Ramsey I** Wales
35F6 **Ramsgate** Eng
65D2 **Ramtha** Jordan
76D1 **Ramu** *R* PNG
56E1 **Ranau** Malay
28A2 **Rancagua** Chile
3B1 **Rancheria** *R* Can
11A3 **Ranchester** USA
61C3 **Rānchi** India
61B3 **Rānchi Plat** India
74D2 **Randburg** S Africa
32F7 **Randers** Den
74D2 **Randfontein** S Africa
14A1 **Randolph** New York, USA
13E2 **Randolph** Vermont, USA
20D3 **Randsburg** USA
78B3 **Ranfurly** NZ
61D3 **Rangamati** Bang
16A1 **Rangely** USA
78B2 **Rangiora** NZ
78C1 **Rangitaiki** *R* NZ
78B2 **Rangitate** *R* NZ
78C1 **Rangitikei** *R* NZ
55B2 **Rangoon** Burma
61C2 **Rangpur** India
62B2 **Rānībennur** India
61C3 **Rānīganj** India
7J3 **Rankin Inlet** Can
75C2 **Rankins Springs** Aust
60B4 **Rann of Kachchh** *Flood Area* India
55B4 **Ranong** Thai
56A2 **Rantauparapat** Indon
57A3 **Rantepao** Indon
12B2 **Rantoul** USA
29B1 **Ranuro** *R* Brazil
53C2 **Raohe** China
36D2 **Raon-l'Etape** France
77H3 **Raoul** *I* NZ
37C2 **Rapallo** Italy
28A2 **Rapel** *R* Chile
7M3 **Raper,C** Can
11B3 **Rapid City** USA
12B1 **Rapid River** USA
13D3 **Rappahannock** *R* USA
57A3 **Rappang** Indon
37C1 **Rapperswil** Switz
14C2 **Raritan B** USA
66C2 **Ras Abū Dâra** *C* Egypt
66C2 **Ra's Abu Madd** *C* S Arabia
66C2 **Ras Abu Shagara** *C* Sudan
64D2 **Ra's al 'Ayn** Syria
67G2 **Ra's al Hadd** *C* Oman
67G1 **Ras al Kaimah** UAE
67E4 **Ra's al Kalb** *C* Yemen
67G1 **Ras-al-Kuh** *C* Iran
67G3 **Ra's al Madrakah** *C* Oman
66D3 **Ras Andadda** *C* Eth
67G3 **Ra's ash Sharbatāt** *C* Oman
66C3 **Ra's Asis** *C* Sudan
66D3 **Ra's at Tarfā** *C* S Arabia
67E1 **Ra's az Zawr** *C* S Arabia
66C2 **Rās Bânas** *C* Egypt
65B3 **Ras Burûn** *C* Egypt
66C4 **Ras Dashan** *Mt* Eth
67G3 **Ra's Duqm** Oman
63B2 **Ra's-e-Barkan** *Pt* Iran
63E3 **Ra's-e-Fasteh** *C* Iran
65A3 **Râs el Barr** *C* Egypt
64A3 **Râs el Kenâyis** *Pt* Egypt
65C4 **Ras el Nafas** *Mt* Egypt
65B4 **Râs El Sudr** *C* Egypt
65C4 **Ras en Naqb** *Upland* Jordan
67F3 **Ra's Fartak** *C* Yemen
66B1 **Râs Ghârib** Egypt
72D2 **Rashad** Sudan
66C2 **Ras Hadarba** *C* Egypt
65C3 **Rashādīya** Jordan
64B3 **Rashîd** Egypt
63B1 **Rasht** Iran
65C1 **Ra's ibn Hāni** *C* Syria
63E3 **Ra's Jaddi** *C* Pak
67G2 **Ra's Jibish** *C* Oman
63E3 **Rāsk** Iran
66C3 **Ra's Kasar** *C* Sudan
72E2 **Ras Khanzīra** *C* Somalia
60B3 **Ras Koh** *Mt* Pak
65B4 **Râs Matarma** *C* Egypt
67F4 **Ra's Momi** *C* Socotra
66B1 **Râs Muhammad** *C* Egypt
70A2 **Ras Nouadhibou** *C* Maur
63E3 **Ra's Nuh** *C* Pak
63E3 **Ra's Ormara** *C* Pak
67F3 **Ra's Sharwayn** *C* Yemen
50J2 **Rasshua** *I* Russian Fed
67F4 **Ra's Shu'ab** *C* Socotra
71E1 **Rass Kaboudia** *Pt* Tunisia
45G5 **Rasskazovo** Russian Fed
67E1 **Ra's Tanāqib** *C* S Arabia
67F1 **Ra's Tannūrah** S Arabia
42B3 **Rastatt** Germany
66D3 **Ra's 'Tsa** *C* Yemen
Ras Uarc = Cabo Tres Forcas
65C4 **Ras Um Seisaban** *Mt* Jordan
69E3 **Ras Xaafuun** *C* Somalia
60C3 **Ratangarh** India
55B3 **Rat Buri** Thai
60D3 **Rath** India
42C2 **Ratherow** Germany
34B4 **Rathlin** *I* N Ire
10B6 **Rat I** USA
10B6 **Rat Is** USA
60C4 **Ratlām** India
62A1 **Ratnāgiri** India
62C3 **Ratnapura** Sri Lanka
43E2 **Ratno** Ukraine
16B2 **Raton** USA
37D1 **Rattenberg** Austria
32H6 **Rättvik** Sweden
3B2 **Ratz,Mt** Can
57C2 **Rau** *I* Indon
56F7 **Raub** Malay
28D3 **Rauch** Arg
78C1 **Raukumara Range** *Mts* NZ
29D3 **Raul Soares** Brazil
32J6 **Rauma** Fin
61B3 **Raurkela** India
63B2 **Ravānsar** Iran

63D2 **Rāvar** Iran
43E2 **Rava Russkaya** Ukraine
14D1 **Ravena** USA
37E2 **Ravenna** Italy
42B3 **Ravensburg** Germany
76D2 **Ravenshoe** Aust
35F4 **Ravenspurn** *Oilfield* N Sea
60C2 **Ravi** *R* Pak
60C2 **Rawalpindi** Pak
64D2 **Rawāndiz** Iraq
42D2 **Rawicz** Pol
76B4 **Rawlinna** Aust
8C2 **Rawlins** USA
25D6 **Rawson** Arg
61E2 **Rawu** China
56D3 **Raya** *Mt* Indon
62B2 **Rāyadurg** India
62C1 **Rāyagada** India
65D2 **Rayak** Leb
7N5 **Ray,C** Can
53B2 **Raychikhinsk** Russian Fed
66D3 **Raydah** Yemen
63D3 **Rāyen** Iran
20C2 **Raymond** California, USA
18D1 **Raymond** Can
14E1 **Raymond** New Hampshire, USA
18B1 **Raymond** Washington, USA
75D2 **Raymond Terrace** Aust
17F4 **Raymondville** USA
10H2 **Ray Mts** USA
22C1 **Rayon** Mexico
67F3 **Raysūt** Oman
63B1 **Razan** Iran
43G3 **Razdel'naya** Ukraine
53C3 **Razdol'noye** Russian Fed
41F2 **Razgrad** Bulg
41F2 **Razim** *L* Rom
35E6 **Reading** Eng
14C2 **Reading** USA
6G3 **Read Island** Can
14D1 **Readsboro** USA
28B2 **Real de Padre** Arg
28C3 **Realicó** Arg
69B2 **Rebiana** *Well* Libya
69B2 **Rebiana Sand Sea** Libya
32L6 **Reboly** Russian Fed
53E2 **Rebun-tō** *I* Japan
76B4 **Recherche,Arch of the** *Is* Aust
43G2 **Rechitsa** Belorussia
27M5 **Recife** Brazil
74D3 **Recife,C** S Africa
29E2 **Recifes da Pedra Grande** *Arch* Brazil
77F2 **Récifs D'Entrecasteaux** Nouvelle Calédonie
36D1 **Recklinghausen** Germany
28D1 **Reconquista** Arg
28C1 **Recreo** Arg
11C2 **Red** *R* Can/USA
17D3 **Red** *R* USA
55C4 **Redang** *I* Malay
14C2 **Red Bank** New Jersey, USA
15B1 **Red Bank** Tennessee, USA
5K3 **Red Bay** Can
3G3 **Redberry L** Can
19B2 **Red Bluff** USA
16B3 **Red Bluff L** USA
35E4 **Redcar** Eng
3F3 **Redcliff** Can
75D1 **Redcliffe** Aust
75B2 **Red Cliffs** Aust
16C1 **Red Cloud** USA
3F3 **Red Deer** Can
3F3 **Red Deer** *R* Can
3H3 **Red Deer** *R* Saskatchewan, Can
3H3 **Red Deer L** Can
18B2 **Redding** USA
11C3 **Redfield** USA
16C2 **Red Hills** USA
9D2 **Red L** USA
7J4 **Red Lake** Can
11C2 **Red Lake** *R* USA
20D3 **Redlands** USA
14B3 **Red Lion** USA
18E1 **Red Lodge** USA
18B2 **Redmond** USA
20D3 **Red Mountain** USA
17C1 **Red Oak** USA
38B2 **Redon** France
20C4 **Redondo Beach** USA
10H3 **Redoubt V** USA
52B5 **Red River Delta** Vietnam
58B3 **Red Sea** Africa/Arabian Pen
10N3 **Redstone** *R* Can
4C3 **Red Sucker L** Can
3F3 **Redwater** Can
3G4 **Redwater** *R* USA
11D3 **Red Wing** USA
20A2 **Redwood City** USA
11C3 **Redwood Falls** USA
12B2 **Reed City** USA
20C2 **Reedley** USA
18B2 **Reedsport** USA
13D3 **Reedville** USA
78B2 **Reefton** NZ
64C2 **Refahiye** Turk
17F4 **Refugio** USA
29E2 **Regência** Brazil
42C3 **Regensburg** Germany
70C2 **Reggane** Alg
40D3 **Reggio di Calabria** Italy
37D2 **Reggio Nell'Emilia** Italy
41E1 **Reghin** Rom
3H3 **Regina** Can
63E2 **Registan** Region, Afghan
22A1 **Regocijo** Mexico
74B1 **Rehoboth** Namibia
13D3 **Rehoboth Beach** USA
65C3 **Rehovot** Israel
26E1 **Reicito** Ven
15D1 **Reidsville** USA
35E6 **Reigate** Eng
36B2 **Reims** France
11D3 **Reinbeck** USA
3H2 **Reindeer** *R* Can
3H2 **Reindeer L** Can
39B1 **Reinosa** Spain
14B3 **Reisterstown** USA
74D2 **Reitz** S Africa
6H3 **Reliance** Can
18E2 **Reliance** USA
71C1 **Relizane** Alg
75A2 **Remarkable,Mt** Aust
56D4 **Rembang** Indon
63D3 **Remeshk** Iran
36D2 **Remiremont** France
36D1 **Remscheid** Germany
14C1 **Remsen** USA
37A2 **Rémuzat** France
12B3 **Rend L** USA
42B2 **Rendsburg** Germany
4F4 **Renfrew** Can
56B3 **Rengat** Indon
28A2 **Rengo** Chile
43F3 **Reni** Ukraine
72D2 **Renk** Sudan
7Q2 **Renland** *Pen* Greenland
75B2 **Renmark** Aust
77F2 **Rennell** *I* Solomon Is
38B2 **Rennes** France
19C3 **Reno** USA
37D2 **Reno** *R* Italy
14B2 **Renovo** USA
14D1 **Rensselaer** USA
18B1 **Renton** USA
57B4 **Reo** Indon
71F3 **Réo** Burkina
63E1 **Repetek** Turkmenistan
43G2 **Repki** Ukraine
29C3 **Représa de Furnas** *Dam* Brazil
29C2 **Représa Três Marias** *Dam* Brazil
18C1 **Republic** USA
16C1 **Republican** *R* USA
33B3 **Republic of Ireland** NW Europe
7K3 **Repulse Bay** Can
4F4 **Réservoir Baskatong** *Res* Can
13D1 **Réservoir Cabonga** *Res* Can
4F4 **Réservoir Decelles** *Res* Can
7L4 **Réservoir de La Grande 2** *Res* Can
7L4 **Réservoir de La Grande 3** *Res* Can
7L4 **Réservoir de La Grande 4** *Res* Can
4F4 **Réservoir Dozois** *Res* Can
7L5 **Réservoir Gouin** *Res* Can
5G4 **Réservoir Pipmouacane** *Res* Can
63C1 **Reshteh-ye Alborz** *Mts* Iran
52A2 **Reshui** China
25E3 **Resistencia** Arg
41E1 **Resita** Rom
7J2 **Resolute** Can
78A3 **Resolution I** NZ
7M3 **Resolution Island** Can
74E2 **Ressano Garcia** Mozam
5H4 **Restigouche** *R* Can
28E1 **Restinga Seca** Brazil
28B2 **Retamito** Arg
36C2 **Rethel** France
41E3 **Réthimnon** Greece
xxviiiD6 **Reunion** *I* Indian O
39C1 **Reus** Spain
37C1 **Reuss** *R* Switz
36E2 **Reutlingen** Germany
37D1 **Reutte** Austria
44K4 **Revda** Russian Fed
3E3 **Revelstoke** Can
21A3 **Revillagigedo** *Is* Mexico
10M4 **Revillagigedo I** USA
36C2 **Revin** France
65C3 **Revivim** Israel
61B3 **Rewa** India
60D3 **Rewari** India
18D2 **Rexburg** USA
32A2 **Reykjavik** Iceland
14A2 **Reynoldsville** USA
21C2 **Reynosa** Mexico
38B2 **Rezé** France
43F1 **Rezekne** Latvia
44L4 **Rezh** Russian Fed
37C1 **Rhätikon** *Mts* Austria/Switz
65C1 **Rhazīr** Republic, Leb
36E1 **Rheda Wiedenbrück** Germany
42B2 **Rhein** *R* W Europe
42B2 **Rheine** Germany
37B1 **Rheinfelden** Switz
38D2 **Rheinland Pfalz** Region, Germany
37C1 **Rheinwaldhorn** *Mt* Switz
Rhine = Rhein
14D2 **Rhinebeck** USA
12B1 **Rhinelander** USA
37C2 **Rho** Italy
13E2 **Rhode Island** State, USA
14E2 **Rhode Island Sd** USA
Rhodes = Ródhos
74D1 **Rhodes Drift** *Ford* S Africa
18D1 **Rhodes Peak** *Mt* USA
38C3 **Rhône** *R* France
35D5 **Rhyl** Wales
27L6 **Riachão do Jacuipe** Brazil
39A1 **Ria de Arosa** *B* Spain
39A1 **Ria de Betanzos** *B* Spain
39A1 **Ria de Corcubion** *B* Spain
39A1 **Ria de Lage** *B* Spain
39A1 **Ria de Sta Marta** *B* Spain
39A1 **Ria de Vigo** *B* Spain
60C2 **Riāsi** Pak
39A1 **Ribadeo** Spain
29B3 **Ribas do Rio Pardo** Brazil
73D5 **Ribauè** Mozam
35D5 **Ribble** *R* Eng
29C3 **Ribeira** Brazil
29C3 **Ribeirão Prêto** Brazil
26E6 **Riberala** Bol
37E3 **Riccione** Italy
13D2 **Rice L** Can
12A1 **Rice Lake** USA
29D1 **Richao de Santana** Brazil
74E2 **Richard's Bay** S Africa
10L2 **Richards I** Can
17C3 **Richardson** USA
3F2 **Richardson** *R* Can
10L2 **Richardson Mts** Can
19D3 **Richfield** USA
14C1 **Richfield Springs** USA
20C3 **Richgrove** USA
5J4 **Richibucto** Can
18C1 **Richland** USA
12C3 **Richlands** USA
20A2 **Richmond** California, USA
74C3 **Richmond** Cape Province, S Africa
12C3 **Richmond** Kentucky, USA
74E2 **Richmond** Natal, S Africa
75D2 **Richmond** New South Wales, Aust
78B2 **Richmond** NZ
76D3 **Richmond** Queensland, Aust
13D3 **Richmond** Virginia, USA
78B2 **Richmond Range** *Mts* NZ
14C1 **Richmondville** USA
4F5 **Rideau Lakes** Can
15C2 **Ridgeland** USA
14A2 **Ridgway** USA
11B1 **Riding Mountain Nat Pk** Can
23D4 **Riecito** Ven
37D1 **Rienza** *R* Italy
42C2 **Riesa** Germany
25B8 **Riesco** *I* Chile
74C2 **Riet** *R* S Africa
40C2 **Rieti** Italy
37B3 **Riez** France
39B2 **Rif** *Mts* Mor
16A2 **Rifle** USA
43E1 **Riga** Latvia
44C4 **Riga,G of** Estonia/Latvia
63D3 **Rigān** Iran
18D2 **Rigby** USA
18C1 **Riggins** USA
7N4 **Rigolet** Can
32J6 **Riihimaki** Fin
40C1 **Rijeka** Croatia, Yugos
54D3 **Rikuzen-Tanaka** Japan
71H3 **Rima** *R* Nig
3F3 **Rimbey** Can
32H7 **Rimbo** Sweden
37E2 **Rimini** Italy
41E1 **Rîmnicu Vîlcea** Rom
5H4 **Rimouski** Can
22B1 **Rincón de Romos** Mexico
32F7 **Ringkøbing** Den
28A3 **Riñihue** Chile
57A4 **Rinja** *I* Indon
72A3 **Rio Benito** Eq Guinea
26E5 **Rio Branco** Brazil
28E2 **Rio Branco** Urug
29C4 **Rio Branco do Sul** Brazil
17F4 **Rio Bravo** Mexico
21B1 **Rio Bravo del Norte** *R* USA/Mexico
29B3 **Rio Brilhante** Brazil
28A4 **Rio Bueno** Chile
26D1 **Riochacha** Colombia
29C3 **Rio Claro** Brazil
23L1 **Rio Claro** Trinidad
28C3 **Rio Colorado** Arg
28C2 **Rio Cuarto** Arg
27L6 **Rio de Jacuipe** Brazil
29D3 **Rio de Janeiro** Brazil
29D3 **Rio de Janeiro** State, Brazil
28D2 **Rio de la Plata** *Estuary* Arg/Urug
25C8 **Rio Gallegos** Arg
25C8 **Rio Grande** Arg
28E2 **Rio Grande** Brazil
22B1 **Rio Grande** Mexico
23A4 **Rio Grande** Nic
21D3 **Rio Grande** *R* Nicaragua
21B2 **Rio Grande** *R* USA/Mexico
17F4 **Rio Grande City** USA
22B1 **Rio Grande de Santiago** Mexico
27L5 **Rio Grande do Norte** State, Brazil
28E1 **Rio Grande do Sul** State, Brazil
xxxG6 **Rio Grande Rise** Atlantic O
23C4 **Riohacha** Colombia
38C2 **Riom** France
26C4 **Riombamba** Ecuador
26E7 **Rio Mulatos** Bol
29C4 **Rio Negro** Brazil
28B4 **Río Negro** State, Arg
25F3 **Rio Pardo** Brazil
28C2 **Rio Tercero** Arg
26F6 **Rio Theodore Roosevelt** *R* Brazil
25B8 **Rio Turbio** Arg
3G2 **Riou L** Can
29B2 **Rio Verde** Brazil
22B1 **Rio Verde** Mexico
29B2 **Rio Verde de Mato Grosso** Brazil
12C3 **Ripley** Ohio, USA
15B1 **Ripley** Tennessee, USA
12C3 **Ripley** West Virginia, USA
35E4 **Ripon** Eng
20B2 **Ripon** USA
53E2 **Rishiri-tō** *I* Japan
65C3 **Rishon le Zion** Israel
14B3 **Rising Sun** USA
36A2 **Risle** *R* France
32F7 **Risør** Nor
62E2 **Ritchie's Arch** Andaman Is
7N3 **Ritenbenk** Greenland
20C2 **Ritter,Mt** USA
18C1 **Ritzville** USA
28B2 **Rivadavia** Arg
28A1 **Rivadavia** Chile
28C3 **Rivadavia Gonzalez Moreno** Arg
37D2 **Riva de Garda** Italy
26A1 **Rivas** Nic
28C3 **Rivera** Arg
28D2 **Rivera** Urug
20B2 **Riverbank** USA
70B4 **River Cess** Lib
20C2 **Riverdale** USA
14D2 **Riverhead** USA
75B3 **Riverina** Aust
71H4 **Rivers** State, Nig
78A3 **Riversdale** NZ
74C3 **Riversdale** S Africa
20D4 **Riverside** USA
3C3 **Rivers Inlet** Can
4B3 **Riverton** Can
78A3 **Riverton** NZ
18E2 **Riverton** USA
37A2 **Rives** France
15E4 **Riviera Beach** USA
7L4 **Rivière aux Feuilles** *R* Can
5G2 **Rivière aux Mélèzes** *R* Can
5H3 **Rivière aux Outardes** *R* Can
7M4 **Rivière de la Baleine** *R* Can
5G4 **Rivière du Lièvre** *R* Can
5H4 **Rivière-du-Loup** Can
7M4 **Rivière du Petit Mècatina** *R* Can
5F2 **Rivière Innuksuac** *R* Can
5G1 **Rivière Lepellé** *R* Can
5H4 **Rivière Pentecôte** Can
5F1 **Rivière Povungnituk** *R* Can
5G1 **Rivière Vachon** *R* Can
36C2 **Rivigny-sur-Ornain** France
54A2 **Riwon** N Korea
67E2 **Riyadh** S Arabia
64D1 **Rize** Turk
52D2 **Rizhao** China
65C1 **Rizokaipaso** Cyprus
32F7 **Rjukan** Nor
7K2 **Roanes Pen** Can
38C2 **Roanne** France
15B2 **Roanoke** Alabama, USA
13D3 **Roanoke** Virginia, USA
13D3 **Roanoke** *R* USA
15D1 **Roanoke Rapids** USA
19D3 **Roan Plat** USA
18D2 **Roberts** USA
19C3 **Roberts Creek Mt** USA
32J6 **Robertsforz** Sweden
17D2 **Robert S Kerr Res** USA
74B3 **Robertson** S Africa
70A4 **Robertsport** Lib
7L5 **Roberval** Can
75B2 **Robinvale** Aust
3H3 **Roblin** Can
3E3 **Robson,Mt** Can
17F4 **Robstown** USA
21A3 **Roca Partida** *I* Mexico
xxxG5 **Rocas** *I* Atlantic O
27M4 **Rocas** *I* Brazil
37D2 **Rocca San Casciano** Italy
28E2 **Rocha** Urug
35D5 **Rochdale** Eng
29B2 **Rochedo** Brazil
38B2 **Rochefort** France
12B2 **Rochelle** USA
6G3 **Rocher River** Can
75B3 **Rochester** Aust
35F6 **Rochester** Eng
11D3 **Rochester** Minnesota, USA
14E1 **Rochester** New Hampshire, USA
14B1 **Rochester** New York, USA
3C1 **Rock** *R* Can
12B2 **Rock** *R* USA
12B2 **Rockford** USA
3G4 **Rockglen** Can
15C2 **Rock Hill** USA
15D2 **Rockingham** USA
12A2 **Rock Island** USA
5H5 **Rockland** Maine, USA
12B1 **Rockland** Michigan, USA
75B3 **Rocklands Res** Aust
15C3 **Rockledge** USA
17F4 **Rockport** USA
11C3 **Rock Rapids** USA
11A3 **Rock River** USA
11A2 **Rock Springs** Montana, USA
16B3 **Rocksprings** Texas, USA
18E2 **Rock Springs** Wyoming, USA
78B2 **Rocks Pt** NZ
75C3 **Rock,The** Aust
14D2 **Rockville** Connecticut, USA
12B3 **Rockville** Indiana, USA
14B3 **Rockville** Maryland, USA
13F1 **Rockwood** USA
16B2 **Rocky Ford** USA
4E4 **Rocky Island L** Can
15D1 **Rocky Mount** USA
3F3 **Rocky Mountain House** Can
16A1 **Rocky Mountain Nat Pk** USA
8B1 **Rocky Mts** Can/USA
10F3 **Rocky Pt** USA
42C2 **Rødbyhavn** Den
5K3 **Roddickton** Can
28B2 **Rodeo** Arg
38C3 **Rodez** France
41F3 **Ródhos** Greece
41F3 **Ródhos** *I* Greece
40D2 **Rodi Garganico** Italy
41E2 **Rodopi Planina** *Mts* Bulg
76A3 **Roebourne** Aust
74D1 **Roedtan** S Africa
36D1 **Roer** *R* Neth
36C1 **Roermond** Neth
36B1 **Roeselare** Belg
7K3 **Roes Welcome Sd** Can
43F2 **Rogachev** Belorussia
17D2 **Rogers** USA
12C1 **Rogers City** USA
20D3 **Rogers L** USA
12C3 **Rogers,Mt** USA
18D2 **Rogerson** USA
4F3 **Roggan L** Can
4F3 **Roggan** *R* Can
74B3 **Roggeveldberge** *Mts* S Africa
18B2 **Rogue** *R* USA
60B3 **Rohn** Pak
60D3 **Rohtak** India
43E1 **Roja** Latvia
29B3 **Rolândia** Brazil

17D2 **Rolla** USA
18D1 **Rollins** USA
75C1 **Roma** Aust
40C2 **Roma** Italy
37D2 **Romagna** Region, Italy
37C2 **Romagnano** Italy
15D2 **Romain,C** USA
5J3 **Romaine** *R* Can
41F1 **Roman** Rom
xxxH4 **Romanche Gap** Atlantic O
57C4 **Romang** *I* Indon
45C6 **Romania** Republic, E Europe
15E4 **Romano,C** USA
38D2 **Romans sur Isère** France
10E3 **Romanzof,C** USA
10K2 **Romanzof Mts** USA
57F8 **Romblon** Phil
Rome = Roma Italy
15B2 **Rome** Georgia, USA
14C1 **Rome** New York, USA
13D2 **Rome** USA
38C2 **Romilly-sur-Seine** France
71A2 **Rommani** Mor
13D3 **Romney** USA
45E5 **Romny** Ukraine
42B1 **Rømø** *I* Den
37B1 **Romont** Switz
38C2 **Romoratin** France
56G7 **Rompin** Malay
56G7 **Rompin** *R* Malay
37D2 **Ronco** Italy
39A2 **Ronda** Spain
26F6 **Rondônia** Brazil
26F6 **Rondônia** State, Brazil
29B2 **Rondonópolis** Brazil
52B4 **Rong'an** China
52B4 **Rongchang** China
52E2 **Rongcheng** China
52B4 **Rongjiang** China
52B4 **Rong Jiang** *R* China
55A1 **Rongklang Range** *Mts* Burma
32G7 **Rønne** Denmark
32H7 **Ronneby** Sweden
79F2 **Ronne Ice Shelf** Ant
36B1 **Ronse** Belg
36A1 **Ronthieu** Region, France
8C3 **Roof Butte** *Mt* USA
60D3 **Roorkee** India
36C1 **Roosendaal** Neth
19D2 **Roosevelt** USA
79E **Roosevelt I** Ant
3C2 **Roosevelt,Mt** Can
10O3 **Root** *R* Can
11D3 **Root** *R* USA
76C2 **Roper** *R* Aust
37A3 **Roquevaire** France
26F3 **Roraima** State, Brazil
26F2 **Roraime** *Mt* Ven
4B3 **Rorketon** Can
32G6 **Røros** Nor
37C1 **Rorschach** Switz
32G6 **Rørvik** Nor
43G3 **Ros'** *R* Ukraine
23Q2 **Rosalie** Dominica
20C3 **Rosamond** USA
20C3 **Rosamond L** USA
22A1 **Rosamorada** Mexico
28C2 **Rosario** Arg
27K4 **Rosário** Brazil
22A1 **Rosario** Mexico
29A3 **Rosario** Par
28D2 **Rosario** Urug
28D2 **Rosario del Tala** Arg
28E2 **Rosário do Sul** Brazil
29A1 **Rosário Oeste** Brazil
14C2 **Roscoe** USA
38B2 **Roscoff** France
33B3 **Roscommon** Irish Rep
35B5 **Roscrea** Irish Rep
23E3 **Roseau** Dominica
4B4 **Roseau** *R* Can/USA
75E3 **Rosebery** Aust
5K4 **Rose Blanche** Can
11A2 **Rosebud** USA
18B2 **Roseburg** USA
17C4 **Rosenberg** USA
42C3 **Rosenheim** Germany
3G3 **Rosetown** Can
20B1 **Roseville** USA
41E2 **Rosiorii de Verde** Rom
32G7 **Roskilde** Den
44E5 **Roslavl'** Russian Fed
44G4 **Roslyatino** Russian Fed
78B2 **Ross** NZ
10M3 **Ross** *R* Can
33B3 **Rossan** *Pt* Irish Rep
40D3 **Rossano** Italy
17E3 **Ross Barnet Res** USA
13D1 **Rosseau L** Can
77E2 **Rossel** *I* Solomon Is
79E **Ross Ice Shelf** Ant
18B1 **Ross L** USA
3E4 **Rossland** Can
35B5 **Rosslare** Irish Rep
78C2 **Ross,Mt** NZ
70A3 **Rosso** Maur
35D6 **Ross-on-Wye** Eng
45F5 **Rossosh** Russian Fed
6E3 **Ross River** Can
79F6 **Ross S** Ant
63C3 **Rostāq** Iran
3G3 **Rosthern** Can
42C2 **Rostock** Germany
44F4 **Rostov** Russian Fed
45F6 **Rostov-na-Donu** Russian Fed
15C2 **Roswell** Georgia, USA
16B3 **Roswell** New Mexico, USA
51H5 **Rota** Pacific O
36E1 **Rotenburg** Hessen, Germany
42B2 **Rotenburg** Niedersachsen, Germany
36E1 **Rothaar-Geb** *Region* Germany
79G3 **Rothera** *Base* Ant
35E5 **Rotherham** Eng
5H4 **Rothesay** Can
34C4 **Rothesay** Scot
57B5 **Roti** *I* Indon
75C2 **Roto** Aust
78B2 **Rotoiti,L** NZ
78B2 **Rotoroa,L** NZ
78C1 **Rotorua** NZ
78C1 **Rotorua,L** NZ
36E2 **Rottenburg** Germany
42A2 **Rotterdam** Neth
36E2 **Rottweil** Germany
77G2 **Rotuma** *I* Fiji
36B1 **Roubaix** France
38C2 **Rouen** France
35F5 **Rough** *Oilfield* N Sea
Roulers = Roeselare
73F6 **Round I** Mauritius
20D1 **Round Mountain** USA
75D2 **Round Mt** Aust
18E1 **Roundup** USA
34D2 **Rousay** *I* Scot
38C3 **Roussillon** Region, France
74D3 **Rouxville** S Africa
4F4 **Rouyn** Can
32K5 **Rovaniemi** Fin
37D2 **Rovereto** Italy
37D2 **Rovigo** Italy
40C1 **Rovinj** Croatia, Yugos
43F2 **Rovno** Ukraine
63B1 **Row'ān** Iran
75C1 **Rowena** Aust
7L3 **Rowley I** Can
76A2 **Rowley Shoals** Aust
57E8 **Roxas** Palawan, Phil
57F8 **Roxas** Panay, Phil
15D1 **Roxboro** USA
78A3 **Roxburgh** NZ
18E1 **Roy** USA
35B5 **Royal Canal** Irish Rep
35E5 **Royal Leamington Spa** Eng
12C2 **Royal Oak** USA
35F6 **Royal Tunbridge Wells** Eng
38B2 **Royan** France
36B2 **Roye** France
35E5 **Royston** Eng
43E3 **Rožňava** Czech
36B2 **Rozoy** France
45G5 **Rtishchevo** Russian Fed
37E2 **Rt Kamenjak** *C* Croatia, Yugos
73D4 **Ruaha Nat Pk** Tanz
78C1 **Ruahine Range** *Mts* NZ
78C1 **Ruapehu,Mt** NZ
67D3 **Rub al Khālī** *Desert* S Arabia
34B3 **Rubha Hunish** Scot
29B3 **Rubinéia** Brazil
48K4 **Rubtsovsk** Russian Fed
10G3 **Ruby** USA
19C2 **Ruby Mts** USA
63D3 **Rudan** Iran
63E2 **Rudbar** Afghan
63B1 **Rūdbār** Iran
53D3 **Rudnaya Pristan'** Russian Fed
43G2 **Rudnya** Russian Fed
53C3 **Rudnyy** Russian Fed
41E2 **Rudoka Planina** *Mt* Macedonia, Yugos
48G1 **Rudol'fa, Ostrov** *I* Russian Fed
52E3 **Rudong** China
12C1 **Rudyard** USA
36A1 **Rue** France
66B4 **Rufa'a** Sudan
38C2 **Ruffec** France
73D4 **Rufiji** *R* Tanz
28C2 **Rufino** Arg
70A3 **Rufisque** Sen
73C5 **Rufunsa** Zambia
35E5 **Rugby** Eng
11B2 **Rugby** USA
32G8 **Rügen** *I* Germany
42B2 **Ruhr** *R* Germany
52D4 **Ruijin** China
41E2 **Rujen** *Mt* Macedonia, Bulg/Yugos
73D4 **Rukwa** *L* Tanz
34B3 **Rum** *I* Scot
41D1 **Ruma** Serbia, Yugos
67E1 **Rumāh** S Arabia
72C3 **Rumbek** Sudan
23C2 **Rum Cay** *I* Caribbean
13E2 **Rumford** USA
37A2 **Rumilly** France
76C2 **Rum Jungle** Aust
54D2 **Rumoi** Japan
73D5 **Rumphi** Malawi
78B2 **Runanga** NZ
78C1 **Runaway,C** NZ
73B5 **Rundu** Namibia
73D4 **Rungwa** Tanz
73D4 **Rungwa** *R* Tanz
73D4 **Rungwe** *Mt* Tanz
59G2 **Ruoqiang** China
50D2 **Ruo Shui** *R* China
56F7 **Rupat** *I* Indon
41F1 **Rupea** Rom
18D2 **Rupert** USA
7L4 **Rupert** *R* Can
36D1 **Rur** *R* Germany
26E6 **Rurrenabaque** Bol
73D5 **Rusape** Zim
41F2 **Ruse** Bulg
12A2 **Rushville** Illinois, USA
11B3 **Rushville** Nebraska, USA
75B3 **Rushworth** Aust
17C3 **Rusk** USA
15E4 **Ruskin** USA
3H2 **Russel L** Can
3H3 **Russell** Can
78B1 **Russell** NZ
16C2 **Russell** USA
4A2 **Russell L** Can
15B2 **Russellville** Alabama, USA
17D2 **Russellville** Arkansas, USA
12B3 **Russellville** Kentucky, USA
19B3 **Russian** *R* USA
44E4 **Russian Federation** *Republic* Europe
49L2 **Russkiy, Ostrov** *I* Russian Fed
64E1 **Rustavi** Georgia
74D2 **Rustenburg** S Africa
17D3 **Ruston** USA
72C4 **Rutana** Burundi
57B4 **Ruteng** Indon
74E1 **Rutenga** Zim
19C3 **Ruth** USA
36E1 **Rüthen** Germany
22C2 **Rutla** Mexico
13E2 **Rutland** USA
62E2 **Rutland** *I* Andaman Is
60D2 **Rutog** China
Ruvu = Pangani
73E5 **Ruvuma, R** Tanz/Mozam
72D3 **Ruwenzori Range** *Mts* Uganda/Zaïre
73D5 **Ruya** *R* Zim
43D3 **Ružomberok** Czech
72C4 **Rwanda** Republic, Africa
44F5 **Ryazan'** Russian Fed
44G5 **Ryazhsk** Russian Fed
32L5 **Rybachiy, Poluostrov** *Pen* Russian Fed
44F4 **Rybinsk** Russian Fed
44F4 **Rybinskoye Vodokhranilishche** *Res* Russian Fed
43F3 **Rybnitsa** Moldavia
3E2 **Rycroft** Can
35E6 **Ryde** Eng
35F6 **Rye** Eng
18C2 **Rye Patch Res** USA
45E5 **Ryl'sk** Russian Fed
45H6 **Ryn Peski** *Desert* Kazakhstan
54A3 **Ryoju** S Korea
53D4 **Ryōtsu** Japan
43F3 **Ryskany** Moldavia
50F4 **Ryūkyū Retto** *Arch* Japan
43E2 **Rzeszów** Pol
44E4 **Rzhev** Russian Fed

S

63C2 **Sa'ādatābād** Iran
66B2 **Saad el Aali** *Dam* Egypt
42C2 **Saale** *R* Germany
37B1 **Saanen** Switz
36D2 **Saar** *R* Germany
36D2 **Saarbrücken** Germany
36D2 **Saarburg** Germany
32J7 **Saaremaa** *I* Estonia
36D2 **Saarland** State, Germany
36D2 **Saarlouis** Germany
28C3 **Saavedra** Arg
65B3 **Saba'a** Egypt
41D2 **Šabac** Serbia, Yugos
39C1 **Sabadell** Spain
54C3 **Sabae** Japan
56E1 **Sabah** State, Malay
10A6 **Sabak,C** USA
57B3 **Sabal** Indon
23C4 **Sabanalarga** Colombia
56A1 **Sabang** Sumatera, Indon
57A2 **Sabang** Sulawesi, Indon
62C1 **Sabari** *R* India
65C2 **Sabastiya** Israel
26E7 **Sabaya** Bol
64C3 **Sab'Bi'ār** Syria
66C3 **Sabderat** Eth
65D2 **Sabhā** Jordan
69A2 **Sabhā** Libya
73D6 **Sabi** *R* Zim
74E2 **Sabie** *R* S Africa
21B2 **Sabinas** Mexico
21B2 **Sabinas Hidalgo** Mexico
17C3 **Sabine** *R* USA
17D4 **Sabine L** USA
67F2 **Sabkhat Maṭṭi** *Salt Marsh* UAE
65B3 **Sabkhet El Bardawîl** *Lg* Egypt
57F8 **Sablayan** Phil
7M5 **Sable,C** Can
15E4 **Sable,C** USA
7N5 **Sable I** Can
63D1 **Sabzevār** Iran
18C1 **Sacajawea Peak** USA
14C1 **Sacandaga Res** USA
11D3 **Sac City** USA
9D1 **Sachigo** *R* Can
4C3 **Sachigo L** Can
54A3 **Sach'on** S Korea
42C2 **Sachsen** State, Germany
42C2 **Sachsen-Anhalt** State, Germany
6F2 **Sachs Harbour** Can
37E2 **Sacile** Italy
37B1 **Säckingen** Germany
5J4 **Sackville** Can
13E2 **Saco** Maine, USA
11A2 **Saco** Montana, USA
20B1 **Sacramento** USA
20B1 **Sacramento** *R* USA
19B2 **Sacramento** *V* USA
16A3 **Sacramento Mts** USA
66D3 **Sa'dah** Yemen
41E2 **Sadanski** Bulg
67G3 **Sadh** Oman
61E2 **Sadiya** India
39A2 **Sado** *R* Port
53D4 **Sado-shima** *I* Japan
60C3 **Sādri** India
Safad = Zefat
60A2 **Safed Koh** *Mts* Afghan
63E2 **Safer** Afghan
32G7 **Saffle** Sweden
19E4 **Safford** USA
64C3 **Safi** Jordan
71A2 **Safi** Mor
63E2 **Safidabeh** Iran
65D1 **Şāfītā** Syria
43G1 **Safonovo** Russian Fed
44H2 **Safonovo** Russian Fed
64E3 **Safwān** Iraq
61C2 **Saga** China
54B4 **Saga** Japan
55B1 **Sagaing** Burma
54C4 **Sagami-nada** *B* Japan
60D4 **Sāgar** India
10J2 **Sagavanirktok** *R* USA
14D2 **Sag Harbor** USA
12C2 **Saginaw** USA
12C2 **Saginaw B** USA
7M4 **Saglek B** Can
54A3 **Sagŏ-ri** S Korea
16A2 **Saguache** USA
23B2 **Sagua de Tánamo** Cuba
23B2 **Sagua la Grande** Cuba
7L5 **Saguenay** *R* Can
39B2 **Sagunto** Spain
65D3 **Sahāb** Jordan
39A1 **Sahagún** Spain
70C2 **Sahara** *Desert* N Africa
60D3 **Saharanpur** India
60C2 **Sahiwal** Pak
64D3 **Şahrā al Hijārah** *Desert Region* Iraq
66B1 **Sahra esh Sharqîya** *Desert Region* Egypt
22B1 **Sahuayo** Mexico
65D1 **Sahyun** *Hist Site* Syria
76D1 **Saibai I** Aust
71C2 **Saïda** Alg
65C2 **Saïda** Leb
63D3 **Sa'īdabad** Iran
39B2 **Saïdia** Mor
61C2 **Saidpur** India
60C2 **Saidu** Pak
54B3 **Saigō** Japan
55D3 **Saigon** Viet
61D3 **Saiha** India
50E2 **Saihan Tal** China
54B4 **Saijo** Japan
53C5 **Saiki** Japan
44D3 **Saimaa** *L* Fin
22B1 **Sain Alto** Mexico
63E3 **Saindak** Pak
34D4 **St Abb's Head** *Pt* Scot
5G4 **St Agapit** Can
5G4 **Ste Agathe-des-Monts** Can
5K4 **St Albans** Can
35E6 **St Albans** Eng
13E2 **St Albans** Vermont, USA
12C3 **St Albans** West Virginia, USA
35D6 **St Albans Head** *C* Eng
3F3 **St Albert** Can
36B1 **St Amand-les-Eaux** France
38C2 **St Amand-Mont Rond** France
37A1 **St-Amour** France
73E5 **St André** *C* Madag
36A2 **St-André-de-l'Eure** France
15B3 **St Andrew B** USA
34D3 **St Andrews** Scot
15C2 **St Andrew Sd** USA
11C2 **Ste Anne** Can
5G4 **Ste Anne de Beaupré** Can
5H4 **Ste-Anne-des-Monts** Can
23H1 **St Ann's Bay** Jamaica
7N4 **St Anthony** Can
18D2 **St Anthony** USA
75B3 **St Arnaud** Aust
5K3 **St Augustin** *R* Can
15C3 **St Augustine** USA
5K3 **St Augustin-Saguenay** Can
35C6 **St Austell** Eng
36D2 **St-Avold** France
35D4 **St Bees Head** *Pt* Eng
4B4 **St Boniface** Can
37B2 **St-Bonnet** France
35C6 **St Brides B** Wales
38B2 **St-Brieuc** France
36A3 **St-Calais** France
4F5 **St Catharines** Can
23M2 **St Catherine,Mt** Grenada
15C2 **St Catherines I** USA
35E6 **St Catherines Pt** Eng
38C2 **St Chamond** France
18D2 **St Charles** Idaho, USA
17D2 **St Charles** Missouri, USA
12C2 **St Clair** USA
12C2 **St Clair,L** USA/Can
12C2 **St Clair Shores** USA
38D2 **St Claud** France
11D2 **St Cloud** USA
37B1 **Ste Croix** Switz
23E3 **St Croix** *I* Caribbean
12A1 **St Croix** *R* USA
13F1 **St Croix** *R* USA/Can
12A1 **St Croix Falls** USA
35C6 **St Davids Head** *Pt* Wales
36B2 **St Denis** France
73F6 **St Denis** Réunion
36D2 **St-Dié** France
36C2 **St Dizier** France
10K3 **St Elias,Mt** USA
10L3 **St Elias Mts** Can
38B2 **Saintes** France
38C2 **St Étienne** France
37B2 **St Étienne-de-Tinée** France
13E1 **St-Félicien** Can
5K4 **St Fintan's** Can
36B2 **St-Florentin** France
16B2 **St Francis** USA
17D2 **St Francis** *R* USA
74C3 **St Francis B** S Africa
74C3 **St Francis,C** S Africa
37C1 **St Gallen** Switz
38C3 **St-Gaudens** France
75C1 **St George** Aust
15C2 **St George** South Carolina, USA
19D3 **St George** Utah, USA
10E4 **St George** *I* Alaska, USA
15C3 **St George I** Florida, USA
36E2 **St Georgen im Schwarzwald** Germany
18B2 **St George,Pt** USA
5H4 **St George** Can
13E1 **St-Georges** Can
23E4 **St George's** Grenada
5K4 **St George's B** Can
35B5 **St Georges Chan** Irish Rep/Wales
77E1 **St Georges Chan** PNG
37A1 **St Germain-du-Bois** France
36A2 **St German-en-laye** France
37B2 **St-Gervais** France
37C1 **St Gotthard** *P* Switz
35C6 **St Govans Head** *Pt* Wales
20A1 **St Helena** USA
xxxH5 **St Helena** *I* Atlantic O
74B3 **St Helena B** S Africa

15C2 **St Helena Sd** USA
75E3 **St Helens** Aust
35D5 **St Helens** Eng
18B1 **St Helens** USA
18B1 **St Helens,Mt** USA
38B2 **St Helier** Jersey
37B1 **St Hippolyte** France
36C1 **St-Hubert** Belg
7L5 **St-Hyacinthe** Can
12C1 **St Ignace** USA
12B1 **St Ignace I** Can
35C6 **St Ives** Eng
11D3 **St James** Minnesota, USA
17D2 **St James** Missouri, USA
3B3 **St James,C** Can
5G4 **St Jean** Can
5J3 **St Jean** *R* Can
38B2 **St Jean-d'Angely** France
37A1 **St-Jean-de-Losne** France
37B2 **St-Jean-de-Maurienne** France
4G4 **St Jérôme** Can
18C1 **St Joe** USA
37E1 **St Johann im Pongau** Austria
7M5 **Saint John** Can
5K3 **St John B** Can
5K4 **St John,C** Can
13F1 **St John** *R* USA Can
19E4 **St Johns** Arizona, USA
7N5 **St John's** Can
12C2 **St Johns** Michigan, USA
15C3 **St Johns** *R* USA
13E2 **St Johnsbury** USA
14C1 **St Johnsville** USA
13E1 **St-Joseph** Can
17D3 **St Joseph** Louisiana, USA
12B2 **St Joseph** Michigan, USA
17D2 **St Joseph** Missouri, USA
23L1 **St Joseph** Trinidad
12C2 **St Joseph** *R* USA
12C1 **St Joseph I** Can
17F4 **St Joseph I** USA
7J4 **St Joseph,L** Can
37B1 **St Julien** France
38C2 **St-Junien** France
36B2 **St-Just-en-Chaussée** France
34A3 **St Kilda** *I* Scot
23E3 **St Kitts-Nevis** *Is* Caribbean
5G4 **St Laurent** Can
37A1 **St-Laurent** France
7M5 **St Lawrence** *R* Can
7M5 **St Lawrence,G of** Can
10D3 **St Lawrence I** USA
13D2 **St Lawrence Seaway** Can/USA
13F1 **St Leonard** Can
5K3 **St Lewis Sd** Can
38B2 **St Lô** France
3G3 **St Louis** Can
70A3 **St Louis** Sen
12A3 **St Louis** USA
36D3 **St-Loup-sur-Semou** France
23E4 **St Lucia** *I* Caribbean
74E2 **St Lucia,L** S Africa
34E1 **St Magnus** *B* Scot
38B2 **St Malo** France
37A2 **St Marcellin** France
5H3 **Ste Marguerite** *R* Can
73E6 **Ste Marie** *C* Madag
36D2 **Ste-Marie-aux-Mines** France
18C1 **St Maries** USA
23E3 **St Martin** *I* Caribbean
4B3 **St Martin,L** Can
37B2 **St-Martin-Vésubie** France
76D1 **St Mary,Mt** PNG
75A2 **St Mary Peak** *Mt* Aust
75E3 **St Marys** Aust
13D2 **St Marys** USA
35B7 **St Marys** *I* UK
15C2 **St Marys** *R* USA
5L4 **St Mary's B** Can
5L4 **St Mary's,C** Can
76E1 **Saint Mathias Group** *Is* PNG
10D3 **St Matthew I** USA
5G4 **St Maurice** *R* Can
37A3 **St-Maximin** France
36C2 **Ste-Menehould** France
10F3 **St Michael** USA
14B3 **St Michaels** USA
37B2 **St-Michel** France
36C2 **St-Mihiel** France
37C1 **St Moritz** Switz
38B2 **St-Nazaire** France
36C1 **St-Niklaas** Belg
36B1 **St-Omer** France
5H4 **St Pacôme** Can
5H4 **St Pascal** Can
3F3 **St Paul** Can
11D3 **St Paul** Minnesota, USA
16C1 **St Paul** Nebraska, USA
10D4 **St Paul** *I* USA
5K3 **St Paul** *R* Can
70A4 **St Paul** *R* Lib
71G4 **St Paul,C** Ghana
5H4 **St Paul du Nord** Can
11D3 **St Peter** USA
15C3 **St Petersburg** USA
7N5 **St Pierre** *I* Can
13E1 **St Pierre,L** Can
36B1 **St-Pol-Sur-Ternoise** France
42D3 **St Pölten** Austria
36B2 **St Quentin** France
38D3 **St Raphaël** France
73E5 **St Sébastien** *C* Madag
5H4 **St Siméon** Can
15C2 **St Simons I** USA
5H4 **St Stephen** Can
15C2 **St Stephen** USA
5G4 **Ste Thérèse-de-Blainville** Can
10O3 **Ste Thérèse,L** Can
4E5 **St Thomas** Can
37B3 **St-Tropez** France
36C1 **St Truiden** Belg
36A2 **St-Valéry-en-Caux** France
36A1 **St-Valéry-sur-Somme** France
11C2 **St Vincent** USA
73E6 **St Vincent** *C* Madag
23E4 **St Vincent** *I* Caribbean
75A2 **St Vincent,G** Aust
36D1 **St-Vith** Germany
36D2 **St Wendel** Germany
51H5 **Saipan** *I* Pacific O
60B2 **Saiydabad** Afghan
26E7 **Sajama** *Mt* Bol
74C3 **Sak** *R* S Africa
53D5 **Sakai** Japan
54B4 **Sakaidi** Japan
54B3 **Sakaiminato** Japan
64D3 **Sakākah** S Arabia
11B2 **Sakakawea,L** USA
4F3 **Sakami** *R* Can
73C5 **Sakania** Zaïre
73E6 **Sakaraha** Madag
45E7 **Sakarya** *R* Turk
43E1 **Sakasleja** Latvia
53D4 **Sakata** Japan
71G4 **Saketé̀l** Benin
53E1 **Sakhalin** *I* Russian Fed
53E1 **Sakhalinskiy Zaliv** *B* Russian Fed
50F4 **Sakishima gunto** *Is* Japan
74C3 **Sakrivier** S Africa
70A4 **Sal** *I* Cape Verde
45G6 **Sal** *R* Russian Fed
32H7 **Sala** Sweden
28D1 **Saladas** Arg
28D3 **Saladillo** Arg
28C2 **Saladillo** *R* Arg
28D3 **Salado** *R* Buenos Aires, Arg
28B3 **Salado** *R* Mendoza/San Luis, Arg
25D3 **Salado** *R* Sante Fe, Arg
71F4 **Salaga** Ghana
55C3 **Sala Hintoun** Camb
72B2 **Salal** Chad
67F3 **Şalālah** Oman
28A2 **Salamanca** Chile
22B1 **Salamanca** Mexico
39A1 **Salamanca** Spain
14A1 **Salamanca** USA
72B3 **Salamat** *R* Chad
51H7 **Salamaua** PNG
65B1 **Salamis** *Hist Site* Cyprus
56E2 **Salang** Indon
32H5 **Salangen** Nor
25C2 **Salar de Arizaro** Arg
25C2 **Salar de Atacama** *Salt Pan* Chile
26E7 **Salar de Coipasa** *Salt Pan* Bol
26E8 **Salar de Uyuni** *Salt Pan* Bol
37C2 **Salasomaggiore** Italy
44K5 **Salavat** Russian Fed
76C1 **Salawati** *I* Indon
57B4 **Salayar** Indon
xxixO6 **Sala y Gomez** *I* Pacific O
28C3 **Salazar** Arg
38C2 **Salbris** France
10J3 **Salcha** *R* USA
74B3 **Saldanha** S Africa
65D2 **Saldhad** Syria
28C3 **Saldungaray** Arg
43E1 **Saldus** Latvia
75C3 **Sale** Aust
71A2 **Salé** Mor
57C2 **Salebabu** *I* Indon
44M2 **Salekhard** Russian Fed
12B3 **Salem** Illinois, USA
62B2 **Salem** India
14E1 **Salem** Massachusetts, USA
14C3 **Salem** New Jersey, USA
14D1 **Salem** New York, USA
18B2 **Salem** Oregon, USA
12C3 **Salem** Virginia, USA
56D4 **Salembu Besar** *I* Indon
32G6 **Salen** Sweden
40C2 **Salerno** Italy
35D5 **Salford** Eng
41D1 **Salgót** Hung
43D3 **Salgótarjan** Hung
27L5 **Salgueiro** Brazil
16A2 **Salida** USA
41F3 **Salihli** Turk
73D5 **Salima** Malawi
32K6 **Salimaa** *L* Fin
17C2 **Salina** Kansas, USA
19D3 **Salina** Utah, USA
40C3 **Salina** *I* Italy
22C2 **Salina Cruz** Mexico
26E8 **Salina de Arizato** Arg
28B3 **Salina Grande** *Salt pan* Arg
28B4 **Salina Gualicho** *Salt pan* Arg
28B2 **Salina La Antigua** *Salt pan* Arg
29D2 **Salinas** Brazil
22B1 **Salinas** Mexico
20B2 **Salinas** USA
20B2 **Salinas** *R* USA
28B3 **Salinas de Llancaneb** *Salt Pan* Arg
28C1 **Salinas Grandes** *Salt Pan* Arg
16A3 **Salinas Peak** *Mt* USA
17D3 **Saline** *R* Arkansas, USA
16B2 **Saline** *R* Kansas, USA
23M2 **Salines,Pt** Grenada
20D2 **Saline V** USA
27J4 **Salinópolis** Brazil
37A1 **Salins** France
35E6 **Salisbury** Eng
13D3 **Salisbury** Maryland, USA
15C1 **Salisbury** North Carolina, USA
7L3 **Salisbury I** Can
35E6 **Salisbury Plain** Eng
32K5 **Salla** Fin
28C1 **Salladillo** *R* Arg
37B2 **Sallanches** France
17D2 **Sallisaw** USA
7L3 **Salluit** Can
61B2 **Sallyana** Nepal
63A1 **Salmas** Iran
32L6 **Salmi** Russian Fed
18C1 **Salmo** Can
18D1 **Salmon** USA
18C1 **Salmon** *R* USA
3E3 **Salmon Arm** Can
18C1 **Salmon River Mts** USA
32J6 **Salo** Fin
37D2 **Salò** Italy
38D3 **Salon-de-Provence** France
Salonica = Thessaloníki
41E1 **Salonta** Rom
32K6 **Salpausselka** Region, Fin
28B2 **Salsacate** Arg
45G6 **Sal'sk** Russian Fed
65C2 **Salt** Jordan
74C3 **Salt** *R* S Africa
19D4 **Salt** *R* USA
25C2 **Salta** Arg
25C2 **Salta** State, Arg
21B2 **Saltillo** Mexico
18D2 **Salt Lake City** USA
28C2 **Salto** Arg
28D2 **Salto** Urug
26D3 **Salto Angostura** *Waterfall* Colombia
29E2 **Salto da Divisa** Brazil
29B3 **Salto das Sete Quedas** Brazil
26F2 **Salto del Angel** *Waterfall* Ven
25E2 **Salto del Guaira** *Waterfall* Brazil
26D4 **Salto Grande** *Waterfall* Colombia
19C4 **Salton S** USA
29B4 **Saltos do Iguaçu** *Waterfall* Arg
60C2 **Salt Range** *Mts* Pak
23H2 **Salt River** Jamaica
15C2 **Saluda** USA
57B3 **Salue Timpaus** *Str* Indon
62C1 **Sālūr** India
37B2 **Saluzzo** Italy
27L6 **Salvador** Brazil
17D4 **Salvador,L** USA
22B1 **Salvatierra** Mexico
67F2 **Salwah** Qatar
55B1 **Salween** *R* Burma
45H8 **Sal'yany** Azerbaijan
12C3 **Salyersville** USA
37E1 **Salzach** *R* Austria
42C3 **Salzburg** Austria
37E1 **Salzburg** Province, Austria
42C2 **Salzgitter** Germany
37E1 **Salzkammergut** *Mts* Austria
42C2 **Salzwedel** Germany
50C1 **Samagaltay** Russian Fed
57F9 **Samales Group** *Is* Phil
23D3 **Samaná** Dom Rep
64C2 **Samandaği** Turk
60B1 **Samangan** Afghan
54D2 **Samani** Japan
65A3 **Samannûd** Egypt
57G8 **Samar** *I* Phil
44J5 **Samara** Russian Fed
76E2 **Samarai** PNG
56E3 **Samarinda** Indon
58E2 **Samarkand** Uzbekistan
64D3 **Sāmarrā'** Iraq
57F8 **Samar S** Phil
61B3 **Sambalpur** India
56C2 **Sambas** Indon
73F5 **Sambava** Madag
60D3 **Sambhal** India
56E3 **Samboja** Indon
43E3 **Sambor** Ukraine
36B1 **Sambre** *R* France
53B4 **Samch'ŏk** S Korea
54A4 **Samch'ŏnp'o** S Korea
54A3 **Samdŭng** N Korea
72D4 **Same** Tanz
37C1 **Samedan** Switz
36A1 **Samer** France
73C5 **Samfya** Zambia
67F4 **Samhah** *I* Yemen
55B1 **Samka** Burma
55C1 **Sam Neua** Laos
77H2 **Samoan Is** Pacific O
41F3 **Sámos** *I* Greece
56A2 **Samosir** *I* Indon
41F2 **Samothráki** *I* Greece
28C2 **Sampacho** Arg
57A3 **Sampaga** Indon
57B3 **Sampara** *R* Indon
56D3 **Sampit** Indon
56D3 **Sampit** *R* Indon
17D3 **Sam Rayburn Res** USA
55C3 **Samrong** Camb
42C1 **Samsø** *I* Den
54A2 **Samsu** N Korea
64C1 **Samsun** Turk
57D4 **Samulaki** Indon
71F3 **San** Mali
55D3 **San** *R* Camb
43E2 **San** *R* Pol
66D3 **Şan'ā'** Yemen
72B3 **Sanaga** *R* Cam
25C4 **San Agustín** Arg
57G9 **San Agustin,C** Phil
10F5 **Sanak I** USA
57C3 **Sanana** Indon
57C3 **Sanana** *I* Indon
63B1 **Sanandaj** Iran
20B1 **San Andreas** USA
16A3 **San Andres Mts** USA
21C3 **San Andrés Tuxtla** Mexico
16B3 **San Angelo** USA
40B3 **San Antioco** Sardegna
40B3 **San Antioco** *I* Medit S
28C1 **San Antonio** Arg
28A2 **San Antonio** Chile
16A3 **San Antonio** New Mexico, USA
57F7 **San Antonio** Phil
16C4 **San Antonio** Texas, USA
20B2 **San Antonio** *R* California, USA
17F4 **San Antonio** *R* Texas, USA
39C2 **San Antonio Abad** Spain
21D2 **San Antonio,C** Cuba
16B3 **San Antonio de Bravo** Mexico
23A2 **San Antonio de los Banos** Cuba
28C4 **San Antonio Este** Arg
20D3 **San Antonio,Mt** USA
28B4 **San Antonio Oeste** Arg
20B3 **San Antonio Res** USA
20B2 **San Ardo** USA
28D3 **San Augustin** Arg
28B2 **San Augustin de Valle Féril** Arg
60D4 **Sanawad** India
22B1 **San Bartolo** Mexico
21A3 **San Benedicto** *I* Mexico
17F4 **San Benito** USA
20B2 **San Benito** *R* USA
20B2 **San Benito Mt** USA
20D3 **San Bernardino** USA
28A2 **San Bernardo** Chile
19C4 **San Bernardo Mts** USA
22A1 **San Blas** Mexico
15B3 **San Blas,C** USA
28A3 **San Carlos** Chile
22C1 **San Carlos** Mexico
26B1 **San Carlos** Nic
57F7 **San Carlos** Phil
28E2 **San Carlos** Urug
19D4 **San Carlos** USA
25B6 **San Carlos de Bariloche** Arg
50F4 **San-chung** Taiwan
44H4 **Sanchursk** Russian Fed
28A3 **San Clemente** Chile
20D4 **San Clemente** USA
19C4 **San Clemente I** USA
28C2 **San Cristóbal** Arg
21C3 **San Cristóbal** Mexico
26D2 **San Cristóbal** Ven
77F2 **San Cristobal** *I* Solomon Is
21E2 **Sancti Spíritus** Cuba
74D1 **Sand** *R* S Africa
56D3 **Sandai** Indon
56E1 **Sandakan** Malay
37E1 **San Daniele del Friuli** Italy
34D2 **Sanday** *I* Scot
16B3 **Sanderson** USA
3G2 **Sandfly L** Can
19C4 **San Diego** USA
64B2 **Sandikli** Turk
61B2 **Sandīla** India
4E4 **Sand Lake** Can
32F7 **Sandnes** Nor
32G5 **Sandnessjøen** Nor
32D3 **Sandø** Faroes
73C4 **Sandoa** Zaïre
43E2 **Sandomierz** Pol
37E2 **San Donà di Piave** Italy
61D4 **Sandoway** Burma
10F4 **Sand Point** USA
18C1 **Sandpoint** USA
38D2 **Sandrio** Italy
3B3 **Sandspit** Can
17C2 **Sand Springs** USA
76A3 **Sandstone** Aust
11D2 **Sandstone** USA
52C4 **Sandu** China
12C2 **Sandusky** USA
32H6 **Sandviken** Sweden
14E2 **Sandwich** USA
5K3 **Sandwich B** Can
3H2 **Sandy Bay** Can
7J4 **Sandy L** Can
4C3 **Sandy Lake** Can
28C2 **San Elcano** Arg
29A3 **San Estanislao** Par
8B3 **San Felipe** Baja Cal, Mexico
28A2 **San Felipe** Chile
22B1 **San Felipe** Guanajuato, Mexico
23D4 **San Felipe** Ven
39C1 **San Feliu de Guixols** Spain
28A2 **San Fernando** Chile
22C1 **San Fernando** Mexico
57F7 **San Fernando** Phil
39A2 **San Fernando** Spain
23E4 **San Fernando** Trinidad
20C3 **San Fernando** USA
26E2 **San Fernando** Ven
22C1 **San Fernando** *R* Mexico
15C3 **Sanford** Florida, USA
13E2 **Sanford** Maine, USA
15D1 **Sanford** N Carolina, USA
9E4 **Sanford** USA
10K3 **Sanford,Mt** USA
28C2 **San Francisco** Arg
23C3 **San Francisco** Dom Rep
20A2 **San Francisco** USA
20A2 **San Francisco B** USA
21B2 **San Francisco del Oro** Mexico
22B1 **San Francisco del Rincon** Mexico
20D3 **San Gabriel Mts** USA
60C5 **Sangamner** India
12B3 **Sangamon** *R* USA
51H5 **Sangan** *I* Pacific O
49O3 **Sangar** Russian Fed
62B1 **Sangāreddi** India
56E4 **Sangeang** *I* Indon
20C2 **Sanger** USA
52C2 **Sanggan He** *R* China
56D2 **Sanggau** Indon
72B3 **Sangha** *R* Congo
60B3 **Sanghar** Pak
57C2 **Sangihe** *I* Indon
37E2 **San Giorgio di Nogaro** Italy
55B3 **Sangkhla Buri** Thai
56E2 **Sangkulirang** Indon
62A1 **Sāngli** India
72B3 **Sangmélima** Cam
8B3 **San Gorgonio Mt** USA
16A2 **Sangre de Cristo** *Mts* USA
28C2 **San Gregorio** Arg
28D2 **San Gregorio** Urug
20A2 **San Gregorio** USA
60D2 **Sangrūr** India
74E1 **Sangutane** *R* Mozam
28A4 **Sanico** Arg
25E3 **San Ignacio** Arg

57F8 **San Isidro** Phil
26D2 **San Jacinto** Colombia
19C4 **San Jacinto Peak** *Mt* USA
28A3 **San Javier** Chile
28D1 **San Javier** Misiones, Arg
28D2 **San Javier** Sante Fe, Arg
28D1 **San Javier** *R* Arg
53D4 **Sanjō** *I* Japan
25H2 **San João del Rei** Brazil
20B2 **San Joaquin** *R* USA
20B2 **San Joaquin Valley** USA
16B2 **San Jon** USA
26B1 **San José** Costa Rica
21C3 **San José** Guatemala
57F7 **San Jose** Luzon, Phil
57F8 **San Jose** Mindoro, Phil
20B2 **San Jose** USA
8B4 **San José** *I* Mexico
26F7 **San José de Chiquitos** Bol
28D2 **San José de Feliciano** Arg
28B2 **San José de Jachal** Arg
28C2 **San José de la Dormida** Arg
28A3 **San José de la Mariquina** Chile
8C4 **San José del Cabo** Mexico
28D2 **San José de Mayo** Urug
22B1 **San José de Raices** Mexico
25G2 **San José do Rio Prêto** Brazil
21B2 **San Joseé del Cabo** Mexico
54A3 **Sanju** S Korea
28B2 **San Juan** Arg
23D3 **San Juan** Puerto Rico
28B2 **San Juan** State, Arg
23L1 **San Juan** Trinidad
20B3 **San Juan** USA
26E2 **San Juan** Ven
23B2 **San Juan** *Mt* Cuba
28B2 **San Juan** *R* Arg
20B3 **San Juan** *R* California, USA
22C2 **San Juan** *R* Mexico
21D3 **San Juan** *R* Nicaragua/Costa Rica
19D3 **San Juan** *R* Utah, USA
22C2 **San Juan Bautista** Mexico
25E3 **San Juan Bautista** Par
20B2 **San Juan Bautista** USA
21D3 **San Juan del Norte** Nic
23D4 **San Juan de los Cayos** Ven
22B1 **San Juan de loz Lagoz** Mexico
22B1 **San Juan del Rio** Mexico
21D3 **San Juan del Sur** Nicaragua
22C2 **San Juan Evangelista** Mexico
18B1 **San Juan Is** USA
16A2 **San Juan Mts** USA
22C2 **San Juan Tepozcolula** Mexico
25C7 **San Julián** Arg
28C2 **San Justo** Arg
44E4 **Sankt Peterburg** Russian Fed
72C4 **Sankuru** *R* Zaïre
20A2 **San Leandro** USA
28E1 **San Leopoldo** Brazil
64C2 **Sanliurfa** Turk
28C2 **San Lorenzo** Arg
26C3 **San Lorenzo** Colombia
24C3 **San Lorenzo** Ecuador
20B2 **San Lucas** USA
28B2 **San Luis** Arg
28B2 **San Luis** State, Arg
19D4 **San Luis** USA
22B1 **San Luis de la Paz** Mexico
28D1 **San Luis del Palma** Arg
20B3 **San Luis Obispo** USA
20B3 **San Luis Obispo B** USA
22B1 **San Luis Potosi** Mexico
22B1 **San Luis Potosi** State, Mexico
20B2 **San Luis Res** USA
40B3 **Sanluri** Sardegna
22D2 **San Magallanes** Mexico
26E2 **San Maigualida** *Mts* Ven
28D3 **San Manuel** Arg
28A2 **San Marcos** Chile
22C2 **San Marcos** Mexico
17C4 **San Marcos** USA
37E3 **San Marino** Republic, Europe
28B1 **San Martin** Catamarca, Arg
28B2 **San Martin** Mendoza, Arg
79G3 **San Martin** *Base* Ant
28A4 **San Martin de los Andes** Arg
37D2 **San Martino di Castroza** Italy
22C2 **San Martin Tuxmelucan** Mexico
20A2 **San Mateo** USA
27G7 **San Matias** Brazil
52C3 **Sanmenxia** China
21D3 **San Miguel** El Salvador
20B3 **San Miguel** USA
20B3 **San Miguel** *I* USA
22B1 **San Miguel del Allende** Mexico
28D3 **San Miguel del Monte** Arg
25C3 **San Miguel de Tucumán** Arg
52D4 **Sanming** China
8B3 **San Nicolas** *I* USA
28C2 **San Nicolás de los Arroyos** Arg
74D2 **Sannieshof** S Africa
70B4 **Sanniquellie** Lib
43E3 **Sanok** Pol
23B5 **San Onofore** Colombia
20D4 **San Onofre** USA
57F8 **San Pablo** Phil
20A1 **San Pablo B** USA
28D2 **San Pedro** Buenos Aires, Arg
70B4 **San Pédro** Ivory Coast
25D2 **San Pedro** Jujuy, Arg
25E2 **San Pedro** Par
19D4 **San Pedro** *R* USA
20C4 **San Pedro Chan** USA
8C4 **San Pedro de los Colonias** Mexico
21D3 **San Pedro Sula** Honduras
40B3 **San Pietro** *I* Medit S
21A1 **San Quintin** Mexico
28B2 **San Rafael** Arg
20A2 **San Rafael** USA
20C3 **San Rafael Mts** USA
37B3 **San Remo** Italy
16C3 **San Saba** *R* USA
28D2 **San Salvador** Arg
24B2 **San Salvador** El Salvador
22B1 **San Salvador** Mexico
23C2 **San Salvador** *I* Caribbean
25C2 **San Salvador de Jujuy** Arg
71G3 **Sansanné-Mango** Togo
39B1 **San Sebastian** Spain
37E3 **Sansepolcro** Italy
40D2 **San Severo** Italy
20B3 **San Simeon** USA
26E7 **Santa Ana** Bol
21C3 **Santa Ana** Guatemala
20D4 **Santa Ana** USA
20D4 **Santa Ana Mts** USA
16C3 **Santa Anna** USA
28A3 **Santa Bárbara** Chile
21B2 **Santa Barbara** Mexico
20C3 **Santa Barbara** USA
20C4 **Santa Barbara,I** USA
20B3 **Santa Barbara Chan** USA
20C3 **Santa Barbara Res** USA
20C4 **Santa Catalina** *I* USA
20C4 **Santa Catalina,G of** USA
25F3 **Santa Catarina** State, Brazil
23B2 **Santa Clara** Cuba
20B2 **Santa Clara** USA
20C3 **Santa Clara** *R* USA
25C8 **Santa Cruz** Arg
26F7 **Santa Cruz** Bol
28A2 **Santa Cruz** Chile
57F8 **Santa Cruz** Phil
25B7 **Santa Cruz** State, Arg
20A2 **Santa Cruz** USA
20C4 **Santa Cruz** *I* USA
77F2 **Santa Cruz** *Is* Solomon Is
19D4 **Santa Cruz** *R* USA
29E2 **Santa Cruz Cabrália** Brazil
20C3 **Santa Cruz Chan** USA
70A2 **Santa Cruz de la Palma** Canary Is
23B2 **Santa Cruz del Sur** Cuba
70A2 **Santa Cruz de Tenerife** Canary Is
73C5 **Santa Cruz do Cuando** Angola
29C3 **Santa Cruz do Rio Pardo** Brazil
28E1 **Santa Cruz do Sul** Brazil
20A2 **Santa Cruz Mts** USA
28D2 **Santa Elena** Arg
26F3 **Santa Elena** Ven
28C2 **Santa Fe** Arg
28C2 **Santa Fe** State, Arg
16A2 **Santa Fe** USA
29B2 **Santa Helena de Goiás** Brazil
52B3 **Santai** China
25B8 **Santa Inés** *I* Chile
28B3 **Santa Isabel** La Pampa, Arg
28C2 **Santa Isabel** Sante Fe, Arg
77E1 **Santa Isabel** *I* Solomon Is
28D2 **Santa Lucia** Urug
20B2 **Santa Lucia** USA
19B3 **Santa Lucia Range** *Mts* USA
70A4 **Santa Luzia** *I* Cape Verde
28C1 **Santa Margarita** Arg
20B3 **Santa Margarita** USA
8B4 **Santa Margarita** *I* Mexico
20D4 **Santa Margarita** *R* USA
37C2 **Santa Margherita** Italy
28E1 **Santa Maria** Brazil
23C4 **Santa Maria** Colombia
20B3 **Santa Maria** USA
70A1 **Santa Maria** *I* Açores
28E2 **Santa Maria** *R* Brazil
16A3 **Santa Maria** *R* Chihuahua, Mexico
22C1 **Santa Maria** *R* Queretaro, Mexico
29D1 **Santa Maria da Vitória** Brazil
22B1 **Santa Maria del Rio** Mexico
26D1 **Santa Marta** Colombia
20C3 **Santa Monica** USA
20C4 **Santa Monica B** USA
29D1 **Santana** Brazil
28D2 **Santana do Livramento** Brazil
26C3 **Santander** Colombia
39B1 **Santander** Spain
39C2 **Santañy** Spain
20C3 **Santa Paula** USA
29B3 **Santa Porto Helena** Brazil
27K4 **Santa Quitéria** Brazil
37E2 **Santarcangelo di Romagna** Italy
27H4 **Santarem** Brazil
39A2 **Santarém** Port
29B2 **Santa Rita do Araguaia** Brazil
28E1 **Santa Rosa** Brazil
20A1 **Santa Rosa** California, USA
21D3 **Santa Rosa** Honduras
28C3 **Santa Rosa** La Pampa, Arg
28B2 **Santa Rosa** Mendoza, Arg
16B3 **Santa Rosa** New Mexico, USA
28B2 **Santa Rosa** San Luis, Arg
20B3 **Santa Rosa** *I* USA
21A2 **Santa Rosalía** Mexico
18C2 **Santa Rosa Range** *Mts* USA
28C1 **Santa Sylvina** Arg
27L5 **Santa Talhada** Brazil
29D2 **Santa Teresa** Brazil
40B2 **Santa Teresa di Gallura** Sardegna
28E2 **Santa Vitoria do Palmar** Brazil
20B3 **Santa Ynez** *R* USA
20B3 **Santa Ynez Mots** USA
15D2 **Santee** *R* USA
37D2 **Santerno** *R* Italy
37C2 **Santhia** Italy
28A2 **Santiago** Chile
23C3 **Santiago** Dom Rep
22A1 **Santiago** Mexico
26B2 **Santiago** Panama
57F7 **Santiago** Phil
26C4 **Santiago** *R* Peru
39A1 **Santiago de Compostela** Spain
23B2 **Santiago de Cuba** Cuba
28C1 **Santiago del Estero** Arg
25D3 **Santiago del Estero** State, Arg
20D4 **Santiago Peak** *Mt* USA
27K7 **Santo** State, Brazil
77F2 **Santo** Vanuatu
29B3 **Santo Anastatácio** Brazil
28E1 **Santo Angelo** Brazil
70A4 **Santo Antão** *I* Cape Verde
29B3 **Santo Antonio da Platina** Brazil
29E1 **Santo Antônio de Jesus** Brazil
29A2 **Santo Antônio do Leverger** Brazil
22B1 **Santo Dominco** Mexico
23D3 **Santo Domingo** Dom Rep
29C3 **Santos** Brazil
29D3 **Santos Dumont** Brazil
19C4 **Santo Tomas** Mexico
28D1 **Santo Tomé** Arg
25B7 **San Valentin** *Mt* Chile
28A2 **San Vicente** Chile
22B1 **San Vicente** Mexico
37E2 **San Vito al Tagliamento** Italy
73B4 **Sanza Pomba** Angola
28D1 **São Borja** Brazil
29C3 **São Carlos** Brazil
29C1 **São Domingos** Brazil
27H5 **São Félix** Mato Grosso, Brazil
29D3 **São Fidélis** Brazil
29D2 **São Francisco** Brazil
27L5 **São Francisco** *R* Brazil
28D1 **São Francisco de Assis** Brazil
25G3 **São Francisco do Sul** Brazil
28E2 **São Gabriel** Brazil
29C2 **São Gotardo** Brazil
73D4 **Sao Hill** Tanz
29D3 **São João da Barra** Brazil
29C3 **São João da Boa Vista** Brazil
29C1 **São João d'Aliança** Brazil
29D2 **São João da Ponte** Brazil
29D3 **São João del Rei** Brazil
29D2 **São João do Paraíso** Brazil
29C3 **São Joaquim da Barra** Brazil
70A1 **São Jorge** *I* Açores
28E2 **São José do Norte** Brazil
29C3 **São José do Rio Prêto** Brazil
29C3 **São José dos Campos** Brazil
29C4 **São José dos Pinhais** Brazil
29A2 **São Lourenço** *R* Brazil
28E2 **São Lourenço do Sul** Brazil
27K4 **São Luis** Brazil
28E1 **Sao Luis Gonzaga** Brazil
29C2 **São Marcos** *R* Brazil
29D2 **São Maria do Suaçui** Brazil
29E2 **São Mateus** Brazil
29D2 **São Mateus** *R* Brazil
70A1 **São Miguel** *I* Açores
29B1 **São Miguel de Araguaia** Brazil
38C2 **Saône** *R* France
70A4 **São Nicolau** *I* Cape Verde
29D1 **São Onofre** *R* Brazil
29C3 **São Paulo** Brazil
29B3 **São Paulo** State, Brazil
28E1 **São Pedro do Sul** Brazil
24H3 **São Pedro e São Paulo** *Is* Brazil
27K5 **São Raimundo Nonato** Brazil
29C2 **São Romão** Brazil
29C3 **São Sebastia do Paraiso** Brazil
28E2 **São Sepé** Brazil
29B2 **São Simão** Goias, Brazil
25G1 **São Simão, Barragem de** *Res* Brazil
29C3 **São Simão** Sao Paulo, Brazil
70A4 **São Tiago** *I* Cape Verde
70C4 **São Tomé** *I* W Africa
70C4 **São Tomé and Principe** Republic, W Africa
70B2 **Saoura** *Watercourse* Alg
29A1 **Saouriuiná** *R* Brazil
29C3 **São Vicente** Brazil
70A4 **São Vincente** *I* Cape Verde
41F2 **Sápai** Greece
57C3 **Saparua** Indon
56E4 **Sape** Indon
71H4 **Sapele** Nig
53E3 **Sapporo** Japan
40D2 **Sapri** Italy
32G7 **Saprsborg** Nor
17C2 **Sapulpa** USA
63B1 **Saqqez** Iran
45H8 **Sarāb** Iran
41D2 **Sarajevo** Bosnia & Herzegovina, Yugos
63E1 **Sarakhs** Iran
45K5 **Saraktash** Russian Fed
49K4 **Sarala** Russian Fed
13E2 **Saranac L** USA
13E2 **Saranac Lake** USA
41E3 **Sarandë** Alb
28E1 **Sarandi** Brazil
28D2 **Sarandi del Yi** Urug
28D2 **Sarandi Grande** Urug
57G9 **Sarangani Is** Phil
44L3 **Saranpaul'** Russian Fed
44H5 **Saransk** Russian Fed
37C2 **Saranza** Italy
71H4 **Sara Peak** *Mt* Nig
44J4 **Sarapul** Russian Fed
15E4 **Sarasota** USA
41F1 **Sărat** Rom
43F3 **Sarata** Ukraine
11A3 **Saratoga** USA
14D1 **Saratoga Springs** USA
56D2 **Saratok** Malay
45H5 **Saratov** Russian Fed
45H5 **Saratovskoye Vodokhranilishche** *Res* Russian Fed
64A2 **Saraykoy** Turk
63E3 **Sarbāz** Iran
63D2 **Sarbīsheh** Iran
37D1 **Sarca** *R* Italy
69A2 **Sardalais** Libya
63B1 **Sar Dasht** Iran
40B2 **Sardegna** *I* Medit S
Sardinia = Sardegna
32H5 **Sarektjåkkå, Mt** Sweden
66C4 **Sarenga** Eth
60C2 **Sargodha** Pak
72B3 **Sarh** Chad
63C1 **Sārī** Iran
65C2 **Sarida** *R* Isreal
64D1 **Sarikamiş** Turk
76D3 **Sarina** Aust
37B1 **Sarine** *R* Switz
60B1 **Sar-i-Pul** Afghan
69B2 **Sarīr** Libya
69A2 **Sarir Tibesti** *Desert* Libya
53B4 **Sariwŏn** N Korea
38B2 **Sark** *I* UK
64C2 **Şarkişla** Turk
51G7 **Sarmi** Indon
25C7 **Sarmiento** Arg
32G6 **Särna** Sweden
37C1 **Sarnen** Switz
4E5 **Sarnia** Can
43F2 **Sarny** Ukraine
60B2 **Sarobi** Afghan
56B3 **Sarolangun** Indon
41E3 **Saronikós Kólpos** *G* Greece
37C2 **Saronno** Italy
41F2 **Saros Körfezi** *B* Turk
44M2 **Saroto** Russian Fed
7N2 **Sarqaq** Greenland
36D2 **Sarralbe** France
36D2 **Sarrebourg** France
36D2 **Sarreguemines** France
36D2 **Sarre-Union** France
39B1 **Sarrion** Spain
60B3 **Sartanahu** Pak
40B2 **Sartène** Corse
36A3 **Sarthe** Department, France
38B2 **Sarthe** *R* France
65D1 **Sārūt** Syria
63E3 **Sarvan** Iran
45J6 **Sarykamys** Kazakhstan
48H5 **Sarysu** *R* Kazakhstan
61B3 **Sasarām** India
53B5 **Sasebo** Japan
6H4 **Saskatchewan** Province, Can
6H4 **Saskatchewan** *R* Can
3G3 **Saskatoon** Can
49N2 **Saskylakh** Russian Fed
74D2 **Sasolburg** S Africa
44G5 **Sasovo** Russian Fed
70B4 **Sassandra** Ivory Coast
70B4 **Sassandra** *R* Ivory Coast
40B2 **Sassari** Sardegna
42C2 **Sassnitz** Germany
37D2 **Sassuolo** Italy
28C2 **Sastre** Arg
54A4 **Sasuna** Japan
62A1 **Sātāra** India
6G2 **Satellite B** Can
56E4 **Satengar** *Is* Indon
32H6 **Säter** Sweden
15C2 **Satilla** *R* USA
44K4 **Satka** Russian Fed
60D2 **Satluj** *R* India
61B3 **Satna** India
60C4 **Sātpura Range** *Mts* India
41E1 **Satu Mare** Rom
28D2 **Sauce** Arg
32F7 **Sauda** Nor
58C3 **Saudi Arabia** Kingdom, Arabian Pen
36D2 **Sauer** *R* Germany/Lux
36D1 **Sauerland** Region, Germany
32B1 **Sauðárkrókur** Iceland
12B2 **Saugatuck** USA
14D1 **Saugerties** USA
3C3 **Saugstad,Mt** Can
11D2 **Sauk Center** USA
12B2 **Sauk City** USA
4E4 **Sault Ste Marie** Can
12C1 **Sault Ste Marie** USA
51G7 **Saumlaki** Indon
38B2 **Saumur** France
73C4 **Saurimo** Angola
23M2 **Sauteurs** Grenada
41D2 **Sava** *R* Serbia, Yugos
77H2 **Savai'i** *I* Western Samoa
71G4 **Savalou** Benin
45H9 **Savan** *R* Iran
15C2 **Savannah** Georgia, USA
15B1 **Savannah** Tennessee, USA
15C2 **Savannah** *R* USA
55C2 **Savannakhet** Laos
23B3 **Savanna la Mar** Jamaica
4C3 **Savant L** Can
7J4 **Savant Lake** Can
55D2 **Savarane** Laos
71G4 **Savé** Benin
73D6 **Save** *R* Mozam
63C2 **Sāveh** Iran
36D2 **Saverne** France
37B2 **Savigliano** Italy
36B2 **Savigny** France
44G3 **Savinskiy** Russian Fed
37E3 **Savio** *R* Italy
38D2 **Savoie** *Region* France
37C2 **Savona** Italy

32K6 **Savonlinna** Fin
10D3 **Savoonga** USA
37E2 **Savudrija Rtič** *Pt* Croatia, Yugos
32K5 **Savukoski** Fin
57B4 **Savu S** Indon
55A1 **Saw** Burma
57C3 **Sawai** Indon
60D3 **Sawai Mādhopur** India
56B2 **Sawang** Indon
55C2 **Sawankhalok** Thai
54D3 **Sawara** Japan
16A2 **Sawatch Mts** USA
5H3 **Sawbill** Can
10J2 **Sawtooth Mt** USA
18C2 **Sawtooth Range** *Mts* USA
76B2 **Sawu** *I* Indon
14A2 **Saxton** USA
71G3 **Say** Niger
60B1 **Sayghan** Afghan
67G3 **Sayh Hajmah** Oman
67F2 **Sayhūt** Yemen
45H6 **Saykhin** Kazakhstan
50D2 **Saynshand** Mongolia
16C2 **Sayre** Oklahoma, USA
14B2 **Sayre** Pennsylvania, USA
22C2 **Sayula** Mexico
22A1 **Sayulita** Mexico
45J7 **Say-Utes** Kazakhstan
14D2 **Sayville** USA
3C3 **Sayward** Can
42C3 **Sázava** *R* Czech
39C2 **Sbisseb** *R* Alg
35D4 **Scafell Pike** *Mt* Eng
34E1 **Scalloway** Scot
34D2 **Scapa Flow** *Sd* Scot
13D2 **Scarborough** Can
35E4 **Scarborough** Eng
23E4 **Scarborough** Tobago
34B2 **Scarp** *I* Scot
40B1 **Schaffhausen** Switz
42C3 **Scharding** Austria
36D1 **Scharteberg** *Mt* Germany
7M4 **Schefferville** Can
36B1 **Schelde** *R* Belg
19D3 **Schell Creek Range** *Mts* USA
14D1 **Schenectady** USA
16C4 **Schertz** USA
36C1 **Schiedam** Neth
37D2 **Schio** Italy
36D1 **Schleiden** Germany
42B2 **Schleswig** Germany
42B2 **Schleswig Holstein** State, Germany
14C1 **Schoharie** USA
76D1 **Schouten Is** PNG
36E2 **Schramberg** Germany
7K5 **Schreiber** Can
19C3 **Schurz** USA
14C2 **Schuylkill** *R* USA
14B2 **Schuylkill Haven** USA
42B3 **Schwabische Alb** *Upland* Germany
74B2 **Schwarzrand** *R* Namibia
36E2 **Schwarzwald** *Mts* Germany
42B3 **Schwarzwald** *Upland* Germany
10G2 **Schwatka Mts** USA
37D1 **Schwaz** Austria
42C2 **Schweinfurt** Germany
74D2 **Schweizer Reneke** S Africa
42C2 **Schwerin** Germany
37C1 **Schwyz** Switz
40C3 **Sciacca** Italy
35B7 **Scilly Isles** *Is* UK
12C3 **Scioto** *R* USA
11A2 **Scobey** USA
75D2 **Scone** Aust
7Q2 **Scoresby Sd** Greenland
xxxF7 **Scotia Ridge** Atlantic O
xxxF7 **Scotia S** Atlantic O
34C3 **Scotland** Country, UK
79F7 **Scott** *Base* Ant
74E3 **Scottburgh** S Africa
3C3 **Scott,C** Can
16B2 **Scott City** USA
79G6 **Scott I** Ant
7L2 **Scott Inlet** *B* Can
3G2 **Scott L** Can
18B2 **Scott,Mt** USA
76B2 **Scott Reef** Timor S
11B3 **Scottsbluff** USA
15B2 **Scottsboro** USA
75E3 **Scottsdale** Aust
19D4 **Scottsdale** USA
14C2 **Scranton** USA
11C3 **Scribner** USA
37D1 **Scuol** Switz
Scutari = Shkodër
74C3 **Seacow** S Africa
4B2 **Seal** Can
6J4 **Seal** *R* Can
75B3 **Sea Lake** Aust
5K3 **Seal Bight** Can
19D3 **Searchlight** USA
17D2 **Searcy** USA
20D3 **Searles** USA
20B2 **Seaside** California, USA
18B1 **Seaside** Oregon, USA
14C3 **Seaside Park** USA
18B1 **Seattle** USA
57B5 **Seba** Indon
13E2 **Sebago L** USA
56B2 **Sebanga** Indon
20A1 **Sebastopol** USA
58B4 **Sebderat** Eth
43F1 **Sebez** Russian Fed
13F1 **Seboomook L** USA
15E4 **Sebring** USA
37D2 **Secchia** *R* Italy
78A3 **Secretary I** NZ
17D2 **Sedalia** USA
36C2 **Sedan** France
10E5 **Sedanka** *I* USA
78B2 **Seddonville** NZ
65C3 **Sede Boqer** Israel
65C3 **Sederot** Israel
70A3 **Sédhiou** Sen
65C3 **Sedom** Israel
19D4 **Sedona** USA
74B2 **Seeheim** Namibia
79E **Seelig,Mt** Ant
36A2 **Sées** France
71B2 **Sefrou** Mor
78B2 **Sefton,Mt** NZ
55C5 **Segamat** Malay
44E3 **Segezha** Russian Fed
39B2 **Segorbe** Spain
70B3 **Ségou** Mali
Segovia = Coco
39B1 **Segovia** Spain
39C1 **Segre** *R* Spain
10D6 **Seguam** *I* USA
10D6 **Seguam Pass** USA
70B4 **Séguéla** Ivory Coast
70A2 **Seguia el Hamra** *Watercourse* Mor
17C4 **Seguin** USA
28C2 **Segundo** *R* Arg
56E2 **Seguntur** Indon
39B2 **Segura** *R* Spain
60B3 **Sehwan** Pak
16C2 **Seiling** USA
36D2 **Seille** *R* France
32J6 **Seinäjoki** Fin
11D2 **Seine** *R* Can
38C2 **Seine** *R* France
36B2 **Seine-et-Marne** Department, France
36A2 **Seine-Maritime** Department, France
72D4 **Sekenke** Tanz
72D2 **Sek'ot'a** Eth
18B1 **Selah** USA
51G7 **Selaru** *I* Indon
56E4 **Selat Alas** *Str* Indon
56C3 **Selat Bangka** *Str* Indon
56B3 **Selat Berhala** *B* Indon
51G7 **Selat Dampier** *Str* Indon
56C3 **Selat Gaspar** *Str* Indon
56E4 **Selat Lombok** *Str* Indon
56A3 **Selat Mentawi** *Str* Indon
56E4 **Selat Sape** *Str* Indon
57B4 **Selat Sumba** *Str* Indon
56C4 **Selat Sunda** *Str* Indon
57C4 **Selat Wetar** *Chan* Indon
57D3 **Selawati** *I* Indon
10F2 **Selawik** USA
10G2 **Selawik** *R* USA
10F2 **Selawik L** USA
35E5 **Selby** Eng
11B2 **Selby** USA
41F3 **Selçuk** Turk
10H4 **Seldovia** USA
74D1 **Selebi Pikwe** Botswana
53C1 **Selemdzha** *R* Russian Fed
53C1 **Selemdzhinsk** Russian Fed
49O3 **Selennyakh** *R* Russian Fed
36D2 **Selestat** France
7O3 **Selfoss** Iceland
11B2 **Selfridge** USA
72C1 **Selima Oasis** Sudan
43G1 **Selizharovo** Russian Fed
6J4 **Selkirk** Can
34D4 **Selkirk** Scot
3E3 **Selkirk Mts** Can
15B2 **Selma** Alabama, USA
20C2 **Selma** California, USA
15B1 **Selmer** USA
37A1 **Selongey** France
39B2 **Selouane** Mor
10M3 **Selous,Mt** Can
56C3 **Selta Karimata** *Str* Indon
28C1 **Selva** Arg
26D5 **Selvas** Region, Brazil
18C1 **Selway** USA
76D3 **Selwyn** Aust
3H1 **Selwyn L** Can
6E3 **Selwyn Mts** Can
56D4 **Semarang** Indon
44G4 **Semenov** Russian Fed
10A5 **Semichi Is** USA
10G4 **Semidi Is** USA
45F5 **Semiluki** Russian Fed
11A3 **Seminoe Res** USA
17C2 **Seminole** Oklahoma, USA
16B3 **Seminole** Texas, USA
15C2 **Seminole,L** USA
48K4 **Semipalatinsk** Kazakhstan
57F8 **Semirara Is** Phil
63C2 **Semirom** Iran
10B6 **Semisopochnoi** *I* USA
56D2 **Semitau** Indon
63C1 **Semnān** Iran
36C2 **Semois** *R* Belg
22C2 **Sempoala** Hist Site, Mexico
56E2 **Semporna** Malay
26E5 **Sena Madureira** Brazil
73C5 **Senanga** Zambia
17E3 **Senatobia** USA
53E4 **Sendai** Honshū, Japan
53C5 **Sendai** Kyūshū, Japan
60D4 **Sendwha** India
14B1 **Seneca Falls** USA
14B1 **Seneca L** USA
16A3 **Senecu** Mexico
70A3 **Senegal** Republic, Africa
70A3 **Sénégal** *R* Maur/Sen
74D2 **Senekal** S Africa
57B3 **Sengkang** Indon
27L6 **Senhor do Bonfim** Brazil
40C2 **Senigallia** Italy
40D2 **Senj** Croatia, Yugos
50F4 **Senkaku Gunto** *Is* Japan
53C3 **Senlin Shan** *Mt* China
36B2 **Senlis** France
72D2 **Sennar** Sudan
7L5 **Senneterre** Can
36D2 **Senones** France
36B2 **Sens** France
41E1 **Senta** Serbia, Yugos
72C4 **Sentery** Zaïre
3D3 **Sentinel Peak** *Mt* Can
60D4 **Seoni** India
Seoul = Soul
78B2 **Separation Pt** NZ
54A3 **Sep'o** N Korea
55D2 **Sepone** Laos
29A2 **Sepotuba** *R* Brazil
7M4 **Sept-Iles** Can
72B1 **Séquédine** Niger
20C2 **Sequoia Nat Pk** USA
65C1 **Serai** Syria
57C3 **Seram** *I* Indon
56C4 **Serang** Indon
56C2 **Serasan** *I* Indon
41D2 **Serbia** *Republic* Yugos
37D2 **Serchio** *R* Italy
45G5 **Serdobsk** Russian Fed
36B3 **Sereín** *R* France
55C5 **Seremban** Malay
72D4 **Serengeti Nat Pk** Tanz
73D5 **Serenje** Zambia
43F3 **Seret** *R* Ukraine
44H4 **Sergach** Russian Fed
53C3 **Sergeyevka** Russian Fed
48H3 **Sergino** Russian Fed
27L6 **Sergipe** State, Brazil
44F4 **Sergiyev Posad** Georgia
56D2 **Seria** Brunei
56D2 **Serian** Malay
41E3 **Sérifos** *I* Greece
5H2 **Sérigny** *R* Can
37C2 **Serio** *R* Italy
69B2 **Serir Calanscio** *Desert* Libya
36C2 **Sermaize-les-Bains** France
7P3 **Sermilik** Greenland
44J5 **Sernovodsk** Russian Fed
44L4 **Serov** Russian Fed
74D1 **Serowe** Botswana
39A2 **Serpa** Port
44F5 **Serpukhov** Russian Fed
29A3 **Serra Amamba** Par
29B1 **Serra Azul** Brazil
29C3 **Serra da Canastra** *Mts* Brazil
39A1 **Serra da Estrela** *Mts* Port
29C3 **Serra da Mantiqueira** *Mts* Brazil
29B2 **Serra da Mombuca** Brazil
29B2 **Serra das Furnas** *Mts* Brazil
29C1 **Serra de Arrajas** *Mts* Brazil
29B4 **Serra de Fartura** *Mts* Brazil
29A3 **Serra de Maracaju** *Mts* Brazil
29A2 **Serra de São Jeronimo** Brazil
28D1 **Serra do Boquairao** *Mts* Brazil
29D2 **Serra do Cabral** *Mt* Brazil
27G5 **Serra do Cachimbo** *Mts* Brazil
29B2 **Serra do Caiapó** *Mts* Brazil
28E2 **Serra do CanguŞcu** *Mts* Brazil
29B3 **Serra do Cantu** *Mts* Brazil
29D3 **Serra do Caparaó** *Mts* Brazil
27K7 **Serra do Chifre** Brazil
29D2 **Serra do Espinhaço** *Mts* Brazil
28D1 **Serra do Espinilho** *Mts* Brazil
29C2 **Serra do Jibão** *Mts* Brazil
29C3 **Serra do Mar** *Mts* Brazil
29B3 **Serra do Mirante** *Mts* Brazil
27H3 **Serra do Navio** Brazil
29C3 **Serra do Paranapiacaba** *Mts* Brazil
29D1 **Serra do Ramalho** *Mts* Brazil
29B1 **Serra do Roncador** *Mts* Brazil
27G6 **Serra dos Caiabis** *Mts* Brazil
29B3 **Serra dos Dourados** *Mts* Brazil
29D1 **Serra do Sincora** *Mts* Brazil
26F6 **Serra dos Parecis** *Mts* Brazil
29C2 **Serra dos Pilões** *Mts* Brazil
29B2 **Serra do Taquaral** *Mts* Brazil
29B2 **Serra Dourada** *Mts* Brazil
29C1 **Serra Dourada** *Mts* Brazil
28E2 **Serra Encantadas** *Mts* Brazil
27G6 **Serra Formosa** *Mts* Brazil
29D2 **Serra Geral** *Mts* Bahia, Brazil
29B4 **Serra Geral** *Mts* Parona, Brazil
29C1 **Serra Geral de Goiás** *Mts* Brazil
29C2 **Serra Geral do Parana** *Mts* Brazil
41E2 **Sérrai** Greece
21D3 **Serrana Bank** *Is* Caribbean
39B1 **Serrana de Cuenca** *Mts* Spain
16B4 **Serranias del Burro** *Mts* Mexico
29B2 **Serranópolis** Brazil
26F3 **Serra Pacaraima** *Mts* Brazil/Ven
26F3 **Serra Parima** *Mts* Brazil
27H3 **Serra Tumucumaque** Brazil
36B2 **Serre** *R* France
37A2 **Serres** France
28B2 **Serrezuela** Arg
27L6 **Serrinha** Brazil
29D2 **Serro** Brazil
29B3 **Sertanópolis** Brazil
52A3 **Sêrtar** China
57D4 **Serua** *I* Indon
74D1 **Serule** Botswana
56A2 **Seruwai** Indon
56D3 **Seruyan** *R* Indon
53B1 **Seryshevo** Russian Fed
4D3 **Seseganaga L** Can
73B5 **Sesfontein** Namibia
73C5 **Sesheke** Zambia
37B2 **Sestriere** Italy
37C2 **Sestri Levante** Italy
53D3 **Setana** Japan
38C3 **Sète** France
29D2 **Sete Lagoas** Brazil
71D1 **Sétif** Alg
66C4 **Setit** *R* Sudan
54C3 **Seto** Japan
54B4 **Seto Naikai** *S* Japan
71A2 **Settat** Mor
35D4 **Settle** Eng
39A2 **Sêtúbal** Port
37A1 **Seurre** France
45H7 **Sevan, Ozero** *L* Armenia
45E7 **Sevastopol'** Ukraine
7K4 **Severn** *R* Can
35D5 **Severn** *R* Eng
44G3 **Severnaya Dvina** *R* Russian Fed
49L1 **Severnaya Zemlya** *I* Russian Fed
44L3 **Severnyy Sos'va** *R* Russian Fed
44K3 **Severnyy Ural** *Mts* Russian Fed
49M4 **Severo-Baykalskoye Nagorye** *Mts* Russian Fed
45F6 **Severo Donets** *R* Ukraine
44F3 **Severodvinsk** Russian Fed
48H3 **Severo Sos'va** *R* Russian Fed
44L3 **Severoural'sk** Russian Fed
19D3 **Sevier** *R* USA
19D3 **Sevier Desert** USA
19D3 **Sevier L** USA
39A2 **Sevilla** Spain
Seville = Sevilla
41F2 **Sevlievo** Bulg
70A4 **Sewa** *R* Sierra Leone
10J3 **Seward** Alaska, USA
17C1 **Seward** Nebraska, USA
10E2 **Seward Pen** USA
3E2 **Sexsmith** Can
68K8 **Seychelles,Is** Indian O
32C1 **Seyðisfjörður** Iceland
64C2 **Seyhan** Turk
45F5 **Seym** *R* Russian Fed
49R3 **Seymchan** Russian Fed
75C3 **Seymour** Aust
14D2 **Seymour** Connecticut, USA
12B3 **Seymour** Indiana, USA
16C3 **Seymour** Texas, USA
37B2 **Seyne** France
37E2 **Sežana** Slovenia, Yugos
36B2 **Sézanne** France
71E2 **Sfax** Tunisia
41F1 **Sfînto Gheorghe** Rom
42A2 **'s-Gravenhage** Neth
52B3 **Shaanxi** Province, China
72C4 **Shabunda** Zaïre
59F2 **Shache** China
79G9 **Shackleton Ice Shelf** Ant
60B3 **Shadadkot** Pak
63C2 **Shādhām** *R* Iran
20C3 **Shafter** USA
35D6 **Shaftesbury** Eng
71G4 **Shagamu** Nig
4D2 **Shagamu** *R* Can
25J8 **Shag Rocks** *Is* South Georgia
63B2 **Shāhābād** Iran
56F7 **Shah Alam** Malay
65D2 **Shahbā** Syria
63D2 **Shahdap** Iran
61B3 **Shahdol** India
63B1 **Shāhīn Dezh** Iran
63D2 **Shāh Kūh** Iran
63E2 **Shahrak** Afghan
63D2 **Shahr-e Bābak** Iran
Shahresa = Qomisheh
63C2 **Shahr Kord** Iran
45J8 **Shahsavār** Iran
44L3 **Shaim** Russian Fed
62B1 **Shājābād** India
60D3 **Shājahānpur** India
60D4 **Shājāpur** India
53E2 **Shakhtersk** Russian Fed
45G6 **Shakhty** Russian Fed
44H4 **Shakhun'ya** Russian Fed
71G4 **Shaki** Nig
11D3 **Shakopee** USA
54D2 **Shakotan-misaki** *C* Japan
10F3 **Shaktoolik** USA
44K4 **Shamary** Russian Fed
72D3 **Shambe** Sudan
14B2 **Shamokin** USA
16B2 **Shamrock** USA
14C1 **Shandaken** USA
20B3 **Shandon** USA
52D2 **Shandong** Province, China
52C5 **Shangchuan Dao** *I* China
52C1 **Shangdu** China
52E3 **Shanghai** China
52C3 **Shangnan** China
73C5 **Shangombo** Zambia
52D4 **Shangra** China
52B5 **Shangsi** China
52C3 **Shang Xian** China
53B2 **Shangzhi** China
33B3 **Shannon** *R* Irish Rep
3H2 **Shannon L** Can
52D3 **Shanqiu** China
53B3 **Shansonggang** China
50G1 **Shantarskiye Ostrova** *I* Russian Fed
52D5 **Shantou** China
52C2 **Shanxi** Province, China
52D3 **Shan Xian** China
52C5 **Shaoguan** China
52E4 **Shaoxing** China
52C4 **Shaoyang** China
34D2 **Shapinsay** *I* Scot
65D2 **Shaqqā** Syria
67E3 **Shaqqat aj Kharitah** Region, S Arabia
67E1 **Shaqra'** S Arabia
67E4 **Shaqrā'** Yemen
67E3 **Sharawrah** S Arabia
52A1 **Sharhulsan** Mongolia
54D2 **Shari** Japan
63D1 **Sharīfābād** Iran
67G1 **Sharjah** UAE
76A3 **Shark B** Aust
63D1 **Sharlauk** Turkmenistan
65C2 **Sharon,Plain of** Israel
14B3 **Sharpsburg** USA

44H4 **Sharya** Russian Fed
72D3 **Shashamenē** Eth
74D1 **Shashani** *R* Zim
74D1 **Shashe** *R* Botswana
52C3 **Shashi** China
18B2 **Shasta L** USA
18B2 **Shasta,Mt** USA
65D1 **Shathah at Tahtā** Syria
64E3 **Shaṭṭ al Gharrat** *R* Iraq
65C3 **Shaubak** Jordan
3G4 **Shaunavon** Can
20C2 **Shaver L** USA
14C2 **Shawangunk Mt** USA
12B2 **Shawano** USA
17C2 **Shawnee** Oklahoma, USA
11A3 **Shawnee** Wyoming, USA
5G4 **Shawinigan** Can
52D4 **Sha Xian** China
76B3 **Shay Gap** Aust
65D2 **Shaykh Miskīn** Syria
66D4 **Shaykh 'Uthmān** Yemen
44F5 **Shchekino** Russian Fed
45F5 **Shchigry** Russian Fed
45E5 **Shchors** Ukraine
48J4 **Shchuchinsk** Kazakhstan
12B2 **Sheboygan** USA
72E3 **Shebele** *R* Eth
72B3 **Shebshi** *Mts* Nig
53E2 **Shebunino** Russian Fed
5J4 **Shediac** Can
10K2 **Sheenjek** *R* USA
34B4 **Sheep Haven** *Estuary* Irish Rep
35F6 **Sheerness** Eng
5J5 **Sheet Harbour** Can
65C2 **Shefar'am** Israel
15B2 **Sheffield** Alabama, USA
35E5 **Sheffield** Eng
14A2 **Sheffield** Pennsylvania, USA
16B3 **Sheffield** Texas, USA
5K3 **Shekalika Bay** Can
60C2 **Shekhupura** Pak
3C2 **Shelagyote Peak** *Mt* Can
5H5 **Shelburne** Can
14D1 **Shelburne Falls** USA
12B2 **Shelby** Michigan, USA
18D1 **Shelby** Montana, USA
15C1 **Shelby** N Carolina, USA
12B3 **Shelbyville** Indiana, USA
15B1 **Shelbyville** Tennessee, USA
11C3 **Sheldon** USA
10M3 **Sheldon,Mt** Can
5J3 **Sheldrake** Can
10H4 **Shelikof Str** USA
3G3 **Shellbrook** Can
18D2 **Shelley** USA
75D2 **Shellharbour** Aust
78A3 **Shelter Pt** NZ
18B1 **Shelton** USA
64E1 **Shemakha** Azerbaijan
17C1 **Shenandoah** USA
13D3 **Shenandoah** *R* USA
14A3 **Shenandoah Mt** USA
13D3 **Shenandoah Nat Pk** USA
71H4 **Shendam** Nig
66B3 **Shendi** Sudan
44G3 **Shenkursk** Russian Fed
52C2 **Shenmu** China
52E1 **Shenyang** China
52C5 **Shenzhen** China
60D3 **Sheopur** India
43F2 **Shepetovka** Ukraine
14B3 **Shepherdstown** USA
75C3 **Shepparton** Aust
36A1 **Sheppey,I of** Eng
7K2 **Sherard,C** Can
35D6 **Sherborne** Eng
70A4 **Sherbro I** Sierra Leone
5G4 **Sherbrooke** Can
14C1 **Sherburne** USA
66B3 **Shereik** Sudan
60C3 **Shergarh** India
17D3 **Sheridan** Arkansas, USA
11A3 **Sheridan** Wyoming, USA
17C3 **Sherman** USA
3H2 **Sherridon** Can
42B2 **s-Hertogenbosh** Neth
10M4 **Sheslay** Can
3B2 **Sheslay** *R* Can
33C1 **Shetland** *Is* Scot
45J7 **Shevchenko** Kazakhstan
53C1 **Shevli** *R* Russian Fed
11C2 **Sheyenne** USA
11C2 **Sheyenne** *R* USA
63C3 **Sheyk Sho'eyb** *I* Iran
50J2 **Shiashkotan** *I* Russian Fed
60B1 **Shibarghan** Afghan
53D4 **Shibata** Japan
54D2 **Shibetsu** Japan
69C1 **Shibin el Kom** Egypt
65A3 **Shibīn el Qanātir** Egypt
4D3 **Shibogama L** Can
54C3 **Shibukawa** Japan
14B2 **Shickshinny** USA
52C2 **Shijiazhuang** China
60B3 **Shikarpur** Pak
47H4 **Shikoku,I** Japan
54B4 **Shikoku-sanchi** *Mts* Japan
54D2 **Shikotsu-ko** *L* Japan
44G3 **Shilega** Russian Fed
61C2 **Shiliguri** India
50E1 **Shilka** Russian Fed
50E1 **Shilka** *R* Russian Fed
14C2 **Shillington** USA
61D2 **Shillong** India
44G5 **Shilovo** Russian Fed
54B4 **Shimabara** Japan
54C4 **Shimada** Japan
53B1 **Shimanovsk** Russian Fed
53D4 **Shimizu** Japan
54C4 **Shimoda** Japan
62B2 **Shimoga** India
53C5 **Shimonoseki** Japan
54C3 **Shinano** *R* Japan
67G2 **Shināṣ** Oman
63E2 **Shindand** Afghan
14A2 **Shinglehouse** USA
4D4 **Shingleton** USA
53D5 **Shingū** Japan
54D3 **Shinjō** Japan
53D4 **Shinminato** Japan
65D1 **Shinshār** Syria
72D4 **Shinyanga** Tanz
53E4 **Shiogama** Japan
54C4 **Shiono-misaki** *C* Japan
52A5 **Shiping** China
5J4 **Shippegan** Can
14B2 **Shippensburg** USA
16A2 **Shiprock** USA
67E3 **Shiqāq al Ma'āṭīf** Region, Yemen
52B3 **Shiquan** China
54D3 **Shirakawa** Japan
54C3 **Shirane-san** *Mt* Japan
54C3 **Shirani-san** *Mt* Japan
63C3 **Shīraz** Iran
65A3 **Shirbīn** Egypt
54D2 **Shiriya-saki** *C* Japan
63C2 **Shīr Kūh** Iran
54C3 **Shirotori** Japan
63D1 **Shirvān** Iran
10F5 **Shishaldin V** USA
10E2 **Shishmaref** USA
10E2 **Shishmaref Inlet** USA
52B2 **Shitanjing** China
12B3 **Shively** USA
60D3 **Shivpuri** India
65C3 **Shivta** *Hist Site* Israel
19D3 **Shivwits Plat** USA
73D5 **Shiwa Ngandu** Zambia
52C3 **Shiyan** China
52B2 **Shizuishan** China
54C3 **Shizuoka** Japan
41D2 **Shkodër** Alb
43G2 **Shkov** Belorussia
49L1 **Shmidta, Ostrov** *I* Russian Fed
75D2 **Shoalhaven** *R* Aust
54B4 **Shobara** Japan
62B2 **Shoranūr** India
62B1 **Shorāpur** India
19C3 **Shoshone** California, USA
18D2 **Shoshone** Idaho, USA
18E2 **Shoshone** *R* USA
18D2 **Shoshone L** USA
19C3 **Shoshone Mts** USA
18E2 **Shoshoni** USA
45E5 **Shostka** Ukraine
66C4 **Showak** Sudan
19D4 **Show Low** USA
17D3 **Shreveport** USA
35D5 **Shrewsbury** Eng
35D5 **Shropshire** County, Eng
53B2 **Shuangcheng** China
52E1 **Shuanglia** China
53C2 **Shuangyashan** China
45K6 **Shubar-Kuduk** Kazakhstan
5J4 **Shubenacadie** Can
10J2 **Shublik Mts** USA
44N2 **Shuga** Russian Fed
52D2 **Shu He** *R* China
52A4 **Shuicheng** China
60C3 **Shujaabad** Pak
60D4 **Shujālpur** India
53B3 **Shulan** China
50C2 **Shule He** China
10G5 **Shumagin Is** USA
41F2 **Shumen** Bulg
44H4 **Shumerlya** Russian Fed
52D4 **Shuncheng** China
10G2 **Shungnak** USA
52C2 **Shuo Xian** China
63D3 **Shūr Gaz** Iran
73C5 **Shurugwi** Zim
3E3 **Shuswap L** Can
44G4 **Shuya** Russian Fed
10H4 **Shuyak I** USA
61E3 **Shwebo** Burma
55B2 **Shwegyin** Burma
61E3 **Shweli** *R* Burma
63E3 **Siahan Range** *Mts* Pak
60A2 **Siah Koh** *Mts* Afghan
60C2 **Sialkot** Pak
Sian = Xi'an
57G9 **Siarao, I** Phil
57F9 **Siaton** Phil
57C2 **Siau** *I* Indon
43E1 **Šiauliai** Lithuania
44K5 **Sibay** Russian Fed
74E2 **Sibayi L** S Africa
40D2 **Šibenik** Croatia, Yugos
56A3 **Siberut** *I* Indon
60B3 **Sibi** Pak
53C3 **Sibirtsevo** Russian Fed
72B4 **Sibiti** Congo
72D4 **Sibiti** *R* Tanz
41E1 **Sibiu** Rom
11C3 **Sibley** USA
57A2 **Siboa** Indon
56A2 **Sibolga** Indon
61D2 **Sibsāgar** India
56D2 **Sibu** Malay
57F9 **Sibuguay B** Phil
72B3 **Sibut** CAR
56E1 **Sibutu Pass** Malay/Phil
57F8 **Sibuyan** *I* Phil
57F8 **Sibuyan S** Phil
52A3 **Sichuan** Province, China
40C3 **Sicilia** *I* Medit S
40C3 **Sicilian** *Chan* Italy/Tunisia
Sicily = Sicilia
26D6 **Sicuari** Peru
60C4 **Siddhapur** India
62B1 **Siddipet** India
61B3 **Sidhi** India
69B1 **Sidi Barrani** Egypt
71B1 **Sidi bel Abbès** Alg
71A2 **Sidi Kacem** Mor
34D3 **Sidlaw Hills** Scot
79F5 **Sidley,Mt** Ant
18B1 **Sidney** Can
11B2 **Sidney** Montana, USA
16B1 **Sidney** Nebraska, USA
14C1 **Sidney** New York, USA
12C2 **Sidney** Ohio, USA
15C2 **Sidney Lanier,L** USA
Sidon = Säida
29B3 **Sidrolândia** Brazil
43E2 **Siedlce** Pol
36D1 **Sieg** *R* Germany
36D1 **Siegburg** Germany
36D1 **Siegen** Germany
37A1 **Sielle** *R* France
55C3 **Siem Reap** Camb
40C2 **Siena** Italy
36C3 **Siene** *R* France
43D2 **Sierpc** Pol
22C2 **Sierra Andrés Tuxtla** Mexico
28B3 **Sierra Auca Mahuida** *Mts* Arg
16A3 **Sierra Blanca** USA
28B4 **Sierra Blanca** *Mts* Arg
28B4 **Sierra Colorada** Arg
39B1 **Sierra de Albarracin** *Mts* Spain
39B2 **Sierra de Alcaraz** *Mts* Spain
28B1 **Sierra de Ancasti** *Mts* Arg
28B2 **Sierra de Cordoba** *Mts* Arg
28B1 **Sierra de Famantina** *Mts* Arg
39A1 **Sierra de Gredos** *Mts* Spain
39A2 **Sierra de Guadalupe** *Mts* Spain
39B1 **Sierra de Guadarrama** *Mts* Spain
39B1 **Sierra de Guara** *Mts* Spain
39B1 **Sierra de Gudar** *Mts* Spain
22C2 **Sierra de Juárez** *Mts* Mexico
28C3 **Sierra de la Ventana** *Mts* Arg
39C1 **Sierra del Codi** *Mts* Spain
28D1 **Sierra del Imán** *Mts* Arg
28B2 **Sierra del Morro** *Mt* Arg
28B3 **Sierra del Nevado** *Mts* Arg
21B2 **Sierra de los Alamitos** *Mts* Mexico
39B2 **Sierra de los Filabres** *Mts* Spain
22B1 **Sierra de los Huicholes** *Mts* Mexico
22C2 **Sierra de Miahuatlán** *Mts* Mexico
22B1 **Sierra de Morones** *Mts* Mexico
39A2 **Sierra de Ronda** *Mts* Spain
28B2 **Sierra de San Luis** *Mts* Arg
39B2 **Sierra de Segura** *Mts* Spain
22C1 **Sierra de Tamaulipas** *Mts* Mexico
39B1 **Sierra de Urbion** *Mts* Spain
28B2 **Sierra de Uspallata** *Mts* Arg
28B1 **Sierra de Valasco** *Mts* Arg
28B2 **Sierra de Valle Fértil** *Mts* Arg
22B1 **Sierra de Zacatécas** *Mts* Mexico
22C2 **Sierra de Zongolica** *Mts* Mexico
28C2 **Sierra Grande** *Mts* Arg
70A4 **Sierra Leone** Republic, Africa
70A4 **Sierra Leone,C** Sierra Leone
57F7 **Sierra Madre** *Mts* Phil
22B2 **Sierra Madre del Sur** *Mts* Mexico
20B3 **Sierra Madre Mts** USA
21B2 **Sierra Madre Occidental** *Mts* Mexico
22B1 **Sierra Madre Oriental** *Mts* Mexico
28B2 **Sierra Malanzan** *Mts* Arg
8C4 **Sierra Mojada** Mexico
39A2 **Sierra Morena** *Mts* Spain
39B2 **Sierra Nevada** *Mts* Spain
19B3 **Sierra Nevada** *Mts* USA
26D1 **Sierra Nevada de santa Marta** *Mts* Colombia
28B2 **Sierra Pié de Palo** *Mts* Arg
19D4 **Sierra Vista** USA
37B1 **Sierre** Switz
29A3 **Siete Puntas** *R* Par
41E3 **Sifnos** *I* Greece
71B1 **Sig** Alg
44E2 **Sig** Russian Fed
56A3 **Sigep** Indon
43E3 **Sighetu Marmaţiei** Rom
41E1 **Sighişoara** Rom
56A1 **Sigli** Indon
32B1 **Siglufjörður** Iceland
36E2 **Sigmaringen** Germany
26A1 **Siguatepeque** Honduras
39B1 **Sigüenza** Spain
70B3 **Siguiri** Guinea
60D4 **Sihora** India
64D2 **Siirt** Turk
50C3 **Sikai Hu** *L* China
3D2 **Sikanni** *R* Can
60D3 **Sīkar** India
60B2 **Sikaram** *Mt* Afghan
70B3 **Sikasso** Mali
57B4 **Sikeli** Indon
17E2 **Sikeston** USA
41F3 **Sikinos** *I* Greece
41E3 **Sikionía** Greece
61C2 **Sikkim** State, India
49O3 **Siktyakh** Russian Fed
39A1 **Sil** *R* Spain
37D1 **Silandro** Italy
22B1 **Silao** Mexico
57F8 **Silay** Phil
61D3 **Silchar** India
4C2 **Silcox** Can
70C2 **Silet** Alg
61B2 **Silgarhi** Nepal
64B2 **Silifke** Turk
65D1 **Silinfah** Syria
59G2 **Siling Co** *L* China
41F2 **Silistra** Bulg
44A3 **Siljan** *L* Sweden
32F7 **Silkeborg** Den
37E1 **Sillian** Austria
17D2 **Siloam Springs** USA
17D3 **Silsbee** USA
72B2 **Siltou** *Well* Chad
43E1 **Šilute** Lithuania
64D2 **Silvan** Turk
29C2 **Silvania** Brazil
60C4 **Silvassa** India
11D2 **Silver Bay** USA
19C3 **Silver City** Nevada, USA
16A3 **Silver City** New Mexico, USA
18B2 **Silver Lake** USA
20D2 **Silver Peak Range** *Mts* USA
14B3 **Silver Spring** USA
3C3 **Silverthrone Mt** Can
75B2 **Silverton** Aust
16A2 **Silverton** USA
37D1 **Silvretta** *Mts* Austria/Switz
56D2 **Simanggang** Malay
55C1 **Simao** China
63B2 **Simareh** *R* Iran
41F3 **Simav** Turk
41F3 **Simav** *R* Turk
4F5 **Simcoe,L** Can
10G5 **Simeohof** *I* USA
56A2 **Simeulue** *I* Indon
45E7 **Simferopol'** Ukraine
41F3 **Simi** *I* Greece
61B2 **Simikot** Nepal
60D2 **Simla** India
16B2 **Simla** USA
36D1 **Simmern** Germany
20C3 **Simmler** USA
74B3 **Simonstown** S Africa
3C3 **Simoom Sound** Can
38D2 **Simplon** *Mt* Switz
37C1 **Simplon** *P* Switz
6C2 **Simpson,C** USA
76C3 **Simpson Desert** Aust
10N2 **Simpson L** Can
3B2 **Simpson Peak** *Mt* Can
7K3 **Simpson Pen** Can
32G7 **Simrishamn** Sweden
50J2 **Simushir** *I* Russian Fed
56A2 **Sinabang** Indon
72E3 **Sina Dhaqa** Somalia
64B4 **Sinai** *Pen* Egypt
22A1 **Sinaloa** State, Mexico
37D3 **Sinalunga** Italy
26C2 **Sincelejo** Colombia
15C2 **Sinclair,L** USA
60D3 **Sind** *R* India
60B3 **Sindh** *Region* Pak
41F3 **Sindirği** Turk
61C3 **Sindri** India
53E2 **Sinegorsk** Russian Fed
39A2 **Sines** Port
72D2 **Singa** Sudan
55C5 **Singapore** Republic, S E Asia
55C5 **Singapore,Str of** S E Asia
56E4 **Singaraja** Indon
36E3 **Singen** Germany
72D4 **Singida** Tanz
61E2 **Singkaling Hkamti** Burma
56C2 **Singkawang** Indon
75D2 **Singleton** Aust
56B3 **Singtep** *I* Indon
55B1 **Singu** Burma
74E1 **Singuédeze** *R* Mozam
54A3 **Sin'gye** N Korea
54A2 **Sinhŭng** N Korea
40B2 **Siniscola** Sardgena
57B4 **Sinjai** Indon
64D2 **Sinjár** Iraq
60B2 **Sinkai Hills** *Mts* Afghan
66C3 **Sinkat** Sudan
59G1 **Sinkiang** Autonomous Region, China
36E1 **Sinn** *R* Germany
27H2 **Sinnamary** French Guiana
54A3 **Sinnyong** S Korea
64C1 **Sinop** Turk
54A2 **Sinpa** N Korea
54A2 **Sinp'o** N Korea
54A3 **Sinp'yong** N Korea
41E1 **Sîntana** Rom
56D2 **Sintang** Indon
17F4 **Sinton** USA
39A2 **Sintra** Port
26C2 **Sinú** *R* Colombia
53A3 **Sinŭiju** N Korea
43D3 **Siofok** Hung
37B1 **Sion** Switz
11C3 **Sioux City** USA
11C3 **Sioux Falls** USA
4C3 **Sioux Lookout** Can
57F9 **Sipalay** Phil
23L1 **Siparia** Trinidad
53A3 **Siping** China
4B3 **Sipiwesk L** Can
79F3 **Siple** *Base* Ant
79F5 **Siple I** Ant
57F8 **Sipocot** Phil
56A3 **Sipora** Indon
15B2 **Sipsey** *R* USA
22A1 **Siqueros** Mexico
57F9 **Siquijor** *I* Phil
62B2 **Sira** India
40D3 **Siracusa** Italy
61C3 **Sirajganj** Bang
3D3 **Sir Alexander,Mt** Can
71G3 **Sirba** *R* Burkina
67F2 **Sīr Banī Yās** *I* UAE
76C2 **Sir Edward Pellew Group** *Is* Aust
41F1 **Siret** *R* Rom
10N3 **Sir James McBrien,Mt** Can
62B2 **Sir Kālahasti** India
3D3 **Sir Laurier,Mt** Can
64D2 **Şirnak** Turk
60C4 **Sirohi** India
62C1 **Sironcha** India
60D4 **Sironj** India
41E3 **Síros** *I* Greece
20C3 **Sirretta Peak,Mt** USA
63C3 **Sirri** *I* Iran
60C3 **Sirsa** India
3E3 **Sir Sandford,Mt** Can
62A2 **Sirsi** India

69A1 **Sirte Desert** Libya
69A1 **Sirte,G of** Libya
40D1 **Sisak** Croatia, Yugos
55C2 **Sisaket** Thai
4A2 **Sisipuk L** Can
55C3 **Sisophon** Camb
20B3 **Sisquoc** USA
20C3 **Sisquoc** *R* USA
11C2 **Sisseton** USA
71F3 **Sissili** *R* Burkina
36B2 **Sissonne** France
63E2 **Sistan** Region, Iran/Afghan
38D3 **Sisteron** France
49L4 **Sistig Khem** Russian Fed
61B2 **Sītāpur** India
41F3 **Sitía** Greece
29C1 **Sitio d'Abadia** Brazil
6E4 **Sitka** USA
10H4 **Sitkalidak I** USA
10H4 **Sitkinak** *I* USA
55B2 **Sittang** *R* Burma
36C1 **Sittard** Neth
61D3 **Sittwe** Burma
56D4 **Situbondo** Indon
53B1 **Sivaki** Russian Fed
64C2 **Sivas** Turk
64C2 **Siverek** Turk
64B2 **Sivrihisar** Turk
69B2 **Siwa** Egypt
60D2 **Siwalik Range** *Mts* India
61B2 **Siwalik Range** *Mts* Nepal
44G3 **Siya** Russian Fed
52D3 **Siyang** China
42C1 **Sjaelland** *I* Den
32G7 **Skagen** Den
32F7 **Skagerrak** *Str* Nor/Den
18B1 **Skagit** *R* USA
18B1 **Skagit Mt** Can
6E4 **Skagway** USA
14B1 **Skaneateles** USA
14B1 **Skaneateles L** USA
32G7 **Skara** Sweden
43E2 **Skarzysko-Kamlenna** Pol
6F4 **Skeena** *R* Can
3C2 **Skeena Mts** Can
6D3 **Skeenjek** *R* USA
35F5 **Skegness** Eng
44B2 **Skellefte** *R* Sweden
32J6 **Skellefteå** Sweden
41E3 **Skíathos** *I* Greece
6E4 **Skidegate** Can
43E2 **Skiemiewice** Pol
32F7 **Skien** Nor
71D1 **Skikda** Alg
53C5 **Skikoku** *I* Japan
35E5 **Skipton** Eng
41E3 **Skíros** *I* Greece
32F7 **Skive** Den
42B1 **Skjern** Den
7O3 **Skjoldungen** Greenland
12B2 **Skokie** USA
41E3 **Skópelos** *I* Greece
41E2 **Skopje** Macedonia, Yugos
32G7 **Skövde** Sweden
49O4 **Skovorodino** Russian Fed
13F2 **Skowhegan** USA
74E1 **Skukuza** S Africa
6C3 **Skwentna** USA
42D2 **Skwierzyna** Pol
33B2 **Skye** *I* Scot
32G7 **Slagelse** Den
35B5 **Slaney** *R* Irish Rep
41E2 **Slatina** Rom
56D4 **Slaung** Indon
41D1 **Slav Brod** Yugos
6G3 **Slave** *R* Can
3F2 **Slave Lake** Can
43G2 **Slavgorod** Belorussia
48J4 **Slavgorod** Russian Fed
43F2 **Slavuta** Ukraine
45F6 **Slavyansk** Ukraine
34C3 **Sleat,Sound of** *Chan* Scot
4F2 **Sleeper Is** Can
10G3 **Sleetmute** USA
35B5 **Sleeve Bloom** *Mts* Irish Rep
17E3 **Slidell** USA
14C2 **Slide Mt** USA
33B3 **Sligo** Irish Rep
33B3 **Sligo** *B* Irish Rep
41F2 **Sliven** Bulg
19C3 **Sloan** USA
41F2 **Slobozia** Rom
3E4 **Slocan** Can
43F2 **Slonim** Belorussia
35E6 **Slough** Eng
20B2 **Slough** *R* USA
58C1 **Slovenia** *Republic* Yugos
43D3 **Slovensko** Region, Czech
42C2 **Slubice** Pol
43F2 **Sluch'** *R* Ukraine
42D2 **Słupsk** Pol
43F2 **Slutsk** Belorussia
43F2 **Slutsk** *R* Belorussia
33A3 **Slyne Head** *Pt* Irish Rep
49M4 **Slyudyanka** Russian Fed
7M4 **Smallwood Res** Can
70A2 **Smara** Mor
41E2 **Smederevo** Serbia, Yugos
41E2 **Smederevska Palanka** Serbia, Yugos
45E6 **Smela** Ukraine
14A2 **Smethport** USA
53C2 **Smidovich** Russian Fed
53E2 **Smirnykh** Russian Fed
3F2 **Smith** Can
20C1 **Smith** USA
10O2 **Smith Arm** *B* Can
10H1 **Smith B** USA
3C3 **Smithers** Can
15D1 **Smithfield** N Carolina, USA
74D3 **Smithfield** S Africa
18D2 **Smithfield** Utah, USA
7L3 **Smith I** Can
3C2 **Smith River** Can
3C3 **Smith Sd** Can
4F5 **Smiths Falls** Can
75E3 **Smithton** Aust
3E2 **Smoky** *R* Can
16B2 **Smoky** *R* USA
75D2 **Smoky C** Aust
16C2 **Smoky Hills** USA
3F3 **Smoky Lake** Can
18D2 **Smoky Mts** USA
32F6 **Smøla** *I* Nor
44E5 **Smolensk** Russian Fed
41E2 **Smólikas** *Mt* Greece
41E2 **Smolyan** Bulg
3G3 **Smoothstone L** Can
43F2 **Smorgon'** Belorussia
14C3 **Smyrna** Delaware, USA
15C2 **Smyrna** Georgia, USA
35C4 **Snaefell** *Mt* Eng
32B2 **Snafell** *Mt* Iceland
18C1 **Snake** USA
18D2 **Snake** *R* USA
8B2 **Snake River Canyon** USA
18D2 **Snake River Plain** USA
77F5 **Snares** *Is* NZ
42B2 **Sneek** Neth
20B2 **Snelling** USA
42D2 **Sněžka** *Mt* Pol/Czech
32F6 **Snøhetta** *Mt* Nor
18B1 **Snohomish** USA
18B1 **Snoqualmie P** USA
55D3 **Snoul** Camb
3H1 **Snowbird L** Can
35C5 **Snowdon** *Mt* Wales
35C5 **Snowdonia Nat Pk** Wales
6G3 **Snowdrift** Can
19D4 **Snowflake** USA
6H4 **Snow Lake** Can
14B2 **Snow Shoe** USA
75A2 **Snowtown** Aust
18D2 **Snowville** USA
75C3 **Snowy Mts** Aust
16B3 **Snyder** USA
53B5 **Soan-kundo** *I* S Korea
54A3 **Sobaek Sanmaek** *Mts* S Korea
72D3 **Sobat** *R* Sudan
27K4 **Sobral** Brazil
43E2 **Sochaczew** Pol
45F7 **Sochi** Russian Fed
54A3 **Sŏch'on** S Korea
69A2 **Socna** Libya
16A3 **Socorro** USA
21A3 **Socorro** *I* Mexico
28A2 **Socos** Chile
67F4 **Socotra** *I* Yemen
20C3 **Soda L** USA
32K5 **Sodankylä** Fin
18D2 **Soda Springs** USA
32H6 **Soderhamn** Sweden
32H7 **Södertälje** Sweden
72C2 **Sodiri** Sudan
72D3 **Sodo** Eth
14B1 **Sodus Point** USA
57B4 **Soë** Indon
36E1 **Soest** Germany
Sofala = Beira
Sofia = Sofiya
41E2 **Sofiya** Bulg
53C1 **Sofiysk** Russian Fed
44E2 **Sofporog** Russian Fed
50H4 **Sofu Gan** *I* Japan
26D2 **Sogamoso** Colombia
53C1 **Sogda** Russian Fed
32F6 **Sognefjorden** *Inlet* Nor
54A4 **Sŏgwi-ri** S Korea
59H2 **Sog Xian** China
66B1 **Sohâg** Egypt
77E1 **Sohano** PNG
60D3 **Sohīpat** India
36B1 **Soignies** Belg
36B2 **Soissons** France
60C3 **Sojat** India
53A4 **Sŏjosŏn-man** *B* N Korea
54A3 **Sokcho** S Korea
64A2 **Söke** Turk
71G4 **Sokodé** Togo
44G4 **Sokol** Russian Fed
43E2 **Sokołka** Pol
70B3 **Sokolo** Mali
7Q3 **Søkongens Øy** *I* Greenland
71H3 **Sokoto** Nig
71H3 **Sokoto** State, Nig
71G3 **Sokoto** *R* Nig
78A3 **Solander I** NZ
57F7 **Solano** Phil
62B1 **Solapur** India
57B4 **Solar** *I* Indon
37D1 **Solbad Hall** Austria
37D1 **Sölden** Austria
10H3 **Soldotna** USA
23C4 **Soledad** Colombia
20B2 **Soledad** USA
28E1 **Soledade** Brazil
35E6 **Solent** *Sd* Eng
36B1 **Solesmes** France
43F2 **Soligorsk** Belorussia
44K4 **Solikamsk** Russian Fed
45J5 **Sol'Iletsk** Russian Fed
26D4 **Solimões** Peru
36D1 **Solingen** Germany
74B1 **Solitaire** Namibia
32H6 **Sollefteå** Sweden
37B3 **Solliès-Pont** France
36E1 **Solling** Region, Germany
53D1 **Solnenechnyy** Russian Fed
36A3 **Sologne** *R* France
56B3 **Solok** Indon
77E1 **Solomon Is** Pacific O
12A1 **Solon Springs** USA
37B1 **Solothurn** Switz
44F2 **Solovetskiye, Ostrova** *I* Russian Fed
53A1 **Solov'yevsk** Russian Fed
32F8 **Soltau** Germany
20B3 **Solvang** USA
14B1 **Solvay** USA
34D4 **Solway Firth** *Estuary* Scot/Eng
73C5 **Solwezi** Zambia
54D3 **Sōma** Japan
41F3 **Soma** Turk
58C5 **Somalia** Republic, E Africa
xxviiiD4 **Somali Basin** Indian O
41D1 **Sombor** Serbia, Yugos
62E3 **Sombrero Chan** Indian O
22B1 **Sombretete** Mexico
76D2 **Somerset** Aust
35D6 **Somerset** County, Eng
12C3 **Somerset** Kentucky, USA
14E2 **Somerset** Massachusetts, USA
13D2 **Somerset** Pennsylvania, USA
74D3 **Somerset East** S Africa
7J2 **Somerset I** Can
14D1 **Somerset Res** USA
14C3 **Somers Point** USA
14E1 **Somersworth** USA
14C2 **Somerville** USA
17C3 **Somerville Res** USA
41E1 **Somes** *R* Rom
36B2 **Somme** Department, France
36B2 **Somme** *R* France
36C2 **Sommesous** France
26A1 **Somoto** Nic
61B3 **Son** *R* India
53A4 **Sŏnch'ŏn** N Korea
74D3 **Sondags** *R* S Africa
32F8 **Sønderborg** Den
7N3 **Søndre Strømfjord** Greenland
7N2 **Søndre Upernavik** Greenland
37C1 **Sondrio** Italy
55D3 **Song Ba** *R* Viet
55D3 **Song Cau** Viet
54A3 **Sŏngch'on** N Korea
73D5 **Songea** Tanz
54A2 **Songgan** N Korea
53B2 **Songhua Jiang** *R* China
52E3 **Songjiang** China
54A3 **Songjŏng** S Korea
55C4 **Songkhla** Thai
53B4 **Songnim** N Korea
55C5 **Sŏng Pahang** *R* Malay
52A3 **Songpan** China
54A4 **Sŏngsan-ni** S Korea
53B3 **Sonhue Hu** *L* China
52C1 **Sonid Youqi** China
55C1 **Son La** Viet
60B3 **Sonmiani** Pak
60B3 **Sonmiani Bay** Pak
19D4 **Sonoita** Mexico
20A1 **Sonoma** USA
20B2 **Sonora** California, USA
19D4 **Sonora** State, Mexico
16B3 **Sonora** Texas, USA
21A2 **Sonora** *R* Mexico
8B3 **Sonoran Desert** USA
20C1 **Sonora P** USA
21D3 **Sonsonate** El Salvador
51G6 **Sonsorol** *I* Pacific O
9E2 **Soo Canals** USA/Can
3D4 **Sooke** Can
43D2 **Sopot** Pol
42D3 **Sopron** Hung
5K4 **Sop's Arm** Can
20B2 **Soquel** USA
40C2 **Sora** Italy
65C3 **Sored** *R* Israel
5G4 **Sorel** Can
75E3 **Sorell** Aust
37C2 **Soresina** Italy
64C2 **Sorgun** Turk
39B1 **Soria** Spain
32J5 **Sørkjosen** Nor
48C2 **Sørksop** *I* Barents S
45J6 **Sor Mertvyy Kultuk** *Plain* Kazakhstan
29C3 **Sorocaba** Brazil
44J5 **Sorochinsk** Russian Fed
51H6 **Soroi** *I* Pacific O
43F3 **Soroki** Moldavia
54D2 **Soroma-ko** *L* Japan
51G7 **Sorong** Indon
57D3 **Sorong** Province, Indon
72D3 **Soroti** Uganda
32J4 **Sørøya** *I* Nor
40C2 **Sorrento** Italy
32K5 **Sorsatunturi** *Mt* Fin
32H5 **Sorsele** Sweden
57F8 **Sorsogon** Phil
44E3 **Sortavala** Russian Fed
53B4 **Sŏsan** S Korea
43D2 **Sosnowiec** Pol
37B3 **Sospel** France
44L4 **Sos'va** Russian Fed
71G3 **Sota** *R* Benin
22C1 **Soto la Manna** Mexico
72B3 **Souanké** Congo
70B4 **Soubré** Ivory Coast
14C2 **Souderton** USA
23P2 **Soufrière** St Lucia
23N2 **Soufrière** *V* St Vincent
38C3 **Souillac** France
71D1 **Souk Ahras** Alg
71A2 **Souk Larbat Gharb** Mor
53B4 **Soul** S Korea
39C2 **Soummam** *R* Alg
Sour = Tyr
74D2 **Sources,Mt aux** Lesotho
11B2 **Souris** Manitoba, Can
5J4 **Souris** Prince Edward I, Can
11B2 **Souris** *R* USA/Can
27L5 **Sousa** Brazil
71E1 **Sousse** Tunisia
73C7 **South Africa** Republic, Africa
14C2 **South Amboy** USA
4E5 **Southampton** Can
35E6 **Southampton** Eng
14D2 **Southampton** USA
7K3 **Southampton I** Can
62E2 **South Andaman** *I* Indian O
7M4 **South Aulatsivik I** Can
76C3 **South Australia** State, Aust
xxviiiH6 **South Australian Basin** Indian O
17E3 **Southaven** USA
16A3 **South Baldy** *Mt* USA
15E4 **South Bay** USA
12C1 **South Baymouth** Can
12B2 **South Bend** Indiana, USA
18B1 **South Bend** Washington, USA
13D3 **South Boston** USA
4E5 **South Branch** USA
14E1 **Southbridge** USA
South Cape = Ka Lae
9E3 **South Carolina** State, USA
51E5 **South China S** S E Asia
8C2 **South Dakota** State, USA
14D1 **South Deerfield** USA
35E6 **South Downs** Eng
75E3 **South East C** Aust
10E3 **Southeast C** USA
xxixO7 **South East Pacific Basin** Pacific O
3H2 **Southend** Can
35F6 **Southend-on-Sea** Eng
78A2 **Southern Alps** *Mts* NZ
76A4 **Southern Cross** Aust
4B2 **Southern Indian L** Can
15D1 **Southern Pines** USA
23H2 **Southfield** Jamaica
xxixK6 **South Fiji Basin** Pacific O
35F6 **South Foreland** *Pt* Eng
16A2 **South Fork** USA
10H3 **South Fork** *R* Alaska, USA
20B1 **South Fork** *R* California, USA
20B1 **South Fork American** *R* USA
20C3 **South Fork Kern** *R* USA
24G9 **South Georgia** *I* S Atlantic O
35D6 **South Glamorgan** County, Wales
12B2 **South Haven** USA
6J3 **South Henik L** Can
13D3 **South Hill** USA
xxviiiJ3 **South Honshu Reige** Pacific O
78A2 **South I** NZ
14D2 **Southington** USA
4B2 **South Knife** *R* Can
53B4 **South Korea** Republic, S E Asia
19B3 **South Lake Tahoe** USA
xxviiiD6 **South Madagascar Ridge** Indian O
79G8 **South Magnetic Pole** Ant
15E4 **South Miami** USA
14B3 **South Mt** USA
6F3 **South Nahanni** *R* Can
23G1 **South Negril Pt** Jamaica
xxxF8 **South Orkney** *Is* Atlantic O
24B5 **South Pacific O**
16B1 **South Platte** *R* USA
79E **South Pole** Ant
12C1 **South Porcupine** Can
35D5 **Southport** Eng
23Q2 **South Pt** Barbados
14C2 **South River** USA
34D2 **South Ronaldsay** *I* Scot
xxxG7 **South Sandwich Trench** Atlantic O
20A2 **South San Francisco** USA
3G3 **South Saskatchewan** *R* Can
4B2 **South Seal** *R* Can
34E4 **South Shields** Eng
78B1 **South Taranaki Bight** *B* NZ
4F3 **South Twin I** Can
34B3 **South Uist** *I* Scot
76D5 **South West C** Aust
10D3 **Southwest C** USA
xxviiiD6 **South West Indian Ridge** Indian O
xxixM6 **South West Pacific Basin** Pacific O
xxxD5 **South West Peru Ridge** Pacific O
35E5 **South Yorkshire** County, Eng
74D1 **Soutpansberg** *Mts* S Africa
43E1 **Sovetsk** Russian Fed
53E2 **Sovetskaya Gavan'** Russian Fed
44L3 **Sovetskiy** Russian Fed
74D2 **Soweto** S Africa
54D1 **Sōya-misaki** *C* Japan
73B4 **Soyo Congo** Angola
43G2 **Sozh** *R* Belorussia
36C1 **Spa** Belg
39 **Spain** Kingdom, Europe
Spalato = Split
35E5 **Spalding** Eng
12C1 **Spanish** *R* Can
19D2 **Spanish Fork** USA
23B3 **Spanish Town** Jamaica
19C3 **Sparks** USA
12A2 **Sparta** USA
15C2 **Spartanburg** USA
41E3 **Spartí** Greece
53C3 **Spassk Dal'niy** Russian Fed
11B3 **Spearfish** USA
16B2 **Spearman** USA
23Q2 **Speightstown** Barbados
10J3 **Spenard** USA
11C3 **Spence** Iowa, USA
12B3 **Spencer** Indiana, USA
7J3 **Spencer Bay** Can
75A3 **Spencer,C** Aust
75A2 **Spencer G** Aust
7L3 **Spencer Is** *Is* Can
78B2 **Spenser Mts** NZ
34B4 **Sperrin** *Mts* N Ire
36E2 **Spessart** Region, Germany
34D3 **Spey** *R* Scot
42B3 **Speyer** Germany
23K1 **Speyside** Tobago
37B1 **Spiez** Switz
10K2 **Spike Mt** USA
37E1 **Spilimbergo** Italy
18C1 **Spirir Lake** USA
6G4 **Spirit River** Can
Spitsbergen = Svalbard
48C2 **Spitsbergen, I** Barents S
42C3 **Spittal** Austria
37E1 **Spittal an der Drau** Austria
32F6 **Spjelkavik** Nor
40D2 **Split** Croatia, Yugos

4B2 **Split L** Can
37C1 **Splügen** Switz
18C1 **Spokane** USA
12A1 **Spooner** USA
41F3 **Sporádhes** *Is* Greece
18C2 **Spray** USA
42C2 **Spree** *R* Germany
74B2 **Springbok** S Africa
5K4 **Springdale** Can
17D2 **Springdale** USA
16B2 **Springer** USA
19E4 **Springerville** USA
16B2 **Springfield** Colorado, USA
12B3 **Springfield** Illinois, USA
14D1 **Springfield** Massachusetts, USA
11C3 **Springfield** Minnesota, USA
17D2 **Springfield** Missouri, USA
12C3 **Springfield** Ohio, USA
18B2 **Springfield** Oregon, USA
15B1 **Springfield** Tennessee, USA
13E2 **Springfield** Vermont, USA
74D3 **Springfontein** S Africa
5J4 **Springhill** Can
19C3 **Spring Mts** USA
74D2 **Springs** S Africa
14A1 **Springville** New York, USA
19D2 **Springville** Utah, USA
14B1 **Springwater** USA
18D2 **Spruce Mt** USA
35F5 **Spurn Head** *C* Eng
33D3 **Spurn Head** *Pt* Eng
18B1 **Spuzzum** Can
3D4 **Squamish** Can
49R3 **Sredhekolymsk** Russian Fed
49S4 **Sredinnyy Khrebet** *Mts* Russian Fed
44F5 **Sredne-Russkaya Vozvyshennost'** *Upland* Russian Fed
49M3 **Sredne Sibirskoye Ploskogorye** *Tableland* Russian Fed
44K4 **Sredniy Ural** *Mts* Russian Fed
55D3 **Srepok** *R* Camb
50E1 **Sretensk** Russian Fed
55C3 **Sre Umbell** Camb
62C1 **Srīkākulam** India
59G5 **Sri Lanka** Republic, S Asia
60C2 **Srīnagar** Pak
62A1 **Srīvardhan** India
42D2 **Sroda** Pol
34C2 **Stack Skerry** *I* Scot
42B2 **Stade** Germany
34B3 **Staffa** *I* Scot
35D5 **Stafford** County, Eng
35D5 **Stafford** Eng
14D2 **Stafford Springs** USA
Stalingrad = Volgograd
3D2 **Stalin,Mt** Can
74B3 **Stallberg** *Mt* S Africa
7J1 **Stallworthy,C** Can
43E2 **Stalowa Wola** Pol
14D2 **Stamford** Connecticut, USA
14C1 **Stamford** New York, USA
16C3 **Stamford** Texas, USA
74B1 **Stampriet** Namibia
74D2 **Standerton** S Africa
12C2 **Standish** USA
18D1 **Stanford** USA
74E2 **Stanger** S Africa
20B2 **Stanislaus** *R* USA
41E2 **Stanke Dimitrov** Bulg
75E3 **Stanley** Aust
25E8 **Stanley** Falkland Is
18D2 **Stanley** Idaho, USA
11B2 **Stanley** N Dakota, USA
62B2 **Stanley Res** India
Stanleyville = Kisangani
21D3 **Stann Creek** Belize
50F1 **Stanovoy Khrebet** *Mts* Russian Fed
37C1 **Stans** Switz
75D1 **Stanthorpe** Aust
34B3 **Stanton Banks** *Sand-bank* Scot
16B1 **Stapleton** USA
43E2 **Starachowice** Pol
41E2 **Stara Planiná** *Mts* Bulg
44E4 **Staraya Russa** Russian Fed
41F2 **Stara Zagora** Bulg
42D2 **Stargard** Pol
17E3 **Starkville** USA
42C3 **Starnberg** Germany
43D2 **Starogard Gdanski** Pol
43F3 **Starokonstantinov** Ukraine
35D6 **Start Pt** Eng
45F5 **Staryy Oskol** Russian Fed
14B2 **State College** USA
14C2 **Staten I** USA
15C2 **Statesboro** USA
15C1 **Statesville** USA
13D3 **Staunton** USA
32F7 **Stavanger** Nor
36C1 **Stavelot** Belg
45G6 **Stavropol'** Russian Fed
75B3 **Stawell** Aust
42D2 **Stawno** Pol
18B2 **Stayton** USA
16A1 **Steamboat Springs** USA
10F3 **Stebbins** USA
10K3 **Steele,Mt** Can
14B2 **Steelton** USA
3E2 **Steen** *R* Can
3E2 **Steen River** Can
18C2 **Steens Mt** USA
7N2 **Steenstrups Gletscher** *Gl* Greenland
6H2 **Stefansson I** Can
74E2 **Stegi** Swaziland
37D1 **Steinach** Austria
4B4 **Steinbach** Can
32G6 **Steinkjer** Nor
74B2 **Steinkopf** S Africa
3D3 **Stein Mt** Can
74C2 **Stella** S Africa
5J4 **Stellarton** Can
74B3 **Stellenbosch** S Africa
22C2 **Stemaco** Mexico
36C2 **Stenay** France
42C2 **Stendal** Germany
45H8 **Stepanakert** Azerbaijan
11C2 **Stephen** USA
78B2 **Stephens,C** NZ
75B2 **Stephens Creek** Aust
12B1 **Stephenson** USA
10M4 **Stephens Pass** USA
7N5 **Stephenville** Can
16C3 **Stephenville** USA
10F4 **Stepovak B** USA
74D3 **Sterkstroom** S Africa
16B1 **Sterling** Colorado, USA
12B2 **Sterling** Illinois, USA
16C2 **Sterling** Kansas, USA
11B2 **Sterling** N Dakota, USA
16B3 **Sterling City** USA
12C2 **Sterling Heights** USA
44K5 **Sterlitamak** Russian Fed
3F3 **Stettler** Can
12C2 **Steubenville** USA
4B3 **Stevenson L** Can
12B2 **Stevens Point** USA
6D3 **Stevens Village** USA
3B2 **Stewart** Can
19C3 **Stewart** USA
10L3 **Stewart** *R* Can
10L3 **Stewart Crossing** Can
78A3 **Stewart I** NZ
77F1 **Stewart Is** Solomon Is
6E3 **Stewart River** Can
14B3 **Stewartstown** USA
11D3 **Stewartville** USA
74D2 **Steyn** S Africa
74D3 **Steynsburg** S Africa
42C3 **Steyr** Austria
74C3 **Steytlerville** S Africa
37D3 **Stia** Italy
10L4 **Stika** USA
3B2 **Stikine** *R* Can
10M4 **Stikine Ranges** *Mts* Can
11D2 **Stillwater** Minnesota, USA
17C2 **Stillwater** Oklahoma, USA
19C3 **Stillwater Range** *Mts* USA
4E4 **Stimson** Can
16B2 **Stinett** USA
75A2 **Stirling** Aust
34D3 **Stirling** Scot
36E3 **Stockach** Germany
14D1 **Stockbridge** USA
42D3 **Stockerau** Austria
32H7 **Stockholm** Sweden
35D5 **Stockport** Eng
20B2 **Stockton** California, USA
35E4 **Stockton** Eng
16C2 **Stockton** Kansas, USA
17D2 **Stockton L** USA
35D5 **Stoke-on-Trent** Eng
4E4 **Stokes Bay** Can
32A2 **Stokkseyri** Iceland
32G5 **Stokmarknes** Nor
49P2 **Stolbovoy, Ostrov** *I* Russian Fed
32K8 **Stolbtsy** Belorussia
43F2 **Stolin** Belorussia
14C3 **Stone Harbor** USA
34D3 **Stonehaven** Scot
17C3 **Stonewall** USA
10H3 **Stony** *R* USA
5K3 **Stony I** Can
3J2 **Stony L** Can
4E3 **Stooping** *R* Can
32H5 **Storavan** *L* Sweden
32G6 **Støren** Nor
75E3 **Storm B** Aust
11C3 **Storm Lake** USA
34B2 **Stornoway** Scot
43F3 **Storozhinets** Ukraine
14D2 **Storrs** USA
32G6 **Storsjön** *L* Sweden
32H5 **Storuman** Sweden
11A3 **Story** USA
3H4 **Stoughton** Can
14E1 **Stoughton** USA
36A1 **Stour** *R* Eng
35F5 **Stowmarket** Eng
53C1 **Stoyba** Russian Fed
34B4 **Strabane** N Ire
75E3 **Strahan** Aust
42C2 **Stralsund** Germany
74B3 **Strand** S Africa
32F6 **Stranda** Nor
32H7 **Strängnäs** Sweden
34C4 **Stranraer** Scot
38D2 **Strasbourg** France
13D3 **Strasburg** USA
20C2 **Stratford** California, USA
4E5 **Stratford** Can
14D2 **Stratford** Connecticut, USA
78B1 **Stratford** NZ
16B2 **Stratford** Texas, USA
35E5 **Stratford-on-Avon** Eng
75A3 **Strathalbyn** Aust
34C4 **Strathclyde** Region, Scot
3F3 **Strathmore** Can
13E1 **Stratton** USA
12B2 **Streator** USA
37C2 **Stresa** Italy
40D3 **Stretto de Messina** *Str* Italy/Sicily
40D3 **Stroboli** *I* Italy
28C4 **Stroeder** Arg
34D2 **Stromness** Scot
32D3 **Strømø** Faroes
17C1 **Stromsburg** USA
32H6 **Stromsund** Sweden
32G6 **Ströms Vattudal** *L* Sweden
34D2 **Stronsay** *I* Scot
35D6 **Stroud** Eng
14C2 **Stroudsburg** USA
41E2 **Struma** *R* Bulg
35C5 **Strumble Head** *Pt* Wales
41E2 **Strumica** Macedonia, Yugos
43E3 **Stryy** Ukraine
43E3 **Stryy** *R* Ukraine
75B1 **Strzelecki Creek** *R* Aust
15E4 **Stuart** Florida, USA
11C3 **Stuart** Nebraska, USA
3D3 **Stuart** *R* Can
10F3 **Stuart I** USA
3D3 **Stuart L** Can
37D1 **Stubaier Alpen** *Mts* Austria
32H8 **Stubice** Pol
55D3 **Stung Sen** Camb
55D3 **Stung Treng** Camb
4C2 **Stupart** *R* Can
40B2 **Stura** *R* Italy
79G7 **Sturge I** Ant
12B2 **Sturgeon Bay** USA
4F4 **Sturgeon Falls** Can
4C4 **Sturgeon L** Can
12B3 **Sturgis** Kentucky, USA
12B2 **Sturgis** Michigan, USA
11B3 **Sturgis** S Dakota, USA
76B2 **Sturt Creek** *R* Aust
75B1 **Sturt Desert** Aust
74D3 **Stuttemeim** S Africa
17D3 **Stuttgart** USA
42B3 **Stuttgart** Germany
32A1 **Stykkishólmur** Iceland
43F2 **Styr'** *R* Ukraine
49M4 **Styudyanka** Russian Fed
29D2 **Suaçui Grande** *R* Brazil
66C3 **Suakin** Sudan
54A3 **Suan** N Korea
52E5 **Su-ao** Taiwan
28C2 **Suardi** Arg
56C2 **Subi** *I* Indon
41D1 **Subotica** Serbia, Yugos
45D6 **Suceava** Rom
22C2 **Suchixtepec** Mexico
26E7 **Sucre** Bol
29B2 **Sucuriú** R, Brazil
72C2 **Sudan** Republic, Africa
4E4 **Sudbury** Can
35F5 **Sudbury** Eng
72C3 **Sudd** *Swamp* Sudan
27G2 **Suddie** Guyana
65B4 **Sudr** Egypt
72C3 **Sue** *R* Sudan
10M4 **Suemez I** USA
64B4 **Suez** Egypt
64B3 **Suez Canal** Egypt
64B4 **Suez,G of** Egypt
14C2 **Suffern** USA
35F5 **Suffolk** County, Eng
13D3 **Suffolk** USA
13E2 **Sugarloaf Mt** USA
75D2 **Sugarloaf Pt** Aust
3H3 **Suggi L** Can
49R3 **Sugoy** *R* Russian Fed
67G2 **Suhār** Oman
50D1 **Sühbaatar** Mongolia
60B3 **Sui** Pak
53C2 **Suibin** China
52C2 **Suide** China
53C3 **Suifenhe** China
53B2 **Suihua** China
53B2 **Suileng** China
52B3 **Suining** China
36C2 **Suippes** France
33B3 **Suir** *R* Irish Rep
52C3 **Sui Xian** China
52E1 **Suizhong** China
60C3 **Sujāngarth** India
56C4 **Sukabumi** Indon
56D3 **Sukadana** Borneo, Indon
56C4 **Sukadana** Sumatra, Indon
53E4 **Sukagawa** Japan
56D3 **Sukaraya** Indon
44F5 **Sukhinichi** Russian Fed
44G4 **Sukhona** *R* Russian Fed
45G7 **Sukhumi** Georgia
7N3 **Sukkertoppen** Greenland
7N3 **Sukkertoppen Isflade** *Gl* Greenland
32L6 **Sukkozero** Russian Fed
60B3 **Sukkur** Pak
62C1 **Sukma** India
53D2 **Sukpay** *R* Russian Fed
73B6 **Sukses** Namibia
54B4 **Sukumo** Japan
3D2 **Sukunka** *R* Can
45F5 **Sula** *R* Russian Fed
60B3 **Sulaiman Range** *Mts* Pak
34B2 **Sula Sgeir** *I* Scot
57B3 **Sulawesi** *I* Indon
57B3 **Sulawesi Sulatan** Prov, Indon
57B3 **Sulawesi Tengah** Prov, Indon
57B3 **Sulawesi Tenggara** Prov, Indon
57B3 **Sulawesi Utara** Prov, Indon
64E3 **Sulaymānīyah** Iraq
71H4 **Suleja** Nig
34C2 **Sule Skerry** *I* Scot
41F1 **Sulina** Rom
32H5 **Sulitjelma** Nor
26B4 **Sullana** Peru
17D2 **Sullivan** USA
3C3 **Sullivan Bay** Can
3F3 **Sullivan L** Can
36B3 **Sully-sur-Loire** France
40C2 **Sulmona** Italy
17D3 **Sulphur** Louisiana, USA
17C3 **Sulphur** Oklahoma, USA
17C3 **Sulphur Springs** USA
4E4 **Sultan** Can
45E8 **Sultan Dağlari** *Mts* Turk
61B2 **Sultānpur** India
57F9 **Sulu Arch** Phil
51E6 **Sulu S** Philip
36E2 **Sulz** Germany
25D3 **Sumampa** Arg
56A2 **Sumatera** *I* Indon
57B4 **Sumba** *I* Indon
56E4 **Sumbawa** *I* Indon
56E4 **Sumbawa Besar** Indon
73D4 **Sumbawanga** Tanz
34E2 **Sumburgh Head** *Pt* Scot
56D4 **Sumenep** Indon
45H7 **Sumgait** Azerbaijan
73B5 **Sumbe** Angola
50H3 **Sumisu** *I* Japan
3E4 **Summerland** Can
5J4 **Summerside** Can
3B2 **Summer Str** USA
6F4 **Summit Lake** Can
19C3 **Summits Mt** USA
78B2 **Sumner,L** NZ
54B4 **Sumoto** Japan
15C2 **Sumter** USA
45E5 **Sumy** Ukraine
18D1 **Sun** *R* USA
54D2 **Sunagawa** Japan
54A3 **Sunan** N Korea
14B2 **Sunbury** USA
28C2 **Sunchales** Arg
28C1 **Suncho Corral** Arg
53B4 **Sunch'ŏn** N Korea
53B5 **Sunch'ŏn** S Korea
11B3 **Sundance** USA
61B3 **Sundargarh** India
61C3 **Sunderbans** *Swamp* India
34E4 **Sunderland** Eng
3F3 **Sundre** Can
13D1 **Sundridge** Can
32H6 **Sundsvaall** Sweden
56E3 **Sungaianyar** Indon
56B3 **Sungaisalak** Indon
56F6 **Sungai Siput** Malay
56F6 **Sungei Petani** Malay
57A4 **Sungguminasa** Indon
18C1 **Sunnyside** USA
19B3 **Sunnyvale** USA
12B2 **Sun Prairie** USA
49N3 **Suntar** Russian Fed
63E3 **Suntsar** Pak
18D2 **Sun Valley** USA
53B2 **Sunwu** China
71F4 **Sunyani** Ghana
44E3 **Suojarvi** Russian Fed
54B4 **Suō-nada** *B* Japan
32K6 **Suonejoki** Fin
61C2 **Supaul** India
19D4 **Superior** Arizona, USA
17C1 **Superior** Nebraska, USA
12A1 **Superior** Wisconsin, USA
12B1 **Superior,L** USA/Can
55C3 **Suphan Buri** Thai
64D2 **Süphan Dağ** Turk
51G7 **Supiori** *I* Indon
57C2 **Supu** Indon
66D3 **Sūq 'Abs** Yemen
64E3 **Suq ash Suyukh** Iraq
65D1 **Suqaylibīyah** Syria
52D3 **Suqian** China
Suqutra = Socotra
67G2 **Sūr** Oman
44H5 **Sura** *R* Russian Fed
56D4 **Surabaya** Indon
54C4 **Suraga-wan** *B* Japan
56D4 **Surakarta** Indon
65D1 **Sūrān** Syria
75C1 **Surat** Aust
60C4 **Sūrat** India
60C3 **Sūratgarh** India
55B4 **Surat Thani** Thai
60C4 **Surendranagar** India
14C3 **Surf City** USA
48J3 **Surgut** Russian Fed
62B1 **Suriāpet** India
38D2 **Sürich** Switz
57G9 **Surigao** Phil
55C3 **Surin** Thai
27G3 **Surinam** Republic, S America
20B2 **Sur,Pt** USA
35E6 **Surrey** County, Eng
37C1 **Sursee** Switz
69A1 **Surt** Libya
32A2 **Surtsey** *I* Iceland
56B3 **Surulangan** Indon
37B2 **Susa** Italy
54B4 **Susa** Japan
54B4 **Susaki** Japan
19B2 **Susanville** USA
37D1 **Süsch** Switz
10J3 **Susitna** *R* USA
14C2 **Susquehanna** USA
14B3 **Susquehanna** *R* USA
14C2 **Sussex** USA
35E6 **Sussex West** Eng
3C2 **Sustut Peak** *Mt* Can
74C3 **Sutherland** S Africa
16B1 **Sutherland** USA
60C2 **Sutlej** *R* Pak
19B3 **Sutter Creek** USA
12C3 **Sutton** USA
4E3 **Sutton** *R* Can
54D2 **Suttsu** Japan
10G4 **Sutwik I** USA
77G2 **Suva** Fiji
53D4 **Suwa** Japan
43E2 **Suwałki** Pol
15C3 **Suwannee** *R* USA
65C2 **Suweilih** Jordan
53B4 **Suwŏn** S Korea
52D3 **Su Xian** China
54C3 **Suzaka** Japan
52E3 **Suzhou** China
53D4 **Suzu** Japan
54C4 **Suzuka** Japan
54C3 **Suzu-misaki** *C* Japan
48C2 **Svalbard** *Is* Barents S
43E3 **Svalyava** Ukraine
7N2 **Svartenhuk Halvø** *Region* Greenland
32G5 **Svartisen** *Mt* Nor
55D3 **Svay Rieng** Camb
32G6 **Sveg** Sweden
32G7 **Svendborg** Den
7J1 **Sverdrup Chan** Can
6H2 **Sverdrup Is** Can
53D2 **Svetlaya** Russian Fed
43E2 **Svetlogorsk** Russian Fed
32K6 **Svetogorsk** Russian Fed
41E2 **Svetozarevo** Serbia, Yugos
41F2 **Svilengrad** Bulg
43F2 **Svir'** Belrussia
44E3 **Svir'** *R* Russian Fed
42D3 **Švitavy** Czech
53B1 **Svobodnyy** Russian Fed
32G5 **Svolvaer** Nor
77E3 **Swain Reefs** Aust
77H2 **Swains** *I* American Samoa
15C2 **Swainsboro** USA
74B1 **Swakop** *R* Namibia

74A1 Swakopmund Namibia
35E4 Swale R Eng
56D1 Swallow Reef I S E Asia
62B2 Swāmihalli India
21D3 Swan I Honduras
35E6 Swanage Eng
75B3 Swan Hill Aust
3E3 Swan Hills Can
3E3 Swan Hills Mts Can
23A3 Swan I Caribbean
4A3 Swan L Can
6H4 Swan River Can
35D6 Swansea Wales
35D6 Swansea B Wales
74C3 Swartberge Mts S Africa
74D2 Swartruggens S Africa
4E4 Swastika Can
Swatow = Shantou
74E2 Swaziland Kingdom, S Africa
32G7 Sweden Kingdom, N Europe
71F4 Swedru Ghana
18B2 Sweet Home USA
16B3 Sweetwater USA
11A3 Sweetwater R USA
74C3 Swellendam S Africa
42D2 Świdnica Pol
42D2 Swidwin Pol
42D2 Swiebodzin Pol
43D2 Swiecie Pol
3G3 Swift Current Can
11A1 Swift Current Creek R Can
3B1 Swift River Can
35E6 Swindon Eng
42C2 Świnoujście Pol
38D2 Switzerland Federal Republic, Europe
35B5 Swords Irish Rep
32D3 Syderø Faroes
75D2 Sydney Aust
7M5 Sydney Can
11D1 Sydney L Can
5J4 Sydney Mines Can
44J3 Syktyvkar Russian Fed
15B2 Sylacauga USA
32G6 Sylarna Mt Sweden
61D3 Sylhet Bang
42B1 Sylt I Germany
12C2 Sylvania USA
3D2 Sylvia,Mt Can
22B1 Symon Mexico
79G11 Syowa Base Ant
Syracuse = Siracusa
16B2 Syracuse Kansas, USA
14B1 Syracuse New York, USA
13D2 Syracuse USA
48H5 Syrdar'ya R Kazakhstan
64C2 Syria Republic, S W Asia
44L4 Sysert' Russian Fed
44H5 Syzran' Russian Fed
42C2 Szczecin Pol
42D2 Szczecinek Pol
43E2 Szczytno Pol
43E3 Szeged Hung
43D3 Székesfehérvar Hung
43D3 Szekszard Hung
43D3 Szolnok Hung
42D3 Szombathely Hung
42D2 Szprotawa Pol

T

74D3 Tabankulu S Africa
76E1 Tabar Is PNG
63D2 Tabas Iran
22B1 Tabasco Mexico
22D2 Tabasco State, Mexico
26E4 Tabatinga Brazil
70B2 Tabelbala Alg
55C3 Tabeng Camb
3F4 Taber Can
57F8 Tablas I Phil
74B3 Table Mt S Africa
10K2 Table Mt USA
17D2 Table Rock Res USA
56C3 Taboali Indon
42C3 Tábor Czech
72D4 Tabora Tanz
44L4 Tabory Russian Fed
70B4 Tabou Ivory Coast
71D1 Taboursouk Tunisia
63B1 Tabrīz Iran
64C4 Tabūk S Arabia
22B2 Tacámbaro Mexico
59G1 Tacheng China
57G8 Tacloban Phil
26D7 Tacna Peru
19D4 Tacna USA
8A2 Tacoma USA
14D1 Taconic Range USA
28E2 Tacuan R Urug
28D2 Tacuarembó Urug
29A3 Tacuati Par
72E2 Tadjoura Djibouti
66D4 Tadjoura,G of Djibouti
4B2 Tadoule L Can
5H4 Tadoussac Can
62B2 Tādpatri India
53B4 Taebaek Sanmaek Mts S Korea
54A3 Taech'on S Korea
54A3 Taedong R N Korea
54A3 Taegang-got Pen N Korea
53B4 Taegu S Korea
53B5 Taehūksan I S Korea
54A2 Taehung N Korea
53B4 Taejŏn S Korea
56G7 Taesek Dampar L Malay
39B1 Tafalla Spain
70C2 Tafasaset Watercourse Alg
35D6 Taff R Wales
65C3 Tafila Jordan
20C3 Taft USA
45F6 Taganrog Russian Fed
70A3 Tagant Region, Maur
61E3 Tagaung Burma
57F9 Tagbilaran Phil
3B2 Tagish L Can
37E1 Tagliamento R Italy
70B2 Taguenout Hagguerete Well Maur
77E2 Tagula I Solomon Is
57G9 Tagum Phil
Tagus = Tejo
70C2 Tahat, Mt Alg
xxixM5 Tahiti I Pacific O
63E3 Tahlab R Iran
17C2 Tahlequah USA
19B3 Tahoe City USA
19B3 Tahoe,L USA
16B3 Tahoka USA
70C3 Tahoua Niger
66B1 Tahta Egypt
57C2 Tahulandang I Indon
57C2 Tahuna Indon
52D2 Tai'an China
52B3 Taibai Shan Mt China
52D1 Taibus Qi China
52E5 T'ai-chung Taiwan
78B3 Taieri R NZ
52C2 Taihang Shan China
78C1 Taihape NZ
52E3 Tai Hu L China
54D2 Taiki Japan
53A2 Tailai China
56A3 Taileleo Indon
75A3 Tailem Bend Aust
34C3 Tain Scot
52E5 T'ai-nan Taiwan
29D2 Taiobeiras Brazil
52E5 T'ai pei Taiwan
55D2 Taiping Malay
54D3 Taira Japan
56B3 Tais Indon
54B3 Taisha Japan
25B7 Taitao,Pen de Chile
52E5 T'ai-tung Taiwan
32K5 Taivelkoski Fin
50F4 Taiwan Republic, China
Taiwan Haixia = Formosa Str
65C3 Taiyiba Jordan
52C2 Taiyuan China
52D3 Taizhou China
66D4 Ta 'izz Yemen
59E2 Tajikistan Republic Asia
39B1 Tajo R Spain
55B2 Tak Thai
53D4 Takada Japan
54B4 Takahashi Japan
78B2 Takaka NZ
53C5 Takamatsu Japan
53D4 Takaoka Japan
78B1 Takapuna NZ
53D4 Takasaki Japan
54C3 Takayama Japan
66C4 Takazie R Eth
53D4 Takefu Japan
56A2 Takengon Indon
55C3 Takeo Camb
54B4 Takeo Japan
Take-shima = Tok-do
63B1 Takestān Iran
54B4 Taketa Japan
54D2 Takikawa Japan
54D2 Takinoue Japan
6G3 Takiyvak L Can
72D2 Takkaze R Eth
3C2 Takla L Can
3C2 Takla Landing Can
10F3 Takslesluk L USA
3B2 Taku R Can
10M3 Taku Arm R Can
3B2 Taku Gl USA
71J4 Takum Nig
22B1 Tala Mexico
43D3 Talabanya Hung
57C3 Talaga Indon
60C2 Talagang Pak
28A2 Talagante Chile
62B3 Talaimannar Sri Lanka
70C3 Talak Desert, Region, Niger
56B3 Talangbetutu Indon
26B4 Talara Peru
76E1 Talasea PNG
65B3 Talata Egypt
39A1 Talavera de la Reina Spain
28A3 Talca Chile
28A3 Talcahuano Chile
61C3 Tālcher India
53A1 Talden Russian Fed
59F1 Taldy Kurgan Kazakhstan
57B3 Taliabu Indon
60B1 Taligan Afghan
72D3 Tali Post Sudan
56E4 Taliwang Indon
10H3 Talkeetna USA
10J3 Talkeetna Mts USA
65A3 Talkha Egypt
15B2 Talladega USA
64D2 Tall 'Afar Iraq
15C2 Tallahassee USA
37B2 Tallard France
65D1 Tall Bīsah Syria
44C4 Tallinn Estonia
64C3 Tall Kalakh Syria
17D3 Tallulah USA
50B1 Tal'menka Russian Fed
45E6 Tal'noye Ukraine
43E2 Talpaki Russian Fed
25B3 Taltal Chile
75C1 Talwood Aust
11D3 Tama USA
56E2 Tamabo Range Mts Malay
71F4 Tamale Ghana
70C2 Tamanrasset Alg
70C2 Tamanrasset Watercourse Alg
14C2 Tamaqua USA
Tamatave = Toamasina
22A1 Tamazula Durango, Mexico
22B2 Tamazula Jalisco, Mexico
22C2 Tamazulapán Mexico
22C1 Tamazunchale Mexico
70A3 Tambacounda Sen
28D2 Tambores Urug
45G5 Tambov Russian Fed
39A1 Tambre R Spain
57B3 Tambu Indon
72C3 Tambura Sudan
70A3 Tamchaket Maur
39A1 Tamega R Port
22C1 Tamiahua Mexico
62B2 Tamil Nādu State, India
55D2 Tam Ky Viet
15C3 Tampa USA
15E4 Tampa B USA
32J6 Tampere Fin
22C1 Tampico Mexico
56G7 Tampin Malay
50E2 Tamsagbulag Mongolia
37E1 Tamsweg Austria
61D3 Tamu Burma
22C1 Tamuis Mexico
75D2 Tamworth Aust
35E5 Tamworth Eng
44D1 Tana Nor
72D2 Tana L Eth
72E4 Tana R Kenya
32K5 Tana R Nor/Fin
54C4 Tanabe Japan
32K4 Tanafjord Inlet Nor
10C6 Tanaga I USA
56E3 Tanahgrogot Indon
57B4 Tanahjampea I Indon
51G7 Tanahmerah Indon
57A4 Tanakeke I Indon
10H2 Tanana USA
10J3 Tanana R USA
Tananarive = Antananarivo
10C6 Tananga Pass USA
37C2 Tanaro R Italy
53B3 Tanch'ŏn N Korea
28D3 Tandil Arg
56C2 Tandjong Datu Pt Indon
51G7 Tandjung d'Urville C Indon
56A1 Tandjung Jambuair C Indon
56E3 Tandjung Layar C Indon
56C3 Tandjung Lumut C Indon
56E2 Tandjung Mangkalihet C Indon
56D3 Tandjung Sambar C Indon
56D2 Tandjung Sirik C Malay
51G7 Tandjung Vals C Indon
60B3 Tando Adam Pak
60B3 Tando Muhammad Khan Pak
75B2 Tandou L Aust
62B1 Tāndūr India
78C1 Taneatua NZ
53C5 Tanega-shima I Japan
55B2 Tanen Range Mts Burma/Thai
70B2 Tanezrouft Desert Region Alg
63D3 Tang Iran
72D4 Tanga Tanz
77E1 Tanga Is PNG
72C4 Tanganyika,L Tanz/Zaïre
71A1 Tanger Mor
59H2 Tanggula Shan Mts China
Tangier = Tanger
54A3 Tangjin S Korea
56B2 Tangjungpinang Indon
56G7 Tangkak Malay
59G2 Tangra Yumco L China
52D2 Tangshan China
57F9 Tangub Phil
50D1 Tanguy Russian Fed
53B2 Tangwang He R China
53B2 Tangyuan China
57F9 Tanjay Phil
56D4 Tanjong Bugel C Indon
56C4 Tanjong Cangkuang C Indon
56F7 Tanjong Malim Malay
56D3 Tanjong Puting C Indon
56D3 Tanjong Selatan C Indon
56E3 Tanjung Indon
56A2 Tanjungbalai Indon
57C3 Tanjungbaliha Indon
56B3 Tanjung Jabung Pt Indon
57A4 Tanjung Karossa Indon
57A2 Tanjung Manimbaya Pt Indon
56C3 Tanjungpandan Indon
56C4 Tanjung Priok Indon
56E2 Tanjungredeb Indon
76A1 Tanjung Selatan Pt Indon
56E2 Tanjungselor Indon
57B2 Tanjung Torawitan C Indon
76C1 Tanjung Vals Pt Indon
60C2 Tank Pak
77F2 Tanna I Vanuatu
50C1 Tannu Ola Mts Russian Fed
71F4 Tano R Ghana
70C3 Tanout Niger
22C1 Tanquián Mexico
52E4 Tan-shui Taiwan
61B2 Tansing Nepal
69C1 Tanta Egypt
70A2 Tan-Tan Mor
6B3 Tanunak USA
54A3 Tanyang S Korea
72D4 Tanzania Republic, Africa
53A2 Tao'an China
53A2 Tao'er He R China
52A3 Tao He R China
73E6 Taolañaro Madag
52B2 Taole China
16A2 Taos USA
71B2 Taounate Mor
71B2 Taourirt Mor
44D4 Tapa Estonia
21C3 Tapachula Mexico
56F6 Tapah Malay
27G4 Tapajós R Brazil
56A2 Tapaktuan Indon
28C3 Tapalquén Arg
56B3 Tapan Indon
22D2 Tapanatepec Mexico
78A3 Tapanui NZ
26E5 Tapauá R Brazil
28E2 Tapes Brazil
60D4 Tapi R India
61C2 Taplejung Nepal
71G3 Tapoa R Burkina
13D3 Tappahannock USA
78B2 Tapuaeniku Mt NZ
29C3 Tapuaritinga Brazil
57F9 Tapul Group Is Phil
26F4 Tapurucuara Brazil
29B2 Taquari R Brazil
75D1 Tara Aust
48J4 Tara Russian Fed
48J4 Tara R Russian Fed
41D2 Tara R Bosnia & Herzegovina/Montenegro, Yugos
71J4 Taraba R Nig
71J4 Taraba State Nig
26F7 Tarabuco Bol
Tarābulus = Tripoli Libya
Tarābulus esh Shām = Tripoli Leb
39B1 Taracón Spain
78C1 Taradale NZ
56E2 Tarakan Indon
57B4 Taramana Indon
34B3 Taransay I Scot
40D2 Taranto Italy
26C5 Tarapoto Peru
38C2 Tarare France
78C2 Tararua Range Mts NZ
44H2 Tarasovo Russian Fed
70C2 Tarat Alg
78C1 Tarawera NZ
39B1 Tarazona Spain
34D3 Tarbat Ness Pen Scot
60C2 Tarbela Res Pak
34C4 Tarbert Strathclyde, Scot
34B3 Tarbert Western Isles, Scot
38B3 Tarbes France
15D1 Tarboro USA
76C4 Tarcoola Aust
75C2 Tarcoon Aust
48H4 Tarda Russian Fed
53D2 Tardoki Yani, Gora Mt Russian Fed
75D2 Taree Aust
70A2 Tarfaya Mor
18D2 Targhee P USA
69A1 Tarhūnah Libya
67F2 Tarīf UAE
26F8 Tarija Bol
62B2 Tarīkere India
67E3 Tarīm Yemen
72D4 Tarime Tanz
59G1 Tarim He R China
59G2 Tarim Pendi Basin China
60B2 Tarin Kut Afghan
74D3 Tarkastad S Africa
17C1 Tarkio USA
44J3 Tarko Sale Russian Fed
71F4 Tarkwa Ghana
57F7 Tarlac Phil
26C6 Tarma Peru
38C3 Tarn R France
43E2 Tarnobrzeg Pol
43E3 Tarnów Pol
37C2 Taro R Italy
76D3 Taroom Aust
70B1 Taroudannt Morocco
39C1 Tarragona Spain
75E3 Tarraleah Aust
39C1 Tarrasa Spain
14D2 Tarrytown USA
64B2 Tarsus Turk
34E2 Tartan Oilfield N Sea
37D2 Tartaro R Italy
44D4 Tartu Estonia
64C3 Tartūs Syria
29D2 Tarumirim Brazil
56A2 Tarutung Indon
37E1 Tarvisio Italy
13D1 Taschereau Can
58D1 Tashauz Turkmenistan
61D2 Tashigang Bhutan
59E1 Tashkent Uzbekistan
63E1 Tashkepri Turkmenistan
48K4 Tashtagol Russian Fed
49K4 Tashtyp Russian Fed
56C4 Tasikmalaya Indon
65C2 Tasīl Syria
5H2 Tasiujaq Can
7N2 Tasiussaq Greenland
72B2 Tasker Well Niger
78B2 Tasman B NZ
76D5 Tasmania I Aust
78B2 Tasman Mts NZ
75E3 Tasman Pen Aust
77E4 Tasman S NZ Aust
64C1 Taşova Turk
70C2 Tassili du Hoggar Desert, Region, Alg
70C2 Tassili N'jjer Desert, Region, Alg
70B2 Tata Mor
71E2 Tataouine Tunisia
48J4 Tatarsk Russian Fed
44H4 Tatarskaya Respublika, Russian Fed
53E2 Tatarskiy Proliv Str Russian Fed
54C3 Tateyama Japan
3E1 Tathlina L Can
66D3 Tathlith S Arabia
10J3 Tatitlek USA
3D3 Tatla Lake Can
7J4 Tatnam, Cape Can
43D3 Tatry Mts Pol/Czech
54B4 Tatsuno Japan
60B4 Tatta Pak
29C3 Tatuí Brazil
16B3 Tatum USA
64D2 Tatvan Turk
77H2 Ta'u I American Samoa
27K5 Tauá Brazil
29C3 Taubaté Brazil
36E1 Taufstein Mt Germany
78C1 Taumarunui NZ
74C2 Taung S Africa
55B2 Taungdwingyi Burma
55B1 Taung-gyi Burma
55A2 Taungup Burma
60C2 Taunsa Pak
35D6 Taunton Eng
14E2 Taunton USA
36E1 Taunus Region, Germany

78C1 **Taupo** NZ
78C1 **Taupo,L** NZ
43E1 **Taurage** Lithuania
78C1 **Tauranga** NZ
78C1 **Tauranga Harbour** *B* NZ
78B1 **Tauroa Pt** NZ
7J3 **Tavani** Can
48H4 **Tavda** *R* Russian Fed
77H2 **Taveuni** *I* Fiji
39A2 **Tavira** Port
35C6 **Tavistock** Eng
55B3 **Tavoy** Burma
55B3 **Tavoy Pt** Burma
64A2 **Tavsanli** Turk
78B2 **Tawa** NZ
17C3 **Tawakoni,L** USA
12C2 **Tawas City** USA
56E2 **Tawau** Malay
72C2 **Taweisha** Sudan
57F9 **Tawitawi** *I* Phil
57F9 **Tawitawi Group** *Is* Phil
22C2 **Taxco** Mexico
22C2 **Taxcoco** Mexico
34D3 **Tay** *R* Scot
56D3 **Tayan** Indon
72E3 **Tayeeglow** Somalia
10F2 **Taylor** Alaska, USA
3D2 **Taylor** Can
12C2 **Taylor** Michigan, USA
17C3 **Taylor** Texas, USA
16A2 **Taylor,Mt** USA
12B3 **Taylorville** USA
66C1 **Taymā'** S Arabia
49L3 **Taymura** *R* Russian Fed
49M2 **Taymyr, Ozero** *L* Russian Fed
49L2 **Taymyr, Poluostrov** *Pen* Russian Fed
55D3 **Tay Ninh** Viet
22A1 **Tayoltita** Mexico
49L4 **Tayshet** Russian Fed
50C2 **Tayshir** Mongolia
34D3 **Tayside** Region, Scot
57E8 **Taytay** Phil
63E2 **Tayyebāt** Iran
71B2 **Taza** Mor
54D3 **Tazawako** Japan
54D3 **Tazawa-ko** *L* Japan
3G2 **Tazin L** Can
69B2 **Tazirbu** Libya
10J3 **Tazlina L** USA
48J3 **Tazovskiy** Russian Fed
45G7 **Tbilisi** Georgia
71G4 **Tchaourou** Benin
72B4 **Tchibanga** Gabon
72B1 **Tchigai,Plat du** Niger
70C3 **Tchin Tabaradene** Niger
72B3 **Tcholliré** Cam
43D2 **Tczew** Pol
22A1 **Teacapán** Mexico
78A3 **Te Anau** NZ
78A3 **Te Anua,L** NZ
78C1 **Te Aroha** NZ
78C1 **Te Awamutu** NZ
71D1 **Tébessa** Alg
56A2 **Tebingtinggi** Indon
22B2 **Teboman** Mexico
22B2 **Tecailtlān** Mexico
19C4 **Tecate** Mexico
22B1 **Tecclotlán** Mexico
44L4 **Techa** *R* Russian Fed
22B2 **Tečpan** Mexico
22A1 **Tecuala** Mexico
41F1 **Tecuci** Rom
17C1 **Tecumseh** USA
58E2 **Tedzhen** Turkmenistan
48H6 **Tedzhen** *R* Turkmenistan
35E4 **Tees** *R* Eng
26F4 **Tefé** Brazil
56C4 **Tegal** Indon
56C4 **Tegineneng** Indon
21D3 **Tegucigalpa** Honduras
20C3 **Tehachapi** USA
20C3 **Tehachapi Mts** USA
19C3 **Tehachapi P** USA
6J3 **Tehek L** Can
57C3 **Tehoru** Indon
63C1 **Tehrān** Iran
22C2 **Tehuacán** Mexico
22C2 **Tehuantepec** Mexico
22C2 **Tehuitzingo** Mexico
35C5 **Teifi** *R* Wales
39A2 **Tejo** *R* Port
20C3 **Tejon P** USA
22B2 **Tejupilco** Mexico
11C3 **Tekamah** USA
78B2 **Tekapo,L** NZ
59F1 **Tekeli** Kazakhstan
64A1 **Tekirdağ** Turk
41F2 **Tekir Dağlari** *Mts* Turk
61D3 **Teknaf** Bang
57B3 **Teku** Indon
78C1 **Te Kuiti** NZ
21D3 **Tela** Honduras
45H7 **Telavi** Georgia
65C2 **Tel Aviv Yafo** Israel
3B2 **Telegraph Creek** Can
28B3 **Telén** Arg
19C3 **Telescope Peak** *Mt* USA
27G5 **Teles Pires** *R* Brazil
37D1 **Telfs** Austria
49K4 **Teli** Russian Fed
45F9 **Telkalakh** Syria
65C3 **Tell el Meise** *Mt* Jordan
10E2 **Teller** USA
62B2 **Tellicherry** India
55C5 **Telok Anson** Malay
57C2 **Tělok Buli** *B* Indon
56E2 **Tělok Darvel** Malay
57B2 **Tělok Dondo** *B* Indon
51G7 **Tělok Flamingo** *B* Indon
57C2 **Tělok Kau** *B* Indon
56D3 **Tělok Kumai** *B* Indon
56E1 **Tělok Labuk** *B* Malay
56C4 **Tělok Pelabuanratu** *B* Indon
56E4 **Tělok Saleh** *B* Indon
56D3 **Tělok Sampit** *B* Indon
56C3 **Tělok Sukadona** *B* Indon
22C2 **Teloloapán** Mexico
43E1 **Telziai** Lithuania
56D3 **Telukbatang** Indon
51G7 **Teluk Berau** *B* Indon
56C4 **Telukbetung** Indon
57B3 **Teluk Bone** *B* Indon
51G7 **Teluk Cendrawasih** *B* Indon
56A2 **Telukdalam** Indon
57A3 **Teluk Mandar** *B* Indon
57B3 **Teluk Tolo** *B* Indon
57B3 **Teluk Tomini** *B* Indon
57C2 **Tĕluk Weda** *B* Indon
71F4 **Tema** Ghana
4E4 **Temagami,L** Can
22C2 **Temascal** Mexico
56B3 **Tembesi** *R* Indon
56B3 **Tembilahan** Indon
23E5 **Temblador** Ven
20B3 **Temblor Range** *Mts* USA
55C5 **Temerloh** Malay
48G5 **Temir** Kazakhstan
48J4 **Temirtau** Kazakhstan
13F1 **Témiscouata,L** Can
4F4 **Témiscaming** Can
75C2 **Temora** Aust
19D4 **Tempe** USA
17C3 **Temple** USA
35B5 **Templemore** Irish Rep
20B3 **Templeton** USA
22C1 **Tempoal** Mexico
28A3 **Temuco** Chile
78B2 **Temuka** NZ
26C4 **Tena** Ecuador
62C1 **Tenāli** India
22C2 **Tenancingo** Mexico
55B3 **Tenasserim** Burma
35C6 **Tenby** Wales
25D2 **Tenco** *R* Par
66D4 **Tendaho** Eth
37B2 **Tende** France
37B2 **Tende** *P* Italy
62E3 **Ten Degree Chan** Indian O
71B2 **Tendrara** Mor
72B2 **Ténéré** *Desert Region* Niger
70A2 **Tenerife** *I* Canary Is
71C1 **Ténès** Alg
16A2 **Tenessee P** USA
55B1 **Teng** *R* Burma
48H4 **Tengiz, Ozero** *L* Kazakhstan
56E3 **Tenggarong** Indon
52A2 **Tengger Shamo** *Desert* China
62B3 **Tenkāsi** India
73C5 **Tenke** Zaïre
71F3 **Tenkodogo** Burkina
37E3 **Tenna** *R* Italy
76C2 **Tennant Creek** Aust
9E3 **Tennessee** State, USA
17E2 **Tennessee** *R* USA
28A2 **Teno** Chile
56E1 **Tenom** Malay
21C3 **Tenosique** Mexico
71A2 **Tensift** *R* Mor
57B3 **Tentena** Indon
75D1 **Tenterfield** Aust
15E4 **Ten Thousand Is** USA
22B1 **Teocaltiche** Mexico
29D2 **Teófilo Otôni** Brazil
22C2 **Teotihiucan** Hist Site, Mexico
22C2 **Teotitlan** Mexico
57C4 **Tepa** Indon
22B1 **Tepatitlan** Mexico
21B2 **Tepehuanes** Mexico
22C2 **Tepeji** Mexico
22B1 **Tepic** Mexico
42C2 **Teplice** Czech
78C1 **Te Puke** NZ
22B1 **Tequila** Mexico
22C2 **Tequistepec** Mexico
39C1 **Ter** *R* Spain
70C3 **Téra** Niger
54C3 **Teradomari** Japan
40C2 **Teramo** Italy
70A1 **Terceira** *I* Açores
43F3 **Terebovlya** Ukraine
29B2 **Terenoz** Brazil
27K5 **Teresina** Brazil
29D3 **Teresópolis** Brazil
62E3 **Teressa** *I* Indian O
56G7 **Teriang** Malay
64C1 **Terme** Turk
58E2 **Termez** Uzbekistan
40C2 **Termoli** Italy
57C2 **Ternate** Indon
53D3 **Terney** Russian Fed
40C2 **Terni** Italy
43F3 **Ternopol** Ukraine
20C3 **Terra Bella** USA
3C3 **Terrace** Can
12B1 **Terrace Bay** Can
40C2 **Terracina** Italy
73C6 **Terrafirma** S Africa
79G8 **Terre Adélie** Region, Ant
17D4 **Terre Bonne B** USA
12B3 **Terre Haute** USA
17C3 **Terrell** USA
5L4 **Terrenceville** Can
11A2 **Terry** USA
42B2 **Terschelling** *I* Neth
39B1 **Teruel** Spain
6C2 **Teshekpuk** USA
71G4 **Teshi** *R* Nig
54D2 **Teshikaga** Japan
53E3 **Teshio** *R* Japan
54D2 **Teshio dake** *Mt* Japan
50C2 **Tesiyn Gol** *Mts* Mongolia
10M3 **Teslin** Can
10M4 **Teslin** *R* Can
10M3 **Teslin L** Can
49L5 **Teslyn Gol** *R* Mongolia
70C2 **Tessalit** Mali
70C3 **Tessaoua** Niger
71A2 **Tessaout** *R* Mor
66C3 **Tessenei** Eth
73D5 **Tete** Mozam
22B2 **Tetela** Mexico
43F2 **Teterev** *R* Ukraine
18D1 **Teton** *R* USA
18D2 **Teton Range** *Mts* USA
71A1 **Tetouan** Mor
44H5 **Tetyushi** Russian Fed
26F8 **Teuco** *R* Arg
22B1 **Teúl de Gonzalez Ortega** Mexico
57C4 **Teun** *I* Indon
54D2 **Teuri-tō** *I* Japan
40C2 **Tevere** *R* Italy
34D4 **Teviot** *R* Scot
48J4 **Tevriz** Russian Fed
78A3 **Te Waewae B** NZ
56D3 **Tewah** Indon
75D1 **Tewantin** Aust
52A3 **Têwo** China
17D3 **Texarkana** USA
17D3 **Texarkana,L** USA
75D1 **Texas** Aust
8C3 **Texas** State, USA
17D4 **Texas City** USA
42A2 **Texel** *I* Neth
16B2 **Texhoma** USA
17C3 **Texoma,L** USA
74D2 **Teyateyaneng** Lesotho
60A2 **Teyuarah** Afghan
22C2 **Teziutlán** Mexico
29B2 **Tezouro** Brazil
61D2 **Tezpur** India
55C1 **Tha** Laos
74D2 **Thabana Ntlenyana** *Mt* Lesotho
74D2 **Thaba Putsoa** *Mt* Lesotho
74D1 **Thabazimbi** S Africa
55B3 **Thagyettaw** Burma
55D1 **Thai Binh** Viet
55C2 **Thailand** Kingdom, S E Asia
55C3 **Thailand,G of** Thai
55D1 **Thai Nguyen** Viet
55D2 **Thakhek** Laos
60C2 **Thal** Pak
55C4 **Thale Luang** *L* Thai
75C1 **Thallon** Aust
67F3 **Thamarit** Oman
78C1 **Thames** NZ
35F6 **Thames** *R* Eng
67E3 **Thamūd** Yemen
62A1 **Thāne** India
55D2 **Thanh Hoah** Viet
62B2 **Thanjavur** India
36D3 **Thann** France
60C3 **Thar Desert** India
75B1 **Thargomindah** Aust
61E4 **Tharrawaddy** Burma
41E2 **Thásos** *I* Greece
55B2 **Thaton** Burma
55A2 **Thayetmyo** Burma
61E3 **Thazi** Burma
11B3 **Thedford** USA
67F1 **The Gulf** S W Asia
3G1 **Thekulthili L** Can
6H3 **Thelon** *R* Can
36A1 **The Naze** Eng
76E3 **Theodore** Aust
19D4 **Theodore Roosevelt L** USA
41E2 **Thermaïkós Kólpos** *G* Greece
18E2 **Thermopolis** USA
6F2 **Thesiger B** Can
4E4 **Thessalon** Can
41E2 **Thessaloníki** Greece
35F5 **Thetford** Eng
5G4 **Thetford Mines** Can
74D2 **Theunissen** S Africa
17D4 **Thibodaux** USA
6J4 **Thicket Portage** Can
11C2 **Thief River Falls** USA
18B2 **Thielsen,Mt** USA
38C2 **Thiers** France
70A3 **Thiès** Sen
72D4 **Thika** Kenya
61C2 **Thimphu** Bhutan
38D2 **Thionville** France
41F3 **Thira** *I* Greece
35E4 **Thirsk** Eng
62B3 **Thiruvananthapuram** India
32F7 **Thisted** Den
41E3 **Thívai** Greece
38C2 **Thiviers** France
3G1 **Thoa** *R* Can
20C2 **Thomas A Eddison,L** USA
15C2 **Thomaston** Georgia, USA
13F2 **Thomaston** Maine, USA
35B5 **Thomastown** Irish Rep
15B2 **Thomasville** Alabama, USA
15C2 **Thomasville** Georgia, USA
15D1 **Thomasville** N Carolina, USA
7J2 **Thom Bay** Can
6J4 **Thompson** Can
17D1 **Thompson** USA
18C1 **Thompson Falls** USA
6G3 **Thompson Landing** Can
3D3 **Thompson** *R* Can
14D2 **Thompsonville** USA
15C2 **Thomson** USA
76D3 **Thomson** *R* Aust
55C3 **Thon Buri** Thai
55B2 **Thongwa** Burma
37B1 **Thonon-les-Bains** France
16A2 **Thoreau** USA
34D4 **Thornhill** Scot
38B2 **Thouars** France
13D2 **Thousand Is** Can/USA
18D1 **Three Forks** USA
3F3 **Three Hills** Can
77G4 **Three Kings Is** NZ
12B1 **Three Lakes** USA
55B2 **Three Pagodas P** Thai
20C2 **Three Rivers** California, USA
12B2 **Three Rivers** Michigan, USA
17F4 **Three Rivers** Texas, USA
18B2 **Three Sisters** *Mt* USA
7M2 **Thule** Greenland
37B1 **Thun** Switz
4D4 **Thunder Bay** Can
10F2 **Thunder Mt** USA
37B1 **Thuner See** *L* Switz
55B4 **Thung Song** Thai
37C1 **Thur** *R* Switz
42C2 **Thüringen** State, Germany
42C2 **Thüringen Wald** *Upland* Germany
35B5 **Thurles** Irish Rep
51H8 **Thursday I** Aust
34D2 **Thurso** Scot
79F4 **Thurston I** Ant
37C1 **Thusis** Switz
75B1 **Thylungra** Aust
52B5 **Tiandong** China
52B5 **Tian'e** China
52D2 **Tianjin** China
52B5 **Tianlin** China
53B3 **Tianqiaoling** China
52B3 **Tianshui** China
52A2 **Tianzhu** China
71C1 **Tiaret** Alg
29B3 **Tibagi** *R* Brazil
71J4 **Tibati** Cam
65C2 **Tiberias** Israel
65C2 **Tiberias,L** Israel
Tiber,R = Tevere,R
18D1 **Tiber Res** USA
72B1 **Tibesti** *Mountain Region* Chad
59G2 **Tibet** Autonomous Region, China
75B1 **Tibooburra** Aust
61B2 **Tibrikot** Nepal
21A2 **Tiburón** *I* Mexico
70B3 **Tichitt** Maur
70A2 **Tichla** Mor
37C2 **Ticino** *R* Italy/Switz
13E2 **Ticonderoga** USA
21D2 **Ticul** Mexico
70A3 **Tidjikja** Maur
37C1 **Tiefencastel** Switz
36C1 **Tiel** Neth
53B2 **Tieli** China
53A3 **Tieling** China
36B1 **Tielt** Belg
36C1 **Tienen** Belg
36E3 **Tiengen** Germany
48J5 **Tien Shan** *Mts* China/Kirgizia
52D2 **Tientsin** China
32H6 **Tierp** Sweden
28A1 **Tierra Amarilla** Chile
16A2 **Tierra Amarilla** USA
22C2 **Tierra Blanca** Mexico
22C2 **Tierra Colorada** Mexico
25C8 **Tierra del Fuego** Territory, Arg
24C9 **Tierra del Fuego** *I* Chile/Arg
29C3 **Tietê** Brazil
29B3 **Tiete** *R* Brazil
12C2 **Tiffin** USA
15C2 **Tifton** USA
57C3 **Tifu** Indon
10F5 **Tigalda** *I* USA
49R4 **Tigil** Russian Fed
71J4 **Tignere** Cam
5J4 **Tignish** Can
26C4 **Tigre** *R* Peru
26F2 **Tigre** *R* Ven
64E3 **Tigris** *R* Iraq
22C1 **Tihuatlán** Mexico
19C4 **Tijuana** Mexico
60D4 **Tikamgarh** India
44E4 **Tikhin** Russian Fed
45G6 **Tikhoretsk** Russian Fed
77F2 **Tikopia** *I* Solomon Is
64D3 **Tikrīt** Iraq
49O2 **Tiksi** Russian Fed
57B2 **Tilamuta** Indon
36C1 **Tilburg** Neth
35F6 **Tilbury** Eng
25C2 **Tilcara** Arg
75B1 **Tilcha** Aust
55A1 **Tilin** Burma
70C3 **Tillabéri** Niger
18B1 **Tillamook** USA
62E3 **Tillanchong** *I* Indian O
70C3 **Tillia** Niger
41F3 **Tilos** *I* Greece
75B2 **Tilpa** Aust
26C3 **Tiluá** Colombia
44H2 **Timanskiy Kryazh** *Mts* Russian Fed
78B2 **Timaru** NZ
45F6 **Timashevsk** Russian Fed
41E3 **Timbákion** Greece
17D4 **Timbalier B** USA
70B3 **Timbédra** Maur
Timbuktu = Tombouctou
70B3 **Timétrine Monts,** *Mts* Mali
70C3 **Timia** Niger
70C2 **Timimoun** Alg
41E1 **Timiş** *R* Rom
41E1 **Timişoara** Rom
4E4 **Timmins** Can
76B1 **Timor** *I* Indon
76B2 **Timor S** Aust/Indon
28C3 **Timote** Arg
65B3 **Timsâh,L** Egypt
15B1 **Tims Ford L** USA
57G9 **Tinaca Pt** Phil
23D5 **Tinaco** Ven
62B2 **Tindivanam** India
70B2 **Tindouf** Alg
37B2 **Tinée** *R* France
20C2 **Tinemaha Res** USA
70B2 **Tinfouchy** Alg
70C2 **Tin Fouye** Alg
10F2 **Tingmerkpuk Mt** USA
7O3 **Tingmiarmiut** Greenland
26C5 **Tingo Maria** Peru
70B3 **Tingrela** Ivory Coast
61C2 **Tingri** China
51H5 **Tinian** Pacific O
28B1 **Tinogasta** Arg
41F3 **Tinos** *I* Greece
61E2 **Tinsukia** India
35C6 **Tintagel Head** *Pt* Eng
70C2 **Tin Tarabine** *Watercourse* Alg
75B3 **Tintinara** Aust
70C2 **Tin Zaouaten** Alg
11B2 **Tioga** USA
14B2 **Tioga** *R* USA
20C2 **Tioga P** USA
55C5 **Tioman** *I* Malay

4E4 **Tionaga** Can
37D1 **Tione** Italy
14B1 **Tioughnioga** *R* USA
35B5 **Tipperary** County, Irish Rep
33B3 **Tipperary** Irish Rep
20C2 **Tipton** California, USA
17D2 **Tipton** Missouri, USA
62B2 **Tiptūr** India
22B2 **Tiquicheo** Mexico
41D2 **Tiranë** Alb
37D1 **Tirano** Italy
43F3 **Tiraspol** Moldavia
65A3 **Tir'at el Ismâilîya** *Canal* Egypt
62B2 **Tirchchirāppalli** India
41F3 **Tire** Turk
64C1 **Tirebolu** Turk
34B3 **Tiree** *I* Scot
41F2 **Tîrgovişte** Rom
41E1 **Tîrgu Jiu** Rom
41E1 **Tîrgu Mureş** Rom
60C1 **Tirich Mir** *Mt* Pak
70A2 **Tiris** Region, Mor
44K5 **Tirlyanskiy** Russian Fed
41E1 **Tîrnăveni** Rom
41E3 **Tirnavos** Greece
60D4 **Tirodi** India
37D1 **Tirol** Province, Austria
40B2 **Tirso** *R* Sardegna
62B3 **Tiruchchendūr** India
62B3 **Tirunelveli** India
62B2 **Tirupati** India
62B2 **Tiruppattūr** India
62B2 **Tiruppur** India
62B2 **Tiruvannamalai** India
3H3 **Tisdale** Can
17C3 **Tishomingo** USA
65D2 **Tisīyah** Syria
43E3 **Tisza** *R* Hung
61B3 **Titlagarh** India
41D2 **Titograd** Montenegro, Yugos
41E2 **Titova Mitrovica** Serbia, Yugos
41D2 **Titovo Užice** Serbia, Yugos
41E2 **Titov Veles** Macedonia, Yugos
72C3 **Titule** Zaïre
15C3 **Titusville** USA
35D6 **Tiverton** Eng
40C2 **Tivoli** Italy
22C2 **Tixtla** Mexico
22C2 **Tizayuca** Mexico
21D2 **Tizimin** Mexico
71C1 **Tizi Ouzou** Alg
70B2 **Tiznit** Mor
22B1 **Tizpan el Alto** Mexico
22C2 **Tlacolula** Mexico
22C2 **Tlacotalpan** Mexico
22B2 **Tlalchana** Mexico
22C2 **Tlalnepantla** Mexico
22C2 **Tlalpan** Mexico
22B1 **Tlaltenago** Mexico
22C2 **Tlancualpicán** Mexico
22C2 **Tlapa** Mexico
22C2 **Tlapacoyan** Mexico
22B1 **Tlaquepaque** Mexico
22C2 **Tlaxcala** Mexico
22C2 **Tlaxcala** State, Mexico
22C2 **Tlaxiaco** Mexico
10M5 **Tlell** Can
71B2 **Tlemcem** Alg
73E5 **Toamasina** Madag
28C3 **Toay** Arg
54C4 **Toba** Japan
60B2 **Toba and Kakar Ranges** *Mts* Pak
23E4 **Tobago** *I* Caribbean
3D3 **Toba Inlet** *Sd* Can
57C2 **Tobelo** Indon
4E4 **Tobermory** Can
34B3 **Tobermory** Scot
51G6 **Tobi** *I* Pacific O
3H3 **Tobin L** Can
19C2 **Tobin,Mt** USA
54C3 **Tōbi-shima** *I* Japan
48H4 **Tobol** *R* Russian Fed
57B3 **Toboli** Indon
48H4 **Tobol'sk** Russian Fed
Tobruk = Tubruq
44J2 **Tobseda** Russian Fed
27J4 **Tocantins** *R* Brazil
15C2 **Toccoa** USA
37C1 **Toce** *R* Italy
25B2 **Tocopilla** Chile
25C2 **Tocorpuri** Bol
26E8 **Tocorpuri** *Mt* Chile
26E1 **Tocuyo** *R* Ven
60D3 **Toda** India
57B3 **Todeli** Indon
37C1 **Tödi** *Mt* Switz
54B3 **Todong** S Korea
8B4 **Todos Santos** Mexico
3F3 **Tofield** Can
3C4 **Tofino** Can
77H2 **Tofua** *I* Tonga
10F4 **Togiak** USA
10F4 **Togiak B** USA
57B3 **Togian** *I* Indon
66C3 **Togni** Sudan
71G4 **Togo** Republic, Africa
52C1 **Togtoh** China
66C3 **Tohamiyam** Sudan
16A2 **Tohatchi** USA
57B3 **Tojo** Indon
10K3 **Tok** USA
53E3 **Tokachi** *R* Japan
54C3 **Tokamachi** Japan
66C3 **Tokar** Sudan
50F4 **Tokara Retto** *Arch* Japan
64C1 **Tokat** Turk
53B4 **Tŏkchŏk-kundo** *Arch* S Korea
54B3 **Tok-do** *I* S Korea
77H1 **Tokelau** *Is* Pacific O
59F1 **Tokmak** Kirgizia
78C1 **Tokomaru Bay** NZ
10M4 **Toku** *R* Can/USA
56D3 **Tokung** Indon
50F4 **Tokuno** *I* Japan
53C1 **Tokur** Russian Fed
53C5 **Tokushima** Japan
54B4 **Tokuyama** Japan
53D4 **Tōkyō** Japan
78C1 **Tolaga Bay** NZ
27H8 **Toledo** Brazil
28A1 **Toledo** Chile
39B2 **Toledo** Spain
12C2 **Toledo** USA
17D3 **Toledo Bend Res** USA
37E3 **Tolentino** Italy
73E6 **Toliara** Madag
26C2 **Tolima** Colombia
22C1 **Toliman** Mexico
57B2 **Tolitoli** Indon
37E1 **Tolmezzo** Italy
37E1 **Tolmin** Slovenia, Yugos
43F2 **Toločin** Belorussia
39B1 **Tolosa** Spain
54A4 **Tolsan-do** *I* S Korea
28A3 **Toltén** Chile
28A3 **Toltén** *R* Chile
22C2 **Toluca** Mexico
44H5 **Tol'yatti** Russian Fed
53C1 **Tom** *R* Russian Fed
12A2 **Tomah** USA
12B1 **Tomahawk** USA
53E3 **Tomakomai** Japan
56E2 **Tomani** Malay
53E2 **Tomari** Russian Fed
43E2 **Tomaszów Mazowiecka** Pol
22A2 **Tomatlán** Mexico
15B2 **Tombigbee** *R* USA
73B4 **Tomboco** Angola
57B3 **Tomboli** Indon
29D3 **Tombos** Brazil
70B3 **Tombouctou** Mali
19E4 **Tombstone** USA
73B5 **Tombua** Angola
74D1 **Tomburke** S Africa
28A3 **Tomé** Chile
39B2 **Tomelloso** Spain
39A2 **Tomer** Port
54A4 **Tomie** Japan
57B2 **Tomini** Indon
76B3 **Tomkinson Range** *Mts* Aust
49O4 **Tommot** Russian Fed
41E2 **Tomorrit** *Mt* Alb
48K4 **Tomsk** Russian Fed
14C3 **Toms River** USA
21C3 **Tonalá** Mexico
18C1 **Tonasket** USA
57C2 **Tondano** Indon
33B2 **Tory** *I* Irish Rep
77H3 **Tonga** *Is* Pacific O
74E2 **Tongaat** S Africa
77H3 **Tongatapu** *I* Tonga
77H3 **Tongatapu Group** *Is* Tonga
77H3 **Tonga Trench** Pacific O
53B2 **Tongbei** China
54A2 **Tongchang** N Korea
52D3 **Tongcheng** China
52B2 **Tongchuan** China
52A2 **Tongde** China
36C1 **Tongeren** Belg
55E2 **Tonggu Jiao** *I* China
52A5 **Tonghai** China
53B2 **Tonghe** China
53B2 **Tonghua** China
53C2 **Tongjiang** China
53B4 **Tongjosŏn-man** N Korea
55D1 **Tongkin,G of** Viet/China
52E1 **Tonglia** China
52D3 **Tongling** China
54A3 **Tongnae** S Korea
75B2 **Tongo** Aust
28A2 **Tongoy** Chile
52B4 **Tongren** Guizhou, China
52A2 **Tongren** Qinghai, China
61D2 **Tongsa** Bhutan
55B1 **Tongta** Burma
50C3 **Tongtian He** *R* China
34C2 **Tongue** Scot
11A2 **Tongue** *R* USA
52D2 **Tong Xian** China
52B2 **Tongxin** China
53A3 **Tongyu** China
52B4 **Tongzi** China
8C4 **Tónichi** Mexico
72C3 **Tonj** Sudan
60D3 **Tonk** India
17C2 **Tonkawa** USA
55C3 **Tonle Sap** *L* Camb
36C3 **Tonnerre** France
54D3 **Tono** Japan
19C3 **Tonopah** USA
10J3 **Tonsina** USA
18D2 **Tooele** USA
75D1 **Toogoolawah** Aust
75B1 **Toompine** Aust
75D1 **Toowoomba** Aust
20C1 **Topaz L** USA
17C2 **Topeka** USA
8C4 **Topolobampo** Mexico
44E2 **Topozero, Ozero** *L* Russian Fed
18B1 **Toppenish** USA
19D4 **Toppock** USA
72D3 **Tor** Eth
41F3 **Torbali** Turk
63D1 **Torbat-e-Heydarīyeh** Iran
63E1 **Torbat-e Jām** Iran
10H3 **Torbert,Mt** USA
39A1 **Tordesillas** Spain
42C2 **Torgau** Germany
36B1 **Torhout** Belg
50H3 **Tori** *I* Japan
37B2 **Torino** Italy
72D3 **Torit** Sudan
29B2 **Torixoreu** Brazil
39A1 **Tormes** *R* Spain
3F4 **Tornado Mt** Can
32J5 **Torne** *L* Sweden
32H5 **Torneträsk** Sweden
7M4 **Torngat Mts** Can
32J5 **Tornio** Fin
28C3 **Tornquist** Arg
57B3 **Torobuku** Indon
71G3 **Torodi** Niger
53D1 **Torom** *R* Russian Fed
4F5 **Toronto** Can
44E4 **Toropets** Russian Fed
72D3 **Tororo** Uganda
64B2 **Toros Dağlari** *Mts* Turk
28E2 **Torquato Severo** Brazil
35D6 **Torquay** Eng
20C4 **Torrance** USA
39A2 **Torrão** Port
39C1 **Torreblanca** Spain
40C2 **Torre del Greco** Italy
39B1 **Torrelavega** Spain
39B2 **Torremolinos** Spain
75A2 **Torrens,L** Aust
28D1 **Torrent** Arg
21B2 **Torreón** Mexico
37B2 **Torre Pellice** Italy
77F2 **Torres Is** Vanuatu
76D2 **Torres Str** Aust
39A2 **Torres Vedras** Port
14D2 **Torrington** Connecticut, USA
11B3 **Torrington** Wyoming, USA
32D3 **Torshavn** Faroes
37C2 **Tortona** Italy
39C1 **Tortosa** Spain
63D1 **Torūd** Iran
43D2 **Toruń** Pol
33B2 **Tory** *I* Irish Rep
44E4 **Torzhok** Russian Fed
54B4 **Tosa** Japan
53C5 **Tosa-shimizu** Japan
53C5 **Tosa-wan** *B* Japan
37D3 **Toscana** Region, Italy
54C4 **To-shima** *I* Japan
32L7 **Tosno** Russian Fed
28C1 **Tostado** Arg
54B4 **Tosu** Japan
64B1 **Tosya** Turk
57B3 **Totala** Indon
44G4 **Tot'ma** Russian Fed
35D6 **Totnes** Eng
27G2 **Totness** Surinam
22C2 **Totolapan** Mexico
39B2 **Totona** Spain
28A1 **Totoral** Chile
28C1 **Totoralejos** Arg
75C2 **Tottenham** Aust
53C4 **Tottori** Japan
70B4 **Touba** Ivory Coast
70A3 **Touba** Sen
70B1 **Toubkal** *Mt* Mor
36B3 **Toucy** France
71F3 **Tougan** Burkina
71D2 **Touggourt** Alg
70A3 **Tougué** Guinea
36C2 **Toul** France
5H3 **Toulnustouc** *R* Can
38D3 **Toulon** France
38C3 **Toulouse** France
70B4 **Toumodi** Ivory Coast
55B2 **Toungoo** Burma
36B1 **Tourcoing** France
70A2 **Tourine** Maur
36B1 **Tournai** Belg
36A2 **Tourouvre** France
38C2 **Tours** France
74C3 **Touws** *R* S Africa
53E3 **Towada** Japan
53E3 **Towada-ko** *L* Japan
14B2 **Towanda** USA
20D2 **Towne P** USA
11B2 **Towner** USA
18D1 **Townsend** USA
76D2 **Townsville** Aust
63E1 **Towraghondi** Afghan
14B3 **Towson** USA
35D6 **Towy** *R* Wales
16B3 **Toyah** USA
54D2 **Toya-ko** *L* Japan
53D4 **Toyama** Japan
54C3 **Toyama-wan** *B* Japan
10D2 **Toygunen** Russian Fed
54C4 **Toyohashi** Japan
54C4 **Toyonaka** Japan
54B3 **Toyooka** Japan
53D4 **Toyota** Japan
71D2 **Tozeur** Tunisia
36D2 **Traben-Trarbach** Germany
64C1 **Trabzon** Turk
5J4 **Tracadie** Can
11C3 **Tracy** Minnesota, USA
28A3 **Traiguén** Chile
3E4 **Trail** Can
33B3 **Tralee** Irish Rep
35B5 **Tramore** Irish Rep
32G7 **Tranås** Sweden
55B4 **Trang** Thai
51G7 **Trangan** *I* Indon
75C2 **Trangie** Aust
28D2 **Tranqueras** Urug
10J2 **Transalaskan Pipeline** USA
79E **Transantarctic Mts** Ant
11C2 **Transcona** Can
74D3 **Transkei** Self-governing homeland, S Africa
74D1 **Transvaal** Province, S Africa
Transylvanian Alps = Muntii Carpaţii Meridionali
40C3 **Trapani** Italy
75C3 **Traralgon** Aust
70A3 **Trarza** Region, Maur
55C3 **Trat** Thai
10M2 **Travaillant L** Can
75B2 **Traveller's** *L* Aust
42C2 **Travemünde** Germany
12B2 **Traverse City** USA
10G2 **Traverse Peak** *Mt* USA
78B2 **Travers,Mt** NZ
16C3 **Travis,L** USA
37C2 **Trebbia** *R* Italy
42D3 **Třebíč** Czech
41D2 **Trebinje** Bosnia & Herzegovina, Yugos
42C3 **Trebon** Czech
28E2 **Treinta y Tres** Urug
25C6 **Trelew** Arg
32G7 **Trelleborg** Sweden
35C5 **Tremadog B** Wales
13E1 **Tremblant,Mt** Can
3D3 **Trembleur L** Can
14B2 **Tremont** USA
18D2 **Tremonton** USA
43D3 **Trenčin** Czech
28C3 **Trenque Lauquén** Arg
35E5 **Trent** *R* Eng
37D1 **Trentino** Region, Italy
37D1 **Trento** Italy
4F5 **Trenton** Can
17D1 **Trenton** Missouri, USA
14C2 **Trenton** New Jersey, USA
5L4 **Trepassey** Can
28C3 **Tres Arroyos** Arg
29C3 **Tres Corações** Brazil
29B3 **Três Irmãos, Reprêsa** *Res* Brazil
25F2 **Três Lagoas** Brazil
28C3 **Tres Lomas** Arg
28E1 **Tres Passos** Brazil
22D2 **Tres Picos** Mexico
20B2 **Tres Pinos** USA
29D3 **Três Rios** Brazil
37A3 **Trets** France
37C2 **Treviglio** Italy
37E2 **Treviso** Italy
36E1 **Treysa** Germany
37C2 **Trezzo** Italy
16B2 **Tribune** USA
62B2 **Trichūr** India
75C2 **Trida** Aust
36D2 **Trier** Germany
40C1 **Trieste** Italy
37E1 **Triglav** *Mt* Croatia, Yugos
65B1 **Trikomo** Cyprus
35B5 **Trim** Irish Rep
62C3 **Trincomalee** Sri Lanka
xxxG6 **Trindade,I** Atlantic O
26F6 **Trinidad** Bol
28D2 **Trinidad** Urug
16B2 **Trinidad** USA
28C3 **Trinidad** *I* Arg
23E4 **Trinidad** *I* Caribbean
23E4 **Trinidad & Tobago** *Is Republic* Caribbean
17C3 **Trinity** USA
8D3 **Trinity** *R* USA
7N5 **Trinity B** Can
10H4 **Trinity Is** USA
15B2 **Trion** USA
37B2 **Triora** Italy
65C1 **Tripoli** Leb
69A1 **Tripoli** Libya
41E3 **Trípolis** Greece
61D3 **Tripura** State, India
xxxH6 **Tristan da Cunha** *Is* Atlantic O
43D3 **Trnava** Czech
76E1 **Trobriand Is** PNG
5H4 **Trois Pistoles** Can
5G4 **Trois-Rivières** Can
44L5 **Troitsk** Russian Fed
44K3 **Troitsko Pechorsk** Russian Fed
53D2 **Troitskoye** Russian Fed
32G7 **Trollhättan** Sweden
32F6 **Trollheimen** *Mt* Nor
68K9 **Tromelin** *I* Indian O
74D3 **Trompsburg** S Africa
32H5 **Tromsø** Nor
20D3 **Trona** USA
32G6 **Trondheim** Nor
32G6 **Trondheimfjord** *Inlet* Nor
65B1 **Troödos Range** *Mts* Cyprus
34C4 **Troon** Scot
xxxJ3 **Tropic of Cancer**
xxxK6 **Tropic of Capricorn**
70B2 **Troudenni** Mali
3D1 **Trout** *R* Can
4F4 **Trout Creek** Can
3D1 **Trout L** Northwest Territories, Can
7J4 **Trout L** Ontario, Can
18E2 **Trout Peak** *Mt* USA
5K4 **Trout River** Can
14B2 **Trout Run** USA
36A2 **Trouville-sur-Mer** France
15B2 **Troy** Alabama, USA
18C1 **Troy** Montana, USA
14D1 **Troy** New York, USA
12C2 **Troy** Ohio, USA
14B2 **Troy** Pennsylvania, USA
41E2 **Troyan** Bulg
36C2 **Troyes** France
19C3 **Troy Peak** *Mt* USA
67F2 **Trucial Coast** Region, UAE
19B3 **Truckee** *R* USA
21D3 **Trujillo** Honduras
26C5 **Trujillo** Peru
39A2 **Trujillo** Spain
26D2 **Trujillo** Ven
19D3 **Trumbull,Mt** USA
75C2 **Trundle** Aust
7M5 **Truro** Can
35C6 **Truro** Eng
51G6 **Trust Territories of the Pacific Is** Pacific O
3D2 **Trutch** Can
16A3 **Truth or Consequences** USA
50C2 **Tsagaan Nuur** *L* Mongolia
50C1 **Tsagan-Tologoy** Russian Fed
73E5 **Tsaratanana** Madag
73C6 **Tsau** Botswana
72D4 **Tsavo** Kenya
72D4 **Tsavo Nat Pk** Kenya
11B2 **Tschida,L** USA
48J4 **Tselinograd** Kazakhstan
74B2 **Tses** Namibia
50D2 **Tsetserleg** Mongolia
71G4 **Tsévié** Togo
74C2 **Tshabong** Botswana
74C1 **Tshane** Botswana
45F7 **Tshcikskoye Vdkhr** *Res* Russian Fed
72B4 **Tshela** Zaïre
73C4 **Tshibala** Zaïre
72C4 **Tshikapa** Zaïre
72C4 **Tshuapa** *R* Zaïre
73E6 **Tsihombe** Madag

45G6 **Tsimlyanskoye Vodokhranilishche** *Res* Russian Fed
Tsinan = Jinan
Tsingtao = Qingdao
73E5 **Tsiroanomandidy** Madag
3C3 **Tsitsutl Peak** *Mt* Can
43F2 **Tsna** *R* Belorussia
52B1 **Tsogt Ovoo** Mongolia
74D3 **Tsomo** S Africa
50D2 **Tsomog** Mongolia
54C4 **Tsu** Japan
54C3 **Tsubata** Japan
53E4 **Tsuchira** Japan
53E3 **Tsugaru-kaikyō** *Str* Japan
73B5 **Tsumeb** Namibia
73B6 **Tsumis** Namibia
54C3 **Tsunugi** Japan
53D4 **Tsuruga** Japan
53D4 **Tsuruoka** Japan
54C3 **Tsushima** Japan
53B5 **Tsushima** *I* Japan
Tsushima-Kaikyō = Korea Str
53C4 **Tsuyama** Japan
39A1 **Tua** *R* Port
56A2 **Tuangku** *I* Indon
45F7 **Tuapse** Russian Fed
78A3 **Tuatapere** NZ
19D3 **Tuba City** USA
25G3 **Tubarão** Brazil
65C2 **Tubas** Israel
57E9 **Tubbataha Reefs** *Is* Phil
42B3 **Tübingen** Germany
69B1 **Tubruq** Libya
14C3 **Tuckerton** USA
19D4 **Tucson** USA
25C3 **Tucumán** State, Arg
16B2 **Tucumcari** USA
28B2 **Tucunuco** Arg
26F2 **Tucupita** Ven
39B1 **Tudela** Spain
10N2 **Tudenet L** Can
64C3 **Tudmur** Syria
28C2 **Tuerto** Arg
74E2 **Tugela** *R* S Africa
75D2 **Tuggerah** *L* Aust
10H4 **Tugidak** *I* USA
57F7 **Tuguegarao** Phil
49P4 **Tugur** Russian Fed
53D1 **Tugur** *R* Russian Fed
52D2 **Tuhai He** *R* China
71F3 **Tui** *R* Burkina
10M2 **Tuktoyaktuk** Can
43E1 **Tukums** Latvia
73D4 **Tukuyu** Tanz
60B1 **Tukzar** Afghan
22C1 **Tula** Mexico
44F5 **Tula** Russian Fed
22C1 **Tulancingo** Mexico
56B3 **Tulangbawang** *R* Indon
20C2 **Tulare** USA
20C2 **Tulare Lake Bed** USA
16A3 **Tularosa** USA
26C3 **Tulcán** Colombia
45D7 **Tulcea** Rom
43F3 **Tul'chin** Ukraine
20C2 **Tule** *R* USA
73C6 **Tuli** Zim
74D1 **Tuli** *R* Zim
16B3 **Tulia** USA
10E5 **Tulik V** USA
65C2 **Tulkarm** Israel
15B1 **Tullahoma** USA
35B5 **Tullarnore** Irish Rep
38C2 **Tulle** France
37A2 **Tullins** France
17D3 **Tullos** USA
35B5 **Tullow** Irish Rep
14B1 **Tully** USA
17C2 **Tulsa** USA
64C3 **Tulūl ash Shāmīyah** *Desert Region* Syria/S Arabia
49M4 **Tulun** Russian Fed
56D4 **Tulungagung** Indon
26C3 **Tumaco** Colombia
49R3 **Tumany** Russian Fed
75C3 **Tumbarumba** Aust
26B4 **Tumbes** Ecuador
75A2 **Tumby Bay** Aust
53B3 **Tumen** China
62B2 **Tumkūr** India
63E3 **Tump** Pak
55C4 **Tumpat** Malay
60D4 **Tumsar** India
71F3 **Tumu** Ghana
75C3 **Tumut** Aust
75C3 **Tumut** *R* Aust
23L1 **Tunapuna** Trinidad
64C2 **Tunceli** Turk
73D4 **Tunduma** Zambia
73D5 **Tunduru** Tanz
41F2 **Tundzha** *R* Bulg
62B1 **Tungabhadra** *R* India
50E4 **Tung-Chiang** Taiwan
32B2 **Tungnafellsjökull** *Mts* Iceland
10N3 **Tungsten** Can
62C1 **Tuni** India
71E1 **Tunis** Tunisia
68E4 **Tunisia** Republic, N Africa
26D2 **Tunja** Colombia
14C2 **Tunkhannock** USA
10F3 **Tuntutuliak** USA
5H2 **Tunulik** *R* Can
10F3 **Tununak** USA
5J2 **Tunungayualok I** Can
28B2 **Tunuyán** Arg
28B2 **Tunuyán** *R* Arg
52D4 **Tunxi** China
20C2 **Tuolumne Meadows** USA
29B3 **Tupã** Brazil
29C2 **Tupaciguara** Brazil
28E1 **Tupanciretã** Brazil
17E3 **Tupelo** USA
43G1 **Tupik** Russian Fed
26E8 **Tupiza** Bol
20C3 **Tupman** USA
13E2 **Tupper Lake** USA
28B2 **Tupungato** Arg
25C4 **Tupungato** *Mt* Arg
61D2 **Tura** India
49M3 **Tura** Russian Fed
44L4 **Tura** *R* Russian Fed
66D2 **Turabah** S Arabia
63D1 **Turān** Iran
49L4 **Turan** Russian Fed
64C3 **Turayf** S Arabia
63E3 **Turbat** Pak
26C2 **Turbo** Colombia
41E1 **Turda** Rom
48K5 **Turfan Depression** China
48H5 **Turgay** Kazakhstan
49L5 **Turgen Uul** *Mt* Mongolia
4F3 **Turgeon** *R* Can
64A2 **Turgutlu** Turk
64C1 **Turhal** Turk
32K7 **Türi** Estonia
39B2 **Turia** *R* Spain
Turin = Torino
44L4 **Turinsk** Russian Fed
53C2 **Turiy Rog** Russian Fed
72D3 **Turkana,L** Kenya/Eth
58E1 **Turkestan** Region, C Asia
59E1 **Turkestan** Kazakhstan
64C2 **Turkey** Republic, W Asia
48G5 **Turkmenistan** *Republic* Asia
63C1 **Turkmenskiy Zaliv** *B* Turkmenistan
23C2 **Turks Is** Caribbean
32J6 **Turku** Fin
72D3 **Turkwel** *R* Kenya
20B2 **Turlock** USA
20B2 **Turlock L** USA
3C2 **Turnagain** *R* Can
78C2 **Turnagain,C** NZ
21D3 **Turneffe I** Belize
14D1 **Turners Falls** USA
36C1 **Turnhout** Belg
3G2 **Turnor L** Can
41E2 **Turnu Măgurele** Rom
41E2 **Turnu-Severin** Rom
49K5 **Turpan** China
23B2 **Turquino** *Mt* Cuba
58E1 **Turtkul'** Uzbekistan
17C2 **Turtle Creek Res** USA
3G3 **Turtle L** Can
49K3 **Turukhansk** Russian Fed
50D1 **Turuntayevo** Russian Fed
29B2 **Turvo** *R* Goias, Brazil
29C3 **Turvo** *R* São Paulo, Brazil
43E2 **Tur'ya** *R* Ukraine
17E3 **Tuscaloosa** USA
Tuscany = Toscana
14B2 **Tuscarora Mt** USA
12B3 **Tuscola** Illinois, USA
16C3 **Tuscola** Texas, USA
15B2 **Tuscumbia** USA
63D2 **Tusharík** Iran
14A2 **Tussey Mt** USA
Tutera = Tudela
62B3 **Tuticorin** India
41F2 **Tutrakan** Bulg
42B3 **Tuttlingen** Germany
77H2 **Tutulia** *I* American Samoa
22C2 **Tututepec** Mexico
50D2 **Tuul Gol** *R* Mongolia
77G1 **Tuvalu** *Is* Pacific O
49L4 **Tuvinskaya** Respublika, Russian Fed
65C4 **Tuwayilel Haj** *Mt* Jordan
66C2 **Tuwwal** S Arabia
22B2 **Tuxpan** Jalisco, Mexico
22A1 **Tuxpan** Nayarit, Mexico
22C1 **Tuxpan** Veracruz, Mexico
22C2 **Tuxtepec** Mexico
21C3 **Tuxtla Gutiérrez** Mexico
39A1 **Túy** Spain
3B2 **Tuya** *R* Can
55D3 **Tuy Hoa** Viet
64B2 **Tuz Gölü** *Salt L* Turk
64D3 **Tuz Khurmātū** Iraq
41D2 **Tuzla** Bosnia & Herzegovina, Yugos
44F4 **Tver'** Russian Fed
34D4 **Tweed** *R* Scot/Eng
75D1 **Tweed Heads** Aust
34D4 **Tweedsmuir Hills** Scot
19C4 **Twentynine Palms** USA
7N5 **Twillingate** Can
18D1 **Twin Bridges** USA
16B3 **Twin Buttes Res** USA
18D2 **Twin Falls** USA
78B2 **Twins,The** *Mt* NZ
4B4 **Twin Valley** USA
20B3 **Twitchell Res** USA
12A1 **Two Harbors** USA
18D1 **Two Medicine** *R* USA
12B2 **Two Rivers** USA
49O4 **Tygda** Russian Fed
17C3 **Tyler** USA
53E1 **Tymovskoye** Russian Fed
50F1 **Tynda** Russian Fed
34E4 **Tyne** *R* Eng
34E4 **Tyne and Wear** Metropolitan County, Eng
34E4 **Tynemouth** Eng
32G6 **Tynset** Nor
10H4 **Tyonek** USA
65C2 **Tyr** Leb
Tyre = Tyr
53C1 **Tyrma** Russian Fed
53C1 **Tyrma** *R* Russian Fed
34B4 **Tyrone** County, N Ire
16A3 **Tyrone** New Mexico, USA
14A2 **Tyrone** Pennsylvania, USA
4B3 **Tyrrel** Can
75B3 **Tyrrell,L** Aust
40C2 **Tyrrhenian S** Italy
45J7 **Tyuleni, Ostrova** *Is* Kazakhstan
48H4 **Tyumen'** Russian Fed
49O3 **Tyung** *R* Russian Fed
35C5 **Tywyn** Wales
41E3 **Tzoumérka** *Mt* Greece
74E1 **Tzaneen** S Africa

U

29D3 **Ubá** Brazil
29D2 **Ubaí** Brazil
29E1 **Ubaitaba** Brazil
72B3 **Ubangi** *R* CAR
37B2 **Ubaye** *R* France
54B4 **Ube** Japan
39B2 **Ubeda** Spain
7N2 **Ubekendt Ejland** *I* Greenland
29C2 **Uberaba** Brazil
29C2 **Uberlândia** Brazil
55D2 **Ubon Ratchathani** Thai
43F2 **Ubort** *R* Belorussia
72C4 **Ubundi** Zaïre
26D5 **Ucayali** *R* Peru
60C3 **Uch** Pak
53E3 **Uchiura-wan** *B* Japan
49P4 **Uchar** *R* Russian Fed
18A1 **Ucluelet** Can
49L4 **Uda** *R* Russian Fed
60C4 **Udaipur** India
61C2 **Udaipur Garhi** Nepal
28D3 **Udaquiola** Arg
32G7 **Uddevalla** Sweden
32H5 **Uddjaur** *L* Sweden
62B1 **Udgir** India
60D2 **Udhampur** India
37E1 **Udine** Italy
44J4 **Udmurtskaya** Respublika, Russian Fed
55C2 **Udon Thani** Thai
49P4 **Udskaya Guba** *B* Russian Fed
53C1 **Udskoye** Russian Fed
62A2 **Udupi** India
53D1 **Udyl', Ozero** *L* Russian Fed
49N2 **Udzha** Russian Fed
54C3 **Ueda** Japan
72C3 **Uele** *R* Zaïre
49U3 **Uelen** Russian Fed
42C2 **Uelzen** Germany
72C3 **Uere** *R* Zaïre
44K5 **Ufa** Russian Fed
44K4 **Ufa** *R* Russian Fed
73B6 **Ugab** *R* Namibia
72D4 **Ugaila** *R* Tanz
10H4 **Ugak B** USA
72D3 **Uganda** Republic, Africa
10G4 **Ugashik B** USA
10G4 **Ugashik L** USA
37B2 **Ugine** France
66D1 **'Uglat as Suqūr** S Arabia
53E2 **Uglegorsk** Russian Fed
44F4 **Uglich** Russian Fed
53C3 **Uglovoye** Russian Fed
44F5 **Ugra** *R* Russian Fed
34B3 **Uig** Scot
73B4 **Uige** Angola
54A3 **Ŭijŏngbu** S Korea
45J6 **Uil** Kazakhstan
18D2 **Uinta Mts** USA
54A3 **Ŭiryŏng** S Korea
54A3 **Uisŏng** S Korea
74D3 **Uitenhage** S Africa
5J2 **Uivak,C** Can
43E3 **Ujfehértó** Hung
54C4 **Uji** Japan
72C4 **Ujiji** Tanz
25C2 **Ujina** Chile
60D4 **Ujjain** India
57B4 **Ujung** Indon
76A1 **Ujung Pandang** Indon
72D4 **Ukerewe** *I* Tanz
61D2 **Ukhrul** India
44J3 **Ukhta** Russian Fed
19B3 **Ukiah** California, USA
18C1 **Ukiah** Oregon, USA
8A3 **Ukiah** USA
43E1 **Ukmerge** Lithuania
45D6 **Ukraine** *Republic* Europe
54A4 **Uku-jima** *I* Japan
50D2 **Ulaanbaatar** Mongolia
50C2 **Ulaangom** Mongolia
52C1 **Ulaan Uul** Mongolia
59G1 **Ulangar Hu** *L* China
52B1 **Ulansuhai Nur** *L* China
50D1 **Ulan Ude** Russian Fed
50C3 **Ulan Ul Hu** *L* China
28B2 **Ulapes** Arg
49Q3 **Ul'beya** *R* Russian Fed
53B4 **Ulchin** S Korea
41D2 **Ulcinj** Montenegro, Yugos
50E2 **Uldz** Mongolia
50C2 **Uliastay** Mongolia
43F1 **Ulla** Lithuania
75D3 **Ulladulla** Aust
34C3 **Ullapool** Scot
32H5 **Ullsfjorden** *Inlet* Nor
35D4 **Ullswater** *L* Eng
53C4 **Ullung-do** *I* S Korea
42C3 **Ulm** Germany
53C2 **Ul'ma** *R* Russian Fed
75A1 **Uloowaranie,L** Aust
53B4 **Ulsan** S Korea
35B4 **Ulster** Region, N Ire
57C2 **Ulu** Indon
48K5 **Ulungur He** *R* China
48K5 **Ulungur Hu** *L* China
34B3 **Ulva** *I* Scot
35D4 **Ulverston** Eng
75E3 **Ulverstone** Aust
49Q4 **Ulya** *R* Russian Fed
43G3 **Ulyanovka** Ukraine
44H5 **Ul'yanovsk** Russian Fed
16B2 **Ulysses** USA
45E6 **Uman** Ukraine
7N2 **Umanak** Greenland
61B3 **Umaria** India
60B3 **Umarkot** Pak
75A1 **Umaroona,L** Aust
18C1 **Umatilla** USA
44E2 **Umba** Russian Fed
72D4 **Umba** *R* Tanz
37E3 **Umbertide** Italy
76D1 **Umboi I** PNG
32H6 **Ume** *R* Sweden
32J6 **Umea** Sweden
74E2 **Umfolozi,R** S Africa
10H2 **Umiat** USA
74E3 **Umkomaas** *R* S Africa
67G1 **Umm al Qaiwain** UAE
67G2 **Umm as Samīm** *Salt Marsh* Oman
72C2 **Umm Bell** Sudan
66B3 **Umm Inderaba** Sudan
72C2 **Umm Keddada** Sudan
66C1 **Umm Lajj** S Arabia
72D2 **Umm Ruwaba** Sudan
67F2 **Umm Sa'id** Qatar
66B4 **Umm Saiyala** Sudan
73C5 **Umnaiti** *R* Zim
10E5 **Umnak I** USA
18B2 **Umpqua** *R* USA
60D4 **Umred** India
74D3 **Umtata** S Africa
29B3 **Umuarama** Brazil
74D3 **Umzimkulu** S Africa
74E3 **Umzimkulu** *R* S Africa
74D3 **Umzimvubu** *R* S Africa
74D1 **Umzingwane** *R* Zim
29E2 **Una** Brazil
40D1 **Una** *R* Bosnia & Herzegovina/Croatia, Yugos
14C1 **Unadilla** USA
14C1 **Unadilla** *R* USA
29C2 **Unai** Brazil
10F3 **Unalakleet** USA
10E5 **Unalaska** *I* USA
66D1 **Unayzah** S Arabia
14D2 **Uncasville** USA
16A2 **Uncompahgre Plat** USA
74D2 **Underberg** S Africa
11B2 **Underwood** USA
44E5 **Unecha** Russian Fed
65C3 **Uneisa** Jordan
10G4 **Unga** *I* USA
7M4 **Ungava B** Can
25F3 **União de Vitória** Brazil
10F5 **Unimak Bight** USA
10F5 **Unimak I** USA
10E5 **Unimak Pass** USA
28B3 **Unión** Arg
17D2 **Union** Missouri, USA
15C2 **Union** S Carolina, USA
13D2 **Union City** Pennsylvania, USA
15B1 **Union City** Tennessee, USA
74C3 **Uniondale** S Africa
15B2 **Union Springs** USA
13D3 **Uniontown** USA
67F2 **United Arab Emirates** Arabian Pen
30E3 **United Kingdom** Kingdom, W Europe
2H4 **United States of America**
7K1 **United States Range** *Mts* Can
3G3 **Unity** Can
18C2 **Unity** USA
16A3 **University Park** USA
36D1 **Unna** Germany
61B2 **Unnão** India
54A2 **Unsan** N Korea
34E1 **Unst** *I* Scot
57B3 **Unuana** *I* Indon
3B2 **Unuk** *R* USA
64C1 **Ünye** Turk
44G4 **Unzha** *R* Russian Fed
26F2 **Upata** Ven
73C4 **Upemba Nat Pk** Zaïre
7N2 **Upernavik** Greenland
74C2 **Upington** S Africa
20D3 **Upland** USA
77H2 **Upolu** *I* Western Samoa
3E3 **Upper Arrow L** Can
78C2 **Upper Hutt** NZ
18B2 **Upper Klamath L** USA
18B2 **Upper L** USA
35B4 **Upper Laugh Erne** *L* N Ire
23L1 **Upper Manzanilla** Trinidad
11D2 **Upper Red L** USA
14B3 **Upperville** USA
Upper Volta = Burkina
32H7 **Uppsala** Sweden
11D2 **Upsala** Can
11B3 **Upton** USA
52B1 **Urad Qianqi** China
67E1 **Urairah** S Arabia
54D2 **Urakawa** Japan
45J5 **Ural** *R* Kazakhstan
75D2 **Uralla** Aust
45J5 **Ural'sk** Kazakhstan
48G4 **Uralskiy Khrebet** *Mts* Russian Fed
29D1 **Urandi** Brazil
6H4 **Uranium City** Can
51G8 **Urapunga** Aust
16A2 **Uravan** USA
54C3 **Urawa** Japan
44L3 **Uray** Russian Fed
12B2 **Urbana** Illinois, USA
12C2 **Urbana** Ohio, USA
37E3 **Urbino** Italy
35D4 **Ure** *R* Eng
44H4 **Uren'** Russian Fed
48J3 **Urengoy** Russian Fed
53C1 **Urgal** Russian Fed
58E1 **Urgench** Uzbekistan
60B2 **Urgun** Afghan
53B1 **Urkan** *R* Russian Fed
41F3 **Urla** Turk
53C2 **Urmi** *R* Russian Fed
71H4 **Uromi** Nig
41E2 **Urozevac** Serbia, Yugos
27J6 **Uruaçu** Brazil
29C1 **Uruacu** Brazil
22B2 **Uruapan** Mexico
29C2 **Urucuia** *R* Brazil
28E1 **Uruguai** *R* Brazil
28D1 **Uruguaiana** Brazil
25E4 **Uruguay** Republic, S America
25E4 **Uruguay** *R* Urug
63B1 **Urumīyeh** Iran
59G1 **Ürümqi** China
50J2 **Urup** *I* Russian Fed
49Q5 **Urup, Ostrov** *I* Russian Fed
67E3 **'Urūq al Awārik** Region, S Arabia
53A1 **Urusha** Russian Fed
60B2 **Uruzgan** Afghan
54D2 **Uryū-ko** *L* Japan
45G5 **Uryupinsk** Russian Fed
44J4 **Urzhum** Russian Fed
41F2 **Urziceni** Rom

59G1 **Usa** China
54B4 **Usa** Japan
44L2 **Usa** *R* Russian Fed
64A2 **Uşak** Turk
74B1 **Usakos** Namibia
48J1 **Ushakova, Ostrov** *I* Russian Fed
72D4 **Ushashi** Tanz
48J5 **Ush Tobe** Kazakhstan
25C8 **Ushuaia** Arg
49O4 **Ushumun** Russian Fed
35D6 **Usk** *R* Wales
64A1 **Üsküdar** Turk
36E1 **Uslar** Germany
44H3 **Usogorsk** Russian Fed
49M4 **Usolye Sibirskoye** Russian Fed
28B2 **Uspallata** Arg
53C2 **Ussuri** *R* Russian Fed
53C3 **Ussuriysk** Russian Fed
49T3 **Ust'Belaya** Russian Fed
49R4 **Ust'Bol'sheretsk** Russian Fed
37C1 **Uster** Switz
40C3 **Ustica** *I* Italy
42C2 **Ústi nad Labem** Czech
48J4 **Ust'Ishim** Russian Fed
42D2 **Ustka** Pol
49S4 **Ust'Kamchatsk** Russian Fed
48K5 **Ust'-Kamenogorsk** Kazakhstan
44L2 **Ust'Kara** Russian Fed
49L4 **Ust Karabula** Russian Fed
44K5 **Ust'Katav** Russian Fed
49M4 **Ust'-Kut** Russian Fed
45F6 **Ust Labinsk** Russian Fed
49P3 **Ust'Maya** Russian Fed
44K3 **Ust'Nem** Russian Fed
49Q3 **Ust'Nera** Russian Fed
49O4 **Ust'Nyukzha** Russian Fed
49M4 **Ust'Ordynskiy** Russian Fed
44J2 **Ust'Tsil'ma** Russian Fed
49P4 **Ust'Umal'ta** Russian Fed
44G3 **Ust'ya** *R* Russian Fed
44M2 **Ust' Yuribey** Russian Fed
54B4 **Usuki** Japan
21C3 **Usumacinta** *R* Guatemala/ Mexico
74E2 **Usutu** *R* Swaziland
43G1 **Usvyaty** Russian Fed
8B3 **Utah** State, USA
19D2 **Utah L** USA
57C2 **Utara** *I* Indon
43F1 **Utena** Lithuania
60B3 **Uthal** Pak
14C1 **Utica** USA
39B2 **Utiel** Spain
3E2 **Utikuma L** Can
42B2 **Utrecht** Neth
74E2 **Utrecht** S Africa
39A2 **Utrera** Spain
32K5 **Utsjoki** Fin
53D4 **Utsunomiya** Japan
55C2 **Uttaradit** Thai
61B2 **Uttar Pradesh** State, India
29C2 **Utucuia** *R* Brazil
10F2 **Utukok** *R* USA
48H4 **Uvat** Russian Fed
77F3 **Uvéa** *I* Nouvelle Calédonie
72D4 **Uvinza** Tanz
72C4 **Uvira** Zaïre
7N2 **Uvkusigssat** Greenland
16C4 **Uvlade** USA
32J6 **Uvsikaupunki** Fin
50C1 **Uvs Nuur** *L* China
53C5 **Uwajima** Japan
56A2 **Uwak** Indon
52B2 **Uxin Qi** China
49O3 **Uyandina** *R* Russian Fed
49L4 **Uyar** Russian Fed
26E8 **Uyuni** Bol
65B4 **Uyûn Mûsa** *Well* Egypt
58E1 **Uzbekistan** *Republic* Asia
38C2 **Uzerche** France
43F2 **Uzh** *R* Ukraine
43E3 **Uzhgorod** Ukraine
44F5 **Uzlovaya** Russian Fed
64A1 **Uzunköprü** Turk

V

74C2 **Vaal** *R* S Africa
74D2 **Vaal Dam** *Res* S Africa
74D1 **Vaalwater** S Africa
32J6 **Vaasa** Fin
43D3 **Vác** Hung
25F3 **Vacaria** Brazil
29B3 **Vacaria** *R* Mato Grosso Do Sul, Brazil
29D2 **Vacaria** *R* Minas Gerais, Brazil
28B1 **Va Castell** Arg
19B3 **Vacaville** USA
74C3 **Vacca,C** S Africa
60C4 **Vadodara** India
32K4 **Vadsø** Nor
37C1 **Vaduz** Leichtenstein
44G3 **Vaga** *R* Russian Fed
25E5 **Va Gesell** Arg
32D3 **Vågø** Faroes
43D3 **Váh** *R* Czech
65C3 **Vahel** Israel
62B2 **Vaigai** *R* India
77G1 **Vaitupu** *I* Tuvalu
53E1 **Val** Russian Fed
45C6 **Vâlcea** Rom
25C6 **Valcheta** Arg
37D2 **Valdagno** Italy
44E4 **Valday** Russian Fed
44E4 **Valdayskaya Vozvyshennost'** *Upland* Russian Fed
26E2 **Val de la Pascua** Ven
39B2 **Valdepeñas** Spain
10J3 **Valdez** USA
28A3 **Valdivia** Chile
36B2 **Val d'oise** *Department* France
13D1 **Val-d'Or** Can
15C2 **Valdosta** USA
18C2 **Vale** USA
3E3 **Valemount** Can
29E1 **Valença** Bahia, Brazil
29D3 **Valença** Rio de Janeiro, Brazil
38C3 **Valence** France
39B2 **Valencia** Region, Spain
39B2 **Valencia** Spain
26E1 **Valencia** Ven
39A2 **Valencia de Alcantara** Spain
36B1 **Valenciennes** France
11B3 **Valentine** Nebraska, USA
16B3 **Valentine** Texas, USA
37C2 **Valenza** Italy
26D2 **Valera** Ven
32K7 **Valga** Estonia
35F5 **Valiant** *Oilfield* N Sea
41D2 **Valjevo** Serbia, Yugos
32J6 **Valkeakoski** Fin
22B1 **Valla de Sannago** Mexico
21D2 **Valladolid** Mexico
39A1 **Valladolid** Spain
37B2 **Valle d'Aosta** Region, Italy
23D5 **Valle de la Pascua** Ven
37B2 **Valle d'Isére** France
26D1 **Valledupar** Colombia
70C3 **Vallée de l'Azaouak** *V* Niger
70C3 **Vallée Tilemis** *V* Mali
26F7 **Valle Grande** Bol
20A1 **Vallejo** USA
28A1 **Vallenar** Chile
29D1 **Valle Pegueno** *V* Brazil
71E1 **Valletta** Malta
11C2 **Valley City** USA
18B2 **Valley Falls** USA
4G4 **Valleyfield** Can
3E2 **Valleyview** Can
37E2 **Valli di Comacchio** *Lg* Italy
39C1 **Valls** Spain
3G4 **Val Marie** Can
43F1 **Valmiera** Latvia
29B3 **Valparaiso** Brazil
28A2 **Valparaiso** Chile
22B1 **Valparaiso** Mexico
15B2 **Valparaiso** USA
74D2 **Vals** *R* S Africa
60C4 **Valsād** India
45F5 **Valuyki** Russian Fed
39A2 **Valverde del Camino** Spain
32J6 **Vammala** Fin
64D2 **Van** Turk
49M3 **Vanavara** Russian Fed
17D2 **Van Buren** Arkansas, USA
13F1 **Van Buren** Maine, USA
36C2 **Vancouleurs** France
3D4 **Vancouver** Can
18B1 **Vancouver** USA
10E3 **Vancouver,C** USA
6F5 **Vancouver I** Can
10L3 **Vancouver,Mt** Can
12B3 **Vandalia** Illinois, USA
12C3 **Vandalia** Ohio, USA
4E4 **Vanderbilt** USA
3D3 **Vanderhoof** Can
51G8 **Van Diemen,C** Aust
76C2 **Van Diemen G** Aust
5G4 **Vandry** Can
22B1 **Vanegas** Mexico
32G7 **Vänern** *L* Sweden
32G7 **Vänersborg** Sweden
14B1 **Van Etten** USA
73E6 **Vangaindrano** Madag
64D2 **Van Gölü** *Salt L* Turk
55C2 **Vang Vieng** Laos
16B3 **Van Horn** USA
13D1 **Vanier** Can
77F2 **Vanikoto** *I* Solomon Is
53E2 **Vanino** Russian Fed
49U3 **Vankarem** Russian Fed
32H6 **Vännäs** Sweden
38B2 **Vannes** France
37B2 **Vanoise** *Mts* France
74B3 **Vanrhynsdorp** S Africa
7K3 **Vansittart I** Can
77F2 **Vanua Lava** *I* Vanuatu
77G2 **Vanua Levu** *I* Fiji
xxixK5 **Vanuatu** *Is* Pacific O
12C2 **Van Wert** USA
74C3 **Vanwyksvlei** S Africa
37B2 **Var** *R* France
37C2 **Vara** *R* Italy
37C2 **Varallo** Italy
63C1 **Varāmīn** Iran
61B2 **Vārānasi** India
44K2 **Varandey** Russian Fed
32K4 **Varangerfjord** *Inlet* Nor
32L4 **Varangerhalvøya** *Pen* Nor
40D1 **Varazdin** Croatia, Yugos
37C2 **Varazze** Italy
32G7 **Varberg** Sweden
32F7 **Varde** Den
32L4 **Vardø** Nor
43E2 **Varéna** Lithuania
37C2 **Varenna** Italy
37C2 **Varese** Italy
29C3 **Varginha** Brazil
32K6 **Varkaus** Fin
41F2 **Varna** Bulg
32G7 **Värnamo** Sweden
44K2 **Varnek** Russian Fed
15C2 **Varnville** USA
29D2 **Várzea da Palma** Brazil
37C2 **Varzi** Italy
28E2 **Vasconcelos** Brazil
39B1 **Vascongadas** Region, Spain
63E2 **Vāshīr** Afghan
44H3 **Vashka** *R* Russian Fed
45E5 **Vasil'kov** Ukraine
12C2 **Vassar** USA
32H7 **Västerås** Sweden
32H7 **Västervik** Sweden
40C2 **Vasto** Italy
48J4 **Vasyugan** *R* Russian Fed
32B2 **Vatnajökull** *Mts* Iceland
32A1 **Vatneyri** Iceland
41F1 **Vatra Dornei** Rom
32G7 **Vättern** *L* Sweden
16A3 **Vaughn** USA
28B1 **Va Unión** Arg
17F4 **Va Unión** Coahuila, Mexico
22B1 **Va Union** Durango, Mexico
22A1 **Va Union** Sinaloa, Mexico
26D3 **Vaupés** *R* Colombia
3F3 **Vauxhall** Can
77H2 **Vava'u Group** *Is* Tonga
62C3 **Vavunija** Sri Lanka
32G7 **Växjö** Sweden
48G2 **Vaygach, Ostrov** *I* Russian Fed
28C2 **Vedia** Arg
16B2 **Vega** USA
32G5 **Vega** *I* Nor
10B6 **Vega Pt** USA
3F3 **Vegreville** Can
39A2 **Vejer de la Frontera** Spain
32F7 **Vejle** Den
28E2 **Velázquez** Urug
74B3 **Velddrif** S Africa
40D2 **Velebit** *Mts* Croatia, Yugos
40D1 **Velenje** Serbia, Yugos
29D2 **Velhas** *R* Brazil
49T3 **Velikaya** *R* Russian Fed
43F1 **Velikaya** *R* Russian Fed
53D2 **Velikaya Kema** Russian Fed
44E4 **Velikiye Luki** Russian Fed
44H3 **Velikiy Ustyug** Russian Fed
41F2 **Veliko Tŭrnovo** Bulg
70A3 **Vélingara** Sen
43G1 **Velizh** Russian Fed
77E1 **Vella Lavella** *I* Solomon Is
62B2 **Vellore** India
36E1 **Velmerstat** *Mt* Germany
44G3 **Vel'sk** Russian Fed
11B2 **Velva** USA
62B3 **Vembanad L** India
53E2 **Vemor'ye** Russian Fed
25D4 **Venado Tuerto** Arg
29C3 **Vençeslau Braz** Brazil
36C2 **Vendeuvre-sur-Barse** France
38C2 **Vendôme** France
10J2 **Venetie** USA
37D2 **Veneto** Region, Italy
37E2 **Venezia** Italy
37E2 **Venezia** Region, Italy
26E2 **Venezuela** Republic, S America
62A1 **Vengurla** India
10G4 **Veniaminof V** USA
Venice = Venezia
62B2 **Venkatagiri** India
42B2 **Venlo** Neth
43E1 **Venta** *R* Latvia
74D2 **Ventersburg** S Africa
43E1 **Ventspils** Latvia
26E3 **Ventuari** *R* Ven
20C3 **Ventura** USA
44E3 **Vepsovskaya Vozvyshennost'** *Upland* Russian Fed
28C1 **Vera** Arg
39B2 **Vera** Spain
22C2 **Veracruz** Mexico
22C1 **Veracruz** State, Mexico
60C4 **Verāval** India
37C2 **Verbania** Italy
37C2 **Vercelli** Italy
37A2 **Vercors** *Plat* France
29A1 **Vérde** *R* Brazil
29B2 **Verde** *R* Goias, Brazil
22B1 **Verde** *R* Jalisco, Mexico
29B2 **Verde** *R* Mato Grosso do Sul, Brazil
22C2 **Verde** *R* Oaxaca, Mexico
19D4 **Verde** *R* USA
Verde,C = Cap Vert
29D2 **Verde Grande, R** Brazil
28C3 **Verde,Pen** Arg
38D3 **Verdon** *R* France
5G4 **Verdun** Can
36C2 **Verdun** France
37A1 **Verdun-sur-le-Doubs** France
74D2 **Vereeniging** S Africa
44J4 **Vereshchagino** Russian Fed
70A3 **Verga,C** Guinea
28D3 **Vergara** Arg
28E2 **Vergara** Urug
37D2 **Vergato** Italy
39A1 **Verin** Spain
49N4 **Verkh Angara** *R* Russian Fed
49K3 **Verkheimbatskoye** Russian Fed
44K5 **Verkhneural'sk** Russian Fed
49O3 **Verkhnevilyuysk** Russian Fed
44H3 **Verkhnyaya Toyma** Russian Fed
49P3 **Verkhoyansk** Russian Fed
49O3 **Verkhoyanskiy Khrebet** *Mts* Russian Fed
44H3 **Verkola** Russian Fed
29B2 **Vermelho** *R* Brazil
36B3 **Vermenton** France
3F3 **Vermilion** Can
4C4 **Vermilion Bay** Can
11C3 **Vermillion** USA
11D2 **Vermillion L** USA
9F2 **Vermont** State, USA
18E2 **Vernal** USA
20B2 **Vernalis** USA
36A2 **Verneuil** France
74C3 **Verneuk Pan** *Salt L* S Africa
3E3 **Vernon** Can
36A2 **Vernon** France
16C3 **Vernon** USA
15E4 **Vero Beach** USA
41E2 **Verola** Greece
37D2 **Verolanuova** Italy
37D2 **Verona** Italy
28D3 **Verónica** Arg
36B2 **Versailles** France
74E2 **Verulam** S Africa
36C1 **Verviers** Belg
36B2 **Vervins** France
43G3 **Veselinovo** Ukraine
36C2 **Vesle** *R* France
38D2 **Vesoul** France
32G5 **Vesterålen** *Is* Nor
32G5 **Vestfjorden** *Inlet* Nor
32A2 **Vestmannaeyjar** Iceland
40C2 **Vesuvio** *Mt* Italy
43D3 **Veszprém** Hung
32H7 **Vetlanda** Sweden
44G4 **Vetluga** *R* Russian Fed
36B1 **Veurne** Belg
37B1 **Vevey** Switz
36B2 **Vexin** Region, France
37A2 **Veynes** France
36C2 **Vézelise** France
39A1 **Viana do Castelo** Port
37D3 **Viareggio** Italy
32F7 **Viborg** Den
40D3 **Vibo Valentia** Italy
36A2 **Vibraye** France
Vic = Vich
79G2 **Vice-commodoro Marambio** *Base* Ant
40C1 **Vicenza** Italy
39C1 **Vich** Spain
26E3 **Vichada** *R* Colombia
44G4 **Vichuga** Russian Fed
38C2 **Vichy** France
17D3 **Vicksburg** USA
29D3 **Vicosa** Brazil
76C4 **Victor Harbor** Aust
28C2 **Victoria** Arg
72A3 **Victoria** Cam
3D4 **Victoria** Can
28A3 **Victoria** Chile
56E1 **Victoria** Malay
75B3 **Victoria** State, Aust
17F4 **Victoria** USA
76C2 **Victoria** *R* Aust
76D4 **Victoria** *State* Aust
4B3 **Victoria Beach** Can
23B2 **Victoria de las Tunas** Cuba
73C5 **Victoria Falls** Zambia/Zim
6G2 **Victoria I** Can
75B2 **Victoria,L** Aust
72D4 **Victoria,L** C Africa
79F7 **Victoria Land** Region, Ant
61D3 **Victoria,Mt** Burma
51H7 **Victoria,Mt** PNG
72D3 **Victoria Nile** *R* Uganda
78B2 **Victoria Range** *Mts* NZ
76C2 **Victoria River Downs** Aust
6H3 **Victoria Str** Can
5G4 **Victoriaville** Can
74C3 **Victoria West** S Africa
28B3 **Victorica** Arg
19C4 **Victorville** USA
28A2 **Vicuña** Chile
28C2 **Vicuña Mackenna** Arg
15C2 **Vidalia** USA
41F2 **Videle** Rom
41E2 **Vidin** Bulg
60D4 **Vidisha** India
43F1 **Vidzy** Belorussia
25D6 **Viedma** Arg
23A4 **Viéjo** Costa Rica
Vielha = Viella
39C1 **Viella** Spain
Vienna = Wien
12B3 **Vienna** Illinois, USA
12C3 **Vienna** W Virginia, USA
38C2 **Vienne** France
38C2 **Vienne** *R* France
55C2 **Vientiane** Laos
37C1 **Vierwaldstätter See** *L* Switz
38C2 **Vierzon** France
40D2 **Vieste** Italy
51D5 **Vietnam** Republic, S E Asia
55D1 **Vietri** Viet
23P2 **Vieux Fort** St Lucia
37A2 **Vif** France
57F7 **Vigan** Phil
37C2 **Vigevan** Italy
38B3 **Vignemale** *Mt* France
39A1 **Vigo** Spain
62C1 **Vijayawāda** India
41D2 **Vijosë** *R* Alb
32B2 **Vik** Iceland
41E2 **Vikhren** *Mt* Bulg
3F3 **Viking** Can
35G5 **Viking North** *Oilfield* N Sea
35G5 **Viking South** *Oilfield* N Sea
32G6 **Vikna** *I* Nor
73D5 **Vila da Maganja** Mozam
57C4 **Vila de Manatuto** Indon
57C4 **Vila de Salazar** Indon
73D5 **Vila Machado** Mozam
73D6 **Vilanculos** Mozam
Vilangchan = Vientiane
39C1 **Vilanova i la Geltrú** Spain
39A1 **Vila Real** Port
73D5 **Vila Vasco da Gama** Mozam
29D3 **Vila Velha** Brazil
28C1 **Vilelas** Arg
43F2 **Vileyka** Belorussia
32H6 **Vilhelmina** Sweden
27G6 **Vilhena** Brazil
43F2 **Viliya** Belorussia
44D4 **Viljandi** Estonia
74D2 **Viljoenskroon** S Africa
43F3 **Vilkovo** Ukraine
16A3 **Villa Ahumada** Mexico
28C1 **Villa Angela** Arg
28C1 **Villa Atamisqui** Arg
28B2 **Villa Atuel** Arg
39A1 **Villaba** Spain
22B2 **Villa Carranza** Mexico
40C1 **Villach** Austria
28B2 **Villa Colon** Arg
28C2 **Villa Constitución** Arg
22B1 **Villa de Cos** Mexico
28C1 **Villa de Maria** Arg
22B1 **Villa de Reyes** Mexico
28B2 **Villa Dolores** Arg
22D2 **Villa Flores** Mexico
37D2 **Villafranca di Verona** Italy
28C2 **Villa General Mitre** Arg
28B2 **Villa General Roca** Arg
28D3 **Villa Gesell** Arg
22C1 **Villagran** Mexico
28D2 **Villaguay** Arg

28D1 **Villa Guillermina** Arg
29A4 **Villa Hayes** Par
21C3 **Villahermosa** Mexico
22B1 **Villa Hidalgo** Mexico
28C2 **Villa Huidobro** Arg
28C3 **Villa Iris** Arg
28C2 **Villa Maria** Arg
26F8 **Villa Montes** Bol
22B1 **Villa Neuva** Mexico
39A1 **Villa Nova de Gaia** Port
39A2 **Villanueva de la Serena** Spain
39C1 **Villanueva-y-Geltrú** Spain
28C1 **Villa Ojo de Agua** Arg
28B3 **Villa Regina** Arg
39B2 **Villarreal** Spain
28A3 **Villarrica** Chile
25E3 **Villarrica** Par
39B2 **Villarrobledo** Spain
28D2 **Villa San José** Arg
28C1 **Villa San Martin** Arg
28C2 **Villa Valeria** Arg
26D3 **Villavicencio** Colombia
38C2 **Villefranche** France
7L5 **Ville-Marie** Can
39B2 **Villena** Spain
36B2 **Villeneuve-St-Georges** France
38C3 **Villeneuve-sur-Lot** France
36B2 **Villeneuve-sur-Yonne** France
17D3 **Ville Platte** USA
36B2 **Villers-Cotterêts** France
38C2 **Villeurbanne** France
74D2 **Villiers** S Africa
36E2 **Villingen-Schwenningen** Germany
62B2 **Villupuram** India
43F2 **Vilnius** Lithuania
49N3 **Vilyuy** *R* Russian Fed
49O3 **Vilyuysk** Russian Fed
36A2 **Vimoutiers** France
71J4 **Vina** *R* Cam
28A2 **Viña del Mar** Chile
39C1 **Vinaroz** Spain
12B3 **Vincennes** USA
28B1 **Vinchina** Arg
32H5 **Vindel** *R* Sweden
60D4 **Vindhya Range** *Mts* India
14C3 **Vineland** USA
14E2 **Vineyard Haven** USA
55D2 **Vinh** Viet
55D3 **Vinh Cam Ranh** *B* Viet
55D4 **Vinh Loi** Viet
55D3 **Vinh Long** Viet
17C2 **Vinita** USA
41D1 **Vinkovci** Croatia, Yugos
43F3 **Vinnitsa** Ukraine
79F3 **Vinson Massif** *Upland* Ant
11D3 **Vinton** USA
74B2 **Vioolsdrift** S Africa
37D1 **Vipiteno** Italy
57C4 **Viqueque** Indon
57F8 **Virac** Phil
62B2 **Virddhāchalam** India
11B2 **Virden** Can
73B5 **Virei** Angola
29D2 **Virgem da Lapa** Brazil
19D3 **Virgin** *R* USA
74D2 **Virginia** S Africa
9F3 **Virginia** State, USA
11D2 **Virginia** USA
13D3 **Virginia Beach** USA
19C3 **Virginia City** USA
23E3 **Virgin Is** Caribbean
12A2 **Viroqua** USA
40D1 **Virovitica** Croatia, Yugos
36C2 **Virton** Belg
62B3 **Virudunagar** India
40D2 **Vis** *I* Croatia, Yugos
20C2 **Visalia** USA
57F8 **Visayan S** Phil
32H7 **Visby** Sweden
6H2 **Viscount Melville Sd** Can
41D2 **Vişegrad** Bosnia & Herzegovina, Yugos
39A1 **Viseu** Port
62C1 **Vishākhapatnam** India
44K3 **Vishera** *R* Russian Fed
37B1 **Visp** Switz
38C1 **Vissingen** Neth
19C4 **Vista** USA
Vistula = Wisla
42C3 **Vitavia, R** Czech
62A1 **Vite** India
43G1 **Vitebsk** Belorussia
40C2 **Viterbo** Italy
39A1 **Vitigudino** Spain
77G2 **Viti Levu** *I* Fiji
49N4 **Vitim** *R* Russian Fed
39B1 **Vitora** Spain
27L8 **Vitória** Brazil
27K6 **Vitória da Conquista** Brazil
38B2 **Vitré** France
36C2 **Vitry-le-Francois** France
32J5 **Vittangi** Sweden
36C2 **Vittel** France
40C3 **Vittoria** Italy
37E2 **Vittorio Veneto** Italy
50J2 **Vityaz Depth** Pacific O
Viveiro = Vivero
39A1 **Vivero** Spain
49L3 **Vivi** *R* Russian Fed
28D3 **Vivorata** Arg
49M4 **Vizhne-Angarsk** Russian Fed
62C1 **Vizianagaram** India
37A2 **Vizille** France
44J3 **Vizinga** Russian Fed
41E1 **Vlādeasa** *Mt* Rom
45G7 **Vladikavkaz** Russian Fed
44G4 **Vladimir** Russian Fed
43E2 **Vladimir Volynskiy** Ukraine
53C3 **Vladivostok** Russian Fed
42A2 **Vlieland** *I* Neth
36B1 **Vlissingen** Neth
41D2 **Vlorë** Alb
42C3 **Vöcklabruck** Austria
37E2 **Vodnjan** Croatia, Yugos
55D3 **Voeune Sai** Camb
71J4 **Vogel Peak** *Mt* Nig
36E1 **Vogelsberg** Region, Germany
37C2 **Voghera** Italy
Vohémar = Vohimarina
73E5 **Vohibinany** Madag
73F5 **Vohimarina** Madag
72D4 **Voi** Kenya
70B4 **Voinjama** Lib
38D2 **Voiron** France
41D1 **Vojvodina** *Aut Republic* Serbia, Yugos
11A2 **Volborg** USA
23A5 **Volcán Baru** *Mt* Panama
22C2 **Volcán Citlaltepetl** *Mt* Mexico
26E8 **Volcán Lullaillaco** *Mt* Chile
28A3 **Volcáno Copahue** *Mt* Chile
28A3 **Volcáno Dumuyo** *Mt* Arg
Volcano Is = Kazan Retto
28A3 **Volcáno Lanin** *Mt* Arg
26E8 **Volcán Ollagüe** *Mt* Chile
28A3 **Volcáno Llaima** *Mt* Chile
28B2 **Volcáno Malpo** *Mt* Arg
28A3 **Volcáno Peteroa** *Mt* Chile
28B3 **Volcáno Tromen** *V* Arg
28A3 **Volcáno Villarrica** *Mt* Chile
22B2 **Volcán Paracutin** *Mt* Mexico
26C3 **Volcán Puraće** *Mt* Colombia
28A2 **Volcán Tinquiririca** *Mt* Chile/Arg
44K4 **Volchansk** Russian Fed
45H6 **Volga** *R* Russian Fed
45G6 **Volgodonsk** Russian Fed
45G6 **Volgograd** Russian Fed
45H5 **Volgogradskoye Vodokhranilishche** *Res* Russian Fed
44E4 **Volkhov** Russian Fed
44E4 **Volkhov** *R* Russian Fed
43E2 **Volkovysk** Belorussia
74D2 **Volksrust** S Africa
49L2 **Volochanka** Russian Fed
44G4 **Vologda** Russian Fed
38B2 **Volognes** France
41E3 **Vólos** Greece
45H5 **Vol'sk** Russian Fed
20B2 **Volta** USA
71G4 **Volta** *R* Ghana
71F3 **Volta Blanche** *R* Burkina
71F4 **Volta,L** Ghana
71F3 **Volta Noire** *R* Burkina
29D3 **Volta Redonda** Brazil
71F3 **Volta Rouge** *R* Burkina
37D3 **Volterra** Italy
37C2 **Voltri** Italy
45G6 **Volzhskiy** Russian Fed
10H3 **Von Frank Mt** USA
44F3 **Vonguda** Russian Fed
7R3 **Vopnafjörður** Iceland
37C1 **Voralberg** Province, Austria
37C1 **Vorder Rhein** *R* Switz
42C1 **Vordingborg** Den
45C8 **Voriái** *I* Greece
44L2 **Vorkuta** Russian Fed
32G6 **Vorma** *R* Nor
45F5 **Voronezh** Russian Fed
32M5 **Voron'ya** *R* Russian Fed
32K7 **Võru** Estonia
36D2 **Vosges** Department, France
38D2 **Vosges** *Mts* France
32F6 **Voss** Nor
53E2 **Vostchnyy** Russian Fed
53E1 **Vostochnyy** Russian Fed
49L4 **Vostochnyy Sayan** *Mts* Russian Fed
79F9 **Vostok** *Base* Ant
44J4 **Votkinsk** Russian Fed
36C2 **Vouziers** France
36A2 **Voves** France
11D2 **Voyageurs Nat Pk** USA
44K3 **Voy Vozh** Russian Fed
45E6 **Voznesensk** Ukraine
63E1 **Vozvyshennost' Karabil'** *Desert Region* Turkmenistan
49T2 **Vrangelya, Ostrov** *I* Russian Fed
41E2 **Vranje** Serbia, Yugos
41E2 **Vratsa** Bulg
41D1 **Vrbas** Serbia, Yugos
40D2 **Vrbas** *R* Serbia, Yugos
40C1 **Vrbovsko** Bosnia & Herzegovina, Yugos
74D2 **Vrede** S Africa
74B3 **Vredendal** S Africa
27G2 **Vreed en Hoop** Guyana
37F2 **Vrhnika** Slovenia, Yugos
41E1 **Vrzac** Serbia, Yugos
40D2 **Vrtoče** Bosnia & Herzegovina, Yugos
74C2 **Vryburg** S Africa
74E2 **Vryheid** S Africa
10E5 **Vsevidof,Mt** USA
41D1 **Vukovar** Croatia, Yugos
44K3 **Vuktyl'** Russian Fed
3F3 **Vulcan** Can
35G5 **Vulcan** *Oilfield* N Sea
40C3 **Vulcano** *I* Italy
55D3 **Vung Tau** Viet
32J5 **Vuollerim** Sweden
44E3 **Vyartsilya** Russian Fed
44J4 **Vyatka** *R* Russian Fed
53C2 **Vyazemskiy** Russian Fed
44E4 **Vyaz'ma** Russian Fed
44G4 **Vyazniki** Russian Fed
44D3 **Vyborg** Russian Fed
44F3 **Vygozero, Ozero** *L* Russian Fed
44J3 **Vym** *R* Russian Fed
35D5 **Vyrnwy** *R* Wales
44E4 **Vyshniy Volochek** Russian Fed
42D3 **Vyzkov** Czech
53D1 **Vysokogornyy** Russian Fed
44F3 **Vytegra** Russian Fed

W

71F3 **Wa** Ghana
36C1 **Waal** *R* Neth
3F2 **Wabasca** Can
6G4 **Wabasca** *R* Can
3F2 **Wabasca L** Can
12B2 **Wabash** USA
12B3 **Wabash** *R* USA
12C1 **Wabatongushi L** Can
6J4 **Wabowden** Can
7M4 **Wabush** Can
15C3 **Waccasassa B** USA
14E1 **Wachusett Res** USA
17C3 **Waco** USA
5H3 **Wacouno** *R* Can
60B3 **Wad** Pak
69A2 **Waddān** Libya
6F4 **Waddington,Mt** Can
3H3 **Wadena** Can
11C2 **Wadena** USA
65D3 **Wadi Abu 'Amūd** *V* Jordan
65B4 **Wadi Abu Tarfa** *V* Egypt
66D2 **Wadi ad Dawāsin** *Watercourse* S Arabia
67E3 **Wadi Adhanah** *Watercourse* Yemen
67F3 **Wadi al Amilhayt** *Watercourse* Oman
64E4 **Wadi al Bātin** *Watercourse* Iraq
64D3 **Wadi al Ghudāf** *Watercourse* Iraq
65D2 **Wadi al Harīr** *V* Syria
67F3 **Wadi al Masīlāh** *Watercourse* Yemen
64D3 **Wadi al Mirah** *Watercourse* S Arabia/Iraq
64D3 **Wadi al Ubayyid** *Watercourse* Iraq
67F3 **Wadi Aman** *Watercourse* Yemen
65C3 **Wadi 'Araba** *V* Israel
64D3 **Wadi Ar'ar** *Watercourse* S Arabia
67E2 **Wadi as Hsabā'** *Watercourse* S Arabia
64C3 **Wadi as Sirhān** *V* Jordan/ S Arabia
45G8 **Wadi ath Thamhar** *R* Iraq
65D2 **Wadi az Zaydi** *V* Syria
66D2 **Wadi Bishah** *Watercourse* S Arabia
65D3 **Wadi edh Dhab'i** *V* Jordan
65C4 **Wadi el'Aqaba** *V* Egypt
65B3 **Wadi el 'Arish** *V* Egypt
65B3 **Wadi el Brûk** *V* Egypt
65A3 **Wadi el Gafa** *V* Egypt
65D3 **Wadi el Ghadaf** *V* Jordan
65C3 **Wadi el Hasa** *V* Jordan
65B3 **Wadi el Higayib** *V* Egypt
65D3 **Wadi el Janab** *V* Jordan
65C3 **Wadi el Jeib** *V* Israel/ Jordan
65D4 **Wadi el Khush Shah** *V* Jordan
72C2 **Wadi el Milk** *Watercourse* Sudan
64A3 **Wadi el Natrun** *Watercourse* Egypt
65B4 **Wadi el Saheira** *V* Egypt
65B4 **Wadi el Siq** Egypt
65C3 **Wadi es Sir** Jordan
65C3 **Wadi Fidan** *V* Jordan
66D3 **Wadi Habawnāh** *Watercourse* S Arabia
66B2 **Wadi Haifa** Sudan
65C3 **Wadi Hareidin** *V* Egypt
65B3 **Wadi Hasana** *V* Egypt
64D3 **Wadi Hawrān** *R* Iraq
72C2 **Wadi Howa** *Watercourse* Sudan
72C2 **Wadi Ibra** *Watercourse* Sudan
67E3 **Wadi Jawf** *Watercourse* Yemen
65D2 **Wadi Luhfi** *Watercourse* Jordan
67E3 **Wadi Makhay** *Watercourse* Yemen
66D3 **Wadi Mawr** *Watercourse* Yemen
67F3 **Wadi Mugshin** *Watercourse* Oman
65C3 **Wadi Mujib** *V* Jordan
65C3 **Wādi Mūsa** Jordan
66B1 **Wadi Ouena** *Watercourse* Egypt
65D4 **Wadi Qa'ash Shubyk** *V* Jordan
67F3 **Wadi Qināb** *Watercourse* Yemen
65C3 **Wadi Qîtaiya** *V* Egypt
66D2 **Wadi Ranyah** *Watercourse* S Arabia
65D4 **Wadi Ratiyah** *V* Jordan
65D4 **Wadi Ruweila** *V* Jordan
66B2 **Wadi Sha'it** *Watercourse* Egypt
67F3 **Wadi Shihan** *Watercourse* Oman
66D2 **Wadi Tathlith** *Watercourse* S Arabia
66D2 **Wadi Turabah** *Watercourse* S Arabia
65C3 **Wadi Ugeiqa** *V* Jordan
72D2 **Wad Medani** Sudan
54A3 **Waegwan** S Korea
64E4 **Wafra** Kuwait
36C1 **Wageningen** Neth
7K3 **Wager B** Can
7J3 **Wager Bay** Can
75C3 **Wagga Wagga** Aust
76A4 **Wagin** Aust
11C3 **Wagner** USA
57C3 **Waha** Indon
20E5 **Wahaiwa** Hawaiian Is
17C1 **Wahoo** USA
11C2 **Wahpeton** USA
62A1 **Wai** India
20E5 **Waialua** Hawaiian Is
78B2 **Waiau** NZ
78A3 **Waiau** *R* NZ
78B2 **Waiau** *R* NZ
57C3 **Waigama** Indon
51G6 **Waigeo** *I* Indon
78C1 **Waihi** NZ
57A4 **Waikabubak** Indon
78C1 **Waikaremoana,L** NZ
78C1 **Waikato** *R* NZ
57A4 **Waikelo** Indon
75A2 **Waikerie** Aust
78B3 **Waikouaiti** NZ
20E5 **Wailuku** Hawaiian Is
78B2 **Waimakariri** *R* NZ
78B2 **Waimate** NZ
20E5 **Waimea** Hawaiian Is
76B1 **Waingapu** Indon
3F3 **Wainwright** Can
10F1 **Wainwright** USA
78B2 **Waipara** NZ
78C2 **Waipukurau** NZ
78C2 **Wairarapa,L** NZ
78B2 **Wairau** *R* NZ
78C1 **Wairoa** NZ
78C1 **Wairoa** *R* NZ
78B2 **Waitaki** *R* NZ
78B1 **Waitara** NZ
78C1 **Waitomo** NZ
78B1 **Waiuku** NZ
54C3 **Wajima** Japan
72E3 **Wajir** Kenya
54C3 **Wakasa-wan** *B* Japan
78A3 **Wakatipu,L** NZ
3G3 **Wakaw** Can
53D5 **Wakayama** Japan
16C2 **Wa Keeney** USA
35E5 **Wakefield** Eng
23H1 **Wakefield** Jamaica
12B1 **Wakefield** Michigan, USA
14E2 **Wakefield** Rhode Island, USA
55B2 **Wakema** Burma
53E2 **Wakkanai** Japan
75B3 **Wakool** *R* Aust
57D3 **Wakre** Indon
5H2 **Wakuach L** Can
42D2 **Walbrzych** Pol
75D2 **Walcha** Aust
42D2 **Walcz** Pol
36D1 **Waldbröl** Germany
14C2 **Walden** USA
36E3 **Waldshut** Germany
35D5 **Wales** Country, UK
10E2 **Wales** USA
7K3 **Wales I** Can
71F3 **Walewale** Ghana
75C2 **Walgett** Aust
79F4 **Walgreen Coast** Region, Ant
72C4 **Walikale** Zaïre
11D2 **Walker** USA
20C1 **Walker L** USA
20C3 **Walker Pass** USA
12C2 **Walkerton** Can
11B3 **Wall** USA
18C1 **Wallace** USA
75A2 **Wallaroo** Aust
75C3 **Walla Walla** Aust
18C1 **Walla Walla** USA
36E2 **Walldürn** Germany
14D2 **Wallingford** USA
xxixK5 **Wallis and Futuna** *Is* Pacific O
18C1 **Wallowa** USA
18C1 **Wallowa Mts** *Mts* USA
75C1 **Wallumbilla** Aust
17D2 **Walnut Ridge** USA
78C1 **Walouru** NZ
14D1 **Walpole** USA
35E5 **Walsall** Eng
16B2 **Walsenburg** USA
15C2 **Walterboro** USA
15B2 **Walter F George Res** USA
16C3 **Walters** USA
14E1 **Waltham** USA
14C1 **Walton** USA
68F9 **Walvis Bay** Namibia
74A1 **Walvis Bay** S Africa
xxxJ6 **Walvis Ridge** Atlantic O
71H4 **Wamba** Nig
72B4 **Wamba** *R* Zaïre
17C2 **Wamego** USA
57C3 **Wamsasi** Indon
18E2 **Wamsutter** USA
60B2 **Wana** Pak
75B1 **Wanaaring** Aust
78A2 **Wanaka** NZ
78A2 **Wanaka,L** NZ
4E4 **Wanapitei L** Can
53C2 **Wanda Shan** *Upland* China
54A4 **Wando** S Korea
75C1 **Wandoan** Aust
75B3 **Wanganella** Aust
78B2 **Wanganui** NZ
78C1 **Wanganui** *R* NZ
75C3 **Wangaratta** Aust
57B4 **Wangiwangi** *I* Indon
53B2 **Wangkui** China
71F4 **Wango Fitini** Ivory Coast
53B3 **Wangqing** China
68G9 **Wankie** Zim
72E3 **Wanlaweyne** Somalia
55E2 **Wanning** China
62B1 **Wanparti** India
52B3 **Wanxian** China
52B3 **Wanyuan** China
3H3 **Wapawekka L** Can
3D3 **Wapiti** *R* Can
17D2 **Wappapello,L** USA
14D2 **Wappingers Falls** USA
11D3 **Wapsipinicon** *R* USA
71J3 **Wara Nat Pk** Cam
62B1 **Warangal** India
75E3 **Waratah** Aust
75C3 **Waratah B** Aust
36E1 **Warburg** Germany
75C3 **Warburton** Aust
75A1 **Warburton** *R* Aust
75C1 **Ward** *R* Aust
74D2 **Warden** S Africa
72E3 **Warder** Eth
60D4 **Wardha** India
78A3 **Ward,Mt** NZ
3C2 **Ware** Can

14D1 **Ware** USA
14E2 **Wareham** USA
36D1 **Warendorf** Germany
75D1 **Warialda** Aust
55D2 **Warin Chamrap** Thai
74B2 **Warmbad** Namibia
73C6 **Warmbad** S Africa
14C2 **Warminster** USA
19C3 **Warm Springs** USA
42C2 **Warnemünde** Germany
18B2 **Warner Mts** USA
15C2 **Warner Robins** USA
75B3 **Warracknabeal** Aust
75A1 **Warrandirinna,L** Aust
76D3 **Warrego** *R* Aust
17D3 **Warren** Arkansas, USA
75C2 **Warren** Aust
11C2 **Warren** Minnesota, USA
12C2 **Warren** Ohio, USA
4E5 **Warren** Michigan, USA
13D2 **Warren** Pennsylvania, USA
14E2 **Warren** Rhode Island, USA
35B4 **Warrenpoint** N Ire
17D2 **Warrensburg** USA
74C2 **Warrenton** S Africa
13D3 **Warrenton** USA
71H4 **Warri** Nig
75A1 **Warrina** Aust
35D5 **Warrington** Eng
15B2 **Warrington** USA
75B3 **Warrnambool** Aust
11C2 **Warroad** USA
Warsaw = Warszawa
14A1 **Warsaw** USA
72E3 **Warshiikh** Somalia
43E2 **Warszawa** Pol
43D2 **Warta** *R* Pol
75D1 **Warwick** Aust
35E5 **Warwick** County, Eng
35E5 **Warwick** Eng
14C2 **Warwick** New York, USA
14E2 **Warwick** Rhode Island, USA
19D3 **Wasatch Range** *Mts* USA
74E2 **Wasbank** S Africa
20C3 **Wasco** USA
11D3 **Waseca** USA
3G2 **Wasekamio L** Can
63E3 **Washap** Pak
12A1 **Washburn** USA
6H2 **Washburn L** Can
18D2 **Washburn,Mt** USA
60D4 **Wāshīm** India
9F3 **Washington** District of Columbia, USA
15C2 **Washington** Georgia, USA
12B3 **Washington** Indiana, USA
11D3 **Washington** Iowa, USA
17D2 **Washington** Missouri, USA
15D1 **Washington** N Carolina, USA
14C2 **Washington** New Jersey, USA
12C2 **Washington** Pennsylvania, USA
8A2 **Washington** State, USA
19D3 **Washington** Utah, USA
12C3 **Washington Court House** USA
7M1 **Washington Land** *Region* Can
13E2 **Washington,Mt** USA
16C2 **Washita** *R* USA
35F5 **Wash,The** Eng
60A3 **Washuk** Pak
10J3 **Wasilla** USA
7L4 **Waskaganish** Can
23A4 **Waspán** Nic
20C1 **Wassuk Range** *Mts* USA
36C2 **Wassy** France
4F4 **Waswanipi L** *L* Can
57B3 **Watampone** Indon
57A3 **Watansoppeng** Indon
74D3 **Waterberge** *Mts* S Africa
14D2 **Waterbury** USA
3G2 **Waterbury L** Can
35B5 **Waterford** County, Irish Rep
33B3 **Waterford** Irish Rep
35B5 **Waterford Harbour** Irish Rep
36C1 **Waterloo** Belg
4E5 **Waterloo** Can
11D3 **Waterloo** USA
12B1 **Watersmeet** USA
18D1 **Waterton-Glacier International Peace Park** USA
13D2 **Watertown** New York, USA
11C3 **Watertown** S Dakota, USA
12B2 **Watertown** Wisconsin, USA
74E2 **Waterval-Boven** S Africa
13F2 **Waterville** Maine, USA
14C1 **Waterville** New York, USA

14D1 **Watervliet** USA
6G4 **Waterways** Can
35E6 **Watford** Eng
11B2 **Watford City** USA
14B1 **Watkins Glen** USA
16C2 **Watonga** USA
8C1 **Watrous** Can
16B2 **Watrous** USA
72C3 **Watsa** Zaïre
10N3 **Watson Lake** Can
20B2 **Watsonville** USA
3E2 **Watt,Mt** Can
57B3 **Watukancoa** Indon
51H7 **Wau** PNG
72C3 **Wau** Sudan
75D2 **Wauchope** Aust
15E4 **Wauchula** USA
12B2 **Waukegan** USA
12B2 **Waukesha** USA
12B2 **Waupaca** USA
12B2 **Waupun** USA
17C3 **Waurika** USA
12B2 **Wausau** USA
12B2 **Wauwatosa** USA
76C2 **Wave Hill** Aust
35F5 **Waverey** *R* Eng
11D3 **Waverly** Iowa, USA
14B1 **Waverly** New York, USA
12C3 **Waverly** Ohio, USA
36C1 **Wavre** Belg
7K5 **Wawa** Can
71G4 **Wawa** Nig
69A2 **Wāw Al Kabīr** Libya
69A2 **Wāw an Nāmūs** *Well* Libya
20C2 **Wawona** USA
17C3 **Waxahachie** USA
57C2 **Wayabula** Indon
15C2 **Waycross** USA
11C3 **Wayne** USA
15C2 **Waynesboro** Georgia, USA
17E3 **Waynesboro** Mississippi, USA
14B3 **Waynesboro** Pennsylvania, USA
13D3 **Waynesboro** Virginia, USA
17D2 **Waynesville** Missouri, USA
15C1 **Waynesville** N Carolina, USA
60B2 **Wazi Khwa** Afghan
35F6 **Weald,The** *Upland* Eng
34D4 **Wear** *R* Eng
16C2 **Weatherford** Oklahoma, USA
17C3 **Weatherford** Texas, USA
18B2 **Weaverville** USA
12C1 **Webbwood** Can
14B1 **Webster** New York, USA
11C2 **Webster** S Dakota, USA
14E1 **Webster** USA
11D3 **Webster City** USA
12A3 **Webster Groves** USA
57C2 **Weda** Indon
25D8 **Weddell I** Falkland Is
79G2 **Weddell S** Ant
3D3 **Wedge Mt** Can
5H5 **Wedgeport** Can
18B2 **Weed** USA
14A2 **Weedville** USA
74E2 **Weenen** S Africa
75C2 **Wee Waa** Aust
52D1 **Weichang** China
42C3 **Weiden** Germany
52D2 **Weifang** China
52E2 **Weihai** China
52C3 **Wei He** *R* Henan, China
52C2 **Wei He** *R* Shaanxi, China
75C1 **Weilmoringle** Aust
36E2 **Weinheim** Germany
52A4 **Weining** China
76D2 **Weipa** Aust
12C2 **Weirton** USA
18C2 **Weiser** USA
52D3 **Weishan Hu** *L* China
42C2 **Weissenfels** Germany
15B2 **Weiss L** USA
3G2 **Weitzel L** Can
4B3 **Wekusko** Can
12C3 **Welch** USA
72E2 **Weldiya** Eth
20C3 **Weldon** USA
74D2 **Welkom** S Africa
13D2 **Welland** Can
35E5 **Welland** *R* Eng
76C2 **Wellesley Is** Aust
10L3 **Wellesley L** Can
14E2 **Wellfleet** USA
35E5 **Wellingborough** Eng
75C2 **Wellington** Aust
16B1 **Wellington** Colorado, USA
17C2 **Wellington** Kansas, USA
20C1 **Wellington** Nevada, USA
78B2 **Wellington** NZ
74B3 **Wellington** S Africa
16B3 **Wellington** Texas, USA

7J2 **Wellington Chan** Can
3D3 **Wells** Can
35D6 **Wells** Eng
18D2 **Wells** Nevada, USA
14C1 **Wells** New York, USA
14B2 **Wellsboro** USA
78B1 **Wellsford** NZ
76B3 **Wells,L** Aust
4A2 **Wells L** Can
14B1 **Wellsville** USA
42C3 **Wels** Austria
35D5 **Welshpool** Wales
3E2 **Wembley** Can
7L4 **Wemindji** Can
18B1 **Wenatchee** USA
18C1 **Wenatchee** *R* USA
71F4 **Wenchi** Ghana
52E2 **Wenden** China
18D2 **Wendover** USA
52E4 **Wenling** China
52A5 **Wenshan** China
76D4 **Wenthaggi** Aust
75B2 **Wentworth** Aust
3F2 **Wentzel L** Can
52A3 **Wen Xian** China
52E4 **Wenzhou** China
52C4 **Wenzhu** China
74D2 **Wepener** S Africa
74C2 **Werda** Botswana
10L2 **Wernecke Mts** Can
42C2 **Werra** *R* Germany
75D2 **Werris Creek** Aust
36D1 **Wesel** Germany
42B2 **Weser** *R* Germany
16B2 **Weskan** USA
17F4 **Weslaco** USA
7N5 **Wesleyville** Can
76C2 **Wessel Is** Aust
36E1 **Wesser** *R* Germany
36E1 **Wesserbergland** Region, Germany
11C3 **Wessington Springs** USA
12B2 **West Allis** USA
xxviiiF5 **West Australian Basin** Indian O
xxviiiF6 **West Australian Ridge** Indian O
17E3 **West B** USA
61C3 **West Bengal** State, India
14C1 **West Branch Delaware** *R* USA
14A2 **West Branch Susquehanna** *R* USA
35E5 **West Bromwich** Eng
13E2 **Westbrook** USA
12A2 **Westby** USA
14C3 **West Chester** USA
20D3 **Westend** USA
36D1 **Westerburg** Germany
42B2 **Westerland** Germany
14E2 **Westerly** USA
76B3 **Western Australia** State, Aust
62A1 **Western Ghats** *Mts* India
34B3 **Western Isles** Scot
70A2 **Western Sahara** Region, Mor
77H2 **Western Samoa** *Is* Pacific O
36B1 **Westerschelde** *Estuary* Neth
36D1 **Westerwald** Region, Germany
38D1 **Westfalen** Region, Germany
25D8 **West Falkland** *I* Falkland Is
14D1 **Westfield** Massachusetts, USA
13D2 **Westfield** New York, USA
14B2 **Westfield** Pennsylvania, USA
12B3 **West Frankfort** USA
75C1 **Westgate** Aust
35D6 **West Glamorgan** County, Wales
13F1 **West Grand L** USA
xxxE4 **West Indies** *Is* Caribbean S
12C3 **West Liberty** USA
3F3 **Westlock** Can
12C2 **West Lorne** Can
35B5 **Westmeath** County, Irish Rep
17D2 **West Memphis** USA
35E5 **West Midlands** County, Eng
35E6 **Westminster** Eng
14B3 **Westminster** Maryland, USA
15C2 **Westminster** S Carolina, USA
74D1 **West Nicholson** Zim
56E1 **Weston** Malay
12C3 **Weston** USA
35D6 **Weston-super-Mare** Eng
15E4 **West Palm Beach** USA

17D2 **West Plains** USA
20B1 **West Point** California, USA
17E3 **West Point** Mississippi, USA
11C3 **West Point** Nebraska, USA
14D2 **West Point** New York, USA
10K3 **West Point** *Mt* USA
78B2 **Westport** NZ
4A3 **Westray** Can
33C2 **Westray** *I* Scot
3D3 **West Road** *R* Can
35F5 **West Side** *Oilfield* N Sea
9E3 **West Virginia** State, USA
20C1 **West Walker** USA
75C2 **West Wyalong** Aust
18D2 **West Yellowstone** USA
35E5 **West Yorkshire** County, Eng
57C4 **Wetar** *I* Indon
3F3 **Wetaskiwin** Can
72D4 **Wete** Tanz
36E1 **Wetter** *R* Germany
36E1 **Wetzlar** Germany
Wevok = Cape Lisburne
76D1 **Wewak** PNG
17C2 **Wewoka** USA
35B5 **Wexford** County, Irish Rep
35B5 **Wexford** Irish Rep
6H5 **Weyburn** Can
35D6 **Weymouth** Eng
14E1 **Weymouth** USA
78C1 **Whakatane** NZ
78C1 **Whakatane** *R* NZ
34E1 **Whalsay** *I* Scot
78B1 **Whangarei** NZ
35E5 **Wharfe** *R* Eng
17C4 **Wharton** USA
11A3 **Wheatland** USA
14B3 **Wheaton** Maryland, USA
11C2 **Wheaton** Minnesota, USA
3G2 **Wheeler** *R* Can
19D3 **Wheeler Peak** *Mt* Nevada, USA
16A2 **Wheeler Peak** *Mt* New Mexico, USA
20C3 **Wheeler Ridge** USA
5H2 **Wheeler** *R* Can
12C2 **Wheeling** USA
3D3 **Whistler** Can
35E4 **Whitby** Eng
4F5 **Whitby** Can
17D2 **White** *R* Arkansas, USA
10K3 **White** *R* Can
16A1 **White** *R* Colorado, USA
12B3 **White** *R* Indiana, USA
11B3 **White** *R* S Dakota, USA
7N4 **White B** Can
11B2 **White Butte** *Mt* USA
75B2 **White Cliffs** Aust
33C2 **White Coomb** *Mt* Scot
3E3 **Whitecourt** Can
18D1 **Whitefish** USA
4D4 **Whitefish B** Can/USA
12B1 **Whitefish Pt** USA
7M4 **Whitegull L** Can
13E2 **Whitehall** New York, USA
14C2 **Whitehall** Pennsylvania, USA
12A2 **Whitehall** Wisconsin, USA
35D4 **Whitehaven** Eng
10L3 **Whitehorse** Can
78C1 **White I** NZ
17D4 **White L** USA
75E3 **Whitemark** Aust
20C2 **White Mountain Peak** *Mt* USA
10J2 **White Mts** Alaska, USA
20C2 **White Mts** California, USA
13E2 **White Mts** New Hampshire, USA
72D2 **White Nile** *R* Sudan
4C4 **White Otter L** Can
14D2 **White Plains** USA
7K5 **White River** Can
11B3 **White River** USA
13E2 **White River Junction** USA
White S = Beloye More
3C3 **Whitesail L** Can
18B1 **White Salmon** USA
3H3 **Whitesand** *R* Can
4B3 **Whiteshell Prov Park** Can
18D1 **White Sulphur Springs** USA
15D2 **Whiteville** USA
71F4 **White Volta** *R* Ghana
12B2 **Whitewater** USA
3H3 **Whitewood** Can
34C4 **Whithorn** Scot
15C2 **Whitmire** USA
4F4 **Whitney** Can
20C2 **Whitney,Mt** USA
10J3 **Whittier** Alaska, USA
20C4 **Whittier** California, USA
6H3 **Wholdaia L** Can
75A2 **Whyalla** Aust

12C2 **Wiarton** Can
71F4 **Wiawso** Ghana
11B2 **Wibaux** USA
17C2 **Wichita** USA
16C3 **Wichita** *R* USA
16C3 **Wichita Falls** USA
16C3 **Wichita Mts** USA
34D2 **Wick** Scot
19D4 **Wickenburg** USA
35B5 **Wicklow** County, Irish Rep
35B5 **Wicklow** Irish Rep
35B5 **Wicklow** *Mts* Irish Rep
75C1 **Widgeegoara** *R* Aust
36D1 **Wied** *R* Germany
43D2 **Wielun** Pol
42D3 **Wien** Austria
42D3 **Wiener Neustadt** Austria
43E2 **Wieprz** *R* Pol
36E1 **Wiesbaden** Germany
36D3 **Wiese** *R* Germany
35D5 **Wigan** Eng
17E3 **Wiggins** USA
34C4 **Wigtown** Scot
34C4 **Wigtown B** Scot
37C1 **Wil** Switz
18C1 **Wilbur** USA
75B2 **Wilcannia** Aust
19C3 **Wildcat Peak** *Mt* USA
37B1 **Wildhorn** *Mt* Switz
3F4 **Wild Horse** Can
37D1 **Wildspitze** *Mt* Austria
15C3 **Wildwood** Florida, USA
14C3 **Wildwood** New Jersey, USA
16B2 **Wiley** USA
74D2 **Wilge** *R* S Africa
76D1 **Wilhelm,Mt** PNG
42B2 **Wilhelmshaven** Germany
14C2 **Wilkes-Barre** USA
79F8 **Wilkes Land** Ant
3G3 **Wilkie** Can
18B2 **Willamette** *R* USA
75B2 **Willandra** *R* Aust
18B1 **Willapa B** USA
19E4 **Willcox** USA
23D4 **Willemstad** Curaçao
3G2 **William** *R* Can
75A1 **William Creek** Aust
75B3 **William,Mt** Aust
19D3 **Williams** Arizona, USA
19B3 **Williams** California, USA
13D3 **Williamsburg** USA
3D3 **Williams Lake** Can
12C3 **Williamson** USA
14B2 **Williamsport** USA
15D1 **Williamston** USA
14D1 **Williamstown** Massachusetts, USA
12C3 **Williamstown** W Virginia, USA
14D2 **Willimantic** USA
14C2 **Willingboro** USA
3E3 **Willingdon,Mt** Can
76E2 **Willis Group** *Is* Aust
15C3 **Williston** Florida, USA
11B2 **Williston** N Dakota, USA
74C3 **Williston** S Africa
3D2 **Williston L** Can
11C2 **Willmar** USA
75A3 **Willoughby,C** Aust
3D3 **Willow** *R* Can
11A2 **Willow Bunch** Can
74C3 **Willowmore** S Africa
18B2 **Willow Ranch** USA
19B3 **Willows** USA
17D2 **Willow Springs** USA
75A2 **Wilmington** Aust
14C3 **Wilmington** Delaware, USA
15D2 **Wilmington** N Carolina, USA
14D1 **Wilmington** Vermont, USA
16C2 **Wilson** Kansas, USA
15D1 **Wilson** N Carolina, USA
14A1 **Wilson** New York, USA
9F3 **Wilson** USA
16C2 **Wilson** *L* USA
75B1 **Wilson** *R* Aust
7K3 **Wilson,C** Can
20C3 **Wilson,Mt** California, USA
16A2 **Wilson,Mt** Colorado, USA
18B1 **Wilson,Mt** Oregon, USA
75C3 **Wilsons Promontory** *Pen* Aust
35E6 **Wiltshire** County, Eng
36C2 **Wiltz** Lux
76B3 **Wiluna** Aust
12B2 **Winamac** USA
74D2 **Winburg** S Africa
14D1 **Winchendon** USA
13D1 **Winchester** Can
35E6 **Winchester** Eng
12C3 **Winchester** Kentucky, USA
14D1 **Winchester** New Hampshire, USA
13D3 **Winchester** Virginia, USA

18E2 **Wind** *R* USA
14A2 **Windber** USA
11B3 **Wind Cave Nat Pk** USA
35D4 **Windermere** Eng
74B1 **Windhoek** Namibia
11C3 **Windom** USA
76D3 **Windorah** Aust
18E2 **Wind River Range** *Mts* USA
75D2 **Windsor** Aust
14D2 **Windsor** Connecticut, USA
35E6 **Windsor** Eng
5K4 **Windsor** Newfoundland, Can
15D1 **Windsor** N Carolina, USA
7M5 **Windsor** Nova Scotia, Can
4E5 **Windsor** Ontario, Can
5G4 **Windsor** Quebec, Can
15C2 **Windsor Forest** USA
14D2 **Windsor Locks** USA
23E4 **Windward Is** Caribbean
23C3 **Windward Pass** Caribbean
3F2 **Winefred L** Can
15B2 **Winfield** Alabama, USA
17C2 **Winfield** Kansas, USA
75D2 **Wingham** Aust
4E5 **Wingham** Can
28C3 **Winifreda** Arg
4D2 **Winisk** Can
7K4 **Winisk** *R* Can
7K4 **Winisk L** Can
55B2 **Winkana** Burma
18B1 **Winlock** USA
71F4 **Winneba** Ghana
11D3 **Winnebago** USA
12B2 **Winnebago,L** USA
18C2 **Winnemucca** USA
11C3 **Winner** USA
17D3 **Winnfield** USA
11D2 **Winnibigoshish L** USA
6J4 **Winnipeg** Can
6J4 **Winnipeg,L** Can
4B3 **Winnipeg** *R* Can
6J4 **Winnipegosis** Can
4A3 **Winnipegosis,L** Can
13E2 **Winnipesaukee,L** USA
11D3 **Winona** Minnesota, USA
17E3 **Winona** Mississippi, USA
13E2 **Winooski** USA
19D4 **Winslow** USA
14D2 **Winsted** USA
15C1 **Winston-Salem** USA
36E1 **Winterberg** Germany
15C3 **Winter Garden** USA
15C3 **Winter Park** USA
20B1 **Winters** USA
36D1 **Winterswijk** Neth
37C1 **Winterthur** Switz
11D3 **Winthrop** USA
76D3 **Winton** Aust
78A3 **Winton** NZ
35F5 **Wisbech** Eng
9E2 **Wisconsin** State, USA
12A2 **Wisconsin** *R* USA
12B2 **Wisconsin Dells** USA
7K5 **Wisconsin Rapids** USA
10H2 **Wiseman** USA
43D2 **Wisla** *R* Pol
42C2 **Wismar** Germany
36D2 **Wissembourg** France
27H2 **Witagron** Surinam
74D2 **Witbank** S Africa
8D3 **Witchita Falls** USA
35E5 **Witham** *R* Eng
35F5 **Withernsea** Eng
35E6 **Witney** Eng
36D1 **Witten** Germany
42C2 **Wittenberg** Germany
76A3 **Wittenoom** Aust
36D1 **Wittlich** Germany
74B1 **Witvlei** Namibia
43D2 **Wladyslawowo** Pol
43D2 **Włocławek** Pol
43E2 **Włodawa** Pol
75C3 **Wodonga** Aust
37C1 **Wohlen** Switz
51G7 **Wokam** Indon
35E6 **Woking** Eng
14B1 **Wolcott** USA
51H6 **Woleai** *I* Pacific O
12B1 **Wolf** *R* USA
36E2 **Wolfach** Germany
18B2 **Wolf Creek** USA
16A2 **Wolf Creek P** USA
3B1 **Wolf L** Can
11A2 **Wolf Point** USA
42C3 **Wolfsberg** Austria
42C2 **Wolfsburg** Germany
3H2 **Wollaston L** Can
3H2 **Wollaston Lake** Can
6G3 **Wollaston Pen** Can
75D2 **Wollongong** Aust
74D2 **Wolmaransstad** S Africa
42D2 **Wolow** Pol
57B4 **Wolowaru** Indon
75B3 **Wolseley** Aust
35D5 **Wolverhampton** Eng
14B2 **Womelsdorf** USA
75D1 **Wondai** Aust
53B4 **Wŏnju** S Korea
75B2 **Wonominta** *R* Aust
3D2 **Wonowon** Can
53B4 **Wŏnsan** N Korea
75C3 **Wonthaggi** Aust
75A2 **Woocalla** Aust
14C3 **Woodbine** USA
13D3 **Woodbridge** USA
3F2 **Wood Buffalo Nat Pk** Can
75D1 **Woodburn** Aust
18B1 **Woodburn** USA
14C3 **Woodbury** USA
10K2 **Woodchopper** USA
20C1 **Woodfords** USA
3H2 **Wood L** Can
20C2 **Woodlake** USA
19B3 **Woodland** California, USA
20B1 **Woodland** USA
18B1 **Woodland** Washington, USA
77E1 **Woodlark** *I* PNG
76C4 **Woodmera** Aust
76C3 **Woodroffe,Mt** Aust
5H3 **Woods L** Can
12B2 **Woodstock** Illinois, USA
13F1 **Woodstock** New Brunswick, Can
4E5 **Woodstock** Ontario, Can
14A3 **Woodstock** Virginia, USA
14C3 **Woodstown** USA
78C2 **Woodville** NZ
17D3 **Woodville** USA
16C2 **Woodward** USA
75A2 **Woomera** Aust
13E2 **Woonsocket** USA
12C2 **Wooster** USA
35D5 **Worcester** Eng
74B3 **Worcester** S Africa
14E1 **Worcester** USA
37E1 **Wörgl** Austria
35D4 **Workington** Eng
18E2 **Worland** USA
36E2 **Worms** Germany
35C6 **Worms Head** *Pt* Wales
35E6 **Worthing** Eng
11C3 **Worthington** Minnesota, USA
12C2 **Worthington** Ohio, USA
11B3 **Wounded Knee** USA
57B3 **Wowoni** *I* Indon
10M4 **Wrangell** USA
10A5 **Wrangell,C** USA
10M4 **Wrangell I** USA
10K3 **Wrangell Mts** USA
33B2 **Wrath,C** Scot
16B1 **Wray** USA
35D5 **Wrexham** Wales
19D4 **Wrightson** USA
15C2 **Wrightsville** USA
20D3 **Wrightwood** USA
6F3 **Wrigley** Can
42D2 **Wrocław** Pol
43D2 **Wrzésnia** Pol
53B3 **Wuchang** China
55E1 **Wuchuan** China
52E2 **Wuda** China
67E3 **Wuday'ah** S Arabia
71H3 **Wudil** Nig
52C2 **Wuding He** *R* China
52A3 **Wudu** China
52C4 **Wugang** China
52B2 **Wuhai** China
52C3 **Wuhan** China
52D3 **Wuhu** China
52D5 **Wuhua** China
60D2 **Wüjang** China
52B1 **Wujia He** *R* China
52B4 **Wu Jiang** *R* China
71H4 **Wukari** Nig
57D4 **Wuliaru** *I* Indon
52B4 **Wuling Shan** *Mts* China
71J4 **Wum** Cam
52A4 **Wumeng Shan** *Upland* China
4D3 **Wunnummin L** Can
61E3 **Wuntho** Burma
36D1 **Wuppertal** Germany
52B2 **Wuqi** China
52D2 **Wuqing** China
42B3 **Würzburg** Germany
42C2 **Wurzen** Germany
53C2 **Wusuli Jiang** *R* China
52C2 **Wutai Shan** *Mt* China
51H7 **Wuvulu** *I* Pacific O
52A2 **Wuwei** China
52E3 **Wuxi** China
52E3 **Wuxing** China
52C2 **Wuyang** China
53B2 **Wuyiling** China
52D4 **Wuyi Shan** *Mts* China
52B1 **Wuyuan** China
53B2 **Wuyur He** *R* China
55D2 **Wuzhi Shan** *Mts* China
52B2 **Wuzhong** China
52C5 **Wuzhou** China
12C2 **Wyandotte** USA
75C1 **Wyandra** Aust
35D6 **Wye** *R* Eng
35D6 **Wylye** *R* Eng
35F5 **Wymondham** Eng
76B2 **Wyndham** Aust
17D2 **Wynne** USA
6G2 **Wynniatt B** Can
75E3 **Wynyard** Aust
3H3 **Wynyard** Can
8B2 **Wyoming** State, USA
12B2 **Wyoming** USA
18D2 **Wyoming Peak** *Mt* USA
18D2 **Wyoming Range** *Mts* USA
75D2 **Wyong** Aust
12C3 **Wytheville** USA

X

60D1 **Xaidulla** China
52D1 **Xai Moron He** *R* China
74E2 **Xai Xai** Mozam
22C2 **Xaltinguis** Mexico
73B5 **Xangongo** Angola
36D1 **Xanten** Germany
41E2 **Xánthi** Greece
74C1 **Xau,L** Botswana
12C3 **Xenia** USA
50C4 **Xiaguan** China
52A2 **Xiahe** China
52D5 **Xiamen** China
52B3 **Xi'an** China
52B4 **Xianfeng** China
52C3 **Xiangfan** China
52C4 **Xiang Jiang** *R* China
52C4 **Xiangtan** Province, China
52C4 **Xianning** China
52B3 **Xianyang** China
53A2 **Xiao'ergou** China
52C4 **Xiao Shui** *R* China
52D4 **Xiapu** China
52A4 **Xichang** China
22C1 **Xicoténcatl** Mexico
22C1 **Xicotepec** Mexico
55C2 **Xieng Khouang** Laos
52B4 **Xifeng** China
61C2 **Xigazê** China
52A1 **Xi He** *R* China
52B2 **Xiji** China
52C5 **Xi Jiang** *R* China
52E1 **Xiliao He** *R* China
52B5 **Xilin** China
22C1 **Xilitla** Mexico
52D4 **Xinfeng** China
52C1 **Xinghe** China
53C2 **Xingkai Hu** *L* China/ Russian Fed
52D5 **Xingning** China
52B4 **Xingren** China
52C2 **Xingtai** China
27H4 **Xingu** *R* Brazil
50C2 **Xingxingxia** China
52A4 **Xingyi** China
53B3 **Xinhan** China
52A2 **Xining** China
52E2 **Xinjin** Liaoning, China
52A3 **Xinjin** Sichuan, China
53A3 **Xinkai He** *R* China
52D2 **Xinwen** China
52C2 **Xin Xian** China
52C2 **Xinxiang** China
52C3 **Xinyang** China
52C5 **Xinyi** Guangdong, China
52D3 **Xinyi** Jiangsu, China
52D1 **Xi Ujimqin Qi** China
53A3 **Xiuyan** China
22C2 **Xochimilco** Mexico
52D3 **Xuancheng** China
52B3 **Xuanhan** China
52D1 **Xuanhua** China
52A4 **Xuanwei** China
52C3 **Xuchang** China
72E3 **Xuddur** Somalia
52A2 **Xunhua** China
52C5 **Xun Jiang** *R* China
53B2 **Xunke** China
52D5 **Xunwu** China
52C4 **Xupu** China
55E1 **Xuwen** China
52B4 **Xuyong** China
52D3 **Xuzhou** China

Y

52A4 **Ya'an** China
75B3 **Yaapeet** Aust
72B3 **Yabassi** Cam
53E2 **Yablochnyy** Russian Fed
50D1 **Yablonovyy Khrebet** *Mts* Russian Fed
65D2 **Yabrūd** Syria
18B2 **Yachats** USA
26F8 **Yacuiba** Bol
62B1 **Yādgīr** India
69A1 **Yafran** Libya
54D2 **Yagishiri-tō** *I* Japan
43G2 **Yagotin** Ukraine
28D2 **Yaguari** *R* Urug
28E2 **Yaguaron** *R* Urug
22B1 **Yahualica** Mexico
72C3 **Yahuma** Zaïre
54C3 **Yaita** Japan
54C4 **Yaizu** Japan
52A4 **Yajiang** China
18B1 **Yakima** USA
18B1 **Yakima** *R* USA
71F3 **Yako** Burkina
72C3 **Yakoma** Zaïre
53C5 **Yakujima-kaikyō** *Str* Japan
53E3 **Yakumo** Japan
53C5 **Yaku-shima** *I* Japan
10L4 **Yakutat** USA
10L4 **Yakutat B** USA
49O3 **Yakutsk** Russian Fed
49N3 **Yakutskaya** Respublika, Russian Fed
55C4 **Yala** Thai
22C2 **Yalalag** Mexico
18B1 **Yale** Can
72C3 **Yalinga** CAR
75C3 **Yallourn** Aust
50C3 **Yalong** *R* China
52A4 **Yalong Jiang** *R* China
41F2 **Yalova** Turk
45E7 **Yalta** Ukraine
53A2 **Yalu He** *R* China
53B3 **Yalu Jiang** *R* China
54D3 **Yamada** Japan
53D4 **Yamagata** Japan
53C5 **Yamaguchi** Japan
48J2 **Yamal, Poluostrov** *Pen* Russian Fed
50E1 **Yamarovka** Russian Fed
75D1 **Yamba** New S Wales, Aust
75B2 **Yamba** S Australia, Aust
72C3 **Yambio** Sudan
41F2 **Yambol** Bulg
57D4 **Yamdena** *I* Indon
61E3 **Yamethin** Burma
Yam Kinneret = Tiberias,L
75B1 **Yamma Yamma,L** Aust
16A1 **Yampa** *R* USA
49R4 **Yamsk** Russian Fed
60D3 **Yamuna** *R* India
61D2 **Yamzho Yumco** *L* China
49P3 **Yana** *R* Russian Fed
75B3 **Yanac** Aust
54B4 **Yanagawa** Japan
62C1 **Yanam** India
52B2 **Yan'an** China
66C2 **Yanbu'al Bahr** S Arabia
75B2 **Yancannia** Aust
52E3 **Yancheng** China
52B2 **Yanchi** China
75B1 **Yandama** *R* Aust
72C3 **Yangambi** Zaïre
50B2 **Yangbi** China
54A3 **Yanggu** S Korea
52C1 **Yang He** *R* China
52C5 **Yangjiang** China
Yangon = Rangoon
52C2 **Yangquan** China
54A3 **Yangsan** S Korea
52C5 **Yangshan** China
52C3 **Yangtze Gorges** China
52E3 **Yangtze,Mouths of the** China
54A3 **Yangyang** S Korea
52D3 **Yangzhou** China
52B4 **Yanhe** China
53B3 **Yanji** China
75C3 **Yanko** Aust
49P2 **Yankskiy Zaliv** *B* Russian Fed
11C3 **Yankton** USA
59G1 **Yanqqi** China
52D1 **Yan Shan** *Hills* China
75B1 **Yantabulla** Aust
52E2 **Yantai** China
52D2 **Yanzhou** China
72B3 **Yaoundé** Cam
51G7 **Yapen** *I* Indon
28D1 **Yapeyú** Arg
51G6 **Yap Is** Pacific O
21B2 **Yaqui** *R* Mexico
44H4 **Yaransk** Russian Fed
44H3 **Yarenga** Russian Fed
44H3 **Yarensk** Russian Fed
26D3 **Yari** *R* Colombia
53D4 **Yariga-dake** *Mt* Japan
59F2 **Yarkant He** *R* China
61D2 **Yarlung Zangbo Jiang** *R* China
66D4 **Yarmin** Yemen
7M5 **Yarmouth** Can
65C2 **Yarmūk** *R* Syria/Jordan
44F4 **Yaroslavl'** Russian Fed
65C2 **Yarqon,R** Israel
75C3 **Yarram** Aust
75D1 **Yarraman** Aust
75C3 **Yarrawonga** Aust
44N2 **Yar Sale** Russian Fed
44E4 **Yartsevo** Russian Fed
49L3 **Yartsevo** Russian Fed
26C2 **Yarumal** Colombia
77G2 **Yasawa Group** *Is* Fiji
71H3 **Yashi** Nig
71G4 **Yashikera** Nig
45G6 **Yashkul'** Russian Fed
60C1 **Yasin** Pak
43E3 **Yasinya** Ukraine
53B1 **Yasnyy** Russian Fed
75C2 **Yass** Aust
75C2 **Yass** *R* Aust
54B3 **Yasugi** Japan
17C2 **Yates Center** USA
6J3 **Yathkyed L** Can
72C3 **Yatolema** Zaïre
53C5 **Yatsushiro** Japan
65C3 **Yatta** Israel
26D4 **Yavari** Peru
60D4 **Yavatmāl** India
53C5 **Yawatahama** Japan
55D2 **Ya Xian** China
63C2 **Yazd** Iran
63C2 **Yazd-e Khvāst** Iran
17D3 **Yazoo** *R* USA
17D3 **Yazoo City** USA
55B2 **Ye** Burma
43F3 **Yedintsy** Moldavia
75A2 **Yeelanna** Aust
44F5 **Yefremov** Russian Fed
45G6 **Yegorlyk** *R* Russian Fed
72D3 **Yei** Sudan
71F4 **Yeji** Ghana
44L4 **Yekaterinburg** Russian Fed
53B1 **Yekaterinoslavka** Russian Fed
45F5 **Yelets** Russian Fed
33C1 **Yell** *I* Scot
62C1 **Yellandu** India
Yellow = Huang He
6G4 **Yellowhead P** Can
6G3 **Yellowknife** Can
75C2 **Yellow Mt** Aust
50F3 **Yellow Sea** China/Korea
8C2 **Yellowstone** *R* USA
18D2 **Yellowstone L** USA
18D2 **Yellowstone Nat Pk** USA
43G2 **Yel'nya** Russian Fed
43F2 **Yel'sk** Belorussia
7K1 **Yelverton B** Can
71G3 **Yelwa** Nig
58C4 **Yemen** Republic, Arabian Pen
55C1 **Yen Bai** Viet
71F4 **Yendi** Ghana
55B1 **Yengan** Burma
48K3 **Yenisey** *R* Russian Fed
49L4 **Yeniseysk** Russian Fed
49L3 **Yeniseyskiy Kryazh** *Ridge* Russian Fed
48J2 **Yeniseyskiy Zaliv** *B* Russian Fed
10H3 **Yentna** *R* USA
35D6 **Yeo** *R* Eng
75C2 **Yeoval** Aust
35D6 **Yeovil** Eng
49M3 **Yerbogachen** Russian Fed
45G7 **Yerevan** Armenia
19C3 **Yerington** USA
44J2 **Yermitsa** Russian Fed
19C4 **Yermo** USA
49O4 **Yerofey-Pavlovich** Russian Fed
65C3 **Yeroham** Israel
49S3 **Yeropol** Russian Fed
45H5 **Yershov** Russian Fed
Yerushalayim = Jerusalem
64C1 **Yeşil** *R* Turk
49M3 **Yessey** Russian Fed
65C2 **Yesud Hama'ala** Israel
75D1 **Yetman** Aust
70B2 **Yetti** Maur
61E3 **Yeu** Burma
45H7 **Yevlakh** Azerbaijan
45E6 **Yevpatoriya** Ukraine
52E2 **Ye Xian** China
45F6 **Yeysk** Russian Fed
28D2 **Yi** *R* Urug
65C1 **Yialousa** Cyprus
53B2 **Yi'an** China
41E2 **Yiannitsá** Greece
52A4 **Yibin** China
52C3 **Yichang** China
53B2 **Yichun** China
52B2 **Yijun** China
64C2 **Yıldızeli** Turk
53A1 **Yilehuli Shan** *Upland* China
52A5 **Yiliang** China
52B2 **Yinchuan** China

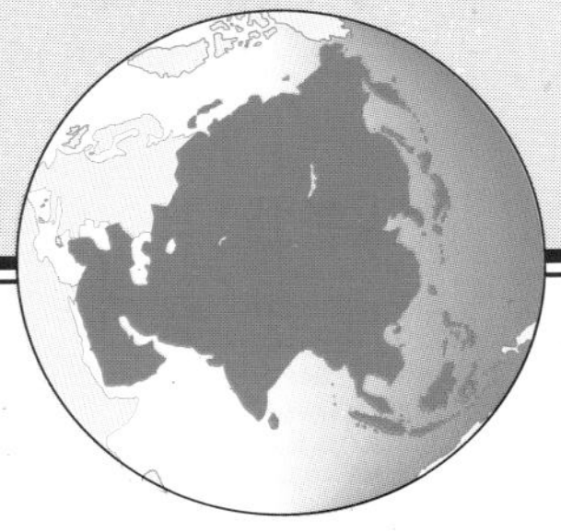

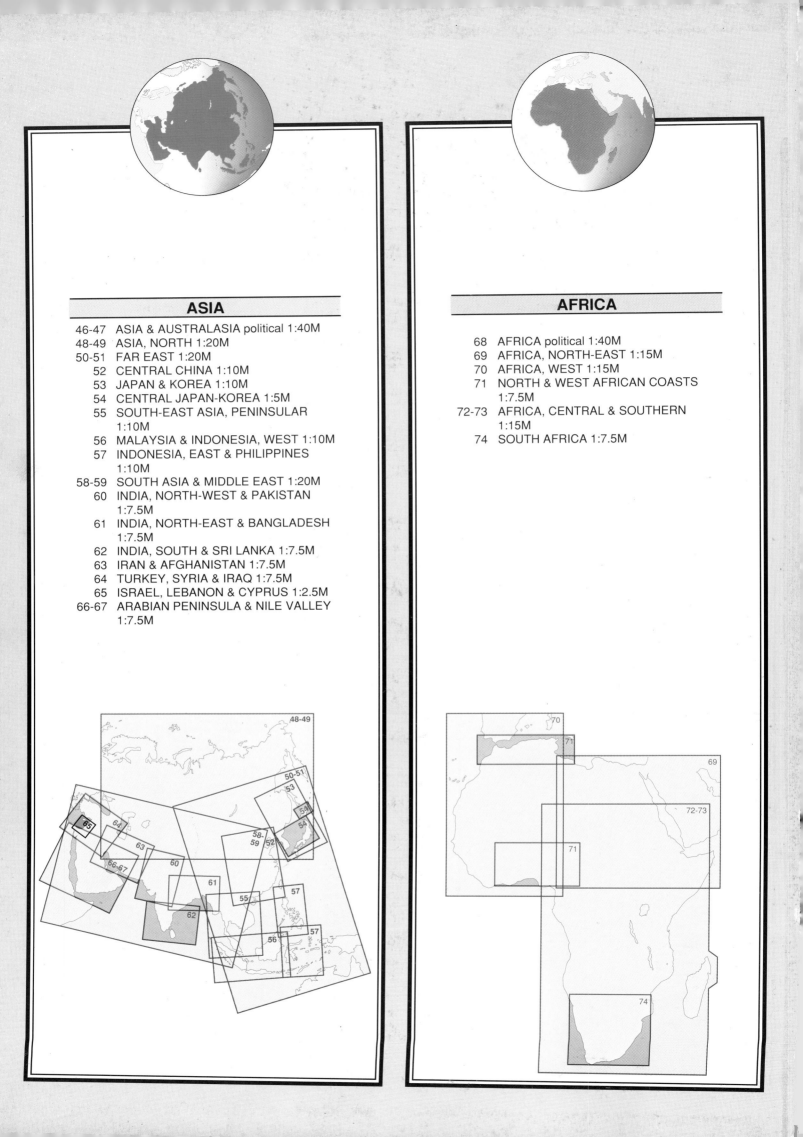

ASIA

46-47 ASIA & AUSTRALASIA political 1:40M
48-49 ASIA, NORTH 1:20M
50-51 FAR EAST 1:20M
52 CENTRAL CHINA 1:10M
53 JAPAN & KOREA 1:10M
54 CENTRAL JAPAN-KOREA 1:5M
55 SOUTH-EAST ASIA, PENINSULAR 1:10M
56 MALAYSIA & INDONESIA, WEST 1:10M
57 INDONESIA, EAST & PHILIPPINES 1:10M
58-59 SOUTH ASIA & MIDDLE EAST 1:20M
60 INDIA, NORTH-WEST & PAKISTAN 1:7.5M
61 INDIA, NORTH-EAST & BANGLADESH 1:7.5M
62 INDIA, SOUTH & SRI LANKA 1:7.5M
63 IRAN & AFGHANISTAN 1:7.5M
64 TURKEY, SYRIA & IRAQ 1:7.5M
65 ISRAEL, LEBANON & CYPRUS 1:2.5M
66-67 ARABIAN PENINSULA & NILE VALLEY 1:7.5M

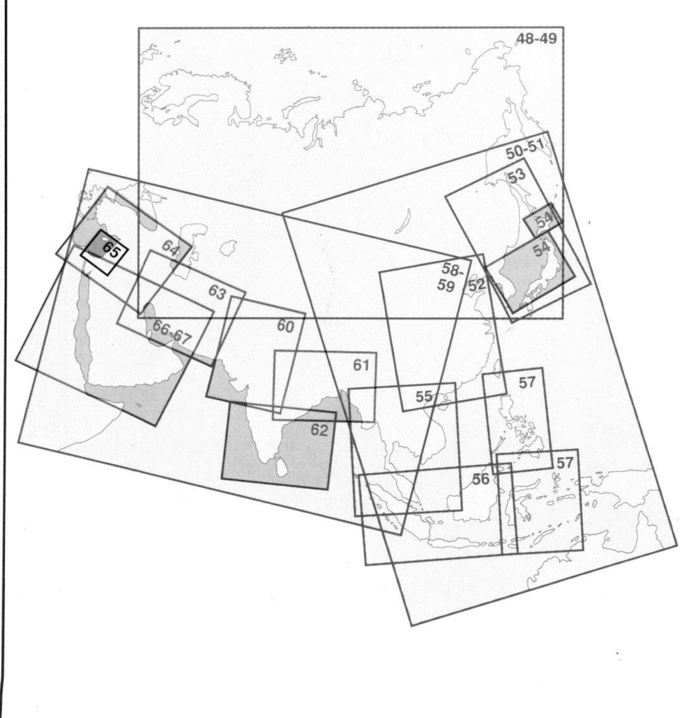

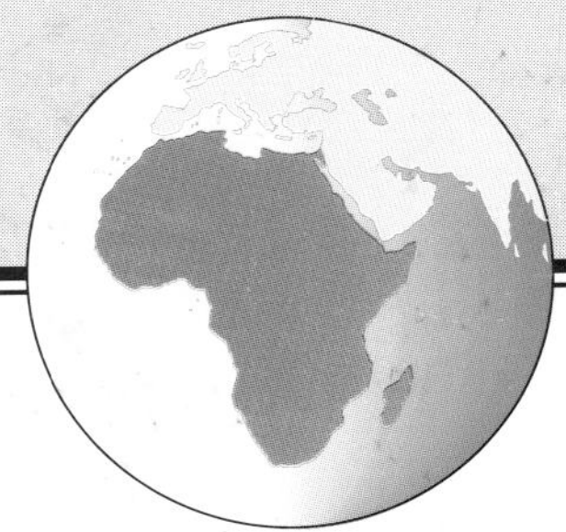

AFRICA

68 AFRICA political 1:40M
69 AFRICA, NORTH-EAST 1:15M
70 AFRICA, WEST 1:15M
71 NORTH & WEST AFRICAN COASTS 1:7.5M
72-73 AFRICA, CENTRAL & SOUTHERN 1:15M
74 SOUTH AFRICA 1:7.5M

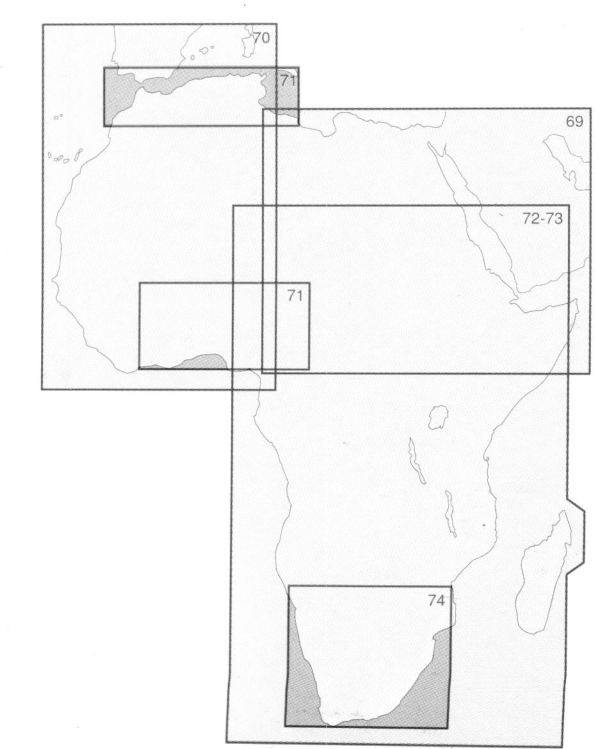